THE CLINICAL ASSESSMENT OF CHILDREN AND ADOLESCENTS: A PRACTITIONER'S HANDBOOK

THE CLINICAL ASSESSMENT OF CHILDREN AND ADOLESCENTS: A PRACTITIONER'S HANDBOOK

Steven R. Smith
University of California, Santa Barbara

Leonard Handler
University of Tennessee

LEA LAWRENCE ERLBAUM ASSOCIATES, PUBLISHERS
2007   Mahwah, New Jersey   London

Editorial Director: Steven Rutter
Executive Assistant: Nicole Buchmann
Cover Design: Tomai Maridou
Full-Service Compositor: MidAtlantic Books & Journals, Inc.

This book was typeset in 10/12 pt. Times Roman, Italic, Bold, and Bold Italic.

Lawrence Erlbaum Associates, Inc., Publishers
10 Industrial Avenue
Mahwah, New Jersey 07430
www.erlbaum.com

CIP information for this volume can be obtained from the Library of Congress.

ISBN: 0-8058-6075-4 (paperback)

ISBN: 0-8058-5791-5 (case)

Books published by Lawrence Erlbaum Associates are printed on
acid-free paper, and their bindings are chosen for strength and durability.

Printed in the United States of America

10 9 8 7 6 5 4 3 2 1

To my wife, Suzanne Smith, PhD, for love, patience, and support.
—SRS

This book is dedicated to my grandson, Oliver William Oppenheim.
Ollie, this book's for you.
—LH

Contents

PREFACE

In both psychological assessment and psychotherapy practice, work with younger populations tends to lag behind that of adults. Innovations in assessment tend to be thoroughly examined and explored in the literature before they are "extended downward" to children. For this reason, child and adolescent psychologists are often left to their own devices when it comes to understanding and applying psychological testing techniques in an informative and ethical manner. The present volume, constructed to be a handbook for the clinical practice of assessment, brings the newest and most empirically valid means of assessment to practicing clinicians by the leaders in child and adolescent personality and behavioral assessment.

Most available books on child assessment proceed from one of two standpoints; first, several texts examine the use of a particular test (e.g., the Rorschach) for assessing various presentations or disorders. For example, in this "test specific" approach, readers may learn how children with depressive features, conduct problems, or ADHD may score on a particular behavior rating scale. Conversely, other texts begin with a focus on a diagnosis and outline the ways in which clinicians may confirm or disconfirm that diagnosis. These "diagnosis specific" books may have chapters exploring how a child with depression may score on projective measures, behavior rating scales, self-report measures, etc.

As clinicians, we felt that these two perspectives on child and adolescent assessment are too narrow and do not reflect "real-world" clinical decision-making. The "test specific" approach does not allow the clinician to explore or make use of the rich variety and combination of tests and assessment measures that are available. The "diagnosis specific" approach presumes that the clinician only uses assessment to arrive at a diagnostic formulation, rather than understand the complexity of personality dynamics, family functioning, and psychopathology. We believe that the best use of assessment is one that draws from both of these perspectives—an appreciation and understanding of the tests, how and when they are the most useful, and the best way to interpret and integrate test results. It is this void in the literature that is filled by this volume.

This book was written specifically for practitioners and graduate students who seek specific information about the clinical practice of assessment. All chapter authors provide clinicians with the tools and guidance they will need in making the day-to-day decisions about test choice and interpretation. Although each chapter includes empirical information, the ultimate focus is on pragmatics and how each topic can be useful to practicing clinicians and advanced graduate students. To this end, each chapter includes a comprehensive case study to illustrate the practical implications.

The present volume has four primary sections:

- In section one, *Issues and Concepts in Child and Adolescent Assessment,* chapters provide a review of such major topics as multimethod assessment, therapeutic assessment, personality assessment in the schools, providing feedback, and integrating neuropsychology and personality assessment.
- In the section on *Assessment Techniques,* chapter authors will detail the use of several well-known and new measures, techniques, and procedures. In addition to two chapters

on using the Rorschach, chapters in this section discuss drawing techniques, story telling techniques, the MMPI-A, the BASC-2, the CBCL, and the Personality Inventory for Youth. Other chapters explore play assessment, family assessment, and quality of life assessment techniques.

- The book's third section, *Specific Syndromes, Issues, and Problem Areas,* will begin from a diagnosis-specific approach and examine the utility of various assessment techniques in diagnostic decision-making. Chapters include such topics as depression, anxiety, ADHD, delinquency, and trauma.

- The fourth section of the book, *Special Populations*, will examine assessment techniques and procedures among underrepresented youth including racial and ethnic minorities as well as pediatric patients and children struggling with a mentally ill parent.

A Practitioner's Handbook will be a useful text for practicing clinicians, school psychologists, and advanced graduate students. Each chapter makes extensive use of the authors' expertise on both empirical issues as well as clinical implications. Unlike other texts, each chapter in the book relies heavily on material from actual clinical cases. Readers will be able to learn about particular assessment techniques as well as see how those techniques could be used in their day-to-day practices. Likewise, students will learn the empirical basis for particular tests while having the test demonstrated in a clinically relevant manner.

We would like to thank the many clinical researchers who have contributed chapters to this volume. Their willingness to give life to their topics in a way that is both readable and applicable helps to continue bridging the gap between researcher and clinician. At LEA, Steve Rutter and Nicole Buchmann have been extremely helpful in shepherding us through the process and providing us support and encouragement as the deadline approached. Special thanks to Susan Milmoe, formerly of LEA, for her initial support.

Steve Smith's personal acknowledgments: I would like to primarily acknowledge my co-editor, Len Handler. Without him, this work is a mere kernel of an idea borne of my frustration as a clinician looking for practical resources on assessing children and adolescents. Len gave this work a deep perspective and a soft clinical touch. A bulldog of an editor, he was the consummate *Dd* to my *W.* I would also like to acknowledge the particular contributions of my spectacular graduate students Jenss Chang, Jessica Little, Lisa Nowinski, Roxanna Rahban, and Katrina Schnoebelen in their various roles in the preparation of this project. Also noteworthy is the support of the faculty, staff, and graduate students of the Department of Counseling, Clinical, and School Psychology at UCSB. Vital in the initiation of this and other "projects" was Wendy Epstein, Ph.D. of Brookline, Massachusetts. Last, I owe a continuous debt of gratitude to my two greatest mentors, teachers, and supervisors, Drs. Mark Blais and Mark Hilsenroth (the latter of whom advised me to never edit a book).

Len Handler's personal acknowledgments: I would like to thank our editor at Erlbaum and Associates, Steve Rutter, and my co-editor, Steve Smith, whose focus on this book was unswerving. I would also like to thank my department head, James E. Lawler, for allowing me the time to devote to this project and others like it, and Lotte Weinstein, for her editorial assistance. Most of all, I want to thank my wife, Barbara, our children, and their spouses, Amy and Phil Oppenheim, Anne Churchill, and Charles Handler, for their patience, support, and encouragement, and for filling my life with joy.

CONTRIBUTORS

Abraham, Pamela, Psy.D., NCSP, Associate Professor and Coordinator, Psy.D. Program in School Psychology, Department of Graduate Psychology, Immaculata University.

Achenbach, Thomas L., Ph.D., Professor and Director, Research Center for Children, Youth, and Families, Department of Psychiatry, University of Vermont.

Archer, Robert P., Ph.D., ABPP, Professor and Director, Psychology Division, Department of Psychiatry, Eastern Virgina Medical School.

Barry, Melissa, M.Ed., Department of Educational Psychology and Instructional Technology, University of Georgia.

Bensaheb, Arva, M.A., Department of Psychology, University of Nevada, Las Vegas.

Braaten, Ellen B., Ph.D., Department of Psychiatry, Massachusetts General Hospital, Harvard Medical School.

Brueggemann, Amber, M.Ed., Department of Educational Psychology and Instructional Technology, University of Georgia.

Butcher, Brianne, B.A., Department of Educational Psychology, University of Texas, Austin.

Cashel, Mary Louise, Ph.D., Associate Professor, Department of Psychology, Southern Illinois University Carbondale.

Clemence, A. Jill, Ph.D., Erik H. Erikson Institute for Education and Research, The Austen Riggs Center.

Cook, William L., Ph.D., Associate Director, Department of Psychiatry, Maine Medical Center.

De Thomas, Courtney, M.A., Doctoral Program in Clinical Psychology, Child/Adolescent ADHD Clinic, Fairleigh Dickinson University.

Dollinger, Stephen J., Ph.D., Professor and Director of Clinical Training, Department of Psychology, Southern Illinois University Carbondale.

Erdberg, Philip, Ph.D., ABPP, Private Practice, Corde Madera, California.

Gee, Christina, Ph.D., Assistant Professor, Department of Psychology, George Washington University.

Gilman, Rich, Ph.D., Assistant Professor, Department of Counseling and Educational Psychology, University of Kentucky.

Goldenring Fine, Jodene, M.S., Department of Educational Psychology, University of Texas, Austin.

Handler, Leonard, Ph.D., ABAP, Professor and Associate Director, Clinical Training Program, Department of Psychology, University of Tennessee.

Hanzel, Elise, Ph.D., Postdoctoral Intern, Center for Autism Research, Evaluation and Service.

Harris, Benjamin H., M.A., Doctoral Program in Clinical Psychology, City University of New York.

Huebner, E. Scott, Ph.D., NCSP, Professor, Department of Psychology, University of South Carolina.

Johnson, Jeannette, Ph.D., Friends Research Institute, Inc.

Kamp, John, Ph.D., Senior Psychologist, Pearson Assessments, Thousand Oaks, California.

Kamphaus, Randy W., Ph.D., Distringuished Research Professor, Department of Educational Psychology and Instructional Technology, University of Georgia.

Kearney, Christopher A., Ph.D., Professor and Director, UNLV Child School Refusal and Anxiety Disorders Clinic, Department of Psychology, University of Nevada, Las Vegas.

Kelly, Francis D., Ed.D., Clinical Director, Poet Seat School, Greenfield, Massachusetts.

Killilea, Ben, M.A., Department of Psychology, Southern Illinois University Carbondale.

Krishnamurthy, Radhika, Psy.D., Professor and Director of Clinical Training, School of Psychology, Florida Institute of Technology.

Lachar, David, Ph.D., Professor and Director, Psychological Assessment Clinic, Department of Psychiatry and Behavioral Sciences, University of Texas Medical School at Houston.

Leffard, Stacie A., M.A., Doctoral Program in School Psychology, Duquesne University.

Leong, Fredrick T.L., Ph.D., Professor, Department of Psychology, Michigan State University.

Levy, Jacob, Ph.D., Assistant Professor, Department of Psychology, University of Tennessee.

Lincoln, Alan, Ph.D., Professor and Director, Center for Autism Research, Evaluation and Service, Clinical Ph.D. Program, Alliant International University.

Loving, James L., Psy.D., Private Practice, Philadelphia, Pennsylvania.

Masterson, Patricia J., Ph.D., Northcoast Behavioral Healthcare, BART's Place, Private Practice, Cleveland, Ohio.

Matto, Holly C., Ph.D., LCSW-C, Assistant Professor, School of Social Work, Virginia Commonwealth University.

Meehan, Kevin B., M.A., Doctoral Program in Clinical Psychology, City University of New York.

Michaelidis, Tamara, Psy.D., Departments of Psychiatry & Behavioral Sciences and Pediatrics, Children's National Medical Center, The George Washington University School of Medicine.

Miller, Jeffrey A., Ph.D., ABPP, Associate Professor and Program Director, School Psychology, Department of Counseling, Psychology, and Special Education, Duquesne University.

Millon, Theodore, Ph.D., D.Sc., Dean and Scientific Director, Institute for Advanced Studies in Personology and Psychopathology, Coral Gables, Florida.

Pearson, Beth L., M.A., Department of Psychology, Case Western Reserve University.

Pogge, David L., Ph.D., Director of Psychology, Four Winds Hospital, Katonah, New York.

Price, Jennifer L., Ph.D., Assistant Professor, Department of Psychology, Georgetown College.

Quirmbach, Linda, M.A., Doctoral Student, Clinical Ph.D. Program, Alliant International University.

Reddy, Linda A., Ph.D., Associate Professor and Director, Child/Adolescent ADHD Clinic, School of Psychology, Fairleigh Dickinson University.

Reynoso, Joseph S., M.A., Doctoral Program in Clinical Psychology, City University of New York.

Rothschild, Lily, Ph.D., Lecturer, Graduate Program in Child and Adolescent Clinical Psychology, Bar-Ilan University, and Chief Psychologist, Safra Children's Hospital, Sheba Medical Center, Israel.

Russ, Sandra, Ph.D., Professor, Department of Psychology, Case Western Reserve University.

Sacha, Tori J., M.A., Department of Psychology, Case Western Reserve University.

Semrud-Clikeman, Margaret, Ph.D., Professor and Program Director, School Psychology, Department of Educational Psychology, University of Texas, Austin.

Sivec, Harry J., Ph.D., Director, BART's Place, and Adjunct Assistant Professor of Psychology, Northcoast Behavioral Healthcare, Case Western Reserve University.

Smith, Steven R., Ph.D., Assistant Professor and Director, Psychology Assessment Center, Deparment of Counseling, Clinical, and School Psychology, University of California, Santa Barbara.

Stokes, John M., Ph.D., Professor, Psychology Department, Pace University and Four Winds Hospital.

Stredny, Rebecca V., Psy.D., Forensic Team Psychologist, Central State Hospital, Petersburg, Virginia.

Streisand, Randi, Ph.D., CDE, Assistant Professor and Diabetes Team Director of Psychology Research and Service, Departments of Psychiatry & Behavioral Sciences and Pediatrics, Children's National Medical Center, The George Washington University School of Medicine.

Suldo, Shannon M., Ph.D., Assistant Professor, School Psychology Program, College of Education, University of South Florida.

Tibon, Shira, Ph.D., ABAP, Senior Lecturer, Graduate Program in Clinical Psychology, The Academic College of Tel-Aviv-Yaffo, and Tel-Aviv University, Israel.

Tringone, Robert J., Ph.D., Senior Psychologist, Division of Child and Adolescent Psychiatry, North Shore LIJ Health System.

Tuber, Steve, Ph.D., ABPP, Professor, Doctoral Program in Clinical Psychology, City University of New York.

Ueng-McHale, Jasmine, M.A., Doctoral Program in Clinical Psychology, City University of New York.

VanDeventer, Meghan, M.Ed., Department of Educational Psychology and Instructional Technology, University of Georgia.

Waehler, Charles A., Ph.D., Associate Professor and Co-Training Director, Collaborative Program in Counseling Psychology, University of Akron.

Yalof, Jed, Psy.D., ABPP, ABSNP, Professor and Chair, and Coordinator, PsyD Program in Clinical Psychology, Department of Graduate Psychology, Immaculata University.

The Clinical Assessment of Children and Adolescents: A Practitioner's Handbook

1

THE CLINICAL PRACTICE OF CHILD AND ADOLESCENT ASSESSMENT

Steven R. Smith

University of California, Santa Barbara

Leonard Handler

University of Tennessee

The use of tests and measures to understand our patients is one of the hallmarks of applied psychology. Unlike the practices of psychiatry, social work, and other allied mental health disciplines, psychologists rely on measurement to quantify patient cognitive functioning, psychopathology, behavior, strengths, neuropsychological performance, aptitudes, attitudes, and social contexts. Following the empiricist's creed, much of applied psychological assessment rests on the assertion of Thorndike (1918) that "whatever exists at all exists in some amount" (p. 16).

However, the clinical practice of psychological assessment with children and adolescents is different from the mere nomothetic measurement ideal proposed by Thorndike. In fact, a distinction must be made between psychological assessment and psychological testing. Although psychological assessment includes testing, it is far more complex and rife with clinical challenges. Handler and Meyer (1998) clarify the important distinction between psychological testing and psychological assessment, and they emphasize that these are hardly synonymous activities. They state:

> Testing is a relatively straightforward process wherein a particular test is administered to obtain a specific score. Subsequently, a descriptive meaning can be applied to the score based on normative, nomothetic findings. For example, when conducting psychological testing, an IQ of 100 indicates a person possesses average intelligence . . . Psychological assessment, however, is a quite different enterprise. The focus here is not on obtaining a single score, or even a series of test scores. Rather, the focus is on taking a variety of test-derived pieces of information, obtained from multiple methods of assessment, and placing these data in the context of historical information, referral information, and behavioral observations in order to generate a cohesive and comprehensive understanding of the person being evaluated. These activities are far from simple; they require a high degree of skill and sophistication to be implemented properly. (pp. 4–5)

A comprehensive psychological assessment includes information from the referring individual; from the child's or adolescent's parent(s) (including a thorough interview and history); from the child or adolescent himself or herself; and from his or her teacher(s) and other relevant informants, such as physicians, relatives, or friends. In addition, to complete a thorough and meaningful assessment, the clinician must help the child's or adolescent's caretakers, the child or adolescent, and perhaps the referring individual to formulate relevant referral questions to be answered by the assessment. After all this activity, including testing the child or adolescent, the clinician then aggregates and integrates the data, writes the report, and provides feedback to the referral source, as well as to the parents and the child or adolescent tested. Compared with this complex series of activities, psychological testing is a far more simple procedure.

UNIQUE CHALLENGES IN THE ASSESSMENT OF CHILDREN AND ADOLESCENTS

It is often the complexity of psychological assessment, rather than psychological testing, that poses several challenges to the assessor, particularly when he or she is working with younger patients. The range of cognitive, affective, and contextual variables that affect a child's or adolescent's performance is seemingly limitless and calls upon a wide array of clinical skills on the part of the assessor. Next follows a discussion of the more important issues that assessment psychologists often face when they work with younger patients.

1.   Children (and many adolescents) lack the ability to describe their feelings and experiences. They lack the adult's ability to conceptualize and contextualize their experiences and the ability to describe them to adults. It is difficult to use traditional interviews in the assessment of children, especially young children (although this is less true with adolescents) because children also lack the words with which to express their thoughts and feelings. For example, asking a child how he or she feels about an issue will often result in a response of "I don't know." The examiner might erroneously conclude that the child is defensive or is withholding information, even though the child's response is probably accurate—he or she may not really know how to answer this question. Therefore, poor performance by children may not reflect a lack of knowledge, but, rather, a lack of the capacity to comprehend the complexity of their world and the relevance of various activities to their well-being.

In addition, although children may be able to say, for example, "my teacher is mean," they will typically be unable to describe why they feel that way, or may not be able to explain what the teacher does that makes the teacher "mean." To make matters even more complicated, this opinion of the teacher, or of other people in the child's life, may be transitory, changing with the next positive interaction he or she has with this person.

2.   Siegel (1987) makes a very important point concerning the assessment of children. She states, "Children do not appear for a psychological evaluation of their own volition" (p. 15). She adds, "During the early stages of the examination [and perhaps in later stages as well] the child communicates, in open or hidden ways, feelings of trepidation about the unfamiliar experience that awaits him [her]" (p. 23).

Children and some adolescents have little ability to conceptualize the reasons they are being assessed. They typically compare the assessment process with the only similar experience they have had—school testing. Therefore, they come to the assessment sessions with anxiety and concern about giving correct answers. This is especially so if the child or adolescent has one or another kind of learning problem, because the child fears even more the possibility that he or she will "fail" the examiner's tests. In addition, given that the examiner is not to provide feedback concerning whether the child's response is correct or incorrect, the child cannot determine whether he or she has responded successfully. Most often, however, children conclude that their answers are incorrect, and they often feel "dumb" or "retarded."

This problem is especially troublesome when the child takes a projective test, such as the Rorschach or a storytelling test, because there are few or no right or wrong answers. Therefore, the child is left guessing even more so about whether his or her responses were correct. This situation therefore engenders even more anxiety than the child had upon first entering what was already experienced as an unusual and strange situation. Often, children take a defensive stance to deal with their underlying anxiety, calling the tests and/or the examiner "stupid" or otherwise criticizing the tests.

3.   The assessor must work quite hard to assist the child or adolescent with his or her anxiety, providing a "holding environment" (a setting of safety and comfort; Winnicott, 1965), as much as this is possible to do with a relative stranger. Schafer (1954, 1956) indicates that even adults find the assessment relationship stressful, and they respond with regressive and self-blaming behavior. Thus, the assessor must make every effort to make the assessment process more like play rather than like school-related work and tests. In addition, the assessor must accomplish this feat without changing the standardized administration directions. Although this is possible to do with some tests (e.g., the Draw-A-Person Test, the House-Tree-Person Test, the Kinetic Family Drawing Test, and some storytelling tests), it is more difficult to make some tests, such as the Rorschach or some self-report measures, playful.

4.   Often, to maintain rapport and cooperation, examiners must process the child's experience with each test the child experienced as problematic or anxiety-producing. In addition, in order to decrease resistance, some examiners provide for the child or adolescent posttest exploration of his or her responses, finding ways in which the child can derive more successful answers to questions he or she had previously failed (see Handler, 1998, 1999, 2002, 2004b, 2005 for a discussion of this approach). This gives the child a feeling of success and provides the examiner additional clues concerning the child's problems.

It is also important to note that the children and adolescents we test are typically children with emotional and social problems of different kinds and therefore they are more vulnerable to the pressures engendered in the assessment situation. These children and adolescents tend to degrade themselves when they feel they have missed test items, and often berate themselves. Children and some adolescents have a poorly developed sense of self. Therefore, they are very sensitive to what they might perceive as their poor performance, especially because the examiner cannot offer them feedback concerning the adequacy of their responses. Children evaluate their success by focusing on the adult's feedback to them (Kohut, 1977). If this is not forthcoming, they almost automatically believe they are wrong or at fault.

5.   Children and many adolescents do not understand why they are being assessed, despite the fact that parents and/or assessors attempt to explain the reason(s) they are being tested. What they are aware of is that their parents or their teachers are unhappy with some aspect of their performance or their behavior. However, they do not see the relevance of the assessment, nor can they comprehend that by these procedures the answers to their problem issues will be understood. Therefore, they are often not ego-involved in the process, which can make them even more restless and avoidant during the assessment sessions.

6.   Some children and adolescents somehow understand that the assessor is someone who might help fix the problem they are having and will sometimes be able to tell the asses-

sor directly, but more often indirectly, through metaphor, what is wrong. However, in traditional assessment, because the assessor needs time to evaluate the data and write a report, the child or adolescent leaves without helpful feedback. Therefore, because the child or adolescent cannot comprehend the complexity of the assessment process for the assessor, he or she leaves the assessment sessions disappointed and might well view the experience as an empathic failure. D. W. Winnicott writes about this problem in the following quote:

> It often happens that we find a child has given all to the psychologist who is performing an intelligence test, and the fact that the material presented has not led to understanding (this not being included in the psychologist's aims) has proved traumatic to the child, leading to a strengthening of suspicion and unwillingness to give the appropriate clues [about his or her problem]. This especially applies in TAT tests in which the patient has reached to unexpected ideas, fears, states. For this reason I have always seen my patients first, referring them to the psychologist where necessary, after I have come to grips with the case by doing something significant in the first interview or first few interviews. (Winnicott, 1989, pp. 319–320)

7.   Many children have separation anxiety as one of their problems. They might therefore refuse to separate from the parent or parents who bring them for the assessment. Although most children accompany the assessor without any apparent problem, many others are fearful, with feelings ranging from mild uneasiness to complete terror about separating from the parent. These emotions can persist in the assessment room, permeating the relationship, affecting test results, and making the assessment experience tolerable at best.

Although most children and adolescents will comply, albeit reluctantly, with the examiner, there are nevertheless a significant number of children and adolescents who are very difficult to test because of resistance or behavioral noncompliance. They resist the examiner in various ways, both directly and indirectly. Although this resistance may be due to the cognitive issues, interpersonal problems, or anxiety discussed above, children and adolescents who are behaviorally difficult call for the utmost creativity, flexibility, and clinical skill on the part of the assessor.

Case examples illustrate this point nicely. For example, Roxanna was a 16-year-old girl I (SRS) saw on an acute-care inpatient psychiatric unit. A full assessment was requested in order to assess for disordered thinking or other serious mental illness that might help to explain her erratic and self-destructive behavior prior to hospitalization. She struck a tough pose with me, her peers, and the other clinical staff and referred to all of the assessment materials as "kid stuff" and "bullshit." When I would encourage her and praise her performance during cognitive testing, she would sarcastically respond, "Yeah, like I was really trying."

The Rorschach was particularly difficult for Roxanna. The unstructured and somewhat "mysterious" nature of the test brought about the anxiety normally masked by her somewhat antisocial presentation. She immediately rejected Card I, and it was clear that she would not be a willing participant in the assessment. The following day, I met again with Roxanna, but this time, I brought along some paint and paper. Although initially reluctant (because this was "bullshit," too), she agreed to make inkblots with me, using lots of color and eagerly folding each paper in half to see what she had made. After "defusing" the inkblots in this manner, I was able to convince her to give the Rorschach another try.

The reason for her initial anxiety about engaging in the Rorschach task was immediately clear, because she produced a profile that was rife with aggressive and personalized responses with very poor form and reality testing (e.g., on Card VI, she responded, "This is my father hitting my mother; I'm down here trying to stop him."). It was evident from her responses and score profile that she was struggling with a psychotic process that was tinged with primitive aggression. After completion of the Inquiry portion, she asked if we could make inkblots again, and I agreed to do so. As a way of taking ownership of her fears, she kept these "home-made" blots and hung them on the walls of her room at the hospital.

Another case example is provided by Kelly (1999):

> When the examiner came to get Virginia, [an eight year-old girl, she announced] that she was busy and that [the examiner needed] to wait. From the outset Virginia attempt[ed] to be in control [of the assessment process], want[ed] to know if she [was] giving the right answers [to the WISC-R [questions], and pout[ed] when the examiner suggest[ed] she just try and do her best. At times she [was] distractible, inattentive, hyperactive, and markedly impulsive. Her ability to tolerate frustration [was] frequently taxed and she [responded] with derisive comments about the test and the examiner (e.g., "Your dress is ugly and so are your earrings."). The examiner [found] it necessary to allow frequent breaks so [Virginia could] play with a nearby doll house.
>
> Virginia did better on structured tests, but had increasingly more difficulty with the unstructured tests. For example when she saw the first Rorschach card she shielded her face with it and impulsively stated, "A stupid, dumb, dumb bat with holes in its body." She threw the card across the table, announced she would not look at any more cards, and walked around the room, and then [stared] out the window. The examiner invited her to return to the testing, telling her the evaluation would not take much longer, but Virginia still refused to continue. The examiner expressed to Virginia that she understood how difficult the testing was for her, but suggested it would be nice to finish the testing that same day, and told her she could get a snack when the testing was completed. She told Virginia she could keep track of the time and could work the stopwatch, and could take another break if it was necessary. In addition, the examiner told Virginia that other girls also found the testing difficult, but that most of them found the testing to be interesting because there were no right or wrong answers. Although Virginia did complete the test, she continued to periodically protest, orally deprecated the tests, and complained angrily. (pp. 132–133)

Such difficulties are thankfully infrequent, but they illustrate the often stressful nature of the assessment process for children and adolescents, just as the process is stressful for adults. Managing such problems involves an appreciation of the child's needs and problems, along with the ability to devise solutions designed to employ the child's predominant interactive style to effectively re-interest him or her in the assessment process.

Judging from the examples just cited, the examiner of potentially highly resistant children, in some selected cases, might want to modify the test instructions in order to obtain or increase cooperation and to obtain meaningful data. The issue of modification of standardized instructions must be compared, in each case, with the possibility of obtaining poor or inadequate data. For example, presenting the Rorschach or storytelling test as games, in which the child is invited to have fun making up stories; seeing interesting things on the cards; playing "an imagination game"; or telling a child who is taking an IQ test that he or she is smart, cheering him or her on, or even alternating easy items with more difficult ones might result in far better cooperation of the child or adolescent, compared with reliance on standardized instructions.

The decision whether to violate standardization is a difficult one to make and should not be made casually. Indeed, such a violation of standardized procedures is not recommended in forensic cases, such as custody evaluations, where the violation of standardized testing will likely result in the dismissal of the psychologist's entire report. Even some learning disability evaluations provided for schools can become quite "heated" and contentious, making any violation of standardization potentially very problematic. In all cases where a violation in standardization has occurred, the psychologist should indicate in the report that it was necessary to violate standardization in order to gain the child's or adolescent's cooperation.

Testing children or adolescents can be difficult for assessors who erroneously define their job as obtaining responses to tests. The goal is not to merely obtain responses, but to develop an understanding of the child's or adolescent's prevailing problem(s). Merely obtaining responses such as "I don't know" to a variety of questions gives the examiner little understanding of the child or adolescent. The examiner might also want to use a Testing of the Limits procedure, first suggested by Klopfer (Klopfer, Ainsworth, Klopfer, & Holt, 1954), to clarify Rorschach scoring, after the test is concluded, to obtain more meaningful responses. In this procedure, the examiner might return to missed items and provide the child or adolescent with a series of graded hints to determine whether the child is capable of generating better data. A fuller explanation of this approach is available in Handler (1998, 1999) and in his chapter on therapeutic assessment in this volume.

A DEVELOPMENTAL PERSPECTIVE ON ASSESSMENT

It is because of this complexity that most psychologists look to psychological assessment to aid in diagnosis and treatment planning. Although survey results suggest that 80% of clinical psychologists spend less than 5 hours per week providing assessment services (Camara, Nathan, & Puente, 2000), these services are particularly important for assessment psychologists who work with younger patients because child and adolescent psychological symptoms tend not to occur or be obvious in the clinical setting (House, 2002). Clemence and Handler (2001) conducted a study of assessment practices in APA-accredited internship settings. Although it may not be representative of what happens in all clinical settings, they found that in settings where assessors work primarily with children, 29% of assessors reported that all patients receive some type of psychological assessment. Another 29% indicated that at least half of their patients received psychological assessment. These rates were higher than all other internship settings surveyed (Clemence & Handler, 2001).

The assessment of children is complicated by myriad overlapping issues in cognitive and emotional development. Specifically, there appear to be three primary cognitive and object relational issues that are most salient for child assessment: self-concept, affective labeling, and concepts of others. Research on the development of self-concept reveals a consistent and cross-cultural progression from infancy to adolescence (Damon & Hart, 1982). First, self-concept shifts from mere physical descriptors and experiences to those that are more psychological in nature. Second, self-concept gradually comes to be based more on internal and self-reflective descriptors, rather than on characterizations by others. Third, the child develops a stable and complex social characterization of the self that is unique and multifaceted. Last, a unified self system develops from disparate, contradictory, or fragmentary self-descriptors.

At the age of three, children begin to have a linguistic understanding of affect (Stone & Lemanek, 1990). General broad categories of affective labels are increasingly refined and honed from early to mid-childhood. Next, as cognitive complexity increases, children are increasingly able to rely on a mental concept of affect rather than rely on physiological or environmental cues. As affective labels become more differentiated, and complex, children and adolescents are able to assert control over affective expression.

Like both self and affective development, social and relational functioning change from external or behavior-based appraisals to desires and preferences that are based on psychological constructs (Lenhart & Rabiner, 1995; McHale, Dariotis, & Kauh, 2003; Westen et al., 1991). The self-other development of mature object relations involves a progression from a state of infantile narcissism and undifferentiated object states to a more complex and differentiated understanding of self and others. Furthermore, young children tend to understand social relationships primarily by similarity in interest and behavior. Thus a child who enjoys sports might have a social network made up primarily of other children who play sports. Similarities and differences proceed from these behavioral comparisons, as well as from concrete likes and dislikes. As they progress into adolescence, children are more apt to look to psychological factors in others, such as honesty or extraversion, as important factors in relationships. The onset of puberty and development of sexuality shift the child's focus away from relations with caregivers to other social relationships that set the stage for future long-term, reciprocal partnerships.

Psychologists who work with children must understand the normative developmental context in which an assessment takes place. Although a nomothetic approach will involve the use of normative comparisons, the interpretation of test results must accompany a keen understanding of each child's place along a developmental continuum. Developmental and cognitive issues also dictate the choice of tests that psychologists have at their disposal at any particular time. What follows is a discussion of self, affective, and relational development at four ages: preschool, early school age, late childhood, and adolescence. Furthermore, the assessment choices for each stage are highlighted.

Preschoolers

Psychoanalytic and object relations theorists (Fairbairn, 1954; Kernberg, 1976; Kohut, 1977, 1987; Winnicott, 1958, 1971) have posited that this period of development is vital to the creation of a stable concept of self and complex representations of others. For instance, Kohut theorized that an infant is innately driven to find reciprocal and valuable relationships with others who will care for him or her. The infant relies on these significant others not only for proper and healthy physical development, but for psychological development as well. At first, the infant self is characterized by a poor differentiation between the self and others (Kohut, 1977). The self is unstable and without boundaries. For this reason, infants require others to help maintain structure or stability of the self over time. Because others are required to help maintain the infant's sense of self, he or she is unable to differentiate him- or herself from others.

Object relations theory (e.g., Winnicott, 1971) states that a child's sense of self is derived and formed by gradual and inevitable but mild failures of empathy. From time to time, even the best parents will fail to mirror their child or to provide access to idealization. Through this process, the child forms solid and stable internalizations of others and their functions. The child begins to see others in his or her life as real and complex, differentiated, and apart from the child's self-organization. Thus, a child who is imperfectly soothed learns to soothe him/herself; a child who grows hungry learns to cry or seek sustenance on his/her own. The boundaries between "me" and "not me" become clearer, and a self is born.

Research suggests that by age three, most children are able to describe, in at least rudimentary terms, their own physical states (Damon & Hart, 1982). The ability to label hunger, sleepiness, and pain is a vital process that can alert caregivers to the internal states of the child. The labeling of these experiences is not only important for helping the child communicate those needs that are most important for his or her physical survival, but they also ensure continued close contact with primary caregivers. Similar to the situation in the development of self-concept, very young children have a limited ability to label affective experience. As children progress linguistically, they become able to label basic mood states, such as "happy" and "sad," as well as interpret the emotions expressed by others. During this period of development, the child's ability to understand and express behavioral correlates of emotion increases in accuracy and complexity (Bretherton, Fritz, Zahn-Waxler, & Ridgeway, 1986).

Related to the assessment needs of young children is the observation that, although they are not able to express self and affect constructs verbally, they are extremely expressive in their play and behavior. Underlying both play therapy and play assessment is the assumption that children will enact, demonstrate, and project their internal experience onto the toys and objects around them. Although they may lack the ability to label their internal experience, they are quick to enact their internal struggles, fears, and fantasies in whatever manner is available to them. Despite being clinically rich, the play messages of children must be read and interpreted by skilled clinicians who are able to weave theory, context, and the idiographic nature of the child's history and presentation to accurately read the child's message. In addition, more and more assessments are available that quantify the parents' concerns about their child's affective and behavioral functioning. Several behavior rating scales are available for parents of very young children, some as young as 2 years old (see chapters by Achenbach, and Kamphaus, VanDeventer, Brueggemann, & Barry in this volume).

Early School Age

Between the ages of four and six, children are able to express aspects of self-concept through physical descriptors, behaviors, and activities. Harter (1990) notes that children of this age make reliable appraisals of their cognitive, physical, and social competence, as well as their general behavior and conduct. When asked, "What are you like?" a child at this age might respond with descriptors such as "I'm a boy," "I have long hair," or "I'm a fast runner." Self-concept at this age tends to be rather concrete and "black and white." Therefore, children will assume that their personal attributes are absolute and unchanging. For example, one is either a fast runner or a slow runner. Moreover, the labels children choose for themselves are often based on what they hear from others. A child who is frequently told that she is smart may begin to label herself as smart, without a full appreciation of what this really means, other than that it is a positive attribute.

Affective labeling becomes much more accurate during this period of development. Children's repertoires of affective labels continue to increase beyond "happy," "sad," and "glad," to include descriptors of anticipatory anxiety, longing, anger, and frustration (Sprinthall & Burke, 1985). Furthermore, as they develop during this period, children are able to more fully understand their emotional experience beyond that of mere physical sensation. There is increasing consideration of others' internal experience, and they begin to understand that others may express emotion that is inconsistent with their internal experience, in order to manipulate the affect of others (i.e., deceit and humor). This cognitive and affective development results in a dichotomy that is so often intriguing or troublesome to parents: although the child has a wonderful and newfound appreciation of humor, he or she also has a newfound ability to lie.

Given these changes, children can be increasingly called upon to give voice to their internal and private experiences in a clinical setting. Although limitations in reading preclude self-report measures, oral sentence completion tasks and structured projective techniques such as the Rorschach (Exner, 2003) and Roberts-2 (Roberts & Gruber, 2005) are particularly useful. The ability to deceive or to hide one's true feelings and intentions has implications for assessment. As children age, they become more and more sophisticated at reporting partial truths or deliberate distortions, due to perceived risks of embarrassment or punishment. Thus, the clinician must be adept at communicating a sense of safety in the assessment relationship with a child. In addition, the use of projective techniques becomes important here because they are less sensitive to deliberate distortion, compared with various self-report measures or interviews.

Late Childhood

During the latency years (ages seven to eleven years), children gain an experience of "sometimes" (Harter, 1990). That is, they begin to see that sometimes they can possess a particular attribute or characteristic (such as honesty), but that at other times they may not. Furthermore, latency-aged children begin to incorporate psychological and social processes into their self-concept. The notion of being "caring" or "shy" begins to emerge, as does a more complex manner of social comparison. Specifically, although younger children often have an unrealistically positive self-appraisal, latency-age children are able to use social comparison to modify and alter their self-understanding and self-concept. Therefore, one is not merely a fast runner, but the "fastest runner in class" or "faster than Jenss, but slower than Katrina."

Emotionally, latency children have a greater appreciation for emotional complexity and personal control. They begin to understand that more than one emotion can be simultaneously held or that some emotions are more transient than others (Burgess & Rubin, 2000). The child gains some understanding of the relationship between feelings and thoughts. The object relations literature suggests that there are several developmental affective tasks during latency: the development of a sense of self, the ability to tolerate affect and manage internal urges, and the refinement of an internal, affective locus of control (Freedman, 1996). In some ways, this period is highlighted by a newfound ability to regulate affective experiences and their expression. From an Eriksonian perspective, the child turns his or her affective focus outward so as to learn about and explore the world in preparation for more mature relationship development during adolescence (Erikson, 1993). As Anna Freud (1968) noted, children tend to focus outward and are not typically predisposed to introspection. This is particularly true for emotional development during latency.

Latency-aged children become better descriptors of their social selves than are younger children. They continue to look to activities in which they participate to help in social definition. Thus, if a child participates in an activity (e.g., sports) that is seen as socially positive, the child will describe him- or herself positively. However, as latency-aged children continue to make social comparisons (at both micro and macro levels), self-appraisal suffers. Research indicates that self-esteem diminishes from ages 9 to 13 because children have become more and more socially reflective and self-aware. This trend has even been found to be robust cross-culturally (Gray-Little & Hafdahl, 2000; Rhodes, Roffman, Reddy, & Fredriksen, 2004). Awareness of social functioning and cognitive comparison seem to have a painful consequence for many latency-aged children, because they struggle to reconcile their own sense of fallibility with the perceived positive attributes of others.

Developments in cognitive, linguistic, and reflective capacities allow for the use of self-report measures at this age. The convergence of reading ability and some capacity for self-reflection allows child clinicians to assess these self-reported behaviors, feelings, and thoughts. However, as Woolley, Bowen, and Bowen (2004) asserted, the major assumption of child self-report measures is that children interpret the items in a manner that the test designers intended. Although not generally convergent with parent or teacher reports (Achenbach, McConaughy, & Howell, 1987), the addition of self-reported symptoms is an important addition to the assessment battery. Furthermore, the ability to write and understand the assessment task allows for the use of sentence completion tests with children of this age.

Adolescence

Because of increased complexity of cognitive processing, adolescents are increasingly able to use several different categories for self-description (Harter, 1990; Nurmi, 2004). As their vocabulary and self-reflection abilities increase, they gain the ability to engage in comparisons with others. Furthermore, they are able to note that seemingly contradictory self-descriptions can be truly contingent upon internal states and social setting (e.g., sometimes one can be gregarious and outgoing, whereas, at other times, he or she is shy and reserved). These conflicting descriptions are a source of distress for middle adolescents. At a time when adolescents are working to understand who they are, they are also able to understand that identity is complex and multifaceted. By late adolescence, teenagers are less distressed by seeming contradictions in self-descriptors and may even be able to look to this as a marker of complexity in a unified whole self-perspective.

As adolescents develop, their understanding of emotion continues to be refined and integrated. It has been hypothesized that adolescents revisit a state of egocentrism because their observations turn increasingly inward, toward their own emotional and cognitive experiences (Bjorklund & Green, 1992; Elkind, 1967). Thus, early to middle adolescents often will be emotionally showy and express affect in transient and superficial ways. Unlike younger children, they are also more able to label affect and reflect on their affective experiences.

As adolescents' ability to express affect increases, so does the complexity of their social relationships. As self-reflection increases, so does anxiety around social comparison. Early adolescence is usually marked by extreme adherence to social rules and mores, trying to fit in with others, and anxiety around any perceived differences (Harter, 1990; Nurmi, 2004). As they grow older and their self-concept grows more complex, teenagers are able to tolerate social differences and adopt a social identity and a self-identity that are based more on choice than on social consequence.

During adolescence, the assessment options available to clinicians are even more varied than they are for adult patients. As is true for younger children, teacher and parent reports can augment self-report and projective test data. Although teenagers are generally seen as important informants about their internal experience (Loeber, Green, & Lahey, 1990), they may be more clandestine about their behavioral issues, particularly when assessment takes place in an inpatient or detention facility (MacLeod, McNamee, Boyle, Offord, & Friedrich, 1999; Stanger & Lewis, 1993). However, clinicians assessing adolescent patients should rely in particular on a multimethod-multirater-multidomain (Campbell & Fiske, 1959) approach to assessment.

MULTIMETHOD-MULTITRAIT ASSESSMENT

Although a major portion of this book contains specific information about an array of different tests, the reader should understand that these tests are merely tools with which the clinician develops his or her comprehensive understanding of the child or adolescent. The various authors of individual chapters in this volume caution the reader that no particular test should be used alone to answer referral issues. As was stated by Verhulst (1995), "Essential for the assessment and diagnosis of child psychopathology is the recognition that there is no single approach to assessment and diagnosis that is superior to all others. Instead we need different approaches and different data sources to arrive at a comprehensive picture of a child's functioning" (p. 209).

The history of this practice requires a bit of a story, taken from part of Len Handler's (2004b) presidential address to the Society for Personality Assessment in 2004, which was reprinted in the *SPA Exchange* (Winter, 2004):

> During World War II the Office of Strategic Services, the forerunner of the CIA, was given the task of selecting men and women to spy for the allies. It seems that previously, those chosen for various espionage duties were failing in the field. Henry Murray, along with a number of psychologists, psychiatrists and anthropologists, got together at Station S (for secret), and constructed a three and a half day evaluation procedure consisting of interviews, some of which were conducted under pressure; observations; self-report measures; projective measures; situational tests; intellectual measures; almost 70 measures in all, many with multiple parts. The data for each candidate were then aggregated by a small group of experts, who wrote an evaluation of the candidate's strengths and weaknesses. This evaluation was then discussed in a full staff meeting, where a final decision was made concerning the candidate's suitability as a spy.
>
> In 1948 Murray and his associates published a book about the program, called *Assessment of Men* (Office of Strategic Services Assessment Staff, 1948). The book gives the reader a vivid and detailed description of the entire program. Murray and his co-authors made several recommendations to future assessors worth repeating here because they have relevance for assessment today.
>
> 1. Conduct the assessment program within a social matrix in which it is possible to have *frequent* informal contacts and *many* opportunities to observe candidates' responses.
> 2. Use many different kinds of evaluation techniques—interview data, self-report measures, projective techniques, and situational tests.
> 3. Employ life-like complicated tasks in a real environment, so that their solution requires high-level integration.
> 4. Enough data should be collected and enough time should be taken so that the chief components of the personality are identified.
> 5. The data should be systematically recorded so they will lend themselves to statistical comparisons.
> 6. Attention should be given to perfecting appraisal techniques to increase reliability and validity.
>
> One of the members of the OSS evaluation team, by the way, was Donald Fiske. Murray and Fiske must have influenced each other because eleven years after the publication of *Assessment of Men,* Campbell and Fiske (1959) described the Multi-trait, Multi-Method approach to test validation, demonstrating that there could be significant error in validity findings due to the use of similar methods. The validity coefficient could be due to the error caused by using measures that employed *similar* methodology. The implication of this approach is that more than one assessment method must be included in a research design to reduce error and that more than one trait should be measured, as well.

There are a number of clinical advantages of multimethod/multitrait assessments. First, multiple sources of assessment enhance the quality of the assessments by creating a more comprehensive picture of the child's functioning than could be possible through the examination of the results from each informant alone. As stated by Meyer (1996), "Recognizing the limitations and biases associated with each personality assessment method and understanding the ways in which each method is sensitive to different external realities would help to understand how two or more of these incomplete and imperfect tools can be used together to gain a more accurate picture of clinical phenomena" (pp. 560–561). Furthermore, in the Psychological Assessment Work Group (PAWG) Report, Meyer et al. (2001) reported a number of studies that clearly showed a dramatically high number of diagnostic errors when only one instrument or only one method of measurement was used, instead of multiple measures. The validity of empirical research is compromised when information is derived from a single method of measurement, or from a single construct that has been operationally defined in a single way. The report points out that just as these two sources of bias produce less valid research, they will also compromise the validity of individual assessments. They make the point that "Assessments will be less valid and accurate to the extent that they rely on a single method for gathering patient information and they will be less valid to the extent that they rely on constructs that have been defined according to a single format or set of principles" (p. 14). The logical conclusion, therefore, is that a test battery that is constructed with the use of multiple methods provides a means of avoiding method bias.

Moreover, such a battery represents the standard for good clinical practice. The *Standards of Practice* (1999), authored jointly by the American Educational Research Association, the American Psychological Association, and the National Council on Measurement in Education, has the following to say about assessment:

> The interpretation of tests or test battery results generally should be based upon multiple sources of convergent and collateral data and an understanding of the normative, empirical and theoretical foundations as well as the limitations of such tests (Standard 12.18).

> The interpretation of test scores or patterns of test battery results should take cognizance of the many factors that may influence a particular testing outcome. Standard 11.20 states: In educational, clinical or counseling settings, a test taker's score should not be interpreted in isolation; collateral information that may lead to alternative explanations for the examinee's test performance should be considered (Standard 12.19).

Despite the clinical utility of this model, research has indicated that the correlations between measurement types are often poor (Achenbach, Dumenci, & Rescorla, 2002; Achenbach et al., 1987; De Los Reyes & Kazdin, 2005; Krishnamurthy, Archer, & House, 1996; McCrae, 1994). This does not limit the utility of a multimethod assessment model, nor does it indicate that any of the pieces of data are necessarily less correct than others (Achenbach et al., 2002; Ferdinand et al., 2003; Meyer, 1996; Verhulst, Dekker, & Van der Ende, 1997; Verhulst & Van der Ende, 1992). However, this lack of correlation forces clinicians to make decisions about the relative weights of assessment data and about how to integrate disparate pieces of information.

SUMMARY

Assessment approaches should match the developmental level of the child or adolescent. As children develop more and more cognitive, affective, and interpersonal resources, an assessor can increasingly rely on the child to provide information. Although projective techniques and the reports of others can be useful for all child and adolescent patients, as children age, they become invaluable reporters of their own affective and cognitive experiences.

It is important that child and adolescent clinicians approach assessment from a multimethod-multirater-mutidomain perspective at all ages. The availability of multiple forms and methods of assessment allows for an integration of data that yields a rich clinical picture. Data obtained from cognitive assessment, self-report, projective data, interviews, and reports from others may often be discrepant (Achenbach et al., 2002; Achenbach et al., 1987; De Los Reyes & Kazdin, 2005), but it is this discrepancy that broadens the clinical picture and enhances the validity of the conclusions drawn (Meyer, 2002). Although it may go without saying, it is vital that clinicians use multiple sources of data, particularly when making diagnostic decisions and classifications that will be meaningful for treatment.

ACKNOWLEDGMENTS

The authors acknowledge the work of Jenss Chang and Katrina Schnoebelen in the preparation of this chapter.

REFERENCES

Achenbach, T. M., Dumenci, L., & Rescorla, L. A. (2002). Ten-year comparisons of problems and competencies for national samples of youth: Self, parent and teacher reports. *Journal of Emotional and Behavioral Disorders, 10*, 194–203.

Achenbach, T. M., McConaughy, S. H., & Howell, C. T. (1987). Child/adolescent behavioral and emotional problems: Implications of cross-informant correlations for situational specificity. *Psychological Bulletin, 101*, 213–232.

American Educational Research Association, American Psychological Association, & National Council on Measurement in Education. (1999). Standards for educational and psychological testing. Washington, DC: American Educational Research Association.

Bjorklund, D. F., & Green, B. L. (1992). The adaptive nature of cognitive immaturity. *American Psychologist, 47*, 46–54.

Bretherton, I., Fritz, J., Zahn-Waxler, C., & Ridgeway, D. (1986). Learning to talk about emotions: A functionalist perspective. *Child Development, 57*, 529–548.

Burgess, K. B., & Rubin, K. H. (2000). Middle childhood: Social and emotional development. In A. E. Kazdin (Ed.), *Encyclopedia of psychology* (Vol. 5, pp. 234–239). Washington, DC: American Psychological Association.

Camara, W. J., Nathan, J. S., & Puente, A. E. (2000). Psychological test usage: Implications in professional psychology. *Professional Psychology: Research and Practice, 31*, 141–154.

Campbell, D. T., & Fiske, D. W. (1959). Convergent and discriminant validation by the multitrait-multimethod matrix. *Psychological Bulletin, 56*, 81–105.

Clemence, A. J., & Handler, L. (2001). Psychological assessment on internship: A survey of training directors and their expectations for students. *Journal of Personality Assessment, 76*, 18–47.

Damon, W., & Hart, D. (1982). The development of self-understanding from infancy through adolescence. *Child Development, 53*, 841–864.

De Los Reyes, A., & Kazdin, A. E. (2005). Informant discrepancies in the assessment of childhood psychopathology: A critical review, theoretical framework, and recommendations for further study. *Psychological Bulletin, 131*, 483–509.

Elkind, D. (1967). Egocentrism in adolescence. *Child Development, 38*, 1025–1034.

Erikson, E. H. (1993). Eight stages of man. In E. H. Erikson (Ed.), *Childhood and society* (pp. 247–269). New York: W. W. Norton.

Exner, J. E. (2003). *The Rorschach: A comprehensive system* (4th ed.). New York: Wiley.

Fairbairn, W. R. D. (1954). *An object relations theory of personality*. New York: Basic Books.

Ferdinand, R. F., Hoogerheide, K. N., van der Ende, J., Heijmens Visser, J., Koot, H. M., Kasius, M. C., et al. (2003). The role of the clinician: Three-year predictive value of parents', teachers', and clinicians' judgment of childhood psychopathology. *Journal of Child Psychology and Psychiatry, 44*, 867–876.

Freedman, S. (1996). Role of selfobject experiences in affective development during latency. *Psychoanalytic Psychology, 13*, 101–127.

Freud, A. (1968). Indications and contraindications for child analysis. *Psychoanalytic Study of the Child, 23*, 37–46.

Gray-Little, B., & Hafdahl, A. R. (2000). Factors influencing racial comparisons of self-esteem: A quantitative review. *Psychological Bulletin, 126*, 26–54.

Handler, L. (1998). The clinical interpretation of the Wechsler Intelligence Tests as personality instruments. In L. Handler & M. Hilsenroth (Eds.), *Teaching and Learning Personality Assessment* (pp. 295–324). Mahwah, NJ: Lawrence Erlbaum Associates.

Handler, L. (1999). Assessment of playfulness: Hermann Rorschach meets D. W. Winnicott. *Journal of Personality assessment, 72,* 208–217.

Handler, L. (2002, July). *Non-traditional approaches to the administration and interpretation of projective tests.* Paper presented at the XVII Congress of Rorschach and other Projective Methods, Rome, Italy.

Handler, L. (2004a, Winter). Presidential Address. *SPA Exchange, 14,* 1–3.

Handler, L. (2004b, August). *A changing paradigm in personality assessment.* Paper presented at the Annual Meeting, European Rorschach Society, Stockholm, Sweden.

Handler, L. (2005, July). *A Rorschach assessment amplified: Using play in testing of the limits.* Paper presented at the XVIII Congress of Rorschach and Other Projective Methods, Barcelona, Spain.

Handler, L., & Meyer, G. J. (1998). The importance of teaching and learning personality assessment. In L. Handler & M. J. Hilsenroth (Eds.), *Teaching and learning personality assessment.* Mahwah, NJ: Lawrence Erlbaum Associates.

Harter, S. (1990). Issues in the assessment of the self-concept of children and adolescents. In A. M. LaGreca (Ed.), *Through the eyes of the child: Obtaining self-reports from children and adolescents.* Needham Heights, MA: Allyn & Bacon.

House, A. (2002). *The first session with children and adolescents: Conducting a comprehensive mental health evaluation.* New York: Guilford Press.

Kelly, F. (1999). *The psychological assessment of abused and traumatized children.* Mahwah, NJ: Lawrence Erlbaum Associates.

Kernberg, O. F. (1976). *Object relations theory and clinical psychoanalysis.* New York: Aronson.

Klopfer, B., Ainsworth, M. D., Klopfer, W. G., & Holt, R. R. (1954). *Developments in the Rorschach technique: Vol. I. Technique and theory.* Oxford, England: World Book.

Kohut, H. (1977). *The restoration of the self.* Madison, CT: International Universities Press.

Kohut, H. (1987). In M. Elson (Ed.), *The Kohut seminars on self psychology and psychotherapy with adolescents and young adults.* New York: Norton.

Krishnamurthy, R., Archer, R. P., & House, J. J. (1996). The MMPI-A and Rorschach: A failure to establish convergent validity. *Assessment, 3*, 179–191.

Lenhart, L. A., & Rabiner, D. L. (1995). An integrative approach to the study of social competence in adolescence. *Development and Psychopathology, 7*, 543–561.

Loeber, R., Green, S., & Lahey, B. B. (1990). Mental health professionals' perception of the utility of children, mothers, and teachers as informants on childhood psychopathology. *Journal of Clinical Child Psychology, 19*, 136–143.

MacLeod, R. J., McNamee, J. E., Boyle, M. H., Offord, D. R., & Friedrich, M. (1999). Identification of childhood psychiatric disorder by informant: Comparisons of clinic and community samples. *Canadian Journal of Psychiatry, 44*, 144–150.

McCrae, R. R. (1994). The counterpoint of personality assessment: Self-reports and observer ratings. *Assessment, 1*, 159–172.

McHale, S. M., Dariotis, J. K., & Kauh, T. J. (2003). Social development and social relationships in middle childhood. In R. M. Lerner, M. A. Easterbrooks & J. Mistry (Eds.), *Handbook of psychology: Developmental psychology* (Vol. 6, pp. 241–265). Hoboken, NJ: Wiley & Sons.

Meyer, G. J. (1996). The Rorschach and MMPI: Toward a more scientifically differentiated understanding of cross-method assessment. *Journal of Personality Assessment, 67*, 558–578.

Meyer, G. J. (2002). Implications of information-gathering methods for a refined taxonomy of psychopathology. In L. E. Beutler & M. L. Malik (Eds.), *Rethinking the DSM: A psychological perspective* (pp. 69–105). Washington, DC: American Psychological Association.

Meyer, G. J., Finn, S. E., Eyde, L. D., Kay, G. G., Moreland, K. L., Dies, R. R., et al. (2001). Psychological testing and psychological assessment: A review of evidence and issues. *American Psychologist, 56*, 128–165.

Nurmi, J. E. (2004). Socialization and self-development. In R. M. Lerner & L. Steinberg (Eds.), *Handbook of adolescent psychology* (2nd ed.). Hoboken, NJ: John Wiley & Sons.

Office of Strategic Services Assessment Staff. (1948). *Assessment of men.* Oxford, England: Rinehart.

Rhodes, J., Roffman, J., Reddy, R., & Fredriksen, K. (2004). Changes in self-esteem during middle school years: A latent growth curve study of individual and contextual influences. *Journal of School Psychology, 42,* 243–261.

Roberts, G. E., & Gruber, C. P. (2005). *Roberts-2 manual.* Los Angeles: Western Psychological Services.

Schafer, R. (1954). Some applications of contemporary psychoanalytic theory to projective testing. *Journal of Projective Techniques, 18,* 441–447.

Schafer, R. (1956). Transference in the patient's reaction to the tester. *Journal of Projective Techniques, 20,* 26–32.

Siegel, M. (1987). *Psychological testing from early childhood through adolescence.* Madison, CT: International Universities Press.

Sprinthall, N. A., & Burke, S. M. (1985). Intellectual, interpersonal, and emotional development during childhood. *Journal of Humanistic Counseling, Education and Development, 24,* 50–58.

Stanger, C., & Lewis, M. (1993). Agreement among parents, teachers, and children on internalizing and externalizing behavior problems. *Journal of Clinical Child Psychology, 22,* 107–115.

Stone, W. L., & Lemanek, K. L. (1990). Developmental issues in children's self-reports. In A. M. LaGreca (Ed.), *Through the eyes of the child: Obtaining self-reports from children and adolescents* (pp. 18–56). Needham Heights, MA: Allyn & Bacon.

Thorndike, E. L. (1918). The nature, purposes, and general methods of measurements of educational products. In G. M. Whipple (Ed.), *Seventeenth yearbook of the national society for the study of education* (Vol. 2, pp. 16–24). Bloomington, IL: Public School Publishing.

Verhulst, F. C. (1995). Recent developments in the assessment and diagnosis of child psychopathology. *European Child and Adolescent Psychiatry, 11,* 203–212.

Verhulst, F. C., Dekker, M. C., & Van der Ende, J. (1997). Parent, teacher, and self-reports as predictors of signs of disturbance in adolescents: Whose information carries the most weight? *Acta Psychiatrica Scandinavica, 96,* 75–81.

Verhulst, F. C., & Van der Ende, J. (1992). Agreement between parents' reports and adolescents' self-reports of problem behavior. *Journal of Child Psychology and Psychiatry, 33,* 1011–1023.

Westen, D., Klepser, J., Ruffins, S. A., Silverman, M., Lifton, N., & Boekamp, J. (1991). Object relations in childhood and adolescence: The development of working representations. *Journal of Consulting and Clinical Psychology, 59,* 400–409.

Winnicott, D. W. (1958). *Collected papers.* New York: Basic Books.

Winnicott, D. (1965). The theory of the parent-infant relationship. In D. W. Winnicott, *The maturational processes and the facilitating environment* (pp. 37–55). New York: International Universities Press.

Winnicott, D. W. (1971). Mirror-role of mother and family in child development. In D. W. Winnicott (Ed.), *Playing and reality.* London: Tavistock.

Winnicott, D. W. (1989). The squiggle game. In C. Winnicott, R. Shepard, & M. Davis (Eds.), *D. W. Winnicott: Psycho-analytic explorations.* Cambridge, MA: Harvard University Press.

Woolley, M. E., Bowen, G. L., & Bowen, N. K. (2004). Cognitive pretesting and developmental validity of child self-report instruments: Theory and applications. *Research on Social Work Practice, 14,* 191–200.

ISSUES AND CONCEPTS IN CHILD AND ADOLESCENT ASSESSMENT

2

PERSONALITY ASSESSMENT
IN SCHOOLS

Jed Yalof and Pamela Abraham
Immaculata University

In this chapter, we present an overview of core issues that are associated with conducting personality assessments in schools. We recognize that most psychologists who work in schools have the education, training, and credentialing specific to the "school psychologist" title, but we also appreciate that there are psychologists whose primary employment and professional role identification are not with the school district. As such, we designated the interface between psychologists and schools as primary, secondary, or tertiary, depending on the degree to which employment and work activities are dedicated specifically to the school system. By "primary work activities" we refer to psychologists who are employed full-time either by a school district or by a private school. By "secondary work activities" we refer to psychologists who work as contracted or on a per diem basis in the schools. By "tertiary work activities" we refer to psychologists in non-school settings (e.g., private practice, residential-psychiatric, forensic) whose personality assessments of school-age children might bring them into contact with the school system.

The chapter proceeds as follows. First, we discuss Section 504 of the 1973 Civil Rights Act and the Individuals with Disabilities Education Act (Section 504, 1973 and IDEA 1997, as discussed in Miller & Newbill, 1998 and Jacob & Hartshorne, 2003, and referenced as a citation in Jacob & Hartshorne, 2003) because of their particular relevance to students with behavior, social-emotional, and ideational problems that warrant special education consideration. Both Section 504 and IDEA are very familiar to psychologists who work primarily in school districts, but are possibly less familiar to psychologists whose personality assessment work only occasionally overlaps with the educational system. Second, we present a framework for personality assessment and discuss different tests and measures that are useful in the identification of referral issues and for conducting personality assessments in schools that lead to decisions about eligibility for special education services. Third, we discuss some of the professional climate issues in school psychology that can affect personality assessment in schools. Fourth, we discuss school psychology training in personality assessment. Fifth, we present a case study.

SECTION 504 AND IDEA

Miller & Newbill (1998) and Jacob and Hartshorne (2003) provide information about Section 504 and IDEA and Section 504 of the 1973 Civil Rights Act. Section 504 is designed to protect the rights of individuals who participate in programs or activities that receive federal funding (Jacob & Hartshorne, 2003; Miller & Newbill, 1998). Included among individuals protected by Section 504 are school-age children who have been determined to have a handicapping condition. A student is defined as handicapped if he or she has "a physical or mental impairment which substantially limits one or more of a person's major life activities; has a record of such impairment, or is regarded as having such an impairment" (Miller & Newbill, 1998, pp. 2–3). Included among Section 504 handicapping conditions are ADD/ADHD, anxiety, dysthymia, dyslexia, eating disorders, emotional disorders, post-traumatic stress disorders, drug and alcohol dependency, learning disabilities, and suicidal tendencies (Jacob & Hartshorne, 2003; Miller & Newbill, 1998). Thus, Section 504 provides broad antidiscrimination protection for students whose mental health or learning needs have been determined to reflect a handicapping condition. A 504 Service/Accommodation Plan, coordinated by school personnel knowledgeable about a child or adolescent, can be implemented even when the handicap does not adversely affect the student's educational performance (e.g., an adolescent with bulimia who excels academically, but would benefit from school-based, group-oriented psycho-educational counseling led by a consulting psychologist who is hired and funded by the district).

IDEA is one subcategory of Section 504. Under IDEA, special education services are available to students whose disability adversely affects their performance (Miller & Newbill, 1998). There are 13 possible disabilities under IDEA: autism, deaf-blindness, deafness, emotional disturbance, hearing impairment, mental retardation, multiple disabilities, orthopedic impairment, other health impairment, specific learning disability, speech or language impairment, traumatic brain injury, and visual impairment. If a student is designated as having a disability under IDEA, then an Individualized Educational Program (IEP) is required and developed in order to provide the student with an individually designed instructional program (e.g., specialized reading program, supplemental math support, extended school year, extended testing time, behavioral intervention, individual counseling, group counseling). The IEP is a written plan of intervention, short-term objectives, and measurable, annual goals that emerge from an evaluation by a multidisciplinary team (i.e., qualified professionals and the parent[s]) and reflects district compliance with the law (Jacob & Hartshorne, 2003; Miller & Newbill, 1998).

The one IDEA category that has particular relevance to the personality assessor is emotional disturbance (ED). ED is defined by the Federal Code of Regulations, Title 34, Section 300.7 (Jacob & Hartshorne, 2003) as follows:

> (i) The term means a condition exhibiting one or more of the following characteristics over a long period of time and to a marked degree that adversely affects a child's educational performance. (A) An inability to learn that cannot be explained by intellectual, sensory, or other health factors. (B) An inability to build on or maintain satisfactory interpersonal relationships with peers and teachers. (C) Inappropriate types of behavior or feelings under normal circumstances. (D) A general or pervasive mood of unhappiness or depression. (E) A tendency to develop physical symptoms or fears associated with personal or school problems. (ii) The term includes schizophrenia. The term does not apply to children who are socially maladjusted unless it is determined that they have an emotional disturbance. (pp. 128–129)

In the next section, we offer a brief framework for conceptualizing and organizing the school psychological evaluation that includes personality assessment and offers an overview of the range of tests and measures that are useful when one is considering how to respond conscientiously to a referral concern.

A FRAMEWORK FOR PERSONALITY ASSESSMENT

The school psychologist makes decisions about assessment strategies based on referral information within the context of constraint or latitude provided by the school district. Districts vary in the flexibility they afford psychologists to select measures. There may be some school districts, for example, where there is a preference for certain types of achievement tests, certain types of behavior ratings, and/or a very cautious attitude toward such tests as the Rorschach because of concerns that may range from fear of misuse, invasion of privacy (e.g., Jacob & Hartshorne, 2003), and relevance to school-related problems. Within this framework of flexibility or constraint, the tests that the psychologist uses will vary, depending on the child/adolescent referral information. School reports, case history, previous evaluations, and treatment/intervention information need to be considered when the test battery is being designed.

Understanding the referral question helps to determine the choice of methods and the areas to be assessed. During the referral, it is important to obtain information about the child's context from an ecological point of view (home, family, community, culture, classroom, peers, teachers, school). It is necessary to clarify whether the child/adolescent is a language minority student and determine his or her level of acculturation if the child/adolescent or parent/guardian is from another country. It is important for school psychologists to understand the risk factors for the development of mental problems for culturally different children. These risk factors include immigration, family role changes, and the experience of racism and prejudice (Gopaul-McNicol & Thomas-Presswood, 1998). Pre-referral intervention responses serve as pivotal information in understanding what methods may be chosen to further delineate a child/adolescent's needs. Strengths and weaknesses from prior assessments also serve as baseline information for the determination of progress, change, and the child's outcome. Learning about research on the variability of different raters in different settings and ways to integrate discrepant data is an important preliminary step prior to obtaining data from rating scales (Prevatt, 1999). Familiarity with educational laws and terms (e.g., Jacob & Hartshorne, 2003) that are used to define eligibility for services is also important for understanding how conclusions from test data will address the referral issues. Following the collection of referral information, the evaluator obtains a developmental, medical, and educational history and conducts observations of the child within the school setting and interviews with the child/adolescent, parents, and teachers.

We appreciate the evolving nature of available tests from which psychologists can select when coordinating an assessment battery. Given the many available tests from which to choose, we offer a categorical matrix of selected assessment instruments (Appendix). Our decision to include these particular tests is based mainly on direct clinical and/or teaching experience with the instrument and is not meant as a negative evaluation of other tests and measures we have excluded. There are single as well as multiple domain measures represented. The list is not exhaustive and will only represent a sampling of those tests that may be beneficial in clarifying some of the more common child/adolescent problematic areas. The choice of tests should coincide with the referral questions. As can be seen from this matrix, there are many different areas that a psychologist who conducts personality assessments in schools needs to consider when prioritizing test selection relative to referral information. In addition, there are other issues that carry weight and influence the assessment process in schools. We have identified several such issues and discuss them in the next section.

PROFESSIONAL CLIMATE ISSUES AND SCHOOL PSYCHOLOGY PERSONALITY ASSESSMENT

Lehr and Christenson (2002) provide a description of a positive school climate, focusing on the importance of an interpersonal ambience generated by the quality of school community, personnel, and spirit that permeates the learning environment. They discuss the school's ecology (e.g., cleanliness, equipment), milieu (e.g., teacher and student morale), social system (e.g., administrative organization, community school relations), and culture (e.g., norms, values, and belief systems of different groups within the school) as variables that shape school climate. The school psychologist has to consider not only climate issues that affect the particular school in which he or she works (or is testing for), but also broader, more general issues that are part of the professional climate in school psychology.

Building on the description of "school climate" offered by Lehr and Christenson (2002), several professional climate issues that affect personality testing in schools are highlighted: (1) The overrepresentation of minorities in special education. (2) The relationship between ED, social maladjustment (SM), conduct disorders (CD), internalizing-externalizing disorders, and comorbidity. (3) The relevance of the *Diagnostic and Statistical Manual of Mental Disorders,* 4th edition [DSM-IV-TR] (American Psychiatric Association, 2000) to school psychology practice. (4) Paradigm shift from classification to early identification and intervention. These issues are discussed below.

Increased Incidence of Minority Representation in Special Education

In 2000, Black children made up 22% of all children in public school with one of three disabilities (specific learning disability [LD], ED, and mental retardation [MR]), even though they were only 17% of the total public school population (National Center for Education Statistics [NCES], 2001). In addition, Black children disproportionately represented 27% of all children with an emotional disturbance. Interestingly, 5% of all students have serious emotional disturbance; however, in 2001 under IDEA, less than 1% qualified for services (Koyanagi, 2003). Not only are minority children, particularly Black children, overidentified as ED, but many children with disabilities are not identified or perhaps are misidentified. As suggested by the Elementary and Middle School Technical Assistance Center (EMSTAC) (2005), the overidentification of Black children may be viewed as racial segregation, leading to removal of these children from mainstream classrooms, lower teacher expectations, and less challenging instruction. On the other hand, children not identified or misidentified may be mislabeled as LD, seen as exhibiting disruptive behaviors, and considered to be SM, and therefore not ED. These children are at increased risk for being expelled as opposed to being identified as ED (Koppelman, 2004; Olympia et al., 2004).

Wagner (1995) noted that African American youths, particularly males, were overdiagnosed with social emotional disturbance (SED), along with two other disabilities, deafness and visual impairment. He hypothesized that poverty contributed significantly to these impairments. Wagner also speculated that poverty was an important variable that needed additional attention when the high rates of ED classification among minority youth are being considered.

Several authors have addressed issues related to overidentification and increased incidence of minority representation in special education (Cullinan, Epstein, & Sabornie, 1992; Harry, 1994; Hughes & Bray, 2004; Kehle et al., 2004; Reddy, 2001; Shaafombabi, 2005; Wagner, 1995). Yet, despite their overidentification for SED in schools, minority children are less likely to receive mental health services (Surgeon General, 1999), and culturally diverse children are often underserved and are at high risk for psychosocial problems, welfare dependency, and low job productivity (Cross, Bazron, Dennis, & Isaacs, 1989; Pumariega & Cross, 1997). School psychologists must keep abreast of the statistical findings regarding educational outcomes for minority youth, acquire competence in cultural assessment issues, understand the current advantages and disadvantages of classification problems, and, as Wagner (1995) highlighted, search for more appropriate assessment tools and methods for identifying children with SED.

Kehle et al. (2004) offered an "alternative nonenvironmental" genetic reason, "heterosis," for the increase in prevalence of ED/SM characteristics. *Heterosis* is a genetic term used to explain that "secular changes in several cognitive, physical, and psychological characteristics may have the same nonenvironmental etiology" (p. 861). This explanation unfortunately forecloses causality, promoting a polarized view with regard to the dichotomous genetics vs. environmental argument and lowers expectations for those identified as ED/SM. The position of Kehle and colleagues (2004) also contradicts a more current view of understanding psychological problems that are multidimensional and examines multiple vulnerabilities that are environmentally and biologically based (i.e., neurological factors and temperament) (Ingram & Price, 2001).

Relationship Between ED, SM, Internalizing-Externalizing Disorder, and Comorbidity

There are several classification issues that affect personality assessment in schools. For instance, ED, as described above, accounted for less than 1% of all students qualified under IDEA in 2001, even though 5% of all children actually have a serious emotional disturbance (Koyanagi, 2003). Thus, there are more students in need of emotional support than receive it, and there are issues that might complicate this problem. For example, the internalizing (e.g., depression, anxiety)–externalizing (e.g., conduct) dichotomy is popular and has empirical support at the level of factor analysis (Knoff, 2002) but may contribute to overidentification of youngsters with conduct problems and possibly underestimate the presence of comorbid disorders.

Price and Lento (2001) reviewed the prevalence studies on diagnostic categories of disorders and found rates of comorbidity to be in the 50% range, even within the internalizing and externalizing clusters. They emphasized the importance of examining the "constellation of comorbid conditions" with less focus on just problematic behaviors.

Olympia and colleagues (2004) appeared to address this point by noting that the federal interpretation of ED at state and local levels, and the choice and interpretation of tests used to measure internalizing or externalizing disorders can affect classification of SM as well as ED. Olympia and colleagues (2004) also noted some SM/ED definition misconceptions about youngsters with externalizing disorders that might eliminate them from special educational consideration. Examples of these misconceptions are that externalizing disorders do not have high comorbidity, behaviors of those that are disruptive are intentional and can be controlled (whereas ED's are unable to regulate and control behaviors), and children with externalizing behaviors do not have guilt, in contrast to the ED child, who is thought to have guilt. Skiba and Grizzle (1991) addressed concerns about inadequate measures to differentiate SM from ED, including lack of operationally defined definitions of ED and SM, overrepresentation of conduct disorders (CD) in special education, language inconsistencies between IDEA and DSM, misuse of scales identifying students as externalizers vs. internalizers, lack of understanding and training about coexisting disorders, and limited resources related to classification. Other authors indicate that minority children with SED tend to be diagnosed as having an externalizing disorder and conduct disorder, perhaps to the neglect of recognizing internalizing disorders (Carron & Rutter, 1991; Kilgus, Pumariega, & Cuffe, 1995). Difficulties and challenges associated with identifying ED in a school setting have been noted (Skiba & Grizzle, 1991; Skenkovich, 1992; Skiba & Grizzle, 1992; Forness, 1992).

In summary, there is a need for more attention to the comorbidity of disorders and the externalizing/internalizing dichotomy and understanding the overlap of disorders and patterns of adaptation. Assessors' knowledge of overlapping conditions when identifying children for special education may contribute to more accurate decisions about classification, effective prevention strategies, intervention planning, and successful outcomes. There are youngsters who are not readily classified as ED and therefore are unable to access special education because of SM/CD problems that do not meet the ED threshold. The psychologist who evaluates youngsters with ED/SM/CD would benefit the child by obtaining increased training in coexisting disorders and including specific measures of emotional disturbance that highlight primary affect states (e.g., anger, depression, anxiety) and personality characteristics (Lounsbury, 2003) when ruling out ED.

DSM-IV in Schools

DSM-IV-TR represents standard diagnostic language in mental health, but not in school psychology. Despite exposure to DSM in classes (Culross & Nelson, 1997), school psychologists are dedicated primarily to the classification schemas of IDEA. Yet students who qualify under Section 504 for educational accommodations because of an identified disability may be diagnosed as such with the use of DSM-IV, as might be the case when dysthymia or attention deficit disorder is diagnosed. However, Knoff (2002) has questioned the value of using DSM-IV as it pertains to school psychology personality assessment. Knoff identifies five problems with DSM-IV: reliance on the medical model of pathology and disease classification; emphasis on signs, symptoms, and syndromes compared with functional assessment of why a problem occurs; too many diagnostic categories; psychometric issues; and problems in the application of definitions of some diagnosis across settings and their lack of fit with ED as described in IDEA.

An alternative position has been offered by Sattler (1983), who stated over 20 years ago that knowledge of the DSM would help a school psychologist understand mental disorders and communicate with community resources such as psychiatrists and community service centers. Power and DuPaul (1996) also support the importance of having knowledge of the DSM, given the recognition by the National Association of School Psychology (NASP) that school psychologists need to become involved in mental health problems in the schools. Similarly, McBurnett (1996) reviewed the relevance of DSM-IV and found this version to be very useful to psychologists working in schools. Atkins et al. (1996), for example, indicated that the DSM-IV was more empirically sound than other versions and was helpful in the attempt to operationalize the definitions of conduct disorder and ODD.

Moving from Classification to Early Identification and Intervention

Koppelman, in the *National Health Policy Forum* (2004), highlights the need for early intervention to improve the chances for a successful educational outcome. However, the emphasis placed on early identification, proposed by the President's Commission on Excellence in Special Education (PCESE) (2002), recommended screening for learning and/or behavioral problems. Limiting the focus of early identification to behavioral problems without also considering and incorporating emotionality into the matrix of assessment promotes the premise that behaviors can operate independently of other personality features, including the affective domain. School psychologists in practice are frequently required to negotiate this tendency to focus on behaviors to the exclusion of the other components of a functioning child, but it is critical to consider the child holistically (i.e., thought, affect, behavior, culture, race/ethnicity, spirituality) during personality assessments to minimize potential slights to the totality of the child's experience.

Child assessments that give consideration to as many aspects of the child's life as possible, or which use this model as an ideal for which to strive, create opportunities for expanding or evolving the potential for beneficial interventions that are responsive to the assessment process. Sattler (2002) has supported this view by noting that measures of behavioral, social, and the emotional competencies are beneficial for school assessment, recommendations, and evaluation of interventions. The term "evolving context" has been used by Truscott, Catanese, and Abrams (2005) to describe the changes in the special education classification system as these changes pertain to service delivery. Concern regarding lack of coordination among mental health providers and current assessment practices (Hatzichristou, 2002) is central to an understanding of the terminology of Truscott et al. because of the increased attention paid to the importance of dovetailing assessment with interventions that are pragmatic, titrated, and in the child's best interest relative to referral concerns.

Hughes and Bray (2004) support focusing on empirically based treatment as opposed to the continuing focus on classification. This position reflects an earlier recommendation by Ysseldyke and Christenson (1988) for a paradigm shift from viewing assessment as classification to linking assessment to effective interventions. Likewise, current supporters of this thinking (Reschly & Ysseldyke, 1995, 2002) recommended that assessment be linked to outcome so that children could be more effectively understood across treatment and educational settings. Likewise, Truscott et al. (2005) recommended a focus on interventions across contexts. This recommended intervention focus also represents the positions of NASP (2004) and PCESE (2002) on program effectiveness.

TRAINING ISSUES IN SCHOOL PSYCHOLOGY AND PERSONALITY ASSESSMENT

In this section we present a sampling of surveys to show some of the trends that have evolved over the years with respect to school psychology training and practice in the area of personality assessment. Application of personality assessment to school psychology practice and intervention covers the range of exceptionalities, including gifted students (e.g., Pfeiffer, 2001), students with a neuropsychologically based disability (Domingos & Yalof, 2002; Rothstein, Benjamin, Crosby, & Eistenstadt, 1988), emotional disorders that are comorbid with ADHD (e.g., Demaray, Schaefer, & Delong, 2003), and students with learning disabilities (e.g., Martinez & Semrud-Clikeman, 2004). A summary of key survey research is presented to illustrate the evolving trend among school psychologists toward the application of emotional and behavior rating measures in the identification social-emotional adjustment.

Goh and Fuller (1983) surveyed 274 practicing school psychologists about their personality assessment practices. Their results indicated that a majority of school psychologists used projective techniques. The percentages of school psychologists using individual personality tests were reported as follows: 88% used the Bender-Gestalt, which was classified as a projective technique; 87% used the Sentence Completion; 73% used the House-Tree-Person; 65% used the Thematic Apperception Test (TAT); 59% used the Children's Apperception Test (CAT); 45% used the Draw-A-Person and Rorschach; 16% used the Hand Test; 11% used Kinetic Family Drawing Scales; and 5% used the Rosenzweig Picture Frustration Study. Among self-report measures, the two most commonly used instruments were self-concept scales (44%) and the Minnesota Multiphasic Personality Inventory (MMPI) (25%). For the individual behavior rating scales, the most commonly used measures were informal ratings (59%) and the Devereux Behavior Rating Scales (33%). The authors noted that school psychologists did not view personality and behavior ratings as incompatible with each other and were likely to use both measures in their work.

Prout (1983) surveyed school psychology practitioners and directors of school psychology training programs to learn about their training and assessment practices. Results showed that a very high percentage of respondents (94.1%) used a combination of assessment techniques. Over one half of the assessments school psychologists conducted included an evaluation of social-emotional functioning. Social-emotional assessment techniques were rank-ordered, with clinical interview, informational classroom observation, human figure drawings, Bender-Gestalt (emotional indicators), and Incomplete Sentences, respectively, as the top five measures. Behavior rating scales were ranked ninth on the list. Other tests and measures, including the TAT, CAT, Rorschach, and MMPI, were ranked below tenth on the list. Practitioners ranked behavioral observation, clinical interview, projective tests, behavior rating scales, and objective tests, respectively, as the top five measures in terms of their importance and utilization. Practitioners reported that the TAT received the most attention in terms of their professional training, followed by human figure drawings, the Bender-Gestalt, clinical interviewing, and the CAT. Trainers ranked clinical interviewing, followed by informal classroom observation, human figure drawings, Bender-Gestalt, and structured classroom observation, as the top five assessment techniques in terms of training emphasis.

Stinnett, Havey, and Oehler-Stinnett (1994) surveyed 400 randomly selected members from NASP about their typical assessment practice techniques. They found that interviews were more popular than projective tests and self-report measures. Overall, results indicated that respondents spent approximately 50% of their practice hours doing assessments. Interview and behavioral observation were considered the most important techniques. The authors emphasized the identified preferences among school psychologists for informal assessment techniques compared with formal assessment techniques.

Wilson and Reschly (1996) surveyed 251 school psychology practitioners and found that the Draw-A-Person technique was the most frequently used projective measure. The authors reported that "at least two-thirds" (p. 16) of respondents were giving the Draw-A-Person, House-Tree-Person, or Kinetic-Family-Drawing "every month" (p. 16). The TAT was the fourth most common measure. The Achenbach-Edelbrock Child Behavior Checklist (CBCL) was the most popular behavior rating scale.

Culross and Nelson (1997) surveyed NASP programs offering specialist level training and asked faculty who taught personality assessment courses to respond to questions about how students were trained. Results indicated that 71% of programs offered a course in personality assessment and 30% offered more than one course in this area. The majority of programs taught both child and adult assessment but focused primarily on child assessment. The six most commonly taught measures were clinical interviewing, behavioral assessment, Bender-Gestalt, classroom observation, and the TAT. Over 80% of the programs offered clinical training (e.g., administration, scoring, interpretation) compared with a smaller percentage of programs whose instruction was primarily didactic versus clinical. The Rorschach was taught by only 38% of the programs that offered clinical training. The authors noted, however, that "practitioners routinely use tests with questionable validity and reliability" (p. 123), noting in particular the limitation of the Bender-Gestalt and figure drawings. The three topics most commonly taught in personality assessment classes were report writing (68%), ethical and professional issues (44%), and diagnostic classification systems (32%). More recently, Brown, Kissell, and Bolen (2003) surveyed 61 APPIC internship directors in order to better understand internship training in school psychology in non-school settings. They found that school psychology interns devoted most of their time to individual and group counseling, with the next highest percentage of time devoted to psychological assessment. The potential value of additional coursework in personality assessment was identified as being important for students who seek pre-doctoral internships in non-school settings.

Shapiro and Heick (2004) surveyed 684 NASP members, focusing on their recent and evolving assessment experiences, and found that 89.6% used rating scales (teacher and/or parent) and 75.3% used student self-ratings in 4 of their last 10 assessments. Ratings were more popular than projective tests, supporting the trend identified by Kamphaus, Petoskey, and Rowe (2000), who summarized research on test practices among child psychologists and indicated that behavior ratings scales would continue to grow in popularity over time.

In summary, a preference appears to have emerged in the education and training of school psychologists for the use of objective scales in identifying social-emotional disturbances.

CASE STUDY

The following case material is a composite case designed to illustrate the value of personality assessment during evaluation of a child for school and clinical purposes. The case highlights the impact of cognitive deficits on personality functioning while also providing insights about the child's inner life that are hard to extrapolate from self-report and observer rating scales. The overlapping nature of internalizing and externalizing disorders, for example, is often overlooked when rating scales are unidimensional.

B.J. (a pseudonym), a teenager, was referred for an assessment by his foster parents because of problems in school (e.g., fighting, impulsivity, disrespect toward teachers, poor academic performance) and at home (acting out against parental limits) and because his therapist requested a comprehensive assessment to assist with treatment interventions. B.J.'s natural mother (father's whereabouts were unknown) abandoned him at an early age, and he has been with his foster parents, who adopted him, since he was two years old. B.J. was diagnosed with attention deficit hyperactive–impulsive disorder (ADHD) combined type, in preschool. He was also diagnosed with a reading disability. There were many disciplinary issues in school and at home, and recently both school and B.J.'s parents had been considering an alternative, out-of-state school placement. School focus has been on supporting B.J.'s academic needs and providing teacher recommendations for classroom management through his IEP. B.J. had been unsuccessful with private therapists, but his most recent therapist felt that he was struggling with issues that went beyond the externalizing behaviors noted in school reports, and requested both cognitive and personality testing. On interview B.J. reported repetitive dreams of being harmed, some ritualistic behaviors, anxiety, and sleep difficulty.

Cognitive assessment revealed low average intelligence (WISC IV), with significant deficiencies in working memory and processing speed. Academic achievement testing (WIAT II) supported the presence of both reading and arithmetic disabilities. There were consistent deficits in both executive functioning (Category Test; Trail Making Test) and sustained attention (Conners Continuous Performance; Seashore Rhythm Test), as well as several below average scores on tests of visual and verbal learning and memory (Wide Range Assessment of Memory and Learning; California Verbal Learning Test; Rey Complex Figure Design and Recognition Trial). Thus, B.J.'s cognitive needs interfaced clearly with his behavior problems, but what was missing from the overall picture was a thorough understanding of B.J.'s personality beyond rating scales (BASC, Conners' Rating Scale) highlighting problems with conduct, attention, impulsivity, and externalizing behavior. On a depression self-report scale (Children's Depression Inventory), he scored above average for negative mood. On an anxiety self-report scale (Multidimensional Anxiety Scale for Children), he scored above average for tense-restless behavior.

B.J. was administered the Roberts Apperception Test and Rorschach to further understand his personality. Several of his stories to the Roberts stimuli were indicative of self-blame, vulnerability to making mistakes, and a desire to receive help. These inferences provided an appreciation for B.J.'s internal, personal struggle in a way that was neither verbalized nor observed during history taking and interview. Rather than casting him only as a poorly controlled ADHD youngster with language-based learning needs, B.J.'s stories suggested a more dynamic internal process in which he was possibly feeling a sense of remorse for bad behavior, experienced anxiety about decreased self-control, and had an underlying desire to receive help. These story themes, combined with B.J.'s difficulty interacting and communicating, could motivate him to subvert the helping efforts of others as a way of avoiding a repetition of the early abandonment trauma. His distancing behavior was evidenced at home as well as in therapy and school.

B.J.'s Rorschach (Exner, 2003) results are abstracted here to further illustrate the importance of conducting a comprehensive personality assessment when there are significant and overlapping disorders that manifest behaviorally with symptoms affecting full access to the curriculum. We emphasize the structural response variables in the following analysis. For example, although B.J. was characterized as an impulsive, externalizing student on rating scales, his Rorschach revealed that he tried very hard to minimize stimulation as a way of keeping himself controlled (Lambda = 3.0). Efforts at internal control were rigid, designed to minimize distressing or anxiety-provoking thoughts (FM = 0) that could contribute to nightmares. B.J. was very self-protective of his personal space (HVI positive). However, he did not have an adaptive coping style (EB = 2.0:2.0). As a result, he was vulnerable to strong emotions (Pure C = 1), confusion, and anger, resulting in judgment errors ($S - 3$; $X - \%$ =.35). B.J.'s self-image was lower than expected ($3r + 2/R$ = .25), and he was not comfortable initiating contact with other people in a positive way ($T = 0$). His interpersonal perceptions indicated that while he expected negative outcomes, he also hoped for positive outcomes (GHR:PHR = 7:5).

In summary, B.J. has features of an anxiety disorder as well as ADHD and a learning disability. It is the overlap between B.J.'s externalizing (i.e., ADHD; Combined Type) and internalizing (i.e., anxiety) problems, rather than just his externalizing issue, that contributes to a broader understanding of his problems. His cognitive deficits interfere with his ability to fully anticipate, attend, manage, and respond thoughtfully to potential conflict situations. These deficits placed B.J. at a coping disadvantage. His ADHD is an externalizing disorder and represents the focus of the school but does not explain the full diagnostic picture. He is anxious, fearful, and angry, with lowered self-image and a desire for positive relationships, even though manifest behaviors are distancing. These insights from personality assessment can be useful to parents, therapist, and teachers as they develop strategies for helping B.J. improve his cognitive, social-emotional, and behavioral adjustment.

CONCLUSION

The practice of personality assessment in school psychology requires an appreciation of points of convergence and divergence with traditional clinical psychology personality assessment practices. Psychologists who work in private settings and whose work products are used by school districts have to be familiar not only with DSM nomenclature, but with IDEA, Section 504, and the prevailing climate of personality assessment in the particular school setting. There are a multitude of referral issues that present either in isolation or comorbidly with other disorders. Assessment requires skillful application and integration of interview, observation, history, and tests and measures with an eye toward functional interventions that serve the student's programmatic goals in relation to the curriculum. Attention to examining dimensions of personality as manifested through cognition, behavior, affect, and social experiences may better determine problematic areas identified for prevention and intervention as well as high rates of comorbidity.

APPENDIX

Referral domain	Test/measure & source	Ages/range*
Observation/interview	Behavioral Assessment System for Children-Student Observation System (BASC-SOS; Reynolds & Kamphaus, 1992). AGS.	School-aged children
	Direct Observation Form (CBC-DOF). Achenbach System of Empirically based Assessment (ASEBA) Research Center for Children, Youth, & Families.	5–14
	Structured Observation of Academic & Play Settings (Milich, Loney, & Landau, 1982)	Children
	Semistructured Interview for Children & Adolescents (SCICA.) ASEBA Research Center for Children, Youth & Families.	6–18
School climate/ ecological	Reynolds Bully Victimization Scales for Schools (RBVS; Reynolds 2003); Includes: Bully-Victimization Scale (BVS), Bully Victimization Distress Scale (BVDS), & School Violence Anxiety Scale (SVAS). PsychCorp.	BVS: Grades 3–12; BVDS: Grades 3–12; SVAS: Grades 5–12
	Social Experience Questionnaire Self-Report (SEQ-S; Crick & Bigbee, 1998) & the Social Experience Questionnaire Peer Report (SEQ-P; Crick & Bigbee, 1998). See http://vinst.umdnj .edu/VAID/TestReport.asp?Code=SEQP	9–11

(continued)

Referral domain	Test/measure & source	Ages/range*
Personality	Student Styles Questionnaire (SSQ;) Oakland, Glutting, & Horton, 1996). PsychCorp.	8–17
	The Kid's Coolidge Axis II Inventory (KCAT) (Coolidge et al., 1990)	5–11
	Personality Inventory for Children, Second Edition (PIC-2; Lachar & Gruber)	5–19 4th–12th grades
	Personality Inventory for Youth (PIY; Lachar & Gruber, 1995). Western Psychological Services.	
	Student Behavior Survey (SBS; Lachar, Wingenfeld, Kline, & Gruber). Western Psychological Services.	5–18
	Minnesota Multiphasic Personality Inventory–Adolescent (MMPI-A; Butcher, Williams, Graham, Archer, Tellegen, Ben-Porath & Kaermmer, 1992). Pearson Assessments.	14–18
	Millon Adolescent Personality Inventory (MAPI; Millon, Green, & Meagher, 1982). Pearson Assessments.	13–19
	BarOn Emotional Quotient-Inventory: Youth Version (BarOn EQ-i:YV; Bar-On & Parker). Multi-Health Systems, Inc.	7–18
Self-concept	Piers Harris Self-Concept Scale, Second Edition (Piers, Harig, & Herzberg). Western Psychological Services.	7–18
Trauma	Trauma Symptom Checklist for Children (TSCC; Briere, 1996). Psychological Assessment Resources, Inc.	8–16
	Clinician Administered PTSD for Children and Adolescents (CAPS-CA; Newman, Weathers, Nadar, Kaloupek, Pynoos, Blake, & Kraiegler). Western Psychological Services.	8–15
	Children's PTSD Inventory (ChPTSD; Saigh). PsychCorp.	6–18
Depression	Children's Depression Inventory (CDI; Kovacs, 1992). Multi-Health Systems, Inc.	7–17
	Reynold's Adolescent Depression Scale Second Addition (RADS-2; Reynolds). Psychological Assessment Resources, Inc.	11–20
	Beck Depression Inventory–II (BDI–II; Beck, Steer, & Brown, 1996). PsychCorp.	13–18
Anxiety	Multidimensional Anxiety Scale for Children (MASC; March, 1997). Multi-Health Systems, Inc.	8–19
	Revised Children's Manifest Anxiety Scale (RCMAS; Reynolds, & Richmond, 1985). Western Psychological Services.	6–19
	State-Trait Anxiety Inventory for Children (STAIC; Spielberger, 1973). MindGarden, Inc.	6–14
	The Fear Survey Schedule for Children–Revised, (FSSC-R) (Ollendick, 1983)	Children & adolescents

(continued)

Referral domain	Test/measure & source	Ages/range*
	Multidimensional Anxiety Scale for Children, (MASC; March, 1996). Multi-Health Systems, Inc.	8–19
	Beck Youth Inventories of Emotional & Social Impairment (BYI; Beck, Beck, & Jolly, 2001). PsychCorp.	7–14
	Adolescent Anger Rating Scale (AARS; Burney). Western Psychological Services.	11–19
	Children's Inventory of Anger (ChIA; Nelson & Finch). Western Psychological Services.	6–16
	Navaco Anger Scale & Provocation Inventory (NAS-PI; Novaco). Western Psychological Services.	9+
Anger	State-Trait Anger Expression Inventory-II (STAXI-II; Spielberger & Vagg, 2002). Psychological Assessment Resources, Inc.	16 and older
OCD	Children's Yale-Brown Obsessive Compulsive Scale (CY-BOCS; Goodman, 1986) In *OCD in children & adolescents: Cognitive-Behavioral Treatment Manual* (1998) by J. March & K. Mulle.	6–17
	Leyton Obsessional Inventory (Williams & Wilkins, 1988) In *OCD in children & adolescents: Cognitive-Behavioral Treatment Manual* (1998) by J. March & K. Mulle	Children & adolescents
	Clark-Beck Obsessive-Compulsive Inventory (CBOCI; Clark & Beck). PsychCorp.	17 and older
Eating	Eating Disorder Inventory–3 (EDI-3; Garner, Olstead, & Polivy, 2004). Psychological Assessment Resources, Inc.	13–53
	Overeating Questionnaire (OQ; O'Donnell & Warren, 2004). Western Psychological Services.	9 years +
Psychopathology	Children's Interview for Psychiatric Syndromes (ChIPS; Rooney, & Fristad, Weller, & Weller). American Psychiatric Publishing, Inc.	6–18
	Adolescent Psychopathology Scale (APS; Reynolds, 1998) and Adolescent Psychopathology Scale– Short Form (APS-SF; Reynolds, 2000). Psychological Assessment Resources, Inc.	APS 12–19 APS-SF 12–19
	Devereux Scales of Mental Disorder (DSMD; Naglieri, LeBuffe, & Pfeiffer, 1994). PsychCorp.	Child: 5–12 Adolescent: 13–18
	Behavior and Emotional Rating Scale-2 (BERS; Epstein & Sharma, 1998). pro-ed.	5–18.11
Social skills	Social Rating System (SSRS; Gresham & Elliot, 1990). AGS.	3–18
Substance abuse	Substance Abuse Subtle Screening Inventory (SASSI-3; Miller, Roberts, Brooks, Lazowski, & the SASSI Institutes, 1997). SASSI Institute.	12–18

(*continued*)

Referral domain	Test/measure & source	Ages/range*
Parent information	Parent Stress Index–Third Edition (PSI-3; Abidin, 1995). Psychological Assessment Resources, Inc.	Parents of children 1 month–12 years
Sentence completion	Rotter Incomplete Sentences Blank, Second Edition (RISB; Rotter, Lah, & Rafferty, 1992). PsychCorp.	High school to adult
Behavior	The Behavior Assessment System for Children, Second Edition (Reynolds & Kamphaus); Parent Rating Scales Preschool (PRS-P), child (PRS-C), & Adolescent (PRS-A); Teacher Rating Scales Preschool (TRS-P), child (TRS-C), & adolescent (TRS-A); self report-child (SRP-C) & self report adolescent (SRP-A). AGS.	PRS-P = 2–5 PRS-C = 6–11 PRS-A = 12–21; TRS-P = 2–5, TRS-C = 6–11 & TRS-A = 12–21; SRP-C = 8–11 & SRP-A = 12–21
	Child Behavior Checklist (CBCL), Teacher's Report Form (TRF), and Youth Self-Report (YSR). ASEBA Research Center for Children, Youth & Families.	CBCL/11/2–5 & C-TRF = 2–5 CBCL & TRF = 6–18; YSR: 11–18
	Conners' Rating Scales–Revised (CRS-R; Conners, 1997); Parent/teacher rating forms and self report. Multi-Health Systems, Inc.	3–17 self-report 12–17
Apperception & thematic methods	Rorschach Technique (Rorschach, 1921). PsychCorp.	5–adult
	Roberts–2 (Roberts). Western Psychological Services.	6–18
	TEMAS (Tell-Me-A-Story) (Costantino, Malgady, & Rogler, 1988). Western Psychological Services.	5–18
	Thematic Apperception Test (TAT: Murray, 1943). PsychCorp.	Children & adolescents
	Children's Apperception Test (C.A.T.; Bellak & Bellak, 1949). PsychCorp.	5–12

* The population is defined as designated in the test manual or primary source.

REFERENCES

American Psychiatric Association. (2000). *Diagnostic and statistical manual of mental disorders* (4th ed., text revision). Washington, DC: Author.

Atkins, M. S., McKay, M. M., Talbott, E., & Avanitis, P. (1996). DSM-IV Diagnosis of Conduct Defiant Disorders: Implications and guidelines for school mental health teams. *School Psychology Review, 25*, 274–283.

Bellak, L., & Bellak, S. (1949). *The Children's Apperception Test*. Larchmont, NY: CPS.

Brown, M. B., Kissell, S., & Bolen, L. M. (2003). Doctoral school psychology internships in non-school settings in the United States. *School Psychology International, 24*, 394–404.

Carron, C., & Rutter, M. (1991). Co-morbidity in child psychopathology: Concepts, issues, and research strategies. *Journal of Child Psychology and Psychiatry, 32*, 1063–1080.

Coolidge, F. L., Philbrick, P. B., Wooley, M. J., Bunting, E. K., Hyman, J. N., & Stager, M. A. (1990). The KCATI: Development of an inventory for the assessment of personality disorders in children. *Journal of Personality & Clinical Studies, 8*(1), 7–13.

Cross, T., Bazron, B., Dennis, K., & Isaacs, M. (1989). *Towards a culturally competent system of care for children with serious emotional disorders*. Washington, DC: Georgetown Technical Assistance Center for Children's Mental Health.

Cullinan, D., Epstein, M. H., & Sabornie, E. J. (1992). Selected characteristics of a national sample of seriously emotionally disturbed adolescents. *Behavioral Disorders, 17*, 273–280.

Culross, R. R., & Nelson, S. (1997). Training in personality assessment in specialist-level school psychology programs. *Psychological Reports, 81*, 119–124.

Demaray, M. K., Schaefer, K. & Delong, L. K. (2003). Attention-deficit/hyperactivity disorder (ADHD): A national survey of training and current assessment practices in the schools. *Psychology in the Schools, 40*, 583–597.

Domingos, B. W., & Yalof, J. (2002). Neuropsychological assessment of high risk adolescents. *The School Psychologist, 56*, 126–130.

Elementary and Middle Schools Technical Assistance Center (EMSTAC) (2005). *Disproportionality: The disproportionate representation of racial and ethnic minorities in special education*. Retrieved on July 1, 2005, from http://www.emstac.org/registered/topics/disproportionality/faqs.htm

Exner, J. E., Jr. (2003). *The Rorschach: A comprehensive system: Vol. I. Basic foundations* (4th ed.). New York: Wiley.

Forness, S. R. (1992). Legalism versus professionalism in diagnosing SED in the public schools. *School Psychology Review, 21*, 29–34.

Goh, D. S., & Fuller, G. R. (1983). Current practices in the assessment of personality and behavior by school psychologists. *School Psychology Review, 12*, 240–243.

Gopaul-McNicol, S., & Thomas-Presswood, T. (1998). *Working with linguistically and culturally different children: Innovative clinical and educational approaches*. Needham Heights, MA: Allyn & Bacon.

Harry, B. (1994). *The disproportionate representation of minority students in special education: Theories and recommendations*. Alexander, VA: Project FORUM, National Association of State Directors of Special Education.

Hatzichristou, C. (2002). A conceptual framework of the evolution of school psychology: Transnational considerations of common phrases and future perspectives. *School Psychology International, 23*, 266–282.

Hughes, T. L., & Bray, M. A. (2004). Differentiation of emotional disturbance and social maladjustment: Introduction to the special issue. *Psychology in the Schools, 41*, 819–821.

Individuals with Disabilities Education Act (1997). (Pub. L. No. 101-476), 20 U.S.C. Chapter 33. Amended by Pub. L. No. 105-17 in June, 1997. Regulations appear at 34 C.F.R. Part 300.

Ingram, R. E., & Price, J. M. (2001). The role of vulnerability in understanding psychopathology. In R. E. Ingram & J. M. Price (Eds.), *Vulnerability to psychopathology* (pp. 3–19). New York: Guilford Press.

Jacob, S., & Hartshorne, T. S. (2003). *Ethics and law for school psychologists* (4th ed.). Hoboken, NJ: John Wiley & Sons.

Kamphaus, R. W., & Frick, P. J. (1996). *Clinical assessment of child and adolescent personality and behavior*. Needham, MA: Allyn & Bacon.

Kamphaus, R. W., Petoskey, M. D., & Rowe, E. (2000). Current trends in psychological testing of children. *Professional Psychology: Research & Practice, 31*, 155–164.

Kehle, T. J., Bray, M. A., Theodore, L. A., Zhou, Z., & McCoach, D. B. (2004). Emotional disturbance/social maladjustment: Why is the incidence increasing? *Psychology in the Schools, 41*, 861–865.

Kilgus, M., Pumariega, A. J., & Cuffe, S. (1995). Influence of race on diagnosis in adolescent psychiatric inpatients. *Journal of the American Academy of Child and Adolescent Psychiatry, 35*, 67–72.

Knoff, H. M. (2002). Best practices in personality assessment. In A. Thomas & J. Grimes (Vol. Eds.), *Best practices in school psychology* (pp. 1281–1302). Bethesda, MD: National Association of School Psychologists.

Koppelman, J. (2004). Children with mental disorders: Making sense of their needs and the systems that help them. *National Health Policy Forum, 799*, 1–24.

Koyanagi, C. (2003). Failing to qualify: The first step to failure in school? Issue Brief, Judge David L. Brazelon Center for Mental Health and Law, Washington, DC. Retrieved July 9, 2005, from http://www.bazelton.org/issues/education/publications/failingtoqualify.htm

Lehr, C. A., & Christensen, S. L. (2002). Best practices in promoting a positive school climate. In A. Thomas & J. Grimes (Vol. Eds.), *Best practices in school psychology* (pp. 929–948). Bethesda, MD: NASP Publications.

Lounsbury, J. W., Tatum, H., Gibson, W., Park, S., Sundstrom, E. D., Hamrick, F., et al. (2003). The development of a big five adolescent personality inventory. *Journal of Psychoeducational Assessment, 21*, 111–133.

Martinez, R. S., & Semrud-Clikeman, M. (2004). Emotional adjustment and school functioning of young adolescents with multiple versus single learning disabilities. *Journal of Learning Disabilities, 37*, 411–420.

McBurnett, K. (1996). Development of the DSM-IV: Validity and relevance for school psychologists. *School Psychology Review, 25*, 259–273.

Milich, R., Loney, J., & Landau, S. (1982). The independent dimensions of hyperactivity and aggression: A validation with playroom observations. *Journal of Abnormal Psychology, 91*, 183–198.

Miller, L., & Newbill, C. (1998). Section 504 in the classroom: How to design & implement accommodation plans. Austin, TX: PRO-ED.

Murray, H. A. (1943). *Thematic Apperception Test manual.* Cambridge, MA: Harvard University Press.

National Association for School Psychologists (2004). Position statement on periodic reevaluations for students with disabilities. Retrieved on July 7, 2005, from http://www.nasponline.org/information/pospaper_tye.html

National Center for Education Statistics (NCES) (2002). *Participation in education: Children with selected disabilities in public schools.* Retrieved July 1, 2005, from http://nces.ed.gov/programs/coe/2005/section1/indicator06.asp

Olympia, D., Farley, M., Christiansen, E., Pettersson, H., Jenson, W., & Clark, E. (2004). Social maladjustment and students with behavioral and emotional disorders: Revisiting basic assumptions and assessment issues. *Psychology in the Schools, 41*, 835–847.

Ollendick, T. H. (1983). Reliability & validity of the Revised Fear Survey Schedule for Children (FSSC-R). *Behavior Research & Therapy, 21*(6), 685–692.

Pfeiffer, S. I. (2001). Professional psychology and the gifted: Emerging practice opportunities. *Professional Psychology: Research & Practice, 32*, 175–180.

President's Commission on Excellence in Special Education (2002). *A new era: Revitalizing special education for children and their families.* Jessup, MD: U.S. Department of Education.

Prevatt, F. F. (1999). Personality assessment in schools. In C. R. Reynolds and T. B. Gutkin (Eds.), *The handbook of school psychology* (pp. 434–451). New York: John Wiley & Sons.

Price, J. M., & Lento, J. (2001). The nature of child and adolescent vulnerability: History and definitions. In R. E. Ingram & J. M. Price (Eds.), *Vulnerability to psychopathology* (pp. 20–38). New York: Guilford Press.

Prout, H. T. (1983). School psychologists and social-emotional assessment techniques: Patterns in training and use. *School Psychology Review, 12*, 377–383.

Pumariega, A. J., & Cross, T. (1997). Cultural competence in child psychiatry. In J. Noshpitz & N. Alessi (Eds.), *Handbook of child and adolescent psychiatry* (Vol. 4, pp. 473–484). New York: Wiley.

Reddy, L. (2001). Serious emotional disturbance in children and adolescents: Current status and future directions. *Behavior Therapy, 32*, 667–691.

The Rehabilitation Act of 1973 (Pub. L. No. 93-112), 29, U.S.C., 794. Regulations implementing Section 504 appear at 34 C.F.R. Part 104 (1996).

Reschly, D. J., & Ysseldyke, J. E. (1995). School psychology paradigm shift. In A. Thomas and J. Grimes (Eds.), *Best practices in school psychology III* (pp. 17–31). Washington, DC: National Association of School Psychologists.

Reschly, D. J., & Ysseldyke, J. E. (2002). Paradigm shift: The past is not the future. In A. Thomas and J. Grimes (Eds.), *Best practices in school psychology IV* (pp. 3–20). Washington, DC: National Association of School Psychologists.

Rothstein, A., Benjamin, L., Crosby, M., & Eisenstadt, K. (1988). *Learning disorders: An integration of neuropsychological and psychoanalytic considerations.* Madison, CT: International Universities Press.

Sattler, J. M. (1983). Identifying and classifying disturbed children in the schools: Implications of DSM-III for school psychology. *School Psychology Review, 12*, 884–890.

Sattler, J. M. (2002). *Assessment of children: Behavioral and clinical applications* (4th ed.). San Diego: Jerome M. Sattler.

Shafombabi, D. E. (2005, Spring/Summer). Over-identification and placement of minorities in special education: No child left behind? *Insight, 25,* 6–10.

Shapiro, E. S., & Heick, P. F. (2004). School psychologist assessment practices in the evaluation of students referred for social/behavioral/emotional problems. *Psychology in the Schools, 41,* 551–561.

Skenkovich, J. E. (1992). Can the language "social maladjustment" in SED definition be ignored? *School Psychology Review, 21,* 21–22.

Skiba, R., & Grizzle, K. (1991). Qualifications v. logic and data: Excluding conduct disorders from the SED definition. *School Psychology Review, 21,* 23–28.

Skiba, R., & Grizzle, K. (1992). The social maladjustment exclusion: Issues of definition and assessment. *School Psychology Review, 20,* 580–598.

Stinnett, T. A., Havey, M. J., & Oehler-Stinnett, J. (1994). Current test usage by practicing school psychologists: A national survey. *Journal of Psychoeducational Assessment, 12,* 331–350.

Truscott, S. D., Catanese, A. M., & Abrams, L. M. (2005). The evolving context of special education classification in the United States. *School Psychology International, 26,* 162–177.

U.S. Department of Health and Human Services (DHHS). (1999). Mental health: A report of the Surgeon General (pp. 123–124). Rockville, MD: National Institute of Mental Health. Retrieved July 7, 2005, from www.surgeongeneral.gov/library/mentalhealth/pdfs/

Wagner, M. (1995). Outcomes for youth with serious emotional disturbance in secondary school and early adulthood. *The Future of Children: Critical Issues for Children and Youths,* 5, 90–112.

Wilson, M. S., & Reschly, D. J. (1996). Assessment in school psychology training and practice. *School Psychology Review, 25,* 9–23.

Ysseldyke, J. E., & Christenson, S. L. (1988). Linking assessment to intervention. In J. L. Graden, J. E. Zins, & M.-J. Curtis (Eds.), *Alternative educational delivery systems: Enhancing instruction options for all students* (pp. 91–109). Washington, DC: National Association of School Psychologists.

3

INTEGRATING NEUROPSYCHOLOGY AND PERSONALITY ASSESSMENT WITH CHILDREN AND ADOLESCENTS

Steven R. Smith
University of California, Santa Barbara

There is an Indian parable of six blind men who encounter different parts of a large elephant and are asked to describe what it is they are feeling. The man who grasps the trunk reports that he's holding a snake; the next man, who is holding one of the large tusks, insists that it is a spear; another man, grasping one of the animal's large legs, says that it is a tree. The point of the parable is that incomplete evidence results in incomplete conclusions and a narrow perspective of the entire beast.

As applied psychology becomes increasingly specialized, psychologists also run the risk of drawing incomplete conclusions about patients and their functioning. Understanding something as complex as human phenomenology through only one narrow lens guarantees that our perceptions and conclusions will be similarly narrow. I argue, as have others (Meyer, 2002; Ready, Stieman, & Paulsen, 2001; Wilson, 1993), that we can and should have both breadth and depth as our goal in all clinical activities, including psychological assessment.

In this chapter, I discuss the current division between neuropsychology and personality assessment. I examine differences in training, test usage, and scientific literature that give rise to somewhat different (and perhaps incomplete) perspectives of our patients. I then discuss the neuropsychological challenges posed by traditional personality assessment and behavioral measurement of children and adolescents and the types of "lessons" that personality assessors can learn from neuropsychology. Similarly, I explore ways in which neuropsychology practice can inform the assessment of child and adolescent personality and behavior. Last, I present a case example and provide some recommendations for clinicians who wish to move toward integrating neuropsychological and personality assessment in practice. Throughout, I argue that the meaning of a given personality or neuropsychological test score should be seen as contingent upon the full array of patient functioning.

ON SEPARATENESS

The separation between neuropsychology and personality assessment begins early in training. Neuropsychologists receive extensive specialized training in cognitive neuroscience, neuropsychological assessment, and psychometrics, in addition to generalist training in clinical psychology (Hannay et al., 1998). The ultimate goal of neuropsychological training is a board certification that would attest to the clinician's expertise in the field. Those who conduct personality assessments, on the other hand, are not required to engage in a specified course of training, but do need to be well versed in their particular tools and instruments as well as the complexity of human personality, psychopathology, and interpersonal dynamics. Although the Society for Personality Assessment has outlined some training guidelines and board certification in assessment is available through the American Board of Assessment Psychology, these are not as tied to clinical training experience as is seen in neuropsychology. This does not imply, however, a lack of rigor in personality assessment training; my point here is merely that the foci, guidelines, and certification processes of clinical psychologists who identify themselves as personality assessors versus neuropsychologists are different and may result in different perspectives about patient functioning.

In addition to training experiences, there are substantial differences in the types of tests used in neuropsychology and personality assessment. For example, Rabin, Barr, and Burton (2005) conducted a survey of the membership of the National Academy of Neuropsychology, International Neuropsychological Society, and APA's Division 40 (Clinical Neuropsychology) to determine what measures are most commonly given by neuropsychologists. In this survey, respondents were asked to rate their top three assessment measures. A similar survey was conducted by Camara, Nathan, and Puente (2000), who surveyed both neuropsychologists and clinical psychologists in APA. The results of both surveys are displayed in Table 3.1. The question asked by the two surveys was slightly different (i.e., "top three" in Rabin et al. [2005] versus "most common" in Camara et al. [2000]), but it seems that neuropsychologists appear quite unlikely to use traditional measures of personality and psychopathology (e.g., the Rorschach was listed as 34th) and that most assessment by clinical psychologists is focused on either personality or cognitive functioning.

TABLE 3.1.
Test Usage by Clinical Neuropsychologists and Clinical Psychologists

Neuropsychologists[a]	*Clinical psychologists*[b]
1. WAIS-III	1. WAIS-R/III
2. WMS-III	2. MMPI-2
3. Trail making test	3. WISC-III
4. CVLT-II	4. Rorschach
5. WISC-III	5. Bender-Gestalt
6. Halstead-Reitan battery	6. TAT
7. Wisconsin card sort	7. Wide range achievement test-R/III
8. Rey-Osterrieth complex figure	8. H-T-P
9. MMPI-2	9. WMS-III
10. Rey auditory verbal learning test	10. MCMI

[a]From Rabin et al. (2005). Neuropsychologists were asked to rate top three assessment measures given.
[b]From Camara et al. (2000). Clinical psychologists were asked to list most common assessment measures given.

To determine whether this difference in clinical practice was reflected in the empirical literature, I conducted a brief keyword search in the *Journal of Personality Assessment* (*JPA*) and the *Archives of Clinical Neuropsychology* (*ACN*). These two journals were chosen as exemplars of their respective disciplines; *JPA* is the official journal of the Society for Personality Assessment and *ACN* is the journal for the National Academy of Neuropsychology. In *ACN*, I searched for the terms "Rorschach," "TAT," and "MMPI-2." There were no articles in which either the Rorschach or TAT was used. As expected, the MMPI-2 was frequently represented, yielding a list of 25 publications. In *JPA*, I ran a search for the words "neuropsychology" and "cognition." This search found only two articles in *JPA* that addressed the integration of personality assessment and neuropsychology (Acklin & Wu-Holt, 1996; Sliverstein & McDonald, 1988), and one of these (Acklin & Wu-Holt, 1996) is not an empirical article.

The point of this discussion is to highlight the fact that although the neuropsychologist and the personality assessor are generally charged with assessing different aspects of patient functioning and so should have different backgrounds and experiences, these differences may not only signal that they are examining different parts of the elephant, but that they do so with a different perspective of how to interpret what they observe. I agree with Ready, Stieman, and Paulsen (2001) that neither assessment approach in isolation can capture the completeness of patient functioning. After all, our patients have complex cognitive, psychological, interpersonal, and intra-psychic lives, and it stands to reason that more information will yield a more complex understanding of patients and their particular profile of strengths and difficulties.

Current Integrations

I am certainly not the first person who has raised this issue of fully integrating neuropsychology and personality assessment. There is some literature reporting on the utility of using personality assessment in combination with neuropsychological assessment. The large majority of this literature organizes its theses into one of two categories: a) personality assessment measures can be used to aid in the assessment of neuropsychological dysfunction (Colligan, 1997; Perry & Potterat, 1997; Perry, Potterat, Auslander, Kaplan, & Jeste, 1996; Piotrowski, 1937a, 1937b; Reitan, 1955), and b) personality assessment measures can be used to assess personality and psychopathology in patients with neurological impairments (Ellis & Zahn, 1985; Exner, Colligan, Boll, Stischer, & Hillman, 1996.; Malmgren, Bilting, Frobarj, & Lindqvist, 1997; Sliverstein & McDonald, 1988; Wilson, 1993) and learning disabilities (Acklin, 1990). A full summary of these issues is beyond the scope of this chapter, but the reader is directed to an excellent review by Minassian and Perry (2004).

Despite these two areas of overlap and a general consensus that all test scores should always be interpreted in light of all relevant data (Weiner, 2003), little has been done to examine how different forms of assessment can help inform the interpretation of tests. For example, how might a particular personality assessment test score *modify* how we interpret a neuropsychological test score? Similarly, how does a particular profile of neuropsychological deficit change our interpretation of personality assessment scores? In most of the literature, it appears as though the *meaning* of all test scores is held constant, despite the pattern of test findings. That is, two patients who have elevated scores on a Rorschach measure of thought disorder (such as the Perceptual-Thinking Index [PTI]) might both be seen as having cognitive distortions reflective of thought disorder. However, one patient's elevated PTI score may be due to a psychotic cognitive process, whereas the other patient's score may be due to a neuropsychological processing problem, linguistic issue, etc. This level of perspective, crucial to understanding the patient, would not be possible if the assessment did not include a neuropsychological component. In clinical practice, test scores would give us a much more complete understanding of the patient if they were interpreted and understood by the integration of several different forms of measurement, both neuropsychological and personality. With only a narrow pool of data, there is an increased likelihood of overlooking or over-interpreting something of importance. In short, we should not describe the elephant's tail after only examining its legs.

THE NEUROPSYCHOLOGY OF PERSONALITY ASSESSMENT

In this section, I discuss the neuropsychological implications of traditional personality and behavioral assessment of children and adolescents. Generally speaking, the assessment of youth typically involves using interviews, behavior ratings, self-report measures, and pro-jective techniques. All of these measurement techniques pose unique neuropsychological challenges for younger patients. Particularly relevant is the use of projective techniques, such as the Rorschach Inkblot Test (Exner, 2003). Among clinicians treating children and ado-lescents, the Rorschach remains one of the most commonly used means of assessing psy-chopathology and personality (Archer & Newsom, 2000). The test allows for the explo-ration of psychological resources, coping, affective style, and interpersonal resources and behavior (Acklin, 1990; Archer & Krishnamurthy, 1997; Exner, 2003; Exner & Weiner, 1995; Holaday, 2000; Stokes et al., 2003).

Interestingly, one of the first uses of the test, namely as a measure used to diagnose psychosis and other forms of thought disorder, may remain one of the test's greatest strengths (Hilsenroth, Fowler, Padawer, & Handler, 1997; Holaday, 2000; Ilonen et al., 1999; Kleiger, 1999; Smith, Baity, Knowles, & Hilsenroth, 2001; Stokes, Pogge, Grosso, & Zaccario, 2001; Wood, Nezworski, Lilienfeld, & Garb, 2003). Although the question remains as to how the Rorschach is able to assess these types of distorted cognitive functions, it seems fair to hypothesize that, on some level, the Rorschach is assessing neurocognitive functions such as cognitive organization, reasoning, working memory, and inhibition. Because the Ror-schach represents a complex visuospatial stimulus that must be effectively organized and understood by patients, it presents a neuropsychological challenge of sorts. Certainly, any derailment in this organization process can result in a distorted Rorschach profile that may identify patients as psychotic or otherwise thought disordered. Without an appreciation of the patient's neuropsychological profile, clinicians may falsely conclude that the patient is more disturbed than is the case or that the disturbance is due to personality issues rather than physiological problems. In short, some patients just don't see the ink in the same way.

Self-report measures pose another neuropsychological challenge. At the most basic level, patients must possess the ability to read and interpret the test statements. Although many self-report measures for youth are written at a second-grade reading level, those with learning dis-abilities or other lexical processing issues might struggle with such measures. What might first appear as defensive responding, inattention to test items and other response styles that might be reflected in validity scales, may merely be the result of reading or comprehension issues. When children and adolescents have difficulty translating their thoughts and feelings into words, their ability to fully respond to self-report measures of personality or psy-chopathology may be compromised. Such children may respond to test items in a way that is overly concrete or idiosyncratic. For example, I once tested a child who responded "True" to a self-report item, "I often hear voices that others do not hear." When asked about this, he responded, "When [my friend] whispers to me at school, the teacher can't hear him, but I can." Follow-up, clarification, and questioning are an integral part of good clinical practice.

Probably the most common form of assessing children and adolescents is the behavior rating scale (BRS; Cashel, 2002). The BRS offers the clinician several advantages, including ease of administration, scoring, and interpretation; cost effectiveness; speed; and convenience. It is important to note that the constructs purportedly measured by the BRS are generally psychological in nature. That is, if a child or adolescent is withdrawn and has flat affect, these might be codified as symptoms of depression. Similarly, if a child displays unusual stereotyped behavior and perseverative interests, these might be interpreted as signs of an autism-spectrum disorder. However, all of these symptoms are seen in patients with brain injury or other neurocognitive disorders. The distinction between "organic" and "psychiatric" may not be as useful as once thought (Semrud-Clikeman, Kamphaus, Teeter, & Vaughn, 1997), and clinicians need to be aware that the labels for the behavioral clusters assessed by behavior rating scales may be incomplete or misleading.

How Neuropsychology Can Inform Personality Assessment

To briefly summarize these global ideas:

1. Not all brains are created equal, and some people just don't see the ink in the same way. That is, depending on a person's given profile of cognitive functions, the very stimulus used in personality assessment may have different meanings and functions. This is true for all forms of assessment, but may be particularly relevant for projective techniques such as the Rorschach.

2. Similarly, children and adolescents with limited verbal capacity, dyslexia, or an inability to recognize and label their internal experience may appear withdrawn, resistant, concrete, or inconsistent on self-report measures of personality. Children may be given psychopathology diagnoses, but they may be mislabeled because of cognitive problems that are not primarily psychiatric in origin.

3. Behavior rating scales are measures of behavior, not of psychopathology necessarily. Clinicians should be sensitive to the fact that the BRS assesses a wide array of child and adolescent functioning that might be "organic" rather than psychiatric or psychological in nature. Instead of relying on the labels that the test authors assign to individual scales, clinicians should concern themselves with the behaviors those scales measure and use alternative sources of data to determine etiology.

4. Brain injury or cognitive dysfunction leads to changes in personality and higher rates of psychopathology. Both children and adults who have sustained some type of cognitive insult (including prenatal events) are at risk for developing emotional and behavioral disorders. Again, what might be seen as a primarily psychological or psychiatric issue may be more neurocognitive in origin. Personality assessment alone may not accurately capture these types of issues.

5. Neurodevelopmental issues are important for assessment of youth of any age. When we assess children and adolescents, we are taking a snapshot of their position along a developmental continuum. The neurocognitive and, therefore, the psychological world of a child is constantly changing.

6. Cognitive capacities are important to an understanding of a person's reality. That is, other things being equal, an individual with an IQ of 80 typically has a very different

experience of the world than does someone with an IQ of 120. In interpreting personality assessment results, we must always be mindful of such differences in subjective
experience.

Overall, it appears as though neuropsychological functioning not only affects how we should
interpret each score, but rather, the entire meaning of personality assessment stimuli and data
is contingent upon the cognitive functioning of a patient. Different cognitive functions result
in different interpretations of test stimuli, resulting in a different meaning of the entire assessment experience.

THE PERSONALITY OF NEUROPSYCHOLOGY

The impact of different forms of assessment is not unidirectional, however. Although little
research has examined the relationship of personality to neuropsychological test performance
(Rosselli, Ardila, Lubomski, Murray, & King, 2001), a large body of work has examined
the relationship of affect to neuropsychology. For example, it is commonly believed that
patients who are depressed will score worse on measures of processing speed and visuomo-
tor integration, such as Block Design (Wechsler, 2004). However, it is difficult to evaluate
this literature, because most of it involves adult patients with head trauma (Kaufman, Grossman, & Kaufman, 1994; MacNiven & Finlayson, 1993; Ruttan & Heinrichs, 2003). In a
review of this literature, Reitan & Wolfson (1997) concluded that "there seems to be strong
evidence that emotional disorders do not directly cause poor neuropsychological test performance" (p. 8). They go on to suggest that when patients have elevated scores on measures of affective disturbance and neuropsychological impairment, it is the neuropsychological impairment that is causing the affective disturbance. Echoing these sentiments, a
recent study of cocaine-abusing adults found that personality variables, as measured by the
Personality Assessment Inventory (Morey, 1991), were not related to scores on neuropsychological tests (Rosselli et al., 2001). Yet recent research has implicated the role of affect
in the neuropsychological test performance in children. For example, in a study of evoked
emotion in young children, where positive, negative, and neutral emotions were evoked
through the reading of stories, researchers found that those children who heard positive stories performed better on Block Design than did children in the neutral or negative conditions (Rader & Hughes, 2005).

Thus, it appears as though affective state may play a role in some forms of neuropsychological test performance. But affect does not equate with personality per se. A line of research
is emerging in neuropsychology that seeks to understand the ecological validity of neuropsychological test scores (Wilson, 1993). That is, this work seeks to understand what types of
real-world impairments can be predicted based on neuropsychological test scores. This work
has shown that using neuropsychological and personality assessment test scores in concert
allows clinicians to predict different aspects of impairment in patient behavior. For example,
like previous researchers, Zillmer and Perry (1996) and Ready et al. (2001) found little relationship between neuropsychological measures and personality in a sample of college students. However, these researchers found that the two measurement types were significantly
related to different aspects of patient behavior. Specifically, neuropsychological test results
predicted work and school achievement behaviors, whereas personality assessment measures
predicted risk-taking, substance abuse, and aggression. They concluded that their results
"highlight the importance of including personality measures in standard neuropsychological
assessment in order to maximize predictive validity of external behaviors" (p. 320).

Although we can conclude that administering both personality and neuropsychological measures will improve the content and ecological validity of our assessment (Ready et al., 2001; Wilson, 1993), no research to date has explored how different personality characteristics affect a child or adolescent's performance on measures of neuropsychology. We know from clinical experience that a child's motivation, engagement, degree of perseverance, and frustration tolerance, all variables related to personality, are important to test performance. Although we have little research to draw on at this point, we can conclude that neuropsychologists should be watchful for affective, motivational, and dispositional variables that might affect the quality and nature of their test results. Thus, personality exerts a substantial impact on how test scores are interpreted and understood as part of a battery.

How Personality Assessment Can Inform Neuropsychology

In the same way that neuropsychological assessment can inform personality assessment, personality assessment can add much to a neuropsychological test battery. For example:

1. A child or adolescent who is unmotivated, oppositional, depressed, anxious, or fearful is not an optimal neuropsychological testing patient. Although perhaps such a consideration is obvious, the clinician must consider the role of the youth's internal state as he or she attempts to solve complex neuropsychological problems. In addition to these psychological states, personality traits, such as an overly introverted interpersonal style, poor frustration tolerance, and neediness, can change the extent to which the child is able to fully engage with the test materials and the examiner.
2. Neuropsychological test scores alone can only tell us about some forms of real-world behavior. The overall picture of the child's or adolescent's day-to-day functioning is broadened by a consideration of affective, interpersonal, and intrapsychic variables as well. Personality assessment adds more predictive validity to the evaluation.
3. Personality assessment allows us to assess how a child or adolescent might be coping with cognitive issues. Research shows that children with learning disabilities suffer with significant issues of self-esteem and poor self-image (Martinez & Semrud-Clikeman, 2004). By coupling personality assessment with neuropsychological evaluations, clinicians can evaluate not only the presence of significant cognitive issues, but also their consequences for the child's internal world.

INTEGRATING NEUROPSYCHOLOGY AND PERSONALITY ASSESSMENT

From this discussion, we can conclude that not all test scores are created equal. One patient's scores may be interpreted quite differently than another patient's scores, depending on neuropsychological or personality factors. I am advocating a somewhat ideographic approach where nomothetic scores are made relevant for each child by the incorporation of interpretation based on all factors, both personality-based and neurocognitive. From the above discussion, it appears as though there are two ways in which the complexity of a child's cognitive and personality profile may result in differences in the way we understand a particular test score. First, personality affects neuropsychology at the level of interpretation. That is, motivation, affect, perseverance, and other personality variables primarily influence how we *interpret* scores on measures of neuropsychology. For example, affective dysregulation might affect scores on timed measures, or transient feeling states and motivation might distort "true" ability.

The second level at which we must consider the interaction between test scores is at the level of *meaning*. This level is far more fundamental than mere interpretation and relates primarily to the way in which neuropsychological functions affect personality assessment. Neuropsychological issues alter the patient's fundamental ability to understand him- or herself, express his or her thoughts and feelings, and interact with the test stimuli. For example, poor left hemisphere (linguistic) functioning may result in an inability to effectively describe or capture internal experience. Similarly, differences in cognitive functioning may alter a child's or adolescent's understanding and experience of the very meaning of being evaluated. Therefore, although personality assessment may change the way we think of a particular test score, neuropsychology suggests that the entire meaning of a test or a testing experience may be slightly (or radically) different for each patient. Without a full assessment of both neurocognitive and personality factors, a clinician is only seeing one part of the elephant, and important information may be overlooked or underinterpreted.

Case Study: Jessica

Jessica is a 10-year-old Caucasian girl referred for a comprehensive neuropsychological and personality assessment by her treating psychiatrist. Questions remained as to Jessica's diagnosis, although she was being aggressively treated pharmacologically for bipolar disorder. Jessica achieved her developmental milestones on time and even talked a little earlier than average. She showed some difficulty in learning how to ride a bike, and her parents described her as "clumsy." She attended a private school and was doing well academically in fourth grade, but she had a history of poor social interactions and disruptive behavior in the classroom. Both Jessica and her parents report that she had a history of explosive and unmodulated affect: "Sometimes she just flies off the handle." She was also known as being "hard to discipline" and aggressive toward her younger siblings.

At the time that I saw her, Jessica was taking a mood stabilizer (Depakote), an antipsychotic (Seroquel), and an anxiolytic (Buspar). Interpersonally, she was somewhat distant and hard to reach. She was oppositional with a female psychometrician but subdued with me. She displayed very poor eye contact and seemed uninterested in the normal give-and-take of social interactions. Specifically, she would speak for extended periods of time on seemingly unrelated topics and would ignore me when I asked questions or tried to redirect her.

The assessment plan called for a full neuropsychological battery and personality assessment. To assess personality, Jessica was administered the Rorschach and the Personality Inventory for Youth (PIY, a 270-item self-report measure for children and adolescents; Lachar & Gruber, 1995). These personality assessment results, shown in Table 3.2, paint a picture of Jessica as a child who may have some serious perceptual and cognitive issues (as indicated by Rorschach scores of unusual perception and distorted cognition, e.g., PTI, Xu%, and FAB2). Her Rorschach scores, which reflected no use of texture (T) and whole human percepts [H:(H)], are congruent with her self-report of poor social skills on the PIY (e.g., Social Introversion, Feelings of Alienation). Certainly this profile of scores alone might begin to suggest some type of serious mental illness, such as bipolar or psychosis. Were we to have stopped at this point in the assessment, these might have been some of the conclusions we would have tentatively drawn.

TABLE 3.2.

Jessica's Personality Assessment Scores

Rorschach	Score
R	24
Lambda	.8
EA	7, extratensive
D, adjusted D	0, 0
T	0
M	3
FM	5
PTI	4
X+%, Xu%, X−%	35, 50, 15
FAB2	3
H: (H)	0:4

Personality Inventory for Youth	T–score
Noncompliance	65
Feelings of alienation	67
Social introversion	58
Social skill deficit	71
Limited peer status	61

Note. T-scores have a mean of 50, with a standard deviation of 10.

However, I also administered neuropsychological tests for a full investigation of global cognitive functioning, achievement, visual-motor processing, and executive functions. To assess global cognitive functioning, I administered the Differential Ability Scales (DAS; Elliot, 1990). The Cognitive Battery of the DAS is organized into a set of core subtests that yield a General Conceptual Ability (GCA) score, as well as Verbal, Nonverbal Reasoning, and Spatial Cluster Scores. Although these scores are not identical to IQ scores from the WISC-IV (Wechsler, 2004), they are reasonably comparable to (and correlate highly with) such measures, inasmuch as they are normed with the same scale (i.e., mean of 100 and standard deviation of 15) and test similar content areas. The GCA can be compared with a Full Scale IQ score, whereas the Verbal, Nonverbal, and Spatial Clusters can be compared with Verbal and Performance IQ, respectively (with Performance IQ component analogs further subdivided between those that explicitly require spatial processing and those that do not).

Second, I administered the Wechsler Individual Achievement Test (2nd Edition; Wechsler, 2002) to examine Jessica's profile of academic strengths and weaknesses. A substantial portion of Jessica's evaluation, however, was spent on assessments of executive functions such as attention, abstraction, inhibition, and set switching. For example, she completed the Wisconsin Card Sorting Test (WCST; Heaton, Chelune, Talley, Kay, & Curtiss, 1993), a measure of abstract concept formation and ability to change cognitive set based on environmental feedback, and the Stroop Color-Word Test (Golden, 1978), a test of the patient's ability to inhibit prepotent cognitive responses. Jessica also completed the computerized Conners' Continuous Performance Test (Epstein et al., 2003), a measure of sustained attention and distractibility. Last, Jessica completed two measures of visual-motor processing, including the Beery-Buktenica Developmental Test of Visual-Motor Integration (VMI; Beery, 1997) and the Rey-Osterrieth Complex Figure (Osterrieth, 1944; Waber & Holmes, 1985). These two latter measures assess the patient's ability to copy complex geometric shapes and designs.

Results of neuropsychological tests, listed in Table 3.3, indicate that Jessica is functioning in the Low Average range of psychometric intelligence. With relatively intact executive functions (e.g., Wisconsin Card Sorting Test, Conners' CPT, and Stroop) and achievement mechanics (i.e., Numerical Operations, Spelling, and Word Reading), Jessica has some very specific areas of deficit: nonverbal and spatial reasoning (e.g., DAS Nonverbal Ability Cluster), academic comprehension (i.e., Mathematics Reasoning and Reading Comprehension), and visual-motor processing (i.e., Beery VMI and Rey Copy).

These deficits seem to implicate a right-hemisphere disorder that limits her visuospatial integration and nonverbal reasoning and comprehension. This profile, in addition to her reported social difficulties, is suggestive of a neuropsychological condition such as a nonverbal learning disability (NLD; Rourke, 1989). Children with NLD often have difficulty understanding nonverbal information and communication. They appear socially odd and have pronounced difficulties with comprehension, organization, and visuospatial processing. The understanding and expression of affect may present particular difficulties. Jessica's history and profile of neuropsychological test scores are certainly suggestive of this type of dysfunction.

Now let us revisit her personality assessment scores. The self-report PIY results are consistent with the social deficits seen in children with NLD and thus add some support for that diagnosis. However, the results of the neuropsychological testing recast the Rorschach results in a somewhat different light. Specifically, some of the perceptual distortion seen on the Rorschach may be due to difficulties processing the Rorschach as a visuospatial image. That is, as a visuospatial stimulus, Jessica's perception of the blots may be somewhat unusual compared with others her age. In the same way that she had difficulty organizing the Rey

TABLE 3.3.
Jessica's Neuropsychological Test Scores

Global cognitive ability		Achievement test results	
Differential ability scales	*Standard scores*	Wechsler individual achievement test–II	*Standard Scores*
General conceptual ability	87	Numerical operations	115
Verbal ability cluster	105	Spelling	128
Nonverbal ability cluster	85	Word reading	127
Spatial ability cluster	78	Mathematics reasoning	77
		Reading comprehension	75
Executive functioning		*Visual-motor functioning*	
Wisconsin card sorting test			*Standard Scores*
Error standard score	106	Beery VMI	35
Conners' CPT		Rey complex figure copy	55
Clinical confidence index	35%		
Stroop color-word test	*Standard scores*		
Word	88		
Color	86		
Color-word	89		

Note. All standard scores have a mean of 100, with a standard deviation of 15.

Complex Figure and solving nonverbal and spatial tasks, Jessica's basic ability to process the Rorschach stimulus appears to be weak.

Therefore, although an examination of personality assessment scores alone would have forced us to conclude that Jessica's perceptions of reality are distorted such that she may be psychotic or have poor reality testing, the addition of neuropsychological test data confirms that Jessica's cognitive processing is distorted, but that it may be distorted because of neuropsychological rather than psychiatric processes. The difference in these interpretations is important from the perspective of labeling and treatment in that treatment for NLD usually consists of social skills training, occupational therapy, and academic supports— a program that is very different from what would be implemented for Jessica were she to be labeled psychotic.

SUGGESTIONS FOR CLINICAL PRACTICE

Some suggestions for clinicians evaluating children can be made based on the above discussion:

A.   Conduct a comprehensive history interview

When patients are referred for an evaluation of psychological functioning, clinicians should be sure to conduct a full review of their medical and neuropsychological history. Although most clinicians will include these types of questions in their evaluations, this type of information should be used to help guide personality test interpretation. Questions that might be relevant include the following:

a.   Has the child repeated grades? Are there any problems with reading or reading comprehension? Learning disabilities? What types of relationships does he or she have with teachers?

b.   Has the child ever been knocked unconscious?

c.   Were developmental milestones achieved on time?

d.   Did the child have trouble learning how to ride a bicycle? Walk down/up stairs? Tie his or her shoes? Drink through a straw? Is the child clumsy or uncoordinated? Is he or she right or left handed?

e.   When was the child's most recent medical checkup? Vision screening? Hearing test?

f.   Has the child had any significant illnesses? Hospitalizations? Surgeries?

Similarly, clinicians should be aware of any family history of neuropsychological illness, degenerative disease, psychosis, or learning disabilities. It is also important to assess for any parental history of alcohol or drug abuse, so that prenatal toxicity can be ruled out.

B.   Regardless of the reason for referral, plan a battery with both cognitive and personality elements

Understandably, conducting lengthy batteries of cognitive and personality assessment presents a clinical challenge, especially given the atmosphere of managed mental health care, which may make pursuing reimbursement for such services difficult or unlikely (Cashel,

2002; Piotrowski, 1999). However, the validity of an assessment is improved by more points of data that can be increased by the addition of even slightly more assessment (Meyer, 2002). A narrow perspective in an evaluation can lead to premature conclusions that reduce the effectiveness and usefulness of the testing.

For clinicians assessing for cognitive and educational concerns, the addition of an omnibus self-report measure of personality and a guardian-completed behavior rating scale will provide important information without adding too much time or effort. Such measures can be used to screen for more substantial issues that might require further assessment using additional measures and behavior-based (projective) assessment. Even the initial self-report and behavioral measures can be used to augment and aid in the interpretation of cognitive, neuropsychological, and educational assessments by allowing the clinician to assess for pathological issues related to depression and anxiety. Moreover, the assessment of the child's personality will allow the clinician to evaluate such characteristics as frustration tolerance, relationships with authority, social skills, and oppositionality, all of which might substantially affect the interpretation of the obtained cognitive test scores.

Similarly, for clinicians conducting assessment of personality and affective functioning, some measure of cognitive functioning is recommended. Although recent surveys have suggested that most child and adolescent clinicians do this as part of their practice (Archer & Newsom, 2000; Cashel, 2002), it is important to emphasize the importance of a cognitive screen in the interpretation of personality assessment measures. A measure of global cognitive functioning (IQ) seems like an appropriate addition to any assessment of personality or psychopathology and will allow clinicians to more fully characterize and understand the relationship the patient may have with his or her environment. The recent development of shorter measures of IQ (e.g., Wechsler Abbreviated Scale of Intelligence; Wechsler, 1999) makes such a cognitive screen less time consuming. Moreover, such an analysis will allow the clinician to fully determine whether the patient has adequate ability to process the test stimuli, read the test items, and adequately formulate responses. If there are significant signs from cognitive testing (such as a large discrepancy between verbal and nonverbal reasoning), this might be an indication that further testing is needed.

C. Observe behavior

Clinicians conducting assessments should be sensitive to the child's or adolescent's motivation, engagement in the tasks, and receptivity to the assessment process. A child who lacks motivation or is oppositional with the evaluator will produce a profile of scores that is not reflective of his true ability or functioning. Like all testing data, observations can and should shape the way in which test scores are interpreted.

D. Balance ideographics with nomothetics

Modern psychological and neuropsychological assessment allows us to assume a nomothetic approach to understanding patient functioning. That is, by using normative databases and making comparisons with a normative sample, we can determine whether patient functioning significantly deviates from the norm. From these deviations (or lack thereof), we are able to make interpretations about personality characteristics, psychopathology, neurocognitive functions, learning disabilities, etc. But, as the above discussion argues, a purely nomothetic approach to understanding test scores may be somewhat misleading, given each patient's unique profile of test scores. If personality partly determines how we interpret neuropsychological test scores and if neuropsychology partly determines how patients make meaning of the personality measures, then we must be aware of these issues and make the effort to interpret tests accordingly. The art of assessment lies in the intersection of the clinician, patient, and test score.

SUMMARY

Although neuropsychological assessment and personality assessment are seemingly distant fields in terms of training models, research base, and clinical orientation, both use the tools and procedures of assessment and measurement to more fully understand patient functioning. Despite a reliance on the psychometric method, there is little available research that can be drawn on to specifically examine how these forms of assessment can be meaningfully integrated. I have attempted to outline thoughts and ideas related to the integration of neuropsychology and personality assessment in clinical practice with children and adolescents. From my perspective, the integration of these measurement techniques occurs at the level of interpretation (the effect of personality on neuropsychological measurement) and the deeper level of meaning (the effect of neuropsychology on personality assessment). When done well, integration of neuropsychological and personality assessment results yields a more complex and comprehensive picture of patient functioning that can significantly alter how we understand our patients. To do less runs the risk of drawing conclusions about only one part of the elephant.

REFERENCES

Acklin, M. W. (1990). Personality dimensions in two types of learning-disabled children: A Rorschach study. *Journal of Personality Assessment, 54*, 67–77.

Acklin, M. W., & Wu-Holt, P. (1996). Contributions of cognitive science to the Rorschach technique: Cognitive and neuropsychological correlates of the response process. *Journal of Personality Assessment, 67*, 169–178.

Archer, R. P., & Krishnamurthy, R. (1997). Mmpi-a and rorschach indices related to depression and conduct disorder: An evaluation of the incremental validity hypothesis. *Journal of Personality Assessment, 69*, 517–533.

Archer, R. P., & Newsom, C. R. (2000). Psychological test usage with adolescent clients: Survey update. *Assessment, 7*, 227–235.

Beery, K. E. (1997). *The Beery-Buktenica developmental test of visual-motor integration: Administration, scoring, and teaching manual* (4th ed.). Parsippany, NJ: Modern Curriculum Press.

Camara, W. J., Nathan, J. S., & Puente, A. E. (2000). Psychological test usage: Implications in professional psychology. *Professional Psychology: Research and Practice, 31*, 141–154.

Cashel, M. L. (2002). Child and adolescent psychological assessment: Current clinical practice and the impact of managed care. *Professional Psychology: Research and Practice, 33*, 446–453.

Colligan, S. C. (1997). The neuropsychology of the Rorschach: An M.D. With M.B.D. In J. R. Meloy, M. W. Acklin, C. B. Gacono, J. F. Murray, & C. A. Peterson (Eds.), *Contemporary Rorschach interpretation* (pp. 535–547). Mahwah, NJ: Lawrence Erlbaum Associates.

Elliot, C. D. (1990). *Differential ability scales*. San Antonio, TX: The Psychological Corporation.

Ellis, D. W., & Zahn, B. S. (1985). Psychological functioning after severe closed head injury. *Journal of Personality Assessment, 49*, 125–128.

Epstein, J. N., Erkanli, A., Conners, C. K., Klaric, J., Costello, J. E., & Angold, A. (2003). Relations between continuous performance test performance measures and ADHD behaviors. *Journal of Abnormal Child Psychology, 31*(5), 543–554.

Exner, J. E. (2003). *The Rorschach: A comprehensive system* (4th ed.). New York: Wiley.

Exner, J. E., Colligan, S. C., Boll, T. J., Stischer, B., & Hillman, L. (1996.). Rorschach findings concerning closed head injury patients. *Assessment*, 317–326.

Exner, J. E., & Weiner, I. B. (1995). *The Rorschach: A comprehensive system: Vol. 3. Assessment of children and adolescents* (2nd ed.). New York: Wiley.

Golden, C. J. (1978). *Stroop Color and Word Test: Manual for clinical and experimental uses.* Chicago: Stoetling.

Hannay, H. J., Bieliauskas, L., Crosson, B. A., Hammeke, T. A., Hamsher, K. D., & Koffler, S. (1998). Proceedings of the Houston Conference on Specialty Education and Training in Clinical Neuropsychology [Special issue]. *Archives of Clinical Neuropsychology, 13*, 157–250.

Heaton, R. K., Chelune, G. J., Talley, J. L., Kay, G. G., & Curtiss, G. (1993). *Wisconsin Card Sorting Test manual: Revised and expanded.* Odessa, FL: Psychological Assessment Resources.

Hilsenroth, M. J., Fowler, J. C., Padawer, J. R., & Handler, L. (1997). Narcissism in the Rorschach revisted: Some reflections on empirical data. *Psychological Assessment, 9*, 113–121.

Holaday, M. (2000). Rorschach protocols from children and adolescents diagnosed with posttraumatic stress disorder. *Journal of Personality Assessment, 75*, 143–157.

Ilonen, T., Taiminen, T., Karlsson, H., Lauerma, H., Leinonen, K.-M., Wallenius, E., et al. (1999). Diagnostic efficiency of the Rorschach schizophrenia and depression indices in identifying first-episode schizophrenia and severe depression. *Psychiatry Research, 87*, 183–192.

Kaufman, A. S., Grossman, I., & Kaufman, N. L. (1994). Comparison of hospitalized depressed patients and matched normal controls on tests that differ in their level of cognitive complexity. *Journal of Psychoeducational Assessment, 12*, 112–125.

Kleiger, J. H. (1999). *Disordered thinking and the Rorschach: Theory, research, and differential diagnosis.* Hillside, NJ: Analytic Press.

Lachar, D., & Gruber, C. P. (1995). *Personality Inventory for Youth manual: Technical guide.* Los Angeles: Western Psychological Services.

MacNiven, E., & Finlayson, M. A. (1993). The interplay between emotional and cognitive recovery after closed head injury. *Brain Injury, 7*, 241–246.

Malmgren, H., Bilting, M., Frobarj, G., & Lindqvist, G. (1997). A longitudinal pilot study of the Rorschach as a neuropsychological instrument. In A. M. Carlsson (Ed.), *Research into Rorschach and projective methods* (pp. 117–139). Stockholm: Swedish Rorschach Society.

Martinez, R. S., & Semrud-Clikeman, M. (2004). Emotional adjustment and school functioning of young adolescents with multiple versus single learning disabilities. *Journal of Learning Disabilities, 37*, 411–420.

Meyer, G. J. (2002). Implications of information-gathering methods for a refined taxonomy of psychopathology. In L. E. Beutler & M. L. Malik (Eds.), *Rethinking the DSM: A psychological perspective* (pp. 69–105). Washington, DC: American Psychological Association.

Minassian, A., & Perry, W. (2004). The use of projective tests in assessing neurologically impaired populations. In M. J. Hilsenroth & D. L. Segal (Eds.), *Comprehensive handbook of psychological assessment: Vol. 2. Personality assessment* (pp. 539–552). Hoboken, NJ: Wiley.

Morey, L. C. (1991). *The Personality Assessment Inventory Professional manual.* Odessa, FL: Psychological Assessment Resources.

Osterrieth, P. A. (1944). Le test de copie d'une figure complexe. *Archives de Psychologie, 30*, 206–356.

Perry, W., & Potterat, E. (1997). Beyond personality assessment: The use of the Rorschach as a neuropsychological instrument in patients with amnestic disorders. In J. R. Meloy, M. W. Acklin, C. G. Gacono, J. F. Murray, & C. A. Peterson (Eds.), *Contemporary Rorschach interpretation.* Mahwah, NJ: Lawrence Erlbaum Associates.

Perry, W., Potterat, E., Auslander, L., Kaplan, E., & Jeste, D. (1996). A neuropsychological approach to the Rorschach in patients with dementia of the Alzheimer's type. *Assessment, 3*(3), 351–363.

Piotrowski, C. (1999). Assessment practices in the era of managed care: Current status and future directions. *Journal of Clinical Psychology, 55*, 787–796.

Piotrowski, Z. (1937a). The Rorschach inkblot method in organic disturbances of the central nervous system. *Journal of Nervous and Mental Disease, 86*, 525–537.

Piotrowski, Z. (1937b). Rorschach studies of cases with lesions of the frontal lobes. *British Journal of Medical Psychology, 17,* 105–118.

Rabin, L. A., Barr, W. B., & Burton, L. A. (2005). Assessment practices of clinical neuropsychologists in the United States and Canada: A survey of INS, NAN, and APA division 40 members. *Archives of Clinical Neuropsychology, 20,* 33–65.

Rader, N., & Hughes, E. (2005). The influence of affective state on the performance of a block design task in 6- and 7-year-old children. *Cognition & Emotion, 19,* 143–150.

Ready, R. E., Stieman, L., & Paulsen, J. S. (2001). Ecological validity of neuropsychological and personality measures of executive functions. *Clinical Neuropsychologist, 15,* 314–323.

Reitan, R. M. (1955). Evaluation of the postconcussion syndrome with the Rorschach test. *Journal of Nervous and Mental Disease, 121,* 463–467.

Reitan, R. M., & Wolfson, D. (1997). Emotional disturbances and their interaction with neuropsychological deficits. *Neuropsychology Review, 7*(1), 3–19.

Rosselli, M., Ardila, A., Lubomski, M., Murray, S., & King, K. (2001). Personality profile and neuropsychological test performance in chronic cocaine-abusers. *International Journal of Neuroscience, 110,* 55–72.

Rourke, B. P. (1989). *Nonverbal learning disabilities: The syndrome and the model.* New York: Guildford.

Ruttan, L. A., & Heinrichs, R. W. (2003). Depression and neurocognitive functioning in mild traumatic brain injury patients referred for assessment. *Journal of Clinical and Experimental Neuropsychology, 25,* 407–419.

Semrud-Clikeman, M., Kamphaus, R. W., Teeter, P. A., & Vaughn, M. (1997). Assessment of behavior and personality in the neuropsychological diagnosis of children. In C. R. Reynolds & E. Fletcher-Janzen (Eds.), *Handbook of clinical child neuropsychology* (2nd ed., pp. 320–341). New York: Plenum Press.

Sliverstein, M. L., & McDonald, C. (1988). Personality trait characteristics in relation to neuropsychological dysfunction in schizophrenia and depression. *Journal of Personality Assessment, 52,* 288–296.

Smith, S. R., Baity, M. R., Knowles, E. S., & Hilsenroth, M. J. (2001). Assessment of disordered thinking in children and adolescents: The Rorschach perceptual-thinking index. *Journal of Personality Assessment, 77,* 447–463.

Stokes, J. M., Pogge, D. L., Grosso, C., & Zaccario, M. (2001). The relationship of the Rorschach schizophrenia index to psychotic features in a child psychiatric sample. *Journal of Personality Assessment, 76,* 209–228.

Stokes, J. M., Pogge, D. L., Powell-Lunder, J., Ward, A. W., Bilginer, L., & DeLuca, V. A. (2003). The Rorschach ego impairment index: Prediction of treatment outcome in a child psychiatric population. *Journal of Personality Assessment, 81,* 11–19.

Waber, D. P., & Holmes, J. M. (1985). Assessing children's copy production of the Rey-Osterrieth complex figure. *Journal of Clinical and Experimental Neuropsychology, 7,* 264–280.

Wechsler, D. (1999). *Wechsler Abbreviated Scale of Intelligence.* San Antonio, TX: The Psychological Corporation.

Wechsler, D. (2002). *Wechsler Individual Achievement Test* (2nd ed.). San Antonio, TX: Psychological Corporation.

Wechsler, D. (2004). *Wechsler Intelligence Scale for Children manual* (4th ed.). San Antonio, TX: Psychological Corporation.

Weiner, I. B. (2003). Making Rorschach interpretation as good as it can be. *Journal of Personality Assessment, 74,* 164–174.

Wilson, B. A. (1993). Ecological validity of neuropsychological assessment: Do neuropsychological indexes predict performance in everyday activities? *Applied and Preventive Psychology, 2,* 209–215.

Wood, J. M., Nezworski, M. T., Lilienfeld, S. O., & Garb, H. N. (2003). *What's wrong with the Rorschach? Science confronts the controversial inkblot test.* San Francisco: Jossey-Bass.

Zillmer, E. A., & Perry, W. (1996). Cognitive-neuropsychological abilities and related psychological disturbance: A factor model of neuropsychological, Rorschach, and MMPI indices. *Assessment, 3,* 209–224.

4

THE USE OF THERAPEUTIC ASSESSMENT WITH CHILDREN AND ADOLESCENTS

Leonard Handler
University of Tennessee

WHAT IS THERAPEUTIC ASSESSMENT?

Therapeutic assessment is an approach to assessment in which the assessment process itself is considered to be a potential therapeutic intervention (Finn, 1996; Finn & Tonsager, 1992, 1997; Finn & Martin, 1996). The goal of therapeutic assessment is not just the collection of information *about* a patient/client, but rather, the assessment procedure itself is designed to be transformative. The term "Therapeutic Assessment" (TA) refers to a set of specific techniques developed by Finn and his associates. However, there have been a number of related assessment approaches developed by others that differ somewhat in procedure, but not in the goal of providing a transformational experience for the patient/client. These approaches are designated as "therapeutic assessment" (ta), preserving Finn's specific approach as "Therapeutic Assessment." In this chapter I describe the differences between Therapeutic Assessment (TA) and therapeutic assessment (ta) on the one hand, compared with traditional assessment. This is followed by a description and discussion of several therapeutic assessment approaches for children and adolescents, and a case study employing one such approach.

HOW DOES THERAPEUTIC ASSESSMENT DIFFER FROM TRADITIONAL ASSESSMENT?

Finn and Tonsager (1997) refer to traditional psychological assessment as the "information-gathering model," typically used to facilitate communication among professionals, to help make decisions about a patient (e.g., medication decisions, treatment decisions) or diagnostic decisions. In sharp contrast to the information-gathering approach, TA and ta models are designed to provide the client/patient[1] with a view of himself or herself that becomes truly transformative, leading to an awareness of personal problems or issues and, eventually, to their resolution. A more detailed discussion of the differences between TA (ta) and collaborative assessment, on the one hand, and the traditional assessment approach appears in Finn and Tonsager (1997), Fischer (1985/1994), and Handler (in preparation).

I became disenchanted with the traditional model rather quickly in graduate school when I realized that the assessments I labored over had little impact on patients' lives. Typically, they were used only to diagnose the patient. When I gave feedback to patients I recognized how little they took away from my efforts to explain their problems. I became aware that patients were having a variety of experiences during the "data collection" phase of the assessment that were vitally important in understanding them, and so I began to collaborate with them during the assessment process. We discussed important thoughts and feelings that were stimulated by the various tests I administered, and I found that this approach resulted in a dramatic change in what the patient took away from the assessment process. Many clients also developed an understanding of themselves that sharply illuminated their life issues, thereby giving them important self-knowledge. I compared this collaborative approach with the traditional (information-gathering) approach and realized that the latter approach offered little benefit to the patient/client, whereas the former approach seemed to motivate patients/clients to deal with their identified life issues.

Connie Fischer (1985/1994) developed a collaborative approach to therapeutic assessment, based on human science psychology and grounded in the European existential-phenomenological philosophy of science. She responds to the client with interventions, either during the assessment process itself or shortly thereafter. These interventions are constructive, illuminating for the client some important aspect of his or her functioning. Furthermore, these interventions provide for the client an awareness of areas of possible growth and development. Fischer states, "These interventions into the client's ways of moving through situations are intended both to evaluate the client's current possibilities and to try out different ones. Psychologists too often have acted as though individualized understanding and intervention should be reserved totally for a separate enterprise, that of therapy" (p. 47).

The following example is from Fischer's book, *Individualizing Psychological Assessment* (1985/1994); it illustrates how she actually collaborates with clients in the assessment process, relating performance (behavior) on psychological tests with the patient's important life issues and possibilities.

The client is a 6-year-old girl, referred for "gifted student" evaluation:

Assessor:	I'm going to tell you two things you said, and you tell me what's different about them: (1) "I don't know. There's some. Is it five pennies?" and "It's when there's snow. It's a season." What's different about you in those two answers?
Client:	I was smart about winter.
Assessor:	And what about the number of pennies in a nickel?
Client:	I was ignorant about pennies.
Assessor:	Ignorant? Who says "ignorant"?
Client (giggling):	Eddie, he's my brother. He's in fifth grade.
Assessor:	But you knew the right answer; five is correct. What's ignorant about that?
Client:	I didn't know if I was sure. I didn't know ahead of time if it was right.
Assessor:	If I hadn't kept at you, do you think you would have guessed by yourself?
Client:	Nope, I mighta made a mistake.

Assessor:	Here's a new test [Stanford-Binet]. This time the rules are that you're supposed to guess, even if you might be wrong. Okay? [Assessor continues with the S-B, documenting that [the] client in fact has been earning misleadingly low scores because of her fear of looking ignorant.] Marie, you know what? I think you were "smart" when you guessed. I'm going to suggest to your mother and father that they tell Eddie that sometimes it's "ignorant" not to guess. What do you think about that?
Client:	Eddie says you're not allowed to guess at school or kids'll make fun of you.
Assessor:	Maybe they do sometimes, especially if you're being silly. Let's practice some more guessing, and see if you can tell when it's silly and when it's not (p. 97).

ADVANTAGES OF THERAPEUTIC ASSESSMENT WITH CHILDREN AND ADOLESCENTS

The advantages of Therapeutic Assessment (and therapeutic assessment) are that both approaches accomplish the following:

1. They can be used to build rapport quickly with children and adolescents. Patients/ clients view the TA (ta) process more as a game and less like a test.

2. Patients' problems and life issues become obvious very quickly, allowing the clinician to evaluate and treat a child or adolescent in the same session, or soon thereafter. Many of the approaches described later in this chapter can be completed in one session or less.

3. When used periodically in the treatment of a child or adolescent, the assessments can allow the clinician to track a patient's/client's progress, measuring his or her acceptance of various aspects of the treatment process.

4. TA (ta) approaches save time and money; because the techniques bridge the gap between assessment and therapy, the child or adolescent benefits from the assessment and treatment processes without an arduous period spent waiting for the assessor to administer and score the tests. Because rapport has been established, and the assessor has provided therapeutic feedback to the child, it is often appropriate for the assessor to continue treating the child after the initial assessment session, making the transition from assessment to treatment smoothly and efficiently.

5. TA (and ta) procedures provide important information to parents or other caretakers, so that they obtain a first-hand appreciation of their child's or adolescent's problems. When they observe the TA (ta) process or review the assessment results the clinician shares with them, parents develop a new understanding about their child's problem(s). They come to view the(se) problem(s) from a very different perspective. Parents can be enlisted more directly in cooperative efforts in problem resolution, because they, like the child or adolescent, can understand the problem better.

6. Integrating assessment with therapy into an ongoing treatment approach can yield specific information to insurance companies and managed care organizations, to demonstrate improvement and provide focused efforts toward future treatment goals.

THE PROBLEM WITH TRADITIONAL ASSESSMENT
PROCEDURES FOR CHILDREN AND ADOLESCENTS

Traditional psychological assessment has often been described as quite stressful, often leaving the patient feeling anxious, angry, or confused (Barber, 1996; Beutler & Berren, 1996; Schafer, 1954, 1956). Psychological testing can be especially stressful for children and adolescents, because the testing sessions are often perceived by children to be much like classroom exams. Although examiners often make heroic efforts to build rapport and to support and encourage the child or adolescent, the examiner must nevertheless administer the tests in a standardized manner, with a minimum of guidance or explanation. The results, according to Schafer, often engender feelings of frustration or abandonment, along with a great deal of apprehension and stress.

Children referred for assessment are often more at risk of developing negative emotions surrounding their experience with assessors who adhere to the traditional testing model because they have typically been referred for emotional problems. In my own experience with the traditional approach, support and rapport-building were typically not enough to prevent the appearance of negative emotions, often causing interference in how the child or adolescent dealt with the test, and therefore resulting in damaged test results. Conversely, TA and ta approaches are quite enjoyable for children and adolescents. They are typically quite engaged in the process and do not feel pressured or anxious. With the use of collaborative assessment procedures, the clinician can investigate reasons for a child's or adolescent's poor performance, can determine, by judicious discussion with the patient, why he or she was not successful and can demonstrate how the child can be successful. Examples of this approach can be seen in the work of Fischer (1985/1994) and Handler (1988, 1998).

Failure experiences are actually built into some assessment instruments, such as the various Wechsler intelligence tests and various achievement tests. The examiner is to stop testing only after a prescribed number of failures. Because many of the children and adolescents we typically test have some type of emotional problem, failures, especially if they are repeated, can be extremely distressing and demoralizing for them, with negative effects that interfere with performance throughout the assessment process (Handler, 1998).

Similarly, whereas the Free Association phase of the Rorschach is often enjoyable for children, the Inquiry can easily engender feelings of failure, especially if the child finds it difficult to tell the examiner why it looked like his or her percept. Asking the examiner for guidance or additional information does not result in much reassurance to allay these feelings or to find direction in a (sometimes) confusing Inquiry question, because the examiner is not allowed to provide the guidance and direction the child seeks.

During my graduate school training, as I tested more and more children and adolescents, I became aware of their discomfort with the standardized testing approach. Nevertheless, I recognized the importance of adhering to standardized procedures in relation to the use of available norms. Gradually, I developed an expanded Testing of the Limits phase (Handler, 1998, 2005a), based on the work of Klopfer (Klopfer, Ainsworth, Klopfer, & Holt, 1945), employed *after* the test was administered in the standardized manner. I went back over the items the patient missed, modifying them in various ways, in order to facilitate the child's or adolescent's success with each item. This approach gave the child/adolescent more confidence, and it helped me understand why he or she failed the item and what experiences or information he or she needed in order to perform better. These discussions were included in the report, and they allowed me to be more specific in crafting focused recommendations for remediation.

If, in the testing session, the child or adolescent became frustrated or despondent over a difficult item, I typically said to him or her, "Do you remember that you got upset when I asked you_____? Well, now that the test is over, let's see if you can be more relaxed and let me ask you that question again." For example, on the Vocabulary subtest of the WISC, I might ask if he or she had ever heard that word before, and if so, I might ask, in what way they had heard it. I might ask what the word reminded him or her of. If these hints were not enough, I might offer additional clues, until the correct answer was elicited, whereupon we might "celebrate" his or her success, or, at the very least, the child/adolescent would be praised. "See," I might say, "look how you figured out the right answer; you really do know your stuff." Actually, I have found that such efforts help the child/adolescent build a search process that he or she then learns to employ in the future.

The children, adolescents, and adults I tested in this way seemed much more open and willing to collaborate, following this approach to their assessment; I found that the transition from assessment to the actual therapy, with me or with someone else, was quite smooth. Although many clinicians frown upon taking patients for therapy whom they have previously assessed, I found the procedure to be quite productive. Therapy proceeded more rapidly and with fewer problems.

Gradually, I became more and more troubled about the formal structure of the traditional assessment procedure, which required a great deal of time and effort, and which delayed actual treatment for weeks or months. I wondered what the children who were tested in this manner thought when they came to see "the doctor" about their problems and were then required to wait so long to actually begin treatment to deal with their ever-present problems. These children probably initially thought they were already *in* therapy, only to have the "doctor" merely ask them a bunch of puzzling, irrelevant questions, and then weeks or months passed with no other contact.

When I discovered D. W. Winnicott's book, *Therapeutic Consultations in Child Psychiatry* (1971), I began to recognize the possibility of using some more collaborative assessment procedures that could be therapeutic as well. In this way the assessment and the treatment could be integrated into the same session. Such an approach would be much more meaningful to the child or adolescent because it would provide him or her with at least initial information and perhaps a solution to their painful problems. Later on I recognized that my approach to assessment with patients/clients was in many ways similar to what Finn and Fischer were doing and writing about. I began searching for more flexible assessment methods for children and adolescents, and now I employ a therapeutic assessment approach with most of the children and adolescents I see in therapy. This approach is especially useful with children and adolescents who at least appear to be unaware of their problem(s) or are unaware of the roots of their problem(s). Therapeutic assessment approaches can be used as a one-time intervention, or such approaches can be used intermittently, to track the progress of the patient in therapy. In this chapter I describe therapeutic assessment methods that can be used either in a one-time consultation or in an ongoing assessment and treatment procedure.

THEORETICAL SUPPORT FOR THERAPEUTIC ASSESSMENT

Narrative therapy (McAdams, Josselson, & Lieblich, 2001; McAdams, 1985, 1993; McLeod, 2001) concepts fit the therapeutic assessment paradigm quite well, especially the Fantasy Animal Drawing Game and Gardner's Mutual Storytelling Game, to be described later. A central theme of narrative therapy is that of enabling a person to reauthor his or her life story (Lieblich, McAdams, & Josselson, 2004). These narratives are formed by the child's dominant culture and family members. Mutual storytelling approaches offer an opportunity for the child or adolescent to tell his or her narrative to the clinician, and, then, the therapist's story offers the child a chance to reauthor the narrative and/or to see himself or herself in a different (more positive) manner. McLeod (cited in Lieblich, McAdams, & Josselson, 2004) describes the theory and process of narrative therapy as follows:

> The person seeking help is a narrator and actually tells and reauthors stories [about him or herself and others] that enable him or her to convey a sense of identity and to make sense of problematic experiences by integrating them into a coherent and complex story. The idea of the narrative therefore includes within it a personal dimension in terms of the unique life stories that make up the teller's autobiography. Narrative also implies an interpersonal process. Telling a story is a performance, shaped by the responses of the audience. (p. 15)

Of course this definition, written with adults in mind, is only partially descriptive of the employment of narratives with children and adolescents, because most of them will not yet have formed a coherent sense of identity. The troubled children and adolescents tell stories that present their problems, but they typically do so in metaphor. It is very probable that narratives of children and adolescents that are fraught with pain and strife eventually become the building blocks of the narratives of the adult self, unless intervention takes place to alter the developing narrative. As indicated above, this process can take place in two ways: by responding therapeutically to the painful narrative, and/or by alerting and informing the parents or caretakers and helping them assist in reauthoring the child's or adolescent's narrative. This would best be done by helping parents or caretakers change the way they view the child/adolescent and his or her problem(s).

Another theory that is consistent with therapeutic assessment approaches is the intersubjective psychoanalytic approach developed by Stolorow and his associates (Mitchell & Aron, 1999; Orange, Atwood, & Stolorow, 1997; Stolorow, Brandchaft, & Atwood, 1987). This approach emphasizes the interactive vision of the patient-therapist relationship and its powerful reciprocal nature. Stolorow (2001) states, "In this view, psychoanalytic therapy is no longer an archeological excavation of deeper layers of an isolated unconscious mind. Instead, it is a dialogical exploration of the patient's experiential world, conducted with an awareness of the unavertable contributions of the therapist's experiential world to the ongoing exploration" (p. xi). This quote fits quite well the interactive approach to assessment I describe as therapeutic assessment (Finn, 2002; Handler, 2004, 2005a,b).

A CAVEAT

To successfully employ TA (ta) approaches to assessment, the clinician must set aside some of his or her traditional training and instead focus on being more playful and imaginative. In one respect, success in TA (ta) with children is facilitated if the assessor allows himself/herself to engage playfully in the assessment process with the children. This was brought home to me in my first attempt to use Winnicott's Squiggle Game as a therapeutic assessment procedure. In this attempt I used the Squiggle Game as I might have used a standardized "test"; the result was that it was of no use in helping to understand a child. In my second attempt, many years later, I used the Squiggle Game as a real game, playing back and forth with a child, without censoring my responses. This time the squiggle results were quite helpful in understanding the child and in providing symbolic feedback.

SOME THERAPEUTIC ASSESSMENT APPROACHES

In the following section I describe some TA (ta) approaches I employ in working with children and adolescents. Although space considerations prevent me from discussing all of the different ta approaches I have devised or have been devised by others, I describe some selected approaches and games I use with children and adolescents. Almost any board game, any test, and most play activities can be used in therapeutic assessment with children and adolescents.

The Squiggle Game

This "game" was often used by D. W. Winnicott, the British psychoanalyst, in his clinical work with children and adolescents. Although the Squiggle Game has typically been identified as an approach Winnicott used with children, I discovered a number of cases where he used the game with adolescents as well (Winnicott, 1971, 1972, 1989).

Winnicott viewed the game as a way of communicating ("getting into contact") with children/adolescents. In the process of squiggling with the patient, he was able to free up the child and help him or her symbolically express problems. He would say to a child or adolescent he was seeing, usually for the first time, something like "I have a game I'd like us to play. Here's how we play it. I close my eyes and I make a mark [on the paper], and you turn it into something. Then you close your eyes and make a mark and I turn it into something" (Winnicott, 1971, p. 3). This interactive process continues, many times, with patient and therapist squiggling, back and forth. Winnicott states, "What happens in the game . . . depends on the use made of the child's experience, including the material that presents itself" (1971, p. 3). The effective squiggle game resembles a play scene, with the child/adolescent and Winnicott commenting on each other's productions and on their own productions. Sometimes Winnicott arranged all the squiggles on the floor, so that he and/or the child could discern a pattern. Based on the content of the squiggles, the child's/adolescent's comments, and an estimation of whether the child/adolescent could handle the insight, Winnicott would sometimes make a direct interpretation concerning what he believed was troubling the patient. At other times the interpretations were made metaphorically. An example of Winnicott's direct interpretation comes from the case of Robin, a five-year-old boy from a farm community, who was showing signs of school refusal. The following quote comes from the middle of a session with Winnicott and the boy. Winnicott states:

> We had all the drawings spread out on the floor in a line beside the table where we were playing or working together so that we could see them all at once, and we found that we had a farm—the snakes, the spider, the earth, the duck and the goose and a fish for the pond and a pig—and we began to wonder whether [squiggle] No 9 was something lying around on the ground. He suggested it was a bit of wire. He added: "And we have got a farmer" referring to my drawing 6. I said: "Would you like to be a farmer?" and he said: "Well yes, but the trouble is there is a lot of work to be done on a farm." It will be remembered that he had come from a farm to the consultation. . . . In my mind was the question of making some kind of interpretation such as: "You wonder whether to go out in the world and be a farmer and work or be where you can get back to mother's lap and curl up like the snake, and touch her when you feel like it, for pleasure." He accepted this idea without any apparent difficulty. (p. 36)

Winnicott's goal with the Squiggle Game was to help the child or adolescent communicate with him through play. Typically, at first, the child's or adolescent's squiggles are rather specific and concrete. Eventually, as the game continues, the child's/adolescent's squiggles become less concrete and more imbued with fantasy. From this point Winnicott would often ask the child or adolescent about his or her dreams, because he felt the dreams were more focused fantasies. He states, "I have a definite intention in these interviews to get to the real dream material; that is to say, to dreams dreamed and remembered. Dream contrasts with fantasying, which is unproductive, shapeless, and to some extent, manipulated" (1971, p. 32). The child's or adolescent's problem is further illuminated by his or her dream material. Winnicott's casebook, *Therapeutic Consultations in Child Psychiatry"* (1971), is filled with many remarkable cases, presented in detail and with the squiggles reproduced as well.

The Fantasy Animal Game

I devised the Fantasy Animal Game (Handler & Hilsenroth, 1994) one day about 25 years ago when I found myself face to face with a frightened five-year-old girl who stood inside my office, at the door, frozen and silent. She would not respond to the efforts I made to communicate with her. Her mother had been hospitalized for over a year, when the child was two or three, because of severe depression. After she returned to her family she attempted to make up for the time she was away by very actively involving herself in the child's life. I had been experimenting with Winnicott's Squiggle Game (Winnicott, 1971), with little success. I also experimented with various drawing activities, including drawing animals, as methods to involve children in enjoyable assessment approaches. I marveled at how Winnicott could facilitate the child's or adolescent's use of fantasy using the Squiggle Game, but, as I described above, I was disappointed when I found his approach and the drawing tests I devised were of little use to me or the patient in assessment or therapy.

Watching my young client standing far from me, close to the office door, I asked her if she liked to draw. To my surprise, she nodded "Yes." "Well," I said, "would you like to draw?" Again she nodded in the affirmative. I invited her to sit next to me at my desk and asked her to "draw a make-believe animal, one that no one has ever seen or heard of before." Asking for a fantasy or make-believe animal was my latest attempt to have the child become involved in fantasy, a method, Winnicott emphasized, to access unconscious processes in a symbolic manner.

To my surprise, she literally attacked the paper, scribbling over the entire sheet. In one of the scribbled loops she placed a small dot. Surprised by this explosive reaction from this formerly frozen child, I recognized that a transformation had occurred. I took a chance that she would now be more open and asked her to tell me a story about her make-believe animal. She replied with the following narrative: "This little fishie [pointing to the dot inside one of her scribbled loops] is stuck inside the momma fishie and she can't breathe and she's drowning." One need not be a rocket scientist to be able to interpret the story she told. She was telling me how she was experiencing her mother's attempts to reconnect with her daughter.

I felt she needed a response from me, but I doubted I could address the child directly. Rather, I felt, a metaphorical response was necessary, using the child's own metaphor. I asked her if I could tell her a story about the fishies and she again nodded, "Yes." Here is the story I told her: "This little baby fishie [pointing to the dot] is stuck inside the momma fishie and she can't breathe; she's dying. But along comes a big helper fishie and he makes an opening in the momma fishie and the baby swims out, and she's free." Suddenly, the child brightened. "Can I sit in your lap?" she asked. As I picked her up, she asked if I could tell her the story again, and so I did. This change in the child's attitude and her responsiveness indicated to me that some important change had occurred in this child. Her continued drawing and storytelling in later sessions affirmed my opinion. In the following sessions the child was more active and spontaneous, as we dealt with her problem. In addition, I shared the child's drawing and story with her mother and collaborated with her to modify her "smothering" behavior. Additional case material concerning the Fantasy Animal game can be found in a paper by Mutchnick and Handler (2002), and in a forthcoming book, *Therapeutic Assessment with Children and Adolescents* (Handler, in preparation).

The idea behind such an unusual request to draw a make-believe animal is to help the child or adolescent use fantasy in drawing and storytelling, thereby allowing him or her more access to and expression of unconscious processes. In addition, the use of storytelling allows the clinician to assess the child's/adolescent's self-narrative and allows the therapist to collaborate with the child (and the family) to co-create a healthier, more adaptive narrative. Sharing the child's or adolescent's drawing and story with parents is important in effecting change in their view of the child and changing their narrative of their child/adolescent to a more positive and constructive story. This aspect of TA (ta) is very important because it coincides with and amplifies the clinician's work with the child or adolescent Thus, for example, parents often view their child or adolescent and describe him or her negatively, using some very pejorative terms (e.g., "sneaky," "spiteful," "bad," "lazy," "selfish," "provocative"). When parents are made aware of the child's or adolescent's problem, they typically begin to see him or her in a new light, and they change these negative labels.

The clinician who uses one or another type of mutual storytelling must be able to interpret the metaphors used by the child or adolescent to describe his or her problems, so that the clinician can respond with a story, metaphorically presented, that offers the child or adolescent a reauthored version of the problem. Gradually, over time, but occasionally quite rapidly, the clinician's reauthored stories begin to develop more meaning for the patient, until the altered, more positive narrative becomes internalized.

Developing a Helpful Narrative

It is typically useful to begin the story told to the child or adolescent in the same manner as the story was told to you, using the same setting and the same characters. The therapeutic assessment clinician then continues to construct a story that helps to provide some antidote to the child's or adolescent's emotional pain. Lacking that for some reason, typically because there might be no real solution to offer, the story is constructed so that it expresses the clinician's recognition of the child's/adolescent's discomfort or pain. Sometimes, in these difficult situations, the therapeutic assessor gives voice, metaphorically of course, to the client's pain by expressing it in the story. In one such situation, a child could not get her schizoid and depressed mother to respond emotionally to her. She told a story about a similar situation with an imaginary animal. I told a story in response, about the animal who shouted at her mother "and gave her mother hell" for not showing such interest. The immediate effect was that the child felt more at ease and became more cheerful; the long-range effect was that she turned instead to her father, who was much more emotionally available.

Some clinicians use the Fantasy Animal Game during the first session, as I did with the first client, described above. Ordinarily, during the first session, I ask the child or adolescent if he or she is interested in playing a "make-believe animal game," in which they would invent a make-believe animal, "one that no one else had ever seen or heard of before." If the child or adolescent is not interested in the game, we go on to do something else, which may or may not be a therapeutic assessment activity. Sometimes the child/adolescent wants to draw but does not want to engage in the fantasy that is required to play the game effectively. I, of course, allow him or her to draw, and sometimes the child produces a fantasy animal. At other times the child draws interesting animals or people and we discuss these drawings. If a child/adolescent seems anxious and/or resistant during the first session, I wait a session or two, or as many sessions as are necessary before suggesting the Fantasy Animal game. I use a trial-and-error approach, allowing the child to make the choices. Sometimes a child/adolescent is interested in making a Fantasy Animal drawing but is reluctant to tell a story and, therefore, I offer several different types of assistance. First, I might say, "I'll help you get started: Once upon a time, a long, long time ago. . . ." Then I motion to the patient to continue. If this does not help, I suggest we tell the story together. I ask the child/adolescent to begin, and when he or she wants me to pick up the story, I suggest that he or she point or gesture to me, or say, "your turn." Thus, a symbolic dialogue is established. Sometimes the patient asks me to take over when he or she wants to avoid some aspect of the story. When this occurs I suggest the child continue for a while.

In this back-and-forth approach, the clinician is able to respond quickly to a portion of the child's/adolescent's story in an attempt to see what kinds of interventions are effective in facilitating problem resolution. For example, a very arrogant six-year-old boy who ignored the authority figures in his life told Fantasy Animal stories about his (benevolent) domination of animals in a variety of jungle settings. He pointed to me with an air of authority and insisted I take over and continue the story he was telling, which involved his control of all the jungle animals. I quickly introduced the lion, who I identified as the king of the jungle, and I gave the lion the authority to be in charge of the jungle setting. The child was surprised, but after several additional story exchanges with similar themes, in other sessions, he no longer challenged the authority of the lion. This was soon followed by his ability at home to begin responding more appropriately to his parents' directions.

While the Fantasy Animal Game is an excellent instrument for use with latency-age children, many adolescents enjoy participating as well. I have even used the approach with young adults, with excellent results. Many adolescents enjoy the playful aspects of the game, and they enjoy listening to the created stories of the clinician as much as do children.

Gardner's Mutual Storytelling Approach

No one has done more clinical work with storytelling techniques than Richard Gardner (1971, 1975, 1986, 1993). He has used the approach by itself and has incorporated it into several board games (described later in this chapter). Gardner uses the Mutual Storytelling approach separately, as a diagnostic tool, and later, after a "diagnosis" is made, he uses the approach therapeutically. He does not advocate the use of his approach in therapeutic assessment and warns against using it therapeutically before the diagnostic phase, because he feels it interferes with the free flow of unconscious material, which "contaminates" the child's unconscious message. My view is quite the opposite, and I have used storytelling approaches in therapeutic assessment with excellent results, often in the very first session. Although Gardner recommends using this approach primarily with latency-age children, in some cases immature adolescents will benefit from its use.

Gardner also recommends asking the child to produce a moral derived from the child's story or from the assessor's story. Although this approach is helpful to children who need superego messages, I believe it is counterproductive for use with a child with whom uncovering work is necessary. Focusing on a moral makes the entire storytelling process much more conscious, which interferes with the symbolic or metaphorical expression, which is much more unconscious. Except for my disagreement about these two issues, I recommend Gardner's publications describing the mutual storytelling approach. He reports that this approach is especially useful with resistant children, which has also been my experience.

Gardner has a very novel way of introducing the approach, which I find works quite well with most children. Using a tape recorder, he makes believe he is a radio show host, or, with a video camera, a TV host. He introduces the child as a guest and tells the audience the child will be telling a story. Although a few children might be frightened by the idea of being on the radio or TV, most of the children with whom I have used this approach were enthralled by having this "opportunity." They engage enthusiastically and often insist on hearing themselves during playback time. New information often comes up during the playback time.

Engleman and Allyn (2005, July) devised a very unusual storytelling approach as a therapeutic assessment intervention. Engelman uses one or several of a child's Rorschach responses and, together with a creative writer, develops an elaborate and quite detailed story for the child or adolescent that is metaphorically relevant and which becomes part of the treatment. The story incorporates important life history data about the patient and basic mental health messages that are important to communicate, metaphorically, to the patient. The story is shared with the child, who has input in revising it. The story is actively employed in the treatment process itself.

Projective Tests

Almost any projective test can be adapted for use in therapeutic assessment, including the Rorschach (Exner, 2003), the TAT (Morgan and Murray, 1935), and other narrative tests (e.g., the Children's Apperception Test [CAT; Bellak & Bellak, 1949], the Roberts Test [McArthur & Roberts, 1982], the Tasks of Emotional Development [TED; Pollack, Cohen, & Weil, 1982]), the Tell Me a Story Test (Costantino, Malgady, & Rogler, 1988), the Draw-A-Person Test (DAP; Machover, 1949), and other drawing tests, such as the Kinetic Family Drawing test (K-F-D), the Hand Test (Young & Wagner, 1999), and many others. All that is necessary is that the examiner ask the child or adolescent to tell a story to the stimulus, and for the examiner/therapist to respond with his or her own therapeutic story. In the case of the Rorschach, the child or adolescent is asked to make up a story about one or more of his or her percepts (Handler, 1996, 2002, 2004, 2005a). Ordinarily it is helpful to choose those percepts that are unusual or idiosyncratic. The clinician would then respond with a relevant therapeutic story. Sometimes a child's story has little or no meaning to the clinician. When this occurs I usually ask the patient to tell me another story about the same response. Very often the second story does have important meaning. If the second story has no symbolic meaning for the clinician, he or she should move on to another response.

For the Hand Test (Young & Wagner, 1999; also see the chapter by Clemence in this volume for a description of the test) the examiner/therapist first administers the test by presenting each card, which contains a picture of a hand in position, and asks, "What is this hand doing?" After finishing the administration of the 10 cards I ask the patient to make up a story about his or her response to one or more of the stimulus cards. The clinician might then respond by making up his or her own story, one that is helpful in responding to the child's metaphorically expressed problem.

One additional way to use the Hand Test is to consider the child's or adolescent's responses as interpersonal responses to the clinician. In this approach, the patient first gives his or her response to each card, and the therapist then gives his or her response, in an attempt to respond to the implicit or symbolic message the child/adolescent is offering. It is sometimes also interesting to reverse the process, where the therapist first gives his or her response, and then the patient gives his or her response.

When using tests such as the TAT, or other related tests, the examiner might respond with his or her own story immediately after the patient tells a story to each card. Although this approach may skew findings for the later cards, it is also possible that each story the patient tells is a symbolic response to the previous story by the clinician. Therefore, what may be developed here is a series of card-by-card communications from the patient to clinician, and from the clinician to the patient. It is perfectly appropriate, however, for the clinician to first obtain the patient's responses to all the cards before he or she begins responding to the child's or adolescent's stories.

Usually, when I use the TAT or related tests I listen carefully for themes that represent difficulties or problems in each story as the child or adolescent tells it and as I write it. Typically I wait to respond until the test is completed. However, sometimes, with younger children, I respond with my story as soon as I identify a problem theme. I also ask the child or adolescent what he or she thought of my story and ask the child to identify his or her favorite part. Sometimes, in order to determine how my story affected the child or adolescent, after I tell my story I ask him or her to tell another story to the card. The changes in the story often reflect the effects of my communication. For example, if the child's or adolescent's story concerns anger at a parent and my story deals with resolution of that problem, the patient's story might include a section about his or her affection for the parent.

Board Games

Gardner devised a number of interesting board games that are based on his mutual storytelling approach, such as the Pick and Tell game, in which the child/adolescent and assessor/therapist move a pawn around the board, using the traditional method of throwing the dice. When the patient lands on a specific space, he or she, without looking, must pick an item out of one of four different bags—the bag of faces, the bag of toys, the bag of words, or the bag of acts—and must then tell a story about the item chosen. The exception is the bag of acts, where the child must perform the act indicated on the card. The client is rewarded with chips if he or she tells a story, and with fewer chips if the story is less well developed. The game may be played by the patient alone, in an assessment phase, or the child/adolescent and the therapist can play together, each telling a story about the object they chose from the bag. A clinician using this game for therapeutic assessment should feel free to modify the approach, such as, for example, having the clinician tell a story in response to the child's/adolescent's story rather than having the clinician tell a story to his or her own selected card.

Another game designed by Gardner is the Thinking, Feeling, Doing Game, in which the client and assessor/therapist move around the board, using a throw of the dice, landing on different colored spaces. Depending on the color of the square on which the mover lands, the player selects a talking card, a feeling card, or a doing card. The child/adolescent or the therapist must read the card and respond to it. For example, one card reads, "Everyone in the class was laughing at a boy. What had happened?" When a child expresses a feeling or thought the therapist thinks is important to discuss, he or she helps the child express these thoughts and feelings. I tried using this game with children and young adolescents. However, I didn't feel we made any therapeutic progress, but other therapists sing its praises.

Another game devised by Gardner is the Storytelling Card Game, which is a cleverly disguised version of the Make a Picture Story Test (MAPS), a test devised by Shneidman (1952), but which is no longer published or available. In the MAPS, as in the Storytelling Card Game, there are a variety of typical scenes or backdrops, with no people or animals in them, and a variety of human and animal figures available to place in the scenes. The client is asked to make up a story using one of the backdrops and several people and/or animals. Recently, I found an old copy of the MAPS test in a storage closet at the university and realized that the backgrounds and people looked quite dated. Gardner's cards are much more up to date. According to Gardner, the clinician can respond to the child's story by making up his or her own story. The patient's story can also be used for exploration. Doing the latter would not be a therapeutic assessment approach, but doing the former would certainly be consistent with the therapeutic assessment paradigm.

There are a number of board games produced and marketed by a wide variety of sources, many available online, that purport to provide behavioral or emotional change. For example, Peacetown purports to teach children and adolescents how to resolve conflict; Exploring My Anger, Angry Animals, Furious Fred, Breaking the Chains of Anger, the Conduct Management Game, and From Rage to Reason are purported to help a child or adolescent learn to control anger; and the Social Conflict Game is designed to be used with children and adolescents who experience frequent conflict with peers. There are games for dealing with sexual abuse and domestic violence (The Peace Path); for helping a child or adolescent deal with personal loss (The Good Mourning Game); games to stimulate the child or adolescent's creativity and problem solving (Imagine, the Ungame, the Nurturing Game); and even games to help a child or adolescent give up self-defeating behaviors (the Use, Abuse, and Recovery Game). In sum, there is almost no limit to the games available that purport to deal with children's and adolescents' emotional problems and life and living problems. Most of these games could be used in a therapeutic assessment paradigm. They are available from such online sources as, for example, childtherapytoys.com, selfhelpwarehouse.com, feelingcompany.com, childwork.com, and creativetherapystore.com. Although I do not endorse these websites, they seemed to have available a wide variety of the games mentioned above, along with many others.

The Use of Photography in Therapeutic Assessment

Wolf (1976) indicates that the use of various photographic techniques stimulates significant progress in psychotherapy with resistant patients. He used a Polaroid camera, an early "instant" film version of the digital camera, to help children and adolescents take a closer look at themselves and focus on aspects of their personality that had previously been too anxiety-provoking to discuss openly. He states, "We have found that the photo itself often serves to initiate those important discussions which ultimately elicit significant material. This brings new energy and interest into our therapeutic sessions" (p. 198). Such use of photographs can also be incorporated at the beginning of therapy.

In this approach the clinician introduces a Polaroid, digital, or traditional film camera and asks the adolescent to take a picture of himself/herself, either pretending to do something, making a silly face, or giving his or her feelings a bodily or facial expression. He asks the client to cut the picture away from its background and then invites him or her to "play" with the photos by drawing whatever they wish to add, cut out whatever they wish to eliminate, and elaborate upon the photo in any way they choose. The therapist then collaborates with the client in exploring underlying content.

Stephen Finn (personal communication, November 20, 2004) describes an alternative way of using photography in therapeutic assessment. He cites the case of an eight-year-old boy in the third grade. He was acting up a great deal, both in school and at home. This behavior problem began about a year before his parents brought him for an evaluation. When asked about anything that had happened in the family or at school at about that time, the parents could not think of anything that would have produced this acting-out behavior.

The boy was given some standard assessment instruments, but nothing remarkable came through, except that he showed some depression on the Rorschach. As part of the assessment the boy was given a disposable camera that was capable of taking 12 pictures and was asked to take it home to take pictures of the 12 most important people and things in his life. After he brought the camera back, Finn had two identical sets of pictures made, one for him and one for the boy.

At the next session the boy was asked to tell what each picture was and why it was important to him. Finn then asked him to take the pictures and put them on the table and arrange them from the most important to least important. The boy arranged the 12 pictures as follows: his cat, his dog, his mom, his dad, and *eight* pictures of a photograph of his mother's brother, who had died a year before, of AIDS.

The family was a Christian family and the parents were very embarrassed that the uncle had been gay and had died of AIDS. The boy was very close to his uncle and had spent a great deal of time with him. The boy was not allowed to see him as he was dying, or even to go to the funeral. The family had not talked about the uncle's death at all.

The parents watched from a separate room, over a video link, as Finn and the boy discussed the loss of his uncle. They were shocked when they heard their son tell Finn about his loss and sorrow. Finn later told the parents he did not think the boy had had a chance to grieve over the loss of his uncle, and the parents admitted that they did not know what to say to the boy or what to do when the uncle died. He planned with the parents a way to talk to the boy about his uncle's death.

At the next session, Finn planned a ceremony with the entire family, to say goodbye to the uncle. During the ceremony the mother cried uncontrollably about her brother's death. Follow-up sessions revealed that the boy's acting out had stopped, both at home and at school.

This case vignette illustrates the importance of using the information acquired in the assessment session to inform the parents about the source of the child's problem and to plan with them a way to repair the problem. Of course the child must also be made aware, either directly or indirectly (e.g., metaphorically), of the source of the problem and of the solution. However, it is important that both the child and the parents be made aware of the source of the problem and the solution planned.

Yet another way of using photographs is to ask the patient to bring in unposed (candid) family pictures, without sorting them first. We examine the pictures together and compare our impressions of them and then discuss what they might signify about the relationship of the people in the pictures. For example, a 17-year-old boy who enjoyed a close, positive relationship with his father felt his father had stopped loving him because he had increasingly become remote and distant from the boy. The boy blamed himself for the damaged relationship, and he believed the father preferred a younger brother, or his baby sister. The early photographs seemed to confirm the boy's impression that he and his father had a close, positive connection. For example, in many of the pictures the father had his arm around the boy's shoulder and in one picture the father was proudly displaying his son to a large group of friends and family.

As we continued to look at later pictures, I noted fewer of them showed this loving pattern. Instead, the father, who seemed to have aged dramatically in a very short time, showed up in group pictures detached from everyone, and now standing in the back of the group rather than in the forefront. Now the boy was standing alone, detached from the group. I asked the boy what was happening in the family in that picture. To my surprise he said, "I think that was about the time my father started getting sick." I was surprised at his comment, because he had not mentioned his father's illness before this interaction. "What do you think was going on at the time this picture was taken?" I asked. The boy began to cry, realizing, for the first time, that his father had withdrawn from everyone, including him, after the initial diagnosis of his serious illness. The family had placed a premium on keeping things as they were before the illness, and everyone in the family was in denial of the seriousness of the father's illness. It was at this point the boy began to actually mourn his father's death, some two years after his father had died.

CHOOSING SUITABLE THERAPEUTIC ASSESSMENT APPROACHES

The decision concerning which ta approach to use should not be determined by age alone. In fact, I believe the decision concerning which approach to use should instead be made on the basis of the child's or adolescent's level of emotional development. Any of the ta approaches described in this chapter can be used with both children and adolescents, but some are more appropriate than others if the child's age and developmental levels are congruent. The lower the adolescent's developmental level, the more he or she will be happy with those approaches that are less challenging and less complex. For example, a very immature 14-year-old boy chose to play Chutes and Ladders, or Candyland, two games based on chance alone. He also loved to draw fantasy animals and tell stories about them.

Although it is true that any of the approaches described in this chapter are appropriate for children and adolescents, it is important to recognize that some children and adolescents are very threatened or even traumatized by the possibility of losing a game based on skill alone. However, they are typically not so disturbed by losing a game based on chance alone. Therefore, modifications must be made in each of the approaches described herein, to match the developmental level of the child or adolescent. Most adolescents whose developmental level is age-appropriate would prefer to play checkers, chess, or some other game of skill, such as Stratego, whereas latency-age children prefer games based on chance alone. Some older latency-age children are often comfortable playing games based on both chance and skill, such as Monopoly. The game Monopoly for Juniors has been modified so that the skill component has been reduced; it is primarily now a game of chance.

The Fantasy animal approach is typically appropriate for children, but, as indicated above, many adolescents enjoy it. The same may be said of the Squiggle Game. I have used it with adolescents who do not think it is stupid to play in this manner. Winnicott (1971, 1972, 1989) cites a number of case studies in which he and the adolescent patient squiggled.

Various approaches to Drama therapy, Gestalt therapy, and Psychodrama are more useful with adolescents, but children enjoy them as well (e.g., Brooks, 2002). The same is true for the use of various photographic techniques discussed in this chapter. Art techniques are useful with children and adolescents because the approaches can be modified to suit the developmental level of the child or adolescent. All the projective tests and photography methods can be used effectively with children and adolescents

Case Study

Lisa is a blond, blue-eyed, eight-year-old girl whose parents came from Kansas to work in Knoxville's tourist industry. Lisa's mother died after a long illness, about six months before Lisa came for therapy; her father has custody of her, but the mother's parents also want custody of Lisa and her five-year-old brother. Lisa's father does not recognize her feelings of abandonment and extreme vulnerability. She clings to her father and has announced to everyone that she wants to live with him, rather than with her grandparents, who live nearby. Lisa's father said she had not shown any sadness concerning the loss of her mother and felt this was a good thing because it meant she was getting over the loss. Even though I explained this was not a good sign because she was not expressing her loss and was containing it, he nonetheless still felt it was a sign of progress.

During the first three sessions the child appeared distant and irritable. She was moody and did not relate to me very much. She spent most of her time playing alone, with one toy or game, or another, but spent only a few minutes with each one. She was arrogant and demanding, refusing to discuss anything with me, and certainly not her mother's death. Instead, she assumed an air of pseudo-independence and criticalness, expressed mainly through her negative evaluation of the toys. Lisa's hyperactivity seemed to me to be part of the way she dealt with the loss, literally hurling herself into action and moving rapidly from activity to activity. She soon began to settle down, spending most of the sessions drawing. She rarely responded to my questions about what she was drawing, and when she did, it was with much irritation.

Lisa soon became more responsive, and so I asked her, during one session, if she would "draw a make-believe animal, one that no one has ever seen before." She turned away from me and drew a picture of a boy, next to a fox, shouting "Help, help!" Lisa said someone was saying, "Booga-booga-boo," as if to frighten the fox away. She told the following story: "There once was a fox with a tail that is short and it had no whiskers. The fox lived in the woods. His mom died. One day *I* was in the forest. I saw it. It was big, but friendly. It had a sister and a brother. His dad, he went to get food one day and a hyena came and killed him. The kids were sad but they knew they loved him, so they went to a cave and they lived happily ever after."

The story appeared to be autobiographical, especially because Lisa personally entered the story. She showed obvious concern about her father and the feeling that she would lose him as well, and then denied the loss, as she had been doing previously (i.e., "they went in a cave and they lived happily ever after").

I then began to tell my story, in response to her story: "Once upon a time there was a fox in the woods and his mom died and the dad was with them. The kids were all sad, and they were scared, too. 'What will happen if you die, too?', they asked the dad. 'Oh children,' he said, '*I* am strong and healthy and I will be alive for many, many years, and I will always be with you and take care of you.' The children started to smile and then they laughed, and they climbed on their dad and kissed and hugged them." At this point Lisa corrected me, "hugged and kissed," she said. This correction indicated that she was paying close attention to my story. I continued, "and they all laughed together and then the dad made dinner for everyone to eat."

At this point Lisa interrupted again, and said, "You forgot to say, 'Don't worry, I will always be with you.' Then she got sick and had to die." Lisa was obviously referring to a conversation she had had with her mother when her mother became ill. But then she quickly returned to the story again, saying, "She died because of the hyena—no, a mountain lion."

Somewhat startled, and with sadness in my heart, I constructed the remainder of my story, modified by Lisa's input: "Then the children said to the dad, 'Mama promised us she would always be with us, but then she died. She promised but she couldn't keep her promise, because the hyena-the mountain lion killed her.' 'Well', said the dad, 'I can beat up any mountain lion or any other animal in the woods or the jungle. No animal can hurt me or kill me, so I can, can, can promise you I will be there whenever you need me. If you close your eyes and see a picture of your mother, she can always be with you in your mind. So the kids all closed their eyes and got pictures of their mama in their minds, and they said, 'Hi mom, I'm so, so, so, so, glad to see you.' And they were happy."

As I told my story, Lisa became better connected with me, more cooperative, and quite a bit friendlier. She asked me to repeat the stories. I soon felt her hard shell softening, which I felt was definitely due to my story and her ability to begin telling me how hurt she was that her mother promised she would always be with Lisa, and then had disappointed her. She was also able to tell me, in her narrative, that she felt she would lose her father as well, and would retreat from interpersonal relationships from then on. As we were about to end the session, she spoke to me directly for the first time. In a soft voice I had not heard before she said, "My momma died and I live with my daddy. He takes good care of me; I love him."

The reader might notice how Lisa personalized the story about an animal, both in content and in the personalization, when she used the word "I" in placing herself in the forest. I believe the child was relieved that she could begin talking about her mother's death, and about the possibility she could also lose her father as well. I inadvertently said, in my story, what Lisa's mother had told her, in an effort to protect and soothe the child. I had not been aware that Lisa's mother told her daughter she would not die, even though she was very ill, or that the child believed her. Imagine the shock and the anger she felt at her mother for telling her something that was not true. When I shared Lisa's story with her grandparents, they indicated that their daughter had indeed told Lisa she would not die.

In the two sessions after the interaction reported above, Lisa was much less hyperactive. She and I were able to complete an entire game, and she was now much more verbal. Her grandmother indicated she was still quite bossy, even arrogant, with family members. I decided to address the issue metaphorically, by telling her a story. I told her a story about Roger, the dog, who needed to learn how to get along with his family. Therefore, the owner took Roger to dog school, where the teacher told Roger she would help him get along by using treats and not punishment. So the teacher said "sit" to Roger, and when he sat down, she gave him a delicious doggie treat.

Suddenly, Lisa got down on all fours, saying she wanted to be Roger. She made believe she was eating the doggie treat. Then I described another scene where Roger was given a doggie treat when he would lie down. Again Lisa gobbled up the imaginary doggie treat and wagged her behind. I ended the story by saying, "Roger, you are a wonderful doggie," and Lisa "trotted" over to me to be petted. I then asked Lisa if she would tell a story about Roger. She told the following story:

"Roger came to a neighbor and said, 'My owner—she's a little three-year-old girl with pigtails—was kidnapped.' So the neighbor and Roger went to find her. So they went into the woods and they saw her lying on the ground, with her eyes closed, and they thought she was dead. But she wasn't; she was just sleeping." I felt this was Lisa's denial again of her mother's death. I felt she could now handle a more reality-based intervention, so I said, "So sometimes people who are sleeping look like they're dead and sometimes people who are dead look like they're just sleeping." Lisa immediately said, "Yes!" and added, "I wish my momma was sleeping and not dead. I think about it all the time. I wish she was really just sleeping." I asked, "Do you dream about your momma?" "Yes!" she replied, "I get scared sometimes. I dream about her being dead and being here. Sometimes I dream I die and I go to Heaven and see Jesus and her in Heaven. I dreamed I got hurt and she took care of me. I miss her. I dream about Swiper, the evil fox [from a TV show, she says, called Dora the Explorer], took my momma and I never saw her again. When she was sick I said, 'I'm afraid you'll die.' " I asked Lisa what her mother answered. Lisa replied, "She said, 'that will never happen. Think of happy things.' " I then told Lisa that her momma wanted to stay with her, but she got sick, really sick. "It's very sad that she died," I said, "but she can be there for you in your memories and in your thoughts and in your dreams. She was a good momma and she took good care of you. Now your grandparents want to take care of you and your daddy wants to take care of you, too."

In this second story Lisa was continuing to work out her feelings about the loss of her mother, dealing with the sadness, but not yet approaching the underlying anger related to her mother's breaking her promise not to die. The second story allowed me to evaluate the progress we had made in therapy and the direction of future goals.

SUMMARY

This chapter describes a paradigm shift in the clinical use of assessment, called therapeutic assessment, which is more consistent with an intersubjective psychoanalytic approach and narrative therapy approach, compared with the traditional psychoanalytic and psychometric assessment traditions. The approach highlights a more collaborative method of clinical application, in which assessment and treatment are combined. The combination of assessment and therapy, often in a single session, has been effective in facilitating significant therapeutic change in the patient/client. Several methods of adapting traditional assessment techniques for use in this paradigm were described, as were nontraditional approaches. Finally, a case study was included to illustrate the application of one storytelling approach.

ACKNOWLEDGMENTS

I thank Stephen Finn for reading and commenting on an earlier draft of this chapter.

NOTE

1. Many clinicians who do therapeutic assessments use the term "client" rather than the term "patient." They make good arguments for using "client," as do those who use "patient." Therefore, I have decided to use the two terms interchangeably in this chapter.

REFERENCES

Barber, R. (1996). The experience of being psychologically evaluated: A phenomenological inquiry (Doctoral dissertation, University of Tennessee, Knoxville).

Bellak, L., & Bellak, S. (1949). *The Children's Apperception Test.* Larchmont, NY: C.P.S.

Beutler, L., & Berren, M. (Eds.). (1996). *Integrative assessment of adult personality.* New York: Guilford Press.

Brooks, R. (2002). Creative characters. In C. Schaefer & D. Canglosi (Eds.), *Play therapy Techniques* (2nd Ed.) (pp. 269–282). Lanham, MD: Jason Aronson.

Costantino, G., Malgady, R., & Rogler, L. (1988). *TEMAS (Tell-Me-A-Story) manual*. Los Angeles: Western Psychological Services.

Engelman, D., & Allyn, J. (2005, July). *Use of a Rorschach percept to construct a therapeutic story*. Paper presented at the XVIII International Congress of Rorschach and other Projective Methods, Barcelona, Spain.

Exner, J. (2003). *The Rorschach: A comprehensive system* (4th Ed.). Hoboken, NJ: John Wiley.

Finn, S. (1996). *Manual for using the MMPI–2 as a therapeutic intervention*. Minneapolis, MN: University of Minnesota Press.

Finn, S. (2002, March). *Challenges and lessons of intersubjectivity theory for psychological assessment*. Paper presented at the Annual Meeting, Society for Personality Assessment, San Antonio, TX.

Finn, S., & Martin, H. (1996). *Therapeutic assessment with the MMPI–2 in managed healthcare*. In J. Butcher (Ed.), Personality assessment in managed healthcare: Using the MMPI–2 in treatment planning (pp. 131–152). New York: Oxford University Press.

Finn, S., & Tonsager, M. (1992). Therapeutic effects of providing MMPI-2 test feedback to college students awaiting therapy. *Psychological Assessment, 4*, 278–287.

Finn, S., & Tonsager, M. (1997). Information-gathering and therapeutic models of assessment: Complementary paradigms. *Psychological Assessment, 9*, 374–385.

Fischer, C. (1985/1994). *Individualizing psychological assessment*. Hillsdale, NJ: Lawrence Erlbaum Associates.

Gardner, R. (1971). *Therapeutic communication with children: The mutual storytelling technique*. New York: Jason Aronson.

Gardner, R. (1975). *Therapeutic approaches to the resistant child*. New York: Jason Aronson.

Gardner, R. (1986). *The psychotherapeutic techniques of Richard Gardner*. Creskill, NJ: Creative Therapeutics.

Gardner, R. (1993). *Storytelling in psychotherapy with children*. Northville, NJ: Jason Aronson.

Handler, L. (1988, March). *The use of Inquiry and Testing of the Limits in WISC and WAIS Interpretation*. Paper presented at the Annual Meeting, Society for Personality Assessment, New York.

Handler, L. (1996, March). *Single projective test responses which illuminate therapeutic issues*. Paper presented at the Annual Meeting, Society for Personality Assessment, Denver, CO.

Handler, L. (1998). The clinical interpretation of the Wechsler Intelligence Tests as personality instruments. In L. Handler & M. Hilsenroth (Eds.), *Teaching and learning personality assessment.* (pp. 245–324). Mahwah, NJ: Lawrence Erlbaum Associates.

Handler, L. (1999). The assessment of playfulness: Herman Rorschach meets D. W. Winnicott. Invited Special Series, The Assessment of Psychological Health. *Journal of Personality Assessment, 72*, 208–217.

Handler, L. (2002, July). *Non-traditional approaches to the administration and interpretation of projective techniques*. Paper presented at the XVII International Congress of Rorschach and Other Projective Methods, Rome, Italy.

Handler, L. (2004, August). *A changing paradigm in personality assessment*. Annual Meeting, European Rorschach Society, Stockholm, Sweden.

Handler, L. (2005, July-a). *A Rorschach assessment amplified, using play in Testing of the Limits*. Paper presented at the XVIII International Congress of Rorschach and Other Projective Methods, Barcelona, Spain.

Handler, L. (2005, July-b). *The administration and interpretation of the Rorschach in light of changes in psychoanalytic theory*. Paper presented at the XVIII International Congress of Rorschach and Other Projective Methods, Barcelona, Spain.

Handler, L. (in preparation). *Therapeutic assessment with children and adolescents*. Mahwah, NJ: Lawrence Erlbaum Associates.

Handler, L., & Hilsenroth, M. (1994, April). *The use of a fantasy animal drawing and storytelling technique in assessment and psychotherapy*. Paper presented at the Annual Meeting, Society for Personality Assessment, Chicago.

Klopfer, B., Ainsworth, M., Klopfer, W., & Holt, R. (1945). *Developments in the Rorschach technique* (Vol. 1). Oxford, England: World Book.

Lieblich, A., McAdams, D., & Josselson, R. (Eds.) (2004). *Healing plots: The narrative basis of psychotherapy*. Washington, DC: American Psychological Association.

Machover, K. (1949). *Personality projection in the drawing of the human figure*. Springfield, IL: Charles Thomas.

McAdams, D. (1985). *Power, intimacy, and the life story: Personological inquiries into identity*. New York: Guilford Press.

McAdams, D. (1993). *The stories we live by: Personal myths and the making of the self*. New York: William Morrow.

McAdams, D., Josselson, R., & Leiblich, A. (Eds.) (2001). *Turns in the road: Narrative studies of lives in transition*. Washington, DC: American Psychological Association.

McArthur, D., & Roberts, G. (1982). *Roberts Apperception Test for Children manual*. Los Angeles: Western Psychological Services.

McLeod, J. (1997). *Narrative and psychotherapy*. London: Sage.

Mitchell, S., & Aron, L. (1999). *Relational psychoanalysis: The emergence of a tradition*. Hillsdale, NJ: Analytic Press.

Morgan, C., & Murray, H. (1935). A method for investigating fantasies: The Thematic Apperception Test. *Archives of Neurology and Psychiatry, 34*, 289–306.

Mutchnick, M., & Handler, L. (2002). Once upon a time . . . : Therapeutic interactive stories. *Humanistic Psychologist, 20*, 75–84.

Orange, D., Atwood, G., & Stolorow R. (1997). *Working intersubjectively: Contextualism in psychoanalytic practice*. Hillsdale, NJ: Analytic Press.

Pollack, J., Cohen, H., & Weil, G. (1982). The Tasks of Emotional Development test: A survey of research applications. *Psychology—A Journal of Human Behavior, 18*(4), 2–11.

Schafer, R. (1954). Some applications of contemporary psychoanalytic theory to projective testing. *Journal of Projective techniques, 18*, 441–447.

Schafer, R. (1956). Transference in the patient's reaction to the tester. *Journal of Projective Techniques, 20*, 26–32.

Schneidman, E. (1953). Manual for the Make A Picture Story Test. *Projective Techniques Monographs, No. 2*.

Stolorow, (2001). Foreword to Buirski, P., & Haglund, P. *Making sense together*. Northville, NJ: Jason Aronson.

Stolorow, R., Brandchaft, B., & Atwood, G. (1987). *Psychoanalytic treatment: An intersubjective approach*. Hillsdale, NJ: Analytic Press.

Winnicott, D. (1971). *Therapeutic consultations in child psychiatry*. New York: Basic Books.

Winnicott, D. (1972). Basis for self and body. *International Journal of Child Psychotherapy, 1*, 7–16.

Winnicott, D. (1989). Two further clinical examples. In C. Winnicott, R. Shepherd, & M. Davis (Eds.), *Psychoanalytic explorations* (pp. 272–283). Cambridge, MA: Harvard University Press

Wolf, R. (1976). The Polaroid technique: Spontaneous dialogues from the unconscious. *Art Psychotherapy, 3*, 197–214.

Young, G., & Wagner, E. (Eds.). (1999). *The Hand Test: Advances in application and research*. Malabar, FL: Kreiger.

5

PERSONALITY ASSESSMENT
FEEDBACK WITH PARENTS

Ellen B. Braaten
Massachusetts General Hospital and Harvard Medical School

Little is known about how child psychologists are formally prepared to perform one of their most challenging professional roles, the sharing of test data with their patients' families. Although much time and energy is justifiably invested in mastering test procedures and using tests to describe personality characteristics and reach differential diagnoses, there is little formal training in how to convey this information to parents, and most psychologists learn these skills by observation or through trial and error. Although providing feedback to parents is often challenging for clinicians, providing feedback regarding personality assessment can be particularly difficult, as the results of personality assessments frequently involve judgments regarding children's individual attributes, place in the family, the quality of their relationships with parents and siblings, and potential causes of behavior problems. Thus, the results of the evaluation frequently relate to the parents' investment in their view of their child and their relationships, which may elicit intense personal feelings in the parents when they hear this information.

Complicating this issue is the fact that results from personality assessments can be somewhat ambiguous, which can leave parents feeling as if they do not have succinct answers to their questions. In addition, the results may reveal personal, intimate details about the child and his or her parents that can make parents—and clinicians—feel uncomfortable. Thus, it is critical that this feedback be offered in a way that is informative, empathic, and supportive of parental emotional expression. Although there are no clear guidelines for this process, this chapter examines this issue by discussing possible techniques and means of explaining complicated and, at times, contradictory psychological test results to parents, so that parents are best able to plan for treatment and support strengths.

CONVEYING RESULTS TO PARENTS: REVIEW OF THE LITERATURE

There are no published studies on how best to convey psychological test results to parents. However, there is a body of literature that has examined effective communication between pediatric clinicians and parents, as well as research examining parent preferences for the communication of "bad" or sensitive news. Some of this research can be useful in the development of general guidelines for sharing psychological test results with parents.

Hasnat and Graves (2000) investigated the level of satisfaction parents felt when first provided a diagnosis of developmental disability in their child. The authors found that parents were more likely to be satisfied if they received a large amount of information, and if the disclosing professional had an understanding of parental concerns, yet was direct in the manner in which the information is presented. Krahn, Hallum, and Kime (1993) interviewed mothers and fathers of infants with a recently diagnosed disability regarding their preferences for how they would prefer to hear the news of their child's disability. Nine themes of parental preferences for how to communicate difficult information emerged, seven of which might be applicable to the sharing of personality measures, including: (1) *communication of information*, which indicated parents preferred direct and understandable language, including positive as well as negative characteristics; (2) *diagnostician*, where parents preferred hearing the information from a familiar person; (3) *communication of affect*, whereby the parents preferred an empathic approach from a person who was comfortable with the expression of emotions; (4) *pacing of process*, where the information was presented gradually in a step-by-step fashion that left time for questions throughout the meeting; (5) *when told*, with parents preferring to be told as soon as problems are suspected; (6) *where told*, with parents expressing strong preferences for being told personally (as opposed to over the phone), in a private, uninterrupted setting; and (7) *support persons present*, with most parents preferring to be told together, or with a support person.

In an outcome analysis that attempted to identify and categorize whether support for parents by clinicians led to positive changes in mothers (Wasserman, Inui, Barriatua, Carter, & Lippincott, 1984), the results indicated that mothers who received more clinician empathy were more satisfied with their care and had greater reductions in their level of concern. Some research has also found that parents value a sympathetic and caring approach (Girvin, 2002; Quine & Pahl, 1986; Sharp, Strauss, & Lorch, 1992), and other studies have suggested a desire for parents to know how well the child will function in the home and strategies for facilitating his or her growth (Lynch & Staloch, 1988). Cross-cultural studies on the sharing of bad news with parents (Krauss-Mars & Lachman, 1994) indicated that the use of a language other than the parents' tends to have a negative influence on the communication between doctors and parents, and that an attempt should be made to understand the family's own cultural views about diagnosis and treatment, because various cultures may have different ways of understanding or responding to certain disabilities or diagnoses (Ahmann, 1994).

SHARING INFORMATION WITH PARENTS: THE FEEDBACK CONFERENCE

Feedback is typically provided to parents after all of the assessments, interviews, and observations have been completed. Whether the evaluation included only projective and personality measures, or whether the use of personality measures occurred in the context of a broader evaluation, the feedback session should be approached as a therapeutic intervention that has the potential to significantly influence parents' emotions, beliefs, and attitudes toward their child and their child's future. Finn and Tonsager (1997) have theorized that the assessment process with adults is therapeutic because it provides the patient with self-verification, self-enhancement, and self-efficacy/discovery. In the evaluation of child patients, the assessment process has the added result of providing parents with verification of their concerns about their child, enhancing their relationship with their child, and providing them with recommendations that enable them to be efficacious when they seek services for their child. Overall, the feedback process should be a collaborative and individualized process in which the patient(s) (i.e., the parents and/or child) and evaluator work together to develop productive understandings (Fischer, 2000).

It is hoped that a positive, supportive clinician-patient/family relationship built on trust emerges through the process of evaluating the child. However, even in the best of situations, parents may be quite anxious about receiving the results of the assessment, and it is sometimes helpful to reflect on the parents' anxiety, and to make them as comfortable as possible. Similarly, clinicians may be anxious about sharing information, which can cause them to lose focus during the feedback session; thus it is typically helpful for the examiner to spend some time thinking about the case before the appointment. In thinking about a case, it is best to identify the most important information that needs to be conveyed. In other words: What is the most crucial information that this family needs to know? How can I best share this information with them in a way they will understand, that will be useful to them? and What next steps are important?

Because parents are frequently anxious about hearing feedback about their children, I often begin the feedback session by saying a few things about what is best about their child, how much I enjoyed working with their child, and why it was enjoyable. Once that is said, I will remind the parent to keep these aspects of their child in mind, because much of what we will discuss will not pertain to their child's strengths, but instead to their concerns about their child. Periodically throughout the feedback session, I will bring up these strengths, so that they do not get "lost" in our discussion of the child's areas of weakness or concern. Once the parents are comfortable and have been reminded of at least a few of their child's positive qualities, it is typically most helpful to begin by restating the referral question, preferably in the parents' own words. For example, "You sought an evaluation for Jim because you were concerned about possible reasons for his increased oppositionality at home, which included stealing and bullying." It is then helpful to check in with the parents about whether that indeed was their understanding. Assuming that there is a commonly "shared" view of the purpose of the assessment, provide the parents with the most salient information that they need to know, including a diagnosis (if there is one). It is not uncommon for parents to tune out much of what comes next, so it is important that the initial information be provided briefly, directly, and sensitively.

Once the essential information has been conveyed, it is helpful for the clinician to check in with the parents, by saying something such as "Does this information fit with how you see Jim?" or "Is there anything that is surprising in these results?" Most often, the parent will state that there is little that is surprising. In fact, there may be a relief that the cause of the problem has been identified. At this point in the process, it is helpful to review the test results more specifically, helping the parent understand the evidence for your conclusions.

However, there are also times when parents disagree with the initial feedback information and the evaluator should allow for, and not be defensive about, questioning, resistance, and denial. What can be most helpful is to spend a little time talking about what is not a "fit" with how they see their child. Sometimes parents are angry or embarrassed about their child; other times they may be using denial of the problem as a defense mechanism that has allowed them to cope with their child's disability; still other times (though much less frequently if the evaluation has been properly completed), the clinician may have not come to the correct conclusion and the parents' input can be crucial in a balanced view of the child. In any case, it is helpful to review the parents' perception of the problem, as well as their present state of knowledge. For example, Theo was a 15-year-old depressed adolescent who was referred for testing because his grades had dropped considerably and he frequently missed school. The results of the projective measures clearly showed a very significant depression. When this information was shared with his parents, his father immediately disagreed, stating, "He's just lazy; if he'd just get out of bed in the morning and get to school, he'd get better grades." At this point, it was clear that Theo's father had a number of misconceptions about depression in adolescents, and it was the evaluator's role to help him get a more accurate comprehension of the problem. As is frequently the case, Theo's father had some issues of his own, as he had also experienced depression as an adolescent (and as an adult) and tended to think he could "work" himself out of a depression. Helping Theo's father gain a better understanding of depression and giving him time to talk about his own depression (as well as how his ways of coping were frequently maladaptive) ultimately helped him gain an understanding of Theo.

After the initial impressions are shared with the parents, and provided the examiner has done a good job of communicating his or her diagnostic formulations in language the parents understand, the evaluator should provide the evidence for his or her conclusions. Rating scales are frequently easy for parents to understand, and parents tend to feel this is "real data" when compared with projective measures. Thus, if rating scales have been completed, it is sometimes useful to begin by sharing parents' ratings (and teacher ratings, if available). In contrast, parents do not typically have an understanding of what projective or personality testing entails, and they usually respond well to simple information on what it entails and how it is used. For example, "The Rorschach, Thematic Apperception Test, Sentence Completion Test, and Kinetic Family Drawing, etc., are psychological tests in which the person's responses are assumed to be a reflection of his personality." In describing individual tests, parents may have misconceptions about what the tests can and cannot do. Many parents (and children) have heard about the Rorschach or seen it used in cartoons or comedy movies, but have no idea what it measures. A very short explanation of the test can include the following: "The Rorschach is a series of inkblots where the child is asked to describe what they look like to him. His responses can then be compared with others' responses and the responses can provide an overview of how he sees the world, handles emotions, and the kinds of emotional resources available to him." Similarly, the TAT can be explained by saying, "The Thematic Apperception Test consists of a series of stories based upon viewing pictures. Responses can be analyzed in terms of important themes and conflicts and how the child manages emotional material."

Some measures of personality can be particularly difficult for parents to hear. The Sentence Completion Test and the Kinetic Family Drawing are two tests that have the potential to make parents feel uncomfortable because the responses often relate to their relationship with their child. In describing the Sentence Completion Test, it is helpful for parents to know that the child's responses can provide insights into how the child views him/herself and others, as well as to identify important areas of preoccupation or conflict. It is not necessarily an accurate document of what is actually occurring in the child's life. For example, a child might respond to the sentence stem, "My father and I . . ." by saying, "never spend time together." If this response is shared with the parents, the parents may indicate that they spend quite a bit of time with their child and that they are baffled as to why their child perceives this differently. This is where they need to be reminded that this is not an accurate reflection of what is actually occurring, but may be an accurate reflection of how their child feels. The child may be feeling lonely, excluded, depressed, or needy, and the parents need to understand that it is the *feeling* that is reflected in his response. Conversely, the child's response may be completely accurate and parents may become defensive or guilt-ridden. In either case, it is helpful to keep the focus on the child's inner experiences and world, reminding the parents that no parent is perfect and that the goal is not to blame, but to identify the problems and fix them. Similarly, the Kinetic Family Drawing can also make parents defensive. In fact, regardless of the picture, parents are frequently uncomfortable seeing their family "doing something together," particularly if it is obvious that the family does not appear to be engaged. This can be a springboard for discussing family issues that may be contributing to their child's problem.

Throughout the feedback session, it is important to repeat major concepts by summarizing the information initially, going back over it in detail, and summarizing it again. It is also important to stop periodically to allow parents to ask questions of you and for you to ask questions of them regarding their comprehension of the information (without making them feel as if they are being "put on the spot"). Paying attention to parents' nonverbal cues and emotions is key. Some parents may freely express their emotions, others may listen stoically to the information, and when there are two parents in the room there are often two different emotional styles that need to be validated. Blaming of one parent by another is all too frequent (i.e., "He's just like you" or "She's just as crazy as your mother"), and one way to diffuse this tension is to remind the parents of the differences between their child's experiences and the experiences of the similar relative. For example, sharing with them the fact that mental health services have changed considerably since they were children, or that positive prognosis is associated with early identification and treatment (something which Grandmother may not have had) reframes the issue to one of hope as opposed to one of helplessness.

There are a couple of specific instances where the feedback process can be particularly difficult. One of these occurs when one (or both) parents have significant mental health issues of their own. If the evaluator is aware of these issues, he or she should anticipate that such parents may be frustrating and may have trouble understanding what is being said, and thus the feedback session should be tailored to address not only the needs of the child, but also the parent(s). Another instance that can make for a difficult feedback process occurs when there is no clear diagnosis. This situation can result in feelings of anxieties in both parents and professionals, with the parents feeling there is no clear answer and professionals feeling they have not adequately done their job.

For example, Susan was an intelligent 15-year-old who had begun to exhibit symptoms of psychosis. She had a normal appearance, was still getting relatively good grades in school, and was exhibiting adequate memory skills. In contrast, she admitted hearing voices, became obsessive about certain topics, and had begun to make comments within conversations that had no relevance to the topic being discussed. She had also made a recent suicide attempt. In reviewing the test results, the parents understandably preferred to focus on the fact that she was bright and that, although her grades were not as strong as they had been in the past, she was able to complete much of her homework and still seemed "like their little girl." Unfortunately, the examiner could not offer a succinct diagnosis, as it was unclear whether the behaviors were a sign of an emerging thought disorder, a psychotic depression, or an OCD with psychotic features. Susan's areas of "normal" ability had the potential of giving her parents false hope, and it was difficult for the evaluator to contradict their views, because no clear reason for the behaviors could be determined from the test data. In this situation, it was important to help the parents understand that Susan's behaviors were not mutually contradictory; that is, she had areas of functioning that did appear developmentally appropriate and others that were outside the realm of appropriate behaviors, and that both could describe

Susan at different times. Although this uneven pattern of abilities can be confusing to parents, keeping the focus on "where to go from here" can be most helpful.

In certain situations, a lack of a clear diagnosis can be a sign of a child who is idiosyncratic, who "marches to his or her own drummer." These children may not meet criteria for any psychological disorder, but may be struggling because they see the world in a different way. These individual differences may result in a child with significant difficulties in the elementary school years, but these children often come into their own later in life with support and understanding. Indeed, many of the most valuable contributors to society have been exceptional people who would not appear "ordinary" on childhood measures of personality. In this case, it is important to highlight the positive aspects these traits may have for the child's future, while validating the difficulties they may currently present for the child and providing guidance to the parents in how best to support their child in his or her development.

Regardless of whether there is a clear diagnosis, the end of the feedback meeting should not leave parents feeling helpless. Although the feedback session should be thought of as a therapeutic intervention, it is not the type of intervention where issues should be left "hanging" (as they frequently are in the therapeutic process). In other words, it is important to have a feeling of closure at the end of the session. The examiner should leave adequate time for discussing the steps that are needed to modify the course of the child's behavior and a plan for following through with these steps. Making appropriate referrals is important, and it is helpful for the evaluator to give the parents names of clinicians who are available to see them, and/or their child. Inevitably, parents will have questions after the session is completed, and there should be a plan for how their questions can be answered, such as letting parents know that the examiner is available to talk by phone, giving them the option of a follow-up visit in a few months' time, or advising them to ask questions of their treatment team (if they are qualified to answer them). Following up the session with a report of the findings is also key and allows parents the opportunity to grasp the details of the findings more specifically.

THE PERSONALITY ASSESSMENT REPORT

Much has been written about what constitutes a good psychological report (e.g., Sattler, 2001), yet there is little empirical evidence on whether these qualities actually benefit consumers. Reports are frequently difficult to comprehend (Weddig, 1984), but reports that provide detailed descriptions of the child's strengths and weaknesses, as well as detailed recommendations, are more easily comprehended by parents than shorter reports that present conclusions and brief recommendations (Weiner, 1987; Weiner & Kohler, 1986). Sattler (2001) indicated that the purposes of the psychological report include providing accurate assessment information to the referral source and parents, serving as a source of clinical hypotheses and appropriate interventions, furnishing baseline information, and serving as a legal document.

There are two schools of thought regarding the timing of receiving the report, with some favoring providing the report to parents before the feedback session and others favoring sending the report after the feedback session has occurred. Still other professionals will provide parents with a copy of the report at the feedback conference. There are no data on when it is best for parents to receive this information, and in clinical practice any of the above options can be helpful, depending upon the case, the parents' needs, and the findings. When the findings indicate significant and/or unexpected difficulties, it is often best to meet before the report is presented to the parents, as there are data indicating that parents prefer to hear "bad" news about their child in person (Garwick, Patterson, Bennett, & Blum, 1995). Some parents are quite insistent on receiving the report first, in that they want time to digest the report and generate questions before the meeting. In this situation, the examiner needs to rely on his or her clinical judgment about what might be in the parents' best interest. There are many cases in which it is totally appropriate for parents to receive the report before the feedback conference, but in cases where the examiner expects the results to be quite disturbing, it might be best to offer the parents two feedback sessions—one that occurs before the parents receive the report and another after they have had time to review the report after receiving it in the mail.

Regardless of when the report is shared with the parents, there are a number of goals that should be addressed in the Personality Assessment Report. First, and most important, *the report should answer the referral question(s)*. When personality is being assessed, there is the temptation for the examiner to discuss aspects of the child's character or family dynamics (among other things) that are not pertinent to the referral questions. Because the report is frequently shared with the school, there is the possibility that the report will be read by people (i.e., teacher aides, teachers, and office support staff) who are not bound by the same ethical and confidentiality guidelines that are followed by psychologists. In addition, the people who may have access to the report frequently live in the community with the family, and it can be embarrassing for them to know certain types of information about a parent or child. In contrast, information from the evaluation may have to be shared with the child's therapist (for whom specific, personal information is important for treatment) and the school. In this case, it is best to have two versions of the report—one for the therapist and one for the school—or to have one version of the report that includes only necessary information, but includes additional information in an accompanying letter to the therapist. For example, Don was a 13-year-old who was exhibiting truant behavior and whose test results indicated an undiagnosed ADHD that predisposed him to impulsive acts. This information was helpful for the school to hear. However, the evaluation also indicated that Don had a number of sexual fantasies (and sexualized behavior) that the truant behavior only symbolized. Whereas it would be important for Don's therapist to know about these fantasies, it is not necessary for Don's teachers to know about these issues, and, thus, that information does not need to be shared with the school. In fact, it is rarely helpful for information about sex, drug/alcohol use, or personal family issues to be shared with the school, unless the issues are directly related to the referral question.

In terms of what should be included in the report's contents, the personality assessment report should do more than just discuss the referral question—it should provide an analysis of the intra- and interpersonal issues that cause, support, or maintain the child's behaviors and affect. At a minimum, the report should include: (1) a report heading and identifying information (child's name, date of birth, date of evaluation, age at testing, parents names, etc.); (2) the reason for referral; (3) background information; (4) a listing of the tests administered; (5) behavioral observations; (6) test results and interpretation of the results; and (7) a summary and recommendations. The most important goal of the report may be to assist in effecting change in the child's environment—in other words, to assist those working with the child in understanding the child's problems and needs, and for identifying what can to be done to address those needs.

CASE STUDY: KYLE

Kyle was a 14-year-old boy who had exhibited significant emotional, behavioral, and academic concerns since the age of 10. He attended a therapeutic school, which had been helpful to some extent, but he had recently begun to exhibit escalated oppositionality, aggression, and truancy, such as using his mother's credit card, stealing $200 from a neighbor's purse, and threatening his brother with a knife. At school, he was noted to have significant social skill difficulties, such as making rude, sexualized, and/or grandiose statements. His thinking frequently appeared be tangential, and at times he acted like an "Anime" (e.g., cartoon) character. All of these concerns were noted to interfere with his ability to make friends.

Kyle was adopted at birth, but his adoptive parents divorced when he was in first grade. Kyle had been diagnosed with ADHD and was taking Concerta. He had been treated with antipsychotics, because there was question of a formal thought disorder, but with little positive effects. Because of his poor response to antipsychotics, Kyle's psychiatrist wanted more information about whether Kyle did meet criteria for a thought disorder before attempting other psychopharmacological interventions.

Kyle presented as a small, physically immature boy whose level of cooperation varied throughout the testing. His affect and behavior were consistent with severe emotional disturbance and included extreme impulsivity, rapid and intense shifts in mood, significant anxiety, periodically talking like a cartoon character when angered or stressed, easily entering graphic violent and sexualized fantasy, fluid thinking, loose associations, delusional ideation, suicidal and homicidal ideation including a plan, and sexualized comments and gestures.

Results of tests of intellectual functioning indicated a WISC-IV Verbal Comprehension Index of 92, a Perceptual Organization Index of 123, a Processing Speed Index of 84, and a Full Scale IQ of 104. Tests of academic functioning indicated reading skills at current grade level, but significantly weak mathematical calculation and writing skills. Kyle's language skills indicated he had difficulty organizing his ideas in verbal and written formats, but it was difficult to determine whether this was a function of true expressive language problems or a result of his thought disorder with highly associative thinking. Tests of executive function skills indicated significant problems with effective organization of visual and auditory material, variable sustained auditory attention, and poor impulse control. Results from the measures of emotional and personality functioning were consistent with a thought disorder characterized by loose associations, delusional and fluid thinking, rapid shifts from reality to fantasy especially when stressed, and poor affect modulation.

Both of Kyle's parents arrived for the feedback session, although it was clear that they did not enjoy being in each other's presence. Kyle's father had the attitude that "there is nothing wrong with Kyle other than his mother babies him." In contrast, Kyle's mother was extremely anxious, fearing that Kyle would never lead a normal life. In presenting the results, I briefly reviewed the tests of cognitive and academic functioning. These were not a surprise to Kyle's parents, as they knew he was an intelligent child who frequently struggled with writing and organizational issues. I felt it was important to review Kyle's intellectual resources before telling his parents that he did meet criteria for a Psychotic Disorder, NOS. This was not a surprise for Kyle's mother to hear, but his father understandably had difficulty comprehending this information. He benefited from some brief information about what psychosis entails, remarking, "Does this mean he's schizophrenic?" Because the test results did indicate that Kyle is indeed at risk for schizophrenia, particularly paranoid, I felt it necessary to address this issue directly, by saying that he did not yet appear to meet criteria for schizophrenia, but that the possibility exists that he might in the future, and that Kyle would need to be closely monitored for further symptoms. This had a sobering effect on Kyle's father, who was then more willing to hear about the results.

In describing the test results, I felt the most important information that Kyle's parents needed to understand involved his significant risk for harming others, including himself. In reviewing the test data, I was able to provide parents with some specific details about Kyle's inner world. For example, there were numerous instances in which Kyle alluded to highly sexual fantasies. His responses on the Rorschach, TAT, and Incomplete Sentences indicated he tended to dehumanize people, and this tendency was quite alarming, given his propensity toward violence, poor impulse control, unmodulated anger/rage, and tendency to become even more disorganized in his thinking/judgment. Consistent with failing to recognize others as "real" and not just as objects of gratification or disposal, Kyle was found to lack empathy and to take pleasure in other people's misfortune. In addition to highly sexualized fantasies, Kyle also shared highly detailed plans for murdering various family members, most notably his birth parents, who he said, "had no right to abandon me!" This was quite difficult for his parents to comprehend, and it was important for them to see these fantasies as a component of Kyle's thought disorder. It was also important for them to see these fantasies in the context of an adolescent whose neuropsychological functioning indicates he has difficulty inhibiting his behavior and organizing his world, which increases the risk that he might act on these fantasies.

What made this particular feedback session quite difficult was that his parents could not "lean" on each other for support. There were unspoken regrets about having adopted a child who so clearly did not meet their expectations and a tendency to blame both themselves and each other for Kyle's problems. Despite these issues, it was also clear that Kyle's parents wanted things to be better, and this was the area in which it was possible for them to find common ground. Once the results were shared and it was clear they had some understanding, the remainder of the session focused almost exclusively on helping them realize that they did share a common perspective and that the evaluation could be used to help them determine what would best meet Kyle's needs. It was clear that Kyle needed a therapeutic school placement that included after-school and/or residential services as needed. Kyle's parents clearly saw the need for continued psychopharmacological interventions and were open to seeking parental counseling, in order to promote consistency between the approaches used during the school day and at their homes. The session ended by reiterating Kyle's strengths and by giving the parents hope that structure, consistency, and therapeutic interventions could promote a sense of safety in Kyle that in turn would facilitate psychological, social, and academic growth.

SUMMARY

Although there are few empirical data on how to best share personality assessment results with parents, results from studies that have examined effective communication between pediatric clinicians and parents, as well as clinical experience, indicate that there are some general guidelines that should be considered:

1. Parents should be informed of the results in the context of a clinician-patient relationship that is built on a sense of trust and support and a genuine sense of caring.
2. There are no clear guidelines as to whether it is most important for parents to receive the written report before or after the feedback session, and, thus, clinicians should

rely on their clinical judgment in deciding what would be most helpful for a particular family.

3. In a two-parent family, it is ideal to have both parents present for the feedback session. In one-parent households, the parents should be invited to have a supportive adult present if they so choose.

4. Results should be shared with parents as soon as possible.

5. Before the feedback session, the professional should identify the most important information that needs to be conveyed. This information should be conveyed early in the session in a manner that is brief, sensitive, and direct. Once this information is given, the examiner should check in with the parents to determine whether they understand what has been said, whether it fits with their understanding of their child, and whether they have any initial questions. Attention to the parents' cognitive and emotional reactions is important in determining where to go next.

6. The results should acknowledge the child's strengths and positive personal characteristics, as well as limitations, and simple, direct language with as little psychological jargon as possible.

7. The professional should be empathic and supportive of the parents' emotional reactions, which can include anger, defensiveness, sadness, or a lack of outward emotions. All of these can be a normal part of the process. Inviting affect into the process by asking parents questions such as "How does it feel to hear this information?" can let parents know that discussing feelings can be part of the process. Conversely, it is also important to keep the focus of the session on the child. In other words, affect should be validated, but the focus should not be on the parents' affect, but on giving the parents an opportunity to express their feelings in the hope that this will allow them to better understand and cope with their child's issues.

8. Answer questions directly and do not be afraid to say "I don't know" when there is no clear answer (e.g., "Will my child always be like this?").

9. Parents should be informed of the findings in their own language and should be able to ask questions in their own language. The clinician should attempt to understand the family's cultural views about diagnosis and treatment.

10. Conclude the session with a discussion of plans for the future and recommendations. Make arrangements for further therapeutic and educational services.

REFERENCES

Ahmann, E. (1994). "Chunky stew": Appreciating cultural diversity while providing health care for children. *Pediatric Nursing 20*(3), 320–324.

Finn, S. E., & Tonsager, M. E. (1997). Information-gathering and therapeutic models of assessment: Complementary paradigms. *Psychological Assessment, 9*, 374–385.

Fischer, C. T. (2000). Collaborative, individualized assessment. *Journal of Personality Assessment, 74*(1), 2–14.

Garwick, A. W., Patterson, J., Bennett, F. C., & Blum, P. W. (1995). Breaking the news: How families first learn about their child's chronic condition. *Archives of Pediatric and Adolescent Medicine, 149*(9), 991–997.

Girvin, J. M. (2002). The communication of neurological bad news to parents. *Canadian Journal of Neuroscience 29*(1), 78–82.

Hasnat, M. J., & Graves, P. (2000). Disclosure of developmental disability: A study of parent satisfaction and the determinants of satisfaction. *Journal of Paediatric Child Health, 36*, 32–35.

Krahn, G. L., Hallum, A., & Kime, C. (1993). Are there good ways to give "bad news"? *Pediatrics, 91*(3), 578–582.

Krauss-Mars, A. H., & Lachman, P. (1994). Breaking bad news to parents with disabled children—a cross-cultural study. *Child Health Care and Development 20*(2), 101–113.

Lynch, E. C., & Staloch, N. H. (1988). Parental perceptions of physicians' communication in the informing process. *Mental Retardation 26*, 77–81.

Quine, L., & Pahl, J. (1986). First diagnosis of severe mental handicap: Characteristics of unsatisfactory encounters between doctors and parents. *Social Science Medicine, 22*, 53–62.

Sharp, M. C., Strauss, R. P., & Lorch, S. C. (1992). Communicating medical bad news: Parents' experiences and preferences. *The Journal of Pediatrics, 121*(4), 539–546.

Wasserman, R. C., Inui, T. S., Barriatua, R. D., Carter, W. B., & Lippincott, P. (1984). Pediatric clinicians' support for parents makes a difference: An outcome-based analysis of clinician-parent interaction. *Pediatrics, 74*(6), 1047–1053.

Weddig, R. R. (1984). Parental interpretation of psychoeducational reports. *Psychology in the Schools, 21*, 477–481.

Weiner, J. (1987). Factors affecting educators' comprehension of psychological reports. *Psychology in the Schools, 24*, 116–126.

Weiner, J., & Kohler, S. (1986). Parents' comprehension of psychological reports. *Psychology in the Schools, 24*, 265–270.

PART

II

Assessment Techniques

6

PLAY ASSESSMENT

Sandra W. Russ, Beth L. Pearson, and Tori J. Sacha
Case Western Reserve University

Why is the assessment of pretend play important? Although clinicians understand the importance of play in child development and use play in a variety of ways in psychotherapy, a formal assessment of play has not been a standard part of child psychological assessment.

The purpose of this chapter is to discuss the ways in which play assessment could contribute to treatment planning and evaluation of treatment effectiveness. We review several play assessment measures. In addition, the Affect in Play Scale (APS) is one possible instrument to utilize in a clinical setting. We briefly review the current research status of the APS and present case material to illustrate how the scale could be used. We also describe a new brief rating version of the scale that rates the child's play as it occurs and does not require videotaping.

IMPORTANCE OF PLAY ASSESSMENT

Children's pretend play is important in child development and in psychotherapy (Russ, 2004; Singer & Singer, 1990). Children's play provides a window on both cognitive and affective processes. Russ (2004, pp. 2–5) categorized different play processes that can be observed and measured in play. They are:

Cognitive Processes

- Organization—the ability to tell a story with a logical time sequence and indications of cause and effect
- Divergent thinking—the ability to generate a number of different ideas, story themes, and symbols
- Symbolism—the ability to transform objects (blocks, Legos) into representations of other objects (e.g., a block becomes a telephone)
- Fantasy/make-believe—the ability to engage in "as if" play behavior; to pretend to be in a different time and space

Affective Processes

- Expression of emotion—the ability to express positive and negative affect states and actual emotions in a pretend play situation
- Expression of affect themes—the ability to express affect content and images in play A doll becomes a monster, which is aggressive or scary content, even if no emotion accompanies it
- Comfort and enjoyment in the play experience—the ability to be involved in play
- Emotion regulation and modulation of the affect in the play—the ability to contain the emotion within a narrative

Interpersonal Processes

- Empathy—The ability to express concern for others and to take the role of the other
- Communication—the ability to express ideas and emotions to others
- Interpersonal schema—capacity for self-other differentiation and trust in others

Play processes relate to important areas of adaptive functioning in children. For example, play has been found to relate to creative problem solving (Dansky, 1980; Russ & Grossman-Mckee, 1990); perspective-taking (Fisher, 1992), and coping (Christiano & Russ, 1996).

In child therapy, play is often used as a form of communication with the therapist. In addition, children use play for expression of thoughts and feelings, and for working through and processing emotional material. Assessment of play skills can help determine whether and how a child can use play in therapy.

MEASURES OF CHILDREN'S PLAY

There are play measures that have been developed that could be used for assessment for therapy. We review a few of these measures here, but for a comprehensive review, see Gitlin-Weiner, Sangrund, and Schaefer (2000).

Play Therapy Observation Instrument

The Play Therapy Observation Instrument (PTOI) was originally developed by Howe and Silvern (1981) and adapted by Perry (Perry & Landreth, 1991) to assess children's play behavior in a way that would meaningfully inform diagnosis, treatment planning, and outcome measurement. Three areas of functioning are assessed with 13 items: (a) social inadequacy, (b) emotional discomfort, and (c) use of fantasy. Six items do not fall onto the three domains. The first item on the social inadequacy subscale refers to incoherent or bizarre content. This refers to disjoined, psychosis-like trains of thought or statistically infrequent play behavior. Other items on the social inadequacy scale include the exclusion of the therapist from the child's activities, responding to the therapist's interventions with hostility or withdrawal, and the degree of body stiffness that the child exhibits in gross and fine movements. One aspect of the emotional discomfort subscale includes the quality and intensity of affect that the child expresses; this refers to the child's mood, not the affect-theme within the play. Other areas of the emotional discomfort scale include aggression toward the therapist, conflicted play, and anxiety as expressed by talk about concerns or by disruption of the play. The use of the fantasy subscale includes items such as the amount of time spent in fantasy versus reality, time spent concentrating on characters rather than things, number of different fantasy stories, and number of different roles enacted.

The PTOI was designed to be used in rating 12-minute segments of a videotaped play therapy session. For each subscale item, the rater chooses a descriptive number that best represents the frequency and/or intensity of the child's play behavior as it occurred over the 12 minutes. In the original development study (Howe & Silvern, 1981) two undergraduate students who were not therapists were reliably trained on the PTOI after 20 hours by use of a training manual and by observation of videotaped sessions of play therapy and live play therapy sessions.

The PTOI has been found to discriminate adjusted from maladjusted children most strongly on the emotional discomfort subscale (Perry & Landreth, 1991). Rosen, Faust, and Burns (1994) used the PTOI with children participating in either psychodynamic or client-centered play therapy and found no significant differences between children's play in the two approaches. This may have been due to the study's small n ($n = 6$). Changes were found, however, in the fantasy play and quality of interaction subscale scores from the first therapy session to the eighth session. This suggests that the PTOI may be a useful instrument for detecting changes in a child's functioning during treatment, as it identifies changes in both process and content.

There are some limitations to the PTOI. As Perry and Landreth (1991) note, there are only two published studies of the PTOI. There is a need for developmental norms and a standardized administration (Perry & Landreth, 1991). They suggest that future research examine the use of the PTOI in direct observation of a session, rather than through the use of a videotape. This step may be particularly important for therapists who wish to assess play behaviors, but who have limited space or funds for video equipment.

NOVA Assessment of Psychotherapy

The NOVA Assessment of Psychotherapy (NAP) was also designed to assess the play therapy process and outcome by capturing components of the child's and therapist's behavior during play (Faust & Burns, 1991). This scale was intended for use in both clinical and research settings. As such, there is a longer, more comprehensive scale intended for research use and a shorter, more convenient version intended for clinical use. In the long version, 17 child behaviors and 12 therapist behaviors are coded in 7-second intervals. Raters tally the presence of any of the scale codes during each 7-second segment. These behaviors fall into four categories: (a) child verbal, (b) child nonverbal, (c) therapist facilitating, and (d) therapist channeling. "Therapist facilitating" refers to behaviors such as reflecting, interpreting, modeling, or imitating. "Therapist channeling" refers to questioning, suggesting, responding, confronting, setting limits, or demanding. Some of the relevant aspects of the child's play that are coded include valence of affect expressed (i.e., positive or negative), cooperative behavior, and aggressive behavior. The scale can be scored during live interaction or from videotape. Initial single case studies of the validity and reliability of the scale suggest that, like the PTOI, the NAP may be useful for assessing affective and behavioral changes during the treatment process (Faust & Burns, 1991).

Faust and Burns' (1991) description of preliminary data from pilot studies indicates that the NAP shows promise, like the PTOI, for assessing affective and behavioral changes during the treatment process. There are several limitations to the NAP at this time, however.

To our knowledge, there are no published studies describing the psychometric characteristics of the instrument and no normative data for the different scales. The authors report that there is psychometric information available in the manual (Burns & Faust, 1989). Although there is a manual that can be used for training and the authors report interrater reliability for a single case study (Faust & Burns, 1991), it is not clear how long training of clinicians in the field would take and how easily adequate agreement would be obtained.

Children's Play Therapy Instrument

Like the other two play therapy instruments described thus far, the Children's Play Therapy Instrument (CPTI; Kernberg, Chazan, & Normandin, 1998) was designed to measure change and outcome in child treatment. In addition, it is intended to be used as an aid in diagnosis. The CPTI assesses play comprehensively; the domains within it contain a number of psychodynamic constructs. The CPTI comprises three levels: 1) Segmentation of Child's Activity, 2) Dimensional Analysis of the Play Activity, and 3) Pattern of Child Activity over Time.

In the first level, *Segmentation*, the therapist/observer identifies segments of the therapy session as either Non-Play (in which the child is engaged in an activity other than play), Pre-Play (in which toys are arranged and the child prepares for play), Play, or Interruption (in which the play stops because of a distraction). The second level of the CPTI, the *Dimensional Analysis* of the play, has three domains, each with its own subcomponents. One of the dimensional aspects of the CPTI is the *Descriptive Analysis*. In this domain, the category of play is described (e.g., gross motor, fantasy, game play, etc.), the script is described (this assesses the child's autonomy and reciprocity and the therapeutic alliance), and the sphere of play is described (where the play takes place). The next domain under the Dimensional Analysis of the play is the *Structural Analysis*. When the structure of the play is analyzed, affective components (types of affect and modulation), cognitive components (how objects and people are depicted), narrative components (topic and theme of play and use of language), and developmental components (estimated developmental level, gender identity, and social level) are all assessed. The final domain included in the Dimensional Analysis of the play is the *Functional Analysis*. In the Functional Analysis, the therapist assesses coping and defensive strategies, as well as a rating of the degree of the child's subjective awareness of herself as a player. The third level of the CPTI assesses *Patterns over Time* (e.g., the sequence and length of the different segments of Pre-Play, Play, Non-Play, and Interruption).

In the initial reliability study (Kernberg et al., 1998), three raters were trained for 15 hours to use the CPTI to assess 8 videotaped play therapy vignettes. On the majority of the domains the raters reached agreement ranging from acceptable to excellent. There were a few subscales, however, in which adequate agreement was not obtained. The authors concluded from this that further development of some of the scales was needed. The CPTI has been used to assess changes in play over the course of 7 months in a single case study of a 2-year, 5-month-old child with autistic features (Chazan, 2000). Chazan (2000) noted an increase in time spent in play and a decrease in non-play and pre-play activities. Changes were also observed in the child's affect expression, cognitions, use of language, developmental ratings, and adaptive functioning

The CPTI appears to be a clearly conceptualized, theory-based measure that shows promise for comprehensive assessment of a child's play activities in therapy. The CPTI is still in the preliminary stages of development. Although preliminary interrater reliability has been established for the measure, further work must be done to establish its reliability definitively. In addition, construct validation has to occur. Kernberg et al. (1998) state that they plan to validate the CPTI as a diagnostic tool that distinguishes among diagnostic categories and is sensitive to changes occurring over time.

Affect in Play Scale

The Affect in Play Scale is a measure of pretend play that assesses both cognitive and affective play processes with a standardized play task, instructions, and coding system (Russ, 1987, 2004). The APS is appropriate for children from 6 to 10 years of age. The task consists of puppets and blocks, and the child is asked to play with them any way he wants to for 5 minutes. The play is videotaped and then coded on variables of organization of play, imagination, comfort, amount of affect, and variety of affect content categories. There are 6 negative affect categories (i.e., aggression, sadness) and 5 positive affect categories (i.e., happiness, nurturance). Each unit of affect expression is scored. A detailed coding manual has been developed (Russ, 2004). The APS attempts to measure the cognitive and affective play processes described earlier in this chapter.

A large number of validity studies have been carried out with the APS (see Russ, Niec, & Kaugars, 2000, for a review). The APS has been related to theoretically relevant criteria such as creativity, coping, and emotional understanding. In a recent study by Russ and Schafer (in press) the amount of affect in play related to the amount of affect in descriptions of memories in first and second graders. This finding has implications for therapy in that the expression of emotion in play is related to the ability to think about and describe emotional events in memory.

Although the APS has engendered a significant amount of research in the field of children's play, the fact that the play sessions must be videotaped for later scoring and that the raters must be well trained in scoring the APS limits its utility in the world of managed care. It would be beneficial to both clinicians and the field of play research if there were an instrument that could be used to more easily assess children's play. An easier measure would serve the dual purposes of breaking the ice and making the child comfortable, as well as allowing the clinician to gain immediate information about the affective and cognitive dimensions of the child's play. It could also be used as a measure of change in the treatment process and as an outcome measure.

In the development of this more efficient, brief rating scale version of the APS (Affect in Play Scale–Brief Rating; APS-BR), the main consideration was to produce a version of the APS that could be substituted for the APS and scored quickly during observation, while maintaining the integrity of the original scale. A new version in the familiar form of a behavioral rating scale would allow clinicians to easily add a measure of play to an assessment. Because of the ease with which this assessment could be carried out, it could encourage the use of play in more child-directed research. Unlike the original APS, the brief behavioral rating version does not require the use of videotape of the play. This will make the assessment more manageable and will increase parental consent for studies in which it is used, as no videotaped record will be kept of the children. Furthermore, because a brief rating scale version would not require videotaping the child, it would be considerably less cumbersome and easier to use during therapy.

Like the APS, the APS-BR scores the child's pretend play on both cognitive and affective dimensions. The cognitive scores include Organization, Imagination, and Comfort. The affective scores include Frequency of Affect Expression and Tone of Affect Expression. Though the APS-BR is very similar in format to the original APS, there are some notable differences. A major difference between the original APS and the new APS-BR is the way in which the frequency of affect expression is scored. On the original APS, the rater scores the total frequency of units of affective expression and classifies the content of the affect according to the 11 categories. While feasible for the videotaped version of the APS, classifying the content of affect in terms of 11 categories during a live 5-minute observation is not practical. Therefore, on the APS-BR, the rater is instructed to "attempt to tally each unit of affect expression. The tally should be an estimation, so as not to detract from the other rating." Instead of a total frequency count, the rater is instead asked to rate the total frequency on a 1–4 scale from low to high. In addition, the APS-BR asks the observer to rate the "overall tone of affect in the story, based on the average amount of positive or negative affect expression in the affect units in the child's play." The manual provides the rater with brief descriptions of each of the 4 points on the scale, along with clear examples of each point. Because the focus is on rating the relative positive/negative tone of the affect expression, and not on the specific affect categories, the APS-BR does not produce a variety of affect categories score.

Apart from these changes, the other notable change from the APS to the APS-BR is the Likert scale scoring. On the original APS, scoring for Organization, Imagination, and Comfort was done on 1–5 Likert scales. On the APS-BR, these scales were adapted into 1–4 Likert scales. The Likert scale was simplified because the rater would not have the luxury of pausing and rewinding videotaped observations when using the APS-BR.

The changes made for the APS-BR do not result in a significant deviation from the format of the original APS. The rater is still scoring the child on the total amount of affect expressed during the 5 minutes, as well as the tone of the affect expressed, and the quality of the fantasy in the play. In addition, the same play task, toys, and instructions are used.

A current study (Sacha, Russ, & Short, 2005) began the process of validating this new measure. In this study, the validity of the APS-BR was assessed by a comparison of scores of play sessions using the original APS and the new APS-BR in a sample of first-grade and second-grade children; examination of associations between scores on the APS-BR and scores on theoretically relevant criterion measures of divergent thinking and emotional memories; and comparison of the pattern of correlations between the APS-BR and criterion measures and the APS and the same criterion measures.

This new study, which used existing videotapes of play observations from a previous study of the APS (Russ & Schafer, in press), produced encouraging results. First, interrater reliability, using a stringent absolute agreement intraclass correlation coefficient, was very high. The average scores for the intraclass coefficients were .86 for Organization, .93 for Imagination, .87 for Comfort, .96 for Frequency of Affect Expression, and .89 for Tone of Affect Expression.

Pearson bivariate correlations were used to test the main hypotheses. As hypothesized, the APS-BR scores were very highly correlated with their respective scores on the APS. Organization ($r = .80$), Imagination ($r = .81$), Comfort ($r = .77$), Frequency of Affect Expression ($r = .79$), and Tone of Affect Expression ($r = .75$) were all significantly correlated at the $p < .001$ level. These correlations all meet Cohen's criteria for a large effect size (1995).

Also as hypothesized, significant correlations were found between the APS-BR and the criterion measures of divergent thinking and emotional memories. In addition, the patterns of correlations between the APS-BR and both criterion measures were similar in strength and direction to the patterns of correlations between the APS and these same measures.

The strength of correlations between the APS and the APS-BR, as well as the similarity of the pattern of correlations between the APS and the APS-BR with criterion measures, suggests that the APS-BR functions in a manner similar to that of the original APS. Therefore, the APS-BR might be used in instances where the APS might be cumbersome or incapable of being used. For example, the APS-BR could be used by a clinician wanting a brief rating of a child's play as part of a more comprehensive assessment. In addition, clinicians outside the field of play and unaware of the APS could use the APS-BR without extensive training or knowledge of its background. Because it does not require videotaping or extensive training to score, the APS-BR could be more readily used than the APS as a part of assessment batteries in research. In this way, the study of play could be advanced by the inclusion of the APS-BR into more child research projects.

Future studies will use the APS-BR with a live sample of children, and new criteria measures, including both convergent and discriminant validity, will be incorporated. Another step in this research is to have clinicians unfamiliar with the APS and outside the field of play research use the APS-BR with children, to determine its feasibility with this sample of practitioners. It is hoped that this quicker, easier version of the APS will encourage more clinicians and researchers to incorporate play into their general assessment of children and to measure change in psychotherapy.

PLAY IN CHILD THERAPY

Research from a variety of sources suggests that play helps reduce anxiety in children. For example, play prior to surgery reduced anxiety in children (Rae, Worchel, Upchurch, Sunner, & Dainiel, 1989). Play also reduced separation anxiety in preschoolers (Milos & Reiss, 1982). Research also suggests that children who already have good fantasy and play skills are better able to use play to reduce anxiety. Implications of the research findings are that play should be considered for therapy if the child is experiencing anxiety around internal conflicts or external trauma and when the child has adequate play skills (see Russ, 2004, for a review). Play assessment can determine whether the child has play skills that are adequate for use in order to use play to process emotional material in therapy.

Case Example

What follows is a case example of a child struggling with separation anxiety. This case has been discussed in Russ (2004). However, what we do in this chapter is score the play dialogue in the therapy according to the APS scoring criteria. Although there is no video recording that permits scoring of nonverbal expressions, this scoring attempt is an illustration of how the APS could be used for treatment planning and assessment of change in therapy.

John was a 6-year-old boy who was having trouble staying in school. The conceptualization of the case was that there were internal conflicts that were underlying the separation anxiety. It was also possible that John's past illness or that of his mother had been traumatic for him. Russ did an informal play assessment at the time of intake. John built an Olympic Village from Legos and had people figures talking and interacting in the play. Organization of narrative and imagination would receive a 3 and 4, respectively (on a 5-point Likert scale), suggesting that he should be able to use fantasy and pretend play in therapy. However, there was no expression of affect in the play. Most 6-year-old boys express emotion in the 5-minute play narrative, especially aggressive content. John was constricted in his affect expression, and one goal of therapy was to help him increase his affect expression in the play. We have chosen samples of play dialogue from Russ (2004, pp. 51–54) and have now scored it.

Session 3:

Content:	Affect Category
Therapist (T): What is that you are making?	
Child (C): An alligator.	Aggression
(Turned it into something else).	
T: Now what is it?	
C: A swordfish	Aggression
T: Oh, a swordfish. Now what?	
C: A turtle.	
T: And now?	
C: A hippopotamus.	

John then tried to make a horse with Legos but could not get it built to his satisfaction. I kept repeating that what he had done was OK and he could use it to play, but he was critical. He then went back to the clay and made something else.

T: What is that?	
C: A dinosaur.	Aggression
(He showed it falling off a cliff.)	Sickness/Hurt
Now it is an angel. (He made a halo for it.)	
(He then made something else)	
This is a person who eats too much.	Oral
He is so fat he keeps falling over, because he is so heavy.	Sickness/Hurt
T: He's so heavy and ate so much food, that he keeps falling.	

Then John drew a picture.

T: What's happening there?	
C: This is a giant.	Aggression
He is stomping on the city.	Aggression
Everything is on fire.	Aggression
T: The giant is stomping on everything. Maybe he is mad about something.	

John didn't comment on that. I told him I would see him next week and he seemed happy about coming.

In this play sample, John received a total affect score of 9. There are 6 expressions of aggression, first in the form of aggressive animals (alligator, swordfish, dinosaur). Finally, a giant is stomping on a city. I had tried to give permission for John to express aggression in this session and in previous sessions. His organization of the story in this session was scored a 3 and imagination a 4.

Session 5:

Content	Affect Category
John went right to the clay and made forms and smashed them.	Aggression
I commented on his smashing them: "You really smashed that one."	
Then one clay figure would start to smash another.	Aggression
He would play monster and start to attack and then stop.	Aggression
He would abruptly pull back. This happened repeatedly.	

I tried to support his aggressive play and say things like,
"He is going to attack," or "He is really angry," or
"He is going to smash him." John then took some puppets
and said he would put on a puppet show.

The alligator and hippopotamus puppet were	Oral Aggression

trying to eat the man.
The man escaped. I commented that they were trying to
eat him, but the man escaped. Then John asked me to play
with him. I put on a puppet, but followed his lead.
He was the boy puppet.

C: His nose is growing, because he told a lie (this occurred
   in a previous session).
T: Sometimes it's hard not to lie. Kids lie sometimes.
   John immediately stopped playing.

In the initial series of aggressive attacks, first in the clay forms and then in the monster, John was expressing much aggression. Although he received 3 aggressive units here, because a long series of non-verbal aggressive attacks occurred, he would have received a higher frequency of aggressive units, if the play had been videotaped. Then the alligator and hippo tried to eat the man, receiving an oral aggression score.

Session 6:

Content	Affect Category
John began by making clay figures.	
First he made a flower, which he smashed.	Aggression
Then he made a ring, which he put on his finger.	
Then he made a play set with slides and caves and	
had clay figures go down the slide.	
They were having fun.	Happiness/Pleasure
John then moved to the puppets and put on a puppet show.	
There was a father puppet and a boy puppet. First,	
the boy got shocked by an electric wire and fell on the ground.	Sickness/Hurt
Then a frog came along and said, "I'll cook you for supper."	Oral Aggression
Then a snake came and started to eat his hand.	Oral Aggression
Then the father puppet came and chased the creatures away.	Aggression
He took the boy to the hospital.	Nurturance
Father talked to the doctors and asked what they would do.	Nurturance
The doctors operated on the boy.	Sickness/Hurt
The boy got better.	Nurturance
Father took him home.	Nurturance
Then father and the boy went on a trip.	Nurturance
They climbed a mountain and got to the top.	
They jumped up and down and cheered.	Happiness/Pleasure

T: The dad took care of the boy. He took him to the hospital
   and talked to the doctors. The boy got better. Then they
   climbed the mountain and were happy and proud.

Then John asked me to put on a puppet show with him.
He made cars out of clay and his puppet and my puppet
rode on them.

The cars went fast and the puppets were having a good time.	Happiness/Pleasure

There was a total of 14 affect units in this play sample. There was a wide range of affect (aggression, happiness, nurturance/affection, sadness/hurt). What was new in this session was the expression of positive affect in the play (happiness, nurturance/affection). We also scored organization and imagination, and both received a 5. There was good organization of the story and much imagination.

In just focusing on the play, John became less constricted in his expression of affect over six sessions. He became freer in expressing aggression in play and even, eventually, expressed positive affect as well. He also used the play to resolve internal conflicts. The expression of aggressive ideation in his play was central to the conflict resolution. He became more comfortable with his aggressive impulses, and anxiety around aggression was lessened. It is hard to know for sure whether anxiety around aggressive impulses was responsible for the separation anxiety or whether early trauma around his hospitalization or that of his mother was responsible. In his story, the father rescues the boy and the boy gets better in the hospital. He might have resolved issues around his father and now sees him as a protector. Anxiety reduction probably occurred in several ways in the therapy.

In this case, John did improve outside of the therapy. When school began in the fall, he was able to stay in school. The therapy ended shortly thereafter, since he was doing well in school. Factors other than the play contributed to improvement as well (firm message from parents that he would have to stay in school), but the changes in the play process could be seen in the play sessions. This is the type of case where repeated measures of play processes before, during, and after therapy could have measured change. In this case, the goal of increased affect expression and a wider range of affect expression would probably have been met if they had been carefully measured.

If a therapist is working with a different type of child, a child who has low organization play skills and high emotional content, but has some imaginative ability, (such as a child with borderline features), then a goal of therapy would be to increase the organization of the narrative. Better organization skills would place the emotional material in a more meaningful context and could help with emotion regulation. The amount of coherence and logic in the narrative could be measured over time.

CONCLUSION

In conclusion, by including an assessment of play in the diagnostic interview or testing process, we can better determine whether and how play should be used in treatment. We can also measure change in play processes throughout the therapy and relate changes in play processes to changes in behavior and other internal processes. Because children frequently play during intake interviews and therapy, it should be relatively easy to include a play assessment. By including play assessment, we can reduce the gap between research and practice and refine our therapy interventions.

REFERENCES

Burns, W. J., & Faust, J. (1989). *The Nova assessment scale of psychotherapy.* Manuscript in preparation.   [AU3]

Chazan, S. E. (2000). Using the children's play therapy instrument (CPTI) to measure the development of play in simultaneous treatment: A case study. *Infant Mental Health Journal, 21,* 211–221.

Christiano, B., & Russ, S. (1996). Play as a predictor of coping and distress in children during an invasive dental procedure. *Journal of Clinical Child Psychology, 25,* 130–138.

Cohen, J. (1995). A power primer. *Psychological Bulletin, 112*, 155–159.

Dansky, J. (1980). Make-believe: A mediator of the relationship between play and associative fluency. *Child Development, 51*, 576–579.

Faust, J., & Burns, W. J. (1991). Coding therapist and child interaction: Progress and outcome in play therapy. In C. E. Schaefer, K. Gitlin, & S. Sandgrund (Eds.), *Play therapy: Diagnosis and assessment* (pp. 663–689). New York: John Wiley & Sons.

Fisher, E. (1992). The impact of play on development: A meta-analysis. *Play and Culture, 5*, 159–181.

Gitlin-Weiner, B., Sangrund, A., & Schaefer, C. (Eds.). (2000). *Play Diagnosis and Assessment.* New York: Wiley & Sons.

Howe, P. A., & Silvern, L. E. (1981). Behavioral observation of children during play therapy: Preliminary development of a research instrument. *Journal of Personality Assessment, 45*, 168–182.

Kernberg, P. F., Chazan, S. E., & Normandin, L. (1998). The children's play therapy instrument (CPTI): Description, development, and reliability studies. *Journal of Psychotherapy Practice and Research, 7*, 196–207.

Milos, M., & Reiss, S. (1982). Effects of three play conditions on separation anxiety in young children. *Journal of Consulting and Clinical Psychology, 50*, 389–395.

Perry, L., & Landreth, G. (1991). Diagnostic assessment of children's play therapy behavior. In C. E. Schaefer, K. Gitlin, & S. Sandgrund (Eds.), *Play therapy: Diagnosis and assessment* (pp. 643–660). New York: John Wiley & Sons.

Rae, W., Worchel, R., Upchurch, J., Sanner, J., & Dainiel, C. (1989). The psychosocial impact of play on hospitalized children. *Journal of Pediatric Psychology, 14*, 617–627.

Rosen, C., Faust, J., & Burns, W. J. (1994). The evaluation of process and outcome in individual child psychotherapy. *International Journal of Play Therapy, 3*, 33–43.

Russ, S. (1987). Assessment of cognitive affective interaction in children: Creativity, fantasy, and play research. In J. Butcher & C. Spielberger (Eds.), *Advances in personality assessment* (Vol. 6, pp. 141–155). Hillsdale, NJ: Lawrence Erlbaum Associates.

Russ, S. (2004). *Play in child development and psychotherapy: Toward empirically supported practice.* Mahwah, NJ: Lawrence Erlbaum Associates.

Russ, S., & Grossman-McKee, A. (1990). Affective expression in children's fantasy play, primary process thinking on the Rorschach, and divergent thinking. *Journal of Personality Assessment, 54*, 756–771.

Russ, S., Niec, L., & Kaugars, A. (2000). Play assessment of affect—The Affect in Play Scale. In K. Gitlin-Weiner, A. Sangrund, & C. Schaefer (Eds.), *Play diagnosis and assessment* (pp. 722–749). New York: Wiley.

Russ, S., & Schafer, E. (in press). Affect in Play, emotion in memories, and divergent thinking. *Creativity Research Journal.*

Sacha, T. J., Russ, S. W., & Short, E. J. (2005). *Development and validation of the Affect in Play Scale–Brief Rating Version (APS-BR).* Manuscript submitted for publication.

Singer, D. G., & Singer, J. L. (1990). *The house of make-believe: Children's play and the developing imagination.* Cambridge, MA: Harvard University Press.

7

THE ROUND-ROBIN FAMILY ASSESSMENT WITH SOCIAL RELATIONS MODEL ANALYSIS

William L. Cook
Maine Medical Center

The approach to family assessment presented here is based on the notion that a family is a system of interdependent individuals. For many years family therapists, psychiatrists, clinical and developmental psychologists, and social workers have been advocating the view that individual behavior and functioning cannot be understood in isolation from the person's primary social context, usually the family. However, because the family system is a complex organization, the methods for studying interdependence in family relationships are complex as well. Most family assessment instruments have tried to simplify the procedure, obscuring the systemic nature of family relationships in the process. In this chapter I present the Round-Robin Family Assessment with Social Relations Model analysis (RR-SRM), a quantitatively based method for assessing individual families that goes a long way toward revealing the complexity of family systems and how each family member fits within the complex whole (Cook & Kenny, 2004). I begin with a brief discussion of the theoretical framework that underlies the approach. This is followed by an extended presentation of the method and the type of information it provides. Finally, I present a case example of a family seeking treatment for an adolescent who is in the prodromal phase of psychosis.

FAMILIES AS SYSTEMS

There are actually many different perspectives on what it means for a family to be a system, and different models of family therapy are loosely tied to these different conceptualizations. Structural family therapy (Minuchin, 1974), for example, emphasizes the importance of boundaries and structure within the system. When the boundary between the parent and child generations gets either too rigid or too diffuse, the child may develop a problem. Thus, boundaries are defined in terms of patterns of interaction between family members; they are relational. The model of brief family therapy developed by the Palo Alto group (Watzlawick, Weakland, & Fisch, 1974) emphasizes the unhelpful feedback loop that exists when the solutions people attempt exacerbate the problems they were intended to solve. For example, a father may lose his temper in a childish way while trying to get his child to be more responsible and adult-like. One thing that these and most other systems-oriented theories of family have in common is the idea that "a change in one part of the system is followed by compensatory change in other parts of the system" (Bowen, 1982, p. 154). However, whether or not a change in one person will elicit a change in another person depends on whether there is interdependence in the relationship. Thus, interdependence is fundamental to any view of the family as a system. There is interdependence whenever what happens to one person matters (in a positive way or in a negative way) to another person. Much of what happens to us on a day-to-day basis is routine and has no effect whatsoever on those around us. Interdependence is observable only when certain thresholds are reached or when particularly significant events occur. Thus, the measurement of interdependence must be specific to particular variables within particular relationships.

Some forms of interdependence can be described as instrumental. For example, if my wife wins the lottery, it will undoubtedly affect how I spend my time. Other forms of interdependence are emotional. For example, when a child becomes ill, family members become emotionally focused on and behaviorally organized around the child. Often the emotional and functional aspects of interdependence overlap. Not only do a child's illness and distress elicit caretaking and nurturance from his or her parents, but a parent may have to miss work to stay home with the sick child, take the child to the doctor, or otherwise alter the plans for the day. A sibling may temporarily feel neglected because of the focus on the other child. When a parent is the one who becomes ill, the other parent may take on the chores that the ill parent normally performs, expanding his or her usual workload. In some cases, a child may take on adult responsibilities prematurely to compensate for a parent's illness. If it is a chronic illness, the child may forfeit his or her childhood.

The Individual within the System

In some respects, the ability to describe the organization of the family in terms of interpersonal dynamics is a goal in its own right. Thus, it is reasonable to study family variables without a particular focus on the outcomes of any one family member. However, that was not the original goal when psychiatrists and other professionals first began describing families as systems (e.g., Ackerman, 1956; Bateson, Jackson, Haley, & Weakland, 1956; Bowen, Dysinger, Brodey, & Basamania, 1957; Bowlby, 1949). The goal then was to understand how family relationships were affecting the course of illness for psychiatric patients (mostly people with schizophrenia). The ideas that were generated by the early thinkers were so exciting that understanding the system often became all important and the individual became almost insignificant. In this chapter I take the view that the focus of a clinician should be primarily on the outcomes of the identified patient. However, the role of the family should be understood in terms of whether it contributes positively or negatively to the identified patient's (IP's) outcomes and whether the patient's outcomes contribute positively or negatively to family members' outcomes. More radical views of the role of the family in the development of a person's psychological problems, such as the idea that having a member with a psychiatric illness somehow benefits (provides homeostatic balance to) certain types of families (Jackson, 1957), have not to my knowledge been supported empirically.

The Assessment of Family Functioning

Historically, the most common way of assessing the family system quantitatively has been through the use of measures where an individual rates the family as a whole. The Family

Environment Scale (FES; Moos & Moos, 1981) and the Family Adaptability and Cohesion Scales (FACES III; Olson, Portner, & Lavee, 1985) are well-known versions of whole-family assessments. An example of an item from such a scale is "People in my family look out for each other." Such scales are problematic for a number of reasons (Cook & Kenny, 2005). First, each family member may have a different perspective on how the family is functioning (Jacob & Windle, 1999). Because the perspective of the rater is confounded with the target of the rating (i.e., the family system), it is difficult to know in any given case whether an extreme score is due to characteristics of the rater or characteristics of the family. Thus, when the developers of these instruments report validity data showing that the instruments distinguish between clinical and nonclinical families, the differences could be due to rater effects, perhaps reflecting an individually based illness, or it could be because the families are actually different in some way (i.e., a target effect). Summing over the ratings of different family members to create an aggregate score, an attempted solution to this problem, is not adequate. Ratings from as many as seven different family members may be needed to cancel out the effect of one extreme rater (Schwarz, Barton-Henry, & Pruzinsky, 1985).

A second problem with whole-family ratings is that the target of the rating is not as obvious as it might first seem. For example, if a teenage daughter does not get along with her mother, how should one rate the family as a whole? One family member may report that the family as a whole functions well, despite problems in one subsystem in the family. Another family member may believe that the mother-daughter dyad epitomizes the family as a whole, even though other relationships in the family are functioning well. Because the family is not a thing like a tree or a car, it cannot serve as an unambiguous target of an assessment rating. There are too many components of the system that might be differentially salient to different family raters. Because the items measuring whole family functioning have more than one possible meaning, methodologists call them *double-barreled items* (Judd, Smith, & Kidder, 1991). Such items should be avoided in the development of psychological or psychosocial measures.

The third problem is a conceptual one. It has been said that the difference between a group of individuals and a family system is like the difference between a pile of bricks and a house. The number of bricks in a pile and the number used to make a house can be the same, but it is the architecture, the way the bricks fit together, that defines the house. The same is true for the family system. The patterns among the relationships, not the group size or group average, define the proverbial "whole" that is greater than the sum of the parts. Ratings of dyadic and whole family functioning do not reveal the patterns in a family system, that is, how the individuals fit together. In this fundamental regard, measuring families at the group level disregards the defining features of the family system. I suspect that the idea that "the whole is greater than the sum of the parts" has been misunderstood by those who have developed measures of whole-family functioning. Rather than a pattern, they have given us a pile.

Finally, ratings of whole-family functioning assume that family members are similar to each other. Although there are aspects of the environment that family members do share (e.g., the size of the home, the neighborhood, income), family members do not share the same set of family relationships. For example, an overly rebellious child often has a conforming sibling in his or her environment, whereas an overly conforming sibling often lives with a rebellious sibling. A permissive parent often has to co-parent with someone he or she experiences as overly strict, whereas a strict parent often feels the need to compensate for the behavior of a permissive parent (Cook, 2001). The point is that family dynamics often make family members different as they compensate for the behaviors of each other. The existing measures of whole-family functioning do not measure or reveal such patterns.

THE SOCIAL RELATIONS MODEL

The only way to obtain full information on all of the components of the family system is to measure each person's thoughts, feelings, behavior, or perceptions vis-à-vis each of the other family members. Such measures are called *relationship-specific measures* (Cook, 2000). An example of a relationship-specific measure of perceived negativity is "This person criticizes me." When each member of a group reports on his or her relationship to each of the other group members individually—or is observed interacting with each of the individual members—it is called a *round-robin design*. In a round-robin design involving a mother, a father, and a child, there will be six relationship-specific measures (mother-father, mother-child, father-mother, father-child, child-mother, child-father). In a two-parent two-child family there will be 12 such measures, as illustrated by Figure 7–1.

The use of a round-robin design provides a snapshot of the family system from every angle. Moreover, each of these measures can be compared with the mean and standard deviation of a comparison sample to determine whether, relative to that sample, a particular relationship within the family is extreme. Even though this orientation takes very seriously the idea that the family is a system and that the relationships may be interdependent (more will be said about this shortly), it is not assumed that all family relationships defined over all variables of interest are always interdependent with all of the other family relationships. In a particular family, for example, a conflict may be restricted to one relationship. This is what is supposed to happen, in fact, in relatively healthy families. On the other hand, a conflict in one family relationship may be just the tip of the iceberg. It could be that the entire

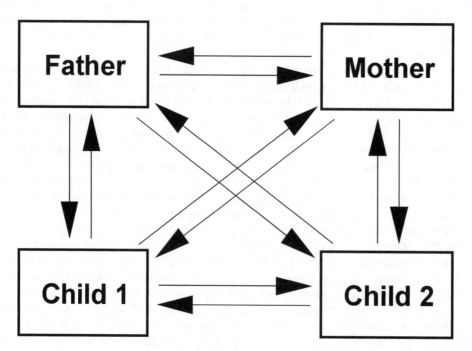

FIGURE 7–1.   The round-robin family design. Each person reports on their relaionship with each of the other family members. The arrows point from the person making the rating to the person being rated. In a 4-person family, 12 relationship measures are collected.

family is embroiled in conflict. One purpose of assessing the whole family is to determine where the conflict lies and who is affected.

It might seem that collecting data on directed family relationships according to a round-robin design and comparing these data with a set of appropriate norms would achieve the desired results of a family assessment; this is not true. Such measures are confounded by both psychological and relational factors that should be central to the psychosocial assessment. For example, if a given husband has a high level of trust for his wife, it could be because he is a trusting person. If we find that he shows a high level of trust in all of his relationships, we could conclude that he is a trusting person. Thus, the measure may reflect a characteristic of the perceiver. On the other hand, the husband may trust his wife because she is very trust-worthy. If she is trusted by everyone, her husband's trust may say more about her than about him—a target effect. It is also possible that his trust of her is unique to his relationship with her. In this case it is not because he trusts everyone (his perceiver effect) and it is not because every-one trusts her (her target effect). Rather, it is a relationship-specific effect, perhaps reflecting the chemistry or goodness of fit of their personalities. Likewise, her trust of him may reflect her general level of trust (perceiver effect), his trustworthiness (target effect), or her unique experience of him (relationship effect). Note that his relationship effect with her is not assumed to be the same as her relationship effect with him. Rather, it is assumed that their relationship is two-sided. Finally, both his trust of her and her trust of him could reflect a characteristic of their family. In this case we would expect everyone in the family to trust everyone else.

As this discussion suggests, when a measure of one person's relationship with another is to be used in an assessment of family functioning, it is important to determine the spe-cific sources of the score. It makes a big difference if we attribute a disturbance in a rela-tionship to the perceiver when it really reflects characteristics of the target. Attributing the problem to the family as a whole when it really reflects a unique, isolated relationship effect is equally problematic. In contrast to other methods for the quantitative assessment of fam-ily functioning (see Cook & Kenny, 2005), the Social Relations Model (SRM; Kenny & La Voie, 1984; Cook & Kenny, 2004) provides the means of making these distinctions. Accord-ing to the SRM, the thoughts, feelings, or behavior of one person toward another are func-tions of four systematic components plus errors of measurement. The systematic components are the actor effect, the partner effect, the relationship effect, and the group effect. Because we focus here on perceptions of family relations, actor effects are called "perceiver effects," partner effects are called "target effects," and the group effect is called the "family effect." Relationship effects are still called "relationship effects."

Procedure

In an RR-SRM assessment, relationship-specific data are collected from each member of the family participating in the assessment. This information is typically collected with ques-tionnaires, but other modes of data collection could be used (e.g., interviewing young chil-dren who cannot complete questionnaires). There is no prescribed set of constructs that must be measured, but there should be a comparison sample for each type of relationship and construct to be assessed. The raw scores from a given family and the SRM effects that explain these raw scores can then be compared with the corresponding measures from the compari-son sample. As in many evaluations, the specific scores are subtracted from the sample mean and divided by the standard deviation to obtain a Z score. The Z score indicates how much the individual deviates from the sample mean. Ideally the comparison sample is representative and the effects of age and sex can be controlled.

The formulas for the SRM effects have been presented elsewhere (Cook & Dreyer, 1984; Cook & Kenny, 2004; Warner, Kenny, & Stotto, 1979). For a two-parent two-child family measured within a round-robin design and assessing one psychosocial construct (e.g., negativity), there will be 1 family effect, 4 perceiver effects (1 for each rater), 4 target effects (1 for each partner), and 12 relationship effects. The Z scores for each of these SRM components can be interpreted, yielding information about family relationships at three levels of analysis. Perceiver and target effects operate at the individual level of analysis. Relationship effects operate at the dyadic level of analysis, and family effects operate at the group level of analysis. As numerous SRM studies have shown, family-, individual-, and relationship-specific factors can all contribute significantly to measures of family relationships (Cook, 1994, 2000, 2001; Cook, Kenny, & Goldstein, 1991; Delsing, Oud, De Bruyn, & van Aken, 2003; Ross, Stein, Trabasso, Woody, & Ross, 2005; Branje, van Lieshout, & van Aken, 2005).

Interpreting the Results

There are two steps in the interpretation phase of the RR-SRM assessment. The first step is to interpret the round-robin raw scores. For each variable (e.g., perceived negativity), there will be 12 raw scores for a 4-person family: Mother-father, Mother-child 1, Mother-child 2, Father-mother, Father-child 1, Father-child 2, Child 1-mother, Child 1-father, Child 1-child 2, Child 2-mother, Child 2-father, and Child 2-child 1. For a 3-person family there will be 6 such scores to interpret. As noted earlier, by comparing the observed scores for a particular family with the mean scores and standard deviations of the same measures observed in an appropriate sample of families, a Z score is obtained for each raw score. Thus, if the mother's report of the father's negativity toward her has a Z of 1.96, she experiences significantly more negativity from her husband than the average mother in the comparison sample. One may choose to interpret any Z score above or below 1.0 as above or below average, respectively, and report Z scores greater or less than 1.96 as "extreme."

The second step is to interpret the SRM effects. For clinical purposes, the primary focus should be the interpretation of the SRM effects that are components of a statistically significant raw score. If the mother reports unusually high levels of negativity from the father (e.g., a Z score > 1.96), one would then inspect the SRM effects that explain it. For the mother's report of the father's negativity, the relevant SRM components are the family effect, the mother perceiver effect, the father target effect, and the mother-father relationship effect. One does not generally need to explain raw scores that are not somewhat extreme. A more detailed introduction to the interpretation of the SRM effects follows.

Family Effects.   The family effect is based on the average of all of the scores from a particular family (for a particular variable). It is the family mean and, therefore, represents the experience of the average member of the family. For perceived negativity a family Z score greater than 1.96 indicates that the average member of the particular family experiences significantly more negativity than the average member of the families in the comparison sample. For example, the mother's experience of negativity from the father may be explained by the fact that she lives in a highly negative family.

Perceiver Effects.   Families are not monoliths, so different family members are likely to report experiences that differ from the average. The perceiver effects reflect the degree to which the experience of each family member differs from the family mean. The calculation of perceiver effects is based on a weighted mean of a given person's ratings of his or her relationship with each of the other family members. The weighting is necessary to adjust for the fact that the person does not have him- or herself as a partner. The perceiver effect would be simply a weighted mean for the rater's experience, except that the family mean is subtracted out (see Cook & Kenny, 2004). Thus, if the mother's perceiver effect for negativity is positive, it means she experiences more negativity than the average member of her family. It is very important to inspect the actual SRM effect prior to interpreting the Z score for the effect. It is possible for a particular mother to have a negative perceiver effect (she experiences less negativity than the average member of her family), but her Z score is positive (her perceiver effect is greater than the perceiver effect for the average mother). A mother who experiences a high level of negativity from her husband may be a mother who experiences a higher level of negativity from all of her family members than does the average mother. Thus, her perceiver effect would provide quite a different explanation of her experience of the father than if it were found that her experience was due to the father's target effect.

Target Effects.   Just as family members differ in terms of their experiences of other family members, so too do they differ in how they are experienced *by* other family members. Target effects reflect the degree to which each family member is experienced as different from the family mean. Like perceiver effects, target effects reflect deviations around the family mean. Consequently, the family member who is experienced as most negative will have a positive target effect for perceived negativity, and the family member who is least negative will have a negative target effect. As with perceiver effects, it is important to inspect the actual SRM effect before interpreting the Z score for the effect. The SRM effect reflects how the person compares with other members of the same family, whereas the Z score reflects how the effect compares with the same effect from the average family in the comparison sample. If the father's target effect for negativity is positive, it means he is experienced as more negative than the average member of his family. If the Z score for his target effect is positive, it means that his target effect is larger than the average target effect for fathers. In this case, the mother's experience of the father's negativity would be explained at least in part by his characteristics.

Relationship Effects.   As mentioned in the discussion of perceiver effects, not all family members have the same experience of the family; thus their scores may differ from the family mean. Similarly, individual family members do not experience each of their partners in the same way. Consequently, a person's scores may vary across partners. Insofar as the perceiver effect reflects a kind of average score for the person's experience of his or her partners, relationship effects reflect deviations around this average score. Thus, relationship effects have the same relation to perceiver effects that perceiver effects have to the family mean. They qualify the perceiver effect by indicating how particular relationships differ from the person's "average" relationship.

The formulas show that a relationship effect is what is left after the family mean, the actor effect of the perceiver, and the partner effect of the target are subtracted from the observed or raw score for a particular relationship (see Cook & Kenny, 2004). One implication of this is that relationship effects qualify target effects. A target effect reflects how the person is experienced on the average (by the perceivers). However, a given person may be experienced differently by different perceivers. For example, the daughter may experience less negativity from the father than the mother does, and the son may experience less negativity from the father than the daughter does. In this scenario, the mother-father relationship effect for negativity will tend to be positive, the daughter-father relationship effect will tend to be near zero, and the son-father relationship effect will tend to be negative.

The formulas for relationship effects (see Cook & Kenny, 2004) have the constraint that all of the relationship effects contributing to a particular perceiver effect must sum to zero, and all the relationship effects that contribute to a target effect must sum to zero. In three-person families, a particular perceiver has only two partners. If these two effects must sum to zero, his or her relationship effect in relation to one partner will be equal to and opposite in sign relative to his or her relationship effect in relation to the other partner. Likewise, the relationship effect for the relationship of one perceiver (e.g., mother) to a particular partner (e.g., father) will be equal to and opposite in sign compared with the relationship effect of the relationship of another family member (e.g., daughter) to that partner. This makes sense when one considers that a relationship effect is a unique adjustment to a partner. When there are only two partners, the unique adjustment reflects the difference between the two relationships after the family, actor, and partner effects have been removed. Another way of saying this is that there is only one degree of freedom for relationship effects in three-person families. In four-person families, there are six degrees of freedom for relationship effects. Consequently one can learn much more about unique family relationships when four or more family members are evaluated.

Assuming that the mother in our example is from a four-person family, we may find that one of the reasons she experiences her husband as high in negativity is her relationship effect in relation to him. If the mother-father relationship effect is positive, it means she experiences him as more negative than she experiences other family members on average. In this respect, it qualifies or moderates her perceiver effect. It also means that he is experienced as more negative by her than by other family members on average. In this respect it qualifies his target effect. If the Z score for the mother-father relationship effect is statistically significant, it means that compared with other mother-father relationships, this mother's unique adjustment to her husband is more pronounced.

Reciprocity.   When the SRM is estimated on a sample of families, reciprocity can be measured for the "average family" at both the individual and dyadic levels of analysis (Cook, 1994). At the individual level, reciprocity is estimated by the correlation of the perceiver effect for a particular role (e.g., mothers) and the target effect for the same role. Thus, if mothers who perceive others as negative are perceived by others as negative, the actor-partner reciprocity correlation will be statistically significant. Actor-partner reciprocity correlations are estimated for each role (mother, father, and each child). At the dyadic level, reciprocity is measured by the correlation of the relationship effects of the two individuals in the relationship. For example, the mother-father relationship effects could be correlated with the father-mother relationship effects to measure reciprocity in marital dyads. Dyadic reciprocity is measured for each of the dyads in the family (mother-father, mother-child, and father-child).[1]

Technically, reciprocity cannot be estimated for a given dyad with the SRM approach. Nonetheless, because reciprocity is so important to the evaluation of family systems (it represents the positive and negative feedback processes that constitute the family's self-organizing capacity), it is worthwhile to use the data to come to some tentative conclusions regarding the presence of reciprocity. Thus, when both the SRM effects that go into a reciprocity correlation are substantially (e.g., one standard deviation) above or below average, we may tentatively conclude that reciprocity has resulted in deviation of the effects from the norms.

Measures

To some degree, the variables one chooses for a family assessment should be determined by the theory of family intervention being practiced. For example, a follower of Boszormenyi-Nagy (Boszormenyi-Nagy & Spark, 1984) would want to use measures of family loyalty (Delsing, Oud, De Bruyn, & van Aken, 2003), and an attachment theorist would be interested in measures of interpersonal attachment security (Cook, 2000; Horowitz, Rosenberg, & Bartholomew, 1993). However, factor analyses of family assessment measures (Gondoli & Jacob, 1993; Jacob & Windle, 1999) and other measures of interpersonal relationships (Kiesler, 1987; Wiggins, 1979) have repeatedly demonstrated that there are two primary domains in the measurement of interpersonal relationships: Affiliation and Control. These dimensions also underlie the major assumptions of Interpersonal Theory (Leary, 1957; Kiesler, 1996), that the needs for control (power, dominance, or autonomy) and affiliation (love, acceptance, friendship) are two of the most basic human motivations. In the present assessment, two dimensions of each domain are used. Affiliation is represented by relationship-specific measures of Positivity (e.g., Person X shows approval or compliments me) and Negativity (e.g., Person X criticizes or complains about me). Both scales consist of four items scaled in a seven-point Likert format. The items were selected from a set of items originally used in the assessment of marital relationships (Wills, Weiss, & Patterson, 1974). Across the 12 family relationships represented in a two-parent two-child family, both scales have average reliabilities (coefficient alpha) of at least .77. The Control domain is measured by the Effectance dimension (e.g., It is easy for me to get person X to change his or her mind.) and the Acquiescence dimension (e.g., Person X can get me to do things I at first did not want to do.) of the Interpersonal Sense of Control scales (Cook, 1993, 2001). The reliabilities averaged across 12 family relationships are .80 for Effectance and .72 for Acquiescence.

The following illustration is written to resemble a written report of a Round-Robin Family Assessment with SRM analysis. It may be that in an actual report the statistics would not be included, in order to make the report more readable. They are included in this report to underscore the fact that the report is based on empirical results.

Illustration

This family was referred to the PIER Program because the daughter had symptoms that may be early signs of psychosis (a drop in functioning, brief auditory hallucinations, and social withdrawal). She has also been depressed and has been diagnosed with ADHD and ODD. She was a patient in an intensive outpatient program from August 2003 to January 2004. The mother (age 49), father (age 45), brother (age 15), and daughter (age 16) participated in the assessment. The questionnaires were completed in May 2004. The family members did not differ significantly in age from the nonclinical sample against which the family was compared.

Family members completed questionnaires concerning their relationships with each other. Two domains of family functioning were assessed, each of which contains two dimensions. The first domain is interpersonal affectivity, consisting of four items measuring Positive Affectivity (e.g., Person X shows approval or compliments me) and four items measuring Negative Affectivity (e.g., Person X criticizes or complains about me). The second domain is the interpersonal sense of control, consisting of six items measuring Interpersonal Effectance (i.e., the sense that one can influence the partner) and five items measuring Interpersonal Acquiescence (i.e., the sense of being influenced by the partner). Differences from the comparison sample were evaluated for the relationship-specific scales measuring each dimension. In addition, for each dimension, four types of Social Relations Model effects were compared with those of the comparison sample: (1) Family effects reflect characteristics of the family as a group; (2) perceiver effects reflect the general experience of the respondent across his or her family relationships, independent of the overall family effect; (3) target effects reflect the general experience of family members in relation to a particular family member, independent of the overall family effect; and (4) relationship effects reflect the unique relationship of the respondent to the partner, independent of family, perceiver, and target effects. Z scores greater than or less than 1.50 are interpreted as "elevated" or "diminished," respectively, and Z scores greater or less than 1.96 are interpreted as "extreme."

Interpersonal Affectivity.   The family mean for positivity, 3.77 on a 7-point (1–7) scale, differs significantly from the norm. Family members on the average report much less positivity from each other than is found in the standard sample (family $Z = -2.12$). The family mean is low because observed scores for three relationships are substantially below the standard score for those relationships. Compared with the standard family, the mother experiences significantly less positivity from her son ($Z = -2.22$), the father experiences significantly less positivity from the daughter (-2.27), and the daughter experiences significantly less positivity from the father ($Z = -2.96$). The low level of positivity the mother experiences from the son is not due to her characteristics as a perceiver, or to her son's characteristics as a partner. It is due primarily to the mother-son relationship effect. In other words, the mother experiences less positivity from the son than she does from other family members in general (relationship effect $= -1.08$, $Z = -2.23$). The father's experience of low positivity from the daughter is explained only by the overall family mean. It cannot be definitively attributed to his perceptions, her traits as an interaction partner, or his unique relationship to her. The low level of positivity the daughter experiences from the father, however, is explained by three factors: (1) she comes from a family that is low in positivity; (2) her father is generally experienced as low in positivity (target effect $= -1.25$, $Z = -1.91$); and (3) her unique relationship with him produces low positivity (relationship effect $= -1.21$, $Z = -2.96$). On the other hand, the mother's target effect for positivity is large on the plus side (effect $= 2.06$, $Z = 2.84$), indicating that she is experienced as more positive than the average member of her family.

The family as a whole does not differ from the average family in the amount of negativity experienced (family mean $= 3.67$ on a 7-point scale), but two of the observed relationship scores are large. The father experiences more negativity from his daughter than does the standard father ($Z = 1.89$), and the daughter experiences more negativity from the father than does the standard daughter ($Z = 2.95$). The negativity the father experiences from the daughter is not explained by his characteristics as a perceiver, but rather by the daughter's characteristics as a partner (target effect $= 1.28$, $Z = 1.68$). The negativity the daughter experiences from the father is partially explained by his being someone who is generally experienced as a negative partner (target effect $= .84$, $Z = 1.90$). However, over and above his generally being experienced as negative, she has unique experience of his negativity (relationship effect $= .90$, $Z = 2.14$). Consistent with being experienced as the most positive family member, the mother is experienced as the least negative family member (target effect $= -1.94$, $Z = -3.35$).

Interpersonal Sense of Control.   In this family, individuals are relatively low, overall, in the sense of control (i.e., Effectance) in their relationships (family mean $= 2.24$ on a 5-point scale, $Z = -2.10$). Four of the observed relationship measures differ substantially from the corresponding means in the standard sample. The father feels a high degree of control in relation to his son ($Z = 1.85$) and a diminished sense of control in relation to his daughter ($Z = -2.20$). Both the son ($Z = -1.54$) and the daughter ($Z = -1.92$) have a diminished sense of control in relation to the father. The father's elevated sense of control in relationship to his son is partially explained by his relatively strong sense of control in the family (perceiver effect $= .50, Z = 1.77$) and partially by his unique sense of control over his son (relationship effect $= .64, Z = 1.89$). His relatively low sense of control in relationship to his daughter is explained by the overall low sense of control of all family members (i.e., the family effect), the low level of control all family members feel in relationship to the daughter (partner effect $= -.75, Z = -1.80$), and his unique relationship to her (relationship effect $= -.65, Z = -2.14$). The daughter's weak sense of control in relationship to her father reflects the overall low level of effectance in the family and the daughter's generally weak sense of control as an individual (perceiver effect $= -.54, Z = -1.52$). The son's weak sense of effectance in relationship to the father is primarily due to the family group effect.

Acquiescence is the sense of being influenced by others. It can be elevated either because one feels controlled by others or because one gives control to others (i.e., one is responsive). In this family only one relationship differed substantially from the standard. The son reports being more acquiescent to the father than is typical of boys his age ($Z = 1.61$). However, the explanation for his relatively high level of acquiescence cannot be attributed to any particular component (family, perceiver, target, or relationship). These four SRM components were each within 1.5 standard deviations of their respective means in the standardization sample, but their cumulative effect resulted in an extreme score. Nonetheless, the SRM analysis reveals two interesting facts about acquiescence in this family. The mother's unique acquiescence to the father was less than in her average family relationship (relationship effect $= -.90$), a substantially smaller mother-father relationship effect than is found in the standard family ($Z = -1.87$). In addition, the father's unique acquiescence to the son is negative (relationship effect $= -.50, Z = -1.67$), indicating that he is relatively less acquiescent to his son than he is to other family members in general. Given that the raw scores for mother-father acquiescence and father-son acquiescence are not significant, we cannot conclude that these relationships are problematic. Nonetheless, the SRM effects do inform us about unique relationships in the family.

Summary

As a group, members of this family experience unusually low levels of positivity and interpersonal effectance. Thus, the daughter's difficulties reflect, in part, the consequences of living in a distressed and distressing social context. Compared with other members of the family, the mother is experienced as relatively more positive and relatively less negative. She experiences relatively less positivity from her son than from other family relationships, and she is relatively less acquiescent to her husband than to other family members. There do not appear to be any relationship-specific problems between her and her daughter. The father is experienced as less positive and more negative than the family average. This pattern appears to be the complement of the pattern observed for the mother, suggesting that she compensates for him. The father reports a relatively high degree of effectance in his family relationships, a sense of control that is even more pronounced in his relationship with his son. He also reports being relatively less acquiescent in relationship to his son. One would expect the father's high effectance and low acquiescence in relationship to the son to make the son feel dominated by his father, but there is nothing in the son's reports to substantiate this. The father experiences relatively less effectance in relationship to his daughter. The daughter is like the father in being experienced as relatively negative by other family members. She experiences him as less positive and more negative than she experiences other family members in general, even after controlling for the father's target effect (i.e., that he is generally perceived as high in negativity). The daughter's family difficulties are not limited to her relationship with her father. She is on both the giving end and receiving end of a diminished sense of effectance, even after controlling for the overall low level of effectance experienced by the average family member. That she neither experiences nor affords others a sense of control is indicative of a reciprocal power struggle and is consistent with her diagnosis of ODD.

Treatment Implications.   In this family the daughter is the "identified patient" and she has also been identified as being at risk for psychosis. Consequently, the highest priority for treatment is to alter family dynamics that might be psychologically distressing for her, because such stressors may precipitate a conversion to psychosis. Negativity directed toward a vulnerable family member, often referred to as Expressed Emotion (Brown, Birley, & Wing, 1972) is known to be a significant psychosocial risk factor for psychosis. In this family, such negativity is most likely to come from the father. He is experienced as negative not just by the daughter, but by all family members. Unfortunately, the daughter experiences even more negativity from him than do other family members. Treatment that reduces the father's overall level of negativity and alleviates the relationship-specific conflict between father and daughter would have the greatest immediate benefit for the daughter.

It would be helpful to assess whether the father's negativity belies an underlying affective disorder. However, treatment of the father-daughter conflict will also need to address the dynamics of control. The degree to which the daughter allows other family members a sense of control (i.e., effectance) is significantly less than what is typical in well-functioning families, and the father experiences even less control in relationship to her than other family members do. His lack of control in relation to her may be a source of his negativity. The daughter also has a very low sense of control in relation to other family members, suggesting a reciprocal exchange characteristic of a power struggle. A diminished sense of control in family relationships can be a source of learned helplessness and depression. For the daughter to feel more control in her relationships, she may have to give more control to others. Control is usually given more freely to those to whom one has a positive affective relationship, so the key to the power struggle might also lie in improving the affective climate. This process may begin by strengthening the mother-daughter relationship, the least problematic of the daughter's family relationships. That the mother, like the daughter, resists influence by the father, may be a point where their bond may be accentuated. However, the mother's resistance of the father's influence also suggests conflict in the marital relationship. It may be that the daughter has been fighting the mother's battle with the father, and that the label of ODD has been her reward for this activity. Further investigation should clarify whether the daughter's behavior is related in any way to marital problems.

DISCUSSION

In this article I describe and illustrate the RR-SRM family assessment. Additional information on this approach can be found in Cook and Kenny (2004) and Cook (2005). The purpose of the RR-SRM family assessment is not to replace other psychological or interpersonal assessments, but rather to complement them with empirically based information regarding the interdependence that exists among family relationships, the interpersonal dynamics that result from interdependence, and the subjective experience these experiences bring to family members.

Clearly the application of the SRM to family assessment is in its infancy, so there is much development yet to take place. In particular, the comparison group of families is a sample of convenience and should not be considered representative (Cook, 2000, 2001). It is also quite likely that some of the decisions about procedures presented at this time will be modified as experience with the approach is gained. For example, a novel aspect of the method presented for the first time in this chapter is the emphasis on SRM explanations of statistically significant raw scale scores of family relationships. Previously all statistically significant SRM components were interpreted as clinically significant regardless of whether they were tied to statistically significant scale scores. Given that the raw scale scores are aggregates of the SRM effects, it is their deviation from the norm that implies clinical significance and makes important the explanations provided by the SRM effects.

Despite the current shortcomings, the RR-SRM approach has numerous advantages over conventional family assessment methods. Instead of treating all of the individuals in the family as if they have the same experience of the family, the SRM approach preserves individual, dyadic, and family-level factors that contribute to whole-family functioning. At both the individual and dyadic levels of analysis, this approach provides information on the direction of effects, clarifying, for example, whether a relationship score should be attributed to characteristics of the perceiver or the target. By investigating both sides of relationships, the presence of reciprocal dynamics can also be preliminarily inferred. Finally, the RR-SRM approach is psychometrically more precise because it does not require the use of ambiguous, double-barreled items.

Although the RR-SRM approach can also be applied to observational data (e.g., Cook & Dreyer, 1984: Stevenson, Leavitt, Thompson, & Roach, 1988), there are several reasons why one might prefer to use a self-report approach to family assessment rather than a more objective, observational approach. Observational approaches to family assessment are much more time and labor intensive. The data must be collected within a standardized observational context (e.g., a problem-solving task), the interactions must be coded with the use of a validated coding system by trained, reliable coders, and the results of these observations must still be compared with some standard against which they can be judged to be unusual or maladaptive. Although observational assessments do not pose a problem for a funded research program, for the ordinary clinician they are not feasible.

Although lacking in objectivity, most clinicians would agree that family members' subjective experiences of each other's behavior is as important as the behavior itself in determining subsequent outcomes. For example, whether one person perceives another to be rejecting can be quite idiosyncratic and may reveal more about the perceiver than about the sender of the comment. However, the perceiver will likely respond according to his or her interpretation of the situation, regardless of the sender's intention. Consequently, the subjective experience of family members is essential to the understanding of family process. Nonetheless, the SRM analysis does add a quasi-objective aspect to the assessment. When all family members have the same experience of a particular partner (i.e., there is a target effect), one can no longer say that an individual's experience of that person is subjective. Minimally, the experience is intersubjective and quite likely reflective of an objective reality. Without the SRM analysis, however, perceivers and targets are totally confounded.

Further support for the RR-SRM family assessment will come from data being collected in a randomized controlled trial of multi-family psycho-educational problem-solving groups

(McFarlane, Cook, Downing, & Robins, 2003). These data will relate the components of the RR-SRM assessment to symptoms of young adults at risk for psychosis and to their responses to both medication and psycho-social treatments. Moreover, plans are under way to computerize the input of family responses to the items, scoring, and interpretation of the results via an internet connection. This will make possible the dissemination of the approach to the treatment community at large. Given its numerous advantages over other approaches, greater accessibility to the assessment procedure plus supporting validity data could make the RR-SRM family assessment the gold standard for the quantitative assessment of family functioning.

ACKNOWLEDGMENTS

This research was supported in part by a grant from the National Institute of Mental Health (MH65367).

NOTE

1. One should not infer reciprocity if two raw scores representing the two sides of a relationship (e.g., husband and wife) are both significantly above or below the mean. Both raw scores could be significant because the family effect is significant. Gottman (1979) has made a similar statement about the correlations between raw scores.

REFERENCES

Ackerman, N. W. (1956). Interlocking pathlogy in family relationships. In *Changing Concepts of Psychoanalytic Medicine*. S. Rado and G. Daniels (Eds.), pp. 135–150. New York: Grune & Stratton.

Bateson, G., Jackson, D. D., Haley, J., & Weakland, J. (1956). Toward a theory of schizophrenia. *Behavioral Science, 1*, 151–164.

Boszormenyi-Nagy, I., & Spark, G. (1984). *Inivisible loyalties: Reciprocity in intergenerational family therapy*. New York: Brunner/Mazel.

Bowen, M. (1982). The use of family theory in clinical practice. In M. Bowen, *Family Therapy in Clinical Practice* (Chapter 9, pp. 147–181). New York: Aronson. Reprinted by permission of Grune & Stratton, from *Comprehensive Psychiatry, 7*, 345–374.

Bowen, M., Dysinger, R. H., Brodey, W. M., & Basamania, B. (1957). *Study and treatment of five hospitalized families each with a psychotic member*. Paper read at annual meeting of the American Orthopsychiatric Association, Chicago, March.

Bowlby, J. (1949). The study and reduction of group tensions in the family. *Human Relations, 2*, 123–128.

Branje, S. J. T., van Lieshout, C. F. M., & van Aken, M. A. G. (2005). Relations between agreeableness and perceived support in family relationships: Why nice people are not always supportive. *International Journal of Behavioral Development, 29*, 120–128.

Brown, G. W., Birley, J. L. T., & Wing, J. K. (1972). Influence of family life on the course of schizophrenic disorders: A replication. *British Journal of Psychiatry, 121*, 241–258.

Cook, W. L. (1993). Interdependence and the interpersonal sense of control: An analysis of family relationships. *Journal of Personality and Social Psychology, 64*, 587–601.

Cook, W. L. (1994). A structural equation model of dyadic relationships within the family system. *Journal of Consulting and Clinical Psychology, 62*, 500–509.

Cook, W. L. (2000). Understanding attachment in family context. *Journal of Personality and Social Psychology, 78*, 285–294.

Cook, W. L. (2001). Interpersonal influence in family systems: A Social Relations Model analysis. *Child Development, 72,* 1179–1197.

Cook, W. L. (2005). The SRM approach to family assessment: An introduction and case example. *European Journal of Psychological Assessment, 21,* 216–225.

Cook, W. L., & Dreyer, A. S. (1984). The social relations model: A new approach to the analysis of family-dyadic interaction. *Journal of Marriage and the Family, 46,* 679–687.

Cook, W. L., & Kenny, D. A. (2004). Application of the Social Relations Model to family assessment. *Journal of Family Psychology, 18,* 361–371.

Cook, W. L., & Kenny, D. A. (2005). An examination of self-report assessments of family functioning: A question of the level of analysis. *Journal of Family Psychology* (in press).

Cook, W. L., Kenny, D. A., & Goldstein, M. J. (1991). Parental affective style risk and the family system: A social relations model analysis. *Journal of Abnormal Psychology, 100,* 492–501.

Delsing, M. J. M. H., Oud, J. H. L., De Bruyn, E. E. J., & van Aken, M. A. G. (2003). Current and recollected perceptions of family relationships: The Social Relations Model approach applied to members of three generations. *Journal of Family Psychology, 17,* 445–459.

Gondoli, D. M., & Jacob, T. (1993). Factor structure within and across three family-assessment procedures. *Journal of Family Psychology, 6,* 278–289.

Gottman, J. M. (1979). *Marital interaction: Experimental investigations.* New York: Academic.

Horowitz, L. M., Rosenberg, S. E., & Bartholomew, K. (1993). Interpersonal problems, attachment styles, and outcome in brief dynamic psychotherapy. *Journal of Consulting and Clinical Psychology, 61,* 549–560.

Jacob, T., & Windle, M. (1999). Family assessment: Instrument dimensionality and correspondence across family raters. *Journal of Family Psychology, 13,* 339–354.

Jackson, D. (1957). The question of family homeostasis. *The Psychiatric Quarterly Supplement, 31,* 79–90.

Judd, C. M., Smith, E. R., & Kidder, L. H. (1991). *Research Methods in Social Relations* (6th Ed.). Fort Worth: Holt, Rinehart and Winston.

Kenny, D. A., & La Voie, L. (1984). The social relations model. In L. Berkowitz (Ed.), *Advances in experimental social psychology* (Vol. 18, pp. 142–182). Orlando: Academic.

Kiesler, D. J. (1987). *Research manual for the Impact Message Inventory.* Palo Alto, CA: Consulting Psychologists Press.

Kiesler, D. J. (1996). *Contemporary Interpersonal Theory and Research: Personality, Psychopathology, and Psychotherapy.* Oxford, England: John Wiley & Sons.

Leary, T. F. (1957). *Interpersonal diagnosis of personality.* New York: Ronald.

McFarlane, W. R., Cook, W. L., Downing, D., & Robins, D. (2003). Family psychoeducation and multi-family groups in prevention of psychosis. Paper presented at the International Prodromal Research Network Annual Meeting, May 1–3, Santa Monica, CA.

Minuchin, S. (1974). *Families and family therapy.* Cambridge, MA: Harvard University Press.

Moos, R. H., & Moos, B. S. (1981). *Family Environment Scale manual.* Palo Alto, CA: Consulting Psychologists Press.

Olson, D. H., Portner, J., & Lavee, Y. (1985). *FACES III.* St. Paul, MN: Family Social Science, University of Minnesota.

Ross, H., Stein, N., Trabasso, T., Woody, E., & Ross, M. (2005). The quality of family relationships within and across generations: A social relations analysis. *International Journal of Behavioral Development, 29,* 110–119.

Schwarz, J. C., Barton-Henry, M. L., & Pruzinsky, T. (1985). Assessing child-rearing behaviors with the CRPBI: A comparison of ratings by mother, father, student, and sibling. *Child Development, 56,* 462–479.

Stevenson, M. B., Leavitt, L. A., Thompson, R. H., & Roach, M. A. (1988). A social relations model analysis of parent-child play. *Developmental Psychology, 24,* 101–108.

Warner, R. M., Kenny, D. A., & Stoto, M. (1979). A new round-robin analysis of variance for social interaction data. *Journal of Personality and Social Psychology, 37,* 1742–1757.

Watzlawick, P., Weakland, J., & Fisch, R. (1974). *Change: Principles of problem formation and problem resolution.* New York: W. W. Norton.

Wiggins, J. S. (1979). A psychological taxonomy of trait-descriptive terms: The interpersonal domain. *Journal of Personality and Social Psychology, 37,* 395–412.

Wills, T. A., Weiss, R. L., & Patterson, G. R. (1974). A behavioral analysis of the determinants of marital satisfaction. *Journal of Consulting and Clinical Psychology, 42,* 802–811.

8

BEHAVIORAL ASSESSMENT

Jeffrey A. Miller
Stacie A. Leffard
Dusquesne University

Behavioral assessment is a primary assessment process for use with children and adolescents and is necessary for all aspects of multimethod child assessment (Merrell, 2003). For example, behavioral assessment methods are included in all four of Sattler's (2001) pillars of assessment: norm-referenced testing, interviews, observations, and informal assessment procedures. Surprisingly, even norm-referenced tests, such as the NEPSY: A Developmental Neuropsychological Assessment (Kemp, Kirk, & Korkman, 2001), include behavioral observation systems. McConaughy and Achenbach (2004) have developed an observational system to be administered during individualized testing. The other three pillars, interviews, observations, and various informal assessment procedures, are all techniques for gathering behavioral assessment data. Despite its broad implications and importance, there is no one universally accepted definition of or procedure for behavioral assessment. The purpose of this chapter is to describe behavioral assessment and its purposes, to explain methods of data collection, and to make procedural recommendations for data integration and interpretation. To begin to clarify the meaning of behavioral assessment, one must compare it with other assessment orientations.

BEHAVIORAL, TRADITIONAL, AND QUALITATIVE-DEVELOPMENTAL ASSESSMENT

Historically, there has been a distinction between behavioral and traditional assessment (Hersen, 1976; Mash & Terdal, 1988). A central assumption accounting for this distinction is that behavioral assessment requires "situational specificity." That is, the particular target behaviors are caused by variables in the immediate settings (Shapiro, 1988). Traditional assessment, on the other hand, focuses on enduring traits resulting in consistent behavior across settings. Furthermore, traditional assessment is linked with making clinical diagnoses rather than describing behavior and its circumstances (Silva, 1993). As behavioral assessment evolves, it is becoming clear that situational specificity is a restrictive assumption. Rather, behavior in a situation can be caused by multimodal variables that are proximal,

115

distal, physiological, or intrapsychic (Haynes & O'Brien, 1990; Miller, Tansy, & Hughes, 1998). As a result of the recognition of the expanding influences on observed behavior, it has been recommended that behavioral assessments measure as many of the modalities as the assessment plan will permit.

There is concern, however, that behavioral assessment has become so encompassing that there are no limits to what behavior and environments need to be evaluated. To help clarify this upper limit, behavioral assessment can be contrasted with Simeonsson's concept of qualitative-developmental assessment (Simmeonsson, Huntington, Brent, & Balant, 2001). Within his approach, like behavioral assessment, problems are thought to be idiosyncratic and complex. However, qualitative-developmental assessment, emerging from the biopsycho-social paradigm, extends focus to sensory, health, and developmental variables with the assumption of a highly integrated and dynamic social context. Thus, clinical decisions are based largely on the association of assessment data with developmental sequences. Qualitative-developmental assessment is important to the field of assessment but appears to go beyond the assumptions of behavioral assessment, which are explained next.

THE NATURE OF BEHAVIORAL ASSESSMENT

Based on the previous discussion, behavioral assessment is a procedure that is utilized by those who employ other assessment approaches, but equally sits beside them as an independent approach for drawing conclusions and making decisions. Behavioral assessment can be contrasted with other approaches in the behavioral tradition. These include behavioral analysis, applied behavioral analysis, and functional analysis. Behavioral analysis suggests systematic observations of behavior within experimental conditions. Applied behavioral analysis extends the term *behavioral analysis* to include socially relevant behaviors in humans (Silva, 1993). Functional analysis is concerned with both the situationally specific reasons for a target behavior and the relationship between these determinants and the behavior. Functional analysis, however, provides no procedures for examining causes of behavior outside the immediate context. The functions of behaviors are far more complex than can be observed in the subject's proximal setting (Haynes & O'Brien, 1990). Nevertheless, in the following description of behavioral assessment it can be seen that functional analysis is one of the central foci of behavioral assessment. Indeed, emphasis on function in behavioral assessment is evidenced by the emergence of the term *functional behavioral assessment.*

Behavioral assessment is a process of systematically gathering observations of a set of target behaviors, examining the relationships between these observations and potential multimodal determinants, and, based on these relationships, generating hypotheses about the important, controllable, causal functions of the behaviors for treatment planning and progress monitoring. Each part of this description can be examined independently. First, behavioral observations are gathered through direct observation, behavior rating scales, and structured interviews. Each technique provides a means for the systematic collection of quantitative and qualitative data. Second, there is a consideration of the potential causes of the target behaviors and how those causes relate to the target behavior. Data about these determinants are also gathered through the assessment procedures listed above. Next, integration and interpretation using clinical judgment are employed to make some conclusions about the nature of functions of the target behavior. Finally, behavioral assessment provides the information necessary to allow the clinician to target the functions of the behavior for treatment and measure the target behaviors to monitor progress.

PURPOSE OF BEHAVIORAL ASSESSMENT

The first purpose of behavioral assessment is to describe the problem behavior and the function of the behavior. In behavioral assessment, there is a focus on obtaining a precise measure of target behaviors. However, there is no assumption that the topography of the behavior is central to understanding the function of the behavior. For example, take the case of a child in school who becomes disruptive after the introduction of math work. A situation-specific interpretation of the behavior may lead to an intervention such as reducing the difficulty of the math work for the child. The function that justifies such an intervention is that the child was escaping from difficult math work. By making this conclusion, the clinician may be missing the real cause of the behavior, which may or may not have anything to do with math work, and possibly committing a disservice to the child. For example, it may be that the child has a skill or performance deficit regarding asking for help, maybe the child is frustrated because of problems he or she is having with peers, maybe the child has a learning disability in mathematics, or maybe the child is controlling the situation to get out of challenging work. It can be seen that there are many potential causes of the child's behavior, some of which are situationally specific and many which are distal to the situation. For each of these hypothesized functions, reducing the difficulty of work not only does not teach the child math or a generalizable skill; rather, it reinforces the escape behavior.

The next central purpose of behavioral assessment is to plan interventions. Interventions are planned in behavioral assessment based on the individualized needs of the client. In traditional assessment, a treatment plan may be devised based on a diagnosis. For example, if an individual was assessed and diagnosed as having depression, then the intervention would be to implement a manualized approach to cognitive-behavioral therapy for depression (Beutler, Clarkin, & Bongar, 2000). This approach has it advantages, but a strict aptitude-by-treatment approach is not flexible enough for children whose behaviors are associated with substantial developmental change and diverse influences from parents, peers, and teachers. Rather, behavioral assessment interventions are based on individual causes or functions of the child's target behaviors (Miller, Bagnato, Dunst, & Mangis, 2006). As an example, for one child exhibiting infrequent social initiation and flat affect, the function of the behavior may be parental discord, and the intervention is logically to intervene at the family-system level. For another child with the same symptoms, there may be a clear skill deficit in social skills that results in the child making depreciative self-statements. For this child the interventions may include direct social skills instruction and psychotherapy.

The final central purpose of behavioral assessment is progress monitoring (Cone, 2001). Evaluation of treatment has not been uniformly agreed upon as a purpose of behavioral assessment, because of debate about the equivalence of assessment and evaluation (Silva, 1993). However, because of the strong emphasis on direct observation of target behaviors, behavioral assessment is uniquely positioned as a procedure for monitoring response to intervention.

TYPES OF BEHAVIOR ASSESSED

Behavior assessment is not limited to motoric responses. Rather, behavior is conceptualized as multidimensional, including motor responses, verbal responses, covert responses (cognitions), and physiological responses (emotions) (Hersen, 1976; Shapiro, 1988). Another way to organize behaviors assessed in behavioral assessment is to use the categories behavioral, social, emotional, and cognitive. As discussed in the next section, sources of emotional and cognitive behavior are most often gathered from self- or other-report sources. However, there is some limitation to the ability of individuals to self-report, as they are often unaware of their feelings or cognitions (DuBois & Silverthorn, 2004; Gladwell, 2005), and this must be taken into consideration in the interpretation of rating scales. Interestingly, there are quite reliable methods of identifying overt behavior that is indicative of feeling and cognitive states (Gottman, Levenson, & Woodin, 2001; e.g., eye rolling as a sign of contemptuous thoughts or hand wringing as a sign of anxious feelings). A clinician skilled in behavioral assessment is able to make systematic observations of client behavior that point to covert behaviors such as thinking and feeling.

SOURCES OF ASSESSMENT DATA

The data required for a complete behavioral assessment emanate from a variety of settings and sources. Behavioral assessment is concerned with the child's functioning in a variety of settings such as home, school, and other social situations. Therefore, sources of data include the child, family members, school personnel, and peers. The referred child is often observed, interviewed, and asked to complete self-report behavior rating scales. "School personnel" refers here to the child's teacher, the principal, other teachers (such as the teacher on duty on the playground), volunteers, trainees, parents of other children in the school, or even the superintendent. Peers are those children with whom the referred child comes in contact. Peers include children in class, students in the lunchroom, a child in the neighborhood, or children at the bus stop. It may not be possible to get data directly from peers. Alternatively, reports about peers from the child or parents and observations of peers' interactions with the child in naturalistic settings are quite revealing. Family sources of data include parents, foster parents, guardians, siblings, blended family members, extended family, or even absent family members.

CONSIDERATIONS FOR CONDUCTING
BEHAVIORAL ASSESSMENT

Nomothetic versus Idiographic

Assessment practices can be thought of as falling along a nomothetic to idiographic continuum. Nomothetic approaches to assessment have come to mean comparison of scores with sample means, aggregation of data, and quantitative analysis. For example, administering a test of cognitive functioning and computing a standard score is nomothetic. Nomothetic practices are relevant to behavioral assessment particularly with regard to behavior rating scales, a core behavioral assessment procedure, in which subject responses are compared with various normative groups. For example, with the *Behavior Assessment System for Children— Second Edition* (Reynolds & Kamphaus, 2004) the clinician can compare a client's scores with a general sample, learning-disabled sample, or an attention-deficit/hyperactivity disorder sample. In contrast to nomothetic approaches, idiographic techniques include interview, direct observation, single-case design, and qualitative procedures. For example, making impressions from the observations made during a clinical interview is idiographic. Direct observation falls somewhere in between nomothetic and idiographic. On one hand, for classroom observations, the referred individual is compared with a peer, which involves some normative comparison. On the other hand, specific behaviors are noted because they have value as markers for underlying problems. Behavioral assessment tends to require a convergence of nomothetic and idiographic assessment approaches (Merrell, 2003).

Quantitative versus Qualitative Interpretation of Assessment Data

Behavioral assessment relies heavily on clinical judgment to determine a course of action. These judgments are based on both quantitative and qualitative data. Data from behavioral rating scales, structured interviews, and frequency counts are quantitative in nature and amenable to measuring change. Other purposes of quantitative data are identification of relative strengths and weaknesses and determination of diagnostic classifications. Qualitative interpretations, on the other hand, provide rich individualized information. As discussed in what follows, the process of direct observation should entail both quantitative summaries, such as percentage of time on task, and qualitative summaries, such as narrative descriptions of actions occurring in the situation.

Level of Inference

Behavioral assessment requires a higher level of inference than behavior analysis. Such a level of analysis is needed because the explanations of behavior are diverse under the behavioral assessment approach. In behavior analysis, it is thought that all of the information necessary is available in the immediate situation. It only requires that the clinician notice the salient aspects of the environment. With behavioral assessment the clinician must keep a wide range of information in mind while observing behavior to generate a useful conclusion. For example, while a child is being observed in the classroom, the clinician must think about the results of the semistructured parent interview and rating scales completed by the parent. Furthermore, after the observation sessions, the clinician must consider what was observed during an interview with the referred child. Finally, the results of the rating scales completed by the child are interpreted in the context of all other observations. Connections and conclusions are formed through sophisticated examination of what is observed from these multiple sources of data.

BEHAVIORAL ASSESSMENT METHODS

Behavioral assessment, as some may conclude, is not only about direct observation in a naturalistic setting. Direct observation can occur in a clinical setting and even during a norm-referenced testing session. Furthermore, to understand the functions of an individual's behavior, the clinician is also interested in what others say about the client's behavior and what the client says about his or her own behavior and the behavior of others. Hence, interviewing and behavior rating scales are important to behavioral assessment. Behavioral assessment methods range from direct to indirect. The most direct is to observe an individual in the naturalistic setting. Indirect methods of behavioral assessment would include asking a child's parent to complete a behavior checklist. Methods of behavioral assessment most often used with children are direct observation, behavior rating scales, and interviewing (Merrell, 2003). Because interviewing and behavior rating scales are covered in other chapters in this volume, they are described only briefly here, and particular attention is given to the process of direct observation.

STRUCTURED INTERVIEWS

Interviewing children and their parents requires a high level of skill on the part of the clinician. Unlike observation and rating scale assessment, interviews require well-developed interpersonal, communication, and thinking-on-your-feet skills. These skills can only be developed through supervised experience and diligent self-evaluation. Interviews are conducted to gather information about the problem; to gather a developmental history; to identify proximal, distal, physiological, and intrapsychic factors associated with the problem behavior; to educate the client and his or her family; and to make observations about the client and the client's interactions with parents. For further information, Merrell (2003) provides an excellent introduction to interviewing techniques. Structured and semistructured interview protocols provide standard questions and a standard sequence for the interview. They have the advantage of providing the structure needed to minimize overlooking important background, behavioral, or interpersonal information. There are several types of structured interviews, such as the *Kiddie Schedule for Affective Disorders and Schizophrenia for School-age Children* (K-SADS; Ambrosini, 2000; Puig-Antich & Chambers, 1978) and the *Diagnostic Interview for Children and Adolescents–Fourth Edition* (DISC-IV; Reich, Welner, & Herjanic, 1997). As can be seen from the titles, these structured interviews have a strong association with diagnosis. For an alternative, Sattler (1998) provides an exhaustive book on structured and semistructured interviews that are designed for numerous types of referral concerns and situations.

BEHAVIOR RATING SCALES

Behavior rating scales augment behavioral assessment by providing clinicians with responses to a standard set of questions with a standard set of response options. These responses are summated and compared with a normative sample for interpretation. A significant difference between rating scales and other behavioral assessment procedures is that they provide indirect assessments of perceptions of behavior (Merrell, 2003). Data from rating scales tend to be interpreted in relation to other assessment data but have been shown to provide evidence-based information about functional impairment (Winters, Collett, & Myers, 2005).

DIRECT OBSERVATION

Observation is the *sine qua non* of behavioral assessment. Clinicians make observations from the moment of meeting a child. Observations are made of the child's gender, height, weight, cleanliness, ethnicity, and interpersonal style. In most cases, one begins to form judgments about a child within seconds of seeing her or him for the first time. Although there is emerging evidence that an expert may be able to make highly reliable conclusions based on a brief observation (Gladwell, 2005), for the purposes of behavioral assessment a more systematic and integrative approach is called for. Direct observation allows the clinician to operationalize problematic behaviors, conduct an observation based on these operational definitions, and use this information to develop interventions (Merrell, 2003). Direct observation is the only form of assessment that simultaneously considers the child's behavior and his or her environmental context (Saudargas & Lentz, 1986) and can therefore be used to resolve any conflicting data from other sources (Reynolds & Kamphaus, 2004). Moreover, direct observation by a clinician is not subject to the same biases that may decrease the validity of rating scales completed by family members or other professionals.

To conduct a direct observation the clinician must consider a wide variety of behaviors assessed across a number of settings and times. In school settings, it is further necessary to compare the referred child with a similar peer in the setting where the referred child is being observed. An example observation form is provided in Figure 8–1. Other commercially available direct observation forms are discussed in the following sections. This form is freely reproducible from http://www.mfba.net/behobsform.pdf. In the following, the procedure for conducting a direct observation of a child in a school classroom, with the use of the form in Figure 8–1, is described.

First the observer documents basic data, such as the name of the child being observed, the context of the observation, and the times of day the observation started and ended. On the

Classroom Observation Record

Date: 05-15-05

Name: John

Age: 14 years old   Grade: 8th

Teacher: Mr. Jones

Times: 8:42 a.m. - 9:02 a.m.

Behavior:

O= OnTask   V= Verbal Off Task

M= Motor Off Task   P= Passive Off Task

Anecdotal Observations:

John walked into class with a group and mocked a female peer in response to other boys mocking her. John was unsure of what to do after she challenged his behavior.

	GC	Peer	Referred	Task Description/Behavior
1	L	O	V	Many students chatting with
2		O	V	peers
3		O	O	Teacher raises voice - John
4		O	O	complies
5		O	P	Staring at peers
6		O	O	
7		O	O	
8		O	O	Answers question, answer
9		O	O	was wrong
10		O	V	Others start talking, John
11		O	V	finds someone to talk to
12		O	O	
13		O	O	
14		O	O	
15		O	V	Several peers off task, he
16		O	V	gets off task (modeling)
17		O	V	Persists with off task despite
18		O	O	others back on task
19		O	O	
20		O	P	Looking at the floor

(Circle Last Interval Observed) 20

Interval Length: 1 minute

Partial   [Time Sample]

Whole   Event/Interval

	Counts		
Counts	20	11	
Intervals	20	20	
Total	100	55	**% On-Task**

Grouping Codes (GC)
L=Large Group
S=Small Group
O=One-to-One
I=Independent
F=Free Time

Summary:
John was modeling other's behavior. He did not seem to take the lead in class disruptions. His work space was disorganized and he was not able to use his materials to help answer a question. He appeared to make contact with peers, but they didn't attempt to interact with him.

FIGURE 8–1. Classroom observation record.

right side of the form there are two columns with 20 rows. This is where observations are recorded. There are two columns in which to record observations of the referred child and a comparison peer. Each row is a period of time, usually 1 minute or 30 seconds. To the right of the two columns there are lines for anecdotal notes about each time period. On the left side of the form there are codes for different types of observations and space for more general anecdotal observations. At the bottom left side there are different methods of behavioral observation that can be used with this form. At the bottom right is an area for total observations and codes for the different types of instructional settings that may be observed. Finally, at the bottom is space for summary statements. Those with experience conducting behavioral observations may note that this form has a lot of space for anecdotal reporting. Copious anecdotal comments are consistent with the notion that behavioral assessment is concerned with both quantitative and qualitative data.

Upon entering the classroom setting, the observer quietly sits in the back of the classroom and identifies the referred student and then a peer for comparison observation. The peer should be of similar gender, ethnicity, and seating placement in the room. That is, if the referred child is sitting in front of the classroom then the comparison peer should be sitting toward the front of the classroom. The goal is to find a peer that is most like the referred peer to reduce differences that may account for discrepancies between the students' behaviors.

Below the Starting Times line is a list of codes that are shorthand for documenting observations. There are four codes provided: O for on-task, V for verbal off-task, M for motor off-task, and P for passive off-task. Verbal off-task includes talking to neighbors, distracting verbalizations, and any noises made with the mouth. Motor off-task includes fidgeting, playing with items on the desk, getting out of one's seat, and turning around in the seat. Passive off-task includes daydreaming or lack of response to classroom stimuli. There is space available to add additional codes. It is particularly helpful to add additional codes when there is a behavior that is frequent and relatively discrete. For example, if there is a particular motor off-task behavior, such as rooting through a notebook, a special code such as N for notebook can be made to code each observation of the behavior. The observer then enters codes into the two columns on the right of the form and anecdotal observations about that time period on the line next to the time interval. In the section called Anecdotal Observations, observations that are not directly related to a specific interval of time should be recorded. For example, the observation that in general the teacher tends not to give reinforcement for correct answers, but is obviously negative toward children for wrong answers, should be documented in this section, as it may have a bearing on the referred child's behavior.

The observation form also includes a space to note the interval length for the observation. It is profitable to use 30- or 60-second intervals for a total observation period of 10 or 20 minutes, respectively. For the 30-second interval, note the sweeping second hand on the classroom clock. When the second hand crosses the 12 on the clock, the observer makes an observation of the peer and then the referred child and notes any specific observations on the line to the right. When the second hand crosses the 6, the observer makes another observation of the children, and so on for 20 intervals. Taking momentary observations is a method of observation called *time sampling*. It allows the observer to observe the whole classroom during the interval, to take qualitative notes on anecdotal observations, as well as make quantitative, systematic observations of the referred child and peer. The process is called time sampling because the child's behavior is sampled only momentarily at set time intervals.

Just below the Length of Interval blank there are four types of observations listed, one of which is time sampling. The other coding methods are partial interval, whole interval, and event/interval. *Partial interval* coding is used to identify behavior that occurs for part of an interval. For example, if the interval is 30 seconds and there is motor off-task behavior for 10 seconds in a particular interval, that interval would receive an M code for motor off-task. *Whole interval coding* is slightly different from partial interval coding. For whole interval coding a code is noted only when the occurrence of the behavior spans the whole interval. Whole interval coding is useful for behaviors that persist for long periods of time and can be summarized in terms of duration by a count of the number of intervals the behavior spanned. The fourth type of coding procedure is called *event/interval* for frequency coding. In *frequency coding* a code is awarded each time a behavior occurs. With this procedure, the frequency of behavior is recorded within each observation interval. For example, during observation of self-injurious behavior, such as hair pulling, a special behavior code could be designated for hair pulling, such as H. Each time the child pulls his or her hair the letter H is entered into the box of the current interval. So if in the second interval the child pulls his or her hair three times, there will be three H's in the box. This is a helpful method for tracking behavior because it allows one to identify increases or decreases in discrete behaviors associated with changes in activities in the classroom.

Other types of observation coding that are not included on the form are called *duration* and *latency*. *Duration coding* is much like whole interval coding, but rather than focus on the number of intervals the behavior spans, the observer times the behavior from start to finish. *Latency coding* is used to determine the time between a cue and the beginning of the behavior. A simple example is measuring the time it takes a child to act following a teacher's request, such as to take out a pencil. More subtle examples include the latency of a child to become engaged in a classroom disruption or to respond to a cue to engage in play with a peer.

For each interval it is important to know whether the activity is in a large group, small group, one-to-one, independent activity, or free time. Group activity is recorded in the column called GC (Grouping Code). Grouping codes are listed at the bottom right of the form. If the observation began in a large group setting, the observer would write a capital L in the GC column for interval 1. Then if in interval 11 there is a transition to small group activity, the observer would mark the letter S in the GC column for interval 11. It is then possible to examine differences in behavior across different classroom groupings. It is not necessary to note the grouping code for each observation; rather, simply indicate the grouping code when transitions occur. In this way it is possible to see the impact transitions have on the child's behavior.

At the end of the observation period the observer computes the referred child's and peer's overall performance. It is traditional to summarize the behavior in the positive, that is, percentage of time on-task. So for the referred child the observer sums all of the intervals marked as on-task and divides by 20 (number of intervals observed), then multiplies by 100. It is appropriate at times to observe only for 10 intervals or 15 intervals, given time demands. To compute a percentage on-task for these shorter observations, the observer simply divides the total number of on-task counts by the total number of intervals observed and multiplies by 100. The observer computes the percentage on-task for both the referred child and the peer. Quantitative summaries facilitate quick comparison of time on-task between the referred child and the peer. After completing all other sections of the classroom observation record, the observer writes a summary of impressions at the bottom of the page.

The above classroom observation process is just one of many direct observation systems. For comprehensive coverage of direct observation approaches, refer to Volpe and McConaughy (2005). In the following section published direct observation systems are discussed.

PUBLISHED DIRECT OBSERVATION ASSESSMENT FORMS

There are several behavioral assessment batteries that include direct observation forms to complement the normative batteries. The following provides a brief description of popular published observation systems. The *Behavior Assessment System for Children, Second Edition, Student Observation System* (BASC–2 SOS; Reynolds & Kamphaus, 2004), was designed for observations of children with significant behavioral or emotional problems that interfere with academic performance. Behaviors are assessed in both adaptive and maladaptive categories. Adaptive categories include Response to Teacher/Lesson, Peer Interaction, Work on School Subjects, and Transition Movement. Problem behavior categories include Inappropriate Movement, Inattention, Inappropriate Vocalization, Somatization, Repetitive Motor Movements, Aggression, Self-Injurious Behavior, Inappropriate Sexual Behavior, and Bowel/Bladder Problems.

There are three components to the SOS. The first is the Behavior Key and Checklist. It provides sample behaviors in each of the adaptive and problematic behavior categories that can be referenced throughout the observation session. At the conclusion of the 15-minute session the observer uses this list to note behavior frequencies (e.g., not observed, sometimes, and frequent). Behaviors on this list are ordered from most frequent to least frequent, as noted by school psychologists surveyed for development of the SOS (Reynolds & Kamphaus, 2004). There is also a space to indicate whether a behavior was disruptive to others during the observation session. The second component of the SOS is a time sample of behavior. The observer uses a 30-second interval and indicates the presence or absence of adaptive and problematic behaviors at the conclusion of the interval. The third and final part of the SOS is the Teacher's Interaction with Student section. This section provides the observer with a place to note specifics about teacher/child interactions and classroom environment. The observer can note what techniques for changing behavior and other classroom characteristics may alter or sustain a child's behavior. This section is designed to facilitate intervention planning (Reynolds & Kamphaus, 2004).

The SOS is available in both paper-pencil and electronic (BASC Portable Observation Program) format with a built-in timer to facilitate accurate recording of behavior in all settings. Test authors suggest that the SOS be used in the diagnostic, treatment-planning, and progress-monitoring stages of treatment. It is designed to be used by anyone who may be part of the treatment or consultative team, including teachers, counselors, and psychologists. Data from the SOS can be used to confirm or dispute data obtained from other reporters (Reynolds & Kamphaus, 2004).

By combining multiple behavioral assessment techniques into a single observation sessions, the BASC–2 SOS provides a comprehensive observation of the referred child within the classroom setting. One weakness of the system is that the form does not have multiple spaces to accommodate data for a comparison student. There is enough space on the time-sample portion of the form to make multiple rows of marks, but practitioners will need to use some means to determine which marks are being used to describe each student. In the Behavior Key and Checklist, there is no space for comparison peer data.

The *Achenbach System of Empirically Based Assessment* (ASEBA; Achenbach & Rescorla, 2001) is another published assessment system that contains a direct observation form. In fact, the ASEBA contains both a Direct Observation Form (DOF) and Test Observation Form (TOF). The DOF is designed for a 10-minute observation session. The form contains a combination of observation techniques utilizing both rating scales for 96 specific behaviors and 1-minute interval recording of on/off-task behaviors. Like the BASC–2 SOS, computer software is available to assist with scoring. Unlike the BASC–2 SOS, the DOF provides space for recording behaviors of two comparison peers. The DOF is also a normed measure with referred and nonreferred samples for comparison (Achenbach & Rescorla, 2001). Both of these options facilitate better interpretation of observation data. Scores are interpreted in the context of multiple scales, including empirically derived syndromes, on-task behavior, Internalizing, Externalizing, and Total Problems.

The Test Observation Form (McConaughy & Achenbach, 2004) is a direct observation tool designed to be used during an individual testing session. It is a normed instrument with samples of both referred and nonreferred children. Norms are gender-specific. Scores are compared with empirically derived syndromes, including Anxious, Oppositional, Withdrawn/Depressed, and others to assist with diagnostic conclusions.

COMPUTER APPLICATIONS

Computer technology is gradually infiltrating all aspects of the field of psychology. Many tasks that were previously completed with paper and pencil are now computerized. These include statistical calculations, stimulus presentation for research, and test score conversion. The next logical step in this progression is to utilize computer software to simplify the collection of behavioral data for clinical purposes. Because paper-and-pencil recording during observation sessions can be distracting to the observer, computer-based recording and analysis tools are being developed to allow the observer to spend more energy focusing on accurate and objective observations and less energy on recording. These computer-based systems are noted to improve reliability and accuracy of recording. They also provide a more efficient method of data analysis and graphing (Kahng & Iwata, 1998). Many computer-based observation systems are now available with a wide variety of features. Some representative computer-based systems are described in the following section.

One available observation system is the *Behavioral Evaluation Strategy and Taxonomy* (BEST) software developed by Educational Consulting Incorporated (Sharpe & Koperwas, 1999). This system, available for both PC and handheld systems, combines data collection and analysis software (Sidener, Shabani, & Carr, 2004). Observers program a configuration file for up to 36 behaviors to be recorded via different keys on the keyboard. An event recorder screen serves as a reminder for how the keyboard is programmed to record responses (Sidener et al., 2004). Types of data that can be recorded include frequency, duration, interval, time sample, latency, interresponse time, and discrete trial (Kahng & Iwata, 1998). Qualitative data can also be entered through a notes feature. Errors in recording can be corrected while the observation session is occurring. Frequency and duration of selected behaviors can be monitored as the session is progressing (Sidener et al., 2004). The included scoring program allows for analysis of multiple observation data files together. Available analyses include qualitative summary, hierarchical ranking of frequencies and duration, sequential analysis, and tables and graphs. Interobserver agreement can also be analyzed.

Another available software program is the *Ecobehavioral Assessment System Software* (EBASS; Greenwood, Carta, Kamps, Terry, & Delquadri, 1994). This system was designed for classroom observation based on feedback about observation instruments from school psychologists. Unlike BEST, EBASS is preprogrammed with existing, empirically supported observation systems for classroom use. The observer simply chooses one of three available systems and selects behaviors that apply to the current observation. The observation systems include the Ecobehavioral System for Complex Analysis of Preschool Environments

(ESCAPE), Code for Instructional Structure and Student Academic Response (CISSAR), and Mainstream CISSAR for students with disabilities who are included in regular education. The system allows for interval data to be collected for more than 100 different responses (Kahng & Iwata, 1998). The interval time is set and a sound can be used to signify a 10-, 15-, or 20-second interval. Data are entered through one of four keyboard keys, and a note feature is also available for observation notes. Analyses are also included for this program. They include percentage of intervals, conditional probabilities, mean, range, and frequency distributions (Kahng & Iwata, 1998). Similar to BEST, interobserver agreement can also be assessed. Data can be stored or graphed and files can be read by SPSS statistical software for further analysis. An additional feature available for EBASS is an included training program complete with a video to train observers to gather reliable data in the preprogrammed observation systems. This system requires a PC or Mac (with emulator) operating system and minimal memory requirements.

In contrast to BEST and EBASS, EthoLog is a freeware program available for observation data collection. It is a visual basic program that runs on PC operating systems. The observer programs the behaviors and the associated key code for data entry, with a keyboard or mouse. Data can be entered as an isolated occurrence or as an occurrence with duration, which are called "instant events" and "state events," respectively, by the software author (Ottoni, 2000). A sound can be programmed as a reminder for interval recording. Similar to BEST and EBASS, notes can be appended to the output file as qualitative data. Analysis is limited in this program; only sequential analysis of instant events is available. However, data can be exported to word processor or spreadsheet programs if further analysis is required (Ottoni, 2000).

Based on the available features of these programs, it is evident that direct observation data can now be more easily collected and analyzed. Computer software allows clinicians to quickly record and organize both qualitative and quantitative data for a variety of referral concerns. With the addition of software that is available for handheld systems, observers can continue to be discrete in their observations while reaping the benefits of computer data collection.

SEARCH STRATEGIES IN DIRECT OBSERVATION

Though behavioral assessment techniques can be used with any theoretical orientation, the thought processes and observation techniques utilized by the clinician during behavioral assessment may lead to broader or more narrow conclusions, depending on one's theoretical orientation. The theoretical orientation of the observer can act as a filter through which information is passed when he or she is forming, confirming, or refuting hypotheses. Specific theoretical orientations influence the clinician to focus on some information while deemphasizing information that clinicians of a different orientation may determine to be important. When conducting behavioral assessment, it is imperative that clinicians are aware of the assumptions they are using to gather and integrate information about a client.

Godoy and Gavino (2003) illustrate these variations in clinical judgment by observing the process of information gathering for hypothesis testing. Based on a contingency table created to categorize information gathered by clinicians, they suggest possible search strategies that are utilized when clinicians are presented with case information. These include (1) behavior-oriented strategy, (2) stimulus-oriented strategy, and (3) complex strategy. The behavior-oriented search strategy is used when the clinician's attention is focused on what happens when a specific behavior occurs. This strategy considers problem behaviors but does not include behaviors that are not considered problematic. The stimulus-oriented strategy is used when a clinician focuses on behavior while a given stimulus is present. This neglects behaviors that result from other stimuli. The complex strategy is simultaneously observing a stimulus when a specific behavior is present and observing behavior when a specific stimulus is present (Godoy & Gavino, 2003). It is obvious that using only one of the above search strategies may lead to a clinician neglecting important information that may be useful to a case. Despite this fact, only 8% of participating clinicians in the Godoy and Gavino (2003) study comprehensively utilized more than one search strategy.

In addition to not using multiple search strategies for comprehensive information gathering, the type of hypothesis tested appears to influence the type of information gathered. Godoy and Gavino (2003) found that if clinicians were testing a hypothesis about a functionally relevant antecedent stimulus, a stimulus-oriented search strategy was used most often. If the clinician was testing a hypothesis about a reinforcing stimulus, the behavior-oriented strategy was used more frequently. Based on these results, it appears that the type of hypothesis and search strategy used greatly influence the judgments made about a case.

During any given observation session, the clinician is provided with a wealth of information. What information the clinician chooses to focus on influences conclusions about the client's behavior made from the observation session. The clinician may focus on the child's behavior, the child's interactions with others, the environment, or any other aspect of the situation. Clinicians should utilize metacognitive processes to monitor the influence of their theoretical orientation on their information gathering and hypothesis testing in order to prevent neglect of important information in behavioral assessment.

ASSESSMENT OF FUNCTION

A critical step in behavioral assessment is to generate hypotheses about the cause or function of the target behavior. Functions of behavior can be defined as "important, controllable, causal functional relationships applicable to a specific set of target behaviors for an individual client" (Haynes & O'Brien, 1990, p. 654). Therefore, there are three characteristics that a potential function of a target behavior must meet. The first characteristic is that a functional relationship must be *important* or not trivial. Identifying and intervening on the most important functions results in more positive and generalized outcomes. The second characteristic is *controllable*, which means that there is a potential through intervention to change the function of the behavior. The final characteristic is *causal*. There must be a causal link between the target behavior and identified determinants. Although *cause* has been used synonymously with *function*, Haynes and O'Brien (1990) clarify that the cause must also be important and controllable to warrant consideration as a function of the target behavior.

Information about the function is gathered through the same assessment approaches described above. That is, while assessing the target behavior, the clinician is also attempting to identify potential determinants of the behavior. Under the assumption of situational specificity, the immediate environment is examined for potential functions of behavior. These include (1) positive reinforcement or obtaining something and (2) negative reinforcement or escaping/avoiding something (Artesani, 2001). For each of these the client may be seeking or avoiding internal stimulation, such as hunger, or external stimulation, such as attention.

Walker and Sprague (1999) argued that the situationally specific functions of behavior should be extended to include nonsituational risk factors such as family dysfunction, emotional dysregulation, and hostile attitudes toward schooling. Miller and colleagues (1998) made a similar argument and identified eight classes of functions of behavior. They are (1) *Affect Regulation/Emotional Reactivity*, including emotional factors, anxiety, depression, anger, and poor self-concept; (2) *Cognitive Distortion*, including distorted thoughts, inaccurate attributions, negative self-statements, and erroneous interpretations; (3) *Reinforcement*, including environmental triggers and payoffs; (4) *Modeling*, including social learning, degree to which behavior is copied, who the behavior is copied from, and why it is being copied; (5) *Family Issues*, including family systems issues, parents, siblings, and extended family; (6) *Physiological/Constitutional*, including physiological and/or personality characteristics, developmental disabilities, or temperament; (7) *Communicate Need*, including functional communication, what the student is trying to say through the behavior; and (8) *Curriculum/Instruction*, including curriculum and educational environment in general and in which the behavior is seen. Each of these areas should be assessed through the various techniques of behavioral assessment to determine if any or several are accounting for the target behaviors.

INTEGRATION AND INTERPRETATION OF ASSESSMENT DATA

Behavioral assessment involves gathering data from a broad range of sources and settings. Furthermore, the problems faced by children are multidimensional and complex. Finally, causes and target behaviors do not necessarily have an obvious one-to-one relationship with each other. These characteristics of behavioral assessment make interpretation a daunting task (Huberty, 2003). In addition, behavioral assessment can be thought of as part of a broader assessment plan that may include measures of cognitive, academic, personality, or neuropsychological functioning.

To make the process of integrating and interpreting assessment data manageable, a stepwise process can be followed. The process proceeds from divergent to convergent thinking within each assessment modality and then proceeds to integration of all assessment modalities (Hughes & Morine, 2005). For example, start with the direct observation results. The task first is (1) to find patterns and (2) to identify inconsistencies among the information sources. When hypotheses about consistencies and discrepancies are being formulated, initial attempts should be divergent. That is, the clinician should be open-minded, considering all possible explanations. This process is repeated with the interview data, behavioral rating data, and, if available, the norm-referenced test results. After each of the assessment modalities has been examined, two assessment modalities are compared. The clinician asks, "Are the consistencies and discrepancies among the two modalities the same or different? Do the two modalities provide any similar interpretations? What revisions to the interpretations are necessary to accommodate the data from both modalities?" This process continues until all assessment data have been examined together. From this process, convergence will emerge in which similar causes or functions of behavior are identified across different assessment modalities.

PROGRESS MONITORING

Direct observation data should be taken at multiple points during the assessment and intervention process. Using direct observation during initial assessment provides a contextual understanding of a child's behavior. Observation after implementation of an intervention allows the clinician to monitor both the child's response to the intervention and the integrity of the intervention implementation. Subsequent observations can be used for progress monitoring to ensure that the intervention is having the desired affect.

In the stage of progress monitoring, it is advantageous for the clinician to employ techniques adapted from single-subject research design to graph and analyze assessment data. Though single-subject research designs are often thought to be a strictly behavioral technique, they can be applied to many situations and theories for the purpose of progress monitoring (Hayes, 1981). Single-subject research designs allow the clinician to track progress and provide clear evidence of an intervention's effectiveness or a client's improvement. In this context, the initial observation data serve as baseline information. From this baseline information, goals for improvement are set. A graph is then constructed that contains the baseline measure and the established goal for improvement. With time designated by the x axis and some measure of behavior by the y axis, an aim line is drawn from the baseline to the goal. This aim line is used in combination with observation after the intervention is implemented. Each observation is then charted and compared with the aim line. If the observation data are above the aim line, then the child is improving faster than expected to meet the goal. If the child's behavior is graphed below the line, then the child is not improving at the needed rate to reach the goal. In either of these cases, the goal should be evaluated for appropriateness and the intervention should be evaluated for appropriateness and integrity of implementation. Using more elaborate single-subject designs, multiple interventions can be tested to determine which is most effective (Elliot, Witt, Kratochwill, & Stoiber, 2002). In each case it is the clinician's responsibility, based on direct observation and all other collected data, to determine the best single-subject design to ensure that the most empirically validated and appropriate intervention is implemented and monitored.

CASE EXAMPLE

John is a 14-year-old boy in eighth grade, referred for assessment because of chronic academic failure and escalating disruptive behavior across school settings. With regard to academic functioning, records indicate a long-standing mathematics learning disability. He exhibits general academic failure, which started around third and fourth grade. John's eighth-grade discipline record is extensive. He appears to be in a cycle of disrupting various settings (classrooms, lunchroom), being assigned detention, missing detention, and then being assigned more detention. He appears to miss both afterschool and lunch detentions. If he does attend detention he tends to receive infractions for disrupting the detention setting as well. By January and February infractions appeared more serious or brazen, including insubordination, insolence, and abusive language. By the end of the year he stopped attending assigned detentions.

Results of the structured interview with John indicate he dislikes school so much that he does not want to go and that his level of effort toward schoolwork varies. He sometimes feels "down," irritable, and like a failure. John reports having close friends he can confide in and being able to communicate with his mother and father, despite mild conflicts. He reports often making careless mistakes, having difficulty getting organized, and finishing what he starts. He often has difficulty concentrating on one thing for very long, is often easily distracted, tends to forget what he is supposed to do, and loses personal belongings. Parent and teacher interview data indicate that John tends to be overreactive to feedback and conflicts tend to quickly escalate into quite disruptive behavior.

Norm-referenced tests, including the Woodcock-Johnson III Tests of Cognitive Abilities (WJ III CA), Woodcock-Johnson III Tests of Achievement (WJ III A), Delis-Kaplan Executive Function System (D-KEFS), and the Conners' Continuous Performance Test (CCPT), indicate that John has average intelligence but has a very slow processing speed and poor sustained attention. Test results are summarized in Table 8.1. He has average reading

TABLE 8.1.

Summary of Test Results

Woodcock-Johnson III Tests of Cognitive Abilities

Composite scores	Standard scores (M = 100, SD = 15)
Global intellectual ability (1–7)	95
Verbal ability (1)	94
Thinking ability (2–5)	103
Cognitive efficiency (6, 7)	82
Processing speed	78
Phonemic awareness	98
Working memory	100

Subtest scores	
1. Verbal comprehension	94
2. Visual-auditory learning	103
3. Spatial relations	107
4. Sound blending	87
5. Concept formation	112
6. Visual matching	75
7. Numbers reversed	94
Incomplete words	117
Auditory working memory	109
Decision speed	87

Woodcock-Johnson III Tests of Achievement

Composite scores	Standard scores (M = 100, SD = 15)	Grade equivalent
Broad reading (1, 2, 9)	91	6.7
Broad mathematics (5, 6, 10)	77	4.7
Math calculation skills (5, 6)	65	3.7
Academic skills (1, 5, 7)	89	6.3
Academic applications (9, 10, 11)	90	6.5

Subtest scores		
1. Letter-word identification	98	8.5
2. Reading fluency	85	5.4
5. Calculation	73	4.1
6. Math fluency	58	2.6
7. Spelling	96	7.1
9. Passage comprehension	96	7.7

(continued)

TABLE 8.1. (*Continued*)

Subtest scores	Standard scores ($M = 100$, $SD = 15$)	Grade equivalent
10. Applied problems	91	6.4
11. Writing samples	84	4.8

D-KEFS

Trail Making Test

Condition scores	Scaled scores ($M = 10$, $SD = 3$)
Condition 1: Visual scanning	12
Condition 2: Number sequencing	12
Condition 3: Letter sequencing	8
Condition 4: Number-letter switching	11
Condition 5: Motor speed	12

Verbal Fluency Test

Condition scores

Letter fluency	12
Category fluency	16
Category switching: correct responses	12
Category switching: switching accuracy	7

Contrast measures

Letter fluency vs. category fluency	12
Category switching vs. category fluency	16

Color-Word Interference Test

Condition scores

Condition 1: Color naming	5
Condition 2: Word naming	8
Condition 3: Inhibition	7
Condition 4: Inhibition/switching	11
Condition 5: Combined naming & reading	7

Tower Test

Condition scores

Total achievement score	9
Mean first move time	10

Conners' Continuous Performance Test

Measure	T scores ($M = 50$, $SD = 10$)
Omissions	48
Comissions	54

(*continued*)

TABLE 8.1. (*Continued*)

Measure	T scores (M = 50, SD = 10)
Hit RT	56
Hit RT std. error	59
Variability	52
Detectability (d')	61
Perseverations	49
Hit RT block change	68
Hit SE block change	62

Behavior Rating Inventory of Executive Function

	T score (M = 50, SD = 10)		
Composite scores	Parent	Teacher 1	Teacher 2
Behavior Regulation Index (BRI)	64	85	79
Metacognition Index (MI)	72	92	100
Global Executive Composite (GEC)	71	95	97
BRI subtest scores			
Inhibit	60	83	83
Shift	47	88	79
Emotional control	75	76	66
MI subtest scores			
Initiate	73	84	84
Working memory	71	101	97
Plan/organize	72	86	98
Organization of materials	69	84	116
Monitor	62	79	82

Behavior Assessment System for Children–Second Edition

	T score (M = 50, SD = 10)		
Composite	Parent	Teacher 1	Teacher 2
Externalizing problems	49	61	57
Internalizing problems	54	68	66
School problems		66	64
Behavioral symptoms index	49	61	66
Adaptive skills	43	41	34
Scale			
Hyperactivity	43	63	61
Aggression	48	54	55
Conduct problems	55	63	55
Anxiety	50	69	58

(*continued*)

TABLE 8.1. (*Continued*)

Scale	T score (M = 50, SD = 10)		
	Parent	*Teacher 1*	*Teacher 2*
Depression	59	53	75
Somatization	51	72	56
Atypicality	44	70	61
Withdrawal	47	51	62
Attention problems	56	66	64
Learning problems		63	61
Adaptability	39	45	37
Social skills	45	48	34
Leadership	51	43	35
Activities of daily living	38		
Study skills		38	36
Functional communication	45	38	38

Minnesota Multiphasic Personality Inventory–Adolescent

T score (M = 50, SD = 10)

Basic	T score	Content	T score
F	44	Anxiety	41
L	41	Obsessiveness	38
K	51	Depression	44
Hs	40	Health concerns	39
D	45	Alienation	42
Hy	46	Bizarre mentation	37
Pd	45	Anger	54
Mf	42	Cynicism	47
Pa	40	Conduct problems	57
Pt	42	Low self-esteem	48
Sc	40	Low aspirations	49
Ma	35	Social discomfort	38
Si	46	Family problems	50
		School problems	78
		Negative treatment indication	45

BarOn EQi: YV

Scale	Standard score (M = 100, SD = 15)
Intrapersonal	92
Interpersonal	77
Stress management	85
Adaptability	73
Total EQ	86
General mood	85
Positive impression	96

comprehension, but his reading fluency is low. There is a convergence of data indicating that any task requiring fast cognitive processing is difficult for him. Mathematics, as suggested from the record review, is low. On the *Minnesota Multiphasic Personality Inventory–Adolescent* (MMPI-A) basic scales, which assess emotional and personality problems such as depression, anxiety, paranoia, and antisocial personality, his responses show no significant problems. The MMPI-A Content and Supplementary scales indicate quite significant school problems and a propensity toward substance abuse as a coping technique.

Parent and teacher ratings on the *Behavior Rating Inventory of Executive Function* (BRIEF) show a convergence of concern about poor initiation, planning, and organization. On the *Behavior Assessment System for Children–Second Edition* (BASC–2) his teachers consistently report inattentive, overactive, impulsive, uncooperative, withdrawn, and inappropriate (nonaggressive) behaviors at school. On the BASC–2 his mother only reports difficulty adapting to change. On the *BarOn Emotional Quotient Inventory: Youth Version* (BarOn EQ-I: YV), a self-report rating scale of emotional intelligence, John appears to experience moderate dysphoria, which would be expected for an individual who has normal intrapersonal emotional intelligence and experiences repeated failure. He appears to have very poorly developed interpersonal emotional intelligence, which can lead an individual to act in various socially inappropriate ways to gain affiliation with peers. John also lacks appropriate skills for coping with academic and social expectations or adapting to change. His primary coping technique is oppositional behavior.

During a classroom observation, John was observed as having more off-task behaviors than another male student who was identified as typical. The observation record is reproduced in Figure 8–1. During the 20-minute time-sample observation, the comparison student was on-task 100% of the time, and John was on-task 55% percent of the time. The primary problem behavior was talking to peers at inappropriate times, and the secondary problem behavior was inattention. Immediately before the inappropriate talking occurred, other peers were engaging in the same behaviors. This suggests that John models the behavior of his peers. Anecdotal observations indicate that John was disorganized and was unable to efficiently use materials, such as a book and his notes, to respond to the teacher's questions. Furthermore, he appeared awkward in his interactions with peers before class started. According to John's teacher, his behavior during the observation was typical for him.

Function of Behavior

John exhibits three primary functions of his disruptive behavior. First, he is not able to meet the demands of the curriculum and probably has not been able to for years. Poor processing speed and sustained attention, accompanied by poor initiation, planning, and organization, interfere with his ability to complete assignments, particularly more complicated, multistep assignments typically found in middle and high school. Second, because of poor interpersonal intelligence and social skills he models the disruptive behavior of others. Furthermore, he has poor insight into when to stop the inappropriate behavior. For example, on the classroom observation form it is noted that he models peers' behavior but perseverates once the rest of the class has stopped and gained control. Finally, John lacks appropriate skills for coping with academic and social expectations or adapting to change. His primary coping technique is oppositional behavior, which likely provides him with a sense of control over a school environment in which he is unable to succeed. It is clear that the consequence of detentions is ineffective and actually seems to provide him with an additional level of control through his success at refusing to attend.

Recommendations

Various interventions are recommended for the first function of his behavior, including direct instruction in organization; instruction in breaking tasks into smaller parts to assist with initiation; modification of assignments that have a high time demand; and coaching from a special education teacher on improving mathematics, processing speed, and sustained attention.

Regarding the second function of the problem behavior, including poor interpersonal emotional intelligence, social skills, coping, and adaptability, it is recommended that he receive weekly individual counseling. Specific targets for counseling include improving insight and acceptance regarding his lack of ability in the above-named areas; reality testing in social situations; social problem solving, including generating a range of alternative and acceptable behaviors with peers; increased insight into the benefits of appropriate social behavior; direct instruction and practice on techniques to remain calm in stressful situations; and increased fluency in coping with unexpected changes in the environment.

Regarding the final function of his behavior, control of his educational environment, John would benefit from a behavioral intervention plan implemented in the short run. It is thought that improvements in the two previous functions will replace his need to take control of the educational environment and, therefore, mitigate the need for an overt reinforcement plan in the long run. A response-cost system related to his extracurricular activities is not recommended, because those activities, including sports, may be a source of school-related success. However, a more proactive, classroom-based approach is indicated. John's classrooms should have clear behavioral expectations for all students and predictable routines and habits, the teacher should frequently scan the classroom and provide supportive feedback to students, and all students should be involved in the lessons throughout the class period. Furthermore, when giving John feedback, the teachers should remain calm, treat John with respect, have a hierarchy of mild consequences, and establish a concurrent plan to reinforce success. Reinforcements that may be effective for an individual in secondary school include complementing the student in front of others, providing tickets to school activities, or coupons to rent a movie or video game.

Commentary on the Case Study

The normative testing was utilized to rule out significant cognitive problems, identify areas of weakness, and examine John's personality structure. This information was useful in beginning to understand some causes of John's disruptive behavior. However, normative test data were insufficient to characterize the complexity of his problems. Behavioral assessment data in the form of interviews and rating scales provided more contextual information and history about the problem. It should be noted that the rating scales resulted in a laundry list of problems that had to be narrowed, based on the totality of the case. Moreover, John rated himself as having appropriate friendships, a rating that was not supported by other data. The proper interpretation of this apparent inconsistency is that John has poor insight into appropriate friendships and thus rates himself inaccurately. The behavioral observation was integral because the quantitative data showed that John is indeed exhibiting more problem behaviors than his peers. More important, the anecdotal information was integrated with other sources of data to provide a convergence of evidence around three main functions of his target behaviors. If this case were examined from a traditional assessment viewpoint, one might conclude that John has attention-deficit/hyperactivity disorder (ADHD). From a behavioral assessment perspective, many of the apparent ADHD behaviors are secondary to more fundamental problems John is facing. To treat John for ADHD with pharmacotherapy would probably not be the best course of action, because it would not provide him with the wealth of new skills and behaviors that would be provided under the above treatment plan.

REFERENCES

Achenbach, T. M., & Rescorla, L. A. (2001). *Manual for ASEBA school age forms and profiles*. Burlington, VT: University of Burlington Center for Children, Youth and Families.

Ambrosini, P. J. (2000). Historical development and present status of the Schedule for Affective Disorders and Schizophrenia for School-aged Children (K-SADS). *Journal of the American Academy of Child and Adolescent Psychiatry, 39*, 49–58.

Artesani, A. J. (2001). *Understanding the purpose of challenging behavior: A guide to conducting functional assessments*. Upper Saddle River, NJ: Merrill Prentice Hall.

Beutler, L. E., Clarkin, J. F., & Bongar, B. (2000). *Guidelines for the systematic treatment of the depressed patient*. New York: Oxford University Press.

Cone, J. (2001). *Evaluating outcomes: Empirical tools for effective practice*. Washington, DC: American Psychological Association.

DuBois, D. L., & Silverthorn, N. (2004). Bias in self-perceptions and internalizing and externalizing problems in adjustment during early adolescence: A prospective investigation. *Journal of Clinical Child & Adolescent Psychology, 33*, 373–381.

Elliot, S. N., Witt, J. C., Kratochwill, T. R., & Stoiber, K. C. (2002). Selecting and evaluating classroom interventions. In M. R. Shinn, H. M. Walker, & G. Stober (Eds.), *Interventions for Academic and Behavior Problems II: Preventive and Remedial Approaches*. Bethedsa, MD: National Association of School Psychologists.

Gladwell, M. (2005). *Blink: The power of thinking without thinking*. New York: Little, Brown.

Godoy, A., & Gavino, A. (2003). Information-gathering strategies in behavioral assessment. *European Journal of Psychological Assessment 19*, 204–209.

Gottman, J., Levenson, R., & Woodin, E. (2001). Facial expressions during marital conflict. *Journal of Family Communication, 1*, 37–57.

Greenwood, C. R., Carta, J. J., Kamps, D., Terry, B., & Delquadri, J. (1994). Development and validation of standard classroom observation systems for school practitioners: Ecobehavioral Assessment Systems Software (EBASS). *Exceptional Children, 61*, 197–210.

Hayes, S. C. (1981). Single case experimental design and empirical clinical practice. *Journal of Consulting and Clinical Psychology, 49*, 193–211.

Haynes, S. N., & O'Brien, W. H. (1990). Functional analysis in behavior therapy. *Clinical Psychology Review, 10*, 649–668.

Hersen, M. (1976). Historical perspectives in behavioral assessment. In M. Hersen & A. S. Bellack (Eds.), *Behavioral assessment: A practical handbook* (pp. 3–22). New York: Pergamon Press.

Hughes, T. L., & Morine, K. (2005, August). *Using creative and critical thinking for psychological report writing*. Paper presented at the American Psychological Association annual conference, Washington, DC.

Huberty, T. J. (2003). Integrating interviews, observations, questionnaires, and test data: Relationships among assessment, placement, and intervention. In M. J. Breen & C. R. Fiedler (Eds.), *Behavioral approach to assessment of youth with emotional/behavioral disorders: A handbook for school-based practitioners* (2nd ed., pp. 587–633). Austin, TX: PRO-ED.

Kahng, S. W., & Iwata, B. A. (1998). Computerized systems for collecting real-time observational data. *Journal of Applied Behavior Analysis, 31*, 253–261.

Kemp, S., Kirk, U., & Korkman, M. (2001). Essentials of NEPSY assessment. New York: Wiley & Sons.

Mash, E. J., & Terdal, L. G. (1988). Behavioral assessment of child and family disturbance. In E. J. Mash & L. G. Terdal (Eds.), *Behavioral assessment of childhood disorders second edition: Selected core problems*. New York: Guilford Press.

McConaughy, S. H., & Achenbach, T. M. (2004). *Manual for the Test Observation Form for ages 2–18.* Burlington, VT: University of Vermont Center for Children, Youth and Families.

Merrell, K. W. (2003). *Behavioral, social, and emotional assessment of children and adolescents.* Mahwah, NJ: Lawrence Erlbaum Associates.

Miller, J. A., Bagnato, S. J., Dunst, C. J., & Mangis, H. (2006). Psychoeducational interventions in pediatric neuropsychiatry. In C. E. Coffey, R. A. Brumback, D. R. Rosenberg, & K. Voeller (Eds.), *Textbook of essential pediatric neuropsychiatry* (pp. 701–714). Philadelphia: Lippincott Williams & Wilkins.

Miller, J., Tansy, M., & Hughes, T. (1998, November 18). Functional behavioral assessment: The link between problem behavior and effective intervention in schools. *Current Issues in Education, 1*(5).

Ottoni, E. B. (2000). EthoLog 2.2: A tool for the transcription and timing of behavior observation sessions. *Behavior Research Methods, Instruments, & Computers, 32,* 446–449.

Puig-Antich, J., & Chambers, W. (1978). *The Schedule for Affective Disorders and Schizophrenia for School-aged Children.* New York: New York State Psychiatric Association.

Reich, W., Welner, Z., & Herjanic, B. (1997). *Diagnostic Interview for Children and Adolescents-IV computer program.* North Tonawanda, NY: Multi-Health Systems.

Reynolds, C. R., & Kamphaus, R. W. (2004). *Behavior Assessment System for Children, Second Edition, Manual.* Circle Pines, MN: AGS Publishing.

Saudargas, R. A., & Lentz, Jr., F. E. (1986). Estimating percent of time and rate via direct observation: A suggested observational procedure and format. *School Psychology Review, 15,* 36–48.

Sattler, J. M. (1998). *Clinical and forensic interviewing of children and families: Guidelines for the mental health, education, pediatric, and child maltreatment fields.* San Diego: Author.

Sattler, J. M. (2001). *Assessment of children: Cognitive approaches* (4th ed.). San Diego: Author.

Shapiro, E. S. (1988). Behavioral assessment. In J. C. Witt, S. N. Elliott, & F. M. Gresham (Eds.), *Handbook of behavior therapy in education* (pp. 67–98). New York: Plenum Press.

Sharpe, T., & Koperwas, J. (1999). *BEST: Behavioral Evaluation Strategy and Taxonomy software, Technical Manual.* Thousand Oaks, CA: Sage/Scolari.

Sidener, T. M., Shabani, D. B., & Carr, J. E. (2004). A review of the behavioral evaluation strategy and taxonomy (BEST) software application. *Behavior Interventions, 19,* 275–285.

Silva, F. (1993). *Psychometric foundations and behavioral assessment.* Newbury Park, CA: Sage Publications.

Simeonsson, R. J., Huntington, G. S., Brent, J. L., & Balant, C. (2001). A qualitative developmental approach to assessment. In R. J. Simeonsson & S. L. Rosenthal (Eds.), *Psychological and developmental assessment: Children with disabilities and chronic conditions.* New York: Guilford Press.

Volpe, R. J., & McConaughy, S. H. (2005). Introduction to the mini-series. *School Psychology Review, 34,* 451–453.

Walker, H. M., & Sprague, J. R. (1999). Longitudinal research and functional behavioral assessment issues. *Behavioral Disorders, 24,* 335–337.

Winters, N. C., Collett, B. R., & Myers, K. M. (2005). Ten-year review of rating scales, VII: Scales assessing functional impairment. *Journal of the American Academy of Child and Adolescent Psychiatry, 44,* 309–338.

9

USING THE RORSCHACH WITH CHILDREN

Philip Erdberg
Corte Madera, California

Among omnibus personality instruments, the Rorschach is the one measure that covers the life span most extensively. By the time children have reached early school age, clinicians can feel comfortable using standard Rorschach variables to help create personality descriptions and plan interventions. From that point on, as Leichtman (1996) put it, "Examiners can now give the test in its most complex forms and expect that children will respond in ways comparable to those of older subjects" (p. 62).

Being able to use the same test across childhood, adolescence, and adulthood brings some distinct advantages. The Rorschach's variables become like old friends as we follow them over the developmental years and beyond. Shifts in the balance of color to form ($FC:CF+C$) track the youngster's increasing ability to modulate behavior when emotion plays a part. The steady decrease in the Egocentricity Index ($3r+2/R$) documents the progressive decentering that Piaget (1952, 1959) identified as an important part of childhood maturation. The stability of form quality ($X+\%$) over the developmental years lets us know that perceptual conventionality is a feature solidly consolidated by early latency (Exner & Weiner, 1995).

This chapter is about using the Rorschach with children. It begins with a description of the stages very young children move through on their way to producing "standard" Rorschachs. It then delineates the domains this multifaceted instrument covers—coping strategies, affect, interpersonal function, self-concept, information processing—and suggests how findings from each of these domains can help clinicians describe youngsters and plan interventions for them. The chapter concludes with an illustrative case example.

EARLY CHILDHOOD: MASTERING THE RORSCHACH

Examining the Rorschachs of very young children, Leichtman (1996) made a tremendously important point. He suggested that their responses "differ in kind from normal Rorschach responses and they lead to doubts that the same modes of thinking underlie their formulation" (p. 19). He goes on to suggest that young children progress through a series of stages on their way, around age seven, to producing Rorschachs that can be interpreted in a "standard" manner. As he put it, "mastery of the test occurs over a considerable period of time—the preschool years and beyond—and is reflected in a series of increasingly sophisticated, qualitatively different patterns of test performance" (p. 35).

Leichtman (1996) suggests that young children pass through three basic stages and two transitional periods between these stages on their way to giving "standard" Rorschachs. He calls the first stage, at around age two, Pervasive Perseveration. During this period, the youngster tends to give the same answer to each of the cards. At around two and a half, during a transitional period Leichtman calls Modified Perseverations, the predominant pattern continues to be a perseverative one, but the youngster may give unique responses to a few of the cards.

Children progress to the second stage, Confabulatory Approaches, around age three. Although some perseverations continue in this stage, it is no longer the predominant way of working through the test. Klopfer, Spiegelman, and Fox (1956) described the confabulatory aspects of this stage, noting that "frequently, the child may choose any of his favorite animals, point out one of its properties . . . and gleefully assign the rest of the blot material to the same concept" (pp. 27–28). Although the youngster's own psychology, as opposed to the stimulus properties of the blot, is still the primary determinant of his or her responses, we can begin to see a shift in the balance, with the external properties of the blot making at least some contribution to the response.

According to Leichtman (1996), between ages four and a half and six, the child moves into a transitional stage, Confabulatory Combinations. This involves a broadening of confabulatory answers in which two details are used to produce an answer that still does not bear much resemblance to the rest of the blot. As Klopfer et al. (1956) expressed, "The concept formation falls short in the way in which the specified elements are organized within a total concept" (p. 28). These confabulatory combinations happen in about half the answers a five-year-old may give, and the other half are likely to be answers that come entirely from the stimulus properties of the blot itself. Again, this pattern represents an increasing shift toward the use of the blot to produce responses.

Leichtman (1996) suggests that as youngsters approach age seven and the third and final stage of his sequence, they become "able to give a varied number of responses to the inkblots, identify their location precisely, and answer questions in ways that permit them to be scored with a reasonable degree of assurance" (p. 61). Children are now responding to the Rorschach with the balance of internal and external input that allows the use of normative data and standard interpretive approaches.

Leichtman's (1995) developmental sequence has important clinical implications. As Klopfer et al. (1956) put it, "If a seven-year-old child still gives responses based on any of the three steps of perseveration, confabulation, and confabulatory combination, we may assume that he functions below his age level" (p. 28). Ames, Learned, Metraux, and Walker (1952) noted that confabulations are typical during ages four through seven, but "their occurrence after these ages at least suggests immaturity if not the pathology which they would imply at later stages" (p. 283).

INTERPRETING CHILDREN'S RORSCHACHS

Once the youngster's responses suggest that he or she is processing the Rorschach with the balance of internal and external guidance that characterizes older children, adolescents, and adults, Rorschach interpretation can proceed in the standard manner. From that point on, as Exner and Weiner (1995) note, "Rorschach behavior means what it means regardless of the age of the subject," (p. 11) and the respondent's age would not modify the interpretive statements we make about any specific Rorschach finding. As an example, we would interpret an *FC:CF+C* value of 2:4 as suggesting that when affect plays a part in the person's processing, the behavior that emerges is likely to be poorly modulated and volatile. That would be our interpretation regardless of whether the person was seven years old or 27 years old. For the seven-year-old, we would then reference normative data to suggest that this is typically how young children handle affectively charged situations. If the person were 27 years old, however, we would note that this level of affective volatility is normatively unexpected and may represent a significant liability.

Because normative data provide useful reference points, it is important that clinicians code Rorschachs according to consistent guidelines. For this reason, coding decisions do not take the age of the respondent into account. As an example, if someone, regardless of age, used the word "smooshed" to describe a flattened animal skin on Card VI, we would code the answer as a deviant verbalization (DV). It is at that point that we would go on to note that deviant verbalizations are very common in seven-year-olds and markedly less so among adults.

As noted previously, the Rorschach is an omnibus instrument that furnishes information about several domains of psychological function. The following sections explore these domains by describing some variables in each that can be useful in assessing children and planning interventions for them.

Coping Strategies

The Rorschach can provide information about two important aspects of coping strategies. The first involves the child's preferred style of solving problems. The majority of younger children are extratensive (their weighted sum of chromatic color exceeds the sum of human movement determinants by two or more points), a style that involves using the interpersonal world as a sounding board. This contrasts with an introversive problem-solving style (human movement exceeds the weighted sum of chromatic color determinants by two or more points), in which the person processes data in a more "internal" manner as he or she copes with stress. Exner and Weiner (1995) report that, by age 12, the distribution of introversive and extratensive styles is more even than at earlier ages. At age seven, only 8% of their nonpatient sample was introversive and 56% was extratensive. By age 12, the distribution had shifted substantially: 32% of the children were introversive and 36% were extratensive.

From an intervention standpoint, information about preferred problem-solving style is important in the planning of therapeutic approaches. The extratensive child is accustomed to involving others as he or she deals with difficulties. The introversive child is much less comfortable in a context that calls for "talking through" problems and may initially appear resistant. Letting the introversive youngster know the therapist realizes that discussing difficulties is not his or her preferred way of developing solutions can be immensely helpful at the beginning of psychotherapy or other intervention.

A second Rorschach variable that provides useful information about a youngster's coping operation is the *adjusted D Score*. Calculated by comparing available problem-solving resources (*EA*) with disruptive ideational and affective demands (*es*) and adjusting for transient stress, *adjusted D Scores* of –2 or lower suggest that the youngster is experiencing a chronic level of overload for which increasing therapeutic support is indicated. Exner and Weiner (1995) report that *adjusted D Scores* of –2 or lower are unusual for nonpatients of any age, with no nonpatient group between ages five and 12 showing more than 7% of children with this finding.

Affect

Questions about impulse control arise frequently in child assessment referrals. A series of Rorschach variables can be helpful in describing the sequence of operations that children experience as they process affectively charged material, beginning with input and ending with behavior. The Affective Ratio (*Afr*), calculated by dividing the number of responses to the three fully chromatic cards (i.e., VIII, IX, X) by the number of responses given to the other seven cards, provides a measure of openness to affectively toned stimuli. This variable shows an appreciable developmental curve, with younger children emerging as more open to such material. Exner and Weiner (1995) report that the mean *Afr* for their nonpatient seven-year-olds is .79, indicating that these children give almost as many answers to the three fully chromatic cards as to all seven of the other cards. By age 12, the *Afr* for the nonpatient sample has decreased to .65, suggesting that the youngster is better able to resist the distraction of emotionally toned material.

Information about a youngster's openness to processing emotionally complex material is important in intervention planning. If the *Afr* is below .50, it is increasingly likely that the child has "closed down" in ways that compromise opportunities for social and interpersonal learning. As an example, Leifer, Shapiro, Martone, and Kassem (1991) report a mean *Afr* of .48 for a group of sexually abused girls, ranging in age from five to 16.

As noted previously, the *FC:CF+C* ratio provides a description of how well the youngster is able to modulate his or her behavior when affect is involved. As with the Affective Ratio, there is a substantial developmental progression, with younger children much less able to bring structure into their affectively toned behavior. Chromatic color dominates in *CF* and *C* responses ("It's a bouquet of flowers, all those bright colors."), whereas *FC* responses are guided primarily by form ("It's a tulip with a bowl-shaped top and a stem, and it's red."). In the Exner and Weiner (1995) sample, it is not until age 13 that *FC* begins to exceed *CF* and *C*. A description of where a particular youngster falls as he or she moves toward more structured affective expression can be helpful for teachers, counselors, and therapists as they plan intervention approaches. As an example, a strategy that emphasizes delay techniques such as the cognitive self-talk approach described by Meichenbaum and Goodman (1971; see also Korhonen, 1986) would be useful for the youngster whose *FC:CF+C* ratio suggests markedly less ability to modulate affect than would be expected at his or her age.

Interpersonal Function

The Rorschach provides two kinds of information about a child's interpersonal life, and both are important in clinical work. The first involves a description of the conventionality of the child's interpersonal field and a prediction of how he or she will be viewed by others. A ratio (*GHR:PHR*) of the number of good human responses (*GHR*) to human responses flawed by distorted form quality or cognitive slippage (poor human responses; *PHR*) is helpful in this regard. If *GHR* is greater than *PHR*, the youngster's conventional reading of the interpersonal field is likely to result in effective behavior that will be seen positively by others. On the other hand, if *PHR* is equal to or greater than *GHR*, unconventional reading of the interpersonal field is likely to bring about maladaptive behavior that others will view negatively. This is a variable that appears to consolidate early. Exner (2003) reports that 78% of his 120 nonpatient seven-year-olds have *GHR* greater than *PHR*. Ninety-one percent of the sample have this finding by age 12.

Information about a youngster's interpersonal competence can be useful in intervention planning. For example, if a child's *PHR* responses are equal to or greater than his or her *GHR* answers, a program that includes social skills training could well be of value. Conversely, a finding of *GHR > PHR* represents a significant strength. It suggests that interventions involving groups are likely to go well and that both adults and other children are likely to respond positively to the individual.

The second kind of information the Rorschach can provide about interpersonal function includes some data about the youngster's expectations about his or her interpersonal field. A cooperative movement code (*COP*) is assigned for answers that include humans or animals in positive or productive interactions (e.g., "two people planning a party"). Aggressive movement codes (*AG*) are assigned for percepts with clearly aggressive interactions (e.g., "two people arguing loudly with each other"). If *AG* is greater than *COP*, the youngster likely views the interpersonal world as a place in which combative, competitive interactions are typical. *COP* equal to or greater than *AG* characterizes youngsters who expect that interpersonal life will involve positive and productive interactions. An understanding of how youngsters see the interpersonal world can be helpful as teachers, counselors, and therapists plan the initial aspects of interventions.

Self-concept

The Rorschach's Egocentricity Index, calculated as three times the number of reflection responses plus the number of pair responses divided by the total number of responses [$3r+(2)/R$], provides data about the balance of importance attributed to self versus others. As noted previously, this balance shifts markedly over the developmental years. Egocentricity Indices greater than .45 suggest that the person is more likely to focus on himself or herself than on others. Those below .33 depict a negative view of self when compared with others. The mean Egocentricity Index for Exner and Weiner's (1995) seven-year-olds is .65; by age 12 it has decreased to .54. It is not until age 15 that the index moves below .45.

We expect younger children to be self-focused, and we worry—with depressed youngsters, for example—when findings suggest a negative view of self in comparison with others. As an example, Acklin (1990) reported that 41% of a group of 9–12-year-old learning-disabled children had Egocentricity Indices less than .30. We can speculate that their ongoing failure experiences in school have led to negative self-assessments when they compared themselves with other students.

Information Processing

Questions about school difficulties are among the most common referrals received by psychologists who assess children. Because the Rorschach is a personality test that collects data by giving respondents a perceptual-cognitive task to solve, it can provide some useful descriptions of how children process data. A strength of the Rorschach task is that clinicians can assess the amount of energy and complexity children bring to information-processing tasks. The Z Frequency (*Zf*) variable provides a count of responses in which the child goes beyond a minimal expenditure of energy, either by using the whole blot or by integrating two or more blot areas (e.g., "two bears climbing up a mountain"). The Z Difference (*Zd*) variable provides a useful description of the youngster's scanning efficiency. By comparing the complexity of his or her answers with normative expectations, we can identify youngsters who are over- or underincorporative. Overincorporative individuals tend to expend more energy than necessary in processing the stimulus features of situations. Underincorporators frequently miss important aspects of situations because of hasty or inefficient scanning. Acklin (1990) reported that 37% of his learning-disabled sample were underincorporative and that 17% were overincorporative.

An important new Rorschach variable, the *X* Appropriate Percent (*XA%*), provides information about the source of a youngster's data, specifically what percentage of it comes from using external stimuli. The *XA%* is the percentage of answers that make appropriate use of the various attributes (shape, color, shading, etc.) of the blot. As such, it provides a description of the balance of internal versus external data a child uses in responding to perceptual-cognitive tasks. Normative data suggest that this variable consolidates quite early in child development. Exner (2003) reported that 78% of his nonpatient seven-year-olds had *XA%* values greater than 89%.

The *X+%* provides data about the conventionality of the youngster's responses. It is the percentage of answers that were seen by approximately 2% or more of Exner's (2003) normative sample. This is another variable that remains very stable throughout childhood. The mean *X+%* for Exner's seven-year-olds is 81%, suggesting that perceptual conventionality can be expected from an early point in the developmental years.

These Rorschach variables provide a fine-grained description of the youngster's data-processing energy and scanning efficiency, as well as information about the internal versus external balance and the conventionality of the data he or she uses in responding to demands. They combine with data from cognitive and academic achievement assessment to provide a comprehensive picture of how a child processes information, allowing education and mental health professionals to design carefully individualized intervention plans.

More current nonpatient data (Hamel, Shaffer, & Erdberg, 2000; Exner & Erdberg, 2005) suggest that the absolute values for form quality and other Rorschach variables have changed since Exner and Weiner first presented cross-sectional data for nonpatient children between five and 16 in 1982. The availability of cross-sectional data allows identification of Rorschach variables that can be expected to change over the developmental years versus those that are consolidated early, and current normative studies provide up-to-date information about responding to the test. It is hoped that additional studies will add to the available normative data for children and adolescents.

CASE EXAMPLE

Jeanne is a 10-year-old Caucasian girl who was referred for psychological assessment because of school behavior problems. She has been stealing food and drinks from her classmates' lockers, a pattern that apparently goes back at least two years. She frequently fights with other students, and although these fights are mostly verbal, some recently have also involved pushing and shoving.

Jeanne and a younger brother, now age eight, lived with their biological parents until Jeanne was about four years old. At that time, an investigation by child protective services, initiated on the basis of neighbors' reports, found that the parents' arguments had become so frequent and volatile as to endanger the two children. The children were removed from the home and placed in a foster setting, where they have remained for the past six years. The parents ultimately divorced and have little contact with either of the children. Both parents are reported to have significant psychiatric and substance abuse problems.

The foster parents initially considered adopting the two children, and although they remain committed to them, they have not raised the topic of adoption for the last few years. They are concerned and perplexed about Jeanne's school difficulties, noting that she presents no behavior problems at home and is compliant about doing her assigned chores.

Academically, Jeanne is doing well at school. Her stealing has alienated her from virtually all her classmates, and her teachers have suggested that placement in another school might allow her to start over with a "clean slate." They find the contrast between Jeanne's good academic performance and her behavior difficulties confusing, and they are requesting consultation on how best to work with her.

Cognitive assessment indicated Jeanne was operating well within the average range with little variability among her scores. She was extremely compliant throughout the evaluation, refusing invitations to get up and stretch or to stop and complete the testing during a second meeting. Her affect was flat, although she did seem quietly pleased by her obvious success during the cognitive testing. She said that arithmetic was her favorite subject, that her teachers were "nice," and that the other children in her class were "okay, but they're not very friendly."

Jeanne worked quietly and methodically through the Rorschach, giving a 23-response record. She emerged as an introversive youngster. Although this is not an unexpected finding for 10-year-olds, it does suggest that she sees herself as her own best resource when it comes to dealing with difficulties. However, her Adjusted D Score of –2 indicates that Jeanne has been experiencing more demands than she has resources to handle. Faced with this overload of demands and a style unaccustomed to involving others in working through difficulties, Jeanne presents a therapeutic challenge. The teachers note that their gentle attempts to talk with her about her behavior problems have been largely unsuccessful and have been met with quiet denial and silence.

It will be important for the psychologist providing assessment consultation to talk with everyone working with Jeanne about the dilemma that these findings represent for her. An approach that describes her introversive style and empathizes with her discomfort at involving another person as a way of solving problems would be an important first step. This sort of initial approach significantly increases the chances that Jeanne will ultimately be able to talk about the overwhelming problems that are provoking her stealing and aggression.

Jeanne's Affective Ratio is .44 and her *FC:CF+C* ratio is 3:0, suggesting that she is working hard to avoid affectively provocative situations and to keep her behavior well controlled when affect plays a part in it. To a large extent, she is succeeding. In the structured contexts of home and classroom, she is less responsive and more stringently controlled than we would expect an average 10-year-old to be. It is only in the more ambiguous and emotionally charged context of interacting with peers that her controls break down, suggesting that Rorschach data about interpersonal function and self-concept will be especially important in the planning of interventions.

Jeanne's *GHR:PHR* ratio is 2:4. She does not read interpersonal data accurately, and it is likely that her interactions with others will provoke a vicious circle in which their negative responses provide little opportunity for self-correction. In addition to individual therapy, a social skills group that emphasizes the accurate interpretation of interpersonal data and teaches appropriate responding will be a critical aspect of an intervention plan.

Interestingly, Jeanne has neither *COP* nor *AG* responses in her Rorschach. Her interpersonal field is largely vacant, with essentially no representation of human interaction, either cooperative or competitive. These findings are suggestive of a significant deficit on Jeanne's part, perhaps a function of the parental neglect that characterized her first four years and that may account for her stealing food as a way of providing her own nurturance. The ambiguity of her relationship with her foster parents may also leave her feeling uncertain about the potential for supportive interaction with others.

It is not surprising that Jeanne's Egocentricity Index is .30. With the exception of the cordial, rather protective relationship she has with her younger brother, her interactions with children have been uniformly negative. When she compares herself with them, she typically feels less competent, less knowledgeable, and very much "out of the loop." There is no direct intervention for improving self-esteem, but it is likely that the combination of individual therapy that helps identify strengths, such as her good academic performance, and social skills training that increases the likelihood of positive interactions will go a long way toward helping Jeanne feel better about herself.

Jeanne works hard to process data, and she does it quite efficiently. Her Z Frequency was 19, notably higher than we would have expected in a 23-response Rorschach. She is neither under- nor overincorporative. However, she is not particularly conventional ($X+\% = 43\%$), and much of her data is not externally grounded ($XA\% = 52\%$). She handles structure and predictable situations easily, but as things become more ambiguous, her conventionality drops and she is more likely to turn to internal as opposed to external guidelines. Again, this may be a result of the likely absence of external input during her first four years.

Given the idiosyncrasy that characterizes Jeanne's psychological functioning, an active treatment approach that works hard to engage her is critically important. As an example, identifying a specific area of strength such as art, music, or writing, and then arranging for Jeanne to attend a summer camp program in which she can interact with children with similar interests would increase the odds of some positive interpersonal experiences.

Although this case example has discussed the use of one instrument, the Rorschach, it is important to remember that competent psychological assessment typically involves multiple methods. Neuropsychological and academic testing would be important for Jeanne, as would a self-report measure of personality, an incomplete sentences technique, parent and teacher behavior ratings, and the opportunity to create stories based on pictures of interpersonal events. Discussions with her foster parents and her teachers would help to put her difficulties in perspective. It is likely that there would be a good deal of overlap among the findings from these multiple approaches, but there would be unique information from each and contradictions as well. It is in the context of this sort of comprehensive assessment that we do best by those youngsters for whom we provide services.

CONCLUSION

The Rorschach allows clinicians to take a developmental perspective, assessing where clients are as they progress through some of the tasks of childhood and adolescence, such as the increasing ability to regulate affect. Simultaneously, as an omnibus measure that provides information about coping style, affect, interpersonal function, self-concept, and information processing, it allows the assessing psychologist to respond to many of the questions that confront professionals in their day-to-day work with children and adolescents. As part of a comprehensive assessment approach, the Rorschach's combination of developmental and descriptive data enhances our ability to plan appropriate interventions.

REFERENCES

Acklin, M. W. (1990). Personality dimensions in two types of learning-disabled children: A Rorschach study. *Journal of Personality Assessment, 54*(1–2), 67–77.

Ames, L. B., Learned, J., Metraux, R. W., & Walker, R. N. (1952). *Child Rorschach responses; developmental trends from two to ten years.* New York: Paul B. Hoeber.

Exner, J. E. (2003). *The Rorschach: A comprehensive system* (4th ed.). New York: John Wiley & Sons.

Exner, J. E., & Erdberg, P. (2005). *The Rorschach: A comprehensive system: Vol. 2. Advanced interpretation* (3rd ed.). Hoboken, NJ: John Wiley & Sons.

Exner, J. E., & Weiner, I. B. (1982). *The Rorschach: A comprehensive system: Vol. 3. Assessment of children and adolescents.* New York: John Wiley & Sons.

Exner, J. E., & Weiner, I. B. (1995). *The Rorschach: A comprehensive system: Vol. 3. Assessment of children and adolescents* (2nd ed.). New York: John Wiley & Sons.

Hamel, M., Shaffer, T. W., & Erdberg, P. (2000). A study of nonpatient preadolescent Rorschach protocols. *Journal of Personality Assessment, 75*(2), 280–294.

Klopfer, B. (1956). *Developments in the Rorschach technique: Vol. II. Fields of application.* New York: World Book.

Klopfer, B., Spiegelman, M., & Fox, J. (1956). The interpretation of children's records. In B. Klopfer (Ed.), *Developments in the Rorschach technique: Vol. II. Fields of application.* New York: World Book.

Korhonen, T. (1986). Some principles of self-instructional training with hyperactive-impulsive children. *Scandinavian Journal of Behaviour Therapy, 15*(4), 179–182.

Leichtman, M. (1996). *The Rorschach: A developmental perspective.* Hillsdale, NJ: Analytic Press.

Leifer, M., Shapiro, J. P., Martone, M. W., & Kassem, L. (1991). Rorschach assessment of psychological functioning in sexually abused girls. *Journal of Personality Assessment, 56*(1), 14–28.

Meichenbaum, D. H., & Goodman, J. (1971). Training impulsive children to talk to themselves: A means of developing self-control. *Journal of Abnormal Psychology, 77*(2), 115–126.

Piaget, J. (1952). *Judgment and Reasoning in the Child.* New York: Humanities Press.

Piaget, J. (1959). *The Language and Thought of the Child.* London: Routledge & Kegan Paul.

10

RORSCHACH CASE FORMULATION IN ADOLESCENTS: A PSYCHOANALYTIC PERSPECTIVE ON THE COMPREHENSIVE SYSTEM

Shira Tibon

The Academic College of Tel-Aviv Yaffo and Tel-Aviv University

Lily Rothschild

Bar-Ilan University and Sheba Medical Center, Israel

For anyone with a psychoanalytically oriented approach, understanding the meaning of a Rorschach protocol constitutes a real challenge: How can we counterbalance the empirical approach of the Comprehensive System (CS; Exner, 2003), with its predominantly empirical focus, by assigning more importance to theoretical psychoanalytic thinking? Many authors, including Exner (1992) and Weiner (2000), have written about the need to employ personality constructs as a conceptual bridge between empirically based CS data, once they have been generated, and clinical inferences.

The integration of theoretical thinking and CS data seems even more important in the study of adolescents, where the clinician deals with the complexity of differentiating reactive issues related to the developmental tasks from chronic factors (Kelly, 1997; Sugarman, 1980; Exner & Weiner, 1995). Being committed to both the empirical rigor of Exner's (2003) CS and to the use of psychoanalytic thinking, this chapter is addressed at understanding an individual Rorschach protocol within the context of the psychic turmoil and the potential difficulties that characterize normative adolescents when they confront developmental tasks.

Based on psychoanalytic thinking that adolescence constitutes a qualitatively new developmental stage of individuation (Bleiberg, 2001; Blos, 1962; Meeks & Bernet, 2001), we suggest adopting some substantial premises in the interpretation of Rorschach findings in adolescents:

A. Normal developmental demands induce regressive experience and primitive defensive reactions. As a result, except for severe psychopathological states (within the schizophrenic or the affectively disordered spectrum), adolescents who show impaired Rorschach protocols might be more reasonably viewed as demonstrating problems evolving from a developmental crisis rather than psychopathological states. These developmental problems, which might include disruptions in control and cognitive, affective, self-perception, and/or interpersonal functioning, can (but do not necessarily) evolve into marked personality disorders in adulthood. Psychosis-like manifestations might thus be revealed in Rorschach protocols of nonpsychotic adolescents.

B   Since there is not yet a well-synthesized and integrated personality style in adolescents and the patterns of defenses may not be fully crystallized, the defensive structure can be more vulnerable to disruption when youngsters are confronted by stress or trauma. When assessing an adolescent with the Rorschach, one must consider the developmental issues related to incomplete development of personality structure, and the vulnerability of existing structures, along with the potential for rapid recovery.

C.   Major mental disorders are often present in atypical forms during adolescence. Thus, for example, manic-depressive disorders appear with dramatic behavioral symptoms, such as severe rebellion, rapid change in function, exaggerated self-esteem with grandiosity, sexual acting out, and mood swings. In addition, depression might be masked by severe conduct disorders. Rorschach interpretation should thus take into account these atypical manifestations of mental disorders.

D.   It might be difficult to distinguish between fixation and regression in adolescence. In some cases there are prolonged psychopathological manifestations that have been precipitated by the developmental tasks, whereas in others these very manifestations might have been developed as a response to an external traumatic event. Distinguishing Rorschach markers of psychopathology that are situational from more trait-like markers is thus essential for understanding the personality of the adolescent.

The interpretative work on an adolescent's Rorschach protocol starts with the question of what constitutes normality in adolescence. Although adaptation to external reality, in its broader sense, can be used as a criterion, it seems quite important to stress that conformity does not necessarily mean normality. Although conformity can be a valid measure of behavioral adaptation, it might hide internal chaos on the one hand, and problems in relating to one's own subjective experience on the other.

Based on our understanding that one of the major developmental tasks in adolescence is associated with the separation-individuation process, as a part of the crystallization of the personality structure, the Rorschach case formulation as presented here is addressed at describing the individual's experience in this process. The case formulation applies Kernberg's (1976) structural diagnosis, which classifies personality organization into three broad levels of functioning: psychotic, borderline, and neurotic. This structural model refers to an overall intrapsychic organization that has stability, continuity, and sameness across different states. It also assumes that the different levels of organization are reflected in the individual's overriding characteristics, particularly with regard to the degree of identity integration, the quality of stress tolerance, the main defense strategies, impulse control, affect modulation, and reality testing.

By using an integrative approach to Rorschach interpretation, where the CS is combined with psychoanalytic conceptualization, we examine Rorschach clues for assessing self-concept, interpersonal relationships, affective and cognitive functioning within the context of the tasks with which the adolescent is confronted at this developmental stage. We further explore these clues in formulating a Rorschach case study.

ASSESSING SELF-CONCEPT

Psychoanalytic conceptualization as explored by self psychology has redefined both developmental theory and clinical technique to reflect the central role of the self (Kohut, 1971).

This conceptualization suggests viewing one's capacity for a sense of cohesiveness, one's sense of personal worth, and one's means of restoring and confirming personal esteem as the dominant categories of analysis, replacing the traditional concepts of drive and defense.

Accordingly, adolescents and adults often might be seen as coming to assessment needing to formulate a conscious sense of who they are. They need to feel understood, mirrored, accepted, and validated in their subjective experiences. In the absence of predefined roles offered by our culture, individuals must derive a sense of self largely from internal integrity and authenticity (McWilliams, 1999). The separation-individuation conflict that dominates the personality picture in adolescence constitutes a significant hurdle in the establishment of a competent and cohesive sense of self.

In normal adolescents the self-regulating functions have already been internalized during childhood and have achieved a degree of automatic activation. Hence, although self-concept can be quite fragile, even for a most confident individual, normal adolescents, particularly from mid-adolescence on, are not subjected to extreme narcissistic vulnerability. Adolescents can build a reflective-symbolic model of achievable tasks and can take steps addressed to these goals, consequently developing a sense of competence, self-esteem, and adaptation.

However, normative narcissistic vulnerability caused by biological, cognitive, sexual, and psychological factors often results in a proneness to embarrassment and shame, acute self-consciousness, shyness, and questions about self-worth and self-esteem (Bleiberg, 2001). These characteristics might reveal themselves in the Rorschach by a significant Depression Index (DEPI), low egocentricity index, elevated number of form-dimensionality (FD) responses, and all types of shading responses, particularly Vista (V), indicating heightened sensitivity and vulnerability to external clues and excessive self-inspection (Exner & Weiner, 1995). In cases where the sensitivity to nuances appears in the context of a parallel regression and/or fixation at an oral level of psychosexual development, it underscores the core problem of adolescence, namely separation-individuation.

However, in Rorschach protocols of adolescents with borderline features, the elevated number of shading responses might be a part of a hyperalert, paranoid style, rather than indicating normative sensitivity to external clues. The paranoid style usually serves a boundary maintenance function and is addressed at avoiding self-disintegration and finding a coherent sense of identity in a developmental phase that involves identity diffusion. This interpretation is validated particularly if the use of shading determinants include only Vista (V) and diffuse-shading (Y), with no texture (T) responses, since T does not typically appear in protocols of patients with character disturbance. Nonetheless, a prematurely developed paranoid character structure reveals itself primarily in a restricted protocol, with a low number of responses that are relatively unelaborated.

The hypothesized borderline level of personality organization might be further validated by an abundance of animal contents, pointing out the childlike quality of object relationships usually found in adolescents who are located at this level of development. Contents involving Anatomy (An), X-ray (Xy), and feelings of emptiness are also common at the borderline level and reflect the potential to discharge affects somatically (Blatt, Tuber, & Auerbach, 1990; Exner & Weiner, 1995; Sugarman, 1980).

The presence of reflection responses (Fr + rF) in mid-adolescence and later on might be an indication that the adolescent has failed to give up the focus on the self, which of course is normative in younger children. This pattern often indicates a proneness to develop narcissistic disorders in adulthood. In some cases, where the youngsters find the solution to narcissistic vulnerability in the illusion of omnipotence and an overinflated sense of self, Rorschach manifestations of grandiosity (e.g., an elevated Egocentricity Index; an elevated number of PER responses; and an abundance of self-aggrandizing and performance-type percepts, such as kings, temples, and crowns) might appear. Sometimes the underlying narcissistic injury might be revealed in devaluated representations (e.g., *two stupid women chatting*) and MOR responses (e.g., *an injured bat*). In other cases, the narcissistic injury is revealed in depression based on what Kohut (1971) called *the depleted self*. In these cases the affect is characterized by feelings of emptiness and reflects a self-perception of weakness, helplessness, and vulnerability. Adolescents who show this type of depression usually provide constricted, nonvital records characterized by simple responses and excessive use of form (F) as the only determinant, resulting in Lambda > .99 and many space (S) responses, to which they attribute contents of emptiness.

When the narcissistic vulnerability develops into a crisis, impaired Rorschach manifestations might be seen, regardless of the adolescent's level of personality organization. However, based on our clinical experience, in neurotic-level adolescents these manifestations (e.g., an elevated number of responses with minus form quality, FQ−) are revealed in specific blots rather than being widespread across the protocol, as they usually are in the protocols of more disturbed adolescents.

In cases where the narcissistic vulnerability of the adolescent is experienced through fears of self fragmentation, a psychotic level of personality organization might be considered. Adolescents at this level of personality organization typically offer Rorschach percepts in which there is concern about the integrity of objects or somatic preoccupations. The experience of a fragmented self might be revealed, as it is at the borderline level, in Anatomy and X-ray responses, but also in images of impaired boundaries (e.g., *a broken glass, holes in clothes,* or *an exploding bug with all the parts scattered*) (Lerner, 1998; Rothschild, 2005; Silverstein, 1999; Sugarman, 1980; Exner & Weiner, 1995).

To sum up, normative narcissistic vulnerability of adolescents might be manifested in the Rorschach by a significant DEPI, a low egocentricity index, an elevated number of form dimension responses, and all types of shading responses, particularly Vista, indicating heightened sensitivity and vulnerability to external cues. Although this configuration of Rorschach markers might characterize the protocols of adolescents at the borderline level of personality organization, the protocols of these adolescents usually include an abundance of animal content, pointing out the child-like quality of object relationships; contents involving Anatomy and X-Ray; and, in some cases, one or more reflection responses. The presence of an elevated number of shading responses that do not include texture further validate the hypothesized borderline level of personality organization. In cases where the configuration of heightened sensitivity and vulnerability appears, together with contents of fragmented objects, the assessment of these adolescents' self-concept might point to a psychotic level of personality organization.

ASSESSING INTERPERSONAL RELATIONSHIPS

The contemporary psychoanalytic perspective on patterns of interpersonal relationships usually refers to these patterns in terms of internalized object relations or object representations. Interactive experiences between the self and others occur in varying degrees of internalization and externalization (Kernberg, 1976; Mitchell, 2000; Ogden, 1986). However, it is assumed that the quality of one's interpersonal relations and various types of psychopathology are affected by the maturity of object representations. Thus, the evaluation of these representations should take into account that relational capacity develops progressively and that in this developmental process fragmented representations gradually turn progressively into complex, differentiated, integrated, and consistent representations of self and others (Blatt, Brenneis, Schimek, & Glick, 1976; Leichtman, 1996). This process takes place within a developmental stage where the adolescent confronts tasks that reactivate the separation-individuation conflict, searching for the balance between autonomy and relatedness, renegotiating the threat of regressing to dependence and reintegrating new cognitive, social, biological, and familial factors. Adolescents who fail to develop mature representations are likely to show any of several interpersonal problems, including a mild form of obsessive isolation, manifestations of paranoid style, conduct disorders, or even a schizotypal disorder (Blatt, Tuber, & Auerbach, 1990; Bleiberg, 2001).

The interpersonal cluster of the CS includes structural variables such as the Coping Deficit Index (CDI), the Hypervigilance Index (HVI), cooperative (COP) and aggressive (AG) responses, the sum of Texture (T) responses, and the sum of human contents. In addition, to assess interpersonal relationships, the contents for M and FM that contain a pair should be explored. Apart from these CS variables, different scales and indices that assess the quality of object representations with the Rorschach, including the Concept of the Object Scale (DACOS; Blatt et al., 1976) and the Mutuality of Autonomy Scale (MOA; Urist, 1977), have been validated by extensive research on adolescents. Some studies used these scales with the Ego Impairment Index (EII–2; Viglione, Perry, & Meyer, 2003), a CS index that incorporates among its subcomponents the variables of Good Human Representation (GHR) and Poor Human Representation (PHR). These studies have explored the object representations in different groups of child and adolescent psychiatric populations (Rothschild & Stein; 2004; Stokes et al., 2003).

In normal youngsters object representations become more articulated and more cohesive from mid-adolescence on. The mature inner objects are revealed in the Rorschach protocol by a predominance of whole and real human percepts, accurately perceived and fully differentiated from each other, integrating both positive and negative aspects, and are well articulated, actively motivated, and involved in mutual activities. This type of response points to the capacity of perceiving the object as constant, multidimensional, and differentiated, and nonetheless related to the self (Blatt et al., 1976; Exner & Weiner, 1995; Kelly 1997; Leichtman, 1996; Sugarman, 1980).

Regression regarding the representational world in neurotic-level cases might be manifested in providing few or even no human responses. Instead, animal and inanimate representations appear, enabling these adolescents to keep themselves distant from experiencing their social ineptness and loneliness. However, in nonregressive adolescents the nonhuman object representations are whole and demonstrate integration, complexity, and articulation, as would the human object representations. Furthermore, when confronted with the testing-of-limits (TOL) procedure, a form of examining the responder's ability to produce obvious percepts (Exner, 2003), these youngsters easily produce a well-developed, mature human response. CS findings in adolescents at the neurotic level of personality organization who are currently experiencing developmental crisis might include a significant Depression Index (DEPI) and Coping Deficit Index (CDI), and an elevated number of food (Fd) responses. Also, the Rorschach protocols of these adolescents usually show overriding passive as compared with active movement responses in general ($p > a + 1$) and in human-movement responses in particular ($Mp > Ma$), reflecting a tendency to escape to fantasy, a sense of helplessness that induces dependency, and vulnerability to the passive dependent avoidant style.

Furthermore, regression in adolescents at the neurotic level of personality organization might also be revealed by an elevated number of texture (T) responses, indicating the potential for forming attachments, which, however, does not guarantee by itself the development of numerous and pleasurable interpersonal relationships, especially in people who become socially fearful, isolated, or withdrawn. Another form of reaction to the developmental crisis among adolescents at this level of personality organization, particularly those adolescents with histrionic features, is the production of human figure responses that are accurately perceived, well differentiated, and highly articulated, and yet are described superficially regarding their feelings or thoughts (Exner & Weiner, 1995; Murray, 1997).

Adolescents who fail to develop mature representations produce Rorschach protocols with partial and impaired objects, which tend to deteriorate over time and with stress. The shift from whole to part figures is consistent with Kernberg's (1976) suggestion that borderline-level patients defensively manage their anxiety by splitting the object representations into good and bad ones, failing to integrate apparently contradictory characteristics in the same object (Lerner, 1998). The undeveloped inner objects are revealed in these protocols by a predominance of part and/or human-like objects that are less articulated and less accurately perceived and are deformed, distorted, and destructive. The interactions are usually malevolent (PHR > GHR) and lacking mutuality; intimate relationships are superficially perceived and chaotic (Blatt et al., 1990; Kelly, 1997; Viglione et al., 2003). Although this type of human response might also appear in protocols of adolescents at the neurotic level of personality organization currently experiencing a developmental crisis, in borderline-level cases they are revealed not as isolated responses but rather as being distributed throughout the protocol.

Furthermore, as noted, adolescents with character disturbance hardly display texture (T) responses because of the lack of adaptive capacity to anticipate and establish close, intimate, and mutually supportive relationships with other people. The excessive degree of preoedipal aggression at the borderline level of organization is revealed in oral aggressive contents, and an elevated number of responses coded with aggressive movement (AG), usually loaded with raw and less controlled aggression than the AG responses of neurotic-level adolescents (Gacono & Meloy, 1994).

CS markers of interpersonal relationships in psychotic-level adolescents differ according to the specific disturbance. Rorschach responses of these adolescents are nonetheless differentiated from those of higher levels of personality organization by their contents, which might frequently be similar to those of young children. Preschoolers often give charming, imaginative responses such as *a tree with feet,* or *a chicken with two heads,* or *even cows that have walked on to the cards, but subsequently walked off.* Concerned with being seen as immature and wishing to avoid ridicule, normal school-age children and adolescents limit the range of responses they allow themselves to produce to more realistic percepts (Leichtman, 1996).

However, in some highly intelligent adolescents, extremely imaginative, nonrealistic object representations might appear without indicating a psychotic level of personality organization, but rather healthy adaptation, creativity, and playfulness (Franklin & Cornell, 1997). In these cases the nonrealistic or even so-called bizarre responses, which could have been perceived as adaptively regressed, are logically "defended" in a realistic, socially or culturally acceptable content.

Overall, the mature inner object world is revealed in the Rorschach protocols of adolescents by a predominance of well-articulated whole and real human percepts, accurately perceived and fully differentiated from each other, integrating both positive and negative aspects, actively motivated and involved in mutual activities. Regression regarding the representational world in neurotic level cases might well be manifested in records with few or even no human responses; an elevated number of food responses; overriding passive as compared with active movement responses in general and human movement responses in particular; and an elevated number of texture responses. The undeveloped inner objects at the borderline level of personality organization would be revealed by part and/or human-like objects that are less articulated, less accurately perceived, and more markedly malevolent and destructive, compared with the neurotic-level protocol. The object representations at the psychotic level would nonetheless be differentiated from those at higher levels of personality organization by contents that lack differentiation between reality and fantasy.

ASSESSING AFFECTS

It is usually accepted that normal adolescents might be characterized by negativism, oppositional tendencies, intense emotionality, and/or withdrawal from emotional situations. The core issue of individuation at this developmental stage, which typically reveals intense affects and separation anxieties, further complicates the picture, challenging the diagnostic task of distinguishing among the different levels of personality organization.

Adolescents at the neurotic level who demonstrate affective difficulties are likely to report dysphoric feelings, to be shy, anxious, fearful, and tense. These personality characteristics are revealed in the Rorschach protocol by a significant Depression Index (DEPI), an elevated number of achromatic color (C') and vista (V) responses, color-shading or multiple shading blends, lowered Affective Ratio (Afr), and an elevated Isolation Index, reflecting painful and internalized affects, defensiveness, reluctance to be engaged in emotional interchange, and anxieties about facing interpersonal situations. Furthermore, protocols of adolescents at the neurotic level typically show an elevated number of inanimate movement (m) and diffuse-shading (Y) responses, indicating the situational stress they experience. Usually the Rorschachs of these adolescents show a minus D score, as might be the case for adolescents at the borderline level. However, the two groups differ concerning the adjusted D score (Adj D). Whereas the records of neurotic-level adolescents typically show a minus Adj D, signifying their persistent sense of inadequacy, often exacerbated by their failure to cope with developmental tasks, the records of borderline-level adolescents rarely show this score, inasmuch as they are not aware of their coping inadequacy.

Although the records of adolescents at the neurotic level might show problems in affect modulation, like impulsivity and lower anxiety tolerance, as revealed by FC < CF + C and the presence of pure C responses, these problems characterize much more the Rorschach protocols of adolescents at lower levels of personality organization. When appearing at the neurotic level, problems in affect modulation are usually associated with an extratensive or an ambient personality style (Exner, 2003; Exner & Weiner, 1995). Furthermore, because neurotic-level adolescents who experience developmental tasks as being difficult to cope with also tend to harbor considerable anger, their protocols might show an elevated number of space responses, frequently resulting in disregard for convention, as revealed by lowered number of popular (P) responses. Nonetheless, S greater than 4 is found more frequently in protocols of patients at the borderline level of personality organization than at the neurotic level. Furthermore, the presence of low anxiety tolerance, indicated by formless shading determinants (V, T, Y), compared with form-shading (FV, FT, FY) responses, and the inability to use sublimatory channels (as revealed by thematic imagery and sequence analysis) sharply differentiate borderline adolescents from their peers at the neurotic level of personality organization (Lerner, 1998; Silverstein, 1999; Exner & Weiner, 1995).

It should be noted that in contrast to the usual conception, CS markers of distress in adolescents should not preclude the possibility of borderline-level organization. Adolescents at the borderline level can thus produce Rorschach protocols with a positive CDI. Nonetheless, a positive CDI with a lowered DEPI is a finding that can usually serve to differentiate adolescents at the borderline level who appear depressed, shy, withdrawn, and socially inept from those at the neurotic level of personality organization. Those at the neurotic level more often display a positive CDI and a significant DEPI (Exner & Weiner, 1995), whereas at the borderline level the pattern of a lowered DEPI; a positive CDI; $S \geq 4$; FC $<$ CF + C; and T = 0 prevail.

While Rorschach manifestations of affective difficulties in protocols of adolescents at the neurotic level are clearly distinguished from those at the lower levels of organization, this is not the case when one is distinguishing between affective difficulties characterizing the borderline and the psychotic levels. Thus, in both groups CS manifestations and thematic imagery of unmodulated, intense, unstable, and inappropriate affect typically appear. In addition, anxiety tolerance is low, and the use of predominantly primary defenses like projective identification and splitting dominates the personality picture. However, the main difference between the two groups concerns impulsivity. Whereas the impulsivity of the borderline-level adolescent, although frequently observed throughout the protocol, appears in response to specifically emotionally loaded stimuli, the impulsivity of those at the psychotic level would be chaotic and unrelated to the stimulus (Acklin, 1997; Sugarman, 1980).

In conclusion, although adolescents at the neurotic level might show problems in affect modulation, such as impulsivity, and lower anxiety tolerance (manifested by FC $<$ CF + C and the presence of pure C), these problems characterize much more the Rorschach protocols of adolescents at lower levels of personality organization. However, the impulsivity at the borderline level is present in responses to specific emotionally loaded stimuli, whereas the impulsivity at the psychotic level appears, regardless of the stimulus presented in the blot.

ASSESSING COGNITIVE FUNCTIONING

Thought disorders are relatively uncommon in adolescents, and the presence of impaired thinking, although not by itself, is a core feature of schizophrenia and is essential to the diagnosis. Thus, in cases where an elevated number of disordered thinking manifestations do appear in adolescents' Rorschach protocols, they usually are associated with severe psychopathological entities, either of the constricted-withdrawal or of the externalizing-impulsive type (Exner & Weiner, 1995).

As the concrete operations that characterize the preadolescence stage are transformed into the formal ones, adolescents are able to differentiate between unrealistic and realistic ideation and to play with symbolic representations in their mind instead of relying mainly on actual experience. The adequate ability of cognitive focusing and reality testing is indicated in the Rorschach protocols of neurotic-level adolescents by a balanced approach of scanning the blot (W:D:Dd) and by displaying a normative percentage of responses where form use fits the form demands of the percepts ($X+\%$). However, in adolescents more than in adults, lowered $X+\%$ might appear with an elevation in Xu%, implying their inclination to demonstrate uniqueness and "stretch" the mental space. As noted, highly creative neurotic-level adolescents might display unrealistic percepts in some of their Rorschach responses, demonstrating illogical reasoning, abstract preoccupation, and vague ego boundaries, thereby resulting in severe special scores and even a positive Perceptual Thinking Index (PTI). Rather than indicating psychopathological manifestations, the special scores and the positive PTI might indicate in these cases the ability to play with reality (the blots) by adaptively regressing to an idiosyncratic cognitive mode (Franklin & Cornell, 1997; Smith, Baity, Knowles, & Hilsenroth, 2001).

The idea that psychotic-like Rorschach manifestations might be a part of a healthy, creative, and playful pattern of coping with the Rorschach blots has been explored in terms of Winnicott's (1971) conceptualization of the ability to play within the transitional space. Handler (1999, 2005) suggests using, in addition to the formal procedure of Rorschach administration, another procedure addressed at revealing the ability to play with the Rorschach response. Smith (1990) describes the Rorschach task as inviting the subject to enter the intermediate space between the external, "objective" reality and the internal "subjective" and personal one and suggests applying Ogden's (1986) formulation of different forms of collapse of potential space as revealing psychopathological manifestations in the Rorschach. The Reality-Fantasy Scale (RFS; Tibon, Handelzalts, & Weinberger, 2005), which explores this model empirically, has been applied in cross-cultural studies in the United States, Italy, and Israel. The findings of these studies provide substantial validation that the scale can be jointly used with the EII–2 (Viglione, Perry, & Meyer, 2003) for distinguishing between healthy and disturbed personality organization in adults and adolescents (Tibon, Porcelli, & Weinberger, 2005).

In borderline-level adolescents, failure to maintain a cognitive focus due to intrusion of irrelevant internal and external stimuli is indicated by Deviant Responses (DR), particularly when the responses are highly confabulated. The fixation on concrete thinking, the overdependence on the environment, the lack of critical objectivity, and the tendency to accept passively the demands of the external world are manifested in responses scored with Incongruent Combination (INCOM) or Fabulized Combination (FABCOM). They frequently point to a lack of self-cohesiveness (*a person without a head*), a false self identity when color is used arbitrarily (*a pink polar bear*), and boundary disturbances, including the failure to preserve distance from the blot (*Oh . . . It's approaching me*). However, a suggested guideline in distinguishing between borderline and psychotic levels of personality organization when CS markers of severe cognitive lapses are presented is to combine the results of the structured WAIS with those of the Rorschach. Although there might be lapses in logical thinking even on the WAIS, borderline patients usually tend to regress and to demonstrate overt signs of thinking disorders that appear less in the WAIS than in the Rorschach (Kleiger, 1999; Lerner, 1998; Sugarman, 1980).

Mediation at the borderline level might be impaired because of impulsivity and the low commitment to reality. However, in contrast to an adolescent at the psychotic level, the Testing of Limits (TOL) procedure (Exner, 2003), which is recommended to be conducted whenever a person fails to provide the popular responses to cards III, V, and VIII, usually improves the performance of the adolescent at the borderline level. The expected polarities between impulsivity and hypervigilance might be revealed on the Rorschach protocols of borderline-level adolescents by the coexistence of opposite scanning approaches in the same protocol (elevated W alongside elevated Dd). However, inasmuch as scanning problems, particularly those associated with impulsivity, are common in cognitive disorders such as ADHD and learning disabilities, the clinician should cautiously distinguish between problems with organic etiology and problems related to a lack of integrative abilities (Bleiberg, 2001).

In adolescents at the psychotic level of personality organization, the Rorschach protocols might show an accumulation of severe special scores, such as Contamination (CONTAM) and inappropriate logic (ALOG), and Level 2 special scores, indicating a substantial manifestation of cognitive slippage. These scores, which offer valuable data about cognitive mismanagement, boundary-less object relations, ideational slippage, and faulty judgment, imply failures in reasoning and concept formation, which characterizes combinative and circumstantial thinking. Also, the impaired ability of establishing cognitive focusing on the most relevant aspect of the stimulus field, which usually characterizes the psychotic level of organization, is indicated by an elevated number of responses with unusual locations (Dd). Furthermore, lack of differentiation between cognitive and affective functioning (as revealed, for example, by an elevated number of pure C responses), strange conceptions regarding human experience ($M- > 0$), excessive escape into fantasy ($Mp > Ma$), excessive use of intellectualization as a defense (Intellectualization Index > 5), inability to integrate percepts as being manifested in pure form response (F) within a blend, and thematic imagery indicating a fragmented self characterize the Rorschach protocols of psychotic-level adolescents more than the protocols of their peers at the borderline and neurotic levels. Other cognitive difficulties, particularly those related to effective dealing with experience, are less specific in psychotic-level adolescents and more frequently characterize Rorschach protocols of adolescents, regardless of the level of personality organization (Exner & Weiner, 1995; Smith et al., 2001).

To sum up, the accumulation of severe special scores rarely appears in Rorschach protocols of adolescents at other than a psychotic level of personality organization. However, isolated markers of disordered thinking might appear in protocols of adolescents with borderline features and even in those at the neurotic level, where developmental crisis produces psychotic-like symptoms. Most likely these protocols also reveal problems in self and object representations and affective difficulties in response to the developmental tasks.

CASE PRESENTATION

Jonathan is a tall, nice-looking, 15-year-old boy who was referred for evaluation by a psychiatrist who questioned the possibility of starting antidepressant medication. Jonathan was born in Israel, the middle child of a three-child family. He has two sisters, superstars at school and extensively involved with their peers, who were 18 and 8 years old at the time of referral. Both parents, in their forties, were born in Israel and work in the high-tech industry. They seem to be extremely ambitious and demanding regarding the academic achievements of their children. The father was diagnosed with ADHD in childhood and so was Jonathan. He is generally an average student at school but is considered a talented musician.

Jonathan presented himself as anxious, depressed, and vulnerable. He admitted to being quite distressed, having problems with attention and concentration, feeling worthless and unsuccessful, and lacking social skills, although he denied thoughts about hurting himself. He asked for professional help and was extremely motivated to start treatment. The parents reported they were very concerned about Jonathan's depressed mood. They also reported that in contrast to both his sisters, he always felt rejected by his peers. However, he is very attached to his sisters and spends hours playing games with the younger one.

Although Jonathan's Rorschach protocol is composed of only 14 responses (see Appendix), the very rich and complicated responses, as well as the lowered Lambda of .08, point to the validity of the protocol and to his intense involvement in the task. Of central concern is the value of 9 on the S-CON, which, of course, was taken as a warning of potential risk for self-destructive behavior. The lowered Lambda, the elevated DEPI of 6, and the significant CDI of 4 further indicated he was at a high suicidal risk and pointed to the need to take active steps in treatment with regard to his self-destructiveness.

The key variable of DEPI > 5 and CDI > 3 reveals an interpretive search starting in the interpersonal relationships cluster, followed by the self-conception cluster (Exner, 2003). Accordingly, it seems that Jonathan's difficulties are primarily in these two realms of functioning, whereas difficulties regarding controls and affect might be secondary to the interpersonal and self-conception problems. Cognitive difficulties, if any, might be caused by the emotional problems and/or by problems associated with the ADHD.

Being needful and dependent (T = 3; Fd = 3), Jonathan constantly looks to others for nurturance, longing for intimate closeness. However, content analysis reveals fears of being controlled, blocked, stuck, and dominated (e.g., *a monster-animal which swallowed a butterfly* [Card III]; *an animal that took control* [Card IV]; *a crab that came about to eat the butterfly and the butterfly has no way to escape* [Card VIII]; and *fish that are searching for a way to go out but they are blocked from all the sides . . . trapped . . .* [Card X]). Clearly, Jonathan is a chronically object-hungry youngster, highly sensitive to separation, yet constantly alert to threatening clues in the environment (elevated number of shading responses). Caught in these conflicting feelings of desiring nurturance yet fearful of being blocked and controlled, he regresses to immature relationships, as revealed by the childish representations of Rorschach animal percepts, as well as by his actual behavior of spending hours playing with his younger sister. Hence, actively searching to cope with both dependency needs and the developmental task of individuation, Jonathan looks for nurturing objects but feels the inappropriateness of showing his desires for nurturance. However, symbiotic, oral, and oral-aggressive responses that focus on swallowing, eating, and food content are predominantly displayed in his protocol, suggesting he is overwhelmed by his dependency needs.

Jonathan's interpersonal difficulties are further dramatically reflected in the absence of human figure responses, the absence of COP, the lowered Affective Ratio (Afr), and the elevated Isolation Index (.43). Like the fish he sees on Card X, needy and dependent, looking for friends, he finds himself in an environment that he feels is hostile, dangerous, and threatening. In this environment he can hardly stand on his own feet independently, like the butterfly he saw on Card V who needs *the two feathers that would fix him in the air.* The few human representations that appear in the protocol are projected into nonhuman percepts and result in poor form quality (FQ−), Poor Human Representations (PHR), and cognitive lapses. However, it should be noted that when being confronted with the TOL procedure on Card III, Jonathan easily responds with a highly elaborated and a good-quality human popular percept of two women involved in a cooperative activity of talking on the phone. This of course provides an indication of available resources that are needed for coping with developmental tasks. Nevertheless, since the communication described in this response (talking on the phone) is not direct, it perhaps suggests Jonathan's ambivalence concerning his desire for closer interpersonal relationships.

Jonathan's negative self-concept is reflected in a rarely found value of zero on the Egocentricity Index. This finding, combined with the three FD and the two Vista responses, points to an intense, painful, and probably disruptive self-focus and self-preoccupation, signifying extremely low self-esteem, critical self-attitudes, and general feelings of psychological inadequacy. His high aspiration level and perfectionistic approach, as revealed in the extremely elevated W:M ratio of 13:1 and the two FQ+ responses, might be associated with his high self-criticism. Jonathan is self-depreciatory, feels threatened, and constantly identifies with small and inferior animals and inanimate objects that need holding and might easily be stepped on. It thus seems that central to this adolescent's experience are his feelings of helplessness in searching for the resolution of parental dependency and attainment of genuine autonomy.

The positive DEPI of 6 points to a likelihood of a depressive disorder, where dysphoric mood and painful affects, as reflected by numerous C' and V responses and by the color-shading and multiple shading blends, dominate the picture. However, the finding of FM + m > sum shading responses suggests that the depressive mood is circumscribed by a stormy internal experience, probably associated with Jonathan's difficulties in self-conception and object relations within the context of the developmental task of separation-individuation. The lowered Afr, which reflects Jonathan's affective guardedness, might thus be a result of his awareness of his overly intense feelings, as well as of his less controlled, though not explosive, expression of affect (FC:CF + C = 0:5; C = 0).

Jonathan's cognitive style seems to be individualistic, as manifested by the elevated Xu% and the low number of popular responses. However, his general cognitive functioning is affected by his difficulties with interpersonal relationships and self-concept, revealing an over-incorporative scanning approach to reality, which at times leads to responses with percepts that do not fit into reality demands, being scored with FQ minus or one of the cognitive special scores. Content analysis of these responses indicates engulfment and aggressive themes that might be related to the separation-individuation conflict, existential anxieties, and identity confusion, which further lead to regression. The exhaustive elaboration of concrete details in his responses might thus exhibit not only a cautious and perfectionistic approach to perception, but also a defensive strategy of coping with his proneness to confabulatory thinking.

Most interesting is Jonathan's response to Card III, where the boundary-less percept of *a bug which swallowed a butterfly* is transferred into an imaginary content of *a monster-animal*, associated with the story of *Peter and the Wolf.* Like Peter, who went to the meadow and by doing so opposed his grandfather's limits, Jonathan experiences the developmental task of separation and the achievement of autonomy as being dangerous for him. However, he defensively transforms the nonrealistic oral-aggressive response into an adaptively regressed one while associatively relating it to a culturally acceptable content. His response to Card X of a coral island where fish are trapped, searching for a way to go out to their friends further reveals the separation-individuation conflict in which staying inside the holding environment is an anxiety-provoking claustrophobic experience, but the outside world is experienced as extremely threatening.

Like preadolescent children, Jonathan produces an abundance of animal movement responses (FM = 10), indicating that consciousness is being overwhelmed and disrupted by intrusive, drive-laden thoughts. The significantly lowered D (–5) and AdjD (–5) scores further point to pervasive stress, which could be a result of the intrusive thinking, intensified by overwhelming dependency needs.

These data raise the possibility that Jonathan's poor concentration might be due to unmet needs and felt helplessness rather than being fully explained by his ADHD problems. The overall diagnostic impression is one of an intelligent and talented adolescent with ADHD who usually functions at the neurotic level of personality organization, but is currently being overwhelmed by feelings of helplessness and neediness, while confronting the developmental tasks he must achieve in the maturation process.

SUMMARY

Rorschach assessment in adolescents as presented in this chapter suggests that the clinician provide a theoretically based structural diagnosis and formulate an experience/near personality description that integrates data and thematic imagery. Although the Rorschach has not been designed to provide the clinician with a DSM (American Psychiatric Association, 2000) diagnosis, most of the referral questions posed by mental health professionals involve diagnostic considerations. Rorschach data constitute a substantial source of information that helps the clinician address these questions. The main question is whether an impaired Rorschach essentially reflects developmental difficulties demonstrated in neurotic-level personality organization, genuine psychopathological manifestations, or characterological disturbances.

This chapter presents our approach to the interpretation of Rorschach data in adolescents, as demonstrated by a case study of a 15-year-old boy with prominent emotional difficulties. The Rorschach protocol of this adolescent is analyzed within the context of developmental lines of self-conception, interpersonal relationships, affect, and cognitive functioning.

When we selected the case to illustrate our approach, it was quite tempting to present a case that was severe in nature and obvious. However, we chose a case study that was not clear-cut and could show the complexity of interaction between level of personality organization and developmental issues. In addition, given the fluidity of personality functioning in adolescents, it has been particularly important to select a case study in which we could have a follow-up to further validate the evaluation.

Exner and Weiner (1995) state that more often than not differential diagnosis revealed by Rorschach assessment of adolescents is based on subtle differences between somewhat overlapping variables. However, Rorschach protocols of adolescents who function within the neurotic level of organization, although frequently demonstrating severe developmental difficulties, are far different from those given by their peers who are located within lower levels of personality organization. Thus, even though neurotic-level protocols might include some psychosis-like manifestations, either expressive or constrictive, obscuring the generally unimpaired, well-adapted personality picture, the overall configuration of variables and the patterns in which psychopathological manifestations are distributed throughout the protocol are substantially different from protocols of patients with lower functioning level.

In line with this suggestion, we analyzed the case study of Jonathan, who clearly showed overwhelming difficulties that blocked his adaptive functioning. Though Jonathan's Rorschach protocol showed some markers of disordered thinking, it also showed that while at the time of assessment he experienced a severe crisis, he had strengths that could locate him at a neurotic level of personality organization. The severe developmental crisis might explain the S-CON of 9, which, together with the elevated DEPI of 6, the lowered Lambda, and the CDI of 4, was construed as a warning that he was at high risk for suicide and pointed to the need to take active steps in treatment with regard to his self-destructiveness. Consequently, psychotherapy and antidepressant medication were recommended, and Jonathan showed significant improvement within a short period of time. At the age of 18 Jonathan was recruited into the Israeli Defense Forces (IDF), and he currently serves in a selective, demanding unit. Being highly evaluated in this unit and involved with his peers, Jonathan can be described as a well-adapted young man who can derive his sense of self from an internal, authentic source.

APPENDIX

Case Study. Rorschach Protocol

Card	No.	Response	Inquiry
I	1	Looks like a crab which has things here (making with the hand a gesture of claws). It has wings. Some kind of a flying crab. It has a body in the middle … open wings, as if it's flying to take something.	The whole blot. Eyes of a crab and two small claws. But I don't see legs. There're wings. Two sides like wings … it's flying. Flying to search something.
	2	A butterfly. It has two things in the form of 8. A wing. Half big and half small. Antennae. Eyes. A basic body and a small tail.	A butterfly. The whole blot. It reminds me of a butterfly because a butterfly has a form of 8. Two big sides. Looks like it's flying. The lower sides are smaller … and two antennae … a tail and a belly. A line in the middle. It's a creature rather than an object.
II	3	A lady-bird which is flying. I'll explain it to you. It's red. When it flies the wings are open and they're in colors, black and red. The legs are relatively in the front. There's a tail behind. Is it possible to turn the card? (He takes the card and holds it).	The whole blot. It's flying. It doesn't stay in one place. It has red spots on the wings. It also has the legs which are spread out. When it's in the air the arms are also spread out … everything is absolutely flat (?). When it stands, it's closed, round. Here it's flat. The reds up there are the arms. It's a view from above. All the drawings are like a view from above.
	4	A bird, a black bird that came and took some fruits from the field. Red fruits. (non-capital strawberries … tomatoes … The two spots are like eyes) … a beak. It might be a certain object that it has taken with the beak.	The whole blot without the red spots up here. One can see a beak and eyes (?) Black sticking out dots. The wings are spread out as if she's flying. Under the bird there's something … legs … but one can't see because the bird is above it … The bird takes something with the legs and brings it to somebody. It brings food. It might be in the field. The red could be … it can't be some spots on the bird … The wings are transparent and one can see what is under the wings, on the ground. Down there's a field. In the center there're red sticking out spots … not in the center.
III	5	This picture is "smallish", smaller than all the other. Looks like a bug, A monster-animal which swallowed a butterfly … scary eyes and teeth and here's the belly of the animal…and the butterfly is inside. Looks like in *Peter and the Wolf*. Like the wolf that ate the duck … looks like this … These two blots might be flowers that the bug is about to eat … (points to the red blots in both sides) … two stalks. It's definitely this. Nothing to add to this.	A bug that ate the butterfly (he turns the card upside down). Scary hands … they take something … and here is the belly … two big eyes and teeth. That's how they eat … It swallowed the whole butterfly … It's in the field … you can tell it by these two spots in both sides. (eyes?) the two black spots in the center between the arms.
IV	6	A two-headed animal. On one side it's a head of a skunk. On the other it looks like a hippopotamus with horns. It's simply lying on the floor. Two very flexible arms … the arms of the skunk … the arms of the hippopotamus are strong and massive … very strong …	Here in the upper part it's a skunk … up to the middle … it has a three-colored nose … grey, white and black. It has two legs which are really adjacent to the nose … very flexible arms which can be seen by the circle … up to the middle … from there on it's an animal that took control. Hippopotamus with horns. Two horns. Nose. Eyes. The whole head is furry … It has also massive arms. They are strong … They are placed on the ground like they should be and here are the nails … these sharp edges on both sides

Card	No.	Response	Inquiry
V	7	It's a butterfly. Mostly similar to a butterfly. As it should be … a tail … two wings … two wings with two feathers that would fix him in the air. The tail holds him well in the air. One can see that he's being held very strongly in the air. He's floating rather than waving the wings.	It looks like he holds itself in the air.
VI	8	A rug … A tiger or synthetic stuff … looks like a head of a fox or a tiger … hairy, with fur. A rug and in the edge there's a head of a tiger.	Like a rug … hairy. Many people have stepped on it. (hairy?) here are those things that are going out … distributed … one can see it's a tiger … here's the head … the nose … it has hair on the nose … it's dead, smashed …
VII	9	A chain of islands. In the middle there's an ocean. Each one is bigger than the other and than it becomes smaller and then like a hoof.	Each one is connected to the other … inside there's the ocean … the islands are not connected to the continent. In the center there's a big sea. (an island?) a continent inside something … there might have been an explosion of a volcano or drying out of water (?) the black spot in the white neighborhood.
	10	A silkworm that might bundle itself up in the center of its belly and then walks … making a turn …	Silkworms … while walking they transfer the whole weigh to the center of the belly (?) the two parts down here … it makes a turn and doesn't go straight.
	11	A foot-print of a horse. A horse stepped on and the foot-print was left in the ground. It looks like that.	A foot-print … not fresh … it didn't step here right now. It's already days ago … not the whole foot-print.
VIII	12	A crab in the red. It has ejected something from the claws and blocked the butterfly. A green butterfly in the center. The crab came about to eat the butterfly and the butterfly has no way to escape through.	The whole red part. These two are the claws. It has ejected some liquid … cobwebs … it seals the butterfly and wants to eat it. The light green is the ejected liquid.
IX	13	It's a head of a dragon that is ejecting fire from its mouth. It is ejecting fire to two different sides. There're eyes…the red…the nose…inside the nose in each nostril there's fire, a big flame.	The head is in the pink part only. It's ejecting orange fire. It's ejecting fire from the nose … (fire?) because it's orange and it's being ejected from the dragon's nose. Like we look on it from above and the dragon is down … looks like we're in the air. The nose is sticking out. One can see that something is being ejected out of the nostrils. A big flame.
X	14	A coral island in the water. There're crabs, scorpions, fish … many fish … and here is their food … green seaweed. Like a triangle and the fish are inside. Those who are outside cannot go out either … These two yellows are like fish that are searching for a way to go out but they are blocked from all the sides … trapped … it wants to get to his brothers … his friends.	The yellows are fish. The green is food. The pink is a triangle. There is something up here. It might be stones in the water. Here are small fish that would probably like to get to something, maybe to his parents or his friends that are outside. This brown here is a crab. These blues are seaweed.

Sequence of Scores

Card	Resp. No	Location and DQ	Loc. No.	Determinant(s) and Form Quality	(2)	Content(s)	Pop	Z Score	Special Scores
I	1	W+	1	FMau		A		4.0	INC
	2	Wo	1	FMao		A	P	1.0	DV, DR
II	3	Wo	1	FMa.CF.FC'.FDu		A		4.5	
	4	D+		FMa.CF.FC'.VF−		Ad,Fd,Ls		5.5	
III	5	WS+	1	FMa.FD−		(A),Fd,Bt		5.5	AG, PHR
IV	6	W+	1	FMp.C'F.FT+		A		4.0	INC2
V	7	Wo	1	FMp+		A	P	1.0	
VI	8	Wo	1	FT.mpo		Ad,Hh	P	2.5	MOR
VII	9	WSv/+	1	FVo		Na		4.0	
	10	Wo	1	FMp−		A		2.5	
	11	Wo	1	Fu		Id		2.5	
VIII	12	W+	1	FMa.mp.CF.TF−		A,Id		4.5	AG, FAB2, PHR
IX	13	WS+	1	FMa.ma.CF.FDu		Fi,(A)		5.5	
X	14	W+	1	Ma.CFo		A,Fd,Na		5.5	FAB, DV, PHR

Structural Summary

Location Features

Zf	=	14
ZSum	=	52.5
ZEst	=	45.5
W	=	13
(Wv	=	0)
D	=	1
W+D	=	14
Dd	=	0
S	=	3

DQ

			(FQ−)
+	=	7	(3)
o	=	6	(1)
v/+	=	1	(0)
v	=	0	(0)

Form Quality

	FQx	MQual	W+D
+	= 2	0	2
o	= 4	1	4
u	= 4	0	4
-	= 4	0	4
none	= 0	0	0

Determinants

Blends	Single	
FM.CF.FC'.FD	M	= 0
FM.CF.FC'.VF	FM	= 4
FM.FD	m	= 0
FM.C'F.FT	FC	= 0
FT.m	CF	= 0
FM.m.CF.TF	C	= 0
FM.m.CF.FD	Cn	= 0
M.CF	FC'	= 0
	C'F	= 0
	C'	= 0
	FT	= 0
	TF	= 0
	T	= 0
	FV	= 1
	VF	= 0
	V	= 0
	FY	= 0
	YF	= 0
	Y	= 0
	Fr	= 0
	rF	= 0
	FD	= 0
	F	= 1
	(2)	= 0

Contents

H	= 0
(H)	= 0
Hd	= 0
(Hd)	= 0
Hx	= 0
A	= 8
(A)	= 2
Ad	= 2
(Ad)	= 0
An	= 0
Art	= 0
Ay	= 0
Bl	= 0
Bt	= 1
Cg	= 0
Cl	= 0
Ex	= 0
Fd	= 3
Fi	= 1
Ge	= 0
Hh	= 1
Ls	= 1
Na	= 2
Sc	= 0
Sx	= 0
Xy	= 0
Idio	= 2

S-Constellation

Yes	FV+VF+V+FD > 2
Yes	Col-Shd Blends > 0
Yes	Ego < .31 or > .44
No	MOR > 3
Yes	Zd > ±3.5
Yes	es > EA
Yes	CF + C > FC
Yes	X+% < .70
No	S > 3
No	P < 3 or > 8
Yes	Pure H < 2
Yes	R < 17
Yes	Total

Special Scores

		Lvl-1	Lvl-2
DV	=	2 x1	0 x2
INC	=	1 x2	1 x4
DR	=	1 x3	0 x6
FAB	=	1 x4	1 x7
ALOG	=	0 x5	
CON	=	0 x7	

Raw Sum6 = 7
Wgtd Sum6 = 22

AB	= 0		GHR	= 0	
AG	= 2		PHR	= 3	
COP	= 0		MOR	= 1	
CP	= 0		PER	= 0	
			PSV	= 0	

Ratios, Percentages, And Derivations

				Affect		Interpersonal	
R = 14		L = 0.08		FC:CF+C = 0 : 5		COP = 0	AG = 2
				Pure C = 0		GHR:PHR = 0 : 3	
EB = 1 : 5.0	EA = 6.0	EBPer = 5.0		SumC' : WSumC = 3 : 5.0		a:p = 9 : 5	
eb = 13 : 8	es = 21	D = -5		Afr = 0.27		Food = 3	
	Adj es = 19	Adj D = -5		S = 3		SumT = 3	
				Blends:R = 8 : 14		Human content = 0	
FM = 10	SumC' = 3	SumT = 3		CP = 0		Pure H = 0	
m = 3	SumV = 2	SumY = 0				PER = 0	
						Isolation index = 0.43	

Ideation		Mediation		Processing		Self-Perception	
a:p = 9 : 5	Sum6 = 7	XA% = 0.71		Zf = 14		3r+(2)/R = 0.00	
Ma:Mp = 1 : 0	Lvl-2 = 2	WDA% = 0.71		W:D:Dd = 13:1:0		Fr+rF = 0	
2AB+(Art+Ay) = 0	WSum6 = 22	X-% = 0.29		W : M = 13 : 1		SumV = 2	
MOR = 1	M- = 0	S- = 1		Zd = +7.0		FD = 3	
	M none = 0	P = 3		PSV = 0		An+Xy = 0	
		X+% = 0.43		DQ+ = 7		MOR = 1	
		Xu% = 0.29		DQv = 0		H:(H)+Hd+(Hd) = 0 : 0	

PTI = 1	DEPI = 6*	CDI = 4*	S-CON = 9*	HVI = No	OBS = No

To sum up, Jonathan appeared in the Rorschach to experience himself as being extremely needy, threatened by the developmental task of separation, and searching for productive solutions to relate to his peers. A devaluated self and ensuing self-destructiveness and dependency were prominent features throughout the Rorschach protocol. The follow-up of Jonathan's psychoanalytically oriented treatment validated the understanding of the Rorschach protocol as revealing normative difficulties rather than indicating manifestations of a mental disorder.

REFERENCES

Acklin, M. A. (1997). Psychodiagnosis of personality structure: Borderline personality organization. In J. R. Meloy, M. N. Acklin, C. B. Gacono, & C. A. Peterson (Eds.), *Contemporary Rorschach interpretation* (pp. 109–122). Mahwah, NJ: Lawrence Erlbaum Associates.

American Psychiatric Association (2000). *Diagnostic and statistical manual of mental disorders, DSM-IV-TR*. Washington, DC: Author.

Blatt, S., Brenneis, C., Schimek, J., & Glick, M. (1976). Normal developmental and psychopathological impairment of the concept of the object on the Rorschach. *Journal of Abnormal Psychology, 85*, 364–373.

Blatt, S. J., Tuber, S., & Auerbach, J. (1990). Representation of interpersonal interaction on the Rorschach and level of psychopathological impairment. *Journal of Personality Assessment, 54*, 711–728.

Bleiberg, E. (2001). *Treating personality disorders in children and adolescents: A relational approach.* New York: Guilford.

Blos, P. (1962). *On adolescence: A psychoanalytic interpretation.* New York: Free Press.

Exner, J. E. (1992). Some Comments on a conceptual critique of the EA:es comparison in the Rorschach Comprehensive System. *Psychological Assessment, 4*(3), 297–300.

Exner, J. E. (2003). *The Rorschach: A Comprehensive System: Volume 1. Basic foundations and principles of interpretation* (4th Ed.). Hoboken, NJ: Wiley.

Exner, J. E., & Weiner, I. B. (1995). *The Rorschach: A Comprehensive System: Vol 3. Assessment of children and adolescents* (2nd ed.). New York: John Wiley.

Franklin, K. W., & Cornell, D. G. (1997). Rorschach interpretation with high-ability adolescent females: Psychopathology or creative thinking? *Journal of Personality Assessment, 68*, 184–196.

Gacono, C. B., & Meloy, J. R. (Eds.). (1994). *The Rorschach assessment of aggressive and psychopathic personalities.* Hillsdale, NJ: Lawrence Erlbaum Associates.

Handler, L. (1999). Assessment of playfulness: Hermann Rorschach meets D. W. Winnicott. *Journal of Personality Assessment, 72*, 208–217.

Handler, L. (2005). *The administration and interpretation of the Rorschach in light of changes in psychoanalytic theory.* Paper presented at the XVIII International Congress of Rorschach and Projective Methods, Barcelona.

Kelly, F. (1997). *The assessment of object relations phenomena in adolescents: TAT and Rorschach measures.* Mahwah, NJ: Lawrence Erlbaum Associates.

Kerenberg, O. (1976). *Object relations theory and clinical psychoanalysis.* New York: Aronson Press.

Kleiger, J. H. (1999). *Disordered thinking and the Rorschach: Theory, research, and differential diagnosis.* Hillsdale, NJ: Analytic Press

Kohut, H. (1971). *The analysis of the self.* New York: International University Press.

Leichtman, M. B. (1996). *The Rorschach: A developmental perspective.* Hillsdale, NJ: Analytic Press.

Lerner, P. (1998). *Psychoanalytic perspectives on the Rorschach.* Hillsdale, NJ: Analytic Press.

McWilliams, N. (1999). *Psychoanalytic case formulation.* New York: Guilford Press.

Meeks, J. E., & Bernet, W. (2001). *The fragile alliance: An orientation to the psychiatric treatment of the adolescent.* Malabar, FL: Krieger.

Mitchell, S. A. (2000). *Relationality from attachment to intersubjectivity.* Hillsdale, NJ: Analytic Press.

Murray, J. F. (1997). The Rorschach and diagnosis of neurotic conditions in children and adolescents: A case study. In J. R. Meloy, M. N. Acklin, C. B. Gacono, & C. A. Peterson (Eds.), *Contemporary Rorschach interpretation* (pp. 301–314). Mahwah, NJ: Lawrence Erlbaum Associates.

Ogden, T. H. (1986). *The matrix of the mind: Object relations and the psychoanalytic dialogue.* Northvale, NJ: Jason Aronson.

Rothschild, L. (2005). *The advantage of integrative approach to Rorschach interpretation for the assessment of primitive modes of experience.* Paper presented at the midwinter meeting for the Society of Personality Assessment, Chicago.

Rothschild, L., & Stein, D. (2004). *Exploring ego functions in two subtypes of eating disorders patients.* Paper presented at the congress of the European Rorschach Association, Stockholm, Sweden.

Silverstein, M. L. (1999). *Self psychology and diagnostic assessment.* Mahwah, NJ: Lawrence Erlbaum Associates.

Smith, B. (1990). Potential space and the Rorschach: Application of object relations theory. *Journal of Personality Assessment, 55*, 756–767.

Smith, S. R., Baity, M. R., Knowles, E. S., & Hilsenroth, M. J. (2001). Asessment of disordered thinking in children and adolescents: The Rorschach Perceptual Thinking Index. *Journal of Paersonality Assessment, 77*, 447–463.

Stokes, J. M., Pogge, D. L., Powell, J., Ward, W., Bilginer, L., & De Luca, V. A. (2003). The Rorschach Ego Impairment Index: Prediction of treatment outcome in a child psychiatric population. *Journal of Personality Assessment 81*, 11–19.

Sugarman, A. (1980). The borderline personality organization as manifested on psychological tests. In J. S. Kwawer, H. D. Lerner, P. M. Lerner, & A. Sugarman (Eds.), *Borderline phenomena and the Rorschach test* (pp. 39–57). New York: International Universities Press.

Tibon, S., Handelzalts, J. E., & Weinberger, Y. (2005). Using the Rorschach for exploring the concept of transitional space within the political context of the Middle East. *International Journal of Applied Psychoanalytic Studies, 2*, 40–57.

Tibon, S., Porcelli, P., & Weinberger, Y. (2005). The Ego Impairment Index and the Reality–Fantasy Scale: Comment on Viglione, Perry, and Meyer (2003). *Journal of Personality Assessment, 84*, 315–317.

Urist, J. (1997). The Rorschach test and the assessment of object relations. *Journal of Personality Assessment, 41*, 3–9.

Viglione, D., Perry, W., & Meyer, G. J. (2003). Refinements in the Rorschach Ego Impairment Index Incorporating the Human Representational Variable. *Journal of Personality Assessment, 81*, 149–156.

Weiner, I. B. (2000). Making Rorschach interpretation as good as it can be. *Journal of Personality Assessment, 74*, 164–174.

Winnicott, D. W. (1971). *Playing and reality.* New York: Basic Books.

11

THE CLINICAL APPLICATION OF THE SOCIAL COGNITION AND OBJECT RELATIONS SCALE WITH CHILDREN AND ADOLESCENTS

Francis D. Kelly

Poet Seat School
Greenfield, Massachusetts

The purpose of this chapter is 1) to briefly describe the Social Cognition and Object Relations (SCORS) scales, 2) to provide the reader with an overview of relevant research relating to child and adolescent populations, and 3) to illustrate the diagnostic and therapeutic interpretive possibilities the SCORS offers when applied to consideration of Thematic Apperception Test (TAT) narratives produced by children and adolescents. To this end, the clinical vignette of a 13-year-old adolescent male with an array of behavioral and affect regulation difficulties is highlighted. The primary emphasis herein is to acquaint the reader with how the SCORS may be used in clinical work to enhance the developmental understanding and assessment of the child and to show how material may be translated into hypotheses that can guide and inform treatment direction and options.

Realizing that TAT narratives offered a potentially rich source of information about an individual's object relations because of the inherent nature of the task—consciously and unconsciously reflecting on one's internal representations of self and others in order to create narratives—Westen and colleagues (Westen, Lohr, Silk, Kerber, & Goodrich, 1985) developed the initial version of an object relations scale designed to tap four main domains of psychological functioning representing cognitive and affective representations of self and others. Integrating information from research, clinical observation and theory, the original Social Cognition Object Relations Scale (SCORS) assessed four dimensions of object relations functioning: Complexity of Representations of People (CR)—the degree to which representations of people are rich, complex, and differentiated; Understanding of Social Causality (USC)—the degree to which attributions about social exchanges and interactions are defined by accurate and logical perceptions; Capacity for Emotional Investment in Relationships (CEI)—the degree to which relationships are defined by need-gratifying versus more mutual, reciprocal involvement; and Affect-Tone of Relationship Paradigms (AT)—the extent to which relationships are viewed as positive and benevolent versus destructive and malevolent.

Brief descriptions of these original four scales and the two more recently added scales (Westen, 2002) are given here, along with responses and scoring examples for each of the scales. Scoring examples for the Dominant Interpersonal Concerns scale, a component of the SCORS-R, is not included, because it is not a social cognition or object relations scale.

THE SOCIAL COGNITION AND OBJECT RELATIONS SCALE–REVISED (SCORS-R)

Complexity of Representations of People

This scale has a developmental trajectory. That is, as children grow older, their representations of self and others become more differentiated from others; adolescents are more likely to be better at distinguishing their own thoughts and feelings from others than are younger children. The sense of self and other becomes richer and more complex. The reasons people act, feel, and think the way they do suggest that as the child gets older, the ability to ascribe psychological motives as explanatory or mediating factors that organize behavior increases. From childhood, through adolescence and into adulthood, the person develops the ability to integrate as opposed to separate discrepant and seemingly incongruous feelings about self and others. At lower scale levels, eccentric, self-absorbed representations prevail. At somewhat higher levels, representations lack complexity and are limited to superficial and stereotypic, albeit conventional, portrayals. At higher levels, there is the indication of psychological awareness and the ability to portray one's self and needs as separate and different from others.

An example of a lower-level response is a 15-year-old, aggressive and schizoid male's narrative to Card 13MF: "He killed her . . . has hands over eyes. Wishing he didn't do it. What the hell? He gets caught by the cops . . . put him in jail. Yep, gets his ass beat in jail. He dies . . . beat to death. Jeffrey Dahmer was beat to death in jail. He used to keep people frozen in his house. I seen the movie, chopped dog's head off, stuck it in the ground on a pole in the woods." The response, in addition to suggesting a world view that is quite terrifying, emphasizes the additional quality of loose and highly idiosyncratic reference to mayhem and primitive violence. The story is scored 2, at best, because the characters are clearly bonded and separate, but there is a definite lack of reference to the respective individual's subjective states or motives. The focus is on describing behavior and not the internal states that direct manifest presentations.

Emotional Investment in Values and Moral Standards

This dimension develops in a manner such that the person is viewed as first governed by external controls and prohibitions, eventually developing a mature stance wherein behavior is guided by internal feelings, thoughts, and principles. SCORS-R lower-level responses given by children and adolescents may suggest a decidedly antisocial and inconsiderate manner of relating; aggressive behavior occurs without suggestion of remorse or regret. Child and adolescent responses occurring at a somewhat higher level are marked by some indication of internalization, not acting badly because of what others might think but with a relative lack of guilt or remorse for wrongdoing. More mature responses suggest some inkling that the child or adolescent has conventional moral views and feels badly about hurting others or violating societal rules.

An example showing age-appropriate response on this dimension is provided by a 9-year-old, withdrawn and depressed girl in her responses to Card 3 BM: *"This girl is put in jail because she did something wrong and she's sitting on the floor. She gets out in 10 years. That's all I can tell you. She's only 10 years old and she stole cigarettes and was smoking and that's wrong."* The story is scored 3 because this child shows clear indication of internalization of standards, expressing the clear message that wrongdoing is dealt with in an incisive, albeit somewhat unrealistic, and excessively punitive manner. There is an indication that she is clearly aware of the difference between right and wrong.

Understanding of Social Causality

This scale assesses the child or adolescent's ability to understand social causality. Again this is a scale that reflects a developmental progression. From early childhood to adulthood the individual's development on this dimension proceeds from a stance wherein the behavior of others is interpreted in a distorted, illogical, and unrealistic manner. At a somewhat later age it is possible to see responses that may be somewhat difficult to interpret because of incongruities, often leaving the examiner with a sense of momentary confusion as to how the person has come up with this sequence of events. Higher-level responses suggest that the person has an accurate and logical understanding of his or her own and other's thoughts, feelings, and behavior.

A scoring example for this dimension is provided by a 16-year-old male who may be showing early signs of cognitive slippage and significant inner conflict. His story to Card 13B is as follows:

A little boy who . . . like a big boy . . . a boy who has to be a man or something like that. I don't know, it's weird. And the boy's like afraid and like mad. He's like afraid of becoming a man, or something and he's mad because he can't do what he wants to do. He wants to be a man so he can have freedom and stuff, but he doesn't want to take the responsibilities.

The narrative is scored 3 because a fairly complex narrative is created but does not lead to any subsequent behavior or response.

Capacity for Investment in Relationships

This scale measures the child's or adolescent's ability to initiate and sustain relationships with others. Proceeding from a stance in which relationships are portrayed as need-gratifying or highly narcissistic, to one which portrays concern, sensitivity, and genuine interest in others, the scale tracks a developmental progression from "me" to "thee." At lower levels narratives are defined by unstable relationships or the absence of connections other than superficial involvement. More intermediate responses are suggested by reference to shared activity and mutual involvement, but a lack of depth or emotional commitment. At higher levels the narrative suggests sentiments of friendship, trust, mutual respect, empathy, and emotional intimacy.

A scoring example for this dimension involves the narrative provided by a 17-year-old male with a history of depression and substance abuse. His response to Card 7BM: "Looks like a father talking to his son. The son made mistakes that father made. Father looks like he's smiling . . . son is worried, not sure what the outcome will be. Son eventually moves on, learns from experience. The two of them gain more trust with one another. The son looks worried . . . anxious maybe. The father looks kind of happy that the son learned a lesson— pleased maybe that he learned a lesson." This narrative scores a 6 for the clear demonstration of reciprocity and reference to caring, reflection, and empathy. The relationship here is defined by mutual sharing, respect, and appreciation of one another.

Affect-Tone of Relationship Paradigms

This is the only scale that does not incorporate a developmental progression but does tap the ways that the child or adolescent experiences relationships, along a continuum from malevolent to benevolent. Psychoanalytic theory (e.g., object relations and attachment theory, as well as social-cognitive research) has underscored the importance of this construct to understanding the inner representational worlds of highly disturbed children, such as those with disorganized and anxious attachments as well as those with severe personality dysfunction (e.g., borderline and narcissistic children), and those who have been subjected to various types of abuse and maltreatment (Ornduff, 1997). The narratives of these latter clinical groups tend to be defined by representations of others as malevolent and intentionally destructive. At somewhat higher levels, portrayals of relationships suggest unpleasant, indifferent, and unhappy ties to others. Narratives suggesting positive and rewarding interpersonal involvement are given by less disturbed children and adolescents.

The narrative provided by a 12-year-old girl, with a history of physical abuse and neglect, is fairly prototypical. Her response to Card 3BM: *"Why do these have to be so depressing? The girl got hit and everyone was laughing at her. And nobody wanted to see if she was O.K. She feels hurt and mad . . . locks herself in room."* The story receives a score of 1 because of the theme introducing abuse and physical maltreatment, with the obvious concern that her expectations of closeness and intimate relationships are defined by malevolence and maltreatment.

Dominant Interpersonal Concerns

This is the newest dimension of the SCORS-R and comprises 50 items—8 positive and 42 negative, which may be found in two sources, Conklin and Westen (2001) and Westen (2002). Some examples of positive Dominant Interpersonal Themes include nurturance, emotional intimacy, affiliation, autonomy, admiration, sexual intimacy, and mastery. Examples of negative Dominant Interpersonal Concerns are themes of rejection, sexual victimization, failure, helplessness, aggression, low self-esteem, suicide, betrayal, self-blaming, punishment, and loneliness.

Several scoring options are possible, but the most efficacious one simply involves evaluating frequency and intensity (e.g., 1 = probably present, but not entirely clear; 5 = clearly present and is a central theme; 7 = the theme is unusual for the card and/or is highly charged emotionally). For example, if a child produces five stories that contain clear victimization themes, the raw score would be 5 for frequency and the intensity scores would vary, according to the story. The introduction of a victimization theme to TAT Card 1 would warrant an intensity score of 7 because this card does not typically elicit such themes. The obvious interpretation would be that expectations in relation to this theme are central to this child's clinical presentation.

ADMINISTRATION AND SCORING

Before considering an overview of scoring issues, it is important to reference several basic assumptions that are central to an understanding of the theoretical tenets that underlie the different scales and direct the clinical application of the original SCORS as well as later revisions, (e.g., Westen, 1995; Conklin & Westen, 2001). First, the nature of the TAT cards is such that they elicit stories that translate into rich and clinically informed material about the person's interpersonal world. Second, the integration of psychoanalytic and social-cognitive developmental theories provides for observation of cognitive, affective, and attributional processes that an individual displays in creating TAT stories. Third, the narratives may be especially informative in articulating implicit working models of self and others that serve as beacons to guide and inform perceptions and representations of self and others and are different from what is obtained when explicit measures of self and others are assessed via self-report, rating scales, and observations of manifest behavior. Fourth, because the study of object relations requires that this construct be viewed as multidimensional as opposed to unitary in nature, it is then important to keep in mind that different dimensions of this construct may have different developmental trajectories, a fact well appreciated by most researchers and clinicians. Therefore, the scoring system must allow for the assessment of multiple dimensions and hence the five domains that currently make up the test.

Which TAT cards should be used with children and adolescents is a matter of some debate, because specific cards have definite pull for certain themes (Cramer, 1996), and clinicians may wish to add or delete certain cards, given the age of the child or the need to address specific interpersonal dynamics (e.g., mother-son relatedness). I generally use most of the 10 cards designated by Bellak and Abrams (1997; i.e., 1, 2, 3BM, 4, 6BM, 7GF, 8 BM, 9 GF, 10 and 13MF), but I usually like to delete two cards and add Cards 12M and 13B. The former card tends to elicit themes that often presage responses to treatment (i.e., transference phenomena) and home in on victim-victimizer themes, whereas the latter is a card with which children resonate and to which they frequently offer material that provides information about the emotional availability of those entrusted with their care (e.g., parents or their surrogates).

In administering the TAT I follow the usual format in which I tell the child or adolescent that I am going to show them some cards and want them to make up a story for each card, including what happened before, what is occurring now, and how things will end up. I tell them that I will be asking them some questions about how the people are feeling and thinking; this is in line with most other opinions regarding administrative procedures (Groth-Marnat, 1997). Responses, as well as extraneous comments (e.g., "This is stupid"; "How do I know what they are feeling, I'm not them"; "This is hard"; etc.), are recorded verbatim. Clinicians should also note changes in nonverbal behavior, because these are often linked to emerging affect regulation shifts and/or underlying conflict material that may be subsequently represented in a narrative.

In scoring TAT stories, the reader is directed to one particular revision of the original instrument, now designated the SCORS-R (i.e., Conklin & Westen, 2001), which assesses six dimensions, compared with the original four. All told, the test now consists of the original four dimensions, Complexity of Representations of People (CR), Understanding of Social Causality (USC), Capacity for Emotional Investment in Relationships (CEI), and Affect-Tone of Relationships Paradigm (AT). The two new additional scales are Emotional Investment in Values and Moral Standards (EIVM) and Dominant Interpersonal Concerns (DIC). Another version, the Social Cognition and Object Relations Scale–Global Ratings (SCORS–G; Westen, 1995), containing three additional scales, has been exclusively employed with adult psychiatric patients, but no current child or adolescent research is available to evaluate the pros and cons of adopting the use of these additional scales with children. In fact, Westen, (2002) urges some caution in implementing these newer scales when they are applied to TAT narratives.

Returning to specific scoring concerns, the six dimensions of the instrument are each separately assessed by assigning a score employing a 7-point scale, anchored at Levels 1, 3, 5, and 7 by reference to specific scoring principles. Comparable to the original SCORS, each of the SCORS-R scales, with the exception of Affect-Tone, follows a developmental trajectory, with Level 1 referring to a developmentally immature story and Level 7 representing a psychologically mature story. Dominant Interpersonal Concerns are rated for frequency and intensity. A 7-point scale is used to rate the intensity of themes. Ultimately, these are rank-ordered for prevalence and emotional valence. Higher-frequency scores point to core conflictual material, and higher-intensity scores relate to the severity of a Dominant Interpersonal Concern. After the scoring process is completed, the scores are collated and summarized in a manner suggested by the presentation in Table 11.1.

TABLE 11.1.
Summary of SCOR-R Responses for Michael

Scale	Card Number					
	1	2	4	8BM	13B	CR mean
Complexity of representations (CR)	3	3	3	2	3	2.8
Affect-tone of relationships paradigms (AT)	3	4	3	1	3	2.8
Capacity for emotional investment (CEI)	3	3	2	1	3	2.4
Investment in values & moral standards (IVMR)	4	3	2	1	4	2.8
Understanding of social causality (USC)	4	4	4	1	4	3.4

Dominant Interpersonal Concerns (DIC)

	Frequency	Intensity
Disappointed authorities	1	5
Failure	1	5
Frustrated by circumstances	1	5
Fears	4	5,6,5,6
Rescue	1	3
Neglect	4	5,6,6,5
Tumultuous relationship	1	6
Victimization	1	5
Fears of losing control	1	3
Aggression	2	5
Loss	1	3

RELEVANT RESEARCH

In this section I review the research that has utilized the SCORS with child and adolescent populations, in both clinical and developmental situations. My recent efforts (Kelly, 1997, 2004) provide a comprehensive overview that addresses reliability and validity concerns in addition to an exhaustive review of relevant research with different clinical populations.

Westen's original contention that the SCORS was a developmental instrument has been validated in many studies. A brief list of adolescent research includes the following. In the first instance, the work of Westen's group (e.g., Westen, Klepser, Ruffins, Silverman, Lifton, & Boekamp, 1991) and the recent effort of Birndoff and Porcerelli (2004) have demonstrated that object relations capacity continues to develop through latency and adolescence, that object representations are multidimensional in nature, and that interpersonal relationships are shaped and molded by past experiences and mediate the processing of social information. In another effort designed to both assess the developmental trajectory of the SCORS and link it to manifest behavior in 8- and 10-year-old children, Niec and Russ (2002) found that the observed developmental differences were consistent with object relations theory and supported the observation that the SCORS internal representation measures provide a means of understanding children's interpersonal functioning, that is, empathic ability. Finally, Raches (2004) found that children aged 7 through 10, with diagnoses of Disruptive Behavior Disorder (DBD), had lower SCORS Affect Tone (AT) mean scores and more physical aggression than did a contrast group. Results suggested that DBD children experienced the world as more threatening and malevolent.

Clinical research has mainly focused on two clinical groups, which upon closer scrutiny are closely related: children who have experienced or are experiencing exposure to varying types of abuse and adolescents with histories of borderline presentations. With respect to the former, the comprehensive work of Ornduff and her colleagues (Ornduff, 1997; Ornduff, Centeno, & Kelsey, 1999; Ornduff, Freedenfeld, Kelsey, & Critelli, 1994; Ornduff & Kelsey, 1996; Pistole & Ornduff, 1994) found that sexually abused children and adolescents score significantly lower on all SCORS scales than do their nonabused counterparts. In related research Freedenfeld and colleagues (Freedenfeld, Ornduff, & Kelsey, 1995) showed that physical maltreatment also has a deleterious impact on the child's object-relations functions. The clinical implications of these findings suggest that treatment efforts should be directed at helping abused children alter malevolent perceptions of self and others and that the clinician should be sensitive to negative transference phenomena, the likely result of damaged and stunted object representations. Ornduff's group (Ornduff, 1997; Ornduff & Kelsey, 1996) generated two particularly important SCORS findings: physically abused children display more pervasive impairment on all SCORS scales, and sexually abused children evidence particular and noteworthy problems on the Affect Tone (AT) scale, because they display the expectation that malevolence and severe mistreatment are to be expected more often than not in their interpersonal dealings; and second, both sexually and physically mistreated children produce more Level 1 scores on the scales that tap more affective (AT, CEI) rather than cognitive (USC, CR) dimensions of object relations. Again, the clinical implications indicate a need to be sensitive to the fact that these children are at risk for developing templates and schemata that adversely mediate and influence subsequent relations, with significant expectation and apprehension that maltreatment, mistrust, and malevolence will characterize close and intimate connections and ties to others.

A population that has been exposed to abuse and maltreatment in earlier childhood in many instances is the borderline adolescent (Westen, Ludolph, Block, Wixom, & Wiss, 1990).

Object relations functioning of borderline female adolescents has been assessed in several investigations with one investigation (Westen, Ludolph, Silk, Kellam, Gold, & Lohr, 1990) demonstrating that borderlines could be differentiated from normal and psychiatrically disturbed counterparts on the basis of SCORS measures. Results underscored the unique nature of the borderline group's developmental functioning: more pathological responses, poorly articulated representations of others, blurred boundaries, and eccentric thinking. Also of importance is the finding that the borderline patients showed relatively intact functioning on the Complexity of Representations of People (CR) scale, leading to the caveat that under certain conditions (i.e., low arousal), the representations of this clinical group may be relatively in line with those of nonborderlines, a fact with which most clinicians would agree. In considering the protocols of borderline children and adolescents, it is frequently the case that considerable intercard variability will be exhibited, thus behooving the clinician to consider potential activating conditions (Westen, 1991) that may precipitate regressive shifts, defensive failures, and the emergence of themes representing key scripts (i.e., Dominant Interpersonal Concerns). A corollary here would be the reminder that clinicians need to be sensitive to conditions and situations that evoke and elicit more adaptive functioning, and deliberate effort should be made to keep this in mind as one sifts through the TAT narratives.

In another investigation, involving female adolescent psychiatric inpatients, Westen and colleagues (Westen, Ludolph, Block, et al., 1990) used the SCORS to illustrate the relationships between developmental history variables and different aspects of these adolescents' object relations. Results supported several conclusions. First, preoedipal experiences and the role of the mother have a cogent influence on the development of later psychopathology. Second, various types of maltreatment (e.g., neglect, sexual abuse, and disruptive family experiences) occurring during the latency years also appear to have an important adverse impact on object relations development. This latter finding provided additional support for the contention and findings of earlier research that object relations continue to develop well into childhood and adolescent years (Westen, 1991). Results illustrated how abuse, neglect, and disrupted attachments are easily detected by various SCORS dimensions. For example, early physical abuse by mothers is reflected in a high percentage of Level 1 responses on all scales, with the exception of Affect Tone; chronic neglect is reflected in low scores (i.e., Levels 1 and 2) on the Understanding of Social Causality scale. Such adolescents often have difficulty understanding their own and others' attributions, motives, and intentions, a finding that has significant implications for treatment planning.

Finally, Conklin and Westen (2001) present the case report of a hospitalized 16-year-old female with anorexia nervosa. Five TAT stories provided the data for the report, which resulted in the illustration of the way in which a dynamic formulation could be generated from the narratives. Offering caveats for administration, scoring and clinical interpretation, the authors conclude that the SCORS-based TAT interpretive paradigm should see additional application in the assessment of patterns of thought, feeling, and motivation in the domain of interpersonal functioning that may not be accessible via other avenues, such as interview material.

Consideration of these varied efforts indicates that the SCORS-R interpretive paradigm can be appropriately used with an array of children and adolescents between the ages of 6 and 20. I have used the SCORS-R (Conklin & Westen, 2001) as the primary interpretive paradigm to evaluate TAT protocols for well over the past decade and find it to be the preferred standardized measure for assessing object relations in children and adolescents. My preference is to use this paradigm as opposed to the more recently developed SCORS-G (Hillesenroth,

Stein, & Pinsker, 2004) because the SCORS-G has been used entirely with adult samples, and it remains to be seen how applicable the three additional scales will be with child and adolescent clients. This is not to say that the additional measures may not be of importance and augment the existing scales, but to date there are no published studies that can serve as reference points. Second, an additional reason for staying the course and employing the six scales promoted by Conklin and Westen (2001) is tied to Westen's (2002) cautionary observations that there may be some difficulty in scoring the three additional scales (i.e., Experience and Management of Aggressive Impulses, Self-esteem, and Identity and Coherence of Self) if TAT stories are the data source.

Finally, concerns that the SCORS-R is difficult to learn and implement are significantly attenuated by referring to the scoring manuals of Hilsenroth et al. (2004) and Westen (2002), which are comprehensive, easily understood, and readily applied in the clinical setting with latency-age children and adolescents.

RATIONALE FOR USING THE SCORS-R
WITH CHILDREN AND ADOLESCENTS

Listed below are some indications for making the SCORS -R the interpretive paradigm when TAT narratives provided by children and adolescents are being evaluated.

- The SCORS-R has well-validated theoretical underpinnings (i.e., object relations, cognitive and developmental psychology, developmental psychoanalysis), grounding the narratives in a matrix that can be translated into meaningful quantitative and qualitative information.
- The results provide the clinician with a source of rich, diversified, implicit information that has significant diagnostic implications. For example, the child's aggressive and oppositional manifest behavior belies drive-defense conflict and tension, as opposed to a more antisocial orientation. Here, results from the USC and CEI domains would provide potential sources of this type of information.
- Object relations information derived from SCORS data may (and should) be juxtaposed against the results of other projective data, for example, Rorschach content object relation measures such as the Mutuality of Autonomy Scale (Urist, 1977; Tuber, 1989, 1992) to provide convergent validation regarding clinical phenomena about object relations capacity. A case in point is the fact that lower-level object relations scores on the MOAS tend to be highly correlated with lower scores on the SCORS. For example, in the case study outlined below (i.e., Michael), there is a suggestion of object relations variability on the SCORS, and this is also the case on the MOAS, where the patient's scores range from Level 2 to Level 6. Hence, there is convergence of results between these two object relations content scale measures, a well-documented phenomenon with adult patients (e.g., Ackerman, Hilsenroth, Clemence, Weatherhill, & Fowler, 2001) and likely the case with children and adolescents as well, based on my clinical experience (i.e., Kelly, 1997).
- Children and adolescents (particularly the more disturbed and/or younger ones) are often reluctant participants in assessment and treatment. Thus, it is difficult to arrive at a point where diagnostic closure is realized. Self-report measures and reports from

others (i.e., teachers, parents, therapists) may be important sources of information about explicit personality traits and attributes, but they inherently fail to capture and pinpoint implicit cognitive and affective factors motivating and sustaining problematic behavior. Here is where the SCORS has a clear and integral role, supplementing the explicit with the implicit, with this in the end providing for a more comprehensive assessment of the child's personality makeup and functioning.

- It is important to evaluate a range of SCORS responses in the final analysis of results. Variations in scores may be associated with more severe clinical states (e.g., borderline states, psychotic conditions, posttraumatic stress disorder). Here, important information may be accessed in relation to Dominant Interpersonal Concerns, activating situations that evoke regressive shifts due to the emergence of conflict material and particular circumscribed deficits (e.g., problems with empathy related to deficits in the processing and understanding of how and why people act, think, and feel the way they do), most likely seen in responses to the Complexity of Representations of People (CR) scale.

- SCORS information readily translates into a multidimensional source of diagnostic information, which may then be ordered into a dynamic cognitive-affective formulation providing a) a succinct statement about the individual's developmental level of functioning across and within the six SCORS-R domains; b) the identification of central areas of conflict and deficit; c) the identification of potential areas of object relations strength; and d) the ability of the clinician to determine what treatment options and directions are indicated or contraindicated. For example, in the consideration of adolescent disorders, it would be important to weigh responses to the CR, USC, EIVM combination and juxtapose these against the CEI and AT results, because the former weigh more on cognitive factors, whereas the latter are more connected with affective determinants. Thus, a therapeutic choice might be slanted more toward a cognitive-behavioral approach, whereas another might emphasize treatment directed more toward an interpersonal, insight-oriented approach.

CASE EXAMPLE: MICHAEL

In this section, TAT stories are presented from the protocol of Michael (not his real name), a 13-year-old boy who attends an alternative therapeutic day school for adolescents with severe emotional and behavioral problems. At the time of the evaluation, he and his two siblings were residing with their mother after briefly living in a homeless shelter. They were relocated because of their father's violent and abusive physical behavior, primarily directed toward the mother, but also inflicted upon Michael and a younger brother. Thus, the history is remarkable for long-standing intermittent exposure to domestic violence and episodes of periodic but unremitting physical abuse. According to his mother, Michael has always been impulsive, hard to parent, and difficult to manage in school, where he can be quite aggressive. When seen for evaluation, questions were raised about what interventions, in addition to the therapeutic day school, were indicated.

Michael's mother reported he had previously been taking Ritalin but was not medicated at the time of testing, because she wanted an updated opinion about whether this intervention was indicated. Michael was not in therapy at the time of testing. He had previously been seen by a psychologist and psychiatrist, which resulted in varying DSM-IV clinical impressions, including Attention-Deficit Hyperactivity Disorder, Posttraumatic Stress Disorder, and Oppositional Defiant Disorder (American Psychiatric Association, 1994). Below are Michael's TAT responses, followed by scoring and interpretive commentary.

TAT Card 1

Michael's response:

> The boy is staring at the violin, thinking how do I play it. He feels disappointed . . . someone bought it for him for a present and he didn't know how to use it. He doesn't want to disappoint . . . make them feel bad. He practices and tries to play it.

Scores for Card 1

Complexity of Representations (CR): Score = 3. Michael provides a relatively elaborate picture of the main character and makes inferences about subjective states, to a minimal extent.

Affect-Tone (AT): Score = 3. Some hint of nervousness and possible guilt; the overall tenor suggests a mildly negative affective quality.

Capacity for Emotional Investment in Relationships (CEI): Score = 3. He considers the wishes and opinions of others in making a decision to try and improve his prowess with the instrument. Relationships are valued.

Emotional Investment in Values and Morals (EIVM): Score = 4. He is invested in moral values and shows signs of experiencing guilt when he feels he is not measuring up or is disappointing significant others.

Understanding of Social Causality (USC): Score = 4. Michael clearly shows a basic understanding of the role of psychological factors in motivating behavior. Internal causality is seen.

Dominant Interpersonal Concerns (DIC): Three predominant concerns are suggested: Disappointed Authorities, Failure, and Frustrated by Circumstance.

Commentary: Michael's concern about wanting to do well and not wishing to disappoint someone who has been good to him suggests a more complicated and emotionally sensitive young adolescent than would be suggested by his manifest presentation. The absence of authority conflict or struggles so frequently elicited from children and adolescents to this card is encouraging. Questions about self-worth are certainly hinted at, but concern about this needs to be held in abeyance until additional information is obtained.

TAT Card 4

Michael's narrative:

> Looks like the girl is about to leave home because they had planted stuff and can't get food out of there. There's not enough water and it doesn't rain and they are not by a stream. She goes out and tries to find help.

Scores for Card 4

Complexity of Representations (CR): Score = 3. There is some complexity, but the overall narrative is defined by a fairly simple and sparse description of only one character and suggests little elaboration or depth.

Affect-Tone (AT): Score = 4. This score is given where the affective quality of representations tends to be bland, neutral, or limited, as is the case here.

Capacity for Emotional Investment in Relationships (CEI): Score = 3. In the narrative the central character is considering not only her own needs, but apparently those of others as well. A helping and caring orientation is also seen in this narrative.

Emotional Investment in Values and Morals (EIVM): Score = 5. The story suggests an investment in clear moral values and a concern for significant others.

Understanding of Social Causality (USC): Score = 4. The story is coherent, logical, and straightforward, but lacks embellishment or explanation at the end.

Dominant Interpersonal Concerns (DIC): Three somewhat interrelated concerns are suggested: Fears (about survival), Rescue, and Neglect (i.e., unmet basic needs). On a positive note, Affiliation is also suggested.

Commentary: Michael's initial narrative raised themes relating to not being capable or competent, being a source of disappointment, and not being good enough. His second narrative speaks to a possible expectation that his world is capricious and not able to provide or meet his and other family members' needs, and it becomes his task to take care of matters, a not unfamiliar scenario for this child. However, this tentative formulation requires additional validation before credence can be given to this interpretation.

TAT Card 4

Michael's narrative:

> Looks like he wants to leave for another girl and she says no! You have kids you have to take care of. He says, Yeah, whatever. He leaves and she's mad. She throws his stuff out on the street. (Am I doing good?).

Scores for Card 4

Complexity of Representations (CR): Score = 3. The representations of the characters are simple, one-dimensional, and limited in complexity. There is little reference to psychological motives mediating behavior.

Affect Tone: (AT): Score = 3. The relationship between the partners is clearly negative and is defined by conflict that has escalated into a momentary dissolution of the relationship because of a breach of trust.

Capacity for Emotional Investment in Relationships (CEI): Score = 2. The situation depicts escalating conflict and an unstable, predominately tumultuous relatedness.

Emotional Investment in Values and Morals (EIVM): Score = 2. The story tends to focus on a selfish, inconsiderate individual who seems poised to place his own needs above those who look to him to provide security and nurturance.

Understanding of Social Causality (USC): Score = 4. The narrative provides a straightforward, basic, and logical rendition of an apparent father figure who leaves his partner and children for another woman.

Dominant Interpersonal Concerns (DIC): One obvious predominant concern, Tumultuous Relationship, overshadows two possible other concerns (i.e., Fears about safety and security) and Neglect (i.e., basic needs are threatened by the environmental chaos and instability).

Commentary: Michael's representation of his world again suggests problems and, in this instance, clear conflict between those entrusted to his care. In this instance one again sees concerns about basic needs and security issues, related to parental conflict and strife. The recurrent theme of a compromised life suggests a youngster who has much on his mind as he attempts to adjust to internal and external demands of early adolescence.

TAT Card 8BM

Michael's story:

> Looks like somebody is getting people to try and kill this man, and he's strapped to the table and they have a gun there in the background. They kill him and then they go on to kill more people. I don't know . . . nothing else.

Complexity of Representations (CR): Score = 2. The response suggests a lack of complexity. The characters are minimally elaborated, and there is no reference to how they feel or think about their malevolent actions

Affect Tone (AT): Score = 1. Michael's narrative quickly escalates into a malevolent and violent scenario. The story, albeit brief, is overwhelmingly about evil and destructive action, meted out by calculating perpetrators.

Capacity for Emotional Investment in Relationships (CEI): Score = 1.There is nothing in the narrative to suggest that any type of gratifying or positive connection is a possibility. Michael appears to anticipate that closeness translates into dire consequence and extreme conflict.

Emotional Investment in Values and Moral Standards (EIVM): Score = 1. There is nothing to suggest that Michael feels or experiences any sense of concern for another's plight or welfare. The narrative suggests an absence of moral values, and there is no suggestion of guilt or remorse.

Understanding of Social Causality (USC): Score = 1. There is no indication of any reasonable rationale or explanation accounting for the heinous actions portrayed or for those in the offing.

Dominant Interpersonal Concerns (DIC): Four concerns are suggested by the story: Victimization, Fears, Fear of Losing Control, and Aggression.

Commentary: This narrative is noteworthy for the sudden introduction of abject violence perpetrated by assailants who possess unknown motives for actions for which they have no remorse. Here one cannot help but speculate that the portrayal of malevolence and mayhem is linked to Michael's apprehension about basic safety and security, given the history of exposure to and the experience of physical abuse and domestic violence.

TAT Card 13B

Michael's story:

> Looks like the kid is waiting on the road for parents and there's nobody around to watch him and he's scared that something happened to his parents. They could have gotten in a car accident. They come home and make him something to eat. He feels good . . . better, that they were only up the street helping someone with car trouble.

Complexity of Representations of People (CR): Score = 3. Depiction of self and others is minimal, with little reference to internal states, other than alluding to the issue of the child being frightened.

Affect-Tone (AT): Score = 3. The initial apprehensive and fearful state warrants this score, even though the final emotional state indicates relief and diminished anxiety. The narrative reveals an anxious quality in relation to expectations that significant others may not be able to provide and take care of him.

Capacity for Emotional Investment in Relationships (CEI): Score = 3. The narrative depicts predominant issues with self-gratification and security and would initially warrant a low score, but the reference to helping others in a selfless way raises this to a final score of 3.

Investment in Emotional in Values and Moral Standards (EIVM): Score = 4. The story suggests an adherence to an inner moral code and value system, as illustrated by the reference to helping others out in time of need.

Understanding of Social Causality (USC): Score = 4. The narrative is logical, coherent, and not difficult to follow. From the narrative one is able to understand why the boy feels the way he does and the reason for parental absence.

Dominant Interpersonal Concerns (DIQ): Three possible concerns are suggested:

> 1) Fears—the representation that dire harm might have come to his parents; 2) neglect—the possible theme that his needs are not being met because of unavailable parents; and 3) loss—or in this case the anxiety and apprehension that he will be left alone because of tragedy.

Commentary: Like the narratives for Cards 2 and 4, there is the suggestion that Michael is apprehensive and concerned about very basic security issues and the ability of his parents to consistently be there for him. In the final scenario, his anxiety is assuaged when his parents arrive to quell his upset.

Table 11.1 summarizes the scoring of the protocol, and this is followed by a formulation based on the results of the six SCORS-R scales.

FINAL FORMULATION

This brief clinical vignette serves to illustrate how TAT responses can be ordered along a developmental continuum, for assessment of social cognition and object relations. The current protocol shows some fluctuations in Michael's object-relational functioning, with a significant regressive shift noted on Card 8BM, where abject aggressivity suddenly becomes the norm. This shift may have something to do with card pull, but a more plausible explanation relates to the fact that much of this youngster's life has seen him exposed to ongoing intermittent domestic violence and subjected to physical abuse. Hence his working model of relationships, particularly those involving encounters with male figures, may be imbued with expectations of mayhem and violence.

Michael's ability to understand his own and others' feelings, thoughts, and intentions suggests a fairly basic and somewhat self-absorbed level of development, which is really not markedly different from that of other young adolescents. The inferences he makes about people's actions suggests that his perceptions are colored to a large extent by his internal concerns and apprehension. Emotionally, his expectations about relationships are for the most part somewhat benign and not particularly negative, but, upon closer scrutiny, they are obviously defined by significant anxiety and worry. Occasional expectations of maltreatment may arise, and this is the likely outgrowth of long-standing abuse and environmental instability.

There is some variability in Michael's capacity to initiate and sustain relationships and ties to others. Situations where angry exchanges or confrontation with adults (more likely with male figures) may occur could precipitate either aggressive responses or withdrawal; at this point it is difficult to be definitive, because the history suggests both types of responses. Aside from the transient regressive shift, which portrays decidedly antisocial behavior, there appears to be every reason to expect that he has a positively defined sense of values and morality; reference to immoral or antisocial themes is lacking in his representations.

Two major themes that recur in Michael's stories about interpersonal transactions concern fears about safety and protection. An attendant issue suggests feelings of being neglected, as well as possible fears of loss and abandonment. It is apparent that diffuse anxiety and worries in relation to these recurrent themes have a major influence on how Michael organizes and defines his perceptions and representations, with this ultimately having a significant influence on his ability to initiate and sustain enduring, positive relationships.

SUMMARY

The goal of this chapter is to provide the reader with an introduction to the use of the SCORS-R in clinical application. The case of a somewhat enigmatic 13-year-old adolescent serves to illustrate how this interpretive paradigm allowed the clinician to view his inner world, which was not otherwise accessible with other sources of information, such as rating scales, observations, or clinical interviews. Overall, this brief introduction to the SCORS-R should provide the reader with a valid and reliable means of assessing patterns of thought, feelings, and motives in relation to self and others. When used in conjunction with other projective instruments and self-report instruments, the potential results offer invaluable information informing assessment and treatment planning.

REFERENCES

Ackerman, S., Hilsenroth, M., Clemence, A., Weatherhill, R., & Fowler, C. (1991). Convergent validity of Rorschach and TAT scales of object relations. *Journal of Personality Assessment, 77*, 295–306.

American Psychiatric Association. (1994). *Diagnostic and statistical manual of mental disorders* (4th ed.). Washington, DC: Author.

Bellak, L., & Abrams, D. (1997). *The TAT, the CAT, and the SAT in clinical use* (6th ed.). Boston: Allyn & Bacon.

Birndoff, S., & Porcerelli, J. (2004). *Development of object relations in children, adolescents and late adolescents.* Unpublished Manuscript, Wayne State University School of Medicine.

Conklin, A., & Westen, D. (2001). Thematic Apperception Test. In J. Dorfman & M. Hersen (Eds.), *Understanding psychological assessment: Perspectives on individual differences* (pp. 107–133). New York: Kluwer/Plenum.

Cramer, P. (1996). *Storytelling, narrative, and the Thematic Apperception Test.* New York: Guilford Press.

Freedenfeld, R., Ornduff, S., & Kelsey, R. (1995). Object relations and physical abuse: A TAT analysis. *Journal of Personality Assessment, 64,* 552–568.

Groth-Marnat, G. (1997). *Handbook of psychological assessment* (3rd ed.). New York: Wiley.

Hilsenroth, M., Stein, M., & Pinsker, J. (2004). *Social Cognition and Object Relations Scale–Global Rating Method (SCORS-G): Training Manual.* Unpublished manuscript, Derner Institute of Advanced Psychological Studies, Adelphi University.

Kelly, F. (1997). *The assessment of object relations phenomena in adolescence: TAT and Rorschach measures.* Mahwah, NJ: Lawrence Erlbaum Associates.

Kelly, F. (2004). Assessment of object representation in children and adolescents: Current trends and future directions. In M. Hersen (Ed.-in-Chief) & M. Hilsenroth & D. Segal (Vol. Eds.), *Comprehensive handbook of psychological assessment: Vol. 2. Objective and projective assessment of personality and psychopathology* (pp. 617–627). New York: John Wiley

Niec, L., & Russ, S. (2002). Children's internal representations, empathy, and fantasy play: A validity study of the SCORS-Q. *Psychological Assessment, 14,* 331–338.

Ornduff, S. (1997). TAT assessment of object relations: Implications for child abuse *Bulletin of the Menninger Clinic, 61,* 1–15

Ornduff, S., Centeno, L., & Kelsey, R. (1999). Rorschach assessment of malevolence in sexually abused girls. *Journal of Personality Assessment, 73,* 100–109.

Ornduff, S., Freedenfeld, R., Kelsey, R., & Critelli, J. (1994). Object relations of sexually abused female subjects: A TAT analysis. *Journal of Personality Assessment, 63,* 223–238.

Ornduff, S., & Kelsey, R. (1996). Object relations of sexually and physically abused female children: A TAT analysis. *Journal of Personality Assessment, 66,* 91–105.

Pistole, D., & Ornduff, S. (1994). TAT assessment of sexually abused girls: An analysis of manifest content. *Journal of Personality Assessment, 63,* 211–222.

Raches, C. (2004). *Children with disruptive behavior disorders: Representations and behaviors with parents.* Unpublished doctoral dissertation, University of Indianapolis, Indiana.

Tuber, S. (1989). Assessment of children's object representations with the Rorschach. *Bulletin of the Menninger Clinic, 53,* 432–441.

Tuber, S. (1992). Empirical and clinical assessments of children's object relations and object representations. *Journal of Personality Assessment, 58,* 179–197.

Urist, J. (1977). The Rorschach test and the assessment of object relations. *Journal of Personality Assessment, 41,* 3–9

Westen, D. (1991). Clinical assessment of object relations using the TAT. *Journal of Personality Assessment, 56,* 56–74.

Westen, D. (1995). *Social Cognition and Object Relations Scale: Q-sort for projective stories.* Unpublished manuscript, Department of Psychiatry, Cambridge Hospital and Harvard Medical School.

Westen, D. (2002). *Current Rating Summary Sheet.* Department of Psychology. Emory University.

Westen, D., Klepser, J., Ruffins, S., Silverman, M., Lifton, N., & Boekamp, J. (1991). Object relations in childhood and adolescence: The development of working relationships. *Journal of Consulting and Clinical Psychology, 59,* 400–409.

Westen, D., Lohr, N., Silk, K., Kerber, K., & Goodrich, S. (1985). *Social Cognition and Object Relations Scale (SCORS): Manual for coding TAT data.* Department of Psychology, University of Michigan at Ann Arbor.

Westen, D., Ludolph, P., Block, J., Wixom, J., & Wiss, F. (1990). Developmental history and object relations in psychiatrically disturbed adolescent girls. *American Journal of Psychiatry, 147,* 1061–1068.

Westen, D., Ludolph, P., Silk, K., Kellam, A., Gold, L., & Lohr, N. (1990). Object relations in borderline adolescents and adults: Developmental differences. In S. C. Feinstein (Ed.), *Adolescent Psychiatry: Developmental and Clinical Studies, 17,* 360–384.

12

INTERPRETATION OF STORYTELLING IN THE CLINICAL ASSESSMENT OF CHILDREN AND ADOLESCENTS

Mary Louise Cashel
Ben Killilea
Stephen J. Dollinger
Southern Illinois University, Carbondale

There are many available methods and procedures for the clinical assessment of children and adolescents. Among them, narrative approaches have long held popularity with practicing clinicians for a variety of reasons. Storytelling is an engaging activity that is familiar and appealing to most children across ages and cultures. Thus, as a task demand, stories are often a welcome addition to a battery of tests. Furthermore, in the process of storytelling, the child or examinee reveals considerable aspects of himself or herself that might not otherwise be communicated. In the broadest sense, children's stories can be analyzed to evaluate thoughts, behaviors, emotions, perceptions of self, relationships with others, and coping and problem-solving skills. As such, they can inform clinical conceptualizations from multitheoretical perspectives, including psychodynamic, behavioral, cognitive-behavioral, interpersonal, and family systems orientations.

This chapter explores the history and theoretical underpinnings of the storytelling approaches. An overview of the Thematic Apperception Test and interpretive systems with applications for children and adolescents is provided. The discussion then focuses on three principal storytelling tests developed specifically for children, namely the Children's Apperception Test (C.A.T; Bellak & Bellak, 1949), the Roberts Apperception Test for Children (RATC; McArthur & Roberts, 1982; Roberts–2; Roberts & Gruber, 2005), and the Tell-Me-A-Story test (TEMAS; Costantino, Malgady, & Rogler, 1988). Finally, a case example is presented, integrating data from social history information, intellectual assessment, behavior report forms, and self-report inventories.

HISTORY OF APPERCEPTIVE APPROACHES
AND THE THEMATIC APPERCEPTION TEST

The theoretical foundation for narrative or thematic approaches is based on the psychoanalytic concept of projection and the projective hypothesis. The projective hypothesis, in essence, states that perception and interpretation of contemporary events is based upon the memory and interpretation of past experiences. This process was labeled "apperception" by Morgan and Murray (1935) and "apperceptive distortion" by Bellak (Bellak, 1944; Bellak & Brower, 1951). Apperception can be thought of as the interpretive process by which the individual makes sense of or understands what he or she sees, hears, or experiences. The way an individual interprets any given experience or situation (or picture) is largely shaped or colored by his or her past experiences. This is the heart of apperception as it applies to storytelling tasks. The assumption is that the story created by an individual in response to a picture with sufficient ambiguity will reflect his or her own conflicts, thoughts, needs, and feelings.

The history of storytelling as a clinical assessment procedure is largely rooted in the development of the Thematic Apperception Test (TAT; Murray, 1943). Henry Murray created the TAT in collaboration with Christiana Morgan at the Harvard Psychological Clinic and published an initial description of the test and its applications (Morgan & Murray, 1935). The TAT is composed of 31 pictures chosen for their stimulating power and ambiguity. Subsequent to its publication, the TAT quickly gained widespread popularity in clinical practice and remains among the most frequently used assessment measures. It has consistently been listed as one of the top four or five ranked measures among practicing psychologists (Camara, Nathan, & Puente, 2000; Geiser & Stein, 1999; Lubin, Larsen, & Matarazzo, 1984; Piotrowksi & Keller, 1989). Surveys conducted specifically of clinicians working with children and adolescents mirrored these findings for many years (Archer, Maruish, Imhof, & Piotrowski, 1991; Elbert & Holden, 1987; Rosenberg & Beck, 1986; Tuma & Pratt, 1982). Most recently, Cashel (2002) found less frequent usage of the TAT and other projective tests in a survey of 162 clinical child (and adolescent) and school psychology practitioners. Nevertheless, over 24.7% of clinicians working with children and 43.2% of clinicians working with adolescents reported that they had incorporated the TAT into their assessment batteries.

The original instructions for administration of the TAT to children are as follows (Murray, 1943, p. 4): "This is a story-telling test. I have some pictures here that I am going to show you, and for each picture I want you to make up a story. Tell what has happened before and what is happening now. Say what the people are feeling and thinking and how it will come out. You can make up any kind of story you please." Murray suggested that these instructions could be modified or repeated as needed. After the first story, the administrator informs the storyteller of any missing elements in the story and encourages the development of longer or more detailed stories, if necessary. For the remaining cards the administrator only briefly queries any critical elements missing for each story (i.e., the beginning, middle, or ending). The most common error the novice clinician is prone to make is failure to sufficiently query for missing elements.

Most clinicians administer 10 or fewer TAT cards in a single testing session, and various researchers have recommended specific sets of cards for use with children. Obrzut and Boliek (1986) stated that the cards best suited for children aged 7 to 11 are 1, 3BM, 7GF, 8BM, 12BM, 13B, 14, and 17BM. These cards tend to elicit themes related to achievement, aggression, parental nurturance, parental rejection, and attitudes toward parents. For adolescents, they recommended cards 1, 2, 5, 7GF, 12F, 12M, 15, 17BM, 18BM, and 18GF. Cooper (1981) developed a set of cards specifically for adolescent males, including 3BM, 4, 6BM, 7BM, 8BM, 10, 13BM, 15, and 18BM. Although the cards are labeled GF and MB for girls/females and men/boys, few if any clinicians adhere strictly to these designations.

In addition to the general projective hypothesis, there are a number of assumptions related to the use of thematic tests, as outlined by Lindzey (1952). In creating a story, the storyteller typically identifies with one character, and the needs, wishes, and conflicts experienced by that character reflect those of the storyteller, either directly or symbolically. However, not all stories will be equally reflective of these needs, conflicts, or impulses. In general, story content that appears most closely related to the pictures on the card will yield less interpretively meaningful information than themes or stories that are not directly inspired by the card material. Repetitive stories and themes occurring across cards are apt to provide the most interpretively meaningful information. Finally, stories can reflect a variety of other factors, including recent situational events, sociocultural determinants, and ethnic group membership. It is thus most important to interpret thematic tests within the context of additional background and assessment information.

INTERPRETIVE SYSTEMS FOR THE TAT

There are many interpretive systems available for the TAT, and most of them are used primarily for research purposes. The interested reader is referred to Shniedman (1951, 1999), Murstein (1963), and Winter (1999) for excellent reviews of these systems. For clinical purposes, four approaches have gained considerable recognition for their utility with children and adolescents; these include the systems developed by Leopold Bellak (1954, 1971, 1975, 1986, 1993), Phebe Cramer (1996), Drew Westen (1991), and Teglasi (1993).

The Bellak Scoring System

Bellak's scoring system, first published in 1947, extended Murray's interpretation to include many aspects of Anna Freud's (1937) ego psychology, namely analysis of defense mechanisms, anxieties and conflicts, and superego (or moral) functioning. As described in the most recent edition of his text, *The T.A.T., the C.A.T., and the S.A.T. in Clinical Use*, 6th Ed. (Bellak & Abrams, 1997), his scoring categories include 10 variables:

1. The Main Theme
2. The Main Hero
3. Main Needs and Drives of the Hero
4. The Conception of the Environment (World)
5. Figures Seen as . . .
6. Significant Conflicts
7. Nature of Anxieties
8. Main Defenses Against Conflicts & Fears
9. Adequacy of Superego
10. Integration of the Ego

The first variable, Main Theme, is essentially a summary of the meaning of the story. Beginning clinicians might think of this as identifying the moral to the story, or what might be generalized from the sequence of events and experiences as they occur in the story. Cognitive psychologists might refer to this as "identifying cognitive schemas," or "learned expectations for interpersonal situations and interactions." The second and third variables in the scoring system assess features of the protagonist or main character, such as basic demographic features and such psychological concepts as sense of adequacy or self-competency, body image, and emotional and behavioral needs. These are largely inferred from the outcome of the stories and from either the introduction or omission of specific figures or characters, items or objects, and problems or circumstances. Generally speaking, story material that is introduced (i.e., that has no obvious or apparent representation on the actual stimulus card) has greater projective value than themes or stories more directly tied to the picture content on the card.

The fourth and fifth variables assess perceptions of the storyteller's environment, social world, and possible interpersonal relationships with family, parents, siblings, peers, and romantic partners. For example, is the world a harsh, unpredictable place where people are rejected, abandoned, or victimized? Alternatively, does the main character experience a supportive environment in which he or she can overcome obstacles and find success and satisfying relationships? The sixth, seventh, and eighth variables focus on possible underlying intrapsychic constructs, namely internal conflicts, such as the need for compliance with authority figures versus maintaining personal autonomy, or the need to pursue achievement and success versus maintaining family relationships, or conflict over sexual guilt. The ninth and tenth variables address specific aspects of ego psychology and may be thought of in terms of coping mechanisms, moral development, thought processing, and reality testing. The integration of the ego is inferred based on the storyteller's ability to perform the task and produce a logical, realistic story that generally conforms to the content on the card. The storyteller's attention, concentration, and thought processes are specifically evaluated, in much the same way they might be assessed in a mental status exam (for coherence, bizarre vs. appropriate content, etc.).

To illustrate this process, read the TAT story below told by a 13-year-old Caucasian male to Card 4. Card 4 depicts a woman clutching the shoulders of a man whose face and body are averted, as if he were trying to pull away from her (Murray, 1943).

> Well, like I have no idea what this picture is supposed to be. There's this guy . . . well, this guy is, this is during the Vietnam times and there's going to be a draft. So he's going to go away on the war for the draft. And yet his wife doesn't want him to do it because she does not want him to get hurt or injured or killed. So, this is sort of a picture of their goodbye before he goes off and gets drafted. He's sort of scared of the situation because he thinks he might be killed. In the end I think he ends up getting drafted, goes to war, comes back—may have been wounded, but he's still alive.

The interpretive theme of this story might be summarized as follows: Although it may be difficult, following through with social responsibilities is important, and such efforts will generally prove successful. The main hero appears to be the male in this story and is essentially a responsible individual who overcomes the obstacle before him (going to war). His behavioral need is to fulfill social expectations or demands, but he also has a need for safety. He could be characterized as "adequate," perhaps with a sense of moral responsibility (he does not dodge or otherwise avoid the draft, despite his fears). The circumstance the boy introduced in this story is the draft. The figure he omitted is the semi-nude individual in the background, which may imply a need to deny sexuality (Bellak, 1993). However, it is our experience that this figure is often omitted by youth. The conception of the world or environment is somewhat precarious and coercive (being drafted to go to war against one's will), and the anxiety is fear of being overcome (killed). But the outcome is somewhat positive on the whole, given that he returns home alive, if wounded. The only other character described in the story is a marital partner, who understandably does not want him to go. With respect to the main defenses against conflicts and fears, there is no evidence of defensive reactions or indication of specific coping behaviors. On the whole, the story is logical, realistic, and reasonably consistent with the content depicted in the picture. Consider now the following story, told by an 18-year-old male to the same card:

> This looks like a married couple whose husband has decided he wants to leave. His wife thinks that they can work things out, but he doesn't. And he's decided that he wants to start his life over again. They end up divorcing [Q-happening in the picture?] He's finally leaving. [Q—thinking?] He looks unconcerned, but she does. [Q-feeling?] Anxious to leave.

The theme in this story might be described as follows. In order to pursue individual aspirations, one must end past relationships and disregard the interests of others. The conflict appears to be one between maintaining a relationship and pursuing ambitions. As in the previous card, this story is quite logical, and the main character is generally successful in fulfilling his needs. However, the story has a more negative tone; the marital relationship is more conflicted and the main character is altogether dismissive of the needs or desires of his wife and ends the relationship.

In such manner, the clinician evaluates each story told with respect to all 10 of these variables and records comments and observations on either the short or long form of the Bellak TAT Analysis Blank and Sheet. Although this system is described as a "scoring" system, it does not generally yield quantitative data or scores. The emphasis for interpretation is on evaluating repetitive patterns across stories. Thus, a storyteller who produced three or more stories in which characters aspired to obtain some degree of success or fame might be said to have a need for achievement. A youth describing numerous hostile interactions between parents and children, or children and teachers, might be said to have conflict with authority figures. Stories in which characters are consistently overwhelmed and overcome by adverse circumstances, depicted as sad, tearful, unable to resolve problems or conflicts, or even suicidal, might be told by a youth struggling with depression, limited problem-solving skills, or poor impulse control. Bellak cautioned against drawing conclusions about the storyteller based on observations made to one story. Furthermore, he recommended corroboration of interpretations made on themes drawn from multiple stories with other testing data.

The principal criticism of the Bellak scoring system, as noted by Abrams (1999), is that "it is a clinical checklist approach to the TAT, a way of summarizing themes and noting different areas of functioning" (p. 151) and is not an empirically based approach. However, a variety of studies over the past 40 or more years examined and supported the construct and concurrent validity of many of the scoring variables, including nature of anxieties (Mandler, Lindzey, & Crouch, 1957), main defenses and defense mechanisms (Blum, 1964; Cramer & Carter, 1978; Haworth, 1963), and morality development and superego functioning (Kohlberg, 1969; Shore, Massimo, & Mack, 1964). This research ultimately laid the empirical foundation for the systems described next.

Cramer's Analysis of Defense Mechanisms

Phebe Cramer extended clinical applications for the TAT through her research on the study of defense mechanisms. Cramer (1987, 1991) proposed a developmental theory of defenses, suggesting that different defenses became salient at different periods of development such that a chronological order for their emergence could be established. Specifically, she found that young children tend to rely more heavily on denial as a coping mechanism, whereas the use of projection is more characteristic of youth in middle adolescence, and the use of identification increases gradually in frequency through late adolescence. As part of her research, she created a scoring system (Cramer, 1982) to assess these defenses in TAT stories. The scoring categories are presented below (Cramer, 1996, p. 89). To score a story, 1 point is given for each manifestation of the criteria, yielding scores for each defense mechanism.

Denial
1. Omission of major characters or objections
2. Misperception
3. Reversal
4. Negation
5. Denial of reality
6. Overly maximizing the positive or minimizing the negative
7. Unexpected goodness, optimism, positiveness, gentleness

Projection
1. Attribution of aggressive or hostile feelings, emotions or intentions to a character or other feelings, emotions or intentions that are normatively unusual
2. Addition of ominous people, ghosts, animals, objects or qualities
3. Magical or circumstantial thinking.
4. Concern for protection from external threat
5. Apprehensiveness of death, injury, or assault
6. Themes of pursuit, entrapment, and escape
7. Bizarre or very unusual story or theme

Identification
1. Emulation of skills
2. Emulation of characteristics
3. Regulation of motives or behaviors
4. Self-esteem through affiliation
5. Work; delay of gratification
6. Role differentiation
7. Moralism

As an example, the TAT story told by the 13-year-old male (above) could be scored as follows: Denial = 0, Projection = 1, Identification = 1. The score for projection would be given for apprehension of death. The main character fulfills his obligation, despite his fears and concerns, resulting in a score of 1 for identification.

Dollinger and Cramer (1990) evaluated the ability of the scoring system to detect the adaptive functioning of defense mechanisms subsequent to real-life trauma. They assessed stories told by a group of 27 boys between the ages of 10 and 13 who had experienced a lightning strike during a soccer game. This was a potentially traumatic event, given that one boy died as a result of the incident. Approximately 1 to 2 months after the lightning strike, the boys were asked to create two stories in response to TAT-like cards, both depicting scenes with a lightning bolt. The stories were scored with the use of the Defense Mechanism Manual (Cramer, 1982), and information regarding youth fears and distress, sleep disturbance, and somatic complaints was also obtained. Youth demonstrating the greatest use of defenses, and especially the age-appropriate use of projection, exhibited the least degree of emotional impairment.

Cramer (1996) also observed that behavioral responses to the TAT sometimes yield clinically useful information, because for some, taking it can be an anxiety-inducing activity. Some individuals may fear what they will reveal about themselves; others may fear that they may not possess sufficient imagination or creativity to produce an interesting story and will appear inadequate; still others may confront their own personal conflicts and become anxious, "sensing that there is a potential psychological threat involved in formulating and voicing a story" (p. 84). Statements made in response to this anxiety may be interpreted in some cases as defensive strategies. For example, denial and/or repression might be manifested in comments such as, "I can't think of anything." The statement "The picture doesn't remind me of anything" incorporates aspects of repression and projection, because the picture is blamed for inadequate content. Some individuals may demonstrate passive resistance, by telling a highly stereotyped story, borrowed from storybooks or the media. In this instance they are copying as opposed to creating a story. Some individuals will use ridicule or denigration, such as "This is a stupid card/test," to distance themselves from any personal connection to the material.

In summary, Cramer's system offers an empirically based approach to evaluating the thought processes and stress and coping behaviors among children. The study of defense mechanisms is a key component of ego (or psychodynamic) psychology, although coping behaviors more broadly construed are also largely the focus of cognitive-behavioral interventions. Next, we briefly examine another empirically supported approach to the clinical analysis of TAT stories developed by Drew Westen (1991).

Westen's Analysis of Social Cognition and Object Relations

Westen's Social Cognition and Object Relations System (SCORS) is an integrative approach to interpretation of the TAT and other storytelling tests that synthesize aspects of cognitive and psychodynamic theories. Social cognition is largely the study of person perception, information processing, attributions, and cognitive schema or expectations of self, others, and interpersonal interactions. The psychodynamic study of object relations is devoted to understanding the development of an individual's sense of self in relation to significant others, typically caregivers. This theory suggests that early experiences with primary caregivers (or "objects") and internal representations of these people form the templates for subsequent interpersonal functioning. In sum, social cognitive and object relations approaches both address the representational and affective processes that mediate interpersonal functioning (Westen, 1991). The SCORS approach is an innovative combination of these theories with an empirically supported, psychometrically sound scoring system. The SCORS scoring system is described in detail by Kelly in another chapter in this volume. Thus, for the sake of brevity, only an overview of the scoring categories or structural dimensions is presented below (Westen, Lohr, Silk, Kerber, & Goodrich, 1985, 1990, 2002).

Complexity of Representations of People: measures the extent to which the subject clearly differentiates the perspectives of self and others; sees the self and others as having stable, enduring, multidimensional dispositions; and sees the self and others as psychological beings with complex motives and subjective experience.

Affect Tone of Relationships Paradigm: measures affective quality of representations of people and relationships. It attempts to assess the extent to which the person expects from the world, and particularly from the world of people, profound malevolence or overwhelming pain, or views social interactions as basically benign and enriching.

Capacity for Emotional Investment in Relationships and Moral Standards: measures the extent to which others are treated as ends rather than means, events are regarded in terms other than need gratification, moral standards are developed and considered, and relationships are experienced as meaningful and committed.

Understanding of Social Causality: measures the extent to which attributions of the causes of people's actions, thoughts, and feelings are logical, accurate, complex, and psychologically minded.

The scoring system was updated in 2002 (SCORS-R; Westen, 2002). The capacity for Emotional Investment in Relationships and Moral Standards was split into Emotional Investment in Values and Moral Standards and Capacity for Investment in Relationships. In addition, a new category was added, Dominant Interpersonal Concerns (see Kelly, in this volume, for details of this change).

Stories told to the TAT are rated for each category on a Likert scale, ranging from very poor to superior development (or in the case of Affect-Tone, from highly malevolent or hostile to benevolent and supportive relationships). Mean scale scores are derived for each category based on the average of the card ratings. Scale scores are derived for the categories with the use of a weighting system described in detail in the manual.

A variety of studies support the reliability and validity of the SCORS system for use with TAT stories completed by children. Scores on the Affect Tone, Capacity for Emotional Investment and Moral Standards, and Understanding of Social Causality successfully discriminated adolescent girls diagnosed with borderline personality disorder from a normal community sample and other psychiatric patients (Westen, Ludolph, Lerner, Ruffins, & Wiss, 1990). Ornduff and her colleagues demonstrated the ability of the SCORS scales to discriminate between groups of sexually and physically abused female children from other clinic-referred children without such histories (Ornduff, Freedenfeld, Kelsey, & Critelli, 1994; Freedenfeld, Ornduff, & Kelsey, 1995). Finally, one recent study demonstrated the convergent validity of SCORS-Q weighted scores with measures of self and teacher ratings of empathy among 8–10-year-olds (Niec & Russ, 2002).

Cognitive, Behavioral, and Multitheoretical Perspectives

Many contemporary clinicians view TAT stories as a modified behavioral sample of cognitive integration, problem solving, affect modulation, self-monitoring, and interpersonal functioning. Such an approach can prove very useful in cognitive-behavioral treatment planning. Even those completely disinterested in the content analysis of stories often find evaluation of the form and process of such material clinically useful. McGrew and Teglasi (1990) adapted scoring categories for the TAT designed to distinguish emotionally disturbed children from normal groups. These included the following (p. 223):

1. Verbalizations Unrelated to the Story: picture criticism, expressions of frustration or disinterest, irrelevant comments, expressions of inadequacy
2. Disruptions to the Internal Logic of the Story: contradictions within the story, perseveration of story content, personal references
3. Judgment and Reality Testing: inappropriate or bizarre actions or verbal expressions that occur during the session, inappropriate, bizarre or highly unlikely story content
4. Actions and Outcome: positive actions, negative actions, no action, with outcome rated on a Likert-scale ranging from 1 to 5 (most adaptive)

Teglasi (1993) discussed in detail how this system can be applied to the assessment of emotional and behavioral and cognitive functioning. Consider the following story told by an eight-year-old Caucasian female referred for behavioral dysregulation and evaluation of a possible Attention Deficit/Hyperactivity Disorder.

> Card 1. Once upon a time a girl wanted to lose a tooth. Her mother and father said, "Noooo." She was wearing a good dress and her mom thought it was unusual for her dad not to let her lose a tooth. She can fix her hair on her own. They are rich. [What led up to this picture? What happened before?] She asked for a, for tweezers to fix her hair. Her dad said, "Whatever would you want tweezers for?" "I want to lose a tooth." "You aren't going to lose a tooth in that good dress!" Well, if she changed clothes she could. Of course she could. She could never lose a tooth unless she had on her aprons. She heard that and decided to go to the kitchen. That's all. [What are they feeling in this picture?] The girl is feeling sad. The dad is feeling mad because she wanted to steal her father's tweezers. And the mom is kind of uncomfortable seeing the daughter very, very sad. [How does the story end?] She gets an apron, she gets tweezers and brushes her hair at the same time. She put on the apron as good as she could, only put it on upside down. Then she decided to change it and it was okay. Next, she took off her dress and then her dad caught her and she said, "My tooth is out!" Her father said, "I should have listened!" The end.

With respect to Teglasi and McGrew's categories, perhaps most striking in this story is the bizarre content and the verbal exchanges between characters. This child demonstrates loose associations, strained and illogical thinking, and cognitive perseveration, namely preoccupation with teeth (which was noted in two additional stories). Although this child was functioning within the average range of intellectual ability with strong verbal skills, her stories gave clear indication of significant thought processing problems and prompted a more thorough evaluation for a psychotic disorder.

APPERCEPTIVE TESTS SPECIFICALLY DESIGNED FOR CHILDREN

Although the TAT gained rapid and enormous popularity for the assessment of adults, many were dissatisfied with it as a tool for the assessment of children. This precipitated the development of measures specifically created with children in mind. The three most widely known measures are the C.A.T. (Bellak & Bellak, 1949), the Roberts Apperception Test for Children (RATC; McArthur, & Roberts, 1982), currently in its second edition (Roberts–2; Roberts & Gruber, 2005), and the Tell-Me-A-Story test (TEMAS; Costantino, Malgady, & Rogler, 1988).

Children's Apperception Test and Children's Apperception Test—Human Figures

In response to concerns that the stimulus materials of the TAT were inappropriate for young children, Bellak and Bellak (1949) created the Children's Apperception Test (C.A.T.). The pictures selected as stimuli involved animals rather than people and were designed to facilitate the understanding of a child's intrapsychic needs, drives, and relationship to important figures. These pictures portrayed themes related to feeding problems, sibling rivalry, attitudes toward parents, and Oedipal feelings and were intended for children 3 to 10 years of age. Subsequent to the publication of the C.A.T., a number of studies compared the narratives of children told in response to animal versus human figure pictures. Whereas some studies found no differences (Budoff, 1960; Biersdorf & Marcuse, 1953), a few suggested that human figures were better (Armstrong, 1954). In response to these studies, Bellak and Bellak (1965) developed a human modification of the C.A.T., the C.A.T.-H. The scene content of the C.A.T.-H cards remained virtually the same, but the animal figures were changed to human figures.

Interpretation of the C.A.T. and C.A.T.-H, as recommended by Bellak and Abrams (1997), is generally consistent with the procedures for the TAT, using either the short or long form. The same 10 variables are considered, and the record is evaluated for repetitive themes, conflicts, needs, and drives. In addition, Mary Haworth (1963) developed a scoring checklist for the evaluation of defense mechanisms in C.A.T. responses, using a methodology very similar to the system that was later developed by Cramer (1982). See Table 12.1 for the complete description. Also noteworthy in her system is the delineation of critical scores per category. Haworth suggested that five or more critical scores would indicate emotional disturbance warranting clinical intervention.

Over the years, many clinicians and researchers voiced clear preferences for the TAT (Cramer, 1996; Teglasi, 1993). However, the results of test usage studies (Cashel, 2002; Hutton, Dubes & Muir, 1992) suggested that the C.A.T. continues to have a following. As many as 24–41.4% of surveyed practicing clinicians endorsed the inclusion of the C.A.T. in test batteries.

Roberts Apperception Test for Children

The Roberts Apperception Test (RATC; McArthur & Roberts, 1982) was developed for the assessment of school-aged children, with the intent of addressing a number of limitations observed in the TAT and C.A.T. The RATC authors asserted that the C.A.T. and TAT were each useful for a limited age range of children and that only very young children would likely respond in a serious manner to animals. They also believed that the original TAT was equally unsuitable for most school-aged youth, given that only 2 of the 31 cards recommended for such use actually depicted children in them. They claimed that the artistry of the TAT cards rendered the scenes unfamiliar and unrealistic, and that they lacked evocative potential. Finally, they noted that no single scoring approach for evaluating children's responses with either the C.A.T. or TAT had gained universal acceptance.

Currently in its second edition, the Roberts–2 is appropriate for children between 6 and 18 years of age. Curiously, as part of the rationale for renaming the measure, the authors suggested that the test assesses social cognition and interpersonal problem-solving skills, and they essentially disavowed its psychodynamic or projective roots. They maintained its recommended use for the assessment of children's perceptions of interpersonal situations and as an aid to clinical decision-making.

The Roberts–2 (and its predecessor) is composed of 27 stimulus cards with realistic illustrations emphasizing everyday interpersonal events as experienced by children and adults in a variety of social situations. The administration procedures for the RATC are explicit and very similar to those for the TAT/CAT. Eleven of the 27 cards have parallel versions for boys and girls, and five are administered to both. For any given child, 16 cards are adminis-

TABLE 12.1.

Content Reflective of Haworth's Adaptive Mechanisms

Defense Mechanisms

Reaction Formation: Exaggerated goodness or cleanliness; oppositional attitudes, rebellion, stubbornness; story tone opposed to picture content

Undoing and Ambivalence: Undoing (changing or contradicting a story line); respondent gives alternatives; balanced phrases (asleep-awake; hot-cold, etc.); indecision by respondent or story character; restating (e.g., "that _____, no this _____"; "He was going to, but _____")

Isolation: Detached attitude toward picture or story ("It couldn't happen," "It's a cartoon"); literal interpretations ("It doesn't show, so I can't tell"); comments on story or picture ("This is hard"; "I told a good one"); laughs at card, exclamations; use of fairy tale, comic-book, or "olden times" themes or characters; describes in detail, logical; "the end"; gives title to story; specific details, names, or quotes ("four hours"; she said, "_____"); character gets lost; character runs away because of anger; subject aligns with parent against "naughty" child character; disapproves of child's actions

Repression and Denial: Child character waits, controls self, conforms, is good, learned lesson; character accepts fate, didn't want it anyway; prolonged or remote punishments; respondent or character states that events were "just a dream"; character forgets or loses something; respondent omits figures or objects from story; omits usual story content; no fantasy or story (describes card blandly); refuses card

Deception: Child character described as superior to adult, laughs at adult, is smarter, tricks adult, sneaks, pretends, hides from, steals from, peeks at or spies on adult; adult character tricks child, is not what appears to be (only one check per story)

Symbolization: Children play in bed; see parents in bed; open window (Cards #5, #9); dig, or fall in a hole; babies born; rope breaks (#2); chair or cane breaks (#3); balloon breaks (#4), tail pulled or bitten (#4, #7); crib broken (#9); rain, river, water, storms, cold; fire, explosions, destruction; sticks, knives, guns; cuts, stings, injuries, actual killings (other than by eating); oral deprivation

Projection and Introjection: Attacker is attacked, "eat and be eaten"; innocent one is eaten or attacked; child is active aggressor (bites, hits, throws; does not include verbal or teasing attacks); characters blame others; others have secrets or make fun of somebody; respondent adds details, objects, characters, or oral themes; magic or magical powers

Phobic Immature or Disorganized

Fears and Anxiety: Child character hides from danger, runs away because of fear; fears outside forces (wind, ghosts, hunters, wild animals, monsters); dreams of danger; parent dead, goes away, or doesn't want child; slips of tongue by respondent

Regression: Respondent exhibits much affect in telling story; personal references; stories of food spilled; bed or pants wet, water splashed; dirty, messing, smelly; person or object falls in toilet; ghosts, witches, haunted house

Controls Weak or Absent: Story content of bones, blood; poison; clang or nonsense words; perseveration of unusual content from a previous story; tangential thinking, loose associations; bizarre content

Identification

Adequate, same-sex: Respondent identifies with same-sex parent or child character; child character jealous of, scolded or punished by same-sex parent; child loves, or is helped by parent of opposite sex

Confused or opposite-sex: Respondent identifies with opposite-sex parent or child character; child character fears or is scolded or punished by opposite-sex character; misrecognition by subject of sex or species; slips of tongue with respect to sex of figures

Adapted from Haworth (1963).

tered in their exact numerical sequence. Querying for missing story elements is restricted to the first two cards. This is important because a child's lack of response after the first two cards is considered clinically significant and influences the scoring of the profile. According to the standardized instructions, querying on the first two cards should be limited to the following five questions: 1) What is happening? 2) What is he/she feeling? 3) What is he/she talking about? 4) What happened before? 5) How does the story end? The current scoring system comprises seven groups of scales:

1. Theme Overview Scales: Popular Pull, Complete Meaning
2. Available Resources scales: Support Self—Feeling, Support Self—Advocacy, Support Other—Feeling, Support Other—Help, Reliance on Other, Limit Setting
3. Problem Identification (PID) scales: PID1—Recognition, PID2—Description, PID3—Clarification, PID4—Definition, PID5—Explanation
4. Resolution (RES) scales: RES1—Simple Closure or Easy Outcome; RES2—Easy and Realistically Positive Outcome; RES3—Process Described in Constructive Resolution; RES4—Process Described in Constructive Resolution of Feelings and Situations; RES5—Elaborated Process with Possible Insight
5. Emotion Scales: Anxiety, Aggression, Depression, Rejection
6. Outcome scales: Unresolved Outcome, Nonadaptive Outcome, Maladaptive Outcome, Unrealistic Outcome
7. Unusual or Atypical Responses: Refusal, No Score, Antisocial, Atypical Categories

The principal changes to the scales in the new edition focused on greater differentiation (elaboration and extension) of the Support-Self, Support-Other, Problem Identification, Resolution, Maladaptive Outcome, and Atypical scales. Each story is scored separately for all scales, and each scale is scored (checked) once per story, if applicable, on the Coding Protocol. Raw scale scores are derived by addition of the number of checkmarks for each scale and are then transferred to the Scoring Profile for the specific age group of the respondent.

In contrast to the original RATC, the standardization sample for the second edition is much more substantial, composed of 1,060 youth, and was stratified according to the U.S. Census for ethnic representation. Interpretation of the Roberts–2 profile is based strictly on T-score analysis, for which scores $\geq 60T$ or $\leq 40T$ are suggested to reflect potential clinical significance. The second edition no longer includes a group of "Clinical" scales. The authors recommended that greatest emphasis be given to evaluating the Outcome scales for clinical relevance. They observed that the Theme Overview, Problem Identification, and Resolution scales are also generally quite reliable, but they suggested using caution in the interpretation of the scales assessing Available Resources and Emotion because these demonstrated much weaker test-retest reliability.

Research with the original RATC demonstrated support for its interrater reliability, with average agreement ranging from 80% to 95% (Kaleita, 1980; McArthur, 1976; McArthur & Roberts, 1982; Muha, 1977) and discriminant validity for identifying clinic referred children and families from children in the normative sample and nonreferred families (Muha, 1977). Moreover, prior studies confirmed the factor structure originally described by the authors (Palomares, Crowley, Worchel, Olson, & Rae, 1991) and supported its discriminant validity for identifying sexually abused children from nonabused samples (Friedrich & Share, 1997; Louw & Ramkisson, 2002). Joiner (1996) found that the RATC was less susceptible to defensiveness than the Children's Depression Inventory (CDI; Kovacs, 1992) and suggested that it may be a good index of depression when this response style is suspected. Finally, the RATC proved to be fairly popular among practicing clinicians, with reported usage ranging from 27.8% to 29% in the most recent surveys (Cashel, 2002; Hutton, Dubes, & Muir, 1992). With regard to the Roberts–2, the authors reported strong interrater reliability, test-retest reliability, and construct validity for the measure in the technical section of the manual. More independent studies evaluating its concurrent, discriminant, and predictive validity are needed.

Tell-Me-A-Story

The third principal storytelling test for children is the Tell-Me-A-Story test (TEMAS) (Costantino, Malgady, & Rogler, 1988), which was originally designed as a multicultural projective test for use with Hispanic youth. The authors observed the need for a psychometrically sound instrument appropriate for minority populations. Prior research evaluating the responses of Hispanic and Black youth to projective tests suggested that these groups of children were less verbally fluent, less mature, and poorly adjusted when compared with nonminority children (Ames & August, 1966; Booth, 1966; Costantino & Malgady, 1983; Dana, 1996; Durret & Kim, 1973). However, as noted by the TEMAS authors, such studies incorporated the use of stimulus materials (primarily the TAT) depicting Anglo-American individuals in scenes with which minority youth were not likely to identify. The authors of the TEMAS thus sought to develop a more culturally sensitive measure with multicultural norms. Similar to the Roberts–2, the TEMAS is intended for school-aged youth, specifically children and adolescents between 5 and 18 years of age.

The TEMAS is composed of 23 cards, with parallel sets for minorities and nonminorities. The minority version depicts Hispanic and Black children in urban settings in scenes intentionally created to represent polarized conflict, for example, between nurturance and rejection or dependence and individuation. The pictures are thus less ambiguous than the TAT or Roberts cards and are presented in color to "facilitate verbalization and projection of emotional states" (Costantino & Malgady, 1999, p. 193). The nonminority version consists of corresponding pictures, identical in design but depicting predominantly White characters. Both versions contain a 9-card short form. The long form includes 11 sex-specific and 12 general cards. The administration instructions are also very similar to those for the TAT/C.A.T.; however, reaction time to each card and the total time for each story are recorded. All cards are administered in numerical order. Each card is designed to pose a dilemma, and the resolutions that children generate reveal information regarding personality dimensions related to emotional, behavioral, and interpersonal functioning. Like the Roberts, a quantitative scoring system was developed for the TEMAS that evaluates 18 cognitive functions, 9 personality functions, and 7 affective functions:

> Cognitive Functions: Reaction Time, Total Time, Fluency, Total Omissions, Main Character Omissions, Secondary Character Omissions, Event Omissions, Setting Omissions, Total Transformations, Main Character Transformations, Secondary Character Transformations, Event Transformations, Setting Transformations, Inquiries, Relationships, Imagination, Sequencing and Conflict

> Personality Functions: Interpersonal Relationships, Aggression, Anxiety/Depression, Achievement Motivation, Delay of Gratification, Self-Concept, Sexual Identity, Moral Judgment, Reality Testing

Affective Functions: Happy, Sad, Angry, Fearful, Neutral, Ambivalent, Inappropriate Affect

The affective and cognitive functions are scored for the presence or absence of related content. A score for Fluency is derived from a count of the number of words per story. The personality functions are rated based on the presence of relevant content with the use of a Likert-type scale. The scoring system was standardized on a sample of 642 children (281 boys and 361 girls), ages 5 to 13, from the New York City area, representing Whites, Blacks, Puerto Ricans, and other Hispanic youth. According to the authors, there were no significant differences in responses, and thus there are no sex-specific norms.

Interpretation of the TEMAS can be made based on a profile analysis using the scoring system. Scores >60T or qualitative indicators exceeding critical levels are considered clinically significant. Alternatively, qualitative strategies as developed for the TAT and other content-based approaches can additionally be used and are necessary for interpretation of adolescent responses. Research with the TEMAS suggests adequate test-retest reliability, content, and predictive validity (Costantino, Malgady, & Rogler, 1988; Costantino, Malgady, Casullo, & Castillo, 1991). Furthermore, discriminant validity has been demonstrated in the ability of the TEMAS scores to distinguish groups of children with Attention Deficit/Hyperactivity Disorder and nondisordered youth, in addition to other clinical and nonclinical groups of African American, Hispanic, and White children (Cardalda, 1995; Costantino, Malgady, Colon-Malgady, & Bailey, 1992; Costantino, Malgady, Rogler, & Tsui, 1988).

The strengths of the TEMAS clearly include its multicultural emphasis and objective scoring system. Also noteworthy is the emphasis on assessing verbal fluency, which is often overlooked in the interpretation of such tests. The TEMAS has been recommended for inclusion in psychological assessment batteries for culturally and linguistically diverse children and adolescents (Dana, 1996) and has been used in the United States, Central America, and South American (Barona & Hernandez, 1990; Bernal, 1991; Walton, Nuttal, & Vaszquez-Nuttal, 1997). The few principal criticisms reflect the small size and regional homogeneity of the standardization sample and the limited independent research conducted by individuals other than the test authors (Flanagan & Giuseppe, 1999). With respect to clinical practice, approximately 12% of survey respondents (Cashel, 2002) indicated use of the TEMAS in test batteries of children. However, the extent to which the respondents worked with ethnic minority children was not queried.

Integration of Storytelling Measures in Psychological Assessment Batteries

There are many factors that must be considered when one decides whether to incorporate a storytelling measure in a psychological assessment battery. These include the purpose of the evaluation, the cognitive and verbal functioning of the youth, and the cultural background of both the youth and the examiner. Flanagan and DiGuiseppe (1999) suggested that assessments conducted strictly for diagnostic purposes are best addressed by administration of "objective," psychometrically validated instruments such as structured diagnostic interviews and behavior report forms. However, Flanagan and DiGuiseppe also suggested that practitioners are often concerned with "why" a problem exists. Projective measures can be helpful in informing "motivations, schema, circumstances and constructs of the individual which drive the emotions" (p. 26). In such manner, they can be very useful for generating hypotheses to inform treatment planning.

Other individual factors related to intellectual functioning, verbal fluency, and ethnic background are equally important. Generally, most clinicians will concede that storytelling tasks are less than useful for youth with borderline or lower levels of cognitive ability. Similarly, interpretation of stories must be made within the context of the child's or adolescent's capacity for verbal expression, cultural background, and sense of familiarity with the card content and the examiner. Costantino and his colleagues effectively demonstrated the significance of these issues (Costantino & Malgady, 1983; Costantino, Malgady, & Vasquez, 1981).

Case Study

The final section of this chapter illustrates the integration of a storytelling measure, the RATC, within a testing battery. For our purposes, we call the referred youth "Jane Smith."

Jane was a 10-year-old Caucasian female referred for evaluation at a university-based clinic for emotional and behavioral problems, which were said to occur primarily at home. Jane was a middle child with three older siblings (two brothers and one sister) and one younger sister. Her developmental history was nonremarkable, and there was no reported history of abuse or neglect. Her parents were married and the family was described as very stable. Her mother, Mrs. Smith, noted that Jane had significant difficulty adjusting to the birth of her younger sister, because Jane had been "the baby" of the family. Her academic history was also generally quite strong. Her mother noted that Jane developed language skills far ahead of age expectancy, and she suspected that Jane was extraordinarily bright. Jane never struggled with academics, although she had periodic difficulties in the classroom related to boredom, testing limits with teachers, "eye-rolling," and "sassing back." Mrs. Smith believed these were successfully addressed with more authoritative teachers. Mrs. Smith indicated that the principal behaviors prompting her to seek evaluation for Jane included the following: being excessively demanding, lying, belligerence, self-defeating behaviors, and difficulties with siblings and peers. Jane had previously participated in a social skills group at school during the previous academic year (fourth grade). She had also participated in individual counseling sessions, but Mrs. Smith did not believe these had been effective, because of Jane's tendency to lie and to manipulate others. With regard to her family history of psychological problems, one of her older brothers was diagnosed with Attention Deficit/Hyperactivity Disorder. Mrs. Smith acknowledged that she had been taking an antidepressant for eight years.

Jane was administered the following tests: Wechsler Intelligence Scale for Children–Fourth Edition (WISC-IV); Beery-Buktenica Developmental Test of Visual Motor Integration (VMI); Woodcock Johnson III Tests of Achievement (WJ-III); Computerized–Diagnostic Interview Schedule for Children (C-DISC); Child Behavior Checklist (CBCL); Behavior Assessment Scale for Children–Second Edition (BASC–2; Parent Rating Scales and the Self Report of Personality); Personality Inventory for Youth; and the Roberts Apperception Test for Children (RATC).

The results of testing revealed the following: Jane was functioning within the Superior range of intellectual ability (FSIQ = 123 ± 4) with consistent development demonstrated between her verbal (VCI = 134 ± 5) and perceptual (PRI = 135 ± 5) skills. However, she obtained significantly lower scores on the two remaining factors, which were in the Low Average and Average range for Working Memory (WMI = 88 ± 8) and Processing Speed (PSI = 103 ± 9). Her performance on the VMI was poor because she completed it quickly and carelessly, making several integration errors and she obtained a score within the borderline range, at the 5th percentile. In contrast, her scores on the Woodcock Johnson–III were consistently within the High Average to Superior range. She particularly excelled in written expression, achieving a score on the Writing Samples test that was above the 99th percentile. Her lowest score was still in the High Average range and was obtained on the Calculation subtest, a test of basic math abilities.

Mrs. Smith's responses to the C-DISC, CBCL, and BASC forms consistently demonstrated that Jane clearly met full criteria for Oppositional Defiant Disorder. Although she did not meet full criteria for a depressive or anxiety disorder, significant elevations were noted on both the CBCL and BASC on scales assessing depressed and anxious behaviors and social problems, in addition to low scores on scales assessing competencies and adaptive functioning. Unfortunately, a Teacher Report Form was not obtained, although Mrs. Smith indicated that Jane's current teacher thought she behaved quite well in the classroom.

Jane's profiles on both the BASC and PIY were considered invalid according to scoring guidelines because of a grossly exaggerated response style. She endorsed highly significant problems across most all scales, including those assessing depression, conduct problems, and attention and social problems. Problems with parental relationships were particularly noteworthy. Perhaps most revealing, however, were her stories on the RATC. A selection of these stories is presented in Table 12.2.

The thematic content was remarkably well developed, with elaborate detail, and suggested that she frequently felt rejected, isolated, unheard, and misunderstood. Most notable are the vivid descriptions she provided of her negative family interactions and her frustration with her parents and siblings. She used her own name in one of the stories and inadvertently referenced herself again in the middle of another. With regard to her coping behaviors, she demonstrated greater tendencies toward help-seeking than youth her age, yet also a good capacity for self-reliance, as illustrated in the success of her characters to ultimately solve their own problems. Alternatively, her stories also suggested tendencies toward engaging in defensive strategies such as withdrawal, isolation, and deception, and it appeared she viewed herself as more clever than her parents or significant others. Her story outcomes indicated that she struggled at times to identify a realistic process for solutions to conflict. When scored according to the RATC manual guidelines, Jane's stories yielded significant elevations on the following scales (T-scores are provided in parentheses): Reliance on Others (65), Support Child (79), Problem Identification (77), Resolution—1 (62), Anxiety (67), Aggression (63), and Rejection (>85).

A clinician making treatment recommendations based on the C-DISC and behavior report forms might appropriately make a referral for parent training interventions for her oppositional defiant children or teens and perhaps individual therapy to address depression or anxiety. However, analysis of Jane's RATC stories suggested that these recommendations alone would be insufficient. Much of Jane's distress and behavioral reactions stemmed from marked dissatisfaction with her family and with her parents' reaction to sibling conflict. This indicated that family-based interventions would perhaps be more effective and were also recommended.

With regard to Jane's relative deficits in specific cognitive and fine motor skill domains, these may have been related to internal preoccupation with emotional distress or anxiety and poor attention to detail. Alternatively, these lower scores may have reflected genuine weaknesses, and further monitoring in the classroom was recommended. Other recommendations included intervention focused on enhancing coping and interpersonal problem-solving skills, based on the results from the behavior report forms and her own responses to the RATC.

TABLE 12.2.
RATC Stories as Told by "Jane Smith"

Card 3

Once there was a girl named Jane who hated math very, very much. She could not stand it. So one day, at school, she had a really hard time at math. She told her teacher this. Her teacher gave her some extra math to do at home for bonus points. That made Jane mad, because she already hated math and she just made it harder for her. She decided to go home, sitting at the kitchen table, trying to do her homework, with her brothers and sisters fighting, the phone ringing, and mom cooking dinner. She decided to go up to her room to do homework on the floor, because she didn't have a desk in her room. She sat there for a while, and got like three problems done. Her little sister came upstairs and started blasting her radio, so she had to move again, so this time she was getting pretty mad, because she had to do her homework. She went into the garage, in the car, and did her homework there. But it got uncomfortable, so she went outside and did her homework there, and she got all but one problem done. The last problem she didn't really understand, so she decided to take it to her teacher the next day. And so what happened is she had her entire family inside, fighting, and she had got away and gotten what she wanted to do in a place they weren't. She got her things done without them bothering her.

Card 12

Makala would always spy on her mom and dad. She would always follow them around, and hide behind corners and walls and furniture. Once her parents were talking about adopting a kid. Her dad didn't want to, and the mom did. Makala really didn't want a little brother, which is what they were talking about. She didn't way to say, "No!" because that would give away her spying and so she had to listen to them talking about getting a little brother. Finally, they decided they would. She was mad that she would have a little brother, because she didn't like little boys very much. But, when they did decide to get one, and they finally got the brother, it turned out that he liked Makala a lot, so they became good friends. And it was actually a good thing that she got a little brother, because she had a little friend to play with all the time. The end.

Card 13

Once a girl named Shannon had a really annoying family. Her brother was always making stupid commentaries about everything that anyone said and always blaming her for everything. Her other brother was always, always, always trying to push people around to make people do what he wanted. Her older sister Rachel always thought that whatever she (Shannon) did was wrong and would never amount to anything and she would always tell her this, and how she was overweight, and all this stuff. And her little sister would always get away with everything she did, and she knew that, and she would bug Jane, no I mean Shannon, especially. One day Shannon couldn't take it anymore and she got really mad, because her sister just called her fat and everyone else was laughing, except for her parents. So she grabbed the chair she was sitting on at the table, picked it up and smashed in on the floor and ran outside yelling how her family was so stupid. But, then she felt bad about it later, and she came back in and her family was all sitting in the exact same places as before and were looking at each other. And she said, "Sorry! I just got a little mad," and so they didn't think about it anymore and didn't care about it anymore, and that's the end.

Card 14

The Smiths were having their house repainted. Little Danielle had taken a bucket of bright red paint into the white living room, and began finger-painting on the wall, and that's what she was doing in class, and she thought that's what you do with paint. She was painting all over the wall; she was painting handprints and everything. Then her mom came in and was so mad. She was like, "What are you doing? Ahhh! (Gasp)." She got in trouble, but after a while her mom actually realized that she liked it. They made a new style of painting, with a white wall, and you put handprints and smears and stuff, so it looked pretty cool, like red clouds on a white background. So that's what they would do, and they started doing that at other people's houses, and they would ask, "Now how did you learn to do this?" The mom and dad would always say, "Well, we can tell you about half of it. The other part you will have to ask Danielle about." So they did a painting business with their own unique style of painting. The mistake she had made actually turned out to be good. So Danielle felt pretty good about what she had done. The mom felt pretty upset with herself because she had yelled at first, but then she rewarded her and felt better.

CONCLUSIONS

Storytelling tests are rooted in a rich psychological history and remain a significant component of psychological testing for many practicing clinicians. Efforts to improve their psychometric properties and to enhance more generally their reliability and validity are continuous. With appropriate use and interpretation, they offer much to improve our understanding of the needs, perceptions, and motivations of children and adolescents.

REFERENCES

Abrams, D. M. (1999). Six decades of the Bellak scoring system, among others. In L. G. Gieser & M. I. Stein (Eds.), *Evocative images: The Thematic Apperception Test and the art of projection* (pp. 143–159). Washington, DC: American Psychological Association.

Ames, L. B., & August, J. (1966). Comparison of mosaic responses of Negro and white primary-school children. *Journal of Genetic Psychology, 109*, 123–129.

Archer, R. P., Maruish, M., Imhof, E. A., & Piotrowski, C. (1991). Psychological test usage with adolescent clients: 1990 survey findings. *Professional Psychology: Research and Practice, 22*, 247–252.

Armstrong, M. (1954). Children's responses to animal and human figures in thematic pictures. *Journal of Consulting Psychology, 18*, 67–70.

Barona, A., & Hernandez, A. E. (1990). Use of projectives in the assessment of Hispanic children. In A. Barona & E. E. Garcia (Eds.), *Children at risk: Poverty minority status and other issues in educational equity* (pp. 297–304). Washington, DC: National Association of School Psychologists.

Bellak, L. (1944). The concept of projection: An experimental investigation and study of the concept. *Psychiatry, 7*, 353–370.

Bellak, L. (1954). *The T.A.T. and the C.A.T. in clinical use*. New York: Grune & Stratton.

Bellak, L. (1971). *The T.A.T. and the C.A.T. in clinical use* (2nd Ed.). New York: Grune & Stratton.

Bellak, L. (1975). *The T.A.T. and the C.A.T. in clinical use* (3rd Ed.). New York: Grune & Stratton.

Bellak, L. (1986). *The T.A.T. and the C.A.T. in clinical use* (4th Ed.). Boston: Allyn & Bacon.

Bellak, L. (1993). *The T.A.T. and the C.A.T. in clinical use* (5th Ed.). Boston: Allyn & Bacon.

Bellak, L., & Abrams, D. M. (1997). *The T.A.T., the C.A.T. and the S.A.T. in clinical use* (6th Ed.). Boston: Allyn & Bacon.

Bellak, L., & Bellak, S. (1949). *The Children's Apperception Test*. Larchmont, NY: C.P.S.

Bellak, L., & Bellak, S. (1965). *The C.A.T.–H–A human modification*. Larchmont, NY: C.P.S.

Bellak, L., & Brower, D. (1951). Projective methods. In *Progress in neurology and psychiatry* (Vol. 6). New York: Grune & Stratton.

Bernal, I. (1991). *The relationship between level of acculturation, the Robert's Apperception Test for Children, and the TEMAS (Tell-Me-A-Story Test)*. Doctoral dissertation, California School for Professional Psychology, Los Angeles.

Biersdorf, K. R., & Marcuse, F. L. (1953). Responses of children to human and animal pictures. *Journal of Projective Techniques, 17*, 455–459.

Blum, G. S. (1964). Defense preferences among university students in Denmark, France, Germany and Israel. *Journal of Projective Techniques and Personality Assessment, 28*, 13–19.

Booth, L. J. (1966). A normative comparison of the responses of Latin American and Anglo American children to the Children's Apperception Test. In M. R. Haworth (Ed.), *The CAT: Facts about fantasy* (pp. 115–138). New York: Grune & Stratton.

Budoff, M. (1960). The relative utility of animal and human figures in a picture story test for young children. *Journal of Projective Techniques, 42*, 347–352.

Camara, W. J., Nathan, J. S., & Puente, A. E. (2000). Psychological test usage: Implications in professional psychology. *Professional Psychology: Research and Practice, 31*, 141–154.

Cardalda, E. (1995). *Socio-cultural correlates to school achievement using the TEMAS (Tell-Me-A-Story) culturally sensitive test with sixth, seventh and eighth graders.* Doctoral dissertation, New School for Social Research, New York.

Cashel, M. L. (2002). Child and psychological assessment: Current clinical practices and the impact of managed care. *Professional Psychology: Research and Practice, 33,* 446–453.

Cooper, A. (1981). A basic set for adolescent males. *Journal of Clinical Psychology, 37,* 411–414.

Costantino, G., & Malgady, R. G. (1983). Verbal fluency of Hispanic, black and white children on TAT and TEMAS, a new thematic apperception test. *Hispanic Journal of Behavioral Sciences, 5,* 199–206.

Costantino, G., & Malgady, R. G. (1999). The Tell-Me-A-Story test: A multicultural offspring of the Thematic Apperception Test. In L. G. Gieser & M. I. Stein (Eds.), *Evocative images: The Thematic Apperception Test and the art of projection* (pp. 191–206). Washington, DC: American Psychological Association.

Costantino, G., Malgady, R., Casullo, M. M., & Castillo, A. (1991). Cross-cultural standardization of TEMAS in three Hispanic subcultures. *Hispanic Journal of Behavioral Sciences, 13,* 48–62.

Costantino, G., Malgady, R. G., Colon-Malgady, G., & Bailey, J. (1992). Clinical utility of the TEMAS with non-minority children. *Journal of Personality Assessment, 59,* 433–438.

Costantino, G., Malgady, R. G., & Rogler, L. H. (1988). *TEMAS (Tell-Me-A-Story) manual.* Los Angeles, CA: Western Psychological Services.

Costantino, G., Malgady, R. G., Rogler, L. H., & Tsui, E. (1988). Discriminant analysis of clinical outpatients and public school children by TEMAS: A thematic apperception test for Hispanic and Blacks. *Journal of Personality Assessment, 52,* 670–678.

Costantino, G., Malgady, R. G., & Vasquez, C. (1981). A comparison of the Murray-TAT and a new thematic apperception test for urban Hispanic children. *Hispanic Journal of Behavioral Science, 3,* 291–300.

Cramer, P. (1982). *Defense mechanism manual.* Unpublished manuscript, Williams College.

Cramer, P. (1987). The development of defense mechanisms. *Journal of Personality, 55,* 597–614.

Cramer, P. (1991). *The development of defense mechanisms: Theory, research, and assessment.* New York: Springer-Verlag.

Cramer, P. (1996). *Storytelling, narrative, and the Thematic Apperception Test.* New York: Guilford Press.

Cramer, P., & Carter, T. (1978). The relationship between sexual identification and the use of defense mechanisms. *Journal of Personality Assessment, 42,* 63–73.

Dana, R. H. (1996). *Multicultural assessment perspectives for professional psychology.* Boston: Allyn & Bacon.

Dollinger, S., & Cramer, P. (1990). Children's defensive responses and emotional upset following a disaster: A projective assessment. *Journal of Personality Assessment, 54,* 116–127.

Durret, M. E., & Kim, C. C. (1973). A comparative study of behavioral maturity in Mexican American and Anglo preschool children. *Journal of Genetic Psychology, 123,* 55–62.

Elbert, J. C., & Holden, E. W. (1987). Child diagnostic assessment: Current training practices in clinical psychology internships. *Professional Psychology: Research and Practice, 18,* 587–596.

Flanagan, R., & Di Giuseppe, R. (1999). Critical review of the TEMAS: A step within the development of thematic apperception instruments. *Psychology in the Schools, 36,* 21–30.

Freedenfeld, R. N., Ornduff, S. R., & Kelsey, R. M. (1995). Object relations and physical abuse: A TAT analysis. *Journal of Personality Assessment, 64,* 552–568.

Freud, A. (1937). *The ego and the mechanisms of defense.* London: Hogarth Press.

Friedrich, W. N., & Share, M. C. (1997). The Roberts Apperception Test for Children: An exploratory study of it use with sexually abused children. *Journal of Child Sexual Abuse, 64,* 83–91.

Geiser, L., & Stein, M. I. (1999). *Evocative images: The Thematic Apperception Test and the art of projection.* Washington, DC: American Psychological Association.

Haworth, M. R. (1963). A schedule for the analysis of C.A.T. responses. *Journal of Projective Techniques and Personality Assessment, 27,* 181–184.

Hutton, J. B., Dubes, R., & Muir, S. (1992). Assessment practices of school psychologists: Ten years later. *School Psychology Review, 21,* 271–284.

Joiner, T. E. (1996). The relations of thematic and nonthematic childhood depression measures to defensiveness and gender. *Journal of Abnormal Child Psychology, 24*, 803–813.

Kaleita, T. A. (1980). *The expression of attachment and separation anxiety in abused and neglected adolescents*. Unpublished doctoral dissertation, California School of Professional Psychology.

Kohlberg, L. (1969). *Stages in the development of moral thought and action*. New York: Holt.

Kovacs, M. (1992). *Children's Depression Inventory Manual*. Los Angeles: Western Psychological Services.

Lindzey, G. (1952). Thematic Apperception Test: Interpretive assumptions and empirical evidence. *Psychological Bulletin, 49*, 1–25.

Louw, A. E., & Ramkisson, S. (2002). The suitability of the Roberts Apperception Test for Children (RATC), the House-Tree-Person (HTP) and Draw A Person (D-A-P) scales in the identification of child sexual abuse in the Indian community: An exploratory study. *Southern African Journal of Child and Adolescent Mental Health, 14*, 91–106.

Lubin, B., Larsen, R. M., & Matarazzo, J. D. (1984). Patterns of psychological test usage in the United States. *American Psychologist, 39*, 451–454.

Mandler, G., Lindzey, G., & Crouch, R. G. (1957). Thematic Apperception Test: Indices of anxiety in relation to test anxiety. *Educational Psychological Measurements, 17*, 466–474.

McArthur, D. (1976). *A comparison of the stimulus influence of three thematic projective techniques with children*. Unpublished doctoral dissertation, California School of Professional Psychology.

McArthur, D. S., & Roberts, G. E. (1982). *Roberts Apperception Test for Children manual*. Los Angeles, CA: Western Psychological Services.

McGrew, M. W., & Teglasi, H. (1990). Formal characteristics of thematic apperception test stories as indices of emotional disturbance in children. *Journal of Personality Assessment, 54*, 639–655.

Morgan, C. D., & Murray, H. M. (1935). A method for investigating fantasies: The Thematic Apperception Test. *Archives of Neurology and Psychiatry, 34*, 289–306.

Muha, T. W. (1977). *A validation study of the Roberts' Apperception Test as a measure of psychological dysfunction in families*. Unpublished doctoral dissertation, California School of Professional Psychology.

Murray, H. A. (1943). *Thematic apperception test manual*. Cambridge, MA: Harvard University Press.

Murstein, B. I. (1963). *Theory and research on projective techniques (emphasizing the TAT)*. New York: Wiley.

Niec, L. N., & Russ, S. W. (2002). Children's internal representations, empathy and fantasy play: A validity study of the SCORS-Q. *Psychological Assessment, 14*, 331–338.

Obrzut, J. E., & Boliek, C. A. (1986). Thematic approaches to personality assessment with children and adolescents. In H. M. Knoff (Ed.), *The assessment of child and adolescent personality* (pp. 183–198). New York: Guilford.

Ornduff, S. R., Freedenfeld, R. N., Kelsey, R. M., & Critelli, J. W. (1994). Object relations of sexually abused female subjects: A TAT analysis. *Journal of Personality Assessment, 63*, 223–238.

Palomares, R. S., Crowley, S. L., Worchel, F. F., Olson, T. K., & Rae, W. A. (1991). The factor analytic structure of the Roberts Apperception Test for Children: A comparison of the standardization sample with a sample of chronically ill children. *Journal of Personality Assessment, 56*, 414–425.

Piotrowski, C., & Keller, J. W. (1989). Psychological testing in outpatient mental health facilities. *Professional Psychology: Research and Practice, 20*, 423–425.

Roberts, G. E., & Gruber, C. (2005). *Roberts–2 manual*. Los Angeles: Western Psychological Services.

Rosenberg, R. P., & Beck, S. (1986). Preferred assessment methods and treatment modalities for hyperactive children among clinical child and school psychologists. *Journal of Clinical Child Psychology, 15*, 142–147.

Shneidman, E. S. (1951). *Thematic test analysis*. New York: Grune & Stratton.

Shneidman, E. S. (1999). The Thematic Apperception Test: A paradise of psychdynamics. In L. G. Gieser & M. I. Stein (Eds.), *Evocative images: The Thematic Apperception Test and the art of projection* (pp. 87–97). Washington, DC: American Psychological Association.

Shore, M. F., Massimo, J. L., & Mack, R. (1964). The relationship between levels of guilt and unsocialized behavior. *Journal of Projective Techniques and Personality Assessment, 28*, 346–349.

Teglasi, H. (1993). *Clinical use of story telling: Emphasizing the TAT with children and adolescents.* Boston: Allyn & Bacon.

Tuma, J. M., & Pratt, M. J. (1982). Clinical child psychology practice and training: A survey. *Journal of Clinical Child Psychology, 11,* 27–34.

Walton, J., Nuttall, R. R., & Vazquez-Nuttall, E. (1997). The impact of war on the mental health of children: A Salvadoran study. *Child Abuse & Neglect, 21,* 737–749.

Westen, D. (1991). Clinical assessment of object relations using the TAT. *Journal of Personality Assessment, 56,* 127–133.

Westen, D. (2002). Current rating summary sheet, Department of Psychology, Emory University, Atlanta, GA.

Westen, D., Lohr, N., Silk, K., Kerber, K., & Goodrich, S. (1985; 1990; 2002). *Measuring object relations and social cognition using the TAT: Scoring manual.* Department of Psychology: University of Michigan.

Westen, D., Ludolph, P., Lerner, H., Ruffins, S., & Wiss, C. (1990). Object relations in borderline adolescents. *Journal of the American Academy of child and Adolescent Psychiatry, 29,* 338–348.

Winter, D. G. (1999). Linking personality and "scientific" psychology: The development of empirically derived Thematic Apperception Test measures. In L. G. Gieser & M. I. Stein (Eds.), *Evocative images: The Thematic Apperception Test and the art of projection* (pp. 107–124). Washington, DC: American Psychological Association.

13

DRAWINGS IN CLINICAL ASSESSMENT
OF CHILDREN AND ADOLESCENTS

Holly C. Matto

Virginia Commonwealth University, School of Social Work, Richmond, Virginia

Good assessment is the cornerstone of mental health services delivery. Mental health clinicians are charged with providing reliable and valid assessment of their clients in order to make ethical and responsible treatment recommendations that competently meet the clinical needs of their client population. Comprehensive data integration is an essential part of good assessment practice, but clinicians must make assessment decisions based on the assessment resources available, while being responsive to their clients' abilities to impart the clinical information solicited. Given the importance and complexity of good assessment, there are several assessment-related questions that continue to challenge clinicians:

1. Are our assessment practices sufficiently clinically comprehensive? That is to say, do they include opportunities to assess all of the relevant clinical domains important to understanding a specific case?

2. Are our assessment practices sufficiently methodologically comprehensive? That is to say, do our assessment tools include the range of methods needed to gather the clinical information we need?

3. Are our assessment practices culturally competent and developmentally appropriate? That is to say, are we tailoring our assessment practices to match the needs of our diverse client populations to reduce the risk of making inaccurate or invalid clinical judgments that have unintended negative consequences for certain groups of youth? And, are our assessment practices congruent with the developmental strengths and limitations of our clients?

A careful review of the research and clinical literature suggests that incorporation of drawings into assessment practices may be beneficial in addressing some of these questions. Drawing methods offer the opportunity to obtain clinical information that may not be easily retrieved through conventional paper-and-pencil verbal tests and, as such, may broaden the range of clinical data to which we have access, as well as broaden the range of informants from whom we can obtain clinical data (e.g., children with reading or language limitations).

Drawings have been used as part of child and adolescent clinical assessment for decades. The use of drawings in assessment practices remains controversial because of persistent concerns about their validity (Garb, Wood, Lilienfeld, & Nezworski, 2002; Roback, 1968; Swensen, 1957, 1968). However, despite these concerns, drawings as assessment tools, and human figure drawings in particular, are psychological tests that continue to be widely used by clinicians (Camara, Nathan, & Puente, 2000; Watkins, Campbell, Nieberding, & Hallmark, 1995). And, over the past decade, the gap between human figure drawing research knowledge and practice use has grown smaller. Perhaps the most appealing clinical aspects of using drawings in assessment is that the nonverbal method transcends language limitations and cultural barriers, which are often encountered with traditional verbal tests, and is a child-focused information-gathering tool, which takes little time to administer and is usually an enjoyable activity. Of course, to focus on method gains at the expense of outcome accuracy would be a little like getting excited about a GPS system without caring about getting to the correct destination. As the saying goes, if you do not know where you are going, all roads lead there. And so the validity admonitions leveraged in the drawing assessment literature have justifiably served to temper enthusiasm for such methods while significantly shaping new empirical inquiry that has led to advancements in instrument development and psychometric refinements of existing drawing tests. This chapter discusses some of these new research developments, presenting a brief historical context of drawing assessment, and includes short clinical illustrations throughout to show how drawings can be used as part of clinical assessment practices.

Historically, drawings have been used to assess intelligence, personality characteristics, and family dynamics. Goodenough (1926) used drawings to assess intelligence or cognitive ability with her Draw-A-Man approach, and Machover (1949) developed the Human Figure Drawing (HFD) approach based on a psychodynamic understanding of personality development manifest through the drawn form, with the HFD representing the child's projected inner emotions, conflicts, and wishes. This Draw-A-Person approach was expanded to encourage the client to elicit a story about the drawing, using prompts such as "What is this person, thinking, feeling, doing?" "How does this person get along with others?" "How does he/she experience sadness?" (Handler, 1996; Machover, 1951).

Hammer (1958) used drawings to assess emotional functioning, and Koppitz's (1968) research identified both emotional and developmental indicators in the drawings of children aged 5–11, with interpretations based on the presence of specific unusual indicators represented in 6% of nonclinical child drawings. From a developmental perspective, Koppitz's research determined that, by age 11, all nonclinical children should include features such as head, eyes, nose, mouth, body, legs, feet, hair, and neck in their human figure drawings. Newer, shorter cognitive tests that employ human figure drawings, such as Naglieri's (1988) Draw-A-Person Quantitative Scoring System, have been found to possess validity relative to the Wechsler Intelligence Scale-Revised (WISC-R) and Wechsler Intelligence Scale-III (WISC-III) (Abell, Wood, & Liebman, 2001), although cautions are given that such tests should never be used in isolation from other intelligence measures.

Other tests that have been developed and that are well utilized by clinicians have taken a more systemic approach to drawing assessment. Buck's (1948) House-Tree-Person (HTP) test assesses an individual's orientation to self and to family life. From a psychodynamic perspective, the house represents home life, and a child's culmination of family experience can be examined; the tree represents the unconscious world, symbolizing how well the child is rooted in reality (i.e., assessing ego strength), the extent to which the child has a propensity toward growth, and the nature of the child's support network (symbolized by the tree's branches reaching out to others). Burns and Kaufman's (1970) Kinetic Family Drawing (KFD) assesses family dynamics and the nature and quality of such interpersonal relationships, asking children to draw a picture of everyone in their family, including the child him/herself, doing an activity. A variation on the traditional KFD is Prout and Phillips' (1974) Kinetic School Drawings, which ask children to "draw a school picture. Put yourself, your teacher, and a friend or two in the picture. Make everyone doing something" (p. 304). Kinetic drawing scoring systems have been developed to assess structural characteristics of the drawn figures and their relationships to the child's drawn self by examining the nature of interpersonal interactions, distance between and among figures, and the placement of the figures on the page.

Some researchers have begun examining alternative scoring methods for diverse cultural groups (see Handler & Habenicht, 1994; Wegmann & Lusebrink, 2000 for brief reviews of KFD cross-cultural studies). Wegmann and Lusebrink (2000) created a revised scoring system, based on the original Burns and Kaufman protocol, comprising subscales such as "family composition" (e.g., figure omissions, figure erasures, extended family additions), "distance and closeness" (e.g., encapsulation of any figure), "interactions and relationships" (e.g., active versus passive action, figures facing each other, level of nurturance depicted), "activities" (e.g., extent of energy expended in activity portrayed), "sexual identification" (e.g., sharing activity with one parent, identification of figures to each other), and "developmental level" (e.g., space organization, body and face completions). These researchers tested their revised KFD scoring protocol across three nonclinical samples of children, 7 to 10 years old, from the United States, Taiwan, and Switzerland, and found that only 7 scoring protocol variables (major figure missing, major figure erasure, extended family added, distance between figures, encapsulation, self sharing an activity with a major figure, and incomplete face) held consistent reliability across these different populations, suggesting limitations in assuming cross-cultural applicability in the KFD's psychometric properties.

Overall, drawing assessment development has garnered some consistent empirical warnings. Knoff (2003) suggests that projective drawings are better used as "hypothesis-generating" tools during assessment, rather than "hypothesis-validating" assessment methods, because of the limitations in the empirical literature on their psychometric functioning (p. 105), although the research is uneven. Others concur that drawing techniques should never be used as a sole assessment tool (nor should any one instrument be used alone), and that the use of global scoring systems, rather than identification of single indicators or small sets of indicators, should be used for assessment interpretations. However, there has been some empirical support for certain drawing indicators' relationship with mental health status. For example, Handler and Reyher's (1965) review of 51 human figure drawing studies on 21 anxiety indicators showed that figure size, omissions, loss of detail, distortion, and head/body simplification were valid indicators of anxiety.

Indeed, there has been considerable controversy over the type of scoring approach that is most valid in the interpretation of drawings for clinical assessment purposes, particularly over whether quantitative or qualitative methods are more suitable. Tharinger and Stark (1990) developed and tested an integrative, holistic scoring system for the DAP and KFD projective drawing protocols, whereby raters were able to offer a general impression of a child's drawing, which was then placed on an overall pathology scale from 1 (absence of psychopathology) to 5 (severe psychopathology). The dimensions that raters used to make their pathology scale general assessments with the human figure drawings included: 1) inhumanness of human figure drawing, 2) lack of agency/ineffectual human figure, 3) indication of lack of well-being, and 4) presence of hollow, vacant, or stilted person in the drawing.

Using the same method, raters also gave general clinical impressions from clients' Kinetic Family Drawings, using the following assessment dimensions: 1) inaccessibility of family members to each other, 2) degree of member engagement/involvement, 3) inappropriate family structure (e.g., roles, boundaries), and 4) inhumanness of family figures (pp. 369–371). Results from the study showed that the researchers' integrative qualitative scoring approach successfully differentiated across mood/anxiety disorder groups and the control group, whereas the traditional Koppitz and Reynolds quantitative scoring systems did not differentiate among the treatment and control groups, with no single indicator showing discriminating ability. Similar support for the use of a holistic-intuitive scoring approach was found in a study of homeless men, psychiatric inpatients, and vocational rehabilitation clients (see Handler, 1996). Integrative impressions of these clients' drawings, with the use of four overall criteria (i.e., Is the person frightened of the world? Does the person in the drawing have intact thinking? Is the person in the drawing comfortable with close relationships? Is this person safe to be around?), significantly differentiated group membership, whereas the individual item scoring approach did not show differentiating ability (Handler, 1996).

Overall, the culmination of research consistently shows that single item indicators are unreliable, and, thus, scoring protocols should use global scores (Handler & Habenicht, 1994; Naglieri, McNeish, & Bardos, 1991; Smith & Dumont, 1995). Handler and Riethmiller (1998), for example, suggest that "configural scoring approaches," or those that combine drawing characteristics, may be more useful in clinical practice than relying on single-item indicators.

In addition to the unreliability, another problem in evaluating drawings with the use of discrete indicators rather than global indicators, is that the single-indicator method increases the risk of culturally insensitive assessment practice. For example, shading may represent an accurate depiction of a child's skin tone, rather than indicating "excessive anxiety" or other behavioral pathologies that have been hypothesized in the literature. Or representing grandparents or extended relatives in a family drawing while excluding the biological parents may be culturally syntonic for a newly immigrated family from a southwest Asian culture, perhaps accurately reflecting the child's current family structure. And yet for other children, for whom the absence of the child's biological parents in the drawing represents family distress, such a drawing may suggest a significant area for clinical focus. Thus, empirical inquiries should investigate the appropriateness of each drawing instrument for diverse groups.

Despite these caveats, drawing assessment tools offer children important opportunities to contribute information to assessment that is not hindered by language difficulties, reading level, or other cultural barriers that exist in traditional emotional/behavioral verbal self-report measures. And new assessment developments have contributed to increased enthusiasm for their use. Three such developments are introduced here.

STANDARDIZED DRAWING TEST DEVELOPMENTS

Draw-A-Person: Screening Procedure for Emotional Disturbance

Knoff (2003) discusses the developments of Naglieri's Draw-A-Person Quantitative Scoring System (QSS) and Screening Procedure for Emotional Disturbance as examples of contemporary expansions on Goodenough-Harris's Draw-A-Man test, attesting to significant improvements shown in their scoring protocols. The Draw-A-Person: Screening Procedure for Emotional Disturbance (DAP:SPED; Naglieri, McNeish, & Bardos, 1991) asks the child to produce three human figure drawings (man, woman, self), which are scored according to 55 item indicators that examine structural and content dimensions such as figure omissions, presence of objects, placement on page, and size of figure. The DAP:SPED standardization sample consisted of 2,355 youths, 6–17 years old, representative of the U.S. population for age, gender, geographic region, race, ethnicity, and socioeconomic status. The global scoring system produces a T-score (mean of 50 and SD of 10), with the use of separate age and gender norms, with higher scores indicative of more emotional/behavioral disturbance. Cronbach's alpha internal reliability estimate of the DAP:SPED is .76 (ages 6–8 years); .77 (ages 9–12 years); and .71 (ages 13–17 years).

The DAP:SPED has demonstrated validity in identifying youths with emotional/behavioral disorders, such as differentiating Conduct/Oppositional Defiant Disorder and control group youths (Naglieri & Pfeiffer, 1992) and special education students with identified emotional disturbance from regular education students (McNeish & Naglieri, 1993). In a recent study, Matto (2002) found the DAP:SPED was better at detecting internalizing as opposed to externalizing behavioral disturbance in a sample of youths receiving clinical services for emotional and behavioral problems, and showed predictive ability for internalization of behavioral disturbance beyond that which a standard pencil/paper instrument measured. Matto and Naglieri (2005) attempted to determine whether there was evidence of construct-irrelevant variance (race-based bias) in the DAP:SPED, using matched Black-White and Hispanic-White samples. Children and adolescents were drawn from a nationally representative sample and matched for gender, grade, and school classroom. No statistically significant differences in the item composites (e.g., large figure items, small figure items, or shading) were found for the race and ethnic comparisons, and DAP:SPED total T-scores did not differ significantly for the Black-White or Hispanic-White matched groups.

Diagnostic Drawing Series

The Diagnostic Drawing Series (DDS) (Cohen, 1983) was developed in the early 1980s; it asks the child to produce three pictures with the use of 12 soft chalk pastels on white $18'' \times 24''$ drawing paper. The first picture is a free drawing, in which clients are directed to "make a picture using these materials" (in Mills, 2003, p. 402). The child is asked to then create a second picture with the directive "draw a picture of a tree" and finally is asked to "make a picture of how you're feeling, using lines, shapes and colors." The child has up to 15 minutes to work on each separate drawing, and all drawings are administered in one session. The technique can be used with children aged 13 and older and is designed to give a graphic profile to assess whether the child's drawings are representative of those drawings produced by clients with certain psychiatric diagnoses. Diagnostic categories have been formed by analysis of the drawings' structural properties (line quality, page coverage, and placement) rather than their symbolic content. According to test developers, the DDS has been normed on 21 different diagnostic groups (e.g., schizophrenia, major depression, eating disorders), based on differences in these structural qualities (see Mills, Cohen, & Meneses, 1993, for reliability of the rating system; and Cohen, Mills, & Kijak, 1994, for further inquiry into this drawing assessment tool).

The Silver Drawing Test

The Silver Drawing Test (SDT) assesses cognitive skills and emotional strengths and is based on Piaget's cognitive development theory. The SDT was first developed in 1983 and has since been revised (see Silver, 2002). The test has been administered to 1,399 unimpaired and impaired (brain injuries, hearing impairment, language difficulties, cognitive and emotional disabilities) children, adolescents, and adults, and norms have been developed for age and gender. Inter-rater reliability has been shown to range from .74 to .98; test-retest reliability from one study (see review, Silver, 2003) was .72. Some large sample standardization studies have been conducted in other countries (e.g., Australia, Brazil, Russia). The test was developed for use with children over age five, and usually takes about 20 minutes to complete. The test employs "stimulus drawings" of people, animals, and objects, using two sets of 15 stimulus drawings to assess cognitive and emotional dimensions such as spatial ability, sequencing, classification, emotions, self-image, and humor (Silver, 2002). Subtests include drawing from imagination, predictive drawing, and drawing from observation. During the drawing from imagination subtest, children are asked to choose two or more stimulus drawings, to imagine that something is happening between the subjects, and to draw what they imagine. Children can add titles to their drawings and are encouraged to discuss their stimulus responses. The technique assesses children's abilities to select, combine, and represent objects and examines emotional themes, self-image identifications, and how humor is used during the process. During the drawing from observation subtest, children are asked to draw three cylinders and a small stone, to assess spatial ability. The predictive subtest, which assesses a child's ability to sequence and conserve, asks the child to draw a sequence of glasses with decreasing liquid volume and to depict how a house might look in various positions on a hill.

Certainly it is wise to reiterate that these new and/or revised developments in standardized drawing assessment techniques should only be used as part of a larger, comprehensive assessment package (Hammer, 1997). Other areas of assessment needed for a complete and more holistic intake evaluation would include a client's full biopsychosocial history and information about the child's family history, a child's developmental and medical history, information about the child in his/her community or neighborhood context, and school-related data on academic functioning and teacher/peer relationships. It may also include additional intelligence testing and personality assessment, if warranted.

DRAWINGS AS TOOLS TO ELICIT THE CLIENT STORY

In addition to the use of drawings as standardized assessment tools, drawing directives can be used quite effectively to facilitate clinical communication between the client and clinician in a way that fosters a productive therapeutic relationship and allows for elicitation of the larger client story (Trombini & Montebarocci, 2004). For example, Trombini and colleagues have used the Drawn Stories Technique, which is a free drawing technique that asks the child to draw a created story in four quadrants on a piece of paper, with the first three quadrants depicting the story sequence and the fourth quadrant illustrating the story's ending. In their technique, these researchers emphasize the importance of an accompanying narrative to the drawn story, examining the positive or negative outcome related to the story sequence. In a nonclinical sample of 211 girls and boys 8–13 years old, Trombini and Montebarocci (2004) found that higher anxiety and depression scores were related to those children's stories with negative outcomes, as compared with those stories with positive outcomes, suggesting that the technique does indeed show promise in identifying psychological distress in children.

As a client story emerges from a drawing directive, it is important to note the dominant themes revealed in the picture. For example, clinicians would want to take note of the interpersonal or intrapersonal conflicts that might be represented, any themes of social isolation, and expression of fears related to uncertainty, unpredictability, or interpersonal rejection. Although the "projective hypothesis," the theoretical space from which drawings as assessment tools originated, has received uneven support (Kaplan, 2003), is it well recognized that clients portray cognitive, affective, and behavioral expressions in their artwork through the selection and placement of color on the page, the selection and elaboration of objects, the verbal meaning assigned to the drawing by the client, and the way in which the client relates to the art process (Kaplan, 2003). In other words, drawings tend to be more clinically useful in gathering meaningful information about a client's current experience (cognitive, affective, behavioral, interpersonal), rather than as a method of interpreting or diagnosing the past. In using drawings as a method to reveal the client's larger current story, it is important to examine how a client relates to the drawn *product* itself, as well as to how a client relates to the *process* of creating the drawings. A verbal processing protocol of the *product* should include clinical observation and a collaborative examination with the client of the following dimensions (see Moon, 1990, and Nucho, 1987, for other protocol elaborations):

Critical Engagement

The clinician engages in a functional analysis of an objective and investigative nature, examining the symbols, shapes, colors, size, art materials used, and objects' placement on the page. This phase allows for an in-depth analysis of the more objective qualities of the drawing. For example, does the drawing contain only red and black, even though 12 different color choices were available? Is the line quality very faint, or dark and emboldened? Is there a thick border that seals the content, or are only very faint pencil figures represented? Where are the figures/objects located on the page, and how much open page space is left? This phase allows the clinician to take a pictorial inventory, without assigning clinical judgment at this stage.

Initial Reactions

The clinician engages in a functional analysis of a subjective and reactive nature, leading to a discussion with the client about the thoughts, emotions, and physical sensations (bodily reactions) evoked during the drawing experience and during the client's subsequent engagement with the completed picture. This phase allows for the introduction of more clinically focused reactions to the drawing content, to direct the client-clinician dialogue. Handler and Reithmiller (1998) write about teaching students the art of engaging with clients' drawings to elicit their own reactions, allowing themselves to identify with the artist/client. The clinician's own subjective reactions, gleaned through identification with the drawn form and by putting oneself in interaction with the drawn form, offer deeper clinical insights into the client's experience (Handler & Reithmiller, 1998). For example, a clinician might ask the child to describe how the dog, abandoned and lost from his family, might be feeling right now. More in-depth examination of the subjective meaning of the colors used would be encouraged. A clinician might say, "I notice there's a lot of fiery colors in your picture— lots of oranges, reds, and yellows. What feelings do you have when you look at these colors?"

Another example of how intense reactions can be evoked from a single drawing was demonstrated in one adolescent's depiction of a hangman's noose with a completed stick figure in its grips and the notation "P_ _ _ _" written at the bottom, near the figure's feet. In discussing his figure drawing, the client described the frustration and despair over the "peace" he has been searching for in living with his depression, and the pressing, current feeling of being at the end of his rope. Another, older (age 19) male client, who was residing on the adult unit of an inpatient substance abuse treatment facility, chose to express his emotions related to his homeless status and intense depression as a tornado ripping through and devastating buildings and trees, illustrating, he said, the lack of control over life's unpredictable circumstances and the resulting empty feeling that is left in the wake of the devastation.

Relational Attributes

The clinician engages in a functional analysis of a relational and interactive nature, helping the client to explore connections to his/her current life situation, the social world, and significant others. For example, one five-year-old child, being seen at a public child guidance clinic for internalizing behavioral disturbance as expressed through withdrawn behaviors in the school environment and social isolation from peers, consistently drew a picture of a very small boy in the bottom corner of the paper, using only very light pencil. He consistently attended individual therapy weekly, each week drawing a very similar picture and talking very little about his drawing. After many weeks, the client came in one morning and produced a significantly different picture—one that incorporated more color and a larger figure. Because the boy's parents scheduled his therapy appointments for very early in the morning, he never saw another child in the waiting room until this particular day. It was revealed that the boy had thought the facility was built for his own problems, having never seen another child in the waiting room, and was delighted to see another child for the first time that particular morning. The relational component of his current perspective of his situation was revealed through the boy's new narrative and changed drawing, demonstrating that external environmental conditions may significantly influence a child's drawing and narrative.

Another example of how current relational dynamics may be expressed in children's drawings is demonstrated in a clinical case where a 16-year-old adolescent female was recently transferred to an outpatient therapy group from an inpatient psychiatric hospital program that she had attended for several months. The client drew, in the first outpatient group, a picture of a girl on top of a very tall building, threatening to jump. Through group (and later individual) therapeutic processing, it was revealed that she had a great deal of anger for the hospital staff about her experiences in the program, perceiving that "no one really cared" about her. The drawing was created to test how the outpatient group members would react and receive her "extreme" clinical history and threatening behavior. During the group processing, when members and the treating clinician dug deeper into the intense pain and hurt she was feeling, she began to cry and her hardened exterior softened.

Another example of the importance of examining the relational dimension in drawings can be seen in the case of a 16-year-old male client being seen in an inpatient hospital-based treatment center for primary polysubstance abuse, with secondary behavioral problems that led to a diagnosis of conduct disorder. In addition, the client was struggling with his own sexual identity. This client had a significantly difficult time on the treatment unit and perpetually isolated himself from the rest of the adolescent inpatient community. One way of furthering his isolation was through his drawings, which were classically disturbing in content (e.g., contained very vivid, graphically detailed violent scenes) and which he chose to leave out in the open for public display in the community space. One of his drawings depicted a person lying on a steel surgical hospital table, with a bright spotlight shining down on his body, with doctors wielding large knives, threatening to "rearrange" him. The client described the person on the table as feeling very vulnerable to those who were trying to rearrange and change him, feeling very much out of control in his surroundings. The content of these drawings and their narratives led to extensive follow-up with the treating psychiatrist and served as an inroad for further evaluation and testing.

Eliciting the client's story can be expanded from the traditional human figure-drawing directives of standardized assessment tools, to include task directives that ask the client to draw a "self-system" representation of multiple components of the self. For example, one technique asks the client to draw four parts of the self system, in quadrants, on a large piece of white paper, each representing the client's perception of his/her *body* self, *achieving* self, *interpersonal/relational* self, and *spiritual* self (Matto, Corcoran, & Fassler, 2003; Nucho, 1987). The verbal instructions and self-system components to be represented can be modified according to developmental level and clinical focus. For example, a clinician might be interested in knowing how an 8-year-old client represents his/her *school* self and *family* self; a clinician working with a 16-year-old juvenile offender on anger management strategies might ask the client to represent his/her *emotional* self and *thinking* self; or a clinician administering this assessment in a group modality might ask early adolescent females to draw their *inside* self (how they perceive themselves) and their *outside* self (how they think others perceive them). In an inpatient substance abuse facility, adolescents may be asked to draw their *addicted* self and their *sober* self. In examining the drawn representation, there are several product and process dimensions to be considered, and the following questions can help direct the inquiry: What self-system component did the client choose to draw first? What was left for last? What, if any, component was left blank? What is the nature of the symbols represented in each quadrant or self-system section? What is the nature of the represented figures? Is the head cut off from the rest of the body?

When this directive was implemented in an inpatient substance abuse treatment facility for adolescents, many common themes emerged from the drawings across adolescent clients. Many left the *interpersonal/relational* and *achieving* selves empty, and one male adolescent depicted his body self covered in a hooded sweatshirt, looking sideways. Another interpersonal self was drawn as a person slouched in a chair, looking down at the floor, with no other objects or figures represented; another male drew a lone car driving through a junkyard, with discarded cars piled high on each side, illustrating the "wrecked relationships" caused by his addiction. Others chose emaciated, alien-like figures to represent the self. One female client encapsulated a brown stick-figure self in a black box with a thick black marker border. The figure had a black bandana covering the eyes, with orange stick figures surrounding the outside of the thick black border, illustrating the disconnect from all other interpersonal relationships. One heroin user expressed his *body* self as a sole head, with a frightened facial expression and one arm, stating that the figure represented his "dirty body." Another adolescent represented his *inside* self as a "sweet, caring, sensitive," full and detailed figure whereas his *outside* self was a picture of a very detailed green gun with the words "I try to hold my anger in, but if you get me mad, I'm somewhat like a gun waiting to go off."

Malchiodi (1990) proposes an evaluation tool to help clinicians attend to the client's engagement in the drawing task. The evaluation includes indicators related to task orientation, product/content, and interaction, with each indicator scored on a scale from 1 to 5:

> *Task orientation* indicators include items such as "waits for directions" versus "shows impulsivity"; "is calm and focused" versus "is restless and agitated"; "sustains involvement" versus "gives up easily"; "demonstrates appropriate concentration" versus "appears distracted"; "follows instruction" versus "cannot follow instruction."

Product/content indicators include items such as "drawn image reflects positive aspects" versus "negative images"; "images are integrated/coherent" versus "disjointed or fragmented"; "shows pride in finished product" versus "devalues product."

Interaction indicators include items such as "maintains own physical space" versus "goes into other's personal space inappropriately"; "responds to limits" versus "has difficulty in responding to limits"; "shares appropriately" versus "is unable to share" (Malchiodi, 1990, pp. 87–90).

Examining how a child engages in the drawing experience can give clinicians in vivo information about the youth's problem-solving capacities. However, it is important to be sensitive to cross-cultural considerations when conducting a process evaluation. Knowing a client's cultural norm for eye contact, general expressiveness, and elaboration would help to more accurately differentiate between culturally prescribed behaviors and those unique to the client's current emotional and behavioral functioning, influencing how the clinician interprets the client's approach to the drawing task.

Drawings and Trauma Work

The use of drawings to facilitate communication in clinical assessment can be particularly appropriate for children who have experienced extreme trauma, when verbal methods break down because of the neurobiological manifestation of the trauma experience at a sensory, rather than verbal, level (see Brewin's [Brewin, Dagleish, & Joseph, 1996; Brewin, 2001] dual representation theory for more on information processing theories that support multimodal assessment practices for children who have experienced trauma). Drawings can be used in crisis evaluation to assess a child's current coping skills, to offer stabilization through a bounded/contained expressive experience, and to facilitate communication of the meaning of the experience, from the child's perspective (Malchiodi, 1990). Clinicians working in domestic violence shelters or other settings that serve children who have experienced traumatic events suggest several clinical uses of drawing tasks. Malchiodi (1990), in her emergency shelter work with children and adolescents who come from violent domestic situations, begins with an initial evaluation that asks the youth to draw a self-portrait, a family drawing, and a free drawing, using markers, crayons, and pencils on 8″ × 10″ white paper. Asking the child to draw one family member, rather than to engage in a traditional KFD, may be more appropriate with this population, as it offers these children more choice and control over their family drawings, because children from violent families may experience overwhelming anxiety at initially being asked to complete a whole-family drawing (Malchiodi, 1990). Eth and Pynoos (1985) developed a semistructured research interview in trauma work with children that utilizes a "draw-a-picture/tell-a-story" technique in the initial session, directing the child to recount his or her experience and worst moment. Using drawing in this initial interview gives the child an opportunity to share his or her own experience of the trauma through symbolism expressed through the art content and through verbalizations that accompany the drawing narrative. Other techniques ask the youth to draw "a favorite kind of day" (AFKD; Manning, 1987) (which has been found to be nonthreatening), with inclement weather scenes associated with physical abuse.

In one sample of youths being treated at a residential facility in a large east coast city, Draw-A-Person assessments were used to elicit stories from the youths in order to gather more in-depth information about their current emotional status. Focused questions were asked of the clients, after they had completed their man, woman, and self drawings; they were asked to 1) describe the person, 2) tell a story about the person, and 3) provide a title for their drawing. Several of the clients' stories related to themes of vulnerability, fear, uncertainty, and distrust of strangers and adults.

One early adolescent male in the study developed a story about his mother and father; the mother was throwing her very large diamond ring onto the ground in anger and distress. Other youths talked about their "bad uncle" or their father who was regularly drinking in the house. Other early adolescents presented overly sexualized portraits of the "draw a woman" figure, and some attributed these pictures to family members or to women they knew or had seen on the streets. Another youth discussed the fear of being invited to get into a stranger's car in his neighborhood, and running away to find help, knowing that he did not want to get into the car. In addition to trust and safety concerns vividly expressed in these children's human figure drawing stories, some youth expressed anxieties about fitting into peer groups and their experiences with peer rejection. Others vividly captured feelings of being different; one child expressed the "self" figure drawing as a "pizza head" with no human features present, suggesting a lack of relational ability and an extreme differentness that kept him isolated from his other non-pizza-head peers.

Among the themes of feeling vulnerable (fear, anxiety) without adequate adult protection and sad in relation to peer rejection, there were themes of competence, with one younger child (age 8) expressing himself as a strong, muscular person with long arms and the necessary capabilities to sufficiently defend himself with confidence. Another youth talked about taking karate classes and being skilled in self-defense, equipped to take on any attackers. Another adolescent represented himself as an "alley cat" because he saw himself as having nine lives, as being able to always land on his feet, and as being able to escape easily.

As illustrated here, implementation of human figure drawings designed to elicit an impromptu story from the youth can lead to the discovery of significant cognitive, affective, and behavioral information about the youth, from the youth's perspective. These drawings and their stories gave the treating clinicians important information about these children's fears and anxieties, born out of their prior traumatic neighborhood and family experiences. These stories offered the treating clinicians entry into the child's world, which allowed the clinician to individually follow up with more detailed questions and/or standardized assessment tools to obtain more precise diagnostic information. For example, in one case where sexual abuse was suspected as a result of the youth's narrative, a follow-up investigation was advanced and allegations were substantiated.

CASE STUDY[1]

Samantha is a five-and-a-half-year-old biracial kindergartner, living with her biological father, her three-year-old sister, and her paternal grandparents. Samantha's biological parents had been divorced for two years, and her mother had limited daily contact and only sporadic emotional involvement with the children, although she lived geographically close in a nearby apartment complex. Samantha has a very strong relationship with her father and feels close to him emotionally. Recently, the public school referred Samantha for an evaluation after her mother died unexpectedly of a heart attack. Teachers at the school reported that, since her mother's death, Samantha has consistently demonstrated defiant and actively resistant behaviors (e.g., not following directions), as well as "clingy" and attention-seeking behaviors (e.g., staying near the teacher despite peer group activities scheduled in the classroom). In addition, Samantha occasionally cried inconsolably, although the teachers reported that these incidents were infrequent. The school staff is uncertain as to what provokes these intense reactions, but when they occurred, they were typically in the early morning hours. The teachers noted that these behaviors were not characteristic of Samantha before her mother's death.

Given the limited involvement that Samantha's mother had in Samantha's daily life prior to her death, there is concern about the potential complicated grief reactions that may arise as she begins processing the "wished for" moments unavailable to her while her mother was alive, in the context of the more immediate acute grief associated with the death. Samantha currently experiences intense fear of loss and abandonment and has been able to verbalize some of those fears. The DSM-IV diagnosis given was Separation Anxiety Disorder—301.21 with early onset, because symptoms occurred before age six years. Specifically, her symptoms manifested as experiencing excessive distress when separated from her father; persistent refusal to take naps at school; and repeated nightmares involving themes of separation. A Bereavement—V62.82 diagnosis was also made, because of Samantha's awareness of her mother's recent death.

In treatment, Samantha wanted to draw pictures "for mommy." Her family drawings consistently depicted a house, showing her bedroom where she said she slept with her sister. She included many details and much color in depicting the bedroom and the two figures— seemingly a safe and happy place in the house where she and her sister were together. In other family drawings, she illustrated an adult female figure sitting in a chair in a corner, occupying a space in the house that was farthest from her own bedroom, stating that this person was "mommy as an angel in heaven." She also drew herself throwing a baby from a window, showing the baby falling through the air, with a man (stating this was her father) waiting to catch the child on the ground. Another picture showed a baby in a stroller, surrounded by a family (stating the people represented her father and his girlfriend) going to the store together.

These family drawings demonstrated how the art process can be used as a relational tool for eliciting information about a client's emotions, such as underlying fears and wishes, as well as illuminating the strengths clients employ in coping with current struggles. For example, Samantha's artwork and dialogue offered a story that was told quite differently from the story by the teacher at school. In Samantha's work there was opportunity and transformation—demonstrating an understanding that her "mommy was an angel" who was removed from the closeness of the bedroom, but who was still "present" in the house and noticed nonetheless. The bright colors and realistic depiction of the remaining family members, their close proximity to each other, and Samantha's story about the drawing all suggested a certain level of comfort and safety. The hope and trust in her father's ability to "save the baby" that was falling from the window reflected characteristics of dealing with loss and fear in ways that still solidified an embedded sense of trust and protection found in her relationship with her primary caregiver. Perhaps Samantha is also testing, through the drawn form, her notion that her father will continue to protect her. Samantha demonstrated ego flexibility, observed through her art expression, in being able to cognitively and emotionally transform her mother into an "angel watching over" her. Yet, core fears of loss and abandonment remain at the fore and affect Samantha's overall functioning. Along these lines, her drawings reveal her need for continuity and emotional support in her current relationships, as she continues to work through her grief.

CONCLUSION

In summary, the current empirical research on the use of drawings in clinical assessment has advanced in several ways. Most notably, human figure drawings have seen developments such as the incorporation of national standardization samples and more objective, global scoring systems using age- and gender-normed measurement templates, eliminating the controversial use of individual item indicators to detect emotional and behavioral disturbance. More attention is being paid to cross-cultural utility and the applicability of scoring protocols and their interpretations for diverse groups. Finally, it is strongly recognized that apart from their use as standardized instruments, drawings can be used as part of comprehensive assessment practices to elicit stories from clients that may offer clinical information not revealed through conventional verbal methods of inquiry. The use of drawings allows the child to be an integral part of the assessment process, affording treatment engagement opportunities that are responsive to the child's developmental stage, cognitive abilities, and different cultural styles and that utilize the child's natural expressive capacities. Furthermore, in implementing drawing methods for assessment purposes, it is critical to assess a child's cognitive development, chronological age, and socioeconomic background/environmental context, as these will influence what is drawn. Along these lines, it is generally accepted that clinicians should solicit multiple drawings that represent a variety of inquiry domains (e.g., self, family, self-in-environment), rather than basing interpretation on one elicited drawing and its narrative. Examining common themes that may emerge across drawings, across stories, and across time in treatment can facilitate a more accurate and comprehensive understanding of the clinical needs to be addressed in treatment.

ACKNOWLEDGMENTS

Special thanks to John C. Russotto, LCSW, a licensed clinical social worker in private practice at the Washington Center for Psychiatry in Washington, DC, and to Dr. Janice Berry-Edwards, DSW, LICSW, assistant professor at Virginia Commonwealth University School of Social Work, for their very insightful clinical consultation for this chapter.

NOTE

1. Clinical material from this case study has been provided by John C. Russotto, LCSW, a clinical social worker in private practice at the Washington Center for Psychiatry in Washington, DC.

REFERENCES

Abell, S. C., Wood, W., & Liebman, S. J. (2001). Children's human figure drawings as measures of intelligence: The comparative validity of three scoring systems. *Journal of Psychoeducational Assessment, 19*, 204–215.

Brewin, C. R. (2001). A cognitive neuroscience account of posttraumatic stress disorder and its treatment. *Behaviour Research and Therapy, 39*, 373–393.

Brewin, C. R., Dagleish, T., & Joseph, S. (1996). A dual representation theory of posttraumatic stress disorder. *Psychological Review, 103*(4), 670–686.

Buck, J. N. (1948). The H-T-P technique: A qualitative and quantitative scoring manual. *Journal of Clinical Psychology, 4*, 317–396.

Burns, R. C., & Kaufman, S. H. (1970). *Kinetic Family Drawing (K-F-D)*. New York: Brunner/Mazel.

Camara, W. J., Nathan, J. S., & Puente, A. E. (2000). Psychological test usage: Implications in professional psychology. *Professional Psychology: Research and Practice, 31*, 141–154.

Cohen, B. M. (Ed.). (1983). *The Diagnostic Drawing Series Handbook*. Available from Barry M. Cohen, P. O. Box 9853, Alexandria, VA 22304.

Cohen, B. M., Mills, A., & Kijak, A. K. (1994). An introduction to the Diagnostic Drawing Series: A standardized tool for diagnostic and clinical use. *Art Therapy, 11*(2), 105–110.

Eth, S., & Pynoos, R. (1985). Psychiatric interventions with children traumatized by violence. In D. H. Shetky & E. P. Benedik (Eds.), *Emerging issues in child psychiatry and the law* (pp. 285–309). New York: Brunner/Mazel.

Garb, H. N., Wood, J. M., Lilienfeld, S. O., & Nezworski, M. T. (2002). Effective use of projective techniques in clinical practice: Let the data help with selection and interpretation. *Professional Psychology: Research and Practice, 33*, 454–463.

Goodenough, F. L. (1926). *Measurement of intelligence by drawings*. New York: Harcourt, Brace & World.

Hammer, E. F. (1958). *The clinical application of projective drawings*. Springfield, IL: Charles C. Thomas.

Hammer, E. F. (Ed.). (1997). *Advances in projective drawing interpretation*. Springfield, IL: Charles C. Thomas.

Handler, L. (1996). The clinical use of drawings. In C. Newmark (Ed.), *Major psychological assessment instruments*. Boston: Allyn & Bacon.

Handler, L., & Habenicht, D. (1994). The Kinetic Family Drawing Technique: A review of the literature. *Journal of Personality Assessment, 62*, 440–464.

Handler, L., & Reyher, J. (1965). Figure drawing anxiety indexes: A review of the literature. *Journal of Personality Assessment, 29*, 305–313.

Handler, L., & Riethmiller, R. (1998). Teaching and learning the administration and interpretation of graphic techniques. In L. Handler & M. Hilsenroth (Eds.), *Teaching and learning personality assessment*. Mahwah, NJ: Lawrence Erlbaum Associates.

Kaplan, F. F. (2003). Art-based assessments. In C. Malchiodi (Ed.), *Handbook of art therapy* (pp. 25–35). New York: Guilford Press.

Knoff, H. M. (2003). Evaluation of projective drawings. In C. R. Reynolds & R. W. Kamphaus (Eds.), *Handbook of Psychological & Educational Assessment of Children* (pp. 91–125). New York: Guilford Press.

Koppitz, E. M. (1968). *Psychological evaluation of children's human figure drawings*. New York: Grune & Stratton.

Machover, K. (1949). *Personality projection in the drawings of a human figure*. Springfield, IL: Charles C. Thomas.

Machover, K. (1951). Drawing of the human figure: A method of personality investigation. In H. Anderson & G. Anderson (Eds.), *An introduction to projective techniques*. New York: Prentice Hall.

Malchiodi, C. A. (1990). *Breaking the silence*. New York: Brunner/Mazel.

Manning, T. M. (1987). Aggression depicted in abused children's drawings. *Arts in Psychotherapy, 14*, 15–24.

Matto, H. C. (2002). Investigating the validity of the Draw A Person: Screening Procedure for Emotional Disturbance: A measurement validity study with high-risk youth. *Psychological Assessment, 14*, 221–225.

Matto, H. C., Corcoran, J., & Fassler, A. (2003). Integrating solution-focused and art therapies for substance abuse treatment: Guidelines for practice. *The Arts in Psychotherapy, 30*(5), 265–272.

Matto, H. C., & Naglieri, J. A. (2005). Race and ethnic differences and human figure drawings: Clinical utility of the DAP:SPED. *Journal of Clinical Child and Adolescent Psychology, 34*(4), 706–711.

McNeish, T. J., & Naglieri, J. A. (1993). Identification of the seriously-emotionally disturbed with the Draw A Person: Screening Procedure for Emotional Disturbance. *Journal of Special Education, 27*, 115–121.

Mills, A. (2003). The Diagnostic Drawing Series. In C. Malchiodi (Ed.), *Handbook of art therapy* (pp. 401–409). New York: Guilford Press.

Mills, A., Cohen, B. M., & Meneses, J. Z. (1993). Reliability and validity of the Diagnostic Drawing Series. *The Arts in Psychotherapy, 20*(1), 83–88.

Moon, B. L. (1990). *Existential art therapy*. Springfield, IL: C. C. Thomas.

Naglieri, J. A. (1988). *Draw-A-Person: A quantitative scoring system*. San Antonio, TX: Psychological Corporation.

Naglieri, J. A., McNeish, T. J., & Bardos, A. N. (1991). *Draw A Person: Screening Procedure for Emotional Disturbance*. Austin: PRO-ED.

Naglieri, J. A., & Pfeiffer, S. I. (1992). Validity of the Draw A Person: Screening Procedure for Emotional Disturbance with a Socially-Emotionally Disturbed Sample. *Psychological Assessment: A Journal of Consulting and Clinical Psychology, 4*, 156–159.

Nucho, A. O. (1987). *The psycho-cybernetic model of art therapy*. Springfield, IL: Charles C. Thomas.

Prout, H. T., & Phillips, P. D. (1974). A clinical note: The Kinetic School Drawing. *Psychology in the Schools, 11*, 303–306.

Roback, H. B. (1968). Human figure drawings: their utility in the clinical psychologist's armamentarium for personality assessment. *Psychological Bulletin, 70*, 1–19.

Silver, R. (2002). *Three art assessments: Silver drawing test of cognition and emotion, draw a story, screening for depression and stimulus drawings and techniques*. New York: Brunner-Routledge.

Silver, R. A. (2003). The Silver Drawing Test of cognition and emotion. In C. Malchiodi (Ed.), *Handbook of art therapy* (pp. 410–419). New York: Guilford Press.

Smith, D., & Dumont, F. (1995). A cautionary study: Unwarranted interpretations of the Draw-A-Person test. *Professional Psychology: Research and Practice, 26*(3), 298–303.

Swenson, C. H. (1957). Empirical evaluations of human figure drawings. *Psychological Bulletin, 54*, 431–466.

Swenson, C. H. (1968). Empirical evaluations of human figure drawings. *Psychological Bulletin, 70*, 20–44.

Tharinger, D. J., & Stark, K. (1990). A qualitative versus quantitative approach to evaluating the Draw-A-Person and Kinetic Family Drawing: A study of mood and anxiety disorder children. *Journal of Consulting and Clinical Psychology, 2*(4), 365–375.

Trombini, E., & Montebarocci, O. (2004). Use of the Drawn Stories Technique to evaluate psychological distress in children. *Perceptual and Motor Skills, 99*, 975–982.

Watkins, C. E., Campbell, V. L., Nieberding, R., & Hallmark, R. (1995). Contemporary practice of psychological assessment by clinical psychologists. *Professional Psychology: Research and Practice, 26*, 54–60.

Wegmann, P., & Lusebrink, V. B. (2000). Kinetic Family Drawing scoring method for cross-cultural studies. *The Arts in Psychotherapy, 27*, 179–190.

14

USE OF THE HAND TEST WITH
CHILDREN AND ADOLESCENTS

A. Jill Clemence

*Erik H. Erikson Institute for Education and Research,
The Austen Riggs Center, Stockbridge, Massachusetts*

Practitioners are often in need of efficient and effective ways of assessing the needs of patients, especially when there are limitations on time, as is often the case. Less time-intensive methods of assessment are increasingly favored among clinicians because of the time demands of clinical practice (Piotrowski, 1999). Such techniques are especially useful in settings in which the time available to produce a report is short (such as medical settings or Employee Assistance Programs), or in settings in which comprehensive psychological testing is unnecessary or unavailable. Thus, brief instruments can greatly add to the clinician's tool chest. The Hand Test is one such instrument.

The Hand Test is a performance-based technique used to aid in the identification and classification of individuals with various emotional and behavioral disorders. The style in which the Hand Test is administered provides several advantages for assessing personality in children and adolescents. Because the test is flexible and less formal, it allows the examiner to establish an assessment atmosphere that is relaxed. This allows the examinee to be less self-conscious and eases tension (Morris, 1993). The informal nature of this test is especially beneficial for building rapport with younger examinees, who often view the procedure as a game (Wagner, 1986). Another advantage of using the Hand Test with children and adolescents lies in its simplicity. The instructions are easy to understand, and there is no need to be concerned about reading ability. Because the test can be administered in approximately 10 minutes, it does not push the limits of a child's attention span (Wagner, 1986). Furthermore, the ambiguous nature of the test makes it very difficult for the examinee to fabricate responses he or she believes will make them appear more or less mentally healthy than they are (Carson, 1990). These factors greatly enhance the clinician's ability to make the most accurate and immediate assessment possible. In general, the Hand Test is a projective technique that is especially well suited for use with children and adolescents.

The Hand Test is made up of nine cards with drawings of hands in various positions, with varying degrees of ambiguity. There is also a tenth card that is blank. The examinee is asked to "tell what it looks like the hands might be doing" on each of the first nine cards. On the tenth card, the examinee is asked to "imagine a hand and tell what it might be doing." Responses are recorded verbatim.

One characteristic that sets the Hand Test apart from other performance-based tests, such as the Rorschach, is its use of hands as stimuli. Hands are undeniably human and thus "pull" for our expectations and impressions of self and others as well as themes of efficacy and action possibilities. Hands are an important component of our relations with other people and with our environment. In interactions with others, we use our hands to relay friendship (high fives, waving), respect (handshakes), approval (thumbs up, pat on the back), anger (fist), and unspoken ideas (sign language). Likewise, hands are probably the most important tools we have for manipulating the immediate environment. We use them to grab, carry, push, pick up, repel, move, and place objects around us. Hands are often central instruments for attaining goals and fulfilling needs. How hands are perceived on the Hand Test reveals much about the examinee's perceptions and action tendencies in the world. These characteristics make hands a very appropriate choice for use as a projective measure and add to the effectiveness and relevance of the Hand Test as an assessment tool.

In addition, the Hand Test task requires the child or adolescent to listen to and follow directions, to collaborate cooperatively with the examiner, to use abstraction, to be creative, to verbalize a response, and to stay on task. Of course, all of these abilities can be discerned by assessment instruments such as the WISC-IV (Wechsler, 2003) and the Rorschach, but if time is an issue, the Hand Test provides an excellent screening instrument for getting a snapshot of all of the above. This can be especially useful when school success or failure can influence a child's reaction to measures like the WISC-IV that appear to the child as "academic-like" tests. Because the Hand Test does not appear similar to the achievement tests children and adolescents often encounter in school settings, it is somewhat less influenced by test anxiety, performance concerns, etc.

Because of its straightforward scoring system and brevity of administration, the Hand Test is considered a logical choice for use as a screening instrument, or as an addition to a standard battery (Goh & Fuller, 1983; Wagner, 1986; Wagner, 1999). Especially noteworthy here is the ability of the test to identify prototypical action tendencies or behaviors that are close to the surface. Moreover, repeated administrations can give the examiner an idea of patient progress and the presence of emerging experiences and needs during the therapy. Its brevity and simplicity make this especially easy to do, given that administration and scoring takes only 15 minutes on average. Furthermore, the use of this simple and straightforward stimulus produces a measure that is more grounded in form and is less complex than other instruments, such as the Rorschach and the CAT. Thus, if used together, these measures supply a gradation of stimulus complexity. For example, if one demonstrates problems with reality testing on the Hand Test, this should be a clear indication of problems in deciphering and management of even very basic perception tasks and most certainly denotes the need for further testing.

DESCRIPTION OF SCORING

Quantitative Scoring

The Hand Test is typically scored with the use of 15 quantitative variables. These are outlined by Wagner (1983) as follows:

> Affection (AFF): Responses involving a warm, positive interchange or bestowal of pleasure (e.g., patting someone on the back).

Dependence (DEP): Responses expressing a need for help or aid from another (e.g., someone pleading for mercy).

Communication (COM): Responses involving a presentation or exchange of information; (e.g., a child saying how old he or she is).

Exhibition (EXH): Responses involving displaying oneself in order to obtain approval or to stress a special noteworthy characteristic of the hand (e.g., showing off muscles).

Direction (DIR): Responses involving dominating, directing, or influencing the activities of others (e.g., giving a command).

Aggression (AGG): Responses involving the giving of pain, hostility or aggression (e.g., (slapping someone).

Acquisition (ACQ): Responses involving an attempt to acquire an as yet unobtained goal or object (e.g., reaching for something on a high shelf).

Active (ACT): Responses involving an action or attitude designed to constructively manipulate, attain, or alter an object or goal (e.g., carrying a suitcase).

Passive (PAS): Responses involving an attitude of rest and/or relaxation with a deliberate withdrawal of energy from the hand (e.g., hand folded in your lap).

Tension (TEN): Responses in which energy is being exerted, but little or nothing is being accomplished; accompanied by a feeling of tension, anxiety or malaise (e.g., hanging on to the edge of a cliff).

Crippled (CRIP): Responses involving a sick, crippled, sore, dead, disfigured, injured, or incapacitated hand (e.g., a hand that is bleeding).

Fear (FEAR): Responses involving the threat of pain, injury, incapacitation or death (e.g., raised up to ward off a blow).

Description (DES): Examinee does little more than acknowledge the presence of the hand (e.g., "just a hand").

Bizarre (BIZ): Responses based on hallucinatory content, delusional thinking, or peculiar, pathological thinking (e.g., a crocodile creeping along the wall).

Failure (FAIL): Scored when no scorable response is given to a particular card.

FAIL reflects the inability of the examinee to respond to the stimuli and may also indicate inappropriate behavioral tendencies manifested under conditions of lowered consciousness.

All of the 15 quantitative variables can be summarized into the following categories for scoring purposes:

Interpersonal (INT): Reflects interactions with others and is therefore made up of six quantitative responses, AFF, DEP, COM, EXH, DIR, and AGG.

Environmental (ENV): Represents an examinee's attitude toward the noninterpersonal world and is a combination of ACQ, ACT, and PAS responses.

Maladjustive (MAL): The combined total of TEN, CRIP, and FEAR responses; suggests difficulty in achieving successful interactions, either interpersonal or environmental.

Withdrawal (WITH): Made up of the total DES, BIZ, and FAIL responses; suggests an inability to establish meaningful and effective life roles.

Pathology (PATH): Estimates the total amount of psychopathology present as reflected in the individual's test protocol. The PATH score is calculated by adding the MAL score to twice the WITH score or MAL + 2 (WITH). For example, if an adolescent's Hand Test protocol contains two TEN responses and a BIZ, the subsequent PATH score will be 4 [(2 TEN) + 2 (1 BIZ)].

Acting Out Ratio (AOR): Reflects aggressive behavior tendencies and is determined by comparing the total number of positive interpersonal responses (AFF + COM + DEP) with the total number of negative interpersonal responses (DIR + AGG). An Acting Out Score can also be created by subtracting the sum of the positive responses from the total of negative responses, with positive scores indicating a tendency for overt, antisocial or aggressive behaviors, and negative scores indicating behavior tendencies that are more socially desirable. For example, if a child's Hand Test protocol contains two AFF, one COM, four AGG, and one DIR response, the subsequent AOS score will be +2 [(4 AGG + 1 DIR) − (2 AFF + 1 COM)].

Average Initial Response Time (AIRT): The average time required for the examinee to provide a scorable response to the test stimuli across the ten cards.

Qualitative Scoring

Wagner (1983) also lists 17 qualitative scoring categories that may be useful to the practitioner when interpreting a Hand Test protocol. These scores serve as a supplementary tool for aiding in the interpretation of the findings but are not necessarily considered a part of the formal scoring system. Wagner (1983) notes that there is little research to support their use at this time. However, he does provide normative data on the qualitative scores and comments on their usefulness in enhancing the meaning of the quantitative scores when used in conjunction.

The qualitative scores are as follows:

Ambivalent (AMB): Responses expressing some hesitation or uncertainty about the action described in the response

Automatic Phrase (AUT): Responses involving stereotypic language of the examinee

Cylindrical (CYL): Responses in which the hand is manipulating a cylindrical object that is large enough to fill the space between the palm and fingers

Denial (DEN): Responses in which the percept is described and then denied

Emotion (EMO): Responses charged with emotion

Gross (GRO): Responses involving action that is primitive, uncontrolled, or unsocialized

Hiding (HID): Responses in which the hand is hiding something

Immature (IM): Responses in which the hand is involved with children or animals

Impotent (IMP): Responses in which the examinee expresses an inability to respond to the card

Inanimate (INA): Responses in which the hand is attributed to an inanimate object such as a statue or a painting

Movement (MOV): Responses involving random, purposeless activity

Oral (ORA): Responses involving food, liquid, or drugs

Perplexity (PER): Responses reflecting the examinee's difficulty responding and sense of puzzlement

Sensual (SEN): Responses involving tactual, sensual experiences

Sexual (SEX): Responses involving sexual activity

Original (O): Responses that are highly unique

Repetition (RPT): Perseverative responses

RESEARCH FINDINGS

Clearly one of the most impressive aspects of the Hand Test is its ability to predict overt behavior. It is this attribute that continues to draw researchers and clinicians to examine its use in a variety of settings. For example, the Hand Test has proved useful in the assessment of behavioral tendencies of children, adolescents (e.g., Clemence, Hilsenroth, Sivec, Rasch, & Waehler, 1998; Sivec & Hilsenroth, 1994; Wagner, Rasch, & Marsico, 1991; Hoover, 1977; Bricklin, Piotrowski, & Wagner, 1962), and adults (see Wagner, 1983, for a review). Other studies have found the Hand Test useful in differentiating behaviorally handicapped and emotionally disturbed children and adolescents from control groups (e.g., Hilsenroth & Sivec, 1990; Smith, Blais, Vangala, & Masek, 2005; Waehler, Rasch, Sivec, & Hilsenroth, 1992; Wagner, Rasch, & Marsico, 1990). In addition, the Hand Test has been found to distinguish between children and adolescents described as aggressive and those described as nonaggressive (Campos, 1968; Clemence, Hilsenroth, Sivec, & Rasch, 1999; Oswald & Loftus, 1967; Selg, 1965; Wagner & Hawkins, 1964). Furthermore, the Hand Test has shown strong interrater reliability among studies with children and adolescents, with scores ranging from 82% (Smith et al., 2005) to 91% (Hilsenroth & Sivec, 1990) across the 15 quantitative variables. Such research has certainly qualified the Hand Test as a valid measure of overt behavioral tendencies and has established this test as an effective instrument for clinical use. Additional reliability data are included in the *Hand Test Manual* (Wagner, 1983) and the *Hand Test Manual Supplement* for children and adolescents (Wagner, Rasch, & Marsico, 1991). The most notable findings regarding this instrument are elaborated in the following sections.

Indicators of Social and Emotional Maladjustment

Past research has found the Hand Test Pathology summary score (PATH) to be a powerful measure of the level of psychopathology present, with higher scores indicating greater pathology, and has been shown to be especially useful in the discrimination of groups demonstrating various levels of social and emotional adjustment. Hilsenroth and Sivec (1990) identified the PATH, AGG, and PAS variables to be useful in the differentiation of socially and emotionally disturbed children from nonclinical children, with the disturbed group scoring higher on each of these variables. These findings were further supported by research reported by Waehler and colleagues (1992), which demonstrates the ability of the PATH and AGG scores to measure the severity of psychological disturbance in children with severe behavior disorders. Clemence et al. (1998) likewise found PATH to be an important screening variable across adolescent patient groups (inpatient, outpatient, and nonpatient). Their findings support the use of a PATH score greater than 3 as indicating at least mild emotional disturbance. In a review of the Hand Test literature concerning children and adolescents, Sivec and Hilsenroth (1994) identified PATH as one of the most robust indicators of problems among adolescents. Likewise, research concerning the prediction of future criminal behavior based on Hand Test scores of adolescents found the PATH score to be significant for both male and female groups (Lie & Wagner, 1996; Lie, 1994). Most recently, Smith et al. (2005)

found the PATH, AGG, and WITH scores to differentiate psychiatric outpatients and medically ill pediatric inpatients, with psychiatric patients scoring significantly higher on each of these variables (Cohen's d = .80, .90, and .74, respectively).

Prediction of Acting Out Behavior

Previous research points to another important indicator of disturbance in adolescents—the Acting Out Score (AOS). Because the Hand Test was designed to assess overt behavioral tendencies, it has been very effective in differentiating adolescents who demonstrate various levels of acting-out behavior (Bodden, 1984). For example, Campos (1968) found that AOS was capable of distinguishing between children described as aggressive and those described as nonaggressive. In addition, research by Oswald and Loftus (1967) showed that institutionalized adolescent males demonstrated higher AOS and AGG scores than the normal group, and Azcarate and Gutierrez (1969) found AOS scores of male adolescent delinquents to be related to the length of time spent in an isolation unit due to disrespectful and assaultive behavior. Hoover (1977) examined Hand Test scores of schoolchildren rated by their teachers as exhibiting maladjustive behaviors and concluded that the Hand Test variables were able to accurately identify overt behavior.

In order to assess the diagnostic efficiency of the Hand Test, several studies have explored the ability of the AOS cutoff scores to discriminate various clinical groups. Using an AOS cutoff score of 0, Wagner and Hawkins (1964) correctly classified 78% of delinquents who were assaultive versus those who were nonassaultive. Clemence, Hilsenroth, Sivec, and Rasch (1999) also found that an AOS of 0 was able to differentiate a group of children identified as aggressive from a nonreferred control group with 66% accuracy, whereas Selg (1965) found an AOS score of 1 was able to classify aggressive children with 86% accuracy. Upon examination of more severely disturbed groups, higher AOS cutoff scores have been found to be useful. For example, an AOS of 2 was used to accurately classify inpatient adolescents versus outpatients and nonclinical participants with 63% accuracy (Clemence et al., 1998) and Wetsel, Shapiro, and Wagner (1967) utilized an AOS cutoff score of 1 to classify chronic offenders with 66% accuracy when the offenders were compared with a group of nonrecidivist delinquents.

Concerning the clinical utility of the AGG variable, Wetsel, Shapiro, and Wagner (1967) found that an AGG score of 2 correctly classified recidivist delinquents with 68% accuracy. Likewise, Clemence et al. (1999) found that an AGG score of 2 was able to differentiate a group of children identified as aggressive by their teachers from a nonreferred control group, with an overall correct classification rate of 69%.

The significant findings of these studies show that children and adolescents who exhibit more aggressive behavior are likely to produce higher AGG and AOS scores. Therefore, it makes sense to use these two variables in the identification of children and adolescents who are prone to act out aggressively. When the Hand Test is used clinically, however, cutoff scores such as these should only be used as very crude guidelines and never as rules. Keep in mind that even though the reported classification rates are high, when 68% of individuals were correctly classified, 32% (almost a third) of those in the sample were misclassified. Therefore, additional data should always be used when clinical decisions or treatment recommendations are being made.

Furthermore, because the Hand Test has been shown to most accurately identify characteristic behavior tendencies that are "close to the surface" (Wagner, 1986, p. 279), Hand Test indicators of acting-out behavior should be considered a reflection of *current* potential for aggression and not for aggressive behavior occurring over longer time periods, such as six months or a year. According to Wagner's (1986) definition, the behavior assessed by the Hand Test is more temporally immediate. Therefore, a more accurate assessment will be made by application of interpretations to behavior that corresponds more closely in time to the administration of the Hand Test.

Usefulness with Other Measures

It is important to remember that the Hand Test alone is not designed to produce a complete description of the child's personality (Wagner, 1986). This instrument is truly best used as one component of a multimethod assessment battery and can easily be incorporated as such (Sivec & Hilsenroth, 1994). Therefore, what does the Hand Test add when used with other instruments? An important but less prolific area of research regarding the Hand Test is that surrounding the incremental validity of the test. Most recently, Smith et al. (2005) found that the Hand Test added significantly to the ability of the Behavior Assessment System for the Children-Parent Report Form (BASC-PRF; Reynolds & Kamphaus, 1992) to differentiate medical inpatients and psychiatric outpatients, increasing the correct classification rate from 66.7% (using the BASC Behavioral Symptoms Index alone) to 77.1% when the AGG and PATH variables were added to the model. Furthermore, when the AGG and PATH variables were entered into a regression on their own, the correct classification of groups was 75%. In addition, the Hand Test showed significant differences when the self-report measures were unable to differentiate between groups, further demonstrating the usefulness of the Hand Test as an addition to a standard battery.

CLINICAL APPLICATIONS

The characteristics just described make the Hand Test useful in a variety of settings. Indeed, the Hand Test has been used clinically with a variety of clients for a variety of purposes. For example, the Hand Test has been used as a workplace screening instrument with employees, as a method for assessing how elderly individuals are coping with age-related changes, as a tool for assessing personality characteristics of those diagnosed with mental retardation, as a screening instrument for brain impairment, as a measure for identifying sexually abused children, and as a diagnostic tool for schizophrenic outpatients, psychiatric inpatients, and individuals suspected of meeting criteria for Dissociative Identity Disorder (see Young & Wagner, 1999, for a discussion of each of these applications).

   Most recently, I have found the Hand Test to be especially useful as part of a consultation and liaison service within a hospital setting. Often the clinician working in a medical setting will have only a few sessions, and at times only a single session, to make contact, assess, and make recommendations for a patient, depending on his or her length of admission and physical condition. Thus, a very brief performance-based instrument that is easy to administer and score is truly needed. Furthermore, brief measures are often sufficient as a screening tool for complementing interviews with the patient, family members, and medical staff and as a method for enhancing the clinician's judgment regarding treatment decisions. The Hand Test fills this need by allowing the clinician to make contact, build rapport, make an initial assessment, and begin to form general ideas about the needs of the patient very efficiently. Because the Hand Test taps into the *current* experience of the patient, not necessarily past or future functioning, it is very useful in this setting. Therefore, the clinician can assess how well the patient appears to be dealing with and adapting to the *current* life stressor, which is the primary focus of the assessment. Thus, the Hand Test, especially when combined with the more typical self-report measures used in medical settings (e.g., pain measures, quality-of-life measures, and coping instruments), supplies the clinician with very useful data to help the treatment team and the patient better manage the demands of the illness and medical treatment.

CASE EXAMPLE

Stacy

Stacy is a 17-year-old single Caucasian female who has a 1-year-old child. She was diagnosed with a serious form of cancer two years before referral. The type of cancer she has is fibrous and grows slowly, encroaching upon various internal organs. This particular form of cancer typically leads to a slow choking of internal organs and often requires years of treatment and several surgeries. At the time of the consultation, Stacy had already had three surgeries to remove parts of the tumor that were threatening major organs. She requires the use of a cane because of the impact of the tumor on her spine, and she is fully aware that her condition is likely to slowly worsen for years. She was referred by the palliative team for a consultation because of symptoms of anxiety, depression, and medical treatment resistance. Several members of the medical staff had reported poor treatment compliance, an inconsistent show rate for outpatient appointments, and a high number of unusual pain complaints that some suspected had psychological rather than entirely physical causes. In addition, an earlier consultation had been attempted a few weeks before this referral, during one of Stacy's hospital admissions, but she adamantly refused to cooperate with the former consultant. He was attempting to teach her self-hypnosis for pain management, but Stacy later reported that she felt she had no need to learn such a technique. The consultant asked that someone else be assigned, because of his strong feelings of frustration with this patient.

Previous school testing indicated that Stacy had a reading disability and was generally functioning below her age level on all areas of cognitive functioning. Interview data with the patient and her mother revealed that Stacy was experiencing an increase in physical pain, concomitant with increases in stress at home, where she lived with her parents, her brother, and her two-year-old daughter. Her home life was described as chaotic because of the numerous stressors that came with her family's low SES (no reliable transportation, inadequate income, dangerous neighborhood, poor housing conditions, etc.). When asked about coping skills, Stacy reported that "hanging out" with her on-again/off-again boyfriend and playing with her daughter seemed to help her deal with her stress.

Upon interview, Stacy presented as disheveled and demonstrated poor hygiene. She was at times friendly in the interview, but also somewhat mischievous, seeming to take pleasure in challenging me. She was generally cooperative, though, and described herself as "tough," saying she could "hold her own against anyone in her neighborhood." Her Hand Test responses are included in the Appendix.

Although this Hand Test is not terribly striking at first glance, it actually reveals a great deal of information about Stacy's functioning. She begins the task with an affiliative COM response, suggesting that she has the capacity to relate in a positive and friendly manner. This response, however, is followed immediately by a socially negative AGG response. Thus, Stacy approaches the task with responses that alternate dramatically in affect tone, which can indicate an individual's tendency toward the use of splitting as a defense (Hilsenroth &

Fowler, 1999). Taking into account observational data regarding Stacy's behavior, it appears that she approached the assessment as she approaches most interpersonal situations, with clear evidence of splitting. For example, team meetings on the palliative unit were characterized by a distinct divide in feelings toward Stacy. Treaters either felt fond of her or they felt completely frustrated by her. Also important to note here is that although she refused to cooperate with the first consultant assigned to her, Stacy responded to my direction by giving a second response to Card I when prompted, suggesting that she is able and willing to cooperate with others from time to time.

Stacy also gave three EXH responses, which is well above the mean for her age [.77 (median = .00)], and which make up 25% of her total responses. Thus, this patient may regularly seek out some form of approval and validation from those around her. Part of her initial focus in interpersonal relationships may also be her need to feel that others find her to be special. This may account for the rejection of her first consultant, who approached her initially with a plan to teach her self-hypnosis for managing her pain. His emphasis on the technique, rather than on the patient, may have left her feeling that she was not special to this treater. Upon transfer, aided by abundant information concerning the problems of the previous consultation, I chose a different approach, which was to take a clear interest in learning about the patient's unique experience and to validate her concerns. This approach proved to make a dramatic difference in Stacy's attitude toward the consultation. She quickly warmed up to me and was immediately compliant with the assessment. Thus, the high production of EXH responses on the Hand Test helps to explain why she responded better to an approach that involved empathic mirroring than she did to a more technical approach that failed to provide her with a sense of specialness. Indeed, some of her acting-out behavior and excessive pain complaints may be linked to attempts to receive special attention from staff. Therefore, this information was included in recommendations for further treatment, which specifically noted that future interactions should begin with an empathic approach involving a sufficient amount of mirroring. It was expected that this approach would provide a foundation from which improved coping skills could be taught, while still allowing Stacy to feel special.

Later, Stacy gave a CRIP response, followed immediately by an AGG response. In addition, a second CRIP on Card IX was immediately followed by an EXH response that had an aggressive tone ("throwing a gang sign"). This suggests that when feelings of inadequacy or damage arise, Stacy quickly moves toward aggression as a defense against these feelings. In fact, her second AGG response had an exhibitive air to it as well (i.e., "shaking the fist" as opposed to actually hitting with the fist). It is as if the hand is waving its aggression in front of others to send a statement, not necessarily to impart injury to someone else, but to show that a person is powerful and strong. Thus, Stacy may rely on a show of aggression (AGG = 2, AOS = 1) in an attempt to signal to others a façade of strength and power in the face of her sense of inadequacy or weakness.

This interpretation is further supported by interview information collected during the assessment. When I asked how she felt about carrying a cane when others her age typically do not, Stacy responded, "It makes a great weapon." She went on to say that nobody "messes" with her because she can even beat up her older brother *and* his friends. Thus, she is clearly saying that when she is perceived as (or perceives herself to be) weak or inferior, she quickly moves to a position of aggressor. This defensive approach is clearly supported by the Hand Test results. Furthermore, Card X (the blank card) is said to reflect how an individual performs when left to rely on his or her own internal resources. Here we see that Stacy may fall back on her use of aggression to seek approval from those around her. This is not surprising, given the tough, inner-city environment in which she lives.

It is important to note that research on the CRIP response with physically ill individuals indicates that CRIP does not necessarily reflect the simple presence of illness or deformity (Smith et al., 2005), but may be more likely to be related to an internalized sense of damage or inferiority (Lenihan & Kirk, 1990; Hilsenroth & Fowler, 1999; Wagner & Young, 1999). Therefore, you might not necessarily see a CRIP response with someone who is ill or injured unless that individual has come to view him- or herself as inadequate or injured in a more personal or psychological way. More research is certainly needed to better understand this variable, but as this case example demonstrates, much can be gleaned from this response when it is taken in context with other available information.

Stacy's low AIRT score (2.9 seconds) denotes a tendency toward impulsivity. Although she is within the range of the normative sample for her age group (2–18 seconds; Wagner, Rasch, & Marsico, 1991), she is on the low end (mean = 6.76; median = 6.30). This impulsivity seems to be sustained throughout the task, demonstrated by a High Minus Low score (H − L, calculated by subtracting the shortest response time from the longest response time across cards) of only four seconds. This also indicates no evidence of card shock and represents a consistent impulsive response style.

By analyzing the card sequence, one can see that Stacy does not produce an environmental response until Card VIII. Thus, she seems to approach the task predominantly with a focus on interpersonal themes and only refers to environmental attitudes later in the test. When she does refer to environmental manipulation, it is in the form of ACQ responses, as opposed to ACT or PAS responses. Thus, she may need to organize herself around relationships before getting to the point where she can begin to consider dealing with environmental demands. Even then she may feel very unsure of her ability to do so, perhaps feeling conflicted about her ability to achieve her goals (ACQ coupled with Ambivalence [AMB]), as opposed to responding with the certainty that her actions will be carried out successfully. Her lack of ACT responses also suggests that she may lack the sense of self-efficacy that goes along with successful manipulation of the environment. It may also be that because of her physical limitations, she has come to question her own constructive abilities and her effectiveness in reaching her goals. In terms of treatment, then, Stacy is likely to respond better if she is in psychotherapy with someone who she feels finds her special and can offer realistic encouragement as well as a stable base from which to plan future behaviors. She will likely need regular help making simple goals and planning clear, effective ways to accomplish them until she is better able to integrate these skills into her daily life.

The Hand Test data, along with interview data (with Stacy, her mother, and staff) and clinical observation, resulted in important treatment recommendations. Because there was no evidence of gross psychotic or organic problems beyond her learning disability, no further testing was recommended. Individual therapy was recommended, with an emphasis on building a strong therapeutic relationship via empathy, mirroring, and validation, from which to begin to form reachable goals for improving Stacy's coping skills, increasing her sense of self-efficacy, and reducing her impulsivity. Furthermore, information gleaned through assessment was useful in helping the staff better manage the patient's use of splitting within the team, which led to a reduction in the amount of chaos that existed around her treatment.

CONCLUSION

Even though Stacy struggles academically and cognitively, performing well below her peers on all areas of academic functioning, she responded very well to the Hand Test, which provided a great deal of information about her personality and her behavior. As is typical of most children and adolescents when they complete the Hand Test, she did not seem at all threatened by the test, instead responding to it almost as a game, which is one of the clear strengths of this instrument in a clinical setting. Thus, the Hand Test is a valuable and effective clinical tool for use with this population.

APPENDIX

Stacy's Hand Test Responses and Scores

CARD	#	TIME	RESPONSE	SCORE
I.	1.	3″	"It's waving." (Q) "You know, saying 'Hi' to a friend." (E: Anything else?)	COM
	2.		"Oh, it could also be like about to slap someone in the face."	AGG
II.	3.	2″	"She's showing off her pretty nails."	EXH
III.	4.	1″	"It's pointing at something." (Q) "Look over there."	DIR
	5.		"Oh, and saying 'I'm number 1'."	EXH
IV.	6.	2″	"Patting someone on the head. Like my dad does to me."	AFF
V.	7.	4″	"This hand doesn't look like it's doing too good. Maybe it got slammed in a car door."	CRIP
VI.	8.	2″	"This is definitely shaking a fist . . . like you're gonna punch somebody out."	AGG
VII.	9.	3″	"He's going to open the door, I guess."	ACQ (AMB)
VIII.	10.	2″	"They're getting ready to pick something up, something very small."	ACQ
IX.	11.	5″	"There's something wrong with that hand. It looks deformed. The thumb is way too big and swollen."	CRIP
X.	12.	5″	"It can be anything? Oh, throwing a gang sign." (D)	EXH

Hand Test Summary Scores for Stacy

INT = 8	R = 12	PATH = 2
ENV = 2	H – L = 4″	AOR = 2:3
MAL = 2	AIRT = 2.9″	AOS = 1
WITH = 0		

REFERENCES

Azcarate, E., & Gutierrez, M. (1969). Differentiation of institutional adjustment of juvenile delinquents with the Hand Test. *Journal of Clinical Psychology, 25*, 200–202.

Bodden, J. L. (1984). The Hand Test. In D. J. Keyser & R. C. Sweetland (Eds.), *Test critique* (Vol. I, pp. 315–321). Kansas City, MO: Test Corporation of America.

Bricklin, B., Piotrowski, Z. A., & Wagner, E. E. (1962). The Hand Test: With special reference to the prediction of overt aggressive behavior. In M. Harrower (Ed.), *American lecture series in psychology*. Springfield, IL: Charles C. Thomas.

Campos, L. P. (1968). Other projective techniques. In A. I. Rabin (Ed.), *Projective techniques in personality assessment: A modern introduction* (pp. 461–520). New York: Springer.

Carson, N. R. (1990). *Psychology: The science of behavior.* Boston: Allyn & Bacon.

Clemence, A. J., Hilsenroth, M. J., Sivec, H. J., & Rasch, M. (1999). The Hand Test AGG and AOS Variables: Relationship with Teacher Rating of Aggressiveness. *Journal of Personality Assessment, 73,* 334–344.

Clemence, A. J., Hilsenroth, M. J., Sivec, H. J., Rasch, M., & Waehler, C. A. (1998). Use of the Hand Test in the classification of psychiatric in-patient adolescents. *Journal of Personality Assessment, 71*(2), 228–241.

Goh, D. S., & Fuller, G. B. (1983). Current practices in the assessment of personality and behavior by school psychologists. *School Psychology Review, 12,* 240–243.

Hilsenroth, M. J., & Fowler, C. (1999). The Hand Test and Borderline Personality Disorder. In G. R. Young & E. E. Wagner (Eds.), *The Hand Test: Advances in application and research* (pp. 59–83). Malabar, FL: Krieger.

Hilsenroth, M. J., & Sivec, H. J. (1990). Relationships between Hand Test variables and maladjustment in school children. *Journal of Personality Assessment, 55,* 344–349.

Hoover, T. O. (1977). Relationships among Hand Test variables and behavior ratings of children. *Dissertation Abstracts International, 37,* 2509B (University Microfilms No. 76-24, 406).

Lenihan, G. O., & Kirk, W. G. (1990). Personality characteristics of eating-disordered outpatients as measured by the Hand Test. *Journal of Personality Assessment, 55,* 350–361.

Lie, N. (1994). Offenders tested with projective methods prior to the first offense. *British Journal of Projective Psychology, 39,* 23–24.

Lie, N., & Wagner, E. E. (1996). Prediction of criminal behavior in young Swedish women using a group administration of the Hand Test. *Perceptual and Motor Skills, 82,* 975–978.

Morris, C. G. (1993). *Psychology: An introduction.* Englewood Cliffs, NJ: Prentice Hall.

Oswald, O., & Loftus, P. T. (1967). A normative and comparative study of the Hand Test with normal and delinquent children. *Journal of Projective Techniques and Personality Assessment, 31,* 62–68.

Piotrowski, C. (1999). Assessment practices in the era of managed care: Current status and future directions. *Journal of Clinical Psychology, 55,* 787–796.

Reynolds, C. R., & Kamphaus, R. W. (1992). *Behavior Assessment System for Children.* Circle Pines, MN: American Guidance Service.

Selg, H. (1965). Der Hand-Test als indikator for offen aggressives verhalten bei kindern. [The Hand Test as an indicator of overt aggressive tendencies in children.] *Diagnostica, 4,* 153–158.

Sivec, H. J., & Hilsenroth, M. J. (1994). The use of the Hand Test with children and adolescents: A review. *School Psychology Review, 23,* 526–545.

Smith, S. R., Blais, M. A., Vangala, M., & Masek, B. J. (2005). Exploring the Hand Test with medically ill children and adolescents. *Journal of Personality Assessment, 85,* 80–89.

Waehler, C. A., Rasch, M. A., Sivec, H. J., & Hilsenroth, M. J. (1992). Establishing a placement index for behaviorally disturbed children using the Hand Test. *Journal of Personality Assessment, 58,* 537–547.

Wagner, E. E. (1983). *The Hand Test manual* (rev. ed.). Los Angeles: Western Psychological Services.

Wagner, E. E. (1986). Hand Test interpretation for children and adolescents. In A. I. Rabin (Ed.), *Projective Techniques for adolescents and children* (pp. 279–305). New York: Springer.

Wagner, E. E. (1999). The Hand Test as a screening technique: Guidelines and examples. In G. R. Young & E. E. Wagner (Eds.), *The Hand Test: Advances in Application and Research* (pp. 59–83). Malabar, FL: Krieger.

Wagner, E. E., & Hawkins, R. (1964). Differentiation of assaultive delinquents with the Hand Test. *Journal of Projective Techniques and Personality Assessment, 28,* 363–365.

Wagner, E. E., Rasch, M. A., & Marsico, D. S. (1990). Hand Test characteristics of severely behavior handicapped children. *Journal of Personality Assessment, 54,* 802–806.

Wagner, E. E., Rasch, M. A., & Marsico, D. S. (1991). *Hand Test manual supplement: Interpreting child and adolescent responses.* Los Angeles: Western Psychological Services.

Wagner, E. E., & Young, G. R. (1999). Hand Test characteristics of pain clinic patients. In G. R. Young & E. E. Wagner (Eds.), *The Hand Test: Advances in application and research* (pp. 59–83). Malabar, FL: Krieger.

Wechsler, D. (2003). *Wechsler Intelligence Scale for Children* (4th ed.). San Antonio, TX: Psychological Corporation.

Wetsel, H., Shapiro, R. J., & Wagner, E. E. (1967). Prediction of recidivism among juvenile delinquents with the Hand Test. *Journal of Projective Techniques and Personality Assessment, 31*, 69–72.

Young, G. R., & Wagner, E. E. (1999). *The Hand Test: Advances in Application and Research* (pp. 59–83). Malabar, FL: Krieger.

15

THE MINNESOTA MULTIPHASIC PERSONALITY INVENTORY–ADOLESCENT

Robert P. Archer
Eastern Virginia Medical School, Norfolk, Virginia

Radhika Krishnamurthy
Florida Institute of Technology, Melbourne, Florida

Rebecca V. Stredny
Central State Hospital, Petersburg, Virginia

SELF-REPORT ASSESSMENT WITH ADOLESCENTS

Questionnaire-based methods of assessing adolescents require careful attention to issues of the adolescent's capacity to provide an accurate self-report and the adequacy of the assessment instrument in providing reliable and valid measurement of psychological functioning during this developmental period. There are relatively few self-report personality measures available for use with adolescents, perhaps in part because of the constraints related to reading/comprehension ability, cognitive/affective developmental status, and motivational level of adolescents in clinical settings. Currently available measures include the Millon Adolescent Clinical Inventory (MACI; Millon, 1993) and the Adolescent Psychopathology Scale (APS; Reynolds, 1998), and an adolescent version of the Personality Assessment Inventory (PAI-A) is currently under development (Morey, 2000). By a large margin, however, the most widely used self-report measure of adolescents' functioning is the Minnesota Multiphasic Personality Inventory–Adolescent (MMPI–A).

Responding to a self-report personality inventory requires some capacity for self-reflection and abstract thinking. Adolescence is a time of rapid cognitive development and, in Piagetian (1975) terms, is the period during which most individuals shift from Concrete Operations to the Formal Operations stage. As this shift occurs, the adolescent acquires the ability to manipulate ideas and concepts, changes that facilitate the adolescent's ability to respond accurately to a self-report personality inventory (Archer, 2005).

In the development of a self-report assessment instrument for adolescents, the reading level of the items is of particular concern. An adolescent's inability to understand items may lead to frustration, inaccurate responses, or omitted items, all of which can jeopardize the validity of test results. There are a number of standardized methods for assessing the reading level of items (for example, computer programs to evaluate item difficulty based on number of syllables per word and number of words per sentence), and the items must be carefully scrutinized in this regard during test development. In addition, the reading level of the individual adolescent test taker must be determined before administration and specifically evaluated with the use of a standardized reading test when deemed necessary.

Finally, it is essential that an adolescent self-report personality inventory use an appropriate item pool to provide adequate content validity. Items must be appropriate to contemporary adolescent experience, as well as to the types of psychopathology and behavior problems most commonly seen in adolescents, such as eating disorders, substance abuse, and problems related to school and family. Likewise, test content should not include areas that are unlikely to be of concern to most adolescents, such as problems with an employer or chronic marital discord.

The Minnesota Multiphasic Personality Inventory (MMPI) and its successor, the MMPI–2, have long been among the most popular assessment instruments for use with adults (e.g., Piotrowski & Keller, 1989). Although the original MMPI was commonly used with adolescents (Archer, Maruish, Imhof, & Piotrowski, 1991), a number of concerns about its appropriateness for use with this population emerged gradually in the late 1970s and 1980s. In order to adequately address issues such as those discussed above, an adolescent form of the MMPI was developed and was eventually introduced as the Minnesota Multiphasic Personality Inventory–Adolescent (MMPI–A: Butcher et al., 1992).

DEVELOPMENT OF THE MMPI, MMPI–2, AND MMPI–A

The MMPI and the MMPI–2

In 1937, Starke R. Hathaway and J. C. McKinley began construction on what eventually became the Minnesota Multiphasic Personality Inventory (MMPI; Hathaway & McKinley, 1940), an objective self-report instrument designed to identify and describe psychological features. The basic clinical scales of the MMPI were developed with the use of a method known as empirical or criterion keying, which at the time was considered revolutionary. Previous personality test development methods had generally relied on rational selection of items, with the use of face validity as the primary criterion; that is, items were selected based on the degree to which they appeared to be related to a given construct. In contrast, the empirical keying approach identifies test items based solely on their ability to differentiate effectively between normal and criterion groups. The criterion groups used for scale development consisted of clinical patients divided into discrete diagnostic categories, including Hypochondriasis (*Hs*; scale *1*), Depression (*D*; scale *2*), Hysteria (*Hy*; scale *3*), Psychopathic Deviancy (*Pd*; scale *4*), Paranoia (*Pa*; scale *6*), Psychasthenia (*Pt*; scale *7*), Schizophrenia (*Sc*; scale *8*), and Mania (*Ma*; scale *9*). Eventually the Masculinity-Femininity (*Mf*; scale *5*) and Social Introversion (*Si*; scale *0*) scales were also added, although these were considered nonclinical scales and were often omitted by early test users (Archer, 2005). A particularly important feature of the MMPI was its validity scales, which evaluated consistency and accuracy in responding. The MMPI was published in 1942 and quickly became established as the most commonly utilized objective personality assessment instrument in the United States across a variety of settings (e.g., Lubin, Larsen, & Matarazzo, 1984; Lubin, Larsen, Matarazzo, & Seever, 1985; Lubin, Wallis, & Paine, 1971; Piotrowski & Keller, 1989). The test was eventually revised and released as the MMPI–2, intended for assessing adults 18 years old and older (Butcher et al., 1989).

The original MMPI normative sample included a small number of adolescents, although no formal adolescent norms were provided (Dahlstrom, Welsh, & Dahlstrom, 1972). In 1972, however, Marks and Briggs used data from 1,766 normal adolescents to generate the most frequently used set of adolescent norms for the original MMPI. During the same time period, Marks, Seeman, and Haller (1974) reported the first actuarially based adolescent personality descriptors for 29 MMPI code types. Their study was based on the responses of approximately 1,250 adolescents, aged 12 though 18, who had undergone at least 10 hours of psychotherapy between 1965 and 1973. The Marks et al. (1974) study was critical in providing the first correlate information for interpreting adolescent code types.

Evidence of the popularity of the MMPI as an adolescent instrument continued to grow. In 1987, Archer produced a comprehensive guide to using the MMPI with adolescents, and the survey conducted by Archer et al. (1991) found that the original MMPI was the most frequently utilized objective personality assessment instrument in the United States for evaluating adolescents. However, survey respondents cited several areas of concern about using the MMPI with adolescents. These included the length of the test, the lack of contemporary norms, the demanding reading level, and the presence of inappropriate or outdated items (e.g., "I used to play drop-the-handkerchief"). In addition, important aspects of adolescent experience were not represented in the original inventory's items because of its focus on adult assessment. These largely omitted content areas included adolescent substance abuse, eating disorders, and school problems.

In July of 1989, an advising committee was appointed by the University of Minnesota Press to develop an adolescent form of the MMPI (Archer, 2005). An overarching goal was to maintain continuity with the original MMPI, including the preservation of basic validity and clinical scales. An effort was therefore made to minimize changes to the basic clinical scales. However, the revision provided an opportunity to make the item pool more appropriate for adolescents and to create several new scales directly relevant to adolescent development and psychopathology. A final goal was the collection of a new normative sample representative of a diverse and contemporary population of adolescents.

The MMPI-A Normative Sample

Data were initially collected from about 2,500 adolescents in Minnesota, Ohio, California, Virginia, Pennsylvania, New York, North Carolina, and Washington. Application of exclusion criteria resulted in a normative sample of 1,620 adolescents including 805 boys and 815 girls. The mean age was 15.5 (SD = 1.7) for boys and 15.6 (SD = 1.18) for girls. The sample participants were 76% Caucasian, 12% African American, and 12% from other ethnic groups. The MMPI–A normative data were a clear improvement over the Marks and Briggs (1972) norms in terms of geographic and ethnic diversity, but the newer norms also have some less desirable characteristics. Many adolescents included in the MMPI–A normative set were children of highly educated parents, as noted by Archer (2005) and Black (1994). For example, about 50% of the adolescents' fathers and about 40% of their mothers reported obtaining a bachelor's degree or higher (in comparison to U.S. census data from 1980, indicating that about 20% of males and 13% of adult females held college degrees). Butcher et al.

(1992) also noted that the MMPI–A norms were less representative of adolescents with histories of truancy, delinquency, or dropping out of school, issues of particular concern when adolescents are evaluated in juvenile detention or correctional facilities.

Structure and Psychometric Characteristics of the MMPI–A

The MMPI–A was adapted from the original MMPI with the following changes: 58 standard scale items were deleted from the basic scales, with 88% of these items coming from scales *F* (Infrequency), *5*, and *0*. Items eliminated from the original MMPI in the development of the MMPI–A typically pertained to religious attitudes and practices, sexual preferences, bowel and bladder functioning, and topics deemed inappropriate for evaluating adolescents (e.g., voting in elections). The MMPI–A includes the original 10 basic clinical scales and 3 basic validity scales, 4 newly developed validity scales, 15 content scales, 6 supplementary scales, 28 Harris-Lingoes subscales (Harris & Lingoes, 1955), and 3 *Si* subscales. The new validity scales included in the MMPI-A are the *F1* and *F2* subscales, the True Response Inconsistency Scale (*TRIN*), and the Variable Response Inconsistency Scale (*VRIN*).

After identifying the items in the MMPI–2 content scales appropriate for the assessment of adolescents, the MMPI–A content scales were refined by the addition or deletion of items based on their relative contributions to the overall scale reliability. A rational review of scales' item content was completed to ensure that items were considered appropriate for measuring underlying constructs. In addition, items that correlated more strongly with a scale or scales other than the one to which they were originally assigned were deleted. The manner in which the MMPI–A content scales were developed resulted in relatively face valid scales, which can be easily influenced by an overreporting or underreporting response style. Therefore, it is important to carefully consider the validity indicators, particularly scores on the Defensiveness or *K* scale, when the content scales are being interpreted. Furthermore, although the MMPI-A content scales have internal consistency, most of the scales also possess one or more content components. Sherwood, Ben-Porath, and Williams (1997) have developed a set of content component scales for 13 of the 15 MMPI–A content scales to assist in the evaluation of specific areas of content endorsement.

The supplementary scales of the MMPI–A include three scales previously developed for the original MMPI: Welsh's Anxiety (*A*) Repression (*R*; Welsh, 1956), and the Mac-Andrew Alcoholism Scale–Revised (*MAC–R*; MacAndrew, 1965). Additional supplementary scales developed specifically for the MMPI–A include the Immaturity (*IMM*) scale developed by Archer, Pancoast, and Gordon (1994), the Alcohol Drug Acknowledgment (*ACK*) scale, and the Alcohol/Drug Problem Proneness (*PRO*) scale developed by Weed, Butcher, and Williams (1994). Finally, the relatively low number of item deletions made to the MMPI–A clinical scales made it possible to retain the Harris-Lingoes and *Si* subscales and extend them to the MMPI–A.

Information on the test-retest reliability, internal consistency, and factor structure of the MMPI–A, as well as correlate information for normal and clinical samples, is provided in the MMPI–A manual (Butcher et al., 1992) and was recently updated by Archer (2005). The MMPI–A exhibits adequate temporal stability, with test-retest correlation values for basic scales ranging from $r = .19$ for the *F1* subscale to $r = .84$ for scale *0*. Similarly, test-retest correlations for the content scales range from $r = .40$ for the Negative Treatment Indicators (*A-trt*) scale to $r = .73$ for the School Problems (*A-sch*) scale. The standard error of measurement for the basic scales on the MMPI–A is typically estimated to be between 2 and 3 raw score points, reflecting good reliability (Butcher et al., 1992). The internal reliability (coefficient alpha) values for the MMPI–A scales range from lower values on scales *5* ($r = .43$) and *6* ($r = .57$), to relatively higher values ($r \geq .80$) for many of the content scales and the *IMM* scale.

Forbey (2003) has estimated that approximately 120 studies of the MMPI–A were completed between 1992 and 2002. A number of these studies have examined the effectiveness of the validity scales in detecting deviant response patterns and have collectively shown that validity assessment is a particular strength of the inventory (Krishnamurthy, 2005). Archer and Krishnamurthy (2002) also note that the MMPI–A has been the subject of numerous master's thesis studies and doctoral dissertations, further reflecting the strong research interest in the inventory. Furthermore, because the MMPI–A retains many characteristics of the MMPI, the research done with adolescents on the original MMPI is largely generalizable to the MMPI–A (Archer, 2005). Research has also shown that correlates for the basic scales and several supplementary scales appear similar for adolescents and adults (e.g., Williams & Butcher 1989; Archer, Gordon, Anderson, & Giannetti, 1989; Archer, Gordon, Giannetti, & Singles, 1988).

One of the areas in which adolescents differ clearly from adults is in their responses to critical items. Archer and Jacobson (1993) examined the endorsement frequency of the Koss-Butcher (1973) and the Lachar-Wrobel (1979) critical items among normative and clinical samples for the MMPI–A and the MMPI–2 and found that adolescents in both the normative and clinical samples endorsed items at a higher frequency than did normal adults. Furthermore, results indicated that adolescents in clinical settings did not generally endorse these critical items more frequently than normal adolescents. In an effort to address this issue, Forbey and Ben-Porath (1998) developed a set of MMPI–A critical items by comparing the item level responses of the MMPI–A normative sample with 419 adolescents receiving treatment in a Midwest residential treatment facility. The result of this effort was a critical item set composed of 82 items grouped into 15 content areas, including aggression, conduct problems, and depression-suicidal ideation.

The *K*-correction procedure used with the original MMPI was not carried over to the MMPI–A. The function of the *K*-correction is to improve the ability of the clinical scales to detect psychopathology by adding varying proportions of *K* scale raw score values to the scales *1, 4, 7, 8,* and *9* (Graham, 2000). Alperin, Archer, and Coates (1996) derived experimental *K*-weights for the MMPI–A to determine whether it could improve test accuracy in adolescent samples. Results indicated that the use of the *K*-correction procedure did not result in any systematic improvement in identifying adolescents with psychological disorders from adolescents from the MMPI–A normative sample.

As noted earlier, a substantial amount of research has been devoted to evaluating the MMPI–A validity scales. Preliminary evaluations of the *VRIN* and *TRIN* validity scales, reported in the test manual (Butcher et al., 1992), indicate that these scales were useful in detecting inconsistent responding (*VRIN*) as well as an acquiescent or nay-saying response style (*TRIN*). The test manual also noted that the *T*-score difference between *F1* and *F2* could prove useful in identifying changes in an adolescent's test-taking approach between the first and second half of the test. Archer (2005) presented a random response pattern on the MMPI–A, with the resulting profile showing elevations on the scales *L* (Lie), *VRIN, F1,* and *F2,* an invalid profile easily detected by most interpreters. Baer, Ballenger, Berry, and Wetter (1997) evaluated varying degrees of random responding on the MMPI–A. Their results demonstrated a pattern of increasing scores on *F1, F2, F,* and *VRIN,* as profile randomness increased. Archer and Elkins (1999) also found that scores on the validity scales *F, F1*, and *F2* were effective in differentiating profiles of a clinical sample of 354 adolescents from randomly generated protocols. Other studies (e.g., Stein & Graham, 1999; Stein, Graham, & Williams, 1995) have shown that standard validity scales discriminate effectively between fake-bad and standard profiles and between fake-good and nonfaked profiles.

MMPI–A ADMINISTRATION AND SCORING

The MMPI–A can be used by clinicians who have training in test theory and test construction as well as adolescent development, personality, psychopathology, and diagnosis. In addition, effective use of the MMPI–A requires a thorough review of the test manual (Butcher al., 1992). The test was essentially designed to assess adolescents aged 14 through 18, although it can be extended downward for use with 12- and 13-year-olds who possess the necessary reading level and cognitive skills. An 18-year-old can potentially be assessed with the use of either the MMPI–A or the MMPI–2, and this decision should be made on an individual basis in consideration of the adolescent's current life context and level of autonomy (Butcher et al., 1992).

Administration

Evaluation of an adolescent's reading ability before administration of the MMPI–A is essential, and failure to do so can result in an invalid protocol due to a high frequency of item omissions (e.g., Ball & Carroll, 1960; Archer and Gordon, 1991). The test manual (Butcher et al., 1992) provides an estimate of reading difficulty for all items, with findings ranging from the 1st to 16th grade levels. The manual recommends that a 7th-grade reading level be considered the necessary standard for completing the test, based on the criterion that at least 80% of the test items should be comprehensible in order to ensure that test results are valid. When there is a question about whether an adolescent's level of academic achievement corresponds to his or her grade level, it may be desirable to administer a brief screening test of reading ability, such as the reading subtest of the Wide Range Achievement Test–Third Edition (WRAT–3; Wilkinson, 1993) or the Gray Oral Reading Test–Fourth Edition (GORT–IV; Wiederholt & Bryant, 2001).

If an adolescent asks for word definitions during the MMPI–A administration, responses should be made in as neutral a manner as possible, preferably by providing dictionary definitions. However, the examiner should avoid providing explanations of items that the adolescent clearly comprehends. It is permissible to instruct the adolescent to respond to the item as it applies to him or her, and to answer in a way that reflects his or her own beliefs or opinions. In cases where reading deficits exist but cognitive ability is sufficient to understand the test items, the MMPI–A can be administered via audiotape. There are translations of the MMPI–A available in Dutch/Flemish, French, and Italian, as well as separate Spanish versions for use in the United States and Mexico, for evaluation of adolescents for whom English is not the primary language.

When administering the MMPI–A, it is important to provide an environment that is sufficiently private but which allows for adequate supervision. In addition, the setting should be as comfortable and as quiet as possible. The MMPI–A should not be left with an adolescent to complete in an unsupervised setting such as a waiting room. Similarly, it should never be sent home for completion. Supervision of the administration should be nonintrusive, while also providing for a proctor to be available at all times to monitor the process and provide help when necessary. In addition, rest periods should be provided whenever needed. It is possible to administer an abbreviated form of the MMPI–A by giving only the first 350 items of the test, which may be useful for evaluation of adolescents who are particularly resistant or low in motivation. However, this format should be considered only as a last resort because neither the validity scales *VRIN, TRIN, F*, and *F2* nor the content and supplementary scales can be scored. When the respondent's test-taking stamina is a concern, it is preferable to divide testing over two sessions, separated by a reasonably short interval, rather than use an abbreviated administration.

There are a number of steps evaluators can take to maximize adolescents' motivation and cooperation with the testing process. Presenting the test in a careful and serious manner increases the likelihood that valid results will be obtained. First, it is important to allow time to develop good rapport before initiation of the test procedure. In addition, the adolescent should be given clear, concise instructions as well as an explanation of the purpose of the testing and how the results will be used. Instructions for completing the test are printed on the inside of the test booklet, and after these have been read, a brief verbal summary should be provided. Time should be taken to answer any questions the adolescent may have about the testing process and purpose. Finally, whenever possible, adolescents should be informed that they will have the opportunity to receive feedback on their test results.

Test Materials

MMPI–A testing materials are available from Pearson Assessments. The necessary materials include testing booklets (available in hardcover or softcover), answer sheets, templates and profile sheets for hand-scoring, and/or a computer scoring program. There are different answer sheets available, depending on whether hand scoring or computer scoring is to be used, and therefore the scoring method must be taken into account when answer sheets are selected. Also available is an audiocassette version of the test and software for computerized test administration.

Scoring

Scoring should begin with a visual scan of the answer sheet to determine whether a significant number of items have been omitted or scored in both the true and false directions. The next step is to obtain the raw score value for each scale, with the use of either the hand-scoring technique or the computer scoring program. The raw scores are then converted to *T*-scores with the use of the appropriate adolescent norm tables (as previously noted, there is no *K*-scale correction procedure used for the MMPI–A). Careful attention should be paid to the gender of the adolescent when raw scores are converted to *T*-scores. The *T*-score values can then be plotted on the MMPI–A profile sheet. When computer scoring is used, the Basic Scale Profile Report provides information for an abbreviated administration, including raw and *T*-scores for four validity scales (*L, F, F1, K*) and the 10 basic clinical scales. The Extended Score Report provides raw scores and *T*-scores for all MMPI–A scales and subscales and a list of omitted items. As an alternative to purchasing the computer scoring program, test users can also utilize the Pearson Assessments mail-in scoring service.

VALIDITY SCALES AND INTERPRETATION

MMPI–A Validity Scales

A significant advantage of the MMPI–A is the information it provides regarding an adolescent's test-taking style and the validity of test results. An initial step in evaluating validity is taken by calculating the Cannot Say (?) score, which is a simple tally of the number of items left unanswered or that were endorsed in both directions. When the total number of such items is 30 or less, it is considered unlikely that the omitted items will significantly affect the test results. Further information regarding validity can be obtained with the Infrequency (*F*) scale. This scale contains items that were endorsed in a deviant direction by less than 20% of the MMPI–A normative sample and is thus a measure of infrequently reported psychopathology. When the *F* scale is elevated, it may indicate an attempt by the adolescent to "fake bad" or overreport symptoms. Elevations may also indicate genuinely severe psychiatric illness or, in some cases, the product of a random response set. The latter possibility can be assessed by examination of other validity scale information, specifically the Variable Response Inconsistency (*VRIN*) scale. An MMPI–A profile is considered to be invalid if the *F* *T*-score is ≥90 (Butcher et al., 1992). *T*-scores ranging from 66 to 89 suggest that other validity indicators should be carefully examined, and if the profile is otherwise valid it is likely that significant psychopathology is present. *F* scale elevations between 60 and 65 are considered moderate and are often produced by adolescents who are experiencing some psychopathology. A normal-range *F* score would be expected to fall at *T* ≤ 59. The *F* scale is also parent to the *F1* and *F2* subscales. The *F1* scale contains 33 items occurring with the first 350 items on the test, and the *F2* scale contains 33 items occurring after item 242. Thus, if the *F1* score is normal while the *F2* is elevated, this might suggest a random response set during the second half of the test (Butcher et al., 1992).

The MMPI–A Lie (*L*) scale contains 15 items that ask about common human faults and is useful in identifying adolescents who portray themselves in an excessively favorable and virtuous manner. When the *L* scale is elevated above a *T*-score of 65, it is also possible (although rare) that an adolescent is using an all-false or "nay-saying" response set. *T*-scores between 56 and 65 on the scale suggest an emphasis on conformity and conventional behaviors, and scores between 46 and 55 are considered to fall in the normal range. When *T*-scores for the *L* scale are 45 or lower, this may reflect an open, confident approach. However, an all-true or "fake-bad" response set is also possible and can be further evaluated by examination of other validity scale data, particularly the *TRIN* scale score.

The Defensiveness (*K*) scale contains 30 items that have empirically identified test-takers who objectively display symptoms of psychopathology but who provide normal-range profiles. This scale identifies more subtle forms of guardedness than the *L* scale. Because most items are scored in the True direction, the *K*-scale score can also help detect an all-true response set. In general, however, elevations on the *K*-scale are associated with defensiveness and the tendency to consciously or unconsciously underreport psychological symptoms or problems. When the *K* scale is elevated to a *T*-score greater than 65, this degree of defensiveness is considered to predict poorer prognosis and longer treatment duration (Archer, 2005). Scores ranging from 56 to 65 may reflect self-reliance and a reluctance to seek help, and scores between 41 and 55 are considered to be normal. *T*-scores of 40 or less may be produced by individuals who have poor self-concepts and limited coping resources.

The configuration of an adolescent's validity scale scores may provide additional insight into the test-taking approach. For example, marked (*T* > 65) elevations of scales *L* and *K*, in combination with an *F* scale below 50, suggest an extremely guarded adolescent who is making a strong attempt to present himself or herself favorably. Conversely, an elevated *F* scale combined with *L* and *K* scales below 50 is indicative of an adolescent who is very openly reporting psychological symptoms or problems. Extreme elevations of the *F* scale relative to *L* and *K*, however, may also suggest a conscious or unconscious attempt to overreport symptoms.

Overreporting is generally easier to detect and typically results in elevations on the *F* scale, with low-range scores on scales *L* and *K*. Underreporting is often suggested by marked elevations on *L* and *K*, combined with low or normal-range scores on *F*. However, some individuals may successfully underreport symptoms without elevating *L* and *K*, making it difficult to ascertain whether an adolescent is merely somewhat guarded and defensive, or is experiencing significant psychopathology that he or she is trying to hide.

Additional validity scales for the MMPI–A include the *VRIN* and *TRIN* scales, both of which examine an individual's tendency to respond in a consistent manner. The *VRIN* scale includes 50 item pairs with similar or opposite content and assesses how frequently an adolescent responds to the item pairs in a logically inconsistent manner. Elevations on the *VRIN* scale suggest that an adolescent responded to the test in a random or inconsistent manner. This hypothesis appears particularly when the *F* scale is also elevated (Wetter, Baer, Berry, Smith, & Larsen, 1992). When *T*-score values equal to or greater than 80 are obtained on the *VRIN* scale, indiscriminate responding renders the profile invalid and uninterpretable (Butcher et al., 1992). *T*-scores between 70 and 79 indicate marginal degrees of inconsistent responding. The *TRIN* scale includes 24 item pairs that are opposite in content, and it is thus sensitive to all-true or all-false response sets. The *T*-score is traditionally followed by a "T" or "F" to indicate whether the responses were skewed in the true or false direction, and all *TRIN* *T*-scores must be ≥50. Interpretation guidelines are similar to those for the *VRIN* scale: *T*-scores between 70 and 79 are considered to indicate marginal validity, and *T*-scores ≥ 80 suggest that the profile should be considered invalid.

BASIC CLINICAL SCALES

Profile Elevation Issues

When a *T*-score of ≥65 is used as the clinical cutoff point for the MMPI–A, many adolescents in clinical settings fail to produce clinically elevated scores. In an effort to address this issue, the MMPI–A utilizes a range of values that serves as a transitional zone between normal-range and clinical-range elevations. Therefore, *T*-scores between 60 and 65 are considered to be marginal elevations on the MMPI–A, and adolescents may be expected to demonstrate some, but not all, of the correlates associated with a scale that is elevated within this range. From a conceptual as well as psychometric standpoint, this transitional zone suggests that the difference between normal adjustment and psychopathology is less clear in adolescence than in adulthood.

Scale 1(Hs): Hypochondriasis

The 33 items on scale *1* are focused on somatic complaints and concerns. Research on adult populations indicates that elevations on this scale are produced by individuals who report numerous and often vague physical complaints, are not psychologically minded, and may use physical complaints as a means of manipulating others (Graham, 2000). Other descriptors for T-scores ≥ 60 include

- Excessive somatic concerns that are likely to be vague in nature
- Somatic responses to stress, which may include eating problems
- Increased likelihood of internalizing problems such as guilt, fears, social withdrawal, perfectionism, dependency, and anxiety
- Demanding, critical, selfish, and whining in interpersonal relationships
- Less likely to engage in delinquent behaviors
- Likely to report school problems, including academic and adjustment difficulties

Scale 2 (D): Depression

The 57 items on this scale are associated with general dissatisfaction, poor morale, and social withdrawal. Adolescents in inpatient settings who show elevations on this scale are also more likely to have depressive symptoms that include histories of suicidal gestures or attempts (Butcher et al., 1992). Descriptors associated with elevations on scale 2 ($T \geq 60$) include

- Feelings of unhappiness, dissatisfaction, and hopelessness
- Apathy and lack of interest in activities
- Feelings of guilty, shame, and despondency
- Social isolation and withdrawal
- Feelings of inadequacy, pessimism, and low self-esteem

Scale 3 (Hy): Hysteria

The 60 items of scale 3 measure a tendency to respond to stressful situations with physical symptoms that do not have an organic basis, with an associated strong need for social acceptance and approval. Personality characteristics of individuals with moderate elevations on this scale may include social extroversion, exhibitionistic behavior, superficial relationships, and self-centeredness. In addition, elevations on scale 3 ($T \geq 60$) may be associated with

- Somatic preoccupations and concerns
- Social involvement and achievement orientation
- Pattern of overreaction to stress that involves the development of physical symptoms
- Self-centered, egocentric, and immature actions
- Strong needs for attention, affection, and social approval

Scale 4 (Pd): Psychopathic Deviate

The 49 items on this scale were chosen based on a clinical sample of adolescents that were court-referred for evaluations because of delinquent behaviors. Content areas covered by this scale include family conflict, social isolation, delinquency, dissatisfaction with life, and problems with authority figures. Elevations on scale 4 ($T \geq 60$) are associated with the following:

- Increased probability of delinquency, oppositional behaviors, and externalizing behavior problems

- Hostility and rebelliousness toward authority figures
- History of poor school adjustment
- Greater likelihood of conduct disorder diagnoses
- Poor planning ability, low frustration tolerance, and impulsivity
- Use of acting out as a primary defense mechanism
- Higher incidence of risk-taking and sensation-seeking behavior
- Higher incidence of use and abuse of drugs and alcohol
- Relative absence of guilt and remorse in regard to wrongdoing

Scale 5 (Mf): Masculinity/Femininity

Scale 5 is a 44-item measure probably best conceptualized as assessing stereotypical gender characteristics, with normal range scores suggesting a relative balance between traditional masculine and feminine features. T-score conversions for this scale are reversed for males and females, so that a high raw score for boys produces a high T-score, whereas a high raw score for girls produces a low T-score. Low scores for both boys and girls are associated with traditional gender roles. Boys who score high on scale 5 ($T \geq 60$) may exhibit the following characteristics:

- Intelligence with aesthetic interests
- Higher levels of academic achievement
- Passivity and submissiveness in interpersonal relationships
- Lower likelihood of delinquent or antisocial behaviors

Girls who score high on scale 5 ($T \geq 60$) may show these characteristics:

- Assertiveness and competitiveness
- Aggressiveness with a greater likelihood of school conduct problems
- Possibility of stereotypically masculine interests in academics and sports

When boys score low on scale 5 ($T \leq 40$), the following characteristics may be observed:

- Masculine emphasis in self-presentation
- Higher frequency of school problems and delinquency
- Relatively narrow range of interests defined by traditional masculine stereotypes

Girls who score low on scale 5 ($T \leq 40$) may exhibit the following characteristics:

- Passivity and submissiveness in interpersonal relationships
- Stereotypically feminine self-presentation
- Higher levels of academic achievement and lower levels of behavior problems

Scale 6 (Pa): Paranoia

Moderate elevations on the 40-item scale 6 are often produced by individuals who are excessively sensitive to the beliefs and actions of others and who are often guarded and suspicious in their interactions. Very high elevations on scale 6 are more typical of individuals with psychotic paranoid symptoms. Traditionally, adolescents have tended to endorse more items on this scale than adults do, largely because of their sense of being controlled and treated unfairly by others. Adolescents who produce marked elevations on scale 6 ($T \geq 70$) may display the following characteristics:

- Use of projection as a primary defense mechanism
- Hostility, anger, and resentment
- Possible disturbances in reality testing
- Delusions of persecution or grandeur
- Ideas of reference

Moderate range elevations (T scores ranging from 60 to 69) may be indicative of the following characteristics:

- Excessive interpersonal sensitivity
- Distrust and suspiciousness in relationships
- Tendencies toward argumentativeness
- Increased disagreements/conflicts with parents
- Difficulty in establishing a trusting relationship with a therapist

Scale 7 (Pt): Psychasthenia

The 48 items of scale 7 cover a variety of content areas, including concentration problems, obsessive thoughts, anxiety and tension, unhappiness and general emotional distress, and physical complaints. This scale was originally designed to measure symptoms of psychasthenia, more recently conceptualized as Obsessive-Compulsive Disorder. Adolescents who score high on scale 7 ($T \geq 60$) may exhibit the following characteristics:

- Perfectionistic and self-critical tendencies
- Tension, apprehension, and anxiety
- Feelings of inadequacy, inferiority, and insecurity
- Tendency to be introspective, ruminative, and lacking in self-confidence
- At marked elevations ($T \geq 70$), obsessive and ruminative thought patterns

Scale 8 (Sc): Schizophrenia

Scale 8 is the longest of the basic clinical scales (77 items) and covers a wide range of content areas relevant to symptoms of schizophrenia (e.g., bizarre thoughts, difficulties in concentration, socially deviant behaviors). Other factors may contribute to elevations on this scale as well, including drug use or experimentation. Elevations on scale 8 ($T \geq 60$) are associated with the following:

- Confused or disorganized thinking
- Withdrawn and seclusive behavior
- Feelings of inferiority, low self-esteem, and incompetence

- Feelings of unhappiness or frustration
- Social rejection and history of being teased by peers
- Vulnerability to stress and tendency to get upset easily
- Possible impairment of reality testing
- Perceived by peers as being odd, unconventional, and socially deviant

Scale 9 (Ma): Hypomania

The 46 items of scale 9 encompass content areas including grandiosity, flight of ideas, irritability, egocentricity, elevated mood, and cognitive and behavioral overactivity. Similar to the pattern found on scale 6, adolescents tend to show elevations on scale 9 more frequently than do adults. The following characteristics are associated with elevated scores ($T \geq 60$) on this scale:

- Talkative, energetic, and outgoing manner
- Rapid personal tempo and tendency to engage in excessive activity
- Preference for action rather than thought and reflection
- Restlessness, distractibility, and impulsiveness
- Grandiosity and unrealistic goal-setting
- Egocentric, self-centered, and self-indulgent actions
- Possibility of flight of ideas, grandiosity and euphoric mood

Scale 0 (Si): Social Introversion

The 62-item scale 0 was originally developed by identification of items that differentiated between introverted and extroverted college students. Like scale 5, scale 0 is considered a nonclinical scale that may measure traits or characteristics relatively independently of psychopathology. Adolescents who produce elevations on scale 0 ($T \geq 60$) may exhibit the following characteristics:

- Social introversion and social discomfort
- Low self-esteem
- Timid, withdrawn, and reserved presentation
- Decreased probability of delinquency or acting out
- Submissive, passive, and compliant demeanor
- Low self-confidence and high levels of insecurity

Adolescents with lower scores on scale 0 ($T \leq 40$) may demonstrate the following characteristics:

- Extroversion, gregariousness, and sociability
- Energetic, talkative, and active mode
- Confident, competent, and socially sensitive stance

CODE TYPE INTERPRETATION

Configural approaches to interpreting the MMPI have generally been viewed as the optimal method for obtaining diagnostic and descriptive information (Graham, 2000). Two-point code types are typically referred to by the numbers of the two basic clinical scales that are most elevated in the profile, with the higher score designated first (e.g., if the highest T-score elevations are on scales *4 [Pd]* and *9 [Ma]*, the profile is referred to as a *4–9* code type). However, most two-point code types are also generally considered to be interchangeable, in that the correlates of *4–9* code type, for example, would be largely equivalent to those of a *9–4* code type. A code type is considered well defined when there is at least a minimum difference of 5 T-score points between the second and third most elevated scales. However, the majority of adolescents do not produce well-defined code types. In such cases, code type descriptors can still be considered relevant but should be used more cautiously.

Among normal adolescents, MMPI–A profiles have an overall congruence rate with profiles generated from the original MMPI of 67.8% for boys and 55.8% for girls (Butcher et al., 1992). These congruences increase to 95.2% for boys and 81.8% for girls for code types defined by at least a 5-point difference between the second and third most elevated scales. Rates of congruence for adolescents in the clinical sample reported in the test manual are quite similar. These congruence estimates fall within the same range as congruence rates between the original MMPI and the MMPI–2 (Butcher et al., 1989). Archer (2005) and Archer and Krishnamurthy (2002) have argued that much of the MMPI research can be generalized to the MMPI–A. There is also a growing body of literature on code types and their associated features for the MMPI–A. For a sampling of the descriptors associated with the most common codetypes see Table 15.1, taken from Archer and Krishnamurthy (2002).

Factors Potentially Affecting Code Type Interpretation

Demographic variables such as ethnicity, gender, and age may have an impact on MMPI–A code type interpretation. Among the MMPI–A normative sample, differences are shown between Black, White, and Other respondents of about 3–5 T-score points on scales *L, F, 4, 6, 7, 8,* and *9* (Archer, 2005). Although these mean differences are relatively small, Archer and Krishnamurthy (2002) have cautioned that clinicians should be "appropriately conservative"

TABLE 15.1.
Key Features of Common MMPI–A Code Types

Code type	Behavioral/emotional correlates
1-3/3-1	Multiple physical complaints, attention-seeking actions, conformity, insecurity, poor insight
2-3/3-2	Emotional overcontrol, passivity, dependence, insecurity, poor peer relationships
2-4/4-2	Poor impulse control, substance abuse, depression, elopement risk
3-4/4-3	Somatic complaints, suicide risk, hostile/aggression, impulses, denial of emotional distress
4-6/6-4	Demands of attention, sympathy, resentment, suspiciousness, parent-child conflicts, hostility
4-8/8-4	Marginal social adjustment; seen as impulsive, odd, and peculiar by others; chaotic family lives and poor school adjustment
4-9/9-4	Defiance, disobedience, acting out, impulsivity, authority conflicts, drug abuse, truancy, running away from home
6-8/8-6	Serious psychopathology including paranoid symptoms, delusions, hallucinations, hostile outbursts, unpredictable behavior
7-8/8-7	Anxiety, depressions, social withdrawal, strong feelings of inadequacy and insecurity, possible thought disorder symptoms including hallucinations

Adapted from *Essentials of MMPI–A Assessment* (2002) by R. P. Archer and Radhika Krishnamurthy. Reprinted with the permission of John Wiley & Sons.

in interpreting profiles from non-White adolescents. Regarding gender, boys and girls respond significantly differently to the MMPI–A, thus requiring separate gender-based norms. The available research on this issue has predominantly been conducted with the original MMPI. In general, the overall gender pattern is for girls to more readily endorse psychological symptoms and complaints than boys. Some researchers have found little impact on code types once T-score conversions have been applied (e.g., Williams & Butcher 1989), although other researchers have found significant gender-related differences in correlate patterns for MMPI scales (e.g., Lachar & Wrobel, 1990; Wrobel and Lachar, 1992). Additional research is still needed to clarify this issue. Finally, in regard to age, although some studies have identified age differences in adult versus adolescent responding to the MMPI (e.g., Lachar, Klinge, & Grissell, 1976), research findings generally suggest that the accuracy of MMPI correlate statements remains relatively constant for profiles across the adolescent age span (e.g., Archer, 1987; Wimbish, 1984). On the whole, although some studies have found demographic differences related to variables such as ethnicity, gender, and age in MMPI and MMPI–A responding, Schinka, Elkins, and Archer (1998) have also recently found that these demographic variables accounted for a small amount of variance in MMPI–A validity, clinical, content, and supplementary scales.

CONTENT AND SUPPLEMENTARY SCALES

Content Scales

Because many of the MMPI basic clinical scales are heterogeneous in terms of content areas, a number of approaches have been taken to assist the evaluator in interpreting elevations on the basic clinical scales. In 1955, Harris and Lingoes constructed subscales for six of the basic scales—*2, 3, 4, 6, 8*, and *9*. Scales *1* and *7* were not included by Harris and Lingoes because these scales are much more homogeneous in their item composition. Scales *5* and *0* were also not included because they were viewed as nonclinical scales. The Harris-Lingoes subscales were carried over from the MMPI to the MMPI–2 and MMPI–A. They are used to narrow interpretations when basic clinical scales are elevated and are considered most useful when the elevation is in a moderate range (T-score ≥ 60 and ≤ 90). For example, a T-score elevation of 70 on the scale *8* could reflect social or emotional alienation, unusual perceptual experiences, dissociative symptoms, feelings of vulnerability, or unusual thought processes. The relative pattern of elevation on the Harris-Lingoes subscales could indicate which areas of difficulty are of greatest concern. The MMPI–A Harris-Lingoes subscales should only be interpreted when there is an elevation of at least T-score $= 60$ on the parent scale, and when the subscale itself is elevated to at least $T \geq 65$. The Harris-Lingoes subscales are generally less helpful when elevations of T-score > 90 are interpreted, because at this level of elevation all content areas will probably have been endorsed. As noted above, Harris and Lingoes did not develop subscales for several MMPI basic clinical scales, including scale *0* (*Si*). Ben-Porath, Hostetler, Butcher, and Graham (1989) developed *Si* subscales for the MMPI–2, which have been carried over to the MMPI–A and are included on the same profile sheet as the Harris-Lingoes subscales. Archer (2005) provides a thorough review of Harris-Lingoes and Si subscale correlates. See Table 15.2 for a list of the Harris-Lingoes and *Si* subscales associated with each of the basic scales.

    There is also a set of 15 content scales specifically developed for the MMPI–A and the content component subscales developed by Sherwood et al. (1997) for 13 of these scales to

TABLE 15.2.
MMPI–A Harris-Lingoes and Si Subscales

Harris-Lingoes subscales (28)

Scale 2 subscales	
D_1	Subjective depression
D_2	Psychomotor retardation
D_3	Physical malfunctioning
D_4	Mental dullness
D_5	Brooding
Scale 3 subscales	
Hy_1	Denial of social anxiety
Hy_2	Need for affection
Hy_3	Lassitude-malaise
Hy_4	Somatic complaints
Hy_5	Inhibition of aggression
Scale 4 subscales	
Pd_1	Familial discord
Pd_2	Authority problems
Pd_3	Social imperturbability
Pd_4	Social alienation
Pd_5	Self-alienation
Scale 6 subscales	
Pa_1	Persecutory
Pa_2	Poignancy
Pa_3	Naivete
Scale 8 subscales	
Sc_1	Social alienation
Sc_2	Emotional alienation
Sc_3	Lack of ego mastery, cognitive
Sc_4	Lack of ego mastery, conative
Sc_5	Lack of ego mastery, defective inhibition
Sc_6	Bizarre sensory experiences
Scale 9 subscales	
Ma_1	Amorality
Ma_2	Psychomotor acceleration
Ma_3	Imperturbability
Ma_4	Ego inflation
Si subscales	
Si_1	Shyness/self-consciousness
Si_2	Social avoidance
Si_3	Alienation—self and others

Adapted from *Essentials of MMPI–A Assessment* (2002) by R. P. Archer and Radhika Krishnamurthy. Reprinted with the permission of John Wiley & Sons.

identify relevant content subdomains. The content scales for which component subscales were developed include Depression (*A-dep*), Health Concerns (*A-hea*), Alienation (*A-aln*), Bizarre Mentation (*A-biz*), Anger (*A-ang*), Cynicism (*A-cyn*), Conduct Problems (*A-con*), Low Self-Esteem (*A-lse*), Low Aspirations (*A-las*), Social Discomfort (*A-sod*), Family Problems (*A-fam*), School Problems (*A-sch*), and Negative Treatment Indicators (*A-trt*). Content scales Anxiety (*A-anx*) and Obsessiveness (*A-obs*) measure relatively homogeneous content areas and therefore do not have component scales. Unlike the Harris-Lingoes subscales, the content scales are not tied to individual or basic clinical parent scales. Less empirical information is available regarding correlates of the MMPI–A content scales than the basic clinical scales, although content scale descriptors have been reported by Williams, Butcher, Ben-Porath, and Graham (1992) and Archer and Gordon (1991). Information about the development of the MMPI–A content scales is presented in Williams et al. (1992), and the relevant literature on these scales was recently reviewed by Archer (2005).

Supplementary Scales

The supplementary scales augment and refine the information obtained from the clinical scales and code types. All of the supplementary scales require that the complete set of test items be administered and thus cannot be scored when an abbreviated administration is given. A brief description of each of the supplementary scales is provided next.

MacAndrew Alcoholism Scale–Revised

This 49-item scale was created by contrasting the item responses of 300 male alcoholics with the responses of 300 male psychiatric patients and selecting the items that best differentiated the groups. The MacAndrew Alcoholism Scale–Revised (*MAC–R*) has been the subject of substantial research involving adolescents, and elevations on this scale appear to be related to an increased likelihood of substance abuse for adolescents in several settings, including public schools, hospital and residential psychiatric facilities, and substance abuse treatment programs. In addition, high *MAC–R* scores are related to the abuse of a variety of drugs besides alcohol. Personality and behavioral characteristics associated with *MAC–R* elevations include assertiveness, self-indulgence, impulsivity, and greater likelihood of conduct disorder diagnoses or law breaking.

Alcohol/Drug Problem Acknowledgment Scale

The 13-item Alcohol/Drug Problem Acknowledgment (*ACK*) scale assesses an adolescent's willingness to acknowledge symptoms, attitudes, or beliefs associated with alcohol or drug abuse. Elevations on this scale indicate the degree to which an adolescent admits alcohol and/or drug-related problems. Research indicates that the *ACK* scale is comparable in sensitivity to the *MAC–R* and *PRO* scales in its ability to identify the presence of substance abuse problems, but the *ACK* scale may prove to be a more specific measure than the other scales because it produces lower correlations with non-substance-abuse-related criteria (Gallucci, 1997).

Alcohol/Drug Problem Proneness Scale

The Alchohol/Drug Problem Proneness (*PRO*) scale consists of 36 items that differentiate between adolescents in alcohol and drug treatment programs, in contrast to adolescents receiving inpatient psychiatric treatment (Butcher et al., 1992). Items cover a wide range of content, including family and peer group characteristics, antisocial behaviors and beliefs, and academic interest and behaviors. *T*-score values of 65 or greater on this scale are associated with increased potential for the development of drug and alcohol problems.

Immaturity Scale

The 43-item Immaturity (*IMM*) scale assesses psychological maturation with the use of Loevinger's (1976) concept of ego development. A high *IMM* score suggests that an adolescent is easily frustrated; is impatient, loud, and boisterous; teases or bullies others; is untrustworthy, defiant, or resistant; is likely to have a history of academic and social difficulties; and/or is likely to have a lower than average verbal IQ and language ability.

Welsh's Anxiety and Repression Scales

Welsh's Anxiety (*A*) and (*R*) scales were originally developed to assess general maladjustment and inhibition, respectively, in response to factor analytic findings that these two dimensions account for a majority of variance on the basic scales (Graham, 2000). Correlates of Welsh's *A* include tension and anxiety; fearfulness and rumination; maladjustment and lack of effectiveness; self-criticism and guilt; and a feeling of being overwhelmed. High scorers on Welsh's *R* may be overcontrolled; show little feeling; be inhibited, constricted, pessimistic, and/or defeated.

INTERPRETIVE STRATEGIES

Steps in Profile Interpretation

A first consideration in interpreting the MMPI–A should be the setting in which the test was administered. The MMPI–A was developed to evaluate adolescent psychopathology in a variety of settings, including outpatient and inpatient psychiatric and alcohol/drug treatment settings, schools, and medical clinics and hospitals. In addition to these educational and/or clinical settings, the MMPI–A can also be given in a variety of forensic settings, including detention and correctional facilities. Each of these settings and contexts may give rise to specific interpretive issues and hypotheses. Similarly, the history and background of the adolescent are relevant for administering and interpreting the MMPI–A and should be taken into account, especially when such issues as motivation, cooperation, and cognitive ability are considered.

The third step in MMPI–A profile interpretation should be an evaluation of the validity of test results. In this regard, Greene (2000) has provided a useful conceptual model involving the use of sequential steps in evaluating profile consistency and accuracy based on validity scale results. After validity has been determined, the basic clinical scales should be examined and a relevant code type or single scale elevations noted. The higher a basic scale elevation, the more likely the individual is to display the symptoms or characteristics associated with the elevation or code type. In addition to basic scale elevations, it can be useful to review any low-range scores (i.e., $T \leq 40$), as some scales (particularly the basic clinical scales) have empirically derived descriptors for low scores.

Following a review of the basic clinical scales, the supplementary scales should be examined to support and refine basic scale interpretation. Welsh's *A* and *R* suggest the overall level of maladjustment and repression, and psychological maturity can be assessed with the *IMM* scale. The remaining three supplementary scales will provide information on alcohol/drug use acknowledgment or risk, and positive scores on these indices indicate the need for more comprehensive evaluation of substance abuse status and potential. The MMPI–A content scales should be examined to further refine the interpretation of basic scales. The content scales may be meaningfully grouped into internalizing (A-anx, A-obs, A-dep, A-hea, A-aln, A-biz, A-lse), externalizing (A-ang, A-cyn, A-con, A-las), and other problem area (A-sod, A-fam, A-sch, A-trt) clusters to aid interpretation. Finally, the Harris-Lingoes subscales may also be used to interpret clinical scales that are elevated to clinical levels, in order to selectively identify the content areas that contribute to the elevation.

As a final stage of profile interpretation, the evaluator could use the MMPI–A Structural Summary form developed by Archer and Krishnamurthy (1994) to profile information. Scale and subscale level test data are organized on this form according to an eight-factor structure identified by Archer, Belevich, and Elkins (1994). The eight dimensions are General Maladjustment, Immaturity, Disinhibition/Excitatory Potential, Social Discomfort, Health Concerns, Naivete, Familial Alienation, and Psychoticism. The Structural Summary is designed to improve the utility of scale findings by reducing the redundancy of data across individual scales and identifying salient, overarching areas of concern. Use of the Structural Summary in case interpretation is illustrated by Archer, Krishnamurthy, and Jacobson (1994).

Computer-Based Interpretation Systems

The MMPI was the first psychological test for which a computer scoring and interpretation system was developed (Butcher, 1987). Computer-generated profile interpretations of the original MMPI for adolescents were introduced by Archer in 1987 and Marks and Lewak in 1991. In addition, an MMPI–A interpretive report developed by Archer was first released in 1992 and most recently revised in a third edition released in 2003, distributed by Psychological Assessment Resources. MMPI–A interpretive reports have also been developed by Butcher and Williams (1992; distributed by Pearson Assessments) and Marks and Lewak (1991; distributed by Western Psychological Services). The development of computer-generated interpretations has sparked debate, and it is important that the clinician using such programs be thoroughly familiar with the test and competent in its use. In addition, computer-generated interpretations should be used only in conjunction with other sources of data and good professional judgment.

CLINICAL APPLICATIONS OF MMPI–A ASSESSMENT

The MMPI–A is most often applied to obtain a comprehensive picture of personality and emotional/behavioral dysfunction of adolescents in outpatient and inpatient psychological treatment facilities. In these settings, the assessment aids in determining diagnosis and identifying favorable treatment directions. MMPI–A-based assessment may also be used as part of school evaluations to facilitate educational placement decisions for adolescents with emotional and behavioral disorders, in juvenile justice system proceedings, and in juvenile case reviews by social service agencies.

Although there are no defined MMPI–A profile patterns associated with specific psychological disorders, it may be noted that the profiles of substance-abusing adolescents often contain a scale *4* elevation, a *4–9* code type, and elevations on supplementary scales *MAC–R*, *ACK*, and *PRO*. Juvenile delinquents often produce elevations on scales *6* and *IMM* in addition to the aforementioned clinical and supplementary scales seen among substance abusers, as well as elevations on content scales *A-ang*, *A-cyn*, *A-sch*, *A-con*, and *A-sod*. Adolescents with eating disorders may show elevations on a number of internalizing scales, including *1,*

2, 3, 7, and *0*, reflecting somatic, emotional, and interpersonal distress. Externalizing scales such as *4, 6, 8*, and *9* may additionally be elevated among those with bulimia nervosa. Multiple scale elevations reflecting emotional and behavioral disruption may also be found among sexually abused adolescents, including elevations on *A-dep, A-ang, A-lse, A-sch*, and *A-fam* (Archer & Krishnamurthy, 2002).

Treatment planning can be usefully informed by MMPI–A results in a variety of ways. For example, indications of defensiveness and guardedness from the validity scales may sensitize the clinician to be patient, develop a strong and reliable interpersonal alliance, and demonstrate trustworthiness before undertaking any interventions. Furthermore, MMPI–A findings may indicate that the treatment plan should be focused, for example, on family interventions when scales *4, A-fam*, and the *Familial Alienation* factor are salient in the profile, or on addressing thought disorder in cases of elevations across scales *8, 6, 6–8*, and *8–9* code types, *A-biz*, and the *Psychoticism* factor (Archer & Krishnamurthy, 2002).

CLINICAL CASE EXAMPLE

Aaron B. is a 16-year-old Caucasian boy who is the only child of an inner city family of low socioeconomic status. His parents were never married. His mother is an alcoholic, and other family members have declined to care for Aaron because of his behavior problems. Aaron was previously evaluated when he was 14 years old. At that time, he had been removed from his mother's care about six months before the evaluation and placed with an aunt and uncle because of a substantiated case of neglect against his mother. However, he frequently ran away from the home of his aunt and uncle in order to stay with his mother. He had also been placed on probation after being charged with petty larceny and subsequently violated his probation by incurring a burglary charge. He was then placed in juvenile detention, and at that point his aunt and uncle relinquished custody of Aaron. He was briefly placed at a residential treatment center, and then in a therapeutic foster home, where he remained for about two months before again violating probation and being returned to juvenile detention.

While in the care of his aunt and uncle, Aaron attended school regularly but often did not come home after school. Previous records indicate that his intellectual ability was within the above-average range. However, his academic progress had been impeded by acting-out behaviors in school and suspensions for fighting. Before his first psychological evaluation, he was court-ordered to receive outpatient psychotherapy at the local community mental health center. He also received substance abuse treatment while at the residential treatment center to address his alcohol and cannabis abuse. Aaron had no history of being prescribed psychotropic medication. He did have a history of legal involvement at the time of his initial evaluation, including charges of petty larceny, burglary, and probation violation.

At the age of 14 Aaron was administered the MMPI–A at the community mental health center as part of a court-ordered evaluation. The evaluation included an extensive clinical interview, a collateral interview with his social worker, and a review of treatment records. Aaron's MMPI–A basic scale profile at the age of 14 can be seen in Figure 15–1.

The first step in the profile interpretation was the assessment of technical validity of this protocol with the use of the validity assessment model proposed by Greene (2000). Aaron produced no item omissions on the Cannot Say (?) scale, and his *T* scores on the *VRIN* ($T = 48$) and *TRIN* ($T = 54$) scales fell well within acceptable ranges provided in the MMPI–A manual (Butcher et al., 1992). Aaron's scores on the defensiveness scales *L* ($T = 50$) and *K* ($T = 51$) indicated a relatively candid and accurate self-report. His scores on scales *F1*

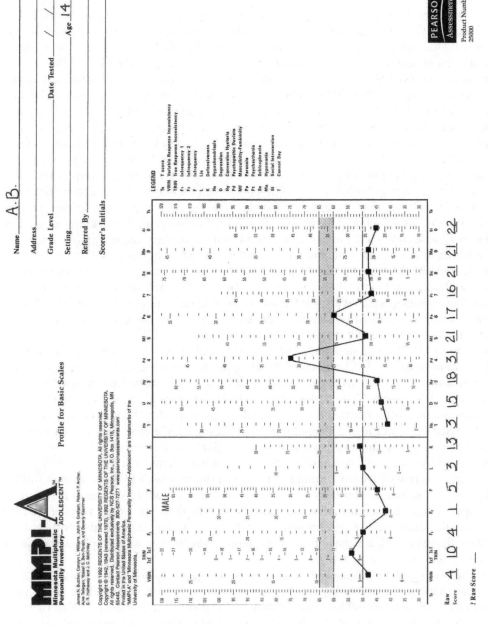

FIGURE 15–1. MMPI–A basic scale profile for Clinical Case Aaron (A.B.). MMPI–A profile sheet reprinted by permission. Copyright © 1992 by the Regents of the University of Minnesota.

($T = 50$) and $F2$ ($T = 42$) also suggested an accurate self-report without evidence of exaggerated or overreported symptoms. Thus, Aaron's validity scale configuration indicated that his responses were both consistent and accurate, and his profile was considered appropriate for meaningful interpretation.

Aaron's basic scale profile showed a single clinical range elevation on the MMPI–A basic scale *4* ($T = 75$), clarified by Harris-Lingoes subscale elevations of $T > 65$ on Pd_1 (Familial Discord) and Pd_2 (Authority Problems) that identified his negative view of family life and resentment of authority. All other basic clinical scales produced T-score values less than or equal to 60. Elevations on scale *4* are common in adolescents in criminal justice and psychiatric settings (Archer, 2005). Scores in this range are typically found for juveniles who are characterized as rebellious, hostile toward authority figures, and defiant. These adolescents often have histories of poor school adjustment and problems in school conduct, and higher elevations on scale *4* are often associated with a variety of overtly delinquent, criminal, and antisocial behaviors. Adolescents who produce scale *4* scores in ranges similar to Aaron's typically have difficulty delaying gratification and are described as impulsive, easily bored, and frustrated (Archer, 2005). The most common diagnosis for adolescents with MMPI–A profiles similar to Aaron's is Conduct Disorder. Their primary defense mechanisms involve acting out, and these acts are often not accompanied by feelings of guilt or remorse. These adolescents may create a good first impression and maintain a relatively extroverted interpersonal style, but they are often viewed by others as self-centered, egocentric, and selfish (Archer & Krishnamurthy, 2002). In detention or correctional facilities, these adolescents are more likely to commit institutional infractions and become involved in conflicts and altercations with other residents. In addition to his clinical range elevation on scale *4*, other basic scale test results produced by Aaron indicate a notable lack of emotional distress (reflected in average range scores on scales *2* and *7*).

Aaron's MMPI–A content and supplementary scale profiles from his first evaluation are shown in Figure 15–2. Aaron's content and supplementary scale profile features were relatively consistent with his basic scale profile in showing little evidence of emotional or affective distress (e.g., *A-anx*; $T = 45$; *A-dep*; $T = 47$). However, he did produce a clinical range elevation on the *MAC–R* scale ($T = 67$), which is characteristic of adolescents who are at an increased risk for drug and alcohol problems. This level of elevation is also characteristic of adolescents who are impulsive, assertive, and likely to be involved in the criminal justice system (Archer & Krishnamurthy, 2002). In contrast, Aaron's scores on the *PRO* and *ACK* scales were well within normal limits. Mixed findings such as these warrant further assessment of substance abuse issues. A review of Aaron's MMPI–A Structural Summary findings revealed the Familial Alienation dimension to be most salient, with two of the four scales in this dimension being elevated at $T \geq 60$. This finding reflects his conflicts with parental figures as well as behaviors such as running away from home, disciplinary problems in school, and externalizing actions.

Aaron was evaluated again two years later, at the age of 16. In the intervening years, he lived in a variety of placements. He spent a brief period in foster care before attending a court-ordered boot camp and subsequently living in a residential treatment center and a group home. Aaron was then placed with his adult sister and had lived with her for about a year before the most recent evaluation. During that time, he was placed in special education classes for behaviorally and emotionally disordered adolescents, but incurred several more suspensions for fighting before being expelled from school. He then began attending an alternative school for behavior-disordered adolescents, where he is currently in the 10th grade. He has continued to incur legal charges, including additional probation violations and charges

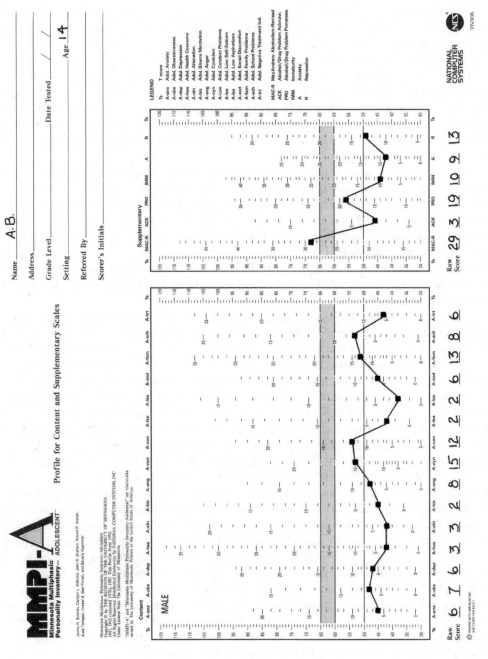

FIGURE 15–2. MMPI–A content and supplementary scale profile for Clinical Case Aaron (A.B.). MMPI–A profile sheet reprinted by permission. Copyright © 1992 by the Regents of the University of Minnesota.

259

for possession of both marijuana and firearms. After the firearms charge, his sister gave notice to the Department of Social Services that she wanted him removed from her home, and an alternative placement is now being sought. Aaron was referred by the Department of Social Services to the community mental health center for a psychological evaluation to obtain a comprehensive view of his current adjustment and secure recommendations for treatment and placement needs.

In the current evaluation, Aaron was again administered the MMPI–A, and the evaluation included the Achenbach Youth Self-Report (*YSR*; Achenbach, 1991), a clinical interview with him, a collateral interview with his sister, and a review of treatment records. His *YSR* responses acknowledged a borderline elevation in the area of Delinquent Behavior, and his MMPI–A profile was congruent with this finding. Aaron's MMPI–A basic scale profile at the age of 16 can be seen in Figure 15–3.

The validity assessment model proposed by Greene (2000) is again the first step in interpretation. Aaron produced no item omissions on the Cannot Say (?) scale, and his T scores on the *VRIN* ($T = 57$) and *TRIN* ($T = 57$) scales fell well within acceptable ranges. Aaron's scores on the defensiveness scales L ($T = 50$) and K ($T = 53$) were quite similar to his scores on these scales in his first evaluation and indicated a relatively open and honest self-report. His scores on scales $F1$ ($T = 55$) and $F2$ ($T = 42$) suggested an accurate self-report without evidence of overreported symptoms. Thus, Aaron's validity scale configuration indicated that his responses were both consistent and accurate, and his profile is considered valid for further interpretation.

In this second evaluation, Aaron's basic scale profile showed a clinical range elevation on MMPI–A clinical scale *2* ($T = 67$), but this time it also showed a clinical elevation on scale *9* ($T = 68$), creating a *4–9* code type. This is a frequently occurring code type among adolescent boys in psychiatric settings (Archer, 2005). Adolescents who endorse this pattern of responses generally have a disregard for social standards and often act out impulsively. Their interpersonal relationships are often shallow, as they often use relationships for manipulative or self-serving reasons without forming meaningful interpersonal connections (Archer & Krishnamurthy, 2002). Adolescents with this code type often receive conduct disorder diagnoses and are described by therapists as narcissistic, impatient, and demanding. In addition, a large proportion of youths with this code type report a history of drug abuse (Marks et al., 1974), consistent with the high-risk, sensation-seeking orientation of this profile type. Among adults this code type has been associated with antisocial personality disorder and a poor prognosis for change, but adolescents with this code type are likely to show more capacity for change and are thus more likely to benefit from treatment than adults (Archer, 2005). Aaron's elevated scores on scales *4* and *9* were elaborated by Harris-Lingoes subscale elevations, once again on Pd_2 (Authority Problems), but also on Ma_1 (Amorality) and Ma_2 (Psychomotor Acceleration), reflecting his heightened disregard of social norms, increased activity and risk-taking tendencies, and overall increase in behavioral dyscontrol relative to the earlier assessment. It may also be noted that Aaron's clinical scale profile again showed a lack of emotional distress (low scores of $T < 40$ on scales *2* and *7*). Furthermore, the low scale *0* score reflects an energized and extroverted presentation, and the low scale *5* score reveals an overly masculine identification with an exaggerated "tough" demeanor.

Aaron's MMPI–A content and supplementary scale profiles from his second evaluation are shown in Figure 15–4. Aaron's content and supplementary scale profile features in this second administration are markedly different from those seen in his first evaluation two years ago. He is now acknowledging some internal experiences of distress, including marginal levels of anxiety (*A-anx*; $T = 63$) and depression (*A-dep*; $T = 62$). This also contrasts with the

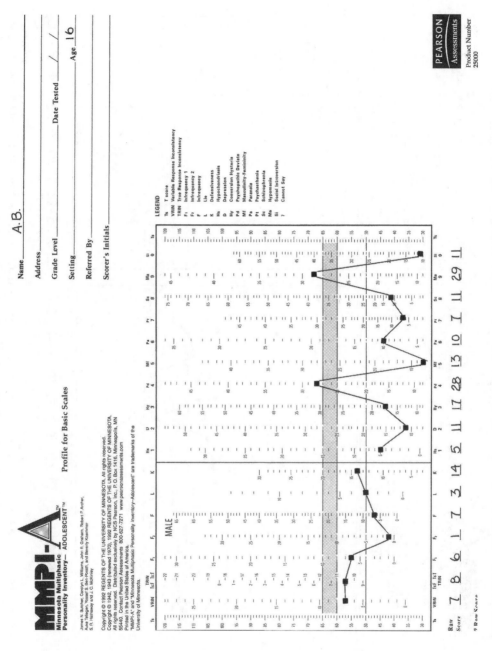

FIGURE 15-3. MMPI–A basic scale profile for Clinical Case Aaron (A.B.). MMPI–A profile sheet reprinted by permission. Copyright © 1992 by the Regents of the University of Minnesota.

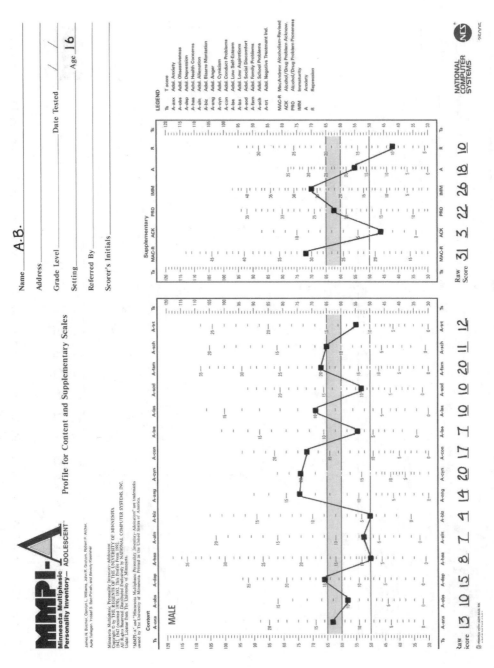

FIGURE 15–4. MMP-A content and supplementary scale profile for Clinical Case Aaron (A.B.). MMPI-A profile sheet reprinted by permission. Copyright © 1992 by the Regents of the University of Minnesota.

current clinical scale profile, but can be understood in terms of the more direct and obvious content scale items being more amenable to endorsement of difficulty. Consistent with the poor behavioral controls and interpersonal manipulativeness suggested by his *4–9* code type, Aaron also produced content scale elevations on scales assessing anger (*A-ang*; $T = 75$) and cynicism (*A-cyn*; $T = 74$). Furthermore, Aaron acknowledged a greater number of problems than he did in his first evaluation two years ago, in both school and family life (*A-sch*; $T = 65$ and *A-fam*; $T = 66$), as well as conduct problems (*A-con*; $T = 72$). In addition, his responses are now more indicative of a lack of goal orientation and achievement motivation (*A-las*; $T = 74$). As in his first MMPI–A profile, Aaron again produced a moderate clinical range elevation ($T = 62$) on the *MAC–R* scale ($T = 72$), and this time he also produced a marginal elevation on *PRO*, suggesting that substance abuse emerges more clearly than before as a significant area of concern for him. An elevation on the *IMM* scale ($T = 70$) underscores the acting-out components of this profile by revealing characteristics of egocentricity, externalization, defiance, and resistance.

Aaron's MMPI–A Structural Summary results were illuminating in revealing the continuities and changes between the first and second assessment. Similarly to the first profile, Familial Alienation emerged as the most salient factor, this time with 75% (vs. the previous 50%) of its scales elevated. In addition, the Disinhibition/Excitatory Potential dimension was significant, with 50% of its member scales elevated at $T \geq 60$, reflecting considerable impulsivity, disciplinary problems, conflicts with adult figures and peers, and wide-ranging acting out. Some increases in the Immaturity dimension (33% vs. the previous 13%) and General Maladjustment (13% vs. the previous 4%) are noteworthy in denoting increased interpersonal and emotional struggles, although these latter dimensions are not prominent enough to define the profile description.

CASE SUMMARY

The MMPI–A findings presented here are consistent with a conduct-disordered adolescent exhibiting worsening behavior problems. Antisocial attitudes evident in his first administration persisted in his second profile and are now accompanied by a greater tendency to act out in an impulsive manner. Coupled with his history of substance abuse and delinquency, these characteristics suggest that Aaron is at very high risk for continuing behavior problems and involvement with the criminal justice system. There are some signs in his current profile, however, that provide guidance on how to approach this adolescent in treatment. Aaron is now more apt to acknowledge his school, family, and conduct problems, making these issues more accessible for therapeutic intervention. In addition, he is now showing some signs of emotional distress (albeit marginally), which may increase the likelihood that he will be motivated to engage in the therapeutic intervention effort. Given his age and lack of family willing to take custody of Aaron, it is recommended that he be placed in a therapeutic foster home and referred for individual psychotherapy. Aaron is still under court supervision under his probation agreement, and he should be held to strict behavioral standards in school and at home, to include regular random drug testing. Aaron may also benefit from mentoring services, preferably from an older male figure who can form a stable relationship with him and encourage him in his schoolwork and interpersonal functioning.

REFERENCES

Achenbach, T. M. (1991). *Manual for the Child Behavior Checklist/4–18 and 1991 profile.* Burlington, VT: University of Vermont Department of Psychiatry.

Alperin, J. J., Archer, R. P., & Coates, G. D. (1996). Development and effects of an MMPI-A K-correction procedure. *Journal of Personality Assessment, 67,* 155–168.

Archer, R. P. (1987). *Using the MMPI with adolescents.* Hillsdale, NJ: Lawrence Erlbaum Associates.

Archer, R. P. (2003). *MMPI-A Interpretive System (Version 3)* [Computer software]. Tampa, FL: Psychological Assessment Resources.

Archer, R. P. (2005). *MMPI-A: Assessing Adolescent Psychopathology* (3rd ed.). Mahwah, NJ: Lawrence Erlbaum Associates.

Archer, R. P., Belevich, J. K. S., & Elkins, D. E. (1994). Item-level and scale-level factor structures of the MMPI-A. *Journal of Personality Assessment, 62,* 332–345.

Archer, R. P., & Elkins, D. E. (1999). Identification of random responding on the MMPI-A. *Journal of Personality Assessment, 73,* 407–421.

Archer, R. P., & Gordon, R. A. (1991, August). Use of content scales with adolescents: Past and future practices. In R. C. Colligan (Chair), *MMPI and MMPI-2 supplementary scales and profile interpretation—content scales revisited.* Symposium conducted at the annual convention of the American Psychological Association, San Francisco.

Archer, R. P., Gordon, R. A., Anderson, G. L., & Giannetti, R. A. (1989). MMPI special scale clinical correlates for adolescent inpatients. *Journal of Personality Assessment, 53,* 654–664.

Archer, R. P., Gordon, R. A., Giannetti, R. A., & Singles, J. M. (1988). MMPI scale clinical correlates for adolescent inpatients. *Journal of Personality Assessment, 52,* 707–721.

Archer, R. P., & Jacobson, J. M. (1993). Are critical items "critical" for the MMPI-A? *Journal of Personality Assessment, 61,* 547–556.

Archer, R. P., & Krishnamurthy, R. (1994). A structural summary approach for the MMPI-A: Development and empirical correlates. *Journal of Personality Assessment, 63,* 554–573.

Archer, R. P., & Krishnamurthy, R. (2002). *Essentials of MMPI-A assessment.* New York: Wiley.

Archer, R. P., Krishnamurthy, R., & Jacobson, J. M. (1994). *MMPI-A casebook.* Tampa, FL: Psychological Assessment Resources.

Archer, R. P., Maruish, M., Imhof, E. A., & Piotrowski, C. (1991). Psychological test usage with adolescent clients: 1990 survey findings. *Professional Psychology: Research and Practice, 22,* 247–252.

Archer, R. P., Pancoast, D. L., & Gordon, R. A. (1994). The development of the MMPI-A immaturity (IMM) scale: Findings for normal and clinical samples. *Journal of Personality Assessment, 62,* 145–156.

Baer, R. A., Ballenger, J., Berry, D. T. R., & Wetter, M. W. (1997). Detection of random responding on the MMPI-A. *Journal of Personality Assessment, 68,* 139–151.

Ball, J. C., & Carroll, D. (1960). Analysis of MMPI Cannot Say scores in an adolescent population. *Journal of Clinical Psychology, 16,* 30–31.

Ben-Porath, Y. S., Hostetler, K., Butcher, J. N., & Graham, J. R. (1989). New subscales for the MMPI-2 Social Introversion (Si) scale. *Psychological Assessment, 1,* 169–174.

Black, K. (1994). A critical review of the MMPI-A. *Child Assessment News, 4,* 9–12.

Butcher, J. N. (1987). Computerized clinical and personality assessment using the MMPI. In J. N. Butcher (Ed.), *Computerized psychological assessment: A practitioner's guide.* New York: Basic Books.

Butcher, J. N., Dahlstrom, W. G., Graham, J. R., Tellegen, A., & Kaemmer, B. (1989). *Minnesota Multiphasic Personality Inventory–2 (MMPI–2): Manual for administration and scoring.* Minneapolis: University of Minnesota Press.

Butcher, J. N., & Williams, C. L. (1992). *The Minnesota Report: Adolescent Interpretive System* [Computer software]. Minneapolis: National Computer Systems.

Butcher, J. N., Williams, C. L., Graham, J. R., Archer, R. P., Tellegen, A., Ben-Porath, Y. S., et al. (1992). *Minnesota Multiphasic Personality Inventory–Adolescent (MMPI-A): Manual for administration, scoring, and interpretation.* Minneapolis: University of Minnesota Press.

Dahlstrom, W. G., Welsh, G. S., & Dahlstrom, L. E. (1972). *An MMPI handbook: A guide to use in clinical practice and research*. Minneapolis: University of Minnesota Press.

Forbey, J. D. (June, 2003). *A review of the MMPI-A research literature*. Paper presented at the 38th Annual Symposium on Recent Developments in the Use of the MMPI–2 and MMPI-A, Minneapolis, MN.

Forbey, J. D., & Ben-Porath, Y. S. (1998). *A critical item set for the MMPI-A (MMPI–2/MMPI-A test reports #4)*. Minneapolis: University of Minnesota Press.

Gallucci, N. T. (1997). Correlates of MMPI-A substance abuse scales. *Assessment, 4*, 87–94.

Graham, J. R. (2000). *MMPI–2: Assessing personality and psychopathology* (3rd ed.). New York: Oxford University Press.

Greene, R. L. (2000). *MMPI–2: An interpretive manual* (2nd ed.). Boston: Allyn & Bacon.

Harris, R. E., & Lingoes, J. C. (1955). *Subscales for the MMPI: An aid to profile interpretation* [Mimeographed materials]. Department of Psychiatry, University of California School of Medicine and the Langley Porter Clinic.

Hathaway, S. R., & McKinley, J. C. (1940). A multiphasic personality schedule (Minnesota): I. Construction of the schedule. *Journal of Psychology, 14*, 73–84.

Koss, M., & Butcher, J. M. (1973). A comparison of psychiatric patients' self-report with other sources of clinical information. *Journal of Research in Personality, 7*, 225–236.

Krishnamurthy, R. (2005). *Minnesota Multiphasic Personality Inventory–Adolescent*. In J. J. Kramer and J. C. Connelly (Eds.), *Test critiques* (Vol. XI, pp. 281–290). Austin, TX: PRO-ED.

Lachar, D., Klinge, V., & Grissell, J. L. (1976). Relative accuracy of automated MMPI narratives generated from adult norm and adolescent norm profiles. *Journal of Consulting and Clinical Psychology, 44*, 20–24.

Lachar, D., & Wrobel, T. A. (1979). Validating clinicians' hunches: Construction of a new MMPI critical item set. *Journal of Consulting and Clinical Psychology, 47*, 277–284.

Lachar, D., & Wrobel, T. A. (1990, August). Predicting adolescent MMPI correlates: Comparative efficacy of self-report and other-informant assessment. In R. C. Colligan (Chair), *The MMPI and adolescents: Historical perspectives, current research, and future developments*. A symposium presented at the American Psychological Association, Boston.

Loevinger, J. (1976). *Ego development: Conceptions and theories*. San Francisco: Jossey-Bass.

Lubin, B., Larsen, R. M., & Matarazzo, J. D. (1984). Patterns of psychological test usage in the United States: 1935–1982. *American Psychologist, 39*, 451–454.

Lubin, B., Larsen, R. M., Matarazzo, J. D., & Seever, M. F. (1985). Psychological test usage patterns in five professional settings. *American Psychologist, 40*, 857–861.

Lubin, B., Wallis, R. R., & Paine, C. (1971). Patterns of psychological test usage in the United States: 1935–1969. *Professional Psychology, 2*, 70–74.

MacAndrew, C. (1965). The differentiation of male alcoholic out-patients from nonalcoholic psychiatric patients by means of the MMPI. *Quarterly Journal of Studies on Alcohol, 26*, 238–246.

Marks, P. A., & Briggs, P. F. (1972). Adolescent norm tables for the MMPI. In W. G. Dahlstrom, G. S. Welsh, & L. E. Dahlstrom, *An MMPI handbook: Vol. 1. Clinical interpretation* (rev. ed., pp. 388–399). Minneapolis: University of Minnesota Press.

Marks, P. A., & Lewak, R. W. (1991). *The Marks MMPI Adolescent Feedback and Treatment Report* [Computer software]. Los Angeles: Western Psychological Services.

Marks, P. A., Seeman, W., & Haller, D. L. (1974). *The actuarial use of the MMPI with adolescents and adults*. Baltimore: Williams & Wilkins.

Millon, T. (1993). *Millon Adolescent Clinical Inventory manual*. Minneapolis: National Computer Systems.

Morey, L. C. (2000, March). *PAI-Adolescent version: Overview of progress to date*. Unpublished report.

Piaget, J. (1975). The intellectual development of the adolescent. In A. H. Esman (Ed.), *The psychology of adolescence: Essential readings* (pp. 104–108). New York: International Universities Press.

Piotrowski, C., & Keller, J. W. (1989). Psychological testing in outpatient mental health facilities: A national study. *Professional Psychology: Research and Practice, 20*, 423–425.

Reynolds, W. (1998). *Adolescent Psychopathology Scale*. Austin, TX: PRO-ED.

Schinka, J. A., Elkins, D. E., & Archer, R. P. (1998). Effects of psychopathology and demographic characteristics on MMPI-A scale scores. *Journal of Pesonality Assessment, 71,* 295–305.

Sherwood, N. E., Ben-Porath, Y. S., & Williams, C. L. (1997). The MMPI-A content component scales:
Development, psychometric characteristics and clinical application. *MMPI–2/MMPI-A Test Report 3.*
Minneapolis: University of Minnesota Press.

Stein, L. A. R., & Graham, J. R. (1999). Detecting fake-good MMPI–A profiles in a correctional facility.
Psychological Assessment, 11(3), 386–395.

Stein, L. A. , Graham, J. R., & Williams, C. L. (1995). Detecting fake-bad MMPI-A profiles. *Journal of Personality Assessment, 65,* 415–427.

Weed, N. C., Butcher, J. N., & Williams, C. L. (1994). Development of the MMPI-A alcohol/drug problem scales. *Journal of Studies on Alcohol, 55,* 296–302.

Welsh, G. S. (1956). Factor dimensions A and R. In G. S. Welsh & W. G. Dahlstrom (Eds.), *Basic reading
on the MMPI in psychology and medicine* (pp. 264–281). Minneapolis: University of Minnesota Press.

Wetter, M. W., Baer, R. A., Berry, D. T. R., Smith, G. T., & Larsen, L. H. (1992). Sensitivity of MMPI–2
validity scales to random responding and malingering. *Psychological Assessment, 4,* 369–374.

Wiederholt, J. L., & Bryant, B. R. (2001). *Gray Oral Reading Test* (4th ed.) (GORT-IV). Austin, TX:
PRO-ED.

Wilkinson, G. S. (1993). *The Wide Range Achievement Test administration manual* (1993 ed.). Wilmington,
DE: Wide Range.

Williams, C. L., & Butcher, J. N. (1989). An MMPI study of adolescents: II. Verification and limitations
of code type classifications. *Psychological Assessment: A Journal of Consulting and Clinical Psychology, 1,* 260–265.

Williams, C. L., Butcher, J. N., Ben-Porath, Y. S., & Graham, J. R. (1992). *MMPI-A content scales: Assessing psychopathology in adolescents.* Minneapolis: University of Minnesota Press.

Wimbish, L. G. (1984). *The importance of appropriate norms for the computerized interpretation of adolescent MMPI profiles.* Unpublished doctoral dissertation, Ohio State University, Columbus.

Wrobel, N. H., & Lachar, D. (1992). Refining adolescent MMPI interpretations: Moderating effects of
gender in descriptions from parents. *Psychological Assessment, 4,* 375–381.

16

CLINICAL UTILITY OF TWO CHILD-ORIENTED INVENTORIES: THE MILLON PRE-ADOLESCENT CLINICAL INVENTORY™ AND THE MILLON ADOLESCENT CLINICAL INVENTORY™

Robert Tringone
Schneider Children's Hospital

Theodore Millon
Institute for Advanced Studies in Personology and Psychopathology

John Kamp
Pearson Assessments

The major tenets of Millon's biosocial learning theory of personality development were first outlined in his *Modern Psychopathology* (1969) text. Subsequent Millon *Disorders of Personality* volumes (1981, 1996) extrapolated on the core components of the theory: 1) three primary polarities from which, combinatorially, the recognized DSM and other personality disorders are derived; 2) eight clinical domains that form the classification system with all personality disorders exhibiting prototypal features within each domain; and 3) perpetuating processes—those behaviors, thought patterns, or affective expressions that a person exhibits in interactions with the outside world that reinforce his or her underlying perceptions, beliefs, and experiences. With the *Toward a New Personology* text (1990), the theory developed and expanded into an evolutionary model, and an entire system of thinking emerged that is most often referred to as the clinical science of personology. Millon (2004) articulated the components that would be necessary to forge a lasting clinical science. The structure of this entity would include a foundation in the universal laws of nature, a comprehensive explanatory psychological theory, a derivable taxonomic classification system, a set of theoretically guided and empirically grounded assessment instruments, and therapeutic interventions that logically follow from those test results and guide coordinated treatment efforts.

The Millon clinical inventories are embedded within this system. Since the 1970s there have been three versions of the adult Millon Clinical Multiaxial Inventory (1977, 1987, 1994). Since the 1980s there have been two versions of the adolescent test (Millon Adolescent Personality Inventory, 1982; Millon Adolescent Clinical Inventory, 1993), and now there is an instrument for the pre-adolescent age group, the Millon Pre-Adolescent Clinical Inventory (2005). This chapter provides a context for considering personality patterns and clinical syndromes with children and adolescents, describes the construction and validation of the M-PACI and MACI tests, discusses some of their key similarities and differences that appear to be grounded in developmental processes, and provides case examples for each test.

TEMPERAMENT AND EMERGING PERSONALITY PATTERNS

Millon's personality theory (1969, 1981, 1990) distinguishes the Millon "family" of inventories from other available measures. These tests, MCMI-III, MACI, and M-PACI, have separate personality pattern scales and clinical syndrome scales. Therefore, an underlying assumption is that clinically significant conditions should be viewed in the context of the person's personality, because these problems are often grounded in early expressions of stable personality traits (Kamp, Millon, & Tringone, unpublished manuscript). In many respects, a child's personality style evolves from his or her inherent temperament, and recent articles link adult personality styles with early temperament (Mervielde, De Clerq, De Fruyt, & Van Leeuwen, 2005; Shiner, 2005).

Over the past four decades, an impressive literature base has developed regarding children's temperament and its role in the development of personality as well as mood and behavior disorders. According to Frick (2004), temperament has certain core features: 1) it is typically seen as an inherited or biologically based process, 2) it is evident early in life, and 3) it is stable over time. The infant arrives in this world with a certain set of dispositions that can be seen as relative supplies of positive or negative affectivity valences. These valences predispose the infant to be expressive toward and responsive to their environment in particular ways (e.g., activity, amplitude, vigor, etc.). Their actions, in turn, elicit counter-reactions, and, with time, reciprocally reinforcing patterns take hold. As the child grows, his/her unique abilities, energies, and interests guide him/her toward preferred ways of gratifying his/her wishes and desires in addition to learning effective ways of avoiding discomforts and distress. Experiences with one's parents, siblings, peers, and other significant figures further shape the child's recognition of what actions are permitted and rewarding as well as those that elicit negative reactions or consequences. With repeated reinforcements, the child develops a repertoire of certain behaviors and reactions that begin to form his or her personality or, in Millon's words, those "ingrained and habitual ways of psychological functioning that emerge from the individual's entire developmental history, and which, over time, come to characterize the child's 'style'" (1981, p. 4).

The child's temperament and emerging personality style interact with their environment. The notion of "goodness of fit" comes into play regarding two important dimensions: adaptability versus vulnerability and protective factors versus risk factors. Adaptability pertains to those characteristics that are a "good fit" with the child's environment. These features may include a calm demeanor, an agreeable social style, a confident sense of self, and others, as long as they are complementary to, in particular, the family system. Vulnerability, on the other hand, speaks to those characteristics that do not enhance one's sense of security, either about themselves or to others, or serve as a buffer to stress. Certain personality styles appear to be associated with sufficient coping resources or resiliency to be able to withstand stress or respond to it in an effective manner, whereas other personality styles wilt under the weight or potentially perpetuate their troubles. Whether one is looking at temperament or more complex emerging personality styles, it is generally recognized that certain characteristics may either increase or decrease the probability of developing a disorder or may mediate or moderate the impact of stress factors in this process (Compas, Connor-Smith, & Jaser, 2004). Significant work has been done in the areas of linking temperament features to common childhood problems. For example, comprehensive review articles have summarized that anxiety disorders appear to be related to high negative affectivity and high physiological hyperarousal (Lonigan, Vasey, Phillips, & Hazen, 2004), depressive disorders are associated with high negative affectivity and low positive affectivity (Clark, Watson, & Mineka, 1994), and conduct disorders are the outcome of a complex array of features that include a difficult temperament, high or low levels of affective reactivity, low levels of fearful inhibitions, high levels of callous-unemotional traits, and poor emotion regulation (Frick & Morris, 2004). Comparable patterns have been reported regarding personality disorders and co-morbid Axis I syndromes. Analyses using the Millon inventories support these findings. For example, the MCMI-III Avoidant, Dependent, and Borderline personality pattern scales show high correlations with the Anxiety Disorder and Dysthymic Disorder scales (Millon, Millon, & Davis, 1994). In a similar manner, MACI and M-PACI Inhibited personality pattern scales have demonstrated strong correlations with their respective anxiety and depression scales. In addition, their Unruly personality pattern scales show high correlations with disruptive behavior related scales.

MILLON INVENTORIES: STAGES OF DEVELOPMENT

All Millon inventories have followed the construction and validation sequence proposed by Loevinger (1957) and Jackson (1970). In her classic monograph, Loevinger suggested substantive, structural, and external stages of test construction and validation that could be followed sequentially. Her schema incorporates the notions of Cronbach and Meehl (1955) on construct validity and of Campbell and Fiske (1959) on convergent and discriminant validity. The intentions of adhering to these principles are to enhance test reliability and validity as well as to maximize its efficiency in measuring personality characteristics and clinical syndromes.

Millon's personality theory is the guiding theory and substantive foundation for all Millon inventories. As noted above, initially proposed as a biosocial learning theory (Millon 1969, 1981), the theory itself has evolved and is now formulated as an evolutionary model (Millon, 1990; Millon & Davis, 1996). At both levels, the theory postulates three primary polarities—self-other, active-passive, and pleasure-pain—that are central to understanding personality organization from this perspective. When personality patterns are conceptualized as learned strategies to secure positive reinforcement and minimize punishment, the self-other polarity represents the *source* to which the individual turns to enhance his or her life and gain satisfaction or to avoid psychic pain and discomfort. Those who look to themselves for gratification and pain avoidance are termed *independent* on the self-other polarity. Those who look to others are termed *dependent*. The term *ambivalent* can be applied to describe those who are conflicted about whether to look to self or to others.

The active-passive polarity represents the *behavior* employed to maximize rewards and minimize pain. Active personalities typically take the initiative and interact with their environment to achieve gratification and avoid distress. Passive personalities are much more reserved and maintain a more accommodating stance vis-à-vis their environment. Finally, the pleasure-pain polarity represents the *nature* of the response elicited from others, which can be positive or negative.

The tripartite model generates and defines personality patterns in a logical and systematic manner when configurations are generated across the three polarities. For the MACI test, the 12 personality pattern scales do not represent personality "disorders" per se because personality disturbances in the adolescent population, on top of their inherent dispositions and life-shaping experiences, may be partially related to their attempts to adjust to and negotiate the many internal and external changes and challenges they face. Adolescent personalities are still evolving and remain malleable to a degree, although evidence is gaining that late adolescents, in particular, demonstrate a high degree of stability in their personalities, and this enduring feature may contribute to significant problems as an adult (Chanen, Jackson, McGorry, Allot, Clarkson, & Yuen, 2004). On the other hand, pre-adolescent personalities appear to be less differentiated and may be more reactive or responsive to influences from their environment. The M-PACI test reflects these notions, inasmuch as it measures seven basic personality patterns. Table 16.1 illustrates the correspondences between the respective personality pattern scales measured by these instruments.

Once the test constructs have been determined, items must be written that illustrate the different facets of these constructs. The item pool must be broad and comprehensive, yet also written at a language level appropriate for the target age group. The MACI test, for instance, has been estimated to be at a sixth-grade reading level, and the M-PACI test has been measured at a third-grade reading level. All of these steps must be taken to satisfy criteria for the theoretical-substantive phase.

The second validation phase, relabeled "internal-structural," pertains to the test's adherence to its underlying theory, where the relationships between the items and scales should be consistent with the theory's predictions. Typically, analyses are conducted regarding the internal consistency of the scales, the correlations between scales, and the test's underlying factor structure. Finally, the third stage, relabeled "external-criterion," requires the comparison of the new test's scores with other measures that have included clinician diagnoses as well as other self-report inventories.

TABLE 16.1.
MACI and M-PACI Test Personality Pattern Scales

Theoretical position	MACI	M-PACI
Passive detached	Introversive	
Active detached	Inhibited	Inhibited
Passive pain	Doleful	
Passive dependent	Submissive	Submissive
Active dependent	Dramatizing	Outgoing
Passive independent	Egotistic	Confident
Active independent	Unruly	Unruly
Passive ambivalent	Conforming	Conforming
Active ambivalent	Oppositional	
Passive discordant	Self-demeaning	
Active discordant	Forceful	
Severe ambivalent	Borderline tendency	Unstable

THE M-PACI TEST

The Millon Pre-Adolescent Clinical Inventory (M-PACI; Millon, Tringone, Millon, & Grossman, 2005) is a multidimensional self-report inventory for use with 9- to 12-year olds seen in clinical settings. It consists of 97 true/false items and has 14 *profile scales* grouped into two sets: Emerging Personality Patterns and Current Clinical Signs. Scores on these scales are reported as base rate (BR) scores, scaled to reflect the relative prevalence of the characteristics they measure. In addition to the profile scales, there are two M-PACI *response validity indicators*. Brief descriptions of the M-PACI profile scales are given in Table 16.2.

With its 14 profile scales, the M-PACI test provides a broad assessment of pre-adolescent psychological issues, distinguishing it from the single-construct assessment instruments that are commonly used with children this age. As would be expected for a multidimensional clinical assessment tool, the M-PACI test includes measures of clinical symptoms that are most prevalent among pre-adolescents. In addition, by measuring emerging personality patterns, the Inventory's reach and usefulness are extended beyond the realm of symptoms alone. The inclusion of the personality scales reflects the view that, even among pre-adolescents, clinically significant psychological problems are often grounded in early expressions of stable personality traits that may be forming.

Specific goals during the development of the M-PACI test were to ensure that most 9- to 12-year-olds would be able to understand the items and complete the Inventory on their own in a reasonable amount of time. Items were crafted to be short and simple, yet interesting and phrased in the language that pre-adolescents use. Most 9- to 12-year-olds can complete the Inventory in 20 minutes or less.

The M-PACI test can help mental health professionals identify, predict, and understand a broad range of psychological issues that are common among 9- to 12-year-olds seen in clinical settings. These settings include private practices, residential treatment facilities, public mental health centers, and family guidance clinics. The Inventory is also appropriate for use in school settings when a child has been referred for evaluation and/or counseling for apparent behavioral and/or emotional problems. Administration of the M-PACI test can be beneficial at many points during the assessment and treatment process: as part of the initial clinical assessment, to gauge progress and reevaluate issues during the course of treatment, and as a treatment outcome measure.

INVENTORY DEVELOPMENT, RELIABILITY, AND VALIDITY

Development of the M-PACI test began with the construction of a research version consisting of 135 items targeting 18 substantive constructs. The normative sample consisted of almost 300 pre-adolescents at more than 50 clinical research sites across the United States. The research subjects were also rated by their clinicians in terms of their most prominent and second most prominent personality patterns, expressed concerns, and clinical signs, and many subjects completed either the Behavior Assessment System for Children: Self-Report of Personality Form C (BASC SRP-C; Reynolds & Kamphaus, 1998), the Children's Depression Inventory (CDI; Kovacs, 2001), or the Revised Children's Manifest Anxiety Scale (RCMAS; Reynolds & Richmond, 2000). Following an iterative process, the inventory was reduced to its 97 items and 14 profile scales. See Table 16.2.

The M-PACI profile scales are relatively short, with between 7 and 12 items each. Their internal consistency values, measured with the coefficient alpha statistic, are moderately

TABLE 16.2.
Descriptions of the 14 M-PACI Profile Scales

Emerging personality patterns scales	*Descriptions*
1 Confident	Passive Independent pattern
	Possess a superior self-image, have an excessive appreciation of their self-worth, believe they are special or have special talents, enjoy positive attention
2 Outgoing	Active Dependent pattern
	Solicit attention and affection, tend to be gregarious and sociable, have high energy and are spirited, often have large social networks, emphasize social appearance
3 Conforming	Passive Ambivalent pattern
	Conscientious, disciplined, responsible, rule-governed, serious-minded, and often emotionally constricted, suppress anger, achievement-oriented
4 Submissive	Passive Dependent pattern
	Attach themselves to others in order to assure themselves of affection, protection, and security; subordinate desires avoid conflicts or taking risks; cooperative; noncompetitive
5 Inhibited	Active Detached pattern
	Limited capacity to experience pleasure, but anticipate pain, tend to be socially ill at ease, apprehensive and sensitive to rejection, may have few friends, and have trouble "fitting in"
6 Unruly	Active Independent pattern
	Project confidence and self-assurance, have learned to mistrust others, typically restless and impulsive, seek immediate gratification, shortsighted, externalize responsibility for their actions
7 Unstable	Conflict Across Polarities
	Experience persistent and intense psychic pain and are more vulnerable to overall psychological problems, less integrated in terms of their personality organization and are less effective in coping with life's demands; notable are their labile moods, unpredictable behaviors, wavering thoughts, "split" object relations, and identity confusion; may engage in self-abusive behaviors

Current clinical signs scales	*Descriptions*
A Anxiety/fears	High scores
	Associated with somatic and cognitive features of an anxiety disorder, may have specific fears or worries
B Attention deficits	High scores
	Associated with attention and concentration issues as well as fidgetiness; suggests impact in the classroom and at home
C Obsessions/compulsions	High scores
	Indicate child has endorsed items associated with both obsessions and compulsions; child identifies some degree of subjective distress
D Conduct problems	High scores
	Represent pattern of noncompliance, poor frustration tolerance, aggressive outbursts, and impaired judgment; considerable underlying anger present
E Disruptive behaviors	High scores
	Associated with poor impulse control, anger, and short temper; often do not "think before they act"; may identify impulsive component with AD/HD
F Depressive moods	High scores
	Indicate presence of sad mood, thoughts of death, despair, and loneliness; clinician must assess time frame and identify stressors
G Reality distortions	High scores
	Identify children who are having unusual perceptual experiences and cognitive distortions; hallucinations or paranoid ideation may be present; child identifies confusion and/or some degree of subjective distress

high, given that the statistic is partly a function of scale length (i.e., a mean of .72 and a median of .71 across the 14 scales). In regard to external validity, the convergent validity coefficients between the M-PACI profile scale BR scores and clinician ratings are robust (i.e., a mean of .38 and a median of .39 across the 14 scales). The M-PACI profile scales also show strong and coherent correlation patterns with the broad-based (BASC-SRP) and single-construct (CDI and RCMAS) measures that were administered.

RESPONSE VALIDITY INDICATORS

Two M-PACI scales provide information about the pre-adolescent's test-taking approach. The first scale, labeled Invalidity, consists of four items that ask the child whether he or she is responding to the items in an honest manner. Two items are keyed True and two items are keyed False in order to detect all-True or all-False response patterns or totally random response patterns. An Invalidity score of 0 is considered *valid*, a score of 1 is considered *questionable*, and a score of 2 or more is considered *invalid*.

Readers who are familiar with the Millon inventories will recall that the MCMI-III and MACI tests employ a set of Modifying Indices that trigger BR adjustments for many scales. No adjustments of this kind are made on the M-PACI test. Instead, a different validity indicator, labeled Response Negativity, was devised. This validity measure consists of 48 items: 34 True-keyed items that have obvious negative or undesirable content and 14 items with obvious positive or desirable content that are False-keyed. Each keyed response adds one raw score point to the scale; therefore, it has a raw score range of 0 to 48. These raw scores are converted to percentile scores based on the raw score frequency distribution of the entire M-PACI normative sample. Very high scores reflect response patterns that are both negative and nonspecific, implying a broad range of problem areas. Very low scores, on the other hand, reflect more positive impressions. Percentile scores that fall within the average range (i.e., 25th to 75th percentiles) suggest it is probable that the child responded to the inventory in an honest or open manner, neither underreporting nor overreporting problems. The more a percentile score diverges, however, from the average range (more specifically the top 10% or the bottom 10%), the more probable it is that some form of distortion has taken place. It is up to the clinician to assess what condition(s) or motivation(s) may have contributed to a potentially exaggerated negative or positive pattern.

INTERPRETIVE PROCESS

M-PACI test interpretation follows a multiple-step sequence. Table 16.3 provides a quick summary.

First, the clinician should review all relevant background information about the child. With the pre-adolescent population, an emphasis should be placed on family interactions, peer relations, and academic achievement, with a thorough look at the child's developmental progressions in all spheres. Second, the M-PACI test interpretation itself should begin with determining whether the profile appears to be reliable and valid. The two response validity indicators, Invalidity and Response Negativity, will provide that information and suggest whether any test-taking distortions may have occurred. The next step is to gauge the overall level of severity. Among the Emerging Personality Patterns scales, the Unstable scale is the primary indicator, because elevations (i.e., BR ≥ 75) are associated with poten-

TABLE 16.3.

Step-by-Step Process for Interpreting M-PACI Test Results

1. Review client information
2. Assess response validity
3. Gauge overall level of severity
4. Identify emerging personality patterns
5. Identify current clinical signs
6. Perform profile integration
7. Review noteworthy responses
8. Integrate M-PACI results with other assessment data

tially severe problems, especially when this scale is the highest one in the set. Among the Current Clinical Signs scales, the Reality Distortions scale must be considered, because an elevation here may suggest the presence of a psychotic disorder. In addition, a large number of high scores may suggest a complex case that will require prioritization of treatment targets. For example, subjects who elevate on the Unstable scale may also elevate on "Internalizing" scales (e.g., Anxiety/Fears, Depressive Moods) as well as "Externalizing" scales (e.g., Conduct Problems, Disruptive Behaviors) at the same time. The fourth step involves identifying the most prominent of the Emerging Personality Patterns scales. Although some profiles may reveal a single scale elevation, it is more common to encounter two prominent scale elevations. In these instances, the interpretation should focus on the *configuration* of the scale scores. The highest scale will identify the primary personality style, and the next highest scale will help define a subtype of that style. After interpreting the Emerging Personality Patterns scale set, the next step is to assess the Current Clinical Signs scales. The scales in this set identify symptom clusters that correspond to many DSM-IV Axis I disorders or conditions (DSM IV; American Psychiatric Association, 1994). The M-PACI test, however, does not offer diagnostic impressions. It is believed that the clinician should utilize these results to help *understand* the child's patterns of thoughts, feelings, and behaviors rather than employ them to pathologize the child's condition and derive diagnostic labels. The M-PACI profile will provide valuable information, and the computer-generated interpretive reports will integrate the results from the scale sets. Nonetheless, an item-by-item review should be conducted, with special emphasis on the Noteworthy Responses. Clinically relevant items may be endorsed, but not lead to a scale elevation. Moreover, some Noteworthy Response items are not a member of a scale. Finally, because no test can stand on its own, it is imperative that the clinician integrate M-PACI test results with the child's history and data from other instruments or techniques that may have been administered.

M-PACI CASE EXAMPLE: 10-YEAR-OLD FEMALE WITH ATTENTION PROBLEMS AND ANXIETY

Sara, a 10-year-old female, was referred for psychological testing because of academic delays, attention problems, and frequent somatic complaints that contributed to school absences. Sara lived with her parents and eight-year-old brother. A history of the paternal side of her family was notable for various members with learning and attention problems, and the maternal family history was remarkable for anxiety and depression.

During the evaluation, Sara was able to establish a positive rapport with the examiner. She was very cooperative and conscientious in her work efforts, although she was hesitant to take chances if she did not know an answer to a question or problem. Her attention span was good while she was interacting with the examiner; however, a popular continuous performance test (Test of Variables of Attention) detected significant problems with sustained attention. Sara's overall intellectual abilities were estimated to reside within the average range, and academic achievement testing did not reveal learning disabilities. Parent-report measures were indicative of significant internalizing problems, particularly anxiety and somatic complaints.

Sara's M-PACI profile is shown in Figure 16–1. She received a score of 0 on the Invalidity scale and scored at the 85th percentile on the Response Negativity scale. The latter score suggests a possible tendency toward overreporting, but not to an extent that would warrant concern about the validity of the test results. At the same time, it is apparent that she

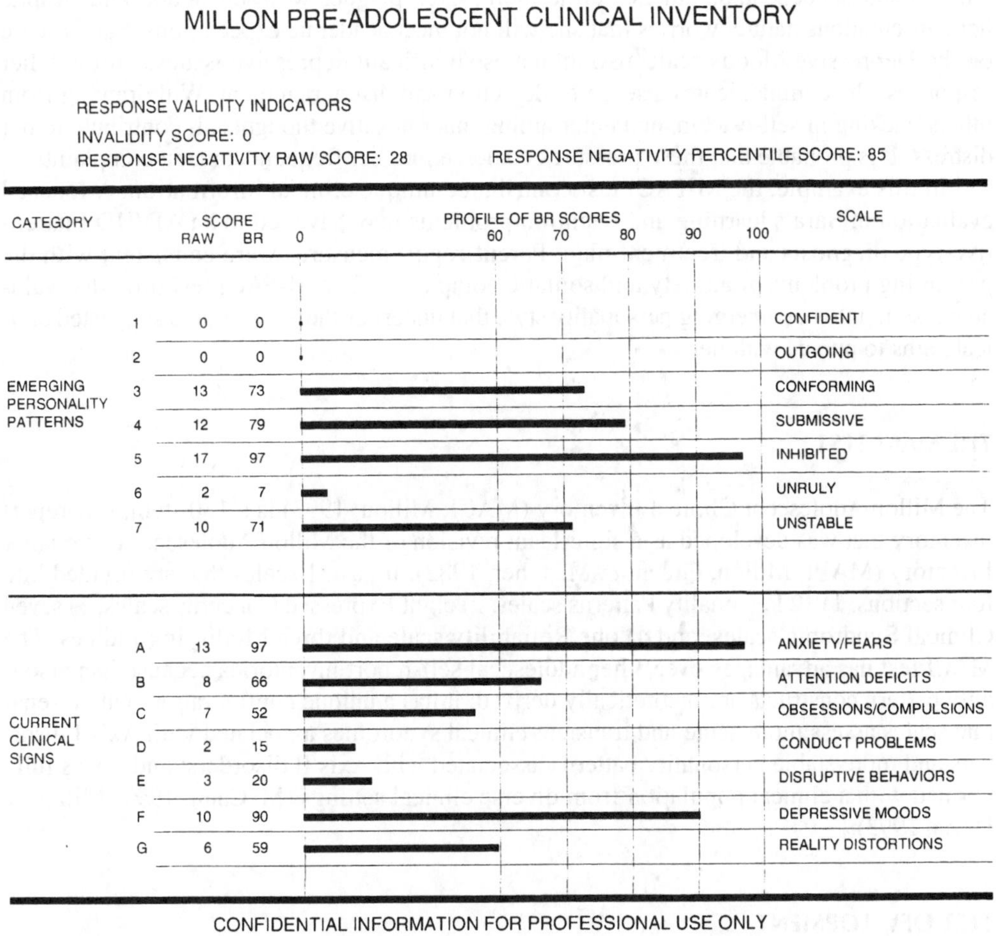

MILLON PRE-ADOLESCENT CLINICAL INVENTORY

RESPONSE VALIDITY INDICATORS

INVALIDITY SCORE: 0
RESPONSE NEGATIVITY RAW SCORE: 28   RESPONSE NEGATIVITY PERCENTILE SCORE: 85

CATEGORY		SCORE RAW	BR	PROFILE OF BR SCORES	SCALE
EMERGING PERSONALITY PATTERNS	1	0	0		CONFIDENT
	2	0	0		OUTGOING
	3	13	73		CONFORMING
	4	12	79		SUBMISSIVE
	5	17	97		INHIBITED
	6	2	7		UNRULY
	7	10	71		UNSTABLE
CURRENT CLINICAL SIGNS	A	13	97		ANXIETY/FEARS
	B	8	66		ATTENTION DEFICITS
	C	7	52		OBSESSIONS/COMPULSIONS
	D	2	15		CONDUCT PROBLEMS
	E	3	20		DISRUPTIVE BEHAVIORS
	F	10	90		DEPRESSIVE MOODS
	G	6	59		REALITY DISTORTIONS

CONFIDENTIAL INFORMATION FOR PROFESSIONAL USE ONLY

FIGURE 16–1.   M-PACI Profile: 10-year-old female with attention problems and anxiety.

endorsed a high number of distressing thoughts, feelings, and behaviors across a broad range of content areas in comparison with the normative sample.

Among the Emerging Personality Patterns scales, the Inhibited and Submissive scales are the most prominent. This configuration suggests that Sara is shy, sensitive, and cautious. She is typically hesitant to elicit attention and slow to initiate social interactions, particularly with her peers. She is generally soft-spoken and nonassertive. A strong tendency to hide or internalize her thoughts and feelings is noted. She relates better to supportive adults, but withdraws from others in a self-protective manner, out of fear that they may make fun of her and as a result of her low self-esteem. Shying away from others, however, limits Sara's opportunities to enhance her peer relations and poor self-image.

Sara's Current Clinical Signs BR scores suggest very significant anxiety problems, significant depressive features, and, to a lesser degree, attention problems. Sara's very high score on the Anxiety/Fears scale is indicative of serious anxiety issues. She experiences heightened nervousness, harbors fears (most notably in a social context), and questions whether she can depend on others. Furthermore, she is plagued with self-doubts and, despite her conscientious nature, worries that she will not meet academic expectations. Sara's score on the Depressive Moods scale also indicates significant depressive issues. Through her responses, she communicates a sense of dejection and discouragement. Withdrawing from others, lacking in self-esteem, and entertaining inner negative thoughts all contribute to her distress. It is probable that these pressures coalesce into her frequent somatic complaints.

In this example, the M-PACI test contributed unique clinical information. A focused evaluation of Sara's learning and attention problems may have led to an AD/HD Inattentive-type diagnosis and treatment plan. Parent-report measures were consistent with the presenting problems of anxiety and somatic complaints. The M-PACI test provided valuable insight into her emerging personality style that underlies these issues and suggested clinical paths to pursue with her.

THE MACI TEST

The Millon Adolescent Clinical Inventory (MACI; Millon, 1993) is a 160-item, self-report inventory that was developed as a significant revision of the Millon Adolescent Personality Inventory (MAPI; Millon, Green, & Meagher, 1982). It has 31 scales that are divided into four sections: 1) 12 Personality Patterns scales, 2) eight Expressed Concerns scales, 3) seven Clinical Syndrome scales, and 4) one Reliability scale and three Modifying Indices. The MACI test has advantages over other adolescent self-report inventories because its personality pattern constructs are theoretically derived; it has a unique configuration, where separate scales assess more acute and transient clinical syndromes associated with Axis I disorders and more stable personality patterns associated with Axis II disorders; and it was fully normed with a clinical population from diverse clinical settings (McCann, 1997; Millon & Davis, 1993).

TEST DEVELOPMENT

The MACI test was also constructed through the validation sequence Loevinger proposed. At the theoretical substantive phase, 11 personality patterns were initially targeted. Eleven represented the mild to moderate variants within Millon's model. Figure 16–2 illustrates those

Sources of Reinforcement					
Behavior Pattern	Independent (Self)	Dependent (Other)	Ambivalent (Conflicted)	Discordant (Reversal)	Detached (Neither)	Detached (Pain)
Active	Unruly	Dramatizing	Oppositional	Forceful	Inhibited	
Passive	Egotistic	Submissive	Conforming	Self-Demeaning	Introversive	Doleful

FIGURE 16–2.   Derivation of personality patterns from active-passive and self-other polarities.

Sources of Reinforcement					
Behavior Pattern	Independent (Self)	Dependent (Other)	Ambivalent (Conflicted)	Discordant (Reversal)	Detached (Neither)	Detached (Pain)
Active	Unruly | Antisocial	Dramatizing | Histrionic	Oppositional | Negativistic	Forceful | Aggressive-Sadistic	Inhibited | Avoidant	
Passive	Egotistic | Narcissistic	Submissive | Dependent	Conforming | Obsessive-Compulsive	Self-Demeaning | Masochistic	Introversive | Schizoid	Doleful | Depressive

FIGURE 16–3.   Continuum of personality patterns to personality disorders.

personality patterns that are derived according to the theory. These names represent the personality patterns the MACI test assesses, and these constructs have correspondences to many of the personality disorders recognized in the DSM-IV. Figure 16–3 illustrates these relationships. The MACI Personality Patterns scales have less severe names and do not represent personality "disorders" per se. Nonetheless, the MACI test assesses more personality patterns than the M-PACI test, which is indicative of the subtle psychological distinctions that tend to emerge as one progresses from childhood into adolescence, toward adulthood.

During this developmental course, it becomes important to differentiate between constructs that share similar features, in particular, because different conditions may warrant different interventions and may also be associated with different prognoses. For example, the M-PACI test assesses one detached personality pattern, Inhibited, which is a style notable in children who may be shy and withdrawn. These children typically have few friends, feel they don't quite "fit in," and often find their way to the periphery of social interactions. On the other hand, the MACI test has three detached personality pattern scales, Introversive, Inhibited, and Doleful, which are differentiated from one another within the active-passive and pleasure-pain polarities.

The Introversive personality, associated with the Schizoid personality, is conceptualized as the passive-detached pattern. Adolescents with high scores on this dimension possess a limited capacity to experience both psychic pleasure and pain and have little motivation to seek out rewards through social interactions. They are not on the periphery for protective reasons or out of disillusion; instead they are internally unmoved and intrinsically underresponsive to stimulation physically, emotionally, and socially.

This pattern can be contrasted with the active-detached pattern, identified as the Inhibited personality pattern, which is associated with the Avoidant personality. Inhibited personalities typically possess a hypersensitivity to anticipated pain that is manifested in an imbalance of diminished psychic pleasure and a sentience for psychic pain. Their social withdrawal is marked with apprehensiveness, and they have learned to avoid social rejection or humiliation by retreating from others. Furthermore, their limited ability to derive pleasure and comfort from any source leads to an undercurrent of tension, sadness, and anger.

The third pattern, the Doleful personality pattern, is formulated as the passive-pain orientation and is associated with the Depressive personality. Doleful personalities experience pain as a persistent companion in their lives. There is an overemphasis on pain and anguish as well as a sense that they have "given up," virtually succumbing to what is believed to be a future filled with more suffering and despair. These adolescents have few friends, because interacting with them is seldom rewarding and is often draining for both parties. These clinical distinctions become more obvious in the adolescent population, occur with sufficient frequency to be clinically important, and can be differentiated with selective item development.

The MACI Borderline Tendency scale was constructed as a measure akin to the DSM-IV Borderline personality and serves as a severity gauge. Whereas the first 11 personality pattern scales have prototype items, this scale does not. It was constructed later in the MACI development process and is a compilation of 21 items from 10 scales that address many of the Borderline personality's core features. Within the Millon schema, the Borderline personality is conceptualized as a more severe pattern where a conflict is present within all three polarities. These conflicts contribute to their intense ambivalence, labile moods, unpredictable behaviors, capricious thoughts, split object relations, and identity diffusion. In addition, these personalities are prone to exhibiting internalizing and externalizing disorders and, similar to the M-PACI Unstable emerging personality style, have shown strong correlations with mood disorders and disruptive behavior disorders.

The MACI test has a central set of Expressed Concerns scales that assess an adolescent's perceptions of important areas in his or her development. While the M-PACI scales demonstrated poor support statistically for their inclusion and were dropped, these MACI scales provide keen insights into adolescent development, and, in some instances, low scores may represent areas of support or, potentially, relative strengths. Two scales, Identity Diffusion and Self-Devaluation, focus on self-image issues, in particular, regarding one's identity and self-esteem. These scales tap one's impressions in terms of the present and the future. Another pair of self-oriented scales, Body Disapproval and Sexual Discomfort, addresses an adolescent's reactions toward his or her physical maturation and the onset of sexual thoughts and urges. Two key areas involve peer relations, measured by the Peer Insecurity scale, and family relations, measured by the Family Discord scale. Whereas pre-adolescent subjects were not able to identify conflicts in these areas, adolescents, perhaps related to the significance of the separation-individuation struggle, communicate frequent elevations, in particular, on the latter scale. The Childhood Abuse scale assesses an adolescent's *emotional reactions* (e.g., shame, disgust) to prior abuse and should *not* be interpreted as a measure of whether or not abuse occurred. Elevations will be found on these scales when an adolescent identifies a scale's target as a subjective concern. The exception to this rule involves the Social Insensitivity scale, which will typically elevate in tandem with the Unruly, Forceful, Delinquent Predisposition, and Impulsive Propensity scales. Serious conduct disorder problems are then indicated.

The MACI Clinical Syndromes scales assess common behavior patterns and mood problems in the adolescent population. Although these syndromes may be distinct in their presentation, it is important to recognize their meaning and significance within the context of the adolescent's personality. The Anxious Feelings and Depressive Affect scales identify key features in the mood realm, and the Suicidal Tendency scale functions as a measure of acute severity and safety risk as it assesses issues related to self-harm and suicidal ideation. As noted above, the Delinquent Predisposition and Impulsive Propensity scales address conduct disorder patterns. The Eating Dysfunctions and Substance Abuse Proneness scales are also important, especially because an elevation on either scale might indicate the need for specialized treatment interventions.

ITEM WEIGHTS AND BASE RATE SCORES

The MACI test utilizes a weighted raw score system of 0 to 3. Prototype items for each scale were assigned a weight of 3, and, according to a series of statistical analyses, nonprototype or subsidiary items were assigned a weight of 2 or 1, depending on the value of their item statistics and their consonance with the underlying theory. All MACI raw scores are transformed into BR scores according to four normative groups (i.e., 13–15-year-old males, 13–15-year-old females, 16–19-year-old males, and 16–19-year-old females). These BR scores extend from 0 to 115 and have anchor points at 75 and 85. The MACI test offers diagnostic impressions, unlike the M-PACI test. On the Personality Patterns scales, those impressions will be reflected as personality *traits* when a BR score is 85 or above on a particular scale and as personality *features* when a BR score falls between 75 and 84. The Clinical Syndromes scales translate into DSM-IV Axis I diagnoses when the BR scores are 75 and above.

MODIFYING INDICES AND BR SCORE ADJUSTMENTS

The MACI test has four scales that assess response style and test-taking attitudes. These scales are Reliability, Disclosure, Desirability, and Debasement. Their relative elevations, both in comparison with the normative group and with one another, indicate whether the adolescents were open and forthcoming in their self-assessment, whether they may have underreported and had a tendency to minimize their troubles, or whether they may have exaggerated their current distress and had a tendency to magnify their troubles.

The Reliability scale is straightforward. It consists of two items that are quite peculiar in their content. If an adolescent endorses one of these items, it challenges the validity of the entire profile, and the clinician should be cautious in interpreting it. A profile is invalid if both items are endorsed.

The Disclosure scale assesses how open and self-revealing or defensive and guarded an adolescent was in responding to the MACI items. The Disclosure scale and the Desirability and Debasement scales are grounded in the research conducted in the development of the MCMI-II (Millon, 1987). BR scores for these scales are anchored at certain percentile ranks and, depending on their relative elevations, may trigger adjustments, upward or downward, for all of the Personality Patterns scales and select Expressed Concerns and Clinical Syndromes scales. In addition, downward BR adjustments are made to select Personality Patterns scales when the Anxious Feelings and/or Depressive Affect scales exceed BR scores of 85, and, depending on the highest Personality Patterns scale in a profile, specific Expressed Concerns and Clinical Syndromes scales may be adjusted upward or downward. These adjustments are all done automatically for the computer-generated reports, with notations given that they have been made.

RELIABILITY

Alpha coefficients were calculated in order to estimate the reliability of the MACI scales. These values are quite strong, which is partially attributable to the large cross-validation group and the length of the MACI scales. The Personality Patterns scales had a mean of .83 and a median of .84, the Expressed Concerns scales had a mean of .79 and a median of .78, and the Clinical Syndromes scales had a mean of .82 and a median of .85. Stability coefficients across all scales, with the test administered twice within a 3–7-day span, had a mean of .81 and a median of .82.

INTERNAL STRUCTURAL VALIDITY

Intercorrelations were calculated between the 30 MACI clinical scales from their BR scores. Among the Personality Patterns scales, strong positive correlations were found between the Egotistic, Dramatizing, and Conforming scales, which were very similar to the M-PACI results. On the MACI test, however, the Conforming scale also demonstrates a strong positive correlation with the Submissive scale. This latter tandem, in turn, shows strong correlations with one Expressed Concerns scale (Sexual Discomfort) and one Clinical Syndromes scale (Anxious Feelings). The Egotistic and Dramatizing scales, presumably through a connection to the Unruly scale, demonstrated strong correlations with the Social Insensitivity and Delinquent Predisposition scales. The Unruly and Forceful scales, linked at a secondary level to the Oppositional scale to form an "anger triad," demonstrate strong associations with conduct problems reflected in the Social Insensitivity, Delinquent Predisposition, and Impulsive Propensity scales, in addition to the Substance-Abuse Proneness scale. The detached scales, Introversive, Inhibited, and Doleful, correlate with one another and demonstrate correlations associated with depressive features, low self-esteem, and peer problems. Finally, the Doleful, Oppositional, Self-Demeaning, and Borderline Tendency scales have their strongest correlations with the Self-Devaluation, Depressive Affect, and Suicidal Tendency scales. The MACI correlation matrix, though more complex, reveals an inner consistency and structure similar to the M-PACI matrix.

EXTERNAL CRITERION VALIDITY

The MACI test manual provides considerable detail regarding external criterion validity results with clinicians' diagnoses and self-report measures that were administered during the data collection phase. Since its introduction, the MACI test has generated much interest, and many studies have targeted the test's clinical utility.

The conduct disorder population has received the most attention. Murrie and Cornell (2000) investigated the MACI test's ability to assess psychopathy in 90 adolescents in a state hospital psychiatric unit. Scores on the Psychopathy Checklist-Revised were utilized to assign the patients into three groups. The top third represented the high-psychopathy (psychopathic) group, and the bottom third represented the low-psychopathy (nonpsychopathic) group. Murrie and Cornell found that the MACI test's Substance-Abuse Proneness, Unruly, Delinquent Predisposition, Forceful, Impulsive Propensity, and Social Insensitivity scales, in descending order, had significant correlations with the PCL-R total score. A discriminant function analysis indicated that the Substance-Abuse Proneness scale was best at distinguishing between high and low groups, followed by the Unruly and Delinquent Predisposition scales. In addition, these investigators constructed a Psychopathy Content Scale that consists of 20 MACI items. The majority of these items are prototype items from the Substance-Abuse Proneness, Delinquent Predisposition, Unruly, and Forceful scales. The new scale had a coefficient alpha of .87 and a correlation of .60 with the PCL-R and distinguished the high- and low-psychopathy groups at an 83% accuracy rate.

In a subsequent study, Murrie and Cornell (2002) tested the accuracy and utility of the Psychopathy Content Scale as a screening device with the Psychopathy Checklist: Youth Version. In a sample of over 100 incarcerated adolescents, the Psychopathy Content Scale showed a high correlation, .49, with the PCL:YV; however, a specific cutoff score that could attain acceptable diagnostic efficiency rates was elusive.

Salekin, Ziefler, Larrea, Anthony, and Bennett (2003) further refined the Murrie and Cornell Psychopathy Content Scale by identifying MACI items that reflected three central components or subscales: callousness, egocentricity, and antisociality. The new content scale, named P–16, was developed to predict recidivism rates in adolescent offenders. Over a two-year course, 55 adolescents were tracked in terms of their general recidivism (any nonviolent crimes), violent recidivism (any violent crimes), and the frequency of their criminal activity. The overall recidivism rate exceeded 60%, with almost one-third of the subjects committing violent crimes. Total P–16 scores correlated with all three measures, the callousness and antisociality subscales correlated with all three measures, and the egocentricity subscale correlated with the violent recidivism only. A Receiver Operating Characteristic (ROC) analysis for the P–16 content scale total score revealed very impressive results for predicting violent recidivism, and the callousness and antisociality subscales were quite adept at predicting general recidivism.

The MACI test's "internalizing" scales have also generated attention. Hiatt and Cornell (1999) examined the concurrent validity of the MACI test with clinician diagnoses in 88 adolescents in a state hospital psychiatric unit. The Doleful Personality Patterns and Depressive Affect Clinical Syndromes scales showed moderate predictive ability and correspondence with clinician diagnoses of depression, as well as strong correlations (Doleful = .67; Depressive Affect = .77) with the CDI.

Velting, Rathus, and Miller (2000) administered the MACI test to clinically referred depressed subjects with and without a history of previous suicide attempts. They reported the mean profiles of the 12 MACI Personality Patterns scales for the two groups. Statistically significant differences were found, with the suicide attempter group scoring higher on the Borderline Tendency scale and the nonattempter group scoring higher on the Submissive and Conforming scales.

Grilo, Fehon, Walker, and Martino (1996) examined the MACI test correlates for psychiatrically hospitalized adolescents with and without substance abuse disorders. Analyses between the mean profiles revealed that adolescents with substance abuse disorders scored at a statistically higher level on the Unruly, Forceful, Social Insensitivity, Delinquent Predisposition, and Substance-Abuse Proneness scales and just below that level on the Oppositional and Impulsive Propensity scales.

In a later study, Grilo, Sanislow, Fehon, Martino, and McGlashan (1999) investigated the impact of childhood abuse in a large, psychiatrically hospitalized adolescent population. Two study groups were created according to their MACI test Childhood Abuse scale BR scores. Subjects who obtained BR scores above 70 were labeled the high-abuse group, and those whose BR scores fell below 30 were labeled the no-abuse group. Analyses controlling for age and depression found statistically significant higher levels of suicide and violence risk, impulse control problems, drug abuse problems, and dependency in the high-abuse group on a series of other self-report measures. The association between abuse and borderline personality was supported in the statistically significant higher mean BR score on the Borderline Tendency scale in the high-abuse group.

Finally, Romm, Bockian, and Harvey (1999) conducted the largest factor analytic study with the MACI test; they tested over 250 adolescents, all referred to a residential treatment facility. Five factors were found, accounting for 77% of the variance. The first factor, labeled Defiant Externalizers, had its primary loadings on the Unruly, Forceful, and Oppositional Personality Patterns scales; the Social Insensitivity and Family Discord Expressed Concerns scales; and the Substance-Abuse Proneness, Delinquent Predisposition, and Impulsive Propensity Clinical Syndromes scales. The second factor, labeled Intrapunitive Ambivalent Types, had its highest loadings on the Doleful, Self-Demeaning, Borderline Tendency, and Oppositional Personality Patterns scales; the Identity Diffusion and Self Devaluation Expressed Concerns scales; and the Depressive Affect and Suicidal Tendency Clinical Syndromes scales. Inadequate Avoidants, the third factor, was identified by its highest loadings on the Inhibited, Introversive, and Peer Insecurity scales. Self-Deprecating Depressives, the label for the fourth factor, was found much more often with females and was marked by primary loadings on the Eating Dysfunctions, Body Disapproval, and Self-Devaluation scales in addition to secondary loadings on the Self-Demeaning, Inhibited, and Depressive Affect scales. The last factor, Reactive Abused Types, was also more common with females and was identified by high loadings on the Childhood Abuse, Sexual Discomfort, Family Discord, and Suicidal Tendency scales.

MACI CASE EXAMPLE: 17-YEAR-OLD FEMALE WITH A FOLIE A DEUX

When clinicians administer self-report inventories in an assessment battery, they face numerous challenges to the reliability, validity, and clinical utility of the information gathered (Tringone, 1999). First, clinicians have to rely on the patient's interpretation of the items. Therefore, these inventories actually are not as "objective" as one might assume. Patients, for example, must decide what the terms *often*, *sometimes*, and so forth mean to them. Although the clinician, as an observer, might set the threshold at one point, the patient may choose a very different point. Second, some patients have very poor self-awareness and insight into their problems. This issue may be global or it may be specific to a particular problem area. In this instance, the patient does not make a conscious effort to deny or withhold information. In other instances, however, patients may make a conscious decision to filter what they are or are not willing to reveal about themselves. Finally, these inventories provide clinical impressions and, with the Millon inventories more specifically, generate detailed interpretive reports without knowing the patient's background history or the immediate context surrounding the assessment. The following case example illustrates how valuable clinical material can be gained in spite of these hurdles.

Maggie, a 17-year-old female, was psychiatrically hospitalized because of a shared psychotic disorder. Two weeks before her admission, she began believing her 18-year-old sister's delusion that a man had been breaking into their home, drugging them, and sexually assaulting them on a daily basis. Maggie stopped attending school in an effort to collect evidence and seek out witnesses, in addition to staying awake at night, waiting to catch the alleged rapist. Despite the fact that the sister underwent medical work-ups that contradicted the story, Maggie maintained her sister was telling the truth.

At the time of her admission, Maggie was living with her parents and sister. Although born in the United States, as an infant, she and her sister were sent together to live in their family's native land with their grandparents. They were raised there until Maggie was about seven years old. Arrangements were made for them to visit "relatives" in the United States; however, they were not informed until some time later that the "relatives" were actually their birth parents. Prior to admission, Maggie was a strong student who had been accepted to a prestigious private university. She had no past psychiatric history. There was no reported history of sexual, physical, or emotional abuse, and she denied drug and/or alcohol abuse.

Maggie's MACI profile is shown in Figure 16–4. Interpretation of a MACI profile essentially follows the same sequence of steps that had been outlined above. Maggie's response pattern indicated that she produced a valid report. She appeared to understand the item content and did not respond in a random manner. A check of the Modifying Indices revealed a tendency toward avoiding self-disclosure, although this could actually be a reflection of her "healthy" premorbid status that had been reported. A comparison of the Desirability and Debasement scales showed a clear leaning toward a self-enhancing response pattern, which, again, could be related to her premorbid status. The Desirability scale has shown positive correlations with the other scales that are elevated in her overall profile. Her BR scores were adjusted according to rules set for the Disclosure Adjustment and the Desirability/Debasement Adjustment.

Maggie's Personality Patterns profile reveals that her highest BR score was obtained on the Submissive scale, followed by the Conforming and Dramatizing scales. She presents as a Submissive personality subtype whose most salient features are her significant dependency needs, a willingness to submit to the wishes and values of others, and a strong sense of compliance with social conventions. She emphasizes a sense of security that she derives from her attachments to others. There is an underlying duty to obey, to meet expectations that others have set for her, and to show respect toward those in authority positions. Cooperative and accommodating, Maggie seeks to avoid conflict with or disapproval from significant others. Strivings for autonomy and acting out are generally suppressed. Especially problematic are impulses of a sexual or aggressive nature. It is probable that, for these reasons, she tends to lead an over-controlled and proper lifestyle, marked by self-discipline and self-restraint. Furthermore, these adolescents often demonstrate limited insight into their feelings.

Although Maggie's BR scores do not exceed 75 on the Expressed Concerns and Clinical Syndromes scales, it is noteworthy, nonetheless, that her highest elevations were obtained on the Sexual Discomfort and Anxious Feelings scales. Their content is consistent with some features of her presenting problems—conflict and confusion over sexual thoughts and impulses that contribute to an undercurrent of anxiety, tension, and confusion.

PERSONALITY CODE: 3** 74*5//-**-*D//-**-*EE//
VALID REPORT

CATEGORY		SCORE		PROFILE OF BR SCORES				DIAGNOSTIC SCALES
		RAW	BR	0	60	75	85	115
MODIFYING INDICES	X	233	15					DISCLOSURE
	Y	12	67					DESIRABILITY
	Z	1	15					DEBASEMENT
PERSONALITY PATTERNS	1	12	36					INTROVERSIVE
	2A	18	53					INHIBITED
	2B	6	32					DOLEFUL
	3	60	87					SUBMISSIVE
	4	40	76					DRAMATIZING
	5	30	63					EGOTISTIC
	6A	7	30					UNRULY
	6B	1	15					FORCEFUL
	7	55	77					CONFORMING
	8A	15	50					OPPOSITIONAL
	8B	12	42					SELF-DEMEANING
	9	2	21					BORDERLINE TENDENCY
EXPRESSED CONCERNS	A	7	24					IDENTITY DIFFUSION
	B	18	39					SELF-DEVALUATION
	C	11	38					BODY DISAPPROVAL
	D	39	73					SEXUAL DISCOMFORT
	E	6	38					PEER INSECURITY
	F	21	51					SOCIAL INSENSITIVITY
	G	11	47					FAMILY DISCORD
	H	3	15					CHILDHOOD ABUSE
CLINICAL SYNDROMES	AA	9	24					EATING DYSFUNCTIONS
	BB	0	2					SUBSTANCE-ABUSE PRONENESS
	CC	17	39					DELINQUENT PREDISPOSITION
	DD	4	12					IMPULSIVE PROPENSITY
	EE	34	73					ANXIOUS FEELINGS
	FF	11	55					DEPRESSIVE AFFECT
	GG	7	25					SUICIDAL TENDENCY

CONFIDENTIAL INFORMATION FOR PROFESSIONAL USE ONLY

FIGURE 16–4.   MACI Profile: 17-year-old female with a folie a deux.

In this example, the MACI test was able to provide some insights into the nature of Maggie's underlying personality style, despite the fact that the test does not assess for severe Axis I conditions (i.e., psychotic symptoms and disorders), and the interpretive report would not be able to explain specifically how she developed a shared psychotic disorder. Thankfully, very few people decompensate into this state, but there is a suspicion that a person's unique history would include significant dependency issues as a vulnerability factor.

Treatment considerations are as follows: 1) In an acute care setting, pharmacotherapy would be recommended to address Maggie's psychotic condition. 2) The treatment team would have to be cognizant of her cultural background, because value and belief systems held by her and her family would be expected to play an integral role in her overall care and progress. These factors provide an important backdrop to the therapeutic suggestions offered by the MACI interpretive report. 3) Eventually, efforts could be directed toward reducing Maggie's level of dependency and submissiveness, because this pattern often interferes with the development of an adolescent's sense of autonomy and competence. It may also preclude experiencing age-appropriate opportunities for psychological growth and maturation. A clinician would need to balance these issues and pace their interventions to gradually enhance the patient's assertiveness, confidence, and independence.

SUMMARY

The M-PACI and MACI tests represent two "generations" within the Millon inventories "family." These tests were constructed and validated in a manner that affirmed their coherence with their guiding theoretical principles and maximized their empirical support. They have separate personality pattern scales and clinical syndrome scales as a function of an underlying assumption that clinically significant conditions should be conceptualized within the context of one's personality.

A connection was made between the notions of temperament and "emerging" personality patterns where both have clear associations with various childhood problems. The M-PACI test measures seven emerging personality pattern scales that represent the more basic cohesive styles. The Confident, Outgoing, and Conforming styles appear to potentially serve as a protective factor or may represent resilient qualities to help cope with or moderate stress. The Submissive, Inhibited, Unruly, and Unstable styles, on the other hand, are associated with various clinical problems and may represent a vulnerability to stress or, in some ways, may actually intensify or perpetuate stress reactions and problems.

The MACI test, as it reflects adolescent development, measures 12 personality pattern scales. During this life phase, inherent dispositions and accumulated life experiences appear to expand the overall repertoire of behaviors, thoughts, and affective expressions that may be seen, yet, at the same time, many adolescents begin to demonstrate preferences for certain modes of expression that represent more refined or circumscribed patterns. Again, these preferred styles may either increase or decrease the probability of developing a disorder.

The unique structure of the M-PACI and MACI tests helps communicate valuable clinical insights that can serve as a guide to enhanced psychotherapeutic interventions. Although Axis I disorders must be primary therapy targets, it is imperative that clinicians also address Axis II traits or features, given their reciprocally reinforcing nature, their associations with clinical problems, and the growing evidence that these patterns, from early on, may be more stable and enduring than once thought.

REFERENCES

American Psychiatric Association. (1994). *Diagnostic and statistical manual of mental disorders* (4th ed.). Washington, DC: Author.

Campbell, D. T., & Fiske, D. W. (1959). Convergent and discriminant validation by the multitrait-multimethod matrix. *Psychological Bulletin, 56*, 81–105.

Chanen, A. M., Jackson, H. J., McGorry, P. D., Allot, K. A., Clarkson, V., & Yuen, H. P. (2004). Two-year stability of personality disorder in older adolescent outpatients. *Journal of Personality Disorders, 18*, 526–541.

Clark, L. A., Watson, D., & Mineka, S. (1994). Temperament, personality, and mood and anxiety disorders. *Journal of Abnormal Psychology, 103*, 103–116.

Compas, B. E., Connor-Smith, J., & Jaser, S. S. (2004). Temperament, stress reactivity, and coping: Implications for depression in childhood and adolescence. *Journal of Clinical Child and Adolescent Psychology, 33*, 21–31.

Cronbach, L. J., & Meehl, P. E. (1955). Construct validity in psychological tests. *Psychological Bulletin, 52*, 281–302.

Frick, P. J. (2004). Integrating research on temperament and childhood psychopathology: Its pitfalls and promise. *Journal of Clinical Child and Adolescent Psychology, 33*, 2–7.

Frick, P. J., & Morris, A. S. (2004). Temperament and developmental pathways to conduct problems. *Journal of Clinical Child and Adolescent Psychology, 33*, 54–68.

Grilo, C. M., Fehon, D. C., Walker, M., & Martino, A. L. (1996). A comparison of adolescent inpatients with and without substance abuse using the Millon Adolescent Clinical Inventory. *Journal of Youth and Adolescence, 25*, 379–388.

Grilo, C. M., Sanislow, C., Fehon, D. C., Martino, S., & McGlashan, T. H. (1999). Psychological and behavioral functioning in adolescent psychiatric inpatients who report histories of childhood abuse. *American Journal of Psychiatry, 156*, 538–543.

Hiatt, M. D., & Cornell, D. G. (1999). Concurrent validity of the Millon Adolescent Clinical Inventory as a measure of depression in hospitalized adolescents. *Journal of Personality Assessment, 73*, 64–79.

Jackson, D. N. (1970). A sequential system for personality scale development. In C.D. Spielberger (Ed.), *Current topics in clinical and community psychology* (Vol. 2, pp. 61–92). New York: Academic Press.

Kamp, J., Millon, T., & Tringone, R. (unpublished manuscript). Development and validation of the Millon Pre-Adolescent Clinical Inventory.

Kovacs, M. (2001). *Children's Depression Inventory (CDI) technical manual*. North Tonawanda, NY: Multi-Health Systems.

Loevinger, J. (1957). Objective tests as instruments of psychological theory. *Psychological Reports, 3*, 635–694.

Lonigan, C. J., Vasey, M. W., Phillips, B. M., & Hazen, R. A. (2004). Temperament, anxiety, and the processing of threat-relevant stimuli. *Journal of Clinical Child and Adolescent Psychology, 33*, 8–20.

McCann, J. T. (1997). The MACI: Composition and clinical applications. In T. Millon (Ed.), *The Millon inventories: Clinical and personality assessment* (pp. 363–388). New York: Guilford.

Mervielde, I., DeClerq, B., DeFruyt, F., & Van Leeuwen, K. (2005). Temperament, personality, and developmental psychopathology as childhood antecedents of personality disorders. *Journal of Personality Disorders, 19*, 171–201.

Millon, T. (1969). *Modern psychopathology: A biosocial approach to maladaptive learning and functioning*. Philadelphia: Saunders.

Millon, T. (1977). *Manual for the Millon Clinical Multiaxial Inventory (MCMI)*. Minneapolis, MN: National Computer Systems.

Millon, T. (1981). *Disorders of personality: DSM-III: Axis II*. New York: Wiley.

Millon, T. (1987). *Manual for the Millon Clinical Multiaxial Inventory-II (MCMI-II)*. Minneapolis, MN: National Computer Systems.

Millon, T. (1990). *Toward a new personology: An evolutionary model*. New York: Wiley.

Millon, T. (1993). *Millon Adolescent Clinical Inventory (MACI) manual*. Minneapolis, MN: National Computer Systems.

Millon, T. (2004). *Masters of the mind: Exploring the story of mental illness from ancient times to the new millennium*. New York: Wiley.

Millon, T., & Davis, R. D. (1993). The Millon Adolescent Personality Inventory and the Millon Adolescent Clinical Inventory. *Journal of Counseling and Development, 71*, 570–574.

Millon, T., & Davis, R. D. (1996). *Disorders of personality: DSM-IV and beyond* (2nd ed.). New York: Wiley.

Millon, T., Green, C. J., & Meagher, R. B. (1982). *Millon Adolescent Personality Inventory manual*. Minneapolis, MN: National Computer Systems.

Millon, T., Millon, C., & Davis, R. (1994). *Millon Clinical Multiaxial Inventory-III manual*. Minneapolis, MN: National Computer Systems.

Millon, T., Tringone, R., Millon, C., & Grossman, S. (2005). *Millon Pre-Adolescent Clinical Inventory manual*. Minneapolis, MN: Pearson.

Murrie, D. C., & Cornell, D. G. (2000). The Millon Adolescent Clinical Inventory and psychopathy. *Journal of Personality Assessment, 75*, 110–125.

Murrie, D. C., & Cornell, D. G. (2002). Psychopathy screening of incarcerated juveniles: A comparison of measures. *Psychological Assessment, 14*, 390–396.

Reynolds, C. R., & Kamphaus, R. W. (1998). *Behavior Assessment System for Children manual*. Circle Pines, MN: American Guidance Service.

Reynolds, C. R., & Richmond, B. O. (2000). *Revised Children's Manifest Anxiety Scale (RCMAS) manual*. Los Angeles: Western Psychological Services.

Romm, S., Bockian, N., & Harvey, M. (1999). Factor-based prototypes of the Millon Adolescent Clinical Inventory in adolescents referred for residential treatment. *Journal of Personality Assessment, 72*, 125–143.

Salekin, R. T., Ziefler, T. A., Larrea, M. A., Anthony, V.L., & Bennett, A. D. (2003). Predicting dangerousness with two Millon Adolescent Clinical Inventory psychopathy scales: The importance of egocentric and callous traits. *Journal of Personality Assessment, 80*, 154–163.

Shiner, R. L. (2005). A developmental perspective on personality disorders: Lessons from research on normal personality development in childhood and adolescence. *Journal of Personality Disorders, 19*, 202–210.

Tringone, R. (1999). Essentials of MACI assessment. In S. Strack (Ed.), *Essentials of Millon inventories assessment* (pp. 92–160). New York: Wiley.

Velting, D. M., Rathus, J. H., & Miller, A. L. (2000). MACI personality scale profiles of depressed adolescent suicide attempters: A pilot study. *Journal of Clinical Psychology, 56*, 1381–1385.

17

Personality Inventory for Children, Second Edition (PIC–2), Personality Inventory for Youth (PIY), and Student Behavior Survey (SBS)

David Lachar
University of Texas–Houston Health Sciences Center

This chapter introduces a family of measures used in the evaluation of school-age children: the Personality Inventory for Children Second Edition (PIC–2), the Personality Inventory for Youth (PIY), and the Student Behavior Survey (SBS). These three questionnaires have been constructed to meet the assessment needs of youth by measuring multiple dimensions of problem behavior; collecting observations from parents, teachers, and youth; and providing standard scores based on contemporary national samples.

AN INTRODUCTION TO MULTIDIMENSIONAL MULTISOURCE ASSESSMENT

Multidimensional objective assessment is both efficient and accurate. Important clinical phenomena are measured with the use of the same format and are evaluated with the same or similar standardization samples (in contrast to an assessment in which a customized selection of narrowband instruments that have different response characteristics and were standardized with different normative samples deliver results that are clinically integrated into a description of a specific child). Clinicians who use multidimensional assessment understand that the documentation of symptom or problem *absence* makes a diagnostic contribution comparable to the documentation of symptom or problem *presence*. They also recognize that a pattern of significant clinical problems is often characteristic of referred children. These problem constellations or patterns of diagnoses are designated "comorbid" and reflect the dynamics

---

Modified with permission from the chapter in Maruish (2004).

of child referral in that the probability of such referrals is determined by the combined like-lihood of referral for separate disorders (Caron & Rutter, 1991). For example, the internal-izing problem dimensions of anxiety and depression are often comorbid (Brady & Kendall, 1992; King, Ollendick, & Gullone, 1991; Lonigan, Carey, & Finch, 1994). Similarly, a variety of externalizing problem dimensions have been found to be comorbid with the diagnosis of attention deficit/hyperactivity disorder (ADHD; Jensen, Martin, & Cantwell, 1997; Pliszka, 1998). Indeed, it has been stated that the measurement and treatment of these comorbid dis-orders are often of comparable importance to the assessment and treatment of ADHD itself (Cantwell, 1996).

Clinicians who routinely apply multidimensional assessment measures to the initial assessment also are aware that children referred for an evaluation often have problems that are different from those originally thought to be present. For example, application of a narrowly focused ADHD measure at the beginning of an evaluation of a child referred because of pos-sible ADHD may be problematic for two reasons. The resulting descriptions from such a mea-sure may not result in clinically elevated scale scores, leaving possible alternative explanations for observed inattention unexplored (e.g., depression, anxiety, situational maladjustment, learning disability, and acquired cognitive deficit). Alternatively, application of such a nar-rowly focused ADHD measure may result in one or more clinically significant scale scores but provide no evidence of the presence or absence of frequently observed comorbid conditions. It would therefore seem most logical and efficient to first apply a multidimensional measure and then subsequently focus on further differentiation of problem areas highlighted by this ini-tial assessment effort. Such a "successive hurdles" approach recognizes the value of initial psychometric information in the design of subsequent evaluative efforts.

Multisource assessment has become the preferred model for the evaluation of child and adolescent emotional and behavioral adjustment and reflects the importance of parent and teacher observation (cf. LaGreca, Kuttler, & Stone, 2001). Unlike the evaluation of adjust-ment in adults, which typically relies on self-report, the evaluation of school-age children usually cannot depend solely on self-description. Indeed, the context of assessment is fun-damentally different for children and adolescents, who are unlikely to refer themselves for evaluation or treatment and may not possess the academic, cognitive, or motivational com-petence to complete a comprehensive self-report instrument. Young children, perhaps from preschool through third grade, may be unable to describe themselves adequately through responses to questionnaire statements (cf. Flavell, Flavell, & Green, 2001). Such children are unlikely to have mastered the range of vocabulary needed to adequately describe dimen-sions of adjustment; such language competence is not usually attained before the fourth or fifth grade.

Another consideration is that youths are most often referred for evaluation because they are either noncompliant with the requests of the significant adults in their lives or exhibit aca-demic problems (often associated with inadequate reading skills). Therefore, completion of a self-report inventory of several hundred items could present quite an assessment chal-lenge, even for a high school student who is referred for an evaluation. Parents and teachers not only refer youth for assessment; they are also the primary sources of useful systematic observation. Certainly adults are the informants who can best report on the noncompliance of a child to their own requests. Parents are the only consistently available source for informa-tion on early childhood development and the child's behavior in the home. Teachers offer the most accurate observations on the age-appropriateness of the child's adjustment in the classroom and academic achievement as well as the attentional, motivational, and social phe-nomena unique to the classroom and to school. It is likely, however, that such observational accuracy decreases following the elementary school grades, as middle-school and high-school teachers have little continuous observation of students, and usually see each student only for 45 minutes a day and in the context of a class consisting of 30 other students. Youth self-description, regardless of the problems that have been documented for this source of information (Greenbaum, Dedrick, Prange, & Friedman, 1994; Jensen et al., 1996), still represents the most direct and accurate expression of personal thoughts and feelings—once the potentially distorting effects of response sets have been identified. [Note that Michael and Merrell (1998) have demonstrated adequate short-term temporal stability for the self-report of third- to fifth-grade students.]

The availability of two or three independent sets of child descriptions provides a compelling opportunity for comparison across informants. Achenbach, McConaughy, and Howell (1987) conducted a comprehensive literature review and found very limited concordance in general between the descriptions of parent, teacher, and youth, although relatively greater between-source agreement was obtained for scales representing externalizing behaviors. A review of similar studies that evaluated the responses to parallel objective interviews of parent and child concluded that greater agreement was obtained for visible behaviors and for child-parent pairs with older children (Lachar & Gruber, 1993).

Although one reasonable approach to the interpretation of differences between parent, teacher, and youth would be to assign such differences to situation-specific variation (e.g., the child is only oppositional at home, not in the classroom), other explanations are equally plausible. Cross-informant variance may reflect the fact that scales with similar names may contain significantly different content. On the other hand, the development and application of valid, strictly content-parallel measures may limit instrument validity. Assignment of only parallel scale content may restrict the diagnostic potential of each informant source by excluding the measurement of attributes that may be uniquely obtained from that source. Such attributes might be measured through a parent-completed measure of developmental delay, a teacher-completed measure of classroom behavior, or a youth-completed measure of self-concept. The PIC–2, PIY, and SBS attempt in their structure and content to provide the opportunity both to compare similar scale content across informants as well as to measure phenomena that may be uniquely obtained from only one informant.

Along with dissimilar scale content, another source of poor across-informant agreement is the substantial effect of response sets on the accuracy of one source of information found to be discrepant when compared with the observations of other informants. The child or adolescent being assessed may not adequately comply with questionnaire instructions, because of inadequate language comprehension, limited reading skills, or lack of sufficient motivation for the task. It is as likely that a youth may wish to hide a personal history of maladaptive behavior and current internal discomfort from mental health professionals, although a negative presentation of parent adjustment and home conflict may be readily provided. Youths may also be motivated in an assessment context to admit to problems and symptoms that are not present. These same motivations and conditions may also influence parent report. Indeed, there has been some concern that poor parent adjustment may compromise the validity of parent report (Achenbach, 1981). Subsequent review (Richters, 1992) and specific analysis of this issue with the Personality Inventory for Children (Lachar, Kline, & Gdowski, 1987) found no empirical support that this is an important concern. The PIC–2 and the PIY incorporate validity scales to identify the effect of response sets. These scales are designed to measure random or inadequate response to scale statements, defensive denial of existing problems, as well as admission of symptoms that are unlikely to be present or the exaggeration of actual problems.

Clinicians may interpret inconsistencies across informants in a variety of ways. At one extreme, a clinician might consider accepting any evidence of symptom presence from any informant source. At the other extreme, a clinician's focus on symptoms may exclude the interpretation of all scale dimensions not demonstrated within the clinical range by at least two or even all three informant sources. Although an optimal approach to the integrative interpretation of multi-informant questionnaires has not been established (which is not to say that the opinions of mental health professionals and parents remain unstudied; Loeber, Green, & Lahey, 1990; Phares, 1997), there is a distinct pragmatic advantage in using an assessment system with comparable parent, teacher, and youth versions. Conditions regularly occur in the conduct of psychological evaluations that make it difficult or impossible to obtain a parent, teacher, or youth report. The child may be too young, uncooperative, or language impaired. The evaluation may occur during the summer vacation, or the child may have not consistently attended one classroom or may have left school permanently. Parents may miss family appointments when their child is hospitalized, or the child may be under agency guardianship. In such instances, a set of comprehensive parent-, teacher-, and self-report measures that can be applied independently of each other provide the flexibility to facilitate psychometric assessment.

THE PERSONALITY INVENTORY FOR CHILDREN SECOND EDITION AND PERSONALITY INVENTORY FOR YOUTH

Development of the PIC–2

Revision of the original PIC began in 1989 with the rewriting of the first 280 items of the PIC booklet in a self-report format for the construction of the Personality Inventory for Youth (Lachar & Gruber, 1993, 1995a, 1995b). Development of the PIY facilitated concurrent critical review of the structure and content of PIC–R scales and the PIC–R profile. Revision efforts have been sensitive to the need to maintain continuity with PIC interpretation principles established over the past 20 years while introducing psychometric changes that improve its efficiency. Over 1,000 clinical protocols have been subjected to considerable statistical analysis. As a consequence, the PIC–R (now the PIC–2) and the PIY have achieved sufficient similarity to facilitate the comparison of parent description and self-description. Their similarity includes a comparable subscale-within-clinical-scale structure. The final PIC–2 administration booklet of 275 statements generates a profile of gender-specific linear T-scores for 3 validity scales, 9 scales, and 21 subscales, as well as a second profile of 8 shortened scales and 4 scale composites used as an abbreviated assessment and for the measurement of treatment effectiveness. The PIC–2 provides a representative normative sample of school-age children (kindergarten through 12th grade). Current efforts are focused on the development of a version of the PIC for preschool children (ages 3–5).

Each of the nine clinical scales was constructed with the use of a uniform iterative process (Lachar & Gruber, 2001). Initial scale composition was based on previous PIC or PIY item placement or substantive item content. Item-to-scale correlation matrices generated from an initial sample of 950 clinical protocols were then inspected to establish the accuracy of the initial item placements. Each inventory statement retained on a final clinical scale demonstrated a significant and substantial correlation to the scale on which it was placed. When an item obtained a significant correlation with more than one clinical scale, it was placed, in almost all cases, on the scale with which it obtained the most substantial correlation.

The PIC–2 gender-specific T-score values are derived from a contemporary national sample of parent descriptions of youths 5 to 18 years of age (n = 2,306); a large sample of referred youths was analyzed to provide evidence of instrument validity (n = 1,551). PIC–2 clinical scales average 31 items in length (range = 19 to 47 items) and obtain a median coefficient alpha of .89 (range = .81 to .95). As would be expected, PIC–2 clinical scales obtain substantial item overlap with PIY scales similarly named (average = 79%, range = 51% to 100%). In spite of this substantial scale similarity, the difference in informants (parent to youth) resulted in only moderate concordance estimates (median correlation = .43, range = .28 to .53). The strongest relationship between parent and youth description was demonstrated for subscales of Delinquency, Family Dysfunction, and Social Skill Deficits.

The items of each PIC–2 adjustment scale have been partitioned into two or three subscales. PIC–2 subscales average 13 items in length (range = 6 to 21 items), with only 3 of 21 subscales incorporating fewer than 10 items. The majority of subscales demonstrate psychometric characteristics comparable to scales on shorter published questionnaires. In all instances, the division of scales into subscales facilitates the interpretation process. For example, the actuarial interpretation of the PIC–R Delinquency scale (Lachar & Gdowski, 1979) identified T-score ranges associated with the dimensions noncompliance, poorly controlled anger, and antisocial behaviors. These dimensions are each represented by different PIC–2 DLQ subscales; their patterns of elevation represent the dominant endorsed content of this adjustment scale. (Note the comparable subscales on the PIY Delinquency scale.) Correlations between PIC–2 scale scores and clinician, teacher, and youth descriptions readily provide actuarial interpretive guidelines for these nine major adjustment dimensions. These interpretive guidelines are detailed in the PIC–2 manual:

Cognitive Impairment (COG). The statements that reflect limited general intellectual ability (COG1), problems in achieving in school (COG2), and a history of developmental delay or deficit (COG3) have been placed on this scale. COG2 elevation has been found to be associated with a broad range of inadequate academic habits and poor achievement in the classroom. Both teacher and clinician ratings demonstrate a strong relation between COG3 elevation and language deficits.

Impulsivity and Distractibility (ADH). The majority of these items (21 of 27) appear on the first dimension. ADH1 (Disruptive Behavior) receives substantial support from teacher ratings: Elevation on this subscale is associated with poor behavioral control and disruptive behavior in the classroom. It is also associated with impulsive, hyperactive, and restless behavior and excessive attention-seeking as reported by clinicians. The second dimension (ADH2, Fearlessness) appears to measure an aspect of bravado that may best be classified as a personality dimension.

Delinquency (DLQ). DLQ1 (Antisocial Behavior) elevation is associated with behaviors suggested by the name of the total scale. DLQ1 subscale elevation predicts admission by both clinician and youth of a variety of unacceptable behaviors: truancy, alcohol and drug misuse, theft, running away from home, deceit, and association with other youths who are similarly troubled. DLQ2 (Dyscontrol) elevation suggests the presence of disruptive behavior associated with poorly modulated anger. Teachers note fighting, and youth admit to similar problems ("I lose friends because of my temper"). Clinicians rate these children as assaultive, defiant, argumentative, irritable, destructive, and manipulative. This lack of emotional control often results in behaviors that demonstrate poor judgment. DLQ3 (Noncompliance) elevation reflects disobedience of parents and teachers, the ineffectiveness of discipline, and the tendency to blame others for problems. Youth agreement with this perception of adults is demonstrated by a variety of PIY item correlates, including "I give my parent(s) a lot of trouble."

Family Dysfunction (FAM). This scale is divided into two meaningful dimensions. FAM1 (Conflict Among Members) reflects conflict within the family ("There is a lot of tension in our home"; "My parents do not agree on how to raise me"). Clinicians note conflict between the child's guardians and concern regarding the emotional or physical abuse of the child. The second FAM dimension more directly measures parent adjustment. Self-report correlates of FAM2 (Parent Maladjustment) include "One of my parents sometimes gets drunk and mean" as well as "My parents are now divorced or living apart."

Reality Distortion (RLT). This content valid scale is considerably different from the empirically keyed PIC–R Psychosis scale, whereas substantial overlap is obtained with the PIY RLT scale (RLT1: 57%, RLT2: 80%). RLT1 (Developmental Deviation) elevation describes a level of intellectual, emotional, and social functioning usually associated with substantial developmental retardation or regression. RLT2 (Hallucinations and Delusions) describes symptoms and behaviors often associated with a psychotic adjustment.

Somatic Concern (SOM). The first dimension of SOM measures a variety of health complaints often associated with poor psychological adjustment. SOM1 (Psychosomatic Preoccupation) elevation is often associated with the self-report of similar complaints ("I feel tired most of the time," "I often have headaches," "I often have an upset stomach"). The second SOM dimension (SOM2, Muscular Tension and Anxiety) appears to measure the somatic components of internalization.

Psychological Discomfort (DIS). This relatively long scale of 39 items is best described as a measure of negative affectivity, divided, as in the PIY, into three meaningful dimensions. The first dimension (DIS1) measures fearfulness and worry and is associated with clinician description of anxiety, fear, and tearfulness as well as self-report of fear and emotional upset. The second dimension (DIS2) is a general measure of depression that obtains considerable correlation with parent, teacher, and youth description. Teachers see students with an elevated DIS2 subscale score as sad or unhappy, moody and serious, and not having fun. Clinicians note many of the classical symptoms of depression, including feelings of helplessness, hopelessness, and worthlessness. Demonstrating inadequate self-esteem, such children are overly self-critical and usually expect rejection. The third DIS subscale is similar to the PIY DIS3 dimension; it combines the report of problematic sleep and a preoccupation with death. Elevation of DIS3 correlates with clinician concern regarding suicide potential and a wide variety of self-reported symptoms, including sleep disturbance, dysphoria, and thoughts about suicide.

Social Withdrawal (WDL). This is the shortest PIC–2 adjustment scale (19 items). The two WDL dimensions parallel those of the PIY. The first WDL subscale (WDL1: Social Introversion) measures the personality dimension social introversion. Most items reflect psychological discomfort in social interactions. Clinician observation and youth self-report describe shyness and an unwillingness to talk with others. The second WDL dimension (WDL2: Isolation) is a brief subscale of eight items that describes intentional lack of contact with others.

Social Skill Deficits (SSK). This scale consists of two dimensions. Both dimensions receive considerable support from self-report correlates in the form of PIY statements. The first SSK subscale reflects limited social influence. SSK1 (Limited Peer Status) elevation relates to self-report of few friends, a lack of popularity with peers, and little social influence. Teachers note avoidance of peers and a lack of awareness of the feelings of others. SSK2 (Conflict with Peers) elevation, in contrast, measures problematic relations with peers. Self-report correlates document these conflicts, and clinicians observe poor social skills and a problematic social adjustment.

Case Study: PIC–2 Standard Form Profile Scales and Subscales

The case of "Cheryl" and the PIC–2 Standard Form profile obtained from Cheryl's mother are introduced here. (Other elements of this case appear as appropriate throughout this presentation of test characteristics.) This teenager was referred for evaluation by her parents to determine if her school performance reflected the presence of a learning disability. Comprehensive evaluation of ability and academic achievement provided no such evidence. As presented in Figure 17–1, this PIC–2 Standard Form profile generated by the personal computer-scoring program available from the test publisher (note specific scale and subscale standard scores above $59T$ that fall within the shaded portion of the profile) demonstrated concern regarding school performance and cognitive status (COG1, COG2, RLT1) and the presence of externalizing symptoms suggesting limited behavioral control (ADH1, ADH2), noncompliance (DLQ3), and conflict with significant adult family members (FAM1). The endorsed critical items (not presented here) provided additional support for the presence of a pattern of problematic behavioral adjustment that would be consistent with inadequate academic motivation and effort.

PIY Scales and Subscales

The majority of PIY items were derived from rewriting of the first 280 items of the PIC–R administration booklet into a first-person format. The PIY self-report scales and subscales were constructed in the same manner as the PIC–2 scales (Lachar & Gruber, 1993, 1995a, 1995b). The nine clinical scales were constructed with a uniform methodology, resulting in the assignment of 231 items to only one scale as well as a high degree of scale content saturation and homogeneity. In addition, each of the nine scales have been further divided into two or three nonoverlapping subscales that represent factor-guided dimensions of even greater content homogeneity. The pattern of scale and subscale elevation is a major focus of the PIY and PIC–2 interpretive process.

Gender-specific linear T-scores have been derived from a national normative sample of 2,327 regular education students in grades 4 through 12, and a variety of analyses have been conducted with a large sample of clinically referred students ($N = 1,178$). PIY clinical scales average 26 items in length (range = 17 to 42 items), and the median coefficient alpha in referred protocols was .85 (range = .74 to .92). The 24 subscales average 10 items in length (range = 4 to 16 items, with 5 subscales less than 8 items in length), and the mean coefficient alpha in referred protocols was .73 (range = .44 to .84, with 8 of 24 subscales less than .70). The PIY administration and interpretation guide (Lachar & Gruber, 1995a) provides empirically derived interpretive guidelines for scales and subscales as well as 15 case studies.

Differences between the character of self-report and parent report are demonstrated when PIY scale and subscale content is compared with PIC–2 equivalents. The PIY Cognitive

Personality Inventory for Children, Second Edition (PIC-2)

A WPS TEST REPORT by David Lachar, Ph.D., Christian P. Gruber, Ph.D.
Copyright ©2003 by Western Psychological Services
12031 Wilshire Blvd., Los Angeles, California 90025-1251
Version 1.110

Child Name: Cheryl
Birthdate: 11-15-87
Age: 15
Respondent: Not Entered
Date Administered: 01/09/03

Gender: Female
Grade: 9

Date Processed: 01/09/03

Child ID: Not Entered
Ethnicity: White

Relationship to Child: Mother
Administered By: David Lachar

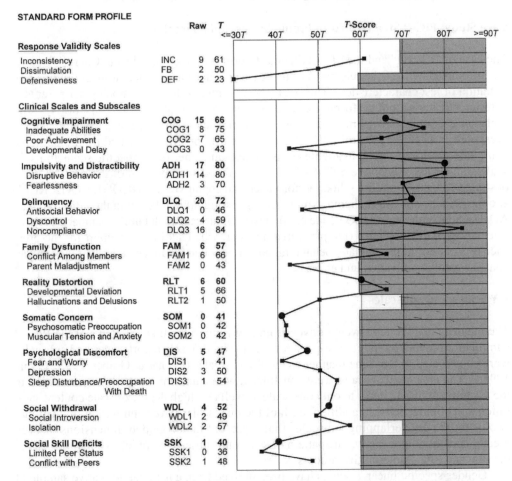

NOTE: Actuarial interpretive guidelines for the scales of the PIC-2 Standard Form Profile are highlighted in chapter 3 (pages 19–53) of the 2001 PIC-2 manual.

FIGURE 17–1.   Cheryl's PIC–2 Results.

Impairment scale includes only half of the items of the comparable PIC–2 scale. This difference reflects the exclusion of developmental or historical items in the self-report format (children are not accurate reporters of developmental delay) as well as the reality that fewer self-report items correlated with this dimension for youth. The PIY Impulsivity and Distractibility scale also incorporated fewer scale items (17) than its PIC–2 equivalent (27). Perhaps the report of ADH disruptive behavior would be more expected from an adult informant, who likely finds such behavior distressful, than from a student, who may not find such behaviors disturbing. Such results predict that the PIC–2 COG and ADH scales will demonstrate superior diagnostic performance in comparison with these PIY scales. In contrast, the other seven PIY clinical scales achieved a significant degree of similarity in content and length with their PIC–2 scale equivalents.

Case Study: PIY Profile Scales and Subscales

Cheryl completed the PIY as part of her evaluation. As demonstrated in Figure 17–2, the resulting scales and subscale scores that fell within the clinical range (shaded area of the profile) reflect acknowledgment of poor school performance (indeed, all COG1 items have been endorsed), and the interpretation of the remaining elevated scales and subscales is relatively straightforward: All of these values reflect problematic externalizing problem behaviors in the form of conflict at home (FAM1), noncompliance with the requests of adults (DLQ3), violation of rules and expectations (DLQ1), and other impulsive and poorly modulated behaviors (ADH3). Representative endorsed critical items support these diagnostic conclusions:

"It is hard for me to make good grades."

"Recently my school has sent notes home about my bad behavior."

"Punishment does not change how I act."

"Teachers complain that I cannot sit still."

"My parent(s) cause most of my problems."

PIC–2 and PIY Screening and Short Forms

The PIY and PIC–2 each incorporate a screening or a shortened assessment procedure. Thirty-two items from the first 80 items of the PIY were selected to form a screening scale (CLASS) intended to provide optimal identification of those regular education students who, when administered the full PIY, produce clinically significant results. These items also include three "scan items" for each clinical scale. Scan items were selected in such a manner that students who endorse at least two of each set of three items would have a high probability of scoring more than $59T$ on the corresponding clinical scale. Shortened versions of three validity scales can also be derived from these items. CLASS has demonstrated its effectiveness with nonreferred elementary school children (Wrobel & Lachar, 1998) as well as with nonreferred adolescents attending high school (Ziegenhorn, Tzelepis, Lachar, & Schubiner, 1994). In the former study, CLASS predicted elevations on PIY adjustment scales and problem descriptions from parents. In the latter study, CLASS significantly correlated with 16 of 18 potential indicators of maladjustment or behavioral risk.

The PIC–2 provides a short form designed specifically to measure change in clinical status associated with therapeutic intervention, the Behavioral Summary. Although PIC and PIC–R scales have demonstrated such sensitivity to change (see the example of treatment-related

Personality Inventory for Youth (PIY)

A WPS TEST REPORT by David Lachar, Ph.D., Christian P. Gruber, Ph.D.
Copyright ©1997-2003 by Western Psychological Services
12031 Wilshire Blvd., Los Angeles, California 90025-1251
Version 1.110

Youth Name: Cheryl
Birthdate: 11-15-87
Age: 15
Date Administered: 01/09/03

Gender: Female
Grade: 9
Date Processed: 01/09/03

Youth ID: Not Entered
Ethnicity: White

Administered By: David Lachar

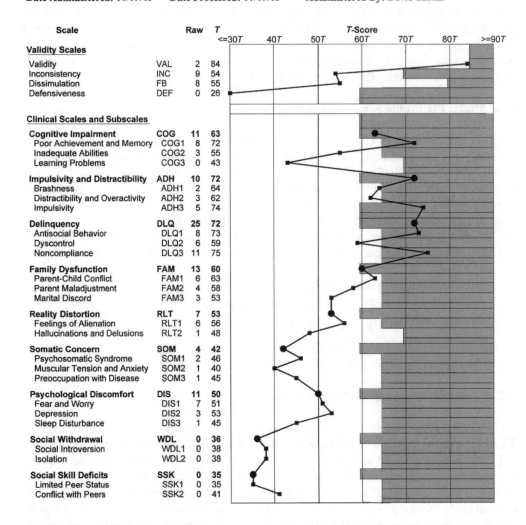

NOTE: Actuarial interpretive guidelines for PIY scales may be found on pages 14–21 of the 1995 PIY Administration and Interpretation Guide.

FIGURE 17–2.   Cheryl's PIY Results.

PIC–R and PIY change in Lachar & Kline, 1994), a brief form tailored specifically for this purpose was constructed by selection of items that are frequently endorsed in the context of clinical assessment and that describe clinical phenomena that are often the focus of short-term interventions. With the use of these guidelines, the 12 most favorable items from each of eight PIC–2 clinical scales were selected. These 96 inventory statements have been placed at the beginning of the 275-item PIC–2 administration booklet to serve as both a short form and a method of efficient reevaluation of a child following a short-term intervention. These statements are also available on a separate form with a self-scoring format. The scale scores and four scale composites may be graphed on the same profile at baseline and at appropriate interim and posttreatment intervals to demonstrate both dimensions of change and dimensions of stability. The Externalization composite is the sum of the ADH and DLQ shortened scales; the Internalization composite is the sum of the RLT, SOM, and DIS shortened scales; the Social Adjustment composite is the sum of the WDL and SSK shortened scales; and all eight scales (representing the response to all 96 items) are combined into a Total Score that is placed at the end of the profile. A similar measure is currently in development for the PIY.

Case Study: PIC–2 Behavioral Summary

Cheryl's Behavioral Summary profile is shown in Figure 17–3. This profile clearly focuses on the presence of poor behavioral control and noncompliance (ADH-S = $80T$, DLQS = $82T$). Family issues are also indicated (FAM-S = $64T$). The pattern of composite scale T-scores (EXT-C = $83T$) provides a single summary measure of this teenager's externalizing problem behaviors and suggests that readministration of the Behavioral Summary would be a useful way to monitor response to treatment.

PIY and PIC–2 Validity Scales

Both PIY and PIC–2 profiles include three comparable validity scales. The first to appear on the profile, Inconsistency, evaluates the likelihood that responses to items are random or reflect in some manner inadequate comprehension of inventory statement content or inadequate compliance with test instructions. The Dissimulation scale identifies profiles that may result from exaggeration of current problems or a malingered pattern of atypical or infrequent symptoms. The third validity scale, Defensiveness, identifies profiles likely to demonstrate the effect of minimization or denial of current problems. The PIY also provides a fourth unique validity measure, which consists of six items written so that, in each case, one of the two possible responses would be highly improbable, such as the false response to "I sometimes talk on the telephone." See Wrobel et al. (1999) for studies of scale performance.

The value of the PIC–2 FB scale is demonstrated in the following vignette. The PIC–2 was completed by the parent of a hospitalized 7-year-old boy in first grade who had a history of multiple psychiatric hospitalizations. This boy had attended a self-contained special education classroom for the emotionally impaired. His current psychiatric hospitalization was due to reported verbal and physical aggression toward family members, noncompliance, auditory and visual hallucinations, agitation, running in front of moving cars, attempting to drown himself, hair pulling, running away from home, and oppositional defiant behavior. His parents were asking for assistance in obtaining an agency placement, as they were unable to cope with his undercontrolled behavior at home. Several psychiatrists had been

Personality Inventory for Children, Second Edition (PIC-2)

A WPS TEST REPORT by David Lachar, Ph.D., Christian P. Gruber, Ph.D.
Copyright ©2003 by Western Psychological Services
12031 Wilshire Blvd., Los Angeles, California 90025-1251
Version 1.110

Child Name: Cheryl
Birthdate: Not Entered **Gender:** Female
Age: 15 **Grade:** 9
Respondent: Not Entered
Date Administered: 01/09/03 **Date Processed:** 01/09/03

Child ID: Not Entered
Ethnicity: White

Relationship to Child: Mother
Administered By: David Lachar

PIC-2: BEHAVIORAL SUMMARY PROFILE (Only first 96 items were completed by respondent.)

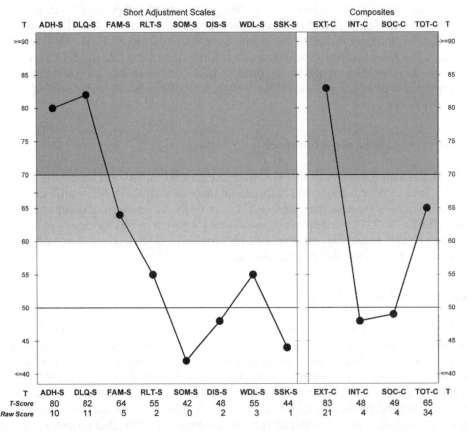

T	ADH-S	DLQ-S	FAM-S	RLT-S	SOM-S	DIS-S	WDL-S	SSK-S	EXT-C	INT-C	SOC-C	TOT-C	T
T-Score	80	82	64	55	42	48	55	44	83	48	49	65	
Raw Score	10	11	5	2	0	2	3	1	21	4	4	34	

ADH-S = Impulsivity and Distractibility - Short
DLQ-S = Delinquency-Short
FAM-S = Family Dysfunction - Short
RLT-S = Reality Distortion - Short

SOM-S = Somatic Concern - Short
DIS-S = Psychological Discomfort - Short
WDL-S = Social Withdrawal - Short
SSK-S = Social Skill Deficits-Short

EXT-C = Externalization - Composite
INT-C = Internalization - Composite
SOC-C = Social Adjustment - Composite
TOT-C = Total Score - Composite

NOTE: Actuarial interpretive guidelines for the scales of the PIC-2 Behavioral Summary Profile are highlighted in chapter 4 (pages 55–66) of the 2001 PIC-2 manual.

FIGURE 17–3. Cheryl's PIC-2 Behavioral Summary Profile.

sufficiently impressed by the parents' reports to have treated this child with a variety of psychotropic medications (stimulants, neuroleptics, mood stabilizers, and antidepressants).

Standing in contrast to the presentation by his parents of severe emotional and behavioral psychopathology was the fact that this young boy had called children's protective services to allege physical and emotional abuse by his parents. In addition, no indication of maladjustment had been observed during his first week of hospitalization. In an attempt to resolve the discrepancy between reported history and current behavior, the treating child psychiatrist made a request for a comprehensive psychological evaluation. The boy's mother completed the PIC–2, his teacher completed the SBS, and the boy himself was administered tests of intellectual ability and academic achievement. An obtained Full Scale IQ of 122 and a SBS profile not indicative of behavioral or emotional maladjustment but rather consistent with his teacher's assessment that the boy was "a bright and cooperative student, obtaining excellent grades" were in remarkable contrast to his mother's description of a severely disturbed child. Although all nine PIC–2 adjustment scales obtained scores above 70T and 18 of 21 subscales were elevated into the clinical range, the pattern of validity scale elevations suggested that little credence should be given to these results (INC = 47T, FB = 127T, DEF = 27T). The Dissimulation raw score of 24, a value equivalent to the top third of the protocols generated by directed malingering, raised serious doubts about the validity of this PIC–2. Subsequent weeks of hospitalization documented in a variety of ways that this child had been the scapegoat in this family and had experienced considerable emotional abuse.

Table 17.1 presents the PIC–2 and PIY profile pairs obtained for three 12-year-old hospitalized patients. Review of Case A's profiles identified PIC–2 and PIY validity scale T-score values that did not suggest that the accuracy of these profiles had been compromised in any systematic manner. It is important to observe that both profiles include clinically elevated scale scores. First, consider the similarities in scale and subscale pattern and scale and subscale clinical elevations. For example, apparent disagreement between PIY and PIC–2 COG3 (53T vs. 85T) actually represents a difference in subscale content. COG3 for parent report reflects developmental issues (Developmental Delay), whereas COG3 for student report represents problems in learning (Learning Problems), a dimension much more similar to PIC–2 COG2 (Poor Achievement). Case A is a 12-year-old who is in his fifth psychiatric hospitalization and had previously attended a self-contained special education classroom for the behaviorally maladjusted. His current diagnoses were ADHD combined type, Oppositional Defiant Disorder, and Conduct Disorder. His behavior at home and in the hospital demonstrated serious behavioral dyscontrol. He had been noncompliant in taking psychotropic medication to improve his emotional and behavioral control. He had threatened to kill himself (see DIS3 scores) and had assaulted his mother, who he said did not want him at home (see PIY FAM1, Parent-Child Conflict, and FAM2, Parent Maladjustment). He attempted to escape from the hospital and required multiple time-outs and seclusions to control his rages, threats, and aggressive and inappropriate behavior (see DLQ2, Dyscontrol). Off of medication, he demonstrated an attention span of less than 15 minutes (see ADH values). He also had a history of impulsive and disruptive behavior, fighting with peers, noncompliance with adults, verbal and physical aggression, and running away from home (see elevated DLQ values for both PIY and PIC–2).

The profiles of Case B, in contrast to those of Case A, document considerable disagreement between parent and child. The only consistency in agreement was in the problem area of academic achievement (PIC–2 COG2, Poor Achievement, PIY COG3, Learning Problems). School history and psychometric assessment documented retention in grade, special class placement, and academic achievement substantially below assessed intellectual abil-

TABLE 17.1.

The Influence of Respondent Defensiveness on PIC–2/PIY Profile Pairs from Three Clinical Evaluations

Scale/Subscale	Case A		Case B		Case C	
	PIC–2	PIY	PIC–2	PIY	PIC–2	PIY
Inconsistency	53	49	67	57	50	68
Dissimulation	60	72	81	48	47	72
Defensiveness	30	39	30	**64**	**65**	50
Cognitive impairment	61	63	67	57	43	47
COG1	56	57	68	52	49	42
COG2	67	50	70	45	41	45
COG3	53	85	48	85	43	67
Impulsivity & distractibility	79	69	81	39	44	64
ADH1	75	77	83	49	46	53
ADH2	81	62	64	37	41	62
ADH3	—	57	—	41	—	66
Delinquency	83	75	86	41	42	49
DLQ1	71	75	63	43	46	49
DLQ2	82	71	98	41	43	56
DLQ3	79	67	76	43	42	42
Family dysfunction	60	69	58	57	67	49
FAM1	58	69	58	52	62	47
FAM2	60	74	54	57	72	49
FAM3	—	53	—	58	—	53
Reality distortion	67	71	73	48	50	79
RLT1	69	64	83	53	55	74
RLT2	62	75	56	41	44	79
Somatic concern	82	75	74	49	41	65
SOM1	82	66	76	38	42	59
SOM2	72	71	65	53	41	65
SOM3	—	73	—	59	—	65
Psychological discomfort	90	59	97	63	53	68
DIS1	70	64	81	64	51	66
DIS2	88	38	92	52	49	58
DIS3	83	70	83	63	63	68
Social withdrawal	47	83	85	41	46	59
WDL1	46	77	72	46	49	53
WDL2	50	78	88	38	42	65
Social skill deficits	57	43	86	56	49	57
SSK1	43	40	68	53	50	56
SSK2	74	50	97	59	48	55

ity. Clearly the PIC–2 most accurately described this 12-year-old male who presented with multiple handicaps. The elevation of the PIY DEF scale ($T = 64$) is the most likely explanation for the fact that this PIY profile is essentially within normal limits. Indeed, this patient's medical record detailed his repeated denial and minimizing of problems during this hospitalization in an attempt to facilitate his early discharge from treatment. This child's psychiatric history was secondary to a traumatic motor vehicle accident. He felt lonely and scared; frequently cried, sobbed, and shook; avoided others; and was preoccupied with excessive worries (DIS, WDL). He externalized his problems (DLQ), had difficulties with peers, and had little insight into his role in these conflicts (SSK2, Conflict with Peers). This pattern of PIY defensiveness is fairly common in inpatient settings.

Case C is quite unusual, in that the PIC–2 completed by this 12-year-old girl's mother is essentially within normal limits, with the exception of FAM1 (Conflict Among Members), FAM2 (Parent Maladjustment), and DIS3 (Sleep Disturbance/Preoccupation with Death), which obtain some elevation. This PIC–2 profile would be quite difficult to interpret without the presence of validity scales, as the mother had referred her daughter for this current hospitalization. Case C presented with suicidal ideation, low self-esteem, depression, crying spells, poor appetite, and associated weight loss (DIS, WDL2, Isolation). She actively demonstrated somatic concern and somatic symptoms (SOM) in response to conflict during this hospitalization and told others that she would not talk about her problems with her mother because she was afraid that she would distress her mother, who was under psychiatric care (PIC–2 FAM2, Parent Maladjustment). The clinicians were sufficiently concerned with this patient's internalizing problems to assign discharge diagnoses of generalized anxiety disorder and depressive disorder and to continue her on antidepressant medication at discharge. Why was the mother defensive in describing her daughter's problems? It was clearly documented in the medical record that she was concerned that she would be seen as an inadequate mother because of her and her daughter's psychiatric problems and that she could thus lose custody of her daughter to another adult family member.

STUDENT BEHAVIOR SURVEY

The development of the Student Behavior Survey (SBS; Lachar, Wingenfeld, Kline, & Gruber, 2000) consisted of several iterations in which the test authors in their review of established teacher rating scales and in the writing of new rating statements focused on content appropriate to teacher observation. SBS items are not derived from the PIY or PIC–2. The SBS items demonstrate a specific school focus. Review of the SBS reveals that 58 of its 102 items specifically refer to in-class or in-school behaviors and to judgments that can be made only by school staff (Wingenfeld, Lachar, Gruber, & Kline, 1998). The SBS items are sorted into 14 scales that are placed onto a profile. The SBS assesses student academic status and work habits, social skills, parental participation in the educational process, and problems such as aggressive or atypical behavior and emotional stress. Norms that generate linear T-scores are gender specific and divided into two age groups, 5 to 11 years and 12 to 18 years.

The SBS consists of three sections. In the first section, the teacher selects one of five ratings options (Deficient, Below Average, Average, Above Average, Superior) to describe eight areas of achievement, such as reading comprehension and mathematics, which are then summed to provide an estimate of current Academic Performance (AP). The remaining 94 items are rated on a four-point frequency scale: Never, Seldom, Sometimes, and Usually. The second section (Academic Resources) presents positively worded statements divided into three scales. The first two of these scales consist of descriptions of positive behaviors that describe the student's adaptive behaviors: Academic Habits (AH) and Social Skills (SS). The third scale, Parent Participation (PP), consists of ratings of the student's parents that are very school specific. Here the teacher is asked to judge the degree to which the parents support the student's educational program. The third SBS section, Problems in Adjustment, provides seven scales consisting of negatively worded items: Health Concerns (HC), Emotional Distress (ED), Unusual Behavior (UB), Social Problems (SP), Verbal Aggression (VA), Physical Aggression (PA), and Behavior Problems (BP). Table 17.2 provides examples of SBS

TABLE 17.2.
SBS Scales and Sample Items

Scale name (Abbr.)	Items	Example of scale item
Academic performance (AP)	8	Reading comprehension
Academic habits (AH)	13	Completes class assignments
Social skills (SS)	8	Participates in class activities
Parent participation (PP)	6	Parent(s) encourage achievement
Health concerns (HC)	6	Complains of headaches
Emotional distress (ED)	15	Worries about little things
Unusual behavior (UB)	7	Says strange or bizarre things
Social problems (SP)	12	Teased by other students
Verbal aggression (VA)	7	Argues and wants the last word
Physical aggression (PA)	5	Destroys property when angry
Behavior problems (BP)	15	Disobeys class or school rules
Attention-deficit/hyperactivity (ADH)	16	Waits for his/her turn
Oppositional defiant (OPD)	16	Mood changes without reason
Conduct problems (CNP)	16	Steals from others

scale items, scale length, temporal stability, interrater reliability, and coefficient alphas based on protocols from students in clinical evaluation or receiving special education services in grades K–12. Initial item and scale performance documented that 99 of 102 items statistically separated the clinical and special education protocols from the protocols of regular education students. It was demonstrated that each item had been placed on the scale with which it obtained the largest correlation. Scale scores of regular education and referred students obtained meaningful three-factor solutions (Wingenfeld et al., 1998).

Additional effort (Pisecco, Lachar, Gruber, Gallen, Kline, and Huzinec, 1999) was applied in the construction of three additional 16-item nonoverlapping scales. These scales consisted of SBS items drawn from several content dimensions that were consensually nominated as representing characteristics that would be associated with youths who obtain one of three *DSM–IV* diagnoses: Attention Deficit Hyperactivity Disorder combined type (9 items from AH, 4 items from BP, and one each from SS, UB, and SP), Oppositional Defiant Disorder (4 items each from ED and VA, 3 items each from SS and BP, and 2 items from SP), and Conduct Disorder (8 items from BP, 5 items from PA, and 3 items from VA). Item-to-scale correlations and a three-factor solution for these 48 SBS items empirically supported the placement of these scale items. The SBS Disruptive Behavior scales are named Attention-Deficit/Hyperactivity (ADH), Oppositional Defiant (OPD), and Conduct Problems (CNP).

Case Study: SBS Profile Scales

To complete this chapter's core case study, we now turn our attention to a teacher description of Cheryl obtained from the SBS. As demonstrated by the SBS profile presented in Figure 17–4, although few scale *T*-scores extend into the interpretable range (shaded, > 59*T*), their interpretive meaning is consistent with the previously discussed clinically elevated PIY self-report and PIC–2 parent-report scales. The low score on AH (40*T*) reflects concern that Cheryl was not effectively engaged in classroom activities and might not be

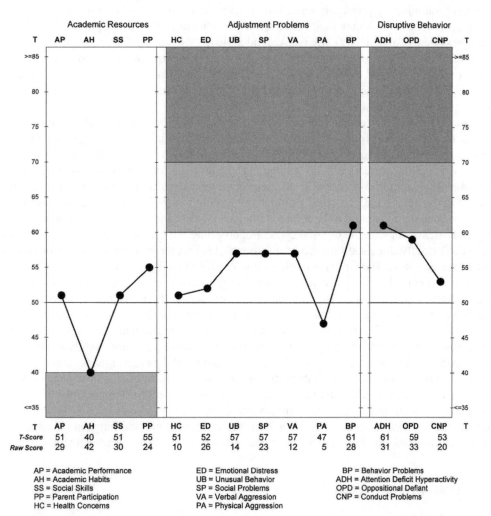

Student Behavior Survey (SBS)

A WPS TEST REPORT by David Lachar, Ph.D., Christian P. Gruber, Ph.D.
Copyright ©2003 by Western Psychological Services
12031 Wilshire Blvd., Los Angeles, California 90025-1251
Version 1.110

Student Name: Cheryl
Birthdate: 11-15-87   **Gender:** Female   **Student ID:** Not Entered
Age: 15   **Grade:** 9   **Ethnicity:** White
Rater: R J Patterson   **Role of Rater:** Teacher   **Months Observing Child:** 3
Date Administered: 12/05/02   **Date Processed:** 01/09/03   **Administered By:** David Lachar

	AP	AH	SS	PP	HC	ED	UB	SP	VA	PA	BP	ADH	OPD	CNP
T-Score	51	40	51	55	51	52	57	57	57	47	61	61	59	53
Raw Score	29	42	30	24	10	26	14	23	12	5	28	31	33	20

AP = Academic Performance
AH = Academic Habits
SS = Social Skills
PP = Parent Participation
HC = Health Concerns

ED = Emotional Distress
UB = Unusual Behavior
SP = Social Problems
VA = Verbal Aggression
PA = Physical Aggression

BP = Behavior Problems
ADH = Attention Deficit Hyperactivity
OPD = Oppositional Defiant
CNP = Conduct Problems

NOTE: Actuarial interpretive guidelines for SBS scales may be found on pages 13–17 of the 2000 SBS manual.

FIGURE 17–4.   Cheryl's SBS Results.

motivated to achieve. Minimal yet significant scale score elevations $(61T)$ on BP and ADH suggest variable noncompliance and rule violation.

EVALUATION OF TREATMENT EFFECTIVENESS

Baseline application of the PIC–2, SBS, and PIY at intake or program admission supports treatment planning by providing an efficient, comprehensive, and expeditious focus on a youth's problems, which may then be placed within a historical or developmental as well as a family systems context. Not only is FAM valuable in this context, but independent administration of the PIC–2 to each parent allows subsequent identification of problem areas on which parents agree and those on which they do not. The provision of feedback to parents from PIC–2 profiles is quite straightforward and usually well received, as these profiles summarize parent observations.

Therapeutic effectiveness is documented through questionnaire readministration after intervention efforts. The focus and form of measure readministration should be guided by both the setting in which therapeutic intervention has occurred and the nature of the identified problem dimensions under treatment. For example, if the problem focus is inattention and disruptive behavior is primarily observed in the classroom, repeated teacher ratings are most appropriate. On the other hand, if a child's individual psychotherapy focuses on current problems that have been demonstrated to be related to negative affect and a problematic self-concept, repeated assessment with the use of a content-appropriate self-report measure should be considered. Certainly the questionnaire or questionnaires that have documented the problems under treatment would be the most likely candidates for readministration.

Of prime consideration is the interpretation of the test differences obtained. The stability of the obtained differences may be judged against the standard error of measurement. These values are provided in each test manual and in general suggest that differences in excess of $5T$ should be stable. Of greater importance in judging the clinical meaning of such differences is the benefit obtained from applying the actuarial interpretive guidelines available for these measures that define the scale scores within the normative and the clinical range as well as gradations within the clinical range. Substantive improvement is most readily documented when scores that appear in the clinical range at baseline and thereby reflect the presence of significant maladjustment fall within the normative range after an intervention. Additional attention should be given to scores that fall within the substantive clinical range at baseline and upon readministration obtain values that suggest only mild levels of maladjustment.

COMMENTARY

The complete 2001 revision of the PIC, the addition of a multidimensional teacher-rating scale, and the collection of a national representative normative sample for each measure have gone a long way to respond to concerns that the PIC was an aging test in need of revision and update (Kamphaus & Frick, 1996; Knoff, 1989; Merrell, 1994). Critical evaluations of the SBS and PIC–2 manuals and investigation of their ability to evaluate emotional adjustment at baseline and quantify response to intervention will continue well into the new century. Indeed, traditional psychometric standards, such as reliability, are inadequate to evaluate such measures. Instead of establishing temporal stability with the use of a test-retest paradigm for the measurement of characteristics that naturally vary over time and are often the focus of intervention, it will be necessary to establish interpretive standards for scales that are sequentially administered over time. To be applied in the evaluation of treatment effectiveness, the degree of scale score change must be found to accurately track some independent estimate of treatment effectiveness (cf. Sheldrick, Kendall, & Heimberg, 2001).

The emphasis on evaluating response accuracy with the use of validity scales and the empirical determination of interpretive guidelines continues to characterize these measures. Many psychologists unconvinced of the importance of these psychometric phenomena might not value their contributions to assessment. Although the PIC has been reduced from 420 to 275 items, into which a set of subscales and a brief 96-item form have been incorporated, some clinicians may still judge the length of these questionnaires to be problematic.

Although I am obviously biased against the view that inventory length is intrinsically a negative attribute, it is certain that the breath and depth of a measure's content establish the potential boundaries of its utility. Even the 270 items of the PIY are easily completed in less than 45 minutes by children in the fourth grade. PIC–2, PIY, and SBS efficiency has been improved by the rejection of any item not actively used in the interpretive process as well as by computer software provided for scoring and interpretation. The value of saving 10 or 15 minutes of teacher, parent, or youth effort should be balanced against what is lost in measure reliability and in the restriction of the variety of dimensions assessed.

The PIC publication history suggests the diagnostic potential of the new and revised measures, especially on the dimensions that retain the greatest similarity from original to revised formats. Continued effort will expand the diagnostic utility of these new and revised forms to achieve the demonstrated performance of the original inventory (Lachar & Kline, 1994). Such efforts have begun (see the PIC–2, PIY, and SBS manuals). For example, demographically matched samples of inpatient adolescents with discharge diagnoses of either conduct disorder or major depression were correctly classified by PIY subscales in 83% of the cases (Lachar, Harper, Green, Morgan, & Wheeler, 1996). In addition, hospitalized adolescents with a diagnosis of conduct disorder obtain PIY profiles similar to those of adolescents incarcerated in a juvenile justice facility (Negy, Lachar, Gruber, & Garza, 2001).

CONCLUSION

This chapter reviews the development and application of a "family" of parent-, teacher-, and self-report multidimensional inventories for use with school-age children and adolescents (grades K–12). These objective questionnaires integrate a variety of psychometric components that improve efficiency and facilitate inventory interpretation, such as validity scales, a subscale-within-scale structure, and screening forms designed to be sensitive to treatment effects. The PIC–2, PIY, and SBS measure dimensions of internalizing and externalizing problem behaviors, social adjustment, family character, and cognitive ability. Each measure incorporates dimensions that are similar across informants as well as dimensions that are unique to a given informant source. The questionnaires can be applied independently or in combination. As this chapter demonstrates, the PIC–2, PIY, and SBS possess instrument validity and can be used in treatment planning and to document treatment effects.

REFERENCES

Achenbach, T. M. (1981). A junior MMPI? [Review of *Multidimensional description of child personality: A manual for the Personality Inventory for Children* and *Actuarial assessment of child and adolescent personality: An interpretive guide for the Personality Inventory for Children profile*]. *Journal of Personality Assessment, 45*, 332–333.

Achenbach, T. M., McConaughy, S. H., & Howell, C. T. (1987). Child/adolescent behavioral and emotional problems: Implications of cross-informant correlations for situational specificity. *Psychological Bulletin, 101*, 213–232.

Brady, E. U., & Kendall, P. C. (1992). Comorbidity of anxiety and depression in children and adolescents. *Psychological Bulletin, 111*, 244–255.

Cantwell, D. P. (1996). Attention deficit disorder: A review of the past 10 years. *Journal of the American Academy of Child and Adolescent Psychiatry, 35*, 978–987.

Caron, C., & Rutter, M. (1991). Comorbidity in child psychopathology: Concepts, issues, and research strategies. *Journal of Child Psychology and Psychiatry, 32*, 1063–1080.

Flavell, J. H., Flavell, E. R., & Green, F. L. (2001). Development of children's understanding of connections between thinking and feeling. *Psychological Science, 12*, 430–432.

Greenbaum, P. E., Dedrick, R. F., Prange, M. E., & Friedman, R. M. (1994). Parent, teacher, and child ratings of problem behaviors of youngsters with serious emotional disturbances. *Psychological Assessment, 6*, 141–148.

Jensen, P. S., Martin, D., & Cantwell, D. P. (1997). Comorbidity in ADHD: Implications for research, practice, and *DSM–IV*. *Journal of the American Academy of Child and Adolescent Psychiatry, 36*, 1065–1079.

Jensen, P. S., Watanabe, H. K., Richters, J. E., Roper, M., Hibbs, E. D., Salzberg, A. D., et al. (1996). Scales, diagnoses, and child psychopathology: II. Comparing the CBCL and the DISC against external validators. *Journal of Abnormal Child Psychology, 24*, 151–168.

Kamphaus, R. W., & Frick, P. J. (1996). *Clinical assessment of child and adolescent personality and behavior*. Boston: Allyn & Bacon.

King, N. J., Ollendick, T. H., & Gullone, E. (1991). Negative affectivity in children and adolescents: Relations between anxiety and depression. *Clinical Psychology Review, 11*, 441–459.

Knoff, H. M. (1989). Review of the Personality Inventory for Children, Revised Format. In J. C. Connolly & J. C. Kramer (Eds.), *The tenth mental measurements yearbook* (pp. 624–630). Lincoln, NE: Buros Institute of Mental Measurements.

Lachar, D., & Gdowski, C. L. (1979). *Actuarial assessment of child and adolescent personality: An interpretive guide for the Personality Inventory for Children profile*. Los Angeles: Western Psychological Services.

Lachar, D., & Gruber, C. P. (1993). Development of the Personality Inventory for Youth: A self-report companion to the Personality Inventory for Children. *Journal of Personality Assessment, 61*, 81–98.

Lachar, D., & Gruber, C. P. (1995a). *Personality Inventory for Youth (PIY) manual: Administration and interpretation guide*. Los Angeles: Western Psychological Services.

Lachar, D., & Gruber, C. P. (1995b). *Personality Inventory for Youth (PIY) manual: Technical guide*. Los Angeles: Western Psychological Services.

Lachar, D., & Gruber, C. P. (2001). *Personality Inventory for Children, Second Edition (PIC–2) Standard Form and Behavioral Summary manual*. Los Angeles: Western Psychological Services.

Lachar, D., Harper, R. A., Green, B. A., Morgan, S. T., & Wheeler, A. C. (1996, August). *The Personality Inventory for Youth: Contribution to diagnosis*. Paper presented at the 104th annual convention of the American Psychological Association, Toronto.

Lachar, D., & Kline, R. B. (1994). The Personality Inventory for Children (PIC) and the Personality Inventory for Youth (PIY). In M. Maruish (Ed.), *Use of psychological testing for treatment planning and outcomes assessment* (pp. 479–516). Hillsdale, NJ: Lawrence Erlbaum Associates.

Lachar, D., Kline, R. B., & Gdowski, C. L. (1987). Respondent psychopathology and interpretive accuracy of the Personality Inventory for Children: The evaluation of a "most reasonable" assumption. *Journal of Personality Assessment, 51*, 165–177.

Lachar, D., Wingenfeld, S. A., Kline, R. B., & Gruber, C. P. (2000). *Student Behavior Survey (SBS) manual*. Los Angeles: Western Psychological Services.

LaCombe, J. A., Kline, R. B., Lachar, D., Butkus, M., & Hillman, S. B. (1991). Case history correlates of a Personality Inventory for Children (PIC) profile typology. *Psychological Assessment: A Journal of Consulting and Clinical Psychology, 13*, 1–14.

LaGreca, A. M., Kuttler, A. F., & Stone, W. L. (2001). Assessing children through interviews and behavioral observations. In C. E. Walker & M. C. Roberts (Eds.), *Handbook of clinical child psychology* (3rd ed., pp. 90–110). New York: Wiley.

Loeber, R., Green, S. M., & Lahey, B. B. (1990). Mental health professionals' perception of the utility of children, mothers, and teachers as informants on childhood psychopathology. *Journal of Clinical Child Psychology, 19*, 136–143.

Lonigan, C. J., Carey, M. P., & Finch, A. J., Jr. (1994). Anxiety and depression in children and adolescents: Negative affectivity and the utility of self-reports. *Journal of Consulting and Clinical Psychology, 62*, 1000–1008.

Maruish, M. (Ed.). (2004). *The use of psychological testing for treatment planning and outcome assessment* (Vol. 2, 3rd ed.). Mahwah, NJ: Lawrence Erlbaum Associates.

Merrell, K. W. (1994). *Assessment of behavioral, social, and emotional problems: Direct and objective methods for use with children and adolescents.* New York: Longman.

Michael, K. D., & Merrell, K. W. (1998). Reliability of children's self-reported internalizing symptoms over short to medium-length time intervals. *Journal of the American Academy of Child and Adolescent Psychiatry, 37*, 194–201.

Negy, C., Lachar, D., Gruber, C. P., & Garza, N. D. (2001). The Personality Inventory for Youth: Validity and comparability of English and Spanish versions for regular education and juvenile justice samples. *Journal of Personality Assessment, 76*, 250–263.

Phares, V. (1997). Accuracy of informants: Do parents think that mother knows best? *Journal of Abnormal Child Psychology, 25*, 165–171.

Pisecco, S., Lachar, D., Gruber, C. P., Gallen, R. T., Kline, R. B., & Huzinec, C. (1999). Development and validation of disruptive behavior scales for the Student Behavior Survey (SBS). *Journal of Psychoeducational Assessment, 17*, 314–331.

Pliszka, S. R. (1998). Comorbidity of attention-deficit/hyperactivity disorder with psychiatric disorder: An overview. *Journal of Clinical Psychiatry, 59*(Suppl. 7), 50–58.

Richters, J. E. (1992). Depressed mothers as informants about their children: A critical review of the evidence for distortion. *Psychological Bulletin, 112*, 485–499.

Sheldrick, R. C., Kendall, P. C., & Heimberg, R. G. (2001). The clinical significance of treatments: A comparison of three treatments for conduct disordered children. *Clinical Psychology: Science and Practice, 8*, 418–430.

Wingenfeld, S. A., Lachar, D., Gruber, C. P., & Kline, R. B. (1998). Development of the teacher-informant Student Behavior Survey. *Journal of Psychoeducational Assessment, 16*, 226–249.

Wrobel, N. H., & Lachar, D. (1998). Validity of self-and parent-report scales in screening students for behavioral and emotional problems in elementary school. *Psychology in the Schools, 35*, 17–27.

Wrobel, T. A., Lachar, D., Wrobel, N. H., Morgan, S. T., Gruber, C. P., & Neher, J. A. (1999). Performance of the Personality Inventory for Youth validity scales. *Assessment, 6*, 367–376.

Ziegenhorn, L., Tzelepis, A., Lachar, D., & Schubiner, H. (1994, August). *Personality Inventory for Youth: Screening for high-risk adolescents.* Paper presented at the 102nd annual convention of the American Psychological Association, Los Angeles.

18

BEHAVIOR ASSESSMENT SYSTEM FOR CHILDREN—SECOND EDITION

Randy W. Kamphaus, Meghan C. VanDeventer,
Amber Brueggemann, and Melissa Barry

University of Georgia

This chapter is devoted primarily to the important clinical task of interpreting the scale scores derived through the administration of the Behavior Assessment System for Children–Second Edition (BASC–2). The BASC–2 manual is exhaustive in its treatment of administration, scoring, validation, norming, Spanish form development, and numerous other important issues. Given this resource, it seems best to prepare this chapter with the distinct aforementioned focus on making diagnostic and treatment decisions based on the considerable validity evidence associated with individual scales. After a brief overview of BASC–2 components and applications, the scales of the teacher (TRS), parent (PRS), and self-report (SRP) are discussed in the context of the considerable amount of available research that supports interpretation efforts.

OVERVIEW OF THE BASC–2

The BASC–2 is a multimethod, multidimensional system used to evaluate the behavior and self-perceptions of children and young adults aged 2 through 25 years. (Reynolds & Kamphaus, 2004, p. 1)

Components

The BASC–2 is considered a *multimethod* instrument because of the inclusion of five separate components that allow clinicians to obtain information in a number of ways from multiple sources and settings. The use of an integrated, multimethod assessment system helps to reduce threats to validity that would be present if only one type of assessment were used (Reynolds & Kamphaus, 2004).

These components include

- A parent rating scale (PRS) that gathers descriptions of the child's observable behavior
- A teacher rating scale (TRS) that gathers descriptions of the child's observable behavior
- A self-report scale (SRP) on which the child or young adult can indicate his or her emotions and self-perceptions
- A structured developmental history (SDH) form that allows the clinician to gather information on the child's background history
- A student observation system (SOS) for recording and classifying directly observed classroom behavior

The PRS and TRS are divided into three age-appropriate forms: a preschool form (ages 2–5), a child form (ages 6–11), and an adolescent form (ages 12–21). The SRP has four separate forms, divided by age: an interview form (ages 6–7), a child form (ages 8–11), an adolescent form (ages 12–21), and a college form (ages 18–25). Across forms, the item content varies to reflect developmental changes in the manifestation of various disorders, and how children and young adults tend to think about themselves and their behavior.

See the BASC–2 manual (Reynolds & Kamphaus, 2004) for a wealth of information concerning the psychometric properties of the measures, including internal consistency, test-retest and interrater reliability, scale intercorrelations, correlations with other measures, multitrait-multimethod validity, as well as profiles of specific clinical groups. A Spanish version of the BASC–2 SRP, SDH, and PRS is also available.

Dimensional Classification

The BASC–2 utilizes a quantitative, *multidimensional* approach to classification rather than a qualitative, *categorical* approach. The categorical approach to classification views diagnosis as dichotomous (one either has the disorder or not) and does not consider subsyndromal pathology (Cantwell, 1996). A well-known example of the application of the categorical approach is the *Diagnostic and Statistical Manual of Mental Disorders* (American Psychiatric Association, 2000). In the *DSM-IV-TR*, the presence of a specific number of marker symptoms or deviant signs defines the disorder. This type of classification fails to take the severity of symptomatology into account. For example, the *DSM-IV-TR* does not distinguish between mild and severe ADHD; rather, an individual either has ADHD or does not.

The dimensional approach, on the other hand, views traits as distributed dimensionally in the population, thus allowing for the assessment of "severity," subsyndromal pathology, and normal variation. A *trait* can be defined as a characteristic feature of mind or character. Because psychological traits cannot be directly perceived through the senses, these traits are referred to as "latent." Rating scales, such as the BASC–2, are indicators or "estimates" of latent traits. The BASC–2 measures multiple dimensions, or traits, including personality and behavioral problems, emotional disturbances, and positive traits such as adaptability.

Applications

The BASC–2 was designed to assist in the differential diagnosis and educational classification of a variety of emotional and behavioral disorders of children, as well as the development of treatment plans (Reynolds & Kamphaus, 2004). Although the multimethod, multidimensional nature of the BASC–2 provides a large, varied store of information, we recommend an integrative approach to assessment. An *integrative approach* emphasizes the collection of many data sources in order to consider context, search for hypotheses that can be corroborated by more than one source of data, make the most parsimonious conclusions, and support conclusions with scientifically based theory and research (Kamphaus, 2001). Therefore examiners are encouraged to integrate BASC–2 results with other information, such as face-to face interviews and test scores, that has been collected as part of a full evaluation.

Clinical Diagnosis and Educational Classification.   The range of dimensions assessed with the BASC–2 helps clinicians to make differential diagnoses of specific categories of disorder, such as those found in the DSM-IV, as well as general categories of problems, such as those addressed by the Individuals with Disabilities Education Act (IDEA, 2004). Because of its dimensional nature as well as its sensitivity, the BASC–2 is also able to identify children at the subsyndromal level of psychopathology. These children do not reach the threshold for a categorical diagnosis, but may still be affected by behavioral and emotional problems.

Before accepting BASC–2 scores as valid representations of client functioning, one must examine the numerous threats to valid measurement, including failure to pay attention to the item content, carelessness, an attempt to portray oneself in a highly negative (malingering) or positive (minimization) light, lack of motivation to respond truthfully, or poor comprehension of the items. The BASC–2 provides examiners with several Validity Indexes to aid in the judgment of the quality of a completed form. The F, or "fake bad" index, is a measure of the respondent's tendency to be excessively negative about his or her self-perceptions and emotions. The L, or "fake good" index, measures a child's tendency to give an extremely positive picture of himself or herself. Last, the V index gives a basic check on the validity of scores in general. This index consists of four or five nonsensical or highly implausible items that, if agreed with, would indicate invalidity. Examiners can also examine the congruence of findings across examiners and contexts and patterns of responding.

After examining validity, clinicians should take a number of steps in utilizing the BASC–2 for assessment and classification (Kamphaus & Frick, 2002):

1. Assess core constructs/symptoms as well as severity of these symptoms (BASC rating scales: TRS, PRS, SRP). Identify all scales with T scores in the at-risk range and confirm the importance of each with available evidence.

2. Assess age of onset (SDH), developmental course (SDH), and multiple contexts (SDH, SOS, and rating scales)

3. Rule out alternative causes for elevated T scores, such as environmental stressors or invalid ratings (SDH, rating scales)

4. Rule in comorbidities or, in other words, the possibility of multiple problems/pathologies (SDH, rating scales)

Treatment/Intervention Planning and Evaluation.   The BASC–2 can also be utilized as a valuable tool for treatment planning and evaluation in the following capacity (Reynolds & Kamphaus, 2004):

1. Define target behaviors via history (SDH), interviews, rating scales (PRS, TRS, SRP), and observations (SOS)

2. Establish baseline adjustment with the use of rating scales and/or observations
3. Assess intervention/treatment effectiveness with a minimum of three rating scales and/or observations
4. Adjust interventions/treatment based on findings

Self-Report of Personality

The Self-Report of Personality (SRP) is a broadband personality inventory consisting of a mixed item-response format. Some of the items require a *True/False* response, whereas others ask for a rating on a four-point scale of frequency, ranging from *Never* to *Almost Always*. The four-point scale, new on the BASC–2, adds reliability and improves measurement at the extremes of the score range. The SRP, which takes about 20 to 30 minutes to complete, has three forms: child (ages 8–11), adolescent (ages 12–22), and young adults attending a postsecondary school (ages 18–25). The latter College form is new to the BASC–2. These levels overlap considerably on scales and item content; the Child and Adolescent forms have identical composite scores: School Problems, Internalizing Problems, Inattention/Hyperactivity, Personal Adjustment, and an overall Composite score titled the Emotional Symptoms Index (ESI). The College level form retains all of these composites, except for School Problems.

Interpretation of the SRP

Interpretation of Scale Scores.   The clinical scales measure maladjustment, and high scores on these scales represent negative characteristics. *T* scores ranging from 60 to 69 are considered At Risk, and scores of 70 or higher are considered Clinically Significant. The BASC–2 forms containing a particular scale are noted in parentheses.

- Alcohol Abuse (SRP-COL) measures the tendency to use alcohol in ways that could lead to impairment of functioning in academic and other settings. The items on this scale are better suited for assessing substance use patterns rather than for surveying patterns of alcohol use that are not associated with impairment. For this reason, high scores on this scale warrant further inquiry and possible additional evaluation for alcohol abuse or other substance abuse problems.
- Anxiety (SRP-C, A, COL) examines generalized fears, nervousness, and worry that typically are irrational and poorly defined in the mind of the individual. It is possible, however, that an individual with anxiety problems will not acknowledge them on an anxiety scale or even during an interview, because of a repressive coping style that is characterized by denial of symptoms. Gil (2005), for example, found that children with irritable bowel syndrome who were classified as "repressors" by a defensiveness scale composed of item content very similar to the SRP L Index, did not acknowledge symptoms such as anxiety, depression, or anger, even when other data showed that such problems may be present. Therefore, it may be wise to use information from other informants to assess for the presence of anxiety, anger, or depression when the L scale is elevated.
- Attention Problems (SRP-C, A, COL) assesses the tendency to report being highly distracted and unable to concentrate. This scale was designed for use in diagnosing the presence of the core symptoms of Attention Deficit/Hyperactivity Disorder (ADHD)

as found in the *DSM-IV-TR*. Prepublication known-group validation evidence for samples of children who have been diagnosed with ADHD (Reynolds & Kamphaus, 2004) has demonstrated that attention problems T scores of 58 and above on the SRP-C and scores of 57 or greater on the SRP-A indicate ADHD. A mean T score of 61 was obtained by a sample of children who were diagnosed with Bipolar Disorder. Attention problems also seem to be symptomatic of the Autism Spectrum Disorders (ASD), with the adolescent clinical sample in the BASC–2 manual producing a mean T score of 58. It seems prudent then to consider an even mildly elevated attention problems score as indicating risk for various forms of child and adolescent maladjustment.

- Attitude to School (SRP-C, A) evaluates how children and youths perceive the utility of school, along with their feelings of alienation or dissatisfaction regarding school. Scores below 41 indicate relative satisfaction and comfort with school. High scores on this scale are often indicative of other clinical problems as well.

- Attitude to Teacher (SRP-C, A) evaluates how the respondent perceives teachers. It is noteworthy that neither this scale nor the Attitude to School scale is associated with specific clinical samples (Reynolds & Kamphaus, 2004), suggesting that children and youths with a wide variety of presenting problems and diagnoses may experience significant problems with schooling and relationships with teachers.

- Atypicality (SRP-C, A, COL) evaluates unusual thoughts and perceptions commonly associated with severe forms of psychopathology such as psychotic disorders. Given that psychotic disorders are relatively rare in childhood, elevations on this scale are more likely to be indicative of the presence of other problems or conditions that are characterized by unusual or developmentally inappropriate behaviors. In this regard, Atypicality scores have been found to be elevated for adolescents diagnosed with ASD (mean T score of 57) (Reynolds & Kamphaus, 2004).

- Depression (SRP-C, A, COL) examines feelings of unhappiness, sadness, negative affectivity, and dejection, as well as feelings that "nothing ever goes right." A score of 55 on the adolescent scale is indicative of depression, as demonstrated by validation evidence found in the BASC–2 manual (Reynolds & Kamphaus, 2004). Children with ADHD also tend to indicate depressive symptoms when filling out the SRP-C (Reynolds & Kamphaus, 2004). Baxter and Rattan (2004) found that a sample of males, aged 9–11, diagnosed with ADHD rated themselves significantly higher than a normative group on the Depression and Anxiety scales of the BASC. This scale has strong reliability, thus indicating that elevated scores should be evaluated carefully before they are interpreted as false positives.

- Hyperactivity (SRP-C, A, COL) measures the tendency to report being overly active, having trouble staying still, and other symptoms of the hyperactivity dimension of ADHD. Mean T scores of 57 for the SRP-C and 56 for the SRP-A were found for the ADHD clinical sample in the BASC–2 manual (Reynolds & Kamphaus, 2004). A mean T score of 59 on the SRP-A was found for the Bipolar clinical sample. Adolescents with ASD also indicated hyperactivity symptoms (mean T score of 58). The latter two findings for clinical samples provide evidence that elevations on this scale are associated with severe forms of psychopathology that are associated with more functional impairment.

- Locus of Control (SRP-C, A, COL) evaluates an individual's perceived control over his or her environment. High scores on this scale indicate a belief that external events or people are in control and may indicate a sense of helplessness on the part of the respondent. Endorsing high levels of external control may indicate mild paranoia and could possibly induce anxiety or depression (Reynolds & Kamphaus, 2004). Children or youths may also express a sense of an external locus of control if they are rejecting of authority figures.

- School Maladjustment (SRP-COL) assesses perceived difficulties and lack of success in a postsecondary educational environment, including feeling overwhelmed and unmotivated. This scale is new to BASC–2 and specific to 18- to 25-year-olds enrolled in a post-secondary educational program. Inasmuch as the items on this scale are limited, high scores should trigger further assessment of educational performance and satisfaction.

- Sensation Seeking (SRP-A, COL) measures an individual's tendency to take risks and seek excitement. This scale was not associated with a specific disorder in the prepublication known group validity studies; however, when accompanied by low Anxiety scores, high Sensation Seeking scores may indicate a conduct-related disorder (Reynolds & Kamphaus, 2004). In general, sensation-seeking tendencies may be associated with a variety of presenting problems and diagnostic conditions. This finding indicates that this scale may be more useful for treatment planning than for making differential diagnostic decisions.

- Sense of Inadequacy (SRP-C, A, COL) evaluates an individual's perceptions of being unsuccessful at school and unable to meet goals, as well as low achievement expectations. As a moderate correlate of the Depression scale, it would not be uncommon for this scale to be jointly elevated with Depression. The school-related content is also useful for assessing the breadth of impairment, as indicated by impairment in school functioning that may be associated with depression or other disorders.

- Social Stress (SRP-C, A, COL) may be considered the inverse of the Interpersonal Relations adaptive scale in that it assesses feelings of stress and tension in interpersonal relations as well as feelings of being excluded. High scores on this scale are found in both children (mean T score of 55) and adolescents (mean T score of 57) with ASD (Reynolds & Kamphaus, 2004). This finding is consistent with the literature on ASD reflecting social relationships as a core deficit of this disorder (American Psychiatric Association, 2000).

- Somatization (SRP-A, COL) measures the tendency to cite minor physical complaints such as headaches, stomachaches, or queasiness as an expression of psychological distress. Depressed adolescents were found to have a mean T score of 56 on this scale (Reynolds & Kamphaus, 2004), as would be suspected given the known vegetative symptoms associated with depression.

In contrast to the clinical scales, adaptive scales measure positive adjustment, and low scores on these scales represent possible problem areas. T scores ranging from 30 to 39 are considered At Risk, and scores below 30 are considered Clinically Significant.

- Interpersonal Relations (SRP-C, A, COL) assesses the respondent's perceptions of his or her relationships with others, especially peers, and the degree of enjoyment derived from these relationships. Low scores on this scale are indicative of an ASD with mean T scores of 45 for the child version and 41 for the adolescent version, as well as Bipolar disorder with a mean T score of 44. In other words, for children with ASD this scale is a mirror image of the Social Stress scale. Given the lawfulness of the inverse relationship among these scales, the lack of same should be suspect and may indicate the presence of a response set.

- Relations with Parents (SRP-C, A, COL) surveys the respondent's perceived importance in the family and the status of the parent-child relationship. Adolescents with Bipolar Disorder scored an average of 43 on this scale (Reynolds & Kamphaus, 2004).

- Self-Esteem (SRP-C, A, COL) assesses the respondent's sense of self-satisfaction. This scale may indicate risk of depression in adolescents, with the Clinical Depression adolescent sample of the BASC–2 manual scoring an average T score of 43. Kamphaus et al. (2003) found one SRP-C cluster from the BASC normative sample that was characterized by a lone low score on this scale. It could very well be that low self-esteem can exist in isolation for some children between 8 and 11 years of age; however, the importance of adequate self-esteem for successful development and adjustment cannot be underestimated, and low self-esteem in children and adolescents should not be ignored.

- Self-Reliance (SRP-C, A, COL) evaluates self-confidence and assurance in one's own ability to make decisions and solve problems. Adolescents with Bipolar Disorder scored an average of 43 on this scale (Reynolds & Kamphaus, 2004).

Interpretation of Composite Scores.   The SRP Composites allow examiners to make more general or global interpretations about a respondent's self-perceptions and emotions. With the exception of Personal Adjustment, scores of 60–69 indicate At Risk and scores of 70 and above indicate Clinically Significant maladjustment. For Personal Adjustment, scores from 31 to 40 are in the At Risk category and scores 30 and below are in the Clinically Significant category.

- School Problems (SRP-C, A) is a broad measure of adaptation to school. Scales on this composite include Attitude to School, Attitude to Teachers, and Sensation Seeking (only SRP-A). As indicated above, school problems can be related to a variety of presenting problems and diagnoses.

- Internalizing Problems (SRP-C, A, COL) is a broad measure of inwardly directed distress. Scales on this composite include Atypicality, Locus of Control, Social Stress, Anxiety, Depression, Sense of Inadequacy, and Somatization (only SRP-A, COL). This scale was formerly known as the Clinical Maladjustment scale on the original BASC. Kamphaus, DiStefano, and Lease (2003) found an Internalizing cluster in the U.S. population with equal gender representation. The individuals in this cluster reported difficulty sustaining relationships with peers and low self-esteem.

- Inattention/Hyperactivity (SRP-C, A, COL) combines the Inattention and Hyperactivity scales in order to identify respondents at risk for an ADHD diagnosis. This composite also appears to be elevated for children and adolescents at risk for an ASD and adolescents with Bipolar Disorder (Reynolds & Kamphaus, 2004).

- Personal Adjustment (SRP-C, A, COL) evaluates problems with interpersonal relationships, self-acceptance, identity formation, and ego strength. Scales include Relations with Parents, Interpersonal Relations, Self-Esteem, and Self-Reliance. Individuals with low scores on this composite are more likely to have adjustment disorders and certain Axis II personality disorders (Reynolds & Kamphaus, 2004).

- Emotional Symptoms Index (SRP-C, A, COL) is the most global indicator of emotional disturbance composed of four scales from the Internalizing composite (Social Stress,

Anxiety, Depression, Sense of Inadequacy) and two scales from the Personal Adjustment composite (Self-Esteem and Self-Reliance). Elevated scores on the ESI will ALMOST ALWAYS signal the presence of serious emotional disturbance that is broad-based in its impact on the thoughts and feelings of the individual (Reynolds & Kamphaus, 2004).

- SAD Triad (SRP-C, A, COL) consists of three of the scales included in the ESI (Social Stress, Anxiety, and Depression) and represents significant emotional distress characterized by Depression with substantial tension.

Parent and Teacher Rating Scales

The Teacher Rating Scale (TRS) is a broadband measure of adaptive and problem behaviors that occur in the school setting. Behaviors are rated on a four-point scale of frequency from *Never* to *Almost always*. The TRS, which requires about 10 to 15 minutes for completion, has three forms: preschool (2–5 years), child (6–11 years), and adolescent (12–21 years). The TRS contributes five composites for children and adolescents, including Adaptive Skills, Behavioral Symptoms Index, Externalizing Problems, Internalizing Problems, and School Problems. The preschool form excludes the School Problems domain, for a total of four composites.

The Parent Rating Scales (PRS) provides a comprehensive measure of a child's adaptive and problem behaviors in the community and home environments. The PRS uses the same four-point scale as the TRS and requires about 10 to 20 minutes to complete. It also has three forms: preschool (2–5 years), child (6–11 years), and adolescent (12–21 years). The PRS composites are the same as those for the TRS, with the exception of School Problems.

Interpretation of the TRS & PRS

Interpretation of Scale Scores.   The clinical scales measure maladjustment, and high scores on these scales represent negative characteristics. T-scores ranging from 60 to 69 are considered At Risk, and scores of 70 or higher are considered Clinically Significant.

- Aggression (TRS-P, C, A; PRS-P, C, A) assesses the tendency to do physical or emotional harm to others or their property. The scale includes verbal and physical aggression but gives greater weight to verbal, or relational, aggression because it occurs more frequently. A Clinically Significant Score represents highly disruptive behavior that will be of great concern to teachers and guardians (Reynolds & Kamphaus, 2004).
- Anxiety (TRS-P, C, A; PRS-P, C, A) measures symptomatic behaviors such as excessive worry, fears and phobias, self-deprecation, and nervousness. During childhood, somatization is a key symptom of anxiety disorders, so a combination of the Anxiety and Somatization scales may be more appropriate for determining whether a child meets diagnostic criteria (Reynolds & Kamphaus, 2004). Baxter and Rattan (2004) also found that both parents and teachers rated a sample of males with ADHD, aged 9–11, significantly higher than a normative group on the Depression and Anxiety scales of the BASC.
- Attention Problems (TRS-P, C, A; PRS-P, C, A) focuses on the core inattention symptoms of ADHD and, when combined with the Hyperactivity scale, can distinguish between the three subtypes of ADHD (Predominantly Inattentive, Predominantly

Hyperactive, and Combined). Attention Problems measures the inability to maintain attention and the tendency to be easily distracted from tasks. The dimensional classification employed by the scale is especially useful, because subclinical problems have been found to cause impairment (Scahill et al., 1999). Children diagnosed with ADHD received a mean score of 61 on the TRS and a mean score of 65 on the PRS (Reynolds & Kamphaus, 2004).

- Atypicality (TRS-P, C, A; PRS-P, C, A) measures a child's tendency to behave in ways that are considered odd or strange. A score in the At Risk range and above could elicit a number of interpretations, such as a psychotic disorder, immaturity, developmental delay, or behavioral or emotional disorders. It is important to interpret this score very carefully, keeping developmental level in mind. Mean Atypicality scores for children diagnosed with ASD were 71 on the TRS and 75 on the PRS (Reynolds & Kamphaus, 2004).

- Conduct Problems (TRS-C, A; PRS-C, A) assesses socially deviant and disruptive behaviors that are characteristic of Conduct Disorder. This scale is not used for the preschool level, as these behaviors rarely occur at that age. Be aware that elevated scores may also occur on other scales, such as Learning Problems and Depression, because of the factors involved in Conduct Disorder. This scale is similar to the Aggression scale but has a greater focus on antisocial and rule-breaking behavior rather than behaviors directed against others. Conduct Problems may also be evident in depressive disorders, as illustrated by the Clinical Depressive Disorders sample's mean T-score of 79 on the PRS-C and 69 on the PRS-A (Reynolds & Kamphaus, 2004).

- Depression (TRS-P, C, A; PRS-P, C, A) is mainly written as quoted statements designed to identify dysphoric mood, suicidal ideation, withdrawal from others, and self-reproach in the target child. In the clinical sample, individuals diagnosed with depression disorders had mean T-scores of 80 on the PRS-C, 76 on the PRS-A, and 65 on the TRS-A (Reynolds & Kamphaus, 2004). As noted above, children with ADHD have also been found to have elevated TRS and PRS Depression scale scores (Baxter & Rattan, 2004).

- Hyperactivity (TRS-P, C, A; PRS-P, C, A) examines the hyperactivity and impulsivity symptoms associated with ADHD. The hyperactivity scale has specific questions regarding interrupting others, poor self-control, inability to wait one's turn, and fiddling with things. This scale has been shown to be qualitatively different from the attention aspect of ADHD through confirmatory factor analysis. The clinical sample means for those diagnosed with ADHD were 66 on the PRS-C, 64 on the PRS-A, and 61 on both the TRS-C and TRS-A (Reynolds & Kamphaus, 2004).

- Learning Problems (TRS-C, A) is a screener for academic difficulty and possible Learning Disabilities. This scale samples information from teachers regarding the child's reading, writing, spelling, and mathematics. Scores in the At Risk range indicate that a follow-up of academic skills is warranted. It is important to note that this scale has a strong relationship with academic achievement outcomes for elementary school children (Hartley, 1999; Oehler-Stinnett & Boykin, 2001). Clinical sample means for those diagnosed with a Learning Disability were 62 on the TRS-C and 61 on the TRS-A (Reynolds & Kamphaus, 2004).

- Somatization (TRS-P, C, A; PRS-P, C, A) assesses the child's verbal complaints regarding physical ailments when there is no true physical cause. Elevated scores on this scale are associated with internalizing disorders, such as Anxiety and Depression (Abelkop,

2001). Adolescents diagnosed with Depressive Disorders had a mean T-score of 68 on this scale (Reynolds & Kamphaus, 2004).

- Withdrawal (TRS-P, C, A; PRS-P, C, A) focuses on the child's avoidance of others and diminished interest in participating in social situations. This scale has been shown to examine a core symptom of Autism and Mental Retardation (Reynolds & Kamphaus, 1992). In addition, slightly elevated scores on this scale are associated with Depression, neglect, and rejection. The clinical sample means for those diagnosed with ASD were 73 on both PRS-C and -A, 71 on TRS-C, and 66 on TRS-A (Reynolds & Kamphaus, 2004).

The Adaptive scales measure positive adjustment, and low scores on these scales represent possible problem areas. T-scores ranging from 30 to 39 are considered At Risk, and scores below 30 are considered Clinically Significant.

- Activities of Daily Living (PRS-P, C, A) screens for adaptive behavior related to acting in a safe manner, performing simple daily tasks, and organizing tasks. This scale may be useful for determining the least restrictive environment for intervention. Scores in the At Risk range and below suggest deficits associated with Mental Retardation, lower-functioning Autism Disorder, and other severe disorders. Based on the clinical samples, one can expect T-scores of about 35 for individuals with Mental Retardation and about 37 for those with motor impairments (Reynolds & Kamphaus, 2004). This is a new scale to the BASC–2 and is available only on the PRS. In the clinical sample, individuals diagnosed with ASD received a mean T-score of 33 on the PRS-C and 31 on the PRS-A.

- Adaptability (TRS-P, C, A; PRS-P, C, A) assesses the temperament variable associated with the ability to adjust to changes in routine, shift from one task to another, and share toys or possessions with other children. Low adaptability scores suggest significant risk and should lead to further evaluation. In the clinical sample, individuals diagnosed with Bipolar Disorder received a mean score of 36 on the TRS-C and -A, 36 on the PRS-C, and 30 on the PRS-A (Reynolds & Kamphaus, 2004).

- Functional Communication (TRS-P, C, A; PRS-P, C, A) examines a child's ability to communicate in ways others can easily understand. This scale is classified as a primary aspect of adaptive-behavior functioning (Doll, 1953; Kamphaus, 1987). Questions in this scale include rudimentary and complex expressive-communication skills, receptive-communication skills, and written skills. Children who score in the At Risk range should be reevaluated in order to rule out an adaptive behavior deficit. It is also important to note that Functional Communication is a new scale introduced in the BASC–2. In the clinical sample, individuals diagnosed with Mental Retardation received mean T-scores of 31 on the PRS-C, 29 on the PRS-A, 32 on the TRS-C, and 39 on the TRS-A. In addition, clinical sample means for those individuals diagnosed with ASD were 30 on the PRS-C and 28 on the PRS-A (Reynolds & Kamphaus, 2004).

- Leadership (TRS-C, A; PRS-C, A) assesses leadership potential and school adaptation. Some items are related to Social Skills items, whereas others include cognitive skills associated with problem solving. On this scale, individuals diagnosed with Mental Retardation received mean T-scores of 36 on the PRS-C, 34 on the PRS-A, 38 on the TRS-C, and 43 on the TRS-A. Clinical sample means for individuals with ASD were 34 on the PRS-C and 33 on the PRS-A (Reynolds & Kamphaus, 2004).

- Social Skills (TRS-P, C, A; PRS-P, C, A) examines interpersonal forms of social adaptation, such as complimenting others and offering assistance when needed. Social skills have been shown to be a key aspect of adequate adaptation and to be necessary in the development of children (Doll, 1953). In addition, the Social Skills scale often distinguishes between children with Autism and Mental Retardation, as the former group is more socially impaired. Clinical sample means for those individuals diagnosed with ASD were 34 on the PRS-C, 38 on the PRS-A, 38 on the TRS-C, and 44 on the TRS-A (Reynolds & Kamphaus, 2004).

- Study Skills (TRS-C, A) focuses on metacognitive problem solving, achievement motivation, and organizational skills. This scale has a strong relationship to the School Problems composite, which suggests that it plays an important role in assessing school adaptation. Clinical sample means for individuals diagnosed with Mental Retardation were 35 on the TRS-C and 40 on the TRS-A (Reynolds & Kamphaus, 2004).

Interpretation of Composite Scores.   The TRS and PRS Composites allow examiners to make more general or global interpretations with respect to how an individual is perceived by parents and teachers. With the exception of Adaptive Skills, scores of 60–69 indicate At Risk and scores of 70 and above indicate Clinically Significant maladjustment. For Adaptive Skills, scores from 31 to 40 are in the At-Risk category, and scores 30 and below are in the Clinically Significant category.

- Adaptive Skills (TRS-P, C, A; PRS-P, C, A) is a broad indicator of the characteristics of adaptive behavior that are important for functioning across environments, such as emotional expression and control, daily living skills, communication skills, and other adaptive skills. This composite is composed of Adaptability, Activities of Daily Living (PRS only), Functional Communication, Social Skills, Leadership, and Study Skills (TRS only).
- Behavioral Symptoms Index (TRS-P, C, A; PRS-P, C, A) provides a measure of the overall level of problem behavior consisting of the Hyperactivity, Aggression, Depression, Attention Problems, Atypicality, and Withdrawal scales. The BSI provides an estimate of the general level of functioning or presence of impairment for an individual with a diagnosed condition (Reynolds & Kamphaus, 2004).
- Externalizing Problems (TRS-P, C, A; PRS-P, C, A) is a broad measure of "uncontrolled" disruptive-behavior problems, such as aggression, hyperactivity, and delinquency (Achenbach & Edelbrock, 1978). This composite includes the Hyperactivity, Aggression, and Conduct Problems scales. Externalizing problems are generally more stable throughout an individual's life span than internalizing problems and, consequently, are associated with a less favorable prognosis (Robins, 1979).
- Internalizing Problems (TRS-P, C, A; PRS-P, C, A) measures "overcontrolled" behavior problems, such as those measured in the Anxiety, Depression, and Somatization scales (Achenbach & Edelbrock, 1978). Although these behaviors are not as disruptive in the classroom, they can still have a substantial negative effect on child adjustment, such as peer relationships (Kamphaus, DiStefano, & Lease, 2003).
- School Problems (TRS-C, A) focuses on academic difficulties, such as motivation, attention, and learning problems. This composite consists of the Attention Problems and Learning Problems scales. A high score on this composite reflects the possibility of low levels of academic achievement. In addition, school problems can be indicative of a variety of problems or diagnoses, including both internalizing and externalizing disorders.

SAMPLE CASE

Sarah is a 10-year-old female referred by her parents for a psychological evaluation because of her apparent low self-esteem, depressed mood, and angry outbursts. Sarah's parents reported that she does well in school academically and excels in mathematics, but they are concerned that Sarah often appears depressed and irritable and expresses feelings of inadequacy. Sarah often remarks that she is "fat and ugly" and that the world would be better off without her. Her teachers reported that Sarah tends to misinterpret the behavior of her peers and does not appear to have many friends. She is very fearful of new situations and becomes unreasonably upset with changes in routine or if things do not go her way.

Parent and teacher ratings on the BASC–2 consistently revealed significant problems with Depression, Anxiety, Withdrawal, and Aggression (see Figure 18–1). One teacher also indicated elevated scores on the Somatization scale. As discussed earlier, both Withdrawal and Somatization have been found to be related to internalizing disorders such as depression (Abelkop, 2001). Adaptability scores were also significantly low, indicating that Sarah exhibits inflexible behavior and is unable to adapt to new situations. Teacher ratings indicated that Sarah engages in behaviors that are considered strange or odd and generally seems disconnected from her surroundings. This behavior is exemplified by acknowledgments of items such as "Seems out of touch with reality," "Does strange things," "Babbles to self," and "Says things that make no sense."

The SRP-C scores provide an in-depth picture of Sarah's thoughts and feelings about herself and others, as well as her overall adjustment (see Figure 18–1). Sarah's ratings on the BASC–2 SRP indicated significant concerns in the areas of School Problems, Internalizing Problems, Emotional Symptoms Index, and Personal Adjustment. Sarah dislikes school intensely and finds her teachers to be unfair, uncaring, and overly demanding. Sarah reports feelings that she has little control over events in her life. She acknowledged feeling isolated and lonely, feeling excessive worry, and feeling sad and misunderstood. Sarah's ratings also indicate a negative self-image, in terms of both personal and physical attributes. Moreover, Sarah appears to have a number of unusual thoughts and perceptions and reported hearing voices in her head that no one else can hear.

The clinicians involved in this case concluded that Sarah's symptoms are consistent with depression, anxiety, and low self-esteem. Issues of anger and hostility are also present. Sarah appears to have chronic doubt about her ability to do well in social situations and on academic tasks, indicating that she is afraid of mistakes, failure, and embarrassment. Sarah tends to cope with these feelings by avoiding tasks that are difficult, withdrawing from group situations, engaging in negative self-talk, and, when directly confronted, reverting to physical aggression and acting out behavior. Sarah is perceived by others as showing characteristics of depression and even recognizes these feelings of sadness, despair, loneliness, hopelessness, and ineffectiveness in coping.

CONCLUSIONS

The BASC, and its successor the BASC–2, has been the fortunate recipient of an ever-expanding research base. It has been used in studies ranging from child cancer to juvenile diabetes, ADHD (Pineda et al., 2005), and a published case study of a child with toxic manganese exposure from drinking water (Woolf, Wright, Amarasiriwardena, & Bellinger, 2002). A relatively extensive BASC research bibliography may be found at the publisher's web

Psychometric Summary for Sarah

<u>BEHAVIOR ASSESSMENT SYSTEM FOR CHILDREN, SECOND EDITION - PARENT RATING SCALES CHILD VERSION (BASC-2 PRS- C)</u>

The BASC 2-PRS is a questionnaire that is filled out by parents in order to assess the behavior problems, emotional problems, and social competence for their children. The BASC 2-PRS yields T-Scores with a mean of 50 and a standard deviation of 10. On the Clinical Scales, scores from 60-69 indicate developing or potentially significant problems while above 70 indicate significant problems. On the Adaptive Scales, scores from 31-40 indicate developing or potential problems while those below 30 are considered significantly low.

	Mother	
Scale	**T Score**	**Percentile**
Clinical Scales		
Hyperactivity	54	72
Aggression	64*	91
Conduct Problems	37	3
Anxiety	79**	99
Depression	85**	99
Somatization	44	33
Atypicality	54	76
Withdrawal	71**	96
Attention Problem	45	37
Adaptive Scales		
Adaptability	32*	5
Social Skills	44	28
Leadership	44	29
Activities of Daily Living	42	20
Functional Communication	55	66
Composites		
Externalizing Problems	52	66
Internalizing Problems	74**	98
Behavioral Symptoms Index	66	93
Adaptive Skills	42	21

<u>Note.</u> * indicates a possible problem. ** indicates a significant problem.

FIGURE 18–1.   Psychometric Summary for Sarah.

BEHAVIOR ASSESSMENT SYSTEM FOR CHILDREN, SECOND EDITION - TEACHER RATING SCALES CHILD VERSION (BASC-2 TRS-C)

The BASC 2-TRS is a questionnaire completed by teachers to obtain ratings of adaptive skills and behavior and emotional problems of students. The BASC 2-TRS yields T-Scores with a mean of 50 and a standard deviation of 10. On the Clinical Scales, scores from 60-69 indicate developing or potentially significant problems while those above 70 indicate significant problems. On the Adaptive Scales, scores from 31-40 indicate developing or potentially significant problems while those below 30 are considered significantly low.

	Teacher #1		Teacher # 2	
Scale	**T Score**	**Percentile**	**T Score**	**Percentile**
Clinical Scales				
Hyperactivity	61*	87	52	69
Aggression	61*	88	61*	88
Conduct Problems	54	76	52	70
Anxiety	89**	99	76**	98
Depression	98**	99	74**	96
Somatization	62*	89	58	84
Attention Problems	48	46	42	26
Learning Problems	58	80	52	66
Atypicality	69*	94	66*	92
Withdrawal	76**	98	60*	85
Adaptive Scales				
Adaptability	25**	1	37*	11
Social Skills	45	33	47	40
Leadership	44	31	47	40
Study Skills	45	33	57	69
Functional Communication	49	40	46	30
Composite Scores				
Externalizing Problems	59	85	55	77
Internalizing Problems	91**	99	74**	97
School Problems	53	67	47	41
Behavioral Symptoms Index	74**	97	61*	88
Adaptive Skills	40*	17	46	35

Note. * indicates a possible problem. ** indicates a significant problem.

FIGURE 18–1. (*Continued*).

BEHAVIOR ASSESSMENT SYSTEM FOR CHILDREN, SECOND EDITION - SELF REPORT OF PERSONALITY CHILD EDITION (BASC-2 SRP-C)

The BASC 2-SRP is a self-report measure designed to evaluate the personality and self-perceptions of children. Two major syndromes make up the Emotional Symptoms Index: Personal Maladjustment and Clinical Maladjustment. In addition, a School Maladjustment Composite is comprised of Attitude to School and Attitude to Teacher. The BASC 2-SRP yields T-Scores with a mean of 50 and a standard deviation of 10.

On the Clinical Scales, scores from 60-69 indicate developing or potentially significant problems while those above 70 indicate significant problems. On the Adaptive Scales, scores from 31-40 indicate developing or potentially significant problems while those below 30 are considered significantly low.

	T-Score	**Percentile**
Clinical Scales		
Attitude to School	77**	99
Attitude to Teachers	83**	99
Atypicality	77**	99
Locus of Control	72**	97
Social Stress	72**	97
Anxiety	73**	98
Depression	63*	88
Sense of Inadequacy	56	76
Attention Problems	53	66
Hyperactivity	63*	88
Adaptive Scales		
Relations with parents	56	67
Interpersonal Relations	32*	7
Self-esteem	15**	1
Self-reliance	50	45
Composite Scores		
School Problems	84**	99
Internalizing Problems	72**	97
Inattention/Hyperactivity	59	82
Emotional Symptoms Index	71**	96
Personal Adjustment	34*	7

Note. * indicates a possible problem. ** indicates a significant problem.

FIGURE 18–1. (*Continued*).

site (agsnet.com). As is the case with all tests, the answer to one research question simply begets another, a process that should ever improve our use of BASC findings in clinical and research settings.

REFERENCES

Abelkop, A. S. (2001). Somatic complaints in young school children: The relationship with internalizing distress, behavior problems, academic achievement, and school adjustment. *Dissertation Abstracts International Section B: Sciences and Engineering, 62*(9-B), 4207.

Achenbach, T. M., & Edelbrock, C.S. (1978). The classification of child psychopathology: A review and analysis of empirical efforts. *Psychological Bulletin, 85*, 1275–1301.

American Psychiatric Association. (2000). *Diagnostic and statistical manual of mental disorders* (4th ed., text revision). Washington, DC: Author.

Baxter, J., & Rattan, G. (2004). Attention deficit disorder and the internalizing dimension in males, ages 9–0 through 11–11. *International Journal of Neuroscience, 114*, 817–832.

Cantwell, D. P. (1996). Classification of child and adolescent psychopathology. *Journal of Child Psychology and Psychiatry, 37*, 3–12.

Doll, E. A. (1953). *The measurement of social competence: A manual for the Vineland social maturity scale.* Circle Pines, MN: American Guidance Service.

Gil, A. (2005). Repressing distress in childhood: A defense against health-related stress. *Child Psychiatry and Human Development, 36*, 27–52.

Hartley, M. M. M. (1999). The relationship among disruptive behaviors, attention, and academic achievement in a clinical referral sample. *Dissertation Abstracts International Section A: Humanities and Social Sciences, 60*(2-A), 0333.

Individuals with Disabilities Education Improvement Act (IDEA) of 2004, Pub. L. No. 108-446.

Kamphaus, R. W. (1987). Conceptual and psychometric issues in the assessment of adaptive behavior. *Journal of Special Education, 21*(1), 27–35.

Kamphaus, R. W. (2001). *Clinical assessment of children's intelligence* (2nd ed.). Needham Heights, MA: Allyn & Bacon.

Kamphaus, R. W., & Frick, P. J. (2002). *Clinical assessment of child and adolescent personality and behavior* (2nd ed.). Needham Heights, MA: Allyn & Bacon.

Kamphaus, R. W., DiStefano, C., & Lease, A. M. (2003). A self-report typology of behavioral assessment for young children. *Psychological Assessment, 15*(1), 17–28.

Oehler-Stinnett, J., & Boykin, C. (2001). Convergent, discriminant, and predictive validity of the Teacher Rating of Academic Achievement Motivation (TRAMM) with the ACTeRs-TF and the BASC-TRS. *Journal of Psychoeducational Assessment, 19*(1), 4–18.

Pineda, D. A., Aguirre, D. C., Garcia, M. A., Lopera, F. J., Palacio, L. G., & Kamphaus, R. W. (2005). Validation of Two Rating Scales for ADHD Diagnosis in Colombian Children. *Pediatric Neurology, 33*(1), 15–25.

Reynolds, C. R., & Kamphaus, R. W. (1992). *Behavior Assessment System for Children.* Circle Pines, MN: American Guidance Service.

Reynolds, C. R., & Kamphaus, R. W. (2004). *The Behavior Assessment System for Children* (2nd ed.). Circle Pines, MN: AGS.

Robins, L. N. (1979). Follow-up studies. In H. C. Quay & J. S. Werry (Eds.), *Psychopathological disorders of childhood* (2nd ed., pp. 483–513). New York: Wiley.

Scahill, L., Schwab-Stone, M., Merikangas, K. R., Leckman, J. F., Zhang, H., & Kasl, S. (1999). Psychosocial and clinical correlates of ADHD in a community sample of school-age children. *Journal of the American Academy of Child and Adolescent Psychiatry*, 38, 976–984.

Woolf, A., Wright, R., Amarasiriwardena, C., & Bellinger, D. (2002). A child with chronic manganese exposure from drinking water. *Environmental Health Perspectives, 110*, 1–4.

19

APPLICATIONS OF THE ACHENBACH SYSTEM OF EMPIRICALLY BASED ASSESSMENT TO CHILDREN, ADOLESCENTS, AND THEIR PARENTS

Thomas M. Achenbach
University of Vermont

The Achenbach System of Empirically Based Assessment (ASEBA) comprises a family of assessment instruments for ages 1½ to 90+ years. The instruments are designed to assess a broad spectrum of problems and adaptive functioning, as reported by the people who are being assessed and by people who know them ("collaterals"), as well as by clinical interviewers, direct observers, and psychological examiners. Data are obtained on standardized rating forms that can be filled out in about 10 to 20 minutes. The forms include both structured items that are scored quantitatively and open-ended items that elicit clinically useful information in the respondent's own words. If a respondent cannot complete a form independently, the items can be read to the respondent by a receptionist or other nonclinician, who then writes the responses on the form.

Each form is tailored to the ages of the people being assessed and to the types of informants who complete the forms. The forms are scored on profiles of scales that enable users to compare the individual being assessed with scores obtained by normative samples of peers. Although this book focuses mainly on children and adolescents, the present chapter includes assessment of parents, because their problems and adaptive characteristics are often closely intertwined with those of their offspring. Clinical assessment of children and adolescents should therefore include assessment of their parents whenever possible. By having parents complete the ASEBA adult forms, clinicians can compare problems reported for parents with those reported for their children. The ASEBA adult forms can also be used to assess "identified patients" who have reached their 18th birthday and may be appropriate for assessing "emancipated minors" who are younger than 18 but live away from parent figures.

ASEBA forms and profiles are designed to help clinicians make direct comparisons between the problems reported for children by multiple informants, including parents, teachers, and the children themselves. Parallel self- and collateral-report forms for adults also enable clinicians to compare parents' views of themselves with how they are viewed by spouses, partners, and other informants. The typical levels of agreement between most combinations of informants are modest, as shown by meta-analyses of cross-informant correlations between reports of both child and adult psychopathology (Achenbach, Krukowski, Dumenci, & Ivanova, 2005; Achenbach, McConaughy, & Howell, 1987; Duhig, Renk, Epstein, & Phares, 2000; Renk & Phares, 2004). This means that no single source of data, including self-reports, is likely to provide a gold standard for assessment. It also means that each informant may add clinically valuable information, both at initial assessments and at subsequent assessments to evaluate the progress and outcome of treatments. Table 19.1 lists ASEBA forms for ages 1½ to 59 years and indicates who completes each form. As referenced in Table 19.1, the manuals for the forms provide extensive reliability, validity, and normative data, as well as clinical and research applications.

DEVELOPMENT OF ASEBA FORMS AND SCALES

The development of the ASEBA began in the 1960s with efforts to determine whether more differentiated patterns of child and adolescent psychopathology could be identified than were evident in the official diagnostic system of the time, which was embodied in the first edition of the American Psychiatric Association's (1952) *Diagnostic and Statistical Manual* (DSM-I). By factor analyzing problems reported in child and adolescent psychiatric case records, Achenbach (1966) found considerably more patterns of problems than were identified in the DSM-I diagnostic categories for children and adolescents. Achenbach also found broad groupings of problems for which he coined the terms *Internalizing* and *Externalizing*. Internalizing problems include those that are primarily within the self, such as anxiety, depression, and somatic complaints without apparent physical causes. Externalizing problems, by

TABLE 19.1.

ASEBA Forms for Ages 1½ to 59 Years

Name of Form	Filled Out By
Child Behavior Checklist for Ages 1½–5 (CBCL/1½–5)	Parents; surrogates
Caregiver-Teacher Report Form for Ages 1½–5 (C-TRF)	Daycare providers; preschool teachers
Child Behavior Checklist for Ages 6–18 (CBCL/6–18)	Parents; surrogates
Teacher's Report Form for Ages 6–18 (TRF)	Teachers; school counselors
Youth Self-Report for Ages 11–18 (YSR)	Youths
Semistructured Clinical Interview for Children and Adolescents for Ages 6–18 (SCICA)	Clinical interviewers
Direct Observation Form for Ages 5–14 (DOF)	Observers
Test Observation Form for Ages 2–18 (TOF)	Psychological examiners
Adult Self-Report for Ages 18–59 (ASR)	Emancipated minors, adults
Adult Behavior Checklist for Ages 18–59 (ABCL)	Spouse, partner, grown children, relatives, friends, roommates, therapists

Note. The primary references for the forms are the Manuals, as follows: CBCL/1½–5 and C-TRF, Achenbach and Rescorla (2000); CBCL/6–18, TRF, YSR, and DOF, Achenbach and Rescorla (2001); SCICA, McConaughy and Achenbach (2001); TOF, McConaughy and Achenbach, (2004); ASR and ABCL, Achenbach and Rescorla (2003). The Manuals provide extensive reliability, validity, and normative data, plus illustrations of clinical and research applications and relations to other instruments.

contrast, include those that involve conflict with other people and with social mores, such as fighting, attacking people, lying, and stealing.

Empirically Based, Bottom-up Syndrome Scales

From the 1970s through the present, the approach embodied in Achenbach's (1966) study has been used to construct instruments for obtaining reports directly from different kinds of informants. The instruments have been developed through iterative stages in which draft items were tried out with samples of the intended informants who completed the items and provided feedback concerning the items and format. When the items were finalized, they were tested for their ability to discriminate between children who were referred for mental health services and demographically similar nonreferred children. Factor analytic procedures were used to identify *syndromes* (i.e., patterns) of problems that tended to co-occur. Syndromes that were found to be statistically robust in a variety of analyses were then used to construct scales of problem items. A syndrome scale consists of problem items that were found to co-occur in ratings by a particular kind of informant.

As an example, on the Child Behavior Checklist for Ages 6 to 18 (CBCL/6–18), factor analyses of ratings of children by their parents yielded eight syndromes (Achenbach, 1991; Achenbach & Rescorla, 2001). One of these syndromes is labeled *Aggressive Behavior*. This syndrome includes items such as *Gets in many fights; Cruelty, bullying, or meanness to others*; and *Physically attacks people*. Each item is rated 0 = *not true*, 1 = *somewhat or sometimes true*, and 2 = *very true or often true*, based on the preceding six months. A child's score on the Aggressive Behavior syndrome scale consists of the sum of the 1 and 2 ratings of the constituent items by the person who filled out the CBCL/6–18.

Profiles of Syndrome Scales

To enable clinicians to quickly see how a child compares with peers on the Aggressive Behavior syndrome and the other syndromes scored from the CBCL/6–18, the syndromes are displayed on a profile in relation to percentiles and standard scores (*T* scores), which are based on scores obtained by a national normative sample of the child's age and gender. Figure 19–1 illustrates a computer-scored CBCL/6–18 profile for 14-year-old Lonnie (not his real name) scored from the CBCL/6–18 completed by his mother. (Hand-scored profiles are also available.)

By looking at the bottom right side of Figure 19–1, you can see abbreviated versions of the problem items that make up the Aggressive Behavior scale. To the left of the items are the numbers the items bear on the CBCL/6–18, and to the left of each number is the 0, 1, or 2 rating given the item by Lonnie's mother. Lonnie's total score of 18 for the Aggressive Behavior syndrome is printed above the list of problem items. This score was obtained by summing the 1 and 2 ratings shown to the left of the items of the Aggressive Behavior syndrome. Beneath the 18, the number 72 is printed. This is the *T* score equivalent of the raw score of 18, based on a national normative sample of 12- to 18-year-old boys who had not received mental health services in the preceding 12 months. The *C* to the right of the *T* score indicates that it is in the clinical range, that is, above a *T* score of 69. Beneath the *T* score of 72, the >97 indicates that Lonnie's syndrome score is above the 97th percentile for the normative sample.

By looking to the left of the Aggressive Behavior scale, you can see Lonnie's scores on the other seven syndromes scored from the CBCL/6–18. The graphic display shows how

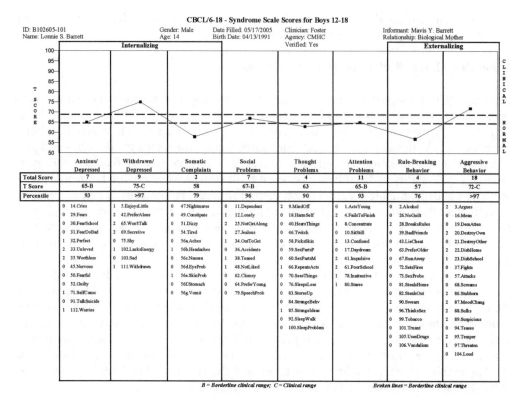

FIGURE 19–1. Computerized syndrome profile scored for 14-year-old Lonnie from CBCL/6–18, completed by his mother. (Hand-scored profiles are also available.)

Lonnie's score on each syndrome compares with the distribution of *T* scores (listed to the left of the profile) for the national normative sample of 12- to 18-year-old boys. Scores that are above the top broken line (above *T* 69) are in the clinical range, which exceeds the 97th percentile for the normative sample. Scores that are between the two broken lines are in the borderline clinical range (*T* 65 through *T* 69; 93rd through 97th percentiles). And scores that are below the bottom broken line are in the normal range (below *T* 65 and the 93rd percentile). In addition to the Aggressive Behavior syndrome, the other syndromes scored from the CBCL/6–18 are designated as *Anxious/Depressed, Withdrawn/Depressed, Somatic Complaints, Social Problems, Thought Problems, Attention Problems,* and *Rule-Breaking Behavior.* Counterparts of the eight syndromes scored from the CBCL/6–18 are also scored from the Teacher's Report Form for Ages 6 to 18 (TRF) and from the Youth Self-Report for Ages 11 to 18 (YSR). The syndromes scored from these three instruments and the other instruments for ages 1½ to 59 years are listed in Table 19.2.

The syndrome scales were derived by factor analyzing problem item ratings for thousands of individuals. The scales were designed to identify actual patterns of co-occurrence among problems, as seen by each type of informant. This approach to constructing scales is known as "empirically based" or "bottom up," because it starts with ratings of many problem items for many individuals and then statistically identifies patterns of co-occurrence among the items.

TABLE 19.2.

Scales Scored from ASEBA Forms for Ages 1½ to 59

Forms	Syndromes	DSM-Oriented Scales	Strengths	Substance use
Ages 1½–5				
CBCL, C-TRF	Emotionally reactive	Affective problems	*Language development Survey*[a]	none
	Anxious/depressed	Anxiety problems	Length of phrases	
	Somatic complaints	Pervasive developmental problems	Vocabulary	
	Withdrawn	Attention deficit/hyperactivity problems		
	Sleep problems[a]	Oppositional defiant problems		
	Attention problems			
	Aggressive behavior			
Ages 5–14				
DOF	Withdrawn-inattentive	None	On-task behavior	None
	Nervous-obsessive			
	Depressed			
	Hyperactive			
	Attention demanding			
	Aggressive			
Ages 6–18				
CBCL, TRF, YSR, SCICA	Anxious/depressed	Affective problems	Activities[b]	None
	Withdrawn/depressed	Anxiety problems	Social[b]	
	Somatic complaints	Somatic problems	School[b]	
	Social problems[d]	Attention deficit/hyperactivity problems[e]	Total competence[b]	
	Thought problems[d]	Oppositional defiant problems	Academic[c]	
	Attention problems[e]	Conduct problems	Adaptive functioning[c]	
	Rule-breaking behavior[f]			
	Aggressive behavior[f]			
	Anxious[g]			
	Language/motor problems[g]			
	Self-control problems[g]			

(*continued*)

TABLE 19.2. (*Continued*)

Forms	Syndromes	DSM-Oriented Scales	Strengths	Substance use
Ages 2–18				
TOF	Withdrawn/depressed	Attention deficit/hyperactivity problems[e]	None	None
	Language/thought problems			
	Anxious			
	Oppositional			
	Attention problems			
Ages 18–59				
ASR,	Anxious/depressed	Depressive problems	Friends	Tobacco
ABCL	Withdrawn	Anxiety problems	Spouse/partner	Alcohol
	Somatic complaints	Somatic problems	Family[h]	Drugs
	Thought problems	Avoidant personality problems	Job[h]	Mean substance use
	Attention problems	Attention deficit/hyperactivity problems	Education[h]	
	Aggressive behavior	Antisocial personality problems	Mean adaptive[h]	
	Rule-breaking behavior			
	Intrusive			

Note. Table 19.1 provides full names of forms. All forms are also scored in terms of the following groupings of problems: Internalizing, Externalizing, and Total Problems. [a]CBCL/1½–5 only. [b]CBCL/6–18 and YSR only (on YSR the mean score for academic performance substitutes for the CBCL/6–18 School scale). [c]TRF only. [d]Not on SCICA. [e]Attention Problems scales have subscales for Inattention and Hyperactivity-Impulsivity. [f]These two syndromes are combined on SCICA. [g]SCICA only. [h]ASR forms only.

Pyramid of Empirically Based Items and Scales

The empirically based, bottom-up approach can be viewed in terms of a pyramid of assessment levels, as illustrated in Figure 19–2. The base of the pyramid consists of many specific problem items, such as those that make up each of the syndromes shown in Figure 19–1. The next level of the pyramid consists of the syndromes that were derived by factor analyzing the correlations among ratings of the problem items for large samples of individuals.

Internalizing and Externalizing.   The level immediately above the syndromes consists of groupings of syndromes that were found to be associated with each other in second-order factor analyses of correlations among the syndromes. ("Second-order" factor analyses are factor analyses of correlations among scores on scales, such as the syndromes, that were themselves derived from "first-order" factor analyses.) As an example, second-order factor analyses of the correlations among the eight CBCL/6–18 syndromes shown in Figure 19–1 yielded a grouping designated as *Internalizing*, which consists of the Anxious/Depressed, Withdrawn/Depressed, and Somatic Complaints syndromes. The second order-factor analyses of the CBCL/6–18 syndromes also yielded a grouping designated as *Externalizing*, which consists of the Rule-Breaking Behavior and Aggressive Behavior syndromes. A child's score for Internalizing is computed by summation of the child's scores for the three Internalizing syndromes. Similarly, the child's score for Externalizing is computed by summation of the child's scores for the two Externalizing syndromes. The Internalizing and Externalizing scores provide broad indices of the degree to which the reported problems are within the self, involve conflict with other people and with social mores, both, or neither. The remaining three syndromes were not found to be consistently associated with either the Internalizing or Externalizing groupings.

Total Problems.   At the top of the pyramid, the Total Problems score consists of the sum of the 1 and 2 ratings of all problem items on a form such as the CBCL/6–18. The

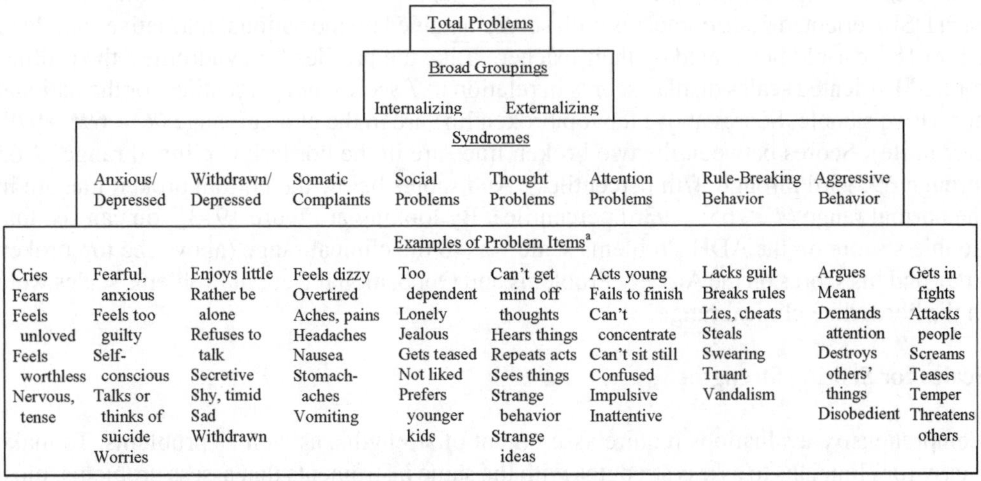

			Total Problems				

Broad Groupings

Internalizing   Externalizing

Syndromes

Anxious/ Depressed	Withdrawn/ Depressed	Somatic Complaints	Social Problems	Thought Problems	Attention Problems	Rule-Breaking Behavior	Aggressive Behavior

Examples of Problem Items[a]

Cries	Fearful, anxious	Enjoys little	Feels dizzy	Too dependent	Can't get mind off	Acts young	Lacks guilt	Argues	Gets in fights
Fears	Feels too	Rather be alone	Overtired	Lonely	thoughts	Fails to finish	Breaks rules	Mean	Attacks
Feels unloved	guilty	Refuses to	Aches, pains	Jealous	Hears things	Can't concentrate	Lies, cheats	Demands attention	people
Feels worthless	Self-conscious	talk	Headaches	Gets teased	Repeats acts	Can't sit still	Steals	Destroys	Screams
Nervous, tense	Talks or	Secretive	Nausea	Not liked	Sees things	Confused	Swearing	others'	Teases
	thinks of	Shy, timid	Stomach-aches	Prefers	Strange	Impulsive	Truant	things	Temper
	suicide	Sad	Vomiting	younger	behavior	Inattentive	Vandalism	Disobedient	Threatens
	Worries	Withdrawn		kids	Strange ideas				others

[a]Abbreviated versions of CBCL/6-18, TRF, and YSR items.

FIGURE 19–2.   Pyramid of empirically based assessment levels provided by the CBCL/6–18, TRF, and YSR.

problem items include all those that are on the eight syndromes, plus problem items that did not load significantly on any syndromes. Some of these other problem items are scored on the DSM-oriented scales that are presented in the following section. Others are not members of any scale except the Total Problems scale, but are intrinsically important in their own right, such as *Cruel to animals*.

DSM-Oriented Scales

In addition to the empirically based scales, the problem items of ASEBA forms are scored in terms of *DSM-oriented scales*. These scales enable clinicians to quickly identify areas in which relatively high problem levels suggest that an individual may qualify for particular DSM diagnoses. The DSM-oriented scales were constructed by enlisting international panels of expert psychiatrists and psychologists to identify ASEBA problem items that are very consistent with particular DSM-IV (American Psychiatric Association, 1994) diagnostic categories (Achenbach, Bernstein, & Dumenci, 2005; Achenbach, Dumenci, & Rescorla, 2003). Items that were identified by a large majority of the experts as being very consistent with a particular DSM-IV diagnostic category were used to construct scales analogous to the syndrome scales that were constructed by factor analysis of the same pools of items. For ages 6 to 18, the following six DSM-oriented scales were constructed from items of the CBCL/6–18, TRF, and YSR: *Affective Problems, Anxiety Problems, Somatic Problems, Attention Deficit Hyperactivity (ADH) Problems, Oppositional Defiant Problems*, and *Conduct Problems*. In addition, subscales for the Inattentive and Hyperactive-Impulsive types of ADH problems were constructed from the TRF. Table 19.2 lists the DSM-oriented scales scored from the ASEBA forms for ages 1½ to 59 years.

The DSM-oriented scales are displayed on profiles analogous to the profiles for the syndrome scales. Figure 19–3 illustrates the hand-scored profile of DSM-oriented scales scored from a TRF completed for 14-year-old Lonnie. (Computer-scored DSM-oriented profiles like those for the syndrome scales are also scored by the same program as the syndrome scales.) The score for a DSM-oriented scale is obtained by summation of the 1 and 2 ratings of its constituent items. The profile in Figure 19–3 indicates how Lonnie's score on each DSM-oriented scale compares with scores obtained by the national normative sample of 12- to 18-year-old boys rated by their teachers. Like the profiles for syndromes, the profiles for DSM-oriented scales display scores in relation to T scores and percentiles for the national normative sample. Scores above the top broken line are in the clinical range ($T > 69$; >97th percentile). Scores between the two broken lines are in the borderline clinical range (T 65 through 69; 93rd through 97th percentiles). And scores below the bottom broken line are in the normal range ($T < 65$; <93rd percentile). By looking at Figure 19–3, you can see that Lonnie's score on the ADH Problems scale was in the clinical range (above the top broken line), and his scores on the Anxiety Problems and Oppositional Defiant Problems scales were in the borderline clinical range.

Scales for Scoring Strengths

Comprehensive evaluations require assessment of strengths, as well as problems. To make it easy for clinicians to assess strengths with the same instruments that assess problems, most ASEBA self-report and other-report forms include sections for competence or adaptive functioning. Table 19.2 lists the names of the competence and adaptive functioning scales scored from the ASEBA instruments for ages 1½ to 59 years.

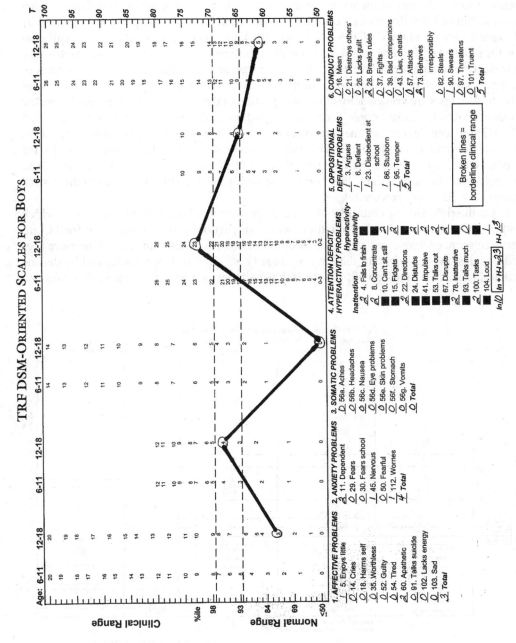

FIGURE 19–3.   Hand-scored profile of DSM-oriented scales scored from a TRF completed by 14-year-old Lonnie's math teacher.

Competence scales for ages 6 to 18.   The CBCL/6–18 and YSR assess competence in terms of items and scales for activities, social relationships, school, and total competence, which is the sum of the scores for the specific kinds of competence scored on the other scales. Figure 19–4 illustrates a computer-scored profile for the competencies reported by Lonnie's mother on the CBCL/6–18. Unlike the high scores that are clinically significant on the problem scales, low scores are clinically significant on the competence scales, because low scores indicate lower levels of competence than are reported for normative samples of peers. If you look at the competence profile scored for Lonnie in Figure 19–4, you can see that broken lines are printed across the lower portion of the graphic display. Scores below the bottom broken line, like Lonnie's score for the School scale, are in the clinical range of $T <$ 31, <3rd percentile, because they are lower than the scores obtained by the upper 97% of the national normative sample. Scores between the two broken lines, like Lonnie's score for the Social scale, are in the borderline clinical range (T 31 to 35; 3rd to 7th percentiles). And scores above the broken lines, like Lonnie's score for the Activities scale, are in the normal range ($T > 35$; >7th percentile).

On the right side of Figure 19–4 you can see Lonnie's Total Competence score, which is the sum of his scores on the Activities, Social, and School scales. Because the Total Competence score encompasses a broader spectrum of competencies than each of the more specific scales, the cutpoints for the clinical range ($T < 37$; <10th percentile) and borderline clinical range (T 37 through 40; 10th to 16th percentiles) are less conservative than those on

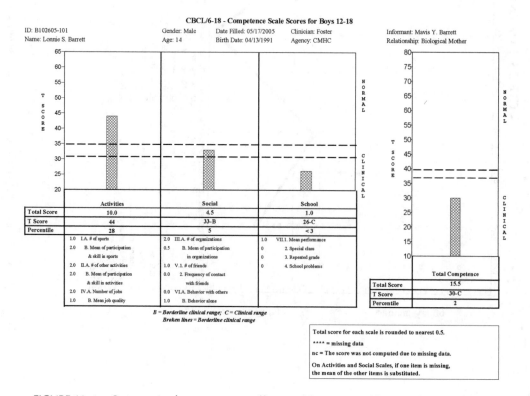

FIGURE 19–4.   Computerized competence profile scored for 14-year-old Lonnie from CBCL/6–18 completed by his mother. (Hand-scored profiles are also available.)

the more specific scales. As Figure 19–4 shows, Lonnie's Total Competence score was in the clinical range. Strengths observed by teachers are scored on TRF scales for academic performance and adaptive functioning.

Adaptive functioning scales for ages 18 to 59.   For ages 18 to 59, the Adult Self-Report (ASR) is scored on normed adaptive functioning scales designated as *Friends, Spouse/Partner, Family, Job*, and *Education*. The Spouse/Partner, Job, and Education scales are scored only for people who, during the preceding six months, were married or living with a partner, had a paid job, or were enrolled in an educational program, respectively. A *Mean Adaptive* score is computed as the average of the *T* scores for all the adaptive scales that are completed for the person being assessed. In addition to the adaptive functioning scales, the ASR and the Adult Behavior Checklist (ABCL) are scored on normed scales for use of tobacco, alcohol, and drugs for nonmedical purposes, and the mean of the specific substance use scales. The adaptive functioning and substance use scales enable clinicians to quickly assess important aspects of adults' functioning that are not tapped by the empirically based problem scales or DSM-oriented scales.

TYPICAL PROCEDURES FOR CLINICAL USE OF THE ASEBA

Children and adolescents seldom refer themselves for mental health services. Instead, parents, teachers, school psychologists, physicians, and other adults typically decide that help is needed. As part of the intake process, clinicians can request that each parent or guardian and other relevant adults complete the CBCL/1½–5 or CBCL/6–18. If a 1½- to 5-year-old child attends day care or preschool, the clinician can request the parents' permission for daycare providers and/or preschool teachers to complete the Caregiver-Teacher Report Form for Ages 1½ to 5 (C-TRF).

For ages 6 to 18, the clinician can request the parents' permission for as many teachers as possible to complete TRFs. These forms provide a great deal of information from multiple perspectives without requiring any of the clinician's time.

With the ASEBA Assessment Data Manager (ADM) computer program, clerical workers can enter and score the data. They can then give the clinician scored profiles, narrative reports, results for critical items, and systematic cross-informant comparisons, which are described in the following sections. To assess progress and outcomes, clinicians can request that the same people complete ASEBA forms on subsequent occasions for comparison with the profiles and scores obtained at intake. To avoid the need for staff to key or hand-score ASEBA forms, machine-readable CBCL/6–18, TRF, and YSR forms are available in both optical mark reading (OMR) and Teleform versions. A client-entry computer program is also available that enables parents and adolescents to key enter their own data at the clinician's office. In addition, ASEBA *Web-Link* makes it possible to send forms electronically from the clinician's computer to web-connected computers elsewhere for direct entry of data by parents, adolescents, and teachers. Web-Link then transmits the data back to the clinician's computer. For respondents who are not computer literate, Web-Link can be used to electronically print paper ASEBA forms on web-connected computers. After respondents fill out the forms, data clerks can enter the data from the paper forms at remote sites. Other options include faxing the completed forms, scanning them for electronic transmission, and mailing them to the clinician.

Cross-Informant Comparisons

When CBCL, C-TRF, TRF, YSR, ASR, and ABCL forms are entered into ADM, forms completed for the same individual can be systematically compared in a variety of ways, as described in the following sections.

Bar Graph Comparisons.   To compare scores from up to eight forms on the empirically based syndromes, ADM prints a page of bar graphs showing the *T* scores obtained for each syndrome from ratings by each informant. ADM also prints bar graphs comparing scores from all informants on the DSM-oriented scales, Internalizing, Externalizing, and Total Problems. The bar graphs enable the clinician to quickly identify areas in which all or most informants report either many or few problems and areas in which there may be important differences between the kinds of problems reported by certain informants. These differences provide clinically valuable data both on how children and adolescents function in different contexts and on how they are perceived by different informants.

For example, Figure 19–5 shows the scores obtained by Lonnie on each DSM-oriented scale from CBCL/6–18 ratings by his mother and father, YSR ratings by Lonnie, and TRF ratings by his math, English, and science teachers. As you can see in Figure 19–5, there were some important variations in scores on the Affective Problems, Attention Deficit Hyperactivity Problems, Oppositional Defiant Problems, and Conduct Problems scales. These are discussed in the case illustration following this section.

Side-by-Side Comparisons of Item Ratings.   In addition to the bar graph comparisons, ADM prints side-by-side comparisons of the 0–1–2 ratings obtained from each informant

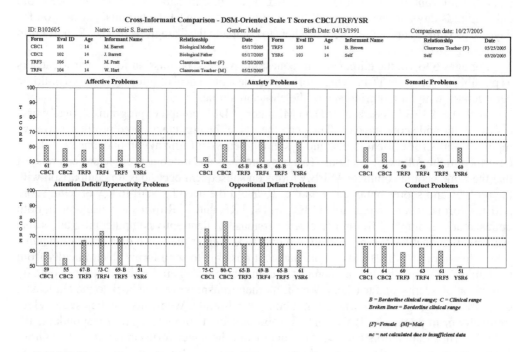

FIGURE 19–5.   Bar graph comparisons of DSM-oriented scale scores for 14-year-old Lonnie from ASEBA forms completed by his mother, father, three teachers, and Lonnie himself.

on each problem item of each scale. By looking at the side-by-side printouts of item scores, the clinician can quickly identify items that are reported by all informants (i.e., are rated 1 or 2), those that are not reported by any informant (i.e., are rated 0), and those that are reported by some informants but not by others.

Correlations between Ratings by Different Informants. Because meta-analyses have shown only modest levels of agreement between most combinations of informants (Achenbach et al., 1987, 2005; Duhig et al., 2000; Renk & Phares, 2004), ADM provides clinicians with guidelines for judging the levels of agreement found between informants for each case. ADM does this by printing Q correlations between the 0–1–2 ratings of each problem item by each pair of informants. ADM then compares these Q correlations with the Q correlations previously found for large reference samples of similar pairs of informants. A Q correlation indicates the degree of consistency between ratings of a large number of items by two different raters. This differs from the more familiar type of correlation (known as R correlation) between two variables, each of which is scored for many individuals, such as the correlation between ability and achievement measured in 100 individuals.

ADM helps the clinician judge the relative magnitude of the Q correlation between two informants, such as a mother and father who each completed the CBCL/6–18. ADM does this by printing the 25th percentile, mean, and 75th percentile of the Q correlations from a large reference sample, such as mothers' and fathers' CBCL/6–18 ratings. On the printout, Q correlations below the 25th percentile of a reference sample are labeled as *below average*, those between the 25th and 75th percentiles are labeled as *average*, and those above the 75th percentile are labeled as *above average*. For example, if the Q correlation between CBCL/6–18 ratings by Lonnie's mother and father were below the 25th percentile of the reference sample, the printout would label the Q correlation between the CBCL/6–18 ratings as "below average." The clinician could then note that the exceptionally low agreement between Lonnie's mother and father warrants exploration. By interviewing the parents, the clinician may learn that the parents hold opposing views of Lonnie's behavior or that one parent has too little contact with Lonnie to be aware of certain problems. Another possible reason for a low Q correlation between parents' ratings is that one parent's relationship with Lonnie tends to trigger certain problem behaviors that are not observed by the other parent.

CASE ILLUSTRATION

Lonnie's mother brought him to a clinician at the urging of the school psychologist at Lonnie's school. Although Lonnie had previously been an excellent student, his academic performance and behavior had become very erratic. The school psychologist said that Lonnie seemed to be preoccupied, failed to pay attention, and had three angry outbursts in class. Lonnie's parents were also concerned about his conflicts with them.

As part of his standard evaluation procedure, the clinician requested that Lonnie's parents each complete the CBCL/6–18. He also requested that each parent complete the ASR to describe their own functioning and the ABCL to describe their spouse's functioning. Because Lonnie's father was away on an extended business trip, the clinician's receptionist used Web-Link to transmit the CBCL/6–18, ASR, and ABCL to him. Lonnie's father then completed and returned the forms to the clinician's office via Web-Link. To obtain a picture of Lonnie's functioning in school, the clinician requested parental permission to have Lonnie's teachers complete TRFs. The TRFs were sent via Web-Link to the school psychologist, who agreed to have Lonnie's teachers complete them.

When the clinician initially met with him, Lonnie was sullen and uncommunicative. However, when the clinician told Lonnie that he'd like to have him complete the YSR and that Lonnie could complete it either on a computer at the office or at home via Web-Link, Lonnie agreed to complete the YSR on the office computer. The clinician's receptionist printed profiles and cross-informant comparisons from the completed CBCL/6–18, TRF, and YSR forms. Figure 19–5 displays the cross-informant comparisons of DSM-oriented scales from the CBCLs completed by each parent, the TRFs completed by three teachers, and the YSR completed by Lonnie. Figure 19–6 displays the syndrome profile scored from Lonnie's YSR.

As you can see in Figure 19–6, Lonnie's YSR ratings yielded scores in the clinical range (above the broken lines) on the Anxious/Depressed and Withdrawn/Depressed syndromes. His scores were in the borderline clinical range (between the two broken lines) on the Social Problems and Thought Problems syndromes. And his scores were in the normal range (below the bottom broken line) on the other syndromes. ADM also prints a narrative report (not shown) that describes the ASEBA results and that lists scores for critical items. These are items that clinicians have judged to be of particular concern. On the critical items, the clinician noted that Lonnie gave item *91, I think about killing myself*, a rating of 2, indicating *very*

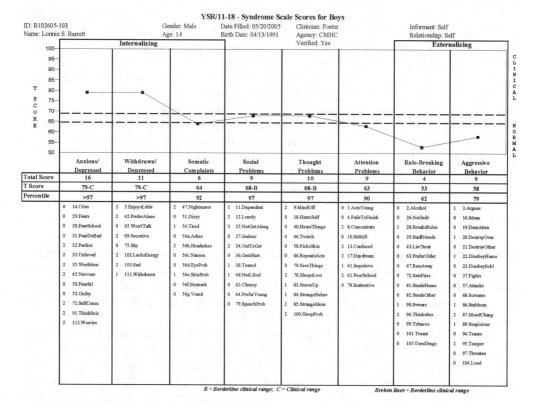

YSR/11-18 - Syndrome Scale Scores for Boys

ID: B102605-103   Gender: Male   Date Filled: 05/20/2005   Clinician: Foster   Informant: Self
Name: Lonnie S. Barrett   Age: 14   Birth Date: 04/13/1991   Agency: CMHC   Relationship: Self
Verified: Yes

	Anxious/ Depressed	Withdrawn/ Depressed	Somatic Complaints	Social Problems	Thought Problems	Attention Problems	Rule-Breaking Behavior	Aggressive Behavior
Total Score	16	11	6	9	10	9	4	9
T Score	79-C	79-C	64	68-B	68-B	63	53	58
Percentile	>97	>97	92	97	97	90	62	79

Item listings by syndrome:

Anxious/Depressed
0 14.Cries
0 29.Fears
0 30.FearSchool
2 31.FearDoBad
2 32.Perfect
2 33.Unloved
2 35.Worthless
2 45.Nervous
0 50.Fearful
0 52.Guilty
0 71.SelfConsc
2 91.ThinkSuic
2 112.Worries

Withdrawn/Depressed
2 5.EnjoysLittle
2 42.PreferAlone
0 65.Won'tTalk
2 69.Secretive
0 75.Shy
2 102.LacksEnergy
2 103.Sad
1 111.Withdrawn

Somatic Complaints
2 47.Nightmares
0 51.Dizzy
1 54.Tired
0 56a.Aches
2 56b.Headaches
0 56c.Nausea
0 56d.EyeProb
1 56e.SkinProb
1 56f.Stomach
0 56g.Vomit

Social Problems
1 11.Dependent
2 12.Lonely
2 25.NotGetAlong
0 27.Jealous
2 34.OutToGet
1 36.GetsHurt
1 38.Teased
1 48.NotLiked
0 62.Clumsy
0 64.PreferYoung
0 79.SpeechProb

Thought Problems
2 9.MindOff
0 18.HarmSelf
0 40.HearsThings
2 46.Twitch
0 58.PicksSkin
0 66.RepeatsActs
0 70.SeesThings
2 76.SleepLess
1 83.StoresUp
1 84.StrangeBehav
2 85.StrangeIdeas
2 100.SleepProb

Attention Problems
0 1.ActsYoung
0 4.FailsToFinish
2 8.Concentrate
0 10.SitStill
2 13.Confused
2 17.Daydream
1 41.Impulsive
2 61.PoorSchool
0 78.Inattentive

Rule-Breaking Behavior
0 2.Alcohol
0 26.NoGuilt
1 28.BreaksRules
0 39.BadFriends
0 43.LieCheat
0 63.PreferOlder
0 67.RunAway
0 72.SetsFires
0 81.StealsHome
0 82.StealsOther
1 90.Swears
2 96.ThinksSex
0 99.Tobacco
0 101.Truant
0 105.UsesDrugs

Aggressive Behavior
1 3.Argues
0 16.Mean
1 19.DemAtten
1 20.DestroyOwn
0 21.DestroyOther
0 22.DisobeyHome
0 23.DisobeySchl
0 37.Fights
0 57.Attacks
0 68.Screams
1 86.Stubborn
1 87.MoodChang
1 89.Suspicious
0 94.Teases
2 95.Temper
0 97.Threaten
0 104.Loud

B = Borderline clinical range;   C = Clinical range   Broken lines = Borderline clinical range

FIGURE 19–6. Computerized syndrome profile scored from YSR completed by 14-year-old Lonnie.

true or often true. In the spaces provided for answering open-ended items that request youths to report any concerns about school and any other concerns, Lonnie had entered "Since I changed school, I can't seem to keep up with the work," "My parents arguments are really getting to me," and "Kids at my new school are out to get me."

As Figure 19–7 shows, the cross-informant comparisons of syndrome scale scores revealed that Lonnie's YSR was the only form that yielded a score in the clinical range on the Anxious/Depressed syndrome. The CBCL/6–18 completed by Lonnie's mother yielded scores in the clinical range on the Withdrawn/Depressed and Aggressive Behavior syndromes, and the CBCL/6–18 completed by Lonnie's father yielded a score in the clinical range only on the Aggressive Behavior syndrome. The TRFs completed by two of Lonnie's teachers yielded scores in the clinical range on the Attention Problems syndrome, and the third TRF yielded a score in the borderline clinical range. Similarly, two of the TRFs yielded scores in the clinical range on the Social Problems syndrome, and the third yielded a score in the borderline clinical range.

The side-by-side comparisons of the 0–1–2 ratings of individual problem items showed that item *91* regarding suicidal thoughts and item *103* regarding being unhappy, sad, or depressed were endorsed only by Lonnie. Lonnie's suicidal thoughts and unhappiness were thus evidently not apparent to his parents or teachers. The relatively high CBCL/6–18 scores for Withdrawn/Depressed and Aggressive Behavior indicated that Lonnie's parents saw his problems mainly in terms of withdrawn and aggressive behavior. The aggressive behavior was especially marked in his fathers' ratings. Ratings by Lonnie's teachers, on the other hand, reflected deviance mainly in social and attentional problems. As shown previously in Figure 19–4, the CBCL/6–18 completed by Lonnie's mother yielded scores for the Activities scale in the normal range, the Social scale in the borderline clinical range, and the School scale in the clinical range. The YSR completed by Lonnie and the CBCL/6–18 completed by his father also indicated greater strength on the Activities scale than in social relations or school. On the TRF, scores were relatively low for academic performance and for adaptive functioning.

Profiles scored from the ASRs and ABCLs completed by Lonnie's parents revealed marked differences between their self-descriptions and how they were described by their spouse. Lonnie's mother's self-ratings on the ASR yielded a score in the clinical range on the Anxious/Depressed syndrome and in the normal range on the other syndromes. The ABCL completed by Lonnie's father to describe his wife, by contrast, yielded scores in the clinical range on the Somatic Complaints and Aggressive Behavior syndromes. The ASR completed by Lonnie's father yielded scores in the clinical range on the Withdrawn syndrome and scores in the normal range on the other syndromes. However, the ABCL completed by his wife yielded scores in the clinical range on the Attention Problems, Aggressive Behavior, Rule-Breaking Behavior, and Intrusive syndromes. The profiles of DSM-oriented scales scored from the two ASRs and ABCLs also revealed disparities between relatively high self-reported depression and social withdrawal versus spouse-reported problems in other areas.

Based on the cross-informant comparisons of problems reported for Lonnie and for his parents, the clinician inferred that the social and attentional problems reported by Lonnie's teachers and the decline in his grades were probably by-products of the suicidal thoughts and depressive affect that Lonnie was experiencing. Lonnie's recent move to a much bigger school and the negative affectivity and conflicting views of each other that were evident in Lonnie's parents' ASR and ABCL profiles, and in the arguments reported by Lonnie on the YSR, were likely factors in Lonnie's problems. The clinician decided that a possible cornerstone for work with Lonnie and his family would be to discuss with Lonnie's parents their contrasting views of each other and the consequences for Lonnie. If each parent granted

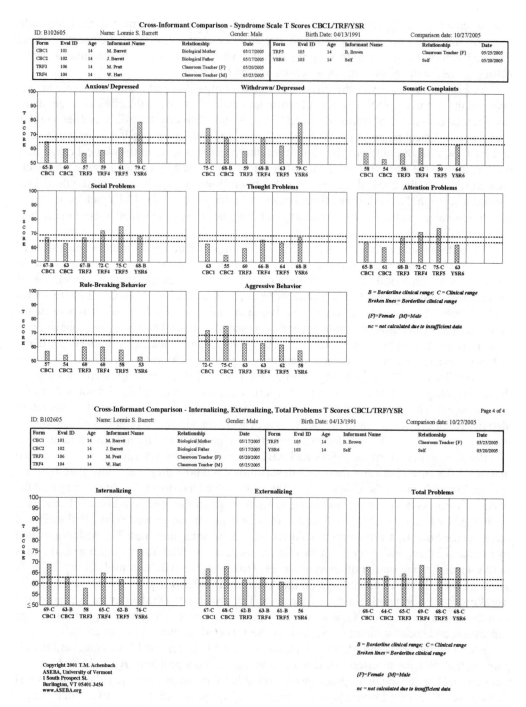

FIGURE 19–7. Bar graph comparisons of syndrome, internalizing, externalizing, and total problems scale scores for 14-year-old Lonnie from ASEBA forms completed by his mother, father, three teachers, and Lonnie himself.

permission, the clinician planned to show the ASR and ABCL profiles to both parents and to encourage a therapeutic alliance for improving their communication with each other and with Lonnie. Depending on how they responded, he would then propose the options of couples therapy for them with another therapist while he saw Lonnie for treatment or conjoint family therapy in which he would meet with Lonnie and both parents together. If the parents seemed unwilling or unable to work together in either of these modalities, he would suggest that they each obtain treatment for themselves while he worked primarily with Lonnie. Whichever treatment modality was selected, he would plan to have the ASEBA forms completed again in six months to evaluate progress.

The clinician's initial treatment goals were to improve communication and cooperation between the parents, to improve their communication with Lonnie, and to help Lonnie adapt to his new school. Accomplishing these goals seemed necessary to reduce Lonnie's depressive affect and suicidal ideation, which, in turn, interfered with his social and academic functioning. Progress could be measured in terms of improved social and school scores on the CBCL/6–18 and YSR competence scales, improved academic and adaptive functioning scores on the TRF, and reductions in scores on the DSM-oriented and syndrome scales that were deviant on the CBCL/6–18, TRF, and YSR forms completed during the initial evaluation, as shown in Figures 19–5 and 19–7. The problems reported for Lonnie and the evidence for impairment in academic and social functioning were consistent with a DSM-IV diagnosis of Dysthymic Disorder (American Psychiatric Association, 1994, 2000).

SUMMARY AND CONCLUSIONS

This chapter outlined the ASEBA and its applications to clinical assessment of children, adolescents, and their parents. ASEBA forms are tailored to the ages of the people being assessed, to different types of informants, and to the contexts in which they see the people who are being assessed. Because no one source of data can serve as a gold standard, the ASEBA is designed to obtain and systematically compare data from multiple informants. Differences between informants' reports are as clinically valuable as similarities, because they can reveal contextual variations in functioning and in informants' perspectives. Not only initial assessments but reassessments to evaluate the course and outcome of treatment should include data from self-reports and reports from multiple informants. Assessment of children and adolescents should also include assessment of parent figures whenever possible. Parents can easily be assessed via standardized self-reports and reports by people who know each parent, especially the parent's spouse or partner.

ASEBA forms are scored on profiles that display scores for items and scales, including strengths, syndromes, DSM-oriented, Internalizing, Externalizing, and Total Problems scales. The scale scores are displayed in relation to norms that are age-, gender-, and informant-specific. Percentiles, T scores, and cutpoints for normal, borderline, and clinical ranges are based on the norms. Clinical applications of the ASEBA were illustrated in the evaluation of 14-year-old Lonnie, as seen by each parent, three teachers, and Lonnie himself. As an important part of the evaluation of Lonnie, Lonnie's parents each completed the Adult Self-Report (ASR) to describe their own functioning and the Adult Behavior Checklist (ABCL) to describe the other parent's functioning. Without any cost in clinical time to obtain these assessments, they provided valuable information for understanding the family dynamics and for planning interventions.

REFERENCES

Achenbach, T. M. (1966). The classification of children's psychiatric symptoms: A factor-analytic study. *Psychological Monographs, 80* (No. 615).

Achenbach, T. M. (1991). *Manual for the Child Behavior Checklist/4–18 and 1991 Profile.* Burlington, VT: University of Vermont, Department of Psychiatry.

Achenbach, T. M., Bernstein, A., & Dumenci, L. (2005). DSM-oriented scales and statistically based syndromes for ages 18 to 59: Linking taxonomic paradigms to facilitate multi-taxonomic approaches. *Journal of Personality Assessment, 84,* 47–61.

Achenbach, T. M., Dumenci, L., & Rescorla, L. A. (2003). *DSM*-oriented and empirically based approaches to constructing scales from the same item pools. *Journal of Clinical Child and Adolescent Psychology, 32,* 328–340.

Achenbach, T. M., Krukowski, R. A., Dumenci, L., & Ivanova, M. Y. (2005). Assessment of adult psychopathology: Meta-analyses and implications of cross-informant correlations. *Psychological Bulletin, 131,* 361–382.

Achenbach, T. M., McConaughy, S. H., & Howell, C. T. (1987). Child/adolescent behavioral and emotional problems: Implications of cross-informant correlations for situational specificity. *Psychological Bulletin, 101,* 213–232.

Achenbach, T. M., & Rescorla, L. A. (2000). *Manual for the ASEBA Preschool Forms & Profiles.* Burlington, VT: University of Vermont, Department of Psychiatry.

Achenbach, T. M., & Rescorla, L. A. (2001). *Manual for the ASEBA School-Age Forms & Profiles.* Burlington, VT: University of Vermont, Research Center for Children, Youth, and Families.

Achenbach, T. M., & Rescorla, L. A. (2003). *Manual for the ASEBA Adult Forms & Profiles.* Burlington, VT: University of Vermont, Research Center for Children, Youth, and Families.

American Psychiatric Association. (1952). *Diagnostic and statistical manual of mental disorders.* Washington, DC: Author.

American Psychiatric Association. (1994). *Diagnostic and statistical manual of mental disorders* (4th ed.). Washington, DC: Author.

American Psychiatric Association. (2000). *Diagnostic and statistical manual of mental disorders* (4th ed. text rev.). Washington, DC: Author.

Duhig, A. M., Renk, K., Epstein, M. K., & Phares, V. (2000). Interparental agreement on internalizing, externalizing, and total behavior problems: A meta-analysis. *Clinical Psychology Science and Practice, 7,* 435–453.

McConaughy, S. H., & Achenbach, T. M. (2001). *Manual for the Semistructured Clinical Interview for Children and Adolescents* (2nd ed.). Burlington, VT: University of Vermont, Research Center for Children, Youth, and Families.

McConaughy, S. H., & Achenbach, T. M. (2004). *Manual for the Test Observation Form for Ages 2–18.* Burlington, VT: University of Vermont, Research Center for Children, Youth, and Families.

Renk, K., & Phares, V. (2004). Cross-informant ratings of social competence in children and adolescents. *Clinical Psychology Review, 24,* 239–254.

SPECIFIC SYNDROMES, ISSUES, AND PROBLEM AREAS

20

ASSESSING PERCEIVED QUALITY
OF LIFE IN CHILDREN AND YOUTH

E. Scott Huebner
University of South Carolina

Rich Gilman
University of Kentucky

Shannon M. Suldo
University of South Florida

A number of prominent psychologists have articulated calls for a science of "positive psychology" to complement psychology's traditional focus on psychopathological conditions (e.g., Seligman & Csikszentmihalyi, 2000). Rather than focusing exclusively on the origins, nature, and treatment of psychological symptoms, such a science would include attention to the study of psychological wellness. In this manner, psychological wellness is conceptualized to reflect more than the absence of symptoms. Comprehensive psychological evaluations must thus expand to incorporate individual and environmental *strengths* as well as psychological difficulties (Wright & Lopez, 2002). A variety of psychological strengths have been considered; however, the classification and measurement of many psychological strengths is in the early stages of development (Peterson & Seligman, 2004), precluding clinical applications of many constructs and measures at present.

One positive psychology construct, perceived quality of life (PQOL) or life satisfaction, has received considerable research attention among adults and children and youth (Diener, Suh, Lucas, & Smith, 1999; Huebner, Suldo, & Gilman, 2006). PQOL has been defined as a cognitive evaluation by a person of the degree of positivity of his or her life (Diener, 1994). It has also been defined as "a person's subjective evaluation of the degree to which his or her most important needs, goals, and wishes have been fulfilled" (Frisch, 1998, p. 24). PQOL reports have been differentiated with respect to evaluation of the quality of overall life and/or major, specific life domains, such as family, friendships, and school, and generally incorporate the complete spectrum of psychological well-being, ranging from very low satisfaction (e.g., terrible) to neutral to very high life satisfaction (e.g., delighted). Such "life satisfaction" measures have been differentiated from measures of psychopathology, such as anxiety, depression, and externalizing problems. Subjective or PQOL reports have also been differentiated from objective quality-of-life measures (e.g., ranging from measures of socioeconomic status, health indexes, access to community resources, etc.). Studies of the relationship between objective and subjective measures have revealed modest relationships at best (Diener et al., 1999), along with evidence of cognitive mediation in many cases (Frisch, 1999).

The incremental contribution of PQOL judgments to traditional symptom-focused psychological assessments of children and youth has been demonstrated in research by Greenspoon and Saklofske (2001). These researchers provided support for a dual-factor model of mental health in elementary school students through the identification of four distinct groups of children: high psychopathology (PTH)–low subjective well-being (SWB) (as measured by PQOL), high PTH–high SWB, low PTH–low SWB, and low PTH–high SWB. The identification of the low PTH–low SWB group particularly challenges traditional models of mental health in which psychological wellness is limited to the absence of psychopathological symptoms.

High *global* PQOL, in particular, appears to operate as a psychological strength or asset in many children and youths. Significant correlations have been revealed between global PQOL reports and many intrapersonal and interpersonal measures of psychological problems, such as low self-esteem, hope, anxiety, depression, external locus of control, and malaptive attributional style. Significant relationships between PQOL reports and a variety of youth risk behaviors, such as suicide, alcohol and drug use, sexual risk taking, and dieting and exercise behavior have been shown (see Gilman & Huebner, 2003). Also, PQOL reports and physical illness indicators (Zullig, Vallois, Huebner, & Drane, 2005) as well as academic problems (Huebner, Suldo, & Gilman, 2006) have been found. Furthermore, PQOL reports have been shown to mediate the relationship between stressful life events and internalizing behavior problems in adolescence, as well as moderate the relationship between stressful life events and adolescent externalizing behaviors (McKnight, Huebner, & Suldo, 2002; Suldo & Huebner, 2004). That is, high life satisfaction has acted as a buffer against the effects of stressful life events. Among adults, a substantial body of research demonstrates that PQOL assessments show predictive utility with respect to psychological disorders, physical illness, health-related expenditures, and academic problems (see Frisch et al., 2003, for a review).

Raphael, Brown, Renwick, and Rootman (1997) discuss four benefits of quality-of-life research for health promotion programs that are applicable to the context of child clinical assessment as well. First, they suggest that quality-of-life information integrates psychosocial perspectives with medical and rehabilitation perspectives. For example, expanded definitions of health, such as that of the World Health Organization (1948), necessitate the consideration of optimal states of physical, mental, and social well-being and not merely the absence of disease. Thus, quality-of-life concerns, including PQOL, are increasingly evaluated along with symptomatic status in determining the effectiveness of health care interventions (see also Frisch, 1998). Second, Raphael et al. highlight the breadth of quality-of-life data, that is, the manner in which quality-of-life data emphasize environmental (e.g., family, school, community) as well as individual determinants of mental and physical health. Multidimensional PQOL reports, which yield indexes of children's perceptions of crucial life contexts (e.g., family, friends, school, community, self) provide an estimate of the "goodness of fit" between a child and the objective conditions of her/his life (Schalock, Keith, Hoffman, & Karan, 1989). Third, quality-of-life data connect with health promotion and evaluation perspectives, given that such data (e.g., PQOL reports) reflect determinants and and/or moderators (e.g., buffering strengths) of adaptive and maladaptive behavior. As noted earlier, low PQOL has been linked with a wide variety of difficulties in psychosocial, physical, and educational functioning (Huebner, Suldo, & Gilman, 2006). Furthermore, high PQOL may operate as a protective buffer promoting resilience in the face of adverse live circumstances. Fourth and finally, quality-of-life measures, including PQOL, can provide important information related to the effects of illness (e.g., psychopathology) or risk behavior and associated interventions. Ethical concerns (e.g., do no harm) could be interpreted so that mental health professionals and others (e.g., medical personnel, educators) should routinely assess PQOL to ensure that their interventions (e.g., psychosocial, medical, educational, etc.) do not negatively affect the PQOL of children and youth, particularly their longer-term PQOL. To date, however, few systematic efforts have been undertaken to monitor and safeguard children's PQOL before, during, or after intervention services have been delivered. Indeed, Frisch (1998) asked whether it is ethical to introduce new treatments without first assessing their impact on clients' quality of life.

Positive psychology researchers have thus concluded that comprehensive psychological assessments should include attention to traditional psychological "symptom" data as well as positive psychological "strengths" data, which includes PQOL reports. For example, Wright and Lopez (2002) propose a four-front approach that includes assessment of (a) individual strengths (e.g., strong self-satisfaction), (b) individual weakness (e.g., symptoms), (c) environmental assets and resources (e.g., strong quality of family life), and (d) environmental stressors and deficits (e.g., poor peer relations). Applying the fourfold model to DSM, Wright and Lopez suggest intriguing modifications of Axes IV and V (along with the introduction of an Axis VI) to guide clinicians in identifying strengths-based data to include "what is working in the client's life" (p. 40), in addition to data related to what is not working. Wright and Lopez argue that such a framework increases intervention possibilities by encouraging the discovery of personal and environmental resources that can enhance intervention efficacy and prevent future problems and/or relapses. Frisch (1998) also discusses the shortcomings of psychological assessments based exclusively on symptom-based measures, concluding that both symptom-based and PQOL measures are essential first-order components of comprehensive assessment plans that provide the strongest foundation for case conceptualization and treatment plans. He further speculates that "in the future, psychological and medical 'checkups' may routinely involve QOL assessments" (p. 36), given their potential cost-effectiveness and predictive validity.

REVIEW OF PQOL MEASURES

PQOL measures have been developed for use with children from grades 3–12. As with adults' PQOL assessment, all measures are self-reports, which is not too surprising, considering that the construct reflects *subjective* experiences of life quality. Extant measures are based on different conceptual underpinnings, and three conceptual models are most commonly reported in the literature. Two models follow the more traditional way in which PQOL has been measured among adults (e.g., Kamman, Farry, & Herbison, 1984; Pavot & Diener, 1993), implying that a single score can reflect the absolute level of PQOL. The models differ in how this score is derived. Global PQOL is assessed through one or more indicators that are context free (e.g., "I have a good life"). In contrast, general PQOL measures aggregate responses across specific life domains (e.g., quality of school, family, *and* peer experiences) to form a composite score. Both types of measures are most useful in cases where descriptive information on absolute levels of PQOL is preferred, or in situations where time and/or resource limitations preclude gathering more differentiated information on life quality within specific domains. The third conceptual model assesses multidimensional PQOL, where mean scores are provided for each domain. There has been some discussion regarding the number and types of domains to be included in multidimensional measures (Gilman & Huebner, 2000). For example, the Multidimensional Students' Life Satisfaction Scale assesses PQOL specific to school, living environment, self, family, and friends, whereas the Comprehensive Quality of Life Scale assesses material well-being, health, productivity, intimacy, safety, place in community, and emotional well-being. Nevertheless, it has also been noted that PQOL has a validity of its own (Frisch, 1999), in that any domain could be included and be considered as a valid indicator. In a larger sense, multidimensional instruments thus tend to reflect the degree to which specific domains are felt to be most pertinent to assess by the designers.

Substantial progress has been made in the construction of various child PQOL measures designed for use with general (i.e., nonclinical) populations as well as specific populations, such as children with psychiatric illness (Bastiaansen, Koot, Bongers, Varni, & Verhulst, 2004), and medical conditions such as diabetes (Ingersoll & Marrero, 1991). Although general PQOL measures have been administered to clinical samples on occasion (Gilman & Handwerk, 2001), there has been little overlap, most likely because of the specificity of the items that may not be generalized across settings. Given the recent interest in PQOL assessment overall, most validation studies have focused on instruments for use with general samples of children. In keeping with this focus, findings reported in this section will be based on general PQOL measures that have undergone relatively rigorous empirical evaluations, including work by independent investigators. For a discussion of measures designed for pediatric populations, the reader should consult recent reviews by Quittner, Davis, and Modi (2003) and Matza, Swensen, Flood, Secnik, and Leidy (2004).

Our description followed many of the previous inclusionary criteria when both adult (Cummins, 1996) and adolescent (Gilman & Huebner, 2000) PQOL measures were reviewed. First, considering the conceptual ambiguity of many PQOL instruments (Wallander, Schmitt, & Koot, 2001), only those instruments based on clear and accepted definitions of PQOL were included. Scales that measured related but more broadly defined constructs such as happiness (e.g., Hills & Argyle, 2002), joy (e.g., Barnett, 1991), and creativity (Torrance, 1990) were excluded. Second, each PQOL instrument was required to reflect either a undimensional (global or general) or multidimensional framework; instruments that restricted PQOL to a specific life domain (e.g., school) were excluded. Finally, only those instruments that had undergone empirical scrutiny beyond its initial validation stage were included. With the use of these selection criteria, six PQOL measures were reviewed. Two instruments, the *Satisfaction with Life Scale* (SWLS; Diener, Emmons, Larsen, & Griffin, 1985) and the *Students' Life Satisfaction Scale* (SLSS; Huebner, 1991), assess global life quality, and a separate unidimensional instrument, the *Perceived Life Satisfaction Scale* (PLSS; Adelman, Taylor, & Nelson, 1989), assesses general PQOL. The remaining two instruments assess PQOL across a variety of life domains. These are the *Multidimensional Students' Life Satisfaction Scale* (MSLSS; Huebner, 1994) and the *Comprehensive Quality of Life Scale, Fifth Edition* (ComQol-S5; Cummins, 1997).

Global PQOL Measures

Satisfaction with Life Scale.   First developed for adults, the Satisfaction with Life Scale (SWLS) also has been used on occasion with adolescents. The scale comprises of five items, and responses are made via a 7-point response scale (1 = strongly disagree, 2 = disagree, 3 = slightly disagree, 4 = neither agree nor disagree, 5 = slightly agree, 6 = agree, 7 = strongly agree). Scoring of the instrument largely consists of adding the items and dividing by the total number to derive a global score. Higher mean scores denote higher levels of PQOL.

The SWLS has been administered to numerous independent samples representing a broad array of cultures, including Chinese (Leung & Leung, 1992), Portuguese (Neto, 1993), Hong Kong (Shek, 1998), Spanish (Atienza, Balaguer, & Garcia-Merita, 2003), and Israeli and Arabic youth (Abdallah, 1998). Interestingly, although the SWLS has been the most frequently used instrument in cross-cultural studies, few studies have investigated the psychometric properties among American youth. The instrument yields reliabilities ranging from .67 (Leung & Leung, 1992) to .78 (Neto, 1993), which are somewhat lower than those obtained from European (Arrindell, Heesink, & Feij, 1999) and American (Diener et al., 1985) adults. Such findings suggest cultural and/or maturational differences in item interpretation. No stability data have been reported, and thus the short- and long-term consistency of the SWLS remains unclear.

The SWLS has demonstrated evidence of convergent validity for children and adolescents, including moderate to strong correlations with measures of self-efficacy and happiness (see Neto, 1993). Furthermore, the scale has demonstrated a moderate relationship with a one-item satisfaction measure (Leung & Leung, 1992). Evidence of discriminant validity has been found via significant and negative correlations with measures of loneliness and shyness (Neto, 1993) and family difficulties (Shek, 1998). Finally, data from both exploratory (Neto, 1993) and confirmatory (Atienza, Balaguer, & Garcia-Merita, 2003; Pons, Atienza, Balaguer, & Garcia-Merita, 2000) factor analyses have supported the underlying factor structure of the instrument.

In summary, the SWLS appears to yield adequate psychometric characteristics across a variety of youths from different cultural backgrounds. Ironically, no studies have used the instrument among American youth, and additional research is necessary to determine cross-cultural invariance with respect to a sample of youths from the country of origin. Other limitations include limited normative data and lack of test-retest information for youths.

Students' Life Satisfaction Scale.   The Students' Life Satisfaction Scale (SLSS) is a seven-item self-report scale that is designed for use with youths ranging between ages 8 and 18. Although scoring of the scale may vary (Gilman & Huebner, 1997), the predominant scoring option is based on a 6-point rating scale (1 = strongly disagree, 2 = moderately disagree, 3 = mildly disagree, 4 = mildly agree, 5 = moderately agree, 6 = strongly agree). Scores thus range from 7 and 42; the items are summed and divided by the total number of items to derive a global scale score. In contrast to the SWLS, the SLSS was designed to be used with children as young as grade 3. Thus, the SLSS items were written at a very simple conceptual level so that the instrument could be administered to younger children as well as to youth with poor reading abilities.

The SLSS has been administered to a variety of samples (e.g., Gilman & Huebner, 1997; Fogle, Huebner, & Laughlin, 2002; McKnight, Huebner, & Suldo, 2002), although most samples have come from the southeastern region of the United States. Recent studies have used samples from other U.S. regions (e.g., Gilman & Barry, 2003), as well as from disparate countries such as Canada (Greenspoon & Saklofske, 1997), Croatia and Ireland (Langknecht, Gilman, Lili, Schiff, & Sverko, 2005), Israel (Schiff, Nebe, & Gilman, in press), and Korea (Park, Huebner, Laughlin, Valois, & Gilman, 2004). Coefficient alphas for American samples have generally been in the .80–.88 range (Dew & Huebner, 1994; Huebner, Drane, & Valois,

2000), and the internal consistency has ranged from .74 (Croatia) to .84 (Canada). These estimates, although roughly consistent, nevertheless indicate that youths from different cultures may interpret the SLSS items in a somewhat different manner. Test-retest coefficients have ranged from .64 across a four-week period (Gilman & Huebner, 1997) to .53 across a one-year interval (Huebner, Funk, & Gilman, 2000), indicating a moderate degree of stability across various time frames.

The SLSS has yielded strong evidence of construct validity, including significant, moderate, and positive correlations with measures of global self-esteem (Huebner, Gilman & Laughlin, 1999), hope (Gilman, Dooley, & Florell, 2006), extraversion (Fogle, Huebner, & Laughlin, 2002), and internal locus of control (Ash & Huebner, 2001). Significant and negative correlations have been found for measures of anxiety and depression (Huebner, Funk, & Gilman, 2000), loneliness (Huebner & Alderman, 1993), and neuroticism (Huebner, 1991). Finally, support for the unidimensional factor structure has been found via exploratory factor analysis (Gilman & Huebner, 1997).

In summary, the psychometric properties of the SLSS indicate that the scale is an adequate measure of PQOL among youths. Studies of the internal consistency and test-retest reliability suggest that the instrument yields reliable information regarding the life quality of children. Furthermore, there is enough evidence for the construct validity of the instrument to suggest that the SLSS assesses what it purports to measure. Nevertheless, some limitations are of note. First, there are limited normative data for the scale, and thus global scores are dependent upon the sample from which they were obtained. Second, although the item content of the SLSS does not overlap with the SWLS, no cross-validation studies with the two scales have been conducted.

Perceived Life Satisfaction Scale.   The Perceived Life Satisfaction Scale (PLSS) is a 19-item self-report measure designed to yield *a total* (general) PQOL score based on items covering material and physical well-being, relationships, environment, personal development and fulfillment, and recreation/entertainment. Each item is rated on a 6-point rating scale (1 = not at all, 2 = not much, 3 = a little, 4 = somewhat, 5 = a lot, 6 = extremely). Youths are asked to respond to how important each item is to their life ("the type of clothes you wear"), and to rate their satisfaction with that particular item. All items are summed to derive the general PQOL score. Scoring of the scale is somewhat different from what is computed for the global measures, as the items are categorized into three groups (1 and 2 ratings are scored as a 2, 3 and 4 ratings are scored as a 1, and 5 and 6 ratings are scored as a 0). Thus, higher scores are indicative of lower PQOL.

The PLSS has been administered to several samples (Adelman et al., 1989; Huebner & Dew, 1993; Smith, Adelman, Nelson, Taylor, & Phares, 1987). Coefficient alphas have ranged from .74 to .80 (Smith et al., 1987), and a test-retest estimate of .85 has been obtained, although the time frame is unspecified (Adelman et al., 1989). There is evidence of convergent validity, with positive and significant correlations with measures of perceived control and positive school attitudes (Adelman et al., 1989) and global self-concept (Huebner & Dew, 1993). Validity has been supported via significant and negative correlations with measures of depression (Adelman et al., 1989) and internal locus of control (Huebner & Dew, 1993). Nevertheless, evidence regarding the unidimensional factor structure has not been found. For example, Huebner and Dew (1993) conducted a principal components analysis with oblique rotation. The results found support for a four-factor solution, suggesting that the PLSS may be multidimensional.

In summary, the PLSS has yielded adequate reliability and test-retest stability, and some evidence for its convergent and discriminant validity with similar/dissimilar measures. Nevertheless, the construct validity of the measure is unclear. Additional factor analyses using confirmatory methods are necessary, as are additional normative data.

Multidimensional PQOL Instruments

Comprehensive Quality of Life Scale. The Comprehensive Quality of Life Scale (ComQoL) is a 35-item multidimensional measure that has been primarily used with Australian samples. Originally constructed to assess PQOL among adults, a downward extension of the scale is available for youth ranging in age between 11 and 18. Seven domains are represented by the ComQol: material well-being, health, productivity, intimacy, safety, place in community, and emotional well-being. The instrument is one of the few that assesses both objective (frequency of participation in each domain) and subjective (satisfaction X importance of each domain) dimensions. Only the subjective dimension of the Com-Qol is described here. For younger children (early to middle elementary school), the child responds to satisfaction items by pointing to a set of five faces ranging from very sad to very happy, and importance items are reflected by a series of drawings of children standing on five steps of increasing height, with the height indicating the relative level of importance (see Marriage & Cummins, 2004). For older youths, satisfaction items are responded to on a 7-point Likert-type rating scale (1 = delighted, 2 = pleased, 3 = mostly satisfied, 4 = mixed, 5 = mostly satisfied, 6 = unhappy, 7 = terrible), and importance items are responded to on a five-point scale (1 = could not be more important, 2 = very important, 3 = somewhat important, 4 = slightly important, 5 = not important at all). There is one satisfaction and one importance item for each PQOL domain. The product of the importance and satisfaction ratings is then calculated for each of the seven domains. Responses are also recalculated to a common metric, so that higher scores reflect both high satisfaction and importance on a particular life domain (Cummins, 1997)

At least three samples have been administered the ComQol since its construction (Bearsly & Cummins, 1999; Gullone & Cummins, 1999; Marriage & Cummins, 2004). The reliability of the combined satisfaction X importance total score has ranged from .64 for younger children (Marriage & Cummins, 2004) to .81 for adolescents (Gullone & Cummins, 1999). Presumably, the difference in reliability estimates for the total score is due to age differences in interpretation of the items. One-week test-retest stability for the combined importance X satisfaction ratings has ranged from .40 (health) to .74 (emotion) across specific domains, and .79 was obtained for the total score.

Evidence for the construct validity of the scale has been demonstrated by significant positive correlations with a sense of personal control (Marriage & Cummins, 2004; Petito & Cummins, 2000), and significant predictions with self-esteem (Marriage & Cummins, 2004). Evidence for the validity of the instrument has also been supported by negative correlations with measures of anxiety and fear (Gullone & Cummins, 1999).

In summary, the ComQol appears to yield adequate reliability and stability estimates for both domain specific and total scores. The ComQol contains a unique scoring feature in that both the importance of and the satisfaction with a particular life domain are considered when PQOL is assessed among youth. Although this scoring feature may lead to more sensitive and accurate understanding of PQOL among youth, it remains to be seen whether assessing the importance of a particular domain yields unique information above that of assessing satisfaction about that domain (see Andrews & Robinson, 1991, for a discussion).

Multidimensional Students' Life Satisfaction Scale.   The Multidimensional Students' Life Satisfaction Scale (MSLSS) is a 40-item self-report instrument that assesses family, friends, school, self, and living environment. In addition, the instrument computes an overall (total) assessment of PQOL by combining all items together. The scale is designed and has been used for youths from ages 8 to 18 (Huebner & Gilman, 2002). The items that make up the MSLSS are responded to on a 6-point rating scale (1 = strongly disagree, 2 = moderately disagree, 3 = mildly disagree, 4 = mildly agree, 5 = moderately agree, 6 = strongly agree). Scoring of each domain consists of summing and dividing by the total number of items making up each domain. Mean scores can range from 6 to 36 for each domain, with higher scores indicating higher levels of PQOL.

Of the multidimensional measures, the MSLSS has been the one most used for American youth (see Huebner & Gilman, 2002), and additional samples have been derived from Korean (Park et al., 2004), Israeli (Schiff, Nebe, & Gilman, in press), Irish (Gilman et al., 2006), and Croatian cultures (Gilman, Ashby, Sverko, Florell, & Varjas, 2005). The instrument has yielded adequate internal consistency coefficients across all samples and across all domains. For example, coefficient alphas for the total score have consistently been in the .90 range. Internal consistency estimates have also consistently ranged in the .80 to .89 range for most domains. Finally, the test-retest coefficient for the total score was .81 across a four-week period, while domain stability coefficients have ranged from .53 (self) to .81 (living environment) across the same time frame (Huebner, Laughlin, Ash, & Gilman, 1998).

The MSLSS has demonstrated evidence of convergent and discriminant validity through significant and expected relationships with various similar and dissimilar measures. For example, significant and positive correlations across domains have been obtained with similar constructs such as self-esteem, positive family and school relationships, and positive peer experiences (see Huebner, 2004, for a review). Likewise, the MSLSS has demonstrated significant and negative correlations with measures of depression and anxiety (Gilman, Huebner, & Laughlin, 2000), social stress (Huebner, Gilman, & Laughlin, 1999) and maladaptive perfectionism (Gilman et al., 2005). Finally, results of separate factor analyses have supported the multidimensional model for students in the United States (Gilman et al., 2005), Korea (Park et al., 2004), Spain (Casas, Alsinet, Rosich, Huebner, & Laughlin, 2001), and Canada (Greenspoon & Saklofske, 1997). In summary, the MSLSS has yielded adequate psychometric properties across a variety of age ranges and cultural groups. Although the instrument appears to assess multidimensional PQOL on a reliable and valid basis, differences in reliability coefficients across cultural groups suggest that the items are interpreted differently. Additional studies are necessary to determine how significant the universality of PQOL is with respect to different cultures (see Oishi & Diener, 2001, for a discussion). Furthermore, studies investigating the MSLSS among Canadian children (Greenspoon & Saklofske, 1997) have questioned the meaningfulness of the living environment subscale, especially among youth in sparsely populated areas.

Alternative Forms of PQOL Measurement

Methodological concerns are noted for any research interest that bases its findings primarily on self-reports (Paulhus, 2002), and PQOL assessment is not different in this respect (Jobe, 2003; McColl, Meadows, & Barofsky, 2003). The main concern is the possibility of social desirability, or the tendency to respond to PQOL items that are based on the perceived expectations of others. Although limited research has investigated the relationship between self-reported PQOL and social desirability, the correlations obtained are mild to moderate (rs of .05–.32) (Gilman & Barry, 2003; Huebner, 1991; Huebner et al., 1998). Furthermore, it has been noted that social desirability may be less of a concern for PQOL research and may reflect substantive individual differences (Diener et al., 1999; Huebner et al., 1998). For example, research among adults (Kozma & Stones, 1988) and adolescents (Dew, 1996) finds that controlling for social desirability does not improve the correlations between PQOL and external criteria.

Nevertheless, alternative forms of PQOL measurement have been proposed and implemented, albeit on a smaller scale than what has been implemented among adults. One method is experience sampling methodology (ESM), which allows for repeated QOL assessment at random moments throughout the course of a youth's day. Although the majority of ESM studies have been conducted among adult populations, the method has been advocated and used for children (see Larson, 1989) and has yielded important information regarding life quality across many domains. For example, using ESM to assess the quality of school experiences among a large sample of adolescents, Shernoff, Csikszentmihalyi, Shneider, and Shernoff (2003) reported that positive school experiences were significantly associated with type of curriculum instruction, classroom management strategies, and perceived school support. Other studies have used the method to investigate the types of activities that children participate in that directly correlate with PQOL (Asakawa & Csikszentmihalyi, 1998; see also Larson, 2000), quality of child and family interactions (Rathunde, 1997), and qualitative differences among children living with single versus married parents (Asmussen & Larson, 1991). Thus, the use of ESM could complement traditional approaches to PQOL assessment and may yield unique information not obtained by a single self-report. Nevertheless, although technological advances have helped to alleviate some previous concerns, such as cost of materials, other limitations, such as attrition, motivation to continually respond to the prompts, and sampling concerns, are noted (Scollon, Kim-Prieto, & Diener, 2003). Nevertheless, the method may be useful for understanding how different facets of life contribute to PQOL. Furthermore, the use of ESM may be useful for moving research beyond highlighting correlates contributing to PQOL to identifying specific mechanisms and causal influences (Schimmack & Diener, 2003).

The use of reports by others (e.g., peers, parents) have also been used to substantiate PQOL self-reports. Bearing in mind that correlations between self- and other-reports and observable behaviors are moderate at best (e.g., $r = .22$; see Achenbach, McConaughy, & Howell, 1987), it is to be expected that the convergence of reports on PQOL measures would be comparable. Findings are generally positive and above expectations. For example, Dew and Huebner (1994) obtained a correlation of .48 between high school students and their parents with use of the SLSS, whereas Gilman and Huebner (1997) reported a correlation of .55 between middle school students and their parents on the same scale. A recent study using the MSLSS found correlations between adolescent and parent reports ranging from .41 to .55 across the five domains of the scale (Huebner, Brantley, Nagle, & Valois, 2002). Although further studies are clearly needed, the findings obtained support the convergent validity of PQOL reports.

Some PQOL measures have received considerably more empirical scrutiny than others, but all measures are generally in the early stages of development and validation. If they were to be evaluated by standards used for norm-referenced instruments to be used for making clinical decisions with individuals (e.g., large nationally representative samples, reliability coefficients greater than .80, numerous validation studies conducted by independent researchers), then all extant PQOL measures would be considered inadequate. Future research with PQOL measures in general is clearly needed with respect to psychometric properties, influence of response distortions, number of domains, usefulness of "importance" ratings, developmental issues, and use with special populations, such as children with mental disabilities (see Gilman & Huebner, 2000, for an extended discussion). Nevertheless, when combined with a relevant battery of traditional psychological tests, background information, interview, and observation data, extant PQOL measures should contribute to more comprehensive psychological assessments of children and youth. Although such measures await further development for some uses (e.g., norm-referenced comparisons), we believe that some of the more well-validated existing scales can be employed in a criterion-referenced fashion, that is, interpreting the levels of satisfaction-dissatisfaction in a qualitative manner, so as to provide clinically useful information (see case study below). For example, it can be helpful to know that an adolescent male describes his satisfaction with family and school experiences as "very dissatisfied," his satisfaction with peer experiences as "very satisfied," and his community experiences as "neutral" before a psychosocial, medical, or educational intervention is considered (e.g., psychotropic medication, special education placement). One aspect of treatment effects could be determined via subsequent "very satisfied" ratings across all domains. In this regard, PQOL information would provide potentially valuable diagnostic, prescriptive, and intervention impact information. When used in a multitrait-multimethod fashion, incorporating multiple measures of the constructs (e.g., self-reports and teacher observations of students' school behavior, sociometric data) along with experienced clinicians' judgments, PQOL measures should be able to yield useful "clinical hypotheses" (including sources of individual and environmental "strengths"). These hypotheses can then be tested against other information to provide incremental information that goes above and beyond that provided by traditional, pathology-focused measures. In this manner, PQOL measures may contribute to enhanced assessment, intervention planning, and health promotion efforts for *all* children and youth, including but not limited to children and youth with clinical levels of behavioral or academic problems.

APPLICATIONS OF PQOL MEASUREMENTS TO ASSESSMENT AND INTERVENTION PLANNING

For reasons presented earlier in this chapter, attending to children's quality of life through direct measurement of their life satisfaction is a first step to ensuring complete psychological wellness. The brevity of the above-described self-report measures of PQOL lends to their utility in screening, progress monitoring, and outcomes assessment. As screening devices, PQOL scales administered to groups of children, such as student bodies, can quickly provide information on average levels among the group. If multidimensional measures (e.g., MSLSS, ComQol) are utilized, schools and other agencies may be able to identify trends in setting-specific strengths and concerns. Group-level administration of brief global measures (e.g., SLSS, SWLS) also results in the identification of students reporting low PQOL, which may facilitate provision of interventions before the onset of clinically significant levels of psychopathology.

Regarding progress monitoring, PQOL measures are useful in assessing the impact of individual interventions such as counseling and special education programming, as well as school-wide programs such as anti-bullying and social skills curricula, on children's well-being. Gilman and Barry (2003) have demonstrated the utility of monitoring children's PQOL as an indicator of their adjustment to residential treatment settings. When used as an outcome measure, PQOL scales provide a means for demonstrating the effects of interventions on adaptive outcomes and measuring improvements in various domains of positive functioning.

In addition to group-level screening and progress monitoring, PQOL assessments are also a useful addition to individual psychoeducational evaluations conducted, in part, to determine students' eligibility for special education. Traditionally, such evaluations have consisted primarily of norm-referenced assessment instruments intended to delineate areas of personal weakness. Commonly used behavior rating scales, for example, indicate the degree to which a student displays psychopathology relative to a standardization sample. Although the addition of subscales that measure areas of adaptive functioning (for example, leadership, social skills, family relations) reflect an improvement in the purposes of rating scales, these instruments continue to focus on symptoms with relatively less information on positive functioning.

Including measures of global and domain-specific PQOL in psychoeducational evaluations partly ameliorates these concerns. For instance, administration and scoring of the MSLSS quickly gathers information about children's satisfaction with multiple systems in their ecology. Rather than comparing children's responses with a normative sample, scores are interpreted in an ipsative manner. After reversing scoring and averaging items within a given domain, subscale scores are first judged to reflect either satisfaction (scores from 4 to 6) or dissatisfaction (scores from 1 to 3) within an important domain of life. Next, an individual's subscale scores are examined together in order to reveal domains of life that are relative strengths/assets or concerns.

In addition to providing an avenue for detecting and gauging personal and environmental strengths, MSLSS scores direct attention to those situations that are most disconcerting to the individual. This focus is in stark contrast to traditional assessment instruments that assess the degree to which the individual is disruptive to his or her environment.

Case Study

The following is a brief case study of A.J., a 12-year-old female who was identified with a learning disability at the age of 10. A.J. was referred to the school psychologist for a reevaluation because of a lack of academic progress despite 18 months of remedial services in a special education classroom with a 6:1 student-to-teacher ratio. Indeed, a norm-referenced achievement test administered during the reevaluation indicated grade-equivalent gains of 0–2 months in various academic skill areas during the 18 months since the initial evaluation.

During an interview, A.J.'s teacher reported that A.J. was well liked by her peers, compliant and attentive during class, and persistent during seatwork. Regarding concerns, the teacher reported that A.J. completes less than 50% of homework assignments, quietly expresses self-doubt and nervousness when presented with assignments (for example, says, "I'm not good at this," and "I'm afraid I will fail this quiz"), and is extremely hesitant to provide answers in front of the class. This information was consistent with results of a teacher-completed behavior rating scale that suggested clinical levels of anxiety.

As part of a comprehensive assessment of A.J.'s social and emotional functioning, she was administered the MSLSS in order to assess her PQOL in several key areas. Her total score ($M = 4.4$) suggested that, despite A.J.'s struggles at school, her perceived quality of life was in the positive range. An examination of the scores from MSLSS subscales (see Figure 20–1) suggested that A.J. is most happy with her family; she responded to such items as "My family gets along well together" and "I like spending time with my parents" with "Strongly Agree."

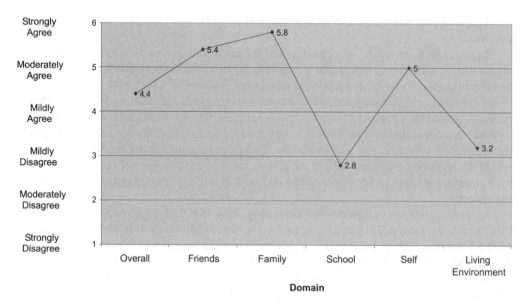

FIGURE 20–1.   MSLSS Scores for A. J.

Despite family support, A.J.'s mean score of 3.2 on the Living Environment subscale was low relative to her satisfaction in most other domains of life in which $1 =$ strongly disagree and $6 =$ strongly agree. She responded "Strongly Agree" to the item "I wish I lived in a different house" (item reverse scored) and strongly disagreed with the item "I like where I live." In response to follow-up questions during an interview with the student, A.J. cautiously shared that her house was "crowded." She later elaborated that she lives in a two-bedroom apartment with eight people. The constant noise and frequent interruptions by A.J.'s two young nieces and nephew (with whom she shared a bedroom) interfered with A.J.'s ability to study and sleep.

Another area of concern suggested by the MSLSS involved A.J.'s dissatisfaction with school ($M = 2.8$). She strongly disagreed with such items as "I learn a lot at school," and "I like being in school," and moderately agreed with "I wish I didn't have to go to school." In response to follow-up questions, A.J. admitted she was frequently tired at school and probably focused more on pretending to be alert and mentally rehearsing articulate responses to questions than on comprehending lessons and practicing skills. A.J. also expressed worries that her peers would pity her if they were aware of her housing situation, and conveyed similar anxiety regarding peer knowledge of her severe academic delays.

Despite fearing negative evaluation by her peers, A.J.'s satisfaction with her friendships ($M = 5.4$) was an area of personal strength. She strongly agreed with such statements as "My friends are nice to me," and "My friends will help me if I need it." Her ability to maintain strong interpersonal relationships may contribute to her positive view of self ($M = 5.0$). A.J.'s perceptions of herself and total life satisfaction score were helpful for understanding the extent to which her academic struggles affected the quality of her life; in this case, low scores in the school satisfaction domain supported the importance of implementing tertiary interventions targeted at academic difficulties. Fortunately, these academic problems had yet to permeate other important domains of life.

Information gleaned from the MSLSS was instrumental in forming data-based recommendations for appropriate interventions. Increasing the amount of collaboration between home and school was considered crucial to increasing A.J.'s success in the classroom. When assessment results were shared at a multidisciplinary meeting, A.J.'s parents were surprised to learn of her fatigue at school, stating she "rarely complains about anything." A.J.'s teachers were similarly unaware of her challenges at home. The school psychologist framed A.J.'s sensitivity and composure as strengths that contributed to her likeability and adaptability but could also result in undue personal sacrifice. Suggestions for home-based interventions included rearranging the family's living arrangement to limit her proximity to small children at night and availability of adult assistance during a protected "study time" during the early evening. A.J. was receptive to these changes, especially regarding the opportunity for additional contact with her parents, who volunteered to assist her with homework.

Recommendations for school-based interventions included implementation of a regular schedule of contact with A.J.'s family, increased frequency of positive attention contingent on academic effort vs. success, and decreased requirements for verbal participation in group lessons. Recommendations for individual interventions included individual therapy consisting of assertion training and cognitive-behavioral strategies to decrease anxiety. Capitalizing on A.J.'s strength in interpersonal functioning, it was recommended that A.J. increase her time spent with peers by joining an extracurricular activity such as chorus or band, an intervention that might also improve her overall feelings toward school. The school psychologist planned to readminister the MSLSS periodically to assess A.J.'s response to these interventions.

SUMMARY

PQOL measures incorporate the full range of positive and negative subjective experiences, from "very low" levels of PQOL, through "neutral" and "very high" levels. Consistent with the premises of a developing science and practice of positive psychology, POQL measures extend beyond those measures that are based upon the assumption that psychological "wellness" is merely the absence of psychopathological symptoms. Although multidimensional measures of PQOL measures assess a broad, multifaceted construct (i.e., quality of life across multiple domains), it should be noted that such measures represent only *one* construct of potential importance to positive psychology (cf. the 24 psychosocial strengths of Peterson & Seligman, 2004, e.g., social intelligence, kindness, curiosity, hope). Nevertheless, multidimensional measures of perceived "goodness of fit" across major environmental and self domains of life should provide an important step in achieving the overarching goal of clinical work with children and youth, that is, the enhancement of the quality of life of children (Frisch, 1998; Kazdin, 1993).

REFERENCES

Abdallah, T. (1998). The Satisfaction with Life Scale (SWLS): Psychometric properties in an Arabic-speaking sample. *International Journal of Adolescence and Youth, 7,* 113–119.

Achenbach, T. M., McConaughy, S. H., & Howell, C. T. (1987). Child/adolescent behavioral and emotional problems: Implications of cross-informant correlations for situational specificity. *Psychological Bulletin, 101,* 213–232.

Adelman, H. S., Taylor, L., & Nelson, P. (1989). Minors' dissatisfaction with their life circumstances. *Child Psychiatry and Human Development, 20,* 135–147.

Andrews, F. M., & Robinson, J. P. (1991). Measures of subjective well-being. In J. P. Robinson, P. R. Shaver, & L. Wrightsman (Eds.), *Social Psychological Attitudes: Vol. 1. Measures of Personality and Social Psychological Attitudes* (pp. 61–114). San Diego, CA: Academic Press.

Arrindell, W. A., Heesink, J., & Feij, J. A. (1999). The Satisfaction With Life Scale (SWLS): Appraisal with 1700 health young adults in the Netherlands. *Personality and Individual Differences, 26,* 815–826.

Asakawa, K., & Csikszentmihalyi, M. (1998). The quality of experience of Asian American adolescents in academic activities: An exploration of educational achievement. *Journal of Research on Adolescents, 8,* 241–262.

Ash, C., & Huebner, E. S. (2001). Environmental events and life satisfaction reports of adolescents: A test of cognitive mediation. *School Psychology International, 22,* 320–336.

Asmussen, L., & Larson, R. (1991). The quality of family time among young adolescents in single-parent and married-parent families. *Journal of Marriage and the Family, 53,* 1021–1030.

Atienza, F. L., Balaguer, I., & Garcia-Merita, M. (2003). Satisfaction with Life Scale: Analysis of factorial invariance across sexes. *Personality and Individual Differences, 35,* 1255–1260.

Barnett, L. A. (1991). The playful child: Measurement of a disposition to play. *Play and Culture, 4,* 51–74.

Bastiaansen, D., Koot, H. M., Bongers, I. L., Varni, J. W., & Verhulst, F. C. (2004). Measuring quality of life in children referred for psychiatric problems: Psychometric properties of the PedsQL-super™ 4.0 generic core scales. *Quality of Life Research: An International Journal of Quality of Life Aspects of Treatment, Care, and Rehabilitation, 13,* 489–495.

Bearsley, C., & Cummins, R. A. (1999). No place called home: Life quality and purpose of homeless youths. *Journal of Social Distress and the Homeless, 8,* 207–236.

Casas, F. C., Alsinet, M., Rosich, E. S., Huebner, E. S., & Laughlin, J. E. (2001). *Cross-cultural investigation of the Multidimensional Students' Life Satisfaction Scale with Spanish adolescents.* Paper presented at the Third Conference of the International Society for Quality of Life Studies, Girona, Spain.

Cummins, R. A. (1996). The domains of life satisfaction: An attempt to order chaos. *Social Indicators Research, 38,* 303–328.

Cummins, R. A. (1997). *Manual for the Comprehensive Quality of Life Scale-Student* (Grades 7–12): ComQol-S5 (5th ed.). School of Psychology, Deakin University, Melbourne, Australia.

Dew, T. (1996). *The preliminary development and validation of a multidimensional life satisfaction scale for adolescents.* Unpublished doctoral dissertation, University of South Carolina, Columbia.

Dew, T., & Huebner, E. S. (1994). Adolescents' perceived quality of life: An exploratory investigation. *Journal of School Psychology, 33*(2), 185–199.

Diener, E. (1994). Assessing subjective well-being: Progress and opportunities. *Social Indicators Research, 31,* 103–157.

Diener, E., Emmons, R. A., Larsen, R. J., & Griffin, S. (1985). The Satisfaction With Life Scale. *Journal of Personality Assessment, 49,* 71–75.

Diener, E., Suh, E. M., Lucas, R. E., & Smith, H. L. (1999). Subjective well-being: Three decades of progress. *Psychological Bulletin, 125,* 276–302.

Fogle, L., Huebner, E. S., & Laughlin, J. E. (2002). The relationship between temperament and life satisfaction in early adolescence: Cognitive and behavioral mediation models. *Journal of Happiness Studies, 3,* 373–392.

Frisch, M. B. (1998). Quality of life therapy and assessment in health care. *Clinical Psychology: Science and Practice, 5,* 19–40.

Frisch, M. B. (1999). Quality of life assessment/intervention and the Quality of Life Inventory (QOLI). In M. R. Maruish (Ed.), *The use of psychological assessment for treatment planning and outcome assessment* (2nd ed., pp. 1227–1331). Mahwah, NJ: Lawrence Erlbaum Associates.

Frisch, M. B., Clark, M. P., Rouse, S. V., Rudd, M. P., Paweleck, J., Greenstone, A., et al. (2003). Predictive validity and sensitivity to change in quality of life assessment and life satisfaction: Further studies of the Quality of Life Inventory of QOLI in mental health settings. In M. J. Sirgy et al. (eds.), *Advances in quality of life theory and research* (pp. 191–210). The Netherlands: Kluwer Academic Press.

Gilman, R., Ashby, J., Sverko, D., Florell, D., & Varjas, K. (2005). A study of perfectionism among Croatian and American youth. *Personality and Individual Differences, 39,* 155–166.

Gilman, R., & Barry, J. (2003). Life Satisfaction and Social Desirability Among Adolescents in a Residential Treatment Setting: Changes Across Time. *Residential Treatment for Children and Youth, 21,* 19–42.

Gilman, R., Dooley, J., & Florell, D. (2006). Relative levels of hope and their relationship with academic and psychological indicators among adolescents. *Journal of Social and Clinical Psychology, 25,* 166–178.

Gilman, R., & Handwerk, M. L. (2001). Changes in life satisfaction as a function of stay in residential setting. *Residential Treatment for Children and Youth, 18,* 47–65.

Gilman, R., & Huebner, E. S. (1997). Children's reports of their life satisfaction: Convergence across raters, time, and response formats. *School Psychology International, 18,* 229–243.

Gilman, R., & Huebner, E. S. (2000). Review of life satisfaction measures for adolescents. *Behavior Change, 17,* 178–195.

Gilman, R., & Huebner, E. S. (2003). A review of life satisfaction research with children and adolescents. *School Psychology Quarterly, 18,* 192–205.

Gilman, R., Huebner, E. S., & Laughlin, J. E. (2000). A first study of the Multidimensional Students' Life Satisfaction Scale with adolescents. *Social Indicators Research, 52,* 135–160.

Gilman, R., Langknecht, H., Lili, T., Schiff, M., & Sverko, D. (2006). *Validation of the Multidimensional Students' Life Satisfaction Scale across multiple cultures.* Manuscript submitted for publication.

Greenspoon, P. J., & Saklofske, D. H. (1997). Validity and reliability of the Multidimensional Students' Life Satisfaction Scale with Canadian children. *Journal of Psychoeducational Assessment, 15,* 138–155.

Greenspoon, P. J., & Saklofske, D. (2001). Toward an integration of subjective well-being and psychopathology. *Social Indicators Research, 54,* 81–108.

Gullone, E., & Cummins, R. A. (1999). The Comprehensive Quality of Life Scale: A psychometric evaluation with an adolescent sample. *Behaviour Change, 16,* 127–139.

Hills, P., & Argyle, M. (2002). The Oxford Happiness Questionnaire: A compact scale for the measurement of psychological well-being. *Personality and Individual Differences, 33,* 1071–1082.

Huebner, E. S. (1991). Initial development of the Students' Life Satisfaction Scale. *School Psychology International, 12,* 231–240.

Huebner, E. S. (1994). Preliminary development and validation of a multidimensional life satisfaction scale for children. *Psychological Assessment, 6,* 149–158.

Huebner, E. S. (2004). Research and assessment of life satisfaction of children and adolescents. *Social Indicators Research, 66,* 3–33.

Huebner, E. S., & Alderman, G. L. (1993). Convergent and discriminant validation of a children's life satisfaction scale: Its relationship to self- and teacher-reported psychological problems and school functioning. *Social Indicators Research, 30,* 71–82.

Huebner, E. S., Brantley, A., Nagle, R., & Valois, R. (2002). Correspondence between parent and adolescent ratings of life satisfaction for adolescents with and without mild mental disabilities. *Journal of Psychoeducational Assessment, 20,* 20–29.

Huebner, E. S., & Dew, T. (1993). Is life satisfaction multidimensional? The factor structure of the Perceived Life Satisfaction Scale. *Journal of Psychoeducational Assessment, 11,* 345–350.

Huebner, E. S., Drane, W., & Valois, R. F. (2000). Levels and demographic correlates of adolescent life satisfaction reports. *School Psychology International, 21,* 187–198.

Huebner, E. S., Funk, B. A., & Gilman, R. (2000). Cross-sectional and longitudinal psychosocial correlates of adolescent life satisfaction reports. *Canadian Journal of School Psychology, 16,* 53–64.

Huebner, E. S., & Gilman, R. (2002). An introduction to the Multidimensional Students' Life Satisfaction Scale. *Social Indicators Research, 60,* 115–122.

Huebner, E. S., Gilman, R., & Laughlin, J. E. (1999). A multimethod investigation of the multidimensionality of children's well-being reports: Discriminant validity of life satisfaction and self-esteem. *Social Indicators Research, 46,* 1–22.

Huebner, E. S., Laughlin, J. E., Ash, C., & Gilman, R. (1998). Further validation of the Multidimensional Students' Life Satisfaction Scale, *Journal of Psychoeducational Assessment, 15,* 118–134.

Huebner, E. S., Suldo, S. M., & Gilman, R. (2006). Life satisfaction. In G. G. Bear & K. M. Minke (Eds.), *Children's Needs III: Development, prevention, and intervention* (pp. 357–368). Bethesda, MD: National Association of School Psychologists.

Ingersoll, G. M., Marrero D. G. (1991). A modified Quality of Life measure for youths: Psychometric properties. *Diabetes Educator, 17*, 114–118.

Jobe, J. B. (2003). Cognitive psychology and self-reports: Models and methods. *Quality of Life Research: An International Journal of Quality of Life Aspects of Treatment, Care, and Rehabilitation, 12*, 219–227.

Kamman, R., Farry, M., & Herbison, P. (1984). The analysis and measurement of happiness as a sense of well-being. *Social Indicators Research, 15*, 91–116.

Kazdin, A. (1993). Adolescent mental health: Prevention and treatment programs. *American Psychologist, 48*, 127–141.

Kozma, A., & Stones, M. J. (1988). Social desirability in measures of subjective well-being: Age comparisons. *Social Indicators Research, 20*, 1–14.

Larson, R. (1989). Beeping children and adolescents: A method for studying time use and daily experience. *Journal of Youth and Adolescence, 18*, 511–530.

Larson, R. W. (2000). Toward a psychology of positive youth development. *American Psychologist, 55*, 170–183.

Leung, J., & Leung, K. (1992). Life satisfaction, self-concept, and relationship with parents in adolescence. *Journal of Youth and Adolescence, 21*, 653–665.

Marriage, K., & Cummins, R. A. (2004). Subjective quality of life and self-esteem in children: The role of primary and secondary control in coping with everyday stress. *Social Indicators Research, 66*, 107–122.

Matza, L. S., Swensen, A. R., Flood, E. M., Secnik, K., & Leidy, N. K. (2004). Assessment of health-related quality of life in children: A review of conceptual, methodological, and regulatory Issues. *Values in Health, 7*, 72–92.

McColl, E., Meadows, K., & Barofske, I. (2003). Cognitive aspects of survey methodology and quality of life assessment. *Quality of Life Research: An International Journal of Quality of Life Aspects of Treatment, Care, and Rehabilitation, 12*, 217–218.

McKnight, C. G., Huebner, E. S., & Suldo, S. M. (2002). Relationships among stressful life events, temperament, problem behavior, and global life satisfaction in adolescents. *Psychology in the Schools, 39*(6), 677–687.

Neto, F. (1993). The Satisfaction with Life Scale: Psychometric properties in an adolescent sample. *Journal of Youth and Adolescence, 22*, 125–134.

Oishi, S., & Diener, E. (2001). Goals, culture, and subjective well-being. *Personality and Social Psychology Bulletin, 27*, 1674–1682.

Park, N., Huebner, E. S., Laughlin, J. E., Valois, R. F., & Gilman, R. (2004). A cross-cultural comparison of the dimensions of child and adolescent life satisfaction reports. *Social Indicators Research, 66*, 61–79.

Paulhus, D. L. (2002). Socially desirable responding: The evolution of a construct. In D. N. Jackson, H. I. Braun, and D. E. Wiley (Eds.), *The role of constructs in psychological and educational measurement* (pp. 49–69). Mahwah, NJ: Lawrence Erlbaum Associates.

Pavot, W., & Diener, E. (1993). Review of the Satisfaction With Life Scale. *Psychological Assessment, 5*, 164–172.

Peterson, C., & Seligman, M. E. P. (2004). *Character strengths and virtues: A handbook and classification*. Oxford: Oxford University Press.

Petito, F., & Cummins, R. A. (2000). Quality of life in adolescence: The role of perceived control, parenting style and social support. *Behaviour Change, 17*, 196–207.

Pons, D., Atienza, F. L., Balaguer, I., & Garcia-Merita, L. (2000). Satisfaction with Life Scale: Analysis of factorial invariance for adolescents and elderly persons. *Perceptual and Motor Skills, 91*, 62–68.

Quittner, A. L., Davis, M. A., & Modi, A. C. (2003). Health-Related Quality of Life in Pediatric Populations. In Roberts, M. C. (Ed.), *Handbook of pediatric psychology* (3rd ed., pp. 696–709). New York: Guilford Press.

Raphael, D., Brown, I., Renwick, R., & Rootman, I. (1997). Quality of life: What are the implications for health promotion? *American Journal of Health Behavior, 21*, 118–128.

Rathunde, K. (1997). Family context and the development of undivided interest: A longitudinal study of family support and challenge and adolescents' quality of experience. *Applied Developmental Science, 5*, 158–171.

Schalock, R. L., Keith, K. D., Hoffman, K., & Karan, O. C. (1989). Quality of life, its measurement, and use in human service programs. *Mental Retardation, 27*, 25–31.

Schiff, M., Nebbe, S., & Gilman, R. (in press). Life satisfaction among Israeli children in residential treatment care. *British Journal of Social Work.*

Schimmack, U., & Diener, E. (2003). Experience Sampling Methodology in happiness research. *Journal of Happiness Studies, 4*, 1–4.

Scollon, C. N., Kim-Prieto, C., & Diener, E. (2003). Experience Sampling: Promises and pitfalls, strengths and weaknesses. *Journal of Happiness Studies, 4*, 5–34.

Seligman, M. E. P., & Csikszentmihalyi, M. (2000). Positive psychology: An introduction. *American Psychologist, 55*, 5–14.

Shek, D. T. (1998). Adolescent positive mental health and psychological symptoms in a Chinese context. *Psychologia, 41*, 217–225.

Shernoff, D. J., Csikszentmihalyi, M., Shneider, B., & Shernoff, E. S. (2003). Student engagement in high school classrooms from the perspective of flow theory. *School Psychology Quarterly, 18*, 158–176.

Smith, D. C., Adelman, H. S., Nelson, P., Taylor, L., & Phares, V. (1987). Students' perceptions of control at school and problem behavior and attitudes. *Journal of School Psychology, 25*, 167–176.

Suldo, S. M., & Huebner, E. S. (2004). Does life satisfaction moderate the effects of stressful life events on psychopathological behavior during adolescence? *School Psychology Quarterly, 19*, 93–105.

Torrance, E. P. (1990). *Torrance Tests of Creative Thinking*. Bensenville, IL: Scholastic Testing Service.

Wallander, J. L., Schmitt, M., & Koot, H. M. (2001). Quality of life measurement in children and adolescents: Issues, instruments and applications. *Journal of Clinical Psychology, 57*, 571–585.

World Health Organization. (1948). Charter. Geneva: Author.

Wright, B. A., & Lopez, S. J. (2002). Widening the diagnostic focus: A case for including human strengths and environmental resources. In C. R. Snyder & S. J. Lopez (Eds.), *Handbook of positive psychology* (pp. 26–44). New York: Oxford University Press.

Zullig, K., Valois, R. F., Huebner, E. S., & Drane, W. J. (2005). Adoeslcent health-related quality of life and perceived life satisfaction. *Quality of Life Research, 14*, 1573–1584.

21

ASSESSMENT OF ATTENTION-DEFICIT/ HYPERACTIVITY DISORDER WITH CHILDREN

Linda A. Reddy
Courtney De Thomas
Fairleigh Dickinson University

Attention-deficit/hyperactivity disorder (ADHD) is one of the most common childhood disorders referred to mental health professionals. ADHD, a complex neurodevelopmental disorder, is seen in approximately 3–7% of school-aged children, with higher rates found among boys than girls (6:1 in clinical settings, 3:1 in community settings) in the United States (e.g., Barkley, 1998; Pastor & Reuben, 2002). In a review of estimates over a four-year period, Rowland, Leswesne, and Abramowitz (2002) found that prevalence rates varied substantially, based on presenting symptoms, assessment approaches used, and setting in which the child was evaluated. Furthermore, lack of consensus on what constitutes a core set of symptomology for ADHD children complicates the screening and assessment process (e.g., Brown et al., 2001; Elia, Ambrosini, & Rapoport, 1999). Researchers contend that a coherent set of symptoms and causal factors does not exist, and this disorder represents a heterogeneous group of separate disorders (Neul, Applegate, & Drabman, 2003). For example, Goodman and Poillion (1992) identified 69 separate characteristics of ADHD, with 38 associated causes.

Etiological considerations focus on neurobiological differences, heredity, and environmental influences as causal agents of ADHD (e.g., Barkley, 1998; Pearl, Weiss, & Stein, 2001). Brain differences between ADHD children and controls represent the most widely researched and theorized variable (DuPaul & Stoner, 2004). Tannock (1998) reported that the fronto-striatal networks and the prefrontal cortex showed anomalies (i.e., smaller quantities of dopamine and norepinephrine in the prefrontal cortex) among ADHD samples. The prefrontal cortex controls behavior inhibition and responses to environmental stimuli, two essential variables of ADHD symptomatology. Tannock asserted that the causes of these neurobiological abnormalities may center on genetic, hormonal, and/or environmental factors.

ADHD has the highest rate of hereditability among children with emotional and behavioral disorders (Pearl et al., 2001). Research has suggested that a genetic component exists in approximately 80% of ADHD cases. Moreover, research on "clusters" of ADHD in families provides further evidence for the hereditary influence (Johnston & Mash, 2001). However, it is unknown whether the high rates of ADHD among relatives are due to heritability factors or shared environments among individuals who are related. Research has found that environmental toxins such as poor nutrition, lead poisoning, smoking during pregnancy, and prenatal exposure to drugs or alcohol may be related to the development of ADHD symptoms and impairments (e.g., Mick, Biederman, Faraone, Sayer, & Kleinman, 2002; Mick, Biederman, Prince, Fischer, & Faraone, 2002). However, environmental toxins affect only symptom severity and do not cause the disorder (e.g., DuPaul & Stoner, 2004; Rowland et al., 2002).

The evaluation process is also guided by theoretical models of ADHD that focus on how deficits in behavior inhibition lead to impairments in brain functioning and subsequent emotional and behavioral difficulties (e.g., Barkley, 1997; Logan, 1994; Quay, 1988; Schachar, Tannock, & Logan, 1993). A child's failure to inhibit responses to stimuli triggers maladaptive reactions that can culminate in ADHD symptoms and impairments. The DSM IV-TR (2000; DSM-IV-TR) describes ADHD as a "persistent pattern of inattention and/or hyperactivity–impulsivity that is more frequently displayed and more severe than is typically observed in individuals at a comparable level of development" (p. 85). This description does not capture the complex brain functions and emotional and behavioral difficulties of those with ADHD. For example, Bronowski (1967, 1977) argued that inhibition and how language is internalized affect children's working memory and responses to stimuli in the environment. Language skills create an ability to think intuitively about the past and future and modulate responses to the environment based on that information.

Based on Bronowski's work (1967, 1977) and Fuster's theory of prefrontal function (1989, 1995), Barkley (1997) proposed a hybrid model of ADHD that details inhibition and its complex impact on executive functions (i.e., working memory, internalization of speech, self-regulation of affect-motivation-arousal, and reconstitution). He outlined three activities inherent in the behavioral inhibition process (i.e., the ability to inhibit initial response, the ability to stop an ongoing response, and skill in controlling interference) and proposed that the four executive functions depend largely on successful enactment of these activities. The inability to control responses, in turn, leads to manifestations of ADHD symptomatology. ADHD symptoms are described as the failure to inhibit task-irrelevant responses, execute goal-directed persistence, incorporate feedback from the environment, re-engage in tasks following disruption, and control behavior through internally represented information (Barkley, 1997). Thus, disinhibition can negatively affect children's attention, motor control, impulsivity, and emotional and behavioral development.

This chapter provides an overview of the assessment practices for children and adolescents with ADHD. The comorbidity and differential diagnosis of ADHD and ADHD-related disorders are presented. A description of some of the major cognitive/neuropsychological and social/emotional assessment approaches used with this population is offered. Finally, a case study is presented to illustrate the application of these measures with an ADHD child.

COMORBIDITY AND DIFFERENTIAL DIAGNOSIS

When evaluating a child with symptoms of ADHD, it is critically important for the practitioner to consider the overlapping symptomology with other childhood disorders (Neul et al., 2003). All too often, children are misdiagnosed with ADHD when they have other related psychiatric disorders (e.g., learning disabilities, anxiety, depression) and/or child/family-focused conditions (e.g., medical conditions, sensory integration disorder). The evaluation process is further complicated by the fact that children with ADHD exhibit high rates of comorbidity (e.g., 74–79% among 4 to 9-year-olds; Wilens et al., 2002).

Learning Disabilities.   Research has reported that the comorbidity of ADHD and specific learning disabilities (LD) ranges from 25% to 70% (Kellner, Houghton, & Douglas, 2003). When ADHD children exhibit reading difficulties, an assessment of phonological awareness, verbal working memory, verbal retrieval, and processing speed is needed to determine whether LD or ADHD, if not both, is the primary source(s) of the child's reading difficulties (Hale & Fiorello, 2004). For example, Ghelani, Sidhu, Jain, and Tannock (2004) compared the reading comprehension skills of reading-disabled (RD), ADHD, and ADHD/RD children. Results indicated that the three clinical groups scored significantly lower on silent reading, took longer to read aloud, and articulated fewer words correctly than controls. On each task, the ADHD children performed better than the RD and ADHD/RD children. However, Toplak, Rucklidge, Hetherington, John, and Tannock (2003) found that both ADHD and ADHD/RD children had difficulties discriminating between intervals of sound and replicating intervals of sound in comparison with controls. Thus, multiple reading assessments may be helpful in the evaluation of ADHD children at risk for RD.

Children with ADHD and LD have interpersonal difficulties. For example, Kellner et al. (2003) found that children with ADHD-Combined Type/LD reported more problems relating to others, anxiety when socializing, and less confidence in social situations than children with ADHD-Inattentive Type and controls. ADHD-Inattentive Type/LD children expressed more negative thoughts and fears of peer interactions than children with ADHD-Inattentive Type and controls. Furthermore, both parents and teachers reported that ADHD children tend to have difficulties participating in recreational activities and waiting their turn and are more socially withdrawn and disruptive than LD children (Stanford & Hynd, 1994).

ADHD children exhibit characteristics often seen in children with nonverbal learning disorders (NLD), such as difficulties following directions, organizing materials, focusing, and interrupting others during individual and group activities (e.g., Rouke, 1995; Thompson, 1997). However, NLD children tend to take a long time to complete tasks, have difficulties waiting their turn in class, become overwhelmed with social situations, become extremely focused ("stuck") on tasks, and struggle to acquire new skills (especially motor skills). In contrast, ADHD children rush through tasks, have difficulties waiting their turn in class, easily approach social situations, and rapidly switch tasks (e.g., Rouke, 1995; Thompson, 1997).

Depressive Disorders.   Depression and ADHD symptoms can present in analogous ways, such as inattention, difficulties in concentration, and irritability (Wasserstein, 2005), and, in some cases, children may meet the diagnostic criteria for both disorders. Reported comorbidity rates for children with ADHD and depressive disorders vary from 10.3% (Souza, Pinheiro, Denardin, Mattos, & Rohde, 2004) to approximately 33–50% (Pfiffner et al., 1999). Research has shown that ADHD children may be more susceptible to developing depressive symptoms than non-ADHD children (LeBlanc & Morin, 2004), and there is evidence that children with ADHD-Combined Type and ADHD-Inattentive Type reflect similar levels of depression and anxiety (Power, Costigan, Eiraldi, & Leff, 2004). Children diagnosed with ADHD and depressive disorders may also present with milder hyperactive/impulsive symptoms and fewer conduct problems (e.g., Perrin & Last, 1996; Pliszka, Carlson, & Swanson, 1999) but more social and emotional difficulties (Karustis, Power, Rescorla, Eiraldi, & Gallagher, 2000) than children diagnosed with ADHD only.

Children with ADHD or Bipolar Disorder (BD) often display inattention, memory issues, distractibility, restlessness, racing thoughts, rapid/pressured speech, impulsivity, and irritability (e.g., Dunn & Kronenberger, 2003; Sax et al., 1999; Shear et al., 1999). Research has shown that approximately 60–80% of children and adolescents with BD have ADHD (Shear, DelBello, Rosenberg, & Strakowski, 2002), whereas 22% of ADHD youth have BD (Butler, Arredondo, & McCloskey, 1995). Shear et al. (2002) reported that ADHD/BD children were significantly less depressed than children with symptoms of BD alone, but ADHD/BD youth demonstrated less self-control skills than the children with BD.

Anxiety-Related Disorders.   ADHD children and children with high levels of anxiety exhibit similar symptoms, such as problems concentrating and/or excessive motor activity (Wasserstein, 2005). Approximately one-third of youth with ADHD have been diagnosed with anxiety disorders (e.g., Perrin & Last, 1996; Safren, Lanka, Otto, & Pollack, 2001; Souza et al., 2004). Children with ADHD and anxiety disorders are more likely to have difficulties with memorization than children with ADHD alone (Perrin & Last, 1996). Furthermore, adolescents with ADHD-Combined Type and anxiety tend to exhibit more oppositional defiant disorder symptoms than adolescents with ADHD-Combined Type alone (Kashani & Orvaschel, 1990).

Comorbidity rates for specific anxiety disorders are disparate. For example, Safren et al. (2001) found that 32% of children with Generalized Anxiety Disorder also met criteria for ADHD, but only 3% of children with Social Phobia demonstrated ADHD symptoms. Furthermore, parent reports of Social Phobia and Separation Anxiety Disorder are found more among children with ADHD-Combined Type and Dysthymia than children with ADHD-Combined Type alone (Vance, Harris, Boots, Talbot, & Karamitsios, 2003). Vance et al. indicated that adolescents with ADHD-Combined Type and Dysthymia are at higher risk for suicide, behavior problems, and alcohol and drug abuse than adolescents who are diagnosed with one of these conditions.

ADHD children can exhibit obsessive-compulsive behaviors (OCB). Arnold, Ickowicz, Chen, and Schachar (2005) reported that 11% of an ADHD sample exhibited OCB (e.g., need for rigid routines, recurrent and persistent thoughts about topics of interest). Children with ADHD/OCB display more educational, emotional, and behavioral issues than children with ADHD alone. Although parents and teachers report similar levels of hyperactivity among children with ADHD/OCB and ADHD alone, parents report that ADHD/OCB children exhibit higher levels of perfectionism than the ADHD children alone.

Children with OCB who meet criteria for Obsessive Compulsive Disorder (OCD) are also found in this population. For example, Geller et al. (2002) reported an average of 30% of ADHD children meeting criteria for OCD. Geller et al. (2004) also evaluated the extent to which "the inattention, distractibility and restlessness in these children may represent internal distraction from obsessional ideation or anxiety and not true ADHD at all" (p. 83) and concluded that children with such symptoms have two distinct comorbid conditions.

Other Disruptive Behavior Disorders.   Comorbidity rates among ADHD children and oppositional defiant disorder (ODD) and/or conduct disorder (CD) children are approximately 40–90% (Pfiffner et al., 1999). ADHD children with aggressive behavior patterns tend to have more family and peer interpersonal conflicts than ADHD children without aggressive behavior patterns (e.g., Harada, Yamazaki, & Saitoh, 2002; Johnston & Mash, 2001). Children diagnosed with ADHD and ODD tend to have higher rates of teacher conflict, school refusal, depression, and anxiety than children with ADHD or ODD alone (Harada et al., 2002).

Language-Based Disorders.   Language processing significantly affects children's learning, social, and behavior opportunities (Irwin, Carter, & Briggs-Gowan, 2002). Language-based disorders are challenging to evaluate because of the overlapping impairments (e.g., auditory processing, attention, and executive functioning) often found among children with ADHD and other disorders (Barkley, 1990; Moss & Sheiffele, 1994). For example, Love and Thompson (1988) reported that 48.3% of children referred for mental health treatment met criteria for ADHD and speech/language disorders. Similarly, Riccio, Hynd, Cohen, Hall, and Molt (1994) found that 50% of children in their sample with central auditory processing disorder (CAPD) met criteria for ADHD. ADHD/CAPD and CAPD children performed comparably on cognitive and language processing measures. However, ADHD/CAPD children scored higher on measures of inattention, impulsivity, and hyperactivity, as well as measures of anxiety, social problems, aggression, and internalizing and externalizing behaviors, than children with CAPD alone. Thus, it is recommended that ADHD evaluations incorporate assessment of language functioning to determine whether auditory problems may be causing or intensifying behavioral issues (Sundheim & Voeller, 2004).

Child/Family-Focused Conditions and Factors.   A number of child and family-focused conditions and factors must be carefully considered when children at risk for ADHD are evaluated. For example, the overall health status of children must be examined (Pearl et al., 2001). Common medical conditions (e.g., constipation, ear infections, asthma, allergies, poor nutrition) can profoundly affect children's learning, emotional, and behavioral functioning. Furthermore, hearing and vision impairments, head injuries, lead toxicity, thyroid disorders, Pediatric Autoimmune Neuropsychiatric Disorders Associated with Streptococcal Infections (PANDAS), and/or seizure disorders can manifest in clinical levels of inattention, impulsivity, insomnia, hyperactivity, anxiety, and/or depression (e.g., Koger, Schettler, & Weiss, 2005; Wasserstein, 2005). In addition, ADHD children exhibit higher rates of allergies, asthma, stomachaches, ear infections (Schnoll, Burshteyn, & Cea-Aravena, 2003), sleep difficulties (Ball, Tiernan, Janusz, & Furr, 1997), and resistance to thyroid hormone (Pearl et al., 2001) than controls.

The symptoms of sensory integration disorder (SID) can resemble ADHD characteristics. Research has shown that ADHD children have more sensory processing deficits than controls (e.g., Mangeot et al., 2001; Yochman, Parush, & Ornoy, 2004). For example, children's heightened awareness of their tactile sense can be distracting and lead to disruptive behaviors such as fidgeting, restlessness, and/or out-of-seat behavior at school. Children with SID often exhibit a strong desire for physical contact with peers and/or a need to touch items, resembling the impulsivity often seen in ADHD children. Both ADHD and SID children have difficulties with auditory processing and may be seen to be highly distracted by background noise in class when their teachers are speaking (Kranowitz, 1998). As treatment options for ADHD and SID are different, an accurate diagnosis is essential for effective intervention.

Child and family-focused factors such as the child's gender, culture, and family psychiatric history are important variables for the evaluation process. Research on gender differences among ADHD children has emerged. For example, parent and teacher ratings of ADHD symptomology are higher in general among males than females (Newcorn et al., 2001). However, teachers report that females exhibit significantly more inattentive behaviors than hyperactive and impulsive behaviors, and males exhibit significantly more inattentive behaviors than hyperactive behaviors. Females are more likely to meet the criteria for ADHD-Inattentive Type, whereas males are more likely to meet criteria for ADHD-Hyperactive-Impulsive or Combined Type (e.g., Biederman & Faraone, 2004). Research has also found that

ADHD females have more intellectual deficits and lower ratings of hyperactivity than ADHD males (e.g., Abikoff et al., 2002; Gaub & Carlson, 1997). Furthermore, ADHD females report more somatic concerns than ADHD males (Graetz, Sawyer, & Baghurst, 2005).

The cultural background of the family can affect ratings of symptom severity among ADHD children. Prevalence rates of ADHD vary across cultures from less than 1% to 20% (Bird, 2002). Research has shown that parents provided lower ratings of impulsivity for Mexican American than Puerto Rican children (Schmitz & Velez, 2003), and teachers provided higher ratings of inattention, impulsivity, and hyperactivity for African American than Caucasian children (Reid et al., 1998). When viewing a videotaped ADHD child, teachers from China provided significantly higher ratings of hyperactivity, impulsivity, inattention, and social impairment than teachers from Hong Kong and the United Kingdom (Alban-Metcalfe, Cheng-Lai, & Ma, 2002). Similar findings have been found with Chinese, Indonesian, Japanese, and English teachers (Mann et al., 1992).

Family psychiatric history is related to ADHD symptoms in children. For example, parents and relatives of ADHD children have higher rates of learning disabilities, depression, antisocial tendencies, and alcohol abuse than controls (Edwards, Schulz, & Long, 1995; Johnston & Mash, 2001). Chi and Hinshaw (2002) found an association between the severity of ADHD symptoms and mothers' levels of anger, depression, and negative discipline style. Symptom severity is also related to parental stress and perceived control over their children's behavior (Harrison & Sofronoff, 2002) as well as maternal responsiveness (i.e., affection toward and approval of the child, authoritative control; Johnston, Murray, Hinshaw, Pelham, & Hoza, 2002). In addition, marital disruption and abuse substantially increase ADHD symptoms in adolescents in comparison with nonabused adolescents (Cohen, Adler, Kaplan, Pelcovitz, & Mandel, 2002).

ADOPTING AN IDIOGRAPHIC ASSESSMENT APPROACH

Because of the pervasive, multicontext nature of problems related to ADHD and its high comorbidity with other childhood disorders, a thorough neurocognitive, developmental, social/emotional, and behavioral evaluation is warranted. Before a full evaluation, a *pretesting assessment* (i.e., intake) is strongly recommended to assess whether a set of tests and/or a full evaluation is appropriate for each individual child. Educating parents and children on the assessment process and goals is advised to increase comfort and motivation during testing. Pretesting can take a variety of forms, such as a parent interview that includes developmental, social, and educational history; review of school records (i.e., report cards, behavior data, current academic assignments); classroom-based observations; teacher consultation; and the completion of parent and teacher behavior rating scales. Observation of parents' and children's responses (i.e., verbal and nonverbal) during pretesting provides valuable data on the parents' and children's social, emotional, and behavioral functioning and comfort with testing. Collaboration with other professionals (e.g., physicians, social workers, and school personnel), family members, and coaches is encouraged.

It is difficult to recommend a core battery of standardized assessments for evaluating children for ADHD. Like all evaluations, a comprehensive ADHD evaluation rests on the type of referral provided, referring agent or agency, and the constellation of unique child, family, and school system factors. Practitioners are encouraged to adopt an idiographic assessment approach that includes multiple methods, informants, and contexts to assess a child's unique learning, social/emotional, cultural/linguistic, and adaptive/maladaptive functioning. Evaluators are also encouraged to select methods that assess the (1) clinical nuances in comorbid externalizing and internalizing disorders; (2) previous assessment and/or treatment experience; (3) teacher observations/feedback; (4) child's view of him/herself, family, school, and community; (5) parent observations/feedback; (6) parent-child interactions (e.g., Parent-Child Interaction Play Assessment, Smith 2000); (7) teacher-child interactions, (8) social/emotional adjustment (e.g., Behavior Assessment System for Children–2, Reynolds & Kamphaus, 2004); (9) speech/language skills (e.g., Clinical Evaluation of Language Fundamentals–4, Semel, Wiig, & Secord, 2003); (10) cognitive abilities (e.g., Woodcock Johnson Tests of Cognitive Abilities; Woodcock, McGrew, & Mather, 2001); and (11) achievement/basic skills (e.g., Woodcock Johnson Tests of Achievement; McGrew & Woodcock, 2001).

It is important that practitioners recognize the relationship between cognition, achievement, and social/emotional functioning. The assessment of ADHD children's emotional and behavioral functioning requires an understanding of the interplay of biological, cognitive, and environmental factors on brain development. Thus, when children interact with their environment, the behaviors they exhibit in a specific situation are related to their previous and current experiences, environmental conditions, and their cognitive and affective templates in which they experience their world. For a detailed discussion on the integration of neurocognitive and emotional and behavioral assessment, see Smith in this volume.

Some of the well-known cognitive/neuropsychological and social/emotional assessment approaches are briefly reviewed next to illustrate the range of measures that can be used with this population. The following section was *not* intended to be an exhaustive list.

COGNITIVE/NEUROPSYCHOLOGICAL ASSESSMENT

There are a number of well-designed, theoretically rich cognitive/neuropsychological assessment instruments that aid practitioners in forming hypotheses about ADHD children's cognitive strengths and needs. Probably the most popularly used intelligence instrument is the *Wechsler Intelligence Scale for Children, 4th Edition* (WISC-IV; Wechsler, 2003). The WISC-IV has moved beyond the Verbal-Performance dichotomy and now more closely follows a neuropsychological model of cognitive functioning that includes a psychometrically strong, four-factor model (i.e., Verbal Comprehension, Perceptual Reasoning [formerly Perceptual Organization], Working Memory [formally Freedom from Distractibility and Processing Speed Indices]). The WISC-IV possesses considerable evidence of reliability and validity, including concurrent validity with the WISC-III (Wechsler, 2003). Large practical (i.e., effect sizes) group differences were reported between ADHD/LD children and controls on Full Scale IQ, Processing Speed, and Working Memory Indices, whereas moderate effect sizes were reported between ADHD children and controls on the Processing Speed Index (Wechsler, 2003). Given its recent release, independent research on the clinical utility of the WISC-IV for ADHD children is limited but anticipated.

Based on the Cattell-Horn-Carroll theory of cognitive abilities, the *Woodcock Johnson Tests of Cognitive Abilities* (WJ III COG) is a comprehensive cognitive assessment battery that consists of 20 tests, classified into three categories: verbal ability, thinking ability, and cognitive efficiency (Woodcock et al., 2001). The WJ III COG also includes five clinical clusters that measure aspects of executive functioning (i.e., Phonemic Awareness, Working Memory, Broad Attention, Cognitive Fluency, and Executive Processes). Details of the reliability and validity indices of the WJ III COG can be found in the technical manual (Woodcock et al., 2001). Studies on the clinical utility of the WJ III COG for ADHD children have been mixed.

For example, Ford, Keith, Floyd, Fields, and Schrank (2003) reported that the seven WJ III COG tests significantly predicted ADHD status and that the two most significant test predictors were Auditory Working Memory and Planning. With a comorbid ADHD sample, the WJ III COG Five Clinical Clusters accurately classified 71.2% of the sample, the seven WJ III COG Tests accurately classified 82.7% of the sample, and the two most significant predictors were Auditory Attention and Rapid Picture Naming (Reddy, Dumont, & Bray, 2005).

An increasingly popular, soon to be revised cognitive assessment measure is the *Differential Ability Scales* (DAS, Elliott, 1990a). The DAS is composed of 17 cognitive subtests designed to produce a composite General Conceptual Ability (GCA) score based on the Horn Cattell Gf-Gc Theory. The subtests produce Verbal, Nonverbal, and Spatial Clusters that correspond to the verbal, fluid, and visualization factors in the Gf-Gc model. The DAS includes three Diagnostic subtests (i.e., Recall of Digits, Recall of Objects, and Speed of Information Processing). The DAS school-aged version is reported to have good reliability and validity (see Elliott, 1990a, 1990b). The DAS Sequential and Quantitative Reasoning subtest and the Recall of Digits subtest correctly discriminate ADHD only and controls 72.5% of the time (Gibney, McIntosh, Dean, & Dunham, 2002). With a comorbid ADHD sample, Reddy, Braunstein, and Dumont (2005) found that the four Diagnostic Subtests accurately classified 67% of the sample, and the Recall of Digits was the most significant predictor for ADHD status.

A number of neuropsychological tests are available to assess the cognitive processes link to children with ADHD and learning issues. Based on Luria's model of neuropsychological processing, the *Cognitive Assessment System* (CAS; Naglieri & Das, 1997) includes a full-scale score, four clusters referred to as the PASS model (i.e., planning, attention, simultaneous processing, and successive processing), and 12 subtests. Reliability and validity indices are good, and most subscales show good technical characteristics (Naglieri & Das, 1997). Naglieri, Goldstein, and Iseman (2003) reported that the ADHD sample exhibited lower CAS Planning scores than anxiety/depressed and control samples, whereas no group differences were found on the WISC-III. In a sample of 119 children (i.e., 48 ADHD, 23 reading disabled, 48 regular education), the ADHD group had lower Planning and Simultaneous scores than the regular education group, and the reading-disabled group had lower Successive scores than the regular education group (Naglieri, Salter, & Edwards, 2004). Cross-battery analyses have suggested that the Planning and Attention factors should be combined and not interpreted separately (Keith, Kranzler, & Flanagan, 2001). Despite some interpretation difficulties, the CAS offers the first substantial treatment validity studies of any cognitive measure (e.g., PREP; see Das, Carlson, Davidson, & Longe, 1997), and several of the CAS scales can be used for hypothesis testing with this population.

The *NEPSY: A Developmental Neuropsychological Assessment* is a comprehensive instrument designed to assess neuropsychological development in children between the ages of 3 and 12 (Korman, Kirk, & Kemp, 1998). It consists of 14 subtests that assess five core domains: Attention/Executive Functions, Language, Sensorimotor Functions, Visuospatial Processing, and Memory and Learning. The NEPSY includes a Core Assessment, which provides an overview of a child's neuropsychological status; an Expanded or Selective Assessment, which provides an analysis of specific cognitive disorders; and a full assessment for a comprehensive neuropsychological evaluation. The authors reported good reliability and concurrent and criterion-related validity (Korman et al., 1998). In comparison with a matched control sample, ADHD children yielded lower Attention/Executive Function Core Domain scores and performed more poorly on the Tower, Auditory Attention and Response Set, Statue, and Knock and Tap subtests, suggesting vigilance, motor persistence, and inhibition difficulties. The ADHD sample also demonstrated impaired performance on all language subtests except Speeded Naming, highlighting the role of attention underlying language tasks. They also performed lower on the Sensorimotor Functions Core Domain, particularly when required to replicate complicated integrated movements, fine-motor control, and tactile localization. The ADHD group exhibited decreased List Learning, Sentence Repetition, and Narrative Memory within the Memory and Learning Domain. Perner, Kain, and Barchfeld (2002) found lower Tower and Statue scores in a sample of children at risk for ADHD (age 4.5 to 6.5 years) than controls. Although limited independent research is available for ADHD children, the NEPSY offers a unique and flexible assessment tool that taps basic and complex cognitive processes for this population.

The *Delis–Kaplan Executive Function System* (D-KEFS; Delis, Kaplan, & Kramer, 2001) consists of nine tests that assess executive functions such as flexibility of thinking, inhibition, attention, language, perception, and abstract thought. The nine tests (i.e., Trail Making, Verbal Fluency, Design Fluency, Color-Word Interference, Sorting, Twenty Questions, Word Context, Tower, and Proverb) can be administered individually or to groups of children and adults aged 8 to 89 years. The D-KEFS allows practitioners to "pick and choose" tests to evaluate clinical hypotheses on executive functioning by comparing and contrasting a child's performance on multiple tests and testing conditions. The D-KEFS manual offers extensive information on the test's technical characteristics and interpretation strategies (Delis et al., 2001). However, validation studies on children with ADHD are missing. Despite this limitation, the D-KEFS offers practitioners the first set of executive tests co-normed on a large national sample and an efficient and flexible approach for assessing children's executive functions.

Although not a neuropsychological test, the Behavior Rating Inventory of Executive Function (BRIEF; Gioia, Isquith, Guy, & Kenworthy, 2000) serves as the first scale for parents and teachers that assesses children's executive function behaviors. The BRIEF consists of eight clinical scales (i.e., Inhibit, Shift, Emotional Control, Initiate, Working Memory, Plan/Organize, Organization of Materials, and Monitor) and two validity scales (i.e., Inconsistency, Negativity). The clinical scales comprise a Global Executive Composite and two indexes, Behavioral Regulation and Metacognition. The BRIEF's strong psychometric properties are detailed in the manual (Gioia et al., 2000). The authors found that the Working Memory and Inhibit scales accurately distinguish ADHD subtypes from controls. In one study, parents rated ADHD children with significantly more problems on all of the BRIEF scales than controls. The Behavioral Regulation Index differentiated ADHD-Inattentive Type from ADHD-Combined Type children (Pratt, Campbell-La Voie, Isquith, Gioia, & Guy, 2000). Similarly, teachers rated ADHD children with significantly more problems on the BRIEF scales than controls. Also, the Inhibit, Shift, Emotional Control, and Monitor scales differentiated ADHD-Inattentive from Combined Type children, with the Combined Type children scoring higher on all scales.

Continuous performance tests (e.g., Test of Variables of Attention, TOVA [Greenberg, 1988–1999]; Conners' Continuous Performance Test-II, CPT-II [Conners & MHS Staff, 2000]) designed to measure attention and the ability to inhibit impulsive responses have gained popularity among practitioners. Considerable research has been conducted on continuous performance tests (CPT) with ADHD and ADHD-related disordered children (Riccio & Reynolds, 2003). Although these measures have high positive predictive power (i.e., a child's poor performance strongly confirm the presence of ADHD-related symptoms), these measures tend to possess poor negative predictive power (i.e., a child's passing performance yields inconclusive results). CPT results are further complicated by the high rate of comorbidity found in this population. Like all measures, CPT results must be used in conjunction with a multifaceted assessment approach.

In the next section, some of the common social, emotional, and behavioral assessments used with ADHD children are outlined. Following this section, a case study is presented to illustrate the application of these measures with this population.

SOCIAL-EMOTIONAL ASSESSMENT

Behavior Rating Scales.   Behavior Rating Scales (BRS) that assess ADHD children's social, emotional, and behavior functioning across informants (i.e., parent, teacher) and settings (i.e., home, school) are helpful for differential diagnosis (Pelham, Fabiano, & Massetti, 2005). The following BRS are described because they have strong psychometric properties, are well researched, and are considered "gold standards" of assessment for children and adolescents. There are other excellent measures (e.g., Brown Attention-Deficit Disorder Scales for Children; Brown, 2001), but these are not presented here because of space limitations.

The *Achenbach System of Empirically Based Assessment* (ASEBA; Achenbach & Recorla, 2001) evaluates the adaptive and maladaptive functioning of children aged 1.5 to 18 years. The ASEBA includes parent (Child Behavior Checklist), teacher (Teacher Report Form), and child (Youth Report Form) forms. The CBCL and TRF include preschool (1.5 to 5 years) and school-aged forms (6 to 18 years) that assess teachers' and parents' perceptions of children's externalizing and internalizing behaviors. The CBCL includes a total scale, two composite scales (i.e., Externalizing and Internalizing), eight clinical scales (i.e., Anxious/Depressed, Withdrawn/Depressed, Somatic Complaints, Social Problems, Thought Problems, Attention Problems, Rule Breaking Behavior, and Aggressive Behavior), and three competence scales (i.e., Activities, Social, and School). Like the CBCL, the TRF includes the same composite and clinical scales, as well as four competency scales (i.e., Working Hard, Behaving, Learning, and Happy). The CBCL and TRF are well researched and have extensive reliability and validity information across a broad range of child clinical populations, including ADHD children (e.g., Achenbach & Rescorla, 2001; Doyle, Ostrander, Skare, Crosby, & August, 1997; Eiraldi, Power, Karustis, & Goldstein, 2000).

One of the most widely used and soon to be revised BRS for ADHD children is the *Conners' Parent and Teacher Rating Scales–Revised* (CPRS-R, CTRS-R; Conners, 1997a). The CPRS-R and CTRS-R assess childhood psychopathology for children aged 3 to 17 years. The CPRS-R has seven primary factors (i.e., Oppositional, Inattention, Hyperactivity, Anxious-Shy, Perfectionism, Social Problems, and Psychosomatic). The CTRS-R has six primary factors (i.e., Oppositionality, Inattention, Hyperactivity-Impulsivity, Anxious-Shy, Perfectionism, and Social Problems). The CPRS-R and CTRS-R have excellent reliability and concurrent and criterion-related validity with ADHD children (Conners, 1997a). For example, the CPRS-R scales correctly distinguished ADHD from nonreferred children 92.3% of the time (Conners, Sitarenios, Parker, & Epstein, 1998a), and the CTRS-R scales correctly distinguished ADHD from nonreferred children 78.1% of the time (Conners, Sitarenios, Parker, & Epstein, 1998b).

The *Behavior Assessment System for Children–2* (BASC–2; Reynolds & Kamphaus, 2004) evaluates the adaptive and maladaptive behaviors of children and adults aged 2 to 25 years. The BASC–2 includes: a Teacher Rating Scale (TRS), Parent Rating Scale (PRS), and Self-Report of Personality (SRP; discussed in the personality inventory section). The PRS and TRS have Preschool (2 to 5 years), Child (6 to 12 years), and Adolescent (12 to

21 years) forms that assess parents' and teachers' perceptions of children's adaptive and problem behaviors. The TRS includes all of the composites and primary scales in the PRS, as well as a composite on school problems and two scales on learning problems and study skills. (For details on the BASC–2 scales, see Kamphaus et al. in this volume.) The authors reported good reliability and concurrent (i.e., ASEBA, BRIEF, CPRS-R, CTRS-R) and criterion-related validity with nonclinical and clinical groups (e.g., ADHD, LD, Depressive Disorders; Reynolds & Kamphaus, 2004). Research has found that the BASC (Reynolds & Kamphaus, 1992) accurately differentiates ADHD from non-ADHD children (e.g., Manning, 2001; Pizzitola, Riccio, & Siekierski, 2005).

The *Social Skills Rating System* (SSRS; Gresham & Elliot, 1990) provides an important strength-based assessment tool for ADHD children. The SSRS assesses children's social behaviors and includes Parent (PF), Teacher (TF), and Student Forms (SF). The SSRS-PF and SSRS-TF have Preschool, Elementary, and Secondary forms, and the SSRS-SF has forms for grades 3 through 6 and grades 7 through 12. The SSRS-PF and SSRS-TF assess parents' and teachers' perceptions of children's social skills and behavioral difficulties. Both the PF and TF include Social Skills and Problem Behaviors Scales, and the TF also includes an Academic Competence Scale (i.e., Elementary and Secondary Forms only). The Social Skills Scale includes five subscales (i.e., Cooperation, Assertion, Responsibility, Empathy, and Self-Control), and the Problem Behaviors Scale includes three subscales (i.e., Externalizing Problems, Internalizing Problems, and Hyperactivity). The Academic Competence Scale includes nine items that assess concerns regarding student academic functioning. The test authors reported good reliability, concurrent validity (e.g., TRF), and criterion-related validity with clinical and nonreferred children (Gresham & Elliot, 1990). Bain and Pelletier (1999) reported that the SSRS differentiates African American preschoolers who are at low and high risk for ADHD.

Personality Inventories.   Personality inventories offer valuable information on the social/emotional functioning of children with ADHD. There are many excellent child and adolescent personality inventories, such as the Minnesota Multiphasic Personality Inventory–Adolescents (MMPI-A Butcher, 1992), the Millon Adolescent Personality Inventory (Millon, Green, & Meagher, 1982), the Personality Inventory for Children–II (Lachar & Gruber, 2001), the Personality Inventory for Youth (PIY; Lachar & Gruber, 1995), and the Student Behavior Survey (SBS; Lachar, Wingenfeld, Kline, & Gruber, 2000). In this volume, several chapters exclusively describe each of these inventories (see Archer, Krishnamurthy, & Stredny, Trigone, Millon, & Kamp, and Lachar).

A noteworthy, new child self-report measure of personality is the Self Report of Personality (SRP) of the BASC–2 (Reynolds & Kamphaus, 2004). The SRP has Child (8 to 11 years), Adolescent (12 to 21 years), and College (18 to 25 years) levels that assess perceptions of personality (detailed information is provided by Kamphaus). The SRP is reported to have good reliability, concurrent validity (ASEBA-YRF; Achenbach & Rescorla, 2001; Conners-Wells Adolescent Self-Report Scale, Conners, 1997b; Children's Depression Inventory, Kovacs, 2003; Revised Children's Manifest Anxiety Scale, Reynolds & Richmond, 2000), and criterion-related validity with clinical groups such as ADHD, depressive disorders, LD, and mentally retarded children (Reynolds & Kamphaus, 2004). The application of personality inventories with this population is presented in the case study.

Projective Assessment.   Projective techniques, a child-focused assessment of his/her "inner life" and the quality of his or her relationships, offer an adjunct to direct and objective methods for social/emotional assessment of ADHD children. Projective techniques provide practitioners with a flexible, nonthreatening venue to evaluate ADHD children's perceptions of their world, themselves, and adults and peers around them. Like all children, ADHD youngsters have difficulties expressing their feelings and thoughts about emotionally laden materials or events. Projective techniques offer indirect ways to obtain data on interpersonal conflicts and motivations without directly assessing memory, verbal comprehension, psychomotor coordination and speed, verbal rehearsal, and/or concept formation difficulties often seen in this population.

Projective techniques for children have received much scrutiny and criticism because of their lack of normative data, reliability and validity characteristics, and empirical support for interpretation guidelines (Barnett, Macmann, & Lentz, 2003). Despite the controversy surrounding their use, projective techniques remain very popular among practitioners (Chandler, 2003). One of the most widely used projective techniques for children is the Draw-A-Person test (e.g., Naglieri, McNeish, & Bardos, 1991; Wilson & Reschly, 1996). The Kinetic Family Drawing (Burns & Kaufman, 1972) and the Kinetic School Drawing (Prout & Phillips, 1974) tests are also used. Popular thematic approaches for children include the Thematic Apperception Test (TAT; Murray, 1943), Child Apperception Test (CAT; Bellak & Abrams, 1997), Tell-Me-A-Story Test (TEMAS; Costantino, Malgady, & Rogler, 1988), and The Roberts-2 (Roberts, 2005). A variety of sentence completion tasks have been developed as well (see Hart, Kehle, & Davies, 1983; Rotter, Lah, & Rafferty, 1992). For an in-depth review of each of these techniques, the reader is referred to the citations listed above. Also in this volume, Erdberg presents the use of the Rorschach with children and Tuber et al. present the application of Rorschach Indices with ADHD children. The application of projective techniques with ADHD children is presented in the case study.

CASE STUDY

Jason is a 7½-year-old Caucasian male, referred by his parents for an evaluation following several recent incidents at school. Since the start of the school year, Jason has become increasingly impulsive and aggressive toward adults and peers and emotional (e.g., tearful, nervous). For example, Jason walked off school grounds during recess, stomped on his teacher's foot (a foot she had had surgery on recently), and threatened a substitute teacher and a classmate with scissors. Difficulties with transitions, following directions, and changes in home and school routines were noted. Because of his behavior pattern, Jason was restricted from lunch and recess with peers and then eventually placed on home instruction for a brief period of time.

Pretesting consisted of a parent interview that included educational, developmental, and medical history, including extended family histories, as well as consultation with school personnel. Jason resides with his parents and 5-year-old sister. He performed well academically in preschool and elementary school. He enjoys learning and school and desires relationships with peers and adults. However, Jason has had a history of difficulties with family, peer, sibling, and teacher relationships. Jason's parents have been married for 13 years and reported having a strong marriage. Jason's mother described him as having an "intensive personality" and as "very active and alert" since birth. His mother had an uneventful full-term pregnancy (i.e., two weeks late); however, labor was induced, and some fetal distress was reported. His apgar test was in the normal range, but the Rh factor was incompatible.

Developmental milestones (including language), vision, and hearing were normal. He has no major medical conditions or accidents, but has seasonal allergies and numerous ear infections (not requiring surgery).

Behavioral issues were first noted when Jason started daycare at 2½ years, with some separation anxiety noted. Jason was described by his teachers as "very active, stubborn at times, bright, and often getting stuck on activities." At the end of pre-kindergarten, Jason's tantrums (e.g., crying), difficulties with peers, and impulsive behavior increased at home and school. During kindergarten and first grade, Jason's behavioral issues continued. For example, he would become aggressive with peers when he perceived them as rejecting him or treating him unfairly, and afterward, he would become tearful and accepted responsibility for his actions. When distressed, Jason's impulsive behavior intensified, his speech increased and became pressured, he preferred to do things with his hands, and interrupted others. Because of his behavior, his teacher and parents encouraged him to "count to 10" and occasionally implemented negative consequences (i.e., time outs, withdrawal of privileges). Jason acts younger than his age, has few friends (i.e., plays one hour per week with peers), and plays primarily with his sister.

Based on pretesting, an evaluation that included neuropsychological, achievement, and social emotional functioning was conducted. Jason initially appeared nervous and shy, as evidenced by his refusal to look at or speak to the evaluator. However, he soon began whispering and "writing" with his fingers the answers to the evaluator's questions. Once the conversation turned to soccer, Jason became relaxed and animated. From this point onward, Jason followed directions and conversed with and maintained eye contact with the evaluator. He frequently fidgeted and was restless during testing; however, his level of activity did not appear to affect his performance. Jason's mood fluctuated from anxious to happy, depending on the difficulty he was having with a given task. For example, when Jason appeared to understand and perform well on a task, his mood was bright, and when Jason struggled with a task, he became anxious and unhappy. He often asked the evaluator if he performed tasks correctly.

Jason performed High Average on the CAS Full Scale IQ score (i.e., 112, 85th percentile). Jason exhibited cognitive deficits in generating and using effective strategies for problem solving (Planning = 82, 11th percentile), focusing on essential details, sustaining attention over time, and resisting distraction (Attention = 75, 5th percentile). Jason exhibited cognitive strengths in his ability to integrate parts into a whole, see several things at one time, work with spatial information (Simultaneous = 132, 98th percentile), and articulate and work with sounds in a specific order (Successive = 128, 97th percentile). Jason's performance on the Woodcock-Johnson III Tests of Achievement (McGrew & Woodcock, 2001) was superior, with clusters and tests ranging in the 70th to 98th percentile. Jason's performance on the Developmental Test of Visual-Motor Integration–Fifth Edition (VMI–5; Beery, Buktenica, & Beery, 2004) was above average.

Jason's parents and teacher were asked to complete several BRS to assess his emotional and behavioral functioning. Overall, Jason's parents and teacher rated him as having significant externalizing and internalizing difficulties on the ASEBA CBCL and TRF, and Conners' rating scales (i.e., CPRS-R, CTRS-R). For example, clinically elevated scale scores (i.e., *T*-scores of 65 and above) were found on the CBCL and TRF Externalizing and Internalizing composites, as well as the Anxious/Depressed, Social Problems, Thought Problems, Attention Problems, and Aggressive Behavior scales. Likewise, clinically elevated scale scores were found on many of the CPRS-R and CTRS-R (i.e., Global Index, ADHD Index, DSM-IV: Total and Hyperactive-Impulsive, Emotional Lability, Restless-Impulsive, Oppositional, Hyperactivity, Anxious-Shy, Perfectionism, and Social Problems). Both his parents and teacher rated Jason as having poor social skills (SSRS-PF and TF Social Skills scale scores of 82, 12th percentile and 70, 2nd percentile) and high problem behaviors (SSRS-PF and TF Problem Behavior scale scores of 122, 93rd percentile, and 130, 98th percentile). In addition, Jason's parents and teacher rated him as having significant executive function behaviors (i.e., a T-score of 65 and above) on several BRIEF scales. For example, Jason has difficulties stopping his own behavior (Inhibit scale), modulating emotional responses (Emotional Control scale), moving from one situation to the next (Shift scale), holding information in his mind for the purpose of completing a task (Working Memory scale), and planning out a long-term project or carrying out tasks in a systematic manner (Plan/Organize scale).

Jason's parents were asked to complete the PIC–2 (standard form) to assess Jason's personality. Jason's parent produced a valid profile. His mother rated his academic and cognitive status (i.e., Cognitive Impairment, Inadequate Abilities, Poor Achievement, and Developmental Delay, Developmental Deviation Scales) in the normative range. Clinically elevated scales were found on the Impulsivity and Distractibility (ADH ≥ 70T), Disruptive Behavior (ADH1 ≥ 70T), Fearlessness (ACH2 ≥ 60T), and Noncompliance (DLQ3 ≥ 60T) scales, suggesting undercontrolled behavior that may appear as inattention, impulsivity, irritability, tantrums, and anger. At times, Jason opposes adults and peers, shows off, disrupts class, and has difficulties socializing with peers. Ratings do not suggest a pattern of delinquent, assaultive, and bullying behavior, and/or a general dislike for school and learning.

Examples of critical items include "My child often acts without thinking," "My child cannot keep attention on anything," and "My child cannot sit still in school because of nervousness."

Parental frustration in managing Jason's behaviors was evidenced on the Coping Among Members (FAM1 ≥ 60T) scale. "One of the child's parents often gets very angry with the child," "One of the parents does not understand the child," and "There is a lot of tension in the home" are examples of critical items endorsed.

Jason exhibits overcontrolled behavior, as evidenced by clinically elevated scores on the Muscular Tension and Anxiety (SOM2 ≥ 70T), Psychological Discomfort (DIS ≥ 70T), Fear and Worry (DIS1 ≥ 60T), and Depression (DIS2 ≥ 60T) scales. Jason's overcontrolled behavior may manifest in anxiety, emotional lability, tension, nervousness, feeling misunderstood, being overly self-critical, and unhappiness. "Little things upset my child" and "My child tends to feel sorry for himself" are examples of critical items endorsed.

Inadequate social skills and conflicts with peers were indicated by clinically elevated scores on the Social Skills Deficits (SSK ≥ 70T), Limited Peer Status (SSK1 ≥ 70T), and Conflict with Peers (SSK2 ≥ 70T) scales, suggesting poor peer relations, few friends, and social isolation. Examples of endorsed critical items include "My child is usually rejected by peers," "Most of my child's friends are younger than he is," and "Other children often get mad at my child."

Jason was asked to complete two self-report measures, the Children's Depression Inventory (CDI; Kovacs, 2003) and the Revised Children's Manifest Anxiety Scale (RCMAS; Reynolds & Richmond, 2000), to further assess levels of depression and anxiety. The evaluator remained in the room with Jason to answer his questions while he was completing the measures. Jason did not asked questions when completing the CDI. His CDI Total T-score of 54 (71st percentile) was in the average range. His Negative Mood score of 59 (84th percentile) was in the slightly above average range, and his Interpersonal Problems score of 64 (90th percentile) was above average. For the Negative Mood scale, Jason indicated, "I am sad many times," "Things bother me many times," and "It is hard to make up my mind about things." For the Interpersonal Problems scale, Jason indicated, "I am bad many times," "I like being with people," "I do not do what I am told most times," and "I get into fights many times." Jason scored in the average range on the Ineffectiveness (54, 69th percentile), Anhedonia (48, 50th percentile), and Negative Self-esteem (46, 39th percentile) scales.

When completing the RCMAS, Jason asked the evaluator questions related to the instructions and items (e.g., What do "fussed at," "getting my breath" mean?). Jason also suggested that "sometimes" should be an answer (yes and no response format is provided only). Jason produced a valid profile. His Total Scale T-score of 59 (82nd percentile) and Physiological Anxiety subscale score of 8 (26th percentile) fell in the normative range. Jason reported clinically elevated scores on the Worry/Oversensitivity (13, 90th percentile) and the Social Concern/Concentration (14, 94th percentile) subscales. Results suggested that Jason is anxious and highly sensitive to environmental pressures at home and/or school (Worry/Oversensitivity Scale). Examples of endorsed items include "I get nervous when things do not go the right way for me" and "I worry about what my parents will say to me." Jason's responses indicated he feels anxious about living up to the expectations of peers and adults and has some difficulties concentrating on tasks (Social Concern/Concentration Scale). "I feel that others do not like the way I do things" and "I feel someone will tell me I do things the wrong way" are examples of endorsed items.

Three projective techniques, the TAT (Murray, 1943), Sentence Completion Test (Hart, Kehle, & Davies, 1983), and the Draw-A-Person test (Koppitz, 1968) were administered to further assess Jason's personality, needs, and motivations. When Jason was presented a TAT card and told his responses would be written down, he became anxious and initially refused to devise a story. Once the evaluator offered him the option of tape-recording his own responses, he happily agreed. Jason was administered cards 1, 3BM, 7GF, 8BM, 12M, 13B, 14, and 17BM, as recommended for children 7 to 11 years of age (Obrzut & Boliek, 1986). Jason's stories reflected impulsivity, anxiety, peer rejection, and a strong desire for peer and adult affiliation. Examples of themes can be seen on Cards 1, 3 BM, 7 GF, and 13 B. For Card 1, Jason's story was, "A boy wanted to play the violin with his friends. He practiced a lot to get it right. They did not want him to play and left. He started to play it and threw it down. His parents yelled at him for breaking his violin." (*What happened next in the story?*) "He had to clean up the mess. The end." For card 3 BM, Jason's story was, "There was a boy who was jumping on his bed with his friends, bouncing and bouncing. They were bouncing too high and got scared. Then his mother saw them and told them to stop. He saw her coming and got worried. He fell off the bed. She spanked him for not listening. He was sent to his room and his friends went home." (*How does he feel?*) "He wants to spank his mother and he is mad no one is left." For Card 7 GF, Jason's story was, "The girl's mom had a baby. She wants to hold the baby, but is worried she'll drop it and get in trouble. She gets to feed the baby since it is lunch time. Her friends have babies at home. She gets to feed the baby at dinner time too but does not hold the baby." For card 13 B, Jason's story was, "This boy is watching his friends play. He is trying to figure out when to play with them. He is worried their basketball game will take too long and he will not get a chance to play before the bell. He waits for a long time and then the bell rings."

Similar themes were noted in Jason's projective drawings and sentence completion test responses. For example, when Jason was asked to draw a person, he paused, appeared nervous, and said, "I don't know how" and handed the paper back to the evaluator. After being encouraged, Jason restated, "I don't know" and then wrote down math problems and facts on the paper. He handed it to the evaluator and said, "I can do math good, see?" As with the TAT, it appears that Jason has more difficulties with completing unstructured and unfamiliar tasks. Jason completed the sentence completion test easily and spontaneously read his responses aloud. His responses reflect achievement, anxiety, impulsivity, and need for peers relations. For example, Jason's responses were *I read* "books," *I feel sorry* "when I mess up," *I am happy when* "I am with my friends," *My feelings get hurt when* "friends do not play with me," *I feel proud when* "do well in school and get a goal!" *I feel ashamed when* "I drop things," and *I worry over* "getting along."

In summary, Jason is a bright 7-year-old boy who has a history of temperamental difficulties, high activity, inattention, poor impulse control, anxiety, and aggressive behavior. Current evaluation results reflect that Jason has functional impairments in attention, planning/organization, working memory, peer relations, and emotional regulation (anxiety, anger). Jason's developmental history, past school performance, behavioral observations, and current neurocognitive and emotional and behavioral results are suggestive of the diagnoses of ADHD-Combined Type and Anxiety Disorder NOS. Similar to Jason, children with ADHD-Combined Type and anxiety tend to exhibit more memory problems (Perrin & Last, 1996) and ODD symptoms than children with ADHD-Combined Type alone (Kashani & Orvaschel, 1990).

CONCLUSION

Children with ADHD represent a heterogeneous mix of neurocognitive, achievement, social/emotional and behavioral difficulties (Reddy & Hale, in press). Practitioners are encouraged to adopt an idiographic assessment approach that selects assessment methods tailored to the unique child's needs. Given the high comorbidity of ADHD with other childhood disorders and conditions, evaluations that integrate both neurocognitive and social/emotional assessments are warranted.

REFERENCES

Abikoff, H. B., Jensen, P. S., Arnold, L. L. E., Hoza, B., Hechtman, L., Pollack, S., et al. (2002). Observed classroom behavior of children with ADHD: Relationship to gender and comorbidity. *Journal of Abnormal Child Psychology, 30*(4), 349–359.

Achenbach, T. M., & Rescorla, L. A. (2001). *Manual of the Achenbach System of Empirically Based Assessment–Child Behavior Checklist, Teacher Report Form, and Youth Report.* Burlington, VT: University of Vermont, Research Center for Children, Youth, and Families.

Alban-Metcalfe, J., Cheng-Lai, A., & Ma, T. (2002). Teacher and student teacher ratings of attention-deficit/hyperactivity disorder in three cultural settings. *International Journal of Disability, Development, and Education, 49*(3), 281–299.

Arnold, P. D., Ickowicz, A., Chen, S., & Schachar, R. (2005). Attention-deficit hyperactivity disorder with and without obsessive-compulsive behaviors: Clinical characteristics, cognitive assessment, and risk factors. *Canadian Journal of Psychiatry, 50*(1), 59–66.

Bain, S. K., & Pelletier, K. A. (1999). Social and behavior differences among a predominately African American preschool sample. *Psychology in the Schools, 36*(3), 249–259.

Ball, D., Tiernan, M., Janusz, J., & Furr, A. (1997). Sleep patterns among children with attention deficit hyperactivity disorder: A reexamination of parent perceptions. *Journal of Pediatric Psychology, 22,*

389–398.

Barkley, R. A. (1990). *Attention-deficit hyperactivity disorder: A handbook for diagnosis and treatment.* New York: Guilford Press.

Barkley, R. A. (1997). Behavioral inhibition, sustained attention, and executive functions: Constructing a unifying theory of ADHD. *Psychological Bulletin, 12*(1), 65–94.

Barkley, R. A. (1998). *Attention-deficit hyperactivity disorder: A handbook for diagnosis and treatment.* New York: Guilford Press.

Barnett, D. W., Macmann, G. M., & Lentz, F. E. (2003). Personality assessment research: Applying criteria of confidence and helpfulness. In C. R. Reynolds & R. W. Kamphaus (Eds.), *Handbook of psychological and educational assessment of children: Personality, behavior, and context* (2nd ed., pp. 3–29). New York: Guilford Press.

Beery, K. E., Buktenica, N. A., & Beery, N. A. (2004). *Beery-Buktenica Developmental Test of Visual-Motor Integration–Fifth Edition (VMI–5).* Cleveland, OH: Modern Curriculum.

Bellak, L., & Abrams, D. M. (1997). *The T.A.T., C.A.T., and S.A.T. in clinical use* (6th ed.). New York: Allyn & Bacon.

Biederman, J., & Faraone, S. V. (2004). The Massachusetts General Hospital studies of gender influences on attention-deficit/hyperactivity disorder in youth and relatives. *Psychiatric Clinics of North America, 27*(2), 225–232.

Bird, H. R. (2002). The diagnostic classification, epidemiology, and cross-cultural validity of ADHD. In P. S. Jensen & J. R. Cooper (Eds.), *Attention deficit hyperactivity disorder: State of the science-best practices* (pp. 17–33). Kingston, NJ: Civic Research Institute.

Bronowski, J. (1967). Human and animal languages. In *To honor Roman Jakobson* (Vol. 1). The Hague, Netherlands: Mouton.

Bronowski, J. (1977). Human and animal languages. In J. Bronowski (Ed.), *A sense of the future* (pp. 104–131). Cambridge, MA: MIT Press.

Brown, R. T., Freeman, W. S., Perrin, J. M., Stein, M. T., Amler, R. W., Feldman, H. M., et al. (2001). Prevalence and assessment of attention-deficit/hyperactivity disorder in primary care settings. *Pediatrics, 107,* 241–252.

Brown, T. E. (2001). *Attention-Deficit Disorder Scales for Children.* San Antonio, TX: Psychological Corporation.

Burns, R., & Kaufman, S. (1972). *Kinetic Family Drawing (K-F-D): An introduction to understanding children through kinetic drawings.* New York: Brunner/Mazel.

Butcher, J. N. (1992). *Essential of MMPI–2 and MMPI–A interpretation.* Minneapolis, MN: University of Minnesota Press.

Butler, F. S., Arredondo, D. E., & McCloskey, V. (1995). Affective comorbidity in children and adolescents with attention deficit hyperactivity disorder. *Annals of Clinical Psychiatry, 7*(2), 51–55.

Chandler, L. A. (2003). The projective hypothesis and the development of projective techniques for children. In C. R. Reynolds & R. W. Kamphaus (Eds.), *Handbook of psychological and educational assessment of children: Personality, behavior, and context* (2nd ed., pp. 51–65). New York: Guilford Press.

Chi, T. C., & Hinshaw, S. P. (2002). Mother-child relationships of children with ADHD: The role of maternal depressive symptoms and depression-related distortions. *Journal of Abnormal Child Psychology, 30*(4), 387–400.

Cohen, A. J., Adler, N., Kaplan, S. J., Pelcovitz, D., & Mandel, F. S. (2002). Interactional affects of marital status and physical abuse on adolescent psychopathology. *Child Abuse and Neglect, 26,* 277–288.

Conners, K. (1997a). *Conners' Parent and Teacher Rating Scale-Revised.* North Tonawanda, NY: Multi-Health Systems.

Conners, K. (1997b). *Conners' Adolescent Self-Report Scale.* North Tonawanda, NY: Multi-Health Systems.

Conners, K., & MHS Staff. (2000). *Conners' Continuous Performance Test–II user's manual.* Toronto: Multi-Health Systems.

Conners, C. K., Sitarenios, G., Parker, J. D. A., & Epstein, J. N. (1998a). The revised Conners' Parent Rating Scale (CPRS-R): Factor structure, reliability, and criterion validity. *Journal of Abnormal Child Psy-*

chology, 26(4), 257–268.

Conners, C. K., Sitarenios, G., Parker, J. D. A., & Epstein, J. N. (1998b). The revised Conners' Teacher Rating Scale (CTRS-R): Factor structure, reliability, and criterion validity. *Journal of Abnormal Child Psychology, 26*(4), 279–291.

Costantino, G., Malgady, R., & Rogler, L. H. (1988). *Tell-Me-A-Story TEMAS manual.* Los Angeles: Western Psychological Services.

Das, J. P., Carlson, J., Davidson, M. B., & Longe, K. (1997). *PREP: PAS remedial program.* Seattle, WA: Hogrefe.

Delis, D. C., Kaplan, E., & Kramer, J. H. (2001). *Delis-Kaplan Executive Function System.* San Antonio, TX: Psychological Corporation.

Doyle, A., Ostrander, R., Skare, S., Crosby, R. D., & August, G. J. (1997). Convergent and criterion-related validity of the Behavior Assessment System for Children–Parent Rating Scale. *Journal of Clinical Child Psychology, 26*(3), 276–284.

Dunn, D. W., & Kronenberger, W. G. (2003). Attention-deficit/hyperactivity disorder in children and adolescents. *Neurologic Clinics, 21*(4), 933–940.

DuPaul, G. J., & Stoner, G. (2004). *ADHD in the schools: Assessment and intervention strategies.* New York: Guilford Press.

Edwards, M. C., Schulz, E. G., & Long, N. (1995). The role of the family in the assessment of attention deficit hyperactivity disorder. *Clinical Psychology Review, 15*(5), 375–394.

Eiraldi, R. B., Power, T. J., Karustis, J. L., & Goldstein, S. G. (2000). Assessing ADHD and comorbid disorders in children: The child behavior checklist and the Devereux scales of mental disorders. *Journal of Clinical Child Psychology, 29*(1), 3–16.

Elia, J. K., Ambrosini, P. J., & Rapoport, J. L. (1999). Treatment of attention-deficit hyperactivity disorder. *New England Journal of Medicine, 11,* 780–788.

Elliott, C. D. (1990a). *Differential Ability Scales: Administration and scoring manual.* San Antonio, TX: Psychological Corporation.

Elliott, C. D. (1990b). *Differential Ability Scales: Introductory and technical handbook.* San Antonio, TX: Psychological Corporation.

Ford, L. Keith, T. Z., Floyd, R., Fields, C., & Schrank, F. J. (2003). WJ III and children with ADHD. In F. Schrank & Flanagan. D. (Eds), *The Woodcock-Johnson III: Clinical Use and interpretation.* San Diego, CA: Academic Press.

Fuster, J. M. (1989). *The prefrontal cortex.* New York: Raven Press.

Fuster, J. M. (1995). Memory and planning: Two temporal perspectives of frontal lobe function. In H. H. Jasper, S. Riggio, & P. S. Goldman-Rakic (Eds.), *Epilepsy and the functional anatomy of the frontal lobe* (pp. 9–18). New York: Raven Press.

Gaub, M., & Carlson, C. L. (1997). Gender differences in ADHD: A meta-analysis and critical review. *Journal of the American Academy of Child and Adolescent Psychiatry, 36*(8), 1036–1045.

Geller, D. A., Biederman, J., Faraone, S. V., Cradock, K., Hagermoser, L., Zaman, N., et al. (2002). Attention-deficit/hyperactivity disorder in children and adolescents with obsessive-compulsive disorder: Fact or artifact? *Journal of the American Academy of Child and Adolescent Psychiatry, 41*(1), 52–58.

Geller, D. A., Biederman, J., Faraone, S. V., Spencer, T., Doyle, R., Mullin, B., et al. (2004). Re-examining comorbidity of obsessive compulsive and attention-deficit hyperactivity disorder using an empirically derived taxonomy. *European Child and Adolescent Psychiatry, 13,* 83–91.

Ghelani, K., Sidhu, R., Jain, U., & Tannock, R. (2004). Reading comprehension and reading related abilities in adolescents with reading disabilities and attention-deficit/hyperactivity disorder. *Dyslexia, 10,* 364–384.

Gibney, L. A., McIntosh, D. E., Dean, R. S., & Dunham, M. (2002). Diagnosing attention disorders with measures of neurocognitive functioning. *International Journal of Neuroscience, 112,* 539–564.

Gioia, G. A., Isquith, P. K., Guy, S. C., & Kenworthy, L. (2000). *Brief Rating Inventory of Executive Function: Professional manual.* Lutz, FL: Psychological Assessment Resources.

Goodman, G., & Poillion, M. J. (1992). ADD: Acronym for any dysfunction or difficulty. *Journal of Spe-*

cial Education, 26, 37–56.

Graetz, B. W., Sawyer, M. G., & Baghurst, P. (2005). Gender differences among children with DSM-IV ADHD in Australia. *Journal of the American Academy of Child and Adolescent Psychiatry, 44*(2), 159–168.

Greenberg, L. M. (1988–1999). *The Test of Variables of Attention (TOVA).* Los Alamitos, CA: Universal Attention Disorders.

Gresham, F. M., & Elliott, S. N. (1990). *Social Skills Rating System.* Circle Pines, MN: American Guidance Service.

Hale, J. B., & Fiorello, C. A. (2004). *School neuropsychology: A practitioner's handbook.* New York: Guilford Press.

Harada, Y., Yamazaki, T., & Saitoh, K. (2002). Psychosocial problems in attention-deficit hyperactivity disorder with oppositional defiant disorder. *Psychiatry and Clinical Neurosciences, 56,* 365–369.

Harrison, C., & Sofronoff, K. (2002). ADHD and parental psychological distress: Role of demographics, child behavioral characteristics, and parental cognitions. *Journal of the American Academy of Child and Adolescent Psychiatry, 41*(6), 703–711.

Hart, D. H., Kehle, T. J., & Davies, M. V. (1983). Effective of sentence completion techniques: A review of the Hart Sentence Completion Test for Children. *School Psychology Review, 12,* 428–434.

Irwin, J. R., Carter, A. S., & Briggs-Gowan, M. J. (2002). The social-emotional development of "late-talking" toddlers. *Journal of the American Academy of Child and Adolescent Psychiatry, 41*(11), 1324–1332.

Johnston, C., & Mash, E. J. (2001). Families of children with ADHD: Review and recommendations for future research. *Clinical Child and Family Psychology Review, 4*(3), 183–207.

Johnston, C., Murray, C., Hinshaw, S. P., Pelham, W. E., & Hoza, B. (2002). Responsiveness in interactions of mothers and sons with ADHD: Relations to maternal and child characteristics. *Journal of Abnormal Child Psychology, 30*(1), 77–88.

Karustis, J. L., Power, T. J., Rescorla, L. A., Eiraldi, R. B., & Gallagher, P. R. (2000). Anxiety and depression in children with ADHD: Unique associations with academic and social functioning. *Journal of Attention Disorders, 4,* 133–149.

Kashani, J. H., & Orvaschel, H. (1990). A community study of anxiety in children and adolescents. *American Journal of Psychiatry, 147,* 313–318.

Keith, T. Z., Kranzler, J. H., & Flanagan, D. P. (2001). What does the Cognitive Assessment System (CAS) measure? Joint confirmatory factor analysis of the CAS and Woodcock-Johnson tests of Cognitive Ability (3rd edition). *School Psychology Review, 30,* 89–119.

Kellner, R., Houghton, S., & Douglas, G. (2003). Peer-related personal experiences of children with attention-deficit/hyperactivity disorder with and without comorbid learning disabilities. *International Journal of Disability, Development and Education, 50*(2), 119–136.

Koger, S. M., Schettler, T., & Weiss, B. (2005). Environmental toxicants and developmental disabilities. *American Psychologist, 60*(3), 243–255.

Koppitz, E. M. (1968). *Psychological evaluation of children's human figure drawings.* Boston: Allyn & Bacon.

Korman, M., Kirk, U., & Kemp, S. (1998). *NEPSY: A Developmental Neuropsychological Assessment Manual.* San Antonio, TX: Harcourt Assessment.

Kovacs, M. (2003). *Children's Depression Inventory.* North Tonawanda, NY: Multi-Health Systems.

Kranowitz, C. S. (1998). *The out-of-sync child: Recognizing and coping with sensory integration dysfunction.* New York: Penguin Putnam.

Lachar, D., & Gruber, C. P. (1995). *Personality Inventory for Youth (PIY).* Los Angeles: Western Psychological Services.

Lachar, D., & Gruber, C. P. (2001). *Personality Inventory for Children (PIC–2)* (2nd ed.). Los Angeles: Western Psychological Services.

Lachar, D., Wingenfeld, S. A, Kline, R. B., & Gruber, C. P. (2000). *Student Behavior Survey manual.* Los Angeles: Western Psychological Services.

LeBlanc, N., & Morin, D. (2004). Depressive symptoms and associated factors in children with attention deficit hyperactivity disorder. *Journal of Child and Adolescent Psychiatric Nursing, 17*(2), 49–55.

Logan, G. D. (1994). On the ability to inhibit thought and action: A user's guide to the stop signal para-digm. In D. Dagenbach & T. H. Carr (Eds.), *Inhibitory processes in attention, memory, and language* (pp. 252–265). San Diego, CA: Academic Press.

Love, A. J., & Thompson, M. G. (1988). Language disorders and attention deficit disorders in young chil-dren referred for psychiatric services: Analysis of prevalence and a conceptual synthesis. *American Journal of Orthopsychiatry, 58*, 52–64.

Mangeot, S. D., Miller, J. L., McIntosh, D. N., McGrath-Clarke, J., Simon, J., Hagerman, R. J., et al. (2001). Sensory modulation dysfunction in children with attention-deficit-hyperactivity disorder. *Developmental Medicine and Child Neurology, 43*, 399–406.

Mann, E. M., Ikeda, Y., Mueller, C. W., Takahashi, A., Tao, K. T., Humris, E., et al. (1992). Cross-cultural differences in rating hyperactive-disruptive behaviors in children. *American Journal of Psychiatry, 149*, 1539–1542.

Manning, S. C. (2001). Identifying ADHD subtypes using the Parent and Teacher Rating Scales of the Behavior Assessment Scale for Children. *Journal of Attention Disorders, 5*(1), 41–51.

Mather, N., & Woodcock, R. W. (2001). *Woodcock-Johnson III Tests of Achievement: Examiner's manual.* Itasca, IL: Riverside Publishing.

McGrew, K. S., & Woodcock, R. W. (2001). *Technical Manual. Woodcock-Johnson III Tests of Cognitive Abilities.* Itasca, IL: Riverside.

Mick, E., Biederman, J., Faraone, S. V., Sayer, J., & Kleinman, S. (2002). Case control study of attention-deficit hyperactivity disorder and maternal smoking, alcohol abuse, and drug use during pregnancy. *Journal of the American Academy of Child and Adolescent Psychiatry, 41*, 378–385.

Mick, E., Biederman, J., Prince, J., Fischer, M. J., & Faraone, S. V. (2002). Impact of low birth weight on attention-deficit hyperactivity disorder. *Journal of Developmental and Behavioral Pediatrics, 23*, 16–22.

Millon, T., Green, C. J., & Meagher, R. B. (1982). *Millon Adolescent Personality Inventory.* Minneapolis, MN: National Computer Systems.

Moss, W. L., & Sheiffele, W. A. (1994). Can we differentially diagnose an attention deficit disorder without hyperactivity from a central auditory processing problem? *Child Psychiatry and Human Development, 25*(2), 85–96.

Murray, H. A. (1943). *Thematic Apperception Test manual.* Cambridge, MA: Harvard University Press.

Naglieri, J. A., & Das, J. P. (1997). *Das-Naglieri Cognitive Assessment System administration and scoring manual.* Itasca, IL: Riverside.

Naglieri, J. A., Goldstein, S., & Iseman, J. (2003). Performance of children with attention deficit hyper-activity disorder and anxiety/depression on the WISC-III and Cognitive Assessment System (CAS). *Journal of Psychoeducational Assessment, 21*(1), 32–42.

Naglieri, J. A., McNeish, T. J., & Bardos, A. N. (1991). *Draw A Person: Screening procedure for emotional disturbance.* Austin, TX: Pro-Ed.

Naglieri, J. A., Salter, C., & Edwards, G. (2004). Assessment of children with attention and reading diffi-culties using the PASS theory and Cognitive Assessment System. *Journal of Psychoeducational Assessment, 22*(2), 93–105.

Neul, S., Applegate, H., & Drabman, R. (2003). Assessment of attention-deficit/hyperactivity disorder. In C. R. Reynolds & R. W. Kamphaus (Eds.), *Handbook of psychological and educational assessment of children: Personality, behavior, and context* (2nd ed., pp. 320–334). New York: Guilford Press.

Newcorn, J. H., Halperin, J. M., Jensen, P. S., Abikoff, H. B., Arnold, L. E., Cantwell, D. P., et al. (2001). Symptom profiles in children with ADHD: Effects of comorbidity and gender. *Journal of the American Academy of Child and Adolescent Psychiatry, 40*(2), 137–146.

Obrzut, J. E., & Boliek, C. A. (1986). Thematic approaches to personality assessment with children and ado-lescents. In H. M. Knoff (Ed.), *The assessment of child and adolescent personality* (pp. 173–198). New York: Guilford Press.

Pastor, P. N., & Reuben, C. A. (2002). Attention deficit disorder and learning disability: United States, 1997–98. In *National Center for Health Statistics: Vital Health Statistics* (DHHS Publication No.

PHS 2002-1534). Hyattsville, MD: Department of Health and Human Services.

Pearl, P. L., Weiss, R. E., & Stein, M. A. (2001). Medical mimics: Medical and neurological conditions simulating ADHD. In J. Wasserstein, L. E. Wolf, & F. F. Lefever (Eds.), *Annals of the New York Academy of Sciences: Vol. 931. Adult attention deficit disorder: Brain mechanisms and life outcomes* (pp. 97–112). New York: New York Academy of Sciences.

Pelham, W. E., Fabiano, G. A., & Massetti, G. M. (2005). Evidenced-based assessment of attention deficit hyperactivity disorder in children and adolescents. *Journal of Clinical Child and Adolescent Psychology, 34*(3), 449–476.

Perner, J., Kain, W., & Barchfeld, P. (2002). Executive control and higher-order theory of mind in children at risk of ADHD. *Infant and Child Development, 11,* 141–158.

Perrin, S., & Last, C. G. (1996). Relationship between ADHD and anxiety in boys: Results from a family study. *Journal of the American Academy of Child and Adolescent Psychiatry, 35*(8), 988–996.

Pfiffner, L. J., McBurnett, K., Lahey, B. B., Loeber, R., Green, S., Frick, P. J., et al. (1999). Association of parental psychopathology to the comorbid disorders of boys with attention-deficit hyperactivity disorder, *Journal of Consulting and Clinical Psychology, 67,* 881–893.

Pizzitola, J. K., Riccio, C. A., & Siekierski, B. M. (2005). Assessment of ADHD using the BASC and BRIEF. *Applied Neuropsychology, 12*(2), 83–93.

Pliszka, S. R., Carlson, C. L., & Swanson, J. M. (1999). *ADHD with comorbid disorders: Clinical assessment and management.* New York: Guilford Press.

Power, T. J., Costigan, T. E., Eiraldi, R. B., & Leff, S. S. (2004). Variations in anxiety and depression as a function of ADHD subtypes defined by DSM-IV: Do subtype differences occur or not? *Journal of Abnormal Child Psychology, 32*(1), 27–37.

Pratt, B., Campbell-La Voie, F., Isquith, P. K., Gioia, G., & Guy, S. (2000). *Behavior Rating Inventory of Executive Function parent ratings in children with ADHD.* Unpublished raw data.

Prout, H. T., & Phillips, P. D. (1974). A clinical note: The kinetic school drawing. *Psychology in the Schools, 11,* 303–306.

Quay, H. C. (1988). Attention deficit disorder and the behavioral inhibition system: The relevance of the neuropsychological theory of Jeffrey A. Gray. In L. M. Bloomingdale & J. Sergeant (Eds.), *Attention deficit disorder: Criteria, cognition, intervention* (pp. 117–125). Oxford: Pergamon Press.

Reddy, L. A., Braunstein, D. J., & Dumont, R. (2005). *Use of the Differential Ability Scale for children with attention-deficit/hyperactivity disorder.* Presented at the American Psychological Association Conference in Washington, DC.

Reddy, L. A., Dumont, R., & Bray, N. (2005). *Use of the Woodcock Johnson Tests of Cognitive Abilities for children with attention-deficit/hyperactivity disorder.* Presented at the American Psychological Association Conference in Washington, DC.

Reddy, L. A., & Hale, J. (in press). Inattentiveness. In A. R. Eisen (Ed.), *Clinical Handbook of Childhood Behavioral Problems.* New York: Guilford Press.

Reid, R., DuPaul, G. J., Power, T. J., Anastopoulos, A. D., Rogers-Adkinson, D., Noll, M., et al. (1998). Assessing culturally different students for attention deficit hyperactivity disorder using behavior rating scales. *Journal of Abnormal Child Psychology, 26*(3), 187–198.

Reynolds, C. R., & Kamphaus, R. W. (1992). *Behavior Assessment System for Children–2 (BASC–2).* Circle Pines, MN: American Guidance Services.

Reynolds, C. R., & Kamphaus, R. W. (2004). *Behavior Assessment System for Children–2 (BASC–2).* Circle Pines, MN: American Guidance Services.

Reynolds, C. R., & Richmond, B. D. (2000). *Revised Children's Manifest Anxiety Scale.* Los Angeles: Western Psychological Services.

Riccio, C. A., Hynd, G. W., Cohen, M. J., Hall, J., & Molt, L. (1994). Comorbidity of central auditory processing disorder and attention-deficit hyperactivity disorder. *Journal of the American Academy of Child and Adolescent Psychiatry, 33*(6), 849–857.

Riccio, C. A., & Reynolds, C. R. (2003). The assessment of attention via continuous performance tests. In C. R. Reynolds & R. W. Kamphaus (Eds.), *Handbook of psychological and educational assess-*

ment of children: Personality, behavior, and context (2nd ed., pp. 291–319). New York: Guilford Press.

Roberts, G. E. (2005). *The Roberts–2*. Los Angeles: Western Psychological Services.

Rotter, J. B., Lah, M. I., & Rafferty, J. E. (1992). *Rotter Incomplete Sentences Blank Manual* (2nd ed.). Antonio, TX: The Psychological Corporation.

Rouke, B. P. (1995). *Syndrome of nonverbal learning disabilities: Neurodevelopmental manifestations*. New York: Guilford Press.

Rowland, A. S., Leswesne, C. A., & Abramowitz, A. J. (2002). The epidemiology of attention-deficit/hyperactivity disorder (ADHD): A public health view. *Mental Retardation and Developmental Disabilities Research Reviews, 8*, 162–170.

Safren, S. A., Lanka, G. D., Otto, M.W., & Pollack, M. H. (2001). Prevalence of childhood ADHD among patients with generalized anxiety disorder and a comparison condition, social phobia. *Depression and Anxiety, 13*, 190–191.

Sax, K., Strakowski, S., Zimmerman, M., DelBallo, M., Keck, P. J., & Hawkins, J. (1999). Frontosubcortical neuroanatomy and the continuous performance test in mania. *American Journal of Psychiatry, 156*, 139–141.

Schachar, R., Tannock, R., & Logan, G. (1993). Inhibitory control, impulsiveness, and attention-deficit hyperactivity disorder. *Clinical Psychology Review, 13*, 721–739.

Schmitz, M. F., & Velez, M. (2003). Latino cultural differences in maternal assessments of attention deficit/hyperactivity symptoms in children. *Hispanic Journal of Behavior Sciences, 25*(1), 110–122.

Schnoll, R., Burshteyn, D., & Cea-Aravena, J. (2003). Nutrition in the treatment of attention-deficit hyperactivity disorder: A neglected but important aspect. *Applied Psychophysiology and Biofeedback, 28*(1), 63–75.

Semel, E., Wiig, E. H., & Secord, W. (2003). *Clinical Evaluation of Language Fundamentals–Fourth Edition*. San Antonio, TX: Psychological Corporation.

Shear, P. K., DelBello, M. P., Rosenberg, H. L., & Strakowski, S. M. (2002). Parental reports of executive dysfunction in adolescents with bipolar disorder. *Child Neuropsychology, 8*(4), 285–295.

Shear, P. K., Duis, C., Larson, E. R., Fleck, D., Krikoarian, R., & Strakowski, S. M. (1999). Verbal learning and memory in mania [Abstract]. *Journal of the International Neuropsychological Society, 5*, 131.

Smith, D. T. (2000). Parent-child interaction play assessment. In K. Gitlin-Weiner, A. Sanguard, & C. Schaefer (Eds.), *Play diagnosis and assessment* (pp. 340–370). New York: Wiley.

Souza, I., Pinheiro, M. A., Denardin, D., Mattos, P., & Rohde, L. A. (2004). Attention-deficit/hyperactivity disorder and comorbidity in Brazil: Comparisons between two referred samples. *European Child and Adolescent Psychiatry, 13*(4), 243–248.

Stanford, L. D., & Hynd, G. W. (1994). Congruence of behavioral symptomatology in children with ADD/H, ADD/WO, and learning disabilities. *Journal of Learning Disabilities, 27*(4), 243–253.

Sundheim, S. T. P., & Voeller, K. K. S. (2004). Psychiatric implications of language disorders and learning disabilities: Risk and management. *Journal of Child Neurology, 19*, 814–826.

Tannock, R. (1998). Attention deficit hyperactivity disorder: Advances in cognitive, neurobiological, and genetic research. *Journal of Child Psychology and Psychiatry, 29*, 65–99.

Thompson, S. (1997). *The source for nonverbal learning disorders*. East Moline, IL: LinguiSystems.

Toplak, M. E., Rucklidge, J. J., Hetherington, R., John, S. C. F., & Tannock, R. (2003). Time perception deficits in attention-deficit/hyperactivity disorder and comorbid reading difficulties in child and adolescent samples. *Journal of Child Psychology and Psychiatry, 44*(6), 888–893.

Vance, A., Harris, K., Boots, M., Talbot, J., & Karamitsios, M. (2003). Which anxiety disorders may differentiate attention deficit hyperactivity disorder, combined type with dysthymic disorder from attention deficit hyperactivity disorder, combined type alone? *Australian and New Zealand Journal of Psychiatry, 37*, 563–569.

Wasserstein, J. (2005). Diagnostic issues for adolescents and adults with ADHD. *Journal of Clinical Psychology, 61*(5), 535–547.

Wechsler, D. (2003). *Manual for the Wechsler Intelligence Scale for Children–Fourth Edition*. San Antonio,

TX: The Psychological Corporation.

Wilens, T. E., Biederman, J., Brown, S., Tanguay, S., Monuteaux, M. C., Blake, C., et al. (2002). Psychiatric comorbidity and functioning in clinically referred preschool children and school-age youths with ADHD. *Journal of the American Academy of Child and Adolescent Psychiatry, 41*(3), 262–268.

Wilson, M. S., & Reschly, D. J. (1996). Assessment in school psychology training and practice. *School Psychology Review, 26*, 9–23.

Woodcock, R. W., McGrew, K. S., & Mather, N. (2001). *Woodcock-Johnson III Tests of Cognitive Abilities.* Itasca, IL: Riverside Publishing.

Yochman, A., Parush, S., & Ornoy, A. (2004). Responses of preschool children with and without ADHD to sensory events in daily life. *American Journal of Occupational Therapy, 58*(3), 294–302.

22

DELINQUENT AND ANTISOCIAL BEHAVIOR

James L. Loving
Private Practice, Philadelphia, Pennsylvania

All mental health professionals who work with children and adolescents encounter delinquency in one form or another. Even professionals who do not assess or treat acting-out youth often come into contact with the havoc they wreak on the lives of loved ones and other victims. In fact, acting-out behavior, broadly defined, is routinely cited as being among the most common reasons youths are referred to mental health professionals in any setting. In one recent sample of 1.3 million children participating in mental health services (Pottick et al., 2002), the disruptive behavior disorders collectively represented the most frequent category of diagnoses (30.8% of the overall sample). Aggression was among the most common presenting problems overall and, not surprisingly, was the single most prevalent presenting problem in both inpatient and residential settings (accounting for 48.7% and 66.2% of referrals, respectively).

Conversely, delinquent youth as a group are rife with diagnosable behavioral and emotional problems. Although precise data are difficult to collect, it has been estimated that youths in the juvenile justice system are at least twice as likely to qualify for a psychiatric diagnosis as are their counterparts within the general population (Otto, Greenstein, Johnson, & Friedman, 1992). This is especially true in detention settings, where the presence of one or more psychiatric disorders is the rule rather than the exception. In one of the largest and most systematic studies available (Teplin, Abram, McClelland, Dulcan, & Mericle, 2002), nearly three quarters of detained juveniles met criteria for at least one disorder, and comorbidity was commonplace. Even after eliminating Conduct Disorder from consideration, roughly 60% of males and roughly 70% of females met criteria for other mental health disorders.

Unfortunately, these youths are often misunderstood and consequently mismanaged. This is not only due to the complexity of some cases, but also to the emotional reactions that many of them can stir in us as clinicians. At one extreme, there is a risk of prematurely dismissing patients as untreatable, especially when certain reprehensible actions impede our capacity to remain objective. At the other extreme, there is a risk of naively underestimating risk while overinferring traits and experiences that certain patients do not possess. We may misunderstand the patient's underlying personality structure and then presume or project our own empathy, capacity for guilt, need to attach, and other qualities, when in reality these features are absent or impaired. For all of these reasons, working with delinquent youth requires the most comprehensive and systematic assessment that circumstances will permit.

This chapter presents overarching concepts and specific methods for conducting psychological assessment in cases of delinquent or antisocial behavior. First, I present a conceptual overview of Conduct Disorder and related conditions that are most relevant to youthful antisociality. Next I discuss general assessment guidelines intended to help overcome obstacles typically encountered with this population. The primary focus of the chapter then consists of an outline of traditional assessment methods as they relate to these cases, as well as an introduction to several specialized instruments that have been developed for specific use with delinquent populations. I conclude with an illustrative case example, before touching on some areas in need of further research.

CONDUCT DISORDER AND RELATED CONDITIONS

Before delving into a discussion of assessment strategies, it is necessary to narrow and define our terms. The focus of this chapter is on delinquent and antisocial conduct. Here these terms are used in an essentially interchangeable fashion, as both are associated with behavior that disregards societal norms and/or the rights of other people. However, it might be more precise to restrict the term "delinquency" to arrestable behavior, or actions that directly violate existing laws. In slight contrast, antisociality refers to behavior that is fueled by a lack of consideration of, or indifference to, the rights and needs of others. Antisocial behavior may or may not be delinquent, depending on whether it violates the local laws that apply to the juvenile in question. This broad collection of behaviors may or may not include violence, which could be simply defined as physical aggression carried out against other people. What follows is not a specific discussion of juvenile violence, although many of the concepts included here obviously apply to and overlap greatly with that specific form of behavior.

Delinquency is a multidetermined behavior carried out by a tremendously diverse array of individuals. The professional literature contains many efforts to disentangle this population into meaningful subgroups, for the sake of understanding, predicting, and managing behavior. A lengthy discussion is not necessary for the purposes of this chapter. However, it would be helpful to discuss the most relevant categories that are outlined in the latest *Diagnostic and Statistical Manual* (*DSM-IV-TR*; American Psychiatric Association, 2000), given its pervasive use and its centrality to our practice.

Conduct Disorder (CD) is defined by a repetitive, persistent pattern of behavior that violates the rights of others or major age-appropriate societal norms. The *DSM-IV-TR* offers 15 wide-ranging behavioral criteria that are divided into four categories: aggression toward people and animals, destruction or property, deceitfulness or theft, and serious violation of rules. The conceptual essence of CD is budding psychopathic personality, whose phenomenology has been described extensively in the literature (e.g., Cleckley, 1976; Hare, 1993; Meloy, 1988). For the prototypical psychopath, interpersonal relations are superficial and dismissive, usually characterized by parasitic and/or blatantly aggressive interactions. Affect is shallow and primitive. Behavior tends to be erratic, short-sighted, and independent of societally defined rules. Conceptually, the antisocial behavior of psychopaths is perpetuated by the interpersonal and affective traits that underlie the disorder, although these are more difficult to assess directly and sometimes must be inferred to some degree from the behavior itself. In criminal adult populations, psychopathy (as measured with the Revised Psychopathy Checklist or PCL-R; Hare, 1991, 2003) has been identified as one of the most robust predictors of both general and violent re-offending, and its presence is strongly correlated with many other negative outcomes (see, e.g., Hart & Hare, 1997, for a review). As discussed extensively elsewhere (e.g., Hare, 1996), psychopathy is closely related to, but importantly distinct from, adult Antisocial Personality Disorder (APD; American Psychiatric Association, 2000). Psychopathy is a more homogenous and higher-risk construct, which is present in perhaps only one third of APD individuals. This is critically important, because although many professionals use the terms *antisocial* and *psychopathic* interchangeably, many APD patients are not truly psychopathic; they carry out persistent antisocial behavior because of factors that are minimally related to underlying personality (e.g., substance dependence; subcultural pressures).

CD is a necessary childhood precursor to APD and adult psychopathy. Both of these adult conditions are conceptualized as having early developmental origins, and both require retrospective evidence of CD as a defining criterion. In fact, many features inherent in APD and psychopathy are listed in the *DSM-IV-TR* as associated features of CD, such as lack of empathy, lack of guilt, callousness, and overly inflated self-image (American Psychiatric Association, 2000). However, these are not required diagnostic criteria for CD, and CD is not synonymous with juvenile psychopathy. Because of the tremendously wide range of diagnostic criteria, most of which are exclusively behavioral in nature, it is common for a juvenile to qualify for the CD diagnosis in cases where the characterological features of psychopathy are only partially formed or even essentially absent. Some distinctions between psychopathy and CD and limitations of the latter have been discussed elsewhere (e.g., Loving & Gacono, 2002). There is an asymmetrical relationship between CD and psychopathy, in that most psychopathic youth meet the criteria for CD, whereas only a subset of conduct-disordered individuals are truly psychopathic. In many cases, the psychopathic personality is still crystallizing, and numerous individual and environmental factors may still prevent the further development of the condition before adulthood. This view is supported by the fact that CD has high rates of comorbidity not only with other externalizing disorders but also with various internalizing disorders (Zoccolillo, 1992). In cases where conduct disorder is accompanied by symptoms of depression and anxiety, for example, the antisocial personality structure is very likely in a nascent stage, with at least vestiges of emotional vulnerability and attachment capacity still present.

In community samples, prevalence estimates for CD cover a fairly wide range, from less than 1% to more than 10% (American Psychiatric Association, 2000). In these general populations, CD implies a relatively severe and high-risk condition. However, in any setting where base rates for delinquency and violence are higher, the prevalence of CD reaches such high levels (upwards of 95% or higher in some samples; e.g., Forth, 1995; Loving & Russell, 2000) that the presence of the condition is arguably rendered useless for differentiating subtypes of offenders. Especially within these extreme populations, despite the tendency of many clinicians to view this diagnosis as an end-point to assessment, the CD diagnosis should be viewed as a starting point for understanding a youth's personality and behavior (Grisso, 1998).

CD has at least short-term implications for risk of re-offending, risk for violence, and other negative outcomes. However, clinicians often mistakenly inflate the disorder's associations with adult criminality, APD, and psychopathy. It has been estimated that only 40% of CD youth progress to diagnosable adult APD (Zoccolillo, Pickles, Quinton, & Rutter, 1992), and that proportion is almost certainly even lower when adult psychopathy is predicted from CD. This is in line with the often-cited literature on adolescence-limited versus life-course-persistent delinquency (Moffitt, 1993), which points out that most delinquent youths can be expected to desist once they pass through early adulthood. Some of the most effective predictors can be obtained simply through a thorough behavioral history, as outlined later in this chapter.

Closely related to, but importantly distinct from, CD is Oppositional Defiant Disorder (ODD; American Psychiatric Association, 2000). ODD is defined by a lasting pattern of negativistic, hostile, and defiant behaviors, meeting at least four of eight criteria (e.g., active defiance of rules; frequent loss of temper; deliberate annoyance of others). The features of ODD are typically noticeable in cases where CD is present, so when both are diagnosable, only CD is assigned.

At the most simplistic level, ODD might be seen as a nonaggressive or less severe variant of CD. However, these two conditions could arguably be viewed as qualitatively distinct constructs that are strikingly different in terms of interpersonal relatedness. That is, the truly conduct-disordered, or psychopathic, individual is interpersonally indifferent and dismissive, unable to attach in any deep or meaningful manner. In contrast, the ODD child often acts out in ways that actually initiate and perpetuate human contact, albeit in dysfunctional and conflict-ridden ways. When the ODD child defies rules, he is typically acting out *against* or *in spite of* some personally meaningful authority (especially a caregiver), whereas the CD child acts out because of a blatant *disregard for* the people who surround him. When aggression is present with ODD, it is often seen as provocation toward, or a reaction to, significant others, whereas aggression in true CD is more often indiscriminant, including opportunistic violence against unknown victims. Although both groups are heterogeneous, this conceptual distinction may be helpful in differentiating between ODD and CD and would have meaningful implications for managing behavior in specific cases.

Developmentally, onset of ODD is typically earlier than that of CD, and although nearly all youth diagnosed with CD (at least those in the early-onset subtype) have behavioral histories consistent with ODD, most ODD children "outgrow" these behaviors, rather than progressing toward eventual CD (Lahey, Loeber, Quay, Frick, & Grimm, 1992; Loeber, Keenan, Lahey, Green, & Thomas, 1993). There appears to be a great deal of variability in the long-term course of ODD, with numerous factors, such as certain parenting styles and peer alienation, influencing the ultimate outcome. Although ODD could be distinguished from CD as an inherently relational disorder, one can understand how a prolonged period of social conflict and repeated rejection could lay the groundwork for interpersonal disconnection that allows CD to evolve.

Other conditions that can play a role in establishing and perpetuating delinquent behavior include Attention-Deficit/Hyperactivity Disorder (ADHD; American Psychiatric Association, 2000). Strong evidence shows that children with comorbid CD and ADHD are at substantially higher risk for violence, delinquency, and general long-term maladjustment than are children with either condition alone (Lynam, 1996). This mix of conduct-disordered features, coupled with the impulse control deficits and/or hyperactivity of ADHD, is a particularly volatile recipe for long-term antisociality. Even in the absence of a specific ADHD diagnosis, youth who display problems with impulsivity are at heightened risk for delinquency and other long-term negative outcomes.

Although not a focus of this chapter, numerous other conditions must be considered as part of an assessment of delinquent behavior. These include the presence of underlying (and possibly undiagnosed) mood disorders or other internalizing disorders, which are being expressed behaviorally in the form of irritable, reactive, or disorganized conduct. As already noted, internalizing disorders are comorbid in a substantial proportion of CD and ODD cases;

however, conceptually, one would not expect to find substantial depression or anxiety in cases where a psychopathic personality is already fairly well crystallized.

Also worth considering are patterns of conduct that are primarily fueled by social or subcultural influences. Especially in cases where antisocial behavior has an adolescent-onset or is fairly circumscribed in nature, even a cursory social history may reveal obvious social factors (e.g., poverty, substance use, pervasive peer influences). In these cases, a thorough assessment will probably rule out the presence of psychiatric or characterological factors. These statements may seem obvious to the reader, but in actual practice, many clinicians are quick to overlook contextual factors while quickly turning attention to presumed pathology inherent in the child. Testing can provide idiographic findings with respect to personality structure, interpersonal dynamics, and emotional functioning, but traditional models of assessment run the risk of overfocusing on individual factors, while underappreciating the significance of environmental variables that play a tremendous role in the understanding and prediction of antisocial behavior.

GUIDEPOSTS FOR ASSESSMENT IN DELINQUENCY CASES

Many of the core features that characterize antisocial youth directly interfere with information-gathering, thus undermining effective evaluation. As examples, delinquent youth commonly approach the assessment process with a posture that is at best defensive and at worst overtly hostile and aggressive. Adversarial dynamics are magnified by the court-involved contexts where many of these youth are encountered. Furthermore, information-gathering can be sabotaged by overt deception and more subtle distortion of information, not to mention pervasive defensive maneuvers (e.g., externalization, rationalization) that function to ward off self-blaming experiences that would otherwise threaten the youth's sense of comfort with the self.

In court-involved settings, clinicians adopt a forensic assessment framework to guide method selection and case conceptualization. Even outside of court contexts, professionals would benefit from adopting such a framework to help combat the obstacles that many delinquent youth pose. Evaluators who adhere to a traditional clinical model are at risk of gathering incomplete and unreliable findings, because some fundamental clinical assumptions and practices do not translate effectively to our work with antisocial populations. As one example, the clinician may intellectually understand the need to be on the alert for deception and noncooperation, but because of deeply engrained expectations about an inherent, mutually felt assessment alliance, he may naively overlook evidence of distortion or manipulation.

One guideline that is inherent in forensic assessment and applicable to working with delinquent populations is to view multimethod assessment as critically important (American Academy of Child and Adolescent Psychiatry, 1997, 2005; Heilbrun, 2001). Of course, a battery approach is typically desirable in any clinical context, but within a forensic model, reliance on multiple relevant tests, as well as background-gathering from multiple parties, is absolutely essential. Ideally, background and impressions are collected not only from the youth and his caregiver(s), but also from involved professionals. Advance review of records is critical, so that the evaluator can be as informed as possible before facing a potentially vague, inarticulate, or obfuscating interviewee. The testing battery ideally includes multiple routes for data-gathering, including self-report measures, parent/caregiver rating scales, and performance-based instruments. At the same time, tests must be limited to those that are both relevant to the referral question and empirically supported for the application at hand (Heilbrun, 1992).

A second suggested guideline is to anticipate and assess unusual response styles. In voluntary clinical settings, self-descriptions are colored by various motives, but in the broadest sense, the clinician presumes that the patient's self-descriptions are reasonably balanced and accurate. In forensic situations, and in delinquent evaluations, the presumption is quite different. Because of engrained interpersonal tendencies and obvious secondary gains, a distorted response set can drastically affect data that are collected throughout interviews and testing. This presumption has two specific corollaries. First, interview data should be corroborated by outside accounts, behavioral observations, and testing results. Second, whenever possible, the test battery should be composed of instruments that include validity scales to help objectively assess the patient's degree of dissimulation. In the absence of validity scales, tests must be interpreted conservatively, especially when there is behavioral evidence of response distortion or when test results appear highly implausible in relation to outside data.

For adults, several instruments have been developed for the specific purpose of assessing forms of deception, particularly malingering. Unfortunately, no such instruments have yet been developed specifically for younger populations, and little validation research has been conducted to show that adult instruments can be applied to adolescent populations. Some authors (e.g., McCann, 1998b) suggest that well-validated adult malingering tools (e.g., the Structured Interview of Reported Symptoms; Rogers, Bagby, & Dickens, 1992) can be cautiously applied to adolescents. In reality, clinicians more often rely on traditional instruments that have been validated with younger populations, using those tests' validity scales to assess response styles.

A third guideline for these cases is to employ rigorous empirical standards for method selection. Although true for all clinical settings, this concern is magnified in forensic cases and in work with delinquent youth. Among other reasons, evaluations in these cases are likely to have greater ramifications than in other settings. Also, evaluators are more likely to face close scrutiny in the courtroom. As discussed elsewhere (see, e.g., Heilbrun, Marczyk, & DeMatteo, 2002, for an overview of key issues), clinicians must select only those assessment methods that are empirically supported, both in general and for the specific application at hand. In court-involved cases, the assessor must possess an updated working knowledge of her tests' psychometric properties and important current literature. She must also be aware of applicable legal standards for admissibility, in order to help ensure that she is not using tests or other methods that could be excluded from the court's consideration.

In this regard, the test that has by far been subjected to the most detailed and heated debate has been the Rorschach (Rorschach, 1921; Exner, 2002), so a few brief points about this instrument deserve mention here. First, several separate authors have offered cogent arguments to show that the Rorschach should be deemed admissible, using the *Daubert* standard and other tests of admissibility (Gacono, Evans, & Viglione, 2002; Hilsenroth & Stricker, 2004; McCann, 1998a; Ritzler, Erard, & Pettigrew, 2000a, 2000b), whereas others have reached the opposite conclusion (Grove & Barden, 1999; Grove, Barden, Garb, & Lilienfeld, 2002). Second, traditionally, Rorschach evidence has rarely been subject to serious legal challenges or excluded from testimony (Meloy, Hansen, & Weiner, 1997; Weiner, Exner, & Sciara, 1996). More recently, this finding has found at least preliminary post-*Daubert* replication (Owens, Patrick, Packman, & Greene, 2004). At present, professionals who use the Rorschach appropriately should be able to draw on its findings in court-involved cases, although they should also expect more frequent and sophisticated challenges than they faced a decade ago.

As one final guideline, when these cases are in fact court-involved, the reader should keep in mind the many practical considerations that impinge upon preferred practice. As one example, clinicians should be cognizant of the tremendous caseloads and burdens that weigh on juvenile courts. As a concrete illustration, to expedite huge numbers of cases, it is not unusual for juvenile court judges to demand that evaluation be completed and reports submitted within one week of referral (National Council of Juvenile & Family Court Judges, 2005). Anecdotally, it seems that one of the greatest adjustment difficulties experienced by many clinical psychologists who venture into court work is related to this demand for rapid turnaround time, after having grown accustomed to the more liberal time constraints that are afforded in most other settings.

Along the same lines, Grisso and Underwood (2004) offered several guidelines to help address the practical needs of delinquent populations. These include anticipating low reading levels for the typical examinee and selecting tests with appropriately low reading levels; choosing tests that are empirically supported for application to clients with diverse ethnic, cultural, or linguistic backgrounds; and, when possible, using tests that have been specifically validated within juvenile justice populations.

SPECIFIC ASSESSMENT METHODS

Collecting the Behavioral History: Interviews and Collateral Input

In delinquency cases, the cornerstone of assessment is the collection of a detailed, informative behavioral history. In cases where referral questions are elementary, this sort of data collection may be sufficient, without the addition of psychological testing. Even in cases where issues are more complex and numerous methods are employed, the behavioral history remains key. This is true for several reasons, including the fact that much of the available longitudinal research identifies certain behavioral variables as being most strongly predictive of negative short- and long-term outcomes. Specific historical data crucial in these cases include, to name a few:

- Early/preadolescent onset (of CD symptoms, of delinquent activity, of violence)
- Callous, malicious, or purposefully destructive behavior (e.g., cruelty to animals and/or people, intentionally destructive fire setting)
- Recurrent pattern of delinquency, which is especially telling if the youth has been subjected to serious deterrents but then has persisted in the same behaviors
- Wide variety or versatility of delinquent behavior (versus a more circumscribed behavior problem)
- Instances of instrumental delinquency or violence (e.g., assault in the context of armed robbery), versus only reactive incidents (e.g., provoked assault)
- Substance abuse and/or dependence

These data points are most relevant to risk assessment but also help more generally in the understanding of the nature and progression of the youth's conduct problems. Every effort must be made to collect behavioral data from multiple credible sources, including not only the examinee and caregivers, but also involved professionals or professional records.

Although not as numerous as in adult clinical work, structured and semistructured interviews are available for use with delinquent populations. One example is the semistructured interview guide that is available as an adjunct to the Psychopathy Checklist: Youth Version (PCL:YV; Forth, Kosson, & Hare, 2003; discussed later here). Despite the advantages of these systems of inquiry, most evaluators employ an individualized semistructured interview format that takes into account the wide-ranging needs of various evaluations with this population.

Traditional Personality Testing

Psychological testing data can play an important role in elucidating findings that are available through more direct means; corroborating or refuting statements made by the examinee or others; and generating important hypotheses that might otherwise be overlooked based on interviews alone. Already mentioned but worth reiterating, a comprehensive evaluation takes into consideration a wide variety of factors, including not only features of the individual but also aspects of his family, community, and broader environment. In some cases, the behavioral history and environmental factors are of critical importance, but testing can shed light on individual factors that speak to risk, guide case conceptualization, and inform treatment decisions. Testing in these cases involves a search for individual variables that bear on risk for delinquency, such as various traits associated with psychopathic personality, impulsivity, presence of comorbid internalizing symptoms and other psychiatric conditions, aspects of the self image and object relations that feed into confrontational interactions, and so on.

Self-report measures, especially the Minnesota Multiphasic Personality Inventory–Adolescent (MMPI–A; Butcher et al., 1992), are the most widely used to assess adolescents (Archer & Newsome, 2000). Broad-band instruments such as the MMPI–A and the Millon Adolescent Clinical Inventory (MACI; Millon, 1993) hold an important place in the delinquent test battery, for at least two reasons. First, they provide in-depth descriptions of personality and overall functioning that contribute to assessment of those features that are tied to risk and planning. Second, most of these multiscale instruments include validity scales that are invaluable for reasons already noted. Even in cases where clinical findings appear to be unremarkable, validity scale profiles can shed light on the examinee's test-taking approach, in turn supporting or refuting impressions of his overall veracity during the evaluation.

Of all broad-band self-report instruments, the MMPI–A has been subjected to the most empirical attention by far, followed by the MACI. Although neither test was originally normed on delinquent populations, both have garnered a large amount of research to identify common elevations and their correlates within this population. The descriptive findings yielded by these tests can aid diagnosis and can identify specific traits that are strengths or areas of concern.

Despite their strengths, these instruments also pose challenges for this population. Reading levels can be prohibitive, and even if options are available to bypass reading deficits (e.g., audiotaped administration), test length still taxes many delinquent youths' attentional capabilities. There are other problems—for example, the undesirably high rate of within-normal-limits MMPI–A profiles within delinquent and other clinical adolescent samples (Archer, Handel, & Lynch, 2001). Moreover, when elevations are present, descriptions may be unhelpfully over-inclusive, unless other scales are available to help refine the findings, as in the case of Adam:

> When Adam, age 14, completed the MMPI–A, his most pronounced elevation was on Scale 4, or
> Pd. The most common basic scale elevation among delinquent samples (and most other adolescent

groups), high Scale 4 yields a wide variety of potential inferences. Some reflect observable behaviors (e.g., high probability of delinquent, externalizing, and/or aggressive behaviors), while some are tied to associated personality traits (e.g., relative absence of guilt and remorse). A cursory scanning of Scale 4 correlates does not help us to decide which of these features apply to Adam. In this case, inspection of the Harris-Lingoes subscales for Scale 4 revealed that much of the basic scale elevation was accounted for by two of its five subscales: Family Problems and Self-Alienation. Collectively, these elevations suggested a great deal of interpersonal conflict and dissatisfaction at home, as well as more generalized unhappiness and negatively-tinged affect. A potential error in this case would be to infer core antisocial attitudes and traits based on an elevated Scale 4, when in fact Adam's actual pattern of responses suggested acting-out primarily in the context of emotional distress and familial conflict.

Brief, symptom-focused self-report measures can play a complementary role in the delinquent battery, especially when specific problem areas are of interest. In the case of the adolescent who describes severe adjustment problems and apparent depressive symptoms in reaction to being arrested and held in detention, tools such as the Beck Depression Inventory (BDI–II; Beck, Steer, & Brown, 1996) can not only help pinpoint specific symptoms but also provide a nomothetic frame of reference for assessing the overall level of symptom severity. Unfortunately, because of most of these measures' transparency and lack of validity scales, they must be interpreted conservatively. These results must be viewed as reflecting the examinee's *self-reported* experiences, which may be distorted by secondary gains. Even when we appreciate this point and interpret cautiously, there is the risk of failing to convey the same cautions to nonpsychologists who receive our results. Counselors, judges, and others run the risk of inferring that these test scores are direct reflections of psychological functioning, so the evaluator must be explicit in describing findings as being reflections of the examinee's self-presentation.

A second broad category of applicable tests is caregiver rating scales. Varying in length and specificity, these instruments are typically multiscale, broad-band tools but may be focused on one or more specific domains of functioning. These instruments allow many of the benefits of self-report measures, but also allow for much-needed input from outside sources. Arguably the most useful feature of these instruments, when available, is the opportunity for cross-informant comparisons. Administering the same instrument to both parents and discovering striking discrepancies can be informative as to the parents' differing perceptions of their child. In fact, in the context of feedback in these cases, comparing profiles can be a concrete, eye-opening experience for parents, who may not have realized how widely divergent their views are. In many cases, parallel forms are also available for the youth himself and for other involved parties (e.g., teachers). Again, cross-informant comparison is potentially useful in these cases, especially when the child's self-report can be compared directly with those of an outside party.

Probably the most widely recognized instrument in this category is the Child Behavior Checklist (CBCL; Achenbach & Rescorla, 2001) and its parallel forms, the Youth Self-Report (YSR) and Teacher's Report Form (TRF). This family of instruments illustrates many of the key strengths and drawbacks that are seen with other caregiver rating systems. The CBCL is conceptually useful and immediately understandable, as it taps into general categories of internalizing and externalizing behavior problems, while also assessing numerous specific subcategories. CBCL items were selected with an effort to correspond closely to items on the YSR and TRF, which facilitates cross-informant comparisons. On the negative side, this instrument (and many others like it) lacks validity scales or any systemic means for detecting unusual response sets. Because these scales are typically fairly face valid, they are susceptible to intentional distortion of results, similar to concerns noted above for brief self-report measures (see the chapter by Achenbach in this volume).

A third broad category of tests for consideration in delinquent cases is performance-based techniques, such as the Rorschach, storytelling tasks, and projective figure drawings. These tools provide for indirect means of data collection that can complement more direct measures described above. Because these methods do not rely on a pencil-and-paper format, reading delays and other deficits are not direct threats to validity. Moreover, given delinquent youths' proclivity for defensiveness and distortion, it is ideal to include varying testing formats. In cases where children are verbally limited or simply resistant to traditional methods, performance-based tasks sometimes afford freedoms that allow for more open expression of their internal experiences. Having said this, psychologists sometimes need to disabuse referral sources of the erroneous notion that these tests have unique powers to elicit "the truth" from otherwise reticent clients. Just as he is able to sabotage the interview and invalidate self-report measures, the resistant client is able to approach projective methods in such an underproductive manner that he essentially prevents detailed, accurate interpretation.

Of these instruments, the Rorschach stands out as the method with the most widely used systematic approach to administration, scoring, and interpretation (Exner, 2005). The Rorschach's nomothetic approach and its extensive research base make it a suitable option when test selection standards are rigorous, including in court-involved contexts (see above). The Rorschach has been applied extensively to various antisocial populations (see Gacono & Meloy, 1994, for the best source). However, efforts to identify variables associated with CD or juvenile psychopathy have been promising but not consistently replicated. Rorschach findings can potentially yield rich individualized descriptions of the youth's personality characteristics, but they must be interpreted conservatively and in conjunction with data from other sources.

> Ben, a 9-year-old with early-onset conduct problems, completed the Rorschach as part of an evaluation to guide treatment. The Rorschach provided detailed hypotheses about Ben's internal experiences, including his sense of self and his perception of social interactions. As an example, his Mediation cluster scores (e.g., very low X+ and Pop, high Xu and X−) suggested that he misperceives incoming information much of the time. Considered alongside Ben's pervasive aggressive imagery (elevated AG, plus striking aggressive content in several responses), his proneness to distorting input from the world around him could be understood in terms of a hostile attribution bias, where neutral actions are perceived as implying malicious intent. With this idea in mind, his therapist was able to help Ben's parents to build empathy for his perception that the world is filled with hostility and potential threats, making them better able to understand why he was so quick to respond to the slightest gestures with self-protective aggression. They were also helped to appreciate the need for concrete, unambiguous communication as one strategy for reducing Ben's aggression at home.

Along the same lines, traditional projective methods can offer supportable hypotheses with regard to self-perception, perception of social interactions, and other areas of functioning. Empirically driven scoring and interpretation systems are available for some of these instruments, and case examples are available to illustrate the effective blending of formalized scoring systems with rich, idiographic interpretation (see, e.g., Porcerelli, Abramsky, Hibbard, & Kamoo, 2001, for applications of the TAT). However, in routine practice, most evaluators find formalized scoring systems to be overly cumbersome and instead rely on less systematic procedures. Given their potential for misapplication, it has been argued convincingly that projectives on the whole should not be deemed admissible under commonly used legal standards (e.g., Lally, 2001, in relation to the human figure drawings). It is reasonable to conclude that, with the exception of the Rorschach, projectives would be most useful in purely clinical contexts, where detailed descriptions can be offered to further the treatment and integrated with convergent sources of data without running the risk of misuse in high-stakes psycho-legal contexts. In the case of Ben, above, for instance, TAT stories included a jarring amount of extreme and arbitrary violence, which dovetailed with findings from the Rorschach to help understand his perceptions of the world as a hostile, unpredictably threatening place.

Specialized Test Instruments

Traditional assessment methods may be supplemented by more contemporary, specialized instruments that have been developed for specific application to delinquent populations. A handful of such tests are currently available, with varying degrees of empirical support to date. These tests could be broadly categorized into three types: Broad-band or multiscale inventories developed specifically for delinquent populations, risk assessment guides, and tests of psychopathy or antisocial personality. A selection of the most widely available and most promising instruments is outlined next.

The Massachusetts Youth Screening Instrument (MAYSI–2; Grisso & Barnum, 2001) is a 52-item self-report measure intended to screen for a variety of psychiatric difficulties commonly encountered in juvenile justice populations. Not surprising, given its brief format, is the fact that the MAYSI–2 does not include validity scales. It is not intended as a substitute for comprehensive assessment, but it is suitable for use by mental health professionals and allied staff, for example, to assist with screening youths at the time of intake to juvenile facilities. Seven scales tap into the following domains: alcohol/drug use, anger/irritability, depression/anxiety, somatic complaints, suicidal ideation, thought disturbance, and traumatic experiences. Despite being developed fairly recently, the MAYSI–2 has amassed empirical support for its factor structure, reliability, and validity (see, e.g., Archer, Stredny, Mason, & Arnau, 2004). It is currently available for use by mental health professionals and juvenile justice professionals.

Another multiscale test for use specifically with delinquent samples is the Jesness Inventory (JI–R; Jesness, 2003). Initially developed in 1965 but updated more recently, the JI–R is a 160-item self-report test intended to provide broad-band personality descriptions that can be applied to classifying and managing juvenile offenders. It has been normed on both the general adolescent population and delinquents (half male and half female). It includes rudimentary validity scales designed to detect underreporting and random responding. The JI–R is composed of numerous clinical scales, covering areas such as immaturity, social anxiety, manifest aggression, and several others. The instrument has been criticized on certain grounds, most notably some limitations of the standardization samples, which probably limit generalizability of findings (e.g., delinquent sample predominantly African American but nondelinquent sample overwhelmingly Caucasian; delinquent sample collected mostly from one site). On the other hand, strengths include the recent inclusion of scales designed to aid in the diagnosis of CD and ODD (Rhoades, 2005; Yetter, 2005).

Juvenile risk assessment is a topic that remains in its empirical infancy. To date, a small number of instruments have been developed for the purposes of drawing from that small but growing literature, in order to guide risk assessment in juvenile justice cases. One such instrument is the Youth Level of Service/Case Management Inventory (YLS/CMI; Hoge & Andrews,

1999). This is a guided risk assessment protocol that is clinician-rated, based on the juvenile's known history and characteristics. It consists of 42 items, falling into eight categories, such as offense characteristics, family circumstances, peer relations, and substance abuse. Drawing from the major risk factors identified in the literature, the YLS/CMI assists the rater in reaching global conclusions about the examinee's level of re-offense risk. It is a straightforward, conceptually useful instrument that essentially serves as an *aide-mémoire* for systematically considering major risk factors. However, it does not possess (or claim to possess) adequate empirical support for use as a precise predictor or measure of re-offense risk. Its authors clearly describe the YLS/CMI as a tool to be used to guide risk assessment decisions.

Not unlike the YLS/CMI, the Structured Assessment of Violence Risk in Youth (SAVRY; Borum, Bartel, & Forth, 2002) is a guided risk assessment protocol, completed by the clinician after the collection of relevant information from interview and collateral sources. Its format is borrowed from comparable adult tools, such as the HCR–20 (Webster, Douglas, Eaves, & Hart, 1997). Unlike the YLS/CMI, the SAVRY draws from the literature specific to violence risk, rather than re-arrest risk. It is composed of 24 items, each representing an empirically supported risk factor associated with youth violence, and these items are grouped under the general rubric of historical, social/contextual, and individual factors. Six protective factors are also scored.

SAVRY research is under way but still relatively limited. At present, it is most prudent to use the SAVRY to identify specific risk factors to be targeted and protective factors to be capitalized upon, but not to draw firm or precise conclusions as to level of risk. It appears to be a useful aide to case conceptualization but is likely to undergo adjustments to items before it becomes more widely available and used.

Finally, a great deal of attention has been directed toward assessing psychopathy in youth, as an extension of the voluminous literature base that has accumulated with adult psychopathy and the PCL–R (Hare, 1991, 2003). A small number of instruments have been developed to assess antisocial and/or psychopathic features in youth (see, e.g., Frick & Hare, 2001). The tool that has been subject to the most attention by far has been an adolescent adaptation of the PCL–R: The Psychopathy Checklist: Youth Version (PCL:YV; Forth, Kosson, & Hare, 2003). This clinician rating scale consists of 20 items, each associated with behavioral, affective, and interpersonal features that are conceptually and empirically associated with the prototypical psychopathic personality. PCL:YV scoring is predicated upon a lengthy semi-structured interview and collateral record review. The "checklist" itself appears deceptively simple to use, but its authors urge caution about participating in formal training and practice in order to appreciate the specific scoring criteria for each item. This issue raises the potential for abuse of the PCL:YV, which mirrors concerns that have been discussed extensively with the adult version of the instrument (e.g., Gacono & Hutton, 1994).

Though only recently published for clinical and forensic purposes, the PCL:YV has undergone extensive empirical study and has been shown to demonstrate excellent psychometric properties. As with its adult counterpart, high PCL:YV scores have been associated with violence, recidivism, and other negative outcomes. However, longer-term predictive studies are not yet completed, so a major point of contention centers on the question of whether high scores on the PCL:YV predict adult psychopathy, criminality, and violence. At present, the most prudent approach is to use the instrument to assist with shorter-term decision-making, but to withhold conclusions that have a long-term impact on juveniles' sentences and other matters.

In fact, the central issues of identifying and labeling psychopathy in youth have been the focus of vigorous debate, before and since the release of the PCL:YV. For an excellent treatment from various points of view, see the journal series that includes Frick (2002); Hart, Watt, & Vincent (2002); Lynam (2002); and Seagrave & Grisso (2002); see also Edens, Skeem, Cruise, & Cauffman (2001). Despite its potential benefits, the PCL:YV carries with it a great potential for misapplication and misunderstanding. Even more so than with any of the other newly developed instruments, users of the PCL:YV will need to be familiar with conceptual and practical issues surrounding its use.

CASE ILLUSTRATION: MICHAEL

Michael Jones (name and all identifying data disguised) is a 16-year-old African American male who was referred for a psychological evaluation by his juvenile probation officer. Michael had recently been arrested in connection with an armed robbery. He and three male acquaintances were accused of ordering a pizza to be delivered to an unoccupied address and, upon his arrival, taking the deliveryman's cash (and the pizza) at gunpoint. All four teens were arrested a short time later, and Michael was soon released to his mother on bail. As of this evaluation, his case was still open in juvenile court. He admitted his involvement in the robbery, but by all accounts his role was merely to serve as lookout. The evaluation was requested to help gain a better understanding of Michael's treatment needs, including whether he was appropriate for placement in a residential facility.

This was Michael's third arrest. He incurred his first two arrests at ages 14 and 15, both times for assault in connection to fights with peers. It is worth noting that both fights took place in large social contexts. The first arrest occurred after Michael recruited a group of peers to retaliate against several boys after they "jumped' his younger cousin. Charges were ultimately dismissed. The second involved a large melee that broke out on school grounds. Several peers were involved, but only Michael was arrested, as he had severely injured another student. He was remanded to probation, but within three months he was arrested for the robbery incident.

Michael is the only child of long-separated parents. He has always been in the care of his mother, and they have always remained in the same high-risk urban neighborhood (marked by high rates of crime, drug use and sales, poverty, and other risk factors). His father has been uninvolved, and there have been no other male figures in his home. Michael and his mother both report a strong, positive relationship but acknowledge that it has been increasingly strained over the past two years, mainly because of his worsening behavior.

Ms. Jones reports that her son was always an active, energetic, exhausting child. She feels he has always been sweet and kind, but he has also been overly sensitive to any perceived slights or threats. As early as preschool, he sporadically fought with other boys, and in his mother's view, this was always after he felt provoked by some comment or gesture. In elementary school, his conduct and performance varied widely. Ms. Jones has always worked very long hours, and when Michael was young, he was usually watched by various relatives. By age 12, he was alone for much of his free time, and it was at this age that he began to gravitate toward delinquent peers. Ms. Jones reported being concerned about his friends and activities since then, but she has felt very little control, because of both her work schedule and her sense of guilt over being so often absent. Also of concern to her is her son's marijuana use. He reports smoking almost daily with friends, although there is no evidence of use of any other substances.

Michael's mental health treatment history has been limited, consisting of one failed attempt at conjoint individual and family therapy. Treatment was prompted by probation and was intended to help Michael manage his anger more effectively and to make better social decisions, as well as to help his mother manage his behavior. Mother and son attended a small number of sessions but then failed to comply, citing scheduling problems.

Assessment in this case included input from four main sources: interviews with Michael and his mother; review of probation records (which were fairly detailed in this case); and psychological testing. As is often the case, Michael had been involved with multiple professionals through probation and mental health, but because of his noncompliance and staff turnover, none of those individuals knew him well enough to provide any detailed impressions.

The behavioral history, arguably the most important source of data in cases like this, was notable in many ways. As one example, Michael displayed lifelong temperamental factors that predisposed him to active behavior and sensation-seeking. He did not meet specific criteria for ADHD, but he did experience chronic, subdiagnosis levels of impulsivity that made it difficult for him or his mother to manage his behavior consistently. These problems were magnified by his mother's inability to provide much consistent adult oversight or household structure. In many ways, Michael was undersocialized and was left to learn the basics of self-discipline and emotional regulation on his own. Second, descriptions from all sources provided strong evidence for attachment capacity, even though Michael's most important relationships were strained. As a preadolescent, he would have met criteria for ODD, although most hallmark symptoms of CD were absent. Third, Michael's behavior began deteriorating at age 12, in relation with his new peer contacts and escalating marijuana use. The history portrays Michael as an adolescent-onset conduct-disordered youth, with some positive prognostic indicators, even despite the seriousness of his behaviors and significant risk for re-arrest.

Test results are summarized in the Appendix. Some selected findings are discussed here, organized for our purposes in a test-by-test manner. The Achenbach scales were completed by Michael and his mother, not only to provide a screening of major behavioral and emotional problem areas, but also to allow for a comparison of their respective views of his presenting problems. Both mother and son acknowledged significant difficulties in terms of externalizing behaviors, although Michael endorsed more symptoms and higher levels of difficulty in nearly all areas. More striking is their pattern of discrepancies on the internalizing scales. A working hypothesis at this point is that he experiences internalizing symptoms that are discomforting for him, but that his mother fails to recognize. If borne out, this finding would be important not only to bring to Ms. Jones's attention but also to share with professionals, who would also be at risk of overlooking important emotional difficulties while they focus on his overt conduct problems.

MMPI–A results add further evidence for undetected emotional discomfort. Michael approached the testing in a fairly open and candid manner, and I was able to point to the MMPI–A's validity scale findings (as well as elevations on scales that acknowledge problems with family, school, and substance use) to support this same impression from the interview. MMPI–A results included pronounced elevations on scales 4 and 9, as is very commonly seen with this population. However, as with the case of Adam above, a closer inspection of subscales helped to individualize these findings. For instance, Michael acknowledged a significant amount of family conflict and problems with authority, but there was little evidence for the emotional toughness or insensitivity that characterize some of his more antisocial peers. Also notable are his scale elevations tied to depression and emotional discomfort. We might expect Michael to vacillate between instances of acting out and periods of regret and self-deprecation. Coupled with the behavioral history, a portrait begins to emerge of a youth who recognizes his actions have painful consequences, but who is too impulsive and short-sighted to change his patterns without help.

The Rorschach in this case adds more support for hypotheses related to underlying depression-like symptoms and emotional control problems. Although content (not included here) was simplistic, bland, and unremarkable, structural scores suggest a great deal of emotional discomfort and confusion. Also suggested are long-standing, serious social coping difficulties. Michael appears to lack basic socialization skills and is prone to become passive in situations when he would be better served by asserting himself. Rorschach findings point to the need for basic social skills and assertiveness training, in addition to therapeutic interventions to address emotional difficulties that may be unseen. This echoes findings from the YSR and MMPI–A.

In this case, ample records and interview time made use of the PCL:YV possible. At its most global level, this instrument revealed an overall severity of psychopathy features that is normative for other juveniles on probation. Inspecting Michael's scores on the PCL:YV's subscales was more informative. Although he does have a notable history of irresponsible, even parasitic life-style features, as well as a concerning history of aggression and antisocial conduct, what is relatively absent is evidence for strong interpersonal and affective traits that underlie the psychopathic character. Like many conduct-disordered youth, Michael is certainly at risk for progressing to more pervasive patterns of antisociality, but at this point, he still displays attachment capacity and affective accessibility that can be capitalized upon in treatment efforts.

The YLS/CMI points out several features unique to Michael and his environment that place him at a roughly moderate overall risk for re-arrest at the time of evaluation. This instrument, as a way of formalizing and organizing the behavioral history and interview data, helps to identify several domains in need of intervention in order to mitigate Michael's risk.

Recommendations for Michael were guided in large part by a knowledge of what had been attempted (successfully or not) in the past, and what is currently available within his jurisdiction. In this case, a reputable and fairly effective treatment program was available to provide multisystemic treatment for Michael and his mother, offering intensive home-based and community-based professional supports. Individual therapy was also recommended to help Michael recognize his emotional difficulties, to see how they might feed into his problematic conduct, and to get his needs met without resorting to acting out. Without this assessment, and in a jurisdiction with different resources, Michael might have been viewed as a poor candidate for treatment. In reality, the evaluation identified numerous strengths that could be capitalized upon, while also making clear that Michael continued to pose a significant risk for re-offense if certain factors were not addressed with professional interventions.

CONCLUSIONS AND FUTURE DIRECTIONS

Although there is an extensive literature on delinquency, antisociality, and their assessment, several areas remain in need of development. As one pressing example, female delinquency is currently receiving increasing attention but continues to be understudied. It is unclear to what degree our male models of violence and delinquency actually generalize to females and in what ways we should conceptualize girls differently. Furthermore, the subfield of juvenile risk assessment (with respect to violence, recidivism, and other specific outcomes) is still emerging. This will evolve into a fuller appreciation for the multitude of risk factors and protective factors that interplay at various levels.

As for testing instruments, attention is likely to be focused on developing and refining specialized tools, including those outlined in this chapter. As the field's model for risk assessment grows more precise, so will related assessment methods. Today, these tools are essentially loose frameworks for guiding interviewing and case conceptualization, but in the coming years, these will undoubtedly be supplanted by more precise efforts to quantify and classify levels of risk.

In the meantime, evaluators have access to a large arsenal or assessment methods, each with particular strengths and shortcomings, which should complement each other as part of a well-integrated, multimethod approach to assessing these challenging youth.

APPENDIX

Selected Test Data for Michael

Achenbach Scales (T scores and percentiles)

	CBCL	YSR
Anxious/depressed	50 (≤50%)	65 (93%)
Withdrawn/depressed	50 (≤50%)	54 (65%)
Somatic complaints	50 (≤50%)	51 (54%)
Social problems	50 (≤50%)	50 (≤50%)
Thought problems	66 (95%)	62 (89%)
Attention problems	52 (58%)	57 (76%)
Rule-breaking behavior	64 (92%)	68 (97%)
Aggressive behavior	54 (65%)	75 (>97%)
Internalizing problems	34 (6%)	59 (81%)
Externalizing problems	59 (81%)	73 (>98%)
Total problems	52 (58%)	66 (95%)

MMPI–A (T scores)

Selected validity scales		Basic scales				Selected supplementary scales	
VRIN	51	1/Hs	54	6/Pa	60	MAC-R	61
TRIN	57F	2/D	69	7/Pt	58	ACK	67
F	49	3/Hy	56	8/Sc	64	PRO	66
L	62	4/Pd	75	9/Ma	68		
K	59	5/Mf	37	0/Si	42		

Harris-Lingoes subscales for elevated basic scales

D1/Subjective depression	65	Pd1/Familial discord	68	Ma1/Amorality	58
D2/Psychomotor retardation	35	Pd2/Authority problems	73	Ma2/Psychomotor acceleration	66
D3/Physical malfunctioning	41	Pd3/Social imperturbability	42	Ma3/Imperturbability	49
D4/Mental dullness	72	Pd4/Social alienation	46	Ma4/Ego inflation	53
D5/Brooding	51	Pd5/Self-alienation	53		

Selected content scales

A-dep	57	A-fam	64
A-ang	54	A-sch	65
A-cyn	59	A-trt	57
A-con	58		

Rorschach (selected raw scores)

Validity		Constellations			
R	17	PTI	0	S-CON	7
Lambda	1.13	DEPI	5(+)	HVI	No
		CDI	4(+)	OBS	No

Controls				Affect	
EB	1 : 4	FM	4	FC : CF + C3	0:3
EA	5.0	m	0	Pure C	2
eb	4 : 2	SumC'	2	Afr	0.42
es and Adj es	6	SumV	0	S	1
D and Adj D	0	SumT	0	Blends : R	3 : 17
		SumY	0		

Interpersonal perceptions				Self perception	
COP	0	SumT	0	Egocentricity Index	0.24
AG	0	Pure H	0	Fr + rF	0
GHR : PHR	2 : 0	PER	0	SumV	0
a : p	2 : 3	Isolate Index	0.12	FD	1
Food	0			An + Xy	0
				MOR	0

Processing		Mediation		Ideation	
Zf	10	XA%	0.82	a : p	2 : 3
W : D : Dd	10:6:1	WDA%	0.81	Ma : Mp	0 : 1
W : M	10:1	X−%	0.00	Intell. Index	4
Zd	−4.0	P	6	MOR	0
PSV	1	X+%	0.53	WSum6	6
		Xu%	0.29	M- and Mnone	0

PCL:YV: (T scores and percentiles, vs. male probationers)

Total Score = 20	46 (49%)
Factor 1/Interpersonal	14 (36%)
Factor 2/Affective	36 (44%)
Factor 3/Lifestyle	84 (58%)
Factor 4/Antisocial	78 (56%)

YLS/CMI (risk levels)

Overall total risk level	Moderate
Prior and current offenses/dispositions	Moderate
Family circumstances/parenting	Moderate
Education/employment	Moderate
Peer relations	High
Substance abuse	High
Leisure/recreation	High
Personality/behavior	Moderate
Attitudes/orientation	Moderate

REFERENCES

Achenbach, T., & Rescorla, L. (2001). *Manual for the ASEBA school-age forms and profiles.* Burlington, VT: University of Vermont, Research Center for Children, Youth, and Families.

American Academy of Child and Adolescent Psychiatry. (1997). Practice parameters for the assessment and treatment of children and adolescents with conduct disorder. *Journal of the American Academy of Child and Adolescent Psychiatry, 36*(10), 122S–139S.

American Academy of Child and Adolescent Psychiatry. (2005). Practice parameters for the assessment and treatment of youth in juvenile detention and correctional facilities. *Journal of the American Academy of Child and Adolescent Psychiatry, 44*(10), 1085–1098.

American Psychiatric Association (2000). *Diagnostic and statistical manual of mental disorders* (4th ed., text revision). Washington, DC: American Psychiatric Association.

Archer, R., Handel, R., & Lynch, K. (2001). The effectiveness of MMPI-A items in discriminating between normative and clinical samples. *Journal of Personality Assessment, 77*(3), 420–435.

Archer, R., & Newsom, C. (2000). Psychological test usage with adolescent clients: Survey update. *Assessment, 7,* 227–235.

Archer, R., Stredny, R., Mason, J., & Arnau, R. (2004). An examination and replication of the psychometric properties of the Massachusetts Youth Screening Instrument–Second Edition (MAYSI–2) among adolescents in detention settings. *Assessment, 11*(4), 290–302.

Beck, A., Steer, R., & Brown, G. (1996). *Beck Depression Inventory manual: Second edition.* Boston: Harcourt-Brace.

Borum, R., Bartel, P., & Forth, A. (2002). *Manual for the Structured Assessment of Violence Risk in Youth (SAVRY).* Tampa, FL: University of South Florida.

Butcher, J., Williams, C., Graham, J., Archer, R., Tellegen, A., Ben-Porath, Y., & Kaemmer, B. (1992). *MMPI-A manual for administration, scoring, and interpretation.* Minneapolis, MN: University of Minnesota Press.

Cleckley, H. (1976). *The mask of sanity* (5th ed.). St. Louis, MO: Mosby.

Edens, J., Skeem, J., Cruise, K., & Cauffman, E. (2001). Assessment of "juvenile psychopathy" and its association with violence: A critical review. *Behavioral Sciences and the Law, 19,* 53–80.

Exner, J. (2003). *The Rorschach: A comprehensive system: Vol. 1. Basic foundations and principles of interpretation* (4th ed.). New York: Wiley.

Forth, A. (1995). *Psychopathy and young offenders: Prevalence, family background, and violence.* Ottawa: Ministry of the Solicitor General of Canada.

Forth, A., Kosson, D., & Hare, R. (2003). *Hare Psychopathy Checklist: Youth Version (PCL:YV). Technical manual.* Toronto: Multi-Health Systems.

Frick, P. (2002). Juvenile psychopathy from a developmental perspective: Implications for construct development and use in forensic assessments. *Law and Human Behavior, 26*(2), 247–254.

Frick, P., & Hare, R. (2001). *The Antisocial Process Screening Device.* Toronto: Multi-Health Systems.

Gacono, C., Evans, B., & Viglione, D. (2002). The Rorschach in forensic practice. *Journal of Forensic Psychology Practice, 2*(3), 33–53.

Gacono, C., & Hutton, H. (1994). Suggestions for the clinical and forensic use of the Hare Psychopathy Checklist-Revised (PCL-R). *International Journal of Law and Psychiatry, 17*(3), 303–317.

Gacono, C., & Meloy, J. R. (1994). *The Rorschach assessment of aggressive and psychopathic personalities.* Hillsdale, NJ: Lawrence Erlbaum Associates.

Grisso, T. (1998). *Forensic evaluation of juveniles.* Sarasota, FL: Professional Resource Press.

Grisso, T., & Barnum, R. (2001). *The Massachusetts Youth Screening Instrument: Second Version (MAYSI–2).* Worcester, MA: University of Massachusetts Medical School.

Grisso, T., & Underwood, L. (2004). *Screening and assessing mental health and substance use disorders among youth in the juvenile justice system: A resource guide for practitioners.* Washington, DC: Office of Juvenile Justice and Delinquency Prevention, Office of Justice Programs.

Grove, W., & Barden, R. (1999). Protecting the integrity of the legal system: The admissibility of testimony from mental health experts under *Daubert/Kumho* analyses. *Psychology, Public Policy, and Law, 5*(1), 224–242.

Grove, W., Barden, R., Garb, H., & Lilienfeld, S. (2002). Failure of Rorschach-Comprehensive-System-based testimony to be admissible under the *Daubert-Joiner-Kumho* standard. *Psychology, Public Policy, & Law, 8*(2), 216–234.

Hare, R. (1991). *Hare Psychopathy Checklist–Revised manual.* Toronto: Multi-Health Systems.

Hare, R. (1993). *Without conscience: The disturbing world of psychopaths among us.* New York: Pocket Books.

Hare, R. (1996). Psychopathy and Antisocial Personality Disorder: A case of diagnostic confusion. *Psychiatric Times, 13*, 39–40.

Hare, R. (2003). *Hare Psychopathy Checklist–Revised manual* (2nd ed.). Toronto: Multi-Health Systems.

Hart, S., & Hare, R. (1997). Psychopathy: Assessment and association with criminal conduct. In D. Stoff, J. Breiling, & J. Maser (Eds.), *Handbook of antisocial behavior* (pp. 22–35). New York: Wiley.

Hart, S., Watt, K., & Vincent, G. (2002). Commentary on Seagrave and Grisso: Impressions of the state of the art. *Law and Human Behavior, 26*(2), 241–246.

Heilbrun, K. (1992). The role of psychological testing in forensic assessment. *Law and Human Behavior, 16*, 257–272.

Heilbrun, K. (2001). *Principles of forensic mental health assessment.* New York: Kluwer.

Heilbrun, K., Marczyk, G., & DeMatteo, D. (2002). Juvenile competence to stand trial. In K. Heilbrun, G. Marczyk, & D. DeMatteo (Eds.), *Forensic mental health assessments: A casebook.* New York: Oxford University Press.

Hilsenroth, M., & Stricker, G. (2004). A consideration of challenges to psychological assessment instruments used in forensic settings: Rorschach as exemplar. *Journal of Personality Assessment, 83*, 141–152.

Hoge, R., & Andrews, D. (1999). *The Youth Level of Service/Case Management Inventory user's manual.* Toronto: Multi-Health Systems.

Jesness, C. (2003). *The Jesness Inventory manual.* Toronto: Multi-Health Systems.

Lahey, B., Loeber, R., Quay, H., Frick, P., & Grimm, J. (1992). Oppositional defiant and conduct disorder: Issues to be resolved for DSM-IV. *Journal of the American Academy of Child and Adolescent Psychiatry, 31*, 539–546.

Lally, S. (2001). Should human figure drawings be admitted into court? *Journal of Personality Assessment, 76*(1), 135–149.

Loeber, R., Keenan, K., Lahey, B., Green, S., & Thomas, C. (1993). Evidence for developmentally based diagnoses of oppositional defiant disorder and conduct disorder. *Journal of Abnormal Child Psychology, 21*, 377–410.

Loving, J., & Gacono, C. (2002). Psychopathy in juveniles: Clinical and forensic applications. In N. Ribner (Ed.), *Handbook of juvenile forensic psychology* (pp. 292–317). San Francisco: Jossey-Bass.

Loving, J., & Russell, W. (2000). Selected Rorschach variables of psychopathic juvenile offenders. *Journal of Personality Assessment, 75*(1), 126–142.

Lynam, D. (1996). Early identification of chronic offenders: Who is the fledgling psychopath? *Psychological Bulletin, 120*, 209–234.

Lynam, D. (2002). Fledgling psychopathy: A view from personality theory. *Law and Human Behavior, 26*(2), 255–259.

McCann, J. (1998a). Defending the Rorschach in court: An analysis of admissibility using legal and professional standards. *Journal of Personality Assessment, 70*(1), 125–144.

McCann, J. (1998b). *Malingering and deception in adolescents: Assessing credibility in clinical and forensic settings.* Washington, DC: American Psychological Association.

Meloy, J. R. (1988). *The psychopathic mind: Origins, dynamics, and treatment.* Northvale, NJ: Aronson.

Meloy, J. R., Hansen, T., & Weiner, I. (1997). Authority of the Rorschach: Legal citations during the past 50 years. *Journal of Personality Assessment, 69*(1), 53–62.

Millon, T. (1993). *Millon Adolescent Clinical Inventory (MACI) manual.* Minneapolis, MN: NCS Assessments.

Moffitt, T. (1993). Adolescence-limited and life-course persistent antisocial behavior: A developmental taxonomy. *Psychological Review, 100*(4), 674–701.

National Council of Juvenile & Family Court Judges. (2005). Juvenile delinquency guidelines: Improving court practice in juvenile delinquency cases. Washington, DC: Office of Juvenile Justice and Delinquency Prevention, Office of Justice Programs.

Otto, R., Greenstein, J., Johnson, M., & Friedman, R. (1992). Prevalence of mental health disorders among youth in the juvenile justice system. In J. Cocozza (Ed.), *Responding to the mental health needs of youth in the juvenile justice system* (pp. 7–48). Seattle, WA: National Coalition for the Mentally Ill in the Criminal Justice System.

Owens, S., Patrick, K., Packman, W., & Greene, R. (2004). *Is the Rorschach still welcome in the courtroom?* Poster presented at the annual meeting of the Society for Personality Assessment, Miami, FL.

Porcerelli, J., Abramsky, M., Hibbard, S., & Kamoo, R. (2001). Object relations and defense mechanisms of a psychopathic serial sexual homicide perpetrator: A TAT analysis. *Journal of Personality Assessment, 77*(1), 87–104.

Pottick, K., Warner, L., Isaacs, M., Henderson, M., Milazzo-Sayre, L., & Manderscheid, R. (2002). Children and adolescents admitted to specialty mental health care programs in the United States, 1986 and 1997. In R. Mandersheid & M. Henderson (Eds.), *Mental health, United States.* Rockville, MD: U. S. Department of Health and Human Services.

Rhoades, E. (2005). Review of the Jesness Inventory-Revised. In Buros Institute of Mental Measurement: Test reviews online. Retrieved September 25, 2005, from http://buros.unl.edu/buros/jsp/lists.jsp

Ritzler, B., Erard, R., & Pettigrew, G. (2002a). A final reply to Grove and Barden: The relevance of the Rorschach Comprehensive System for expert testimony. *Psychology, Public Policy, and Law, 8*(2), 235–246.

Ritzler, B., Erard, R., & Pettigrew, G. (2002b). Protecting the integrity of the Rorschach expert witnesses: A reply to Grove and Barden (1999) regarding the admissibility of testimony under *Daubert/Kumho* analyses. *Psychology, Public Policy, and Law, 8*(2), 201–215.

Rogers, R. Bagby, R., & Dickens, S. (1992). *Structured Interview of Reported Symptoms (SIRS): Professional manual.* Odessa, FL: Psychological Assessment Resources.

Rorschach, H. (1921). *Psychodiagnostik.* Bern: Ernest Bircher.

Seagrave, D., & Grisso, T. (2002). Adolescent development and the measurement of juvenile psychopathy. *Law and Human Behavior, 26*(2), 219–240.

Teplin, L., Abram, K., McClelland, G., Dulcan, M., & Mericle, A. (2002). Psychiatric disorders in youth in juvenile detention. *Archives of General Psychiatry, 59*, 1133–1143.

Webster, C., Douglas, K., Eaves, & Hart, S. (1997). *The HCR–20 scheme: Assessing risk for violence, version 2.* Burnaby: Mental Health, Law, and Policy Institute, Simon Fraser University.

Weiner, I., Exner, J., & Sciara, A. (1996). Is the Rorschach welcome in the courtroom? *Journal of Personality Assessment, 67*(2), 422–424.

Yetter, G. (2005). Review of the Jesness Inventory-Revised. In Buros Institute of Mental Measurement: Test reviews online. Retrieved September 25, 2005, from http://buros.unl.edu/buros/jsp/lists.jsp

Zoccolillo, M. (1992). The co-occurrence of conduct disorder and its adult outcomes with depressive and anxiety disorders: A review. *Journal of the American Academy of Child and Adolescent Psychiatry, 31*, 547–556.

Zoccolillo, M., Pickles, A., Quinton, D., & Rutter, M. (1992). The outcome of childhood conduct disorder: Implications for defining adult personality disorder and conduct disorder. *Psychological Medicine, 22*(4), 971–986.

23

ASSESSMENT OF THINKING PROBLEMS
IN CHILDREN

John M. Stokes
Pace University & Four Winds Hospital

David L. Pogge
Four Winds Hospital

The assessment of thinking problems in children requires a clear conceptual definition of thinking disturbance. It then requires a careful understanding of the role developmental factors play in the manifestation of the thought processes covered under the term *thought disturbance*. Alternative methods of assessing thought disorder can then be reviewed in an effort to evaluate the advantages and disadvantages each presents. These can be evaluated both in principle, as a function of the nature of the phenomenon, and as they relate to the capabilities and characteristics of different age groups. In this chapter we attempt to examine each of these issues. We then attempt to present some descriptive data concerning psychometric manifestations of thinking disturbance in a sample of psychiatrically hospitalized children. Finally, we present a case example of a child for whom psychometrically measurable thinking disturbance was found to be a predictor of the eventual emergence of a more severe psychiatric disorder.

ISSUES DEFINING DISORDERED THINKING

Kleiger (1999) has comprehensively reviewed the problems that arise in the attempt to assess disordered thinking. These include the distinction between the more traditional notion of thought disorder and that of communication problems or discourse failures (Andreason, 1982; Harvey, 1983; Docherty, 2005); differentiating positive and negative manifestations of thought disorder (Andreason, 1982, 1984a, 1984b); and the implications of unifactorial versus multifactorial, or dichotomous versus continuous, models of thought disorder. Klieger (1999) observes that, despite the general agreement that disordered thinking exists along a continuum of severity, the dichotomizing and categorical term *thought disorder* continues to appear in both clinical discussion and scholarly writing.

Klieger notes that although it has been generally acknowledged that qualitatively different manifestations of disturbed thinking have been identified by almost every investigator who has studied thought disturbance, and some of these appear to have differential diagnostic or prognostic significance, as yet there is no consensus as to the types or kinds of disturbed thinking that exist. Many of the terms that are used for classifying and quantifying thought disturbance continue to be used differently by different authors. It appears that most authors include within their definitions of disordered thinking thought processes marked by illogical reasoning, connections among ideas that are difficult for the listener to follow, and the combination of ideas in ways that are unconventional, unrealistic, or bizarre. It appears that adequate thinking is defined, by implication, as thinking that is logically conventional and coherent, indicated by speech that moves from topic to topic in a manner that is not misleading or confusing to the audience, and is based on ideas that are drawn in an acceptable manner from the real world. To the extent that one's thinking lacks these characteristics, it is more likely to be seen as disordered.

Obviously, definitions of thought disorder that include these elements imply that the quality of one's thinking at any point in time can be thought of as falling along a continuum that ranges from unassailably logical, conceptually conventional, and clearly articulated thought to logically incoherent and bizarre thinking that is communicated in an arbitrary and confusing manner. Although the latter is characteristic of individuals who are in a psychotic state, the former, at its extreme, would appear to constitute an ideal that few people consistently manifest. Within such a conceptualization the issue becomes one of adequately identifying one's position on this hypothetical continuum and determining its diagnostic, prognostic, and therapeutic implications. The precise boundary between "disordered thinking" and thinking that is not disordered becomes somewhat arbitrary, and the term *thought disorder* becomes nothing more than a convenient term for a level of severity of thinking problems, and not a categorical distinction.

Developmental Considerations

If thinking disturbance is conceptualized as one's position on a continuum of conventionality, logical coherence, and clarity of communication of one's thinking, then the primary developmental issue related to thinking disturbance in children is whether or not there are normal developmental changes in an individual's position on that continuum. In other words, in normal children, does the coherence of the logic of their thinking, the conventionality of their concepts and ideas about the world, and the adequacy with which they communicate their thinking change significantly and systematically as a function of their chronological age and psychological maturity? A secondary developmental issue is the impact that an individual's age has on the methods of assessment that may be used to quantify these aspects of thinking.

Theoretical works from varying perspectives (e.g., Athey, 1986; Leichtman, 1986; Caplan & Sherman, 1990), normative data (Exner, 2003; Exner & Weiner, 1995), and studies of children using thought disorder measures (e.g., Arboleda & Holzman, 1985) typically show that the frequency of occurrence of thinking problems changes significantly as a function of normal development. Many authors believe, and empirical data suggest, that normal children are prone to combine concepts and engage in less logical thinking to a greater extent than normal adults. As normal children develop, it appears that the frequency and severity of these kinds of thinking problems steadily decline. This then implies that the threshold for distinguishing normal from clinically disordered thinking must be empirically adjusted to account for this developmental trend. Data supporting this point of view can be found in the work of Arboleda and Holzman (1985). Using the Thought Disorder Index (TDI), which rates verbalizations for the presence of categories of mild to serious thinking problems, they found that age accounted for 6.73% of the thought disorder variance in scored Rorschach protocols. A similar developmental change in the level of disturbed thinking in normal children is observed in the age norms for the Comprehensive System for the Rorschach test (Exner & Weiner, 1995; Exner, 2003). The Weighted Sum Six (WSUM6) is the weighted index of thinking disturbance in the Comprehensive System. Although less complex and lacking the fine gradations of the TDI, the WSUM6, which is intended primarily for clinical use, declines fairly steadily in the nonpatient sample from a mean of 11.08 (SD = 1.92) in 5-year-olds to a mean of 2.30 (SD = 1.34) in nonpatient 16-year-olds. Given that the mean for nonpatient adults is 1.91 (SD = 1.47), this suggests that the frequency of verbalizations that fulfill the operational definition of *thought disorder* within the Comprehensive System is normally significantly higher for young children and declines steadily with normal growth and development. It is this normal age-related decline in thought disorder in normal children that led to the development of an age-adjusted weighting for this variable in both the Schizophrenia Index (SCZI) and the Perceptual and Thinking Index (PTI), which are the indices of psychosis in the Comprehensive System.

Both the TDI and the WSUM6, which are based on coding of verbalizations by a subject to a standard stimulus, elicit measurable lapses in thinking in nonpatient children that decline in frequency and severity with increasing age. However, not all methods for assessing thinking disturbance show this developmental trend. For example, Berstein and Loucks (1989) did not find a decrease in more global appraisals of bizarre content, contradiction of reality, and cluster thinking on the Rorschach between the ages of 5 and 12. Bolton, Dearsley, Madronal-Luque, and Baron-Cohen (2002) developed the Magical Thinking Questionnaire (MTQ) to assess disturbed thinking in children. This measure uses a forced choice format (i.e., yes/no/maybe) to assess beliefs concerning whether it is possible to make an event occur just by thinking about it, or to make things happen through an action that is rationally or causally unrelated to the event. A study of 127 children (ages 5–17) who were above the 50th percentile in ability revealed excellent test-retest reliability and a normal distribution for each age group. Unlike the data obtained from nonquestionnaire measures, the incidence of magical thinking observed with the MTQ did not decrease between the ages of 5 and 17.

As these examples suggest, not all psychometric methods are equally likely to elicit evidence of disturbed thinking or to show a developmental trend in the thinking of normal children. If one accepts the conclusion that thinking normally does become more coherent and conventional, and is more adequately communicated as children mature, then measures of thinking in children should reflect this trend. This then calls into question the validity and utility of those assessment methods that do not reflect this developmental trend.

Diagnostic Considerations

Thinking disturbance is often treated as though it were nearly synonymous with schizophrenia or the schizophrenic-spectrum disorders. Although disturbed thinking constitutes one of the DSM-IV criteria for this diagnosis, it clearly represents a measurable form of psychological dysfunction that occurs across a wide range of diagnostic entities. With the use of such diverse measures of thinking disturbance as the TDI (Johnson & Holzman, 1979), the Rorschach (Comprehensive System; Exner, 2003), the Kiddie Formal Thought Disorder Rating Scale (K-FTDS; Caplan, Guthrie, Tanguay, Fish, & David-Lando, 1989), and the Bizarre-Idiosyncratic Thinking Scale (BITS; Marengo, Harrow, Lanin-Kettering, & Wilson, 1986), disturbed thinking has been documented in children with early-onset schizophrenia (Caplan, Foy, Asarnow, & Sherman, 1990; Caplan, Guthrie, & Foy, 1992; Caplan & Sherman, 1990) and children with schizotypal personality disorder (Asarnow & Ben-Meir, 1988; Caplan & Guthrie, 1992; Russell, Bott, & Sammons, 1989; Tompson, Asarnow, Goldstein, & Miklowitz, 1990). It has also been reported in nonhospitalized, nonpsychotic children of mothers hospitalized with affective psychotic disorders and other children at high risk with schizophrenic mothers (Arboleda & Holzman, 1985).

Clinically significant elevated WSUM6 has also been identified in children with post-traumatic stress disorder (Holaday, 2000), with mildly elevated levels also found in sexually abused girls (Leifer, Shapiro, Martone, & Kassem, 1991). Even gifted children have been found to have higher levels of thought disorders as measured by CS WSUM6 than the children in nonpatient comparison samples (Gallucci, 1989), although a review of this study indicates significantly fewer instances of more severe critical special scores. Children with Asperger's Disorder and High Functioning Autism have not been found to demonstrate impaired WSUM6 levels (Holaday, Moak, & Shipley, 2001; Ghaziuddin, Leininger, & Tsai, 1995). Although one study employing Exner's WSUM6 found no elevation in children with Attention Deficit Hyperactivity Disorder (ADHD; Cotugno, 1995), Caplan's (K-FTDS) method indicated that children with ADHD have been found to demonstrate significantly higher levels of thought disorder than normal children, but lower levels of thought disorder than schizophrenic children (Caplan, Guthrie, Tang, Nuechterlein, & Asarnow, 2001). Using this method, these authors have also found elevated levels of thought disorder in children with seizure disorders (Caplan, Guthrie, Shields, & Mori, 1992; Caplan et al., 2002). Clearly, problems in thinking, although frequent and severe in psychotic disorders, are not limited to schizophrenic-spectrum disorders or to psychotic conditions per se.

There are at least three different ways of conceptualizing the diagnostic significance of thinking problems. From a psychodynamic perspective, disturbed thinking represents the emergence of primary process thinking (Blatt & Wild, 1976; Cameron, 1938; Holt, 1977; Rapaport, Gill, & Shafer, 1968). As Russ (1987) has pointed out, when this occurs one must determine whether primary process thinking and difficulties distinguishing reality from fantasy occur as a result of structural deficits, failures in ego development, and a lack of adequate repressive barrier, as opposed to more transitory disruption or adaptive regression. From this perspective, the reason for the emergence of disturbed thinking then determines its diagnostic implications. The challenge this perspective presents is to arrive at an empirically sound method for differentiating these hypothetical etiologies.

From the trait perspective, as articulated in Meehl's (1962) theory of schizophrenia, disturbed thinking signals the presence of the underlying dimension of schizotypy. The extent or severity of thought disturbance manifested by an individual reflects one's place on that dimension. Psychosis is viewed as a continuum, and thought disorder is one of several components of psychological functioning that are assessed to determine where, if at all, one falls on that continuum. Theoretically, significant thinking disturbance in childhood would imply a higher level of schizotypy and a greater long-term risk for the emergence of a schizotypal personality disorder or schizophrenia. Methods for assessing schizotypy in children have been developed (e.g., Rawlings & MacFarlane, 1994; Eysenck & Eysenck, 1976). As Rawlings, Claridge, and Freeman (2001) point out, these scales index a diverse range of characteristics.

They are not intended to specifically assess thinking, although it would be expected that children who are more "schizotypal" on these measures would be more likely to have problems in thinking.

From a neuropsychological perspective, the problems in logic and conceptualization that fall within the rubric of *thought disorder* are among the many problems in cognition that are found in many psychiatric disorders, particularly the schizophrenic-spectrum disorders. Psychopathologists studying schizophrenia have argued that the term *thought disorder* is in itself misleading and should be re-labeled as *communication failure* (Docherty, 2005). These authors feel that this change in terminology helps to clarify the cognitive nature of these problems. When these communications failures occur in conjunction with the other cognitive impairments that have been associated with schizophrenia, they form a neuropsychological constellation consistent with that diagnosis. These include problems in complex attention, executive functioning, working memory, and verbal learning (Asarnow, Brown, & Strandburg, 1995; Asarnow, 1999; Cornblatt & Obuchowski, 1997; Ehrlenmeyer-Kimling, 2000; Ehrlenmeyer-Kimling et al., 2001; Kumra et al., 2000).

From the neuropsychological point of view the assessment of cognition, including the assessment of thought disorder, is central to the differential diagnosis of psychiatric conditions. The presence of the characteristic neuropsychological impairments of schizophrenia would suggest the presence of that disorder, regardless of the age of the patient. As fewer of the neuropsychological deficits associated with schizophrenia are detected, that diagnosis is less likely to apply. Although thought disorder, or communication failure, is one such impairment, neither its presence nor absence would, by itself, confirm or rule out a diagnosis of schizophrenia. Rather, it merely provides one additional piece of the picture that defines that syndrome. At the same time, thought disorder, like any other cognitive impairment, could potentially occur in conjunction with many other conditions, or it could occur in isolation as a focal problem. It is neither pathognomonic nor exclusive of any particular diagnostic entity.

Methods of Assessment

If thought disorder is defined by the degree to which thinking is logical, conceptually clear and conventional, and comprehensibly communicated, then the assessment of thought disorder would ideally tap each of these elements in a reliable and valid manner. If thought disorder is seen as a continuum, then any method of assessment would ideally span as much of that continuum as possible in as fine a gradation as is practical and appropriate. Efforts to assess thinking disturbance have included interview methods, observer ratings, and performance-based procedures.

Interview.   In evaluating the choice of interview techniques, one must differentiate between interview procedures designed to elicit symptoms of a psychotic disorder, such as the Diagnostic Interview Schedule for Children (DISC; Shaffer, Fisher, Lucas, Dulcan, & Schwab-Stone, 2000) or Childhood Interview for Psychiatric Syndromes (ChIPS; Rooney, Fristad, Weller, & Weller, 1999) versus those that are specifically designed to elicit, observe, and quantify disordered thinking. Although there is inevitably a correlation between diagnoses of psychotic disorders assigned on the basis of diagnostic interviews and the presence of disturbed thinking, this correlation simply reflects the fact that disturbed thinking is one symptom of psychosis. Since disordered thinking occurs outside of psychotic disorders, and a psychotic disorder can be diagnosed in the absence of disturbed thinking, this correlation provides an inadequate basis for the specific measurement of thinking disturbance.

The use of structured interview methods may present problems when applied to children, who are least reliable when reflecting on their own thoughts (Fallon & Schwab-Stone, 1994). The adequacy of response to a structured interview may vary as a function of verbal skills and language development, independently of the quality of that child's thinking. It will also be affected by the child's ability to recognize the difference between "real" and "make-believe." Both language skills and cognizance of the difference between reality and fantasy develop with age and may present problems for structured interviews that do not make use of developmental norms and therefore lack a psychometric method of accounting for these factors. Interviews also have demand characteristics that may affect children somewhat differently than they affect adults. One finding among those attempting to assess thought disorder per se appears to be that interviews that elicit conversational speech from patients appear to provide a more adequate basis for quantifying thought disorder than do those that more narrowly limit a subject's range of verbalization (Griffith, Mednick, Schulsinger & Diderichsen, 1980).

Because of perceived limitations of interviews with children due to limited speech samples, immature conversational skills, and the resistance commonly displayed by children below the age of nine when responding to interview questions probing for psychotic symptoms, Caplan and colleagues (1989, 1990, 2001) developed and refined the K-FTDS. This technique utilizes a game-like storytelling format to rate the presence of three independent thought disorder components: illogical thinking, loose associations, and cohesion. One problem noted by the authors with respect to the clinical use of the K-FTDS was the differing reliabilities obtained, depending upon the transcription method. The highest interrater reliabilities were obtained for written transcripts, then videotaped interviews, with the lowest reliability for audiotaped interviews (Caplan, Guthrie, Tanguay, et al., 1989). Thus, although analysis of children's discourse with the use of these methods does appear to provide meaningful measures of thinking disturbance, the requirement of the method may, as yet, be impractical for clinical use.

One structured interview that assesses disordered thinking along a continuum that includes both unusual beliefs (e.g., "Both ghosts and monsters are only make-believe") and psychotic symptoms is the Childhood Unusual Beliefs Scale (CUBSCALE; Viglione, 1996). This interview format combines the advantages of self-report and structured interview in that it contains some items that are merely answered in a yes/no format, and others where more probing is required to determine whether criteria have been met. The scale has been found to be moderately related to the presence of disordered thinking as measured by the Rorschach WSUM6 (Viglione, 1996).

Rating Scales.   An alternative method that is often utilized in the assessment of children, particularly those who are not yet old enough to be assessed with common questionnaire instruments, is the use of rating scales based upon the responses of parents, teachers, clinicians, and other trained observers (see Fields et al., 1994; Guy, 1976; Spencer, Alpert, & Pouget, 1994; Thakur, Jagadheesan, & Sinha, 2003). Behavior ratings by parents are often used in the assessment of various aspects of psychopathology in children. However, the accuracy of parent ratings will inevitably vary with the parents' ability to observe subtle aspects of behavior and to recognize that they are abnormal. It appears, however, that parents are not always equally adept at observing and rating all forms of psychological and behavioral disturbance. For example, Russell (1994) found that it is not unusual for schizophrenic children to have been experiencing psychotic symptoms that had not been obvious to parents or teachers.

Although parents, teachers, and others may be quite reliable in their observation of problems in overt behavior (e.g., aggression, bed-wetting, hyperkinetic behavior, etc.), their ratings of events that are inherently private (e.g., hallucinations) may be much less accurate. Their rating of phenomena that can only be observed through the child's verbal behavior (e.g., delusional beliefs, bizarre or illogical thinking) appears to be less accurate (e.g., Ferdinand, Van der Ende, & Verhulst, 2004) and depends upon both the child's level of verbal activity in general and their specific inclination to verbalize strange beliefs, peculiar ideas, and illogical reasoning. Parent ratings are also limited by the extent to which they attend to the things their children say and have the ability to recognize thinking that is developmentally abnormal or pathological. Both the presence of unusual thoughts and the child's willingness to verbalize strange ideas appear to be age-related, and this may differentially affect the sensitivity of parent ratings of thought disturbance. Parents who are unclear about the extent to which unusual thinking is common in children may overrate that symptom, whereas others may dismiss pathological thinking verbalized by a child on the mistaken assumption that this is common in that age group. To the extent that children are less likely to clearly articulate disturbed thinking in their daily life and parents lack a clear sense of the quality of thinking that is developmentally normal, rating scales are likely to be a less sensitive method of detecting and quantifying disturbed thinking in children.

In addition to the inherent problems in using observer ratings to quantify subjective phenomena, most behavior rating scales are aimed at providing information relevant to the diagnosis of the most commonly occurring psychiatric disorders. For this reason, thinking disturbance is often not afforded the range of coverage required for adequate measurement. Moreover, because factor structures and scales are developed in populations with relatively low incidence of psychosis, disturbed thinking, hallucinations, delusions, bizarre behaviors, and other symptoms of psychosis are often lumped into one heterogeneous scale or distributed across other scales that share some aspects of the construct. Clinicians attempting to synthesize data from different instruments are faced with the prospect of interpreting parent ratings with heterogeneous item content, labeled somewhat misleadingly as "Thought Problems" (Achenbach, 1991), "Autism" (Naglieri, Lebuffe, & Pfeiffer, 1994), or "Reality Distortion" (Lachar & Gruber, 2001), which typically contain some item content related to disordered thinking, but also include other item content related to the occurrence of other symptoms ordinarily reflective of psychotic levels of disturbance. Although research has supported the ability of rating scales to differentiate children with psychotic disorders (Kline, Lachar, & Godowski, 1987; Lachar, Godowski, & Snyder, 1984; Smith & Reddy, 2002; Smith, Reddy, & Wingenfield, 2002), the applicability of these scales to the more precise problem of identifying thinking disturbance has not been as adequately studied.

Performance-Based Methods.   Although rating scales and interview methods have their place in the assessment process, some psychological phenomena can best be assessed by presenting an individual with a task that challenges a psychological process, and then measuring his or her performance in response to that challenge. For example, one could assess vocabulary by rating the level of complexity of the subject's language during an interview, or by asking parents or teachers to rate the subject's vocabulary on a scale. It is likely that these would correlate with each other and that both would correlate with the breadth and sophistication of the subject's actual vocabulary. However, even more precise measurement might be achieved with a standardized vocabulary test. Challenging the specific area of functioning in this fashion can at times provide a more accurate index of an attribute of interest. Few would argue that speed at running is better assessed by remarks during an interview or ratings by parents, than by actual timing of an individual as he or she attempts to run a fixed distance. Moreover, the structure of this method allows for the development of increasingly effective procedures for eliciting the performance of interest and allows for the development of normative data sets. Normative data, in turn, provide a more precise estimate of the extent to which a performance is unusual, and allow the paradigm to take into account age, gender, or any other characteristic that is critical to understanding the significance of the performance.

Performance-based measures have been developed for the assessment of thought disorder. These measures include interview procedures such as the K-FTDS (Caplan et al., 1989), as well as ratings such as BITS (Marengo, Harrow, Lanin-Kettering, & Wilson, 1986) and TDI (Johnson & Holzman, 1979), which have been applied to disturbed thinking elicited in response to the Wechsler Scales (Skelton, Boik, & Madero, 1995; Armstrong, Silberg, & Parente, 1986) and Thematic Apperception Test stories (McCarthy et al., 2003). Although comparison of severity of thought problems across different types of measures has been found to have diagnostic significance in adolescents (Weiner, 1966; Skelton, Boik, & Madero, 1995; Armstrong, Silberg, & Parente, 1986), no studies appear to have examined such differences in children. The Rorschach test appears to be the most widely used performance-based measure of disturbed thinking. Within the CS (Exner, 2003), which is the most frequently used method of administering and scoring the Rorschach in clinical settings, the subject is asked to provide responses to the 10 standard inkblot stimuli and is then asked to show the examiner what part or parts of the inkblot were used in the response and to explain which characteristics of the inkblot (e.g., color, shape, shading, etc.) were the basis for the response. This paradigm challenges the subject with a cognitive demand (i.e., What might this [inkblot] be?) and then requires an articulation of the basis for his or her thinking (i.e., What made it look like that?). The Rorschach allows for articulation of a broad range of responses, thereby enabling the subject to display the conventionality of his or her conceptualizations, the logic of his or her thinking, and the adequacy of his or her communications. At the same time, it requires a response to standardized stimuli in the context of a standardized presentation procedure and provides the examiner with specific operational rules for coding the occurrence and severity of a specific set of problems in thinking. The frequency and severity of those problems are then calculated and can be compared with a variety of normative samples, beginning at age five and continuing up to adulthood.

The thought disorder variables of the CS can be coded reliably (Exner, 2003; Exner & Weiner, 1995; McGrath et al., 2005) in clinical settings. The composite variables that index thought disorder, such as the Perceptual and Thinking Index (PTI; Exner, 2003) and Ego-Impairment Index (EII–2; Viglione, Perry, & Meyer, 2003) in the CS are correlated in the expected manner in child samples with the presence of psychotic disorders (Smith, Baity, Knowles, & Hilsenroth, 2001; Stokes, Pogge, Grosso, & Zaccario, 2001) and relapse of psychotic symptoms (Stokes et al., 2003). Thus, this method would appear to have particular advantages in the clinical assessment of thinking disturbance in general and in the assessment of thought disorder in children and adolescents in particular.

THE FOUR WINDS STUDY

In order to explore the relationship among thought disorder variables and between thought disorder variables and global indicators of psychosis, we analyzed archival data from the child inpatient assessment service at Four Winds Hospital. Four Winds is a private psychiatric facility in the suburbs of New York City that specializes in the treatment of children and adolescents. More than 300 of the over 1500 children and adolescents hospitalized at Four

Winds each year undergo comprehensive psychological testing as part of their standard clinical care. The cases used in the following analyses were extracted from those archival data of the psychological assessment service of the hospital from children between the ages of 5 and 12 years ($M = 9.73$; SD = 1.9) who had been administered the CUBSCALE. The sample was predominantly male (72%) with heterogeneous discharge chart diagnoses, including Schizophrenia (<1%), Psychotic Disorder NOS (17.5%), Mood Disorder with Psychotic Symptoms (3.5%), Mood Disorders without Psychotic Symptoms (50.6%), and disruptive behavior disorders, including Oppositional Defiant Disorder, Conduct Disorder, Intermittent Explosive Disorder, and Impulse Control Disorder NOS (24.3%), Pervasive Developmental Disorders (1%), and Post-Traumatic Stress Disorder (2.5%).

The measures that were analyzed included the Rorschach, Devereux Scales of Mental Disorders (DSMD), ChIPS, and the CUBSCALE. With respect to the Rorschach, the reader is referred to Exner (2003) for a description of the development and characteristics of the critical special scores, and to Exner and Weiner (1995) for a description of their use in making clinical inferences with children. These include scores for deviant verbalizations (DV), which represent the strange or unconventional use of words; deviant responses (DR) for tangential or irrelevant commentary introduced in ways that disrupt communications; incongruous combinations (INCOM), fabulized combinations (FABCOM), and contaminations (CONTAM) for the combination of ideas in unconventional and inappropriate ways; and illogical reasoning (ALOG). Each of these is specifically defined, and DV, DR, INCOM, and FABCOM are all further coded for greater (e.g., DV2, DR2, INCOM2, FABCOM2) and less (e.g., DV1, DR1, INCOM1, FABCOM1) severity. The DSMD was studied with the use of those scales identified most closely with psychotic disorders (i.e., Autism, Acute Problems, and Critical Pathology), as well as item content that specifically relates to the construct of thought problems (Lebuffe, Naglieri, & Pfeiffer, 1996) (i.e., items 79, 97, 92, 94, 84) and hallucinations (item 106). The ChIPS, which is a structured interview, elicited clinical judgments with respect to the presence in this sample of auditory hallucinations (14.3%), visual hallucinations (7.8%), or delusional symptoms (10.4%), with 19.5% of the children in the sample ($N = 114$) meeting criteria for a psychotic disorder. This rate was consistent with the base rates of psychotic disorders within the larger child inpatient sample.

Relationships among Global Indicants of Psychosis

Table 23.1 indicates that the structured interview (ChIPS) and medical chart diagnoses of psychosis were correlated at lower levels than would be anticipated, perhaps revealing some limitations of the interview technique with children. Aside from intercorrelations within components of each assessment method, there were only modest relationships among various global indicators of psychosis. None of the DSMD scales correlated with either ChIPS or chart diagnosis of a psychotic disorder. However, PTI and EII–2 showed significant correlations with both chart and ChIPS diagnoses of psychotic disorders.

Relationships among Global Measures of Thought Disorder

In order to study the phenomenon of parent ratings of thinking disturbance more closely, a composite scale was developed from those DSMD items that are typically described as measuring "thought problems." A review of Table 23.2 reveals that this scale is correlated significantly with the child's report of delusional symptoms on the ChIPS but did not correlate significantly with the CUBSCALE. The Rorschach WSUM6 was significantly correlated

TABLE 23.1.
Correlations among Global Measures of Psychotic Symptoms

	DSMD		Rorschach		ChIPS	Chart
	Acute	*Crit. path.*	*PTI*	*EII-2*	*Dx*	*Dx*
DSMD						
Autism	.66**[a]	88**[a]	−.27[b]	−.22[b]	.04[c]	−.09[a]
Acute prob.	—	.94**[a]	.12[b]	.21[b]	.08[c]	.13[a]
Crit. path.		—	−.07*[b]	−.06[b]	.08[c]	.02[a]
Rorschach						
PTI			—	.75**[d]	.22*[d]	.33**[d]
EII				—	.34**[d]	.24**[d]
ChIPS Dx					—	.25*[e]

[a]$N = 49$; [b]$N = 38$; [c]$N = 28$; [d]$N = 114$; [e]$N = 92$.

with both the ChIPS and the CUBSCALE but was not correlated with DSMD ratings on items specifically rating elements of disturbed thinking.

Relationships between Thought Disorder Measures and Indicants of Psychosis

Table 23.3 presents a more comprehensive pattern of relationships between thought disorder and psychosis measures. In reviewing the specific DSMD item content rated by parents, it is important to note that most of the items measuring thought problems were correlated with ratings of hallucinations. However, none of the DSMD items or scales were significantly related to any finding of psychotic symptoms on structured interview or to the chart diagnoses.

Before interpreting the findings related to the Rorschach test, it is important to note that for the sample ($N = 114$), there were significant intercorrelations among all of the variables that make up the PTI. As has been found for adult samples, WSUM6 was correlated ($r = .27$) with perceptual inaccuracy (X−%). Although the procedure for coding poor human representations (PHR) and good human representations (GHR) may artificially inflate the correlations, it is important to note that WSUM6 also correlated strongly ($r = .40$) with the presence of PHR and less strongly ($r = −.22$), in an inverse fashion, with the presence of GHR. These findings are consistent with those obtained for adult subjects that indicate moderate relationships among the constructs of perceptual accuracy, thinking disturbance, and

TABLE 23.2.
Correlations among Global Measures of Thought Disorder

	Rorschach WSUM6	*CIPS thinking problems*	*CUBSCALE Total*
DSMD thought prob. items	.07[b]	.44*[c]	.26[f]
WSUM6	—	.21*[g]	.25*[d]
ChIPS thinking	—	—	.47**[e]

[a]$N = 49$; [b]$N = 38$; [c]$N = 28$; [d]$N = 114$; [e]$N = 92$; [f]$N = 48$; [g]$N = 87$.

TABLE 23.3.
Correlations among Thought Disorder Measures and Psychosis Indicators

	DSMD halluc	ChIPS aud hall.	ChIPS vis. hall.	ChIPS del. Sx	ChIPS psy dx	Chart psy dx
DSMD	(N = 48)	(N = 28)	(N = 28)	(N = 28)	(N = 28)	(N = 48)
Dis. speech	.18	.02	.17	.23	.13	−.12
Real/fantasy	.39**	.08	.27	.34	.15	−.10
Sp. powers	.39**	−.05	.23	.19	.23	.17
Confused	.05	−.17	.01	.04	−.03	−.01
Makes up words	.29*	.14	.25	.28	.26	−.06
Autism scale	.37*	−.09	−.05	−.09	.04	−.09
Rorschach	(N = 37)	(N = 87)	(N = 87)	(N = 87)	(N = 87)	(N = 114)
Sum level 1	.09	.14	.16	.16	.11	.15
DV2	.12	−.03	.02	.26*	.16	.27**
DR2	−.06	.09	.04	.26*	.02	.06
INC2	−.04	.16	.09	.09	.12	.02
FAB2	.53**	.40**	.20	.17	.33**	.34**
ALOG	.36**	.04	.20	.03	.03	.38**
CONTAM	.18	.09	.19	.27	.24*	.41**
WSUM6	.31	.31**	.25*	.25*	.26*	.34*
M minus	.19	.35**	.19	.25*	.32**	.02
X minus %	.19	.10	.21*	.26*	.16	.15
PTI	.25	.24*	.19	.19	.22*	.33**
EII-2	.26	.36**	.31**	.31**	.34**	.25**
	(N = 48)	(N = 92)	(N = 92)	(N = 92)	(N = 92)	(N = 151)
CUBSCALE	.53**	.56**	.40**	.47**	.52**	.20*

*p < .05; **p < .01.

object representations (Berg, Packer & Nunno, 1993; Quinlan, Harrow, and Tucker, 1972). However, in the entire child inpatient sample, ($N = 665$), only 6.2% of the Rorschach protocols included impaired thinking (WSUM6 above cutoff) without impaired perceptual accuracy (X−% GT .29), whereas 43.1% demonstrated impaired perceptual accuracy without thinking problems. A careful understanding of the presence of all components is most likely to elucidate diagnostic status.

A review of Table 23.3 indicates that the components of the PTI are related to parent ratings and child self-report of hallucinations, and both ChIPS and chart diagnosis of psychotic disorder. The variables contained within the mild levels of thinking disturbance did not independently predict the presence of psychotic symptoms. Thinking problems, more precisely defined by WSUM6, were related to parent ratings of both hallucinations and delusional symptoms, as well as the determination of all psychotic symptoms in the structured interview. By contrast, perceptual inaccuracy (X−%) was only related to the presence of delusional symptoms. However, an analysis of the composite measure (PTI) reveals that only 3.1% of those with PTI = 0 were rated as displaying frequent hallucinations or very frequent hallucinations on the DSMD, whereas 34.4% of children with PTI = 5 were rated as such. Although the general trend is for the composite variables (i.e., PTI, EII–2) to be more strongly related to psychotic symptoms, some variables, such as FAB2 and M−, appear to be capable of independently predicting status across a range of psychotic symptom indicators. These data additionally lend support to the CUBSCALE as a measure of disordered thinking, since it was significantly correlated with WSUM6 ($r = .25$) as well parent ratings, and both ChIPS and chart ratings of Psychotic disorder.

These findings illustrate the value of a multicomponent assessment, the low convergence among various methods for assessing the presence of thinking problems, and the difficulties associated with relying solely on interview or behavior ratings in the attempt to assess thinking problems in children. They demonstrate the clinical value of utilizing performance-based measures such as the Rorschach, which was more strongly related to discharge chart diagnoses of psychotic disorders than either interview or parent ratings. They also suggest the need for clinicians to develop more refined ways of examining the subcomponents of more global rating scales measuring psychotic behaviors. Finally, although these data clearly indicate that thinking problems are moderately related to the presence of other psychotic behaviors, they also highlight the value of viewing thinking problems as a separate construct that needs to be understood within a context of other features in order to determine diagnostic and prognostic significance.

Case Example

This case concerns Barbara, an eight-year-old female child who was hospitalized twice within a two-month period. Because she was enrolled in a hospital quality assurance study at the time of her first hospitalization, she received the typical clinical evaluations that occurred during these hospitalizations, as well as additional evaluations included in that quality assurance project. These included parent ratings using the DSMD at the time of her first admission to the hospital, and at 30 and 120 days after her discharge from that admission. During both admissions Barbara's symptoms were rated by her treating physician. Her behaviors were also rated by the nursing staff at the end of her first hospital stay. A structured diagnostic interview (i.e., K-SADS) involving both Barbara and her mother was completed by the quality assurance research team during her first hospitalization. Finally, during her second hospitalization, which took place four weeks after her discharge from her first hospitalization, a psychological test battery was completed that included the Rorschach test. At the end of her initial hospital stay, which was approximately one week in duration, her diagnosis by the clinical treatment team was (DSM-IV 299.33) major depressive disorder, recurrent, severe, without psychotic symptoms. At neither the beginning nor the end of that hospitalization did Barbara's therapist rate her as displaying any hallucinations, delusions, or thought disturbance. The K-SADS, completed independently by the research team, also diagnosed a major depressive episode and indicated neither psychotic symptoms nor any evidence of thought disturbance at that time. Thus, neither interview nor clinical observation suggested any disturbance in thinking at that time. Ratings on the DSMD are presented in Table 23.4.

The mother's ratings, which reflect the child's behavior in the four weeks before her hospitalization, indicate significant depressive symptomatology and a host of odd behaviors, but no endorsement of any items that specifically refer either to disturbed thinking or to clear symptoms of psychosis. These ratings were different from nursing staff ratings obtained during Barbara's first hospitalization, which indicate no clinically significant problems within the highly structured setting provided by the hospital, nor any behaviors reflecting either disturbed thinking or psychosis.

TABLE 23.4.
Ratings on the Devereaux Scale of Mental Disorders (DSDM)

Scale/composite T-score	Mother 1st admission	Nursing staff 1st admission	Mother 2nd admission
Conduct	67	40	75
Attention	63	40	73
Externalizing	66	40	76
Anxiety	49	43	47
Depression	80	60	58
Internalizing	65	51	52
Autism	48	40	65
Acute problems	83	46	46
Critical pathology	67	42	56
Total	68	43	63

Three weeks after discharge from her first hospitalization, Barbara was readmitted to the hospital because of increasingly aggressive and disruptive behaviors, both at home and at school. Neither psychotic symptoms nor evidence of disturbed thinking was noted by the admitting physician. Diagnoses of bipolar disorder, major depressive disorder, oppositional defiant disorder, and borderline personality disorder were considered. Mother's DSMD ratings of Barbara's behavior during that time indicate more severe problems in conduct and odd and socially inappropriate behaviors, with no signs of anxiety or depression. For the first time, her ratings also include an endorsement of one of the eight items on the DSMD that refer to problems in thinking. To the item "have difficulty separating fact from fantasy" the mother assigns a rating of "Occasionally." No other psychotic-like behaviors were noted.

On the ninth day of her second hospitalization, Barbara completed a comprehensive psychological test battery. This was requested in response to the treatment team's continuing uncertainty regarding this child's diagnosis. Her test performance included a WISC–III Full Scale IQ of 109, Verbal IQ of 113, and Performance IQ of 103. Variable attention was observed on some of the neuropsychological tests in that battery, including the Wisconsin Card Sorting Test (Heaton, Chelune, Talley, Kay, & Curtiss, 1993) and the Continuous Performance Test (see Borgaro, Pogge, DeLuca, & Stokes, 2003, for description), but no significant or consistent impairment was evident. Both reading and math achievement were in the average range. The CS Rorschach yielded a valid and interpretable record (R = 14; Lambda = 0.00). Her score on the depression index (DEPI = 6) was reflective of the likelihood of a mood disorder and was consistent with her symptomatic presentation. As these data indicate, she displayed a pattern of disturbed thinking in the context of intact perceptual accuracy, which is unusual for inpatient samples. Her Rorschach scores on the variables critical to the assessment of thinking disturbance and psychosis are presented in Table 23.5.

To this point few psychotic symptoms had been observed by the patient's mother, her psychiatrist, or the nursing staff. No evidence of thinking disturbance had been elicited or observed in either of her hospitalizations or in the structured diagnostic interview completed by a trained research team. Little consideration was being given to the possibility of a psychotic disorder. However, in response to the stimuli of the Rorschach, this child's thinking,

TABLE 23.5.
Summary of Key Rorschach Structural Summary Findings

Sum 6	*= 17*	*DV2*	*= 0*	*XA%*	*= 0.57*	*PTI*	*= 4*
Level 2	= 8	DR2	= 6	WDA%	= 0.57	SCZI	= 4
Wsum6	= 88	INC2	= 1	X−%	= 0.21	GHR	= 0
M−	= 2	FAB2	= 1	X+%	= 0.21	PRH	= 10
M none	= 0	ALOG	= 5			EII	= 5.39
		CONTAM	= 1				

as reflected in her Wsum6 of 88, was markedly more disturbed than is normative at her age (eight-year-old Wsum6: $M = 14.33$; $SD = 5.10$). Thus, this performance-based procedure elicited evidence of a thinking disturbance not readily detected by other means.

At 120 days after discharge from her first hospitalization (approximately two months after completion of her second hospitalization), Barbara's mother again rated her behavior during the prior 30 days. Her DSMD ratings are presented in Table 23.6.

At this point, four months after the completion of her first hospitalization, every scale was significantly elevated, with conduct problems and depression most prominent, but with the mother now rating three of the disturbed thinking items as occurring (i.e., have difficulty separating fact from fantasy, say that people were against him/her, and appear obsessed or preoccupied with a specific object or idea). Subsequent to the completion of this quality assurance study, this child was hospitalized for a third time. At that time, Barbara was determined to be actively psychotic by the admitting psychiatrist.

Initially clinical observation, parent ratings, and structured interviews failed to detect problems in thinking that emerged quite prominently in response to a performance-based measure (i.e., Rorschach). Diagnoses formulated prior to the performance-based assessment tended to focus on Barbara's distress (i.e., major depressive disorder) and behavior problems (i.e., rule out oppositional defiant disorder). Both of these sets of problems clearly disappeared within the structured and supportive environment of the hospital, only to reemerge each time with greater severity very shortly after she left that setting. Only several months later did Barbara's problems in thinking and reality testing become sufficiently severe to be detected by clinical interview or parent observation, although the trajectory of

TABLE 23.6.
Barbara's Parent DSMD Ratings at 120-day Follow-up

Scale T-scores	120-day follow-up	120-day follow-up	
	T-scores	*Composite*	*T-scores*
Conduct	79	Externalizing	74
Attention	65	Internalizing	77
Anxiety	70	Critical pathology	70
Depression	80	Total	76
Autism	66		
Acute problems	69		

this case suggests that these thinking problems, and the psychiatric condition underlying them, are likely to have been critical to her distress, her behavior problems, and her repeated failure to respond to treatment.

SUMMARY

The adequacy of thinking is a critical facet of psychological functioning. Disordered thinking is an important symptom too often assumed to be subsumed within diagnostic categories (e.g., schizophrenia) or related constructs (e.g., psychosis), and as a result its contribution to an individual's functioning is obscured. However, it is neither specific to any diagnosis nor an inevitable feature of any condition. Moreover, assessment of this crucial clinical construct in children is complicated by the developmentally normal evolution of thinking with age. Methods for assessing thinking in children must incorporate some means of addressing these developmental trends.

While rating scales, structured interviews, and performance-based methods have been developed for the assessment of thinking problems, they do not always show the desired convergence; the demands those methods place on younger patients may sometimes make them less suitable for children. The clinical significance of detectable thinking problems in children highlights the need for additional research aimed at improving existing assessment methods and developing new technologies for the detection and quantification of thought disorder in children. Reliable measurement of thought disorder will inevitably precede an understanding of its causes and the development of more effective treatments.

REFERENCES

Achenbach, T. M. (1991). *Manual for the Teacher's Report Form and 1991 Profile*. University of Vermont Department of Psychiatry, Burlington, VT.

Andreason, N. C. (1982). Should the term "thought disorder" be revised? *Comprehensive Psychology, 23*, 291–299.

Andreason, N. C. (1984a). *The Scale for the assessment of negative symptoms (SANS)*. Iowa City, University of Iowa.

Andreason, N. C. (1984b). *The Scale for the assessment of positive symptoms (SAPS)*. Iowa City, University of Iowa.

Arboleda, C., & Holzman, P. S. (1985). Thought disorder in children at risk for psychosis. *Archives of General Psychiatry, 42*, 1004–1013.

Armstrong, J., Silberg, J., & Parente, F. (1986). Patterns of thought disorder on psychological testing. Implications for adolescent psychopathology. *Journal of Nervous and Mental Disease, 174*(8), 448–456.

Asarnow, J. R. (1999). Neurocognitive impairments in schizophrenia: A piece of the epigenetic puzzle. *European Child & Adolescent Psychiatry, 8*, 5–8.

Asarnow, J. R., & Ben-Meir, S. (1988). Children with schizophrenia spectrum and depressive disorders: A comparative study of premorbid adjustment, onset pattern, and severity of impairment. *Journal of Child Psychology and Psychiatry, 29*, 477–488.

Asarnow, J. R., Brown, W., & Strandburg (1995). Children with a schizophrenic disorder: neurobehavioral studies. *European Archives of Psychiatry and Clinical Neuroscience, 245*, 70–79.

Athey, G. I. (1986). Implications of memory impairment for hospital treatment. *Bulletin of the Menninger Clinic, 50*(1), 99–110.

Berg, J., Packer, A., & Nunno, V. (1993). A Rorschach analysis: Parallel disturbance in thought and in self/object representation. *Journal of Personality Assessment, 61*(2), 311–324.

Berstein, A. G., & Loucks, S. (1989). *Rorschach Test: Scoring and interpretation.* New York: Hemisphere Publishing.

Blatt, S., & Wild, C. (1976). *Schizophrenia: A developmental analysis.* New York: Academic Press.

Bolton, D., Dearsley, P., Madronal-Luque, R., & Baron-Cohen, S. (2002). Magical thinking in childhood and adolescence: Development and relation to obsessive compulsion. *British Journal of Developmental Psychology, 20*(4), 479–495.

Borgaro, S., Pogge, D. L, DeLuca, V. A., & Stokes, J. (2003). Convergence of different versions of the Continuous Performance Test: Clinical and scientific implications. *Journal ofClinical and Experimental Neuropsychology, 25*(2), 283–292.

Cameron, N. (1938). Reasoning, regression, and communication in schizophrenia. *Psychological Monographs, 50*(1).

Caplan, R., Foy, J., Asarnow, R., & Sherman, T. (1990). Information processing deficits of schizophrenic children with formal thought disorder. *Psychiatry Research, 31*(2), 169–177.

Caplan, R., & Guthrie, D. G. (1992). Communication deficits in childhood schizotypal personality disorder. *Journal of the American Academy of Child and Adolescent Psychiatry,* 961–967.

Caplan, R., Guthrie, D., & Foy, J. (1992). Communication deficits and formal thought disorder in schizophrenic children. *Journal of the American Academy of Child and Adolescent Psychiatry, 31*(1), 151–159.

Caplan, R., Guthrie, D., Komo, S., Siddarth, P., Chayasirisobhon, S., Kornblum, & Sankar, R. (2002). Social communication in pediatric epilepsy. *Journal of Child Psychology, Psychiatry and Allied Disciplines, 43*, 245–253.

Caplan, R., Guthrie, D., Shields, W. D., & Mori, L. (1992). Formal thought disorder in pediatric complex partial seizure disorder. *Journal of Child Psychology and Psychiatry, 32*, 604–611.

Caplan, R., Guthrie, D., Tang, B., Nuechterlein, K. H., & Asarnow, R. F. (2001). Thought disorder in attention-deficit hyperactivity disorder. *Journal of the Academy of Child and Adolescent Psychiatry, 40*(8), 965–972.

Caplan, R., Guthrie, D., Tanguay, P. E., Fish, B., & David-Lando, G. (1989). The Kiddie Formal Thought Disorder Scale (K-FTDS): Clinical assessment, reliability and validity. *Journal of American Academy of Child Psychiatry, 28*, 408–416.

Caplan, R., & Sherman, T. (1990). Thought disorder in the childhood psychoses. In B. Lahey & A. Kazdin (Eds.), *Advances in Clinical Child Psychology* (Vol. 1, pp. 175–206). New York: Plenum Press.

Cornblatt, B., & Obuchowski, M. (1997). Update of high-risk research: 1987–1997. *International Review of Psychiatry, 9*, 437–447.

Cotugno, A. (1995). Personality attributes of attention deficit hyperactivity disorder (ADHD) using the Rorschach test. *Journal of Clinical Psychology, 51*, 554–562.

Docherty, N. (2005). Cognitive impairments and disordered speech in schizophrenia: Thought disorder, disorganization, and communication failure perspectives. *Journal of Abnormal Psychology, 114*, 269–278.

Ehrlenmeyer-Kimling, I. (2001). Early neurobehavioral deficits as phenotypic indicators of the schizophrenia genotype and predictors of later psychosis. *American Journal of Medical Genetics, 105*, 23–24.

Ehrlenmeyer-Kimling, I., Rock, D., Roberts, S., Jamal, M., Destenbaum, C., Cornblatt, B., et al. (2000). Attention, memory, and motor skills as childhood predictors of schizophrenia-related psychoses: The New York high-risk project. *American Journal of Psychiatry, 157*, 1416–1422.

Exner, J. E. (2003). *The Rorschach: A comprehensive system: Vol. 1. Basic foundations and principles of interpretation.* New York: John Wiley & Sons.

Exner, J. E., & Weiner, I. (1995). *The Rorschach: A comprehensive system: Vol. 3. Assessment of children and adolescents* (2nd ed.). Oxford, England: John Wiley & Sons.

Eysenck, H. J., & Eysenck, S. B. G. (1976). *Psychoticism as a personality dimension.* London: Hodder & Stoughton.

Fallon, T., & Schwab-Stone, M. (1994). Determinants of reliability in psychiatric surveys of children aged 6–12. *Journal of Child Psychology & Psychiatry & Allied Disciplines, 35*, 1391–1409.

Ferdinand, R., van der Ende, J., & Verhulst, F. (2004). Parent-adolescent disagreement regarding psychopathology in adolescents from the general population as a risk factor for adverse outcome. *Journal of Abnormal Psychology, 113*(2), 198–207.

Fields, J. H., Grochowski, B. A., Lindenmayer, J. P., Kay, S. R., Grosz, D., Hyman, R. B., & Alexander, G. A. (1994). Assessing positive and negative symptoms in children and adolescents. *American Journal of Psychiatry, 151*(2), 249–253.

Gallucci, N. (1989). Personality assessment with children of superior intelligence: Divergence versus psychopathology. *Journal of Personality Assessment, 53*(4), 749–761.

Ghaziuddin, M., Leininger, L., & Tsai, L. (1995). Brief Report: Thought disorder in Asperger Syndrome: Comparison with high-functioning Autism. *Journal of Autism & Developmental Disorders, 25*, 311–317.

Griffith, J. J., Mednick, S. A., Schulsinger, F., & Diderichsen, B. (1980). Verbal associative disturbances in children at high risk for schizophrenia. *Journal of Abnormal Psychology, 89*, 125–131.

Guy, W. (Ed.). (1976). *ECDEU Assessment Manual for psychopharmacology, revised. DHEW Pub. No. ADM 76-338.* Rockville, MD: National Institute of Mental Health.

Harvey, P. D. (1983). Speech competence in manic and schizophrenic psychoses: The association between clinically rated thought disorder and performance. *Journal of Abnormal Psychology, 92*, 368–377.

Heaton, R. K., Chelune, G. J., Talley, J. L., Kay, E. G., & Curtiss, G. (1993). *Wisconsin Card Sorting Test Manual: Revised and Expanded.* Odessa, FL: Psychological Assessment Resources.

Holaday, M. (2000). Rorschach protocols from children and adolescents diagnosed with posttraumatic stress disorder. *Journal of Personality Assessment, 75*(1), 143–157.

Holaday, M., Moak, J., & Shipley, M. A. (2001). Rorschach protocols from children and adolescents with Asperger's Disorder. *Journal of Personality Assessment, 76*, 482–495.

Holt, R. R. (1977). A method for assessing primary process manifestations and their control in Rorschach responses. In M. Rickers-Ovsinkina (Ed.), *Rorschach Psychology* (pp. 375–420). Huntington, NY: Krieger.

Johnson, M. H., & Holzman, P. S. (1979). *Assessing schizophrenic thinking: A clinical and research instrument for measuring thought disorder.* San Francisco: Jossey-Bass.

Kleiger, J. (1999). *Disordered thinking and the Rorschach: Theory, research, and differential diagnosis.* Hillsdale, NJ: Analytic Press.

Kline, R. B., Lachar, D., & Godowski, C. L. (1987). Convergence and concurrent validity of the DSM-III diagnoses and the Personality Inventory for Children (PIC). *Canadian Journal of Behavioral Sciences Review, 20*, 250–154.

Kumra, S., Wiggs, E., Bedwell, J., Smith, A. K., Arling, E., Albus, K., et al. (2000). Neuropsychological deficits in pediatric patients with childhood-onset schizophrenia and psychotic disorder not otherwise specified. *Schizophrenia Research, 42*, 135–144.

Lachar, D., Godowski, C. L., & Snyder, D. K. (1984). External validation of the Personality Inventory for Children profile and factor scales: Parent, teacher, and clinician ratings. *Journal of Consulting and Clinical Psychology, 52*, 155–164.

Lachar, D., & Gruber, C. (2001). *Personality Inventory for Children (PIC–2), Second Edition.* Los Angeles, CA: Western Psychological Services.

Lebuffe, P., Naglieri, J. A., & Pfeiffer, S. I. (1996). *The Devereux Scales of Mental Disorders: Computerized Scoring Assistant* [Computer Software]. San Antonio, TX: Psychological Corporation.

Leichtman, M. (1988). When does the Rorschach become the Rorschach? Stages in the mastery of the test. In H.D. Lerner & P.M. Lerner (Eds.), *Primitive mental states and the Rorschach* (pp. 559–600). Madison, CT: International Universities Press.

Leifer, M., Shapiro, J., Martone, M. W., & Kassem, L. (1991). Rorschach assessment of psychological functioning in sexually abused girls. *Journal of Personality Assessment, 56*(1), 14–28.

Marengo, J., Harrow, M., Lanin-Kettering, I., & Wilson, A. (1986). Evaluating bizarre-idiosyncratic thinking: A comprehensive index of positive thought disorder. *Schizophrenia Bulletin, 12*, 497–513.

McCarthy, J., Loewenthal, L., Leonard, N., Herdsman, L., Bluestone, C., & Gorman, B. (2003). Evaluation of bizarre-idiosyncratic thinking scale as a measure of thought disorder in children and adolescents with severe psychiatric disorders. *Perceptual and Motor Skills, 97*, 207–214.

McGrath, R., Pogge, D., Stokes, J., Cragnolino, A., Zaccario, M., Hayman, J., Piacentini, T., & Wayland-Smith, D. (2005). Field reliability of comprehensive system scoring in an adolescent inpatient sample. *Assessment, 12*(2), 199–209.

Meehl, P. E. (1962). Schizotaxia, shizotypy, and schizophrenia. *American Psychologist, 17*, 827–838.

Naglieri, J. A., Lebuffe, P., & Pfeiffer, S. I. (1994). *The Devereux Scales of Mental Disorders-Manual.* San Antonio, TX: Psychological Corporation.

Quinlan, D., Harrow, M., & Tucker, G. (1972). Varieties of "disordered" thinking on the Rorschach: Findings in schizophrenic and nonschizophrenic patients. *Journal of Abnormal Psychology, 79*(1), 47–53.

Rapaport, D., Gill, M., & Schafer, R. (1968). The Rorschach test. In R. R. Holt (Ed.), *Diagnostic Psychological Testing.* New York: International Universities Press.

Rawlings, D., Claridge, G., & Freeman, J. (2001). Principal components analysis of the Schizotypal Personality Scale (STA) and the Borderline Personality Scale (STB). *Personality & Individual Differences, 31*(3), 409–419.

Rawlings, D., & MacFarlane, C. (1994). A multidimensional schizotypal traits questionnaire for young adolescents. *Personality and Individual Differences, 17*, 489–496.

Rooney, M. T., Fristad, M. A., Weller, E. B., & Weller, R. A. (1999). *Administration manual for the ChIPS.* Washington, DC: American Psychiatric Press.

Russ, S. (1987). Assessment of cognitive affective interaction in children: Creativity, fantasy, and play research. In J. Butcher & C. Spielberger (Eds.), *Advances in personality assessment* (Vol. 6, pp. 141–155). Hillsdale, NJ: Lawrence Erlbaum Associates.

Russell, A. (1994). The clinical presentation of childhood-onset schizophrenia. *Schizophrenia Bulletin, 20*(4), 631–646.

Russell, A., Bott, L., & Sammons, C. (1989). The phenomenology of schizophrenia occurring in childhood. *Journal of the American Academy of Child and Adolescent Psychiatry, 28*(3), 399–407.

Shaffer, D. F., Fisher, P., Lucas, C. P., Dulcan, M. K., & Schwab-Stone, M. E. (2000). NIMH Diagnostic Interview Schedule for Children Version IV (NIMH DISC-IV): Description, differences from previous versions, and reliability of some common diagnoses. *Journal of the American Academy of Child and Adolescent Psychiatry, 39*, 28–38.

Skelton, M., Boik, R., & Madero, J. (1995). Thought disorder on the WAIS–R relative to the Rorschach: Assessing identity-disordered adolescents. *Journal of Personality Assessment, 65*(3), 533–550.

Smith, S., Baity, M., Knowles, E., & Hilsenroth, M. (2001). Assessment of disordered thinking in children and adolescents: The Rorschach perceptual thinking index. *Journal of Personality Assessment, 77*(3), 447–464.

Smith, S. R., & Reddy, L. A., (2002). The concurrent validity of the Devereux Scales of Mental Disorders. *Journal of Psychoeducational Assessment, 20*, 112–127.

Smith, S. R., Reddy, L. A., & Wingenfeld, S. A. (2002). Assessment of psychotic disorders in inpatient children and adolescents: Use of the Devereux Scales of Mental Disorders. *Journal of Psychopathology and Behavioral Assessment, 24*, 269–273.

Spencer, E. K., Alpert, M., & Pouget, E. R. (1994). Scales for the assessment of neuroleptic response in schizophrenic children: Specific measures derived from the CPRS. *Psychopharmacology Bulletin, 30*(2), 199–202.

Stokes, J., Pogge, D., Grosso, C., & Zaccario, M. (2001). The relationship of the Rorschach Schizophrenia Index to psychotic features in a child psychiatric sample. *Journal of Personality Assessment, 76*(2), 209–229.

Stokes, J., Pogge, D., Powell-Lunder, J., Ward, A., Bilginer, L., & DeLuca, V. (2003). The Rorschach Ego-Impairment Index: Prediction of treatment outcome in a child psychiatric population. *Journal of Personality Assessment, 81*, 11–20.

Thakur, A., Jagadheesan, K., & Sinha, V. (2003). Psychopathological dimensions in childhood and adolescent psychoses: A confirmatory factor analytic study. *Psychopathology, 36*, 190–194.

Tompson, M. C., Asarnow, J. R., Goldstein, M. J., & Miklowitz, D. J. (1990). Thought disorder and communication problems in children with schizophrenia spectrum and depressive disorders and their parents. *Journal of Clinical Child Psychology, 19*, 159–168.

Viglione, D. (1996). Data and issues to consider in reconciling self-report and the Rorschach. *Journal of Personality Assessment, 67*(3), 579–588.

Viglione, D., Perry, W., & Meyer, G. (2003). Refinements in the Rorschach Ego Impairment Index incorporating the human representational variable. *Journal of Personality Assessment, 81*(2), 149–157.

Weiner, I. (1966). *Psychodiagnosis in schizophrenia*. New York: Wiley.

24

COMPREHENSIVE ASSESSMENT OF YOUTH EXPOSURE TO TRAUMA AND ITS MYRIAD CONSEQUENCES

Jennifer L. Price
Georgetown College

Joseph, an 8-year-old boy, presents with behavioral problems at school and is argumentative at home. Maria, a 6-year-old girl, was observed engaging her dolls in simulated sexual acts at school, but otherwise appears to be experiencing no psychological distress. Austin, a 16-year-old boy, presents with low mood, fatigue, and difficulty concentrating. Shana, a 12-year-old girl, complains of nightmares and difficulty concentrating and has trouble experiencing happiness. Which of these youth has a trauma history? The answer is: all of them.

Nearly half of all children will experience a traumatic event at some point during their childhood (Giaconia et al., 1994). Typical traumatic experiences include natural disasters, exposure to war/terrorism, chronic/life-threatening illness, community violence (e.g., school shootings), and interpersonal violence, such as witnessing domestic violence and experiencing sexual and physical abuse (Davis & Siegel, 2000). Many children experience some degree of psychological distress in the aftermath of trauma, although specific prevalence rates are difficult to determine because of the varied nature of symptom presentations in children (Nader, 1997).

Assessing the effects of trauma in children and identifying a history of trauma exposure are complex tasks because of the varied responses to trauma. In the case examples just mentioned, Shana presents with some of the typical symptoms of post-traumatic stress disorder (PTSD). A meta-analysis of samples of traumatized children revealed that approximately 36% of children who are exposed to trauma develop PTSD (Fletcher, 1996a). Cohen (1998) notes that "as children mature, they are more likely to exhibit adult-like PTSD symptoms" (p. 7S). However, like Maria in the case example just mentioned, younger children may engage in reenactment of the trauma in play and artwork and may not display the numbing and active avoidance symptoms typical of adult PTSD (Cohen, 1998).

As presented in the cases of Joseph and Austin, traumatized children often present with symptoms other than those consistent with PTSD (Nader, 1997). Children can present with depression, generalized anxiety, behavioral problems, concentration and attention difficulties, and physical symptoms, and they may show no signs of psychological disorder (Nader, 1997). In addition, children diagnosed with disruptive behavior disorders are at higher risk for exposure to trauma as well as development of PTSD subsequent to trauma (Ford et al., 2000). Problems with regulation of emotions, as well as disorganized early attachment patterns and unhealthy subsequent relationships, are especially likely among victims of child maltreatment (Van der Kolk & Fisler, 1994). Thus, knowing a child has a trauma history is useful information, but the presentation can vary greatly, depending on the manifestation of symptoms for a particular child. Assessment of children is even more complex when the trauma history is unknown. Moreover, children with an unknown traumatic experience as the underlying cause of their psychological distress can be characterized as "treatment resistant," when in reality, a thorough assessment to uncover that trauma history would have changed the treatment strategies used with the child.

The purpose of this chapter is to provide clinicians with information regarding models of trauma assessment, ways to detect the presence of a trauma history in youth, as well as strategies for assessing potential behavioral and psychological symptoms common after a trauma, with the use of both global personality measures and trauma-specific assessment tools. Readers should consider this information an introduction, understanding that specialization in this area would certainly require additional training. Useful resources to aid in this training are referenced as appropriate, including reviews of many of the measures being presented (e.g., Ohan, Myers, & Collett, 2002; Strand, Sarmiento, & Pasquale, 2005). In addition, case examples are integrated into each section as illustrations of the measurement strategies being presented.

MODELS OF TRAUMA ASSESSMENT

When faced with assessing the intricacies of a child's reaction to trauma, it is helpful to have an organizing framework. Multiple researchers and clinicians have proposed models of trauma assessment (e.g., Fletcher, 1996a; Webb, 2004). These models generally include three components: understanding the nature of the traumatic event (e.g., type, duration, severity), assessing the variety of individual responses (e.g., posttraumatic symptoms) and influences on those responses (e.g., age/developmental stage, coping style), and evaluating factors in the support system/recovery environment (e.g., social support, culture). These three components provide the organizing framework for the current chapter as well.

Identifying and Understanding the Traumatic Event

The most common approach to assessing a history of trauma in children involves interviewing the identified child and his or her primary caregiver(s). Ideally, each interview should include direct inquiries about the occurrence of potentially traumatic events (Cohen, 1998). In cases where a caregiver is suspected of abuse, only the child and the nonoffending parent should be the interviewees. Generally, it is important to ask about history of exposure to a variety of events (e.g., all forms of abuse and neglect, natural disasters and accidents, serious illness/injury, etc.). For the child interview, developmentally appropriate language should be used to describe the trauma. Specific information about the nature of the trauma(s) should be gathered, including frequency, duration, and severity. Clinicians should also ask about the child's emotional state during and after the trauma as well, specifically referencing fear, helplessness, horror, and emotional numbing or "shock." Extensive guidelines for conducting this type of interview are available in numerous clinician handbooks (e.g., Cohen, 1998; Newman, 2002; Wilson & Keane, 2004).

Because of the number of details required to comprehensively assess the nature of the trauma, the use of structured interviewing and/or a written report is strongly recommended in lieu of or in addition to clinician-designed interviews. Several clinician-administered caregiver interviews and self-report measures for older children and adolescents have displayed sound psychometric properties. Of these, some include both assessment of exposure to trauma and subsequent PTSD symptoms. Thus, they are only listed here and are discussed more fully in the section on assessment of individual reactions, because that is their primary focus. These measures include the Children's PTSD-Reaction Index (CPTS-RI; Pynoos, Rodriguez, Steinberg, Stuber, & Frederick, 1998); the Childhood PTSD Interview (CPTSDI; Fletcher, 1996b); and the Children's PTSD Inventory (CPTSDI; Saigh et al., 2000).

Unlike these dual-purpose tools, the sole purpose of the Traumatic Events Screening Inventory (TESI; Ribbe, 1996) is to identify the presence of a trauma history in children aged 4 to 18. The TESI measures exposure to a wide variety of traumatic events, with the use of DSM-IV (American Psychiatric Association, 1994) criteria. The TESI has self-report and parent-report versions, both of which have shown excellent psychometric properties in preliminary studies (Ribbe, 1996).

Other measures have been designed to assess specific types of childhood traumas. For assessing various forms of child maltreatment (i.e., emotional abuse, physical abuse, sexual abuse, emotional neglect, and physical neglect), the Childhood Trauma Questionnaire (CTQ; Bernstein & Ahluvalia, 1997) was originally developed with adults who were maltreated as children, but has been modified for use down to 12 years of age. This measure has excellent psychometric properties and is an efficient way of assessing various forms of childhood maltreatment (Ohan et al., 2002).

The use of anatomically detailed (AD) dolls to assess exposure to sexual abuse has been empirically supported as well (Maan, 1991). The use of AD dolls is particularly useful with very young children or even older youths with limited language skills. However, researchers are clear that the use of AD dolls requires training in standardized assessment procedures (see Maan, 1991, for a summary of these procedures). Although they are not widely used, other measures have been proposed to assess additional specific types of trauma, such as exposure to community violence (Cooley, Turner, & Beidel, 1995) and sexual abuse (Levy, Markovic, Kalinowski, Ahart, & Torres, 1995; Spaccarelli, 1995).

Clearly, age is a factor in the selection of a measure of trauma exposure. For young children, caregiver reports are very important. However, it is critical that children who are verbal are also interviewed, to maximize the likelihood of disclosure. For older children and adolescents, written self-report questionnaires can be helpful, especially because of their brevity and ease of administration. As indicated previously, several options for assessment of exposure have not yet been presented because they are built into broader symptom measures. In cases where trauma history is highly likely (e.g., in an at-risk population, or when trauma exposure is already documented and the assessment is intended to gather additional information), one of those measures would be a logical choice because the need for assessing symptoms is likely. For a true screening tool, the TESI is an excellent option for clinicians because of the wide range of applicable ages and the ease of administration.

Case Example: Six-year-old Maria was referred to a community mental health center after her school counselor observed her engaging her dolls in simulated sexual acts. According to the counselor, she displayed no other signs of psychological distress. During the intake interview, Maria was asked if any bad things had ever happened to her. She initially denied this, but then added "Well, one time I got in trouble for yelling at my mom." Maria's mother was also asked a general question about the possibility of Maria experiencing any traumatic events, but her mother also denied a trauma history. Because of the school counselor's suspicions of sexual abuse, the TESI was administered separately to Maria and her mother. Although her mother continued to deny knowledge of Maria experiencing any traumatic events, Maria acknowledged that her neighbor had "touched [her] private parts" on several occasions. Thus, her trauma history was revealed and the clinician was able to follow up with additional investigation of her posttraumatic reactions.

ASSESSING INDIVIDUAL RESPONSES TO TRAUMA

Making note of factors affecting individual responses is also important during a trauma assessment. In particular, clinicians need to attend to a child's level of knowledge, language skills, memory development, emotion regulation, and social cognition (Salmon & Bryant, 2002). In addition to the impact of these developmental factors, clinicians should consider the varying individual responses to trauma. Though his research focuses on the effects of sexual abuse, Friedrich's (1994) concepts can be applied to other types of trauma as well. He recommends assessment of three main types of problems, including attachment difficulties (e.g., disorganization, rejection), dysregulation of emotion (e.g., PTSD symptoms, dissociation), and problems with self-representation (e.g., low self-esteem, shame). Various techniques have been used to assess posttraumatic reactions in these areas. In this section, I briefly review some of the most common and empirically sound measures of trauma-based reactions.

Assessment of Posttraumatic Symptoms.   Once it is determined that a child has been exposed to a traumatic event, it is important to assess a variety of potential posttraumatic reactions. Because PTSD is the only DSM diagnosis directly linked to trauma, many measures emphasize these symptoms. However, as previously discussed, people respond to trauma in many different ways. Thus, a number of these measures include assessment of other commonly experienced symptoms, such as depressed mood, anxiety, and interpersonal difficulties. Though assessment of posttraumatic symptoms in adults is far more advanced, numerous measures have been developed to offer developmentally appropriate assessment of symptoms. Structured interviews of children and caregivers, teacher and caregiver rating scales, and self-reports completed by older children have each been successfully used to evaluate symptoms in children and adolescents. In some instances, measures include two or more parallel versions (e.g., parent-report plus self-report), so these cases are noted.

Clinician-Administered Scales.   As indicated previously, some clinician-administered measures of PTSD for children and adolescents include trauma exposure assessment as well. These measures are discussed first. The Children's PTSD-Reaction Index (CPTS-RI; Pynoos et al., 1998) includes evaluation of exposure to 12 potentially traumatic events, including assessment of the child's emotional state during and after the events. When exposure is identified, the CPTS-RI measures symptoms of PTSD based on DSM criteria. The CPTS-RI has excellent psychometric properties and has been applied to children of diverse cultures (Ohan et al., 2002). It is unique in that it can also be used as a self-report measure for children nine years old and older.

The Childhood PTSD Interview (CPTSDI; Fletcher, 1996b) includes parallel parent and child (ages 7–18) versions. In the CPTSDI, interviewees are asked to identify specific traumatic events; then the interviewer assesses PTSD symptoms as well as anxiety, depression, dissociation, and various other symptoms likely to occur after a trauma. Though the original validation study was limited by a small sample, the scale has moderate to high convergent validity with other measures and is useful in that it connects symptoms with a specific traumatic event (Strand et al., 2005).

The Children's PTSD Inventory (CPTSDI; Saigh et al., 2000), also based on DSM-IV criteria, is a third option for a clinician-administered scale for youth who are 7 to 18 years old. The CPTSDI includes an assessment of trauma exposure in addition to items concerning PTSD symptoms. Excellent psychometric properties, appropriate developmental modifications to the wording of items, and use of dimensional as well as categorical assessment of symptoms make it an excellent option for clinicians and researchers (Ohan et al., 2002).

Moving on to measures of individual responses to trauma that do not include measurement of trauma exposure: the Clinician Administered PTSD Scale for Children and Adolescents (CAPS-CA; Nader et al., 2002) is a standardized interview solely of PTSD symptoms based on DSM-IV criteria. It measures the frequency and intensity of PTSD symptoms for youth aged 8 to 18. The few studies of reliability and validity are promising, and the CAPS-CA appears to be sensitive to changes in symptoms over the course of treatment, a great advantage to therapists (Ohan et al., 2002).

Whereas the measures discussed thus far can be applied to any trauma type, the Children's Impact of Traumatic Events Scale-Revised (CITES-R; Wolfe, Gentile, Michienzi, Sas, & Wolfe, 1991) is designed to measure the impact of child maltreatment by assessing PTSD symptoms as well as cognitive symptoms related to PTSD (e.g., perception of social support after disclosure of abuse).

Self-Report Measures.   Numerous self-report measures have been developed to assess posttraumatic symptoms in older children and adolescents. Several of these have very strong empirical support. The Child PTSD Symptom Scale (CPSS; Foa, Johnson, Feeny, & Treadwell, 2001) measures PTSD symptoms and functional impairment according to DSM-IV criteria for youth aged 8 to 15. It has excellent psychometric properties, is brief, and is easy to administer and score (Foa et al., 2001). Another self-report measure with extensive psychometric support, especially in the assessment of sexually abused children, is the Trauma Symptom Checklist for Children (TSCC; Briere, 1996). Appropriate for children ages 7 to 16, the TSCC is unique in that it not only measures PTSD symptoms, but consists of six clinically derived subscales (Anxiety, Depression, Anger, Posttraumatic Stress, Dissociation, and Sexual Concerns) as well as two validity scales used to detect under- and overresponding. Among its advantages are its large normative sample and sensitivity to changes in symptoms over the course of treatment (Ohan et al., 2002).

Several other self-report measures show promise for various specific purposes, though their empirical support to date is less extensive. The When Bad Things Happen Scale (WBTH; Fletcher, 1996c) is appropriate for children aged 7 to 14. This measure was validated with the Childhood PTSD Interview (Fletcher, 1996b); thus, it is limited by the same small sample. However, its self-report style, minimal requirements for reading ability, and brief completion time offer some advantages (Strand et al., 2005).

The Impact of Events Scale (IES; Horowitz, Wilner, & Alvarez, 1979) has been applied to adolescents and children as young as 8 years, though it was originally developed to measure symptoms in adults. The Children's Reaction to Traumatic Events Scale (CRTES; Jones,

2002) is a self-report measure modified from the IES to be more developmentally appropriate for children aged 8 to 12. It assesses avoidance and intrusive symptoms of PTSD, and though it has limited psychometric data, based on the extensive research with the IES, the CRTES shows promise as an alternative for younger victims (Ohan et al., 2002).

The Child Report of Posttraumatic Symptoms (CROPS; Greenwald & Rubin, 1999) and the corresponding Parent Report of Posttraumatic Symptoms (PROPS) include assessment of various posttraumatic reactions, not limited to PTSD. With good reliability data and brevity to its advantage, this pair of measures is promising (Strand et al., 2005).

Unique as a self-report measure for young children, the Angie/Andy Cartoon Trauma Scales (ACTS; Praver, DiGiuseppe, Pelcovitz, Mandel, & Gaines, 2000) was designed to measure the impact of chronic trauma such as child abuse and community violence by utilizing cartoon images to help young children describe their responses. The ACTS is broad in that it measures six areas typically affected by chronic trauma: dysregulation of affect and impulses, attention or consciousness, self-perception, relations with others, somatization, and systems of meaning. The ACTS has preliminary support for reliability and concurrent validity, and it has good sensitivity and specificity in discriminating youth with and without histories of trauma (Praver et al., 2000).

Caregiver and Teacher Ratings.   Another alternative for assessing reactions in young children is the use of an external rater, typically a primary caregiver, although teachers may also be used. For children under the age of 13, the Trauma Symptom Checklist for Young Children (TSCYC; Briere, 2001) is a caregiver report of various posttraumatic stress symptoms, as well as anxiety, depression, anger, and abnormal sexual behavior. The TSCYC has shown adequate reliability and construct validity in a large sample of maltreated children (Briere et al., 2001).

Also designed to assess symptoms in young children (aged 2–10), the Pediatric Emotional Distress Scale (PEDS; Saylor, Swenson, Reynolds, & Taylor, 1999) consists of three subscales: anxious/withdrawn, fearful, and acting out. Its psychometric properties are good, and it has a normative sample that can be used to assess severity of symptoms. Though the PEDS appears to have good sensitivity in discriminating between children with and without trauma exposure, it should not be used clinically to determine history of trauma, because it measures many symptoms consistent with psychiatric conditions *not* caused by trauma (Ohan et al., 2002).

The PTSD Checklist for Children-Parent Report (PCL/C-PR; Ford & Rogers, 1997) is a modified version of the adult PTSD Checklist, a measure designed to assess severity of DSM-IV PTSD symptoms. The PCL/C-PR has been used with children from age 6 to 17. Preliminary studies have demonstrated good reliability and criterion validity (Daviss et al., 2000). Because of the ease of use and brevity of the PCL-PR, it is likely to appeal to clinicians.

In addition to using measures specifically designed for trauma-exposed populations, various other tools can measure reactions to trauma. The Child Behavior Checklist (CBCL; Achenbach, 1991) is appropriate for ages 4 to 18 and has excellent psychometric properties (Achenbach & Edelbrock, 1983). It does have a PTSD subscale, although studies are equivocal on its usefulness with traumatized children. Wolfe and Gentile (1993) found that the PTSD subscale differentiated sexually abused children from nonabused children drawn from the measure's normative sample. In addition, Dehon & Scheeringa (2005) recently reported that the CBCL-PTSD scale predicted PTSD diagnosis in young traumatized children. However, others have questioned the concurrent and discriminant validity of the CBCL-PTSD scale (Ruggiero & McLeer, 2000). Studies on the recently revised CBCL (Achenbach & Rescorla, 2001) have not yet been conducted.

Other broad behavior rating scales (e.g., Behavior Assessment Scale for Children; Reynolds & Kamphaus, 1992) as well as disorder-specific scales (e.g., Children's Depression Inventory; Kovacs, 1981) may also be used with traumatized children in order to assess a wide variety of symptoms. It is also important to keep in mind that many non-trauma-specific self-report measures designed for use with adults have been used with adolescent populations, so the options for clinicians are quite numerous (e.g., Foy, Wood, King, King, & Resnick, 1997). The only difference in strategies for using these non-trauma-specific measures with traumatized children and adolescents is the implication that the symptoms are somehow connected to the trauma. Thus, subsequent treatment strategies may be trauma-focused rather than disorder-specific.

Another option for evaluating the global diagnostic picture for a child is to administer a non-trauma-specific interview that covers multiple diagnoses (e.g., Child and Adolescent Psychiatric Assessment [CAPA; Angold et al., 1995]). The Life Events Interview, a section of the CAPA that is part of the PTSD module, assesses a youth's exposure to a wide variety of potentially traumatic events. The reliability and discriminant validity for this interview are supported (Costello, Angold, March, & Fairbank, 1998). In this measure, parents and children/adolescents are interviewed separately, starting with the trauma exposure questions, then PTSD screening questions, followed by detailed questions about PTSD symptoms. Thus, this trauma module could be used independently, or the entire interview could be used to assess multiple psychiatric disorders because trauma victims' responses vary so widely.

Overall, the process of selecting a measure of posttraumatic symptoms is a complicated one. If trauma exposure needs to be assessed, one of the measures that combines assessment of exposure and symptoms is efficient. If the trauma is already known or a measure such as the TESI was used to assess exposure, it is important to utilize as many methods and sources as possible. Thus, if time allows, using clinician-administered interviews of caregiver and child as well as a written self-report and a caregiver report is ideal. If time is limited, the brief self-report options do seem to function reliably, although some researchers have found that children and adolescents may underreport symptoms. In cases where the child is too young to complete a self-report, using a written caregiver report and a brief interview with the child is a reasonable option.

Case Example: Shana, a 12-year-old girl, had recently experienced a severe motor vehicle accident in which her cousin (the driver) was killed. Her mother brought her to a mental health clinic because she was concerned about how Shana was responding to this tragic event. Shana initially minimized her difficulties. She reported that she had "a few nightmares," "sometimes can't concentrate at school," and "just [doesn't] feel happy." However, the clinician utilized several strategies to investigate Shana's mental health status, including a clinician-administered interview (CAPS-CA), a self-report measure (CPSS), and a caregiver report measure (PCL-PR). Though the three reports differed slightly, with Shana's self-report indicating the lowest severity of symptoms and the caregiver report indicating the highest degree of severity, the clinician readily discovered that Shana was suffering from moderate to severe symptoms of PTSD. This example points to the need to utilize multiple methods and sources to gain the most comprehensive collection of information.

Assessment of Dissociation. Dissociation is a well-established reaction to trauma and an associated feature of PTSD. In addition, dissociative symptoms strongly influence the effectiveness of many therapeutic strategies and generally require special attention in therapeutic settings. Thus, measures of dissociation are also essential in assessing trauma reactions in children and adolescents. For young children, the Child Dissociative Checklist (CDC; Putnam, Helmers, & Trickett, 1993) is a caregiver or adult-observer report scale with good reliability as well as normative data. It measures six dimensions of dissociation, including dissociative amnesia, rapid shifts in demeanor and abilities, spontaneous trance states, hallucinations, identity alterations, and aggressive or sexualized behaviors. For older youth, the Adolescent Dissociative Experiences Scale (A-DES; Armstrong, Putnam, Carlson, Libero, & Smith, 1997) is a self-report option that assesses four aspects of dissociation, including dissociative amnesia, absorption and imaginative involvement, passive influence, and depersonalization/derealization. The A-DES has excellent internal reliability and has shown good sensitivity and specificity in discriminating between adolescents with and without dissociative disorders (Armstrong et al, 1997).

Case Example: To illustrate the influence of a measure of dissociation, consider the case of Austin, a 16-year-old boy who presented with attentional difficulties. Austin also acknowledged low mood and fatigue, but said his biggest problem was "losing concentration at school." He said he had read about ADHD on the Internet and thought he might have it. In a routine trauma history screening, Austin acknowledged a history of sexual molestation by an uncle but said he was "over it" and didn't want to discuss it. In spite of his insistence that attention and concentration were his only difficulties, the young man completed the A-DES as part of a standard battery for traumatized adolescents, and his extensive dissociative symptoms were revealed. This finding strongly influenced the clinician's strategies in therapy, causing her intervention to be trauma-focused rather than behaviorally focused on attention/concentration strategies. Austin eventually acknowledged the larger role his abuse history played in his life that he was previously unable to recognize.

Assessment When Trauma History Is Unknown

Although it is advisable to utilize a measure to identify the presence of a trauma history in assessment of all children, at times this is not feasible. In addition, children may be unwilling to acknowledge a history of trauma, or the caregivers being interviewed may be unaware of a trauma history. Thus, it is also useful to identify characteristics of traumatized children that might be considered "red flags" on commonly used global personality measures (e.g., Rorschach, Minnesota Multiphasic Personality Inventory–Adolescents [MMPI–A]).

Global Self-Report Measures.   Few studies have examined the utility of the MMPI-A (Butcher et al., 1992) for identification of trauma symptoms (Cashel, Ovaert, & Holliman, 2000; Forbey, Ben-Porath, & Davis, 2000; Scott, Knoth, Beltran-Quiones, & Gomez, 2003). These studies suggest that no clinical scales of the MMPI–A can consistently differentiate adolescent trauma victims from nonvictims. However, some researchers have suggested that the PTSD subscale of the MMPI–2 (PK; Keane, Malloy, & Fairbank, 1984) can identify adolescents with trauma symptoms as it has with adults (Berton & Stabb, 1996), and others have adapted this scale for the MMPI–A (Cashel, Ovaert, & Holliman, 2000). Moreover, although the MMPI–A and even the MMPI–2 can be extremely useful in identifying symptomatology in adolescent patients, there does not seem to be a consistent profile that will assist clinicians with identifying trauma victims when the trauma history is unknown. Similarly, some evidence shows that though the Personality Inventory for Youth (PIY; Lacher & Gruber, 1995) is moderately correlated with the TSCC, it is less sensitive to PTSD status than trauma-focused measures (Fricker & Smith, 2001). Thus, although omnibus self-report personality tests can be quite useful in identifying areas of distress for patients, clinicians likely cannot rely on them to distinguish when symptoms are trauma-based. Clinicians may find it useful to use such measures as initial screening tools, following with trauma-specific measures when potentially trauma-related symptoms are evident.

Projective Techniques.   The most commonly used projective technique, the Rorschach, scored with the use of Exner's Comprehensive System (CS; Exner, 2003), can be used clinically as part of a multisource, multimethod personality assessment to identify interpersonal and intrapersonal reactions to trauma. Moreover, several response characteristics have shown promise in differentiating traumatized children from nontraumatized children.

An early exploratory study identified several CS variables on which traumatized youth were significantly more impaired compared with Exner's normative data for children and adolescents (Holaday, Armsworth, Swank, & Vincent, 1992). Specifically, the variables that differentiated the traumatized group included the use of Space, Texture, W:SumC Ratio, D Score, the presence of Inanimate Movement, Form Quality, and Egocentricity. On a number of variables, the traumatized children scored significantly lower than the mean, indicating poorer form accuracy (F+%), a more negative self-image (EgoC), more impaired interpersonal relatedness (Texture), poorer ability to tolerate stress (D score), and greater situational anxiety (m). The traumatized group scored significantly higher than the mean on two variables, indicating more anger (Space) and problems with integration of affects and open expression of feelings (W:SumC Ratio).

In a study of children traumatized by severe burns, Holaday and Whittenberg (1994) also found more impaired structural summaries. In particular, this group differed from the normative sample in that most had a negative self-image (lower scores on EgoC), poor perceptual accuracy (lower X+% scores), and problems tolerating intimacy and closeness (fewer Texture responses). In addition, half the traumatized youth experienced coping deficits (higher mean on CDI), and a quarter showed signs of depression (higher mean on DEPI). A quarter of the participants were also positively identified on the Schizophrenia Index (SCZI), but no other evidence indicated thought disturbance. Consistent with previous research (e.g., Cerney, 1990), the group seemed to consist of two unique subgroups (high or low Lambda). The high Lambda group presented as emotionally constricted, and the low Lambda group appeared emotionally flooded (Holaday & Whittenberg, 1994). Thus, the authors concluded that clinicians should be aware of these two possible extreme reactions to trauma, a finding that has been observed in other research and clinical settings as well. A follow-up study with the sample three years later revealed that the traumatized youth continued to differ from the normative sample on the same variables (Holaday, 1998).

A later study comparing children diagnosed with PTSD with children diagnosed with Oppositional Defiant Disorder (ODD) is critically important because it differentiates a traumatized sample from a clinical sample rather than comparing the traumatized sample solely to Exner's normative data (Holaday, 2000). This study demonstrated that although both clinical groups differed from the normative sample on a variety of CS variables, the PTSD group had more impaired scores on several variables. The PTSD group showed evidence of distorted thinking (higher mean for SCZI and a greater number special scores (Raw Sum SS and Wgt Sum SS) as well as poorer perceptual accuracy (lower scores on X+%). The author suggested that the PTSD group's elevated score on SCZI is reflective of the irrational thinking and impaired perceptions that often result from trauma. She advised, "Psychologists should be aware that a positive SCZI might indicate that a history of trauma has been censored either to protect the child or adolescent or to safeguard a perpetrator" Holaday,

2000, p. 152). Future research is needed to determine the relationship between PTSD diagnosis and the Perceptual Thinking Index (PTI), a revision of SCZI that measures different aspects of thought disturbance.

In addition to these findings with the Comprehensive System, researchers have also investigated the use of the Mutuality of Autonomy scale (MOA; Urist, 1977), which measures interpersonal relationship capacities derived from Rorschach protocols, in order to identify impairment in object relations functioning in traumatized children and adolescents. For example, Kelly (1995, as cited in Kelly, 1999) found that abused children had more impaired object relations functioning than children in a nonabused, clinical control group. This finding is consistent with the results of self-report personality measures with interpersonally traumatized youth (Haviland, Sonne, & Woods, 1995).

Studies of the specific population of sexually abused children and their patterns of Rorschach responding have been equivocal. An early exploratory study found 17 Comprehensive System variables that differentiated sexually abused children and adolescents from a nonabused group (Clinton & Jenkins-Monroe, 1994). Using the CS and the MOA, Leifer, Shapiro, Martone, and Kassem (1991) also found that sexually abused girls exhibited higher levels of thought disorder, had less tolerance for stressful situations, experienced human interactions as more malevolent, and displayed more sexual preoccupation than the nonabused comparison group. Others have failed to replicate such pervasive differences but have confirmed higher frequency of responses, with trauma content among sexually abused children as a consistent predictor (Billingsley, 1995; Friedrich, Einbender, & McCarty, 1999; Welner, 2001). Others have found no differences between sexually abused and nonabused groups with the use of Comprehensive System variables (Arenella & Ornduff, 2000).

Overall, the Rorschach is useful in terms of identifying aspects of personality and perception negatively influenced by trauma. CS variables can be used to identify bodily concerns, disorganized thinking, impaired self-perception, interpersonal difficulty, and emotion dysregulation. Clearly, as is the case with other measures, the presence of a trauma history cannot be determined solely by administration of the Rorschach. Rather, clinicians who use the Rorschach regularly may recognize "red flags" for possible trauma exposure by noting the presence of certain protocol patterns, such as sexual preoccupation (for sexual abuse). Impairment in interpersonal relatedness, perceptual inaccuracies, and emotional constriction or flooding is also consistent with a trauma history, although trauma is certainly not the only cause of these difficulties.

In terms of other commonly used projective techniques that may assist in the assessment of childhood trauma, the Thematic Apperception Test (TAT; Murray, 1971) shows some promise. Its primary function in assessing traumatized children has been in determining the effect of trauma on object relations functioning, a particular area of disturbance in interpersonally victimized children (Kelly, 1999). In particular, several studies have investigated the impact of child maltreatment on object relations, with the use of the Social Cognition and Object Relations Scale (SCORS; Westen, Lohr, Silk, Kerber, & Goodrich, 1985) applied to TAT protocols. Ornduff, Freedenfeld, Kelsey, & Critelli (1994) found that sexually abused girls had lower levels of functioning on all four SCORS object relations scales: complexity of representations of people, affect-tone of relationship paradigms, capacity for emotional investment in relationships and moral standards, and understanding of social causality. Similarly, physically abused children tend to have lower levels of capacity for emotional investment in relationships, a less developed understanding of social causality, and more malevolent views of relationships (Freedenfeld, Ornduff, & Kelsey, 1995).

Consistent with the treatment literature with this population, other studies have also identified object relations impairment in physically and sexually abused children, with the use of the SCORS (Ornduff & Kelsey, 1996) as well as other scoring methods for the TAT (Stovall & Craig, 1990). Some researchers have suggested noting the manifest content of children's responses (e.g., preoccupation with sexual behaviors) to identify those with a possible history of sexual abuse (Pistole & Ornduff, 1994).

As discussed with clinical rating scales and with the Rorschach, no one instrument should ever be used to determine presence of a trauma history. Taking these research results into account, when using the TAT in a clinical situation where trauma history is unknown, using the SCORS as a standardized scoring procedure may help clinicians identify children with impaired object relations that may be a result of some form of child maltreatment or other trauma. However, a lack of significant findings on any measure does not indicate an absence of trauma exposure.

Research using other projective techniques is less advanced; however, some authors have suggested that various measures have potential for identifying traumatized children. For example, the Roberts Apperception Test for Children (McArthur & Roberts, 1982) may be useful in distinguishing sexually abused children in that they tend to report more sexual content than non-sexually abused children (Friedrich & Share, 1997). Others have found utility in projective techniques such as human figure drawings (Peterson, Hardin, & Nitsch, 2001), the Hand Test (Rasch & Wagner, 1989), and the Expectations Test (Gully, 2003). However, research on these measures should be considered preliminary until the studies have been replicated.

Though this section has focused primarily on using projective techniques in identifying traumatized children when the trauma history is unknown, it is also important for clinicians to keep known trauma histories in mind when assessing children with projective techniques. Clinicians must be careful not to overpathologize in situations where a child's pattern of responding may be highly unusual under normal circumstances, but understandable when the child's trauma history is taken into account. For example, imagine a child repeatedly seeing broken, bloody body parts on Rorschach cards. Although this is clearly cause for concern, such responses become quite understandable when one considers the child's recent exposure to his or her community being ravaged by war or natural disaster. The morbidity of the responses remains, but they might be conceptualized as a reexperiencing of symptoms consistent with PTSD.

Case Example: Joseph, an 8-year-old boy, was brought, reluctantly, to an outpatient mental health clinic by his parents. They indicated that Joseph's teacher complained about his behavior at school. His parents agreed that he was argumentative at home, but said they didn't think therapy would help. As part of a standard assessment battery, Joseph completed the PIY, Rorschach, and TAT, to which the SCORS was applied. Joseph's responses on the PIY indicated problems with Impulsivity and Distractibility, Delinquency, Social Skill Deficits, and Family Dysfunction. Although none of these elevations could determine trauma exposure because they could certainly be elevated in the absence of a trauma history, the projective measures Joseph completed added significantly to the clinical picture.

Among other things, his Rorschach structural summary revealed significant difficulty regulating his emotions (elevated W:SumC) and potential problems with interpersonal closeness (no Texture responses). Joseph's structural summary also showed his difficulty coping with life stressors (positive CDI). Use of the MOA scale on the Rorschach and the SCORS on the TAT both revealed impairment in object relations functioning. In addition, the content of his TAT stories centered on conflictual family relationships. For example, for Card 5, he described a mother "bursting in to her son's bedroom" to punish him for making too much noise. He ended the story with the child being beaten by his father with a belt. It was through this assessment that Joseph first began to reveal his experience of physical abuse and neglect at home.

Based on these findings, a structured interview regarding trauma exposure (TESI) was added to the assessment in order to ascertain the specifics about this abuse history. Although Joseph was hesitant at first, he eventually acknowledged that his parents were verbally and emotionally abusive, and his father was physically abusive. In order to ascertain the presence of trauma-based reactions to this abuse, Joseph also completed the TSCC, which revealed elevations on Anxiety, Depression, Anger, and Posttraumatic Stress. Discovery of this trauma exposure and subsequent symptoms was critical, not only for allowing for intervention to ensure Joseph's safety at home, but also for establishing a treatment plan that would address the underlying issues rather than focusing solely on modifying his maladaptive behaviors.

Evaluating the Recovery Environment

In terms of the third component of child and adolescent trauma assessment, assessing factors in the support system/recovery environment is quite important. Several characteristics typify children most likely to readily adapt to trauma. Clinicians should ask about factors in the recovery environment, such as the availability of family or peer support, particularly immediately after disclosure of the trauma, as well as preexisting coping skills. Degree of psychological distress, particularly self-worth, has been shown to be mediated by parental support and coping strategies in victims of child sexual abuse (Guelzow, Cornett, & Dougherty, 2002). Family and peer support is also associated with mental health in victims of child physical abuse (Ezzell, Swenson, & Brondino, 2000). Clinicians may wish to utilize a measure that includes assessment of social support, such as the CITES-R, in order to adequately evaluate these aspects of the recovery environment.

Clinicians should also consider the influence of culture on individual responses and subsequent recovery, such as traditions regarding expression of emotions and acceptance of mental health care. Multicultural issues, although not widely researched, can greatly influence the process and outcome of trauma assessment (Rabalais, Ruggiero, & Scotti, 2002). Although there is little, if any, literature on the role of religion/spirituality in youth's responses to trauma, such issues are also important to address if they are relevant for a particular child.

RECOMMENDATIONS/CONCLUSION

Of the many important messages within this chapter, the most important is the recommendation for clinicians to consistently screen all youth for a history of trauma. Many of the standardized measures presented are brief, easy to use, and highly effective in identifying children who may benefit from more in-depth assessment of posttraumatic reactions. In situations where assessment time is limited, screening for symptoms related to trauma can also be extremely useful. The Screen for Child Anxiety Related Emotional Disorders (SCARED; Muris, Merckelbach, Schmidt, & Mayer, 1999) is a self-report questionnaire measuring DSM-IV-defined anxiety disorder symptomatology in children. Its four questions screening for traumatic stress have been shown to identify children who could benefit from additional assessment to determine their level of trauma exposure and symptomatology

(Muris, Merckelbach, Körver, & Meesters, 2000). The measures of posttraumatic reactions discussed in this chapter offer many options for this type of follow-up for children with a positive screening.

Overall, clinicians should be aware of the great importance of identifying children with a trauma history. Although non-trauma-specific measures may be highly accurate diagnostic tools, they cannot inform clinicians of the traumatic experience that is the origin of the symptoms. Being unaware of this trauma leads to therapeutic interventions designed to treat the symptoms rather than assist children in coping with the underlying trauma. Moreover, in order to provide the most beneficial treatment available, clinicians must be aware of a child's trauma history and have detailed information about the child's individual response, as well as factors in the recovery environment.

REFERENCES

Achenbach, T. M. (1991). *Manual for the Child Behavior Checklist/4–18 and 1991 Profile.* Burlington, VT: Department of Psychiatry, University of Vermont.

Achenbach, T. M., & Edelbrock, C. (1983). *Manual for the Child Behavior Checklist and Revised Child Behavior Profile.* Burlington, VT: Department of Psychiatry, University of Vermont.

Achenbach, T. M., & Rescorla, L. A. (2001). *Manual for the ASEBA School-Age Forms and Profiles.* Burlington, VT: University of Vermont, Research Center for Children, Youth, and Families.

American Psychiatric Association (1994). *Diagnostic and statistical manual of mental disorders* (4th ed.). Washington, DC: American Psychiatric Press.

Angold, A., Prendergast, M., Cox, A., Harrington, R., Simonoff, E., & Rutter, M. (1995). The Child and Adolescent Psychiatric Assessment (CAPA). *Psychological Medicine, 25*, 739–753.

Arenella, J., & Ornduff, S. R. (2000). Manifestations of bodily concern in sexually abused girls. *Bulletin of the Menninger Clinic, 64*(4), 530–542.

Armstrong, J. G., Putnam, F. W., Carlson, E. B., Libero, D. Z., & Smith, S. R. (1997). Development and validation of a measure of adolescent dissociation: The Adolescent Dissociative Experiences Scale. *Journal of Nervous and Mental Disease, 185*, 491–497.

Bernstein, D. P., & Ahluvalia, T. (1997). Validity of the Childhood Trauma Questionnaire in an adolescent psychiatric population. *Journal of the American Academy of Child & Adolescent Psychiatry, 36*(3), 340–348.

Berton, M. W., & Stabb, S. D. (1996). Exposure to violence and post-traumatic stress disorder in urban adolescents. *Adolescence, 31*(122), 489–498.

Billingsley, R. C. (1995). Indicators of sexual abuse in children's Rorschach responses: an exploratory study. *Journal of Child Sexual Abuse, 4*(2), 83–98.

Briere, J. (1996). *The Trauma Symptom Checklist for Children (TSCC) Professional Manual.* Odessa, FL: Psychological Assessment Resources.

Briere, J. (2001). *The Trauma Symptom Checklist for Young Children (TSCYC) Professional Manual.* Odessa, FL: Psychological Assessment Resources.

Briere, J., Johnson, K., Bissada, A., Damon, L., Crouch, J., Gil, E., Hanson, R., & Ernst, V. (2001). The Trauma Symptom Checklist for Young Children (TSCYC): reliability and association with abuse exposure in a multi-site study. *Child Abuse and Neglect, 25*, 1001–1014.

Butcher, J. N., Williams, C. L., Graham, J. R., Archer, R., Tellegen, A., Ben-Porath, Y. S., et al. (1992). *MMPI-A Manual for Administration, Scoring, and Interpretation.* Minneapolis, MN: University of Minnesota Press.

Cashel, M. L., Ovaert, L. B., & Holliman, N. G. (2000). Evaluating PTSD in incarcerated male juveniles with the MMPI-A: An exploratory analysis. *Journal of Clinical Psychology, 56*(12), 1535–1549.

Cerney, M. S. (1990). The Rorschach and traumatic loss: Can the presence of traumatic loss be detected from the Rorschach? *Journal of Personality Assessment, 55*, 781–789.

Clinton, G. T., & Jenkins-Monroe, V. (1994). Rorschach responses of sexually abused children: An exploratory study. *Journal of Child Sexual Abuse, 3*(1), 67–84.

Cohen, J. A. (1998). Practice parameters for the assessment and treatment of children and adolescents with posttraumatic stress disorder. *Journal of the American Academy of Child and Adolescent Psychiatry, 37*(10 Supplement), 4S–26S.

Cooley, M. R., Turner, S. M., & Beidel, D. C. (1995). Assessing community violence: The children's report of exposure to violence. *Journal of the American Academy of Child and Adolescent Psychiatry, 34*, 201–208.

Costello, E. J., Angold, A., March, J., & Fairbank, J. (1998). Life events and post-traumatic stress: The development of a new measure for children and adolescents. *Psychological Medicine, 28*(6), 1275–1288.

Davis, L., & Siegel, L. J. (2000). Posttraumatic stress disorder in children and adolescents: A review and analysis. *Clinical Child and Family Psychology Review, 3*(3), 135–154.

Daviss, W. B., Mooney, D., Racusin, R., Ford, J. D., Fleischer, A., & McHugo, G. (2000). Predicting posttraumatic stress after hospitalization for pediatric injury. *Journal of the American Academy of Child and Adolescent Psychiatry, 39*, 576–583.

Dehon, C., & Scheeringa, M. S. (2005) Screening for preschool posttraumatic stress disorder with the Child Behavior Checklist. *Journal of Pediatric Psychology*. Retrieved on 7/28/05 from Journal of Pediatric Psychology Advance Access, doi:10.1093/jpepsy/jsj006.

Exner, J. E. (2003). *The Rorschach: A comprehensive system. Basic foundations and principles of interpretation* (4th ed.). New York: Wiley.

Ezzell, C. E., Swenson, C. C., & Brondino, M. J. (2000). The relationship of social support to physically abused children's adjustment. *Child Abuse and Neglect, 24*(5), 641–651.

Fletcher, K. E. (1996a). Childhood posttraumatic stress disorder, In E. J. Mash & R. A. Barkley (Eds.), *Childhood Psychopathology* (pp. 242–276). New York: Guilford Press.

Fletcher, K. (1996b). Psychometric review of the Childhood PTSD Interview. In B. H. Stamm (Ed.), *Measurement of stress, trauma, and adaptation* (pp. 87–89). Lutherville, MD: Sidran Press.

Fletcher, K. (1996c). Psychometric review of the When Bad Things Happen Scale (WBTH). In B. H. Stamm (Ed.), *Measurement of stress, trauma, and adaptation* (pp. 435–437). Lutherville, MD: Sidran Press.

Foa, E. B., Johnson, K. M., Feeny, N. C., & Treadwell, K. R. H. (2001). The Child PTSD Symptom Scale: A preliminary examination of its psychometric properties. *Journal of Clinical Child Psychology, 30*(3), 376–384.

Forbey, J. D., Ben-Porath, Y. S., & Davis, D. L., (2000). A comparison of sexually abused and non-sexually abused adolescents in a clinical treatment facility using the MMPI-A. *Child Abuse and Neglect, 24*(4), 557–568.

Ford, J. D., Racusin, R., Ellis, C. G., Daviss, W. B., Reiser, J., Fleischer, A., et al. (2000). Child maltreatment, other trauma exposure, and posttraumatic symptomatology among children with oppositional defiant and attention deficit hyperactivity disorders. *Child Maltreatment, 5*(3), 205–217.

Ford, J. D., & Rogers, K. (1997, November). *Empirically-based assessment of trauma and PTSD with children and adolescents*. Paper presented at the Annual Convention of the International Society for Traumatic Stress Studies, Montreal, Canada.

Foy, D. W., Wood, J., King, D., King, L., & Resnick, H. (1997). Los Angeles Symptom Checklist: Psychometric evidence with an adolescent sample. *Assessment, 4*(4), 377–384.

Freedenfeld, R. N., Ornduff, S. R., & Kelsey, R. M. (1995). Object relations and physical abuse: A TAT analysis. *Journal of Personality Assessment, 64*, 552–568.

Fricker, A. E., & Smith, D. W. (2001). Trauma specific versus generic measurement of distress and the validity of self-reported symptoms in sexually abused children. *Journal of Child Sexual Abuse, 10*(4), 51–66.

Friedrich, W. N. (1994). Assessing children for the effects of sexual victimization. In J. Briere (Ed.), *Assessing and treating victims of violence* (pp. 17–28). San Francisco, CA: Jossey-Bass.

Friedrich, W. N., Einbender, A. J., & McCarty, P. (1999). Sexually abused girls and their Rorschach responses. *Psychological Reports, 85*(2), 355–362.

Friedrich, W. N., & Share, M. C. (1997). The Roberts Apperception Test for Children: An exploratory study of its use with sexually abused children. *Journal of Child Sexual Abuse, 6*(4), 83–91.

Giaconia, R. M., Reinherz, H. Z., Silverman, A. B., Pakiz, B., Frost, A. K., & Cohen, E. (1994). Ages of onset of psychiatric disorders in a community population of older adolescents. *Journal of the American Academy of Child and Adolescent Psychiatry, 33*, 706–717.

Greenwald, R., & Rubin, A. (1999). Assessment of posttraumatic symptoms in children: Development and preliminary validation of parent and child scales. *Research on Social Work Practice, 9*, 61–75.

Guelzow, J. W., Cornett, P. F., & Dougherty, T. M. (2002). Child sexual abuse victims' perception of paternal support as a significant predictor of coping style and global self-worth. *Journal of Child Sexual Abuse, 11*(4), 53–72.

Gully, K. J. (2003). Expectations Test: Trauma scales for sexual abuse, physical abuse, exposure to family violence, and posttraumatic stress. *Child Maltreatment, 8*(3), 218–229.

Haviland, M. G., Sonne, J. L., & Woods, L. R. (1995). Beyond posttraumatic stress disorder: Object relations and reality testing disturbances in physically and sexually abused adolescents. *Journal of the American Academy of Child and Adolescent Psychiatry, 34*(8), 1054–1059.

Holaday, M. (1998). Rorschach protocols of children and adolescents with severe burns: A follow-up study. *Journal of Personality Assessment, 71*(3), 306–321.

Holaday, M. (2000). Rorschach protocols from children and adolescents diagnosed with posttraumatic stress disorder. *Journal of Personality Assessment, 75*(1), 143–157.

Holaday, M., Armsworth, M. W., Swank, P. R., & Vincent, K. R. (1992). Rorschach responding in traumatized children and adolescents. *Journal of Traumatic Stress, 5*(1), 119–129.

Holaday, M., & Whittenberg, T. (1994). Rorschach responding in children and adolescents who have been severely burned. *Journal of Personality Assessment, 62*(2), 269–279.

Horowitz, M., Wilner, N., & Alvarez, W. (1979). Impact of Events Scale: A measure of subjective stress. *Psychosomatic Medicine, 41*, 209–218.

Jones, R. T. (2002). *The Child's Reaction to Traumatic Events Scale (CRTES): A self-report traumatic stress measure.* Blacksburg, VA: Virginia Polytechnic University.

Keane, T. M., Malloy, P. F., & Fairbank, J. A. (1984). Empirical development of an MMPI subscale for the assessment of combat-related posttraumatic stress disorder. *Journal of Consulting and Clinical Psychology, 52*, 888–891.

Kelly, F. D. (1999). *The psychological assessment of abused and traumatized children.* Mahwah, NJ: Lawrence Erlbaum Associates.

Kovacs, M. (1981). Rating scales to assess depression in school-aged children. *Acta Paedopsychiatrica, 46*, 305–315.

Lacher, D., & Gruber, C. P. (1995). *Personality Inventory for Youth (PIY) Manual: Technical guide.* Los Angeles, CA: Western Psychological Services.

Leifer, M., Shapiro, J. P., Martone, M. W., & Kassem, L. (1991). Rorschach assessment of psychological functioning in sexually abused girls. *Journal of Personality Assessment, 56*(1), 14–28.

Levy, H., Markovic, J., Kalinowski, M., Ahart, S., & Torres, H. (1995). Child sexual abuse interviews: The use of anatomical dolls and the reliability of information. *Journal of Interpersonal Violence, 10*(3), 334–353.

Maan, C. (1991). Assessment of sexually abused children with anatomically detailed dolls: A critical review. *Behavioral Sciences and the Law, 9*, 43–51.

McArthur, D. S., & Roberts, G. E. (1982). *Roberts Apperception Test for Children (RATC) Manual.* Los Angeles, California: Western Psychological Services.

Muris, P., Merckelbach, H., Körver, P., & Meesters, C. (2000). Screening for trauma in children and adolescents: The validity of the Traumatic Stress Disorder Scale of the Screen for Child Anxiety Related Emotional Disorders. *Journal of Clinical Child Psychology, 29*(3), 406–413.

Muris, P., Merckelbach, H., Schmidt, H., & Mayer, B., (1999). The revised version of the Screen for Child Anxiety Related Emotional Disorders (SCARED–R): Factor structure in normal children. *Personality and Individual Differences, 26*, 99–112.

Murray, H. A. (1971). *Thematic Apperception Test manual.* Cambridge, MA: Harvard University Press.

Nader, K. O. (1997). Assessing traumatic experiences in children. In J. P. Wilson & T. M. Keane (Eds.), *Assessing Psychological Trauma and PTSD* (pp. 291–348). New York: Guilford Press.

Nader, K. O., Kriegler, J., Blake, D., Pynoos, R., Newman, E., & Weathers, F. (2002). *The Clinician-Administered PTSD Scale, Child and Adolescent Version (CAPS-CA)*. White River Junction, VT: National Center for PTSD.

Newman, E. (2002). Assessment of PTSD and trauma exposure in adolescents. *Journal of Aggression, Maltreatment and Trauma, 6*(1), 59–77.

Ohan, J. L., Myers, K., & Collett, B. R. (2002). Ten-year review of rating scales. IV: Scales assessing trauma and its effects. *Journal of the American Academy of Child and Adolescent Psychiatry, 41*(12), 1401–1422.

Ornduff, S. R., Freedenfeld, R. N., Kelsey, R., & Critelli, J. (1994). Object relations of sexually abused female subjects: A TAT analysis. *Journal of Personality Assessment, 63*, 223–238.

Ornduff, S. R., & Kelsey, R. M. (1996). Object relations of sexually and physically abused female children: A TAT analysis. *Journal of Personality Assessment, 66*(1), 91–105.

Peterson, L. W., Hardin, M., & Nitsch, M. J. (2001). The use of children's drawings in the evaluation and treatment of child sexual, emotional, and physical abuse. *Trauma and Loss: Research and Interventions, 1*(2), 29–36.

Pistole, D. R., & Ornduff, S. R. (1994). TAT assessment of sexually abused girls: An analysis of manifest content. *Journal of Personality Assessment, 63*(2), 211–222.

Praver, F., DiGiuseppe, R., Pelcovitz, D., Mandel, F. S., & Gaines, R. (2000). A preliminary study of a cartoon measure for children's reactions to chronic trauma. *Child Maltreatment, 5*, 273–286.

Putnam, F. W., Helmers, K., & Trickett, P. K. (1993). Development, reliability, and validity of a child dissociation scale. *Child Abuse and Neglect, 17*, 731–741.

Pynoos, R., Rodriguez, N., Steinberg, A., Stuber, M., & Frederick, C. (1998). *The UCLA PTSD reaction index for DSM IV (Revision 1)*. Los Angeles: UCLA Trauma Psychiatry Program.

Rabalais, A. E., Ruggiero, K. J., & Scotti, J. R. (2002). Multicultural issues in the response of children to disasters. In A. M. La Greca, W. K. Silverman, E. M. Vernberg, & M. C. Roberts (Eds.), *Helping children cope with disasters and terrorism* (pp. 73–99). Washington, DC: American Psychological Association.

Rasch, M. A., & Wagner, E. E. (1989). Initial psychological effects of sexual abuse on female children as reflected in the Hand Test. *Journal of Personality Assessment, 53*(4), 761–769.

Reynolds, C. R., & Kamphaus, R. W. (1992). *Behavior Assessment System for Children: Manual*. Circle Pines, MN: American Guidance.

Ribbe, D. (1996). Psychometric review of Traumatic Event Screening Instrument [*sic*] for Children (TESI-C). In B. H. Stamm (Ed.), *Measurement of stress, trauma, and adaptation* (pp. 386–387). Lutherville, MD: Sidran Press.

Ruggiero, K. J., & McLeer, S. V. (2000). PTSD Scale of the Child Behavior Checklist: Concurrent and discriminant validity with non-clinic-referred sexually abused children. *Journal of Traumatic Stress, 13*(2), 287–299.

Saigh, P. A., Yasik, A. E., Oberfield, R. A., Green, B. L., Halamandaris, P. V., Rubenstein, H., et al. (2000). The Children's PTSD Inventory: Development and reliability. *Journal of Traumatic Stress, 13*(3), 369–380.

Salmon, K., & Bryant, R. (2002). Posttraumatic stress disorder in children: The influence of developmental factors. *Clinical Psychology Review, 22*, 163–188.

Saylor, C. F., Swenson, C. C., Reynolds, S. S., & Taylor, M. (1999). The Pediatric Emotional Distress Scale: A brief screening measure for young children exposed to traumatic events. *Journal of Child Clinical Psychology, 28*(1), 70–81.

Scott, R. L., Knoth, R. L., Beltran-Quiones, M., & Gomez, N. (2003). Assessment of psychological functioning in adolescent earthquake victims in Colombia using the MMPI-A. *Journal of Traumatic Stress, 16*(1), 49–57.

Spaccarelli, S. (1995). Measuring abuse, stress, and negative cognitive appraisals in child sexual abuse: Validity data on two new scales. *Journal of Abnormal Child Psychology, 23*(6), 703–726.

Stovall, G., & Craig, R. J. (1990). Mental representations of physically and sexually abused latency-aged females. *Child Abuse and Neglect, 14*(2), 233–242.

Strand, V. C., Sarmiento, T. L., & Pasquale, L. E. (2005). Assessment and screening tools for trauma in children and adolescents. *Trauma, Violence, and Abuse, 6*(1), 55–78.

Urist, J. (1977). The Rorschach test and the assessment of object relations. *Journal of Personality Assessment, 41*, 3–9.

Van der Kolk, B. A., & Fisler, R. E. (1994). Childhood abuse and neglect and loss of self-regulation. *Bulletin of the Menninger Clinic, 58*(2), 145–168.

Webb, N. B. (2004). *Mass trauma and violence: Helping children and families cope.* New York: Guilford Press.

Welner, A. (2001). Rorschach correlates of sexual abuse: Trauma content and aggression indexes. *Forensic Panel Letter, 5*(2), 8–9.

Westen, D., Lohr, N., Silk, K., Kerber, K., & Goodrich, S. (1985). *Social cognition and object relations scale (SCORS): Manual for coding TAT data.* University of Michigan, Ann Arbor.

Wilson, J. P., & Keane, T. M. (2004). *Assessing Psychological Trauma and PTSD* (2nd ed.). New York: Guilford Press.

Wolfe, V. V., & Gentile, C. (1993). Psychological assessment of sexually abused children. In W. T. O'Donohue & J. H. Geer (Eds.), *Sexual Abuse of Children* (pp. 143–187). Hillsdale, NJ: Lawrence Erlbaum Associates.

Wolfe, V. V., Gentile, C., Michienzi, T., Sas, L., & Wolfe, D. A. (1991). The Children's Impact of Traumatic Events Scale: A measure of post-abuse PTSD symptoms. *Behavioral Assessment, 13*, 359–383.

25

RORSCHACH CONFIGURATIONS
OF CHILDREN WITH ADHD

Steve Tuber
Benjamin H. Harris
Kevin B. Meehan
Joseph S. Reynoso
Jasmine Ueng-McHale
City University of New York

This chapter presents both idiographic and nomothetic data describing patterns of responses from the Rorschach Inkblot Method (RIM) for a group of children diagnosed with Attention Deficit Hyperactive Disorder (ADHD). We begin by briefly reviewing an object representational approach to children's Rorschach performance and then shift to a description of the nature and consequences of ADHD in young children. We then describe a recent study that examines the quality of Rorschach object representational paradigms in children with this disorder. We conclude with two case illustrations of children with ADHD that both amplify the nomothetic findings and suggest a possible prototype for how young children with ADHD may present on the Rorschach and why.

Psychodynamic theory and clinical practice over the past 50 years have emphasized the heuristic value of the study of the intrapsychic templates of interpersonal behavior, that is, the "object relations" of both adults and children. Within the realm of psychological testing, these relations have been examined via an assessment of the object representational paradigms expressed on projective tests, especially the RIM. In a number of studies with child populations, Tuber and his colleagues (Goddard & Tuber, 1989; Meyer & Tuber, 1989; Tuber, 1983, 1989, 1992; Tuber & Coates, 1989; Tuber, Frank, & Santostefano, 1989) found that the quality of human movement (M), animal movement (FM), and inanimate movement (m) responses on the Rorschach relate in significant ways to the quality of children's internal representations of self and others and their social functioning. Tuber (1983) found that children whose highest object relations responses, as measured by the Mutuality of Autonomy Scale (MOAS), were more adaptive and benign and were significantly more likely to require no further psychiatric services after discharge from an inpatient residential treatment center, compared with peers who had less benign scores. Similarly, children with more malevolent Rorschach MOAS responses were more likely to require psychiatric rehospitalization over a 20-year follow-up period. Tuber and Coates (1989) reported that boys diagnosed with Gender Identity Disorder had many more malevolent Rorschach responses than a control sample, and Goddard and Tuber (1989) found that boys with Separation Anxiety Disorder also had more disturbed object representational scores, compared with a control group, with a particular emphasis on clinging, and fewer autonomous responses. Tuber (1989) found that Rorschach object representational responses could be meaningfully linked to core relational conflicts in their psychotherapy, and Tuber et al. (1989) found that short-term changes in object representational paradigms could be linked to the trauma of impending hernia surgery in boys. Meyer and Tuber (1989) reported that very young children with imaginary companions had far more plentiful human movement responses than similarly aged children without such "companions" (see Tuber, 1992, for a more in-depth review of these studies). In more recent work, Tuber (2000) extended the use of this type of Rorschach assessment to the vicissitudes of child and adult psychoanalysis. That study depicted the manner in which child Rorschach object representational responses evidenced a striking continuity with intrapsychic themes in both the child and adult treatment of the same subject.

The present chapter extends this work to another common clinical syndrome in childhood, to children diagnosed with ADHD. Although the ADHD diagnosis has received widespread interest from both the scientific community and mainstream media, it remains a clinical picture that has not been thoroughly examined with the use of projective tests, guided by psychoanalytic thinking. A psychoanalytic perspective that assesses aspects of unconscious fantasy, conflict, and defense may be especially equipped to move beyond the behavioral/symptom-dominated outlook of the DSM, which does not sufficiently take into account the mental experience of the ADHD individual and does not give enough attention to the child's quality of relationships.

In a psychoanalytic context it is important to understand the severe social and interpersonal limitations of the ADHD child in light of his or her intrapsychic and affective experience difficulties (see Nixon, 2001, or Stormont, 2001, for a review). As Gilmore (2000, 2002) noted in her conceptualization of ADHD from an ego-psychological approach, with low affect and anxiety tolerance, children with ADHD can become so dysregulated by unexpected changes in their environment that they may appear either hyperexcitable and anxious, or strikingly lacking in anxiety. Children diagnosed with ADHD are often dysregulated by mutual social exchange, where there is a potential for surprise and loss of control, such as those situations experienced at school and with families. The child's reaction to overstimulation is often found to be confusing or frustrating to loved ones, and, as a result, such children may internalize experiences of significant others as frustrated, confused, and angry with them (Yeschin, 2000).

Children with ADHD symptomatology are often maladaptively sensitive to stimuli and have profound difficulty regulating their affect, arousal level, and behavioral inhibition. As such, it is expected that these ego impairments would be reflected in Rorschach variables sensitive to such vulnerabilities, namely movement and color variables, as well as ratios that depict the relationship between these variables. These include ratios that capture children's access to internal resources or ego strengths. Because children with ADHD evidence impairments in their capacity for delay and self-regulation, which impinge on their social fluency, it is also expected that that these children would respond with fewer representations of social interactions through the use of human and animal movement (M, FM) as well as depictions of human (or human-like) figures in general [H, (H), Hd, (Hd)].

An assessment of the use of color on the Rorschach is also expected to relate to impairments in affect regulation seen in children with ADHD. Schachtel (1966/2001) argued four decades ago that an individual's responsiveness to the stimulation of the bold colors in the Rorschach is indicative of one's responsiveness to one's own internal affectivity. He hypothesized that a lack of responsiveness to color may reflect an aversion to strong, passionate affects. Because children with ADHD can become easily dysregulated by affective stimulation, it is expected that these children would tend to have one of two types of responses to color stimuli: 1) they may constrict their responses and avoid using color to form their percepts (e.g., few FC, CF, and C responses) or 2) they may include color in their responses, but swamped by the intensity of the color stimuli, they may fail to actively impose form on their percepts (e.g., CF and C dominating over FC responses). In terms of the first of these two strategies, children may seek to avoid the feeling state of being overstimulated by simplifying the stimulus demands of the blot and focusing excessively on form in order to organize their percepts, resulting in high Lambda scores. The second strategy toward affect regulation would acknowledge affective intensity, but flood and overwhelm the child.

In addition, a number of ratios that include movement and color may be relevant to assessing children's access to the internal resources or ego strengths central in ADHD impairments. Exner (1993) argues that the ability to represent human movement and color indicates an overall capacity to access internal resources, represented by a variable termed the Experience Actual (EA) score. The EA score represents the sum of the total number of human movement responses and a weighted sum of the chromatic color responses.

Exner also evaluates the capacity to access internal resources in relation to the individual's current stimulus demands, as represented by nonhuman movement determinants, shading and achromatic determinants (D score). The D score represents the EA score minus the sum of all nonhuman movement determinants, the shading and achromatic determinants. Stimulus demands are understood by Exner as externally or internally originating from and drawing on the emotional or mental activity of the person. Thus, as a measure of the difference between one's available resources and one's experienced demands, a person's D score can be thought of as indicative of capacities of control and stress tolerance. Because, as Barkley (1997) argues, children with ADHD have an impaired ability to draw on inner resources to delay gratification, inhibit behavior, and regulate emotional responses, it is expected that these children would be found to have lower scores on variables signifying resources and capacities of control and stress tolerance (EA, D score).

The small body of research on assessments of children with ADHD using the RIM (Bartell & Solanto, 1995) is consistent with these hypotheses. In one such study, Gordon and Oshman (1981) evaluated 40 boys (ages 6 to 11) and found that boys designated as hyperactive produced fewer M responses and Human Content (H) responses and more Animal Content (A) responses, compared with the nonhyperactive group. Similarly, in a sample of 24 children (ages 5 to 11) diagnosed with ADHD, Bartell and Solanto (1995) found that these children produced fewer M responses, poorer form quality (X+%), and a lower EA score in comparison with Exner's (1993) norms for children of the same age. Cotugno (1995) compared the protocols of 120 children (ages 5 to 6) who comprised an ADHD group, a non-ADHD clinical control group, and a normal control group. He found that, compared with the normal control group, children in both the ADHD and clinical groups produced a higher frequency of pure form responses (Lambda), fewer color responses (FC+CF+C), more shading responses, fewer popular responses, fewer depictions of whole humans (H), and overall fewer accurate responses (X+%).

In a recent study (Reynoso et al., under review) we sought to assess ego impairments and access to internal resources in children with ADHD symptomatology, using the Rorschach. We predicted that children with ADHD would produce 1) fewer responses with human movement (M), 2) fewer representations of human figures [H+Hd+(H)]+ (Hd)], 3) fewer representations of color (FC+CF+C), 4) fewer form-dominated color responses compared with other color responses (greater CF+C: FC), 5) poorer form quality (X+%), 6) a greater percentage of high Lambda responses, and 7) lower EA and D scores.

The participants for this study were 36 children (14 females and 22 males) between the ages of 7 and 10 years (M = 99.63 months; SD = 10.52 months). All children were referred to a National Institute on Deafness and Other Communication Disorders (NIDCD) funded project at the City College of New York examining attention and language in community children (Gomes et al., 2001). Most children were referred for either behavioral or reading problems in school. All of the children were fluent English speakers enrolled in English-only classrooms, but 8 of the children came from bilingual households. Self-reported ethnicity/ race was as follows: 21 African American children, 9 Latino children, 5 Caucasian children, and 1 child with no information provided. Children were excluded from the larger NIDCD study if they had a chronic medical, psychiatric, or neurological illness; were taking systemic medication; or were not attending school. Normal hearing and vision and a Performance IQ of 85 or better were all requirements for inclusion.

Children were categorized as ADHD with a "best estimate" procedure in which information from schoolteachers, parents, and tester was integrated (Schaughency & Rothlind, 1991). With the use of this procedure, 23 children were found to meet the criteria for ADHD and 13 children were found to meet criteria for the comparison group. Of the 23 ADHD children, 16 were boys, and 6 boys and 7 girls were in the comparison group. Interrater reliability for two coders was computed by kappa coefficients, with correlations of 0.90 for Location, 0.89 for Determinants, 0.70 for Form Quality, and 0.87 for Content, indicating solid interrater agreement. Scores of the more experienced rater (ST) were used in the data analysis when discrepancies between the raters occurred.

As we predicted, with regard to ratios reflecting children's access to internal resources, the ADHD group was found to have significantly lower EA scores than the comparison group ($F(1,34) = 5.895, p = .021$). There were trends in the ADHD group toward lower D scores ($F(1,34) = 3.643, p = .065$) and Adjusted D scores ($F(1.34) = 2.85, p = .10$), compared with the comparison group. With regard to movement variables, as predicted, the ADHD group was found to have significantly fewer M scores than the comparison group ($F(1,34) = 6.36$, $p = .017$). Similarly, as predicted, the ADHD group was found to have significantly fewer human content scores [H+(H)+(Hd)+Hd] ($F(1,34) = 5.369, p = .027$) than the comparison group. There were no significant differences between the groups on color responses. It is noteworthy that there were so few color responses overall that a comparison of form-dominated color responses with other color responses (CF+C: FC) was not possible. Finally, there were no significant differences between the groups in terms of accuracy (X+%) or percentage of pure form responses (Lambda).

Thus the ADHD group had less access to overall resources (EA, D, Adj D) and specifically less access to human percepts (M and H+(H)+(Hd)+Hd). These findings were consistent with the notion that children with ADHD have difficulty accessing internal resources in the face of high stimulus demand in order to organize, process, and represent their experience. The fact that children with ADHD evidenced specifically less access to human percepts may reflect impairments in their capacity for delay and ideational resources, as Rapaport, Gill, and Schafer (1968) would suggest. It also may be the case that children with ADHD who are easily dysregulated by mutual social exchange may tend to shy away from percepts of an interpersonal nature. Last, less access to human percepts in children with ADHD may reflect impairments in their internal representations of self and others. Contrary to our predictions, the ADHD group did not differ on color variables, accuracy of percepts (X+%), or percentage of pure form responses (Lambda). However, these findings suggest that children with many ADHD symptoms perform in distinct ways on the Rorschach in comparison with children with other kinds of difficulties. Specifically, children struggling with many ADHD symptoms may be distinct in comparison with children with other learning or behavioral problems in that they probably have less access to internal ego resources and to human percepts in their fantasy lives, thus impairing their capacity for self-regulation.

Problems in the self-regulation of arousal and affect and deficits in executive functions disrupt the normal developmental progress that shifts sources of self-control from the external world of the child to the internal world (cf. Ruff & Rothbart, 1996). This problem complicates the internalization of experiences of coregulation with caregivers. It also leaves children with a diminished capacity to evaluate their own actions and undermines their ability to draw on inner resources to delay gratification, inhibit behavior, and regulate emotional responses, abilities that are crucial to engaging in mutual social interactions. These disruptions may result in a reciprocal cycle in which the child's dysregulation of arousal, attention, and affect; disruptions in the internalization of coregulatory experiences with caregivers; and impairments in internal resources inhibit healthy ego development and negatively affect a child's capacity to understand and represent object relations.

In terms of the nonsignificant comparison between groups on the frequency of color responses, it is also possible that the dynamic interplay between children's deficits in executive function and affect regulation as represented in color responses was not captured in the current data analyses. It may be, for example, that children who have problems with attention and impulsivity have a more complicated relationship with color stimuli that is not reflected in whether the child simply represents color or not, over the entire protocol. For children who are highly reactive to intense stimuli, it may be important to focus not only on the frequency of color scores overall, but also on the child's performance on chromatic cards relative to achromatic cards. Similarly, although it was not found that children with ADHD symptoms differed with the comparison group in the percentage of pure form responses (Lambda), it may be the case that the degree to which the child relies on a strategy of simplifying the stimulus by focusing excessively on form is dependent upon the complexity and intensity of stimuli. In this conceptualization a child may have a bimodal way of coping with the world: one strategy of simplification and constriction, and a second strategy of acknowledgment of some vitality and affect, which is then overwhelming. Thus the quality of the child's response would be heavily influenced by the stimuli in the environment, as likely occurs for the child in different contexts.

To further illustrate the thinking behind our approach and to demonstrate a way to use both nomothetic and idiographic research to inform clinical practice, we now present the RIM protocols of two of our ADHD participants. These cases provide an important complement to the empirical analysis in that they vividly illustrate how dynamic and context-dependent a child's responses can be, as opposed to a static and narrow view of ADHD children as having little access to human representations and internal resources across all settings.

Case 1: Terri

Terri, an eight-year-old African American girl, was found to meet criteria for ADHD, Inattentive Type. We present Terri as an example of an ADHD child whose attentional difficulties significantly affected her ability to draw upon internal resources to organize her responses to the Rorschach blots. Accordingly, her protocol is marked by mostly pure form responses, which are of varying quality.

Behaviorally, Terri was remarkably distracted throughout the two days of testing. She had a Full Scale IQ of 85 on the WASI, although the examiner noted that because of her distractibility during the administration of the test, this score did not likely represent her full potential. During the administration of the Rorschach she would continually climb under the table to pick at lint and fuzz on the carpet, or hang off her chair to play with wires under the table. She did not spontaneously give responses to the Rorschach cards placed in front of her, but rather required a prompt almost every time. She also spun many of the cards on the table, sending them flying to the ground.

As can be seen in Table 25.1, Terri's record contains 14 responses, two fewer than a typical girl of her age (Ames, Metraux, Rodell, & Walker, 1974). When one compares her record with that of a typical child her age, it quickly becomes apparent that hers is impoverished. With the notable exception of shading, Terri used no other determinants on any of her responses. Although typical eight-year-olds do not tend to use a large number of determinants other than form, one can expect to see at least a minimal range of determinants in their responses.

In addition, subtle yet significant differences from a normative sample were noted in Terri's performance on the chromatic and achromatic cards. As can be seen in Table 25.2, on the five color cards, every one of her responses used only form, and all were of poor form quality. In contrast, on the five achromatic cards more than half of her responses were of good form quality. Furthermore, of the four responses using texture, the three responses that occurred on color cards were all of poor form quality. In contrast, the one texture response that occurred on an achromatic card was of good form quality. Thus it seems that

TABLE 25.1.
Entire Record for Terri

Determinant	Terri	Typical 8-year-old
R	14	15.9
M	0	1.3
FM	0	1.5
M	0	.4
FC+CF+C	0	1.7
FC'+CF'+C'	0	.9
Texture	4	.2
H+Hd+(H)+(Hd)	1	2.6
A+Ad+(A)+(Ad)	12	7.3
Lambda	2.5	1.37
X+%	29%	78%

Note: All Norms are derived from Ames et al. 1974.

TABLE 25.2.
Achromatic vs. Chromatic Cards for Terri

Determinant	Achromatic cards	Chromatic cards
R	6	8
M	0	0
FM	0	0
m	0	0
FC+CF+C	0	0
FC'+CF'+C'	0	0
Texture	1	3
H+Hd+(H)+(Hd)	1	0
A+Ad+(A)+(Ad)	4	8

Note: Achromatic cards are I, IV, V, VI, & VII; chromatic cards are II, III, VIII, IX & X.

although Terri has adequate ability to perceptually organize a response when presented with achromatic stimuli, she is unable to organize a good form level response in the face of color.

This difference suggests that despite the fact that Terri did not use color in her responses, the presence of the color nonetheless had a significant impact on her performance. It seems she expended so much "intrapsychic capital" attempting to be organized in the face of the color stimuli that she appeared like a much less integrated child in her responses. Indeed, Terri reacted to the cards with marked cognitive rigidity and inflexibility, in the manner of a child four or five years old (Leichtman, 1996). After expending a great deal of energy on the first few cards, Terri struggled to elaborate upon or explain her responses. A close examination of some of her responses will help to flesh out this dynamic.

Table 25.3 contains Terri's Free Association and Inquiry. On Card I she gave the responses of a "cat," an "elephant," and a "ghost." Thus she began with a well-formed object, a cat, but she was then drawn to the white space and provided a poor form quality response for which she could not account, an elephant. She then tried to organize the entire percept in a single response, but she was able to provide only a vague, global response of "the face, the face, the face," which illustrates her less developmentally appropriate, uninterested responsiveness.

On Card II, she appeared to experience color shock, exclaiming, "Ugh! What's that?" After struggling to organize her first two responses, "bat" and "snake," she provided a shading response (a thought disordered furry fish), which seemed to suggest marked inner disruptiveness. It is important to note that even though color is not explicitly mentioned by her, and thus is not reflected in the scoring of this card, Terri appeared to have had a strong reaction to this stimulus.

When given Card VI, a card that often elicits shading responses, Terri initially asked whether she was finished, perhaps in recognition of the unpleasant affect the shading was stirring up in her. Nonetheless, she provided two responses, a "lion" and a "head," although it is not clear from the Inquiry whether or not the head was part of the lion. She was clearly drawn to the shading, as she made reference to a "lion rug," but then became angry with the examiner and yelled that the "fur" and the "fug rug" make it look like a fur coat. Although shading responses are relatively common on this card (she rejected Card IV, another common shading response card), this shading response provokes anger at the examiner, a disrupted move outside the frame of her test responses. Notably, she then rejected Card VII (another card

TABLE 25.3.
Terri's Rorschach Record

I.

1. A cat
[Anything else?]

1. [Where do you see a cat?] Right here (points to the middle) no; right here (points to right corner). These things, the, the ears. [What makes it look like a cat?] The ears. [Take your finger and show me where you see the cat.] (She taps the card on the ear.) [Only this part or the whole thing?] The whole thing.

2. An elephant
[Anything else?]

2. [Where do you see the elephant?] The face. [Can you use your finger and show me?] These, these. The white things. [What makes it look like an elephant?] The white things.

3. Mm, it look like a ghost
[Anything else or is that it?] (No response)

3. [Where do you see the ghost?] The face. [What makes it look like a ghost?] The face, the face, the ears.

II.

Ewe! What's that?
4. (Rotates card 360 degrees) Oo, this looks like a cat. The other one was a bat. (She goes under the table. We have an exchange where I ask her to sit up in her seat. She picks at things on the rug. She gets up again, holding a Lego piece.)
[Anything else?]

4. [Where do you see a cat?] Right here. [Can you use your finger and trace it for me?] (unclear what she's pointing to) [Is it the whole part or. . .] The whole part. [What makes it look like a cat?] (She doesn't answer) [What makes it look like a cat?] The whole face. (She's sitting with her face covered in her arms on the table.)

5. A fish

5. [Where do you see a fish?] The bat eyes. [Where do you see the fish?] (She points to the bottom.) [Just this part?] And this, the fur (points to black section). [The fur of the fish?] (She agrees.)

6. A bat
[Is that it?]

6. (She may not have responded to this inquiry or we got side-tracked. She had shown me the bat eyes earlier.)

7. A snake

7. [Where do you see the snake?] Here in the middle (points to the white space). [What makes it look like a snake?] Because his face. [Where do you see the face?] Right here (points).

III.

8. Tiger [Hm-hm. Is that it?] (Nods)

8. [Where do you see the tiger?] (Points) The whole thing, the face, and the eyes, and these are the gorillas. These are the monkeys.

IV.

I don't know what's this. (Turns card around)
9. It's a pig, a piggy, a piggy, I don't know what's that. I don't want to make a sentence about this one.

(continued)

TABLE 25.3. (*Continued*)

V.

10. A bat.
[Anything else?] (No response)

10. The wings. [What makes it look like?] (No response.)
[Additional response:]
A sword. [Where?] This part, the line.

VI.

Are we done? Aw, I want to be done now.
11. A lion. [Anything else?] A head. [Is that part of the lion or a different thing?] (She doesn't respond and has gone under the table. She doesn't want to come out.)

11. [Where do you see the lion?] (points to top D) This top part, this part.
[What makes it look like a lion?] Yes. And it looks like a lion coat, wait and a lion rug.
[What makes it look like a lion coat or rug?] Because the, (rubs card), the fur. [Where do you see the head?] (Points to top D). [What makes it look like?] It looks like a fur coat. [What makes it look like a head?] I said a fur! A fur coat b/c it's furry and a rug b/c it has fur.

VII.

I don't know what this one is! (Shrugs) What are you writing? (She puts her face down in her arms on the table.)

VIII.

12. A lion, no, not, not, not a lion. A, a, a, cheaper, cheetah (∨).

12. The mouth. [Where?] This, the re—no, this.
[What makes it look like?] B/c it has spots.
[Where are the spots?] Here. (points)

IX.

13. What is that? Oo, I know, this is a zebra. (sings zebra, zebra, zebra)
[Anything else?] (No response)

13. It has stripes. [Where?] (She gestures vaguely toward the card.) Right here. [Can you touch the picture and show me?] I don't know where the eyes, right here. There's the eyes.
[What makes it look like?] Because it has stripes and strips with whit stripes, too, and it got some hair on the back. [Where is the hair?] Right here (unclear where she's pointing). And it has a tail with some hair on the tail.

X.

14. What is that? There it, this way. (∨) It's a gorilla.

14. This is the hair and it's black and it eats bananas.
[What makes it look like a gorilla?] Because gorillas sometimes they get mad, and sometimes they get a mad face and they're black and they stink and they like bananas. (The examiner is wearing black.)

that often elicits shading responses) and put her head down on the table. On the last four cards, she provided two more shading responses, both of which were of poor form level.

Clearly, Terri was both drawn to and overwhelmed by the shading of the cards. This conflict appears so central that it precluded her access to other determinants (i.e., movement or color), which are often reflective of the possible wealth of internal resources a child can bring to bear on this test. It seems as if she was experiencing so much inner confusion that she could not help but be preoccupied by this tension. On achromatic cards she was successfully able to screen out inner dysphoria, whereas on the chromatic cards this strategy was less successful. Unfortunately, this left her with minimal access to other internal resources. In the absence of further investigation, including but not limited to psychotherapy, it is difficult to assess whether Terri has access to an untapped store of resources upon which to draw.

Case 2: Henry

Henry, a seven-year-old boy of Haitian descent, met criteria for ADHD, Combined type, and was found to have a Full Scale IQ of 94. At the time of the referral, Henry was exhibiting disruptive behavior at school that included kissing girls against their will and looking up their skirts. Henry's mother noted that his teacher described him as "very active and impulsive." His mother also described a pattern of disruptive behavior at home, unsolicitedly stating that Henry was "always on the go."

As can be seen in Table 25.4, with one notable exception, Henry's overall Rorschach record does not differ dramatically from that of a typical seven-year-old. He matches or approximates norms on most determinants, with the notable exception of inanimate movement (m).

However, upon closer inspection (see Table 25.5), Henry's Rorschach record also reveals a bimodal way of viewing and interacting with the world, which is particularly highlighted by the ways in which he dealt with color and blackness.

Five of Henry's total of 23 responses occurred on the five achromatic cards, all of which were whole responses. On the achromatic cards all of his responses used only pure form, but his form quality on these cards was quite good ($X+\%_{black} = 0.83$). He did not represent animate interaction in any way and rejected one of the cards (VII) altogether. In sum, on these five achromatic cards he provided a bland, deadened, and constricted record. Yet, on the five color cards, Henry responded like a different child. He gave 18 responses to the color cards, only two of which were whole responses. He provided very few pure form responses, and his form quality on these cards is significantly lower ($X+\%_{color} = 0.33$), compared with the achromatic cards.

Whereas Henry's responses to the achromatic cards were sparse, his responses to the color cards were quite full and alive. In fact, the total number of words he used on the first

TABLE 25.4.
Entire Record for Henry

Determinant	Henry	Typical 7-year-old
R	23	18.3
M	1	1.4
FM	2	2.0
m	8	0.8
H+Hd+(H)+(Hd)	1	2.6
A+Ad+(A)+(Ad)	7	7.6
FC+CF+C	4	2.9
FC'+CF'+C'	1	1.1
Texture	0	0.5

Note: All norms are derived from Ames et al. (1974).

TABLE 25.5.

Achromatic vs. Chromatic Cards for Henry

Determinant	Achromatic Cards	Chromatic Cards
R	5	18
M	1	0
FM	0	2
M	0	8
H+Hd+(H)+(Hd)	1	0
A+Ad+(A)+(Ad)	4	3
FC+CF+C	0	4
FC'+CF'+C'	0	1
Texture	0	0

Note: Achromatic cards are I, IV, V, VI, & VIII; Chromatic cards are II, III, VIII

all-color card with which he was presented (VIII) surpassed the total number of words he used on the previous four cards combined (Cards IV–VI; Card VII was rejected). His responses to the color cards contained an enormous amount of movement, especially inanimate movement (m), and CF responses. Although he provided six form-dominated responses, the remaining 12 responses were all of vague form level, a less developmentally advanced type of response, or, as Mayman (1970) writes, "(the) cheapest form level available."

A disparity between achromatic and chromatic cards was also noted with regard to content. With one exception, the responses to achromatic cards contained very ordinary content: two bats and a butterfly. There is one response of "a human, inside" and one rejection, but those seem tame when compared with the content on the color cards: explosions, fire, volcanoes, lava, fiery chaos, speed, motion, and electricity.

Thus, Henry's presentation was quite varied, depending upon the type of stimuli presented to him. It is only when one compares the chromatic and achromatic cards that the full picture of his Rorschach comes to light. Although Henry attempted to rely on a strategy of simplifying the stimulus by focusing excessively on form when presented with achromatic cards, the stimulation of the color cards seemed to be too great for him, leading to a "fiery chaos" of inanimate movement and vague forms. It should be noted that an assessment of children like Henry, without regard to this chromatic versus achromatic dichotomy, would lump all of his responses together, thus failing to depict his markedly different responses, depending on the degree of bold color he must wrestle with on the RIM.

Henry's RIM protocol can be seen in Table 25.6.

On Card I, Henry began with the responses of "butterfly" and "bat," each a pure form response. However, when the examiner presented him with Card II, with the first hints of color, he responded with "explosion" and "volcano lava." When the examiner inquired about these responses, Henry provided a flood of color, unbound by form. Clearly Henry was overstimulated by this card, and he reacted to it accordingly. Unable to find the words to describe his reaction, he turned to action language ("Poom!"). His shift from an explosion to the slower moving "lava" seemed to be an attempt on his part to slow down the speed with which he was experiencing the percepts (although the inanimate movement was clearly still present) and to retreat somewhat by invoking distance. Whatever anxiety and/or affect had been stimulated by the color in this card seemed to be breaking through, just like the lava; his language deteriorated, his capacity to self-modulate nearly vanished, and he perseverated

TABLE 25.6.
Henry's Rorschach Record

I.

1. A butterfly.
[Anything else?]

1. [What makes it look like a butterfly?] (points) This (a) and these things (b). [What makes those things look like a butterfly?] The eyes and the feelers. [Show the therapist feelers.] Not feelers, the decoration; these are the eyes, the little hands poking up, these are the decorations.

2. A bat, that's all.
[Anything else?] No

2. [What makes it look like bat?] It has these for the wings, and these things (b) up there, and this (a). [What makes these things look like a bat?] I don't know what that is but it looks like a bat with those. [That (a)?] The feet.

II.

3. Explosion.

3. [What makes it look like explosion?] (points to top and bottom D). [Explosion?] This happens, poom! (top D exploding) and this thing that's littler (bottom D) goes like that (motions lava coming out). This thing is from far distance you can see these, so from close distance it's big like that. [?] When this thing goes it's little from far distance (bottom D) but you can see this (top D) from close distance.

4. Volcano lava . . . I don't know any more.

4. [What makes it look like volcano lava?] (points to everything) [Volcano lava?] Because the volcano lava has this (bottom D and this thing breaks sometimes through that (top D) [?] This is the lava (the red under the black D) and this thing breaks (black D) and looks just like that (red coming out looks like top D), like you see its there and it's breaking on the side. [Breaking as if?] It has this (red) inside of it, and you can see its poking out, because you made it just like what I wanted. [?] Yeah, I know I was gonna see something like that.

III.

5. That one looks like a bug, cause look it has a bow, a bow on it, and these are the eyes, the feelers, and these things are the back of it.

5. [What makes it look like bug?] The eyes, the mouth, the back of it, that leads to the . . . foot, the feelers.
How many more do he and the therapist have to do?
Do he and the therapist have to do all of these, how about one more?

IV.

6. This one looks like a bat too, upside down.

6. Cause it has this . . . are the ears, the head, the little eyes, look the little eyes, the wing, and the legs upside down, and this is the bottom.

V.

7. Bat again.

7. It looks like a bat because of the legs, the ears, and the wings, and this is the little hands. Why do so many look like a bat?

(continued)

TABLE 25.6. (*Continued*)

VI.

8. I don't know what that looks like . . . a human being, inside.

8. Cause of the hands, the head, and . . . I don't know, this, the hand, the feet. [Human being inside?] Just this (center D). [What about it makes it look inside?] I don't know.

VII.

9. I don't know what that is. [Take you time, it's hard sometimes but I think you'll see something.] I don't see nothing . . . (15 sec) I don't see nothing. [Nothing?] No.

VIII.

10. A picture, cause of the colors, colors of a picture.

10. [What makes it look like picture?] The colors, and this little line, and that's it. [Lines?] These lines and the shape. [Show the therapist the shape] (points around perimeter) The shapes . . . this one looks like a cat, and this, I don't know what that looks like, but this looks like a spaceship lighting off the back of it going up, that's it. [Back of it going up?] Back of it, no, this is the spaceship, but the back has the fire, this is the fire. No, this whole thing is a spaceship, this is the front, this is the back, this is space animals, space cats, and this is the fire, this is the back of a thing, and this is the front. This is the missiles. [What makes it look like space cats?] No I just say space cats, they're not space cats, but I say it because I don't know what, I just put something there. [Going up?] The space things are climbing up the ship. [As if?] To . . . cause they're the enemies from the sky and he's gonna be brave and take out the missiles so they can shoot it. This is the missile. [What makes it look like fire?] That this goes down and this is smoke. [What makes it look like smoke?] This is the fire, this is the smoke going up, it's kinda grayish.

IX.

11. [Take you time, I know it's hard.] Dragonfly.

11. This is the speed that's pushing the air out. This is the fire that's behind it because he's going fast, cause he's going super fast, and this is the dragon in the middle, this is the wings. [Super fast as if?] It was a rocket. [What makes it look like fire?] Cause it's yellow, no orange. [Speed?] It's pushing the speed. [What makes it look like speed?] Cause you see how fast he's going? This is him, and this is where he's, the air is coming, this drops of water cause he's going fast and he's sweating, and this is the air cause, to show how fast he's going. [Sweating?] (points) [What makes it look like water?] It's little.

(*continued*)

TABLE 25.6. (*Continued*)

X.

12. It's an electro-clip. [?] An electro-clip.

12. Cause it's got this (points to large D) and this is the clipper (top D). [What's an electro-clip?] You know when you put those electro-clips in the car (jumper cable clips)? Or if it's a toy one, you know Operation, the toy where you put the batteries in and then you pick up those little pieces? [Yes. Show the therapist again now.] This opens, and this you squeeze to go like this (imitates squeezing handles) and this whole thing is a clip, but leave this out (side D). This closes, this is the opening thing, and then this is the the thing that's like this (motions) and this has a line going across like that (center D) [?] So when it's apart, to keep it together, not to fall apart. And this things, this, looks like screws, and that's it. [Squeeze as if?] To, pretend this is what you are squeezing this, like if your taking a splinter out, that's sort of it.

from the explosion to the lava. The experience of seeing the color rendered him passive (Schachtel, 1966/2001) in that he was unable to actively impose good form on the percept.

On Card III, Henry recovered by successfully avoiding the color stimuli, resulting in responses that were bland and simple. This suggests that on the RIM, just as in his everyday life, there may be moments when he can avoid affective dysregulation by screening out stimuli that threaten to overwhelm him. With the absence of bold color on the following four cards, Henry provided relatively sparse responses to this sequence, registering only 109 words on these four cards, including a rejection of Card VII. Thus, judging from the responses on the five achromatic cards, we are left with little sense of Henry's potential resources. He does not appear to be able to access achromatic color, movement, or shading, leaving the impression that his world is quite deadened. There is no mention of human connection or affect.

On Card VIII, Henry again seemed to become derailed by the vivid color in the stimulus. He provided the vague, formless response of "a picture" and when asked about this, he again became overwhelmed by his associations. Although he initially attempted to employ the same strategy used on Card III, in which he avoided engaging color by providing a vague response (here, "a picture"), as the Inquiry progressed his associations became more idiosyncratic. A popular response, the "cats," deteriorated into a vague, achromatic color-dominated response, with "smoke" and "fire coming out of a spaceship." Furthermore, the benign cats became "spacecats" that "take out the missiles so they can shoot it." This response illustrates his internal process quite well; although he has the internal resources to form an accurate percept (the commonly seen cats), he nevertheless became overstimulated by the color stimulus and then projected his feelings of attack onto the cats, so that his benign percept then became malevolent.

On Card IX, he provided the response of "dragonfly," which upon Inquiry is understood to be a thought-disordered, contamination response of a dragon and a fly coexisting in the same space on the blot. However, Henry finally achieved some integration of his two modes of response on Card X, which he saw as an "electro-clip," such as a jumper cable that one uses to charge a stalled car battery. On the Inquiry, he provided a vivid reflection of what he must do in the world to contain his affect and anxiety; he tries to screen out potentially overwhelming stimuli by clamping down his electro-clip "to keep it together, not to fall apart." This method of coping with overstimulation has been partially successful for Henry, but it also bespeaks the degree to which he must exert energy to hold this dysphoric stimulation and bodily discomfort at bay. Furthermore, this strategy of screening out potentially overwhelming stimuli pinches off his access to internal resources in general and to human percepts in particular. In this case, an analysis of the sequential and chromatic/achromatic response patterns better allows one to understand Henry's difficulties in the context of unconscious conflict and defense against uncomfortable affect than a simple tallying of response categories.

CONCLUSION

Over the past 25 years, we have used a Rorschach object representational approach to study children's inner experience. Our latest research has been to both nomothetically and idiographically study the Rorschach protocols of children with ADHD. We found a paucity in the production of fully human percepts and human movement and limited access to internal ego strengths important for self-regulation in children with a high number of ADHD symptoms, compared with children who had other learning or behavioral difficulties. Most prior research was content to link these Rorschach limitations to the impulsivity and restlessness of children with the DSM diagnosis, providing a Rorschach analogue to a behavioral description.

Future empirical Rorschach research would benefit from an examination of different patterns of self-regulation seen in these children's responses to the different types of stimuli presented in the RIM. It may be that careful analysis would reveal several strategies or patterns in the ways in which children struggling with ADHD attempt to manage the world around them. This would help to capture the variability we see in these children's functioning at school, home, and the consulting room. This approach to research would also help integrate the pockets of strengths and access to ego resources that these children do possess and identify the conditions that allow these strengths to emerge so beautifully. We might then move beyond our own limitations in empirical, bimodal functioning in which children are seen as either ADHD or normal, with or without associated deficits in total. To this end, the integration of empirical research and case material from Rorschach testing may provide a valuable avenue for understanding the dynamics underlying ADHD children's self-regulatory difficulties. These data may also help us to discern the ways in which these impairments affect these children's capacities to access and make use of their fantasies, to experience and contain affect, and to relate well to their peers and family members.

ACKNOWLEDGMENTS

This work was supported in part by the National Institute on Deafness and Other Communication Disorders (grant DC 04992–02) awarded to Hilary Gomes, Ph.D., and by a PSC-CUNY Award given to Steve Tuber, Ph.D.

The authors are gratefully for the enormous work of Virginia M. Wolfson and Hilary Gomes.

REFERENCES

Ames, L. B., Metraux, R., Rodell, J. L., & Walker, R. (1974). *Child Rorschach responses: Developmental trends from 2–10 years* (rev. ed.). Northvale, NJ: Jason Aronson.

Barkley, R. A. (1997). *ADHD and the Nature of Self-Control.* New York: Guilford Press.

Bartell, S. S., & Soltano, M. V. (1995). Usefulness of the Rorschach inkblot test in assessment of Attention Deficit Hyperactivity Disorder. *Perceptual and Motor Skills, 80,* 531–541.

Cotugno, A. J. (1995). Personality attributes of Attention Deficit Hyperactivity Disorder (ADHD) using the Rorschach inkblot test. *Journal of Clinical Psychology, 51*(4), 554–561.

Exner, J. E. (1993). *The Rorschach: A comprehensive system* (Vol. 1, 3rd ed.). New York: Wiley.

Gilmore, K. (2000). A psychoanalytic perspective on attentional-deficit/hyperactivity disorder. *Journal of the American Psychoanalytic Association, 48*(4), 1259–1293.

Gilmore, K. (2002). Diagnosis, dynamics, and development: Considerations in the psychoanalytic assessment of children with AD/HD. *Psychoanalytic Inquiry, 22*(3), 372–390.

Goddard, R., & Tuber, S. B. (1989). Boyhood separation anxiety disorder: Thought disorder and object relations psychopathology as manifested in Rorschach imagery. *Journal of Personality Assessment, 53*(2), 239–252.

Gomes, H., Halperin, J. M., Tartter, V. C., Ritter, W., Wolfson, V. M., & Mody, M. (2001). *Auditory and visual attention in children with specific language impairment.* NIH/NIDCD Grant.

Gordon, M., & Oshman, H. (1981). Rorschach indices of children classified as hyperactive. *Perceptual and Motor Skills, 52,* 703–707.

Leichtman, M. (1996). *The Rorschach: A developmental perspective.* Hillsdale, NJ: Analytic Press.

Mayman, M. (1970). *Form quality of Rorschach responses.* Unpublished manuscript.

Meyer, J., & Tuber, S. (1989) Intrapsychic and behavioral correlates of the phenomenon of imaginary companions in young children. *Psychoanalytic Psychology, 6,* 151–168.

Nixon, E. (2001). The social competence of children with Attention Deficit Hyperactivity Disorder: A review of the literature. *Child & Adolescent Mental Health, 6*(4), 172–180.

Rapaport, D., Gill, M. M., & Schafer, R. (1968). *Diagnostic psychological testing* (rev. ed.; R. R. Holt, Ed.). New York: International Universities Press.

Reynoso, J., Harris, B., Meehan, K., Ueng-McHale, J., Wolfson, V., Gomes, H., et al. Ego deficits, self-regulation and object relations in children with ADHD. Submitted for publication, *Psychoanalytic Psychology.*

Ruff, H. A., & Rothbart, M. K. (1996). *Attention in early development: Themes and variations.* New York: Oxford University Press.

Schachtel, E. (1966/2001). *Experiential foundations of Rorschach's text.* Hillsdale, NJ: Analytic Press.

Schaughency, E. A., & Rothlind, J. (1991) Assessment and classification of Attention Deficit Hyperactive Disorders. *School Psychology Review, 20*(2), 187–202.

Stormont, M. (2001). Social outcomes of children with AD/HD: Contributing factors and implications for practice. *Psychology in the Schools, 38*(6), 521–531.

Tuber, S. (1983). Children's Rorschach scores as predictors of later adjustment. *Journal of Consulting and Clinical Psychology, 51,* 379–385.

Tuber, S. (1989). Children's Rorschach object representations: Findings for a non-clinical sample. *Psychological Assessment, 1,* 146–149.

Tuber, S. (1992). Empirical and clinical assessments of children's object relations and object representations. *Journal of Personality Assessment, 58,* 179–197.

Tuber, S. (2000). Projective testing as a post-hoc predictor of change in psychoanalysis: The case of Jim. In J. Cohen & B. Cohler (Eds.), *The Psychoanalytic Study of Lives Over Time* (pp. 283–308). New York: Academic Press.

Tuber, S., & Coates, S. (1989). Indices of psychopathology in the Rorschach of boys with severe gender-identity disorder. *Journal of Personality Assessment, 53,* 100–112.

Tuber, S., Frank, M., & Santostefano, S. (1989). Children's anticipation of impending surgery. *Bulletin of the Menninger Clinic, 53*, 501–511.

Yeschin, N. J. (2000). A new understanding of attention deficit hyperactivity disorder: Alternative concepts and interventions. *Child and Adolescent Social Work Journal, 17*(3), 227–245.

26

ASSESSING ANXIETY DISORDERS
IN CHILDREN AND ADOLESCENTS

Christopher A. Kearney
Arva Bensaheb
University of Nevada, Las Vegas

One of the most prevalent and debilitating set of mental disorders among children and adolescents is anxiety disorders. Common anxiety and anxiety-related disorders among youths include separation anxiety disorder, generalized anxiety disorder, social anxiety disorder, specific phobia, school refusal behavior, selective mutism, and mixed anxiety-depressive symptoms. Less common anxiety disorders among youths include panic, obsessive-compulsive, and posttraumatic stress disorders. The symptoms and prevalence of these disorders have been described in great detail elsewhere and are not a critical part of this chapter (see Morris & March, 2004; Ollendick & March, 2004). However, assessment measures that are pertinent to specific disorders are covered here. In addition, some general characteristics regarding anxiety that affect assessment are described next.

Anxiety is a normal emotional state that generally comprises physiological, cognitive, and behavioral components (Vasa & Pine, 2004). A child who refuses to attend school because of high social anxiety, for example, may initially experience intense *physiological* symptoms such as heart palpitations, sweating, trouble breathing, and trembling. These physiological symptoms may then lead to *cognitive* worries about peer rejection and ridicule, mistakes at school, and awkward performance before others. If these cognitive symptoms are sufficiently intense, then certain anxiety-based *behaviors* may become evident, such as avoidance, escape, withdrawal from others, crying, clinginess, temper tantrums, and excessive reassurance-seeking. A good sample of anxiety-based physiological, cognitive, and behavioral components is presented by Barrios and Hartmann (1997). Each of these components should be assessed for any particular case.

Anxiety in children necessarily means that significant others are impinging upon, and reacting to, a child's behaviors. Significant others typically include parents, siblings, extended relatives, peers, dating partners, and teachers, although this is not an exclusive list. Because children interact daily with these people, and because these people are often integral to the treatment process, the assessment of childhood anxiety must include information from multiple sources (Silverman & Kearney, 1991). In addition, because of the internalizing nature of anxiety, a child's subjective report of his or her emotional state must be given considerable credence during assessment.

Human anxiety is a complicated state that likely results from many factors. Common factors implicated in the etiology of anxiety disorders include behavioral inhibition, genetic predisposition, physiological hyperarousal, attachment difficulties, cognitive vulnerabilites, lack of control, problematic parenting styles and family environment, maladaptive learning experiences, and poor development of social, coping, and anxiety management skills (Vasey & Dadds, 2001). A common developmental pathway for childhood anxiety begins with initial biological predispositional factors, such as withdrawal from novel situations, genetic contributions, attachment difficulties, and key brain changes that may produce overarousal to various situations. As a child ages and encounters more challenging situations, he or she may develop psychological vulnerabilities such as alienation from peers and poor social and coping skills. Should family dysfunction and other difficulties such as lack of social support occur as well, a child could be at serious risk for developing an anxiety disorder (Kearney, 2005). Therefore, assessment for a particular child must focus on multiple areas of functioning and development.

In related fashion, children differ greatly with respect to age and cognitive development, gender, race, social status, temperament, and other key variables that can influence treatment. Therefore, a clinician's assessment of a particular child must consider these individual differences. This is most pertinent to cognitive development, where the treatment of an anxious 7-year-old will necessarily differ from the treatment of an anxious 17-year-old. Using instruments that are developmentally sensitive and that assess for cognitive/verbal ability is thus imperative. In addition, use of instruments that are culturally sensitive must be closely considered (Cooley & Boyce, 2004).

Literature regarding the assessment of youth with anxiety disorders has burgeoned in recent years, so we encourage clinicians to avail themselves of techniques with established reliability and validity, such as the ones discussed in this chapter. In addition, we encourage clinicians to choose assessment devices that allow them to chart treatment progress and that are sensitive enough to detect even minor differences in anxiety, avoidance, cognitions, and other sometimes subtle constructs. We begin our discussion of various assessment instruments by covering the technique most common to this population: the interview.

INTERVIEWS

Interviews for assessing youths with anxiety disorders are quite popular among clinicians and researchers and include unstructured and structured dialogues. Unstructured interviews are less reliable than structured ones, but many clinicians prefer an unstructured approach so that they can tailor questions specifically to a given client. If a clinician decides to adopt this approach, then we recommend several general areas to cover. These areas include, among others, physiological, cognitive, and behavioral aspects of anxiety, general symptomatology, effects on a child's and family's daily functioning, current life stressors, coping techniques, family dynamics, pertinent biological variables, factors such as attention-seeking that maintain anxiety, safety and crisis issues such as suicidal behavior or school absenteeism, treatment and other pertinent histories, health status and medications, contextual issues such as marital discord or school-based threats, cultural variables and perspectives, and expectations regarding treatment (Kearney, 2005).

On the other hand, structured interviews are also available to gather information more reliably about symptomatology, primary and comorbid diagnoses, severity, and interference with daily functioning. Examples include the *Child and Adolescent Psychiatric Assessment* (Angold & Costello, 2000), *Child Assessment Schedule* (Hodges, McKnew, Cytryn, Stern, & Kline, 1982), *Diagnostic Interview for Children and Adolescents* (Welner, Reich, Herjanic, Jung, & Amado, 1987), *Interview Schedule for Children* (Kovacs, 1985), *National Institute of Mental Health Diagnostic Interview Schedule for Children* (Shaffer et al., 1996), *Pediatric Anxiety Rating Scale* (Research Units on Pediatric Psychopharmacology Anxiety Study Group, 2002), and *Schedule for Affective Disorders and Schizophrenia for School-Age Children–Present and Lifetime Version* (Kaufman et al., 1997). An advantage of these interviews is that many different childhood disorders, not simply anxiety disorders, can be evaluated.

The most commonly used structured interview for child anxiety disorders, however, is the *Anxiety Disorders Interview Schedule for DSM-IV: Child and Parent Versions* (ADIS for DSM-IV: C/P; Silverman & Albano, 1996). This interview is largely based on diagnostic criteria, although some sections are designed for conditions related to anxiety disorders, such as school refusal behavior. In addition, diagnostic sections are available for assessing externalizing problems such as attention deficit hyperactivity, conduct, and oppositional defiant disorder. Separate child and parent versions allow for information collection from various sources, and information from these sources is combined to arrive at a diagnostic profile. The measure has demonstrated good reliability across child and parent reports (Silverman, Saavedra, & Pina, 2001; Wood, Piacentini, Bergman, McCracken, & Barrios, 2002). Concerns about the ADIS for DSM-IV: C/P include its strict adherence to diagnostic criteria, discrepancies among child and parent reports, and insensitivity to situation-specific behaviors and developmental differences among children (DiBartolo, Albano, Barlow, & Heimberg, 1998; Kearney, 2005).

Other specialized interviews or clinician-administered measures have also been developed for certain child populations, especially youths with posttraumatic stress disorder (PTSD). The most pertinent examples include the *Childhood PTSD Interview* and *Children's PTSD Inventory* (Fletcher, 1996; Saigh et al., 2000). For obsessive-compulsive disorder, the 10-item *Children's Yale-Brown Obsessive Compulsive Scale* (CY-BOCS) is often recommended (Scahill et al., 1997). In addition, specialized questions for youths with school refusal behavior have been proposed by several authors (Huffington & Sevitt, 1989; Kearney, 2001; King, Ollendick, & Tonge, 1995).

CHILD SELF-REPORT MEASURES

As mentioned earlier, a child's report of his or her own internal mood states is important in the assessment of covert behaviors such as fear and anxiety. A plethora of child self-report measures have thus been developed in recent years. Some of these measures focus on general measurements of anxiety, and some have been tailored for very specific populations. In this section, we briefly describe these instruments but do not provide a detailed outline of their psychometric strength. Instead, we concentrate on general suggestions for clinicians who wish to use them. In addition, we do not cover areas of behavior that are commonly *related* to anxiety in children, most notably depression and somatic complaints. However, we encourage clinicians to assess for these and other frequently comorbid conditions.

General Child Self-Report Measures

The earliest child self-report measures of anxiety were fairly general in nature. A well-known example is the *Revised Children's Manifest Anxiety Scale*, a 37-item, yes-no measure of worry/oversensitivity, concentration problems, and physiological symptoms (Reynolds & Richmond, 1985). Another common general measure is the *State-Trait Anxiety Inventory for Children*, which consists of two 20-item scales focusing on a child's anxiety at that particular moment (state) and in general (trait; Spielberger, 1973). Although these scales are generally useful, they are largely downward extensions of adult measures. Therefore, questions remain about their developmental sensitivity. In addition, the measures have been found to overlap with aspects of depression and externalizing behavior problems (Lonigan, Carey, & Finch, 1994; Stark & Laurent, 2001).

More contemporary general child self-report measures of anxiety include the *Multidimensional Anxiety Scale for Children* (MASC), the *Screen for Child Anxiety Related Emotional Disorders* (SCARED), the *Spence Children's Anxiety Scale* (SCAS), and the *Child Anxiety Sensitivity Index* (CASI). The MASC is a 39-item measure of symptoms that surround social anxiety, separation anxiety/panic, physical anxiety, and harm avoidance (March, 1997). The measure has good psychometric strength and is now widely used among clinicians and researchers. The SCARED is a 41-item measure of anxiety symptoms that largely surround factors of somatic/panic, general anxiety, separation anxiety, and school and social phobia (Birmaher et al., 1997, 1999). The scale is also widely used and has been revised (Muris, Merckelbach, Schmidt, & Mayer, 1999).

The SCAS is a 44-item scale also closely aligned to DSM criteria for generalized, social, and separation anxiety, panic attack/agoraphobia, obsessive-compulsive disorder, and physical injury fears (Spence, Barrett, & Turner, 2003). A parent version of this scale has also been developed (Nauta et al., 2004). The psychometric strength of the SCAS has been questioned by some, however, who have modified the scale into the *Revised Child Anxiety and Depression Scales* (RCADS; Chorpita, Moffitt, & Gray, 2005). The RCADS has shown excellent psychometric properties in community and clinical samples and appears to contain six main factors: separation anxiety, social anxiety, obsessive-compulsive, panic, generalized anxiety, and depression.

Finally, the CASI is an 18-item measure designed to assess a child's fear of his or her own internal anxiety sensations, a construct that has been linked to panic and other anxiety-related conditions (e.g., Kearney, Albano, Eisen, Allan, & Barlow, 1997). A factor analysis of the CASI has revealed four main factors: disease concerns, unsteady concerns, mental incapacitation concerns, and social concerns (Silverman, Goedhart, Barrett, & Turner, 2003). The CASI is also a downward extension of an adult measure of anxiety sensitivity but appears to have good utility when it is used to address specific youths with panic and fears of internal sensations.

Clinicians who wish to use these scales should consider their breadth, psychometric strength, and efficiency of administration. As such, the MASC and RCADS represent good choices, as they cover a wide range of anxiety-related symptomatology in a relatively brief fashion. Other clinicians may wish to provide more support for an assigned DSM diagnosis, however, in which case the SCARED/SCARED-R may be helpful.

Social Anxiety

Social anxiety and social anxiety disorder have quickly become a major focus among clinical child psychologists and others. As such, the development of child self-report measures in this area has blossomed. Two of the most well-known and psychometrically strong measures in this area are the *Social Anxiety Scale for Children*, now revised (SASC/SASC-R), and the *Social Phobia and Anxiety Inventory for Children* (SPAIC).

The SASC was originally designed from general measures of anxiety, but with a focus on peer relations (La Greca, Dandes, Wick, Shaw, & Stone, 1988). The instrument was later revised and reflected three primary factors: fear of negative evaluation from peers, social avoidance and distress specific to new situations, and generalized social avoidance and distress (La Greca & Stone, 1993). The measure was later revised to increase developmental sensitivity toward adolescents: the *Social Anxiety Scale for Adolescents* (La Greca & Lopez, 1998). These measures have good psychometric properties and are useful for screening social anxiety among youths and serving as dependent measures in longitudinal analyses and studies of treatment outcome (La Greca, 1998, 1999).

The SPAIC was originally derived from a related adult measure of social anxiety and covers social distress across various general situations as well as situations involving adults and familiar and unfamiliar peers (Beidel, Turner, & Morris, 1995). The SPAIC generally contains five main factors: assertiveness, general conversation, physical and cognitive symptoms, avoidance, and public performance (Beidel, Turner, & Fink, 1996). The scale is quite useful at distinguishing youths with and without social anxiety disorder (Beidel, Turner, Hamlin, & Morris, 2000).

Clinicians who wish to use these scales may opt for the SASC/SAS in situations where a general screening for social anxiety is desired. In cases where a clinician feels that a child does indeed have social anxiety, then the SPAIC may be useful for confirming the diagnosis and for identifying specific problems that need to be addressed. Indeed, these measures do seem to be measuring different aspects of social anxiety (Inderbitzen-Nolan, Davies, & McKeon, 2004; Storch, Masia-Warner, Dent, Roberti, & Fisher, 2004).

In cases of test anxiety, which may be a subset of social anxiety, the *Test Anxiety Scale for Children* is commonly used (Sarason, Davidson, Lighthall, Waite, & Ruebush, 1960). Other measures that may also be pertinent to the assessment of youths with social anxiety include the *Liebowitz Social Anxiety Scale for Children and Adolescents* (Masia, Klein, Storch, & Corda, 2001), *Social Fears Belief Questionnaire* (Field, Hamilton, Knowles, & Plews, 2003), *Social Worries Questionnaire* (and its parent version; Spence, Donovan, & Brechman-Toussaint, 1999), and *Worry Scale* (Perrin & Last, 1997).

Fears and Phobias

For assessing fears and phobias in children, one of the most venerable measures has been the Fear Survey Schedule for Children–Revised (FSSC–R; Ollendick, 1983). The FSSC–R is an 80-item measure of fears that largely surround failure and criticism, the unknown, injury and small animals, danger and death, and medical procedures. In our own work with youths with problematic absenteeism, we have also utilized 12 FSSC–R items that are specifically related to school (Kearney, Eisen, & Silverman, 1995). The FSSC–R has been shown to have good psychometric properties, although its utility for supporting diagnostic decisions is limited. The scale has since been revised by Gullone and King (1992).

Other child self-report measures are also available for fears of spiders, dental procedures, hospital situations, water, and other stimuli (Aartman, van Everdingen, Hoogstraten, & Schuurs, 1998; Barrios & Hartmann, 1997; Kindt, Brosschot, & Muris, 1996). Although these questionnaires have some general clinical utility, the avoidance associated with true phobic conditions is often better measured via behavioral observations (see later section).

Trauma and Posttraumatic Stress Disorder

An increasingly important area of child self-report surrounds trauma and posttraumatic stress disorder (PTSD). This is so because the effects of trauma on children can be quite substantial and because children who have been severely maltreated tend to develop PTSD (McLeer et al., 1998). Common child self-report measures for this population include the *Trauma Symptom Checklist for Children* and *Trauma Symptom Checklist for Young Children* (Briere, 1996; Briere et al., 2001). These measures assess for a child's reactions to trauma, including PTSD symptoms, depression, anxiety, anger, dissociation, and sexual concerns. Other child self-report and related measures concern areas that are related to PTSD, such as sexual maltreatment, violence, and dissociation (see Strand, Sarmiento, & Pasquale, 2005, for a complete review).

In addition, the *Child PTSD Symptom Scale* is a 17-item measure that is linked to DSM criteria for PTSD (Foa, Johnson, Feeny, & Treadwell, 2001). This measure contains three subscales pertaining to reexperiencing symptoms, avoidance, and arousal. The measure has demonstrated excellent psychometric properties and is a good choice for screening childhood PTSD.

Obsessive-Compulsive Disorder

Symptoms of obsessive-compulsive disorder may also be reported by children, most notably via the *Leyton Obsessional Inventory-Child Version*. A short, 11-item form of this scale has been developed with subscales for compulsions, obsessions/incompletness, and cleanliness (Bamber, Tamplin, Park, Kyte, & Goodyer, 2002). This scale has been shown to differentiate youths with obsessive-compulsive disorder (OCD) from youths without obsessions, even among cases involving depression. Clinicians who are assessing for OCD may wish to use the CY-BOCS noted earlier in conjunction with this short form of the Leyton.

School Refusal Behavior

Although not a formal anxiety disorder, school refusal behavior is often linked to anxiety-related conditions. This is because many children with problematic school absenteeism meet diagnostic criteria for separation, generalized, and social anxiety disorders, among other conditions (Kearney & Albano, 2004). As such, many of the general and specific anxiety child self-report measures that have been described here may apply to this population.

Few measures have been designed specifically for youths with school refusal behavior, though one exception is the *School Refusal Assessment Scale–Revised* (SRAS–R; Kearney, 2002). The SRAS–R is a 24-item measure of the relative strength of four functions or factors that serve to maintain school refusal behavior: (1) avoidance of stimuli that provoke negative affectivity, (2) escape from aversive social and/or evaluative situations, (3) pursuit of attention from significant others, and (4) pursuit of tangible reinforcement outside of school. The initial two functions refer to school refusal behavior motivated by negative reinforcement, whereas the latter two functions refer to school refusal behavior motivated by positive reinforcement. Of course, youths could refuse school for a combination of reasons.

Child and parent versions of the SRAS–R have been developed, and the scales appear to have good psychometric strength (Kearney, 2002). In addition, the scales have been shown to be useful for predicting which prescriptive treatment package is best (and not best) for a particular child with school refusal behavior (Kearney, Pursell, & Alvarez, 2001; Kearney & Silverman, 1999). We recommend that clinicians use the SRAS–R as a means of gauging what proximal factors seem to be impinging most on a particular child who is refusing school.

PARENT AND TEACHER MEASURES

Parent and teacher checklists may also be useful for assessing youths with anxiety-related conditions, and many of these checklists cover various internalizing and externalizing behavior problems. Pertinent examples include the wide-ranging *Child Behavior Checklist* and *Teacher Report Form* (CBCL and TRF; Achenbach & Rescorla, 2001), the *Conners Rating Scales* (Parent and Teacher Versions–Revised; Conners, 1997), and the *Child Symptom Inventory–4* (CSI–4; Sprafkin, Gadow, Salisbury, Schneider, & Loney, 2002). Of these, the CBCL and TRF are commonly used to assess for many different internalizing, mixed, and externalizing behavior problems. The factor most closely associated with youths with anxiety disorders is the anxious/depressed subscale, though special attention should also be paid to the withdrawn/depressed and somatic complaints subscales. Subscales from the CSI–4 may be helpful as well, particularly those related to generalized, separation, and social anxiety.

Although parent and teacher data about general behavior problems are helpful, we have found that some parents and many teachers are not accurate reporters of anxiety-related conditions in youth. In fact, peer ratings may be better predictors of a child's social anxiety than teacher ratings, though teachers are good at identifying youths with test anxiety (La Greca, 2001). Although general interview and checklist reports from parents and teachers can be useful, they should be supplemented with observational and monitoring data, which are discussed next.

BEHAVIORAL OBSERVATION AND SELF-MONITORING

Although child self-report and parent/teacher measures are critical for assessing internal fear and anxiety states in children, behavioral observations are also crucial for examining avoidance and other overt aspects of this population. A common method for doing so is the *behavioral assessment test*, sometimes referred to as a behavioral approach test or behavior avoidance test (BATs). This procedure involves asking a child to role-play a given situation, perform some way before others, or approach a feared stimulus. Common examples among children include taking tests, reading a story aloud, engaging in social interactions, approaching others for help, ordering food, or gradually approaching a phobic stimulus such as a dog (Beidel, Turner, & Morris, 1999; King, Muris, & Ollendick, 2005).

During BATs, a child is often asked to provide ratings of fear, anxiety, or urges toward avoidance on a 0–10 or 0–100 scale. Therapists often pay close attention to a child's social and coping skill level as well as degree of avoidance. Such information is useful for developing treatment plans (e.g., fear/avoidance hierarchies for systematic desensitization) and for ruling out specific disorders. With respect to the latter, for example, a child who can eventually pet a dog within several minutes may not qualify for a diagnosis of specific phobia.

Behavioral observations may be of the contrived sort described here, but can also involve more naturalistic procedures. In our work with anxious children who have trouble attending school, for example, we often observe family practices in the morning before school as well as a child's attempt to enter a school building (Kearney & Albano, 2000). Sometimes this is done under specific conditions to test a hypothesis about a particular reason a child is missing school. For example, a child may claim that he or she can attend school if a parent stays with him or her during the school day. If a child can indeed attend school under this condition, then some evidence may be gleaned for separation anxiety or attention-seeking behavior.

Direct observations of behavior may also be used to gather information about family dynamics that impinge upon an anxious child. Some researchers, for example, have asked anxious children and their parents to engage in various tasks. Interactions between the child and his or her parents are then observed and coded along avoidant, aggressive, proactive, withdrawn, controlling, negative, or other categories (Barrett, Rapee, Dadds, & Ryan, 1996; Woodruff-Borden, Morrow, Bourland, & Cambron, 2002). The practicality of these procedures may be limited for many clinical settings, but obtaining a general sense of how parents respond to their child's anxious behaviors is extremely important for designing an effective treatment plan.

A downside to naturalistic behavioral observations is that they take substantial time to arrange and conduct. An alternative, therefore, is to ask children and significant others to monitor a child's behavior along key fronts. Children may be asked, for example, to keep daily diaries of subjective anxiety and depression, physical symptoms, problematic thoughts, and urges to avoid or escape anxiety-provoking situations. Parents may also be asked to record a child's efforts to cope with a given situation as well as any disruptive behavioral problems. Although formal self-monitoring procedures have been developed for youths with anxiety disorders and are often helpful for individual cases, daily compliance can often be problematic and may need to be linked to incentives (Beidel et al., 1999; Beidel, Neal, & Lederer, 1991).

COGNITIVE ASSESSMENT

Behavioral observations are useful for examining overt aspects of anxiety-related conditions, but cognitive assessments are often critical for understanding various thought patterns that influence a particular child's anxiety. One method of doing so is a *thought listing* procedure in which a child maintains a written log of key thoughts before, during, and after entry into an anxiety-provoking situation (Kendall & Chansky, 1991; Spence et al., 1999). For example, a child who is anxious about eating in the school cafeteria could outline specific thoughts immediately prior to sitting down, while eating, and as he or she is exiting the situation. An advantage of this approach is that specific thoughts in actual anxiety-provoking situations are assessed without having to rely on memory. Unfortunately, some youths provide only general thoughts that are not helpful in treatment or they fail to record any thoughts.

As an alternative, *think aloud* procedures may be employed. In this approach, a child is asked to verbalize thoughts and other reactions while engaging in a behavioral assessment test in a clinical setting (Houston, Fox, & Forbes, 1984). In this way, compliance may be enhanced and some thoughts may be gleaned. However, the procedure may be subject to reactivity and a child may provide incomplete answers (Eisen & Kearney, 1995). Thought listing and think-aloud procedures are most useful for anxious youths with more advanced cognitive development, youths who are enthusiastic about the procedures, and youths whose anxiety is clearly associated with cognitive distortions or biases.

Cognitive assessment for youths with anxiety disorders can also come in the form of short stories that are rated for level of perceived threat. Some researchers, for example, have read very short stories to youths that may or may not imply separation or social anxiety or threat (Bogels & Zigterman, 2000; Muris, Merckelbach, & Damsma, 2000). Youths are then asked specific or open-ended questions about their reactions to the stories and how threatening the stories seemed to the main character. This type of assessment is quite useful for children of different ages and does not require much time in a clinical setting.

Cognitions may also be assessed via child self-report questionnaires. Good examples include the *Automatic Thoughts Questionnaire* (Kazdin, 1990), the *Children's Cognitive Assessment Questionnaire* (Zatz & Chassin, 1983), the *Children's Negative Cognitive Error Questionnaire* (Leitenberg, Yost, & Carroll-Wilson, 1986), the *Cognition Checklist* (Ambrose & Rholes, 1993), the *Cognitive Triad Inventory for Children* (Kaslow, Stark, Printz, Livingston, & Tsai, 1992), the *Negative Affect Self-Statement Questionnaire* (Ronan, Kendall, & Rowe, 1994), and the *Thought Checklist for Children* (Laurent & Stark, 1993). These measures provide only general information about cognitive distortions and biases, however, so they may not be highly useful for a particular case.

RECORDS AND DOCUMENTATION

The assessment of youths with anxiety disorders should also involve a perusal of available records and related documentation. Pertinent examples include records of past treatment, school performance, medication history and other medical variables, and hospitalizations. These records are particularly useful in cases of extreme anxiety, comorbid problems such as severe depression, and associated school refusal behavior. In our work with youths with problematic absenteeism, for example, we often rely on school reports of intellectual achievement, behavior problems, attendance, grades, and past attempts to integrate a child into a regular classroom setting (Kearney & Albano, 2000). In particular, knowing what treatments have been unsuccessfully used in the past will help a clinician avoid unproductive practices.

PHYSIOLOGICAL ASSESSMENT

As mentioned earlier, physiological symptoms are a key component of many youths with anxiety disorders. In research settings, physiological assessment is therefore sometimes used to evaluate this population. Such assessment typically consists of monitoring heart rate, blood pressure, skin conductance and resistance, muscle tension, perspiration, and adrenergic activity (Beidel, 1989; King, 1994). However, these practices have not led to consistent or strong results in the literature and have been criticized for their variability, cost, expense, lack of normative data, and poor utility for deriving a treatment plan (Schniering, Hudson, & Rapee, 2000). In general clinical settings, we recommend that clinicians consider a measure of heart rate, but with the understanding that such a measure will not always prove overly helpful.

Other Assessment Measures

Clinicians who address youths with behavior problems know that children and adolescents differ greatly with respect to areas of development and temperament. As such, use of *intel-*

lectual tests may be useful for identifying youths who can handle cognitive therapy procedures. In addition, *personality inventories* such as the *Personality Inventory for Children* or specific measures such as the *Carey Temperament Scales* can be useful for evaluating temperamental issues that could influence treatment (Carey & Jablow, 1997; Wirt, Lachar, Klindinst, & Seat, 1995).

Projective testing may also be considered in cases where anxiety may not have a clear external referent, where an anxious child lacks the vocabulary or self-awareness needed to accurately express his or her internal states, where a child is not forthcoming about anxiety-related issues, or where a child may have suffered trauma. Child temperament and themes of abandonment, threat, aggression, apprehension, and other relevant variables may also be explored (see Gitlin-Weiner, Sandgrund, & Schaefer, 2000, for more information). Research with adults indicates that the Rorschach can be effective for assessing anxiety or internal states of arousal (McCown, Fink, Galina, & Johnson, 1992; Perry et al., 1995). Performance-based measures such as the Rorschach, Roberts Apperception Test, or storytelling or figure-drawing techniques might therefore be important additions to the assessment battery. Readers are directed to chapters in this volume regarding these measures.

CASE EXAMPLE

In this section we present a sample composite case from our clinic to illustrate a typical assessment and conceptualization approach for an anxious youth. Of course, any assessment approach will necessarily have to be tailored to an individual child. In this case example, however, we hope to outline a general strategy that can lead to key decisions about the form and function of problematic behavior as well as treatment direction.

Marshall (not his real name) was a 14-year-old male who was referred for anxiety and episodes of school refusal behavior. Marshall and his parents had been referred to our clinic by the guidance counselor at Marshall's school, who reported via telephone that her student had missed 15 days of school and had been late to school on 23 other days. This attendance record was particularly problematic because Marshall had just started high school and was now at risk for being expelled based on the school district's attendance policy. The guidance counselor also noted that Marshall seemed to be having inordinate difficulty entering the school building in general and his classes in particular.

Our initial assessment in this case consisted of structured diagnostic interviews: the Anxiety Disorders Interview Schedule for DSM-IV: Child and Parent Versions. We interviewed Marshall first as his parents, Mr. and Mrs. M., completed various questionnaires in the waiting room. During this interview process, we generally educate a child about the type of questions that will be asked, the voluntary nature of the questions, and issues regarding confidentiality and other relevant issues. Although we utilize a structured diagnostic interview, we always begin the process by asking general questions about a child's life and why he or she has visited the clinic. This allows a typically anxious youngster to initially choose what topics he or she is most comfortable discussing before more difficult topics are covered.

Marshall indicated that his transition to high school was much more difficult than he expected. In particular, he seemed overwhelmed by the number of new classes, teachers, peers, homework assignments, and buildings. Although he admitted that his attendance record during middle school was not particularly stellar, he was able to pass all of his classes and advance to high school. Upon entry there, however, Marshall said he felt "lost" and generally alienated from others. He had no friends in any of his classes, experienced severe symptoms of "panic" while in class, and eventually found it quite comforting to simply stay home from school.

As the clinician progressed through the interview, she noted that Marshall seemed to meet criteria for generalized anxiety disorder, social anxiety disorder, and, to some extent, panic disorder. The latter was difficult to formalize because Marshall described vague symptoms of anxiety that resembled panic but that did not seem to rise to the level of full-blown panic disorder. For example, he said he often felt "overwhelmed" in class by a sense of suffocation and tension, but he was not describing specific episodes of panic attacks with more sympathetic nervous system activity. In addition, his "panic" was specific only to school-related situations.

Marshall more clearly met criteria for generalized and social anxiety disorders. He reported uncontrollable worry about making mistakes, having to perform before others, and not having any friends in his classes. He also feared being bullied at school, though this had not happened before (Marshall was largely ignored by his peers). In addition, Marshall said he was extremely nervous in social situations with peers, especially those situations that involved classroom performance, walking down hallways and into classrooms, and speaking to others at school. He indicated that he was hoping his parents would enroll him in a home schooling program so that he could simply avoid his high school altogether.

Marshall's parents largely echoed their son's report, but concentrated as well on his oppositional problems about attending school. Both parents said Marshall was highly resistant to going to school as well as social occasions such as birthday parties with friends. They said their son "had always been like this," a largely shy and inhibited child who preferred solitary activities and who did not have good social skills. Though Marshall's introversion was tolerable in the elementary school years, attendance problems and refusal to attend social gatherings had generally increased in severity over the past three years. Mr. and Mrs. M.'s reports supported a diagnosis of generalized and social anxiety disorder as well as oppositional defiant disorder.

Mr. and Mrs. M. were asked to complete the Child Behavior Checklist and School Refusal Assessment Scale–Revised. Scores on these measures reflected their interview reports; Marshall was rated as having severe internalizing behavior problems and moderate externalizing behavior problems. In addition, Marshall was rated high as refusing school to escape aversive social and/or evaluative situations as well as pursuit of attention from his parents.

Marshall completed several self-report measures of general and social anxiety, fear, and depression (Table 26.1). His scores on the State-Trait Anxiety Inventory for Children and the Social Anxiety Scale for Children–Revised were elevated compared with normative values and indicated a specific concern about anxiety in new social situations. In contrast, however, his fear and depression scores were normal. Marshall also completed the child version of the School Refusal Assessment Scale–Revised, endorsing two main functions of his school

TABLE 26.1.
Marshall's Scores on Selected Measures

Child behavior checklist internalizing T	75 (clinical range)
Child behavior checklist externalizing T	60 (nonclinical range)
State-trait anxiety inventory for children (state subscale)	50 (elevated)
Social anxiety scale for children–revised	60 (high)
Fear survey schedule for children–revised	99 (average)

refusal behavior: avoidance of stimuli that provoke negative affectivity and escape from aversive social and/or evaluative situations.

Following this assessment session and after securing necessary releases of information, the clinician contacted Marshall's guidance counselor, two teachers, and a previous therapist who Marshall had visited one year before. Marshall's guidance counselor indicated that the school had decided to delay legal proceedings against Marshall's parents because of their decision to pursue treatment and try to resolve Marshall's attendance problems. She also indicated a desire to assist in treatment, including any exposures that may be conducted. Marshall's teachers reported that their student was relatively shy in the classroom but would comply with requests when asked. Overall, he was withdrawn but polite and a good academic student. Marshall's previous therapist indicated that he had concentrated on relaxation training and other somatic management strategies with Marshall, but that these had proved to be unsuccessful.

In the week-long interim between sessions, Marshall and his parents were also given several instructions. Both parties were asked to rate Marshall's daily level of anxiety, depression, and noncompliance on a 0–10 scale. Marshall's parents were also instructed to attempt to take Marshall to school each day and record any behavior problems encountered in doing so. Marshall was also asked to record his thoughts during this process and in other situations where he felt particularly stressed.

During the second session, this daily information was reviewed. Marshall had attended only 2 of 5 days of school and was reportedly quite nervous about activities during physical education class and walking into full classrooms and the cafeteria. In addition, he reiterated the physical symptoms described previously. Records of thought processes were only somewhat useful, but Marshall did admit to worries about being isolated from others, making mistakes, and being ridiculed. Daily ratings of behavior revealed that Marshall's anxiety was especially problematic on Monday and Tuesday.

The clinician used this information to help Marshall develop a hierarchy of anxiety-provoking situations. Easier items on the list included attending classes where he did not have to perform before others (computer class, for example), family gatherings where he knew everyone, and going to the movies with a neighborhood friend. Moderately anxiety-provoking items included walking into the school building and classrooms, eating lunch in the cafeteria, and handing in homework that might include a mistake. Highly anxiety-provoking items included attending classes where some performance was expected, peer interactions, and social gatherings where he did not know everyone.

The clinician was able to utilize all of this information to develop a treatment plan. Given that Marshall had not previously responded well to somatic management strategies, and because of the urgency of his school attendance situation, the clinician decided to adopt a treatment program that included cognitive therapy and a heavy emphasis on exposure-based practices. The latter initially included a part-time school attendance program that involved easier classes. Over time, more difficult classes were added, with consequences implemented at school and home for compliance and noncompliance. During the exposure process, the clinician worked with Marshall to improve his social skills, manage his anxiety in social and performance situations, enhance his ability to interact with various peers, and handle mistakes with aplomb.

The clinician also worked closely with school officials to sanction this gradual approach and ensure that Marshall's grades would not suffer as a result. In addition, peers who were known to Marshall, and liked by him, were made available in his classes to reduce his sense of isolation. Marshall's parents were also involved, not only in the consequence part of treatment, but also to schedule and encourage Marshall's attendance at social gatherings outside of school. During treatment, the clinician continued to use daily ratings of behavior and relied on parent and teacher observations to adjust the intervention strategies. Marshall was eventually able to resume full-time school attendance while his generalized and social anxiety continued to be addressed.

Adopting a multimethod, multisource approach to assessment is crucial. In addition, information should continue to be gathered throughout treatment not only to gauge treatment progress, but also to identify areas that may be of interest for relapse prevention. The assessment and treatment of youths with anxiety disorders is a fascinating and rewarding area of research and clinical work, and we encourage clinicians who enter this area to keep abreast of rapid developments in the field.

REFERENCES

Aartman, I. H. A., van Everdingen, T., Hoogstraten, J., & Schuurs, A. H. B. (1998). Self-report measurements of dental anxiety and fear in children: A critical assessment. *Journal of Dentistry for Children, 65*, 252–258.

Achenbach, T. M., & Rescorla, L. A. (2001). *Manual for the ASEBA school-age forms & profiles*. Burlington, VT: University of Vermont Research Center for Children, Youth, & Families.

Ambrose, B., & Rholes, W. S. (1993). Automatic cognitions and symptoms of depression and anxiety in children and adolescents: An examination of the content specificity hypothesis. *Cognitive Therapy and Research, 17*, 289–308.

Angold, A., & Costello, E. J. (2000). The Child and Adolescent Psychiatric Assessment (CAPA). *Journal of the American Academy of Child and Adolescent Psychiatry, 39*, 39–48.

Bamber, D., Tamplin, A., Park, R. J., Kyte, Z. A., & Goodyer, I. M. (2002). Development of a short Leyton Obsessional Inventory for Children and Adolescents. *Journal of the American Academy of Child and Adolescent Psychiatry, 41*, 1246–1252.

Barrett, P. M., Rapee, R. M., Dadds, M. M., & Ryan, S. M. (1996). Family enhancement of cognitive style in anxious and aggressive children. *Journal of Abnormal Child Psychology, 24*, 187–203.

Barrios, B. A., & Hartmann, D. P. (1997). Fears and anxieties. In E. J. Mash & L. G. Terdal (Eds.), *Assessment of childhood disorders* (3rd ed., pp. 230–327). New York: Guilford Press.

Beidel, D. C. (1989). Assessing anxious emotions: A review of psychophysiological assessment in children. *Clinical Psychology Review, 9*, 717–736.

Beidel, D. C., Neal, A. M., & Lederer, A. S. (1991). The feasibility and validity of a daily diary for the assessment of anxiety in children. *Behavior Therapy, 22*, 505–517.

Beidel, D. C., Turner, S. M., & Fink, C. M. (1996). Assessment of childhood social phobia: Construct, convergent, and discriminative validity of the Social Phobia and Anxiety Inventory for Children (SPAI-C). *Psychological Assessment, 8*, 235–240.

Beidel, D. C., Turner, S. M., Hamlin, K., & Morris, T. L. (2000). The Social Phobia and Anxiety Inventory for Children (SPAI-C): External and discriminative validity. *Behavior Therapy, 31*, 75–87.

Beidel, D. C., Turner, S. M., & Morris, T. L. (1995). A new inventory to assess childhood social anxiety and phobia: The Social Phobia and Anxiety Inventory for Children. *Psychological Assessment, 7*, 73–79.

Beidel, D. C., Turner, S. M., & Morris, T. L. (1999). Psychopathology of childhood social phobia. *Journal of the American Academy of Child and Adolescent Psychiatry, 38*, 643–650.

Birmaher, B., Brent, D. A., Chiappetta, L., Bridge, J., Monga, S., & Baugher, M. (1999). Psychometric properties of the Screen for Child Anxiety Related Emotional Disorders (SCARED): A replication study. *Journal of the American Academy of Child and Adolescent Psychiatry, 38*, 1230–1236.

Birmaher, B., Khetarpal, S., Brent, D., Cully, M., Balach, L., Kaufman, J., & Neer, S. M. (1997). The Screen for Child Anxiety Related Emotional Disorders (SCARED): Scale construction and psychometric characteristics. *Journal of the American Academy of Child and Adolescent Psychiatry, 36*, 545–553.

Bogels, S. M., & Zigterman, D. (2000). Dysfunctional cognitions in children with social phobia, separation anxiety disorder, and generalized anxiety disorder. *Journal of Abnormal Child Psychology, 28*, 205–211.

Briere, J. (1996). *Trauma Symptom Checklist for Children (TSCC): Professional manual*. Lutz, FL: Psychological Assessment Resources.

Briere, J., Johnson, K., Bissada, A., Damon, L., Crouch, J., Gil, E., et al. (2001). The Trauma Symptom Checklist for Young Children (TSCYC): Reliability and association with abuse exposure in a multi-site study. *Child Abuse and Neglect, 25*, 1001–1014.

Carey, W. B., & Jablow, M. M. (1997). *Understanding your child's temperament*. New York: McMillan.

Chorpita, B. F., Moffitt, C. E., & Gray, J. (2005). Psychometric properties of the Revised Child Anxiety and Depression Scale in a clinical sample. *Behaviour Research and Therapy, 43*, 309–322.

Conners, C. K. (1997). *Conners Rating Scales-Revised*. North Tonawanda, NY: Multi-Health Systems.

Cooley, M. R., & Boyce, C. A. (2004). An introduction to assessing anxiety in child and adolescent multi-ethnic populations: Challenges and opportunities for enhancing knowledge and practice. *Journal of Clinical Child and Adolescent Psychology, 33*, 210–215.

DiBartolo, P. M., Albano, A. M., Barlow, D. H., & Heimberg, R. G. (1998). Cross-informant agreement in the assessment of social phobia in youth. *Journal of Abnormal Child Psychology, 26*, 213–220.

Eisen, A. R., & Kearney, C. A. (1995). *Practitioner's guide to treating fear and anxiety in children and adolescents: A cognitive-behavioral approach*. Northvale, NJ: Jason Aronson.

Field, A. P., Hamilton, S. J., Knowles, K. A., & Plews, E. L. (2003). Fear information and social phobic beliefs in children: A prospective paradigm and preliminary results. *Behaviour Research and Therapy, 41*, 113–123.

Fletcher, K. (1996). Psychometric review of the Childhood PTSD Interview. In B. H. Stamm (Ed.), *Measurement of stress, trauma, and adaptation* (pp. 87–89). Lutherville, MD: Sidran.

Foa, E. B., Johnson, K. M., Feeny, N. C., & Treadwell, K. R. H. (2001). The Child PTSD Symptom Scale: A preliminary examination of its psychometric properties. *Journal of Clinical Child Psychology, 30*, 376–384.

Gitlin-Weiner, K., Sandgrund, A., & Schaefer, C. (2000). *Play diagnosis and assessment* (2nd ed.). New York: Wiley.

Gullone, E., & King, N. J. (1992). Psychometric evaluation of a revised fear survey schedule for children and adolescents. *Journal of Child Psychology and Psychiatry, 33*, 987–998.

Hodges, K., McKnew, D., Cytryn, L., Stern, L., & Kline, J. (1982). The Child Assessment Schedule (CAS) diagnostic interview: A report on reliability and validity. *Journal of the American Academy of Child and Adolescent Psychiatry, 21*, 468–473.

Houston, B. K., Fox, J. E., & Forbes, L. (1984). Trait anxiety and children's state anxiety, cognitive behaviors, and performance under stress. *Cognitive Therapy and Research, 8*, 631–641.

Huffington, C. M., & Sevitt, M. A. (1989). Family interaction in adolescent school phobia. *Journal of Family Therapy, 11*, 353–375.

Inderbitzen-Nolan, H., Davies, C. A., & McKeon, N. D. (2004). Investigating the construct validity of the SPAI-C: Comparing the sensitivity of the SPAI-C and the SAS-A. *Journal of Anxiety Disorders, 18*, 547–560.

Kaslow, N. J., Stark, K. D., Printz, B., Livingston, R., & Tsai, S. L. (1992). Cognitive Triad Inventory for Children: Development and relation to depression and anxiety. *Journal of Clinical Child Psychology, 21*, 339–347.

Kaufman, J., Birmaher, B., Brent, D., Rao, U., Flynn, C., Moreci, P., Williamson, D., & Ryan, N. (1997). Schedule for Affective Disorders and Schizophrenia for School-Age Children-Present and Lifetime Version (K-SADS-PL): Initial reliability and validity data. *Journal of the American Academy of Child and Adolescent Psychiatry, 36*, 980–988.

Kazdin, A. E. (1990). Evaluation of the Automatic Thoughts Questionnaire: Negative cognitive processes and depression among children. *Psychological Assessment, 2*, 73–79.

Kearney, C. A. (2001). *School refusal behavior in youth: A functional approach to assessment and treatment*. Washington, DC: American Psychological Association.

Kearney, C. A. (2002). Identifying the function of school refusal behavior: A revision of the School Refusal Assessment Scale. *Journal of Psychopathology and Behavioral Assessment, 24*, 235–245.

Kearney, C. A. (2005). *Social anxiety and social phobia in youth: Characteristics, assessment, and psychological treatment.* New York: Springer.

Kearney, C. A., & Albano, A.M. (2000). *When children refuse school: A cognitive-behavioral therapy approach/Therapist's guide.* New York: Oxford University Press.

Kearney, C. A., & Albano, A. M. (2004). The functional profiles of school refusal behavior: Diagnostic aspects. *Behavior Modification, 28*, 147–161.

Kearney, C. A., Albano, A. M., Eisen, A. R., Allan, W. D., & Barlow, D. H. (1997). The phenomenology of panic disorder in youngsters: An empirical study of a clinical sample. *Journal of Anxiety Disorders, 11*, 49–62.

Kearney, C. A., Eisen, A. R., & Silverman, W. K. (1995). The legend and myth of school phobia. *School Psychology Quarterly, 10*, 65–85.

Kearney, C. A., Pursell, C., & Alvarez, K. (2001). Treatment of school refusal behavior in children with mixed functional profiles. *Cognitive and Behavioral Practice, 8*, 3–11.

Kearney, C. A., & Silverman, W. K. (1999). Functionally-based prescriptive and nonprescriptive treatment for children and adolescents with school refusal behavior. *Behavior Therapy, 30*, 673–695.

Kendall, P. C., & Chansky, T. E. (1991). Considering cognition in anxiety-disordered children. *Journal of Anxiety Disorders, 5*, 167–185.

Kindt, M., Brosschot, J. K., & Muris, P. (1996). Spider phobia questionnaire for children (SPQ-C): A psychometric study and normative data. *Behaviour Research and Therapy, 34*, 277–282.

King, N. J. (1994). Physiological assessment. In T. H. Ollendick, N. J. King, & W. Yule (Eds.), *International handbook of phobic and anxiety disorders in children and adolescents* (pp. 365–379). New York: Plenum.

King, N. J., Muris, P., & Ollendick, T. H. (2005). Childhood fears and phobias: Assessment and treatment. *Child and Adolescent Mental Health, 10*, 50–56.

King, N. J., Ollendick, T. H., & Tonge, B. J. (1995). *School refusal: Assessment and treatment.* Needham Heights, MA: Allyn & Bacon.

Kovacs, M. (1985). The Interview Schedule for Children (ISC). *Psychopharmacology Bulletin, 21*, 991–994.

La Greca, A. M. (1998). *Social anxiety scales for children and adolescents: Manual and instructions for the SASC, SASC-R, SAS-A (adolescents), and parent versions of the scales.* Miami, FL: Author.

La Greca, A. M. (1999). The social anxiety scales for children and adolescents. *The Behavior Therapist, 22*, 133–136.

La Greca, A. M. (2001). Friends or foes? Peer influences on anxiety among children and adolescents. In W. K. Silverman & P. D. A. Treffers (Eds.), *Anxiety disorders in children and adolescents: Research, assessment and intervention* (pp. 159–186). New York: Cambridge University Press.

La Greca, A. M., Dandes, S. K., Wick, P., Shaw, K., & Stone, W. L. (1988). Development of the Social Anxiety Scale for Children: Reliability and concurrent validity. *Journal of Clinical Child Psychology, 17*, 84–91.

La Greca, A. M., & Lopez, N. (1998). Social anxiety among adolescents: Linkages with peer relations and friendships. *Journal of Abnormal Child Psychology, 26*, 83–94.

La Greca, A. M., & Stone, W. L. (1993). Social Anxiety Scale for Children-Revised: Factor structure and concurrent validity. *Journal of Clinical Child Psychology, 22*, 17–27.

Laurent, J., & Stark, K. D. (1993). Testing the cognitive content-specificity hypothesis with anxious and depressed youngsters. *Journal of Abnormal Psychology, 102*, 226–237.

Leitenberg, H., Yost, L. W., & Carroll-Wilson, M. (1986). Negative cognitive errors in children: Questionnaire development, normative data, and comparisons between children with and without self-reported symptoms of depression, low self-esteem, and evaluation anxiety. *Journal of Consulting and Clinical Psychology, 54*, 528–536.

Lonigan, C. J., Carey, M. P., & Finch, A. J. (1994). Anxiety and depression in children and adolescents: Negative affectivity and the utility of self-reports. *Journal of Consulting and Clinical Psychology, 62*, 1000–1008.

March, J. (1997). *Multidimensional Anxiety Scale for Children*. North Tonawanda, NY: Multi-Health Systems.

Masia, C. L., Klein, R. G., Storch, E. A., & Corda, B. (2001). School-based behavioral treatment for social anxiety disorder in adolescents: Results of a pilot study. *Journal of the American Academy of Child and Adolescent Psychiatry, 40*, 780–786.

McCown, W., Fink, A. D., Galina, H., & Johnson, J. (1992). Effects of laboratory-induced controllable and uncontrollable stress on Rorschach variables *m* and *Y*. *Journal of Personality Assessment, 59*, 564–573.

McLeer, S. V., Dixon, J. F., Henry, D., Ruggiero, K., Escovitz, K., Niedda, T., et al. (1998). Psychopathology in non-clinically referred sexually abused children. *Journal of the American Academy of Child and Adolescent Psychiatry, 37*, 1326–1333.

Morris, T. L., & March, J. S. (2004). *Anxiety disorders in children and adolescents* (2nd ed.). New York: Guilford Press.

Muris, P., Merckelbach, H., & Damsma, E. (2000). Threat perception bias in nonreferred, socially anxious children. *Journal of Clinical Child Psychology, 29*, 348–359.

Muris, P., Merckelbach, H., Schmidt, H., & Mayer, B. (1999). The revised version of the Screen for Child Anxiety Related Emotional Disorders (SCARED-R): Factor structure in normal children. *Personality and Individual Differences, 26*, 99–112.

Nauta, M. H., Scholing, A., Rapee, R. M., Abbott, M., Spence, S. H., & Waters, A. (2004). A parent-report measure of children's anxiety: Psychometric properties and comparison with child-report in a clinic and normal sample. *Behaviour Research and Therapy, 42*, 813–839.

Ollendick, T. H. (1983). Reliability and validity of the Revised Fear Survey Schedule for Children (FSSC-R). *Behaviour Research and Therapy, 21*, 685–692.

Ollendick, T. H., & March, J. S. (2004). *Phobic and anxiety disorders in children and adolescents: A clinician's guide to effective psychosocial and pharmacological interventions*. New York: Oxford University Press.

Perrin, S., & Last, C. G. (1997). Worrisome thoughts in children clinically referred for anxiety disorder. *Journal of Clinical Child Psychology, 26*, 181–189.

Perry, W., Sprock, J., Schaible, D., McDougall, A., Minassian, A., Jenkins, M., et al. (1995). Amphetamine on Rorschach measures in normal subjects. *Journal of Personality Assessment, 64*, 456–465.

Research Units on Pediatric Psychopharmacology Anxiety Study Group (2002). The Pediatric Anxiety Rating Scale (PARS): Development and psychometric properties. *Journal of the American Academy of Child and Adolescent Psychiatry, 41*, 1061–1069.

Reynolds, C. R., & Richmond, B. O. (1985). *Revised Children's Manifest Anxiety Scale manual*. Los Angeles, CA: Western Psychological Services.

Ronan, K. R., Kendall, P. C., & Rowe, M. (1994). Negative affectivity in children: Development and validation of a self-statement questionnaire. *Cognitive Therapy and Research, 18*, 509–528.

Saigh, P. A., Yasik, A. E., Oberfield, R. A., Breen, B. L., Halamandaris, P. V., Rubenstein, H., et al. (2000). The Children's PTSD Inventory: Development and reliability. *Journal of Traumatic Stress, 13*, 369–380.

Sarason, S. B., Davidson, K. S., Lighthall, F. F., Waite, R. R., & Ruebush, B. K. (1960). *Anxiety in elementary school children*. New York: Wiley.

Scahill, L., Riddle, M. A., McSwiggen-Hardin, M., Ort, S. I., King, R. A., Goodman, W. K., et al. (1997). Children's Yale-Brown Obsessive Compulsive Scale: Reliability and validity. *Journal of the American Academy of Child and Adolescent Psychiatry, 36*, 844–852.

Schniering, C. A., Hudson, J. L., & Rapee, R. M. (2000). Issues in the diagnosis and assessment of anxiety disorders in children and adolescents. *Clinical Psychology Review, 20*, 453–478.

Shaffer, D., Fisher, P., Dulcan, M. K., Davies, M., Piacentini, J., Schwab-Stone, M. E., et al. (1996). The NIMH Diagnostic Interview for Children version 2.3 (DISC-2.3): Description, acceptability, prevalence rates, and performance in the MECA study. *Journal of the American Academy of Child and Adolescent Psychiatry, 35*, 865–877.

Silverman, W. K., & Albano, A. M. (1996). *The Anxiety Disorders Interview Schedule for Children for DSM-IV, child and parent versions*. San Antonio, TX: Psychological Corporation.

Silverman, W. K., Goedhart, A. W., Barrett, P., & Turner, C. (2003). The facets of anxiety sensitivity represented in the Childhood Anxiety Sensitivity Index: Confirmatory analyses of factor models from past studies. *Journal of Abnormal Psychology, 112*, 364–374.

Silverman, W. K., & Kearney, C. A. (1991). The nature and treatment of childhood anxiety. *Educational Psychology Review, 3*, 335–361.

Silverman, W. K., Saavedra, L. M., & Pina, A. A. (2001). Test-retest reliability of anxiety symptoms and diagnoses with the Anxiety Disorders Interview Schedule for DSM-IV: Child and Parent Versions. *Journal of the American Academy of Child and Adolescent Psychiatry, 40*, 937–944.

Spence, S. H., Barrett, P. M., & Turner, C. M. (2003). Psychometric properties of the Spence Children's Anxiety Scale with young adolescents. *Journal of Anxiety Disorders, 17*, 605–625.

Spence, S. H., Donovan, C., & Brechman-Toussaint, M. (1999). Social skills, social outcomes, and cognitive features of childhood social phobia. *Journal of Abnormal Psychology, 108*, 211–221.

Spielberger, C. D. (1973). *Manual for the State-Trait Anxiety Inventory for Children*. Palo Alto, CA: Consulting Psychologists Press.

Sprafkin, J., Gadow, K. D., Salisbury, H., Schneider, J., & Loney, J. (2002). Further evidence of reliability and validity of the Child Symptom Inventory–4: Parent checklist in clinically referred boys. *Journal of Clinical Child and Adolescent Psychology, 31*, 513–524.

Stark, K. D., & Laurent, J. (2001). Joint factor analysis of the Children's Depression Inventory and the Revised Children's Manifest Anxiety Scale. *Journal of Clinical Child Psychology, 30*, 552–567.

Storch, E. A., Masia-Warner, C., Dent, H. C., Roberti, J. W., & Fisher, P. H. (2004). Psychometric evaluation of the Social Anxiety Scale for Adolescents and the Social Phobia and Anxiety Inventory for Children: Construct validity and normative data. *Journal of Anxiety Disorders, 18*, 665–679.

Strand, V. C., Sarmiento, T. L., & Pasquale, L. E. (2005). Assessment and screening tools for trauma in children and adolescents: A review. *Trauma, Violence, and Abuse, 6*, 55–78.

Vasa, R. A., & Pine, D. S. (2004). Neurobiology. In T. L. Morris & J. S. March (Eds.), *Anxiety disorders in children and adolescents* (2nd ed., pp. 3–26). New York: Guilford Press.

Vasey, M. W., & Dadds, M. R. (2001). *The developmental psychopathology of anxiety*. New York: Oxford University Press.

Welner, Z., Reich, W., Herjanic, B., Jung, K. G., & Amado, H. (1987). Reliability, validity, and parent-child agreement studies of the Diagnostic Interview for Children and Adolescents (DICA). *Journal of the American Academy of Child and Adolescent Psychiatry, 26*, 649–653.

Wirt, R. D., Lachar, D., Klinedinst, J. K., & Seat, P. D. (1995). *Personality Inventory for Children (PIC)*. Los Angeles, CA: Western Psychological Services.

Wood, J. J., Piacentini, J. C., Bergman, L., McCracken, J., & Barrios, V. (2002). Concurrent validity of the anxiety disorders section of the Anxiety Disorders Interview Schedule for DSM-IV: Child and Parent Versions. *Journal of Clinical Child and Adolescent Psychology, 31*, 335–342.

Woodruff-Borden, J., Morrow, C., Bourland, S., & Cambron, S. (2002). The behavior of anxious parents: Examining mechanisms of transmission of anxiety from parent to child. *Journal of Clinical Child and Adolescent Psychology, 31*, 364–374.

Zatz, S., & Chassin, L. (1983). Cognitions of test-anxious children. *Journal of Consulting and Clinical Psychology, 51*, 526–534.

27

THE ASSESSMENT OF DEPRESSION
IN CHILDREN AND ADOLESCENTS

Margaret Semrud-Clikeman
Jodene Goldenring Fine
Brianne Butcher
University of Texas at Austin

Assessment of depression in children and adolescents requires an understanding of developmental issues that contribute to the expression of depression as well as a firm knowledge of assessment practices. The aim of this chapter is threefold. First a discussion of the models of depression is presented to provide a theoretical framework for understanding depression in children and adolescents. Second, a brief overview of developmental issues that can contribute to depression is provided. Finally, a discussion of the assessment measures as well as their applicability to children and adolescents with depression is presented.

The diagnosis and assessment of childhood depression rests on the symptoms listed in DSM-IV-TR (American Psychiatric Association, 2000), using generally the same symptoms as those used to diagnose adult depression. DSM-IV-TR provides a framework for diagnosing depression in adults. To qualify for a diagnosis of depression under this framework, the child/adolescent must show a depressed mood or loss of interest in pleasurable activities for at least two weeks. In addition, there must be at least four additional symptoms that may include changes in appetite/weight, sleep, or activity level; feelings or worthlessness and/or guilt as well as suicidal ideation; and/or problems with concentration and work completion. In addition to these DSM-IV-TR symptoms, social withdrawal, somatic symptoms, a negative body image, and bodily complaints have been found in children and adolescents with depression (Hammen & Rudolph, 2003). Cantwell (1983) suggests that children can show a unique presentation of depression and that depression in children may be characterized by restlessness and irritability rather than the sad mood and apathy frequently seen in adults. This suggestion is now present in DSM-IV-TR (American Psychiatric Association, 2000).

There are several models of depression that can help to inform the assessment of children and adolescents. The cognitive-behavioral model combines the child's behavior and how the environment shapes this behavior with how the child perceives his/her environment. In contrast, the behavioral model suggests that depression is the result of the child not receiving sufficient reinforcement from his/her environment. This dearth of reinforcement may be due to few reinforcers in the environment or difficulty in obtaining these reinforcers, possibly due to off-putting behaviors. Interpersonal models stress the relationships the child has with peers and parents. Difficulties are found in establishing friendships and connections to others and most particularly with peers (Rudolph, Hammen, & Burge, 1994). In these models the child has difficulty with problem-solving, coping, and emotional regulation (Rudolph, Kurlakowsky, & Conley, 2001). Children with these types of difficulty often ruminate on their difficulties, and this rumination in turn interferes with their ability to utilize active and effective problem-solving strategies. Psychodynamic theories of depression in childhood stress a disruption in caregiving relationships. Object relations theory suggests that the experience of a loss places the child in a vulnerable position for developing depression. This loss may be either literal or figural (death or emotional deprivation/poor parenting). In this model depression stems from anger about the lost object, which is then converted into an internal schema that usually takes the form of self-criticism (Davis & Wallbridge, 1983). Attachment theory can also be a model for depression. When the child is unable to form an attachment to the primary caregiver, a sense of security and trust is not present, and the infant becomes vulnerable to future problems with mood and self-acceptance (Bowlby, 1980).

The psychosocial and developmental contexts in which depression occur are important variables that need to be evaluated when a child or adolescent is being assessed for possible depression (Cicchetti, Gaiban, & Barnett, 1991; Cicchetti & Schneider-Rosen, 1986; Sroufe & Rutter, 1984). Thus, depression in childhood and adolescence is a combination the child's temperament, coping skills, biological heritage, and environmental experiences. A lack of openness to change, often required by environmental demands, and an inability to easily assimilate new experiences may overwhelm a child and are likely associated with depression in early childhood. In addition, difficulties with attachment may contribute to depressive feelings, particularly if there is a disruption in early attachment (Cicchetti & Schneider-Rosen, 1986; Cummings & Cicchetti, 1990; Kobak, Sudler, & Gamble, 1991; Kopp, 1989; Nurcombe, 1994).

The prevalence of depression appears to be increasing with a concomitant decrease in the age when depression is first noted (Stark, Sander, Yancy, Bronik & Hoke, 2000). The estimated rate of depression is approximately 2% of children and 4% of adolescents (American Academy of Child and Adolescent Psychiatry, 1998). Prior to adolescence, there are no gender differences, but during adolescence, girls show an increase; the incidence almost doubles by adulthood (Stark et al., 2000).

The duration of depression in children also varies depending on age. Major depression appears to last for 32 to 36 weeks, whereas dysthymia can last from 3 to 4 years (Kovacs, Akiskal, Gastonis, & Parrone, 1994; Strober, Lampert, Schmidt, & Morrell, 1993). Risk factors include not only the level of severity of depression but also the duration, with those children from dysfunctional families and girls showing more severe and longer episodes of depression (McCauley et al., 1993, Stark et al., 2000). In addition, depression in children and adolescents appears to be recurrent, with a 20% to 60% chance of returning within 1 to 2 years of remission (AACAP, 1998). Risk factors for a relapse include early age of onset, comorbid disorders, and psychosocial stressors (Birmaher et al., 2002; Emslie, Rush, Weinberg, & Gullion, 1997).

Cormorbidity is an important issue during an evalution of a child for depression. Approximately 40% to 70% are reported to have one comorbid disorder, and 20% to 50% have two or more (Birmaher et al., 1996). Common comorbid disorders include anxiety, ADHD, oppositional defiant disorders, and possibly posttraumatic stress disorder (Birmaher et al., 1996; Kilpatrick et al., 2003). Moreover, in late adolescence, personality disorders may arise and complicate the depression assessment as well as treatment (Lewinsohn, Rohde, Seeley, & Klein, 1997). When comorbidity is present, there is more severe impairment, a poorer response to treatment, and an increased risk for suicide (Lewinsohn, Rohde, & Seeley, 1998). How depression expresses itself differs, depending on the developmental level of the child or adolescent (Luby et al., 2002; Weiss & Garber, 2003).

A meta-analysis of 11 empirical studies found developmental effects in 18 of 29 (62%) core and associated depressive symptoms (Weiss & Garber, 2003). Another analysis of empirical research found that some symptoms of depression were consistent across age groups, including depressed mood, decreased concentration, sleep disturbance, and suicidal ideation. The presentation of other symptoms varied by age. Anhedonia (or a depressed mood), variation of symptom severity throughout the day, hopelessness, psychomotor retardation, and delusions increased with age, whereas depressed appearance, low self-esteem, somatic complaints, and hallucinations decreased with age (Borchardt & Meller, 1996; Carlson & Kashani, 1988). The extent to which developmental effects moderate the presentation of depression and the nature of those effects are not yet entirely understood (Goodyer, 1996), but developmental considerations appear to be useful in the assessment of depression. A brief description of empirical knowledge highlighting developmental issues important for the assessment of depression from infancy through early adulthood follows.

INFANCY AND EARLY CHILDHOOD

The diagnosis of depressive disorders in infancy and early childhood continues to be an area of debate, though sadness and core symptoms of depression, including withdrawal, negative affect, irritability, eating disturbances, apathy, abnormal stranger reactions, fussiness, and tantrums, have been observed in children at this developmental level (Garber & Horowitz, 2002; Trad, 1994). Persistent negative evaluations of the self and others are less common at this early stage of development (AACAP, 1997).

Bemporad (1994) suggested that early childhood depression is a reaction to situational factors. Infants may place greater significance on single events because of their limited experiences. This focus may result in global interpretation of singular events such that negative experiences in infancy could be interpreted as a global loss of control (Trad, 1994). Because of the significance of situational variables to the child's internal state, when depression is being assessed in infants and very young children, it is necessary to evaluate the child in the context of a broader environment, including important caregivers, extended family, the school, and the culture (AACAP, 1997).

The relationship between the infant and significant caregivers, or the infant-caregiver bond, has been recognized as an important factor in infant and early childhood sadness (Trad, 1994; Zero to Three/National Center for Clinical Infant Programs, 1994). A number of variables, including parental or caregiver psychopathology, can contribute to a disruption in this bond. Infants are very sensitive to the moods and behaviors of significant caregivers, and they often "mirror" the behavior of their depressed mother (Field, 1984; Zero to Three/ National Center for Clinical Infant Programs, 1994).

Studies involving twins, adoption, and families suggest that environmental and genetic factors combine to contribute to higher rates of depression in children with depressed caregivers (Kendler, 1995). Biological changes in depressed children may begin as early as infancy (Dawson et al., 1999; Luby et al., 2002). Other contributors to infant and early child-hood depression entail repeated negative experiences that the infant interprets as a global loss of control (Trad, 1994). These experiences include abuse or neglect (Barnett, Manly, & Cicchetti, 1991), hospitalization, separation from a significant caregiver, or other prolonged stress-inducing experiences (Trad, 1994).

Currently few instruments are standardized for the assessment of depression in infancy because of the uncertainty regarding the stability of depression at this developmental level (American Academy of Child and Adolescent Psychiatry, 1997). Although the diagnosis of depressive disorder in infancy remains an area of debate, standardized instruments may be used to supplement the clinician's understanding of the infant's biopsychosocial and cultural risk and protective factors (AACAP, 1997). The *Diagnostic Classification of Mental Health and Developmental Disorders of Infancy and Early Childhood* manual (1994) from the Zero to Three/National Center for Infants Clinical Programs diagnostic classification task force is designed to assess mental health difficulties, including depression, in the first four years of life.

PRESCHOOLERS AND EARLY-ELEMENTARY-AGE CHILDREN

Investigations of depression at the preschool and early elementary levels, like those of infants, trail behind exploration of depression in adolescence (Kashani, Allen, Beck, Bledsoe, & Reid, 1997). Luby et al. (2002) suggest that current DSM-IV criteria may not be sufficiently sensitive to capture a substantial portion of preschool children with depression. Luby et al. (2002) speculate that a number of the symptom state criteria are inapplicable to the life experiences of young children. Likewise, the duration requirements are not sensitive to the normatively greater fluctuation of mood states in young children. Thus, modified criteria used to assess age-appropriate manifestations of core symptom states and disregarded duration restrictions is suggested. Examples of modifications to DSM-IV criteria to represent age-appropriate symptom states include describing depressed mood as "irritability or lack of pleasure in activities or play" and including age-appropriate expression of symptoms such as "excessive or inappropriate guilt or suicidal ideation expressed and/or occurring persistently in play." These differences in symptom expression are consistent with Bemporad's (1994) conclusion that the expression of depression may be qualitatively different in young children because of the immaturity of their cognitive and social development.

Although clinical self-report interviews are useful in the assessment of depression for older children, young children have difficulty reporting time-related events and underreport problems (Lous, de Wit, de Bruyn, & Riksen-Walraven, 2000). There are few standardized instruments for the assessment of depression in preschoolers and early-elementary-age children. Lous et al. (2000) suggest that parent reports are valid indicators of overt behaviors but are not as sensitive to the child's depressive thoughts or feelings.

Parent-report measures of psychopathology that contain a depression index such as the Personality Inventory for Children–2 (Wirt, Lachar, Seat, & Broen, 2001), the Child Behavior Checklist (CBCL; Achenbach & Rescorla, 2001), and the Behavior Assessment Scale for Children, Second Edition (BASC–2; Reynolds & Kamphaus, 2004) are outlined in various chapters in this volume. All of these measures can be used with children as young as two years of age.

Assessment of play behavior may be helpful in the identification of depression in preschoolers (Kashani & Carlson, 1987; Lous et al., 2000). Both the type and content of play behavior yield information about the child's psychological functioning. Lous et al. (2000) found that depressed preschoolers showed less play behavior than nondepressed children and more nonplay behavior. They also displayed less coherence of play than nondepressed peers, switching between behaviors more often. Lous et al. (2000) concluded that depressed preschoolers may show "differential activity" rather than depressed activity. This finding is consistent with data indicating that 75% of preschoolers exhibit psychomotor agitation, compared with only 25% exhibiting decreased activity (Kashani et al., 1997). Themes in play may also be significant in the identification of depressed preschoolers. Luby et al. (2002) noted very high levels (61%) of death-related or suicidal themes in the play of depressed preschool children compared with nondepressed peers.

LATE-ELEMENTARY- AND MIDDLE-SCHOOL-AGE CHILDREN

In the preadolescent transitional period, the prevalence of depression rises slightly but remains relatively low compared with adolescent rates of depression. Childhood onset depression has been associated with a more severe and recurrent form of depression than adolescent or adult onset depression (Garland & Weiss, 1995). Kovacs (1996) reported that in a nine-year follow-up of children with major depressive disorder, 50% of the children studied had subsequent depressive episodes.

As was outlined earlier, children of this age often display a unique profile of depressive symptoms (Borchardt & Meller, 1996). Compared with adolescents and adults, children report more irritable mood, temper outbursts, physical aggression, and distractibility. Physical symptoms and somatic complaints are also an integral part of major depression in school-aged children and can be important indicators for identification of depressive disorders (Goodyer, 1996). One study of depressed children and adolescents attending a psychiatric clinic (outpatients and inpatients) in North America reported that around 70% of the patients had significant physical complaints at presentation. Children 6 to 12 years of age reported headaches, sleep problems, abdominal pain, and enuresis more often than adolescents (McCauley, Carlsson, & Calderon, 1991).

For children at this age, the use of self-report measures may be appropriate particularly if the child is forthcoming in discussing his/her feelings. Parent and teacher ratings may become less helpful as the child and preadolescent begin to hide feelings from caregivers. When a child/preadolescent is less forthcoming or possibly less aware of feelings, projective tests are very appropriate. The Rorschach can be very helpful in uncovering feelings of emotional distress as well as concerns about emotional distance and closeness.

HIGH SCHOOL AGE AND ADOLESCENCE

The prevalence of depression increases drastically during adolescence, with high school annual incidence rates of major depressive disorder between 3% and 8% (AACAP, 1997; Lewinsohn & Essau, 2002). Although depression is considerably more common in adolescents, individuals with adolescent-onset depression often have better treatment outcomes with quicker recovery than do depressed children (Garland & Weiss, 1995). The most common symptoms in adolescents meeting criteria for MDD were depressed mood (97.7%), sleep disturbances (88.6%), difficulties thinking or concentrating (81.8%), weight or appetite disturbances (79.5%), and anhedonia (77.3%; Roberts, Lewinsohn, & Seeley, 1995).

Lewinsohn, Seeley, Pettit, and Joiner (2003) found no significant differences in symptom prevalence between adolescence and early adulthood. Although symptom prevalence may not differ between adults and adolescents, expression of symptoms and behavior may take different forms. Maladaptive behaviors, including drug abuse, promiscuity, truancy, and theft, have been associated with depression in adolescents (Gjerde, Block, & Block, 1988). Several studies have reported elevated levels of suicidal behavior among adolescents, especially females (Carlson & Kashani, 1988; Weissman et al., 1999).

Researchers suggest several explanations for the gender differences in depression rates, including socialization practices, hormonal changes in puberty, styles of coping with adversity, and genetic influences (Lewinsohn & Essau, 2002; Silberg et al., 1999). There are also gender differences in the expression of depression. Roberts et al. (1995) found that females were significantly more likely than males to report symptoms of weight/appetite disturbance and worthlessness/guilt.

Important areas of focus in the assessment of childhood and adolescent depressive disorders include depression symptoms, duration, severity, and age of onset (Lewinsohn & Essau, 2002). While parent and teacher reports and behavioral observations are most indicative of early childhood depression, self-reports become increasingly valid in late childhood and adolescence with greater cognitive maturity. Children at later developmental levels can more reliably report duration and severity of depressive symptoms than young children. In addition, self-reports provide better accounts of internalizing symptoms than can be elicited from other sources (Cantwell, Lewinsohn, Rohde, & Seeley, 1997). Although assessment techniques vary in reliability and validity by developmental level, a multimethod, multisource assessment is recommended at all ages for accurate diagnosis of depression (AACAP, 1997). A more comprehensive description of assessment tools for the diagnosis of depression follows in the next section.

ASSESSMENT

Referral Questions

When a child or adolescent is referred for evaluation by his/her teacher for school problems, the behaviors of concern may be symptomatic of many disorders. Inattention, irritability, withdrawal, oppositional behavior, and academic difficulty could be variously attributed to Attention-Deficit Hyperactivity Disorder, Oppositional-Defiant Disorder, Anxiety Disorder, mood disorders (Adjustment Disorder, Depression, Dysthymia, Bipolar, Cyclothymia), or symptoms secondary to Learning Disability. Many of these disorders are comorbid in child and adolescent populations. Thus, the first referral is often a school-based one: the child's grades have fallen, he does not want to go to school, there is difficulty attending class and completing tasks, he doesn't follow directions, he is disruptive, and he gets into fights with his peers or plays alone at recess. Often the referral is related to teacher concern about ADHD or academic failure; oppositional behaviors may be of more concern to parents who have difficulty managing the child at home.

Children have a smaller range of behaviors than do adults (Speier, Sherak, Hirsch, & Cantwell, 1995). For example, a young child experiencing hunger, sadness, fatigue, or fear is likely to demonstrate with identical acting-out behaviors such as tantrums. As the child matures, differential behaviors emerge for each internal state. With this in mind, it is especially important to evaluate child behaviors in the context of home and school environments, patient and family history, and additional situational stressors in order to determine the source of problem behaviors at school. A transactional approach considering interactions among persons, places, and situations against the background of history, medical issues, and development can help tease out the reasons why children and adolescents exhibit worrisome behaviors.

Assessment Methods

Interviews

Interviews can be fully structured, semistructured, or nonstructured. Either trained clinicians or lay administrators can use fully structured interviews, as they require little additional questioning or clinical knowledge. Semistructured interviews, which allow for additional questioning, should be used by trained clinicians. Semistructured interviews can be used to obtain information crucial to current problems, comorbidity, and differential diagnosis. A more comprehensive evaluation can be obtained because a framework for asking questions related to specific problem symptoms is provided, ensuring that no important information is overlooked.

Structured and semistructured interviews may not be appropriate for younger children. Studies suggest that below the age of 10, children's structured interview reporting is unreliable (Edelbrock, Costello, Dulcan, Kalas, & Conover, 1985) because the language is not adequately developed and the introspection required is not available to children so young. For these reasons, Schwab-Stone (1995) reported that children below the age of 12 have difficulty answering questions on one structured interview, the DISC. As children grow older, their ability to reliably respond to questions improves, but the reliability of parental report *decreases* with age as adolescents' internal experience diverges from parent perception and adolescents become more reticent about sharing feelings. When very young children are interviewed, a loosely structured interview allowing for the development of common vocabulary will be best, as would the use of tangible objects to discuss feelings (i.e., dollhouse, coloring).

For interviewing young children, Orvaschel (2004) suggests first asking them what word they use when they feel really bad, like when they're in trouble. Then, ask the child if they always know why they feel that way, using the words given by the child. This method establishes whether there is a depressed/irritable mood in context. To screen for sadness, Orvaschel suggests querying about boredom, making sure that sadness is present even when there are engaging activities available to the child. When establishing a time frame for mood disturbance, start with small time segments and move to larger times anchored in events likely to be noted by children (i.e., birthdays, school, holidays). For example, ask the child "if they feel that way (e.g. bad, sad, cranky, mad, etc.) for a few minutes or a long time, like all morning or all afternoon, or all day at school, and so on. This can be followed with questions about whether this was true today, was true yesterday, the whole week, since school started, since his or her birthday" (p. 305). Young children can answer questions about whether they are hungry, but not about weight loss, so ask whether their clothes have become loose or tight. To assess for suicidality in young children, look for behaviors such as holding breath and putting their head in a pillowcase or under water. Although such behaviors may not be immediately dangerous, they may represent serious intent and should be followed up with a standard suicide evaluation.

When parents and guardians are interviewed, a detailed family history is extremely important. People with close relatives with depression are more likely to be depressed as well

(Kazdin & Marciano, 1998). The heritability of depression has been estimated at 30% to 40% (Middledorp, Cath, Van Dyck, & Boomsma, 2005), with the remaining amount due to environment, including socio-familial factors.

Interviews, like other methods of data gathering, have poor concordance among informants, although consistency of the same informant across measures has been found to be adequate (Semrud-Clikeman, Bennett, & Guli, 2003). As discussed above, age can have an effect on interview reliability. Intellectual ability, age, and gender have also been found to be related to the consistency of child reports (Fallon & Schwab-Stone, 1994). Thus, care must be taken in the interpretation of interview results. Table 27.1 lists the structured and semi-structured interviews currently in use. Noted in the table are the names, type, age range, informants, time to administer, and publisher. Some interviews are omnibus measures, meaning that they screen for a variety of psychiatric diagnoses, including Major Depressive Disorder. The time for administration varies on whether the entire interview is used; some modules may be eliminated as unsuitable for the case at hand.

Rating Scales

Rating scales are checklists that are completed by the child, parent, and often the teacher. They provide an informant's impression about the behaviors of the child or adolescent. They are generally easy to use and can usually be completed by the informant without the assistance of a clinician. When giving a rating scale to a parent or child, be sure that their English language reading ability is high enough to properly interpret the questions. The required reading level is usually available on the publisher's website. It is best for youths to complete the questionnaires in the clinician's office without their parents or caretakers. When a questionnaire is sent home to complete, parent oversight or worries about parents' reactions may influence the responses of the child.

Many rating scales are omnibus measures, having scales for a variety of problems: Attention, Depression, Conduct Disorder, and so forth. It is best for informants to complete all of the questions, even if there is only one area of concern. Some questions contribute to more than one scale, and the questions for each scale are usually scattered across the measure. When scoring a rating scale, be sure to look for unusual patterns, such as all "yes," all "no," or regularly alternating responses indicating that the respondent has not truly considered the questions. Take into consideration respondents who rate at either a low or high extreme. While not necessarily meaning to skew the results, such extremes can reveal the personal style or level of concern of the informant. Table 27.2 shows some of the rating scales commonly in use today.

Keep in mind that self-report rating scales are easily faked because the face validity of the questions is high. Children and adolescents wishing to present as "normal" can easily do so. Intelligent and aware children can also prevent leakage of depressive material on highly structured assessments like the WISC–4 and other cognitive measures. At such times, projective measures have a place in the battery because of the unstructured nature of the tasks.

Projective Measures

Projective measures can be inkblots, thematic storytelling, drawings, or sentence completions. In all of these types of tests, the child is asked to respond to open-ended stimuli for which a free-association response is given. The basis of the projective response is the tendency of people to interpret their inner worlds on the basis of personal experience. Projective

TABLE 27.1.
Structured and Semistructured Interview Measures

Name	Type	Age	Informants	Administration	Publisher
Diagnostic interview for children and adolescents (DICA-IV)	Structured, DSM-IV criteria, Omnibus	6–17	Child Parent	Computer, 20 minutes–2 hours	mhs.com
Diagnostic interview schedule for children (DISC)	Structured, DSM-IV, ICD-10 criteria, Omnibus	9–17 (Y) 6–17 (P) 6–17 (T)	Youth Parent Teacher	Computer, 70 minutes–2 hours	Developed by the National Institute of Mental Health, currently managed by Columbia University, DISC Group disc@worldnet.att.net
Schedule for affective disorders and schizophrenia for school-age children (K-SADS-P) K-SADS-E	Semistructured, DSM-IV criteria P = current episode E = past + current		Youth Parent	Clinician interview	Helen Orvaschel, Ph.D., Center for Psychological Studies, Nova Southeastern University, 3301 College Avenue, Ft. Lauderdale, FL 33314
Interview schedule for children and adolescents (ISCA)	Semistructured, DSM-IV criteria	8–17	Youth Parent Summary	Clinician interview	Maria Kovacs, Ph.D., Western Psychiatric Institute and Clinic, University of Pittsburgh School of Medicine, 3811 O'Hara Street, Pittsburgh, PA 15213

TABLE 27.2.
Rating Scales

Name	Informant	Type	Age	Subscales	Publisher
Children's Depression Inventory (CDI) (Kovacs, 1992)	Youth Parent Teacher	Depression checklist	7–17	Negative mood, interpersonal problems, ineffectiveness, anhedonia, negative self-esteem	parinc.com mhs.com pearsonassessments.com
Beck Youth Inventories (BYI) (Beck, Beck, & Jolly, 2003)	Youth	Multiple checklists	7–14	Separate inventories: depression, anxiety, anger, disruptive behavior, self-concept	harcourtassessment.com
Beck Depression Inventory-II (BDI-II) (Beck, Beck, & Jolly, 2003)	Adolescent	Depression checklist	13–80	DSM-IV criteria	harcourtassessment.com
Reynolds Adolescent Depression Scale–II (RADS-II) (Reynolds, 2005)	Adolescent	Depression checklist	12–18	Dysphoric mood, anhedonia/negative affect, negative self-evaluation, and somatic complaints	parinc.com harcourtassessment.com
Behavior Assessment Scale for Children–II (BASC-2) (Reynolds & Kamphaus, 2004) Self (SRP) Parent (PRS) Teacher (TRS)	Youth Parent Teacher	Omnibus checklist	4–18	Multiple clinical and adaptive scales, critical items	agsnet.com
Achenbach System of Empirically Based Assessment (ASEBA) (Achenbach & Rescorla, 2001) Youth Self-Report (YSR)	Preschool School age	Omnibus checklist	1.5–18	Multiple clinical and adaptive scales, critical items	aseba.org
Child Behavior Checklist (CBCL) (Achenbach et al., 2001) Teacher Report Form (TRF)	Parent Teacher				

tests can be especially useful with children, who are often good candidates for such techniques because they naturally tend to view the world from a very personal, egocentric perspective (Chandler, 2003). For many, explicit verbal expression of internal states may not be the best communication method, either because language is not yet developed enough to reveal problems or, in some cases, because language development and intellect are superior and able to mask them.

Validation studies of the ability of some projective techniques to discriminate between diagnostic groups have shown poor performance (Chandler, 2003), and multiple methods of administration and scoring produce significantly varying results (Weiner, 1986). Thus, like all assessments, projective measures are not a good single source for diagnosis of depression and should never be used alone. They are very useful in cases where the child is not forthcoming or is reluctant to discuss his/her feelings openly. They can also provide a window into the internal life of the child that may not be available through the use of behavioral rating scales or interviews. Finally, projective measures should be among the last items administered in the testing sequence. By that time, the examiner will have a grasp of the intellectual and language abilities of the child, and for children susceptible to emotional distress, the lack of structure could negatively affect their performance on more structured subsequent tasks.

Inkblots.   The Rorschach Inkblot Test is a set of 10 symmetrical inkblots to which the child provides a free-association response. The Exner (2001) *Comprehensive System* of scoring is used most commonly because of its standardized procedures and the relatively large amount of research available for the system. Exner provides normative data based on between 105 and 150 subjects in each age group from ages 5 to 15. One advantage of Exner's *Comprehensive System* is that collection of the protocol is a deliberately defined process, including instructions for how the examiner should sit, query, and record responses. It takes a great deal of time and practice to develop proficiency in the administration and scoring of the Rorschach, and structured training and supervision are strongly recommended.

Rather than producing a diagnosis, the Rorschach is meant to give increased understanding of personality processes (Weiner, 1986), cognitive style (Exner, 1983), and behavioral tendencies (Chandler, 2003). For children, the Rorschach is a snapshot of factors that are naturally developmentally transient, but may reveal the current processes of the child. Thus, although the Rorschach cannot diagnose depression, it can identify personality characteristics associated with depression. See chapters by Tibon and Rothschild, Erdberg, and Tuber et al. (this volume) for more information on using the Rorschach with children and adolescents.

Thematic Storytelling.   Unlike the highly ambiguous figures of the Rorschach, thematic storytelling measures elicit free-association story responses to picture cards designed to engender specific themes, such as aggression, sibling stress, attitude toward parents, and Oedipal issues. Children are asked to view the picture cards and then tell a story with a beginning, middle, and end (see Cashel et al., this volume, for a review). The technique tends to yield the current concerns of the child, motivations, needs, threats, and their perception of significant others (Chandler, 2003). Storytelling techniques, of course, are dependent on the developmental stage of the child, expressive language ability, and intellectual ability. Furthermore, research has shown that cultural differences may affect verbal production and interpretation of storytelling measures (Flanagan & Giuseppe, 1999).

Drawing.   Projective drawings are drawings made by the child at the request of the examiner. Usually human figures are drawn, but projective tests can also include inanimate objects such as trees and houses. The pictures are analyzed for structure and content. Structural aspects include the characteristics of figures, the position of the figures with respect to other figures in the drawing, the drawing style, and actions in the drawing. Structural organization has been used in the past to infer intellectual maturity with the use of various scoring systems, such as the Goodenough-Harris Draw-A-Man Quantitative Scoring System (DAP-QSS: Naglieri, 1988). Content refers to the themes occurring in and across projective drawings. Projective drawings can be static ("*Draw me a man*") or kinetic ("*Draw a picture of everyone in your family doing something*"). See the chapter by Matto (this volume) for a review.

What role can projective drawings play in a multimethod assessment for depression? Knoff (2003) argues that content analysis of projective drawings can be an important part of an assessment when used sparingly and appropriately to assist in generating hypotheses about a referred child. He suggests using the drawings and the conversations with the child about them in a way similar to that used in a thematic perception test, only the stimuli are generated by the child.

Sentence Completion.   Like the projective drawing tests, sentence completion tasks lack reliability and normative standardization, but they can still offer insights into the emotional functioning of a child as an addition to a comprehensive multimethod battery. Sentence completions are cloze tasks: a sentence stem is given and the child completes the sentence. Younger children may have the sentence stems read to them and respond orally, but it is important to read the sentence stems in the most neutral manner possible. Whether the sentences are read orally or the child completes them with pen and pencil, do not stop to comment on responses. Querying is acceptable after the protocol is finished. If a child hesitates to answer, make note of it and wait quietly for the child to respond. Sentence stems may be repeated, but it is best to note the sentences on which repetition was needed.

Haak (2003), the author of one sentence completion protocol, suggests that indicators for depressed children are almost always found in sentence completion tasks. Among the 12 indicators Haak suggests are outright references to depression or sadness, outright reference to self-destruction, responses that confuse anger and sadness (i.e., "When I'm angry, I cry"), consistently negative self-concept, homicidal ideation, and yearning for support from parental figures (Haak, 2003, p. 171–172). Haak further suggests that the format of the sentence completion task aids the expression of low-energy depressed children because it is partially structured.

There are several published sentence completion protocols, but most are for adults and children over the age of 12. One very popular sentence completion test is the Rotter Incomplete Sentences Blank, Second Edition (Rotter, Lah, & Rafferty, 1992), but this measure is for high school students and does not extend downward. The Children's Self-Report and Projective Inventory (CSRPI: Ziffer & Shapiro, 1992) is a multicomponent battery that includes sentence completion protocols for children aged 5 to 12. Many school psychologists have unpublished versions that directly address the concerns of children.

In summary, the instruments available for the assessment of depression in children and adolescents range from interviews, to checklists, to projective techniques. In general, the caregiver checklists are most reliable, but remember that the results are *perceptions* of behaviors. Careful consideration of the source is important. The usefulness of self-report checklists will vary, depending upon the capacity and willingness of the child to accurately report on symptoms. Interviews are essential to obtaining important information that can place the behaviors of concern in the context of family history, school and home environments, and medical issues. Projective measures can be helpful when children are unwilling or unable to talk directly about their internal state, but such methods should be used to enhance or augment information gleaned from other approaches. The thorough assessment will include a variety of the techniques we have discussed.

Multiple Informants and Multiple Methods

As for any psychological assessment, it is considered best to gather information from divergent sources and look for convergence on diagnostic criteria in the data. When information is assembled from different people, the perspective and circumstances of the reporter need to be considered and the data interpreted accordingly. Simply adding up risk factors is not recommended. For example, mothers tend to report more symptoms than do fathers (Mash & Dozois, 1996); parents of young children may be reluctant to share symptoms for fear of appearing to be poor at parenting their child; older children may be fearful of divulging perceived weaknesses.

Each informant will be able to provide special information. Teachers provide information regarding changes in academic performance and attendance and changes in peer relations, whereas parents can provide somatic symptoms and changes in sleep and appetite and the history of symptoms over time (Speier, Sherak, Hirsch, & Cantwell, 1995). The child will be the best source of information on his or her internal emotional state (Orvaschel, 2004), but it will be important to develop a common, age-appropriate vocabulary during the interview, as discussed above. A good understanding of developmental issues will help in the gathering and interpretation of information from children. Additional caretakers, grandparents, counselors, school personnel, and peers can provide useful details concerning the child.

Not only is there a wide variety in symptoms of depression among individuals, but depression may also be observed variously in different environments. In a study using a variety of measures (Leon, Kendall, & Garber, 1980) it was found that, at home, depressed children in third to sixth grades showed more conduct problems, psychosomatic problems, anxiety, impulsivity, and perfectionism than did their nondepressed peers. At school, depressed children were more passive and inattentive than they were at home. Younger children had more behavior problems, and older children had more anxiety. Thus, the age of the child appears to provide different symptoms and behaviors. This finding is different from that of adult depression, where the symptoms are far more common between people.

In addition to assembling information from a variety of persons, multiple types of measures are also part of a broad-based assessment, including interviews (structured or unstructured), behavioral checklists, observations, and projective testing. Moreover, it is important to assess the child's cognitive development, verbal concept formation, and problem-solving ability for the development of an appropriate treatment plan (Semrud-Clikeman et al., 2003). Although using multiple methods and instruments is the best way to assess depression in a child or adolescent, the data alone are not sufficient for diagnosis. The clinician must integrate the information from an ecological perspective, considering each measure in light of environmental, historical, cultural, personal, situational, and developmental influences.

CASE STUDY

Referral Question and Background

JT is a nine-year-old boy attending the fourth grade at Sunnyside Up School. He was referred for assessment with concerns regarding attention, focus, and disruptive behaviors at school and home. JT has been reprimanded for fighting and failure to follow classroom rules seven times during the first three months of this school year. One suspension followed an incident on the school bus during which JT hit a kindergarten child. JT does not complete school tasks, though his teacher feels that he is capable of doing the work. He needs frequent redirection and is alternatively day-dreamy and disruptive.

JT was born full-term following an uneventful pregnancy and birth. He met developmental milestones within normal expectations, and was described by his mother as an alert, active, and easily comforted infant. Preschool was reportedly uneventful, and symptoms of concern are not noted until seven years of age. No major injuries were reported. A medical report by Dr. G notes chest pain for the past two years associated with the onset of school. Dr. G suggested that the pain might be stress-related. Also noted in Dr. G's report is concern about a steady increase in JT's weight over the past few years. JT's mother reports that JT is lethargic and tired most days.

The family therapist, Ms. W., with whom the family is working, diagnosed JT's father with ADHD last year. Family history is also positive for depression (mother). JT's mother describes him as socially isolated, highly sensitive to adult disapproval, and "constantly in motion." He does not follow through on chores and often seems not to hear her. She notes that his father prefers JT's older brother and is especially disapproving of JT.

Case Conceptualization and Assessment

The referring question is ADHD, and there is some evidence to support this problem: high activity level, poor social interaction, classroom disruption, difficulty in task completion, need for frequent redirection, and excessive daydreaming and disruption. Symptoms appear in both the home and school environments. There are a few clues in the background information that are inconsistent with an ADHD diagnosis, including onset at seven years of age. Some information in the background seems to support an alternative hypothesis of depression: chest pain related to school, weight gain, evidence of a parent-child relationship issue, and difficulty with anger management. Other diagnostic possibilities included communication disorder, especially expressive language, learning disability, anxiety, and oppositional defiant disorder.

Test behaviors suggested poor strategy development and difficulty generating alternative approaches. Although JT persisted on difficult items, failure elicited physical signs of distress: red face, frown, and putting his head on the table. JT visibly restrained himself from throwing test items.

Scores on the WISC-IV suggested evenly developed cognitive functioning in the average range. High average scores on processing speed tasks suggested good ability to perform efficiently on attention-demanding, low-cognition tasks. This is notable because children with ADHD tend to do poorly on such tasks. Memory scores on the California Verbal Learning Test for Children (CVLT-C) and Rey Auditory Memory Test were also well within the average range. Several subtests of the Delis-Kaplan Executive Functioning System were used to assess mental flexibility, memory for rules, impulse control, and verbal fluency; all were within the average range. Overall, cognitive symptoms of ADHD failed to emerge from the data. However, behavioral symptoms of ADHD *did* show up on rating scales. Scores for inattention and hyperactivity on the Behavior Rating Scale for Children, Second Edition (BASC–2), at school and home are in the clinical range of concern, as are anxiety, withdrawal, and problems with adaptability. Notably, depression is rated in the extreme range (T-score > 100).

JT was administered the Children's Depression Inventory (CDI), and then the Kiddie SADS was used informally to structure an interview regarding depressive symptoms. JT's CDI responses indicated symptoms of depression within the clinical range (T-score = 83). All scales of the CDI were elevated above the clinical range, with Interpersonal Problems, Anhedonia and Negative Self-Esteem above T-score = 70. Initially, JT was reluctant to talk about his feelings. The examiner moved him to the floor and gave him blocks to play with while talking, which improved his level of response dramatically.

JT revealed that he feels "empty" and sad most of the time. His sad feelings are there when he awakens in the morning and last all day, with relief only when he is sleeping. His mood worsens in the afternoon, but JT cannot identify why. On a scale of 1 (not sad) to 10 (extremely sad), JT rated his mood at 8. When asked what happens when he cannot stand his sadness, JT responded, "I go ballistic." JT also reported that he feels anger much of the time. He cannot remember a time when he did not feel intense sadness and anger. Asked whether he feels better when he is with any particular person, JT reported that he cannot express his feelings to anyone and that his depressive symptoms are not relieved by the presence of his parents. JT did not report feelings of guilt or excessive social isolation. Asked what he would like to change about himself, JT responded, "Everything." When asked to describe himself, JT said, "Nothing, I am nothing." Consistent with prior medical reports, chest pain was reported several times per week, only on school days. Suicidal ideation was present, approximately four times per month, but plan formation was indistinct and unrealistic. Excessive guilt was not endorsed.

JT was also administered the Rorschach Inkblot Test. On this measure, JT showed evidence of long-standing feelings of emotional distress and low self-esteem. Furthermore, the degree of stress that he was experiencing was likely to be preoccupying and disorganizing. Thus, his reality-testing abilities were significantly worsened during periods of affective distress, resulting in misperceptions of events and people. Furthermore, consistent with his self-report that he is "nothing," JT's Rorschach scores suggested that he is prone to negative comparisons with others. In addition, JT may show marked oppositional tendencies that are likely to be related to his underlying feelings of anger, coupled with the cognitive overload he may experience during periods of stress. When integrated with behavior ratings and self-reported symptoms of depression, these Rorschach scores shed light not only on a diagnostic picture, but also on JT's internal experience.

Although ADHD and depression can co-occur, in this case, ADHD-like symptoms or those of any other underlying disorder would be difficult to accurately diagnose until JT's symptoms of depression are alleviated. In this case, the symptoms of depression should first be alleviated, and if symptoms of inattention and hyperactivity persist, further assessment would be warranted.

CONCLUSION

The assessment of childhood and adolescent depression requires an astute clinician who is intimately familiar with the developmental aspects of depression and appropriate measures for interviewing and evaluating a child's depression, and who can relate to the child/adolescent at his/her cognitive levels. The use of rating scales may be helpful for children who are willing to discuss their feelings. For others, the use of projectives may be most appropriate. It is incumbent upon the clinician to be able to select the most appropriate method for the individual child. As such, the method may range from play to interviewing to standardized measurement. The challenge of evaluating depression in children is significant and requires appropriate training.

REFERENCES

Achenbach, T. M., & Rescorla, L. A. (2001). *Manual for the ASEBA School-Age Forms & Profiles.* Burlington, VT: University of Vermont, Research Center for Children, Youth, and Families.

Achenbach, T. M., Rescorla, L. A., McConaughey, S. H., Pecora, P. J., Wetherbee, K. M., & Ruffle, T. M. (2001). *Achenbach System of Empirically Based Assessment.* Burlington, VT: ASEBA Research Center for Children, Youth, and Families.

American Academy of Child and Adolescent Psychiatry (1995). Practice parameters for the psychiatric assessment of children and adolescents. *Journal of the American Academy of Child and Adolescent Psychiatry, 34,* 1386–1402.

American Academy of Child and Adolescent Psychiatry (1997). Practice parameters for the assessment and treatment of children and adolescents with depressive disorders. *Journal of the American Academy of Child and Adolescent Psychiatry, 37,* 63S–83S.

American Academy of Child and Adolescent Psychiatry (1998). Practice parameters for the psychiatric assessment of infants and toddlers (0–36 months). *Journal of the American Academy of Child and Adolescent Psychiatry, 36,* 21S–36S.

American Psychiatric Association. (2000). *Diagnostic and statistical manual of mental disorders: DSM-IV-TR* (4th ed., text revision). Washington, DC: Author.

Barnett, D., Manly, J. T., & Cicchetti, D. (1991). Continuing toward an operational definition of psychological maltreatment. *Development and Psychopathology, 3,* 19–29.

Beck, J. S., Beck, A. T., & Jolly, J. (2003). *Beck Youth Inventories of Emotional and Social Impairment.* San Antonio, TX: Psych Corp, A brand of Harcourt Assessment.

Bemporad, J. R. (1994). Dynamic and interpersonal theories of depression. In W. M. Reynolds & H. F. Johnston (Eds.), *Handbook of depression in children and adolescents* (pp. 81–96). New York: Plenum Press.

Birmaher, B., Ryan, N. D., Williamson, D. E., Brent, D. A., Kaufman, J., Dahl, R. E., Perel, J., & Nelson, B. (1996). Childhood and adolescent depression: Part I. A review of the past 10 years. *Journal of the American Academy of Child and Adolescent Psychiatry, 35,* 1427–1439.

Borchardt, C. M., & Meller, W. H. (1996). Symptoms of affective disorder in pre-adolescent vs. adolescent inpatients. *Journal of Adolescence, 19*(2), 155–161.

Bowlby, J. (1980). *Attachment and loss: Vol. 3. Loss: Sadness and depression.* New York: Basic Books.

Cantwell, D. (1983). Depression in childhood: Clinical picture and diagnostic criteria. In D. Cantwell and G. Carlson (Eds.), *Affective disorders in childhood and adolescence* (pp. 3–18). New York: Spectrum.

Cantwell, B. D., Lewinsohn, P. M., Rohde, P., & Seeley, J. R. (1997). Correspondence between adolescent report and parent report of psychiatric diagnostic criteria. *Journal of the American Academy of Child and Adolescent Psychiatry, 36,* 610–619.

Chandler, L. A. (2003). The projective hypothesis and the development of projective techniques for children. In C. R. Reynolds & R. W. Kamphaus (Eds.), *Handbook of psychological and educational assessment of children* (2nd ed., pp. 51–65). New York: Guilford Press.

Cicchetti, D., Gaiban, J., & Barnett, D. (1991). Contributions from the study of high-risk populations to understanding the development of emotion regulation. In J. Garber & K. Dodge (Eds.), *The development of emotion regulation and dysregulation* (pp. 15–48). New York: Cambridge University Press.

Cicchetti, D., & Schneider-Rosen, K. (1986). An organizational view of affect: Illustration from the study of Down's syndrome infants. In M. Lewis and L. Rosenblum (Eds.), *The development of affect* (pp. 309–350). New York: Plenum Press.

Cummings, E. M., & Cicchetti, D. (1990). Toward a transactional model of relations between attachment and depression. In M. T. Greenberg, D. Cicchetti, and E. M. Cummings (Eds.), *Attachment during the preschool years* (pp. 339–372). Chicago: University of Chicago Press.

Davis, M., & Wallbridge, D. (1983). *Boundary and space: An introduction to the work of D. W. Winnicott.* New York: Brunner/Mazel.

Dawson, G., Frey, K., Panagiotides, H., Yamada, E., Hessl, D., & Osterling, J. (1999). Infants of depressed mothers exhibit atypical frontal electrical brain activity during interactions with mother and with a familiar, nondepressed adult. *Child Development, 70*(5), 1058–1066.

Edelbrock, C., Costello, A. J., Dulcan, M. K., Kalas, R., & Conover, N. C. (1985). Age differences in the reliability of the psychiatric interview of the child. *Child Development, 56*, 265–275.

Emslie, G. J., Rush, A. J., Weinberg, W. A., & Gullion, C. M. (1997). Recurrence of major depressive disorder in hospitalized children and adolescents. *Journal of the American Academy of Child and Adolescent Psychiatry, 36*, 785–792.

Exner, J. E. J. (1983). The Rorschach: A history and description of the comprehensive system. *School Psychology Review, 12*, 407–413.

Exner, J. E. J. (2001). *A Rorschach workbook for the comprehensive system* (5th ed.). Asheville, NC: Rorschach Workshops.

Fallon, T., & Schwab-Stone, M. (1994). Determinants of reliability in psychiatric surveys of children aged 6–22. *Journal of Child Psychology and Psychiatry, 35*, 1391–1408.

Field, T. M. (1984). Early interactions between infants and their postpartum depressed mothers. *Infant Behavior and Development, 7*, 517–522.

Flanagan, R., & Giuseppe, R. D. (1999). Critical review of the TEMAS: A step within the development of thematic apperception instruments. *Psychology in the Schools, 36*(1), 21–30.

Garber, J., & Horowitz, J. L. (2002) Depression in Children. In I. H. Gotlib & C. L. Hammen, *Handbook of depression* (pp. 510–540). New York: Guilford Press.

Garland, E. J., & Weiss, M. (1995). Subgroups of adolescent depression. *Journal of the American Academy of Child and Adolescent Psychiatry, 34*, 831.

Gjerde, P. E., Block, J., & Block, J. H. (1988). Depressive symptoms and personality during late adolescence: Gender differences in the externalization-internalization of symptom expression. *Journal of Abnormal Psychology, 97*, 475–486.

Goodyer, I. M. (1996). Physical symptoms and depressive disorders in childhood and adolescence. *Journal of Psyhosomatic Research, 41*, 1405–1408.

Haak, R. A. (2003). The sentence completion as a tool for assessing emotional disturbance. In C. R. Reynolds & R. W. Kamphaus (Eds.), *Handbook of psychological and educational assessment of children: Personality, behavior, and context* (pp. 159–181). New York: Guilford Press.

Hammen, C., & Rudolph, K. D. (2003). Childhood mood disorders. In E. Mash and R. Barkley (Eds.), *Child psychopathology* (pp. 233–278). New York: Guilford Press.

Kashani, J. H., Allen, W. D., Beck, N. C., Bledsoe, Y., & Reid, J. C. (1997). Dysthymic disorder in clinically referred preschool children. *Journal of the American Academy of Child and Adolescent Psychiatry, 36*(10), 1426–1433.

Kashani, J. H., & Carlson, G. A. (1987). Seriously depressed preschoolers. *American Journal of Psychiatry, 144*(3), 348–350.

Kazdin, A. E., & Marciano, P. L. (1998). Childhood and adolescent depression. In E. J. Mash & R. A. Barkley (Eds.), *Treatment of childhood disorders* (2nd ed., pp. 211–248). New York: Guilford Press.

Kendler, K. S. (1995). Genetic epidemiology in psychiatry: Taking both genes and environment seriously. *Archives of General Psychiatry, 52*, 895–899.

Kilpatrick, D. G., Ruggiero, K. J., Acierno, R., Saunders, B. E., Resnick, H. S., & Best, C. L. (2003). Violence and risk of PTSD, major depression, substance abuse/dependence, and comorbidity: Results from the National Survey of Adolescents. *Journal of Consulting and Clinical Psychology, 71*, 692–700.

Knoff, H. M. (2003). Evaluation of projective drawings. In C. R. Reynolds and R. Kamphaus (Eds.), Handbook of psychological and clinical assessment of children: Personality, behavior, and *context* (2nd ed., pp. 91–158). New York: Guilford Press.

Kobak, R., Sudler, N., & Gamble, W. (1991). Attachment and depressive symptoms during adolescence: A developmental pathways analysis. *Development and Psychopathology, 3*, 461–474.

Kopp, C. B. (1989). Regulation of distress and negative emotions: A developmental view. *Developmental Psychology, 25*, 343–354.

Kovacs, M. (1992). *Child Depression Inventory*. N. Tonawanda, NY: Multi-Health Systems.

Kovacs, M. (1996). The course of childhood-onset depressive disorders. *Psychiatry Annual, 26*, 326–330.

Kovacs, M., Akiskal, H. S., Gatsonis, C., & Parrone, P. L. (1994). Childhood-onset dysthymic disorder: Clinical features and prospective naturalistic outcome. *Archives of General Psychiatry, 51*, 365–374.

Lachar, D., & Gruber, C. P. (1995). *Personality Inventory for Youth*. Los Angeles: Western Psychological Services.

Leon, G. R., Kendall, P. C., & Garber, J. (1980). Depression in children: Parent, teacher, and child perspectives. *Journal of Abnormal Child Psychology, 8*, 221–235.

Lewinsohn, P. M., & Essau, C. A. (2002). Depression in adolescents. In I. H. Gotlib & C. L. Hammen. *Handbook of depression*. (pp. 510–540). New York: Guilford Press.

Lewinsohn, P. M., Rohde, P., & Seely, J. R. (1998). Major depressive disorder in older adolescents: Prevalence risk factors and clinical impressions. *Clinical Psychology Review, 18*, 765–794.

Lewinsohn, P. M., Rohde, P., Seely, J. R., & Klein, D. N. (1997). Axis II psychopathology as a function of Axis I disorders in childhood and adolescence. *Journal of the American Academy of Child and Adolescent Psychiatry, 36*, 1752–1759.

Lewinsohn, P. M., Seeley, J. R., Pettit, J. W., & Joiner, T. E., Jr. (2003). The symptomatic expression of major depressive disorder in adolescents and young adults. *Journal of Abnormal Psychology, 112*, 244–252.

Lous, A. M., de Wit, C. A. M., de Bruyn, E. E. J., & Riksen-Walraven, J. M. (2000). Depression markers in young children's play: A comparison between depressed and nondepressed 3- to 6-year-olds in various play situations. *Journal of Emotional and Behavioral Disorders, 8*(4), 249–261.

Luby, J., Heffelfinger, A., Mrakotsky, C., Hessler, M., Brown, K., & Hildebrand, T. (2002). Preschool major depressive disorder: preliminary validation for developmentally modified DSM-IV criteria. *Journal of the American Academy of Child and Adolescent Psychiatry, 41*, 928–937.

Mash, E. J., & Dozois, D. J. A. (1996). Child psychopathology: A developmental systems perspective. In E. J. Mash & R. A. Barkley (Eds.), *Child psychopathology* (pp. 3–60). New York: Guilford Press.

McArthur, D. S., & Roberts, G. E. (1982). *Roberts Apperception Test for Children: A manual*. Los Angeles: Western Psychological Services.

McCauley, E., Carlsson, G., & R. Calderon. (1991). The role of somatic complaints in the diagnosis of depression in children and adolescents. *Journal of the American Academy of Child and Adolescent Psychiatry, 30*, 631–635.

Middledorp, C. M., Cath, D. C., Van Dyck, R., & Boomsma, D. I. (2005). The co-morbidity of anxiety and depression in the perspective of genetic epidemiology: A review of twin and family studies. *Psychological Medicine, 35*, 611–624.

Naglieri, J. A. (1988). *Draw-A-Person: A quantitative scoring system*. San Antonio, TX: Psychological Corporation.

Nurcombe, B. (1994). The validity of the diagnosis of major depression in children and adolescence. In W. H. Reynolds and H. F. Johnston (Eds.), *Handbook of depression in children and adolescents* (pp. 61–80). New York: Plenum Press.

Orvaschel, H. (2004). Depressive disorders. In M. Hersen (Ed.), *Psychological assessment in clinical practice: A pragmatic guide* (pp. 297–319). New York: Brunner Routledge.

Reynolds, C. R., & Kamphaus, R. W. (2004). *Behavior Assessment System for Children* (2nd ed.). Circle Pines, MN: AGS.

Reynolds, W. M. (2005). *Reynolds Adolescent Depression Scale*. Lutz, FL: Psychological Assessment Resources.

Roberts, R. E., Lewinsohn, P. M., & Seeley, J. R. (1995). Symptoms of *DSM–III–R* major depression in adolescence: Evidence from an epidemiological survey. *Journal of the American Academy of Child and Adolescent Psychiatry, 34*, 1608–1617.

Rotter, J. B., Lah, M., I, & Rafferty, J. E. (1992). *Rotter Incomplete Sentences Blank* (2nd ed.). San Antonio, TX: Psychological Corporation.

Rudolph, K. D., Hammen, C., & Burge, D. (1994). Interpersonal functioning and depressive symptoms in childhood: Addressing the issues of specificity and comorbidity. *Journal of Abnormal Child Psychology, 22*, 355–371.

Rudolph, K. D., Kurlakowsky, K. D., & Conley, C. S. (2001). Developmental and social-contextual origins of depressive control-related beliefs and behavior. *Cognitive Therapy and Research, 25*, 447–475.

Schwab-Stone, M. (1995). Do children aged 9 through 11 years understand the DISC version 2.25 questions? *Journal of the American Academy of Child and Adolescent Psychiatry, 34*, 954–956.

Semrud-Clikeman, M., Bennett, L., & Guli, L. (2003). Assessment of childhood depression. In C. R. Reynolds & R. W. Kamphaus (Eds.), *Handbook of psychological and educational assessment of children: Personality, behavior, and context* (2nd ed., pp. 259–290). New York: Guilford Press.

Silberg, J., Pickles, A., Rutter, M., Hewitt, J., Smonoff, E., Maes, H., et al., (1999). The influence of genetic factors and life stress on depression among adolescent girls. *Archives of General Psychiatry, 56*, 225–232.

Speier, P. L., Sherak, D. L., Hirsch, S., & Cantwell, D. P. (1995). Depression in children and adolescents. In E. E. Beckham & W. R. Leber (Eds.), *Handbook of depression* (2nd ed., pp. 467–566). New York: Guilford Press.

Sroufe, L. A., & Rutter, M. (1984). The domain of developmental psychopathology. *Child Development, 55*, 17–29.

Stark, K. D., Sander, J. B., Yancy, M. G., Bronik, M. D., & Hoke, J. A. (2000). Treatment of depression in childhood and adolescence: Cognitive-behavioral procedures for the individual and family. In P.C. Kendall (Ed.), *Child and adolescent therapy: Cognitive-behavioral procedures* (2nd ed., pp. 173–234). New York: Guilford Press.

Strober, M., Lampert, C., Schmidt, S., & Morrell, W. (1993). The course of major depressive disorder in adolescents: I. Recovery and risk of manic switching in a follow-up of psychotic and nonpsychotic subtypes. *Journal of the American Academy of Child and Adolescent Psychiatry, 32*, 34–42.

Trad, P. V. (1994) Depression in infants. In W. M. Reynolds & H. F. Johnston (Eds.), *Handbook of depression in children and adolescents* (pp. 401–426). New York: Plenum Press.

Weiner, I. B. (1986). Assessing children and adolescents with the Rorschach. In H. M. Knoff (Ed.), *The assessment of child and adolescent personality* (pp. 141–171). New York: Guilford Press.

Weiss, B., & Garber, J. (2003). Developmental differences in the phenomenology of depression. *Development and Psychopathology, 15*, 403–430.

Weissman, M. M., Wolk, S., Goldstein, R. B., Moreau, D., Adams, P., Greenwald, S. Klier, C. M., Ryan, N. D., Dahl, R. E., & Wickramaratne, P. (1999). Depressed adolescents grown up. *Journal of the American Medical Association, 17*, 7–13.

Wirt, R. D. Lachar, D., Seat, P. D., & Broen, W. E., Jr. (2001*). Personality Inventory for Children–2nd edition.* Los Angeles, CA: Western Psychological Services.

Zero to Three/National Center for Clinical Infant Programs (1994). Diagnostic Classification of Mental Health and Developmental Disorder of Infancy and Early Childhood. Arlington, VA: Zero to Three/National Center for Clinical Infant Programs.

Ziffer, R. L., & Shapiro, L. (1992). *Children's Self-Report and Projective Inventory.* Circle Pines, MN: AGS.

SPECIAL POPULATIONS

28

ASSESSMENT IN PEDIATRIC HEALTH

Randi Streisand
Tamara Michaelidis

Departments of Psychiatry & Behavioral Sciences and Pediatrics
Children's National Medical Center
and
The George Washington University School of Medicine, Washington, DC

The increasing effectiveness of medical interventions has led to improved survival rates and diminished morbidity for many children and adolescents with chronic health conditions. Consequently, there are more children alive and living longer with chronic disease today than in years past. Indeed, it is estimated that upwards of 18% of children and adolescents may suffer from one or more chronic health conditions. With this number in mind, clinicians and researchers have increasingly been called upon to assess different areas of pediatric physical and behavioral functioning and well-being.

There are a host of challenges that confront children and adolescents experiencing an acute medical crisis or living with a chronic disease, including the potential for altered neurocognitive, psychosocial, and behavioral status. Many of the factors that underlie normal physical, cognitive, and socioemotional development are often disrupted by illness alone, as well as by the attendant sequelae of inpatient hospitalizations, invasive medical procedures, pharmacologic treatments, days absent from school, and missed social opportunities with peers. The cumulative impact of these influences on development may be difficult to predict or measure. Nevertheless, assessment is essential so that appropriate psychosocial intervention can be applied when indicated.

General and illness-specific assessment tools are used by pediatric health clinicians and researchers to gauge behavioral and psychosocial issues arising in the context of a physical health condition. Because chronic physical conditions can affect the lives of children and adolescents in areas such as physical development, social functioning, cognitive and academic functioning, and emotional well-being, the assessment of youngsters with chronic medical conditions requires careful consideration of multiple outcome domains.

The need for assessment tools specifically relevant to child and adolescent health has been well documented (La Greca & Lemanek, 1996; Rodrigue, Geffken, & Streisand, 2000).

Specifically, it has been noted that there is a relative lack of relevant, reliable, and valid assessment tools for ill children, adolescents, and/or their families. Such measures are thought to be critically important in advancing the field of pediatric heath psychology because they may provide further evidence of the impact of illness on child and family well-being, as well as the need for psychosocial intervention.

More recently, efforts have been expended in developing parent-related pediatric specific measures (Naar-King, Ellis, & Frey, 2004; Rodrigue, Geffken, & Streisand, 2000), such as those assessing maternal worry and stress (DeVet & Ireys, 1999; Streisand, Braniecki, Tercyak, & Kazak, 2001), parental coping strategies (Quittner et al., 1996), and pediatric quality of life (Varni, Seid, & Kurtin, 2001). However, a substantial portion of the scientific findings continue to depend upon general self-report tools primarily intended for physically "healthy" respondents (Radcliffe, Bennett, Kazak, Foley, & Phillips, 1996; Rodrigue, Streisand, Banko, Kedar, & Pitel, 1996). Although general measures are important, continuing to rely solely on them is of limited value, because general measures typically do not take into account critical illness experiences likely to affect the child and family. Furthermore, careful assessment of parent and family well-being is thought to be critical, given that most chronic conditions of childhood require parental participation or supervision in the management of daily illness demands.

However, despite the limitations associated with applying general measures designed for healthy respondents to specialized pediatric populations, it is widely recognized that such measures can and often do provide useful clinical information when combined with illness-specific measures. As such, this chapter highlights both the advantages and the limitations of integrating general measures into the assessment of pediatric illness.

The overriding goal of this chapter is to highlight the complexities associated with evaluating psychosocial factors in pediatric illness, while providing suggestions for how to conduct comprehensive assessments in pediatric populations. Specifically, the chapter initially reviews the relevant developmental and contextual factors to include in evaluations, discusses considerations for selection of instruments, and reviews available assessment tools in pediatric health. Common challenges of using general versus illness-specific measures in pediatric populations are presented, and the chapter concludes with a case presentation of assessment strategies integrating both general and pediatric-specific measures for a child with a chronic medical condition.

DEVELOPMENTAL AND CONTEXTUAL FACTORS

As in assessiment of children and adolescents without chronic medical conditions, assessment of the pediatric patient requires many considerations, including a patient's developmental level, as well as the contextual surroundings. Appropriate developmental factors to consider include achievement of relevant developmental milestones, capacity to appropriately respond to clinical interviewing and assessment measures based on a patient's age and developmental level, and the current life cycle stage of the family (i.e., parenting young children and/or older children, etc.). Contextual factors include all the psychosocial domains influencing the child or adolescent, including school, peer relations, the health care system, and, most critically, the family environment. *Family environment* refers to family composition *and* configuration (patterns of interaction in familial relationships) and any stressors affecting family functioning, such as socioecomonic status, parental separation or divorce, or other emotional, behavioral, or health issues affecting family members.

Understanding psychosocial factors is critical to conducting pediatric assessments because they often have a direct influence on emotional and behavioral functioning, and because psychosocial factors can play a prominent role in the course and prognosis of pediatric illness (Kazak, 1992). For example, consider the role of social modeling and learning, as these principles appear to be central to the acquisition of behavior patterns in children. With regard to pediatric illness, parental and even peer modeling of certain behaviors (i.e., coping), family-held beliefs about health and illness, and parental understanding of illness and its treatment can directly affect a child's emotional and physical well-being (Celano, 2001).

Although the specific nature of the pediatric assessment will certainly vary depending on referral question and type of illness, the aforementioned developmental and contextual factors should always be kept in mind. For further illustration, consider the work of Bronfrenbrenner (1979), who argued in favor of viewing the child as part of a multilevel system, with the illness playing a role in the interaction of the child and family with other systems (e.g., the school, health care team, and community). This approach also highlights the influence that illness has upon the family system and the increased demands often placed on the family in navigating the other systems involved in a child's life. Negotiating the health care system, obstacles to medical treatment such as lack of insurance coverage, and the school's ability to manage chronic medical conditions are just a few of the relevant issues influencing pediatric illness. With the use of this "systems" frame of reference, the characteristics of the child or adolescent, the family, the relevant psychosocial domains influencing both child and family, and the medical treatment should all be ascertained. Table 28.1 outlines five different domains for consideration in pediatric assessments; illness-specific characteristics are described later in the chapter.

Although the previously described issues are worth considering for each evaluation, assessment of the pediatric patient will certainly vary, depending on setting, illness, and available multidisciplinary team. In general, most assessments of the pediatric patient will include a clinical interview, as well as some type of formal testing and assessment of psychological status. Depending on the child's age and developmental level, clinicians may also choose to conduct separate interviews with the parent and child. This may prove particularly useful in the understanding of a patient's knowledge of his/her illness as well as coping and adherence. The role of the clinician to the referring medical team will also help determine the type of assessment conducted. For example, the behavioral care provider may be considered to be part of the medical specialty team (i.e., psychologist with the craniofacial team) or may serve as a consultant for one particular case.

SELECTION OF INSTRUMENTS

The first consideration in selecting appropriate assessment tools in the clinical setting is the referral question. The majority of referrals typically occur as a result of some type of problem

TABLE 28.1.
General Domains of Pediatric Assessment

Developmental level	Cognitive functioning
Emotional and behavioral functioning	Family functioning
Illness-related characteristics	

exhibited by the child or adolescent. For example, parents may be dissatisfied with their child's performance, a teacher may be concerned with a student's behavior, or a child may express displeasure about events in his/her life. Just as the referral may have resulted from various sources within the patient's life, the referral problem may not be significant to each of the individuals in the patient's environment. For example, the patient's view may differ from the views of both the parent and teacher, and the child may not appreciate the need for evaluation. In consideration of the referral question, one should keep in mind the person for whom the referral problem is actually problematic.

In addition to the referral question stemming from some type of problematic behavior, children and adolescents with chronic illnesses are often referred as part of a treatment protocol and not necessarily because of some type of exhibited difficulty. For example, children undergoing bone marrow transplantation are often assessed for both cognitive and psychosocial function before and after treatment, regardless of their premorbid status. This assessment is part of the protocol to assist in determining any effects of the cancer treatment. Other such referrals include assessments before surgery (i.e., solid organ transplantation; Streisand & Tercyak, 2004), or before the transition of children and adolescents to a more intense medical regimen (i.e., insulin pump therapy; Cogen, Streisand, & Sarin, 2002).

When the referral is of a more general nature, and not specific to a treatment or medical protocol, then the problem being considered typically represents some disturbance in a developmental transition. Children and adolescents with chronic illnesses are likely to be assessed for changes from previous functioning, or for difficulties in adapting and adjusting to their illness and treatment. This represents one of the challenges in working with young populations with illnesses: is the referral problem related to the child or adolescent's current illness/ regimen and likely to be transient, or is it more indicative of a developmental change?

It is important to consider the issue of the referral source itself. If the questions under consideration are diagnostic in nature, the health care professional must select instruments that would allow ruling one or more competing diagnoses to be ruled in or out. Several structured or semistructured interviews, in addition to paper-and-pencil checklists and possibly projective measures, allow for an examination of several disorders or diagnoses. Similarly, if the question pertains to strategies that may help the child to better adjust to his/her illness, then the use of an assessment tool that focuses on adjustment is warranted.

TYPES OF MEASURES

Once the referral question has been clarified and prior to selecting measures, one should consider the possible types of assessment instruments for answering the referral question. Sattler (2001) describes four types of information to be gained in child assessment: (1) personal information about the child and his/her family that can obtained from interview and behavioral-checklist reports; (2) information about the child's behavior within different settings (for example, children's behavior may be observed in schools, with other family members, and in peer groups) that comes from observational assessment; (3) information gathered from standardized tests, which are useful for comparing a child to his/her comparison group and allow for the evaluation of changes associated with other aspects of the child's life such as illness; and (4) information related to the child's specialized skills and strengths that may otherwise not be measured by standardized tests. In addition to considering the method most relevant to the assessment question, the health care professional must also consider the availability of respondents, length of time allotted for the assessment, and cost of instruments.

Furthermore, many referral questions as well as behaviors are multidimensional and may require the use of multiple assessment tools and strategies.

USING MEASURES DESIGNED FOR THE GENERAL POPULATION WITH A PEDIATRIC SAMPLE: CHALLENGES AND COMMON PITFALLS

General measures, or those commonly used in psychological assessments of physically "healthy" youngsters, provide useful information about a child or adolescent's normative psychosocial functioning, including mood, behavior across a wide spectrum, and family environment. These measures are also used with pediatric populations and can be an important component of clinical assessment. However, a few issues limit their sensitivity when they are applied to physically ill children and adolescents and should be taken into consideration when measures are selected and results interpreted.

It is important to highlight that general measures are developed and standardized on physically "healthy" children and adolescents (and so are intended for physically "healthy" respondents). Therefore relying only on general measures is of limited value for several reasons. First, unique aspects associated with pediatric illness are not assessed but may influence psychosocial adjustment. For example, issues such as illness-related discomfort, pain, sickness, and worry or fear about health or medical procedures are not evaluated, yet are likely to affect the child (and family). In addition, illness-specific parenting stressors related to managing the medical regimen, financial and care-giving demands, worry about health outcomes, or negotiating the health care system are not assessed by general measures, but are common issues for parents and can directly affect a child's functioning and well-being. Second, validity may be compromised because items intended to measure psychosocial problems may actually be measuring physical symptoms of illness. Specifically, findings on general measures may vary and might be superficially inflated when items describe somatic complaints that are intended to reflect psychological difficulties. For example, items on sleeping problems, fatigue, dizziness, and stomachaches are intended to measure symptoms of anxiety or depression, yet responses may actually be a reflection of a disease process in physically ill children and adolescents

Similarly, items measuring behavioral or externalizing problems may vary or be elevated because of illness-related factors. Items that assess behaviors such as attention, concentration, motor restlessness, disobedience, argumentativeness, or interactions with peers might be elevated because of illness-related discomfort, nonadherence to treatment, or even side effects of treatments. In contrast, measures that yield insignificant or "normal" results may simply not be sensitive enough to identify problems, such as mild adjustment difficulties, often seen in children with chronic illness (Drotar, 2004).

Psychological evaluations and clinical research on physically ill children and adolescents are typically intended to identify behavioral competencies and less severe adjustment problems associated with illness. Yet, general measures were primarily developed to identify psychopathology rather than mild behavioral problems within the normal range (Perrin, Stein, & Drotar, 1991). In addition, researchers have cautioned against interpreting "social competence" items in chronically ill children and adolescents because some general measures (i.e., the Child Behavior Checklist) focus on social *participation* rather than social *capacity* (Perrin et al., 1991). Those authors stress that although some physically ill children may be limited in the number of social activities in which they can participate, this does not suggest they are less socially competent (Perrin et al., 1991). These considerations reflect some of the primary pitfalls of using general measures with special populations: when clinicians are not sensitive to differential interpretation, test results may be misleading and do not always tell the whole or accurate story.

Finally, it is important to note that parent-reported general measures present the very same set of issues. The primary challenge with using general measures is to recognize and account for their limitations by incorporating them into a more comprehensive evaluation that examines how illness affects the child and family and how the family and child cope with, care for, and understand the illness. This can be done through focused clinical interviewing, observation, and illness-specific pediatric and parenting measures.

Examples of General Measures Often Used in Pediatric Evaluations

Although general measures present a number of challenges, they can also provide a starting point for examining overall psychosocial adjustment and for identifying comorbid psychiatric disorders. In addition, these measures have several benefits: they have well-established norms and are psychometrically sound; some provide information on several domains of functioning and from multiple informants; and they can often be used repeatedly over time to measure change without compromising validity. Several general measures also complement one another and are often used together in pediatric research and clinical assessments. The following section briefly reviews several general measures that are frequently used in pediatric populations.

Measures of Child and Adolescent Psychosocial Functioning.   The Child Behavior Checklist (CBCL; Achenbach, 1991) is a measure of psychosocial functioning in children and adolescents (two forms are available: ages 2–3 and 4–18) that provides information on internalizing (i.e., anxiety and depression) and externalizing (i.e., aggression) behaviors and has been widely used, both clinically and for research purposes, in a variety of chronically ill and healthy populations. Examples of clinical uses include incorporating the CBCL into comprehensive evaluations for pretransplant patients, for readiness to transition onto a more intensive diabetes regimen, or as part of a neuropsychological evaluation for cancer survivors. The CBCL has also been used in a variety of pediatric research studies on emotional and behavioral adjustment to illness, including congenital heart disease, cystic fibrosis, childhood obesity, kidney disease, and recurrent abdominal pain (DeMaso, Twente, Spratt, & O'Brien, 1995). For example, the CBCL was utilized to evaluate the impact of maternal perceptions and severity of pediatric congenital heart disease (CHD) on the emotional-behavioral functioning in children with CHD; results showed that maternal perceptions had a greater impact on psychosocial adjustment than illness severity (DeMaso et al., 1995).

A number of studies examining the impact of childhood obesity on psychosocial outcomes have also used the CBCL as a primary measure of emotional-behavioral functioning, and research findings across several studies have shown that obesity is associated with greater social problems and higher scores on the total summary scale of the CBCL (Strauss, 2000).

The widespread use of the CBCL in pediatric research and clinical practice has also led to several papers and studies examining the validity of the CBCL in special populations. Perrin et al., (1991) have outlined several problems in applying the CBCL to the study of pediatric illness based on using the measure in their own research. Problems include the potential bias of interpreting physical symptoms, limited ability to identify mild adjustment problems, and misleading assessment of social competence. The authors emphasized that problems associated with the CBCL relate more to interpretation than to actual weaknesses in the measure. A more recent study examining possible scoring confounds of the CBCL when applied to children with diabetes found that elevated scores were not confounded by physiological symptoms associated with illness (Holmes, Respess, Greer, & Frentz, 1998).

In general, the benefits of this measure include ease of administration and scoring; availability of teacher, parent, and adolescent self-report versions; and the fact that it yields subscale scores on a number of psychosocial domains. However, despite the benefits and risks of using the CBCL, applying this measure to pediatric populations means conducting careful item-by-item inspection of responses. It should not be used by itself and possesses all of the potential pitfalls and challenges reviewed previously.

The Child Depression Inventory (CDI; Kovacs, 1983) is a self-rated assessment of depressive symptoms for school-aged children and adolescents (ages 7–17) and is the most commonly used inventory for child depression (Fristad, Emery, & Beck, 1997). The CDI assesses key symptoms of depression, such as a child's feelings of worthlessness and loss of interest in activities, and covers the consequences of depression as they relate to functioning in school and with peers. The assessment is designed for a variety of situations, including schools, child guidance clinics, pediatric practices, and child psychiatric settings. It is commonly used to support a diagnosis of depression, for treatment planning, and for research purposes.

The CDI has been used to understand the impact of acute and chronic illness on mood in children and adolescents with cancer, asthma, diabetes, juvenile arthritis, sickle cell disease, and traumatic brain injury. Examples of clinical research using the CDI include a study conducted by Kirkwood and colleagues (2000) that incorporated both the CDI and the CBCL to examine the impact of traumatic brain injury and orthopedic injury on depressive symptoms in children (the CBCL was used to measure parental report of child depression). Results showed that traumatic brain injury placed children at increased risk for developing depressive symptoms across time. Another recent study examined the influence of parental distress on depression in juvenile arthritis and found that increased levels of parental distress were associated with greater child depressive symptoms (Wagner et al., 2003).

Although the CDI yields the most comprehensive normative data of childhood depression, researchers have stressed that, like all measures, it should not be used to diagnose depression in isolation. Fristad and colleagues (1997) identified that one third of studies they reviewed used the CDI in isolation and did not provide cautionary statements limiting the findings. The authors noted that although the CDI is a sensitive indicator of distress, it was not designed to identify and diagnose depression. Again, as with the CBCL, the limitations of using the CDI in pediatric populations include the potential confounds of items intended to measure depressive symptoms (fatigue, sleep problems, etc.), but which also may reflect physical symptoms of illness. Similarly, it is recommended that 1) an item-by-item analysis be conducted, 2) significant responses should be followed up by additional interviews, and 3) the measure should be used in conjunction with other measures.

Projective Measures. Projective measures are used less often in pediatric health assessment, usually because results are less definitive, scoring and interpretation can be subjective, and assessments are usually targeted to a specific problem area (i.e., family and patient adherence to medical regimens, ability to manage more intensive regimens, emotional adjustment to illness, etc). Some projective measures also yield limited normative, validity, and reliability data. However, despite their limitations, there are several potential benefits to incorporating projective measures into a comprehensive evaluation. In general, such measures can provide unique clinical information that may not be assessed through observation, clinical interviews, or self-report measures. Projective measures involve presenting a patient with ambiguous stimuli (i.e., asking a patient to draw a picture or respond verbally or nonverbally to images, pictures, unfinished sentences); the theory is that children and adolescents will project their underlying feelings (either unconscious or guarded) onto the stimuli, thereby providing the clinician with greater insight into their thoughts, feelings, beliefs, expectations, wishes, self-concept, emotional conflicts, and interpersonal relationships. Certain projective measures can be useful for patients who cannot communicate their thoughts and feelings verbally because of their age or other developmental issues. These measures can also provide an opportunity to express feelings in the abstract, without having to refer directly to oneself, which may reveal issues that would otherwise not be reported. In conjunction with pediatric health assessments, projective tests such as drawings and sentence completion might yield additional clinical information about how illness affects self-image and self-esteem. Finally, projective measures are usually easy to administer and can be experienced as enjoyable or less demanding to a patient and, most importantly, can help clinicians identify areas that may need further assessment.

Examples of projective measures include the Kinetic Family Drawing and House-Tree Person Drawing (Burns & Kaufman, 1970; Burns, 1987), Roberts Apperception Test (McArthur & Roberts, 1989), sentence completion, and the Rorschach (see Exner, 2003). In addition to the limits of validity and reliability, additional clinical considerations include using caution when interpreting results, using results only to generate hypotheses rather than to identify or confirm clinical diagnoses or problems, and only using projective measures in combination with more psychometrically sound measures. (For additional information on the use of projective measures in children and adolescents, please refer to Rabin, 1986.)

Measures of Family Functioning.   The McMaster Family Assessment Device (FAD; Epstein, Baldwin, & Bishop, 1983) is a brief parent-report measure of family functioning that describes emotional relationships and functioning within the family. The FAD examines Problem Solving, Communication, Family Roles, Affective Responses and Affective Involvement, Behavioral Control, and overall General Functioning in the family. The FAD is one of the most widely used measures of family functioning and has been used successfully in a number of pediatric samples, including children with cancer (Streisand, Kazak, & Tercyak, 2003). Specifically, Streisand and colleagues (2003) utilized the FAD to examine the association between pediatric parenting stress (i.e., parenting stress associated with caring for a chronically ill child) and family functioning in children with cancer. Results showed that families of children undergoing cancer treatment experienced difficulty on almost all areas of the FAD when compared with children who had completed cancer treatment. In addition, several of the FAD scales also correlated with an illness-specific measure of parenting stress (Pediatric Inventory for Parents; Streisand et al., 2001), demonstrating that parents who reported greater pediatric parenting stress also reported poorer family functioning.

Another general family measure is the Family Environment Scale (FES; Moos & Moos, 1986), which was developed to assess social and environmental characteristics of families. The scale provides three separate measures of family environment, such as expressiveness, cohesiveness, and conflict. It is useful in family systems research, for assessing areas of family intervention and identifying family strengths and weaknesses. For example, the FES has been used to examine the effects of family environment on child behavior problems and medical indicators in children with kidney disease (Soliday, Kool, & Lande, 2001). That study also used the CBCL to identify behavioral problems and then compared it with the FES. Results demonstrated that higher family conflicts predicted higher externalizing behavior problems and more prescribed medications, higher family cohesion predicted fewer hospitalizations, and nontraditional family structure predicted more prescribed medications. The FES has also been used to demonstrate that family conflicts are associated with greater behavioral problems in children and adolescents with sickle cell disease (Thompson et al., 1999).

In conclusion, the basic limitations of applying these general measures to families of physically ill children and adolescents is that nonspecific measures of family functioning do not take into account parental and family stress related to illness. For example, as noted by Streisand et al. (2001), even subtle variations in parental stress can influence the well-being of both parent and child, yet critical factors associated with the demands of caring for an ill child are not evaluated by traditional family measures.

Overall, with regard to both family and self-report measures of psychosocial functioning, there are several well-established and psychometrically sound general measures that can provide valuable information for pediatric assessments. However, these measures should not be used in isolation, and additional assessments will usually be required to fully understand the impact of illness on the family and the impact of family on illness.

Review of Illness-Specific Characteristics and Measures in Pediatric Assessment

Given that other chapters in this book describe assessment of children in other domains, the remaining focus of this chapter elaborates on illness-related characteristics that should be assessed within pediatric evaluations, including pain, quality of life, stress and coping, knowledge and expectations, adherence, and family communication/conflict/responsibility. Examples of specific assessment tools are listed in Table 28.2 beside each illness characteristic. For further description of measures and for illness-specific measures (e.g., measures that were designed for use by only one illness group), readers are encouraged to review Naar-King, Ellis, and Frey (2004) and Rodrigue, Geffken, and Streisand (2000).

Pain. Understanding the level of pain experienced by the child or adolescent will provide the clinician with a much deeper understanding of other areas of their functioning. If a child or adolescent is in significant pain, one cannot expect that he or she will be behaving typically, or will follow the health care team's medical advice. In trying to understand the level of pain early in the assessment process, it is likely that both the child and family will be more forthcoming in providing further information. The experience of pain may even affect the assessment process (i.e., a child not feeling well enough to complete self-report questionnaires) and should therefore be assessed early in the pediatric evaluation.

Quality of Life. Within the childhood chronic illness literature, studies report mixed findings on the impact of illness on children and adolescents (Bennett, 1994). Measures of quality of life have now been incorporated into many clinical and research programs and may provide information about the current level of functioning and how the illness has affected the child or adolescent over time. Quality of life has been defined in a variety of ways, yet most health professionals agree that the construct is multidimensional and incorporates both objective and subjective aspects of physical symptoms or disease state, functional status, and psychological and social functioning (Landgraf, Abetz, & Ware, 1996). General measures of quality of life provide global ratings across multiple areas of functioning (e.g.,

TABLE 28.2.
Illness-Specific Domains and Measures

Pain
Behavioral Approach-Avoidance and Distress Scale (Hubert, Jay, Saltine, & Hays, 1988).
Child-Adult Medical Procedure Interaction Scale-Revised (Blount et al., 1997).
Children's Pain Inventory (McGrath et al., 1996).
Faces Pain Scale (Bieri, Reeve, Champion, Addicoat, & Ziegler, 1990).
Observational Scale of Behavioral Distress (Jay & Elliot, 1981).
Perception of Procedures Questionnaire (Kazak, Penati, Waibel, & Blackall, 1996).
Waldron-Varni Pediatric Pain Coping Inventory (Varni et al., 1996).

Quality of life
Child Health Questionnaire Child and Parent forms (Landgraf, Abetz, & Ware, 1996).
Functional Disability Inventory (Walker & Greene, 1991).
Child Health and Illness Profile (Starfield et al., 1995).
Pediatric Quality of Life Inventory (Varni, Seid, & Kurtin, 2001).

Stress/coping
Coping Strategies Inventory (Tobin, Holroyd, Reynolds, & Wigal, 1989).
Kidcope (Spirito, Stark, & Williams, 1988).
Life Events Checklist (Johnson & McCutcheon, 1980).
Coping Health Inventory for Children (Austin, Patterson, & Huberty, 1991).

Knowledge and expectations
Measures are illness-specific and therefore not listed here.

Adherence
Measures are illness-specific and therefore not listed here.

Family communication/conflict/responsibility
Coping Health Inventory for Parents (McCubbin et al., 1983).
Family Coping Scale (Kupst et al., 1984).
Impact on Family Scale (Stein & Riessman, 1980).
Parent Perception Inventory (Samuelson, Foltz, & Foxall (1992).
Parents of Children with Disabilities Inventory (Noojin & Wallander, 1996).
Pediatric Inventory for Parents (Streisand, Braniecki, Tercyak, & Kazak, 2001).

satisfaction with life in general, family, school). Specific measures of quality of life typically ask the child or adolescent to report on how his/her illness affects each of several areas of functioning. A thorough pediatric assessment may incorporate both a general and illness-specific measure, and, in fact, more recently developed quality of life instruments have both general function as well as illness-specific modules (Varni et al., 2001; Landgraf et al., 1996). For more information on assessing quality of life, see Huebner, Gilman, and Suldo in this volume.

Stress and Coping. Stress and coping have received much attention in the pediatric health literature. Although the precise definitions of stress and coping are often debated, most researchers agree that stress is an interaction between internal and external factors (Bernard & Krupat, 1994) and is experienced when a situation or event is appraised as entailing specific demands that exceed one's available resources (Lazarus & Folkman, 1984). Measurement of stress for a pediatric assessment may include child or adolescent self-report, parent or other adult report (e.g., nurse), major life events, observed distress during medical procedures, or even pain. There are several existing assessment tools in each of these domains, all representing some type of distress. In addition, some clinicians or researchers may also use a physiological indicator of stress (e.g., heart rate, blood pressure).

In terms of coping, the pediatric assessment is most likely geared toward how the child or adolescent handles stressful situations (i.e., pain, hospitalization). Types of coping to be assessed typically include problem- and emotion-focused coping. Problem-focused coping strategies attempt to change some aspect of the environment or situation, whereas emotion-focused coping strategies include those efforts used to manage the negative emotions associated with the situation or event. Determining how children and adolescents cope with medical procedures or chronic health conditions has become increasingly important because research findings have linked several coping strategies to more favorable behavioral health outcomes. In general, the literature supports the notion that problem-focused or more active coping styles predict better adjustment in situations where the stressor is changeable. There are several instruments to measure coping in the pediatric patient, with differing foci in their specific assessment. For example, some measures ask the child or adolescent to recall a particular incident or event, whereas others ask them to respond to how they cope in general. The decision of choosing one measure over another should be dependent on the referral question.

Knowledge and Expectations.   Assessment of the child or adolescent's understanding of their medical condition and regimen, as well as expectations related to treatment, is critical to an assessment of the pediatric patient. The child's or adolescent's understanding and expectations will certainly vary, depending on age and cognitive function, as well as where the family is in the illness trajectory (i.e., recently diagnosed versus in treatment for several years). Domains of knowledge to be assessed include the illness itself, and how the medical regimen helps treat or control the illness. If the pediatric evaluation is part of a regimen change evaluation (i.e., pretransplant, or prior to transitioning to a more intensive medical regimen), then expectations are also critical to the assessment process. The evaluation must be able to determine motivations for the surgery or new type of regimen, and the child or adolescent's expectations should play a critical role in the evaluation. It is important that their expectations are realistic. If necessary, other members of the health care team can help the child or adolescent achieve a better understanding of what will follow the surgery or new regimen. Although knowledge or understanding of the medical illness or regimen is typically necessary in order for the child or adolescent to follow the health care team's advice, research has demonstrated that knowledge alone is not sufficient in determining one's adherence (Johnson, 1995).

Adherence.   Adherence to medical treatment is of concern within all pediatric populations. As a multidimensional construct (Rapoff, 1999), adherence behaviors in younger populations are particularly complex because responsibilities for care are often shared by the parent and child. Adherence to medical regimens includes multiple behaviors, including following a medical regimen, attending clinic appointments, following prescribed life-style changes, and avoidance of risky behaviors (Meichenbaum & Turk, 1987). Rates of non-adherence vary across ages and pediatric populations, and overall adherence rates in pediatric samples can rage anywhere from 20% to 80% (Litt & Cuskey, 1980). Poor adherence can lead to a host of difficulties, depending on the particular illness. For example, greater adherence to the medical regimen has been associated with reduced risk for diabetes-related complications (Diabetes Control and Complications Trial Research Group, 1994). Risk factors for poor adherence include the child's age (older children are typically less adherent), side effects of medication (more side effects in children who are less adherent), complexity of the regimen (the more complex the regimen, the less adherent), and poor understanding of the medical treatment. Factors that may promote improved adherence include decreased family stress or two-parent versus one-parent families.

Depending on the illness or illness regimen, adherence or self-care behaviors may be assessed in a variety of ways. There are self-report checklists for many illness groups, recall interviews or adherence diaries, or physician ratings. Evaluating adherence is critical to understanding how the illness is affecting the child and family, and to the likelihood that the child or adolescent will be successful with more complex medical regimens/procedures. For example, when undergoing evaluation prior to transplantation, children and adolescents (with their parents' assistance) must demonstrate committed adherence, given that transplant organs are in short supply and demand is high, and the posttransplant regimen is typically even more rigorous than what the child or adolescent experiences before transplant.

In addition to the more traditional paper-and-pencil and interview formats to assess adherence, the clinical interview should include specific questions about the medical regimen and self-care behaviors. For example, the clinician may inquire about how the child and family remember that it is time for the to take medication, or what happens when the child or adolescent must take medication when he or she is away from the family. Answers to these questions will assist the evaluator in understanding all that is asked of the pediatric patient, and how effective the patient and his/her family are with following through with regimen behaviors.

Family Communication, Conflict, and Responsibility

Understanding the family environment is another critical component of the pediatric evaluation. In addition to assessing family resources, including socioeconomic factors and family social support, it is important to assess the parents' own psychological functioning and how the family functions as a unit. As noted earlier in this chapter, assessment tools that are designed for general family functioning may be appropriate for use, augmented by other measures designed for use with pediatric populations. Illness-specific measures of family communication and conflict assess how the family interacts around illness issues, and which parts of the illness are related to the greatest sources of family conflict. Responsibility refers to the medical regimen or illness-related tasks and who in the family is responsible for which aspects of carrying them out. For example, many illnesses, such as cystic fibrosis, asthma, and diabetes, require that children perform multiple self-care tasks daily. Through the assessment it would be important to understand which medical care aspects are performed independently by the child, which are the responsibility of the parent alone, and which are shared. Division of responsibility for medical tasks may be related to adherence and ultimately to child health outcomes.

CLINICAL CASE STUDY

The following section provides an example of one type of pediatric health assessment (i.e., pediatric consultation) and briefly outlines a case illustration integrating several assessment measures within a consultation-liaison model. Pediatric consultations for children in medical settings are often the result of poor health, suspected poor adherence to medical regimens, and/or difficulty adjusting to illness and typically involve providing comprehensive assessment and treatment recommendations within a limited period of time. Referral questions may be straightforward and discrete or fairly complex in nature, and usually require assessment of behavioral, emotional, and environmental factors supporting and/or interfering with physical health or medical adherence to treatment. Once the reason for referral has been clarified, a number of factors must be considered before the consultation begins. The important domains of functioning to be assessed, the types of instruments or measures that should be included, the psychometric properties and developmental appropriateness of measures, and the time demands and financial costs to the family and the assessors are all examples of relevant clinical considerations (Streisand, 2000).

For the case illustration, assume that you have been asked to consult on "Rita," a 13-year-old girl with a 7-year history of Type 1 diabetes, who was recently hospitalized for diabetes-related reasons (diabetic ketoacidosis). This is Rita's second hospitalization this year, and the referring physician is concerned about poor adherence to her insulin regimen. Rita and her mother have assured the physician that she takes her insulin as recommended, but accidentally "missed" some injections while visiting a relative over the weekend, resulting in her hospitalization. Despite this assurance, the physician indicated that Rita has been experiencing elevated blood sugar levels for the past year, and the referring physician has requested an assessment of potential barriers to adherence and recommendations for treatment before the patient is discharged and goes home later that afternoon. The physician also noted that Rita presented as tearful and withdrawn upon hospital admission, and the physician would therefore like an assessment of Rita's mood.

Recognizing that diabetes is a chronic illness that can generally be managed through behaviors (i.e., taking medications, monitoring blood glucose levels, diet), you prepare to conduct a biopsychosocial assessment that conceptualizes Rita's heath and behavior as being influenced by the family system. It is important to recognize that Rita's illness also has a direct influence on the family system (i.e. care-giving and financial demands, etc). Given the reciprocal relationship between pediatric illness and family variables, you can approach the evaluation with two primary goals: to obtain a global understanding of Rita's psychosocial functioning and family environment and to understand unique aspects relevant to her diabetes.

General areas to investigate likely include Rita's current emotional/behavioral functioning and psychiatric history, her academic and social functioning, the current living situation, sources of social support, Rita's relationship and interactions with family members, and psychosocial stressors affecting the family. Illness-specific areas to investigate include Rita's adjustment to having a chronic illness and her typical coping strategies, pain and discomfort associated with her medical regimen, parenting stress related to caring for diabetes, family knowledge about diabetes, and adherence to Rita's medical regimen. Understanding the daily demands related to treatment and the relevant illness characteristics (i.e., pain, etc.) associated with a particular pediatric illness is essential for informing your assessment approach; this knowledge will help shape your interview questions and selection of standardized measures. Moreover, understanding the particular demands for each patient is critical, as treatment regimens vary across individuals. Because you have a number of variables to assess within a limited time frame, you may consider combining clinical interviews, several self-report measures, and any other available information, such as results from psychoeducational testing or past psychiatric treatment. You have been asked to evaluate Rita's mood; incorporating several general self-report measures should complement clinical interviewing and observation. General self-report measures that assess mood and behaviors are typically easy and quick to administer and score. In the case of pediatric consultations, these general measures are often helpful for clarifying clinical concerns that emerge during interviewing and can provide additional support for specific treatment recommendations. Two commonly used general measures (presented earlier in this chapter) include the CDI and the CBCL. The CDI would provide another forum for Rita to respond to questions about her mood, and the CBCL offers a parent's perspective on Rita's mood and behavior. Rita's CDI score of 10 was in the clinically significant range, suggesting mild depression, and the parent-rated CBCL similarly showed a *t*-score of 65 on the internalizing domain. Both measures provided additional evidence that Rita is struggling with depressed mood. Additional questioning should then focus on whether her mood is related to poor adjustment to diabetes, or whether a primary mood disorder is affecting her adherence behaviors. Additional mood-related measures to administer include an anxiety scale (i.e., Multidimensional Anxiety Scale for Children; March, Parker, Sullivan, Stallings, & Conners, 1997). Rita's score of 34 was well below the clinical cutoff score of 60, which suggested that she does not have an anxiety disorder. Finally, in addition to mood assessments, you also evaluate whether Rita is experiencing body image concerns or disordered eating, as both can also account for elevated blood sugar levels. You administer the Eating Disorders Inventory (EDI; Garner, 1991); results show no significantly elevated scores. Assume that you also have access to a recently conducted psychoeducational evaluation; this information will help your assessment because it may indicate additional stressors and deficits associated with intellectual and educational functioning that may affect Rita's adjustment and adherence to her diabetes regimen. Results of testing showed that Rita has an IQ of 105 (WISC-IV), which places her in the average range of intellectual functioning compared with same-aged peers. Her verbal and nonverbal IQ scores are commensurate also, suggesting evenly developed skills in both areas. Whereas results of achievement testing (i.e., WIAT-II) show average skills in reading (SS = 98 in reading and SS = 103 in spelling), her math score (computational and math reasoning) is in the borderline range of skill compared with her peers (SS = 76). Although psychoeducational testing results show normal functioning in most areas, Rita's relative weakness in math presents several issues that might influence her diabetes management. Specifically, struggling in math might present an additional daily stressor, and basic math skills are critical for Rita's diabetes regimen, as she must count carbohydrates and calculate insulin doses.

With regard to illness-specific variables, such as coping and stress associated with illness, there are several options for assessment. Appropriate questioning might include asking what Rita and her family perceive to be the most stressful or challenging aspect of managing diabetes, how they have responded, and what they think has been effective or not. Keep in mind that diabetes may be just one of several other life stressors the family is coping with, and their emotional and physical resources for addressing a chronic illness may be negatively affected. An illness-specific measure of stress and coping is the Coping Strategies Inventory (CSI; Tobin, Holroyd, Reynolds, & Wigal, 1989). This measure assesses cognitive and behavioral problem-solving approaches, expression of emotion, and social support and includes separate versions for parent and child.

In addition to assessing stress and coping, pain is another important component that can affect adjustment and adherence. Inquiring about Rita's discomfort during procedures such as blood glucose checks, injections, and routine blood draws can provide some information about how she perceives pain. Inquiring about what Rita feels and thinks before and during procedures and how she responds to pain also provides useful information about potential problems. While there are also multiple measures available to assess pain in children, in Rita's case, inquiring about her thoughts, feelings, and responses to pain may be sufficient to identify whether pain is a potential barrier to adjustment or adherence. Through interviewing you established that Rita feels "angry" about having diabetes, is self-conscious about telling peers and performing diabetes-related tasks at school, and experiences pain during injections, which often causes her to "skip" injections at times.

Finally, the assessment of adherence behaviors is fundamental for identifying obstacles to following medical treatments. Adherence is complex and involves not only knowledge about the illness and its treatment, but all of the behaviors the child and family must do to manage the illness. Obtaining an accurate assessment of adherence is further complicated because families and children may feel defensive about their current behaviors. Pediatric consultations require the ability to quickly establish an alliance with family members who might feel anxious, guilty, or even criticized for their child's current health status, as may be the case with Rita.

Clinical interviewing should focus on how the family divides and shares responsibility for diabetes, such as asking what specific responsibilities Rita has each day, how her mother helps her, and how the family addresses diabetes when away from home (who supervises Rita, who is responsible for bringing supplies, etc). In addition to clinical interviewing, there are also specific measures for assessing adherence, including the Self Care Inventory (Greco et al., 1990), which is a quick assessment tool that allows parents and children to self-report self-care behaviors across a variety of regimen tasks. Assume that results of interviewing reveal that Rita is often home alone after school and is largely responsible for her diabetes care because her mother works long hours and cares for Rita's three younger siblings.

In summary, pediatric consultations require a clinician to combine a general psychosocial evaluation with a comprehensive evaluation of multiple illness-specific factors. Conceptualizing the family as one of the most influential social domains of a child's life, and appreciating the reciprocal influence that family functioning and stressors have upon illness and the affect that illness has upon the family is an important starting point. In addition, integrating clinical interviewing with general and illness-specific measures can allow clinicians to assess a wide range of factors in a limited period of time and can provide additional support for treatment recommendations. In Rita's case, a multilevel systems approach to assessment (which incorporated both general and illness-specific measures) revealed that the most significant barriers to adherence and health were lack of adequate parental supervision due to other stressors, depressed mood, a learning disability in math (affecting her ability to manage diabetes and requiring even more parental assistance), and poor adjustment to having a chronic illness. Approaching Rita's assessment by carefully examining all of the aforementioned domains ultimately directed treatment toward obtaining additional in-home services for the family and individual therapy for Rita and providing ongoing family work to increase parental supervision and provide psychoeduation about diabetes management.

SUMMARY AND FUTURE DIRECTIONS

Overall, the review provided by this chapter leads to several general considerations. First, it is clear that evaluation of the pediatric patient is complex and also highly variable, depending on the individual referral or research question. Types of assessments and therefore assessment tools will vary across pediatric populations as well as individual medical settings. Second, although many measurement tools have been designed for specific use with pediatric populations, other, more general measures will continue to be used for these populations, which differ from that in which the measures were designed to be used. As described here, there are many advantages of using such measures, particularly the well-standardized ones.

However, the health care professional must be aware of the challenges and potential pitfalls in relying on such general measures for pediatric evaluations. In conclusion, evaluating the pediatric patient is a complex enterprise and, similar to the assessment of all children, requires careful attention to the multiple domains both affecting and affected by the child's and adolescent's health. Mental health professionals working with pediatric patients have much to offer both the child and family, as well as the pediatric health care team.

ACKNOWLEDGMENTS

Preparation of this chapter was supported by grant DK062161 from the National Institute of Diabetes and Digestive and Kidney Diseases (to R.S.).

REFERENCES

Achenbach, T. M. (1991). *Manual for the Child Behavior Checklist/4–18 and 1991 Profile.* Burlington, VT: University of Vermont Department of Psychiatry.

Austin, J. K., Patterson, J. M., & Huberty, T. J. (1991). Development of the coping health inventory for children. *Journal of Pediatric Nursing, 16,* 166–174.

Bennett, D. S. (1994). Depression among children with chronic medical problems: A meta-analysis. *Journal of Pediatric Psychology, 19,* 149–169.

Bernard, L. C., & Krupat, E. (1994). *Health psychology: Biopsychosocial factors in health and illness.* New York: Harcourt Brace College Publishers.

Bieri, D., Reeve, R. A., Champion, G. D., Addicoat, L., & Ziegler, J. B. (1990). The Faces Pain Scale for the self-assessment of the severity of pain experienced by children: Development, initial validation, and preliminary investigation for ratio scale properties. *Pain, 41,* 139–150.

Blount, R. L., Cohen, L. L., Frank, N. C., Bachanas, P. J., Smith, A. J., Manimala, M. R., & Pate, J. T. (1997). The Child-Adult Medical Procedure Interaction Scale-Revised: An assessment of validity. *Journal of Pediatric Psychology, 22,* 73–88.

Bronfenbrenner, U. (1979). *The ecology of human development.* Cambridge, MA: Harvard University Press.

Burns, R. C. (1987). Kinetic-house-tree-person drawings: an interpretive manual. New York: Brunner Routledge.

Burns, R. C., & Kaufman, S. F. (1970). Kinetic family drawings (K-F-D): An introduction to understanding children through kinetic drawings. New York: Brunner/Mazel.

Celano, M. (2001). Family systems treatment for pediatric asthma: Back to the future. *Families, Systems & Health: The Journal of Collaborative Family Health Care, 19,* 285–290.

Cogen, F. R., Streisand, R., & Sarin, S. (2002). Selecting children and adolescents for insulin Pump therapy: Medical and behavioral considerations. *Diabetes Spectrum, 15,* 72–75.

DeMaso, D. R., Twente, A. W., Spratt, E. G., & O'Brien, P. (1995). Impact of psychological functioning, medical severity, and family functioning in pediatric heart transplantation. *Journal of Heart and Lung Transplant, 14,* 1102–1108.

DeVet, K. A., & Ireys, H. T. (1999). Psychometric properties of the maternal worry scale for children with chronic illness. *Journal of Pediatric Psychology, 23,* 257–266.

Diabetes Control and Complications Trial Research Group (1994). Effect of intensive diabetes treatment on the development and progression of long-term complications in adolescents with insulin-dependent diabetes mellitus: Diabetes Control and Complications Trial. *Journal of Pediatrics, 125,* 177–88.

Drotar, D. (2004). Validating measures of pediatric health status, functional status, and health-related quality of life: Key methodological challenges and strategies. *Ambulatory Pediatrics, 4*, 358–64.

Epstein, L. H., Baldwin, L. M., & Bishop, D. S. (1983). The McMaster family assessment device. *Journal of Marital and Family Therapy, 9*, 171–180.

Exner, J. E. (2003). *The Rorschach: basic foundations and principles of interpretation* (4th ed.). Hoboken, NJ: Wiley.

Fristad, M. A., Emery, B. L., & Beck, S. J. (1997). Use and abuse of the children's depression inventory. *Journal of Consult Clinical Psychology, 65*, 699–702.

Greco, P., LaGreca, A. M., Auslander, W. F., Spetter, D., Skyler, J. S., Fisher, E., & Santiago, J. V. (1990). Assessing adherence in IDDM: A comparison of two methods. *Diabetes, 40*, 108A.

Holmes, C. S., Respess, D., Greer, T., & Frentz, J. (1998). Behavior problems in children with diabetes: Disentangling possible scoring confounds on the Child Behavior Checklist. *Journal of Pediatric Psychology, 23*, 179–185.

Hubert, N. C., Jay, S., Saltine, M., & Hays, M. (1988). Approach-avoidance distress in children undergoing preparation for painful medical procedure. *Journal of Clinical Child Psychology, 17*, 194–202.

Jay, S. M., & Elliot, C. (1981). *Observation Scale of Behavioral Distress-Revised.* Los Angeles: University of Southern California.

Johnson, J. H., & McCutcheon, S. (1980). Assessing life stress in older children and adolescents: Development of the Life Events Checklist. In I. G. Sarason & C. D. Spielbergr (Eds.), *Stress and anxiety* (Vol. 7). Washington, DC: Hemisphere.

Johnson, S. B. (1995). Insulin-dependent diabetes mellitus in childhood. In M. C. Roberts (Ed.), *Handbook of Pediatric Psychology* (2nd ed.). New York: Guilford Press.

Kazak, A. E. (1992). Family systems, social ecology, and chronic illness: Conceptual, methodological, and intervention issues. In J. Akamatsu, M. A. Stephens, S. Hobfoll, & J. Crowther (Eds.), *Family Health Psychology* (pp. 91–109). Washington, DC: Taylor & Francis

Kazak, A. E., Penati, B., Waibel, M. C., & Blackall, G. F. (1996). The Perception of Procedures Questionnaire: Psychometric properties of a brief parent report measure of procedural distress. *Journal of Pediatric Psychology, 21*, 195–207.

Kirkwood, M., Janusz, J., Yeates, K. O., Taylor, H. G., Wade, S. L., Stancin, T., et al. (2000). Prevalence and correlates of depressive symptoms following traumatic brain injuries in children. *Child Neuropsychology, 6*, 195–208.

Kovacs, M. (1983). The child depression inventory (CDI). *Psychopharmacology Bulletin, 21*, 995–999.

Kupst, M. J., Schulman, J. L., Maurer, H., Honig, G., Morgan, E., & Fochtman, D. (1984). Coping with pediatric leukemia: A two year follow up. *Journal of Pediatric Psychology, 9*, 149–163.

La Greca, A. M., & Lemanek, K. L. (1996). Editorial: Assessment as a process in pediatric psychology. *Journal of Pediatric Psychology, 21*, 137–151.

Landgraf, J. M., Abetz, L., & Ware, J. E. (1996). *The CHQ user's manual.* Boston: The Health Institute, New England Medical Center.

Lazarus, R. S., & Folkman, S., (1984) *Stress, appraisal, and coping.* New York: Springer.

Litt, I. F., & Cuskey, W. R. (1980). Compliance with medical regimens during adolescence. *Pediatric Clinics of North America, 27*, 3–15.

March, J. S., Parker, J. D., Sullivan, K., Stallings, P., & Conners, C. K. (1997). The Multidimensional Anxiety Scale for Children (MASC): Factor structure, reliability, and validity. *Journal of the American Academy of Child and Adolescent Psychiatry, 36*(12), 1645–1646.

McArthur, D. S., and Roberts, G. E. (1989). *Roberts Apperception Test for Children: Manual.* Los Angeles: Western Psychological Services.

McCubbin, H. I., McCubbin, M. A., Patterson, J. M., Cauble, A. E., Wilson, L. R., & Warwick, W. (1983). CHIP-Coping Health Inventory for Parents: An assessment of parental coping patterns in the care of the chronically ill child. *Journal of Marriage and the Family, May*, 359–370.

McGrath, P. A., Seifert, C. E., Speechley, K. N., Booth, J. C., Stitt, L., & Gibson, M. C. (1996). A new analogue scale for assessing children's pain: An initial validation study. *Pain, 64*, 435–443.

Meichenbaum, D., & Turk, D. C. (1987). *Facilitating treatment adherence*. New York: Plenum Press.

Moos, R. H., & Moos, B. S. (1986). *Family Environment Scale manual* (2nd ed.). Palo Alto, CA: Consulting Psychologists Press.

Naar-King, S., Ellis, D. A., & Frey, M. A. (2004) *Assessing children's well-being: A handbook of measures*. Mahwah, NJ: Lawrence Erlbaum Associates.

Noojin, A. B., & Wallander, J. L. (1996). Development and evaluation of a measure of concerns related to raising a child with a physical disability. *Journal of Pediatric Psychology, 21*, 483–498.

Perrin, E. C., Stein R. E., & Drotar, D. (1991). Cautions in using the Child Behavior Checklist: Observations based on research about children with a chronic illness. *Journal of Pediatric Psychology, 16*, 11–21.

Quittner, A. L., Tolbert, V. E., Regoli, M. J., Orenstein, D. M., Hollingsworth, J. L., & Eigen, H. (1996). Development of the role-play inventory of situations and coping strategies for parents of children with cystic fibrosis. *Journal of Pediatric Psychology, 21*, 209–235.

Rabin, A.I. (1986). *Projective techniques for children and adolescents*. New York: Springer.

Radcliffe, J., Bennett, D., Kazak, A. E., Foley, B., & Phillips, P. C. (1996). Adjustment in childhood brain tumor survival: child, mother, and teacher report. *Journal of Pediatric Psychology, 21*, 529–539.

Rapoff, M. A. (1999). *Adherence to pediatric medical regimens*. New York: Plenum Press.

Rodrigue, J. R., Geffken, G. R., & Streisand, R. M. (2000). *Child health assessment*. MA: Allyn & Bacon.

Rodrigue, J. R., Streisand, R., Banko, C. G., Kedar, A., & Pitel, P. A. (1996). Social functioning, peer relations, and internalizing and externalizing problems among youths with sickle cell disease. *Children's Health Care, 25*, 37–52.

Samuelson, J. J., Foltz, J., & Foxall, M. J. (1992). Stress and coping in families of children with myelomeningocele. *Archives of Psychiatric Nursing, 6*, 287–295.

Sattler, J. M. (2001). *Assessment of children: Cognitive applications* (4th ed.). San Diego, CA: Author.

Soliday, E., Kool, E., & Lande, M. B. (2001). Family environment, child behavior, and medical indicators in children with kidney disease. *Child Psychiatry and Human Development, 31*, 279–295.

Spirito, A., Stark, L. J., & Williams, C. (1988). Development of a brief checklist to assess coping in pediatric patients. *Journal of Pediatric Psychology, 13*, 555–574.

Starfield, B., Riley, A. W., Green, B. F., Ensminger, M. E., Ryan, S. A., Kelleher, K., Kim-Harris, S., Johnston, D., & Vogel, K. (1995). The adolescent & child health and illnes profile: A population-based measure. *Medical Care, 33*, 553–556.

Stein, R. E. K., & Riessman, C. K. (1980). The development of an Impact-on-Family Scale: Preliminary findings. *Medical Care, 18*, 465–472.

Strauss, R. S. (2000). Childhood obesity and self-esteem. *Pediatrics, 105*, 15.

Streisand, R. (2000). Selecting and administering child health assessment instruments. In J. R. Rodrigue, G. R. Geffken, & R. M. Streisand, *Child health assessment: A handbook of measurement techniques*. Needham Heights, MA: Allyn & Bacon.

Streisand, R. M., Braniecki, S., Tercyak, K. P., & Kazak, A. E. (2001). Childhood illness-related parenting stress: The pediatric inventory for parents. *Journal of Pediatric Psychology, 26*, 155–162.

Streisand, R. M., Kazak, A.E., & Tercyak, K.P. (2003). Pediatric-specific parenting stress and family functioning in parents of children treated for cancer. *Children's Health Care, 32*, 245–256.

Streisand, R., & Tercyak, K. P. (2004). Stress related to caring for a child with an illness: The Scope of impact of pediatric parenting stress. In N. Long & M. Hoghughi (Eds.), *Handbook of parenting: Theory, research, and practice*. London: Sage Publications.

Thompson, R. J., Armstrong, D. F., Kronenberger, W. G., Scott, D., McCabe, M. A., Smith, B., et al. (1999). Family functioning, neurocognitive functioning, and behavior problems in children with sickle cell disease. *Journal of Pediatric Psychology, 24*, 491–498.

Tobin, D. L., Holroyd, K. A., Reynolds, R. V., & Wigal, J. K. (1989). The hierarchical factor structure of the Coping Strategies Inventory. *Cognitive Therapy and Research, 13*, 343–361.

Varni, J. W., Seid, M., & Kurtin, P. S. (2001). PedsQ1 4.0: Reliability and validity of the Pediatric Quality of Life Inventory version 4.0 generic core scales in healthy and patient outcomes. *Medical Care, 39*, 800–812.

Varni, J. W., Waldron, S. A., Gragg, R. A., Rapoff, M. A., Bernstein, B. H., Lindsley, C. B., et al. (1996). Development of the Waldron/Varni Pediatric Pain Coping Inventor. *Pain, 67*, 141–150.

Wagner, J. L., Chaney, J. M., Hommel, K. A., Mullins, L. L., White M. M., & Jarvis, J. N. (2003). The influence of parental distress on child depressive symptoms in juvenile rheumatic diseases: The moderating effect of illness intrusiveness. *Journal of Pediatric Psychology, 28*, 453–462.

Walker, L. S., & Greene, J. W. (1991). The Functional Disability Inventory: Measuring a neglected dimension of child health status. *Journal of Pediatric Psychology, 16*, 39–58.

29

ASSESSING INTELLECTUAL ABILITIES OF CHILDREN AND ADOLESCENTS WITH AUTISM AND RELATED DISORDERS

Alan Lincoln
Elise Hanzel
Linda Quirmbach

*Alliant International University, Center for Autism Research,
Evaluation and Service, San Diego, California*

The goal of this chapter is to familiarize the reader with approaches used to assess the intellectual abilities of persons with autism. In order to evaluate the intellectual abilities of persons with autism it is necessary for the clinician to appreciate what is known about the organization of intellectual abilities that are typically associated with the disorder and to understand how to effectively assess mental retardation because it frequently is present as a comorbid condition. Thus, it is critical that clinicians assessing such individuals have both the understanding and the capacity to evaluate across a range of developmental abilities as well as have at their disposal appropriate instruments that can be employed as part of the evaluation.

Another important factor in assessing individuals with autism and related disorders is the examiner's ability to work with behaviors that may interfere in the assessment process. It is important to evaluate whether the individual is actually taking examinations in a manner that truly allows the sampling of behaviors suggestive of intellectual processes. Successful performance on intellectual tests is probably valid. However, poor performance may or may not be reflective of intellectual ability. Failed items can be due to limited skill, an inability to comprehend instructions, poor cooperation, impulsive behavior, variable attention, or a combination of any of these performance issues. The examiner therefore needs to be experienced in evaluating how such behavioral factors might be affecting the evaluation process and make reasonable attempts to accommodate the individual's compromised capacity to take the test.

AUTISM AND INTELLIGENCE

Infantile Autism or Autistic Disorder (AD) was first described by Leo Kanner in 1943 as a severe developmental disorder that includes severe communication, social, and behavioral disturbances. Furthermore, it is now known that persons with AD suffer from atypical brain development (see Courchesne, 1997, review) as well as atypical and uneven patterns of cognitive development (Lincoln, Courchesne, Kilman, & Elmasian, 1988; Lincoln, Allen & Kilman, 1995, review; Siegel, Minshew & Goldstein, 1996). It is likely that the atypical patterns of cognitive development reflect biologically based differences in brain functions, which are secondary to the brain abnormalities as well as the abnormalities of learning and metacognition. In 1979 Michael Rutter stated: "There is good evidence for the existence of a basic cognitive deficit in autism. This deficit generally involves impaired language, sequencing, abstraction and coding functions. It is also associated with abnormalities in language function and usage which are particularly characteristic of the autistic syndrome" (p. 261). Cognitive deficits also may underlie impaired social and emotional behavior, thus affecting the whole spectrum of functioning (Rutter 1983; Tager-Flusberg, 1999; Tager-Flusberg, Joseph, & Folstein, 2001). In contrast, the abilities of perceptual discrimination, rote memory, and visuospatial skills appear to be essentially intact (Lincoln et al., 1988; Lockyer & Rutter, 1970; Rumsey, 1992; Rutter & Schopler, 1988; Lincoln et al., 1995, review).

Distinctive patterns of cognitive strengths and weaknesses have been observed in high-functioning autistic individuals (e.g., Allen, Lincoln, & Kaufman, 1991; Asarnow, Tanguay, Bott, & Freeman, 1987; Goldstein, Beers, Siegel, & Minshew, 2001; Iverson, 1997; Lincoln et al., 1995; Lockyer & Rutter, 1970; Ventor, Lord, & Schopler, 1992). Although there is still some degree of controversy regarding the full nature of the cognitive impairments in persons with AD (Siegel, Minshew, & Goldstein, 1996), there is general consensus that nonretarded persons with AD typically have better visual-spatial ability than verbal comprehension ability (Lincoln et al., 1988, 1995; Siegel, Minshew, & Goldstein, 1996). Lincoln et al. (1988) suggested that the more intact visual-spatial ability in nonretarded persons with AD might reflect relatively intact functions related to fluid intelligence—specifically, functions related to the processing of visual information that is independent of the evaluation of contextually relevant or language-based information. However, Minshew, Goldstein, & Siegel (1997) suggest that it is the relative complexity of intellectual demands that limits the individual with AD such that they demonstrate "impairments in skilled motor, complex memory, complex language and reasoning domains (and are relatively intact with respect to) performance in the attention, simple memory, simple language and visual-spatial domains" (p. 303).

However, this idea of a weak capacity to process complex information and problems does not fit with the relative efficiency of how well nonretarded persons with autism solve complex matrix reasoning tasks. On matrix reasoning tasks, the individual is required to evaluate multiple relationships or dimensions simultaneously and infer how a pattern can best be completed. On such tasks, all of the information necessary to solve the task is available to the examinee, so that previous experiences with the stimuli are not necessary to recall in order to be successful. However, on the types of verbal reasoning tasks typically employed on formal IQ tests, it is necessary to evaluate contextually relevant information and to use previous knowledge and experience to appropriately infer a correct solution.

The errors in solving verbal comprehension tasks made by individuals with autism often reflect their ability to attend to only one of the dimensions of the problem posed to them and their failure to evaluate the broader context. For example, a young man came to a social skill group dressed in a three-piece green suit and carried a birthday cake with a large "16" candle partially embedded in the frosting. The group leader asked another member why the young man was dressed up. The young man replied, "St. Patrick's Day."

SPECIAL CONSIDERATIONS FOR ASSESSING THE INTELLIGENCE OF AN INDIVIDUAL WITH AUTISM

There is good reason to believe that intelligence tests can be useful in ascertaining cognitive strengths and weaknesses. However, in many instances, individuals with autism will be difficult to assess because of the behaviors associated with the autism, such as language impairments, poor motivation, or limited skills. This requires the examiner to be prepared to adjust the testing situation in order to elicit the highest level of cooperation and valid responses from the examinee. It is critical that the examiner be familiar enough with the testing instruments to be able to make individual accommodations while still maintaining the reliability and validity of the test responses. This approach will provide the most reliable test interpretation, which, when combined with additional assessment data and observations, can be invaluable in the development of the most appropriate treatment plan.

There are several types of avoidant behavior that can interfere with the clinical assessment of individuals with autism. Oftentimes the examinee will be unfamiliar with the examiner and/or testing environment. Since encountering new situations and people is often very stressful for individuals with autism, they may try to run away, crawl under the table, lean back in the chair, or push materials away. We have found several strategies that help facilitate the child's engagement with the test and the examiner. One strategy is to structure the position of the testing table against the wall with the examinee's back to an adjacent wall and the examiner sitting directly across from the examinee. If necessary, assistants or parents can position their chair so that the child would have to go past them in order to get away from the testing table. In some cases, we have found it helpful to test the child with the examiner positioned directly behind the child. However, this approach means that the examiner must be prepared to present the materials from an orientation that would be the opposite of the way in which one would normally present them. Additional strategies we have found to be successful include administering the test while sitting on the floor with the examinee, giving frequent and planned breaks, and utilizing meaningful and compelling reinforcers.

Another source of difficulty that can interfere with the testing situation involves the examinee's idiosyncratic self-stimulatory behaviors, repetitive behaviors, and interest or perseveration in parts of objects. For example, an individual might get very excited over the prospect of spinning blocks when the task actually calls for them to match the designs on each face of the block to a template. They may be motivated to look at the edge of the desk with peripheral eye gaze, thus completely failing to attend to the stimuli relevant to the testing. Often such undesired behaviors are a sign that the expectations of the test are inconsistent with the examinees' level of developmental ability or that they simply do not understand what is expected of them. By titrating the level of difficulty of the tasks, one can sometimes circumvent undesired behavior and improve testing compliance.

It is also possible to use such idiosyncratic interests in the test materials or other aspects of the environment as a reward, contingent on the completion of a task that the examinee is expected to do. This works on the basic principle that any behavior that one frequently engages in is likely to be intrinsically reinforcing and, therefore, can be used to reinforce other, more desired behaviors. For example, one child we tested was very interested in pulling the office blinds up and down. He responded quite well to the prompt, "First work, then blinds." One of the core deficits in autism is significant impairments in verbal comprehension. Those who have developed language tend be relatively able to identify and recall content based on their learning and experience, but often fail to understand such content at a deeper level, which involves the integration of other areas of content, experiences, and context relevancy. This can make it difficult for the examinee to understand the verbal instructions necessary to take tests as well as for the examiner to use language in a manner that facilitates their ability to perform. This is why some children with autism can perform relatively well on subtests assessing rote knowledge, such as the WISC-IV Information subtest, but have great difficulty on Comprehension, a subtest that requires a deeper understanding of what is asked and greater verbal reasoning and judgment to produce an effective solution. It is often necessary to supplement standard tests of intelligence with specific language measures that can assess expressive and receptive speech.

It can often be the case that a major source of behavioral resistance to the test is related to selecting measures that might be age appropriate, but not developmentally appropriate. For example, the WISC-IV might be an age-appropriate test for a moderately retarded six-year-old; however, it may be inappropriate with respect to the individual's developmental level. This can also be true with respect to specific cognitive domains. For example, it is often the case that children with autism perform better on nonverbal intellectual tasks than on verbal intellectual tasks. Thus, if a six-year-old received standard scores in the mid-70s in his strongest skill areas, he might have scores below the floor of the test in his weakest skill areas. In such a case, one would have to either disregard the performance on measures that could not be sampled because the skills were too low or administer additional measures that had greater range within the domain being assessed. Therefore, it is advantageous to select measures that give enough range with respect to the domains they assess so as not to encounter a floor effect. At the minimum, one wishes to avoid obtaining raw scores of zero. At least some raw score credit is needed to consider the subtests valid, even if the standardized score is at a floor level. In general, it is recommended, particularly when young children are being assessed, that the examiner have access to test materials that cover developmental levels, from infancy through childhood. This allows the examiner to titrate the level of task demand and evaluate whether behavior compliance changes with such modification.

Similarly, it is sometimes necessary to use infant measures with an adult or adolescent with mental retardation because their developmental level is too low to be evaluated with *age-appropriate* measures. By testing at a more developmentally appropriate level, it is sometimes possible to increase cooperation and valid response. For example, a severely retarded and nonverbal 14-year-old with autism may have the capacity to stack eight cubes and build a three-block bridge, tasks at approximately the 24–30-month level, but may only demonstrate the receptive and expressive language skills at the 6–8-month level. Developmental tests such as the Bayley Scales for Infant Development II (Bayley, 1993) or the Mullen Scales of Early Learning (1995) may be useful in capturing measurable behavior in such a delayed individual. In most cases, it is mental retardation more than autism that limits the functional capacity of the individual.

INTELLIGENCE TESTING AND AUTISM

The assessment of intellectual abilities has a long history and a scientific foundation beginning as early as the late 1800s. The history of the science of intelligence involves various efforts to define the construct as well as the development of methods used to operationalize and measure various specific skills that were believed to be related to higher-order intellectual operations. The important point here is that we never really directly measure intelligence; rather, we measure specific skills that we believe are theoretically related to higher-order intellectual operations. For example, on the Wechsler Adult Intelligence Scale: III, three subtests, Vocabulary (verbal definitions), Similarities (the ability to express abstract verbal concepts), and Information (the ability to recall specific facts), are each administered. Their raw scores are converted to standard scores, the standard scores are summed, and, subsequently, the sum of the standard scores is converted to a Verbal Reasoning Index (VRI) standard score. This VRI score is considered to be a higher-order intellectual operation that is related to Verbal IQ, a still higher-level intellectual operation. We do not directly sample Verbal IQ; rather, we measure it indirectly by having an individual perform various tasks. Thus, the scores on these tasks allow us to operationalize a construct of verbal intelligence. Wechsler made it very clear that intelligence was not simply measured as a sum of various skills, but also as the successful integration of such skills. The so-called idiot savant or autistic savant may have very strong skills in one or more areas such as calendar memory, the ability to solve puzzles, or photographic memory, but if these isolated abilities are not integrated with other skills necessary to support intellectual functions, they may not support successful adaptation and life skill competency.

Most of our understanding about the nature of human intelligence is based on factor analytic studies that have employed a wide range of measures that assess various aspects of information-processing and problem-solving skills. Horn (1991) recently proposed the Cattell-Horn-Carroll (CHC) model (Carroll, 1997), which describes intelligence through a factor analysis that includes at least four relatively independent or orthogonal intellectual domains. These domains or factors include Fluid intelligence (Gf; one's ability to solve novel problems that does not depend on school-acquired knowledge and acculturation), Crystallized intelligence (Gc; one's school-acquired knowledge and acculturation), Broad Visualization (Gv; one's ability to engage in fluent visual scanning, Gestalt closure, rotate figures, and see reversals), and Auditory Processing (Ga; one's ability to process auditory information). These domains are not believed to be inclusive of all aspects of human intelligence. Rather, they represent the best understanding of how various tasks group together through the statistical process of factor analysis. Thus, subtests that have their greatest correlation with one of the above factors tend to correlate more with each other than with subtests that have their greatest correlation on one of the other orthogonal factors.

The current version of the child and adult versions of the intelligence tests originally developed by David Wechsler, the Wechsler Intelligence Scale for Children: IV (WISC-IV; 2004) and the Wechsler Adult Intelligence Scale: III (WAIS-III; 1997), each have a factor structure consistent with CHC model of intelligence. This is also true of the Kaufman Assessment Battery: 2nd Edition (K-ABC–2; Kaufman & Kaufman, 2004) and the Leiter International Performance Scale–Revised. The WISC-IV and the K-ABC–2 include clinical samples of children diagnosed with autism during the standardization and report information on the performance of these children with respect to the distribution of their IQ scores, index scores, and subtest scale scores. The Leiter-R has been independently studied with respect to the performance of children with autism in two separate studies (Hanzel & Lincoln, submitted; Tsatsanis et al., 2003).

The WAIS-III and the WISC-III and WISC-IV

Factor analytic studies of the Wechsler scales have shown that the Block Design and Object Assembly subtests load primarily on a single factor, referred to as the Perceptual Organization factor, and the Vocabulary and Comprehension subtests load on an orthogonal factor, the Verbal Comprehension factor (Wechsler, 1974, 1986, 1991, 1997; Wechsler et al., 2004). It is further believed that the Perceptual Organization Factor is more related to fluid intelligence, which is believed to be more innate and biologically determined, whereas the Verbal Comprehension factor is more related to crystallized intelligence, which is believed to be influenced by learning, culture, and environment (Kaufman, 1994; Wechsler, 1974, 1986, 1991).

There has been consistent replication in the literature regarding intellectual performance on selected subtests of the various versions of the Wechsler Adult Intelligence Scales (WAIS, WAIS-R, and WAIS-III) and the Wechsler Intelligence Scale for Children (WISC, WISC–R, WISC-III, and WISC-IV), demonstrating that groups of AD individuals perform relatively well on Block Design and Object Assembly subtests (Iverson, 1997; Lincoln et al., 1995; Siegel et al., 1996). Those studies also indicate that persons with AD perform relatively poorly on Vocabulary and Comprehension subtests.

Table 29.1 lists WISC-IV global IQ and subtest scale scores reported in the WISC-IV manual for a cohort of children diagnosed with autism (meeting DSM-IV-TR criteria), ages 7 to 16. There were 2 females and 17 males in the sample (Wechsler et al., 2004). The relative discrepancy among these subtests may be less evident, particularly between Comprehension and Block Design relative to other studies employing various versions of the WISC (see Table 29.3).

Thus, in Table 29.1 there is only a 5.5-point difference between the Verbal Comprehension Index (80.2) and the Perceptual Reasoning Index (85.7). In addition, there is only a

TABLE 29.1.

Descriptive Statistics: Mean WISC-IV Index and Subtest Scores and Standard Deviations for Matched Control (MC) and Autistic Disorder (AD) Group

	Autistic disorder		Matched control	
Verbal Comprehension Index	80.2	(17.4)	106.1	(12.0)
Perceptual Reasoning Index	85.7	(20.6)	101.6	(12.2)
Working Memory Index	76.9	(16.5)	102.9	(13.1)
Processing Speed Index	70.2	(18.3)	96.8	(12.2)
Full Scale IQ	76.4	(19.5)	103.9	(11.1)
Block design	7.9	(3.5)	10.1	(3.2)
Similarities	7.0	(3.3)	11.5	(2.3)
Digit span	6.2	(3.1)	10.6	(3.2)
Picture concepts	7.4	(4.0)	10.3	(2.3)
Coding	4.0	(3.3)	8.5	(3.3)
Vocabulary	7.2	(3.2)	11.2	(2.2)
Letter-number sequencing	5.5	(3.6)	10.8	(2.0)
Matrix reasoning	7.7	(3.9)	10.4	(3.4)
Comprehension	5.3	(4.0)	11.1	(2.6)
Symbol search	5.2	(3.7)	10.2	(2.5)
Picture completion	6.5	(3.8)	10.0	(3.4)
Cancellation	6.3	(3.6)	8.7	(4.1)
Information	7.1	(3.7)	10.2	(2.5)
Arithmetic	8.2	(4.4)	8.7	(1.2)
Word reasoning	6.8	(3.3)	10.8	(3.1)

2.6-point difference between Block Design (7.9) and Comprehension (5.3) subtests. Furthermore, there is only a 0.7-point difference between Block Design (7.9) and Vocabulary (7.2) subtests. There were no significant differences between the groups. However, a more recent study (Quirmbach & Lincoln, submitted) that included 41 children diagnosed with autism demonstrated significant discrepancies among WISC-IV subtests; this corroborates previous research that indicated performance discrepancies in individuals with autism on the Wechsler Intelligence Scales (e.g., Lincoln et al., 1995). In the current study, the WISC-IV was administered to 41 children aged 6–14 (mean age 9.4 years) who were diagnosed with autism according to the DSM-IV-TR criteria and the Autism Diagnostic Observation Schedule (ADOS). The sample included 3 females and 38 males. Participants ranged in Full Scale IQ between 42 and 122. The results are presented in Table 29.2.

Table 29.2 shows a significant ($p < .05$) 18.5-point difference between the Verbal Comprehension Index (75.4) and the Perceptual Reasoning Index (93.9). In addition, there is a significant ($p < .05$) 6.6-point difference between the Block Design (10.9) and Comprehension (4.3) subtests. Furthermore, there is a significant ($p < .05$) 4.7-point difference between the Block Design (10.9) and Vocabulary (6.2) subtests.

In Table 29.3, mean WISC scores for verbal subtests are significantly lower than Block Design subtests for children with autism. The most significant difference is between the Block Design subtest and the Comprehension subtest.

The sample of children with autism included in the WISC-IV manual (Wechsler et al., 2004) all had a Full Scale IQ above 60. Thus, Quirmbach & Lincoln (submitted) also conducted analyses in which seven children with a Full Scale IQ less than 60 were excluded in order to determine whether discrepancies among subtests would still be evident. When the data were analyzed, which included 34 children with autism with a Full Scale IQ of at least 60, there were still discrepancies across subtests. There is a 16.7-point difference between the Verbal Comprehension Index (81.4) and the Perceptual Reasoning Index (98.1). In addi-

TABLE 29.2.

Descriptive Statistics: Mean WISC-IV Index and Subtest Scores and Standard Deviations for Autistic Disorder (AD) Group

	Autistic disorder	
Verbal Comprehension Index	75.4	(25.4)
Perceptual Reasoning Index	93.9	(15.4)
Working Memory Index	79.4	(22.9)
Processing Speed Index	83.4	(18.7)
Full Scale IQ	79.7	(21.3)
Block design	10.9	(3.2)
Similarities	7.5	(4.9)
Digit span	7.3	(4.7)
Picture concepts	7.2	(3.5)
Coding	6.4	(3.0)
Vocabulary	6.2	(4.9)
Letter-number sequencing	5.8	(4.3)
Matrix reasoning	8.9	(3.3)
Comprehension	4.3	(4.0)
Symbol search	7.7	(4.5)

TABLE 29.3.

Descriptive Statistics: Mean WISC Subtest Scores Comparing Different Samples of Children with Autistic Disorder (AD) and Typically Developing Children

Subtest	WISC-IV (Quirmbach & Lincoln, submitted)	WISC-III (Hanzel et al., submitted)	WISC-III (Hanzel et al., submitted)	WISC-III (Iverson, 1997)	WISC-III (Iverson, 1997)	WISC-R (Iverson, 1997)
N	**41**	**20**	**20**	**20**	**22**	**34**
Ages	**6–14**	**7–14**	**7–13**			
Diagnosis	**Autism**	**Autism**	**Normal control**	**Autism**	**Normal control**	**Autism**
Block design	10.9	11.9	11.4	13.8	9.6	11.1
Comprehension	4.3	2.6	12.2	3.2	9.5	1.7
Vocabulary	6.2	5.9	12.3	4.3	8.5	3.9

tion, there is a 6.3-point difference between the Block Design (11.4) and Comprehension (5.0) subtests, as well as a 4.1-point difference between Block Design (11.4) and Vocabulary (7.3). Although discrepancies are evident in this sample, the children included (aged 6–14) were younger than the WISC-IV manual sample, which included children aged 7–16. High functioning children with autism may tend to improve their verbal skills with age. Thus, perhaps the discrepancy between verbal and nonverbal reasoning skills decreases as children get older. However, findings from Quirmbach & Lincoln (submitted) are very similar to the intellectual profile previously identified, demonstrating that children with autism tend to perform significantly better on nonverbal reasoning tasks (i.e., the Block Design subtest) than on verbal tasks (i.e., the Comprehension and Vocabulary subtests; e.g., Lincoln et al., 1995). In Table 29.3, subtest scores demonstrate the discrepancies between verbal subtests, including Comprehension and Vocabulary, and the Block Design subtest.

The Leiter International Performance Scale and the Leiter International Performance Scale-Revised

Disturbances of speech and language have been observed in individuals diagnosed with autism, regardless of age or developmental stage (Lord & Paul, 1997; Simmons & Baltaxe, 1975; Tager-Flusberg, Joseph, & Folstein, 2001). Even with progress in other impaired areas of functioning, the disabilities of speech and language remain major handicaps in later development, with approximately 50% of the population acquiring no language skills at all (Eisenberg, 1956; Eisenberg & Kanner, 1956; Kanner, 1971; Lord & Paul, 1997; Minshew et al., 1997). Thus, encountering individuals of this population in clinical practice can often require the use of assessment instruments that do not depend on verbal language ability (Marcus, Flagler, & Robinson, 2001).

The Leiter International Performance Scale (1948) was originally intended to be a nonverbal version of the Stanford-Binet scale, following the concept of measuring intelligence in terms of developmental age (Sattler, 1992). However, it had severe psychometric limitations as an objective assessment tool. There is little description of the standardization sample, and there are no reliability or validity statistics reported in the manual. Because the most recent revision was created in 1948, items are outdated and the scores at each level appear to be uneven. In spite of these limitations, it had been recommended for use with language-handicapped (Sattler, 1992), hearing-impaired, and various other groups of children with special needs (Roid & Miller, 1997).

The current revision of the Leiter (Leiter-R; Roid & Miller, 1997) was created in order to update and substantiate this unique and significant assessment instrument. The Leiter-R was standardized on a sample of 2,000 children throughout the United States. Extensive tests of reliability and validity have been performed (Gridley, Bos, & Roid, 1996; Madsen, Roid, & Miller, 1996; McLellan & Walton, 1996; Roid, 1996; Roid & Miller, 1997). In keeping with recent advances in research of intelligence theory by Horn (1988, 1994), Gustaffson (1984), and Carroll (1993, 1997), the individual test items were analyzed and reorganized to match the factors of cognitive ability (Roid & Miller, 1997).

Gf/Gc Theory of Intelligence Supporting the Leiter-R

The Leiter-R was designed around a hierarchical model of intelligence that includes a general intelligence factor (g; Gridley et al., 1996). This model includes the theory of fluid (Gf), crystallized (Gc), and broad visualization (Gv) abilities discussed by Horn and Cattell

(Horn & Catell, 1966; Gustafsson, 1984; Carrol, 1993). Extensive factor analyses resulted in the final three-tiered hierarchical model of intelligence: a general (*g*) intelligence factor at the apex; fluid abilities (Gf), crystallized abilities (Gc), and broad visualization (Gv) in the second tier; and numerous smaller factors in the third tier. This model of intelligence provided the theoretical framework for the development of the Leiter-R (Madsen et al., 1996; Roid & Miller, 1997).

Items were designed to measure the primary domains in this theory of intelligence. Fluid reasoning (Gf) tasks included matrix reasoning, sequencing of figural patterns, figural analogy, and functional classification. General visualization (Gv) measures include figural rotation, figural matching, spatial orientation, gestalt closure, and picture completion. Tasks that measure memory (short-term Gsm and long-term Gtsr) include immediate and delayed recognition of pictorial objects, immediate and delayed associative (pictorial) memory, spatial memory (a matrix grid of pictured objects must be recalled in correct spatial order), and memory for sequential orders of pictured objects (the examiner points to the pictures in a prescribed order, and the subject replicates the sequences after a 10-second delay) in both forward and backward sequences. Two subtests were developed to measure attention abilities, one sustained scanning task in which subjects must find all replications of a specific object on a specific page and one divided attention task that requires divided attention between pointing to prescribed objects and concurrently sorting cards. Items and subtests used to measure crystallized ability (Gc) were not included, as it has been defined to measure verbal abilities and knowledge acquired through education (Gustafsson, 1984; Horn, 1994). The Leiter-R was developed as a nonverbal, culture-free battery that did not require the use of verbal skills or skills acquired through verbal ability (Gridley et al., 1996).

Assessment with the Leiter-R

In the original standardization research, 11 categories of atypical children were compared with the standardization sample, including severe speech and language impairment, severe motor delay or deviation, and significant cognitive delay (mental retardation; Roid & Miller, 1997). Since the 1997 release of the Leiter-R, additional research with the Leiter-R has begun to become available on the performance of comparison samples of children in various diagnostic categories as well as children with autism (Hanzel & Lincoln, submitted; Tsatsanis et al., 2003).

Tsatsanis et al. (2003) assessed a "low-functioning" group of children with autism and evaluated their performance on both the current Leiter-R and older version of the Leiter. The sample consisted of 26 children ranging in age from 4 to 16 years. The correlation between the Leiter scales was high (*r* = .87), and there was a difference of 3.7 points between the two mean scores, which is not significant at either the statistical or the clinical level. However, significant intraindividual discrepancies were present in 10 cases, 2 of which were both large (24 and 36 points) and clinically meaningful. The mean profile of performance on Leiter-R subtests is also presented for this sample of children with autism, in order to allow for comparison with other groups. Based on the results of this initial evaluation, together with the current normative data, good psychometric properties, and availability of global and subtest scores with the Leiter-R, the instrument is generally recommended for use with children with autism. However, because of changes in the design of the Leiter-R, there may be greater clinical success with the original Leiter for those children who are very low functioning and severely affected, particularly younger children.

Hanzel and Lincoln (submitted) found similar results with a higher functioning sample of children. The subjects in this study included 20 children with high-functioning Autistic

Disorder (AD-HF), ranging in age from 7 to 14 years, and 20 children without any significant psychological disorders, ranging in age from 7 to 13 years. There were 2 females and 18 males in both the AD-HF group and the Normal Control (NC) group. All subjects were Caucasian. The AD-HF group contained subjects ranging in age from 7 years 8 months to 14 years 4 months, with a mean average of 11 years 3 months. The NC group subjects ranged in age from 7 years 7 months to 13 years 1 month, with a mean average of 10 years 8 months. Subjects in both the AD-HF group and the NC group were from lower-middle-class and middle-class families (see Table 29.4 and Figure 29–1).

Table 29.5 shows correlations among Leiter-R and WISC-III IQ and Index scores. As can be seen in Table 29.5, the significant correlation between the two measures supports the validity of the Leiter-R. The results from this study indicate that the Leiter-R is a valid measure of the domains measured in the more established measures of intelligence and cognitive abilities, with standardization and administration not dependent on any verbal mediation (Roid & Miller, 1997). The strong correlations of the Full Scale and Fluid Reasoning measures with the Full Scale and Performance measures of the WISC-III provide support for its use as an option as a nonverbal measure of cognitive abilities. The confirmatory factor analyses supporting the theoretical model of a hierarchical factor structure of the subtests with single (g) factor and secondary factors of fluid reasoning (Gf) and visualization (Gv) are evidenced in the initial and subsequent validity and reliability research (Bos, Gridley, & Roid, 1996; Bay, 1998).

In general, nonverbal assessment as utilized in the Leiter-R can be particularly important in the assessment of autism. Children with autism have demonstrated unique abnormalities in functions of memory (Ameli, Courchesne, Lincoln, Kaufman, & Grillon, 1988; Lincoln, et al., 1995; Lincoln, Dickstein, Courchesne, Elmasian, & Allen, 1992; Minshew & Goldstein,

TABLE 29.4.

Descriptive Statistics: Leiter-R Visualization & Reasoning Battery Composite Scores and WISC-III Scale and Corresponding Factor Scores Normal Control (NC) Group and High-Functioning Autistic Disorder (AD-HF) Group

Leiter-R Visualization & Reasoning Battery

	NC group		AD-HF group	
	Mean	*SD*	*Mean*	*SD*
Fluid reasoning	106.80	15.51	92.10	21.10
Full scale	108.50	16.41	92.15	20.48

WISC-III

	NC group		AD-HF group	
	Mean	*SD*	*Mean*	*SD*
Verbal	113.75	13.56	74.85	17.27
Performance	103.00	10.87	93.85	16.67
Full scale	108.95	12.85	82.55	15.67
Verbal comprehension (VC)	113.50	13.48	76.90	17.59
Perceptual organization (PO)	104.00	11.67	98.80	15.92

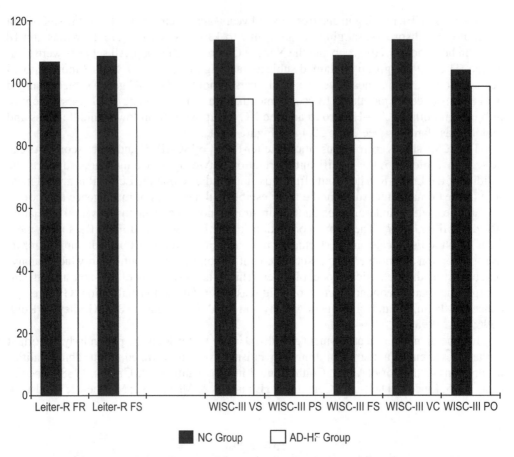

FIGURE 29–1.   Leiter-R fluid reasoning and full scale scores, WISC-III scale and corresponding factor scores, normal control (NC) group, and high-functioning autistic disorder (AD-HF) group.

2001; Prior & Chen, 1976) and attention (Allen & Courchesne, 2001; Courchesne, Lincoln, Kilman, & Galambos, 1985; Courchesne et al., 1994; Garretson, Fein, & Waterhoouse, 1990; Goldstein et al., 2001; Minshew & Goldstein, 2001). The Attention and Memory battery of the Leiter-R contains subtests that measure areas of specific weakness for children with AD-HF, including echoic memory, memory of meaningful and meaningless stimuli, short-term and long-term memory, working memory, and sustained and shifting attention. The Visualization and Reasoning battery also includes measures with socially meaningful stimuli (people, animals, and objects in everyday social context) as well as stimuli not dependent on social context and awareness (shapes and sequences). The variety of measures across both batteries allows for detailed and comprehensive focused evaluation of many of the core features unique to autism.

Disadvantages of the Leiter-R

Although a significant advantage of the Leiter-R is its nonverbal standardization, this feature is likewise a disadvantage in its assessment of children with AD-HF. Children with high-

TABLE 29.5.

Correlations between Leiter-R Fluid Reasoning (Gf) and Full Scale Scores and WISC-III Scale and Corresponding Factor Scores Normal Control (NC) Group High-Functioning Autistic Disorder (AD-HF) Group

	NC group		AD-HF group	
	Corr	p value	Corr	p value
Leiter-R Fluid Reasoning (Gf) Score				
WISC-III Verbal Scale	.506*	.023	.599**	.005
WISC-III Verbal Comprehension Factor	.533*	.016	.549*	.012
WISC-III Performance Scale	.709**	.000	.587**	.007
WISC-III Perceptual Organization Factor	.706**	.001	.513*	.021
WISC-III Full Scale	.735**	.000	.679**	.001
Leiter-R Full Scale Score				
WISC-III Verbal Scale	.499*	.025	.460*	.041
WISC-III Verbal Comprehension Factor	.549*	.012	.404	.078
WISC-III Performance Scale	.608**	.004	.563**	.010
WISC-III Perceptual Organization Factor	.702**	.001	.496*	.026
WISC-III Full Scale	.695**	.001	.582**	.007

*Correlation is significant at the 0.05 level.
**Correlation is significant at the 0.01 level.

functioning autistic disorder (WISC PIQ > 70) have by definition higher language skills than autistic children with a WISC PIQ < 70 (Bartak & Rutter, 1976). This is especially the case if the more stringent definition of high-functioning autistic disorder is used (WISC VIQ and FSIQ > 70; Minshew, Goldstein, Muenz, & Payton, 1992; Siegel et al., 1996). Therefore, the absence of spoken language in relating directions and requests, as well as communicating responses, is potentially confusing and stressful for children with AD-HF. The Leiter-R administration procedures allow for adjustment of the administration to "combine brief verbalizations with the standardized nonverbal pantomime procedures" (Roid & Miller, 1997, p. 3). However, because the Leiter-R was standardized only on complete nonverbal administration, the authors recommend "caution . . . in using the Leiter-R normative scores if standardized administration instructions are radically changed" (Roid & Miller, 1997, p. 76). No instructions are provided for determining when and how to adapt administration as well as how much the normative scores may be affected.

Other difficulties with the nonverbal nature of the Leiter-R may arise because of the general impairment of nonverbal communication (gestural, affective, and facial) and verbal communication (Bartak, Rutter, & Cox, 1975; Marcus et al., 2001; Ohta, 1987) as seen in individuals with autism. On each subtest, the child uses card selection or points to the test stimulus to communicate responses. Instructions are communicated by the examiner initially by imitation. If the child does not understand the task, then it is suggested that the examiner "gently help the child to point to the correct item" (Roid & Miller, 1997, p. 23). Inasmuch as it is common for children with autism to have the associated feature of "odd responses to sensory stimuli . . . oversensitivity . . . to being touched" (DSM-IV-TR, 2000, p. 72), this alternative can be particularly aversive.

The physical test materials of the Leiter-R can also be difficult to manage, especially when adjustments are needed to engage an examinee. Many of the subtests require the use of cards and an easel. This can quickly become problematic when a child starts losing interest, wants to move quickly, and, for example, begins to throw or mix up the cards. The administration format also requires the examiner to score responses by looking over the top of the easels and viewing the stimulus upside down. This can be particularly difficult when a child points to responses quickly and when the sequencing stimuli are presented by the examiner, such as in Forward Memory and Reverse Memory.

The nonverbal standardized administration of the Leiter-R provides a way to limit the inherent bias of instruments requiring spoken language. Though the verbal abilities of children with autism can vary significantly across IQ levels, the hallmark deviance in communication and use of language appears to be pervasive across all levels of functioning of autistic individuals (Lord & Paul, 1997; Tager-Flusberg, 1999). As a result, even when children have some or even significant speech and vocabulary, relying on verbal mediation to access other cognitive abilities can result in inaccurate and misleading data (Marcus et al., 2001).

CASE STUDY: A 12-YEAR-OLD BOY WITH AUTISTIC DISORDER BASED ON THE WISC-IV

Reason for Referral and Behavioral Observations

Tyler was brought in for an assessment by his parents because of current difficulties with his social and academic functioning. Tyler was originally diagnosed with autism at the age of three. Tyler can be characterized as shy and eccentric. He demonstrates poor eye contact, engages in immediate and delayed echolalia, has difficulty sustaining conversation with others, and engages in self-stimulatory behaviors (such as hand-flapping).

Findings

Tyler was administered the Wechsler Intelligence Scale for Children–Fourth Edition (WISC-IV), Autism Diagnostic Observation Schedule (ADOS)–Module 2, and the Reading Recognition and Reading Comprehension subtests of the Peabody Individual Achievement Test–Revised. Tyler's WISC-IV results are presented in the tables.

Tyler's distinctive thinking and reasoning abilities make up an intellectual profile that is difficult to characterize by a single score derived from the WISC-IV. His nonverbal reasoning abilities are much better developed than his verbal reasoning abilities.

Tyler's significant verbal weaknesses include his performance on the Comprehension and Vocabulary subtests. Tyler has difficulty providing oral solutions to everyday problems and explaining the underlying reasons for certain social rules or concepts. For example, when asked, "Why is it important for police to wear uniforms?" Tyler responded, "The police are for to get people when they are bad." Thus, Tyler was unable to answer the question but responded to an association he was familiar with—the importance of having police officers. Similarly, when asked to "Tell me some reasons that you should turn off lights when no one is using them," Tyler responded, "Turn them off." The examiner repeated the question, to which Tyler responded "Turn off the light switch."

Thus, Tyler was unable to answer the question asked; he told the examiner the rule he learned about "turning off the light switch" without understanding the reason behind the rule. Typically, individuals diagnosed with Autistic Disorder have difficulty understanding social situations, comprehending conventional standards of social behavior, and using sound social judgment. In addition, Tyler performed much better on abstract categorical reasoning and concept formation tasks that did not require verbal expression (Picture Concepts) than those that required verbal expression (Similarities).

Tyler performed in the Average range on nonverbal reasoning subtests. His score on Block Design (91st percentile) is a significant strength for Tyler compared with his peers. Thus, Tyler is skilled at mentally organizing visual information and analyzing part-whole relationships when information is presented spatially. It is common for individuals diagnosed with Autistic Disorder to score higher on Block Design than on other subtests. Other strengths for Tyler, compared with his overall mean score on the WISC-IV, include Picture Concepts and Matrix Reasoning. Thus, Tyler demonstrated strengths in fluid visual information processing, fluid reasoning, and abstract reasoning skills.

Tyler had difficulty sustaining attention, concentrating, and exerting mental control, as shown by his performance in the Extremely Low range on the Working Memory Index. This may impede Tyler's performance in a variety of academic areas, but especially on tasks that require him to solve numerical problems in his head. Tyler's ability to process simple or routine visual material without making errors, as measured by the Processing Speed Index, is quite variable. He demonstrated more skill on Symbol Search than Coding. Thus, Tyler demonstrated excellent mental control when information was presented visually (Symbol Search) and had difficulty when asked to complete fine motor tasks (Coding).

Based on the WISC-IV, Tyler's performance demonstrates a profile commonly shown by children diagnosed with autism. His nonverbal skills are significantly better developed than his verbal skills. Specifically, he shows a significant strength on Block Design and significant deficits on the Comprehension and Vocabulary subtests. Similar to his poorly developed verbal skills, Tyler demonstrated reading deficits according to the Peabody Individual Achievement Test–Revised (PIAT–R). Although Tyler is currently in the sixth grade, his reading recognition and reading comprehension are estimated to be at the second-grade level.

Summary and Recommendations

The current evaluation demonstrates that Tyler's overall skills correspond with the profile of autism. He may benefit from social skills interventions, such as social skills groups or social stories, which facilitate improvement in his social awareness and his relationships with others. Based on his intellectual profile, it is very likely that he needs support in academic areas. He may benefit from completing reading comprehension exercises on a regular basis in order to improve his verbal skills. In addition, it is likely that Tyler may benefit from practice with mental arithmetic problems, in order to strengthen his working memory. Thus, a tutor who works with Tyler one on one in the classroom, providing step-by-step instructions through visual means, is likely to benefit Tyler the most. Although it is clear that he is quite capable of effective visual-spatial processing, these abilities are not integrated with his verbal reasoning ability. His significant comprehension deficits and symptoms of autism are likely to be a primary factor in limiting his social adaptation and academic progress.

SUMMARY COMMENTS

The intellectual abilities of individuals with autism can be accurately assessed with standardized tests that are currently available. The current versions of the child and adult Wechsler scales, the Leiter International Performance Test–Revised, and the K-ABC-II are three instruments that have each been researched with respect to the assessment of intelligence in persons with autism. Aside from their excellent psychometric properties, each has a theoretical foundation in the most contemporary theory regarding the nature of human intelligence. A thoughtful and skilled clinician can obtain meaningful data about the individual with autism. This information can be used to describe meaningful individual differences with respect to neurocognitive performance and be useful in the development of treatment and psychoeducational intervention.

REFERENCES

Allen, G., & Courchesne, E. (2001). Attention function and dysfunction in autism. *Frontiers in Bioscience, 1*(6), 105–119.

Allen, M. H., Lincoln, A. J., & Kaufman, A. S. (1991). Sequential and simultaneous processing abilities of high-functioning autistic and language-impaired children. *Journal of Autism and Developmental Disorders, 21*(4), 483–502.

Ameli, R., Courchesne, E., Lincoln, A., Kaufman, A. S., & Grillon, C. (1988). Visual memory processes in high-functioning individuals with autism. *Journal of Autism and Developmental Disorders, 18*(4), 601–615.

Asarnow, R. F., Tanguay, P. E., Bott, L., & Freeman, B.J. (1987). Patterns of intellectual functioning in non-retarded autistic and schizophrenic children. *Journal of Child Psychology and Psychiatry, 28*(2), 273–280.

Bartak, L., & Rutter, M. (1976). Differences between mentally retarded and normally intelligent autistic children. *Journal of Autism and Childhood Schizophrenia, 6*(2), 109–120.

Bartak, L., Rutter, M., & Cox, A. (1975). A comparative study of infantile autism and specific developmental receptive language disorder. *British Journal of Psychiatry, 126*, 127–145.

Bay, M. (1998). An exploratory factor analysis of the Leiter-R. *Dissertation Abstracts International, 58*(8-B), 4513.

Bayley, N. (1993). *Bayley Scales of Infant Development, 2nd Revision.* New York: Psychological Corporation.

Bos, J., Gridley, B. E., & Roid, G. H. (1996). *Factor structure of nonverbal cognitive abilities: Construct validity of the Leiter-R.* Paper presented at the meetings of the American Psychological Association, Toronto, August.

Carroll, J. B. (1993). *Human cognitive abilities: A survey of factor-analytic studies.* New York: Cambridge University Press.

Carroll, J. B. (1997). The three-stratum theory of cognitive abilities. D. P. Flanagan, J. L. Genshaft, & P. L. Harrison (Eds.), *Contemporary intellectual assessment: Theories, tests, and issues* (pp. 122–130). New York: Guilford Press.

Courchesne, E. (1997). Brainstem, cerebellar and limbic neuroanatomical abnormalities in autism. *Current Opinion in Neurobiology, 7*(2), 269–278.

Courchesne, E., Lincoln, A. J., Kilman, B. A., & Galambos, R. (1985). Event-related potential correlates of the processing of novel visual and auditory information in autism. *Journal of Autism and Developmental Disorders, 15*(1), 55–76.

Courchesne, E., Townsend, J., Akshoomoff, N. A., Saitoh, O., Yeung-Courchesne, R., Lincoln, A. J., et al. (1994). Impairment in shifting attention in autistic cerebellar patients. *Behavioral Neuroscience, 108*(5), 848–865.

Eisenberg, L. (1956). The autistic child in adolescence. *American Journal of Psychiatry, 112*, 607–612.

Eisenberg, L., & Kanner, L. (1956). Early infantile autism. *American Journal of Orthopsychiatry, 26*, 556–566.

Garretson, H. B., Fein, D., & Waterhouse, L. (1990). Sustained attention in children with autism. *Journal of Autism and Developmental Disorders, 20*(1), 101–114.

Goldstein, G., Beers, S. R., Siegel, D. J., & Minshew, N. J. (2001). A comparison of WAIS-R Profiles in adults with high functioning autism or differing subtypes of learning disability. *Appl. Neuropsychology, 8*(3), 148–54.

Gridley, B., Bos, J. S., & Roid, G. H. (1996). *Factor structure of a nonverbal cognitive battery: The Leiter International Performance Scale–Revised.* Paper presented at the meetings of the American Psychological Association, Toronto, August.

Gustaffson, J.-E. (1984). A unifying model for the structure of intellectual abilities. *Intelligence, 8*, 179–203.

Hanzel & Lincoln (Submitted). *Journal of Autism & Developmental Disorders.*

Horn, J. L. (1988). Thinking about human abilities. In J. R. Nesselroade & R. B. Cattell (Eds.), *Handbook of Multivariate Experimental Psychology* (2nd ed., pp. 645–686). New York: Plenum Press.

Horn, J. L. (1991). Measurement of Intellectual Capabilities. A review of theory. In K. S. McGrew, J. K. Werder, & R. W. Woodcock (Eds.), *Woodcock-Johnson Technical Manual: A reference on theory and current research* (pp. 197–256). Allen, TX: DLM Teaching Resources.

Horn, J. L. (1994). Theory of fluid and crystallized intelligence. In R. J. Sternberg (Ed.), *Encyclopedia of Human Intelligence* (pp. 443–451). New York: Macmillan.

Horn, J. L., & Cattell, R. B. (1966). Refinement and test of the theory of fluid and crystallized intelligences. *Journal of Educational Psychology, 57*(5), 253–270.

Iverson, Kristen. (1997). *Assessment of reasoning abilities in high-functioning children with autistic disorder.* Unpublished doctoral dissertation, California School of Professional Psychology, San Diego.

Kanner, L. (1943). Autistic disturbances of affective contact. *Nervous Child, 2*, 217–250.

Kanner, L. (1971). Follow-up study of eleven autistic children originally reported in 1943. *Journal of Autism and Childhood Schizophrenia, 1*(2), 119–145.

Kaufman, A. S. (1994). *Intelligent testing with the WISC-III.* New York: Wiley.

Kaufman, A. S., & Kaufman, N. L. (2004). *Kaufman Assessment Battery for Children, Second Ed.* Circle Pines, MN: AGS.

Leiter, R. (1969). *Leiter International Performance Scale.* Chicago: Stoelting Company.

Lincoln, A. J., Allen, M. H., & Kilman, A. (1995). The assessment and interpretation of intellectual abilities in people with autism. In E. Schopler & G. B. Mesibov (Eds.), *Learning and cognition in autism* (pp. 89–117). New York: Plenum Press.

Lincoln, A. J., Courchesne, E., Kilman, B. A., Elmasian, R., & Allen, M. (1988). A study of intellectual abilities in high-functioning people with autism. *Journal of Autism and Developmental Disorders, 18*(4), 505–524.

Lincoln, A. J., Dickstein, P., Courchesne, E., Elmasian, R., & Tallal, P. (1992). Auditory processing abilities in non-retarded adolescents and young adults with developmental receptive language disorder and autism. *Brain and Language, 43*, 613–622.

Lockyer, L., & Rutter, M. (1970). A five-year follow-up study of infantile psychosis: IV. Patterns of cognitive ability. *British Journal of Social and Clinical Psychology, 9*, 152–163.

Lord, C., & Paul, R. (1997). Language and communication in autism. In D. J. Cohen & F. R. Volkmar (Eds.), *Handbook of autism and pervasive developmental disorders* (2nd ed.). New York: Wiley & Sons.

Madsen, D. H., Roid, G. H., & Miller, L. J. (1996). *Nonverbal intellectual assessment: Restandardization of a new measure—the Leiter International Performance Scale–Revised.* Paper presented at the meetings of the American Psychological Association, Toronto, August.

Marcus, L.M., Flagler, S., & Robinson, S. (2001). Assessment of children with autism. In R. J. Simeonsson & S. L. Rosenthal (Eds.), *Psychological and developmental Assessment: children with disabilities and chronic conditions* (pp. 267–291). New York: Guilford Press.

McLellan, M. J., & Walton, M. J. (1996). *Concurrent validation of the Leiter-R and WISC-III with Navajo children.* Paper presented at the meeting of the American Psychological Association, Toronto, August.

Minshew, N. J., & Goldstein, G. (2001). The pattern of intact and impaired memory systems in autism. *Journal of Child Psychology and Psychiatry, 42*(8), 1095–1101.

Minshew, N. J., Goldstein, G., Muenz, L. R., & Payton, J. B. (1992). Neuropsychological functioning in nonmentally retarded autistic individuals. *Journal of Clinical and Experimental Neuropsychology, 14*(5), 749–761.

Minshew, N. J., Goldstein, G., & Siegel, D. J. (1997). Neuropsychologic functioning in autism: Profile of a complex information processing disorder. *Journal of the International Neuropsychological Society, 3*, 303–316.

Mullen, E. M. (1995). Mullen Scales of Early Learning. Circle Pines, MN: AGS.

Ohta, M. (1987). Cognitive disorders of infantile autism: A study employing the WISC, Spatial relationship conceptualization, and gesture imitations. *Journal of Autism and Developmental Disorders, 17*(1), 45–62.

Prior, M. R., & Chen, C. S. (1976). Short-term serial memory in autistic, retarded and normal children. *Journal of Autism and Developmental Disorders, 6*(2), 121–131.

Quirmbach, L. M., & Lincoln, A. J. (submitted) A study of intellectual abilities of children with autism: The application of the WISC-IV.

Roid, G. H., & Miller, L. J. (1997). Leiter International Performance Scale–Revised; Examiner's Manual. In G. H. Roid and L. J. Miller, *Leiter International Performance Scale–Revised*. Wood Dale, IL: Stoelting.

Rumsey, J. M. (1992). Neuropsychological studies of high-level autism. In E. Schopler & G. Mesibov (Eds.), *High-functioning individuals with autism* (pp. 41–64). New York: Plenum Press.

Rutter, M. (1979). Language, cognition, and autism. In R. Katzman (Ed.), *Congenital and acquired cognitive disorders* (pp. 247–264). New York: Raven Press.

Rutter, M. (1983). Cognitive deficits in the pathogenesis of autism. *Journal of Child Psychology and Psychiatry, 24*(4), 513–531.

Rutter, M., & Schopler, E. (1988). Autism and pervasive developmental disorders: Concepts and diagnostic issues. In E. Schopler & G. B. Mesibov (Eds.), *Diagnosis and assessment in autism* (pp. 15–36). New York: Plenum Press.

Sattler, J. M. (1992). *Assessment of children* (3rd ed.). San Diego, CA: Jerome M. Sattler.

Siegel, D. J., Minshew, N. J., & Goldstein, G. (1996). Wechsler IQ profiles in diagnosis of high-functioning autism. *Journal of Autism and Developmental Disorders, 26*(4), 389–406.

Simmons, J. Q., & Baltaxe, C. (1975). Language patterns of adolescent autistics. *Journal of Autism and Childhood Schizophrenia, 5*(4), 333–351.

Tager-Flusberg, H. (1999). A psychological approach to understanding the social and language impairments in autism. *International Review in Psychiatry, 11*, 325–334.

Tager-Flusberg, H., Joseph, R., & Folstein, S. (2001). Current directions in research on autism. *Mental Retardation and Developmental Disabilities Research Reviews, 7*, 21–29.

Tsatsanis, K. D., Dartnall, N., Cicchetti, D., Sparrow, S. S., Klin, A., & Volkmar, F. R. (2003) Concurrent validity and classification accuracy of the Leiter and Leiter-R in low-functioning children with autism. *Journal of Autism and Developmental Disorders, 33*(1), 23–30.

Ventor, A., Lord, C., & Schopler, E. (1992). A follow-up study of high-functioning autistic children. *Journal of Child Psychology and Psychiatry, 33*(3), 489–507.

Wechsler, D. (1974). *Manual for the Wechsler Intelligence Scale for Children (WISC)*. San Antonio, TX: Psychological Corporation.

Wechsler, D. (1986). *Manual for the Wechsler Intelligence Scale for Children-Revised (WISC-R)*. San Antonio, TX: Psychological Corporation.

Wechsler, D. (1991). *Manual for the Wechsler Intelligence Scale for Children-Third Edition (WISC-III)*. San Antonio, TX: Psychological Corporation.

Wechsler, D. (1997). *Manual for the Wechsler Adult Intelligence Scale-Revised (WAIS-R)*. San Antonio, TX: Psychological Corporation.

Wechsler, D., Kaplan, E., Fein, D., Kramer, J., Morris, R., Delis, D., et al. (2004). *Manual for the Wechsler Intelligence Scale for Children–Fourth Edition (WISC IV)*. San Antonio, TX: Psychological Corporation.

30

CLINICAL ASSESSMENT OF ETHNIC MINORITY CHILDREN AND ADOLESCENTS

Frederick T. L. Leong
Michigan State University

Jacob J. Levy
University of Tennessee

Christina B. Gee
George Washington University

Jeannette Johnson
Friends Research Institute

Clinical assessment of ethnic minority children and adolescents should be informed by general information regarding these cultural groups as well as research on the validity and reliability of specific assessment instruments. Therefore, our paper begins with a discussion of some of the cultural factors related to clinical assessment for ethnic minority children and adolescents from the four major racial and ethnic minority groups, namely African Americans, Hispanic Americans, Asian Americans, and Native Americans. A critique of the research with these ethnic minority children and adolescents is also presented. This is followed by a review of specific clinical instruments that are commonly used to assess mental health with these ethnic minority group children and adolescents. Given the different distribution of available literature, the four sections corresponding to the four racial ethnic minority groups do not necessarily use the same organizational framework. Finally, a specific case study of an African American patient is presented to illustrate some important cultural factors in clinical assessment with ethnic minority children and adolescents.

CULTURAL FACTORS IN CLINICAL ASSESSMENT

African Americans

Two issues consistently arise in the discussion of psychological testing of African Americans: a) test bias, meaning that there is a statistical group difference between African Americans and other racial groups, particularly European (White) Americans; and b) test utility, meaning that regardless of whether there is a between-group difference on test results, those differences (or lack of differences) actually represent the true psychological presentation of the groups (Hall & Phung, 2002). Although these issues are paramount with respect to cognitive assessment (the debate of differential cognitive abilities, e.g., IQ, and academic achievement are well documented; see Suzuki, Short, Pieterse, & Krugler, 2002, for a detailed discussion of these issues), racial differences with respect to personality testing have received less attention. The overwhelming majority of multicultural research has focused on the issue of test bias (i.e., examining group difference in test scores and profiles). Recent meta-analytic studies suggest that there are far fewer between-group differences than was once believed (e.g., Hall, Bansal, & Lopez, 1999).

For African Americans, an evaluation of the issues of test bias and between-group difference in test performance and results is certainly a necessary and worthy endeavor. However, examination of between-group differences is only part of what constitutes the multicultural utility of assessment instruments. African Americans not only demonstrate potential significant clinical differences from other racial groups (European Americans in particular), but also manifest a wide variety of within-group differences. It is important to examine the community and societal influences on the individual African American adolescent. For example, are communication problems, both verbal and nonverbal, developing in part because Black English is accepted in the home and community, but is deemed inappropriate at school? What effects have experiences with racism, prejudice, and discrimination had on the adolescent? What are the adolescent's views, perceptions of, and experience with the African American community? Uncovering the individual answers to such questions could lead to great insight into the adolescent's racial identity development. Thus, depending on the nature of the client's racial identity, administering an etic (standard) instrument may be more appropriate for some African Americans, whereas selecting Afrocentric emic (designed for a particular population) instruments may be more appropriate for others.

We propose that Helms's (1990) Racial Identity Development Stages provides a conceptual framework by which to understand the process of developing racial consciousness or identity. She proposes a series of stages that one works through in internalizing and externalizing experiences of racism. The first stage is termed Preencounter, and, as applied to African Americans, is characterized by idealization of the dominant (Eurocentric) worldview and denigration of the Africentric worldview (i.e., pro-White/anti-Black). As the African American individual begins to experience injustices and discriminations based on his or her race, and despite their general positive outlook on the dominant culture, the individual enters the next stage, termed Encounter. This stage is characterized by feelings of confusion and frustration about one's beliefs about society, and a great appreciation for one's own culture (confused White/euphoric Black). In the next stage, Immersion/Emersion, an attempt is made to eliminate this confusion and frustration by physically and emotionally withdrawing into African American culture and adopting, uncritically, all things (and people) perceived as Afrocentric, rejecting all things (and people) viewed as non-African American (i.e., pro-Black/Anti-White). As people begin to critically examine the aspects of African American culture that fit them with those that do not, and open themselves up to experiences outside their culture, the person enters into the final stage of racial identity development, Internalization (internalized Black/accepting White).

Morris (2000) suggests that clinicians choose measures on the basis of clients' stage of racial identity development. For clients in the Preencounter stage, Morris noted that it is generally appropriate to use etic measures. Clients at this stage generally have attitudes, characteristics, and worldviews consistent with the dominant culture and thus wish to be evaluated in a similar manner. Morris also notes that it is appropriate to utilize standard etic measures for people in the Encounter and Internalization stages. However, special modifications are needed, including disclaimers of the test's multicultural limitations, and clarification of salient cultural differences that may affect test interpretation. Specifically, results from children and adolescents in the Encounter stage need to be viewed primarily from a Eurocentric perspective, and results from children and adolescents in the Internalization stage need to be viewed from more of an Afrocentric perspective.

For clients in the Immersion/Emersion stage, Morris (2000) contends that the use of etic measures is inappropriate. Not only might clients who are predominantly Afrocentric mistrust the use of testing, resulting in inaccurate results; their perceptions and behavior may also not fit Eurocentric norms, resulting in faulty clinical decision making. Thus, clients in the Immersion/Emersion stage should only be administered instruments that have been standardized predominantly with African Americans (i.e., emic measures). However, because Afrocentric personality measures are very limited (i.e., the TEMAS is only mainstream personality test with Afrocentric norms), personality testing with these individuals may be counter-indicated.

Several instruments have been developed to assess a client's racial identity. Two of the most widely used are Helms's Racial Identity Attitudes Scale (Helms & Parham, 1996) and the Cross Racial Identity Scale (CRIS; Vandiver et al., 2000). In addition, Jones (1996) provides reviews of a variety of Afrocentic measures, including instruments designed to assess African American adolescents' achievement motivation (Castenell & Levitow, 1996), racial socialization (Stevenson, 1996), and learning styles (e.g., Kern & Coats, 1996).

Hispanic Americans

Hispanic Americans are an ethnic minority group with very diverse backgrounds. They can have their origins in Mexico, Puerto Rico, Cuba, or Nicaragua. In view of this diversity, one of the major issues in the evaluation of the clinical assessment literature for Hispanic Americans is the extent to which important subgroup differences can be masked when a study consists of a general sample of Hispanics. Some studies focus on specific subgroups, but it is also recognized that it may not always be possible to obtain a large enough sample, such as a sample of Mexicans or Puerto Ricans, to conduct a study. The end result is that any review of the clinical literature on Hispanic Americans will tend to contain a mixture of studies that focus on specific subgroups, whereas others have lumped various subgroups together under the rubric of Hispanic Americans. Clinicians referring to this literature need to be cognizant of the set of literature they are relying upon and the limitations created by this problem of comparing apples (studies based on specific subgroups) to fruit salads (studies based on a mixture of subgroups labeled as Hispanics).

One theme that seems quite prevalent in this literature is the importance of examining the effects of acculturation on the reliability, validity, and utility of specific clinical instruments. Many of the studies reviewed in this chapter pertaining to Hispanics had acculturation as a primary or secondary variable and showed the significant moderating effects of this variable. Furthermore, the significant role played by acculturation in the evaluation and application of clinical tests with Hispanics is also further supported by a similar pattern of findings in terms of counseling and psychotherapy with this ethnic minority group. As such, it would be helpful for clinicians to evaluate their patients' acculturation levels when applying the findings from these studies in their clinical practice.

Another significant theme that underlies this literature is that of language. Because many of the Hispanic American participants in the various studies either do not speak English or have a limited command of the language, translations of the instruments are often needed. The use of the gold standard of instrument translation, named the "back-translation method," is not evenly applied in these studies. Sometimes the nature and extent of the translation procedures are not even adequately reported. Furthermore, the effects of using translated instruments on the sensitivity and specificity of these measures have not been systematically evaluated. Yet we know that the use of interpreters can have systematic distortion effects on counseling and psychotherapy. Perhaps meta-analyses of these studies will one day illustrate the differential effects of studies based on translated instruments versus original language instruments and how we should view each type of study.

Finally, there are two interrelated limitations to this literature that need to be pointed out. First, there is a paucity of systematic studies that make up a program of research focused on the clinical assessment of mental health for Hispanic Americans. This problem is further exacerbated by the problem mentioned earlier of studies based on specific subgroups that are combined with studies based on a mixture of groups. For practical reasons, separating out the two sets of studies would only result in very limited information that may be of questionable generalizability. Second, our review discovered that many of the existing studies of various instruments were based on doctoral dissertations that tend not to make their way into the published literature that would be readily available to clinicians. Clearly, there is a great need for more systematic research with the various measures that focus on specific subgroups, so that a reliable and generalizable body of literature would be accumulated that is of use to clinicians.

For further information, readers should refer to the excellent discussion of the major methodological challenges in the assessment of Hispanic children and adolescents provided by Canino and Guarnaccia (1997). In addition to addressing the major cultural influences on children and families in the Hispanic culture, the authors also discuss such issues as case definition, the need to use multiple informants, and the interaction between social class and culture, as well as a recommended method for the translation and adaptation of diagnostic instruments. They also provide recommendations for future research studies in this area.

Asian Americans

Similar to other ethnic minorities, Asian American children and adolescents must deal with the challenges of adolescence as well as the unique issues related to being an ethnic minority within the United States. The typical developmental tasks of childhood and adolescence in Western society do not always converge with the values of traditional Asian culture (Huang, 1994). For example, whereas American culture promotes individuation from parents, traditional Asian cultures value continued deference to, respect for, and dependence on parents. Indian American adolescents, who have not been raised in families that promote individuation and independence, may experience some initial anxiety when leaving home for the first time to attend college (Viswanathan, Shah, & Ahad, 1997).

Culturally competent assessment of Asian American children and adolescents is further complicated by the heterogeneous ethnic groups that fall under the umbrella term of *Asian American*. Asian Americans are made of up a diverse set of over 20 distinct ethnic and cultural groups that include Chinese, Japanese, Korean, Cambodian, Vietnamese, Pacific Islander, and Indian. Although these cultures may share some similarities, they also have their own unique languages and cultures that influence their values and beliefs. For example, clinicians should be familiar with the differences among the various Southeast Asian refugee populations (including Cambodian, Vietnamese, Hmong, and Laotian). Specifically, Hmong and Cambodians tend to have the lowest level of literacy in their native language in comparison with Laotians and Vietnamese (Chung & Lin, 1994). One additional factor that is often not addressed in the literature on assessment of Asian Americans is the increase in bi- and multi-ethnic individuals, particularly among the younger population. Clinicians should be aware that their child and adolescent clients may have equally strong ethnic affiliations to more than one group (Gee, 2004). In addition, given that adolescence is a time when identity issues typically come to the forefront, it is likely that some adolescents may be experiencing confusion or uncertainty about their ethnic identity.

Beyond the differences that exist among ethnic groups, vast differences may be present even within a single ethnic group. For example, the first-wave Vietnamese refugees tended to be more educated in comparison with the second-wave refugees, who were often exposed to unsafe and unsanitary refugee camps, frequently saw relatives killed or tortured, or were separated from loved ones, sometimes without knowledge of their whereabouts (Abueng & Chung, 1996). Thus, clinicians should assess for the reason and circumstances surrounding the child or adolescent and his/her family's migration, because these migration-related traumas may increase the risk of psychological disorders. Indeed, some previous research of Cambodian youth found relatively high rates of posttraumatic stress disorder (PTSD) and depression (e.g., Clarke, Sack, & Goff, 1993). Furthermore, Southeast Asian refugee children and adolescents may feel caught between two cultures, not belonging fully to either one. In addition, they may feel a tremendous amount of pressure to succeed academically and financially in order to support their families if their parents were not able to secure employment because of lack of language skills or education (Tobin & Friedman, 1984).

Age at immigration, generational status, and acculturation status are other important components of a thorough assessment of Asian American child and adolescent mental health. These factors can be indicators of the degree to which adolescents and their families adhere to more traditional Asian value systems or more Western value systems. For example, children and adolescents who were born in the United States, but whose parents immigrated to the United States as adults, may experience a great deal of struggle due to conflicting value systems. Children and adolescents can experience the stress of going between the dominant culture at school and the traditional culture at home (Inman, Constantine, & Ladany, 1999; Tobin & Friedman, 1984). A recent study of U.S. and foreign-born Chinese Americans aged 18 and older suggests that the risk of depression may be higher for recent immigrants and may decrease as length of residence increases (Hwang, Chun, Takeuchi, Myers, & Siddarth, 2005).

In addition, traditional Asian families are commonly patriarchal in nature and tend to have strict role expectations based on age and gender (Huang, 1994). These role relationships can be disrupted as the child or adolescent often speaks more English than the parent and may be put into the position of taking care of adult tasks, such as bill-paying and grocery shopping. In his/her role as a cultural broker, the power dynamic can be reversed, thus causing stress within the family. Furthermore, age at immigration can affect the adolescent's own language proficiency, which may influence the degree to which he/she has the vocabulary to explain feelings or symptoms in English (Okazaki, Kallivayalil, & Sue, 2002; Viswanathan et al., 1997). Children and adolescents should have the option of having an assessment done in his/her native language whenever possible. If the child or adolescent wishes to have an assessment conducted in his/her native language, the clinician should ask which dialect he/she speaks, given that many of the Asian languages comprise many different dialects that may vary dramatically in terminology and grammar (Iwamasa, 1997).

However, clinicians should not assume that age at immigration and generational status are always directly related to level of acculturation. Asian American children and adolescents who live in mostly homogeneous ethnic enclaves may have little exposure to Western ideas and may have little need to learn English. Therefore, they may be less acculturated than adolescents who live in more heterogeneous communities. Moreover, children and adolescents may acculturate more quickly in areas such as fashion and language, while still maintaining core values of their native culture (Sue & Sue, 1987).

The clinical assessment of Asian American children and adolescents should be informed by an awareness of the historical and cultural characteristics of the specific population and the available research on the validity and reliability of assessment measures. Assessment of the child or adolescent requires a thorough assessment of a variety of background factors for both the individual and relevant family members, which often include extended family. Important factors to assess during the clinical interview include immigration-related circumstances, generational status, and degree of acculturation.

Unfortunately, clinicians can rely on little information regarding the appropriateness of using Caucasian American norms for Asian American children and adolescents. In addition, the absence of validity studies that have included Asian American children and adolescents compels clinicians to interpret scores and profiles with caution and examine and explore individual item endorsements (Tsai & Pike, 2000). At the same time, clinicians should also be cautioned against underestimating psychopathology by assuming that various beliefs and symptoms can be explained as being due to the individual's cultural heritage. Lopez (2002) has recommended the practice of "shifting cultural lenses," a process by which the assessor considers the competing hypotheses based on differing specific cultural contexts. As researchers continue to develop new measures and validate existing assessment instruments, clinical assessment of Asian American children and adolescents will improve.

NATIVE AMERICANS

Concern has been expressed regarding the use of conventional evaluation assessment techniques with Native Americans. Exclusive reliance on quantitative techniques may be too reductionistic to adequately portray Indian realities in a manner meaningful to Indian people. That is, if the purpose of assessment is expected to be useful to Native Americans, the purpose must reflect the values, beliefs, and other epistemological assumptions of the Indian community. For this to occur, the assessment process itself should respect the wide range of linguistic, tribal, and cultural differences among American Indians. Nevertheless, most assessments with American Indians are not concerned with the diversity of the population. American Indians might be one racial or ethnic group, but culturally they are many. Very little assessment of American Indians focuses on specific tribal groups, but instead relies on a generic category typically labeled American Indian or Native American. Trimble (1991) refers to this approach as an "ethnic gloss" and argues that it fails to capture the significant differences that exist within most racial and ethnic groups. Using ethnic gloss with American

Indians is especially problematic because of the extreme diversity of the population. Nevertheless, ethnic gloss has been the predominate approach used in assessing American Indians. As a result, little refined work related to measurement is available for this population. Ethnic gloss can be minimized by elaboration of the population descriptions or sample through administration of detailed demographic or ethnic identification measures. In addition, given that the American Indian worldview utilizes a relational framework, assessing American Indians requires moving beyond a framework that uses an individualistic approach to one that utilizes a sociocultural framework that will focus on the individual in context.

In the face of inadequate assessment, three steps can be taken to improve current instrumentation: 1) Improve existing standardized instruments to make them less culturally *inappropriate* than they are currently for all cultural groups in which they are used. 2) Draw upon qualitative/ethnographic research approaches in the development and administration of semistructured assessment formats that permit flexibility in ways in which questions are framed and rephrased. 3) Ensure the valid administration of assessments by professionals who are familiar with the culture and the language and who are skilled in conducting assessments.

Most standardized tests conflict with many aspects of Native American culture. For example:

- The content of standardized assessments measures experiences that may not be common to reservation Indians.
- Native Americans, who value patience in response, may be penalized by timed assessments.
- Native Americans are a visually oriented culture, and tests relying on verbal responses penalize them.
- Native Americans often approach written tasks differently than the dominant culture. For example, individuals who are accustomed to cooperating with each other and sharing information may not be able to proceed readily when faced with the solitary task of writing a response to a written question.

American Indians have been subjected to decades of assessment using assessment tools that are not standardized or normed on the population and have not been tested for their reliability and cultural validity (Dauphinais & King, 1994; LaFromboise & Low, 1997; Manson, Bechtold, Novins, & Beals, 1999). It can be reasonably argued that all assessment is essentially a culturally negotiated product and implies some degree of social compromise. At a practical level, these types of principles are articulated in the works of theorists such as Guba and Lincoln (1989) and Patton (1990). Guba and Lincoln (1989) recommend using naturalistic inquiry methods in order to maintain the cultural integrity of the assessment process and to respect multiple perspectives. Naturalistic inquiry allows for and encourages all stakeholders in the enterprise to tell their story. The authors state that the standardized or survey interview does not take account of multiple worldviews. Wolf and Tymitz (1977) suggest that naturalistic inquiry is aimed at understanding actualities, cultural realities, and perceptions that exist untainted by the obtrusiveness of formal measurement or preconceived questions. Naturalistic inquiry is a more valuable method for assessing Native Americans because it is geared to the uncovering of stories told by real people, about real events, in real and natural ways.

Culturally responsive evaluation can employ semistructured interviews that can be designed to allow individual respondents to "tell their own story," in their own words, minimizing the bias imposed by the method. This means that in the actual conduct of data collection, respondents would not be discouraged from offering whatever they consider important.

Using storytelling as a means of assessment serves the purpose of recognizing that each respondent is, in a very meaningful way, a stakeholder in the process. Storytelling, dialogue, and metaphoric expression enable us to decipher language by entering what Hale (1986) describes as "the kitchen of meaning." In listening to stories we acknowledge the complexities of language and culture. In her essay, "The Moral Necessity of Metaphor," Ozick (1986) writes: "Through metaphor, the past has the capacity to imagine us, and we it. Those who have no pain can imagine those who suffer. Illuminated lives can imagine the borders of stellar fire. We strangers can imagine the familiar hearts of strangers." A metaphor is a type of story that calls upon us to consider a radically different way of knowing. In her book, *The Sacred Hoop: Recovering the Feminine in American Indian Tradition*, Paula Gunn Allen (1986) contends that allowing people to "give voice" to their life journey, that is, telling their story, allows a "holistic image to pervade and shape consciousness, thus providing a coherent and empowering matrix for action and relationship." Zemke (1990) notes that stories can play a stabilizing role in our culture and believes that "without air our cells die, without a story our selves die." A story provides structure for our perceptions and assessments of reality. In many American Indian tribal groups, a story is seen as having a life of its own. Such stories carry an energy—a truth, a lesson, an insight, an evaluative reflection—that can enter our being and connect us to a powerful source of truth making and perceptual affirmation. Many Native healers have often viewed English words as being "cages for ideas" and become frustrated with their ability to express authentically the gestalt of their cultural reality and life experience when non-Native researchers probe for explanations that fit into a structuralist worldview.

REVIEW OF SPECIFIC MEASURES

African American Children and Adolescents

Minnesota Multiphasic Personality Inventory-Adolescent. The Minnesota Multiphasic Personality Inventory-Adolescent (MMPI-A; Butcher et al., 1992) is a revision of the original MMPI (Hathaway & McKinley, 1942) designed to measure personality and psychopathology in adolescents, aged 14 to 18 years. Since the publication of the MMPI-A, only a few studies have examined racial and other cultural differences on the instrument. No published study, to date, has specifically investigated possible between-group differences for African American samples. Although there has been a dearth of multicultural research on the MMPI-A, the same is not true for the adult version. The original MMPI and its current revision, the MMPI–2, have been investigated extensively with regard to cross-cultural equivalence. Early studies comparing African American and European American adolescents found noticeable differences on several MMPI clinical and validity scales (Ball, 1960; McDonald & Gynther, 1962). Subsequent investigations, however, found that when participants were matched on the basis of other salient demographic variables, such as socioeconomic status (SES), there were no significant profile differences between African American and European American adolescent samples (e.g., Archer, 1987). Several studies note mean group difference between African American and European American samples on individual scales, specifically Scales 4 (Psychopathic Deviate), 7 (Psychasthenia), 8 (Schizophrenia), and 9 (Hypomania) (e.g., Hall et al., 1999; Timbook & Graham, 1994). However, these differences typically are less than 5 T-score points. Thus, although the results are statistically significant, they are not clinically meaningful (Greene, 2000; Hall et al., 1999). In addition, meta-analytic investigations comparing African American and European American samples found no substantive differences in profiles as a function of race (e.g., Hall et al., 1999).

In an examination of the profiles of the normative sample for the MMPI-A (Butcher et al., 1992), several individual clinical and validity scales differ on the basis of race. Similar to the adult version, these between-group differences on the MMPI-A are less than 5 T-score points and thus are not clinically meaningful (Baer & Rinaldo, 2004). Although it may be reasonable to assume, similar to the meta-analytic findings of the adult version, that there are no substantial differences between African Americans and other racial groups on the MMPI-A, this question has yet to be investigated with rigor.

Millon Adolescent Clinical Inventory.   The Millon Adolescent Clinical Inventory (MACI; Millon, 1993) is another widely used measure of adolescent personality and psychopathology. The MACI is widely used by school psychologists and other helping professionals in school-based evaluations (e.g., eligibility for special education). One reason for this may be that, compared with the MMPI-A, the MACI is much shorter and can be completed in 20–30 minutes; the MMPI-A typically takes 60–90 minutes to complete. Like all Millon inventories, the MACI is designed to measure personality constructs derived from Millon's theory of personality (see Millon & Davis, 1996), as well as clinical syndromes associated with both Axis I and Axis II disorders identified by the *Diagnostic and Statistical Manual of Mental Disorders Fourth Edition* (*DSM-IV*; American Psychiatric Association, 1994).

Millon's adult inventories (e.g., the Millon Clinical Multiaxial Inventory-III) have been criticized for their lack of ethnic diversity in the normative samples. The same does not hold true with the MACI, which boasts a relatively large number of racially diverse adolescents (8% African American) in its norm group (Strack, 1999). Unfortunately, the MACI has generated little research interest since its introduction, and evidence of its multicultural utility is limited. In one of the few published studies that address potential racial issues with the MACI, Stefurak, Calhoun, and Glaser (2004) found no race effects when exploring typologies based on the Personality Pattern scales of the MACI in a sample of detained male juvenile offenders.

Personality Inventories for Children and Youth.   The Personality Inventory for Children (currently in its 2nd edition—PIC–2; Lacher & Gruber, 2001) is a multidimensional objective measure of behavioral, emotional, cognitive, and interpersonal adjustment of children and adolescents. Normed on an ethnically diverse national sample, the PIC–2 provides standardized norms for the entire public-school age range (grades K through 12). The PIC–2 is completed by a child's parent or parent surrogate. Limited cross-cultural research has been conducted on this instrument. However, in a study conducted by Kline and Lachar (1992), the orginial version of the PIC predicted external criteria (via a symptom checklist) *marginally* better for Whites than for African-Americans, but a particular pattern of race-related effect was difficult to discern.

Similar to the PIC–2, the Personality Inventory for Youth (PIY; Lachar & Gruber, 1995) is a multisource, objective measure of personality and dysfunction for use with children and adolescents in grades 4 through 12. The PIY consists of three questionnaires, one completed by the child or adolescent, one by the child's or adolescent's primary care giver(s), and one by his or her teacher. It is reasoned that examining multisource data will result in a more accurate measure of clinical phenomena, with special attention to accounting for frequency and pervasiveness (Lachar, 2004). The test developers note that the PIY's normative sample was racially diverse, and, in a comparative study, Lachar and Gruber found no evidence of racial differences among African American, Hispanic, and European American students on any of the nine PIY substantive scales.

Similar to the other measures discussed, the PIY has not been the subject of many comparative studies. In fact, other than the aforementioned study found in the PIY manual, no published study has investigated the multicultural utility of this instrument. However, in a dissertation examining the convergent validity of several adolescent personality measures, the PIY tended to classify American participants of European decent as depressed more often than their African American counterparts (Young, 1998). Thus, continued investigation into the utility of this instrument appears warranted.

Achenbach Measures. Achenbach (1991) developed a multiaxial assessment process designed to measure child and adolescent psychological behavior. Similar to the PIY, Achenbach's system gathers data from multiple sources, in an effort to examine behavior across context. Specifically, this assessment includes the Child Behavior Check List (CBCL), which is completed by the child's parent (the CBCL/4–18 is used to assess children aged 4–18); the Teacher Report Form (TRF), which is completed by the teacher based on observations of school-related behavior; and finally the Youth Self-Report (YSR), which is completed by the child or adolescent to describe his or her own perceptions of their behavior.

With regard to the use of Achenbach's system with African American children and adolescents, it is important to become aware of the patterns of discrepancy and agreement among the multiple informants (i.e., parent, teacher, and adolescent report). In their study on patterns of agreement among parents, teachers, and male children and adolescents on Achenbach's measures, Youngstrom, Loeber, and Strouthamer-Loeber (2000) found that teachers reported fewer externalizing and internalizing behaviors than did the youth or their parents. In addition, they found that teacher-child or teacher-adolescent disagreement was higher for African Americans than for European Americans on externalizing behavior.

More recently, Lau and colleagues (2004) conducted a large study examining racial differences in terms of informant report, cross-informant discrepancies, and cross-informant correlations. With regard to informant reports, no racial differences were found in child and adolescent self-reports on either internalizing or externalizing behavior. American parents of European descent reported more internalizing and externalizing behavior problems than African American parents; teachers reported more internalizing behavior problems for European Americans than African Americans, but reported more externalizing behavior problems in African Americans than European Americans.

In the examination of cross-informant discrepancies, there were lower child-parent and adolescent-parent discrepancies existed for European Americans as compared with minority groups on both internalizing and externalizing behavior problems. In addition, lower child-teacher and adolescent-teacher discrepancies were found for European Americans as compared with African Americans on internalizing behavior problems, and lower discrepancies for both European and African Americans on externalizing behavior problems were found compared with Asian Americans. No parent-teacher discrepancy differences were found on internalizing behavior problems, but lower discrepancies were found for European and Asian Americans than for African Americans.

Finally, in terms of significant agreement correlations for African Americans, child-teacher and adolescent-teacher agreements were higher for African American girls than for European American girls on both internalizing and externalizing behavior problems. Parent-teacher agreement was higher for European Americans and Hispanics than for African Americans and Asian Americans on internalizing behavior problems.

What is unclear in the aforementioned studies is whether the racial difference found was the result of unfair test bias or a real disparity in naturalistic observations. Achenbach's measures are simply behavioral checklists. Thus, the issue in question is whether the behaviors listed in his measures are understood and equivalent in meaning across racial groups. Based on the results described above, it appears that continued investigation into the multicultural utility of Achenbach's system is warranted.

Tell-Me-A-Story.   The assessment measures discussed thus far have all been designed, constructed, and normed on a generalized population and are believed to be appropriate for universal application. As indicated earlier, in multicultural assessment, these standard instruments are generally referred to as "etics" (Dana, 1997). A contrasting approach, referred to as the "emic" perspective (Dana, 1997), involves developing an instrument to be applied with a specific cultural or racial group. The rationale for the emic perspective is that minority groups have unique cultural values, behavioral idiosyncrasies, and worldviews that may make inaccurate an assessment of psychopathology that does not directly address these differences and uniquenesses (Ridley, Li, & Hill, 1998). Thus, it is from an emic perspective that tests like the "Tell-Me-A-Story" (TEMAS) test have come to have a prominent presence in personality assessment.

The TEMAS test (Costantino, Malgady, & Rogler, 1988) has been described as "the best example of an apperception test specifically designed for multicultural application" (Ritzler, 2004, p. 578). It was developed as a more culturally sensitive projective measure of personality. Similar to its etic counterpart, the Thematic Apperception Test (TAT; Morgan & Murray, 1935), the TEMAS test includes a series of stimulus cards designed to pull for specific personality, cognitive, and affective functions. The uniqueness of the TEMAS test is that it includes several racial variations of the people represented on the cards in an effort to match the race of the respondent. The TEMAS test provides norms for four racial/ethnic groups: African Americans, European Americans, Puerto Ricans, and other Hispanics. Most, if not all, of the research examining the psychometric properties of the TEMAS has been conducted by its primary developer (Costantino) and his colleagues. Although there is no reason to doubt the findings of Costantino and his colleagues, good science would dictate additional independent investigations. Until additional evidence is available, it is important for users of this test to refer to the TEMAS manual (Costantino, Malgady, & Rogler, 1988) for reports of the reliability estimates for the functions measured by the test, because there is a great deal of disparity in consistency of results for African Americans by function. For example, reliability coefficients ranged from a very low .31 for Setting Transformations to a very high of .97 for Fluency, with a median coefficient of .62 (Costantino & Malgady, 2000). Thus, depending on the reliability of the measurement of a particular function, determinations of its validity will vary greatly, although note that this is a common problem with all projective measures, not just the TEMAS test.

Graphic Techniques.   Three commonly used projective techniques applied clinically with children are the Draw-A-Person Test (DAP; Machover, 1949), the House-Tree-Person Drawing (H-T-P) Test (Buck, 1948), and the Kinetic Family Drawing (K-F-D) Test (Burns & Kaufman, 1970). These techniques are easy to administer and easy for child clients to complete. For the DAP, the child is simply asked to "Draw a person." No parameters are given, and the child is free to draw a person any way he or she likes. After the child draws a picture of one person, he or she is asked to draw a picture of a person of the sex opposite that of the first drawing. The child is then asked to make up stories about the people. The H-T-P test is similar, but in addition to a person, the child is also asked to draw pictures of a house and a tree. The theoretical underpinning of both techniques is that in drawing these ambiguous pictures, the child will unconsciously project his or her underlying personality traits, dynamic, and psychopathology.

The K-F-D is a drawing test in which the child or adolescent is asked to draw his or her family *doing something*. McNight-Taylor (1974) tested 8–12-year-old low-income Black children in the southeastern region of the United States and found the drawings to be rather sparse and primitive. The author explained the poor performance by suggesting that the children had neurological impairment, poor parental care, anxiety, frustration, and aggression. However, Handler and Habenicht disagreed with this conclusion and instead explained the findings as reflecting insecurity in the testing situation, and the fact that this group had few experiences with fine motor tasks, such as drawing, compared with gross motor experiences. This pattern of inexperience with drawing was also reported by Dennis (1966), who demonstrated similar variations in drawing ability and drawing sophistication in a number of cultures where drawing was either not stressed or was otherwise discouraged.

In using graphic techniques cross-culturally, several studies have found significant differences in drawings of children from cultures other than their own (e.g., Gonzales, 1982; Klepsch & Logie, 1982). An early cross-cultural study (Hammer, 1953) used the H-T-P test to determine whether African American children were less well adjusted than European American children and found American children to be less well adjusted on nearly every rating. More recently, however, other research has found that drawing techniques (specifically the DAP) do not yield significantly different results between African Americans and European Americans (Matto & Naglieri, 2005). Probably the most important issue to consider in order to avoid misinterpretation of meanings of clients' drawings is to understand the nature of clients' cultural context, thus helping to differentiate between personal and cultural issues (such as the effects of racism).

Hispanic American Children and Adolescents

Minnesota Multiphasic Personality Inventory-Adolescents. Scott, Butcher, Young, and Gomez (2002) administered the Minnesota Multiphasic Personality Inventory-Adolescent (MMPI-A) to 385 14–18-year-olds in Colombia, Mexico, Peru, Spain, and the United States in order to assess the generalizability of the instrument with various Spanish-speaking adolescents. The results showed a high degree of similarity across the five countries on the basic content and supplementary scales. Specifically, the majority of the scales were within half a standard deviation of the U.S. Hispanic mean and no scale elevations were found to be greater than $T = 65$. Based on these results, the authors concluded that the Hispanic MMPI-A, with its established norms, seems appropriate for adaptation in Spanish-speaking countries other than the United States.

Using a sample of 54 African and Mexican American adolescent first-time offenders (mean age 15 years), Gomez, Johnson, Davis, and Velasquez (2000) examined the MMPI-A with regard to possible ethnic differences. Multivariate analyses by ethnicity and MMPI-A scales (validity, clinical, content, and supplementary scales) were found not to be significant. However, there was a significant univariate difference where African American adolescents scored significantly higher on the Repression scale than the Mexican American group. A greater percentage of within-normal-limits profiles were indicated for African Americans (50%) than for Mexican Americans (25%).

In another study to evaluating the utility of the MMPI-A for Hispanic youth, Gumbiner (1998) compared the validity, clinical, content, and supplementary scale scores of 30 Hispanic 14–18-year-olds with normative data. The results revealed elevated T-score means on F1 (66), F2 (68), F (68), L (61), Hs (61), D (63), Sc (62), A-hea (63), A-biz (63), A-Ise (61), A-las (60), A-scb (61), and IMM (61) scales for the Hispanic boys. Furthermore, scores for low aspirations, low self-esteem, immaturity, and school problems were all interrelated. For the Hispanic girls, none of the scale scores were elevated, but on several scales mean T scores (Hs, Hy, Ma, Si, A-anx, A-obs, A-hea, A-ang, A-las, MAC-R, and ACK) were below average when compared with normative data. The author interpreted these findings as indicating the MMPI-A's tendency to underpathologize girls. Consistent with the literature, the boys scored higher on the Immaturity Scale than the girls. Gumbiner also speculated that the boys' dislike for school and their low aspirations may be related to the lower education and employment of their fathers and that the A-las, A-sch, and IMM scales may prove to be useful in identifying adolescent boys who may be at risk for dropping out of school.

Several studies examined the relationship between the MMPI-A and acculturation among Hispanic youths. In the first of these studies, examining the relationship between the MMPI-A Lie Scale, acculturation and SES, Mendoza-Newman (2000) sampled 65 Hispanic adolescents from the San Francisco Bay Area. The participants completed a demographic questionnaire, the Acculturation Rating Scale for Mexican Americans-II, and the MMPI-A. No significant relationships were found between acculturation or SES as individual variables with those of Scale L (Lie) and Scale 5 (Masculinity-Femininity). However, a significant negative correlation between the combination of acculturation, SES, and Scale L (Lie) was found. The author pointed to the importance of considering acculturation in interpreting results from the MMPI-A Lie Scale.

In another study examining the relationship between acculturation and SES on the Lie Scale of the MMPI-A, Ryan-Arredondo (2002) sampled 300 adolescents (aged 14 to 18). The sample consisted of 100 Mexican American subjects from a small rural town in Texas, 100 Mexican subjects from a large city in Mexico, and 100 White American subjects from a small rural town in Texas. An examination of the two-factor solution within the scale revealed that they were not equivalent across the three ethnic groups. However, the Cronbach's alpha internal consistency estimates indicated that none of the differences in reliability between the ethnic groups were statistically significant. The authors observed that this pattern of results indicated that although the construct measured by the MMPI-A Lie Scale is measured consistently across groups, it is being measured consistently poorly. With the use of partial correlation methods in relation to acculturation and SES, 4 of 14 items (29%) were identified as performing differentially for the ethnic groups. It was found that acculturation and SES levels of the Mexican American, Mexican, and Anglo groups were not statistically significant predictors of the MMPI-A Lie Scale score for any group. The authors concluded that the Lie Scale scores should be interpreted with caution with Mexican and Mexican American adolescents, who do not interpret the questions in the same manner as one another.

Negy, Leal-Puente, Trainor, and Carlson (1997) also investigated the relationship between acculturation and the MMPI-A in a sample of 120 Mexican American 13–18-year-olds. These participants completed the MMPI-A, a short demographic questionnaire, and a five-item version of the Acculturation Rating Scale for Mexican Americans. The results indicated that the current sample of Mexican American adolescents' performance on the Validity, Clinical, and Content scales differed minimally from the national normative group's performance. However, it was found that the Mexican youth's performance on the MMPI-A varied as a function of their levels of acculturation and socioeconomic status.

A chapter by Velasquez, Maness, and Anderson (2002) provides a useful review of MMPI–2 and MMPI-A research with Hispanic populations. In addition to offering practical guidelines for the culturally competent assessment of Hispanics, this chapter also described some of the most recent findings on research with Hispanics with the MMPI–2 and MMPI-A. In addition, the chapter also presents a list of questions that clinicians need to address prior to evaluating Hispanic clients with the MMPI–2, as well as a discussion of key cultural issues for interpretation of certain MMPI–2 scales with this ethnic minority group. Another useful resource is a bibliography provided by Corrales et al. (1998), which presents a comprehensive list of all research conducted on U.S. Latinos, including Puerto Ricans, with the MMPI–2 and MMPI-A, beginning in 1989, covering a total of 52 studies.

Millon Adolescent Clinical Inventory.   The Millon Adolescent Clinical Inventory (MACI) is presented as an alternative to the MMPI-A. However, using PsycInfo, we could locate only one study with the MACI that focused on Hispanic youth. In this study, using the MACI, Barry and Grilo (2002) examined gender and ethnicity patterns in eating and body image disturbances (BID) in 715 12–19-year-old inpatients in a psychiatric facility. There were 553 Caucasians, 77 Latino Americans, and 85 African Americans in the sample. Gender × Ethnicity interactions in the features of eating disorders and BID were examined in this clinical study. Among the three ethnic groups, significant differences were found in their reporting of BID, but not in endorsement of eating disorder features. A significantly higher proportion of Caucasian participants reported body image concerns than did African American and Latino participants. The latter two ethnic groups did not differ significantly from one another. However, significant Gender × Ethnicity interactions were observed, with Caucasian females endorsing higher rates of eating disorder features and BID, compared with African American and Latino females. The authors concluded that among adolescent psychiatric inpatients, although Caucasian females report the highest rates of eating disorder features and BID, such concerns are not uncommon in males or in ethnic minority groups, including Hispanics.

Beck Depression Inventory (BDI).   Gibbs (1986) examined the incidence of depression and whether demographic or psychosocial factors were related to depression in 84 Black, 19 White, 7 Hispanic, and 6 Asian female ninth–twelfth graders. The participants completed the Beck Depression Inventory (BDI), and self-image, biographical, and demographic questionnaires, as well as a problem checklist. Findings revealed that level of depression was significantly correlated with mothers' occupations, household mobility, and self-reported problems. However, no significant differences among racial groups were found. The small number of Hispanic participants in this study severely restricts the generalizability of these findings.

In a study focused on Hispanics, Rotherham-Borus, Piacentini, Van-Rossem, and Graae (1996) investigated outpatient treatment adherence among 140 female adolescent Hispanic suicide attempters (ages 12–18 years) when they received either standard emergency room care or a specialized emergency room program. Participants completed the Beck Depression Inventory (BDI), Suicide Survey, and the Rosenberg Self-Esteem Scale. Their mothers completed the Brief Symptom Inventory and the BDI. Results indicated that attempters receiving the specialized program were more likely to attend one treatment session and were somewhat more likely to attend more sessions than participants receiving standard emergency room care. Participants receiving the specialized program reported reduced psychiatric symptoms, and mothers reported more positive attitudes toward treatment and perceptions of family interactions. Thus, it appears that the BDI exhibited clinical utility with this population.

In another study focused on Hispanics, Alberti (1997) examined the correlations among life stress, self-appraisal of problem-solving ability, depression, and hopelessness in a Latino adolescent population. Participants consisted of 129 Latino adolescents (mean age = 14.7) from a middle school in Los Angeles. Stress was defined as minority-immigrant status, depression was measured by the BDI, hopelessness by Beck's Hopelessness Scale (BHS), and self-appraisal of problem solving by Heppner's Problem Solving Inventory (PSI). Spanish translations of the measures were also provided so that non-English-speaking recent immigrants could participate The findings showed that stress was not correlated with hopelessness or depression in any of the groups, but overall self-appraisal of problem-solving ability was correlated with both depression and hopelessness among participants. Furthermore, a comparison of three factors of problem-solving with depression and hopelessness, by group, revealed that self-assurance while engaging in problem-solving activities was significantly correlated with both depression and hopelessness for all three groups. A tendency to approach problem-solving activities while solving problems was significantly correlated with both depression and hopelessness for subjects born in the United Sttates and long-term immigrants, but not for recent immigrants.

Projective Assessment.   There is a dearth of empirical studies on projective assessment with Hispanic Americans, including children and adolescents. Our review was able to identify only two articles on the topic. In the first article, Malgady, Costantino, Rogler, and colleagues (1984) reported on the development of a Thematic Apperception Test (TEMAS) for urban Hispanic children. They administered a thematic apperception technique (TEMAS) composed of chromatic stimuli depicting Hispanic characters in urban settings to 73 kindergartners to third graders from Puerto Rican backgrounds. These data were then compared with data on 210 (kindergartners to sixth graders) clinical Puerto Rican participants obtained from an earlier study, to investigate the psychometric properties of the instrument. The results showed internal consistency and interrater reliability in scoring TEMAS protocols. Furthermore, TEMAS indices significantly discriminated between the public school and clinical samples, as theoretically expected. The authors argued that these findings provide preliminary support for the clinical utility of the TEMAS for Hispanic children. Despite the dearth of published studies, the Tell-Me-a-Story (TEMAS) measure, as a multicultural thematic apperception test designed for use with minority and nonminority children and adolescents, appears to hold promise and warrants further investigations.

In the second study, which is a dissertation by Sanchez Rosado (2002), the impact of acculturation on the Kinetic Family Drawing (K-F-D) as a tool for use with children of Mexican descent was evaluated. The participants consisted of nonclinical children, 320 of Mexican descent and 114 Caucasian Americans in grades 3 through 6 who were interviewed and than asked to draw K-F-Ds. The drawings were then analyzed qualitatively and quantitatively to ascertain different acculturation levels. The analyses revealed that levels of acculturation were clearly evident in the K-F-Ds of these children. For example, less acculturated Mexican family members were more often drawn engaged in work-related activities with defined roles, whereas more leisure activities were drawn by the more acculturated children and by Caucasian children. Higher levels of communication and interaction levels were also drawn by more acculturated than by less acculturated children.

Asian American Children and Adolescents

Contrary to lay perceptions of Asian Americans as a "model minority," research conducted on these populations indicates that rates of depression and anxiety among Asian Americans are comparable to those found among European American populations (see Lee, Lei, & Sue, 2001, for a review). However, there have been relatively few research studies that have used child or adolescent Asian American populations when validating clinical assessment measures. Studies have primarily focused on adults, aged 18 and older. In addition, the majority of the research on the psychometric properties of various assessment tools has been conducted with Asians living in their native countries. Therefore, the generalizability of these studies to Asian youths living in the United States is unclear. Furthermore, a number of these studies are not published in English-language academic journals, which also limits U.S. researchers' access to potentially relevant information. This chapter covers only a small amount of the research in this area and focuses primarily on ethnic minorities living in the United States; see Leong, Okazaki, and Tak (2003) for a comprehensive review of studies of self-report measures of depression and anxiety for Asians living in East Asia.

Beck Depression Inventory-II.   Of the standardized measures for the assessment of depressive symptoms, the Beck Depression Inventory-II (BDI-II; Beck, Steer, & Brown, 1996) continues to be frequently used. However, the majority of research on the validity of this measure with Asian Americans has been conducted on college students and adult populations. Among U.S. college students, the BDI-II appears to have reasonable reliability for Asian Americans (e.g., Carmody, 2005). The majority of studies of Chinese-translated versions of the BDI have found it to be reliable and valid for use with Chinese populations (for review, see Leong, Okazaki, & Tak, 2003). However, as mentioned previously, many of these studies were conducted in Asia and/or with adult populations, potentially limiting the generalizability of these findings to Asian American children or adolescents. Considering those limitations, one study of Chinese adolescents in Hong Kong using a Chinese-translated version of the original BDI found that the measure had good reliability and validity. However, results indicated that the data were better explained by a two-factor solution that included a factor for general symptoms of depression and a separate factor for somatic symptoms (Shek, 1990).

Center for Epidemiological Studies Depression Scale.   The Center for Epidemiological Studies Depression scale (CES-D; Radloff, 1977) is also a popular self-report assessment tool for depression and has been found to be useful with adolescents (Radloff, 1991). Greenberger and colleagues (1996) used a 16-item abbreviated version of the CES-D with Asian (Chinese and Korean) early adolescents and young adults. Interestingly, although the researchers found that the CES-D demonstrated high internal consistency, an examination of the individual items revealed that Asian Americans reported feeling more frequently that "My life is a failure," reported more disabling symptoms (i.e., "everything was an effort"), and reported more difficultly in coping with distress (i.e., "could not shake off the blues" or "had trouble keeping my mind on things"). Furthermore, the authors found that early adolescents (but not college students) who were first-generation or immigrants reported more symptoms than their American-born counterparts. The study by Greenberger and Chen highlights the need for additional research to understand the correlates and symptom presentation of depression in Asian American adolescents.

A subsequent study by Greenberger, Chen, Tally, and Dong (2000) further supported the validity of using the 20-item CES-D with Chinese high school students between the ages of 15 and 18, living in mainland China. Using confirmatory factor analysis, they found that the U.S. and Chinese samples exhibited the same four-factor structure initially proposed by Radloff (1977) and the same interrelations among factors. They did find differences in the specific factor loadings and variances of individual items, although they suggest that, overall, the structure is sufficiently similar in Chinese and U.S. adolescent populations. Future research should examine whether these results replicate in Chinese American adolescent samples.

Other Depression Measures.   Given that the manifestations of depression may be somewhat different in children and adolescents than in adults, there have been some attempts to validate other measures specifically designed for youth. For example, there has been some research on a Korean-translated version of the Youth Depression Adjective Checklist (Carey, Lubin, & Brewer, 1992). However, despite reasonable internal consistency, this measure's low test-retest reliability suggests that more research is required before the measure can be used widely in clinical assessment of Korean adolescents (Sung, Lubin, & Yi, 1992).

Instead of translating existing measures of depression into other languages, researchers have been developing new culture-specific measures of depression. Several measures, such as the Vietnamese Depression Scale (Kinzie, Manson, Vinh, Tolan, Anh, & Pho, 1982) and the Lao Depression Inventory (Davidson-Muskin & Golden, 1989), have been developed for Southeast Asian populations. For Chinese populations, the Chinese Depression Inventory (Zheng & Lin, 1991) is a measure that was derived from several preexisting self-report measures. Unfortunately, at the present time, none of these culture-specific measures of depression have undergone sufficient psychometric evaluation to determine their validity for Asian American children and adolescents, particularly those living in the United States. Okazaki (2000) has argued that prior to the development of additional new assessment measures designed for particular Asian American groups, ethnographic research should be conducted in order to gain a better understanding of the way in which Asian Americans experience and express psychological distress.

State-Trait Anxiety Inventory.   For the assessment of symptoms of anxiety, clinicians frequently use the State-Trait Anxiety Inventory (STAI; Spielberger, 1983). Hishinuma and colleagues (2000) examined the psychometric properties of the STAI for Asian/Pacific Islander adolescents living in Hawaii. Instead of the originally proposed two-factor model (State vs. Trait), they found that a four-factor model in which those subscales are further subdivided into "anxiety-present" ("I feel anxious") and "anxiety-absent" (e.g., "I feel rested") best fit the data. However, the authors also indicated that one particular item, "I try to avoid facing a crisis or difficulty," should be interpreted with caution, because of low item-remainder correlations. Furthermore, the STAI appears to be less valid for use with Filipino populations, especially Filipino males. In a follow-up study, Hishinuma et al. (2001) examined the STAI as a predictor of anxiety disorders in the Asian/Pacific Islander adolescent population. The authors found that both the STAI-State mean score and the STAI-Trait subfactor using anxiety-present items predicted concurrent and future DSM-III-R anxiety disorders. The implication of the authors' findings is that a subset of STAI items may be used as a brief anxiety screener for Asian American adolescents (Hishinuma et al.).

Other research has attempted to validate a translated version of Spielberger and colleagues' State-Trait Anxiety Inventory for Children (STAIC; Spielberger, Edwards, Lushene, Monturoi, & Platzek, 1973). Using a Hong Kong sample, Li and Lopez (2004a, 2004b) conducted a pair of studies on children aged 7–12 to examine the reliability and validity of a

Chinese-translated version of the STAIC. The STAIC-State demonstrated high internal consistency and high item-total correlations for each item; furthermore, scores were correlated with exposure to stressful situations (Li & Lopez, 2004a). Similarly, the STAIC-Trait demonstrated moderately high internal consistencies and moderately high test-retest reliabilities (Li & Lopez, 2004b).

Additional Considerations in Assessment of Anxiety.   Clinicians should be aware that some behaviors may not be indicative of an anxiety disorder, but instead, should be viewed as part of a religious or cultural practice. For example, many Indian Americans practice Hinduism, which has a number of rituals that can be mistaken for symptoms of obsessive-compulsive disorder. Another area in which clinicians may overpathologize Asian American children and adolescents is in the assessment of social phobia. As mentioned previously, traditional Asian cultures commonly value deference to authority and strict adherence to roles and power hierarchies, including avoidance of sustained eye contact (Viswanathan et al., 1997). As a result, Asian American children and adolescents may have been socialized within their families to respect these more rigid social boundaries and exercise self-restraint in interpersonal contexts. As such, they may appear to lack the assertiveness and extraversion that is valued in Western culture. Indeed, Okazaki, Liu, Longsworth, and Minn (2002) found higher reports of social anxiety on self-report measures for Asian Americans versus White Americans.

Consistent with this, research conducted on the Fear Survey for Children-Revised among Hawaiian children aged 7–16 years (Shore & Rapport, 1998) revealed the presence of an additional social conformity fear subscale for use with Asian American youth. These cultural traits may be exacerbated if the child or adolescent lives (or attends school) in a community with few other Asian Americans. If the child or adolescent were to be observed in another setting with other Asian American peers, he/she might appear to be very assertive and outgoing. Therefore, clinicians should assess the child's or adolescent's behavior across different settings in order to obtain a more accurate assessment.

Another consideration for the assessment of anxiety is that some types of anxiety may be more prevalent among Asian American adolescents than others. For example, test anxiety may be more of an issue for Asian youth, because of the high pressure often placed on adolescents to succeed academically. Many Asian families immigrated to the United States in order to take advantage of educational opportunities. And, as indicated above, the success of children is often perceived as an economic necessity for families in which the parents cannot find sustainable employment, because of language barriers. Furthermore, the cultural value of interdependence among family members often means that academic failure is perceived as bringing shame and disappointment to the entire family (Viswanathan et al., 1997).

Symptom Checklist 90-Revised.   The Symptom-Checklist 90-Revised (SCL–90-R; Derogatis, 1983) is also frequently used to screen for psychopathology. It comprises a number of subscales, including depression, anxiety, and somatization, and provides norms for both normal and clinical populations of adolescents and adults. Although there are no studies that have examined the use of this measure among Asian American adolescents, Takeuchi and colleagues (Takeuchi, Kuo, Kim, & Leaf, 1989) used factor analysis to compare the subscale fit for the original Symptom Checklist–90 (SCL–90; Derogatis, 1977) among Caucasians, Native Hawaiians, Japanese, and Filipino adults in Hawaii. They found that whereas the hypothesized subscales fit the Caucasian populations best, Native Hawaiians demonstrated the worst fit. The authors interpreted their findings to suggest that the traditional interpretation of the SCL–90 subscales may not be appropriate with Asian ethnic populations. In addition, their findings suggested that when assessing depression or anxiety in Asian American populations, clinicians should always assess somatization symptoms (Takeuchi et al., 1989). Unfortunately, there are no available studies of the validity of the revised version of the SCL–90, the SCL–90-R, for use with Asian American adolescents. Therefore, it is unclear whether the U.S. norms and factor structure are valid for this population.

Minnesota Multiphasic Personality Inventory–Adolescent.   Although a growing number of researchers are working toward the development of culturally specific measures of personality and psychopathology that can be used with Asian Americans (e.g., Chinese Personality Assessment Inventory; Cheung et al., 1996), the majority of clinicians use more well-established measures, such as the Minnesota Multiphasic Personality Inventory–Adolescent (MMPI-A). The adult-version MMPI and MMPI–2 have been studied more extensively in Asian countries or with Asian Americans attending U.S. colleges and have been translated into a number of Asian languages (e.g., Hmong, Thai, Japanese, Korean, Chinese). These studies have often been limited by small sample sizes, and a number of articles have not been translated into English (for review, see Okazaki, Kallivayalil, & Sue, 2002). Because there have been no systematic studies of the MMPI-A using Asian American adolescents, it is unclear how generalizable research studies on the MMPI and MMPI–2 are to this younger population. However, research comparing Asian American and Caucasian college students suggests that level of acculturation influences MMPI profiles. For example, although Sue, Keefe, Enomoto, Durvasula, and Chao (1996) found no significant differences in alpha coefficients for scales, they did find that less acculturated Asian Americans had higher scores on several scales than more acculturated Asian American or Caucasian students. It is unclear whether these differences indicate a bias in the measure or accurately reflect cultural differences in symptomatology. Consistent with the findings of Sue and colleagues (1996), Tsai and Pike (2000) found that the Asian American college students who were less acculturated had significantly higher scores on more scales than those Asian Americans who were more acculturated. Furthermore, the highly acculturated Asian Americans had profiles that were similar to the Caucasian students' profiles.

Although Cheung and Song (1989) suggested the joint use of both native and U.S. *T*-score norms, Tsai and Pike simply recommended that clinicians consider responses within the cultural context in order to avoid overpathologizing Asian Americans. They note that specific item endorsements could often be explained by acculturative stress or cultural beliefs. Furthermore, although there were differences between the Asian American and White students on a number of scales, most of the *T*-scores were within the normal limits (Tsai & Pike, 2000).

Projective Assessment.   In comparison with the amount of research that has been conducted on the validity and reliability of objective measures of personality and psychopathology, there has been even less research on projective assessment measures. One criticism of projective assessment measures is that the stimuli can be culturally specific and may not elicit the same reaction in different cultural groups who have different value systems (Gopaul-McNicol & Armour-Thomas, 2002). Dana (1999) made five key suggestions for culturally sensitive picture-story tests, including (1) use culturally recognizable figures that have physical features of that cultural group; (2) use scoring that reflects culturally important characteristics that are independently developed and normed for each cultural group or country; (3) use norms that are stratified by educational level, socioeconomic status, and acculturation level; (4) collaborate with individuals from the cultural group to develop scoring variables; and (5) interpret the data based on culture-specific personality theory and information regarding psychopathology. As mentioned above, the TEMAS meets some of these criteria and has norms for African American, Hispanics, and non-Hispanic whites. However, norms for Asian Americans still do not exist, although Costantino and colleagues are in the process of developing these (Costantino, Tsui, Lee, Flanagan, & Malgady, 1998; cited in Costantino & Malgady, 2000).

In a review of the literature on the Kinetic-Family-Drawing Technique (K-F-D), Cho (1987) found that Taiwanese school children, 10 to 14 years old, were focused more on family ties rather than reflecting individuality, and that the father was depicted as more remote than the mother, who was depicted as the nurturant heart of the family. Similar findings were obtained by Nuttall, Chieh, and Nuttall (1998), where K-F-Ds of Chinese 8–11-year-old children from the People's Republic of China were compared with those of children from the United States. The Chinese drawings reflected the importance of both the nuclear and extended family, whereas the American drawings reflected individualism and independence from their families.

To address the issue of culturally sensitive interpretation of picture-story data, De Vos (1973; cited in Ephraim, 2000) has adapted the scoring of the traditional Thematic Apperception Test (TAT; Murray, 1943) by using a "psychocultural" approach that examines the narratives' content as opposed to their structural features. This scoring system analyzes the respondents' narratives along 10 basic thematic areas that include instrumental concerns (e.g., achievement, cooperation-competition) and expressive concerns (e.g., pleasure, nurturance, harmony). The proponents of the scoring system argue that this practice encourages the development and use of ethnocultural norms (Ephraim, 2000), thus allowing it to be easily adapted to a variety of cultural groups, including Asian Americans. However, to date, there has been limited research examining the validity and reliability of this approach, particularly with children and adolescents. An additional limitation to this approach is the difficulty in training practitioners and the time-consuming application of the scoring method (Dana, 1999). Given the state of research on projective assessments for Asian Americans, caution in their usage is warranted, and, as suggested by Dana (1993), interpretations should be made with consideration of the cultural context.

Native American Children and Adolescents

Intelligence Testing.   Historically, most of the interest in assessing American Indians was directed toward measuring their intelligence. Interest in assessing the intelligence of American Indians can be found in the literature as early as 1922 (Garth, 1921, 1922a,b, 1923). Even given this long history of interest in assessing their intelligence, there has been no discernible progress in developing appropriate norms for existing tests or in the development of culturally sensitive intelligence tests for American Indians. The Wechsler has been used extensively with American Indian children, despite the fact that there are no referenced norms for this group, and despite tribal differences in learning and expression among American Indian children. Dana (1984) reviewed the literature on intelligence testing and concluded that intellectual assessment of American Indian children has utilized tests and assessments that are generally inappropriate for this group, a conclusion made in other reviews of the literature (McShane, 1980). It is not surprising, then, that a disproportionate number of

American Indian youth have been labeled mentally retarded based on the inappropriate use of standardized norm-referenced tests (McShane, 1988). Appropriate norms for American Indians do not exist. The WISC or WISC-R has been used with many different tribal groups, such as the Seminoles (Greene, Kersey, & Prutsman, 1973), Navajos (Mishra, Lord, & Sabers, 1989), Columbia River Basin (McCullough, Walker, & Diessner, 1985), or Papago (Zarske, Moore, & Peterson, 1981). Some researchers, such as McShane and Plas (1982), have developed WISC-R factor structures for Ojibwa children, and others have used the WISC or WISC-R to develop Indian-oriented factor analytic approaches to cognitive processes (Krywaniuk & Das, 1976). Several variables have been found to affect performance, such as reinforcement (Devers, Bradley-Johnson, & Johnson, 1994) or item bias (Mishra, 1982). In general, most studies find significant differences between Verbal and Performance scale tests, with Performance scale scores being one to two standard deviations higher, calling into question the validity of the Full Scale IQ score.

Personality Inventories.   Self-report personality inventories, such as the California Psychological Inventory (CPI) or the MMPI, are used extensively with American Indian populations, but a norm-referenced MMPI for this group does not exist. Several dissertations assessing the validity and reliability of the MMPI in American Indians have recently been published (Fisher, 1998; Smith-Zoeller, 2003), but findings from these dissertations have not appeared in the peer-reviewed literature. Many researchers have studied the utility of the MMPI in several different tribes (Hoffman, Dana, & Bolton, 1985) and have suggested that test bias is minimal (Greene, Robin, Albaugh, Caldwell & Goldman, 2003), whereas others report that the inventory lacks cultural sensitivity and that culture overrides psychopathology (for a review see Dana, 1993; Pollack & Shore, 1980). Dana (1988) suggests caution in using the MMPI with American Indians because minimizing important cultural differences can lead to misinterpretation. Dahlstrom, Lachar, and Dahlstrom (1986) reviewed MMPI patterns of American Indians and concluded that the data were too minimal to make any generalizations. Finally, the CPI has been used in a few studies (Davis, Hoffman, & Nelson, 1990), which have reported a lower profile for American Indians. These profile differences have been attributed primarily to acculturation and role expectations, and the CPI has not been generally recommended for use with American Indians, because of the lack of sufficient norms for this group.

Internalizing and Externalizing Behaviors.   The use of the Child Behavior Checklist (CBCL; Achenbach, 1991) with American Indian children and adolescents is rare. In one study, Ehlers, Wall, Garcia-Andrade, & Phillips (2001) used the existing norms of the CBCL to study American Indian adolescents, and in another study (Wall, Garcia-Andrade, Wong, Lau & Ehlers, 2000), the CBCL was used to study American Indian children of alcoholics. This practice of using existing norms has typically been found to overpathologize the group (Manson, Ackerma, Dick, Baron, & Fleming, 1990). The Center for Epidemiological Studies Depression scale (CES-D; Devins & Orme, 1985) has been widely used with boarding schools for Native American adolescents in five Southwestern tribes (Manson et al., 1990). A factor analysis of the CES-D data resulted in a high false-positive rate. Manson and his colleagues (1990) suggested that caution should be used when the CES-D is employed with American Indian adolescents, because of the wide variation and dimensional structure of the factor analysis, which contributes to ambiguous cutoff rates in the scores. Marsella, Sartorius, Jablensky, & Fenton (1985) suggest that symptom patterns should be evaluated with multivariate techniques and analysis, and that one assessment will not be able to address the multiplicity of issues of internalizing and externalizing behaviors in nondominant cultural groups.

   Projective Assessment.   The most widespread use of projective tests with American Indians has primarily involved using the Rorschach test on American Indian adults. The use of projective techniques with American Indian children has received little attention. As early as 1945, the Rorschach test was widely used in anthropological and psychological studies of adults from different cultural groups, from Moroccans and Samoans, and including American Indians (Abel, 1948; Hallowell, 1945a; Klopfer & Boyer, 1961; Spindler, 1987). Abel (1948) concluded that despite the difficulties in administration, inquiry, and interpretation, this method is a valuable tool in the study of culture. De Vos and Boyer (1989) extended these findings to demonstrate, in their study of Apache Indians, that perceptual organization changes across time, and that alcoholism affects these perceptual changes. Hallowell (1945b) employed the Rorschach with Ojibwa Indians and analyzed the locale, content, and frequency of 3,684 responses from 151 Saulteaux tribe adults and children by comparing their responses with those of White subjects. He discussed the psychological significance of using the Rorschach to study cultural differences between these two groups. One other study (French, 1993) reported on the differences in a multicultural group of Hispanic, Mexican, and American Indian children and found that a combination of two projective tests, the Draw-A-Person/Draw-A-Family and the Thematic Apperception Test, were very useful with this group of children. In a review of the K-F-D test literature, Gregory (1992) tested Native American children from the Potawatomi and Iroquois nations, compared with Caucasian children. Findings reflected the matriarchal family structure of these eastern Native American nations. However, no other conclusions can be made about the use of projective techniques with American Indian children and adolescents, given the scarcity of data reported in the literature.

CLINICAL CASE EXAMPLE: TYRONE

Referral Information and School History

Tyrone is a 16-year-old African American male who was referred for assessment as part of his triennial evaluation for special education eligibility. He was identified as having an Emotional Disturbance in second grade and has received special education services since that time. The primary areas of concern involve Tyrone's behavior when he is frustrated and angry. He is a very sensitive teen who can be very endearing and affectionate, but when frustrated or angry, he becomes highly disruptive, noncompliant, verbally aggressive, and withdrawn. Tyrone was placed into a self-contained classroom during his third- and part of his fourth-grade years. Following an increase in threatening and assaultive behavior, he was hospitalized for one month. Subsequent to his discharge, Tyrone was referred to an Alternative School, where he remained for two years. Following his return to public school, Tyrone was placed primarily in self-contained classrooms during his sixth- and seventh-grade years. During this time Tyrone continued to have behavioral difficulties in school, including intimidation, verbal and physical aggression, and low frustration tolerance. He then returned to the Alternative School for two years. Following improvements in Tyrone's behavior, he returned to a public high school and was placed in mainstream classes, with resource support. He has received special educational resources services since that time.

Family Background

Tyrone currently lives with his mother and younger sister, Stacy (age 10), in Boston. Tyrone's mother works in a Boston hospital medical records department. She suffers from a severe speech impediment, although her ability to understand language and communicate in writing is not impaired. Previous reports indicated that Tyrone has had difficulties coping with his mother's impairment and at times has undermined her efforts as a parent by eliciting support from his maternal grandmother. Tyrone has no contact with his father.

Tyrone's family history is significant for witnessing intense domestic violence, including sexual assault, between his mother and her two husbands, as well as between his maternal grandparents. Also, records indicate that Tyrone placed his younger sister's finger in a pencil sharpener, which necessitated an emergency room visit. In addition, Tyrone was placed in foster care two and a half years ago, after assaulting his mother and committing a sexual offense against a younger male cousin.

Assessment Techniques

The Millon Adolescent Clinical Inventory (MACI), Child Behavior Checklist/4–18 (CBCL/4–18), Child Behavior Checklist-Teacher Report Form (TRF), Child Behavior Checklist-Youth Self-Report (YSR), Racial Identity Attitudes Scale, Interview with Tyrone, and Review of Records were used.

Pretesting Observations and Multicultural Considerations

Tyrone and the examiner (a European American female) met weekly for four weeks, for counseling prior to testing. During the initial session, the examiner and Tyrone discussed his feelings about the testing (especially in relation to how he felt discussing his problem with the assessor). She also had Tyrone complete a Racial Identity Attitudes Scale to assess his stage of racial identity development. According to that measure, Tyrone is in the Encounter stage of racial identity development, indicating in their counseling sessions concerns and uncertainty about the reasons for the testing. He did not initially appear reassured when the reasons for the assessment were discussed. For this reason, testing was delayed until a level of rapport was established, and Tyrone expressed some confidence in the testing process, although he consistently reported that he did not want to "go back to the special school." Also, because of Tyrone's stage of identity development, it was important to view the results of the testing in the context of one who may respond to the materials from a more Eurocentric perspective, rather than from an Afrocentric perspective.

Teacher and Parent Ratings (CBCL/4–18 and TRF)

Both Tyrone's mother and teacher indicated he had clinically significant levels of somatic complaints. High levels of somatization suggest that Tyrone has underlying feelings of anxiety and depression that are manifesting as physical complaints. Items endorsed included "Complains of dizziness," "Complains of pain," and "Complains about health." In addition, the Anxiety subscale and the Internalizing Composite were in the "At-Risk" range. Items endorsed indicative of anxiety include "Expresses self-doubt before tests," "Worries," and "I'm afraid I will make a mistake." The remaining scales were within normal limits.

MACI, YSR, and Clinical Interview

The profile of Tyrone that emerged during testing indicates an intense desire to present himself in a socially desirable manner, as well as a denial of negative thoughts or feelings. Tyrone is not reporting any significant symptoms that are troubling, but one would not expect him to do so, given his high motivation to be seen in a positive light.

This pattern of behavior suggesting Tyrone is motivated to be viewed positively is in stark contrast to those behaviors he has displayed in the past, which have included more overtly aggressive, negative, cruel, and grandiose tendencies, as a way of masking his insecurities. Although negativism and grandiosity continue to be present to a lesser degree, Tyrone has apparently gained more control over his behavior. However, it appears that Tyrone continues to struggle with underlying feelings of anger, anxiety, and low self-esteem, which he now masks through an overly controlled conforming and cooperative demeanor. Tyrone will go to great lengths to maintain his composure, and he has established a fairly rigid and predictable routine to make this possible.

Tyrone tends to avoid engaging in direct confrontations, because they may lead to a loss of control, and thus he will handle conflict in a more passive-aggressive manner, by choosing to minimize or ignore unpleasant events and responding in more indirect ways. In situations where he is highly vulnerable, Tyrone may continue to display angry outbursts. It is more likely, however, that these displays will occur at home, as historically Tyrone's family members have been the recipients of his aggression. In addition, given Tyrone's continued defensiveness and resistance to examining his feelings and past experiences on a deeper level, it is likely that he will continue to endure undercurrents of anxiety and nervousness. These feelings, as is currently the case, will typically manifest as physical complaints, rather than through a more direct presentation of symptoms.

SUMMARY

Tyrone was assessed as part of his triennial evaluation to determine continued eligibility for Special Education. Tyrone's teacher and parental reports indicate Clinically Significant levels of Somatization and At-Risk levels of Anxiety. Tyrone's self-ratings did not produce elevated ratings on any of the clinical scales, but indicated a profile of having an intense desire to be viewed positively. Tyrone appears to have developed an overcontrolled demeanor as a means for masking underlying negative emotions and is likely experiencing regular feelings of nervousness and anxiety.

REFERENCES

Abel, T. M. (1948). The Rorschach test in the study of culture. *Rorschach Research Exchange, 12*, 79–93.

Abueng, F., & Chung, K. (1996). Traumatization stress among Asian and Asian Americans. In A. Marsella, M. Friedman, E. Gerrity, & R. Scurfield (Eds.), *Ethnocultural aspects of posttraumatic stress disorder: Issues, research, and clinical applications* (pp. 285–299). Washington, DC: American Psychological Association.

Achenbach, T. (1991). *Manual for the Child Behavior Checklist/4–18 and 1991 Profile.* Burlington, VT: University of Vermont, Department of Psychiatry.

Alberti, R. (1997). Assessing the reliability and validity of the Bermond-Vorst Alexithymia Questionnaire among U.S. Anglo and U.S. Hispanic samples. *Dissertation Abstracts International Section A: Humanities and Social Sciences, 58*, 1-A, 0091.

Allen, Paula Gunn. (1986). *The sacred hoop: Recovering the Feminine in American Indian tradition.* Boston: Beacon.

American Psychiatric Association. (1994). *Diagnostic and statistical manual of mental disorders* (4th ed.). Washington, DC: Author.

Archer, R. (1987). *Using the MMPI with adolescents.* Hillsdale, NJ: Erlbaum.

Baer, R., & Rinaldo, J. (2004). The Minnesota Multiphaic Personality Inventory-Adolescent (MMPI-A). In M. Hersen (Ed.), *Comprehensive handbook of psychological assessment: Vol. 2. Personality assessment* (pp. 213–223). Hoboken, NJ: John Wiley & Sons.

Ball, J. C. (1960). Comparison of MMPI profile differences among Negro-white adolescents. *Journal of Clinical Psychology, 16*, 304–307.

Barry, D., & Grilo, C. (2002). Eating and body image disturbances in adolescent psychiatric inpatients: Gender and ethnicity patterns. *International Journal of Eating Disorders, 32*(3), 335–343.

Beck, A., Steer, R., & Brown, G. (1996). *BDI-II Manual.* San Antonio, TX: The Psychological Corporation.

Buck, J. (1948). The H-T-P. *Journal of Clinical Psychology, 4*, 151–159.

Burns, R., & Kaufman, S. (1970). *Kinetic Family Drawings (K-F-D): An introduction to understanding children through kinetic drawings.* New York: Brunner/Mazel.

Butcher, J., Williams, C., Graham, J., Archer, R., Tellegen, A., Ben-Porath, Y., et al. (1992). *MMPI-A (Minnesota Multiphasic Personality Inventory-Adolescent): Manual for administration, scoring, and interpretation.* Minneapolis: University of Minnesota Press.

Canino, G., and P. Guarnaccia (1997). Methodological challenges in the assessment of Hispanic children and adolescents. *Applied Developmental Science, 1*, 124–134.

Carey, M., Lubin, B., & Brewer, D. (1992). Measuring dysphoric mood in preadolescents and adolescents: The Youth Depression Adjective Checklist (Y-DACL). *Journal of Clinical Child Psychology, 21*, 331–338.

Carmody, D. (2005). Psychometric characteristics of the Beck Depression Inventory-II with college students of diverse ethnicity. *International Journal of Psychiatry in Clinical Practice, 9*, 22–28.

Castenell, L., & Levitow, J. (1996). Assessing achievement motivation in Black populations: The Castenell Achievement Motivation Scale. In R. Jones (Ed.), *Handbook of achievement motivation* (Vol. 1., pp. 263–268). Hampton, VA: Cobb & Henry.

Cheung, F. M., Leung, K., Fan, R., Song, W., Zhang, J., & Zhang, J. (1996). Development of the Chinese Personality Assessment Inventory. *Journal of Cross-Cultural Psychology, 27*, 181–199.

Cho, M. (1987). *The validity of the Kinetic Family Drawing as a measure of self-concept and parent/child relationship among Chinese children in Taiwan.* Unpublished doctoral dissertation, Andrews University.

Chung, R. C., & Lin, K. (1994). Help-seeking behavior among Southeast Asian refugees. *Journal of Community Psychology, 22*, 109–120.

Clarke, G., Sack, W. H., & Goff, B. (1993). Three forms of stress in Cambodian adolescent refugees. *Journal of Abnormal Child Psychology, 21*, 65–77.

Costantino, G., & Malgady, R. (2000). Multicultural and cross-cultural utility of the TEMAS (Tell-Me-A-Story) Test. In R. H. Dana (Ed.), *Handbook of cross-cultural and multicultural personality assessment* (pp. 481–514). Mahwah, NJ: Lawrence Erlbaum Associates.

Costantino, G., Malgady, R., & Rogler, L. (1988). *Tell-Me-A-Story (TEMAS) manual.* Los Angeles: Western Psychological Services.

Corrales, M., Cabiya, J., Gomez, G., Ayala, G., Mendoza, S., & Velasquez, R. (1998). MMPI-2 and MMPI-A research with U.S. Latinos: A bibliography. *Psychological Reports, 83*, 1027–1033.

Dahlstrom, W. G., Lachar, D., & Dahlstrom, L. E. (1986). *MMPI patterns of American minorities.* Minneapolis: University of Minnesota Press.

Dana, R. H. (1984). Intelligence testing of American Indian children: Sidesteps in quest of ethical practice. *White Cloud Journal, 393*, 35–43.

Dana, R. H. (1988). Culturally diverse groups and MMPI interpretation. *Professional Psychology, 19*(5), 490–495.

Dana, R. H. (1993). *Multicultural assessment perspectives for professional psychology.* Boston, MA: Allyn & Bacon.

Dana, R. H. (1997). Multicultural assessment and cultural identity: An assessment-intervention model. *World Psychology, 3*, 121–141.

Dana, R. H. (1999). Cross-cultural and multicultural use of the Thematic Apperception Test. In L. Gieser & M. Stein (Eds), *Evocative images: The Thematic Apperception Test and the art of projection* (pp. 177–190). Washington, DC: American Psychological Association.

Dauphinais, P. L., & King, J. (1994). Psychological assessment with American Indian children. *Applied & Preventive Psychology, 12*, 97–110.

Davis, G. L., Hoffman, R. G., & Nelson, K. S. (1990). Differences between Native Americans and Whites on the California Psychological Inventory. *Psychological Assessment: A Journal of Consulting and Clinical Psychology, 2*(3), 338–342.

Dennis, W. (1966). *Group values through children's drawings.* New York: Wiley.

Devers, R., Bradley-Johnson, & Johnson. (1994). The effect of token reinforcement on WISC-R performance for fifth- through ninth-grade American Indians. *The Psychological Record, 44*, 441–449.

Devins, G. M., & Orme, C. M. (1985). Center for Epidemiologic Studies Depression Scale. In D. J. Keyser & R. C. Sweetland (Eds.), *Test critiques* (Vol. 2, pp. 144–160). Kansas City, MO: Test Corporation of America.

De Vos, G. A., & Boyer, L. B. (1989). *Symbolic analysis cross-culturally: The Rorschach test.* Berkeley, CA: University of California Press.

Ehlers, C. L., Wall, T. L., Garcia-Andrade, C., & Phillips, E. (2001). Visual P3 findings in Mission Indian youth: relationship to family history of alcohol dependence and behavioral problems. *Psychiatry Research, 105*(1–2), 67–78.

French, L. A. (1993). Adapting projective tests for minority children. *Psychological Reports, 72*, 15–18.

Garth, T. R. (1921). The results of some tests on full and mixed blood Indians. *Journal of Applied Psychology, 5*, 359–372.

Garth, T. R. (1922a). A comparison of mental abilities of mixed and full blood Indians on a basis of education. *Psychological Review, 29*, 221–237.

Garth, T. R. (1922b). The intelligence of Indians. *Science, 56*, 635–636.

Garth, T. R. (1923). A comparison of the intelligence of Mexican and mixed and full blood Indian children. *Psychological Review, 30*, 388–402.

Gee, C. B. (2004). Assessment of anxiety and depression in Asian American youth. *Journal of Clinical Child and Adolescent Psychology, 33*, 269–271.

Gibbs, J. T. (1986). Assessment of depression in urban adolescent females: Implications for early intervention strategies. *American Journal of Social Psychiatry, 6*(1), 50–56.

Gomez, F. C., Jr., Johnson, R., Davis, Q., & Velasquez, R. J. (2000). MMPI—A performance of African and Mexican American adolescent first-time offenders. *Psychological Reports, 87*(1), 309–314.

Gonzales, E. (1982). A cross-cultural comparison of the developmental items of five ethnic groups in the Southwest. *Journal of Personality Assessment, 46*, 26–31.

Greene, H. R., Kersey, H. A., & Prutsman, T. D. (1973). A cross-sectional study of intelligence and achievement in a Seminole Indian reservation school. *Florida Journal of Educational Research, 15*, 37–45.

Greene, R.L. (2000). *The MMPI–2: An interpretive manual* (2nd ed.). Boston: Allyn & Bacon.

Greene, R. L., Robin, R. W., Albaugh, B., Caldwell, A., & Goldman, D. (2003). Use of the MMPI–2 in American Indians: II. Empirical correlates. *Psychological Assessment, 15*(3), 360–369.

Gregory, S. (1992). *A validation and comparative study of Kinetic Family Drawings of Native-American children.* Unpublished doctoral dissertation, Andrews University.

Guba, E. G., & Lincoln, Y. S. (1989). *Fourth generation evaluation.* Newbury Park, CA: Sage.

Gumbiner, J. (1998). MMPI-A profiles of Hispanic adolescents. *Psychological Reports, 82*, 659–672.

Hall, G. C. N., Bansal, A., & Lopez, I. R. (1999). Ethnicity and psychopathology: A meta-analytic review of 31 years of comparative MMPI/MMPI–2 research. *Psychological Assessment, 11*, 186–197.

Hall, G. C. N., & Phung, A. H. (2002). Minnesota Multiphasic Personality Inventory and Millon Clinical

Multiaxial Inventory. In L. A. Suzuki, J. G. Ponterotto, & P. J. Meller (Eds.), *Handbook of multicultural assessment* (2nd ed., pp. 307–330). San Francisco: Jossey-Bass.

Hallowell, A. I. (1945a). The Rorschach technique in the study of personality and culture. *American Anthropologist, 47*, 195–210.

Hallowell, A. I. (1945b). "Popular" responses and cultural differences: An analysis based on   frequencies in a group of American Indian subjects. *Rorschach Research Exchange, 9*, 153–168.

Hammer, E. (1953). Negro and white children's personality adjustment as revealed by a comparison of their drawings (H-T-P). *Journal of Clinical Psychology, 9*, 7–10.

Hathaway, S. R., & McKinley, J. C. (1942). *The Minnesota Multiphasic Personality Schedule.* Minneapolis: University of Minnesota Press.

Helms, J. E. (1990). *Black and White racial identity: Theory, research, and practice.* Westpoint, CT: Praeger.

Helms, J. E., & Parham, T. (1996). The Racial Identity Attitudes Scale. In R. Jones (Ed.), *Handbook of tests and measurements for Black populations* (pp. 167–174). Hampton, VA: Cobb & Henry.

Hirschfelder, A., & Montano, M. (1993). *The Native American almanac.* NJ: Prentice Hall.

Hishinuma, E. S., Miaymoto, R. H., Nishimura, S. T., Goebert, N. Y. C., Makini, G. K., Andrade, N. N., et al. (2001). Prediction of anxiety disorders using the State-Trait Anxiety Inventory for multiethnic adolescents. *Anxiety Disorders, 15*, 511–533.

Hishinuma, E. S., Miyamoto, R. H., Nishimura, S. T., Nahulu, L. B., Andrade, N. N., Makini, G. K., et al. (2000). Psychometric properties of the State-Trait Anxiety Inventory for Asian/Pacific Islander adolescents. *Assessment, 7*, 17–36.

Hoffman, T., Dana, R. H., & Bolton, B. (1985). Measured acculturation and MMPI–168 performance of Native American adults. *Journal of Cross-Cultural Psychology, 16*(2), 243–256.

Huang, L. N. (1994). An integrative approach to clinical assessment and intervention with Asian-American adolescents, *Journal of Clinical Child Psychology, 23*, 21–31.

Hwang, W., Chun, C., Takeuchi, D. T., Myers, H. F., & Siddarth, P. (2005). Age of first onset of major depression in Chinese Americans. *Cultural Diversity and Ethnic Minority Psychology, 11*, 16–27.

Inman, A. G., Constantine, M. G., & Ladany, N. (1999). Cultural value conflict: An examination of Indian women's bicultural experience. In D. S. Sandhu (Ed.), *Asian and Pacific Islander Americans: Issues and concerns for counseling and psychotherapy* (pp. 31–41). Commack, NY: Nova Science.

Iwamasa, G. Y. (1997). Asian Americans. In S. Friedman (Ed.), *Cultural issues in the treatment of anxiety.* New York: Guilford Press.

Jones, R. L. (1996). *Handbook of tests and measurements for Black populations.* Hampton, VA: Cobb & Henry.

Kaestner, E., Rosen, L., and Appel, P. (1977). Patterns of drug abuse: Relationships with ethnicity, sensation seeking, and anxiety. *Journal of Consulting and Clinical Psychology, 45*(3), 462–468.

Kern, D., & Coates, D. L. (1996). The How I Learn and How My Child Learns scales. In R.L. Jones (Ed.), *Handbook of tests and measurements for Black populations* (Vol. 1, pp. 285–296). Hampton, VA: Cobb & Henry.

Klepsch, M., & Logi, L. (1982). *Children draw and tell.* New York: Brunner/Mazel.

Klopfer, B., & Boyer, L. B. (1961). Notes on the personality structure of a North American Indian shaman: Rorschach interpretation. *Journal of Projective Techniques, 25*, 170–178.

Krywaniuk, L. W., & Das, J. P. (1976). Cognitive strategies in Native children: Analysis and intervention. *The Alberta Journal of Educational Research, 22*(4), 34–42.

Lachar, D. (2004). The Personality Inventory for Children, Second Edition (PIC–2), Personality Inventory for Youth (PIY), and Student Behavior Survey (SBS). In M. Hersen (Ed.), *Comprehensive handbook of psychological assessment: Vol. 2. Personality assessment* (pp. 192–212). Hoboken, NJ: John Wiley & Sons.

Lachar, D., & Gruber, C. P. (1995). *Personality Inventory for Youth. Administration and interpretation guide. Technical guide.* Los Angeles: Western Psychological Services.

Lachar, D., & Gruber, C. P. (2001). *Personality Inventory for Children Second Edition (PIC-2) Standard Form and Behavioral Summary manual.* Los Angeles: Western Psychological Services.

LaFromboise, T. D., & Low, K. G. (1997). American Indian children and adolescents. In J. T. Gibbs & L. N.

Huang (Eds.), *Children of color: Psychological interventions with culturally diverse youth* (pp. 112–142). San Francisco, CA: Jossey-Bass.

Lau, A. S., Garland, A. F., Yeh, M., McCabe, K. M., Wood, P. A., & Hough, R. L. (2004). Race/ethnicity and inter-format agreement in assessing adolescent psychopathology. *Journal of Emotional and Behavioral Disorders, 12,* 145–156.

Lee, J., Lei, A., & Sue, S. (2001). The current state of mental health research on Asian Americans, *Journal of Human Behavior in the Social Environment, 3,* 159–178.

Leong, F. T. L., Okazaki, S., & Tak, J. (2003). Assessment of depression and anxiety in East Asia. *Psychological Assessment, 15,* 290–305.

Machover, K. (1949). *Personality projection in the drawing of the human figure.* Springfield, IL: Charles C. Thomas.

Malgady, R. G., Costantino, G., Rogler, L. H. et al. (1984). Development of a Thematic Apperception Test (TEMAS) for urban Hispanic children. *Journal of Consulting and Clinical Psychology, 52,* 986–996.

Manson, S. M., Ackerman, L., Dick, R., Baron, A., & Fleming, C. M. (1990). Depressive symptoms among American Indian adolescents: Psychometric characteristics of the Center for Epidemiologic Studies Depression Scale (CES-D). *Journal of Consulting and Clinical Psychology, 2*(3), 231–237.

Marsella, A. J., Sartorius, N., Jablensky, A., & Fenton, F. R. (1985). Cross-cultural studies of depressive disorders: An overview. In A. Kleinman & B. Good (Eds.), *Culture and depression: Studies in the anthropology and cross-cultural psychology of affect and disorder* (pp. 299–324). Berkeley: University of California Press.

Matto, H., & Naglieri, J. (2005). Race and ethnic differences and human figure drawings: Clinical utility of the DAP: SPED. *Journal of Clinical Child and Adolescent Psychology, 34,* 706–711.

McCullough, C. S., Walker, J. L., & Diessner, R. (1985). The use of Wechsler Scales in the assessment of Native Americans of the Columbia River Basin. *Psychology in the Schools, 23,* 23–31.

McDonald, R. L., & Gynther, M. D. (1962). MMPI norms for southern adolescent Negros. *Journal of Social Psychology, 58,* 277–282.

McNight-Taylor, M. (1974). *Perceptions of relationships in low income Black families.* Unpublished doctoral dissertation, University of Virginia.

McShane, D. A. (1980). A review of scores of American Indian children on the Wechsler Intelligence Scales. *White Cloud Journal, 1*(4), 3–10.

McShane, D. A. (1988). An analysis of mental health research with American Indian youth. *Journal of Adolescents, 11,* 87–116.

McShane, D. A., & Plas, J. M. (1982a). WISC-R factor structures of Ojibwa Indian children. *White Cloud Journal, 2*(4), 18–22.

McShane, D. A., & Plas, J. M. (1982b). Wechsler scale performance patterns of American Indian children. *Psychology in the Schools, 19*(1), 23–34.

Mendoza-Newman, M. C. (2000). Level of acculturation, socioeconomic status, and the MMPI-A performance of a non-clinical Hispanic adolescent sample. *Dissertation Abstracts International: Section B: The Sciences and Engineering, 60,* 9-B, 4897.

Millon, T. (1993). *Millon Adolescent Clinical Inventory manual.* Minneapolis, MN: National Computer Systems.

Millon, T., & Davis, R. D. (1996). *Disorders of personality: DSM-IV and beyond.* New York: Guilford Press.

Mishra, S. P. (1982a). The WISC-R and evidence of item bias for Native American Navajos. *Psychology in the Schools, 19,* 458–464.

Mishra, S. P. (1982b). Reliability and predictive validity of the WISC-R with Native-American Navajos. *Journal of School Psychology, 20*(2), 150–154.

Mishra, S. P., Lord, J., & Sabers, D. L. (1989). Cognitive processes underlying WISC-R performance of gifted and learning disabled Navajos. *Psychology in the Schools, 26,* 31–36.

Morgan, C., & Murray, H. (1935). A method for investigating fantasies: The thematic Apperception Test. *Archives of Neurological Psychiatry, 34,* 289–306.

Morris, E. F. (2000). Assessment practices with African Americans: Combining standard assessment measures within an Africentric orientation. In R. H. Dana (Ed.), *Handbook of cross-cultural and multicultural personality assessment* (pp. 573–604). Mahwah, NJ: Lawrence Erlbaum Associates.

Negy, C., Leal-Puente, L., Trainor, D. J., & Carlson, R. (1997). Mexican American adolescents' performance on the MMPI-A. *Journal of Personality Assessment, 69*(1), 205–214.

Nuttall, E., Chieh, L., & Nuttall, R. (1998). Views of the family by Chinese and U.S. children: A comparative study of Kinetic Family drawings. *Journal of School Psychology, 26,* 191–194.

Okazaki, S., Kallivayalil, D., & Sue, S. (2002). Clinical personality assessment with Asian Americans. In J. N. Butcher (Ed.), *Clinical personality assessment* (2nd ed., pp. 135–153). New York: Oxford University Press.

Okazaki, S., Liu, J. F., Longsworth, S. L., & Minn, J. Y. (2002). Asian American-White American differences in expressions of social anxiety: A replication and extension. *Cultural diversity and Ethnic Minority Psychology, 8,* 234–247.

Ozick, C. (1986). The moral necessity of metaphor. *Harper's Magazine (May),* 64–65.

Patton, M. (1990). *Qualitative evaluation and research methods: 2nd edition.* Newbury Park, CA: Sage.

Pollack, D., & Shore, J. H. (1980). Validity of the MMPI with Native Americans. *American Journal of Psychiatry, 137*(8), 946–950.

Radloff, L. (1977). The CES-D scale: A self-report depression scale for research in the general population. *Applied Psychological Measurement, 1,* 385–401.

Ridley, C. R., Li, L. C., & Hill, C. L. (1998). Multicultural assessment: Reexamination, reconceptualization, and practical application. *The Counseling Psychologist, 26,* 827–910.

Ritzler, B. (2004). Cultural applications of the Rorschach, apperception tests, and figure drawings. In M. Hersen (Ed.), *Comprehensive handbook of psychological assessment: Vol. 2. Personality assessment* (pp. 573–585). Hoboken, NJ: John Wiley & Sons.

Robin, R. W., Greene, R. L., Albaugh, B., Caldwell, A., & Goldman, D. (2003). Use of the MMPI–2 between two tribes and with the MMPI–2 normative group. *Psychological Assessment, 15*(3), 351–359.

Rotherham-Borus, M. J., Piacentini, K., Van-Rossem, R., & Graae, F (1996). Enhancing treatment adherence with a specialized emergency room program for adolescent suicide attempters. *Journal of the American Academy of Child and Adolescent Psychiatry, 35,* 654–663.

Ryan-Arredondo, K. (2002). An evaluation of internal bias as a function of Hispanic status on the Minnesota Multiphasic Personality Inventory-Adolescent Lie Scale. *Dissertation Abstracts International Section A: Humanities and Social Sciences, 63*(4-A), 1258.

Sanchez Rosado, K. A. (2002). Levels of acculturation of children of Mexican descent as perceived in their kinetic family drawings. *Dissertation Abstracts International Section A: Humanities and Social Sciences, 62*(7-A), 2596.

Scott, R. L., Butcher, J. N., Young, T. L., & Gomez, N. (2002). The Hispanic MMPI-A across five countries. *Journal of Clinical Psychology, 58*(4), 407–417

Shek, D. T. L. (1990). Reliability and factorial structure of the Chinese version of the Beck Depression Inventory. *Journal of Clinical Psychology, 46,* 35–43.

Shore, G. N., & Rapport, M. D. (1998). The Fear Survey Schedule for Children-Revised (FSSC-HI): Ethnocultural variations in children's fearfulness. *Journal of Anxiety Disorders, 12,* 437–461.

Smith-Zoeller, M. A. (2003). MMPI–2 subscale 8 responses and Native American traditional worldview: Is there a relationship? *Dissertation Abstracts International: Section B: The Sciences and Engineering, 63*(8-B), 3939.

Spindler, G. (1987). Joe Nepah: A "schizophrenic" Menominee peyotist. *Journal of Psychoanalytic Anthropology, 10,* 1–16.

Stefurak, T., Calhoun, G. B., & Glaser, B. A. (2004). Personality typologies of male juvenile offenders using a cluster analysis of the Millon Adolescent Clinical Inventory. *International Journal of Offender Therapy and Comparative Criminology, 48,* 96–110.

Stevenson, Jr., H. C. (1996). Development of the Scale of Racial Socialization for African American adolescents. In R. L. Jones (Ed.), *Handbook of achievement motivation* (Vol. 1, pp. 309–326). Hampton, VA: Cobb & Henry.

Strack, S. (1999). *Essentials of Millon inventories assessment.* New York: Wiley.

Sue, D., & Sue, S. (1987). Cultural factors in the clinical assessment of Asian Americans. *Journal of Consulting and Clinical Psychology, 55*, 479–487.

Sue, S., Keefe, K., Enomoto, K., Durvasula, R., & Chao, R (1996). Asian American and White college students' performance on the MMPI–2. In J. N. Butcher (Ed.), *International adaptations of the MMPI–2* (pp. 206–220). Minneapolis: University of Minnesota Press.

Sung, H., Lubin, B., & Yi, J. (1992). Reliability and validity of the Korean Youth Depression Adjective Checklist (T-DACL). *Adolescence, 27*, 527–533.

Suzuki, L. A., Short, E. L., Pieterse, A., & Kugler, J. (2002). Ability testing across cultures. In L. A. Suzuki, J. G. Ponterotto, & P. J. Meller (Eds.), *Handbook of multicultural assessment* (2nd ed., pp. 359–382). San Francisco: Jossey-Bass.

Timbook, R. E., & Graham, J. R. (1994). Ethnic differences on the MMPI–2? *Psychological Assessment, 6*, 212–217.

Tobin, J. J., & Friedman, J. (1984). Intercultural and developmental stresses confronting Southeast Asian refugee adolescents. *Journal of Operational Psychiatry, 15*, 39–45.

Trimble, J. E. (1991). Ethnic specification, validation prospects, and the future of drug use research. *The International Journal of the Addictions, 25*(2A), 149–170.

Tsai, D. C., & Pike, P. L. (2000). The effects of acculturation on the MMPI–2 scores of Asian American students. *Journal of Personality Assessment, 74*, 216–230.

Vandiver, B. J., Cross, W. E. Jr., Fhagen-Smith, P. E., Worrell, F. C., Swim, J., & Caldwell, L. (2000). *The Cross Racial Identity Scale.* Unpublished scale.

Velasquez, R. J., Maness, P. J., and Anderson, U. (2002). Culturally competent assessment of Latino clients: The MMPI–2. In James N. Butcher (Ed), *Clinical personality assessment: Practical approaches* (2nd ed., pp. 154–170). London: Oxford University Press.

Viswanathan, R., Shah, M. R., & Ahad, A. (1997). Asian-Indian Americans. In S. Friedman (Ed.), *Cultural issues in the treatment of anxiety*. New York: Guilford Press.

Wolf, R., & Tymitz, B. (1976–1977). Ethnography and reading: Matching inquiry mode to process. *Reading Research Quarterly, 12*, 5–11.

Young, K. I. (1998). *Objective and projective measures: Assessment of depression in adolescents: A convergent validity study.* Unpublished dissertation.

Youngstrom, E., Loeber, R., & Strouthamer-Loeber, M. (2000). Patterns and correlates of agreement between parent, teacher, and male adolescent ratings of externalizing and internalizing problems. *Journal of Consulting and Clinical Psychology, 68*, 1038–1050.

Zarske, J. A., Moore, C. L., & Peterson, J. D. (1981). WISC-R factor structures for diagnosed learning disabled Navajo and Papago children. *Psychology in the Schools, 18*, 402–407.

Zheng, Y., & Lin, K. M. (1991). Comparison of the Chinese Depression Inventory and the Chinese version of the Beck Depression Inventory. *Acta Psychiatrica Scandinavica, 84*, 531–536.

31

HEARING THE SILENT NEED: ASSESSING CHILDREN WHO HAVE A PARENT WITH A SERIOUS MENTAL ILLNESS

Harry J. Sivec
Case Western Reserve University School of Medicine

Charles A. Waehler
The University of Akron

Patricia J. Masterson
Case Western Reserve University School of Medicine

Beth L. Pearson
Case Western Reserve University

Some children do not invite their friends over after school because they are afraid of what their father might say or do. Others wake up during the night and find their mother crying inconsolably with her arms cut and bloody. A youngster can witness her father barricading himself in his room for hours or days while carrying on about unauthorized surveillance that he "knows" is going on. A teenage son may show up at his high school football game exhausted from having to run the four miles to school because his mother is having an "episode" or has one of her doctor's appointments and was not able to transport him to his game.

These are some of the scenarios faced by children who have a parent[1] with a serious mental illness (SMI). These children are at risk; they are at increased genetic risk of inherit-

---

1. Although the authors use the term "parent" in this chapter to refer to an adult who provides a significant caregiving role with a child or adolescent, we recognize that this role is sometimes performed by a person who is not the biological parent or legal parent of a minor (e.g., step-parent, uncle, aunt, grandparent, older sibling). Similarly, many of the issues presented in this chapter relate to concerns that develop when family members other than the parent or primary caregiver (e.g., older sibling, grandparent) have a mental illness.

ing a debilitating mental illness compared with their peers, and they are also more likely than their peers to experience adjustment and relationship problems (Feldman, Stiffman, & Jung, 1987; Gotlib, & Goodman, 1999). Despite the well-known risk factors, the needs of these children often go unheard by even the best-intentioned clinicians. There is often minimal opportunity for assessment (DeChillo, Matorin, & Hallahan, 1987), let alone interventions, until these children begin to manifest their own problems.

The chronic impact of living with a parent with mental illness is well documented (cf. Johnson, 1988; Marsh, 1998). Studies involving the adult children of parents with SMI are rife with examples of the chronic difficulties associated with growing up in these families. Perhaps most common is a pervasive sense of loss and grief, accompanied by chronic sorrow (Marsh, 1998). Many adults who had a parent with a mental illness feel they missed significant parts of their childhood, that they were forced to grow up too early, and that they learned to ignore their own needs. These individuals may also be strongly motivated to "not be like my parent" to the extent that they may neglect their own emotional needs for help and support.

Anywhere between 20% and 57% of individuals with SMI have a minor child in their life (Ostman & Hansson, 2002). However, few health-care systems routinely attempt to determine whether children are present in the home of someone with SMI (DeChillo et. al., 1987). Nicholson, Geller, Fisher, & Dion (1993) indicated that only 16 state mental health authorities routinely collect information pertaining to the parental status of the women in their care. In general, children of the mentally ill tend to be overlooked during the course of their parents' mental illness. These children are challenged because their struggles and needs are great but are too often unheard. When they are referred for attention it is usually because their own emotional or behavior problems have led them to be noticed. Evaluation and intervention services provided to this vulnerable population could address both prevention and intervention functions for families grappling with chronic mental illness in a family member.

Along these lines, there are two ways in which a clinician is most likely to encounter children with a mentally ill parent. One occurs when a clinician is working with a client diagnosed with serious mental illness and learns during the course of intake or treatment that the client has a child. This is probably the most common scenario in inpatient psychiatric units. For many clinicians, this information would barely scratch the surface of an assessment formulation unless evidence of abuse or neglect was suspected, and, in which case, the involvement of a Children's Service agency would be mandated.

The second way in which a clinician is most likely to encounter a child with a mentally ill parent is when the child is referred with her/his own problems being experienced at home and/or school. During an evaluation, the clinician determines that the client has a parent who is diagnosed with a serious mental illness. Although the clinical appraisal will likely include an array of assessments regarding the client and the family, unless the parent's mental illness is identified as a source of immediate concern, little else may be addressed regarding the impact of the parent's illness on the child. In general, identifying a parent or sibling with a mental illness would signal a "risk factor," and the clinician may wonder about the level of chaos or inattention at home, but it usually remains the child's responsibility to voice this concern as a major issue if it is to be addressed.

Noting that a parent has or had a serious mental illness during a child's developmental years should send out a loud call to the sensitive clinician. A conscientious assessor will appreciate that there may be both acute and chronic effects as sequelae to SMI. Three studies directly assessed the immediate impact of a psychiatric emergency/hospitalization on children. Shachnow (1987) was perhaps the first to systematically assess the short-term impact of a parent's psychiatric hospitalization on children in the home. She interviewed patients, their children, and available spouses during the course of hospitalization. The results indicated that most of the children in this study did not have an adult to help them talk about or understand the circumstances of their parent's illness. Most of the children in this study were described as having a strong emotional response to their parent's illness. Some children were overtly symptomatic (labeled "Compromised" 22%), whereas others appeared to cope reasonably well ("Copers" 19%). Features of compromised adjustment for younger children (under 12) included sleep disturbance, diminished appetite, increased clinging behavior, crying near bedtime, and social withdrawal. Older children (12 and older) also experienced sleep disturbance, a decline in school performance, and social withdrawal. It is of note that, unless inquired into directly, these are the kinds of symptoms that can "fly under the radar" of even the most sensitive parent and astute assessor.

In a similar study, Castleberry (1988) interviewed families and their children, ages 12 and under, every 7–10 days during the parent's hospitalization. In contrast to the work by Shachnow (1987), this study did not find major problems in school performance, eating, and play activities, or in the children's relationships with other children. However, bedtime routines were altered, and children tended to ask more questions and seek reassurance at these times. Of particular note, the hospital in this study was described as offering a family-friendly milieu in which the children visited their parent almost every weekend, on the unit, and often shared meals with the parent. In addition, most children remained in their own home, under the care of a non-hospitalized family member. This study helps identify areas important to address in a thorough evaluation (e.g., How often does this child visit with her/his parent, and for how long? Are those visits child-centered or illness-focused?).

In research conducted at the Northcoast Behavioral Healthcare hospital in Cleveland, Ohio, where an intervention program focuses on education and support services for children whose parents are hospitalized in a psychiatric facility (BART's Place; see Katz, Gintoli, & Buckley, 2001), children ($N = 49$) were interviewed and administered standardized, psychological tests of anxiety (MASC: Multidimensional Anxiety Scale for Children; March, 1997) and depression (CDI: Children Depression Inventory; Kovacs, 1992). The parents in this study were hospitalized in a state psychiatric facility for an acute crisis or because they were referred for Restoration to Competency intervention by the courts. Mean composite scores for depression and anxiety fell within the normative range for the entire sample (Sivec, Masterson, Katz, & Russ, 2003). As such, most children appeared to be free of major psychological symptoms measured by the MASC and CDI at the time of hospitalization of the parent. Even so, several children (40%) in this study demonstrated significant signs of anxiety. For example, some endorsed concerns about making sure things are safe and that they have not done anything wrong (i.e., elevated Anxious Coping Scale; March, 1997). Other children in this study indicated they were frightened when alone or in unfamiliar places and that they preferred to stay close to family members (i.e., elevated Separation/Panic Scale; March, 1997). These findings are consistent with the depiction of children of mentally ill parents who are motivated to minimize the potential for harm (see Marsh, 1998). These results also argue for assessment strategies that address specific target behaviors, in addition to overall client functioning.

Other studies have also documented the broad range of social and adjustment problems that can occur when a child lives with a parent who has a mental illness. Downey and Coyne (1990) reported that school-aged children of depressed parents are more likely to show higher levels of internalizing and externalizing symptoms than children of parents without a mental illness. Feldman et al. (1987) reported that more than half of the children in their study identified as "at risk" by virtue of having a parent with mental illness obtained scores on the Child Behavior Checklist (CBCL) suggestive of emotional and/or behavior problems. Similarly, Gotlib and Goodman (1999) reported that two-thirds of children of depressed mothers scored in the clinical range on the CBCL.

In some studies, researchers have asked patients, parents, and other caregivers about the need for services for children who have a mentally ill parent. Wang and Goldschmidt (1996) reported that 34% of the psychiatric inpatients in their study indicated that their children could benefit from additional help. In the same study, a global assessment of the child's situation (e.g., psychiatric status of parent, home/support network of child, etc.) was determined for each child. The investigators found cause for "great child psychiatric concern" for 37% of the children. In another study (Ostman & Hansson, 2002), spouses of mentally ill patients were interviewed regarding the needs of their children. About half (55%) of spouses in this study indicated their children had further need for support. Overall, many children show significant concerns and/or symptoms when a parent is hospitalized with a SMI. Although not all children appear to be compromised by the experience, assessors need to recognize that many child concerns can manifest as subtle and indirect characteristics. The concerns appear to be mainly anxiety related (MASC scores, reports of anxiety, sleep disruption), but other problems are also often present (e.g., depression, acting out).

GENERAL ASSESSMENT FRAMEWORK

Reviewing the studies in the preceding section should help to amplify the issue of listening carefully to the whole patient system when a psychologist is assessing a child who has a parent with SMI. Importantly, given the two ways a clinician is most likely to encounter children with a mentally ill parent—indirectly by working with a client diagnosed with SMI and learning that she/he has a child, or directly when the child is referred with her/his own problems—neither the parent nor the child should be viewed in isolation. The child's presentation must be heard and understood in the context of the parent's illness.

Attending to the child's developmental level and needs as these have been affected by the parent's illness is essential. Issues of gender, cultural norms, and additional social support are individual difference factors that also need to be heeded. For instance, a mother's two-month hospitalization for depression may have quite a different impact on her 3-year-old daughter compared with her 15-year-old son. Many assessors rely on internal norms and then draw upon additional resources (e.g., models proposed by Erickson, Freud, and Piaget) to understand age ranges associated with the development of certain skills and aptitudes. These practitioners can then better appreciate what developmental tasks may have been compromised or neglected by the presence of SMI in the family. Recognizing the challenges within this specific family system, and for this particular child, is paramount.

In preparing to assess the needs of a child dealing with a mentally ill family member, it is helpful for clinicians to have a number of different clinical "amplifiers" to stay attuned to the particular melodies, harmonies, and discords present. We have found it helpful to frame the assessment in terms of understanding the interactions among three different cycles of development: individual (child), family, and the course of illness itself (see Rolland, 1988, 1994; and Marsh, 1998, for specific application to mental illness). Although clinicians are accustomed to hearing their clients on multiple levels (e.g., developmental, family system, and a comprehensive psychological test battery), we hope to enhance the assessment process with the addition of two important elements: a "hearing aid" that tunes the clinician into the specific impact that a parent's mental illness may have on children in both the short term and over time, and a "microphone" to amplify attention to assessing resilient coping processes.

FIRST-LINE AND COMPREHENSIVE ASSESSMENT APPROACHES

It is important to capture the magnitude of distress experienced by children whose parent has a mental illness and the ways in which this distress is likely to be expressed. The available research has focused on the reactions of children whose parent was hospitalized at the time of the evaluation. These research data point to signs of anxiety/distress and possible adjustment problems. Because any single approach can be flawed and incomplete, we recommend a comprehensive evaluation strategy that incorporates child self-report, observations from caregivers, and performance measures.

Of course, a good interview that develops rapport and a connection with a child is indispensable and is the cornerstone of any evaluation. Another way for children to give voice to their concerns is via standardized, self-report measures. Along these lines, brief, psychometrically sound measures of distress are appropriate. For example, the Multidimensional Anxiety Scale for Children (MASC; March, 1997) contains 39 self-report items that are separated into four major scales: Physical Symptoms, Harm Avoidance, Social Anxiety, and Separation/Panic. A Total Anxiety score may also be computed. The MASC is widely used and has demonstrated satisfactory test-retest reliability, internal consistency, and factorial and discriminant validity (ages 8–19; March, 1997).

Another commonly used measure is the 27-item Children's Depression Inventory (CDI; Kovacs, 1992). This self-rated depression scale is suitable for young children and adolescents (ages 7–17). The test is brief, is easily scored, is frequently used by clinicians, and has demonstrated good test-retest reliability, internal consistency, and construct validity (see Kovacs, 1992; Sitarenios & Kovacs, 1999). The CDI provides a total score and five subscales reflecting various aspects of depression: Negative Mood, Interpersonal Problems, Ineffectiveness, Anhedonia, and Negative Self-esteem.

In our research work, we have found the use of the MASC to be more sensitive to reactions in children who have a parent with mental illness relative to the CDI (Sivec et al., 2003). For more in-depth, self-report evaluation with older children and adolescents, the clinician may consider the Personality Inventory for Youth (PIY; Lachar, & Gruber, 1995) or the Minnesota Multiphasic Personality Inventory-Adolescent (MMPI-A; Butcher et al., 1992). These measures are well validated but also require more time on the part of the examinee. In addition, if the initial assessment data point to a major diagnosis, the clinician may consider a structured diagnostic interview (e.g., the Schedule for Affective Disorders and Schizophrenia for School-Age Children: Present and Lifetime Version or K-SADS-PL; Kaufman et al., 1997).

Although self-report tests can be useful, low scores obtained on standardized tests may reflect a defensiveness or unwillingness to divulge symptoms (see Joiner, Schmidt, & Schmidt, 1996). Along these lines, children of mentally ill parents who were later interviewed as adults indicated that they were generally unaware of the impact of the trauma or their unmet needs until they were older (Marsh, 1998). They report that, as children, they felt they must be "good," healthy, and strong because the family already had many problems.

To the extent that children may be generally motivated to minimize their own concerns, other assessment approaches are recommended. One approach is to obtain objective information that reflects the observations of a caregiver. In this regard, the Child Behavior

Checklist/4–18 (CBCL; Achenbach, 1991) is a widely used measure of symptoms and adjustment. Furthermore, this measure has been used specifically with children of parents with mental illness (see Downey & Coyne, 1990; Feldman et al., 1987; Gotlib & Goodman, 1999). This assessment tool can help to provide information about social competence; the seven areas rated include such things as activities and social and school competencies. Problem behaviors are measured by caregiver ratings of 118 items. These ratings are summarized by way of two broadband factors (internalizing/externalizing dimensions) and seven narrowband syndromes (i.e., Withdrawn, Somatic, Anxious/Depressed, Social, Thought, Attention, Delinquent, and Aggressive) and an overall, total problems score (see Achenbach, 1991). It is important to identify a caregiver who knows the child sufficiently so that accurate observations can be obtained. Although no distinct pattern of impact has been identified for children of parents with SMI in the research literature, available studies consistently point to higher levels of problems, compared with children who do not have a parent with mental illness (see Downey & Coyne, 1990; Feldman et al., 1987; Gotlib & Goodman, 1999).

Adult observations are useful, but they have limitations. For instance, observations about the child in question may be distorted by an overwhelmed parent or may be based upon limited observations of an adult who steps in to care for the child. Therefore, it may be more important to undertake performance-based measures by which direct behavioral observations of the child can be made. Two relatively commonly used, quick, and adaptable assessment approaches are the Hand Test (Bricklin, Piotrowski & Wagner, 1962; see also, Sivec, Waehler, & Panek, 2004) and Graphic Techniques (e.g., Draw-A-Person [DAP], House-Tree-Person [HTP], and Kinetic Family Drawing [KFD]; Handler, Campbell, & Martin, 2004).

With its relatively unstructured, somewhat disguised, and ambiguous stimuli (10 cards with drawings of hands on them about which clients are asked, "What might this hand be doing?"), the Hand Test invites an unlimited number of free and qualitatively different responses (Sivec, Waehler, & Panek, 2004). In this way, a premium is placed on generating subjective, idiosyncratic responses, which are subjected to specific scoring criteria meant to assess prototypical attitude and action tendencies of the child. The Hand Test administration is typically brief (about 10 minutes) and is meant to supplement other clinical observations and response material in a test battery (see the chapter by Clemence in this text).

Two Hand Test variables are particularly relevant for this group. The Hand Test Acting-Out Score has consistently identified acting-out potential in children across a number of studies (e.g., Clemence, Hilsenroth, Sivec, Rasch, & Waehler 1998; Clemence, Hilsenroth, Sivec, & Rasch, 1999; see Sivec & Hilsenroth, 1994, for a review). Likewise, the Hand Test Pathology score has been linked to social/emotional maladjustment and acting-out behavior and used as a marker of psychopathology in a number of studies with children (Sivec et al., 2004). A third variable, FEAR, has been found in samples of individuals exposed to abuse and threats (Rasch & Wagner, 1989) and may also provide useful clinical information for this population. In these ways, the Hand Test may help a child express through indirect responses useful information regarding the degree of distress and maladjustment she or he is experiencing.

Graphic techniques also invite the child to engage in a specific behavioral activity that can provide insight into her or his personal functioning. Graphic techniques have their critics (cf. Joiner, Schmidt, & Barnett, 1996), but these performance-based measures can supplement other assessment methods in a test battery (Handler, Campbell, & Martin, 2004). Graphic techniques have the advantage of limiting cultural bias, while also being simple and quick to administer, easy for most children to produce, and useful with clients who are evasive or guarded (Waehler, 1997). They can also offer a natural bridge for discussing specific conflict areas, because, as Reithmiller and Handler (1997) suggest, drawings allow clients to express themselves in intensely personal ways. The content of drawings can also provide a medium for discussing difficult topics in a way that also affords some safe emotional distance. Drawings such as the Kinetic Family Drawing (K-F-D) have also been linked with attachment issues (Pianta, Longmaid, & Ferguson, 1999), which may be relevant for this population.

Rorschach and TAT

For a more in-depth evaluation using performance-based measures, clinicians may also use the Rorschach Inkblot Test and/or the Thematic Apperception Test (TAT; Murray, 1943). As with other measures, the Rorschach Inkblot Test can be used to identify personality strengths and signs of psychopathology (Exner & Weiner, 1995). Both the Rorschach and TAT also offer methods for exploring interpersonal themes and dynamics. For example, Urist's (1977) Mutuality of Autonomy Scale (MOAS) measures a range of adaptive to more pathological object representations (Tuber, 1992). In research with children/adolescents, the MOAS has been shown to be sensitive to changes associated with an acute crisis (Tuber, Frank, & Santostefano, 1989) and to distinguish between clinical and control groups (see Kelly, 2004, for a review). Also relevant for the children described in this section, Tuber (1992) reported that the MOAS appears to have specific relevance for difficulties with separation (see also Goddard & Tuber, 1989). Regarding the TAT, Westen (1995) has developed a method (SCORS) for assessing social-cognitive and affective processes that are considered theoretically important to understanding a person's capacity for relatedness to others. The SCORS has also been used with children/adolescents in clinical situations (see Kelly, 2004, for a review) and shown to be sensitive to developmental changes (Westen et al., 1991). Children whose parents have a mental illness may be particularly vulnerable to disruptions in the ways that they view and experience relationships. In this regard, both the Rorschach and TAT offer theory-based and empirically tested methods for assessing these issues.

Assessing Resilient Processes/Coping

As we have reviewed, having a parent or family member with mental illness can lead to a plethora of negative outcomes for children. Despite this, some children are able to survive and thrive, despite their parent's mental illness (Anthony & Cohler, 1987). These children can be characterized as resilient, because resiliency refers to a positive outcome, despite adverse circumstances (Masten & Coatsworth, 1998). Understanding what processes lead to resiliency in children of mentally ill parents can inform interventions designed to help this special population. Furthermore, it is important to look for resilient coping processes in children with an SMI parent in order to counterbalance the all too common tendency to look for deficits (i.e., confirmation bias) in cases that involve high-risk background variables.

Seifer (2003) proposes a model of resilience processes in young children that includes child characteristics (e.g., positive emotions, physiology, secure attachment), as well as the contextual variables of the family (e.g., economic resources, social supports, few risks) and parent characteristics (e.g., positive thoughts, positive feelings, and self-efficacy). Following along with this model, practitioners' assessment efforts with children of the mentally ill must "hear" the child within his or her developmental context. Recognizing how developmental needs have been interrupted, delayed, neglected, changed, or ignored because of the presence of mental illness in the family is critical to understanding how all family members (and their relations with one another) are being affected.

Take, for example, the situation of a 14-year-old girl whose father is hospitalized at mid-life for a major depressive disorder with psychotic features. She had seen some of the symptoms developing as her father became more and more withdrawn, depressed, and angry. She is too young to visit her father in the hospital, and no one discusses the reality of mental illness with her. She does not need to be told verbally to "Keep this to yourself because we don't want other people to know." She does this automatically by having this behavior modeled for her. The girl is confused and afraid of what might happen to her family. She doesn't want to add more stress to her mother's life by asking questions, so she learns to deny her feelings and channels all of her energy into schoolwork. She becomes the proverbial "good girl" who is afraid to further burden her family with her worries. She is resilient and may not manifest overt symptoms immediately, but her normal developmental tasks of socialization and dating are disrupted, and her family role mutates into being mother's personal helper and confidant in her father's absence. This pattern reflects a common coping strategy for children with mentally ill parents. That is, the child ignores/avoids the issues and/or attempts to reduce stress in the family by taking on more caregiving behaviors (Riebschleger, 2004).

There are many personality characteristics that make resiliency more likely in children. These include intelligence, social skills, problem-solving ability, self-esteem, and self-efficacy (Garmezy, 1981; Rutter, 1987). Assessing these positive characteristics, which might normally go unheard because of the "noise" made by dramatic presenting of clinical concerns, becomes important to making realistic case determinations and recommending interventions.

One area that can be assessed somewhat easily is intelligence. This variable is associated with adjustment and is likely to be related to coping skill development. Although a comprehensive evaluation of intellectual abilities is likely to be too cumbersome, there are brief measures of intelligence available. For example, both the Wechsler Abbreviated Scale of Intelligence (WASI, Psychological Corporation, 1999) and the Kaufman Brief Intelligence Test (K-BIT, Kaufman & Kaufman, 1990) have solid standardization samples/norms and many studies documenting acceptable psychometric properties.

Although some characteristics associated with resilience (e.g. physiology, intelligence) are not easily changed, a child's repertoire of coping strategies is one area that is modifiable. Existing coping strategies can be assessed to reinforce current strategies and to identify other skills to be learned.

Assessing Coping Skills

When we refer to coping we are drawing on Lazarus and Folkman's (1984) definition of "constantly changing cognitive and behavioral efforts to manage specific external and/or internal demands that are appraised as taxing or exceeding the resources of the person" (p. 141). This definition indicates that stress is a subjective experience (e.g., the individual *appraises* the situation as exceeding her resources; the situation is not inherently, objectively stressful). Lazarus and Folkman also make it clear that coping efforts "constantly change." Therefore, when a child's coping strategies are being assessed, it is important to look at many aspects of the situation in order to determine the child's full range of coping abilities and areas needing improvement.

Considering that a situation is stressful based on how it is appraised necessitates determining which aspects of the mental illness a child finds stressful. For example, if you ask, "How did you deal (cope) with things when your mother was taken to the hospital?" children may answer in a variety of surprising ways. A 7-year-old boy may respond by telling what he did to manage his emotions when he was first told his mother was leaving (went and played with toys), or he might say that he was happy to be able to watch all the television he wanted. A 13-year-old girl may remark that a few days after her mother left, she got help from her cousin with her homework because her mother wasn't available to help as usual, or that she was glad that no one was bugging her about her homework being done. When a clinician begins to speak with children about a stressful situation, asking specific, targeted questions about what aspects they, personally, find stressful is important. Abstract questions may lead to children leaving out key coping strategies that they used to manage secondary stressors (Coyne & Racioppo, 2000). Subsequently, asking questions about what they have done to cope with the situation so far becomes more effective. In addition to informal, subjective interviews with a child, standardized assessment methods are also available to assess coping.

Measures Used to Assess Coping

There are several measures that are used to evaluate coping skills in children. We have selected three groups of measures we believe are relevant to working with children who have parents with SMI. The first group includes two measures: the Children's Coping Strategies Checklist (CCSC) and the How I Coped Under Pressure Scale (HICUPS; Ayers, Sandler, West, & Roosa, 1996) ask children ages 9–13 to rate how often they use a given coping strategy when faced with a problem. The CCSC asks children how they cope with stressors in general, whereas the HICUPS asks children how they responded to a specific stressor. The measures are composed of 45 items that form 10 subscales and 4 factors (Active Coping Strategies, Distraction Strategies, Avoidance Strategies, and Support-Seeking Strategies). Items are rated on a 4-point, Likert-type scale. The 10 subscales include Cognitive Decision Making, Direct Problem Solving, Seeking Understanding, Positive Cognitive Restructuring, Physical Release of Emotions, Distracting Actions, Avoidant Actions, Cognitive Avoidance, Problem-Focused Support, and Emotion-Focused Support. These scales have demonstrated good reliability and validity and have been used in studies of children coping with parental divorce and bereavement (Ayers et al., 1996; Sandler, Kim-Bae, MacKinnon, 2000).

In the next group, the Kidcope (Spirito, Stark, & Williams, 1988) is a brief screening measure that consists of 10 items for adolescents aged 13 to 18 and 15 items for children aged 7 to 12. The Kidcope is like the HICUPS in that it asks children to report on how they coped with a specific stressor in the past month. Then children rate the frequency and efficacy of each item. Older children and adolescents use a 4-point Likert-type scale for frequency and a 5-point Likert-type scale for efficacy. Younger children respond yes/no to frequency and use a 3-point Likert-type scale for efficacy. This measure has frequently been used in pediatric populations (e.g., Spirito et al., 1988) and suicide attempters (Spirito, Francis, Overholser, & Frank, 1996).

Finally, the Responses to Stress Questionnaire (Connor-Smith, Compas, Wadsworth, Harding Thomsen, & Salzman, 2000) is a coping measure that is designed to assess both voluntary coping responses and involuntary, automatic reactions. Voluntary coping responses include *primary control engagement coping* (which refers to problem solving, emotional regulation and expression), *secondary control coping* (which refers to positive thinking, cognitive restructuring, acceptance, and distraction), and *disengagement coping* (which refers to avoidance, denial, and wishful thinking). Involuntary responses to stress include *involuntary engagement* (such as rumination, intrusive thoughts, and emotional and physical arousal) as well as *involuntary disengagement* (such as emotional numbing, cognitive interference, inaction, and escape).

The Responses to Stress Questionnaire has been validated on three samples of adolescents (ranging from 11 to 19 years of age) and two samples of parents. There are two versions of the Responses to Stress Questionnaire: an adolescent self-report form and parents' report of their adolescents' responses. Two main sections comprise the questionnaire. The first section assesses how frequently in the past six months the adolescent experienced a given stressor. This first section can be tailored to a specific domain of interest. For example, Jaser et al. (2005) asked adolescents questions specifically pertaining to coping with parental depression. In the second section, adolescents use a 4-point Likert-type scale to indicate the frequency with which the coping strategy or response occurred. This section contains 57 items. It is worth noting that a study by Jaser et al. (2005) found that adolescents' use of startegies such as distraction, cognitive restructuring, positive thinking (i.e., secondary control coping) to cope with family stress was related to lower levels of depression, anxiety, and aggression. Conversely, evidence of involuntary engagement stress responses (i.e., increased arousal, rumination) was associated with higher levels of depression, anxiety, and aggression.

Each of these four measures has strengths and weaknesses. All of them can be adapted to assess specific stressors. All of them assess problem solving, distraction, social support, cognitive restructuring, and wishful thinking. The Kidcope additionally assesses coping strategies that are likely to be maladaptive, such as social withdrawal, self-criticism, and blaming others, whereas the Responses to Stress Questionnaire additionally assesses involuntary stress responses. The HICUPS and the CCSC can be obtained for free on-line through Arizona State University's Prevention Research Center. The HICUPS/CCSC and Responses to Stress Questionnaire are both much longer than the Kidcope, which may be better in terms of the reliability of the measures, but has the cost of being more time-consuming. Each measure has varying degrees of empirical support as a research instrument: More studies that examine the measures as clinical assessment instruments are needed.

Assessing Family Life Cycle and Functioning of the Family Unit

While establishing some sense of developmental achievement, deficits, and coping styles for the child with a parent with SMI, it is also important to examine the functioning of the family unit. Carter and McGoldrick's (1988) model of family development identifies six phases experienced by families:

- Launching of the single person from the family of origin
- Joining of families through marriage
- Becoming parents and adjusting to young children
- Transformation of the family system in adolescence
- Launching children and moving on
- Changes in later life

Imagine the situation of a couple in the throes of early parenthood and all of the adjustments that entails. They married young and are both in their early twenties. They have a three-year-old son and a six-month-old daughter. The father experiences his first episode of mania in what is later diagnosed as a chronic bipolar disorder. The family, located at the stage of "becoming parents and adjusting to children," is thrown into a chaotic state in which the normal task of the family (adjusting to life as parents with children) is significantly complicated by the erratic behavior of one parent. Uncertainties arise about how the family life will be affected and changed and how much energy, time, and money will be available for the normal tasks and activities they had expected. It is important to inquire about the goals and plans the family had hoped to accomplish, in order to understand their grief and loss.

In addition to assessing the impact of SMI on the family's functioning, it is also important to identify the family's positive coping processes. For example, one factor consistently revealed in the literature and in clinical practice regarding the health of the children is the availability of a functional caregiving system in the absence of the SMI parent. Figley (1989) also describes 11 characteristics that tend to differentiate families that cope well with stress from families that struggle when stressors emerge. These might serve as a checklist for the assessor to consider when consulting with the family: (1) clear acceptance of the stressor, (2) family-centered locus of problem, (3) solution-oriented problem solving, (4) high tolerance, (5) clear and direction expressions of commitment and affections, (6) open and effective communication utilization, (7) high family cohesion, (8) flexible family roles, (9) efficient resource utilization, (10) absence of violence, and (11) infrequency of substance use.

Understanding the family unit also requires that the assessor become attuned to which person (or persons) within the system provides care to the particular child in question. This may require setting aside traditional Eurocentric assumptions that the biological mother and/or father is in the best position to provide constructive care. At times having other relatives, "kin," or guardians serving in primary or secondary parental roles can afford optimal development for children. Availability and consistency of the caregiver are two characteristics to assess, in addition to basic relationship, caring, and communication skills, regarding whether productive care can be provided for a child or adolescent (Reid & Morrison, 1983; Schachnow, 1987).

Assessing the Life Cycle of the Illness

In considering the life cycle of the illness itself, Rolland (1988, 1994) developed a model to look at the dimensions of a chronic physical illness. This model has been adapted to mental illness (see Marsh, 1998) and includes four critical dimensions:

I.   Onset—acute or chronic;
II. Course of the illness—progressive, constant, or relapsing/episodic;
III. Outcome/recovery—full, partial, none;
IV. Incapacitation—level of actual impairment and social stigma.

Determining these illness dimensions and the family's understanding of these dimensions (and integrating them with family life cycle and individual coping strategies) can be essential to the comprehensive appreciation of the situation.

The onset (Dimension I) of mental illness varies, depending on the individual: coming on suddenly with little warning for some; developing gradually over time for others. A sudden onset can send a family into shock, denial, anger, paralysis, or other incapacitating emotions. The family can spend a lot of time resisting what they are actually dealing with despite the fact that their loved one is hospitalized in a psychiatric facility. The family's normal life and ways of coping are often shattered by this new kind of crisis. Often, because of the shock and resistance to the idea that they are actually dealing with the stigmatizing reality of a mental illness, their ability to regroup and organize their resources may be delayed or never happen. This pattern may be expected to contribute to anxiety and distress seen in some children. Gradual onset, on the other hand, may lead the family to look away from the growing gravity of the symptoms. They may excuse, rationalize, minimize, or avoid asking dreaded questions. If the illness is masked by the use of substances (legal or illegal), the family may think they are dealing only with a drug problem. Alternatively, sudden angry outbursts, mood swings, insomnia, or isolation may be attributed to various stressors in daily life. With this onset pattern, assessors need to identify the use of avoidance strategies in family members adjusting to a relative's mental illness.

The course of illness (Dimension II) can be described as "progressive, constant, or relapsing/episodic." As in the case of differing onset patterns, each course of illness is laden with its own set of challenges. A "progressive" course, for example, entails persistent symptoms that become more severe and disabling over time. With many serious mental illnesses, the parent's treatment avoidance or noncompliance often leads to a progressive worsening of symptoms. This course can be associated with other complications (e.g., loss of job, relationship disturbance, homelessness), so that assessing this information can lend further understanding to the situation.

The second possible illness course, a constant presence of noticeable symptoms, is commonly seen with individuals who have treatment-resistant illnesses. Families run the risk of giving up hope or distancing themselves from the ill family member. The central issue to assess in this illness course is treatment adherence by the parent-patient.

The Relapsing/Episodic pattern, a third possible illness course, can be the most vexing and frustrating. The fluctuating course of the illness may render families helpless in their efforts to attain stability. They can "put everything on hold" as they wait for the next crisis. The exhaustion, frustration, and disruption to normal functioning can be markers seen in families that are constantly living on the edge of an impending crisis. This pattern may predispose some children to anxiety issues or concerns.

Once the onset and course of illness are identified, it is important to ascertain the family's response. In particular, do the adult caregivers experience significant levels of burden in dealing with the illness (Solomon & Draine, 1995), which leaves them with diminished resources available for the children (Marsh, 2001)? These factors will directly affect the child being assessed. Although they do not always identify this need, children benefit from having concrete information as to what is going to happen to them based on the illness course.

Assessing the type of recovery outcome expected (Dimension III) for the parent—full, partial, or none—makes up the third illness dimension. Once the topic of mental illness is broached in the evaluation, family members will want to know about possible outcomes. Often the reality is that no one can the predict outcome at the outset of an illness. Although there may be identified signs indicating a positive prognosis, it is important for families to seek a balanced perspective offering both hope and a reasonable range of expectations. Listening for the family's method for dealing with uncertainty can be essential to understanding how the child is attempting to cope with the problem.

Incapacitation (Dimension IV; Rolland, 1988, 1994) includes both actual impairment from the illness and social stigma. The greater the degree of incapacitation, the more important it becomes to identify the person who has assumed the primary caregiving role for the child. If the assessor observes a lack of clarity as to who is responsible for the children and how their basic needs are going to be met, he or she can understand the child's lack of safety and trust in the world. It is also important to assess the number and degree of changes the child faces (e.g., changing caregivers, homes, school districts, or friends). These changes can contribute to feelings of distress (e.g., feeling overwhelmed) or maladaptive coping (e.g., emotional numbing; silent, resentful compliance; or acting out). Finally, it is important to gauge the degree to which family members face social stigma associated with mental illness. For example, the family's report of isolation and withdrawal from other people in their lives may reflect the impact of stigma.

Assessing Grief Issues

An assessment of children and family members of the mentally ill would not be complete without a discussion of the issue of grief. Grief is perhaps the most common and poignant issue faced by patients and family members at some stage in their illness and recovery (see Marsh, 1998; Miller, Dworkin, Ward, & Barone, 1990; Solomon & Draine, 1996). As the poet John Greenleaf Whittier declares, "For all sad words of tongue and pen, the saddest are these, 'it might have been.' " Mental illness can mean that the life one thought one was going to have is altered, sometimes drastically, sometimes forever. Assessing how children and families address the reality of the losses that mental illness brings can be essential. Although SMI can be a line of demarcation in a family's life, there is life before and after the illness. One six-year-old child, with wisdom and perceptiveness beyond his years, puts it this way, "Before mommy got sick she was like Christmas. Now she's like Halloween."

Kubler-Ross's (1969) well-known stages of death and dying can be applied to a family struck by mental illness: Denial, Anger, Bargaining, Depression, and Acceptance. The level of grief among family members in relation to a family member with SMI may be comparable to grief felt by families who experience a death in the family (Miller et al., 1990). Acknowledging the family's struggle with grief can do much to understand the situation. Discussion of this area, and any associated guilt, may help to unleash the energy needed to proceed with additional assessment and possible treatment. Not acknowledging the presence of grief and/or not addressing it can lead to distance in the relationship between assessor and family.

Practical Considerations

Another group of factors to take into consideration is the concrete and practical strengths and liabilities of families. When assessing the family system, it is important to assess the following qualities of family members: physical health, financial stability, educational levels, prior or current legal problems, communication skills, level of community involvement and support, availability of extended family, and the safety of their neighborhood. The old adage "Don't assume anything" is important in being sensitive to these families, helping them to maximize their internal and external resources, and not alienating them from the mental health system. Do they have a phone, a car, money for gas, stable housing? Inner-city families may be struggling with some of these issues under the best of circumstances. Mental illness can deplete any family's resources, no matter how wealthy. Especially when the major breadwinners have been struck by an illness, or when divorce has occurred and finances are in disarray, the family may not have ready access to the most basic of resources. Referring to Maslow's (1968) hierarchy of needs may be a useful guide to assessing what level of intervention is required in meeting the most pressing client needs.

CASE EXAMPLE

Ms. X. is a 31-year-old, married Amish woman who was admitted to the hospital with a Major Depressive Disorder, Recurrent with Psychotic Features. She had stopped taking medications six weeks prior to this admission. She became irritable; was sexually preoccupied; reported what seemed to be auditory hallucinations with instructions to scratch her neck and hands; and was reported to have made suicidal threats, the fact that was most prominent in her being brought to the hospital. Ms. X. has a history of Major Depression, Post-partum type, first diagnosed four years ago following the birth of her third child. She was hospitalized at that time and treated with medications and counseling. Her biological mother had been diagnosed with Schizophrenia. Ms. X.'s two children—Susan, age 9, and Joshua, age 7—were referred to assess the impact of the current hospitalization on them. They were seen during a visit with their mother, which she requested after being in the hospital for one week and feeling stabilized on her medication.

In the assessment session, both children completed a K-F-D, the MASC, the Kidcope, and the CDI in addition to an interview. For the K-F-D, they were instructed to draw a picture of their family doing something three months ago "before mommy started acting sick" and then to draw a picture of their family doing something "right before mommy came into the hospital."

The "Before" K-F-D pictures of both children reflected a busy, smiling, and connected family, going about various household tasks. Mom was in the kitchen baking or outside, hanging up the laundry. The children were pictured close to her and involved with her. Dad was also in the pictures, either eating or working in the yard. The "After" pictures provided a striking contrast. Susan's "After" picture did not include her mother: Susan was in the kitchen doing dishes, and her brother was throwing a ball against a wall. Joshua's picture portrayed the family in the kitchen at the table. Mom and Joshua were crying, and he stated that no one was eating.

Drawing Commentary.   These pictures portray some of the common themes experienced by families in this type of situation: the oldest daughter taking on more caretaking responsibilities. Joshua is overidentified with his mother's emotional life and conveys his concern about some needs not being met (no one is eating).

On the MASC, although Susan's total scores were not elevated, she showed a slight elevation in the Perfectionism scale. Otherwise, there were few indices of acute distress identified on MASC or CDI. On the other hand, Joshua produced moderately high elevations on the Negative Mood subscale of the CDI. He also obtained a significantly elevated score on the Anxious Coping subscale and moderate elevations on the Separation/Panic subscale of the MASC. His drawings and self-report indicate issues related to anxiety, distress, and concerns about separation and meeting needs.

Ms. X.'s husband, Susan and Joshua's father, was asked to complete CBCLs for both children. In spite of being involved in interviews with his wife and children, Mr. X. did not complete these instruments for his children—offering no explanation for not doing so. Also, both children appeared to be somewhat insulated from the family distress at this time by the active involvement of grandparents and others in the community.

Coping and resiliency were assessed with both children through interviews and by use of the Kidcope. Susan, who achieved high grades at school, focused more on ways to fix problems. She clearly understood that she did not cause the problem and recognized that the most recent episode could have been prevented had her mother adhered to her medication regime. On the Kidcope she endorsed "I tried to fix the problem by . . . thinking of answers . . . (or) talking to someone." Joshua, on the other hand, was concerned about causing his mother's illness, and on the Kidcope also endorsed "I wished the problem never happened." He appeared to be narrowly focused on causing the problem and hoping that his mother's return home would "make everything go away."

Case Assessment Summary.   Joshua appeared to be more vulnerable than his older sister, showing the most distress across measures. He was concerned about safety and not doing anything wrong. His mood was mildly dysphoric. His method of coping involved self-blame and avoidant behaviors. He presented with internalizing problems and separation concerns. Susan was better adjusted. She has developed outlets at school for success, and she recognized that her mother's symptoms were not her fault. She focused on activities that will help the situation. Her primary risk involved a more insidious process of deferring her own needs at critical points and later experiencing the impact of missed opportunities for age-appropriate challenges and growth.

Contextual variables and frameworks considered in this chapter that applied to this case included *Child Developmental stages.* Susan was age 5 (nearly 6) at the time of illness onset, and she had already begun a successful adaptation to school (beginning the industry/inferiority stage). At the time of her mother's current hospitalization, she was 9 and continued to do well in school (experiencing both academic and social success). Joshua was age 3 at the time of illness onset, and he was at home with his mother during the onset of the illness and her first recovery. He was at the stage of initiative/guilt and dealing with sibling rivalry issues during his mother's first episode. During his mother's most recent hospitalization, he had begun school (age 7) and was facing the developmental challenges of industry/inferiority and socialization tasks.

Family Stage of Development.   The X family would be classified in the "New Family, Raising children" phase at the time of onset and were at the "Raising kids, school-age years" during the relapse. As such, they experienced an ongoing set of changes associated with the school-age years (socialization, intellectual development, increased self-directed behavior, etc.). It is also of note that living in the Amish community meant that they strictly adhered to a family-centered philosophy. Amish culture also tends to be very conservative, and specific roles are clearly defined for men, women, and children. In addition, there is a strong mandate to support family members during any type of illness or hardship.

Illness Life Cycle.   The onset of illness was sudden (past and current episodes). Ms. S's course was relapsing. The outcome was full recovery (in past), and the degree of incapacitation was considered high when Ms. X was off medication. As such, the children are faced with uncertainty about the duration of their mother's "well" or "sick" periods. At the same time, living in a supportive community, with minimal social stigma, helped to buffer the children from some of the effects of a sudden-onset, relapsing illness (e.g., readily available caregivers, few changes in jobs or roles). Also, they may have greater hope in the benefits of interventions because of the positive treatment response achieved by their mother in the past.

CONCLUSION

In summary, there are many issues involved in a thorough assessment of the children and family members of a person experiencing mental illness. Assessors in these situations need to attend to many different client messages: The developmental stages of individual family members that get interrupted, neglected, or denied; the tasks and stages of family life that become even more overwhelming; the dimensions of the illness that need to be addressed and that have ramifications for everyone; the sociological and practical strengths and limitations of individuals and the family as a whole; and the acknowledgment of grief reactions to the presence of mental illness. Unfortunately, very few studies have examined assessment strategies with this particular population. A variety of specific assessment tools may be used to identify common reactions (i.e., anxiety, distress, etc.). In addition, we emphasize the importance of evaluating resilience and coping in children and their families. Along these lines, measures of coping strategies have recently been applied with children in situations involving stress associated with a parent's mental illness (e.g., Jaser et al., 2005). Overall, it is perhaps most important to remember that the assessor is providing a valuable service to the child and family by recognizing that mental illness in a family member affects the child as much, if not more, than anyone else. In this way, the child's silent need is heard.

REFERENCES

Achenbach (1991). *Manual for the Child Behavior Checklist/4–18, YSR, TRF profiles.* Burlington: University of Vermont, Department of Psychiatry.

Anthony, E. J., & Cohler, B. J. (1987). *The Invulnerable Child.* New York: Guilford Press.

Ayers, T. S., Sandler, I. N., West, S. G., & Roosa, M. W. (1996). A dispositional and situational assessment of children's coping: Testing alternative models of coping. *Journal of Personality, 64,* 923–958.

Bricklin, B., Piotrowski, Z. A., & Wagner, E. E. (1962). The Hand Test: A new projective test with special reference to prediction of overt behavior. In M. Harrower (Ed.), *American lecture series in psychology.* Springfield, IL: Charles C. Thomas.

Butcher, J. N., Williams, C. L., Graham, J. R., Archer, R. P., Tellegen, A., Ben-Porath, Y. S., et al. (1992). *Minnesota Multiphasic Personality Inventory-Adolescent (MMPI-A): Manual for administration, scoring, and interpretation.* Minneapolis: University of Minnesota Press.

Carter, B., & McGoldrick, M. (Eds.). (1988). *The changing family life cycle* (2nd ed.). New York: Gardner Press.

Castleberry, K. (1988). Helping children adapt to the psychiatric hospitalization of a parent. *The Psychiatric Hospital, 19,* 155–160.

Clemence, A. J., Hilsenroth, M. J., Sivec, H. J., & Rasch, M. (1999). Hand Test AGG and AOS variables: Relation with teacher rating of aggressiveness. *Journal of Personality Assessment, 73,* 334–344.

Clemence, A. J., Hilsenroth, M. J., Sivec, H. J., Rasch, M., & Waehler, C. A. (1998). Use of the Hand Test in the classification of psychiatric inpatient adolescents. *Journal of Personality Assessment, 71,* 228–241.

Conner-Smith, J. K., Compas, B. E., Wadsworth, M. E., Thomsen, A. H., & Saltzman, H. (2000). Responses to stress in adolescence: Measurement of coping and involuntary stress responses. *Journal of Consulting and Clinical Psychology, 68,* 976–992.

Coyne, J. C., & Racioppo, M. W. (2000). Never the twain shall meet? Closing the gap between coping research and clinical intervention research. *American Psychologist, 55,* 655–664.

DeChillo, N., Matorin, S., & Hallahan, C. (1987). Children of psychiatric patients: Rarely seen or heard. *Health and Social Work, Fall,* 296–302.

Downey, G., & Coyne, J. C. (1990). Children of depressed parents: An integrated review. *Psychological Bulletin, 108,* 50–76.

Exner, J. E., Jr., & Weiner, I. E. (1995). *The Rorschach: A comprehensive system: Vol. 3. Assessment of children and adolescents* (2nd ed.). New York: Wiley.

Feldman, R. A., Stiffman, A. R., & Jung, K. G. (1987). *Children at risk: In the web of parental mental illness.* New Brunswick, NJ: Rutgers University Press.

Figley, C. R. (1989). *Helping traumatized families.* San Francisco: Jossey-Bass.

Garmezy, N. (1981). Children under stress: Perspectives on antecedents and correlates of vulnerability and resistance to psychopathology. In A. I. Rabin, J. Aranoff, A. M. Barclay, & R. Zucker (Eds.), *Further Explorations in Personality.* New York: Wiley-Interscience.

Goddard, R., & Tuber, S. (1989). Boyhood separation anxiety disorder. *Journal of Personality Assessment, 53,* 239–252.

Gotlib, I. H., & Goodman, S.H. (1999). Children of parents with depression. In W. Silverman & T. Ollendick (Eds.), *Developmental issues in the clinical treatment of children* (pp. 415–432). Needham Heights, MA: Allyn & Bacon.

Handler, L., Campbell, A., & Martin, B. (2004). Use of graphic techniques in personality assessment: Reliability, validity, and clinical utility. In M. Hilsenroth & D. Segal (Eds.), *Objective and projective assessment of personality and psychopathology* (pp. 387–404). Volume 2 in M. Hersen (Ed.-in-Chief), *Comprehensive handbook of psychological assessment.* New York: John Wiley & Sons.

Jaser, S. S., Langrock, A. M., Keller, G., Merchant, M. J., Benson, M. A., Reeslund, K., et al. (2005). Coping with the stress of Parental Depression II: Adolescent and Parent Reports of Coping and Adjustment. *Journal of Clinical Child and Adolescent Psychology, 34,* 193–205.

Johnson, J. T. (1988). *Hidden victims: An eight-stage healing process for families and friends of the mentally ill.* New York: Doubleday.

Joiner, T., Schmidt, K., & Barnett, J. (1996). Size, detail, and line heaviness in children's drawings as correlates of emotional distress: (More) negative evidence. *Journal of Personality Assessment, 67,* 127–141.

Joiner, T. E., Schmidt, K. L., & Schmidt, N. B. (1996). Low-end specificity of childhood measures of emotional distress: Differential effects for depression and anxiety. *Journal of Personality Assessment, 67,* 258–271.

Katz, J., Gintoli, G., & Buckley, P. (2001). BART's Place for children and teenagers of parents with serious mental illness. *Psychiatric Services, 52,* 107.

Kaufman, J., Birmaher, B., Brent, D. A., Rao, U., Flynn, C., Moreci, P., et al. (1997). Schedule for Affective Disorders and Schizophrenia for School-Age Children—Present and Lifetime Version (K-SADS-PL): Initial reliability and validity data. *Journal of the American Academy of Child and Adolescent Psychiatry, 36,* 980–988.

Kaufman, A. S., & Kaufman, N. L. (1990). *Manual for Kaufman Brief Intelligence Test (K-BIT).* Circle Pines, MN: American Guidance Service.

Kelly, F. (2004). Assessment of object representation in children and adolescents: Current trends and future directions. In M. Hilsenroth & D. Segal (Eds.), *Objective and projective assessment of personality and psychopathology* (pp. 617–627). Vol. 2 in M. Hersen (Ed.-in-Chief), *Comprehensive handbook of psychological assessment.* New York: John Wiley & Sons.

Kovacs, M. (1992). *Children's Depression Inventory.* North Tonawanda, NY: Multi-Health Systems.

Lachar, D., & Gruber, C. P. (1995). *Personality Inventory for youth. Administration and interpretation guide. Technical guide.* Los Angeles: Western Psychological Services.

Lazarus, R. S., & Folkman, S. (1984). *Stress, appraisal, and coping.* New York: Springer.

March, J. (1997). *Multidimensional Anxiety Scale for Children.* Multi-Health Systems: North Tonawanda, New York.

Marsh, D. T. (1998). *Serious mental illness and the family: The practioner's guide.* New York: Wiley.

Marsh, D. T. (2001). *A family focused approach to serious mental illness: Empirically supported interventions.* Sarasota, FL: Professional Resources Press.

Maslow, A. (1968). *Toward a Psychology of Being.* New York: Wiley.

Masten, A. S., & Coatsworth, J. D. (1998). The development of competence in favorable and unfavorable environments: Lessons from research on successful children. *American Psychologist, 53,* 205–220.

Miller, F., Dworkin, J., Ward, M., & Barone, D. (1990). A preliminary study of unresolved grief in families of seriously mentally ill patients. *Hospital and Community Psychiatry, 41,* 1321–1325.

Murray, H. (1943). *Manual for the Thematic Apperception Test.* Cambridge, MA: Harvard University Press.

Nicholson, J., Geller, J. L., Fisher, W. H., & Dion, G. L. (1993). State policies and programs that address the need of mentally ill mothers in the public sector. *Hospital and Community Psychiatry, 44,* 484–489.

Ostman, M., & Hansson, L. (2002). Children in families with a severely mentally ill member: Prevalence and needs for support. *Social Psychiatry and Psychiatric Epidemiology, 37*, 243–248.

Pianta, R., Longmaid, K., & Ferguson, J. (1999). Attachment-based classifications of children's family drawings: Psychometric properties and relations with children's adjustment in kindergarten. *Journal of Clinical Psychology, 28*, 244–255.

Psychological Corporation. (1999). *Manual for the Wechsler Abbreviated Scale of Intelligence*. San Antonio, TX: Author.

Rasch, M., & Wagner, E. E. (1989). Initial psychological effects of sexual abuse on female children as reflected in the Hand Test. *Journal of Personality Assessment, 53*, 761–769.

Reid, W. H., & Morrison, H. L. (1983). Risk factors in children of depressed parents. In H. L. Morrison (Ed.), *Children of depressed parents*. New York: Grune & Stratton.

Reithmiller, R., & Handler, L. (1997). Problematic methods and unwarranted conclusions in DAP research: Suggestions for improved research procedures. *Journal of Personality Assessment, 69*, 459–475.

Riebschleger, J. (2004). Good days and bad days: The experiences of children of a parent with a psychiatric disability. *Psychiatric Rehabilitation Journal, 28*, 25–31.

Rolland, J. S. (1988). Chronic illness and the family life cycle. In B. Carter & M. McGoldrick (Eds.), *The changing family life cycle* (2nd ed., pp. 433–456). New York: Gardner Press.

Rolland, J. S. (1994). *Families, illness, and disability: An integrative treatment model*. New York: Basic Books.

Rutter, M. (1987). Psychosocial resilience and protective mechanisms. *American Journal of Orthopsychiatry, 57*, 316–329.

Sandler, I. N., Kim-Bae, L., & MacKinnon, D. P. (2000). Coping and appraisal as mediators of the effects of locus of control beliefs on psychological symptoms for children of divorce. *Journal of Clinical Child Psychology, 29*, 336–347.

Seifer, R. (2003). Young children with mentally ill parents: Resilient developmental systems. In Luthar, Suniya, S. (Eds.), *Resilience and vulnerability: Adaptation in the context of childhood adversities* (pp. 29–49). New York: Cambridge University Press.

Shachnow, J. (1987). Preventive intervention with children of hospitalized psychiatric patients. *American Journal of Orthopsychiatry, 57*, 66–77.

Sitarenios, G., & Kovacs, M. (1999). Use of the Children's Depression Inventory. In M. E. Maruish (Ed.), *The use of psychological testing for treatment planning and outcomes assessment* (2nd ed., pp. 267–298). Mahwah, NJ: Lawrence Erlbaum Associates.

Sivec, H. J., & Hilsenroth, M. J. (1994). The use of the Hand Test with children and adolescents: A review. *School Psychology Review, 23*, 526–545.

Sivec, H. J., Masterson, P., Katz, J., & Russ, S. (2003, March). *Psychological characteristics and outcomes for the children of parents/relatives with serious mental illness*. Paper presented at the 6th All-Ohio Institute on Community Psychiatry, Beachwood, OH.

Sivec, H. J., Waehler, C. A., & Panek, P. E. (2004). The Hand Test: Assessing prototypical attitudes and action tendencies. In M. Hilsenroth & D. Segal (Eds.), *Objective and projective assessment of personality and psychopathology* (pp. 405–420). Vol. 2 in M. Hersen (Ed.-in-Chief), *Comprehensive handbook of psychological assessment*. New York: John Wiley & Sons.

Solomon, P., & Draine, J. (1995). Subjective burden among family members of mentally ill adults: Relations to stress, coping and adaptation. *American Journal of Orthopsychiatry, 65*, 419–427.

Solomon, P., & Draine, J. (1996). Examination of grief among family members of individuals with serious and persistent mental illness. *Psychiatric Quarterly, 67*, 221–234.

Spirito, A., Francis, G., Overholser, J., & Frank, N. (1996). Coping, depression, and adolescent suicide attempts. *Journal of Clinical Child Psychology, 25*, 147–155.

Spirito, A., Stark, L. J., & Williams, C. (1988). Development of a brief checklist to assess coping in pediatric patients. *Journal of Pediatric Psychology, 13*, 555–574.

Tuber, S. (1992). Empirical and clinical assessments of children's object relations and object representations. *Journal of Personality Assessment, 58*, 179–197.

Tuber, S., Frank, M., & Santostefano, S. (1989). Children's anticipation of impending surgery. *Bulletin of the Menninger Clinic, 53*, 501–511.

Urist, J. (1977). The Rorschach test and the assessment of object relations. *Journal of Personality Assessment, 41*, 3–9.

Waehler, C. A. (1997). Drawing bridges between science and practice. *Journal of Personality Assessment, 69*, 482–487.

Wang, A. R., & Goldschmidt, V. V. (1996). Interviews with psychiatric inpatients about professional intervention with regard to their children. *Acta Psychiatrica Scandinavica, 93*, 57–65.

Westen, D. (1995). *Social Cognition and Object Relations Scale: Q-sort for projective stories (SCORS-Q).* Unpublished manuscript, Department of Psychiatry, Cambridge Hospital and Harvard Medical School.

Westen, D., Klepser, J., Ruffins, S., Silverman, M., Lifton, N., & Boekamp, J. (1991). Object relations in childhood and adolescence: The development of working representations. *Journal of Consulting and Clinical Psychology, 59*, 400–409.

AUTHOR INDEX

SUBJECT INDEX

Note: Page numbers ending in "f" refer to figures. Page numbers ending in "t" refer to tables.